MW00784965

One God & One Lord
Reconsidering the Cornerstone of the Christian Faith

By
Mark H. Graeser
John A. Lynn
John W. Schoenheit

Fifth Edition
Revised by: John A. Lynn
© ℗ 2011 The Living Truth Fellowship

ISBN: 978-0-9836042-2-8

Note: Most Scriptures quoted in this book are from The New International Version (NIV). References taken from other translations or versions are noted as such, e.g., King James Version = (KJV), New American Standard Bible = (NASB), etc. In verses or quotations from other authors, words in **bold print** indicate our own emphasis and words inside [brackets] from Scripture or from other authors are ours.

All Scripture quotations, unless otherwise indicated, are taken from the Holy Bible New International Version®, NIV®, © 1973, 1978, 1984 by International Bible Society. Used by permission of Zondervan. All rights reserved.

Scripture quotations marked (NASB) are taken from the New American Standard Bible®, © 1960, 1962, 1963, 1968, 1971, 1972, 1973, 1975, 1977 by The Lockman Foundation Used by permission.

Scripture quotations marked (AMP) are taken from the Amplified Bible, © 1954, 1958, 1962, 1964, 1965, 1987 by The Lockman Foundation. Used by permission.

Scripture quotations marked (Moffatt) are from The Bible: James Moffatt Translation, © 1922, 1924, 1925, 1926, 1935 Harper Collins, San Francisco, CA, © 1950, 1952, 1953, 1954, James A. R. Moffatt.

Scripture quotations marked (NRSV) are taken from the New Revised Standard Version Bible, © 1989, Division of Christian Education of the National Council of the Churches of Christ in the United States of America. Used by permission. All rights reserved.

Scripture quotations marked (NKJV) are taken from the New King James Version®, © 1982 by Thomas Nelson, Inc. Used by permission. All rights reserved.

Scripture quotations marked (RSV) are taken from the Revised Standard Version, © 1952 [2nd edition, 1971] by the Division of Christian Education of the National Council of the Churches of Christ in the United States of America. All rights reserved.

Scripture quotations marked (NEB) are taken from The New English Bible, © 1970 by Oxford University Press and Cambridge University Press, printed in The United States of America.

Scripture quotations marked (NLV) are taken from The Holy Bible, New Life Version, © 1969–2003 by Christian Literature International, P.O. Box 777, Canby OR 97013. Used by permission.

Scripture quotations marked (TLB) are taken from The Living Bible, ©1971 by Tyndale House Publishers, Wheaton, Illinois 60187. All rights reserved.

Scripture quotations marked (DRB) are taken from The Douay-Rheims Bible, © 1899 American Edition.

Scripture quotations marked (ASV) are taken from The American Standard Version, 1901.

Scripture quotations marked (YLT) are taken from Young's Literal Translation, by Robert Young, 1898.

The sacred name of God, Yahweh, is indicated by "LORD."

ISBN: 978-0-9836042-2-8
Fifth Edition
Revised by: John A. Lynn
©℗ 2011 The Living Truth Fellowship

All rights reserved. No part of this book may be reproduced, stored in a retrieval system, or transmitted in any form or by any means, electronic, mechanical, photocopying, recording or otherwise, without the prior written permission of the publisher, except in the case of brief quotations embodied in critical articles and reviews, academic papers, and other non-commercial uses. For more information contact us at the address below.

This book was originally written by Mark Graeser, John Schoenheit, and John Lynn while they all worked together in ministry. They are now working in separate ministries, and the one with which John Lynn is now affiliated is The Living Truth Fellowship, Ltd., by whom this book is now being re-published.

The few revisions and additions in this edition were authored by John A. Lynn, as assisted by Bob Maffit and Ken Schleimer, who worked tirelessly to prepare this edition for publication. The beautiful new cover design was done by Franco Bottley.

God bless you as you take this step in your journey of coming unto a knowledge of the truth.

To receive our monthly newsletter, *FRUIT OF D'VINE*, and to be put on our mailing list, contact us at:

The Living Truth Fellowship
7399 N. Shadeland Ave., Suite 252
Indianapolis IN 46250
Phone: (317) 721-4046
Email: admin@tltf.org
Website: www.tltf.org
YouTube Channel: www.youtube.com/justtruthit
Vimeo Channel: www.vimeo.com/justtruthit

Country of origin the United States of America.

Dedication

We would first like to express our deepest love for our heavenly Father and His wonderful Son. We are ever so thankful to be allowed the privilege to study and teach the Word of God to people who hunger and thirst for the truth.

We are also very thankful for the many men and women who have gone before us to make this book possible. Through the ages the people who have held the beliefs espoused in this book have been hated, hunted, persecuted, tortured and killed by professing Christians. Noble and godly men and women suffered terribly, yet went into exile or to their graves rather than deny the Christ they were convinced of from Scripture. The examples of these great men and women are a constant source of courage and conviction to us, and, in part, we dedicate this book to their memory.

Table of Contents

Acknowledgments

We want to especially thank our The Living Truth Fellowship staff for their steadfast daily service, both to us and to the many people around the world in association with us. Although faced with far more work than they would normally be asked to do, they have cheerfully and admirably come through time and again and greatly helped to make it possible for us to complete this work.

We give special thanks to the many individuals who have contributed in specific ways to help us produce this book:

Pat Baird
Brian Bassindale
Jeff Blackburn
Franco Bottley
Eleanor Branch
Gwyn Bowen
Vancy Brown
Sue Carlson
Mike Colombaro
Michael Cutuli
Rachel Darr
Eddie DeBruhl
Rita Fiorentino
Giles Fischer
Cindy Freeman
Nancy Friscia
Vince Friscia
Rick Golko
Robert Hach

Wayne Harms
Craig Heman
Keith Jackson
Matthew Johnson
Barbara Jones
Steve Kilborn
Corban Klug
Judi Klug
Steve LaDieu
Jim Landmark
Steve Lefevers
Jane Lynn
John S. Lynn
Pat Lynn
Ivan Maddox
Bob Maffit
Linda Maffit
Jan Magiera
Ryan Maher

John Michalak
Joe Ramon
Barbara Reeve
Whitney Ricciardi
David Rogers
Ken Schleimer
Don Snedeker
Cynthia Snyder
Suzanne Snyder
Janet Speakes
Michael Steinberg
Richie Temple
Joanna Van Hoose
Jim Vehonsky
Bob Wassung
Doug Wilkin
Dustin Williams

Introduction

Who do *you* say that he is?

One evening Jesus was in a boat with his disciples crossing the Sea of Galilee. A sudden, violent storm enveloped them, high waves filled the boat with water and the disciples were terrified. Jesus, however, remained asleep. They awakened him and said, "Don't you care that we are going to die?" Of course Jesus cared about them, and after all, *he* was on the boat *with* them. He arose, rebuked the storm, and the turbulent sea calmed right down. The terrified disciples said among themselves, "...What manner of man is this, that even the wind and the sea obey him?" They had never seen anyone act with such fearlessness and such authority, nor wield such godly power. In the Greek text, the Apostles' question reads: "Who then is this One?" Indeed, this is the question of the ages, and one that every person must answer for himself.

Some time later, as his ministry developed and his fame grew, Jesus asked his disciples a question of his own: "...Who do people say the Son of Man is?" (Matt. 16:13). After they reported to him the various opinions circulating among the people concerning who they thought he was, Jesus asked them: But what about you? Who do *you* say that I am? Peter's response was "...You are the Christ, the Son of the Living God." Jesus affirmed that not only was that the correct answer, but that Peter knew it because God Himself had revealed it to him.

His question continues to hang in the air even two thousand years later, and it is the question that one day every man and woman will be required to answer. Why? Because God "...has set a day when he will judge the world with justice by **the man** he has appointed..." (Acts 17:31a). There is no more important quest facing mankind than finding out the true identity of Jesus Christ and understanding the significance of his life. The issue is a matter of life and death, both in regard to the quality of one's life now, and his future eternal destiny.

Suffering and Glory

The coming of this Man was first announced in Genesis 3:15, and at that time the two principal aspects of his life were described: suffering and glory. The entire scope of Christological history (that is, "the study of Christ") revolves around these two themes. The multiplicity of misconceptions about him also can be distilled into this paradigm. In general, people have either demeaned him or elevated him inappropriately. Another way to state the problem is that people have either prevented him from truly suffering or prevented him from being truly glorified. Either way, the true significance of his identity and accomplishments has been distorted, and therefore the essence of the Christian Gospel compromised.

At Jesus Christ's first coming to the Jews, many wrongly expected the Messiah to be more than he was at that time. Their one-sided theological conception of him as the conquering, glorified King kept them from recognizing and appreciating who he was and what he was sent to do. There was no room in their theological inn, so to speak, for him to be the suffering Savior of mankind, and when he was manhandled and crucified, many were offended at him and thought him to be a pretender to the throne of David. On the other hand, others saw him only as the bastard son of Joseph, a mere man who died the death of a common criminal.

Subsequent misconceptions about Jesus Christ have run the gamut, either demeaning or exalting him according to man's imagination. Untethered to biblical truth, these musings of men have included bastard child, extraterrestrial, mushroom cult leader, charlatan, mystic or angelic being. Many Christians have been taught that Jesus must be elevated to the status of a "God-man." Others think of him as just a "good man." Some people believe that we cannot really know if there even was an historical figure called Jesus of Nazareth, while others believe him to be a mythological creation. In fact, every Christological position of which we are aware, at some point either artificially elevates or ignorantly degrades the Lord Jesus. Our quest, then, is to find the true and balanced perspective of this remarkable man who in our view is the very focal point of human history. To do so, we will find that many traditional ideas will have to be jettisoned in favor of the clear testimony of the only credible source of information about this Jew from Galilee who was called in his own tongue, *Yeshua ha Mashiyach*, Jesus the Messiah.

A Spiritual Battle

The battle over the true identity of Christ is a very spiritual one with high stakes for mankind. Unquestionably, this Jesus of Nazareth has been the object of more speculation and demonic assault than any other person in the history of man. It is no accident that the name "Jesus Christ" springs spontaneously from the lips of all kinds of people, from the pious priest to the construction worker who has just dropped a cinder block on his foot. Even when Jesus Christ is rejected as an object of faith, he is chosen as an object of derision.

This is predictable based upon what the Bible says is really going on around us. In fact, a major theme of Scripture concerns the ever-raging battle between the true God, the Father of Jesus Christ, and the false god, the "god of this age," whom we now know as Satan, the Devil. He is a shrewd general, directing the main thrust of his attack upon the most vital truths in God's Word. The chief object of his hatred is The Man who now sits at the right hand of God. Accordingly, his primary goal is to blind the minds of men to the truth of the glorious Gospel about *Jesus Christ* (2 Cor. 4:3 and 4). It is sad to say that by a number of means he has been *very* successful in at least distorting, if not totally obscuring, the simple truth of who Jesus Christ is.

As Satan once inspired the evil King Jehoiakim to cut up and then burn the Word of God written by Jeremiah (Jer. 36), so he inspired evil men to destroy the Living Word, Jesus Christ. His relentless assault continues unabated, attempting to undermine the authority and credibility of the written Word of God that makes known the Living Word. His assault is primarily carried out on the battlefield of the *mind*. Today, we see fewer and fewer Christians who actually honor the written Word of God as their only rule of faith and practice. Instead, too many Christians give lipservice to biblical authority but in reality rely upon other standards for faith: the historic position of the Church, the testimony of their favorite preachers, the "leading of the spirit," their own feelings, etc.

But as Satan failed to destroy either the scrolls of Jeremiah or the Living Word, Jesus Christ, so he has failed to destroy the written Word of God. In fact, after the original scroll was destroyed, God told Jeremiah to dictate more words than the first scroll contained. Likewise, after Jesus Christ was killed, God raised him from the dead, highly exalted him and gave him the authority to give to all those who believe on him the power to live like he did, doing the works that he did. Thus, Jesus Christ now exerts far more influence on the world than he did when he walked the earth.

In light of this spiritual battle, it is certainly not surprising that through the centuries the Christian Church could be seduced by Satan's subtlety from the simplicity that is in Christ (2 Cor. 11:3). This is why for the better part of nineteen hundred years the "historic" Christian Church has unwittingly clung to and promoted "a different gospel" about "a Jesus other than the Jesus we preached" (2 Cor. 11:4). The other "Jesus" of historical Christian orthodoxy is a mystical "God-man" who existed before he was born. In this book, we will do our best to provide an alternative to this traditional position, one that we believe fits the evidence and logic of Scripture as a whole. We sincerely believe that a careful, logical and objective consideration of the evidence will lead the reader to the same conclusions that we have reached.

Resetting the Cornerstone

Jesus Christ is, by the agreement of all Christians, the subject of the Bible from Genesis 3:15 to Revelation 22:21. He is the very cornerstone of the edifice of biblical teaching. In Ephesians 2:20 and 1 Peter 2:6, he is called the "chief cornerstone." 1 Corinthians 3:10 and 11 make it very clear that he is also the foundation for the building of the Church. The cornerstone sets the angles and dimensions for an entire building, which can rise only as high as the foundation and cornerstone permit. If the corner is cut inaccurately, the walls of the building will be skewed and its height will be limited. 2 Timothy 2:15 (KJV) cautions the student of the Bible to "rightly divide" (*orthotomeo*) the Word of truth. This Greek word, derived from *orthos*, "right" or "straight," and *temno*, "to cut," literally means a "right or straight cutting."

Cutting the cornerstone accurately, therefore, is of the greatest importance for biblical understanding and exegesis and the furtherance of the Christian Gospel worldwide. We must therefore be diligent and skillful in the choice and application of the tools we will use to accomplish this crucial task. As we will attempt to demonstrate, the history of the Church's Christology is a tale of misdirected zeal and the use of inappropriate tools, in particular theological reflection, Gnostic mysticism and Neoplatonic speculation. Diligent, even *heroic* effort has been made to rationalize the historically "orthodox" position, despite much contrary evidence from the scope of the Bible and logic.[1] In our view, the result is a view of Christ that cannot stand up to rational or scriptural scrutiny, thus emboldening the critics of Christianity, notably Muslims, Jews and intellectuals. Indeed, we speculate that for every person who has embraced the orthodox view and become a Christian, there is at least one who has rejected Christianity because he or she could not believe in its central teaching of the "divinity of Christ." It is for this reason and because we believe that the truth honors both God and Jesus that we propose resetting the cornerstone for the Christian faith in a more biblically tenable and supportable position. We also believe that the truly biblical understanding of Christ's identity is imperative to strengthen the faith of Christians against the onslaughts of the modern and "post-modern" world.

As for the true identity of Jesus Christ, the thesis of this book is as follows: The Jesus of Scripture is the "Last Adam" whom God created as the only possible remedy for the problem of sin and death brought on by the First Adam. What Adam was before his fall is what Jesus was, a man made the way man was intended to be. God's Word tells us that Jesus was "...made like his brothers in every way...." It says he was **touched with the feeling of our infirmities**. It says that he was **tempted in the same ways we are**. It says that he was tired, hungry and thirsty and that he experienced the full range of human emotions. As the "Last Adam," Jesus Christ truly was a one-hundred-percent human being.

---

1. We place quotes around the word "orthodox" because what is considered "orthodox" and "heretical" has changed many times throughout Christian history. As we will point out in Chapter 16 on the beginnings of heresy, what came to be considered "orthodoxy" was in reality a heretical view of Christ that won out. It won out not on the strength of its biblical logic, but by intimidation and force.

As human beings with limited ability and perception, it is impossible for us to accurately conceive of, or identify with, the eternal *God* whose throne is the heavens and footstool is the earth (Isa. 66:1). A blind man might as easily describe the color "yellow." We can, however, conceive of and identify with *The Man* Jesus Christ, who exemplified what God is all about. Jesus Christ perfectly represented his heavenly Father. How? By always saying what God would have said and by doing what God would have done. Remember such statements of Jesus as: **My doctrine is not mine, but His who sent me; The Son can do nothing of himself, but only what he sees the Father do; I always do my Father's will.** Because Jesus perfectly lived the Word and will of God, he could say, **If you've seen me, you've seen the Father.**

The converse is also true—if Jesus Christ is distorted, misrepresented or obscured, the identity of his Father, the "only true God," is also obscured. This is why the title of this book is *One God & One Lord*, because knowing the true identities of both God and Christ hinges on our correct understanding and usage of biblical language. The Bible is very clear in this regard: there is only *One* God, a unitary personal being, and this God is not Jesus Christ, who is His *Son*. And there is only *one Lord*, a separate being who is not God, his Father. He is the *Lord* Jesus Christ.

1 Timothy 2:5 tells us that "...there is one God and one mediator between God and men, **the man** Christ Jesus." Jesus said that no one could truly know the Father except by coming through him. Jesus is "...the way and the truth and the life...." He is *the way* (the Greek word means "the road") to God. He is *the truth* that marks that road, and he is *the life* found by those who choose to follow the road. Thus, if we are to know, love, honor and obey the Creator of the heavens and the earth, it is imperative that we *know* the one He sent to reveal Himself, the Lord Jesus Christ. In fact, it is a matter of life and death, for he is the *only* way to the one true God. We believe that when Jesus' true identity is skewed, those desiring to follow him on the road of life may find themselves disoriented and frustrated. We find it an inescapable conclusion that an erroneous concept of who Jesus is basically leaves Christians with a "you-can't-get-there-from-here" attitude in their quest to be like him. And after all, that is to be the goal of every Christian—to be like him. Any doctrine of Christ that subverts, hinders or obscures this goal in any way should be held suspect and finally discarded.

So how are we to come to know the truth about who Jesus was, and is? There is no way to know Jesus Christ but to rely on the Bible, the written Word of God, and let God tell us the truth about His only-begotten Son. Our entire argument rests upon this premise: the Bible is the revealed Word and Will of God. If it is anything less than that, our argument will fall to pieces. But we believe there has been an abundance of evidence of the precise inspiration of Scripture that will support this premise.

Ultimately, our goal is to rest upon the authority of the testimony of the biblical text itself so precisely that if the Bible is right, we will be right, and if the Bible is wrong, we will be wrong. If our *interpretation* of the Bible is wrong, we will take full responsibility for it and be willing to stand corrected. Our goal is not to be right in order to make others wrong, and thereby make ourselves look good. Our goal is to assist the reader in heeding the two great biblical commandments:

Mark 12:29–31 (NRSV)
(29) Jesus answered, "The first is, 'Hear, O Israel: the Lord our God, the Lord is one;
(30) you shall love the Lord your God with all your heart, and with all your soul, and with all your mind, and with all your strength.'
(31) The second is this, 'You shall love your neighbor as yourself.' There is no other commandment greater than these."

This love for God and Christ will reveal itself in loving obedience, and this obedience will enable Christ to reveal himself to us. Consider the following verse:

John 14:21 (NRSV)
They who have my commandments and keep them are those who love me; and those who love me will be loved by my Father, and I will love them and reveal myself to them."

To know the Lord Jesus Christ, one must first *have* the Word of God, that is, understand it. Then one must also put the Word into practice, that is, *obey* it. To those who do both, the Lord Jesus will make himself real. Knowing the Lord Jesus is the key to loving him, and loving him is the key to serving him. Serving him is the key to a joyous and fruitful life.

In this book, we will allow the Word of God to magnify to us its main subject, Jesus Christ. In order for it to magnify the Lord Jesus to us, we must be careful to pay close attention to the signposts of biblical terminology. If we use words the way God does in His Word, we will not drift into the theological shallows. The Word of God says to be cautious not to add to nor subtract from its words. Extra-biblical vocabulary can easily introduce extra-biblical concepts that are often contradictory to God's original intent. A classic example is the introduction of the Greek word *homoousian* at the council of Nicaea, which we will be exploring in Chapter 18 on the rejection of Scripture and logic. Also, in many cases, equivocation of important terms has led the way to mysticism and incomprehensible dogmas. Therefore, defining words accurately according to their biblical usage will be a major preoccupation of this book.

We will be focusing on the *identity* of Jesus Christ and his relationship with God. Other books could be written on the subject of his *work*, which we will not be focusing on in this book. The foundation for understanding and appreciating Christ's accomplishments lies in properly discerning his identity as "the Last Adam." We are also limiting our historical overview to those ideas, developments and influences that directly bear upon the formation of Christian doctrine concerning his identity and the role that this doctrine has had in Church history. In particular, we will argue that because Christian orthodoxy adopted the means and methods of mysticism, the resulting rejection of reason became a major hindrance to individual spiritual growth and liberation.

In fact, we believe that the historical record shows that the Christian church became an authoritarian and monarchial hierarchy held in place by a set of unintelligible doctrines that needed an elite class of priests to interpret to the masses. The average Christian believer was thus held captive to unquestionable dogmas replete with mystery and paradox until the dawning of the Reformation began to make available intellectual freedom. This book is in line with a historical trajectory begun in the 14th century by John Wycliffe, who began the process of retrieving the Bible from the clutches of spiritual tyrants and returning it to the common sense of the common man. Numerous others since then have reached many of the same conclusions that the reader will encounter in these pages, and most of them have been branded heretics, cultists or blasphemers by the institutional church. Many of them died in pursuit of the truths that the readers of this book will be able to encounter in the safety of modern toleration of religious pluralism and, beyond that, growing indifference to the very idea of "truth." Nevertheless, like grass poking up through cracks in concrete, the living truth of who Jesus Christ is keeps popping up in the pages of Scripture, out from under centuries of misunderstanding, and despite modern indifference.

Part of our intention in writing this book is to acquaint the reader with the large volume of support for our position extant in the literature of modern biblical scholarship, particularly in the past 20 years. Since it does not support traditional theology, much of this work has not found a popular audience and is therefore not found in standard Christian bookstores. We have endeavored to reduce to footnotes most of the references to the work of these scholars in order not to bog down the reader in often tedious and difficult scholarly jargon. But if the reader will be brave and read the footnotes carefully, he will find almost another book within this book.

Our purpose is to strengthen the faith of those who are dissatisfied with traditional Christology by directing them to recognized scholars who have reached the same conclusions as a result of their research. But our fundamental commitment is not to the intellectual stimulation of our readers with the often detached perspective of the scholar or historian. We write as believers, intent upon learning the truth that might set us free and kindle a fire of desire to further the Gospel of Christ to the ends of the earth. For those who think this book too scholarly, we would plead for grace and understanding and a second or third reading if necessary. In our view, it is the scholars whose theological speculations, often little more than pedantic sophistry, have muddied the waters. To clear things up, we have found it necessary to engage the scholars' arguments head on, and that often requires a commitment to logical reasoning that some readers may find difficult or tedious.

This book has actually evolved during a ten-year period beginning with a paper titled "Rethinking Christology" that Mark Graeser presented to a group of Trinitarian ministers who were attempting to dialogue with and minister to "cultists." Mark's paper forms the basis of several of the chapters of this book. In 1990, John Lynn taught an audio seminar called *Jesus Christ: The Diameter of the Ages*.[2] Its colloquial and devotional flavor is preserved in a number of sections of the book, which will appeal to those readers who are looking for the more entertaining, readable and less scholarly material. We would particularly recommend for their readability and devotional appeal Chapters 1–3, the last section of Chapter 8, and Chapters 12 and 13. In 1997, John Schoenheit published a work on the Trinity, the highlights of which are represented in Appendix A, that handles the verses often used to argue for the Trinity.

Thus, this book represents a collaboration of many years, several people and much study. A subject this important, and so complicated by tradition and misunderstanding, could hardly be handled by any one person. As a result of the team approach to the writing of the book, the reader may at times sense a "patchwork" aspect to the style, as it reflects our different thinking and writing. We trust that the book as a whole will not be skewed in the direction of any personal style, but reflect our unified desire to "speak the truth in love."

---

2. To hear this Seminar go to: TheLivingTruthFellowship.org, click on Bible Teachings, then click Audio, then click Bible Seminars. This dynamic 6-hour series is indispensable in understanding the most important subject of the entire Bible: JESUS CHRIST. It deals with his relationship with God, the Church, and Israel. The teaching shows how Jesus saw in the Old Testament the prophecies of his birth, life, suffering, death, resurrection, ascension, exaltation, and his future kingdom. Thus he was obedient to the written Word, all the way to his death on the Cross. This seminar also shows what Jesus is now doing as Lord and Christ, and some of what he will do when he returns to earth to rule his kingdom. The teachings proclaim scriptural truths vital to one's knowing Jesus Christ as Lord on a daily basis, and thereby knowing God, our Father.

Overview

We will now provide an overview of the entire book. In Part 1, we will look at why Jesus Christ is called in Scripture "the Last Adam," and how each of them was the image of God. We will consider the mechanics and the legality of the redemption that the Savior made available to all men. We will consider what Scripture says about man as "the image of God," and how Jesus, the perfect Man, is now fulfilling the intended destiny of mankind. Chapter 3 will examine the way Jesus Christ is literally the "purpose of the ages," and look at his post-resurrection glory.

In Part 2, we will then discuss what the Old Testament tells us about the identity of the Messiah in prophecy from two perspectives. The first is the detailed prophetic portrait that is painted by the Hebrew Scriptures about the coming one, and the second is the way the Jews interpreted these prophecies, which were sometimes ambiguous or difficult to interpret. This helps us understand why even today Jews have difficulty believing that Jesus is the promised Messiah.

Part 3 is a detailed analysis of the Four Gospels, which describe the Savior in person. Chapter 6 is an overview of the Gospels, and explains why there are four, Chapter 7 handles the evidence from the Synoptic Gospels (Matt., Mark and Luke), particularly the view presented there of the apparently "reluctant Messiah" who veiled his identity throughout his life. Chapter 8 will handle the gospel of John in detail, since this is the section of Scripture used to anchor orthodox Christianity. Chapter 9 will look at the relationship between Jesus and the *logos* and handle the first 18 verses of John, called "the prologue," which are often misunderstood and misinterpreted.

Part 4 will look at the evidence of the remainder of the New Testament, which clearly identifies Jesus of Nazareth as both Lord and Christ. The book of Acts, the Church Epistles and the book of Revelation have much to say about who Jesus Christ is and his "functionally equal" relationship with his Father.

Part 5 will focus on the practical aspects of who Jesus Christ is, what he is doing now, and our potential to identify with him to the end that we become like him in thought, word and deed. We will close with a look at the true hope of each Christian, that hope made available by the work of Jesus Christ, the only-begotten Son of God.

Part 6 is an historical perspective on the development of traditional Christology. First we will look at the phenomenon called "the expansion of piety," which explains corruptions of the text of Scripture and the historical tendency to elevate the identity of Christ. We will then identify the beginnings of heresy as addressed in the epistles of 1 and 2 John, where we can see that an illogical, confusing and self-contradictory view of Jesus Christ had already taken root in the first century of Christianity. We will also look at the influence of Gnosticism and Neoplatonism on the development of Christian doctrine in the centuries after Christ.

The doctrine of the "incarnation" of Christ will then be examined in light of the Apostle Paul's prophecy in Timothy that Christian leaders would turn away from the truth unto myths. Then we will see how the rejection of Scripture and logic, a crucial element of true faith, led to the idea that God was beyond reason. To conclude our historical perspective, we examine Socinianism as the historical movement most closely aligned to our position, and one that validated the importance of reason and liberty. We will then consider modern trends in the development of both Trinitarianism and Christian Unitarianism.

Another virtual "book within a book" is the appendices, which are intended to be used for reference more than to be read straight through. Our hope is that this book will be one that is not read only once and then put away to gather dust, but one that continues to edify, enlighten and inspire the reader to pursue his or her relationship with both the Living Word and the written Word.

What Is At Stake

Some readers may take the position that what we are arguing for is just nitpicking over equally probable biblical interpretations that have no significant practical ramifications. From this perspective, it looks like the world is already full of books detailing every possible theological and Christological position, few of which interest the average person. So, they ask, what difference does it make who Jesus really was and is? That is a very good question.

Beyond what we have already asserted about the importance of this subject, we believe there are five ways in which this topic is vitally significant. In the first place, the issue of biblical integrity is at stake. Some interpretations do damage to the integrity of Scripture, even though there may be a few verses that can be squeezed to support them. The question is, does an interpretation fit with Scripture *as a whole*? This is demanded by logic. If the Bible is not to be the foundation for our belief, then we must accept some other basis. If the Bible is taught in such a way that contradictions are ignored, tolerated or created, the Word of God is thus corrupted and made less credible to those people who are unwilling to embrace contradiction in the pursuit of truth.

Second, spiritual tyranny is encouraged when confusing and self-contradictory dogma is required as an object of faith. Rather than honestly persuade people by logically consistent and scripturally sound principles, tradition and man-made "authorities" are set up as lords demanding submission. Spiritual leadership of this sort does not engender authentic discipleship, but in too many cases unquestioning and rigid adherence to incomprehensible doctrines. The shaky underpinnings of their faith are evidenced by their angry and emotional reaction to rational and scriptural challenges. Convictions based in truth empower a patient and loving response toward those who present challenging ideas.

Third, all false interpretations of the identity of Jesus Christ demean both his accomplishments and the nature of the one true God, his Father. Something is inevitably lost when God's people are unable to clearly discern the face of God, for whatever reason. Any doctrinal system that makes it more difficult to understand the nature of God or appreciate the life and work of the Savior is not in the best interests of Christians or of Christianity itself.

Fourth, false teaching concerning Christ makes it difficult for us to identify with him and believe that it is possible to do the works he did. Since we are commanded to walk in his steps, and are told that we can do the works that he did, any doctrine antagonistic to this is suspect. We assert that our ability to identify with Jesus as a man facilitates our following him, and that any doctrine that hinders our identification with him will correspondingly hinder our ability to do what he did.

Lastly, evangelizing the world is made much more difficult by centering the Christian Gospel on a "God-man," who is basically a mythological figure and one who does not harmonize with common sense. It is our contention that children, Jews, Muslims and thoughtful truth-seekers everywhere are hindered from believing in Christ when told that he is "fully God and fully man," "God the Son," or some other unbiblical description. Jesus commanded his followers to "go into all nations and make disciples." There is an implied promise in this commandment, which is that as we obey it, he will open the doors for us. The sad state of the world nearly two thousand years after Christians first received this commandment is most telling—there are billions of people who still need to hear the Gospel of Christ. We believe this is because too few human beings have ever heard the unadulterated

Gospel ("Good News") about the Savior. What they have heard has been a blend of truth and pagan philosophy. How can this be? Please continue reading!

In the process of writing this book, we have found it necessary to aggressively rethink our own Christological position with scriptural diligence, intellectual honesty and rigorous rationality, being everwilling to challenge even our most deeply held convictions, assumptions and beliefs. We now invite the reader to join us in this quest, regardless of how uncomfortable the journey may be for him at times. If our beliefs are scripturally sound, they will hold up to scrutiny. If not, we must let them go in favor of something better, by which both our personal lives and the life of the Church can only be enriched. In the course of accompanying us on this path to the truth, we pray that the reader will clearly recognize that our motivation is fervent love for our heavenly Father and our Lord Jesus, and that our main goal in writing this book is that both would receive all the credit and glory due them.

Preface

The last verse of the gospel of John contains an amazing statement about the life of Jesus Christ:

John 21:25 (NRSV)
But there are also many other things that Jesus did; if every one of them were written down, I suppose that the world itself could not contain the books that would be written.

Just writing about his doings would fill the earth with books, and when there are already innumerable books about him written from almost every conceivable perspective, any new book must be vigorously justified. The vast majority of the books in print about Jesus have been written from the "orthodox" perspective of his "deity" by authors who believe in a "triune Godhead." These folks, called *Trinitarians*, believe that Jesus is "God" the Creator in human flesh and have held the majority position since the Council of Constantinople in 381 A.D.[1] This position is embraced by all mainline denominations of Christendom and constitutes the linchpin of the movement toward ecumenical unity among Christians. For the most part, it is assumed that all true Christians hold this position.

A few books challenging the orthodox view have made it into print, but most of these promote the idea that Jesus was someone less than the unique Son of God, as we believe the Bible clearly identifies him to be. Trinitarian authors then strongly argue that unless a person fully embraces Trinitarian doctrine concerning Christ, he will have a truncated and powerless view of him that threatens the integrity of the Christian message. So closely identified with Christianity is Trinitarianism that few of the major Christian book publishers will publish a book unless its author affirms allegiance to the orthodox view.

Thus, we find ourselves representing a distinct minority position among Christian leaders and teachers. If you are *not yet a Christian*, and have never been able to accept the claims made by "orthodox" Christians concerning the identity of Jesus Christ, we implore you to read this book before you reject him. Perhaps we will be able to communicate his great love and wisdom in such a way that you will be able to say from your heart, like the blind man who was healed in John 9: "Lord, I believe!" We believe that if you read this book with an open mind and careful study, comparing what we say with the Word of God, you may well be persuaded that what we write is true. If not, we would love to have the opportunity to speak with you further. You will find our address and website at the beginning and end of this book. We want to convey to you how much you are loved by God and the Lord Jesus Christ. That is our hope and our passion as we request that you continue to read on. May your eyes be opened, and your heart touched by the life and true identity of the greatest man who ever lived.

If you are already a Christian, and currently hold to "traditional" theology about the identity of Jesus Christ, we promise you that this book will challenge what may be your deepest convictions. We ask you to maintain a mind open to the possibility of being persuaded by greater light from Scripture. It is our experience that many people who say they believe in the "Trinity" do not actually know what the orthodox definition of the Trinity is. When we explain it to them, a typical response is, "Well, I do not believe *that*." The basic tenet of the traditional doctrine of the Trinity is that "the

---

1. The orthodox definition of the Trinity is as follows: There is One God who co-exists in three eternal and co-equal persons, Father, Son and Holy Spirit. The Son, therefore, is fully "God" as much as the Father is. We respectfully dissent from this orthodox position, and the rest of this book will be devoted to explaining why.

Father is God, the Son is God, the Holy Spirit is God, they are co-equal and co-eternal and together the three of them make one God." Many people think the Trinity is simply belief in the Father, the Son and Holy Spirit, but that is not so. Although it may seem to you at first that this book teaches a doctrine that is heretical and dangerous, perhaps you will discover that it is actually teaching something very close to what you already believe.

You may have been taught that Jesus Christ is devalued by any concept of him other than the Trinitarian perspective, and this is understandable. We acknowledge that throughout history many of those who have rejected the Trinity have *also* rejected the uniqueness of Christ as the only-begotten Son of God, reducing him to the level of only a great prophet or teacher. For us, however, Christ is also *devalued by the Trinitarian concept of him*, because "nothing is impossible with God." But for a *man* to do what Jesus did is not only a sterling accomplishment worthy of everlasting merit, it also sets a legitimate standard for what we too can do as we follow his example of faith in God. In this book, you will find a perspective of him that recognizes his uniqueness (his virgin birth, sinless life, resurrection) and emphasizes his exaltation to his God-given position as Lord (Phil. 2:8–11).

We acknowledge the fact that Trinitarian Christians have through the centuries advanced the cause of Christ with millions of people. But, in light of their own admission that the doctrine of the "Trinity" is at best hazy in Scripture, we would ask: has this doctrine limited the outreach of the Gospel? How many more people, in particular staunch monotheists such as Jews and Muslims, as well as those rational thinkers for whom a mystical faith is unsatisfying, could have been reached not only for salvation but also for maturing into committed followers of the Lord Jesus Christ?

Perhaps you have been so persuaded by Trinitarian rhetoric that you are afraid to even consider our views, because you have been told that the only people who espouse a non-Trinitarian Christian gospel are heretics and members of "cults." But, on the other hand, you may still be willing to hear a different perspective. The question is whether or not what you believe corresponds with what the whole of Scripture actually says. If it does not, you cannot lose anything by letting go of beliefs that are not truly grounded in the Word of God. We hope that what you can gain will become evident as you continue to read. We will do our best to show you the biblical evidence for our convictions, and we trust that you will find our position as persuasive and compelling as we do. If not, we invite you to dialogue with us.

Why do we feel compelled to undertake the project of penning yet *another* book about the greatest man ever to draw breath? First and foremost, because we feel that our Lord Jesus Christ has been so misrepresented by traditional or "orthodox" Christianity that countless people have been denied the opportunity to meet the real Jesus as he appears in the pages of God's Word. The second reason we are constrained to write this book is because, although we have not read every book written about Jesus Christ, we know of no other book that says what we say in this one. Yes, we have found some of the ideas in the works of others, but this is the only one we know of that puts all these parts together. As for its validity, we hope that you will hear us out and judge for yourself.

Of course, the most important book ever written about Jesus Christ is the first one written about him—the Bible, which we believe to be authored by the Creator of the heavens and the earth. We will be providing you with a lot of evidence that the Bible is a highly credible document, despite what you may hear to the contrary from many sources today. If you are not even sure that you believe in God, please consider that the value of understanding Jesus Christ's identity and accomplishments is that he is the best representative that God has ever had. He is truly the "image of God." The God revealed by Jesus is "the only **true** God" (John 17:3).

Although some may call this work a "doctrinal treatise," it is far more than that. We write with a burning love for The Man who chose to be obedient unto death, even the death of the Cross, for it is through his death that we have life—life with meaning and purpose now and life everlasting in Paradise with him and our Father, God. Our goal is to help people exalt the Lord Jesus as God has exalted him, no more and no less, to the end that they know, love, trust and obey Jesus as their Lord. Seeing the doctrinal truth from Scripture as to who Jesus Christ is and what he is now doing as Head of the Church is the most effectual means to identify with him to the end of doing the works that he did and thus glorifying our Father in heaven. You may notice that in this book we do not capitalize the pronouns referring to Jesus Christ. We do this in keeping with the editorial practice of the vast majority of Bible translators and publishers, who also do not capitalize the pronouns referring to God, which we do. Nothing should be read into this punctuation practice other than a simple desire to distinguish between God and His Son.

It is of the utmost importance that each person comes to a true understanding of who this person called Jesus Christ is, because understanding who he is gives the unbeliever an open door to everlasting life, and the Christian a blueprint for living life in a fallen world. The truth about the identity and work of Jesus Christ satisfies the deepest longings of the human heart—the desire to be loved, understood and appreciated for who we are. We hope to so vividly set forth the heart of our Savior that you develop an insatiable passion to know him intimately.

Rest assured that we have walked the same path of overturned mindsets that we are asking you now to walk, or at least to consider walking. As long as God's Word marks that path, we need not fear. Our experience during the past thirty years has been that *many* people have been searching the wilderness of religion, philosophy and theology for that path of logic and truth, and that they rejoice when they find it. To us, it is the one that is most scriptural and rational, and it leaves the fewest questions unanswered. Most importantly, it is the perspective that we believe God has revealed in His Word, the primary source of truth about Jesus Christ. Remember that truth is not determined by whether the majority of people believe it, as the once-upon-a-time-widely-held "flat earth" theory so plainly proves. Each person must be willing to subject even his or her most deeply held convictions to the scrutiny of God's written Word.

Everyone applauds accuracy as essential to nearly every field of human endeavor. What endeavor could be more important to a person than accurately understanding the written revelation of his Creator? Such an understanding is the basis of one's whole attitude toward God, and affects nearly every aspect of his or her life. We find it unfortunate that many well-meaning Christians have attempted to characterize, define and understand Jesus Christ more from extra-biblical sources such as Greek philosophy, theological reflection and human speculation than from the Bible alone. All representations of Christ arrived at via these avenues are, to many thoughtful and spiritually hungry people, distorted, unsatisfying and mere caricatures of the real person that he is.

At this point we think it would help you to learn a bit about our own spiritual backgrounds. John Lynn was brought up in a traditional *Presbyterian Church* (actually, he lived at home). John Schoenheit was raised as an atheist. Mark Graeser was exposed to the *Unitarian Universalist Church* as a small child, and received no formal Christian education while growing up. John Schoenheit majored in philosophy and Mark minored in it. John Lynn has heard of it. We have a background in logic and debate. However, we do not intend to be antagonistically argumentative or controversial, but are simply pursuing the truth with everything we have.

At one time we were all spiritual seekers who had been left cold by traditional Christians and "churchianity." We were reached by an unorthodox group called *The Way International*, considered by some to be a "cult," but for us it was a lifesaver. We were very involved in that ministry for the better part of 20 years, serving in a variety of teaching and leadership positions. We were taught a staunchly non-Trinitarian Christian gospel, but one that viewed a personal relationship with Jesus Christ as at best suspect, and at worst idolatrous. We have come to recognize that in our tradition Jesus Christ was not exalted and honored as Scripture indicates, so we have steadily parted company with the teaching of *The Way* in order that we might better follow The True Way, Jesus Christ.

In the process of our spiritual journey, we have realized that many "Trinitarians" do have a dynamic and personal relationship with Jesus, whom they exalt and honor as "God." We have been humbled to see this. Nevertheless, we remain unable to accept the "logic" of the Trinity, and we find it not only unscriptural but also antagonistic to our passionate desire to identify with The Man Jesus Christ and be like him. Furthermore, our study of Church history has shown us that the Trinity is a concept developed through nearly four centuries with the help of extra-biblical concepts and language. As the reader will discover in this book, this fact is widely known by theologians and Church historians. Amazingly, it is still not recognized by the average Christian.

In writing this book, our purpose is not to be controversial or iconoclastic, nor is it to assault Christian orthodoxy or Trinitarianism, *per se*. Rather, it is to herald what we believe is by far the greatest truth in the Bible, the truth about who Jesus Christ is, what he reveals about his Father God and what he has done, is doing and will do for mankind. We will do our best to allow the living Word of God to "jump start" the minds of any readers who are stalled on the off-ramp of impractical religious tradition.

We have written this book for readers to enjoy and utilize in several ways, depending on their interest in the subject. Many of the appendices in the book are for those who are serious students of the Bible and want reference tools to assist them in their personal, ongoing study of God's Word.

If you are of a more scholarly bent, we have left a trail in the footnotes of this book for you to analyze our methods and reasoning and check our sources. We have made every attempt to provide scholarly support for the positions we take in this book because we admit that we are not recognized Bible scholars. We are largely self-taught, primarily because we do not subscribe to the fundamental beliefs of virtually every Christian seminary at which we might pursue advanced degrees. We would ask those who are impressed by worldly credentials to consider that neither Jesus himself (John 7:15) nor his followers (Acts 4:13) were considered properly educated by their contemporaries. The best recommendation of this book is that through logic and Scripture, it enables men and women to be devoted followers of the Lord Jesus Christ. Any other validation is secondary at best.

Though we obviously consider the subject of this book a serious one, we often employ humor or irony both to entertain and to inspire our readers to think logically according to biblical truth. We realize that we will likely offend some of our readers in the process of pursuing truth, but that is not our intention. We simply desire to be faithful teachers of the Word of God, the literature of eternity that is filled with "...exceeding great and precious promises...," chief among which is Jesus Christ, *the Promise*. We pray that what you find herein will engender a passion to *know him, love him* and *be like him*.

PART ONE

The Man, Man's Redeemer

From the classified section of *The Jerusalem Herald*, Nisan 1, A.D. 27:

HELP WANTED
Redeemer for Mankind

Job description: Man needed to pay price for sins of mankind. Must live totally sinless life. Demanding schedule, constantly on the go. No guaranteed home or income. Must be willing to train forgetful staff who tend to quit under pressure. Must totally fulfill law of Old Testament. Must be absolutely obedient to the will of management. Will ultimately be beaten and humiliated and experience indescribable suffering and anguish. Will become sin offering and die on job.

To qualify: Must be male, minimum age 30. Father must be God, mother must be of house and lineage of David, must have been virgin when he was born. Adopted father must also be of house of David. Must have sinless blood and spotless record. Must have been born in Bethlehem and raised in Nazareth. Must be self-motivated, with aggressive personality and burning desire to help people. Must have tremendous knowledge of Old Testament and firm reliance on biblical principles. Must incorporate the foresight of Noah, the faith of Abraham, the patience of Job, the faithfulness of Joseph, the meekness of Moses, the courage of Joshua, the heart of David, the wisdom of Solomon, the boldness of Elijah, the power of Elisha, the eloquence of Isaiah, the commitment of Jeremiah, the vision of Ezekiel and the love of God.

Wages: Holy spirit (without measure) to start. Additional payoff in intimacy with God and receiving revelation as necessary to complete job. Constant on-job training, supervision and guidance by top-level management.

Benefits: Position will lead to highly exalted position in future if job carried out successfully.

Workman's compensation: Injuries sustained on job, including death, well compensated by promotion including new body. Management will highly promote name upon successful completion of job, and entire publicity department will be devoted to getting name before multitudes. Will assume presidency of expanding international venture (The Ministry of Reconciliation), as Head of Body of well-equipped members ready to move dynamic new product on world market. All in all, tremendous eternal potential for growth and rewards in return on initial investment of giving life.

If qualified, management will contact you. No need to apply.

1

Christianity 101: Two Adams

Why did God need to fill this position of Redeemer? Because He had to "fire" the original general manager of His creation for gross impropriety and malfeasance. When God delegated the oversight of Creation to a *man* with *free will*, He anticipated the possibility of that man's failure, and formulated a plan to solve the problem. The plan was for *another man* to rectify the catastrophic situation. Why *another* man, when He had such poor success with the first one? Why did He not just march down here and take care of things Himself? Many Christians believe that is exactly what God did—that He became a man in order to redeem mankind. But since man was in such a sorry state that he could not redeem himself, was the only alternative for *God Himself* to do the job? We think there are a number of problems with this theory.

First of all, one of the most defining attributes of God is His absolute holiness.[1] This means that He transcends His creation the way Henry Ford transcended the automobile that he built. Though God can be intimately involved with His creation, He, by definition as "the Creator," stands distinct and apart from it. He cannot make Himself into a rock or a tree or a frog or a man, because these are all created things. Neither is He "one" with them, as pantheism suggests—that God is "in" the rocks and trees and frogs and men. This is a very basic biblical truth.

---

1. See Leviticus 19:2, 20:7 and 26, 21:8; Joshua 24:19, *et al*.

Because He is so holy, God knew that He Himself could not *legally* redeem mankind by becoming one of us. Neither can He just make up the rules as He goes along. His righteousness and integrity are absolute, and He cannot break the rules that He has established. One of those rules is that He keeps His Word. That is important, because God never promised to send *Himself* to ultimately redeem mankind. Rather, He promised that **the seed of the woman** (Gen. 3:15 - KJV) would come, and that this man would do the necessary work.

Furthermore, there is nothing in the Bible to indicate that God can become a true man, because He is *God*. One of the boundaries of God's nature is given in Numbers 23:19: "God is not a man…" And from the beginning, one of Man's defining boundaries was that the consequence for disobeying God's command was *death*. *Potential mortality*, then, was always a defining part of man's existence. God, therefore, cannot actually *be* a man, because He *cannot* die.[2] He is immortal, by definition.[3] The great pattern of the Bible is that God equips *others* to serve Him and act as His agents. Moses, Gideon, David and Jesus were each sent by God to perform a necessary job. In Jesus' case, the job was the ultimate redemption of mankind and creation. But how could a *man* do such a job? He could do it by following the pattern established by all the men God sent to perform a task—being equipped by God and then precisely obeying His plan. This is exactly how Jesus Christ accomplished his task as Redeemer. Not only *could* a man do the job, but the job *required* that a man do it, since God Himself could not legally do so. To understand why this is so, we will now turn our attention to the source of the problem that necessitated the sending of another Adam to be Man's Redeemer.

The First Adam

Exploring the biblical background of the need for a Redeemer is crucial to understanding both the integrity of the Bible and the identity of Jesus. Before we subject this remarkable man from Galilee to a needless onslaught of theological speculation, we must carefully analyze the biblical relationship between the "First Adam" and the "Last Adam." Even modern biblical scholars are recognizing that this parallel between the two "Adams" was a key element of apostolic Christianity, and is probably the earliest and richest biblical insight concerning the identity of this unique man named Jesus Christ.[4] We, too, have come to the conclusion that this relationship is the key to understanding and appreciating Jesus' identity, and that it establishes the first boundary marker in our survey of this subject.

---

2. However, He can (and occasionally did) "appear" as a man. Regarding the rare examples of God coming into concretion in the form of a man, see Appendix A (Gen. 18:1 and 2). In these cases, however, God did not actually transform Himself into a man, but took on the *appearance* of a man so that He could have fellowship with certain people at crucial times in redemption history.

3. 1 Timothy 1:17 clearly identifies God as being immortal, meaning that He cannot die. In fact, He is the very Author of Life itself. An enormous burden of proof is laid upon those who would argue that God Himself could *die* for our sins. If He *were* able to die, who would raise Him from the dead? See Appendix A (1 Tim. 6:14–16).

4. In theological terms, this is called "Adam Christology," and many scholars acknowledge that this was the "Apostles' doctrine" concerning the identity of Jesus. James D. G. Dunn, *Christology in the Making* (Grand Rapids MI, W. B. Eerdmans, 1989) notes on pp. 114 and 115: "We have…seen how *widespread* [his emphasis] was this Adam Christology in the period before Paul wrote his letters—a fact not usually appreciated by those who offer alternative exegeses of the [Phil. 2:6–13] hymn." Dunn also quotes Young: "It is eschatology, not incarnation, which makes Christ final in the New Testament…Christ is final for Paul, not as God incarnate, but as the Last Adam." The Apostle Paul compares and contrasts Jesus and Adam in three key places in Scripture: Romans 5:12ff, 1 Corinthians 15:22 and 45, and Philippians 2:6–13 (and also Hebrew 2:7 and 8 if Pauline authorship is accepted). We will visit and revisit these passages throughout the book.

Once upon a time—"in the beginning"—God was all by Himself. His heart's desire was, in essence, a family to love and be loved by. First, He created angels and other spirit beings. He then made two people—a man and a woman—and gave them dominion over the earth, their home. God's instructions were simple—He told them to multiply and to fill up the earth with more people after their kind, i.e., *mankind*. He gave them only one prohibition—not to eat of a particular tree in the garden. They chose to disobey their Creator, and thus wreaked havoc not only upon His originally perfect creation, but also upon their own offspring.

The First Adam was part of a creation that God declared to be "very good." His "seed," therefore, was perfectly designed to reproduce "fruit after its kind," even as the plants and animals were. Therefore we can assert that Adam was genetically flawless, but he was not a robot. He had the quality that goes a long way in defining what a human being is, as distinct from animals: freedom of will. Where animals are governed by instinct, man was made with a brain that made him able to be self-aware and govern himself. He was therefore well equipped to understand that he was a being that owed his existence to his Creator. He could learn from his environment and choose his behaviors. It was up to him to make decisions in response to God's commandments, whereas animals receive their "commandments" as a part of their genetic packaging. Raccoons do not choose whether or not to raid a garbage can.

This privilege to choose was not granted only to Adam. The same held true for his "wife," Eve (they never had a formal ceremony—Adam just awoke from a nap and found out he was married!). It is not our purpose here to examine the mechanics of Adam and Eve's original sin, but suffice it to say they did the one and only thing they were not supposed to do—they ate of the tree of the knowledge of good and evil. Though they both partook of it, God held Adam responsible. His disobedience revealed that in the depth of his heart, Adam came to doubt God's true love for him. Thus, he did not believe that God would provide for him what he really needed, and he chose to take matters into his own hands and provide for himself. Of course, the consequences were far reaching—for him, his wife and all their descendants.

In fact, Adam's disobedience set the general pattern of all men's subsequent disobedience to God (Rom. 1:18–21). He also set the pattern for the coming Messiah in other ways as well, in particular as the following Scripture indicates:

Romans 5:14 (NRSV)
Yet death exercised dominion from Adam to Moses, even over those whose sins were not like the transgression of Adam, who is a type of the one who was to come.

There are many people in the Old Testament who could be called "types of Christ." But this is the only place in the New Testament that directly points back to a particular person who would set *the* pattern for who the Messiah would be like. Adam was a "…pattern of the one to come," in that both Adam and Jesus Christ were men who by one act had a universal effect on mankind.

The record of Adam's transgression makes it clear that the verb "to sin" means to disobey the Word of God. By his action of sinning, he introduced "sin" into God's perfect Creation. Thus, a state of corruption was imposed upon God's perfect Creation, which was now indelibly tainted and would require a process of redemption. For the catastrophic consequences of sin to be completely rectified, a new heaven and earth were necessary.

The entrance of sin caused an even greater problem for God to solve—*death*. The following verse clearly illustrates this:

Romans 5:12
Therefore, just as **sin** entered the world through one man, and **death** through **sin**, and in this way **death** came to all men, because all **sinned**—

Thus, the twofold problem that God had to solve was *sin* and *death*. Adam and Eve disobeyed God, which was an individual act of "sin." But by this one unrighteous act, they catalyzed a transformation of Creation from a state of perfection and righteousness to a state of "sin." When they did, they and all their descendants became subject to death, the direct result of sin. After that, the only kind of children they could produce were children "…separated from the life of God…" (Eph. 4:18), and hence, from the moment of their birth, destined to die.

God's Solution: Another Adam

What was God's solution to the problem of sin and death? The only solution legally available: *another Adam!* In fact, if we had to sum up the whole Bible in five seconds, we could say: "It is the story of two men and their effect on mankind. The first man wrecked everything; the second man is fixing it."

Like the First Adam, the Last Adam would have to be, first of all, *genetically* flawless and without a sin nature.[5] It was God's responsibility to create him that way, which He did via the virgin birth. But more than that, the Last Adam had to be *behaviorally* flawless. God could not be responsible for that. He could only hope that, in contrast to the First Adam, the Last Adam would be obedient throughout his life and thus accomplish the redemption of mankind. In essence, God took a risk and trusted that the Last Adam would trust Him. This is love in action: taking a risk, giving second chances, demonstrating commitment to a promise. As the Bible says in 1 John 4:8, God is love, and He has therefore modeled it perfectly. In our view, His plan, as revealed in His Word, exemplifies a far greater love than if He had somehow become a man Himself.

Before looking at God's initial reference in Genesis 3:15 to the special promised offspring of Adam and Eve, we want to get a running start in the broader context of the passage.

Genesis 3:21 (NRSV)
And the LORD God made garments of skins for the man and for his wife, and clothed them.

Were Adam and Eve's outfits the first clothing ever mentioned in the Bible? No, they had earlier become the first tailors in the Bible, as the following verse indicates:

Genesis 3:7
Then the eyes of both of them were opened, and they realized they were naked; so they sewed fig leaves together and made coverings for themselves.

Here we have, in essence, the birth of "religion." After having failed to keep God's commandments and thereby stand righteously before Him, the first humans tried to cover their own sin, to "justify"

---

5. Because the First Adam was genetically flawless, we can safely conclude that the Last Adam was also. Scientific evidence corroborates this truth. In his book, *The Seed of the Woman* (Brockville, Ontario, Doorway Publications, 1980), Arthur Custance does an admirable job on the subject of the genetic perfection of Jesus Christ. Although the entire thesis of the work is important to our point, pp. 282–286 are especially relevant.

themselves. This marked the beginning of a sinful human pattern: man attempting to cover his guilt with the works of his own hands in a self-righteous effort to earn favor with God. The futility of such religious efforts to remove the guilt inherent in all mankind is revealed by the fear that gripped them in the presence of God, as the next verse shows.

Genesis 3:8 (NRSV)
They heard the sound of the Lord God walking in the garden at the time of the evening breeze, and the man and his wife **hid themselves** from the presence of the Lord **God** among the trees of the garden.

We can see that religion is a very poor substitute for a personal relationship with the Creator based on trust in Him, and it failed to produce any confidence or faith in God's loving care. In fact, the first humans tried to *hide* from Him, which is precisely the naked effect of sin—it drives a wedge between God and man!

It is very significant, then, that the first thing God did for mankind, after they sinned but before He ejected them from Paradise, was to get rid of their fig leaf underwear and make them some new clothing. In effect, He said to them, "You *can't* go out looking like that—and you *are* going out!" The clothing they had made for themselves was not a sufficient covering as far as God was concerned. Most significant is the material from which the new clothes were made—animal skins. Did God get the skins from animals who donated their extras? No, animals like to be clothed too. What we have here is the first *shedding of blood* in the Bible. In His grace and mercy, God instituted a substitutionary sacrifice for the sin of Adam and Eve, one that clothed them in a temporary righteousness and allowed them to live until the seeds of death planted in them came to fruition some 900 years later. The blood of animals was shed to provide a covering for mankind that was "suit-able" in God's sight.

Remember that from Genesis 3:15 on, Scripture is pointing toward the coming Redeemer. The shedding of the animals' blood was a foreshadowing of the shedding of the blood of "the Lamb of God," a sacrifice necessary for God to be able to clothe with His righteousness those who would believe on this Redeemer. With the sacrifice of animals, and the subsequent clothing of Adam and Eve in their skins, God made *temporary* atonement for the sin they had just committed. In light of this pattern, we can appreciate that the shed blood of Christ, the "Lamb of God," made *permanent* atonement for mankind, and also made it possible for people to be "...clothed with power from on high" (Luke 24:49). No longer is anyone who believes in Jesus Christ spiritually "naked."

Jesus Christ had to be the Last Adam, a "lamb from out of the flock," but "without spot or blemish" so that he could die as an acceptable sacrifice.[6] By being both genetically *and* behaviorally flawless, the Last Adam's life would be a sufficient sacrifice for the *sin nature* inherent in all men, as well as for all their sinful behavior in the future. We will see in the book of Hebrews that the reason the Last Adam had to be a *true man* was so that he could *die* to pay the price for the sins of all men. We will also see that via his death, he "took the Devil's best punch," and that in his resurrection, he got up "off the canvas."

In Genesis 3:9–13, God questioned both Adam and Eve about their disobedience, and then prophesied concerning the consequences of their sin. But God's harshest judgment was reserved

---

6. We use "lamb from out of the flock" to bring together two concepts—first, that Jesus was the *true* Passover lamb, a lamb taken from the flock of sheep; and second, that there are many Scriptures that say that Jesus was one of us. He was one of the "brothers" (Deut. 18:18; Heb. 2:11), he was a man, the Last Adam, and thus he was like the Passover Lamb in that he was "of the flock," not an outsider, but truly one of us.

for His nemesis, the "Serpent," Satan. He turned to Satan and pronounced the death sentence upon His archenemy, the one who had masterminded the downfall of the first man. How fitting that the first announcement of the coming Redeemer was made "in your face" to the one responsible for the introduction of sin, evil and death into God's creation.

Genesis 3:15 (NRSV)
I will put enmity between you and the woman, and between your offspring [seed] and hers; he will strike your head, and you will strike his heel."

Let us now unpack this verse, which is one of the most loaded-with-truth verses in the entire Bible. Theologians refer to this verse as the "proto-evangelium" because it basically capsulizes all the rest of Scripture by foretelling both the sufferings and glory of the Messiah. It also foretells the "head-to-head" conflict between the Promised Seed and the Serpent, until the destruction of Satan is accomplished in one of the final acts of redemption before Paradise can be restored.[7] To us, this verse stands as a marvel of God's poetic and literary genius. It is no wonder that the Bible has been called "the literature of eternity." In two simple sentences this verse sets forth the promise, the conflict and the destinies of both Christ and Satan, who were to be the two principal antagonists in the great struggle to complete the process of redemption. Today we can view this verse with 20/20 biblical hindsight and see in it truths that those of Old Testament times did not clearly understand.

It is very significant that Satan is presented as a serpent crushed under the foot of the woman's offspring. First of all, we should note how appropriate this image is, because a poisonous snake is best killed by crushing its head so it cannot rear back and strike. But before being crushed, the Serpent would bite "the heel" of the Promised Seed, causing a time of suffering.[8] This was the first prophecy of his suffering and death required for the redemption of mankind.

It is obvious to us today that there is a temporal sequence of events being set forth. This coming seed would *recover* from being struck in the heel and then strike the head of his adversary after that.[9] From our vantage point in the Church Age, we can see that the Serpent's head will be crushed by the exalted one who was raised from the dead with a new, glorious body and made Head, first of the Church and later of the whole earth in his Millennial Kingdom. As we will see in 1 Corinthians 15:24–28, Christ must reign until all God's enemies are subdued, and Satan is "Public Enemy #1."

The next truth in this verse is that the coming one, the solution to the problem of sin and death, would be a *man*. We know this by the reference to him as a "seed." Adam and Eve were the only two people ever to start tall and without navels, that is, they did not begin as seeds in the wombs of their mothers. Of course, Adam and Eve could not be born because there was no one to father and mother

---

7. See Appendix F on the Satan/Christ parallelism, which will also be addressed in Chapter 3.

8. It is significant that only two body parts are mentioned in this verse: the head and the heel. The heel represents the time when the Messiah had a body vulnerable to the Serpent's bite, which caused death. The "head" foretells a time in the future when the Redeemer would be in a place of authority, and able to crush the Serpent's head. God has given the Promised Seed all the authority he needs to complete the job he has been given.

9. The NIV and some other versions make a differentiation in the verbs usually translated "bruise," "strike" or "crush." The Hebrew text uses the same word for both verbs used in this sentence. The Hebrew word is *shup* and it means "to bruise" or "to crush." Although it could be shown from the entire scope of the Word that the Serpent would only "bruise" Jesus' heel, and that Jesus will "crush" his head, that truth is not clearly brought out here. It is more accurate to translate the verb *shup* the same way, either "bruise" or "crush." The Serpent did crush Jesus' heel, but having a crushed heel only put him down for a short time—three days and three nights. When Jesus crushes the Serpent's head, it will put him "down for the count."

them, so God created them. Then He made it plain that they were to "be fruitful and multiply and fill up the earth." God wanted them to do this while they were in their original state, so that their descendants would live forever in the original Paradise. However, as we know, they disobeyed God and thus could produce nothing but a race of mortals—people doomed to die.

Because the Last Adam had to be a man, he had to start as a *seed* and be *born* of a woman. But in order to have the potential to become the Redeemer of mankind, he had to start with a sinless nature like the First Adam did. Genesis 3:15 predicts how God would accomplish this seemingly impossible feat, and that is the next great truth revealed in this verse. Note that God referred to the seed as "her" seed. In retrospect, we see in these words a foreshadowing of the virgin birth.[10] In a normal birth, it is the man who puts the seed into the woman, where it combines with an egg and grows for nine months. When it came to Jesus Christ, however, it was God who put a perfect human seed (the Greek word for "seed" is *sperma*) into the womb of a virgin named Mary.[11] The

---

10. It is often taught, and until recently we also believed, that Genesis 3:15 was a specific prophecy of the virgin birth because of the phrase "her seed." We assumed a literal meaning of the word "seed," equivalent to "sperm," and took that to be a figure of speech to emphasize that God was the author of such a seed, since a woman does not generate "seed" herself. While the Hebrew word *zera*, here translated "seed," occurs more than 200 times in the Hebrew text of the Old Testament, and does mean "seed" (literally, like what is sown in the ground—See Gen. 1:11, etc.), or "semen" (Gen. 38:9; Lev. 15:16), it can also mean "offspring," "descendants," or "children" (Ps. 22:23; Isa. 1:4).

It was quite understandable to the Hebrews, then, that in this sense a woman could have "seed," i.e., *children*. That fact is very clear in the Old Testament. In Genesis 4:25, when Seth was born, Eve comforted herself over the death of one of her children, Abel: "Adam lay with his wife again, and she gave birth to a son and named him Seth, saying, 'God has granted me another child [seed] in place of Abel, since Cain killed him.' " This verse makes it very clear that Eve had "seed." In Genesis 16:10, an angel was talking to Hagar, Abraham's Egyptian slave, about her children: "The angel added, 'I will so increase your descendants [seed] that they will be too numerous to count.' " The angel was talking to Hagar, and spoke about her "seed," yet she was not even in the genealogy leading to Christ. Later, when Abraham wanted a wife for his son, he sent his servant, who found Rebekah. As her family sent her away to Abraham, they blessed her and spoke to her of their hopes for her children: "And they blessed Rebekah and said to her, 'Our sister, may you increase to thousands upon thousands; may your offspring [seed] possess the gates of their enemies' " (Gen. 24:60).

The book of Leviticus also speaks of a woman having seed: "But if a priest's daughter becomes a widow or is divorced, yet has no children [seed], and she returns to live in her father's house as in her youth, she may eat of her father's food. No unauthorized person, however, may eat any of it" (Lev. 22:13). The book of Ruth contains a pertinent reference. The elders of Bethlehem spoke to Boaz, who had just stated that he would marry Ruth. The elders said, "Through the offspring [seed] the LORD gives you **by** this young woman, may your family be like that of Perez, whom Tamar bore to Judah" (Ruth 4:12). In this verse, the offspring, the seed, was the gift of the LORD given **to** Boaz **by** Ruth. Obviously we are not talking about the sperm, but we are talking about the children, because it would be by Ruth that the LORD would give children (seed) to Boaz. This same truth is found in 1 Samuel 2:20: "Eli would bless Elkanah and his wife, saying, 'May the LORD give you children [seed] by this woman to take the place of the one she prayed for and gave to the LORD.' Then they would go home." Again, the husband is being given "seed" by the wife.

From Hebrew lexicons and from the text of Scripture itself, the word "seed" can mean "offspring" or "children." Women did have "seed," not in the sense of "sperm," but in the sense of "children." This fact explains why the Jews were not expecting Christ to be born of a virgin, and even Mary herself, a believer and descendant of David, asked the angel how she could give birth to Israel's Messiah without having a husband (Luke 1:34). We now know that Christ was born of a virgin, and looking back we can see that the possibility is allowed for in Genesis 3:15. However, to say that Genesis 3:15 specifically prophesies a virgin birth is not correct. The verse was written by Israelites for Israelites, and presumably they knew their own language well, yet they read the verse for centuries and understood that it referred to the Messiah, without knowing or believing it foretold a virgin birth.

11. It could be argued that God did not create "seed" or "sperm" in Mary that then fertilized her egg, but rather that He created a zygote, a fertilized egg inside Mary that then grew into the child, Jesus. This latter view is the view of all Trinitarians who argue that Jesus, who pre-existed his birth as some form of spirit being, "incarnated" (literally, "came into flesh") in the womb of Mary. Scripture is not explicit about this, which is not surprising because the conception of Mary occurred long before test tube babies, surrogate mothers and *in vitro* fertilization. Nevertheless, we believe

child resulting from this union, therefore, had the same genetic flawlessness as the First Adam. The following verses make it plain that God was the direct cause of Jesus' conception:

Luke 1:30–35 (NRSV)

(30) The angel said to her, "Do not be afraid, Mary, you have found favor with God.

(31) And now, you will conceive in your womb and bear a son, and you will name him Jesus.

(32) He will be great, and will be called the Son of the Most High, and the Lord God will give to him the throne of his ancestor David,

(33) He will reign over the house of Jacob forever, and of his kingdom there will be no end."

(34) Mary said to the angel, "How can this be, since I am a virgin?"

(35) The angel said to her, "The Holy Spirit will come upon you, and the power of the Most High will overshadow you; therefore the child to be born will be holy; he will be called the Son of God.

Mary asked the angel Gabriel a very logical question: How would a baby be conceived in her womb without a man being involved? Gabriel's reply contains a great truth that many Christians throughout history have overlooked because of their theological assumptions. In verse 35, the Greek conjunction translated "so" (NIV) and "therefore" (KJV) indicates the *cause* responsible for the eventual birth of "the holy one," the Son of God. From the Greek word for "born" (*genao*), we get the word "Genesis," and it denotes the *beginning* of Jesus in the womb of Mary.[12] This makes it very plain that Jesus Christ began in the womb of Mary, just as every human being begins

---

the language of Scripture is still capable of revealing to us what happened. If God created a zygote in Mary's womb, we believe the language of creation would appear somewhere in the records of the conception and birth of Christ. Instead, we find that Christ is called the "seed" (Greek = *sperma*) in the Bible. Also, the Word of God talks of Mary's "conception," which would not really be accurate if she had not in fact conceived. Furthermore, when the angel was explaining to Mary how she would become pregnant, the terminology he used of God's interaction with Mary, i.e., "come over you" and "overshadow you," seems to portray God's role as a father and impregnator, not as a creator. Lastly, we would point out that Jesus is said to be from the line of David through his father and his mother. For us it is easier to understand him being called that if Mary were his mother in the ordinary sense of the word. We do not believe that Mary having a genetic contribution to Jesus would have placed his genetic perfection in jeopardy. This is no doubt at least a large part of what Philippians 2:6 (KJV) means when it says that Jesus was in "the form of God." That is, his body was the result of the direct action of God, even as Adam's was. The difference between the two Adams in this regard was that one awoke fully formed while the other was formed in a woman's womb and went through the entire process of human development.

12. Two similar Greek words, *genesis* and *gennesis*, can be translated "birth." But *genesis* can also mean "creation," "beginning" and "origination." Since these words are very similar, a scribe could have easily changed the one to the other to eliminate the idea that the so-called "eternal" Son of God had a "beginning," which was the position of the "heretical" Arians. Bart Ehrman proposes a reason why the text was corrupted in this way, with *genesis* changed to *gennesis*:

When one now asks why scribes might take umbrage at Matthew's description of the "genesis" of Jesus Christ, the answer immediately suggests itself: the original text could well be taken to imply that this is the moment in which Jesus Christ comes into being. In point of fact, there is nothing in Matthew's narrative [nor Mark's or Luke's, for that matter!], either here or elsewhere throughout the Gospel, to suggest that he knew or subscribed to the notion that Christ had existed prior to his birth. Anyone subscribing to this doctrine [of Christ's "pre-existence" and "incarnation"] might well look askance at the implication that Matthew was here describing Jesus' origination, and might understandably have sought to clarify the text by substituting a word that 'meant' the same thing, but that was less likely to be misconstrued. And so the term *gennesis* in Matthew 1:18 would represent an orthodox corruption. *(continued)*

in the womb of his or her mother. If Jesus Christ is truly a *man*, the Last Adam, he could not possibly have existed prior to his birth. How can one exist before he exists?[13]

The third great truth in Genesis 3:15 is that the Man, man's Redeemer, would suffer. His "heel" would be "struck." This was a prophecy of his suffering and death that was required for the redemption of mankind. The fourth truth in this verse goes hand-in-hand with the third. It is obvious to us today that this coming seed would *recover* from being struck in the heel and strike the *head* of his adversary. What we see foreshadowed here is the *resurrection* of Jesus Christ and his future destruction of the Devil. Revelation 20:10 tells us that the old Serpent will one day be cast into the lake of fire where he will burn for "ages unto ages," and Ezekiel 28:18 tells us that he will eventually be brought "to ashes."[14]

The last truth that we see in Genesis 3:15 is perhaps the *piece de resistance!* It also relates to the other reason why Jesus Christ is called a "seed" in this, the first mention of him in Scripture. What is the purpose of a seed? *To produce fruit after its kind.* This is clearly communicated in the first chapter of the Bible, where we see God establish the fruit—seed—fruit cycle. Every plant produces a "fruit" wherein is "seed," which when germinated will reproduce the same "kind" of plant.

Genesis 1:11–13 (NRSV)
(11) Then God said, "Let the earth put forth vegetation: plants yielding seed, and fruit trees of every kind on earth **that bear fruit with the seed in it**." And it was so.
(12) The earth brought forth vegetation: plants yielding seed of every kind, and **trees of every kind bearing fruit with the seed in it**. And God saw that it was good.
(13) And there was evening and there was morning, the third day.

God also made the animals to reproduce their own "kind." That is, the "seed" of the male would combine with the egg of the female and reproduce the same "kind" of animal. Is not this same principle also being communicated in connection with the Last Adam in the following verse?

John 5:26 (NRSV)
For just as the Father has life in himself, so he has granted the Son also to **have life in himself**;

The chief property of a seed is that it has "life in itself." That is what enables it to reproduce after its kind. One day, as we will see in Chapter 12, Jesus Christ will produce a new race for a new age. He will do this by reproducing himself "after his kind." This truth is clearly communicated in the following verses:

Philippians 3:20 and 21 (NRSV)
(20) But our citizenship is in heaven, and it is from there that we are expecting a Savior, the Lord Jesus Christ.

Bart D. Ehrman, *The Orthodox Corruption of Scripture* (Oxford University Press, N.Y., 1993), pp. 75 and 76. See also Chapter 15 on "The Expansion of Piety."

13. The concept of "the pre-existence" of Christ, and its companion concept, "the incarnation," has caused many problems for theologians. We discuss the issue in detail in Chapter 17.

14. See our book by: Mark Graeser, John Lynn, and John Schoenheit, *Is There Death After Life?* (The Living Truth Fellowship, Indianapolis, IN, 2011), Chapter 4.

(21) He will transform the body of our humiliation that it may be conformed to the body of his glory, by the power that also enables him to make all things subject to himself.

Adam: The Pattern of the Coming Redeemer— Two Men, Two Acts, Two Universal Results

The plan of redemption summed up in Genesis 3:15 is from then on unfolded throughout the rest of Scripture. Another "Adam," who could exist only by means of birth, had to come and live a life of perfect obedience to God, all the way to a torturous death on the Cross. As we have pointed out earlier, some say that the redemption of mankind could have been accomplished only by God becoming a man and laying down His life, and this is known by the non-biblical term, "the Incarnation."[15] The answer to this very common teaching is so important that we must repeat it here. Such a "man" could not be a *true* man, as Adam was. As we are seeing, Scripture makes it plain that the Redeemer had to be a *man* so that he could *die* for the sins of all mankind (Heb. 2:9 and 14; Rom. 5:17). Is it really plausible that *God*, who is the Author and very essence of life, could *die*? Justice required that a representative of the race of those who sinned be the one to die to atone for that sin. This is the irrefutable logic of Romans 5:12–17, to which we will refer many times in discussing who Jesus is.[16]

Jesus Christ's original *genetic* purity, coupled with his subsequent *behavioral* purity, made him the perfect sacrifice for both the *sin nature* all men inherited from the First Adam and the

---

15. "The incarnation" is the phrase some theologians have coined to describe "when God became a man." We assert that the Bible does not teach that God became a man, but rather that He had a Son. Allow us to point out that the word "incarnation" never appears in Scripture. See Chapter 17.

16. It is common for Trinitarians to argue that Christ must be God because "a man could not atone for the sins of mankind." Theologians through the ages have varied greatly in their opinions of exactly how Christ could accomplish redemption for fallen man, and these theological musings can be found in any good theological dictionary under the heading of "Atonement." However, a standard argument goes something like this: "Mankind has sinned against an infinite God, and therefore the sin is infinitely great. It takes an infinite being to atone for infinite sin, and the only infinite being is God. Therefore, since Christ atoned for sin, Christ must be God." This argument, which seems reasonable to some people, is man-made, and nothing like it can be found in Scripture. What can be found in Scripture is simple and straightforward: "For just as through the disobedience of the one **man** the many were made sinners, so also through the obedience of the one **man** the many will be made righteous" (Rom. 5:19). There is not a single verse anywhere in Scripture that hints in any way that "God" was a sacrifice for sin.

"The Church Fathers" tried to explain in great detail how Christ could atone for the sins of mankind, and offered many different theories as to how atonement could be accomplished. Origen, Augustine and others believed that Christ was a payment made by God to Satan. Others taught that Christ was not a substitute for man, but rather a representative of man, and somehow the effect of his sufferings and resurrection extend to all mankind. In the Middle Ages, Anselm taught that mankind's sin offended God, and that Christ's redemption was an act of "satisfaction," to appease God. Abelard explained Christ's atonement in terms of love and the response of love elicited from the sinner due to Christ's example. The list of man's theories about exactly how our atonement was accomplished is long, and entire books have been written on the subject.

The reason for the varying theories is that the New Testament does not set forth a "theory of atonement," it just states the facts of the case, i.e., that Christ's death paid for sin. Scripture makes many and varied references to the atoning work of Christ. Christ is called a "sacrifice" (Eph. 5:2; Heb. 9:26), a "sin offering" (Isa. 53:10; 2 Cor. 5:21 [NIV alternate reading]), a "ransom" (Matt. 20:28; 1 Tim. 2:6; Heb. 9:15) and an "atoning sacrifice" (Rom. 3:25; 1 John 2:2, 4:10). We do not see the need or reason to build a "theory of atonement" when none is offered in the Word of God. The words of the Word are sufficient. As far as the subject of this book is concerned, the most important conclusion that can be drawn from what is revealed in the Word of God is that it is unbiblical to assert that Christ had to be God to pay for the sins of mankind when the Bible explicitly says that payment for sin came "by man." See also Chapters 16 and 17.

corresponding *sinful behavior* of all men who would ever live.[17] Because of His Son's sinless life and substitutionary sacrifice, God then had the legal right to extend grace to mankind. Jesus Christ became the perfect sacrifice and died in place of all men. Thus, those who appropriate unto themselves the benefits of this sacrifice by faith in Christ's atoning death exchange their inherent guilt for his righteousness. Hallelujah!

Not only did the Last Adam have to be able to die; he had to be able to *sin* as well. Many Christians have been taught that it was impossible for Jesus to sin, but, logically, the Last Adam, of necessity, had to have had the same freedom of will that the First Adam had. To say anything less is to devalue Jesus' walk of righteousness. His behavioral perfection was ultimately dependent upon himself alone. He had the choice of whether or not to obey God, and hence he was temptable. Scripture makes it clear that *God* cannot be tempted (James 1:13). If Jesus had not been able to sin like the First Adam, his temptations would have been inauthentic, and his "accomplishment" of perfect obedience would have been a foregone conclusion rather than truly praiseworthy. We will examine this subject further in the next chapter.

Remember that the whole Bible is essentially the story of two men and their effect upon mankind—the First Adam and the Last Adam. It points up the contrast between the First Adam's disobedience, death and production of a race of mortals (people destined to die), and the Last Adam's obedience, life and his production of a race of people who will live forever. This truth is clearly highlighted in the book of Romans, which is the foundational doctrinal treatise of the Church Epistles. The key passage we need to examine is found in Romans 5:12–19, where we see summarized the stark contrast between the First Adam and the Last Adam. Verse 12 delineates the twofold problem of sin and death that all mankind faces due to the sin of the First Adam.

> **Romans 5:12–14 (NRSV)**
> (12) Therefore, just as sin came into the world through one man, and death came through sin, and so death spread to all, because all have sinned—
> (13) Sin was indeed in the world before the law, but sin is not reckoned when there is no law.
> (14) Yet death exercised dominion from Adam to Moses, even over those whose sins were not like the transgression of Adam, who is **a type of the one who was to come**.

There are many people in the Old Testament who could be called "types of Christ." But this is the only place in the New Testament that directly points back to a particular person who would be *the* pattern for who the Messiah would be like. Adam was a "…type (pattern) of the one who was to come," in that both Adam and Jesus Christ had a universal effect on mankind by one act, as the next verses in the context elucidate:

> **Romans 5:15–19 (NRSV)**
> (15) But the free gift is not like the trespass. For if the many died through the **one man's trespass**, much more surely have the grace of God and the free gift **in the grace of the one man**, Jesus Christ, abounded for the many.

---

17. There can be a distinct difference in the usage of the terms "sin" and "sins" in the Word of God. Often, "sins" refers to the "fruit" of the old nature, while "sin" refers to the "root," or the old nature itself. See E. W. Bullinger, *The Church Epistles* (1991 reprint Johnson Graphics, Decatur, MI, 1905) pp. 27 and 28.

(16) And the free gift is not like the effect of **the one man's sin**. For the judgment following **one trespass** brought condemnation, but the free gift following many trespasses brings justification.

(17) If, because of the **one man's trespass**, death exercised dominion through that **one**, much more surely will those who receive the abundance of grace and the free gift of righteousness exercise dominion in life through the **one man**, Jesus Christ.

(18) Therefore just as **one man's trespass** led to condemnation for all, so **one man's act of righteousness** leads to justification and life for all.

(19) For just as by **the one man's disobedience** the many were made sinners, so by **the one man's obedience** the many will be made righteous.

It is easy to see the contrast between the two men in the above verses. This truth about the two Adams is also featured in another Church Epistle closely related to Romans—1 Corinthians. It addresses the practical failure of the Corinthians to adhere to the doctrine set forth in Romans.[18] It is therefore logical that the theme of the Last Adam should be revisited, and it is:

1 Corinthians 15:21 and 22 (NRSV)
(21) For since death came through **a human being**, the resurrection of the dead has also come through **a human being**.
(22) For as all die in Adam, so all will be made alive in Christ.

These verses sum up what we already saw in Romans 5:12–19. The question is, *how* did the Last Adam's "one act of righteousness," his dying on the Cross, make available everlasting life to all who believe in him? First, we will sum up the answer, and then we will look at a magnificent section of Scripture that expands upon it in more detail. The answer in a nutshell is this: only another "Adam," that is, *a man*, could rectify the tragic situation caused by the sin of the First Adam and accomplish the complete redemption of mankind. This is how we know that the Last Adam was a total human being.

As stated earlier, the problem God faced was twofold: *sin* and *death*, not just for the First Adam, but for all his descendants. The way in which the Last Adam would *solve* the problem would be in direct contrast to how the First Adam *caused* it. The First Adam *disobeyed*; the Last Adam was *obedient* unto death, even the death of the Cross. The First Adam's disobedience brought *death*; the Last Adam's obedience unto death brought *life*, via his *resurrection*. The First Adam produced a race of people *born dead* in sin; the Last Adam made it available to be *born again to life*, and he is now in the process of producing an *everlasting* race of perfect people.[19]

God's original plan was to have many sons and daughters living together in Paradise forever. The First Adam was *supposed* to have been the father of that perfect race; the Last Adam *will* be the "father" of such a race. Since the ultimate problem that mankind faced was death, the Last Adam had to defeat this daunting and terrifying enemy. The only way he could do so was by *dying*, so that

---

18. The truth about the position and structure of the Church Epistles is vital for each Christian to understand. See Appendix J.

19. See Chapter 14, and also listen to the following audio teachings on our website: www.TLTF.org, click Bible Teachings, then click Audio, under TLTF Audio Teachings scroll to "*Shining Like Stars in the Universe*," also on the same page click Bible Seminars and scroll to "*Jesus Christ, The Diameter of the Ages*."

God could then *raise him from the dead*, thus conquering death and giving him everlasting life. This truth is clearly conveyed by the following verses:

Romans 6:9 and 10
(9) For we know that since Christ was raised from the dead, he cannot die again; death no longer has mastery over him.
(10) The death he died, he died to sin once for all; but the life he lives [by resurrection], he lives to God.

Hebrews 2:9 and 14 (NRSV)
(9) but we do see Jesus, who for a little while was made lower than the angels [being made a man of flesh and blood who could die], now crowned with glory and honor because of the suffering of death, so that by the grace of God he might taste death for everyone.
(14) Since, therefore, the children [of Adam] share flesh and blood, he himself likewise shared the same things, so that **through death** he might destroy the one who has the power of death, that is, the devil.

What was God's goal? The restoration of His original dream of humans living forever on a perfect earth. The entire Bible points to the one who would be God's agent for bringing this about—Jesus Christ. Jesus Christ saw in the Old Testament Scriptures that if he would be obedient unto death, God would raise him from the dead and give him the power to produce a new race for a new age, an age in which he would rule on earth with God. Jesus Christ defeated our ultimate enemy, death, and he has guaranteed the same victory to all who believe on him.

As we see in the following verses, when Jesus Christ has completely accomplished the restoration of Paradise and produced a new race for a new age, he will report to God, his Father, and say, in essence, "Last Adam reporting; mission accomplished; Paradise regained." Then he will take his place as the Head and Firstborn of a great company of redeemed brothers and sisters in an everlasting family reunion in Paradise with his Father and his spiritual siblings. This awesome truth is communicated clearly in a section of Scripture that we will be visiting often in our journey to understanding the relationship between God and His Son Jesus Christ. It is particularly relevant here in connection with the completion of the Last Adam's work:

1 Corinthians 15:24–28
(24) Then the end will come, when he hands over the kingdom to God the Father after he has destroyed all dominion, authority and power.
(25) For he must reign until he has put all his enemies under his feet.
(26) The last enemy to be destroyed is death.
(27) For he "has put everything under his feet." Now when it says that "everything" has been put under him, it is clear that this does not include God himself, who put everything under Christ.
(28) When he has done this, then the Son himself will be made subject to him who put everything under him, so that God may be all in all.

This magnificent passage attributes the glory for the entire plan of redemption to its original Architect, God.

We have now squared off one aspect of the cornerstone for the Christian faith: *in order for him to redeem mankind, Jesus had to be whatever Adam was before his fall.* Jesus Christ is the Last Adam, a man like Adam who could undo what Adam did. The Last Adam, by dying on the Cross, sacrificed himself as an offering for the sin that the First Adam introduced into the world. This Adamic parallelism establishes one of the most foundational biblical truths regarding Christ, one that allows us to see the entire span of the Bible: two men, two gardens, two commands, two decisions, two deaths, two universal results, two races of people and two Paradises.

With such a simple but profound basis for biblical understanding, why engage in theological speculation about Christ's identity that can only complicate and compromise the beautiful literary symmetry and integrity of Scripture? We will now continue to compare and contrast the two Adams by looking at how both first and last are related to the important phrase, "the image of God." We're wasting precious time. The clock is ticking, I can hear the countdown.

2

The Destiny of Mankind
(Man As "The Image of God")

We will now continue to explore the Adam—Christ parallel as it relates to the original destiny of mankind and the concept of the "image of God." In America, "Madison Avenue" advertising moguls would have us believe that "image is everything." All too often, however, the "images" that advertisers create make people look like something they really are not, enabling them to misrepresent themselves. God, because He is invisible, is especially concerned about His image, but in His case He wants this image to exactly represent His true nature. Who was the *first* "image" of God? The First *Adam*. And, in the beginning, Adam was an able representation or "image" of God.

Genesis 1:26 (NRSV)
Then God said, "Let us make humankind in our image, according to our likeness; and let them have dominion over the fish of the sea, and over the birds of the air, and over the cattle, and over all the wild animals of the earth, and over every creeping thing that creeps upon the earth."

Adam was the absolute pinnacle of God's creative activities during the six days recorded in Genesis 1. In fact, Adam (and therefore mankind) was designed to be "the image of God," the glorious head of a race of people who would serve as the overlords of God's creation, sharing authority and dominion with Him over all that He had made. Man was equipped with godly attributes that enabled him to speak and act on God's behalf. Thus, he began his tenure on earth "...crowned with glory and honor," as the following verses show:

Psalm 8:3–8 (NRSV)
(3) When I look at your heavens, the work of your fingers, the moon and the stars that you have established;
(4) what are human beings that you are mindful of them, mortals that you care for them?
(5) Yet you have made them a little lower than God, and **crowned them with glory and honor**.
(6) You have given them dominion over the works of your hands; you have put all things under their feet:
(7) all sheep and oxen, and also the beasts of the field,
(8) the birds of the air, and the fish of the sea, whatever passes along the paths of the seas.

Sections from these verses are quoted in the book of Hebrews:

Hebrews 2:6–8 (NRSV)
(6) But someone has testified somewhere [Ps. 8], "What are **human beings** that you are mindful of them, **or mortals**, that you care for them?
(7) You have made them for a little while lower than the angels; **you have crowned them with glory and honor**,
(8) subjecting all things under their feet...."

What we read in Psalm 8 (then quoted in Heb. 2) is exactly what Scripture tells us in Genesis 1 and 2, and the writer of Psalms is in awe that God would put "a little dirt man" in charge of His magnificent creation.[1] In other words, that God would have such gracious regard for man is to His glory, and not due to man's intrinsic greatness. It is evident that from God's perspective, man was a lot more than a mere upright, animated dustball with opposable thumbs. God had big plans for him. But this first man, Adam, fell from his glorious position of responsibility and authority and ended up bringing suffering upon himself and all mankind. Thus, God's intention to glorify man was cut short because Adam disobeyed, but it would later be fulfilled and amplified in the Man Jesus Christ. If we are ever going to understand the nature and role of Jesus Christ, we must first clearly understand God's exalted purpose for mankind.

We have found that when we assert that Christ is the Last Adam, a fully human being and not God, orthodox Christians accuse us of making Christ a "mere man."[2] This argument has force, but

---

1. The Hebrew word *adam* literally means "red earth," an economical way of describing man whose body is essentially dust with blood coursing through it.

2. We would call this accusation an example of a logical fallacy called "attacking a straw man." This fallacy is committed when one party in a dispute misrepresents the position of the other in order to make it easier to refute. Just as it is easy

only because of what the word "man" has come to mean. To clarify the issue biblically, we must look past mankind's present sorry state and see the awesome beauty and perfection of what God originally intended "man" to be. He never intended for people to be dominated by sin nature—stubborn and rebellious against Him. God created mankind to be a race that would represent Him well, reflect His character and rule the world in loving submission to Him. Although today we speak of a "mere man" because sin so dominates our lives, God's original intention was not to create a "mere man," but a *masterpiece*.

Adam was intended as a prototype of that new model of creature that God unveiled in Genesis 1. But, like many prototypes, he failed to pass the test. However, God did not throw away the drawings. He hung onto them until the time when He could create another prototype patterned like the first one, a man who would fulfill mankind's destiny to be the crowning achievement of God's creation. Jesus Christ was God's second attempt at creating a masterpiece, the ultimate representation of that "masterpiece race" made in the image of God. There was nothing "mere" about Adam as conceived by God, and nothing "mere" about Christ who was made according to the same design.

Thus, by his sin, Adam turned the image of God into an image of sinful man.[3] Although that ended his rulership and dominion, Adam and his progeny continued to dimly reflect "the image of God." Although mankind no longer really lives up to the title of "image of God," God continued to use it as a reminder of man's destiny and purpose, and to communicate the value of man from His perspective.[4] It also served to point to the coming one, the Messiah, who would ultimately fulfill this destiny. Indicative of this is the following verse in Genesis 9, which occurs many hundreds of years after Adam's sin, in the context of God instructing Noah about the new arrangement He would have with mankind after the Flood.

Genesis 9:5 and 6 (NRSV)
(5) For your own lifeblood I will surely require a reckoning: from every animal I will require it and from human beings, each one for the blood of another, I will require a reckoning for human life.
(6) Whoever sheds the blood of a human, by a human shall that person's blood be shed; for **in his own image God made humankind**.

Immortality is a fundamental aspect of God's being and nature, and man, as "the image of God," was also made to be immortal. Though he lost this privilege, it is clear that man still reflected other aspects of God's "image," no matter how dimly. He can appreciate beauty and manifest artistic and

---

to knock over a straw man, so it is easy to topple an argument that is patently false. The "mere man" argument is a straw man because it does not consider the true biblical significance and destiny of mankind as originally conceived by God. See Appendix K for more detailed listing and explanation of logical fallacies employed in the field of Christology.

3. See Genesis 5:3, where Adam is said to have a son "…in his own likeness, in his own image…." This son, Seth, was made in the image of his sinful father Adam.

4. Only by perceiving mankind as made in the image of God is true human compassion possible. If mankind is merely the leading edge of blind and random evolutionary processes, his value is not patterned after anything, and he has no destiny. So, as a god-like being relative to lower life forms, man creates his own meaning and purpose by the things he chooses to do. He is answerable to no higher being, reflects no higher purpose and is headed toward no glorious or certain future. The concept of man made in the image of God is ultimately the only basis for an ethical system that values humans for their own sake and discourages the abuses of tyrants, murderers and others who see their fellow men as nothing more than a means to their own ends.

musical creativity.[5] He has a moral sense of right and wrong, and can choose to do right. He can reason from the known to the unknown. He can use language and other symbols to communicate his thoughts and intentions. In short, man can exhibit qualities that are more like those that God has than those that animals have.[6]

Because man was still the bearer of His image, God expected him to govern himself in a godly manner. Once all unrighteous people had been eliminated by the Flood, God held man accountable to maintain order by investing him with the ultimate civil authority, that of punishing murderers by putting them to death. God did not tolerate man murdering his fellow man, because He had invested a lot of Himself in man, and was committed to preserving the species. Why? Because it was to be through mankind that the Messiah, true Man, the Last Adam, the Redeemer would come. He would be everything God had hoped for man, fulfill man's destiny of co-rulership of Creation and become God's true and ultimate "image."

From Image Bearer To Image Maker

Sadly, man's spiritually childish inclination is to play God, in ways that range from the subtle to the blatant. Indeed, the essence of "religion" is that man is the *subject*, the "creator," if you will, and what he calls "God" is simply the *object* of his own vain reasonings. Since this "god" comes from the mind of man (often with help from Satan), it usually takes on an image made to look like mortal man" (Rom. 1:23). In other words, man brings God down to his level, or even beneath himself. The irony of this is that man ends up groveling before the very things over which God originally gave him dominion. Because of His love for Man, God strictly forbade the Israelites to make "graven images" of Him, knowing that any such attempt would result in at best a grossly distorted representation of Him. But even the Israelites, like the pagans around them, often made statues and other images of "God."

> **Romans 1:18–23 (NRSV)**
> (18) The wrath of God is revealed from heaven against all ungodliness and wickedness of those who by their wickedness suppress the truth.
> (19) For what can be known about God is plain to them, because God has shown it to them.
> (20) Ever since the creation of the world his eternal power and divine nature, invisible though they are, have been understood and seen through the things he has made. So they are without excuse;
> (21) for though they knew God, they did not honor him as God or give thanks to him, but they became futile in their thinking, and their senseless minds were darkened.
> (22) Claiming to be wise, they became fools;
> (23) and they exchanged the glory of the immortal God for images resembling a mortal human being or birds or four-footed animals or reptiles.

---

5. Some may object to the use of the term "create" in connection with man, but we use it not in the sense of truly "bringing into existence what has not been before," which is only God's domain. Man has "creativity" by virtue of his ability to fill an empty canvas with colorful images, a blank page with noble thoughts, or a concert hall with beautiful sounds.

6. Ephesians 4:24 provides additional insight into the meaning of the term, "the image of God." The "new self" or the "new man" that Christians receive in the New Birth is said to have been "…created to be like God in true righteousness and holiness." Therefore, God has provided the means by which mankind can return to the state of being he had when he was originally created "in the image of God," and reflected the true character of his Creator.

God's incredible handiwork, which is often called "nature," is in reality displaying *His* nature and goodness. The wonders of creation, which beg awe and thankfulness, are God's continual advertising campaign designed to alert people to both His existence and His beneficence (see also Heb. 11:6). No statue is big enough to block out a sunset. Psalm 115:1–8 compares the living God with dead pagan idols:

Psalm 115:1–8 (NRSV)
(1) Not to us, O LORD, not to us, but to your name give glory, for the sake of your steadfast love and your faithfulness.
(2) Why should the nations say, "Where is their God?"
(3) Our God is in the heavens; he does whatever he pleases.
(4) Their idols are silver and gold, the work of human hands.
(5) They have mouths, but do not speak; eyes, but do not see;
(6) they have ears, but do not hear; noses, but do not smell.
(7) they have hands, but do not feel; feet, but do not walk; they make no sound in their throats.
(8) those who make them are like them; so are all who trust in them.

The pagan nations surrounding Israel designed their idols just as we read in Romans—in the image of mortal men. As such, these senseless idols were always idle. No image of God fashioned by human hands would ever be sufficient to make known His glory. Through the Law that God gave to Moses for Israel, He provided a foreshadowing of His magnificent blessings yet to come.

Hebrews 10:1 (KJV)
For the law having a shadow of good things to come, *and* not the very image of the things, can never with those sacrifices which they offered year by year continually make the comers thereunto perfect.

A shadow is only a dark shape, with few defining characteristics. It is not at all a detailed image. This verse compares a shadow to the "very image [*eikon*]." Barclay describes the force of the word *eikon* in this verse: "a real, true, accurate, essential reproduction and representation, as contrasted with that which is shadowy, vague, nebulous, unreal and essentially imperfect. It is the complete perfection of the reproduction…"[7]

The New Testament Greek word *eikon*, translated "image," means "that which resembles an object, or which represents it, hence, image, likeness."[8] Our corresponding English derivative, "icon," is "a sacred image usually painted on wood or metal," or "an object of religious devotion."

---

7. William Barclay, *Jesus As They Saw Him* (Harper and Row, NY, 1962), p. 89.

8. E. W. Bullinger, *A Critical Lexicon and Concordance to the English and Greek New Testament* (Zondervan, Grand Rapids MI, 1976), p. 401. This definition is confirmed by *Thayer's Lexicon*, which says that *eikon* "adds to the idea of likeness the suggestions of representation (as a derived likeness) and manifestation." [Robert H. Thayer, *The New Thayer's Greek-English Lexicon*, (Lafayette, IN, Book Publisher's Press), 1981, p. 175]. Thayer cites Lightfoot's definitive study on Colossians 1:15 that identifies two main ideas in the word *eikon*: representation and manifestation. Barclay, *op. cit.*, *Jesus As They Saw Him*, p. 393: "If when we say that Jesus is the *eikon* of God, it means that Jesus is the *representation* of God; God is the divine archetype and Jesus is the human likeness of Him." The other meaning is *manifestation*. The *eikon* is the visible manifestation of the invisible and the unseen, of that which in itself cannot be seen. Plummer: "Jesus is 'the visible representative of the invisible God.'" W. E. Vine, *Vine's Complete Expository Dictionary Of Old And New*

In the Old Testament, God was adamant that His people not attempt to fashion an image of His likeness. He gave His people His Word, both spoken and written, by way of prophets who represented Him. From His Word they could know about Him and His love for them, yet all His revelation to them was but an introduction to His heart, a foreshadowing of a coming reality. It all pointed toward His ultimate communication to mankind—the Messiah, Jesus, the Christ, the living Word.

Hebrews Two: Christ As True Man

The New Testament book of Hebrews provides an important and foundational understanding of Man as he was made in the image of God, and this insight is crucial to understanding the identity of the Last Adam. Hebrews 1:4–2:4 establishes the superiority of the post-resurrection Christ over the angels.[9] Then, Hebrews 2:5–18 elaborates on the necessity that the Redeemer had to be a true man, another Adam. As we begin to look at this section, the subject in question is who will be in charge in the world to come.

Hebrews 2:5 (NRSV)
Now God did not subject the coming world, about which we are speaking, to angels.

This verse tells us who will *not* be in charge—angels. However, that does not tell us who *will* be in charge. Though we have already looked at these next verses in connection with mankind's original dominion, we now want to examine them more fully.

Hebrews 2:6–8
(6) But there is a place where someone has testified: "What is man that you are mindful of him, the son of man that you care for him?
(7) You made him a little lower than the angels; you crowned him with glory and honor
(8) and put everything under his feet." In putting everything under him, God left nothing that is not subject to him. **Yet** at present we do not see everything subject to him.

We must look at Hebrews 2:8b again carefully: "…In putting everything under him [the First Adam], God left nothing that is not subject to him.[10] Yet at present we do not see everything subject to him [mankind]." By revelation, the writer of the epistle to the Hebrews refers back to Psalm 8, but after quoting it, he makes it clear that something has happened to change things from the way God originally set them up. The word "yet" is a contrasting conjunction, informing us that something has drastically changed. We can see now that mankind no longer has dominion over

---

Testament Words, p. 576: "In Hebrews 10:1, the contrast between the shadow and the very image has been likened to the difference between a statue and the shadow cast by it." The statue is the *eikon*, representing the real thing. The statue is obviously not the person himself.

9. We will discuss the prologue of Hebrews (1:1–3) in the next chapter, because it is a key element in the scriptural depiction of Jesus Christ as "the purpose of the ages."

10. Note in the words "…God left nothing that **is** not subject to him…" the use of the figure of speech *prolepsis* or "anticipation," wherein future events are spoken of as having already occurred in the present. We know that the use of "is" is figurative here because the verse goes on to say that "…at present we do not see everything subject to him," pointing to its future literal fulfillment in Christ. We have a related figure in English that is called the "historic present." This important figure of speech is vital to the proper understanding of the gospel of John, which so anticipates Christ's glory that it speaks of it in the present narrative of the events of his life. For more on this figure, see Chapter 8.

creation, but rather is at its mercy in many ways.[11] Paradise is definitely "lost," and the devastating evidence of that is all around us each day. Thank God that the next verse in Hebrews begins with *another* contrasting conjunction.

Hebrews 2:9
But we see Jesus, who was made a little lower than the angels, now crowned with glory and honor because he suffered death, so that by the grace of God he might taste death for everyone.

What do we have in verses 8 and 9 but, once again, the *two Adams*? The First Adam wrecked everything, and the Last Adam is fixing it. The phrase set off by commas, "...now crowned with glory and honor because he suffered...," ought to be considered as a parenthetical insertion, but let us hold that in abeyance for a moment while we consider the verse by reading around that phrase. What it clearly says is that Jesus Christ had to be a man like the First Adam (each was "made a little lower than the angels") so that he could *die* in place of all men. Had Jesus not been a *man*, he could not have *died*. The parenthesis tells us what we have already seen: *because* Jesus was obedient unto *death*, God has highly exalted him (Phil. 2:8ff). In contrast to Jesus who died, *God* is "immortal" and therefore cannot die.

Not only did Adam die, he brought death upon all men. He also brought suffering to himself and all human beings after him. Adam began in glory and ended in suffering; Jesus began in suffering, but was glorified in his resurrection and thereby led many "sons to glory," as the next verse shows:

Hebrews 2:10
In bringing many sons to glory, it was fitting that God, for whom and through whom everything exists, should make the author of their salvation perfect through suffering.

Here again is the critical truth that we have seen before. The first "son of God," Adam (Luke 3:38), was intended to be the source of *many sons* living a glorious everlasting life, but he disobeyed God and became the "author" of death instead.[12] So it would be the *other* "son of God," Jesus Christ, the Last Adam, who would be the "author of salvation" for people who believe in him. The Greek word *archegos*, here translated "author," means the "first one in line in a rank or file."[13] Jesus Christ has blazed a trail of perfect faith to the heart of God, and thus he has become "the way" to life everlasting.

There is another great truth in verse 10: Jesus was "made perfect" through suffering. Although through the virgin birth Jesus was given *genetic* perfection by his heavenly Father, he was not given *moral* (behavioral) perfection, which he had to learn and earn by obedience, as the following verses make crystal clear:

Hebrews 5:8 and 9 (NRSV)
(8) Although he was a Son, he **learned obedience** through what he suffered;

---

11. As Jesus demonstrated authority over creation ("...Even the winds and the waves obey him!" - Matt. 8:27), so those who believe in him can exercise a measure of authority over fallen creation by obedience and faith in the risen Lord. This is the significance of Mark 16:15–18, which describes the authority the disciples could exercise over poisonous snakes and the like as they went forth to preach the Gospel. This authority is not absolute, however, but relative to faith and particular revelation from God concerning what is available in any given situation.

12. Though Satan is formally labelled "the author of death" (Heb. 2:14), Adam was his agent and unwitting "co-author."

13. Bullinger, *op. cit., Lexicon*, p. 133.

(9) and having been **made perfect** [by overcoming his trials, including death], he became the source of eternal salvation for all who obey him,

The obvious and necessary conclusion of this truth is that it was possible for Jesus to sin. Just as he had to be able to *die* to be the Redeemer, so he had to be *able* to sin, but then resist the temptation to do so. This rounds out the parallel between Adam and Jesus, because if Jesus could not have sinned, he would not have truly been a man like Adam, who could and did sin. Neither Adam nor Jesus had a sin nature from birth, that is, a predisposition to sin, but each had the freedom and responsibility to choose between obedience and sin. Satan knew this, and thus unleashed his full arsenal of temptations upon Jesus.

We must repeat this truth for emphasis: *without having the potential for moral imperfection, Jesus would not have truly been like the First Adam.* Although it was possible for Jesus to have sinned like the First Adam, he chose instead to obey his Father.[14] If Jesus Christ could *not* have sinned, then he could not have genuinely been tempted in **all** ways, as Scripture says, and certainly not in any way that *we*, as human beings, can identify with. God's Word makes it clear that we are to draw strength from his example, so we must be able to relate to his experience of temptation. How could we possibly draw strength from knowing that "God in human flesh" resisted temptation? How could anyone be encouraged to overcome temptation from the example of *God* doing so? God's Word in Hebrews continues to reinforce this point:

Hebrews 4:15
For we do not have a high priest who is unable to sympathize with our weaknesses, but we have one who **has been tempted in every way, just as we are**—yet was without sin.

If Jesus had a "divine side" that equipped him to avoid temptation, as tradition teaches, then he was not tempted "[exactly] as we are." The rest of humanity must face temptation without such an advantage, for *we* are not "100 percent God and 100 percent man." If Jesus were "God," in any sense that affected his experience, could he really have been tempted *just as we are?* James 1:13 says that God *cannot* be tempted, much less succumb to any temptation. If Jesus could not have actually given in to temptation, then his "temptation" is neither *genuine* temptation nor a *real* test of character. In fact, if Jesus were "God," to say that he was able to resist temptation is to say nothing about him at all. In that case, his moral courage and sterling character become presupposed as a necessary part of his "deity," a concept that actually demeans Jesus rather than exalts him. In fact, in our experience, the more the identity of Christ is pushed toward "deity," the less meritorious his accomplishments become. They then become the anticlimactic work of a "God-man" for whom nothing is particularly

---

14. In general, "to sin" biblically means to disobey the will of God. If Jesus were "God," he could not have disobeyed the *will* of "God" because his will, by definition, would *be* "God's" will. Trinitarians will argue that he was fully tempted in his humanity, but not tempted in his "divinity." This "dual nature" doctrine is meant to protect him from the charge that he could have sinned in any way. But this theological device creates a more serious problem: it breaks the logical parallel between the First Adam and the Last Adam. Adam did not have a "dual nature" or a "divine nature" that lessened his ability to be tempted. If Christ had a dual nature, but Adam did not, then Christ is not truly the "Last Adam." Adam had an unblemished human nature, the commandment of God and the free choice of whether to obey it or not. The fact that God directly made Adam from the dust of the ground and spoke to him intimately did not prevent him from sinning. Similarly, the fact that God created the life in Mary's womb and had an intimate relationship with His Son, Jesus, did not prevent Jesus from sinning either. He, too, had an unblemished human nature, the commandment of God and the free choice to obey it or not. Unlike Adam, Jesus *chose to obey.*

difficult, and whose experience is certainly not an authentic struggle against sin to which *we* "mere humans" can relate.[15]

Hebrews 5:8 and 9 is God's Word, and it clearly says that *He made Jesus Christ perfect through suffering.* In other words, Jesus had to go through a process of purification and trial before he could be properly termed "perfected." He did not have this status by virtue of some intrinsic "deity" derived from his "incarnation," independent and transcendent of how he lived and behaved. If that were the case, the monumental heroism of his dogged obedience in the face of relentless, diabolical opposition would fade into mystical insignificance.

Let us continue to follow the logic of Hebrews 2, looking again at verse 14. God's Word continues to hammer home the truth that Jesus Christ had to be a one-hundred-percent, red-blooded human being like Adam was in order to save fallen humanity from the destruction wrought by the first man.

Hebrews 2:14 and 15
(14) Since the children have flesh and blood, he too shared in their humanity so that by his death he might destroy [render powerless] him who holds the power of death—that is, the devil—
(15) and free those who all their lives were held in slavery by their fear of death.

Once again we see that the reason Jesus had to be a man was so that he could *die* in order to conquer death. As the fact of death all around us makes clear, the Devil has not yet been destroyed, but his doom is certain—Jesus Christ is coming again to crush his head.

Hebrews 2:16 and 17 (NRSV)
(16) For it is clear that he did not come to help angels, but the descendants of Abraham.
(17) Therefore he had to become **like his brothers and sisters in every respect**, so that he might **be** a merciful and faithful high priest in the service of God, to make a sacrifice of atonement for the sins of the people.

Verse 17 clearly tells us that Jesus is *not a spirit being* like angels are, but rather *a human being* like unto the "brothers" he came to save. This likeness was not just superficial, or in appearance only. He was made like his brothers *"in every respect."* He was a partaker of man's limitations and need for dependence upon his Maker to avoid sin and find fulfillment. The only exception to this statement is that Jesus did not inherit man's sinful nature.

It is common even for people who do not believe in the Trinity to think there is a big difference between themselves and Jesus Christ, because they know that he did not have the sin nature they inherited from Adam. Most people are so dominated by their sin nature that they cannot even imagine what life would be like without it. But we must remember that the sin nature was not part of our humanity as God designed it. Adam and Eve did not originally have it, yet they were fully human, just as we are. The sin now inherent in us is an intrusion into our lives, like a virus in our blood. Although it is infecting us, it is not an intrinsic part of who we are. It is common for Christians to believe that they are tempted only because of their sin nature, but this is clearly not the case. Both Adam and Jesus Christ were tempted, and Scripture also speaks of things such as "the lust of the

---

15. Dunn, *op. cit., Christology in the Making,* p. xxxiv. "It might be pointed out that a Jesus who makes an Adamic choice is more of a model for Christian behavior (Phil. 2:1–13) than a pre-existent Christ."

flesh" and the "lust of the eyes." The fact that we are in a human body means that we become tempted by hunger, tiredness, wanting more than we need and by many other things as well.

God's Word tells us that as a young man, Jesus "*grew* in wisdom and in stature and in favor with God and men" (Luke 2:52). It also tells us that Jesus "*learned* obedience by what he suffered and, once made perfect, he *became* the source of eternal salvation for all who obey him" (Heb. 5:9). These truths are important in light of the word "become" in Hebrews 2:17 above. It took Jesus living a life of perfect obedience unto his death on the Cross for God to be able to raise him and make him the perfect High Priest who is "…touched with the feeling of our infirmities…" (Heb. 4:15 - KJV). We have now reached the apex of this magnificent section of Scripture describing the true humanity of Christ. It is because he actually suffered when tempted that he can now relate to our suffering and help us in the hour of our need.

> **Hebrews 2:18**
> Because **he himself suffered when he was tempted,** he is able to help those who are being tempted.

The truths of God's Word that we have thus far set forth in these first two chapters are the foundation of our redemption, that is, "Christianity 101." Only a *man* could redeem fallen *mankind*, but that man would have to be a *perfect* sacrifice, one who could fully atone for both the sin nature *and* the sinful behavior of all the descendants of the First Adam. Only one man in history could have filled the bill: Jesus of Nazareth. God created him with genetic perfection just like the First Adam had. In contrast to the First Adam, however, Jesus Christ chose to obey his heavenly Father all the way to his death on the Cross. God then crowned him with glory and honor because of the things he suffered, raising him from the dead. He also made him the perfect High Priest, the Head of the Body of Christ and the Lord over all. Truly, Jesus Christ has blazed a trail of perfect faith for us to follow, and, as the Savior, he invites all men to walk in his steps. Those who accept his invitation are born into the family of God and can mature into dynamic representatives of his character and love.

The Last Adam's "Nature"

Since we have been arguing for a precise parallel between the First Adam and the Last Adam, and have asserted that neither had a "sin nature," we must address the issue of what kind of "nature" each had. This subject has been hotly debated for centuries, before and after the "orthodox" position of the "dual nature" of Christ was formulated at the Council of Chalcedon in 451 A.D.[16] There it was decided that the official position of the Church was that Christ had both a human *and* a divine nature. That is to say, he was 100 percent God and 100 percent man. The orthodox believers asserted his complete humanity against the Gnostics and Docetics, who argued that Christ was not really a man at all, but only appeared to be a man. On the other hand, they asserted his "divinity" against the Arians, who argued that he was not God, but rather a created being. They also defended his divinity against those who questioned his virgin birth and divine Sonship.

We have already discussed some of what is wrong with the "orthodox" position, namely that Jesus could not have been truly tempted if he were in some way "God." But let us add a few other objections to this doctrine before attempting to determine a more biblical and rational alternative. First, the

---

16. See Chapter 19 on the seven Church Councils and their role in the development of Christian doctrine.

Chalcedonian formula is guilty of a logical fallacy called "equivocation." Equivocation involves the changing of the meaning of a term in the middle of an argument.[17] In equivocating the terms "man" and "God," Trinitarians create a separate category of being for Jesus Christ and remove him from the normal and customary meaning of each term as it is understood both biblically and experientially. Furthermore, what is asserted about Jesus Christ could not be asserted about Adam, who was truly the archetypal "man." Unless Jesus' nature before his resurrection was completely comparable to Adam's, he cannot properly and without equivocation be categorized as "man." To teach that Jesus is "100 percent God and 100 percent man" is 200 percent logical equivocation.

But merely to say that both Adam and Jesus had a "human nature" is inadequate, particularly since this term has become identified with the sinful aspects of man's being. We often say, "That's human nature," after someone has just done something wrong. Without getting mystical, theological or too speculative, we need to assess what we know about this thing called "human nature." There are no Scriptures that definitively answer the question, so we must begin our reasoning from a clear conception of what it means that Adam was made in "the image of God."

We know that Adam was designed to represent his Maker and be able to have intimate fellowship with Him. This means that he would have to have known God well enough to act on His behalf. It seems logical that Adam would also had to have been able to relate to who God was by sharing some of His attributes and capabilities. We can see from the context of Genesis 1 that God endowed Adam with the capacity to rule and have dominion over the animals. God gave Adam a personality[18] and a temperament, or disposition.[19] As anyone who has raised animals knows, most have characteristics individual to their personalities. Some are more dominant than others, some are more playful, some more trainable, etc. Every human parent learns that his or her children are each unique from the womb with a particular temperament or "nature" right from "the factory."

Medieval physiology proposed four basic conditions of body and mind: the sanguine, phlegmatic, choleric and melancholic. Each was a basic kind of temperament that human beings manifest, with both good and bad qualities. For instance, one with a choleric temperament is a "take-charge" kind of person. However, he may lack sensitivity toward the feelings of those he attempts to lead. One with a phlegmatic temperament is very calm and unruffled, but may be slow to act, and tend toward laziness. Though the systems vary, human personality research continues to support the basic concept that people fall loosely into these general categories of temperament types. That is, every human being has a particular nature that predisposes him toward certain kinds of behavior. We should note that this "predisposition" does not *cause* one to act in a certain way, but it does mean that in the absence of any determination or will to the contrary, the odds are good that the predisposed behavior will be carried out, often unconsciously.[20]

---

17. See Appendix K for a more complete discussion of logical fallacies, particularly equivocation.

18. "The quality or fact of being a particular person; personal identity; individuality." Also, then, "habitual patterns and qualities of behavior of any individual as expressed by physical and mental activities and attitudes; distinctive individual qualities of a person, considered collectively." *Webster's New Unabridged Universal Dictionary* (Deluxe Second Edition, Simon and Schuster, NY, 1983).

19. *Ibid.,* A disposition is defined as "one's customary frame of mind; one's nature or temperament; as in an amiable or an irritable disposition."

20. The study of personality types goes way back into ancient history. The fourfold models go back at least as far as the Greeks and were often related to air, fire, earth and water. The nine-fold enneagram dates before Christ, and originated in the Middle East, possibly Babylon. The terms we use in the text of this work are Medieval in origin. Books to study these personality types are available in any good library.

These behaviors can be evaluated biblically and morally to determine whether they are right or wrong, but much sinful behavior occurs by impulse without reflection. This is the influence of what Scripture calls "the flesh," that is, the sin nature inherent in all men. In the absence of strong moral training and education as children, humans tend toward selfish and careless behavior that the Bible defines as sinful. Also, we should note that whether people choose the kind of behavior for which they have a predisposition or whether they choose something else is a function of their free choice. Yet there seems to be nearly universal agreement among modern researchers about the influence of the genetic component on human personality and temperament. This "nature versus nurture" debate will continue to rage on, however, because of the intricate and delicate balance that seems to exist within the various aspects of human beings and their environments.

Since a genetic "nature" or "temperament" is so clearly an ongoing part of human being and personality, it stands to reason that it was also a part of the *first* human's being. Before he fell, Adam had a nature perfectly suited to bearing the image of God. Therefore, he had a "divine" nature, meaning that he shared some of the qualities and attributes of God, who was his source. By studying the character of God in His dealings with man, and also in the actions of Jesus and other men representing God, we can conclude that God is loving, peaceful, joyful, slow to anger, kind, good, faithful, gentle and self-disciplined, just to name a few. These qualities must have been in abundance in Adam, who was the son and image of God, as he administered Paradise and carried out the will of his Creator. He had every quality in whatever measure necessary for him to exercise his dominion over the earth. And because there was no sin, there was nothing sinful in his disposition, that is, nothing that would cause him to act contrary to the will of God.

If we think of Adam as a perfect image of God's character, one of the consequences of the Fall was to shatter that "mirror" into pieces. Now, instead of one man exhibiting the totality of God's attributes without sin, mankind would continue to reflect these qualities in a collective way, but mixed with sin. This explains why we continue to see human beings demonstrating compassion, creativity, moral strength, intellectual and scientific brilliance and feats of selfless courage. These godly qualities in man are consistent with what we would predict if mankind were in fact made in the image of God. Obscuring these godly qualities, however, are traits such as sinful self-interest, cruelty and indifference. These seem to often characterize man's behavior and experience, which is predicted by the Bible as a result of the consequences of sin.

Based upon this reasoning then, we believe that Jesus Christ had a perfect human nature, just as Adam originally had before it became fragmented and stained by sin. This means that Jesus exemplified in a single person every godly quality ever seen in mankind collectively. These qualities were present in his nature from his mother's womb, even as our children's temperaments are. He was the perfect blend of qualities and characteristics that God intended for man, as His "image," to manifest. In observing Jesus' behavior, we see his ability to be tough, yet tender; patient and slow to anger, yet appropriately aggressive and passionate. In short, Jesus Christ was a man as Man was intended to be—the reflection of his Creator and his Father—like Father, like Son.

One further note: Jesus Christ did not fulfill his ministry by virtue of some inherently divine nature that he brought with him through an "incarnation." The New Testament makes it very clear how he was able to do the Messianic works that he did—by being anointed with holy spirit at the baptism of John.

Luke 3:21 and 22 (NRSV)

(21) Now when all the people were baptized, and when Jesus also had been baptized and was praying, the heaven was opened,

(22) and the Holy Spirit descended upon him in bodily form like a dove. And a voice came from heaven, "you are my Son, the Beloved; with you I am well pleased."

Luke 4:18 and 19 (NRSV)

(18) "The Spirit of the Lord is upon me, because **he has anointed me** to bring good news to the poor. He has sent me to proclaim release to the captives and recovery of sight to the blind, to let the oppressed go free,

(19) to proclaim the year of the Lord's favor."

Acts 10:38 (NRSV)

how **God anointed Jesus of Nazareth with the Holy Spirit and with power**; how he went about doing good and healing all who were oppressed by the devil, for God was with him.

As wonderful a human being as Jesus was, it is not recorded that he performed any miracle or preached a word until he was empowered by holy spirit. It was this *spirit*, then, and not his temperament, personality or intrinsic "divinity," that enabled him to do the works that he did. This is crucial to understand, and yet few Christians recognize this important point.[21] This is yet another truth that should profoundly encourage us as Christians, because it explains how we can do the works that Jesus Christ did.

> **John 14:12 (NRSV)**
>
> Very truly, I tell you, the one who believes in me will also do the works that I do and, in fact, will do greater works than these, because I am going to the Father.

Jesus Christ received from his Father the promised holy spirit and shed it on his disciples on the Day of Pentecost.

> **Acts 2:33 (NRSV)**
>
> Being therefore exalted at the right hand of God, and having received from the Father the promise of the Holy Spirit, he has poured out this that you both see and hear [i.e., holy spirit].

---

21. One of the main reasons so few understand this is the common teaching that "the Holy Spirit" is one of the persons in a "triune Godhead." Thus, they have difficulty explaining how Christ could be "God in human flesh" through the incarnation, yet still need to be empowered by "the Holy Spirit," another member of the Godhead, before he could begin to do his work. To many orthodox Christians, Christ is in some sense the eternal God from his birth, yet is indwelled at his baptism by another "person" called "the Holy Spirit," another member of the triune God. It is no wonder that some Christians refer to him as the "Christ event," since he was apparently three persons happening at one time. If Christ were "true God" from his birth, would he not have had God's power from his birth and not needed any subsequent anointing? See Appendix I.

The holy spirit enabled them to do the same works that Jesus had been doing. The book of Acts records the disciples doing just that. But if Jesus did his mighty works by being "God," how can we "mere men" hope to do the same?

The Last Adam's Family

Set in the heart of Hebrews 2:5–18 is a profound truth: every Christian is related to Christ in the most intimate, family way. He is not a being of such exalted status that we cannot relate to him. In fact, he is called our "brother." Let us now look at verses 11–13.

> **Hebrews 2:11**
> Both the one [Christ] who makes men holy and those who are made holy **are of the same family** [have the same Father]. So Jesus is not ashamed to call them **brothers**.[22]

This verse is brimming with truth. It clearly states that God is the original author of life for *both* Jesus Christ *and* all who believe in him. Yet Jesus Christ is the one who sanctifies those who believe in him. It was *God* who gave him the authority and the ability to do so. As Jesus is the Son of God, so those whom he sanctifies are "sons." Jesus Christ is not ashamed to call us his brothers. Amen!

In the next two verses from the same context, there are three quotations from the Old Testament about the coming Redeemer.

> **Hebrews 2:12 and 13 (NRSV)**
> (12) saying, "I will proclaim your name to my brothers and sisters, in the midst of the congregation I will praise you."
> (13) And again, "I will put my trust in him." And again, "Here am I and the children whom God has given me."

The first quote is from Psalm 22:22, found in one of the sections of the Old Testament most clearly referring to Jesus Christ. It is a prophecy that the Messiah will one day stand amidst a great congregation and praise God with them. Could those people be the "many sons in glory" of Hebrews 2:10? Absolutely. It is noteworthy that Psalm 22 is a prophecy of both the *suffering* and the glory of Christ. What was Jesus thinking about when the Roman soldiers pounded the first spike into his wrist? No doubt he was thinking about his future destiny, that is, "…the joy that was set before him…" (Heb. 12:2).

The second quote from the Old Testament ("…I will put my trust in him…") is from Isaiah 8:17. Jesus Christ was the first man to perfectly trust God. He was the epitome of faith. Because he put his trust in God, we can put our trust in him. The NIV Study Bible note on Hebrews 2:13 recognizes that the point of this quotation is to assert *the perfect manhood of Christ*: " 'I will put my trust in Him.' An expression of true dependence on God perfectly exemplified in Christ. In him, humanity is seen as it was intended to be." Amen. We could not have said it any better. Jesus Christ was able to do what he did because of his "true dependence on God." Man was originally made to have intimate

---

22. Consider also the following translation of the above verse, which clarifies the distinction between God and Christ: "The truth being that he who bestows the hallowing [Jesus Christ] and those who are being hallowed derive their origin, one and all, from the One [God]. And that is why the Son is not ashamed to call them his brothers." Heinz Cassirer, *God's New Covenant: A New Translation* (William B. Eerdmans, Grand Rapids, MI, 1989).

communion with his Maker, trust in His superior wisdom and love and, through obedience to his Creator, share with Him in the management of His affairs on the earth. Jesus epitomized this dependency on his God, his Maker.

The third quote from the Old Testament in this section of Hebrews comes from Isaiah 8:18, and could hardly be extracted from a more pertinent context, which reveals that Isaiah and the people of God were surrounded by a much larger number of unbelievers bent on their destruction. Death was certain unless God delivered them. God did deliver them by way of Isaiah, who said in essence, "Stick with me and you will be saved." He then referred to them as **the children God has given me**. In that record, Isaiah is a "type" of Christ.[23]

Here we come face to face with a tremendous truth of Scripture not often realized—that those who believe in Christ are, figuratively speaking, his "children."[24] To see this, let us go back to Isaiah 53, another Old Testament passage of Scripture that specifically speaks of the coming Christ. As in the initial revelation about Christ in Genesis 3:15, where God prophesied both his suffering and his glory, so Isaiah 53 portrays both his hideous death and his glorious future life.

Isaiah 53:7–12

(7) He was oppressed and afflicted, yet he did not open his mouth; he was led like a lamb to the slaughter, and as a sheep before her shearers is silent, so he did not open his mouth.

(8) By oppression and judgment he was taken away. **And who can speak of his descendants?** For he was cut off from the land of the living; for the transgression of my people he was stricken.

(9) He was assigned a grave with the wicked, and with the rich in his death, though he had done no violence, nor was any deceit in his mouth.

(10) Yet it was the LORD's will to crush him and cause him to suffer, and though the LORD makes his life a guilt offering, **he will see his offspring** and prolong his days, and the will of the LORD will prosper in his hand.

---

23. A "type" is a specific parallel between two historical entities. Biblical typology involves a correspondence by analogy such that earlier persons, places or events are patterns by which later events can be better understood or interpreted. The study of typology comes out of a study of the Bible itself. The New Testament uses both the words *tupos*, or "type," and *antitupos*, or "antitype." The Greek word *tupos* can refer to the original model, prototype or stamp as well as to the copy, imprint or mark that was left by the original. The word *antitupos* refers only to the copy, imprint or mark and not to the original or stamp. Romans 5:14 calls Adam a "...pattern" (a *tupos*) of "the one to come," i.e., Christ, while Hebrews 9:24 calls the earthly sanctuary a "copy" (*antitupos*) of the real one in the heavens. There has been great debate among Christians as to what are the true types of Christ in the Bible and what is strained imagination and fanciful thinking. For example, just because someone was whipped in the Old Testament does not mean he was a "type" of Christ, but, on the other hand, the clear parallels between Joseph and Christ or Abraham/Isaac and Christ have been recognized for centuries. In this case, the fact that what Isaiah said is quoted in Hebrews as being prophetically spoken by the Messiah makes the type axiomatic and abundantly clear.

24. The spiritual "fatherhood" of great men of God is evident in Scripture. In Romans 4:16, Abraham is called **the father of all of us who believe**. In 2 Kings 2:12, Elisha cries out to Elijah his mentor, "My father, my father." In 2 Kings 13:14, Jehoash the king of Israel called Elisha "My father, my father." Paul refers to his "fatherhood" of the believers in Corinth whom he had led to Christ (1 Cor. 4:15 - KJV), saying that he had "begotten" them through the Gospel. Because of his character and attributes, and being the author of everlasting life, Jesus Christ is obviously the ultimate "father" figure, even though he has no natural children. God's Messiah, Jesus, will conquer the earth (Rev. 19), raise the dead (John 5:25), and reign as king in the Millennium. Thus, in Isaiah 9:6, part of the Messiah's *name* is "Father of the coming age." See Appendix A (Isaiah 9:6).

(11) After the suffering of his soul, he will see the light of life and be satisfied; by his knowledge my righteous servant will justify many, and he will bear their iniquities. (12) Therefore I will give him a portion among the great, and he will divide the spoils with the strong, because he poured out his life unto death, and was numbered with the transgressors. For he bore the sin of many, and made intercession for the transgressors.

Verse 8 asks, "…And who can speak of his descendants?…" What we see here is that Jesus would die without ever having any children. In the Hebrew culture, this was considered a curse. Jesus died with no one to carry on his lineage. But look at verse 10: "…he will see his offspring…." What "offspring"? The "children God has given him," the "many sons in glory." Does this not specifically relate to Christ being called a "seed" in Genesis 3:15? Yes, he is the seed that will bear *much fruit after his kind*. "…We know that when he appears, we shall be like him…" (1 John 3:2). Praise God!

Jesus Christ: The Image of God

With all this background in mind, we can now turn our attention to the phrase "the image of God," as it is used in reference to Jesus of Nazareth. The Last Adam, now highly exalted as Lord and Christ, is the only *true* image of God. Actually, he is not referred to as "the image of God" until after his resurrection, as we shall see. So while Jesus admirably represented God's heart, love and character in his earthly ministry, he is now in a position of such glory that he is functioning "just like God."[25] Man's destiny as the image-bearer of God finds complete fulfillment in the glorification of Jesus Christ, because all those who believe in him will one day be made *like him*.

Even prior to his resurrection and ascension, however, Jesus brought many things to light about his invisible Father, the God who created the heavens and the earth. In fact, of all the "images" and representations that presume to depict the invisible, it is Jesus Christ who most vividly exemplified and made manifest the character of God by the way he lived. The heart and will of God was manifested by his life of obedience. For instance, we know it is God's will to heal those with faith in Him because Jesus healed *everyone* who came to him with faith. So it is for everything that Jesus said and did—he revealed God's heart and will for those who believe in him. As one scholar put it, "Christ is given to us as the image of God by which we may know what God wills and does."[26]

John 1:18 (KJV)
No man hath seen God at any time; the only begotten Son, which is in the bosom of the Father, he hath declared *him*.

The Greek word for "declared" means "to lead or bring out, hence to make known, declare, unfold."[27] By his personality, his character, the spirit that was upon him and by his absolute obedience to his Father, Jesus perfectly exhibited God's heart to mankind. His language, taken as a whole, reveals that he never thought of himself as the source of his wisdom and mighty works. When he said, He "…who has seen me has seen the Father…" (John 14:9), he was not referring to any physical resemblance nor

---

25. Immortality is a large part of what is meant by "the image of God," as is indicated by the fact that this phrase is only used of the *resurrected* Christ, who is now immortal himself.

26. Gerhard Kittel, ed., *Theological Dictionary of the New Testament* (Wm. B. Eerdmans, Grand Rapids, MI, 1964, "*Eikon*"), p. 396.

27. Bullinger, *op. it., Lexicon*, p. 210.

intrinsic deity. He was referring to his obedient way of being, his words and his works. The following are a number of statements Jesus made that help us understand this more clearly:

- "…the Son can do nothing on his own, but only what he sees the Father doing; for whatever the Father does, the Son does likewise" (John 5:19 - NRSV).
- "…the Father who dwells in me does his works" (John 14:10 - NRSV).
- "…I have made known to you everything that I have heard from my Father" (John 15:15 - NRSV).
- "All that the Father has is mine…" (John 16:15 - NRSV).
- "…whoever sees me sees him who sent me" (John 12:45 - NRSV).

Jesus shared with others everything that God showed him. His was a reflective and representative role, honoring his Father at every turn, emptying himself of any need for recognition or approval. His only desire was to do the will of God (John 4:34) and to bring Him glory.

We can learn another important thing about the word *eikon*, "image," by observing the following verses:

Matthew 22:17–21 (KJV)
(17) Tell us therefore, What thinkest thou? Is it lawful to give tribute unto Caesar, or not?
(18) But Jesus perceived their wickedness, and said, "Why tempt ye me, ye hypocrites?
(19) Shew me the tribute money. And they brought unto him a penny.
(20) And he saith unto them, Whose *is* this image [*eikon*] and superscription?
(21) They say unto him, Caesar's; Then saith he unto them, Render therefore unto Caesar the things which are Caesar's; and unto God the things that are God's.

It is clear that the coin-carrying Pharisees did not pull out one with Caesar himself glued to it. The coin had an *image* stamped on it, which was obviously not *identical* to the original.[28] In fact, the image was probably only a crude likeness. The degree of similarity between the archetype or prototype and its image varies, and the uses of *eikon* reflect those variations. The range of use of *eikon* varies from gross misrepresentation (as in the case of false images of God), to similarity (as in Col. 3:10 - KJV), where our new self is being renewed in similarity to Christ), to exact likeness (Heb. 1:3).

Today, through photographic technology, we can reproduce exact images of people.[29] Or can we? A lady friend excitedly shows you a snapshot and proclaims, "This is my fiancé, Henry." You reply, "But

---

28. Logical "identity" is established by the following principle: Whatever is true of A, must also be true of B. And whatever is true of B, must also be true of A. Logically, *similar* things are not *identical*. For example, a statue (image) of George Washington is not identical to George Washington. If it were, George Washington himself would have been made of bronze. See Appendix K.

29. The diminutive form of *eikon—eikonion*—corresponds to the modern photograph. Barclay, *op. cit., Jesus As They Saw Him*, p. 390: "Apion the soldier writes home to his father Epimachus: 'I send you a little portrait (*eikonion*) of myself at the hands of Euctemon.'" Barclay continues: "The word *eikon* becomes the regular word for the identifying description of a person, which was subjoined to official documents, in particular with regard to the buying and selling of slaves. The *eikon* was the official and accurate description of the person involved and the means whereby he or she could be identified. If we take it in this way, we may say that Jesus is the exact portrait and description of God."

he's completely flat! And he's only three inches tall with half a body! I don't think the marriage will work." Obviously, an image, no matter how perfectly it reflects the original thing, is not *identical* to it.[30]

There are two verses in the Church Epistles that clearly and specifically refer to Jesus Christ as "the image of God," and we will now examine them carefully in their contexts. We will see that Christ's being called the "image of God" most specifically refers to his glorious post-resurrection ministry at the "right hand of God" since being crowned with glory and honor. Remember that Hebrews 2:9 says the Last Adam is "…**now** crowned with glory and honor because he suffered death…." In other words, he didn't fully come into his "glory and honor" until after his death and resurrection. We should also point out 1 Corinthians 15:45: "…The first man Adam became a living being, the Last Adam, a life-giving spirit." When did he become "a life-giving spirit"? *After* his resurrection and glorification. Does that mean that he did not represent his Father well during his earthly ministry? No. We have already established that Jesus always did the will of his Father. However, whatever it is to be the complete "image of God" is found in his exaltation and glorification at the right hand of God.

Let us revisit Hebrews 1:3, which communicates this truth powerfully. Although this verse is often applied to the earthly life, ministry and being of Jesus Christ, upon closer examination we can see that it is referring to his post-resurrection life:

Hebrews 1:3a (NRSV)
He [The Son] is the reflection of God's glory and the exact imprint of God's very being, and he **sustains** all things by his powerful word….

Notice that the verbs "is" and "sustains" are in the present tense and refer to his present state of being in glory at the right hand of God. We can understand how Christ would be a better representation of God at the right hand of the Father's glory than hanging from his Cross. In fact, those who saw him thought him smitten and accursed of God (see Deut. 21:23 and Isa. 53:4). While dead, he was as far from radiating the glory of God as a person can get. Nevertheless, he was raised from the dead unto immortality and everlasting life, with a fabulous new body that enables him to act as the Head of the Church and work with all the members of his Body wherever they are in the world. He is now the ultimate representative of God. If people are unable to see him for who he is, it is because they have been blinded by the Adversary, as the following verses show:

2 Corinthians 4:3–6 (KJV)
(3) But if our gospel be hid, it is hid to them that are lost:
(4) In whom the god of this world hath blinded the minds of them which believe not, lest the light of the glorious gospel of Christ, **who is the image of God**, should shine unto them,
(5) For we preach not ourselves, but Christ Jesus the Lord; and ourselves your servants for Jesus' sake.

---

30. Various Trinitarian scholars try to force eikon to mean identity or equality with the original. For example: The use of *eikon* in Colossians 1:15 "is intended to indicate the essential unity of God and Jesus, of the Father and the Son." (*Ibid.*, p. 388 and 389). Kittel, *op. cit., Theological Dictionary*, Vol. II, p. 395: "When Christ is called the image of God, all the emphasis is on the equality of the *eikon* with the original." Trinitarian theologians attempt to force the semantic range of *eikon* to include the concept of identity, but the uses of *eikon*, both biblical and secular, preclude this extrapolation. See Appendix A (Col. 1:15).

(6) For God, who commanded the light to shine out of darkness, hath shined in our hearts, to *give* the light of the knowledge of the glory of God in the face of Jesus Christ.

It is the Gospel, the good news of Christ's accomplishments, that brings to light the glory of Christ, and thereby the glory of God whose plan it was to send him. The written Word makes known the living Word, Jesus Christ, who makes known the one true God. Thus, a "succession of representation" is clearly articulated in the above verses. We preach not ourselves, but the Gospel of Christ. Christ represented not himself, but God. And God "…shined in our hearts, to give the light of the knowledge of the glory of God in the face of Jesus Christ." Because Jesus Christ gave his all to represent God, God is now reciprocating by making known Christ, His perfect representative and "the exact representation of His being."

The other verse that specifically refers to Jesus Christ as the image of God is also in the Church Epistles.

Colossians 1:15 (NRSV)
He is the **image** of the **invisible** God, the firstborn of all creation;

Let us take note of the use of the word "invisible" here. God's invisibility has been the occasion of much rebellion and idolatry on the part of His people throughout history. They wanted something visible to worship and pray to like the pagans had, and this led to all manner of misguided activities, as even the most casual reading of the Old Testament will show. Fallen man has a "lust of the eyes," which drives him to desire a visible object for his devotion. Even though the creation itself so clearly points to the hand of its invisible Designer that man is "without excuse" (Rom. 1:20), he continually fails to make the connection.

Man is in many respects the pinnacle of that creation, his body and mind the most awesome examples of divine handiwork. The human brain has 10 billion cells, with each cell capable of establishing interconnections with some 35,000 other brain cells. The possible interconnections are 10 billion to the some $35,000^{th}$ power, an incomprehensibly huge number. What man's mind is capable of, even in its fallen condition, has yet to be fathomed. The First Adam was the "firstborn" of this magnificent creation described in Genesis 1, but, by virtue of his disobedience, he lost the privileges of the firstborn son. At his resurrection, the Last Adam became the firstborn of a new creation that began with his resurrection. He is the prototype of this new creation, his resurrected body gloriously exemplifying even greater magnificence than what we see in the present creation. That Christ is such a prototype is proven three verses later in Colossians 1, where the term "firstborn" occurs again:

Colossians 1:18 (NRSV)
He is the head of the body, the church; he is the beginning, **the firstborn from the dead**, so that he might come to have first place in everything.

In the context, "…the **firstborn** of all creation" directly correlates with his being "…the **firstborn** from among the dead…." It was in his *resurrection* that he came into his glory. It was then and only then that he was fully able to reflect the entire majesty of God who exalted him. Because he was sinless and obedient during his earthly tenure, Jesus' resurrection and exaltation catapulted him to a glorious dominion and co-rulership of God's creation even exceeding the First Adam's. Only when Jesus Christ was elevated to his present position of dominion and co-rulership, having sat down at the right hand of God with all authority fully delegated to him, was he said to be "the image of God" in all the fullness of the term. Thus, in this position he has fulfilled the destiny of Man, who was made in "the image of God."

Christians: Bearers of Christ's Image

In closing this chapter, we will look at three verses that complete our examination of the phrase, "the image of God," and also shed some valuable light on how this teaching affects us as believers in Christ.

> **Colossians 3:9–11 (NRSV)**
> (9) Do not lie to one another, seeing that you have stripped off your old self with its practices
> (10) and have clothed yourselves with the new self, which is being renewed in knowledge **according to the image of its creator**.
> (11) In that renewal there is no longer Greek and Jew, circumcised or uncircumcised, barbarian, Scythian, slave and free; but **Christ is all and in all!**

Our "new self" is the divine nature of Christ that is a part of what we receive when we obey Romans 10:9 and are born again. This reality, also called the "gift of holy spirit," the "spirit of truth," etc., is "being renewed in knowledge in the image of its creator."[31] Who is its creator? As far as giving us the potential to be like God, Jesus Christ is, because it is he who poured out the gift of God's nature into our hearts (Acts 2:33). He *is* all, and *in* all, and he is working in us to fashion us in his image, even as he is fashioned after God's image (cp. Eph. 1:22 and 23). This same truth is conveyed in the following parallel passage:

> **Ephesians 4:22–24 (NRSV)**
> (22) You were taught to put away your former way of life, your old self, corrupt and deluded by its lusts,
> (23) and to be renewed in the spirit [NIV "attitude"] of your minds,
> (24) and to clothe yourselves with the new self, created **according to the likeness of God** in true righteousness and holiness.

Today each Christian has within himself the absolute guarantee of one day being made totally like Christ (1 Cor. 15:49; Phil. 3:21; 1 John 3:1 and 2). In the meantime, God has given us through Christ the potential to manifest His character to the world. In fact, this is the very purpose of our existence—to represent our Maker well!

> **Romans 8:29 and 30 (NRSV)**
> (29) For those whom he foreknew he also predestined to be **conformed to the image of his Son**, in order that he might be the firstborn within a large family.
> (30) And those whom he predestined he also called; and those whom he called he also justified; and those whom he justified he also **glorified**.

---

31. For further study see our book by: Mark Graeser, John A. Lynn, & John Schoenheit, *The Gift of Holy Spirit: The Power To Be Like Christ* (The Living Truth Fellowship, 7399 N. Shadeland Ave., Suite 252, Indianapolis IN 46250, 2011).

As believers, we are already partial partakers of his heavenly glory, although our final glorification awaits his final appearing. Meanwhile, as we look to him, we are being transformed into "the likeness of His [glorious] Son" more and more, day by day. What an awesome privilege it is to be a Christian! These truths are further established in the following verses:

2 Corinthians 3:17 and 18 (NRSV)
(17) Now the lord is the [life-giving] Spirit, and where the spirit of the Lord is, there is freedom.
(18) And all of us, with unveiled faces, seeing the glory of the Lord as though reflected in a mirror, **are being transformed into the same image from one degree of glory to another;** for this comes from the Lord, the Spirit.

As the resurrected Lord, Jesus Christ is pouring out holy spirit, the spirit that is the basis for our transformation and our sharing in his glory. Now, through the life and ministry of the Last Adam, Jesus Christ, we too participate in the process whereby those of mankind who believe in him are truly able to reflect the image of God. As Perfect Man, he has fulfilled the original destiny of mankind by reclaiming the authority and dominion that the First Adam lost. Is he a *mere* man? Hardly. He is everything God originally intended for man, and more, which includes all glory and honor. And in his exaltation, we who believe on him will be exalted with him and share in his glory. Hallelujah!

3

Jesus Christ:
The Purpose of the Ages

Having established the direct correlation between the First Adam and the Last Adam, we now want to establish another aspect of our cornerstone: the biblical truth that Jesus Christ is the purpose, or the "diameter," of the ages. Perhaps the greatest purpose of Christ was the redemption of *mankind*, which he accomplished by his death on the Cross, as the following Scripture says:

> **Ephesians 1:7 (NRSV)**
> In him [Jesus Christ] **we have redemption through his blood**, the forgiveness of our trespasses, according to the riches of his grace.

Redemption is one of the central themes of the Bible, so it is vital that we understand what it is. Redemption is the entire process of redeeming, or literally "buying back" or "releasing on receipt of a ransom." This word "ransom" evokes images of a kidnapping, which is quite accurate, and leads to the question, *who* kidnapped *what* or *whom*? In a manner of speaking, Satan "kidnapped" God's creation by introducing iniquity into it. By tricking Adam, he plunged mankind into captivity through sin, death and the fear of death (Heb. 2:14 and 15). Although he is not big enough to hold creation for ransom in a literal sense, he has continually hindered (but not stopped) God's purposes, and he continues to exercise the authority he usurped. It was this authority that he offered to share with Jesus when he tempted him in the wilderness.

Luke 4:5–8 (NRSV)
(5) Then the devil led him [Jesus] up and showed him in an instant all the kingdoms of the world.
(6) And the devil said to him, "To you I will give their glory and all this authority; for **it has been given over to me, and I give it to anyone I please**.
(7) If you, then, will worship me, it will all be yours."
(8) Jesus answered him, "It is written, 'Worship the Lord your God, and serve only him.'"

There are two questions raised by the Devil's assertion that he has authority and power to bequeath on whomever he will, and the answers to them help us understand why a complete redemption of creation has become necessary. The first question is: who "gave" Satan authority over "...all the kingdoms of the world" so he could offer it to Jesus?[1] The answer to this takes us back again to Genesis 3. To whom had God given "dominion" over all the world? Adam. Who entered the picture to cause Adam's fall? Satan. So let's put two and two together. What was Satan's motivation to deceive Adam and Eve and cause their fall? Obviously, there had to be something in it for him. He was not just out for a cosmic stroll, playing little tricks on whomever he happened upon. Genesis 3:1 tells us that the serpent was "more crafty" than any other created being. His deliberate purpose was to trip up Adam and usurp his rulership by getting him to default on his responsibility and therefore forfeit his dominion and authority. Satan gambled that after Adam fell from grace, he would become the "top dog," since he was still an "angel of light" (even though a fallen one), and hence "superior" to Adam in spiritual ability.[2]

The testimony of the Bible is that he succeeded, creating a need for the redemption of God's entire creation. This would require someone to "crush" the serpent's head. Though God is his superior, and could have immediately made him dust, He chose only to make Satan "*eat* dust" (Gen. 3:14) until the day that he would be made ashes.[3] God chose to delegate the task of destroying His enemy, Satan, to His Son, the Redeemer and the Purpose of the Ages. The grand purpose of Jesus Christ's life is understandable only in relationship to Satan's rebellion and its consequences in heaven and on earth. As we have already seen, the scope of redemption would require both his suffering *and* glory, for Christ would not be equal to the task of crushing the Serpent's head until he entered his "glory." Not even the archangel Michael, the captain of the army of the host of the Lord, goes head-to-head with his former peer (see Jude 9 and Appendix F).

Though Satan's presence and influence are almost totally veiled in the Old Testament, he is described in the New Testament as a "prince" having a "kingdom," accompanied by "rulers,"

---

1. Theologian John Calvin proposed the idea that God is the one who gave Satan this power in order to glorify Himself and demonstrate His superiority. The Bible never says this, and we believe such a notion seriously compromises God's righteousness.

2. See E. W. Bullinger, The Companion Bible, (reprinted; Zondervan, Grand Rapids, MI, 1974), Appendix 19, for an interesting etymological study of the word "serpent," showing that Satan appeared to Eve as an "enlightened one," spewing out his demented "brilliance." 2 Corinthians 11:14 corroborates this truth: **Satan himself is transformed into an angel of light**.

3. See our book, *op. cit., Is There Death After Life,* Chapter 4.

"authorities," "powers", and "spiritual forces of evil in the heavenly realms" (Eph. 6:12). Jesus Christ totally exposed his kingdom and its effect on people (Luke 10:17–24), and is in the process of "bringing him to ashes" (Ezek. 28:18). Though Satan knows his days are numbered, he is insanely committed to hindering God's purposes and delaying the day of his doom, if he can. He is also trying to deceive as many people as he can so they do not believe in Christ and receive everlasting life in Paradise. As the father of pride and envy, he apparently reasons that if he is going to be destroyed, he will take as many people down with him as possible.

The second question in regard to Satan's authority is: was this authority that he offered to Jesus legitimately *his* to give, or was he lying? He is, after all, the "father of lies" (John 8:44). The most compelling answer to this question is the way Jesus answered the Devil. He did not question the fact that the Devil was making a legitimate offer. He simply recognized that there was too high a price to pay for what he was offering. We have no doubt that the Devil is still in the empire-building business, enrolling everyone he can in the pursuit of worldly fame, fortune, and self-promotion. And those he cannot lure into that trap he discourages and humiliates by setting before them unattainable ideals for "beauty, brains, and bucks." In case those traps fail, he provides counterfeit religious systems for "escaping the world," and persecution of those who choose to resist. He has all the bases covered, because he is the "systematizer" of error.[4] Surveying the state of the world since the time of Adam's fall, we would have to say that there is an invisible conductor orchestrating evil and masterminding events of nature and human history in a manner contrary to the will of God. But we do not have to rely on our experience for an accurate assessment, because God's Word says that this is precisely what is happening behind the scenes:

1 John 5:19 (NRSV)
We know that we are God's children, and that the whole world lies under the power
of the evil one.

So we see that the Redeemer still has a lot of work to do, and that redemption is still being accomplished. This is because not only did Jesus come to redeem *mankind* by giving his life as a sacrifice, God sent him to redeem *all of His creation*.[5] In the first part of his job, his enemy was sin and death, and Jesus' orders were to endure suffering and death caused by the sin of Adam. In the latter part of his assignment, Christ's enemy is Satan (and his demons), and his orders are to rise up in his glory and vanquish all the enemies of God.

This latter aspect of his job description requires that he deal *directly* with the one responsible for the introduction of sin and death into God's creation. Remember that the first time the coming Redeemer is mentioned in Scripture was when God prophesied to Satan in Genesis 3:15 that he would eventually be destroyed, not by God Himself, but by the offspring of the woman. This conflict and parallelism between Christ and the Devil is another aspect of the cornerstone of the Christian faith that must be cut correctly. When we consider this head-to-head fight-to-the-finish, we are

---

4. Satan uses strategy and systematizes error such that it continues generation after generation. The Apostle Paul wrote in Ephesians about people blown about by "craftiness in deceitful scheming" (Eph. 4:14 - NASB). "Craftiness" is from the Greek *panourgia*, and means "craftiness, cunning, unscrupulousness, false wisdom." It is the word used about someone who will use any and all means to achieve an end. The words "deceitful scheming" are translated from the Greek word *methodeia* (from which we get "method") and it means "deceit, craft or trickery" that has a plan or method behind it. Thus, the Adversary has an evil plan and method, and will use any and all means at his disposal to reach his sinister goals.

5. Romans 8:19–21 clearly says that the entire creation awaits the day when it will "...be liberated from its bondage to decay and brought into the glorious freedom of the children of God."

struck with an insight concerning God's righteousness. As God *could* not legally or righteously be the Redeemer of mankind because He could not die, He *would* not be the destroyer of Satan because His righteousness is so pure that it extends even to being fair and just to His archenemy. Though He could destroy Satan as easily as He had drop-kicked him from heaven, God delegated the destruction of Satan to one who would earn the right and the moral authority to do so—Jesus Christ! Though we cannot possibly know all that was in the Father's heart, we know from Philippians 2:8–11 that His plan of redemption is to His glory, and His plan involved *delegating the complete process of redemption to Christ*. God is there to help, guide, and direct as always, but He has invested in Christ **all authority in heaven and earth** (Matt. 28:18), more than enough to get the job done.

Our God is not as interested in getting the job done quickly and efficiently as He is in having it done **right**, as in *righteously*. There is also a majestic poetic justice involved in allowing Christ to be Satan's destroyer, because as Jesus walked the same path of temptation in the flesh that Adam walked, without sinning, so in his glorified position as Lord he is standing where Lucifer once stood, only without iniquity or pride being found in him. Hence, he is uniquely qualified to undo what Lucifer did when he scorned his privileged anointing at God's right hand as "the guardian cherub" in "the holy mount of God" (Ezek. 28:14).

Satan Started as a Star

Let us now look at the privileged position in which Lucifer began his existence, because understanding his relationship with God and the manner in which he lost it will help us appreciate Jesus Christ and his road to glory. Where Jesus began his earthly life in humility and ended it in ignominy, Satan began in glory and will end in ashes. His downfall was his fatally flawed decision to attempt to exalt himself to an even higher position than he was already given, to a position *just like God*.

The following account in Ezekiel 28 is the most detailed reference in the entire Bible to Satan's original state, his decision to leave it and his eventual complete annihilation. Note the use of language in verse 12, making it appear that this passage is addressed only to a particular "King of Tyre." It is evident, however, that though this king may have had a few faults of his own, they pale in comparison to the criminal antics of the one this passage is really being addressed to—the Cosmic Criminal, Satan, the crafty old "Serpent." Note also that God says here that *He* will be the one to destroy Satan, but this is not a contradiction of Genesis 3:15, which says that *the promised seed* would crush his head. There is a common Hebrew idiom being employed here in which the one whose plan it is can speak of doing the work, although he has actually delegated it to an agent.[6]

> **Ezekiel 28:12–19 (NASB)**
> (12) "Son of man, take up a lamentation over the king of Tyre, and say to him: 'Thus says the Lord God, "**You had the seal [i.e., you were the model] of perfection, Full of wisdom and perfect in beauty.**
> (13) "You were in Eden, the garden of God; Every precious stone was your covering: The ruby, the topaz, and the diamond; The beryl, the onyx, and the jasper; The lapis lazuli, the turquoise and the emerald; And the gold, the workmanship of your settings and sockets, Was in you. On the day that you were created They were prepared.

---

6. The Jewish rule of "agency" is explained in Appendices A (Gen. 16:7–13) and D.

(14) "You were the anointed **cherub who covers,** And I placed you *there* . You were on the holy mountain of God; You walked in the midst of the stones of fire.

(15) "You were **blameless in your ways** From the day you were created, Until **unrighteousness was found in you.**

(16) "By the abundance of your trade You were **internally filled with violence, And you sinned;** Therefore I have cast you as profane From the mountain of God. And I have destroyed you, O covering cherub, From the midst of the stones of fire.

(17) "**Your heart was lifted up** because of your **beauty**; You corrupted your **wisdom** by reason of your splendor. I cast you to the ground; I put you before kings [this will happen in the future], That they may see you.

(18) "By the multitude of your iniquities, In the unrighteousness of your trade, You profaned your sanctuaries. Therefore I have brought fire from the midst of you; It has consumed you, And I have turned you to ashes on the earth In the eyes of all who see you [also future, spoken of as past for the certitude of the event—"the lake of fire"—Rev. 19:20, *et al.*].

(19) "All who know you among the peoples Are appalled at you; You have become terrified, And you will be no more."

So we see that the present Adversary of God and His Christ began as "the model of perfection," beautiful and wise beyond comparison. From this description, he seems to have been the most graciously favored of all God's created beings. Would it be going too far to assert that God had given him *everything he could give a created being* without making him *identical to* Himself? We think this is what the above Scriptures are communicating. So it is all the more reprehensible that Lucifer became discontent, actually thinking that he deserved to be even *more* than he already was. Lucifer's pathetic example proves that it is *always* possible to be unthankful, no matter how much one has been given.

At this point let us turn to the description of Lucifer's fall as found in Isaiah. We have highlighted his five "I will" statements to accentuate the deliberate choice he made to reject God's grace (biblically, the number five indicates "grace"). Note that this passage ends with a revealing statement from God's perspective about who Satan really is when stripped of all his lies and pretensions. He is very small indeed, apart from what God has given him through His grace and generosity. When he is finally revealed for who he is, and judged in righteousness by the Son of Righteousness, all will marvel at what a pretender he really is, and how unworthy of notice.

Isaiah 14:12–17 (NASB)

(12) "How you have fallen from heaven, O star of the morning, son of the dawn! [KJV—"Lucifer"[7]] You have been cut down to the earth, You who have weakened the nations!

(13) "But you said in your heart, '**I will** ascend to heaven; **I will** raise my throne above the stars of God, And **I will** sit on the mount of assembly In the recesses of the north.

(14) '**I will** ascend above the heights of the clouds; **I will** make myself like the Most High.'

(15) "Nevertheless, you will be thrust down to Sheol, To the recesses of the pit.

---

7. The Hebrew word translated "Lucifer" in Isaiah 14:12 (KJV) actually means "shining star." The Latin Vulgate translated the Hebrew as "Lucifer," which made its way into the Roman Catholic Douay-Rheims Version and into the King James Version.

(16) "Those who see you will gaze at you, They will ponder over you, *saying*, 'Is this the man who made the earth tremble, Who shook kingdoms,
(17) Who made the world like a wilderness And overthrew its cities, Who did not allow his prisoners to *go* home?'

Remember that in Ezekiel 28 Satan was described as being "*full* of wisdom," until that wisdom was "corrupted…by reason of [his] splendor." Satan was, therefore, the original embodiment of God's wisdom in a created being, and it is not too big a stretch to imagine that he was God's companion in some aspects of creation. But instead of being blessed to participate with God in His divine functions, Satan desired personal "equality" with God, meaning that he would have the same powers and abilities as his Creator. He was apparently close enough to God to "taste" what it would be like to *be* Him, and considered such "equality" enough of a possibility that he thought he could get away with grasping for it. Instead, he lost his relationship with his Creator (because he apparently overlooked the fact that he was *created*), and to this day uses the awesome ability that God gave him to hinder His purposes, promote lies concerning the integrity of God's Word and bombard mankind with a plethora of possibilities for errant belief and worship. His demented goal is to make good look evil, and evil good, and the true God and His Christ look bad in any way he can. But like the primitive man who throws mud at the sun to dim its light, so all his centuries-worth of effort to obscure God and Christ from mankind will be to no avail, for one day "…every tongue [shall] confess that Jesus Christ is Lord, to the glory of God the Father" (Phil. 2:11).

The fall of Lucifer left a big hole in heaven, so to speak, as he vacated his position of authority and power as one of three archangels (along with Gabriel and Michael). He also persuaded one-third of the angels to leave with him in his descent to oblivion. This caused a radical restructuring of heavenly authority, the faithful angels having to fill the void left in the rebels' wake. The position Satan left was not easily filled, for he was "the finished pattern" (mold) when God created him to be his "right hand man."[8] Christ is the new mold, patterning himself exactly after his Father, as Hebrews 1:3 communicates. God had given the position to Lucifer as his "birthright," so to speak, since he just "woke up" one day as a created being equipped to the max. It is clear that God had already formulated a plan for filling this position with another exalted being. But we can surmise that He purposed in His heart that the next time it would be by someone *earning the right to it*, someone who would not try to grasp at equality with Him. The following passage highlights Christ's humility in contrast to Satan's prideful power-grab:

Philippians 2:5–11
(5) Your attitude should be the same as that of Christ Jesus:
(6) Who, being in very nature God, **did not consider equality with God something to be grasped,**
(7) but made himself nothing [KJV—"of no reputation"], taking the very nature of a servant, being made in human likeness.
(8) And being found in appearance as a man, he humbled himself and became obedient to death—even death on a cross!
(9) **Therefore, God exalted him to the highest place** and gave him the name that is above every name,

---

8. Bullinger, *op. cit.,* Companion, text note on Ezekiel 28:12, p. 1145.

(10) that at the name of Jesus every knee should bow, in heaven and on earth and under the earth,

(11) and every tongue confess that Jesus Christ is Lord, to the glory of God the Father.

Clearly, God has exalted His wonderful Son to "the highest place," a place that is "just like God," or functionally equal with God. This is *the very place that Lucifer wanted to be*, but because he grabbed for it, he was cast out of heaven. In contrast, Jesus is not concerned with having personal equality with God as Lucifer was. He is content to serve God in whatever way and in whatever role God gives him. Because of this humility, God has exalted him as high as He can exalt someone—to His own right hand, equal in authority, power and dominion with Himself. As Jesus said in Matthew 28:18, "...**All** authority in heaven and earth has been given to me." The delegation of this authority occurred right after his resurrection, but was realized when he was seated at the right hand of God after his Ascension.

The authority God has given Christ has placed him in a position of *functional equality with God*. Let's look again at 1 Corinthians 15:24–28, paying particular attention to the highlighted phrase in the last verse.

> **1 Corinthians 15:24–28 (NASB)**
> (24) then *comes* the end, when He (**Christ**) delivers up the kingdom to the God and Father, when He (**Christ**) has abolished all rule and all authority and power [by exercising his own].
> (25) For He (**Christ**) must reign until He (**Christ**) has put all His (**Christ's**) enemies under His (**Christ's**) feet.
> (26) The last enemy that will be abolished is death.
> (27) For He (**Christ**) HAS PUT ALL THINGS IN SUBJECTION UNDER HIS (**Christ's**) FEET. But when He (**Christ**) says,[9] "All things are put in subjection," it is evident that He (**God**) is excepted who put all things in subjection to Him (**Christ**).
> (28) And when all things are subjected to Him (**Christ**), **then** [in the future, not now] **the Son Himself also will be subjected to the One** (**God**) who subjected[10] all things to Him (**Christ**), that God may be all in all.

If the Son *will be* subject to God in the future at the end of his Millennial reign on the earth, the time to which this is referring, then what does that say about his *present* relationship with God, his Father? It says that presently Christ is fully authorized as God's appointed agent of redemption, not subordinate to His Father, but in a *functionally equal* position. He is in a relationship with God like the relationship that Joseph had with Pharaoh, personally distinct from Him but reigning with all His authority (we will explore this more fully in the next chapter). As the result of his resurrection

9. God says this in Psalm 8:6. However, in Psalm 8:6 God is not speaking in first person, rather Psalm 8:6 is the narration of the Bible, so it would be more natural for us to say, "it says," which is also a legitimate way to translate the Greek text.

10. The form of the Greek verb *hupotagēsetai* is used for both the passive and middle voice (R. C. H. Lenski, *The Interpretation of 1 and II Corinthians*, Augsburg Publishing House, Minneapolis, MN, 1963, p. 683). In the passive voice, Jesus would "be subjected" to God. In the context, all the enemies are subjected (passive voice) to God and Jesus whether they wanted to be subject or not. They had no choice. That is not the sense of Jesus being subjected to God, however. God will not use force, or the threat of force, to subject Jesus to Himself. Rather, the context and scope of Scripture show us the middle voice proper here: Jesus will voluntarily "subject himself" to God. Thus, verse 28 should read, "And when all things have been subjected to him (**Christ**), then the Son will subject himself to him (**God**) who subjected all things to him (**Christ**), that God may be all in all."

and ascension, Jesus Christ has the privilege to share with God in the dominion of all His Creation, not only in this, the Church Age, but in the coming ages as well.[11]

In reference to his original splendor, Lucifer was called a "morning star," which actually means "shining star." But he became too bright for his britches. Jesus Christ is referred to in Revelation 22:16 as the "**bright** morning star," indicating that he now exceeds Lucifer's original brilliance because of his virtuous character. By never trying to shine in his own light, but being content to reflect the Father's brilliance, Jesus has now been blessed by God to be a luminary of luminaries, shining alongside God at His right hand. God "broke the mold" when He created Lucifer, but Jesus Christ is *patterning himself* after his Father, as we will see later, in Hebrews 1:3. What Lucifer sought for and even grabbed at—equality with God—Jesus never even considered for a moment that it could be his. But since Lucifer's rebellion, God has longed for one to be His companion and share with Him in His many divine functions. Jesus Christ is now such a one, a glorious Lord not in any way competing with the Father, but cooperating with Him to His glory.

The question naturally arises at this point in our discussion: how can Jesus function in this exalted manner, considering that he is still a *man*? (1 Tim. 2:5). To answer that, we have to know something about his new body, and this is what we will explore next.

Two Jobs, Two Bodies

Christ's first body was perfectly suited for carrying out the first aspect of the job of "Redeemer." It was not stained with sin nature and yet it could die. Hebrews speaks of this body.

> **Hebrews 10:5–7 (NRSV)**
> (5) Consequently, when Christ came into the world, he said, "Sacrifices and offerings you have not desired, but **a body you have prepared for me**;
> (6) in burnt offerings and sin offerings you have taken no pleasure.
> (7) Then I said, 'See, God, I have come **to do your will, O God**' (in the scroll of the books it is written about me)."[12]

The "will of God" for Jesus Christ in the "suffering" part of his calling was for him to live an obedient life and then lay down his life for mankind. His body was therefore prepared as the perfect sacrifice. What was the will of God for Jesus Christ *after* his resurrection? It was for him to be highly exalted and actually *reign with God* on high, as King David, the Psalmist, had prophesied.

> **Psalm 110:1 and 2 (NRSV)**
> (1) The LORD says to my Lord, "**Sit at my right hand** until I make **your enemies** [especially Satan] your footstool."
> (2) The LORD sends out from Zion your mighty scepter. **Rule** in the midst of **your foes**.

---

11. Ephesians 1:21 says that Christ has been given authority "...not only in the present age but also in the one to come."

12. Note that the Messiah speaks of "God" in verse 7 as one wholly *other* to himself, and the One whose will he came to do. This is the same truth communicated in Heb. 1:9 (KJV), when it says "thy God," meaning that even in the Messiah's exalted position, he is to recognize God's personal superiority. His position involves only *functional* equality with God. When speaking to Mary Magdalene in one of his post-resurrection appearances, he said, "...I ascend to my Father and your Father, to **my God** and your God" (John 20:17 - NRSV).

The Jews had rightly expected that the Messiah would sit on the throne of *David* in Jerusalem and rule the earth in righteousness. It was this session on the Davidic throne that the Jews were avidly anticipating at the time of Christ's earthly ministry. But Psalm 110 referred to a time of an even greater exaltation—literally *sitting at the right hand of God.*

Clearly, to be able to perform in this exalted capacity, he would need to have a correspondingly exalted body. Reading between the lines of Psalm 110:1 and 2, we see that part of Christ's job is to subdue his "enemies" with God's help, but he did not subdue his enemies when he came the first time. In fact, his enemies subdued him, at least that is how it looked. In his resurrected glorification, however, he is able to subdue all things to himself (Phil. 3:21). He is presently working to destroy the works of his chief enemy, Satan, even as Genesis 3:15 had prophesied. Furthermore, he is empowering his people against the enemy as well. Ephesians 6:10ff indicates that there is a spiritual war raging all about us, and to successfully stand we must be "strong in the Lord," that is, rely on his strength in us.

So it stands to reason that part of what would equip Christ for his next assignment, ruling and reigning with God in heaven itself, was his having a body equal to the task. To begin with, this body would have to be equipped with the ability to transcend the physical limitations of earthbound existence. Five verses in Hebrews and one in Ephesians point to Christ's passage through "the heavens," or the *physical* universe, into "*heaven itself,*" a spiritual place where God and angels dwell.[13]

Hebrews 1:3b (NRSV)
…When he had made purification for sins, he sat down at the right hand of the Majesty **on high [i.e., in heaven]**,

Hebrews 4:14 (NRSV)
Since, then, we have a great high priest **who has passed through the heavens**, Jesus, the Son of God, let us hold fast to our confession.

Hebrews 7:26 (NRSV)
For it was fitting that we should have such a high priest, holy, blameless, undefiled, separated from sinners, and exalted **above the heavens**.

Hebrews 8:1 (NRSV)
Now the main point in what we are saying is this: we have such a high priest, one who is seated at the right hand of the throne of the Majesty **in the heavens**.

Hebrews 9:24 (NRSV)
For Christ did not enter a sanctuary made by human hands, a mere copy of the true one, but **he entered into heaven itself**, now to appear **in the presence of God on our behalf**.

---

13. In Scripture, both the words "heaven" and the plural form, "heavens," can refer to the atmosphere above the earth or to the dwelling place of God and angels. Verses showing that heaven refers to the atmosphere include those that have references to "…the birds of the air…" (2 Sam. 21:10, the word "air" is *shamayim*, literally, "heavens"), the wind blows in heaven (Ps. 78:26 - KJV), the clouds are in heaven (Ps. 147:8 - KJV), the snow comes from heaven (Isa. 55:10), or, the "rain from heaven" (Acts 14:17). The words "heaven" or "heavens" can also refer to the dwelling place of God, as many verses make plain.

Ephesians 4:8–10 (NRSV)
(8) Therefore it is said, "When he ascended **on high**, he made captivity itself a captive; he gave gifts to his people."
(9) (When it says, "He ascended," what does it mean but that he had also descended into the lower parts of the earth?
(10) He who descended is the same one who **ascended far above all the heavens, so that he might fill all things** [NIV "the whole universe"]).

So Christ now reigns in heaven in his resurrected body, which has been perfectly designed for him to function as God's right-hand man. He "fills" the hole in heaven left by the departing Serpent and his brood of vipers. He also now reigns over *the Church* as its Head, and he will appear again from heaven to literally rule *the earth* from Jerusalem for 1000 years. At the end of that time, he will destroy Satan and his associates, cast death and hell into the lake of fire and, having vanquished all enemies, enjoy the Final Paradise that is his reward. Amazingly, we who have believed in him will enjoy it along with him, our wonderful Redeemer.

Jesus Christ: The *Dia*meter of the Ages

The first three verses in the book of Hebrews clearly define the greatness of Jesus Christ as the "purpose of the ages." They are a kind of capsulation of most of the Old Testament and the Four Gospels, summarizing God's communication to mankind from His calling of the nation of Israel to His exaltation of Jesus Christ as Lord. They provide a fitting introduction to our examination of Jesus Christ as he is revealed in the Old Testament and the Four Gospels, as well as in the book of Acts and the Church Epistles. Let us begin with the first two verses:

Hebrews 1:1 and 2 (NRSV)
(1) Long ago God spoke to our ancestors in many and various ways by the prophets,
(2) but in these last days he has spoken to us by a Son, whom he appointed heir of all things, through [*dia*] whom he also created the worlds [ages].[14]

---

14. It is unfortunate that the King James Version usually renders the Greek word *aion* as "world," because it leaves the reader with the idea of place instead of time. The word *aion* generally refers to an age or a period of time (as does our English word, eon, which comes from the Greek *aion*, via Latin). This can be seen quite clearly in the New Testament itself, where *aion* occurs more than 120 times. In all but about a dozen of those, a literal version such as the NASB translates it by "age" or some other word indicating a period of time. About a dozen times "world" is used, but even some of those could be properly understood as referring to a time period, such as Matthew 13:22, which the NASB translates as "…the worry of the world…," but the NIV has as "…the worries of this life…." Galatians 1:4 speaks of Jesus rescuing us from "this present evil age." This brings up two questions: what is the duration of this present age and why is it evil? The answers are closely related. In Luke 4:6 (KJV), while the Devil was tempting Jesus, he told Jesus that all the kingdoms of the world were his to give because they had been "delivered unto him." Jesus did not dispute this claim because he knew it was true. Had it not been true, Satan's offer would not have been a temptation to Christ. When the First Adam originally disobeyed God, he lost his God-given dominion and authority over the Earth. Thus began the "present evil age," and it will not end until the Last Adam comes again and takes back this dominion and authority by force. In the meantime, Satan is referred to as the "god of this age" (2 Cor. 4:4). While living in this present evil age, each Christian is encouraged not to be "conformed to this world [age]" (Rom. 12:2), but to be transformed by the renewing of his mind. In Hebrews 1:2, the NIV mistranslates the Greek word *aion* as "universe," and many other versions mistranslate it as "world." They do that because it agrees with their theology that Jesus is God and He created the world, but the Greek does not have to be translated, or understood, in that way. For a thorough explanation of this verse, see Appendix A.

Clearly, the essence of these verses is that God has communicated to man by the spoken Word, by the written Word and finally by the created and living Word, His Son Jesus Christ. Verse two is sometimes used to attempt to prove that Jesus is the Creator, but a closer look at it in its context reveals the error of this assumption.[15]

Critical to this examination is the key Greek preposition, *dia*, of which E. W. Bullinger states:

> The word "through" is the Greek word *dia*, which when used with the genitive case: "...has the general sense of *through*...From the ideas of space and time, *dia*...denotes any cause *by means of* which an action passes to its accomplishment...hence, it denotes the passing through whatever is interposed between the beginning and end of such action.[16]

Jesus Christ is the "diameter of the ages," the golden thread woven throughout the royal tapestry of truth. He was in the mind and plan of God when Satan rebelled, when the First Adam sinned and all throughout the Old Testament as God patiently worked to preserve and protect his line of descent, the Christ line. Finally, the Redeemer was born and then lived his life flawlessly. As the exalted Lord, he will eventually bring to pass the complete redemption of Creation. Jesus Christ is the fulcrum and focus of history, which is really "His-story." In commissioning His Son as the Redeemer of mankind, God "put all His eggs in one basket," so to speak. Only Jesus Christ, the Last Adam, could do His will of redeeming Creation, and it would require the "ages" to consummate this master plan. As the focal point of the ages, Jesus Christ is the cause or the "means" through (*dia* = by means of) which God's plan is being accomplished.

Regarding God's plan of redemption through Jesus Christ, Hebrews 1:3 magnificently sets forth vital information concerning who, how and what. To see the depth of redemption relative to this

---

15. The phrase "...through whom he made the universe" (NIV) has been repeatedly used to support the doctrine of the Trinity, when it actually does not. The points made by J. S. Hyndman in 1824 are still valid today:

> "Through whom he made the worlds." It is really curious to observe the confidence with which this passage is brought forward in support of the idea that Jesus not only existed before he appeared as a man, but also that he created the material universe. The preposition which is here used in connection with *epoisen* ["he made"] is *dia*, which universally denotes instrumental agency, by way of distinction from *hypo*, which is almost universally used to signify primary or original causation. Supposing, then, that the notion of creation is conveyed by the original of the word translated "made," and supposing also that "world" is a correct translation of the Greek noun which occurs in the passage, what, I ask, would be the doctrine of the words? Would it be that the Son created the world as an original artificer? Surely not; but that God created it by the agency or means of Jesus Christ.

> This verse is parallel in the mode of its phraseology to the first verse. Now, as when it is said, "God spake through the Son," the universal doctrine of the New Testament is expressed respecting the source of our Savior's knowledge, *viz.*, that it was derived from Him who was greater than he, and that he was not the original fountain of his communications. So when it is said, "God made the worlds through his Son," it is no less clear and no less incontrovertible that all that is attributed to Jesus in the passage is an agency that is secondary and subordinate to that of the Supreme. Indeed, as in the former sentence, so in this, the very form and structure of the phraseology are more than sufficient to determine this point...

> Not in fact to admit that the words, "through whom also he made the world," convey the idea of instrumental agency in the Son, is either to make the sentence perfectly unintelligible or absurd...

> The proper and literal rendering of *aiones*, translated "worlds," is *ages* or *dispensations*. This is its natural and only proper meaning. It is so translated in almost all its occurrences in the New Testament, and in many instances must be so as to make sense and coherency in the sentences with which it stands connected.

J. S. Hyndman, *Lectures on the Principles of Unitarianism* (Alnwick, 1824. Reprinted by: Spirit & Truth Fellowship International, Martinsville, IN, 1994), pp. 125–127. (For more information on Hebrews 1:2, see Appendix A).

16. Bullinger, *op. cit.*, Companion, Appendix 104.

entire study, a number of words in verse 3 must be examined. First, we will look at five words in the first sentence:

Hebrews 1:3
The Son is the **radiance** of God's **glory** and the **exact representation** of his **being**, sustaining all things by his powerful word. After he had provided purification for sins, he sat down at the right hand of the Majesty in heaven.

In the above verse, the word "radiance" is translated from the Greek word *apaugasma*, which Thayer translates as "reflected brightness." Thayer goes on to say that Christ is called this because "he perfectly reflects the majesty of God."[17]

The word "glory" is defined as referring to "not the object itself, but the appearance of the object that attracts attention."[18] An apple may be nothing special, but a highly polished, glistening apple would stand out in a bowl of other apples and attract attention. A man may be nothing special, but *The Man* Jesus Christ shined among other men and attracted much attention.

"Exact representation" is *charakter*, which is found only in Hebrews 1:3. The word is derived from the verb *charasso*, meaning "to cut in; to engrave." The word means the exact impression as when metal is pressed into a die, or as a seal upon wax.[19] *Charakter* is "a distinctive sign, trait, type, or form, the image impressed as corresponding exactly with the original or pattern."[20] Jesus Christ has earned and been given the distinction of being the perfect representative of Almighty God. As we saw in Chapter 2 in connection with the Greek word *eikon*, Adam was designed to be the image, or the representative of God, but in large part disqualified himself by his disobedience. In contrast, Christ has, by virtue of his faithful obedience, continued to pattern himself after his Father.

"Being" is translated from the Greek word *hupostasis*, which appears four other places (2 Cor. 9:4, 11:17; Heb. 3:14, 11:1). It means "a substructure, what really exists under *or* out of sight, the essence of a matter in contrast to its appearance."[21] Its use in Greek literature supports this definition, as it indicates "the reality behind appearances." Its use in the Septuagint (a Greek translation of the Hebrew Old Testament) gives it the essence of a "plan" or "purpose."[22] This is added support for the idea that Jesus Christ is the "purpose of the ages."

The first part of Hebrews 1:3 may then be paraphrased as follows:

Jesus Christ is the reflection of God's power. He is the extraordinary Man whose appearance attracts attention. He radiates the character of God to the world, being the exact impression of God's heart. The invisible God is the unseen foundation upon which Jesus Christ built his life. God is the Author of the master plan of salvation, and Jesus Christ is the Agent who is carrying it out.

The remainder of verse 3 illustrates *how* he does so, and what he is accomplishing for mankind. The next clause to consider is, "…sustaining all things by his [Jesus Christ's] powerful word…." Jesus Christ is bringing to pass God's plan by his steadfast adherence to God's Word. He continues to adhere

---

17. Thayer, *op. cit., Thayer's*, p. 55.
18. Bullinger, *op. cit., Lexicon*, p. 323.
19. *Ibid.*, p. 401.
20. *Ibid.*, p. 401.
21. *Ibid.*, p. 582.
22. Kittel, *op. cit., Theological Dictionary*, Vol. VIII, pp. 578–582.

faithfully to God's plan for the Church Age. A mirror turned toward the sun will reflect its light very brightly, but if the mirror is turned away from the source of light, there will be no reflection, even though the sun is still shining. Even at the right hand of God, Jesus Christ keeps the countenance of his life fixed upon his heavenly Father, and always reflects God's light.

The next clause in Hebrews 1:3 "…After he had provided purification for sins…" shows *what* the Redeemer brought to pass by his faithfulness in acting upon the Word of God. When mankind's potential purification was complete, Jesus Christ sat down at the right hand of God. The purification of man's sins, and Jesus Christ taking his seat of authority on high, were completed once and for all. What this action accomplished for those who believe on him will be fully known only at his appearing.

While accomplishing the everlasting redemption of people who choose to believe on his name, Jesus Christ set a unique example of victorious day-by-day living. In so doing, he declared God to the world. Today, Jesus Christ is no longer on the earth, but those who are born again have "Christ" in them by way of holy spirit, his divine nature, and they can by Christlike faithfulness to God's Word manifest a similar attractive radiance. Each believer today can rise above the mediocrity of worldly men and shine extraordinarily to the end that his life is also a glory to God.

It is in the "face" of our Lord Jesus that we most clearly see the glory of God. Though we do not have a physical image of his "face," we are able to study his life and attributes in God's Word and get to know him in that way. We are also able to have a personal relationship with him via the gift of holy spirit. This is why, for successful Christian living, it is absolutely imperative that we dwell in the heart of our wonderful Savior day by day, making his attitude our attitude. The more we know and love the Lord Jesus, the more we know, love and glorify God, our Father.

One God & One Lord

Let us now cite another key passage of Scripture that corroborates the truths we just saw in Hebrews 1:1–3, and which also contains the thesis verse of this book.

> **1 Corinthians 8:4–6**
> (4) So then, about eating food sacrificed to idols: We know that an idol is nothing at all in the world and that there is no God but one.
> (5) For even if there are so-called gods, whether in heaven or on earth (as indeed there are many "gods" and many "lords"),
> (6) Yet for us there is but **one God**, the Father, **from whom all things came and for whom we live**; and there is but **one Lord**, Jesus Christ, **through whom all things came and through whom we live**.

Notice that the context in which verse 6 is found is specifically regarding the worshipping of idols, that is, false gods. Paul states that among the polytheistic heathen there are many gods and many lords, and he then draws a clear contrast between pagan polytheism and Christian monotheism [belief in only one God]. This expression of monotheism involves an absolute distinction between "God" and Jesus Christ, precluding the idea that Jesus Christ could be "God" in the same sense that the Father is "God."[23] In one of many clear identity statements that define who "God" is, verse 6 clearly says

---

23. Of course we do not dispute the fact that theos is apparently used in relation to Christ in a few verses of Scripture, most notably John 1:1, 20:28 and Hebrews 1:8 (for more information on these verses see Appendix A). As Jesus himself acknowledged, in John 10:34 and 35, Scripture employs a usage of "god" that is equivalent to "God's human representative."

that the only true "God" is "the Father."[24] John 17:3 also teaches this truth by recording the words of Jesus himself when he referred to God, his Father, as "the only true God." In light of the clarity of these verses, we marvel that so many Christians can accept the orthodox teaching that Jesus is "true God from true God" as the Nicene Creed propounds. Verse 6 is, in reality, a classic summation of the heart of true Christianity. Let us look at it again, this time in more detail.

1 Corinthians 8:6
Yet for us there is but one God, the Father, from [ek = "out from"] whom all things came and for [eis = "unto"] whom we live; and there is but one Lord, Jesus Christ, through [dia] whom all things came and through [dia] whom we live.

Please bear with us as we review a bit of basic grammar and parts of speech, carefully noticing the precise use of the prepositions in this verse. Prepositions are like signposts that direct the meaning of a passage. Notice the distinct and separate use of the Greek prepositions ek in relation to God and dia in relation to Christ. This should arrest our attention and keep us from speeding past these important signs on our way to a preconceived idea (and maybe getting a ticket for violating the laws of logic). The preposition ek in this context means "from" or "out from," while the preposition dia in this context means "through." The lesson of the verse is simple and clear. All things came from God, through Jesus to the Church.[25]

The NIV translation of the next clause related to God "...and **for whom** we live..." contains a fabulous truth. In the Greek text, there is no word for "live," and the word "for" is the word eis, usually translated "unto." When used with the accusative case, eis means "into, unto, to, implying motion to the interior."[26] It is saying, in essence, that "we were evicted, but He let us move back in." We are reconciled to God. How? Through (dia) the agency of Christ. Jesus is like a rental agent who paid our back rent and restored our relationship with the landlord. Or he is like the sports agent who wins a fabulous contract for us even after we've had a terrible year.

In John 14:6, Jesus said: "...I am the way and the truth and the life. No one comes unto the Father except through [dia] me," i.e., through my agency. In other words, the Holy God is on the other side of an immense chasm separating Him from sinful man. Without the agency of Jesus Christ, the Messiah, spanning the chasm by means of his atoning sacrifice and resurrection, we would be forever consigned to falling short of reaching God with our pathetic religious works and good intentions.

As we have now seen several times, the preposition associated with the Lord Jesus Christ is dia, meaning "through." Are we seeing a pattern here? A diameter is a straight line running all the way from a point on one side of the circle through the center to a point on the other side of the circle. God is the point on one side and man is the point on the other. The Man Jesus Christ is the Mediator, the straight line, between God and men (1 Tim. 2:5). He is "the bridge over troubled waters." He is The Way all the way unto the Father. Lo and behold, that is what the last part of 1 Corinthians 8:6 says,

---

What we object to is the way many Trinitarians equivocate the term "God" to mean "God the Father as distinct from God the Son." In the vast majority of the cases, the word "God" is used of the one-and-only true God who is also the Father of Jesus Christ. Understood without the equivocation, the term "God" logically excludes "the Son" of God," Jesus Christ. Without equivocating the term "God," how can anyone argue that anyone can be both "God" and "the Son of God" at the same time? See Appendix K.

24. See also Rom. 1:7; 1 Cor. 1:3, 15:24; 2 Cor. 1:2 and 3, 11:31; Gal. 1:1, 3 and 4; Eph. 1:2, 3 and 17, 4:6, 5:20, 6:23; Phil. 1:2; 1 Thess. 1:1 and 3; James 3:9, et al.

25. For a much more complete explanation of 1 Corinthians 8:6, see Appendix A.

26. Bullinger, op. cit., Lexicon, p. 403.

that through (*dia*) the one Lord, Jesus Christ, all things come from God to us, and through him we come unto God. How could God make any plainer the truth that He, the Father, is **the one true God**, and that His Son Jesus Christ is **the Lord** through whom He worked to accomplish the redemption of mankind? The Lord Jesus is the one and only agent of redemption, and the one "basket" in which God put all His "eggs."

The "Dynamic Duo"

Since God and Christ are working together so intimately, we have taken the liberty of calling them "the Dynamic Duo." This phrase communicates to us the fact that *both* God and Jesus Christ are involved in our lives and the process of redemption. Building upon the foundation we have laid from 1 Corinthians 8:6, let us see further biblical evidence of this One God, One Lord paradigm.

> **Ephesians 4:4–6 (NRSV)**
> (4) There is one body and one Spirit, just as you were called to the one hope of your calling,
> (5) **one Lord**, one faith, one baptism,
> (6) **one God and Father** of all, who is above all and through all and in all.

This section also marks out a distinct separation between the one Lord, Jesus Christ, and the one God, the Father. We also see the elevation of the Father as the one to whom all glory is due as the Source of "all," and Who is *over*, *through* and *in* "all." Note also the precise identity established between "God" and "the Father." There is no other true God beside "the Father." And the Son is not "God," but he *is* "Lord."

Every one of the Church Epistles begins with the salutation, "Grace and peace from God the Father and the Lord Jesus Christ." This fits with 1 Corinthians 8:6, which states that there is "one God the Father, and one Lord Jesus Christ." One plus one equals two. In Scripture, the number two denotes either division and distinction or establishment and confirmation.[27] In fact, without a distinction between two things, there could be no confirmation of one by the other. Regarding the relationship between God and Christ, the number two indicates both a separation and connection. The connecting word, "and," in itself indicates the distinction between God *and* Christ.

It is very important for us to see clearly the relationship between the one God, the Father, the *Author* of salvation, and the one Lord, Jesus Christ, the *Agent* of salvation.

---

27. E. W. Bullinger discusses the significance of the number two in his classic work on numbers in Scripture:

We now come to the spiritual significance of the number Two. We have seen that *One* excludes all difference, and denotes that which is sovereign. But Two affirms that there is a difference—there is *another*; while ONE affirms that there is not another! This *difference* may be for good or for evil…The number Two takes a two-fold colouring, according to the context. It is the first number by which we can *divide* another, and therefore in all its uses we may trace this fundamental idea of *division* or *difference*. The two may be, though different in character, yet one as to testimony and friendship."

Number In Scripture, Its Supernatural Design And Spiritual Significance, (Kregel Publications, Grand Rapids, MI, 1971), pp. 92–106.

Romans 15:8 (NRSV)
For I tell you that Christ has become a servant of the circumcised [i.e., Jews] on behalf of truth of God in order that he might **confirm the promises** [that God has] given to the patriarchs,

This verse says that Jesus Christ came to *confirm* God's promises to Israel, coming along as Number Two behind God, who is "Numero Uno," and who made the original promises to Israel.

What other verses can we find to clarify the distinction and the cohesion of "the Dynamic Duo?"

1 Timothy 2:5 (NRSV)
For there is **one God**; there is also **one mediator** between God and humankind, Christ Jesus, himself human,

By definition, a "mediator" is a separate person from each of the two parties between whom he mediates (Gal. 3:20). Jesus Christ is separate from God because he is a *man*, and he is separate from sinful mankind because he is God's only-begotten *Son* who had no sin nature and lived a sinless life. If Adam and his descendants had remained sinless, they would have had no need for a mediator. The introduction of sin into the life of mankind necessitated the mediation of a sinless man. Of course, Jesus knew this, as evidenced by what he prayed shortly before his death:

John 17:3 (NRSV)
And this is eternal life [life in the coming age], that they may know you, **the only true God**, and **Jesus Christ** whom you have sent.

Jesus referred to his Father as the *only true God*, and understood that God commissioned him as the agent of salvation. As the Head of the Church, the Lord Jesus works with our heavenly Father to direct the functions of its members and to help us carry them out, as the following verses make clear:

2 Thessalonians 2:16 and 17 (NRSV)
(16) Now may our **Lord Jesus Christ** himself and **God our Father**, who loved us and through grace gave us eternal comfort and good hope,
(17) comfort your hearts and strengthen them in every good work and word.

Another verse, perhaps somewhat "obscure" but nonetheless relevant to our context here, clearly illustrates the distinction and cohesion between God and His Son, as well as the conspicuous absence of a "third person."

2 John 9 (NRSV)
Everyone who does not abide in the teaching of Christ, but goes beyond it, does not have God; whoever abides in the teaching has both the Father and the Son.

Another passage that makes the distinction between God and Christ is 1 Corinthians 15:24–28. The distinction between God and Christ in this section is so abundantly plain that even in the text itself it is called "clear." Here the Word of God vividly declares the relationship between God and Jesus Christ as it relates to Christ having accomplished all the work God sent him to do and finally being made subject to God as His co-ruler on the new earth. We will now quote this passage again from the perspective of the clear separation between the *two*, identifying to whom each pronoun is referring. The way to determine the referent of the pronouns is to remember from Psalm 110:1 and 2 that *God* is the one who puts everything under Christ's feet, including his enemies. He gives Christ the authority to reign for a time, until his enemies are subdued.

1 Corinthians 15:24–28 (NASB)
(24) then *comes* the end, when He (**Christ**) delivers up the kingdom to the God and Father, when He (**Christ**) has abolished all rule and all authority and power.
(25) For He (**Christ**) must reign until He (**Christ**) has put all His (**Christ's**) enemies under His (**Christ's**) feet.
(26) The last enemy that will be abolished is death.
(27) For HE (**Christ**) HAS PUT ALL THINGS IN SUBJECTION UNDER HIS (**Christ's**) FEET. But when He (**Christ**) says, "All things are put in subjection," it is evident that He (**God**) is excepted who put all things in subjection to Him (**Christ**).
(28) And when all things are subjected to Him (**Christ**), then the Son Himself also will be subjected to the One (**God**) who subjected all things to Him (**Christ**), that God may be all in all.[28]

This passage contains echoes of another passage of Scripture that we looked at in the previous chapter in connection with the privilege extended to mankind. The language is applied to Christ, who, as we have discussed, is fulfilling mankind's destiny and privilege.

Psalm 8:3–8 (NASB)
(3) When I consider Thy heavens, the work of Thy fingers, The moon and the stars, which Thou hast ordained;

---

28. One of the reasons we quote this passage repeatedly is that it so clearly defines the relationship between God and Christ in both person and function. As such, it is very difficult for Trinitarian theologians to interpret in a way that is honest to the text. A stunning example of how a Trinitarian bias can color what would otherwise be an obvious interpretation of a passage is found in the NIV Study Bible note on the phrase "…the Son himself will be made subject to him…" (1 Cor. 15:28). The NIV editors attempt to elevate the Son with a distinction between person and function that, in effect, demeans the personal superiority of the Father:

> …The Son will be made subject to the Father in the sense that administratively [i.e., functionally], after he subjects all things to his power, he will then turn it all over to God the Father, the administrative head. This is not to suggest that the Son is in any way inferior to the Father. All three persons of the Trinity are equal in deity and in dignity [i.e., they have *personal* equality]. The subordination referred to is one of function. The Father is supreme in the Trinity [but only in a functional sense]; the Son carries out the Father's will (e.g., in creation, redemption); the Spirit is sent by the Father and the Son to vitalize life, communicate God's truth, apply his salvation to people and enable them to obey God's will (or word)….

This explanation is arbitrary. There is no mention of "equality in deity but difference in function" in these verses. The text is clear as it stands—the Son will be subject to "God" (not "the Father"). Simply reading the verses reveals the separation between "God" and Christ, and also reveals the superiority of God over Christ. The editorial bias of the NIV editors is further revealed when, after the passage in 1 Corinthians 15.24–28 has clearly separated "God" from "Christ," with no mention of "the Holy Spirit," they equivocate the term "God" to mean "the *Triune* God," instead of the God whose identity is "the *Father* of Jesus Christ," who is clearly the one in view. They then comment on the phrase "so that *God* may be all in all," as follows: "*The triune God will be shown to be supreme and sovereign in* all things."

(4) What is man, that Thou dost take thought of him? And the son of man, that Thou dost care for him?

(5) Yet Thou hast made him a little lower than God, And **dost crown him with glory and majesty!**

(6) **Thou dost make him to rule over the works of Thy hands; Thou hast put all things under his feet,**

(7) All sheep and oxen, And also the beasts of the field,

(8) The birds of the heavens, and the fish of the sea, Whatever passes through the paths of the seas.

A verse in the last chapter of the Bible corresponds with the Corinthians verses, and forever fixes the relationship of the "Dynamic Duo."

Revelation 22:3

No longer will there be any curse. The throne of God and of the Lamb will be in the city, and his servants will serve him.[29]

Hebrews 1: Christ's Superiority Over the Angels

Another important aspect of Christ as the cornerstone of our faith is his supremacy in heaven since his resurrection. This idea naturally and logically follows from the idea that Christ is functionally *equal* to God, because since God is obviously the highest authority in heaven, if He delegates that authority to someone, that person will share supremacy with God and reign over everyone else. Because Christ has been resurrected and has ascended into heaven, he now has authority and supremacy over the angels, as the following verses makes clear:

1 Peter 3:21b and 22

(21b) …It saves you by the resurrection of Jesus Christ,

(22) who has gone into heaven and is at God's right hand—**with angels, authorities and powers in submission to him.**

Christ's present superiority over the angels is also the subject of a detailed argument found in Hebrews 1:4–9 and 13, which we will now go through, visiting other corroborating parts of Scripture as appropriate.

Hebrews 1:4 (NRSV)

having **become** as much **superior to angels** as the name he has inherited is more excellent than theirs.

---

29. Certainly, if there were any such thing as a "Trinity," then all three persons should be present on this august occasion. "God the Holy Spirit" would also be included in all of the above verses we have considered, such as greeting the churches, etc. But, absolutely, "He" would have to be there on the final throne, or the "Godhead" would be incomplete. The truth is that there is but **ONE GOD** and **ONE LORD**, and they will together rule over a literal and physical "new creation," in fulfillment of God's original dream and plan.

We know that Christ *became* superior to the angels *after his resurrection*, because of what is written in the very next chapter of Hebrews:

Hebrews 2:9
But we see Jesus, **who was made a little lower**[30] **than the angels, now** [i.e., since his resurrection] crowned with glory and honor because he suffered death, so that by the grace of God he might taste death for everyone.

If he was to perform his earthly ministry as God desired, Jesus had to be made a man and not an angel. But, as he was made "a little lower" than the angels before his resurrection, he was made "a little higher" than they after it. As *spirit* beings, angels are not subject to the laws of physics. They fly without wings, appear and disappear at will, speak from the center of burning shrubs, comfort heroic believers thrown into giant furnaces, and often minister miraculously to those who "will inherit salvation" (Heb. 1:14).[31]

In contrast to angels, the first body that Jesus had was a distinctly *physical* body, and therefore subject to the laws of physics. He was subject to *gravity* because his body had real mass, *hunger* because his body burned food for energy, and *physical exhaustion* because, due to the law of inertia, energy must be continually applied to keep any physical object moving in space. When he wanted to go somewhere, he had to walk, and he got tired from journeying. His body needed rest, food and sleep as any human being's body does. When he got a splinter in his finger while working in his carpentry shop, it hurt, and it bled. When he was beaten and crucified, his body went into shock and he finally died like any other human body.

But, when Christ was raised from the dead, he was given a glorious body that enabled him to do everything that angels do and more. He is apparently no longer limited to the laws of physics as we understand them. He "passed through" the heavens in an instant, rather than at the speed of light. If he were a true "physical" being, as defined by the present laws of physics, he could travel no faster than the speed of light, and would just now be approaching the galaxies that are relatively close to the earth—a mere 2000 light years away! He passed through locked doors to greet the disciples who were huddled there in fear. He transformed his appearance so he would be recognizable or unrecognizable. In short, it appears that he can now do everything that angels do.

Yet, his body retains some kind of physicality, for Jesus specifically said that he is *not* "a spirit" (NIV—"ghost"): For "...a ghost [i.e., a true *spirit* being] does not have flesh and bones, as you see I have" (Luke 24:39). Besides having flesh and bones, he also has a digestive system, because he ate fish with the disciples, and as he stated, he will eat and drink with them again in the future kingdom. He encouraged Thomas to actually touch him to prove to himself that it was really he. And a particularly intriguing aspect of his new, glorious body is that it still bears the wounds of his injuries on the Cross—the nailprints in his hands and feet and the hole in his side, yet without blood.[32]

---

30. Although the KJV and NIV say that Jesus was a "little lower" than angels, that is not the best translation. First of all, what does it mean to be a "little" lower than angels? The Greek is better translated as it is in the RSV, NRSV, NASB. These say Jesus was "lower" than the angels for a "little while," but is now crowned with glory and honor, and is thus now "higher" than them.

31. Despite their various mysterious aspects, we do know one thing about angels biblically—they are *not dead humans!* See our book: *op. cit., Is There Death After Life?*, and our audio teaching: *The Ministry of Angels to Believers*, available to listen to free at: www.TLTF.org under Bible Teachings/audio/TLTF Audio Pod Cast.

32. It is a matter of intriguing speculation as to what animates his new body. We see a connection with 1 Corinthians 15:45 which calls the Last Adam a "life-giving spirit." It appears that he has "life in himself" (John 5:26), instead of having life "in his blood," which is characteristic of human and animal life in this present heaven and earth.

The first stage of Christ's "glory" was his resurrection from the dead, which represented a qualitative new beginning of his life. Every other person who had ever been raised from the dead, like Lazarus in John 11, got up with the same body. Jesus is the only person who got up with a wholly different body. It is highly noteworthy to us that although Jesus had been conceived divinely and born of Mary more than 30 years earlier through the normal processes (her pregnancy, grunting, labor pains, etc.) his resurrection is also spoken of as a *birthday!*[33] This we can see from the next verse in the first chapter of Hebrews:

Hebrews 1:5 (NRSV)
For to which of the angels did God ever say, "You are my Son; today I have begotten you"? Or again, "I will be his Father, and **he will be my Son**"?

The phrase, "…today I have begotten you" is a citation of a phrase that first appeared in the second Psalm, in connection with the Messiah's future rulership of the earth.

Psalm 2:7–9 (NRSV)
(7) I will tell of the decree of the Lord: He said to me, **"You are my son; today I have begotten you.**
(8) Ask of me, and I will make the nations your heritage, and the ends of the earth your possession.
(9) You shall break them with a rod of iron, and dash them in pieces like a potter's vessel."

Though the Jewish commentators at that time would have been hardpressed to see any connection between this phrase and the resurrection of the Messiah, it was clearly referring to it, as is seen in the Apostle Paul's use of it in his discourse to the Jews in Antioch of Pisidia.

Acts 13:32 and 33 (NRSV)
(32) And we bring you the good news that what God promised to our ancestors
(33) he has fulfilled for us, their children, by **raising Jesus** [from the dead]; as also it is written in the second Psalm, '**You are my Son; today I have begotten you.**'

What do we have here but the exulting of a Father at the "birth" of His Son ("Gabriel, Michael, have a cigar!"). Only this time His Son was not "begotten" to be *sacrificed*—he was raised from the dead to *reign*. That was something for the Father to shout about! We will now see from the next verse in Hebrews 1 that the term "firstborn" occurs in connection with his resurrection:

Hebrews 1:6 (NRSV)
And again, when he [God] brings the firstborn into the world, he says, "Let all God's angels worship him."

---

33. Trinitarian theologians who stress the "incarnation" of Christ as the cornerstone of Christianity cannot truly explain why Scripture would place such a high value on his resurrection, new body, seating at the right hand of God and being given "all authority" in heaven. To them, his incarnation represents the defining event of his life in eternity, when he divested himself of his pre-incarnate divinity and took on human flesh for a time. According to this thinking, his resurrection should then be the moment when he *returns to the glory he had before his incarnation,* including the authority that he had in heaven over angels as a co-equal member of the Trinity. We believe that the fact that Scripture places great emphasis on his resurrection is wonderful proof that he did not pre-exist his birth.

How do we know that this particular "birth" is referring to his resurrection? By the overall context, and because Hebrews 1:5 speaks of Christ's "birth" being his resurrection. This sets the context of verse 6, which also speaks of Christ being brought into the world. Also, at his first birth, the angels did not worship the baby. They worshiped **God** who brought him forth! This is evident in the only record in the Four Gospels where angels appeared at Christ's birth.

Luke 2:13 and 14 (NRSV)
(13) And suddenly there was with the angel a multitude of the heavenly host, **praising God** and saying,
(14) **"Glory to God in the highest heaven**, and on earth peace among those whom he favors!"

The "birth" that is spoken of in Hebrews 1:5 and 6 is referring to the resurrection of God's son from the dead. At his first birth, Christ was inferior to angels, whom God made to be glorious messengers and divine representatives:

Hebrews 1:7 (NRSV)
Of the angels he says, "He makes his angels winds, and his servants flames of fire."

Though angels are glorious, Jesus Christ's glory has exceeded theirs ever since he took his place at the right hand of God after his resurrection. As the *Son of God*, he has the rights and privileges of the firstborn, something never offered to the angels, as verse 5 above makes plain. And since, by grace, we believers in Christ are "*joint-heirs*" with him (Rom. 8:17 (KJV); Eph. 3:6), we are therefore entitled to the same rights and privileges— including having the same kind of glorious body in the future—as the following verses indicate:

Philippians 3:20 and 21 (NRSV)
(20) But **our citizenship is in heaven**, and it is from there that we are expecting a Savior, the Lord Jesus Christ.
(21) He will transform the body of our humiliation that it may be conformed to the body of his glory, by the power that also enables him to make all things subject to himself.

Thus, we also share in the benefits of the heavenly citizenship that is now ours because we are members of Christ's figurative "body," the Christian Church (Eph. 1:22 and 23). 1 Corinthians 15:45-49 also speaks of the "splendor" of the heavenly body that Christ received at his resurrection, and which we will receive also. It is a "spiritual" body that is in some ways physical, but nevertheless imperishable—meaning not subject to physical decay.

1 Corinthians 15:40–49 (NRSV)
(40) There are both heavenly bodies and earthly bodies, but the glory of the heavenly is one thing, and that of the earthly is another.
(41) There is one glory of the sun, and another glory of the moon, and another glory of the stars; indeed, star differs from star in glory.

(42) So it is with the resurrection of the dead. What is sown is perishable, what is raised is **imperishable,**

(43) It is sown in dishonor, it is raised in **glory.** It is sown in weakness, it is raised in **power.**

(44) It is sown a physical body, it is raised a **spiritual body.** If there is a physical body, there is also a spiritual body.

(45) Thus it is written, "The first man, Adam, became a living being"; the Last Adam became a **life-giving spirit.**

(46) But it is not the spiritual that is first, but the physical, and then the spiritual.

(47) The first man was from the earth, a man of dust; the second man is from heaven.

(48) As was the man of dust, so are those who are of the dust; and as is the man from heaven, so are those who are of heaven.

(49) Just as we have borne the image of the man of dust, **we will also bear the image of the man of heaven.**

We assume from this passage that in the new heaven and earth, God is going to change the very laws of physics, based upon the prototype of Christ's new body. This new body is based upon new principles and physical laws that are well above our limited capacity to understand in our present bodies. But someday in the future we will know fully even as we are fully known (1 Cor. 13:12).

Hebrews 1 continues to assert the superiority of the Son over angels:

Hebrews 1:8 and 9 (NRSV)
(8) But of the Son he says: "Your throne, O God,[34] is forever and ever [i.e., for a long time], and the righteous scepter is the scepter of your kingdom.
(9) You have loved righteousness and hated wickedness; therefore **God, your God,** has anointed you with the oil of gladness **beyond your companions."**

Christ's "companions" in this context include *angels*, who are subordinate to him and yet dwell with him in heaven in the presence of God. Because he is superior to them, everything that an angel can do, Jesus can do in his new body, and more. But because they are on the same spiritual plane of existence, the idea of companionship is appropriate.

Hebrews 1:13 (NRSV)
But to which of the angels has he [God] ever said, "Sit at my right hand until I make your enemies a footstool for your feet"?

Finally, verse 13 lays the capstone on this magnificent section of Scripture that has by this time firmly established two facts. First, Christ is superior to the angels, and second, this superiority occurred *after* his resurrection, ascension and exaltation. From this exalted position, he is currently in the process of completing the redemption prophesied in Genesis 3:15, wherein we find the purpose

---

34. Hebrews 1:8 is often used to attempt to prove that Jesus is "God" in some intrinsic sense, equal to God by virtue of his "incarnation." But the context is clearly his post-resurrection "Sonship" and exaltation to the right hand of God, where he is granted the privilege to rule and reign alongside God. As God's representative and empowered agent, he is spoken of as "God," following an established biblical pattern. Notice in verse 9 that though Christ is a kind of "God," (meaning "God-like") he still *has* a God to whom he is accountable, namely the one true God, his Father. See Appendix A (Hebrews 1:8).

for which the Redeemer would come, a *purpose of the ages*. This purpose encompasses the entire redemption of heaven and earth, fills the vacuum in heaven created by the loss of an archangel and one third of the angels, and involves Christ sitting in a place that Lucifer could conceive of but did not have the humility to be exalted to—functional equality with God!

These truths are corroborated in Colossians 1 in a section of Scripture that also speaks of the supremacy of Christ, and one to which we will be returning often in this book. This magnificent passage will harmonize with the many verses that we have examined in this chapter, elevate Christ and thus glorify God, his Father.

> **Colossians 1:15–19 (NRSV)**
> (15) He is the image of the invisible God, the **firstborn** [by resurrection] of all creation [i.e., the prototype of the new creation, the new heaven and earth];
> (16) for in [*dia*] him all things in heaven and on earth were created, things visible and invisible, whether [angelic] thrones or dominions or rulers or powers—all things have been created through [*dia*] him [i.e., through his obedient agency] and for him [i.e., with him in mind].
> (17) He himself is before all things [in priority], and in him all things hold together [he sustains all things, as Heb. 1:3 says].
> (18) He is the head of the body [of Christ], the church; he is the beginning, **the firstborn from the dead**, so that he might come to have first place in everything [i.e., he is over the angels and functionally equal to God].
> (19) For in him all the fullness of God was pleased to dwell,

Psalms 8 and 110 prophesied of this culminating glorification of the Son of God, the Messiah. In the next two chapters, we will examine the other Messianic prophecies contained in the Old Testament in order to understand what could and could not be searched out about the Coming One.

PART TWO

The Messiah
in Prophecy

4

A Prophetic Portrait of the Messiah

By the agreement of all Christians, the great subject of the Bible is Jesus Christ, the Son of God. While that truth is evident in the New Testament, it is equally present in the Old, though not as obvious. Furthermore, while it is clear that Jesus was indeed the subject of *general prophecy* throughout the Law of Moses, the Prophets and Psalms (Luke 24:25–27 and 44), a more vigorous study reveals an even richer portrait of the coming Messiah.

The Hebrew word *mashiyach* ("Messiah") means "the anointed one," and its Greek counterpart is *christos* ("Christ"). The Old Testament portrays the coming Messiah in hundreds of ways. He is foretold or foreshadowed both in prophecy and in typology. The Tabernacle and Temple alone depict him in dozens of ways. He is foreshadowed by the priests, the feasts, the sacrifices, the altar, the bread of the presence, the menorah, the mercy seat, the colors, the metals and the very dimensions themselves.

Indeed, God placed in orbit around the person and work of the coming Messiah almost the entire array of characters, images, objects and events in the Old Testament. In some books, the typology is obvious, while in others an application of the greater context of the Messiah's identity is sometimes required. Nonetheless, his prophetic "life" or "presence" courses palpably through every book as the lifeblood that sustained the world until the time when Jesus would actually be born and *physically* manifest the heart of God.

In light of the raging spiritual battle that is continually being waged by Satan against God and His Christ, it is not surprising that coming to a true recognition of the Messiah's identity is challenging. In fact, we must all humbly acknowledge our own capacity to be blinded by Satan, the enemy of Christ, and hindered from seeing this man for who he is. Let us visit a passage that speaks loudly in this regard.

2 Corinthians 4:3 and 4 (NRSV)
(3) And even if our gospel is veiled, it is veiled to those who are perishing.
(4) In their case **the god of this world has blinded the minds of unbelievers**, to keep them from seeing the light of the gospel of the glory of Christ, who is the image of God.

Lucifer has fallen from being a "morning star" to a spiritual "black hole." As such, he does his best to hold back the light of Christ to keep people from seeing and therefore believing. This was certainly true of the time immediately after Jesus' resurrection, when two of his disciples were making the seven mile [about 11 kilometers] trek to Emmaus after being in Jerusalem for the Passover and, as it turned out to their dismay, the *crucifixion* of the one they thought was going to be their Messiah. We think that this record in Luke 24 is a perfect introduction to this section of this book, which will look at what *could* be known about the coming Messiah from the Old Testament. Let us imagine that we were one of these two bewildered and shell-shocked "disciples" who had not yet made the leap to being actual "believers." Cannot we *all* say that we have stood in their places in our own journeys toward understanding and following the *true* Christ?

Luke 24:13–27 (NRSV)
(13) Now on that same day two of them were going to a village called Emmaus, about seven miles [about 11 kilometers] from Jerusalem,
(14) and talking with each other about all these things that had happened.
(15) While they were talking and discussing, Jesus himself came near and went with them,
(16) but their eyes were kept from recognizing him.
(17) And he said to them, "What are you discussing with each other while you walk along?" They stood still, looking sad.
(18) Then one of them, whose name was Cleopas, answered him, "Are you the only stranger in Jerusalem who does not know the things that have taken place there in these days?"
(19) He asked them, "What things?" They replied, "The things about Jesus of Nazareth, who was a prophet mighty in deed and word before God and all the people,
(20) and how our chief priests and leaders handed him over to be condemned to death and crucified him.
(21) But we had hoped that he was the one to redeem Israel. Yes, and besides all this, it is now the third day since these things took place.
(22) Moreover, some women in our group astounded us. They were at the tomb early this morning,
(23) and when they did not find his body there, they came back and told us that they had indeed seen a vision of angels who said that he was alive.

(24) Some of those who were with us went to the tomb and found it just as the women had said; but they did not see him."

(25) Then he said to them, "Oh, how foolish you are, and how slow of heart to believe all that the prophets have declared!

(26) Was it not necessary that the Messiah should suffer these things and then enter his glory?"

(27) Then beginning with Moses and all the prophets, he interpreted to them the things about himself in all the scriptures.

After the sting of his initial rebuke of their lack of diligence passed, imagine the way their hearts leapt and their minds opened as they got a personal tutorial in Old Testament history from the one it was all about![1] Even though at this point they did not realize who he was that was giving them this "short course," Old Testament 101, they were nonetheless thrilled at the insight. Did they wonder for just a second how odd it was that they should just *happen* upon a walking encyclopedia of Old Testament Messianic prophecies at the very time they were gloomily discussing their feelings of disappointment about Jesus? Talk about a coincidence!

Jesus began his teaching with "Moses," which means the first five books of the Bible (called the Pentateuch), expounding first Genesis 3:15 and then moving through the rest of the Hebrew Scriptures unfolding the Messiah's identity and calling along the way. Note how clearly he distinguishes between his "sufferings" and his "glory." Their eyes were finally opened to his identity later while eating with him, and they scampered back to Jerusalem to tell the others what they had seen and heard.

Later, apparently that same day, Jesus addressed a group composed of eleven of the Apostles, the two recent graduates of "The Road to Emmaus School of Old Testament Messianic History," and various others of his disciples. He gave this group a similar lecture he had given the two earlier, sharing portions of the "Law, Prophets and Psalms" pertaining to himself.

Luke 24:44–46 (NRSV)

(44) Then he said to them, "These are my words that I spoke to you while I was still with you—that everything written about me in the law of Moses, the prophets, and the psalms must be fulfilled."

(45) Then he opened their minds to understand the scriptures,

(46) and he said to them, "Thus it is written, that the Messiah is to suffer and to rise from the dead on the third day,

He also opened their minds to the awesome details of the prophecies in the Old Testament that were written about his suffering, death and resurrection—all the things they had been blinded to—so that they would have a *complete* portrait of the Messianic purpose of the ages and would thus be

---

1. Note that he held them responsible for their personal failure to believe *all* that the prophets had spoken, even calling them "fools." Their selective approach to Scripture is what he was addressing, because they clearly had believed *some* of what the prophets said. Like all of us, they had a tendency to gravitate toward the Scriptures that bolstered their Jewish nationalism and ignored the "messy" and embarrassing verses about a suffering Messiah who would be rejected by his own people. Note also that he left them no excuses, such as: "But *everyone* believed you were going to be a political deliverer" or, "But I had too much synagogue training," etc., etc. Though false teaching and teachers abound in every age, God and the Lord Jesus hold each of us responsible for the condition of our hearts, and whether they are "slow to believe," or diligent like the Bereans of Acts 17:11, who "…searched the scriptures daily, whether those things were so" (KJV). This is ultimately the only antidote for the blindness spoken of in 2 Corinthians 4:4.

able to stand with him in the completion of his purposes. So that we can have a similarly complete picture and fully appreciate the miraculous way God worked to accomplish our redemption, we must also carefully read the Old Testament in light of its subject, Jesus Christ. We need to recognize the prophetic "target" that was set up in the corridor of eternity, toward which God, like the master archer, set His bow. Even before releasing the Messianic arrow at the birth of Jesus, He had already established its trajectory by a constellation of carefully crafted prophetic words, set as points of light to guide the arrow as it would eventually streak through the night. Beginning in Genesis 3:15 with the image of the promised seed of the woman, the Old Testament Scriptures lead the diligent seeker to a "bullseye" understanding of the suffering, death and resurrection through which the Messiah had to pass on the way to his glory. If he were to fly straight and true, it was incumbent upon Jesus to learn in detail the entire prophetic course of his life. This he did impeccably, and it is both available and important for us to learn it as well.

What follows is our best understanding of what such a synopsis of the Old Testament would be like, when looked at in light of "all the things" that were written concerning the coming Christ.

The Golden Thread

- In **Genesis** he is the seed of the woman (3:15 - KJV).
- In **Exodus** he is the Passover Lamb (12:11).
- In **Leviticus** he is the High Priest (21:10).
- In **Numbers** he is the one lifted on a pole who gives healing (21:9).
- In **Deuteronomy** he is the prophet from among his brothers (18:15).
- In **Joshua** he is the captain of the LORD's host (5:14 - KJV).
- In **Judges** he is the stone that crushes the heads of his enemies (9:53 - KJV).
- In **Ruth** he is the kinsman-redeemer (3:9).
- In **1 Samuel** he is the ark and mercy seat before whom pagan gods bow (5:3).
- In **2 Samuel** he is the King—declared by prophets and anointed with oil (5:3).
- In **1 Kings** he is the true Temple where people meet God (8:11).
- In **2 Kings** he is the great miracle worker (2:9).
- In **1 Chronicles** he is the descendant of Adam who will rule forever (1:1).
- In **2 Chronicles** he is the child-king hidden and protected from his enemies (22:11).
- In **Ezra** he is the teacher well-versed in the Law of Moses (7:10).
- In **Nehemiah** he is the one who remembers us with favor (5:19).
- In **Esther** he is the gold scepter of mercy in the hand of God the King (5:2).
- In **Job** he is the daysman, the mediator between God and man, whom Job longed for (9:33).
- In **Psalms** he is the stone the builders rejected (118:22).
- In **Proverbs** he is the Word fitly spoken (25:11 - KJV).
- In **Ecclesiastes** he is that which gives life meaning (2:25).
- In **Song of Solomon** he is the lover and our beloved (2:16 - KJV).
- In **Isaiah** he is the son of the virgin (7:14).
- In **Jeremiah** he is the source of living waters (2:13).
- In **Lamentations** he is the hope whose compassions are new every morning (3:23).
- In **Ezekiel** he is the one who gives life to dry bones (37:11).
- In **Daniel** he is the son of man coming in the clouds of heaven (7:13).
- In **Hosea** he is the faithful husband who buys back his unfaithful wife (3:2).

- In **Joel** he is the one who pours out the LORD's spirit on all people (2:28).
- In **Amos** he is God's plumbline, making the straight and crooked obvious (7:8).
- In **Obadiah** he is the deliverance on Mt. Zion (v. 17).
- In **Jonah** he is the sign—three days and nights in the heart of the earth (1:17).
- In **Micah** he is the peace that causes all nations to beat their swords into plowblades (4:3).
- In **Nahum** he is God's refuge to the good and God's vengeance to the wicked (1:7).
- In **Habakkuk** he is the righteous one who lived by faith (2:4).
- In **Zephaniah** he is the one who will restore the fortunes of Judah (3:20).
- In **Haggai** he is the desired of all nations (2:7).
- In **Zechariah** he is the smitten shepherd (13:7 - KJV).
- In **Malachi** he is the "sun of righteousness" risen with healing in his wings (4:2).[2]

Who do *you say* that he is?

And he is so much more:

- Like Abel's sacrifice, he is the sacrifice that is pleasing to God.
- Like Noah's ark, he is the shelter from God's wrath.
- Like Moses' staff, he is the one who makes a way for us in impossible situations.
- Like manna, he is the bread from heaven.
- Like Joshua's pile of rocks, he is the faithful witness.
- Like Shamgar's ox goad, he is our victory against certain death.
- Like Gideon's fleece, he is God's sure sign that gives hope to the hopeless.
- Like Samson's jawbone, he is of little value to the worldly but is the key to victory in life.
- Like Joab's trumpet, he is sounding a clear call to gather his faithful army.
- Like Elijah's mantle, he is both a shelter from the storms of the world and the power of God in the hands of a faithful believer.
- Like the "fourth man" in Daniel, he is our protection from fiery extinction.

Who do *you say* that he is?

The godly characteristics of all Old Testament heroes are embodied in Christ, the ultimate hero:

- Like Noah, he prepared his life before the storm.
- Like Abraham, he obeyed God and went where God led him.
- Like Isaac, he willingly accepted the bride provided by his Father.
- Like Jacob, he learned obedience through the things that he suffered.
- Like Joseph, he kept his heart from bitterness although he was mistreated by those around him.
- Like Moses, he was meek before God.
- Like Joshua, he was a fearless leader.
- Like Othniel, he forsook worldly wealth to deliver God's people.

---

2. The first list like this that we know of was done by Oral Roberts in 1951 in a book titled *The Fourth Man*.

- Like Ehud, he ignored the fact that the world thought him cursed.
- Like Deborah, he did not mind breaking cultural stereotypes.
- Like Gideon, he tore down altars of false religion.
- Like Jephthah, he had family problems but overcame them.
- Like Samson, he was aggressive and sought an occasion against the enemy.
- Like Samuel, he kept himself pure when the priests around him were corrupt.
- Like David, he started with a small, untrained group but trained them faithfully.
- Like Solomon, he grew in wisdom until it was vast.
- Like Elijah, he combined his words with power.
- Like Job, he was a righteous sufferer.
- Like Esther, he concealed his true identity until the proper time.
- Like Isaiah, he continually set before the people the future hope.
- Like Jeremiah, he was passionate, even weeping for his people.
- Like Daniel, he prayed fervently to God.

Who do *you say* that he is?

Jesus Christ is the "golden thread" that holds together the Royal Tapestry of truth. He is the star out of Jacob. He is the "great light" foretold by Isaiah. He is a priest after the order of Melchizedek. He is the one who unites the priesthood with the kingship. He is the king coming with salvation, and the king who comes in the name of the Lord.

The Messiah is pictured in so many ways in the Old Testament that it would be a daunting task indeed to list them. Some of the references to him are very clear and straightforward, while others are veiled to a greater or lesser extent. A brief overview of **Genesis** alone shows that there are many clear prophecies and foreshadowings of the coming Messiah:

- He is the Last Adam, foreshadowed by the First Adam (1:27).
- He is the seed of the woman (3:15).
- He is the one who will shed his blood to cover the sins of man (3:21).
- He is an ark, and those who take refuge in him will not perish in the Judgment (Chapters 6–8).
- He is the Shemite with whom God is most blessed (9:26).
- He is the "seed" of Abraham who will bless all the nations (12:3).
- He is the promised child, as Isaac was (18:10).
- He will destroy the wicked with fire (19:24).
- He is the lamb Yahweh will provide for sacrifice (22:8).
- He is the son willing unto death (22:9).
- He walks with us to make our journey a success (24:40).
- He is the seed of Isaac who will bless all nations (26:4).
- He is the one whom the nations will serve and before whom the people will bow (27:29).
- He is the stairway to God (28:12).
- He is the seed of Jacob who will bless all nations (28:14).
- He is "Judah," the praise of the Lord (29:35).[3]

---

3. "Judah" means "praised."

- He is the faithful witness who witnesses our actions, both good and bad (31:44–52).
- He wrestles with us, shows us our weaknesses, and works to make us into his image (32:24–30).
- He is the one the nations will obey (49:10).
- He, like Joseph, was the favorite son, betrayed by his brethren, tempted with evil, but finally elevated to the right hand of the ruler. Although others meant harm, God turned their actions into good that many might be saved (50:20).

Who do *you say* that he is?

The overview of the Messiah in Genesis that we just read is by no means exhaustive. A similar overview can be done for each book in the Old Testament because Jesus Christ, the Messiah of God, is its grand subject. Noah's ark, Moses' staff, etc., were all literal, physical things. Nevertheless, behind the literal meanings we can also see some of what God is communicating to us about Jesus Christ, His only begotten Son.

The Blueprint: Bloodline and Bloodshed

Let us never forget that Jesus Christ is our perfect example of walking with God. At the beginning of his earthly ministry, when he was tempted by the Devil in the wilderness, he replied each time: "It is written." Jesus Christ's faith in and reliance upon the *written* Word of God formed the foundation of his life. What part of the written Word did Jesus have from which to learn? The Hebrew Scriptures (Genesis through Malachi). He studied them so diligently that, according to the record in Luke 4, when he went into the synagogue at the beginning of his ministry, he unrolled the scroll of Isaiah, which was about 60 feet long with no chapters, verses or punctuation, and found Isaiah 61:1.

> **Isaiah 61:1 (NRSV)**
> The spirit of the LORD God is upon me, because the LORD has anointed me; he has sent me to bring good news to the oppressed, to bind up the brokenhearted, to proclaim liberty to the captives, and release to the prisoners;

How did Jesus know who he was and what his purpose was? He knew it primarily from the Scriptures in the Old Testament, beginning with Genesis 3:15. Through the Word, his heavenly Father mentored him and helped him grow "…in wisdom and stature, and in favor with God and men." Jesus saw that he was the Promised Seed, the only hope for mankind. Once he received holy spirit at his baptism (the start of his ministry), this written revelation was augmented by much on-the-job direct revelation.

The Old Testament was written for our learning today, but it was the blueprint for Jesus Christ to know his identity, his purpose and his destiny, as well as the destiny of mankind. As we look at a number of records in the Old Testament, we want to ask ourselves what God wanted Jesus to learn from these records. Jesus' unshakable conviction about his identity was the underpinning that enabled him to be obedient to carry out his mission, even unto death.

The Old Testament primarily focuses on the people of Israel, the bloodline from which the Redeemer of all men came. We believe that one reason Christianity has been, and still is, relatively ineffective in reaching Jewish people is because it promotes as its foundation the idea of a three-in-one God and, correspondingly, that Jesus is God. This would have been a ludicrous concept to the Jews of the Old Testament, because from Genesis 3:15 through Malachi, the coming Messiah was prophesied to be a *man*, the seed of Abraham and the seed of David. As we saw, he was prophetically referred to as the "seed" of a woman (Gen. 3:15).

The coming Messiah was to be a descendant of Shem, Abraham, Isaac, Jacob, Judah, David, etc. Isaiah 53:3 calls him "a man of sorrows." The wording of Isaiah 52 and 53 stands firmly against the idea that the Messiah would be God. "See, my [God's] servant will act wisely…" (Isa. 52:13) is the start of the great section that describes the suffering, death and exaltation of the Messiah. Scripture is clear: the Messiah was to be a "man" and the "servant" of God. If the Messiah were in fact God in the flesh, he would not be a "servant" of God, but would retain all the honor he would command as God. Zechariah 6:12 does an excellent job of portraying the Messianic expectations of the Jews: "Tell him this is what the LORD Almighty says: 'Here is the **man** whose name is the Branch, and he will branch out from his place and build the temple of the LORD.'" The wording of this verse is very clear, and portrays the Messiah as a man, a "branch" (that is, a sprout, shoot or "offspring" of God), who will build the Temple of the LORD. Because, by definition, an "offspring" is one who arises out from another, it would not be natural to read this verse and understand that this "man," this "branch," would be God Himself.

Moses wrote concerning the Messiah in Deuteronomy 18:15: "The LORD your God will raise up for you a prophet like me from among your own brothers…." This verse set much of the expectation about the coming Messiah. The Christ was to be "a prophet." That in itself shows that he would be a spokesman *for* God, and this would not make sense if he *were* God. The verse goes on to say that this prophet would be "like me." Moses was not a pre-existent being, but was fully human, and we see that God's Christ would be like Moses. The verse also goes on to say that this prophet would be "…from among your own brothers…." "God in human flesh" is hardly "…from among your own brothers…," but a Messiah who was fully human in every way, who existed in God's mind as the plan of redemption and who "became flesh" when Mary became pregnant, would be exactly what Scripture foretold and what Israel expected.

Some Christians attempt to insert the "pre-existent" Christ in the Old Testament, such as the fourth "man" in the fiery furnace (Dan. 3:25) and the "man" who wrestled with Jacob (Gen. 32:24). The Old Testament, however, nowhere even hints that Jesus Christ was alive and functioning in any capacity before his birth, and makes it plain that each of the above "men" were, in fact, *angels* (see Dan. 3:28 and Hosea 12:4).[4]

Isaac: Another Promised Seed

In Genesis 12, God spoke to a man named Abram (whose name was later changed to "Abraham") and told him to "get outta town" and go to a new land, one that God would show him as he went. Abraham was 70 years old when he left Ur of the Chaldees and started out for Canaan. En route, he stopped at Haran for five years. Although the Bible does not tell us why he stopped, we do know

---

4. Many have been taught that Jesus is the "LORD" (Yahweh) in the Old Testament. We will deal with this in Chapter 12. One of the primary reasons for believing this was that in the Old Testament Yahweh would occasionally appear to people. Although this is revolutionary information to many people, it should not be unexpected. God created people to fellowship with them, and so the fact that He would show up in some form should not surprise us. For a detailed explanation, see Appendix A (Gen. 18:1 and 2).

that he resumed his journey after his father, Terah, died. It may be that his father had become too weak or sick to travel. After his father died, God spoke to Abraham again, and he resumed his travel toward Canaan. God said to him:

Genesis 12:2 and 3 (NASB)
(2) And I will make you a great nation, And I will bless you, And make your name great; And so you shall be a blessing;
(3) And I will bless those who bless you, And the one who curses you I will curse. And in you all the families of the earth shall be blessed."

Abraham was about 75 years old (and Sarah was ten years younger than he was) when he received this promise from God. He understood that for all the people on earth to be blessed "in" him, one of his offspring would have to be the promised Messiah. However, by the time Abraham was 86 years old, he still had not fathered a child. After years of trying to conceive the promised child with Sarah, Abraham resorted to a common custom, and had intercourse with Sarah's handmaid, Hagar. That child was named Ishmael. Years later, when Abraham was 99 and Sarah was 89, God made another promise to him, this one more specific. God told him that he would be the father and that Sarah would be the mother of a son (they named him "Isaac"), and that this son would be born in about a year. At their ages, this was an astounding promise!

Thus, Isaac is a "promised seed," and as such he is a "type" of the coming Redeemer. As we look at the record of Abraham and Isaac in Genesis 22, we will clearly see what truth regarding the Redeemer God wanted to communicate. In light of all that led up to the birth of Isaac, would you say that he was a special child? One of the reasons that Isaac is special is because God told Abraham that it was from Isaac's line that the Redeemer would come. So what does Isaac represent? He represents a token, in the senses realm, of the greater One yet to come. Abraham would not live to see all the seed that would come from Isaac, including the Promised Seed, Jesus Christ, but he would live to see Isaac born. Let us now delve into Genesis 22.

Genesis 22:1 (NRSV)
After these things God tested Abraham. He said to him, "Abraham!" And he said, "Here I am."

The word "tested" does not mean that God tempted Abraham with evil to see if He could make him do something wrong. James 1:13 says that God does not tempt people with evil. The Hebrew word simply means, "to prove." God was asking Abraham to do something to prove his allegiance to Him.[5]

Genesis 22:2 (NRSV)
He [God] said, "Take your son, your only son Isaac, whom you love, and go to the land of Moriah, and offer him there as a burnt offering on one of the mountains that I shall show you."

---

5. See our book by: Mark Graeser, John A. Lynn, and John Schoenheit, *Don't Blame God! A Biblical Answer to the Problem of Evil, Sin, & Suffering*, (The Living Truth Fellowship, Indianapolis, IN, 2011), Chapter 14.

What did Abraham understand by the phrase, "a burnt offering"? This was something very familiar to him, and he knew exactly what it meant. He was to build an altar, pile wood on it, tie down the sacrifice (in this case his "only son" Isaac) and kill it by cutting its throat with one thrust of his knife. This is exactly what God told Abraham to do to Isaac and this is exactly what Abraham understood. Put yourself in Abraham's place, and think how you would feel in this situation.

Genesis 22:3 (NRSV)
So Abraham rose early in the morning, saddled his donkey, and took two of his young men with him, and his son Isaac; he cut the wood for the burnt offering, and set out and went to the place in the distance that God had shown him.

Notice that Abraham did not argue with God, despite the magnitude of what God asked him to do. He simply obeyed.

Genesis 22:4 (NRSV)
On the third day Abraham looked up and saw the place far away.

There is no question that this record of Abraham and Isaac is a foreshadowing of God asking His only begotten Son to die as a sacrifice, and of raising him from the dead three days and three nights later. We believe it is significant that it was on the third day that Abraham saw the mountain ahead of him. We believe it took him three days and three nights to get there, and that during that time Isaac was as good as dead, because Abraham had made up his mind to obey God and sacrifice his son.

Genesis 22:5 (NRSV)
Then Abraham said to his young men, "Stay here with the donkey; the boy and I will go over there; **we** will worship, and then **we** will come back to you."

Whoa! (Yes, that's also what Abraham said to the donkey). At the end of the verse, the text reads, "…**we** will come back to you." That is amazing, because what Abraham meant when he said that he and Isaac would "worship" was that he would slit Isaac's throat and then burn him on the altar. How then could he say *we* will come back? That is a very good question, and we do not have to guess at the answer, because the following verses tell us:

Hebrews 11:17–19 (NRSV)
(17) By faith Abraham, when put to the test, offered up Isaac. He who had received the promises was ready to offer up his only son,
(18) of whom he had been told, "It is through Isaac that descendants shall be named for you."
(19) He considered the fact that God is able even to raise someone from the dead— and figuratively speaking, he did receive him back [from death].

Let us first note that God's Word says that Abraham was acting by "faith." One cannot have faith unless he has something to have faith in, that is, the Word of God—a command and/or a promise, spoken or written. "By faith" means that Abraham did exactly what God told him to do. Hebrews 11:19 shows us why Abraham believed he would come back down the mountain with Isaac. It was because he trusted that God would raise Isaac from the dead and, figuratively speaking, that is exactly what happened, as we will see.

Genesis 22:6a (NRSV)
Abraham took the wood of the burnt offering and placed it on his son Isaac, and he himself carried the fire and the knife….

This verse shows us that Isaac is not a little child. In fact, we believe he was about 30 years old. It is significant that Isaac carried the wood on which he would die, just as Jesus did until the soldiers made Simon carry it. Now consider the question that Isaac asked his father.

Genesis 22:7 (NRSV)
Isaac said to his father Abraham, "Father!" And he said, "Here I am, my son." He said, "The fire and the wood are here, but where is the lamb for the burnt offering?"

Isaac so much as said, "Say, Dad, I see the fire and the wood, but don't we usually take an animal along on these trips?" Think about his question: "Where is the lamb?" This question echoed throughout the entire Old Testament until it was answered on the banks of the river Jordan by John the Baptist:

John 1:29 (NRSV)
The next day he [John] saw Jesus coming toward him and declared, "Here is the Lamb of God who takes away the sin of the world!

How would Jesus take away the sin of the world? By his shed blood, for without the shedding of blood there is no remission of sin (Heb. 9:22). Jesus was the "Lamb" that God provided for the sins of mankind, as the following verse typifies:

Genesis 22:8 (NRSV)
Abraham said, "God himself will provide the lamb for the burnt offering, my son."
So the two of them walked on together.

Abraham was confident that God would provide a lamb for the sacrifice and fulfill His promises.

Genesis 22:9
When they reached the place God had told him about, Abraham built an altar there and arranged the wood on it. He bound his son Isaac and laid him on the altar, on top of the wood.

Notice the statement in the above verse that Abraham "bound" Isaac and laid him on the altar. Did Abraham have to chase Isaac around and around the altar and then wrestle him to the ground? Remember that Isaac was 100 years younger than Abraham. It seems apparent that had he wanted to resist, he could have. No, what we see here is the son willing to die at his father's request. Abraham represents the Father willing to give his son. How this record must have touched the heart of Jesus Christ when he first understood it, and how remembering its inherent promise of resurrection must have given him strength as he went to the Cross.

Genesis 22:10–14 (NRSV)
(10) Then Abraham reached out his hand and took the knife to kill his son.
(11) But the angel of the LORD called to him from heaven, and said, "Abraham, Abraham!" And he said, "Here I am."
(12) He said, "Do not lay a hand on the boy or do anything to him; for now I know that you fear God, since you have not withheld your son, your only son, from me."
(13) And Abraham looked up and saw a ram, caught in a thicket by its horns. Abraham went and took the ram and offered it up as a burnt offering instead of his son.
(14) So Abraham called that place "The LORD will provide," as it is said to this day, "On the mount of the LORD it shall be provided."

Remember that Genesis 3:15 prophesied both the *suffering* of the Redeemer and the *glory* that would follow. In the record of Abraham and Isaac, Jesus saw that if he would be obedient unto death, God would raise him from the dead. There is another record in the book of Genesis we will now consider, from which Jesus Christ learned more about the suffering and the glory that would follow, the glory that would be his destiny after his resurrection.

Joseph: Righteous Sufferer to Co-Ruler

It is most significant that of the fifty chapters in the book of Genesis, fourteen of them speak of Joseph, one of the twelve sons of Jacob. Joseph is an important person in the Old Testament record because he is another "type" of Christ, and one whose life very vividly exemplified some great truths about the coming Redeemer. Once again, remember that Jesus Christ read and studied the life of Joseph and learned from it what God wanted him to learn.

Jesus saw in Joseph a man who was innocent but wronged by his own brothers. He saw a man who was thrown in jail as a common criminal and subjected to many hardships. He also saw that because of Joseph's faithfulness to God's Word and his reliance on the power of God, he did something that no other man in Egypt could do. Because of Joseph's obedience to God, he was raised from the status of a common criminal to a governmental position of the highest rank. Because of his deeds, Joseph was exalted to a position second only to the Pharaoh and was given the Pharaoh's signet ring, which represented the authority and power of Pharaoh. In that position of authority, Joseph was able to save the lives of his brothers. In Joseph, Jesus Christ saw himself.

Please allow us some—no, actually a gargantuan amount of—literary license in summarizing the life of Joseph up until Genesis 41. He was the eleventh son of Jacob, a nice boy, but one who tended to shoot off his mouth, at least that's what his ten older brothers thought. One morning at breakfast Joseph said, "Yo, Levi, you want to shoot me those unleavened Wheaties? Hey, you wouldn't believe the dream I had last night. It was awesome. You guys are gonna bow down to me, and I'm going to rule over you. Cool, huh?" They thought to themselves, "Fat chance, twerp," and they were really steamed at their kid brother. Also, they resented that Joseph was their father's favorite son.

Some time after this, they saw Joseph walking along the dusty trail near Dothan and one of them said, "This is our chance, boys. Let's waste this punk and tell dad that an animal ate him." One of the brothers, Reuben, intervened and said, "Let's not kill him, let's just dump him in that pit over there." Reuben's intention was to come back later to rescue Joseph and take him home. This is no doubt why a sandwich was later named after him. The brothers agreed, and threw Joseph into the pit. Then they sat down to have lunch.

While they were eating, a wagon train on the way to Egypt passed by. Judah, one of the brothers, saw an opportunity to make a quick buck and persuaded his brothers to sell Joseph as a slave. When Joseph arrived in Egypt, he was sold to a man named Potiphar, who was greatly impressed with the quality of his life. He also impressed Mrs. P., so much so that she wanted to "hit the sack" with him, but Joseph spurned her advances, saying that he could not sin against God. With all the fervor of a "woman scorned," Mrs. P. framed him, and Joseph was sent to jail. Rather than feel sorry for himself, Joseph continued in his faith, which greatly impressed the prison warden, who put him in charge of the entire prison.

Some time later, Pharaoh's cupbearer dropped his cup, and the chief baker's bread didn't rise. Both were thrown into jail. One night each of them had a dream that they did not understand. By revelation, Joseph interpreted their dreams for them, and his interpretations came to pass. Two years later, Pharaoh had a dream that, much to his consternation, neither he nor his advisers could understand. The reinstated cupbearer remembered the incident with Joseph and told the Pharaoh about him. By revelation, Joseph interpreted Pharaoh's dream for him and also laid out an economic program for the seven years of plenty and the seven years of famine that the dream indicated would come to pass. Joseph's spiritual wisdom and power so impressed the Pharaoh that he elevated him to his second-in-command.

What a record! Think about it—people who are in jail and about to be paroled are very concerned that they have a *job* waiting for them, so they can provide for themselves and not go back to a life of crime. Such people are often glad to have *any* job. But think about the people in Egypt picking up their morning papers and seeing the headline: **"EX-CON BECOMES ASSISTANT PHARAOH!"**

Genesis 41:37 and 38 (NRSV)
(37) The proposal pleased Pharaoh and all his servants.
(38) Pharaoh said to his servants, "Can we find anyone else like this—one in whom is the spirit of God?"

It is significant that Pharaoh, himself considered a "god" in Egypt, did not ascribe such status to Joseph, but instead recognized that Joseph was a unique *man*. Pharaoh understood that it was God who showed Joseph the interpretation of the dream by way of the spirit of God in him. The fact that, in Egyptian culture, the Pharaoh was looked at as a "god" is another element in the parallel between Joseph being exalted to the right hand of Pharaoh and Jesus Christ's future exaltation at the right hand of God. Surely this analogy was not lost on Jesus Christ when he studied this account, and neither should it be lost on us. However, it very well may be if we believe that Jesus is God.

Genesis 41:39 (NRSV)
So Pharaoh said to Joseph, "Since God has shown you all this, there is no one so discerning and wise as you.

In essence, what Pharaoh said was, "I've never seen a man like you before." Doesn't that sound like what people said about Jesus Christ in the Gospels? For example, "No one ever spoke the way this man does…" (John 7:46).

Genesis 41:40 and 41 (NRSV)
(40) You shall be over my house, and all my people shall order themselves as you command; only with regard to the throne will I be greater than you."
(41) And Pharaoh said to Joseph, "See, I have set you over all the land of Egypt."

The Pharaoh said, "Hey, you've earned the promotion I've given you. I'm not only putting you in charge of my house, but also in charge of all of Egypt! Oh, by the way, Joseph, just remember you're not the Pharaoh" ("…only with regard to the throne will I be greater than you"). Look at what Pharaoh did then:

Genesis 41:42 (NRSV)
Removing his signet ring from his hand, Pharaoh put it on Joseph's hand; he arrayed him in garments of fine linen, and put a gold chain around his neck.

Pharaoh's signet ring was the only such ring in all of Egypt. This ring signified the power and authority that Pharaoh gave Joseph. It did not make Joseph the Pharaoh, but *it did enable him to do everything that the Pharaoh could do.* And remember, it was only the Pharaoh who could delegate this authority to him.

Genesis 41:43 (NRSV)
He [Pharaoh] had him [Joseph] ride in a chariot of his [Pharaoh's] second-in-command; and they cried out in front of him [Joseph], "Bow the knee!" Thus he [Pharaoh] set him [Joseph] over all the land of Egypt.

The pronouns in the above verse are very important. We do not want to get the Pharaoh and Joseph mixed up. Obviously, the people had no problem telling the difference between them. The Pharaoh was in the first chariot and Joseph was in the second chariot. They each understood the relationship between them, and so did the people.

Genesis 41:44 and 45 (NRSV)
(44) Moreover Pharaoh said to Joseph, "I am Pharaoh, and without your consent no one shall lift up hand or foot in all the land of Egypt."
(45) Pharaoh gave Joseph the name Zaphenath-paneah; and gave him Asenath daughter of Potiphera, priest of On, as his wife. Thus Joseph gained authority over the land of Egypt.

It is significant that Pharaoh also gave Joseph a new name, a name that was above every other name. Joseph's new name meant "abundance of life." Little did Pharaoh know how much that title really meant, because in his position of authority, Joseph would later save the lives of his brethren and preserve the line of the coming Messiah, who is the "abundance of life" for all men who believe on him. The Pharaoh also gave Joseph a bride, as God will one day do for Jesus. Note also that Joseph did not just sit around the palace at the right hand of Pharaoh, but went throughout the land of Egypt carrying out his responsibilities.

Genesis 41:46 (NRSV)
Joseph was thirty years old when he entered the service of Pharaoh king of Egypt. And Joseph went out from the presence of Pharaoh, and went through all the land of Egypt.

Remember that Jesus Christ was about thirty years old when he began his earthly ministry (Luke 3:23). Let the record show that the position Joseph received from Pharaoh was no "figurehead" position. Joseph was far more than royal window-dressing. This is made clear by what Pharaoh said when the famine did come and the people came to *him* for help.

Genesis 41:55 (NRSV)
When all the land of Egypt was famished, the people cried to Pharaoh for bread. Pharaoh said to all the Egyptians, "Go to Joseph; what he says to you, do."

Obviously, Joseph is a vivid type of Christ. To see the parallels between Joseph's exaltation by Pharaoh and Jesus' exaltation by God, let us look at some verses in Philippians, which we will examine later in more detail.

Philippians 2:5–11
(5) Your attitude should be the same as that of Christ Jesus:
(6) Who, being in very nature God, did not consider equality with God something to be grasped,
(7) but made himself nothing, taking the very nature of servant, being made in human likeness.
(8) And being found in appearance as a man, he humbled himself and became obedient to death—even death on a cross!
(9) Therefore God exalted him to the highest place and gave him the name that is above every name,
(10) that at the name of Jesus every knee should bow, in heaven and on earth and under the earth,
(11) and every tongue confess that Jesus Christ is Lord, to the glory of God the Father.

Although Jesus Christ was the Son of God with the spirit of God upon him without measure, he humbled himself and became a servant unto men. He saw prophesied in the Old Testament that this service meant hardship and suffering in his life, leading to his death on the Cross. As a man, death was his greatest enemy, and his impending torture and horrible death on the Cross made it even worse. Yet, he was obedient unto death and because of that, God highly exalted him and gave him the name that is above every name. Just as it was with Joseph, one day every knee will bow to the Lord Jesus Christ.

Because of Jesus Christ's faithfulness in his earthly ministry, God promoted him to his own right hand and gave him the "whole kingdom" to oversee (just as Pharaoh did for Joseph). One day this future kingdom will be a reality, and Jesus Christ will take his rightful place as the King. The type of Christ set forth in Genesis 41 augments the truth we see clearly in other Scriptures—that God has not delegated to His Son *essential* equality, but rather *functional* equality.[6] God has, so to speak, given Jesus His signet ring so that Jesus now has the authority to do everything that God wills to have done. Just as it was with the Pharaoh and Joseph ("…only with respect to the the throne will I be greater than you"), so it is with the Father and His Son. The following verses that we have mentioned previously make this very plain. How interesting that these most explicit verses keep coming up.

1 Corinthians 15:24–28
(24) Then the end will come, when he [Christ] hands over the kingdom to God the Father after he [Christ] has destroyed all dominion, authority and power [by exercising his own].
(25) For he [Christ] must reign until he [Christ] has put all his [Christ's] enemies under his [Christ's] feet.
(26) The last enemy to be destroyed is death.
(27) For he [Christ] "has put everything under his [Christ's] feet." Now when it says that "everything" has been put under him [Christ], it is clear that this does not include God himself, who put everything under Christ.
(28) When he [Christ] has done this, then [in the future, not now] the Son himself will be made subject to him [God] who put everything under him [Christ], so that God may be all in all.

The above verses hearken back to a key verse in the Old Testament that illustrates this same truth about the relationship between God and Jesus Christ. It is one that we will expand upon later.

Psalm 110:1 (NASB)
The LORD says to my Lord: "Sit at My right hand, Until I make Thine enemies a footstool for Thy feet.

"The LORD" refers to God Almighty, while "my Lord" refers to the Messiah, in whose coming David hoped. In closing this chapter, we want to again set forth two other Old Testament verses that corroborate this same truth:

Daniel 7:13 and 14 (NASB)
(13) "I kept looking in the night visions, And behold with the clouds of heaven One like a Son of man was coming, And he came up to the Ancient of Days And was presented before Him.
(14) "And to him was given dominion, Glory and a kingdom, That all the peoples, nations, and *men of every* language Might serve Him. His dominion is an everlasting dominion Which will not pass away; And His kingdom is one Which will not be destroyed.

---

6. It is very important to recognize the difference between *essential* equality and *functional* equality if we are to have a proper understanding about the Lord Jesus Christ. Trinitarians believe that Jesus is *essentially* God, i.e., that intrinsically, in his very essence and nature, Jesus is God. We believe that Jesus is *essentially* a man, the only begotten Son of God. Nevertheless, God has given Jesus *functional* equality, so that Jesus currently functions as if he were God. God made Jesus "Lord," and now it is he who gives the gift of holy spirit (Acts 2:33), gives out ministries in the Church (Eph. 4:11) and directs and holds together his Body, the Church (Col. 1:17 and 18). In the future, Jesus will raise the dead and judge them (John 5:21 and 22; Acts 17:31). The functional equality of Christ will last until after the final judgment, when even death will be destroyed. Then Christ will be "made subject" to God the Father, as 1 Corinthians 15:24–28 states.

Notice that there are two persons mentioned here: "the son of man" and "the Ancient of Days." This is a prophecy about God exalting Jesus to the position of ruler over his future kingdom.

Because Jesus Christ is the subject of the Old Testament from Genesis 3:15 through the book of Malachi, there are many, many other sections therein that speak prophetically of the coming Messiah and Redeemer. Not one even hints that he would be *God* come down to earth in human form. God's original prophecy about His Son in Genesis 3:15 is consistent with all the others thereafter. It is most significant that at the beginning of his earthly ministry, Jesus Christ read from the Word of God (Isaiah) about himself. He knew who he was, and he continued to think, speak and live out the truths of God's Word that were the foundation of his life.

With all this impressive typology, imagery and prophetic portraiture of the Messiah, the question naturally arises, why then did not the Jews accept Jesus? Did he not fulfill enough of the prophecies to make it clear who he was? Or did the Jews misunderstand the prophecies? We now turn our attention to the way the Jews actually interpreted the prophecies without the benefit of the 20/20 hindsight we have today.

5

The Messiah the Jews Expected

In the previous chapter, we looked with 20/20 hindsight at what was prophesied about the Messiah. In this chapter, we will examine the Messiah from the Jews' perspective looking forward. Although they diligently searched the Hebrew Scriptures for prophecies of their coming Messiah, their understanding of him was incomplete. It is important to remember that what we today see very clearly in our New Testament understanding about the Christ is often quite veiled in the Hebrew Scriptures.[1]

In fact, the people of Israel had a totally different concept of what Christ would be like than most Christians have, and this affected the way they interpreted and recognized Messianic prophecies. The Jews did not apply Scriptures about the virgin birth, the trip to Egypt and death of the Messiah to Christ, and these verses were not as self-evident as Christians tend to think.[2] Most are unaware of

---

1. We use the term "Hebrew Scriptures" here because technically the "Four Gospels" are part of what is called the "Old Testament." Hence we use the term "Hebrew Scriptures" to refer to the Scriptures from Genesis through Malachi. We will continue to refer to the "Old Testament" when we are referring to the time period rather than the Scriptures.

2. Alfred Edersheim has provided a list that he titles, "List of Hebrew Scripture Passages Messianically Applied in Ancient Rabbinic Writings." This list includes the various passages of the Hebrew Scriptures that the ancient rabbis believed applied to the Messiah. It is a wonderful tool from which to build an understanding of what the Jews of Christ's time were looking for. Alfred Edersheim, *The Life and Times of Jesus the Messiah*, Part 2 (Grand Rapids, MI, Wm. B. Eerdmans, 1971).

the tremendous help the New Testament is in interpreting the "Old Testament." For example, how do we know Hosea 11:1 applies to Christ? Matthew says so. How do we know Jeremiah 31:15 applies to Christ? Again, Matthew says so. Many of the Hebrew Scriptures that Christians apply to Christ because of what the New Testament says about him were not applied to him at all by the Jews, and not because they were spiritually blind. In many cases, the references were deliberately veiled. We can gain much insight into the nature of biblical prophecy by understanding the difficulties the Jews faced in properly interpreting the Messianic passages.

Messiah's Suffering and Death

The very different Jewish Messianic expectation is clearly seen in their view of the suffering and death of the Messiah. When Jesus told Peter and the Apostles that he must suffer and die, Peter did not say, "Yes, Lord, we knew from the prophecies written about you that you are going to suffer and die." Rather he said, "…Never, Lord!…'This shall never happen to you!'" (Matt. 16:22). The idea that the Messiah had to *die* was inconceivable to them. When Christ first introduced it, Peter vehemently argued against it. Shortly after that, Jesus said to his disciples that he would be betrayed and put in the hands of men, but the disciples did not understand what he was talking about (Luke 9:44 and 45). Later, Jesus said that he would be mocked, insulted, spit on, flogged and killed. He made it very clear.[3] Yet Scripture says, "The disciples did not understand any of this. Its meaning was hidden from them, and they did not know what he was talking about" (Luke 18:34).

At the "Last Supper," the disciples still did not comprehend the impending suffering and death of the Messiah, and later that night in the Garden of Gethsemane, Peter wanted to fight with the Jews and Romans, sword to sword. Even after the crucifixion, the disciples could not understand why Jesus' tomb was empty. Angels had to remind the women who came to the tomb that Jesus had said he would rise from the dead (Luke 24:6–8). When the women passed on this good news to the rest of the disciples, however, they were not convinced, and when Jesus appeared to them, they thought he was a ghost (Luke 24:37). After his resurrection, Jesus was finally able to get the disciples to understand the Scriptures regarding his death and resurrection (Luke 24:44–46).

Peter and the disciples were not the only ones who were confused about Jesus and his mission. An earlier event in the Gospels that demonstrates the misconceptions that existed about the coming Messiah is when John the Baptist sent his disciples to Christ with the question, "…Are you the one who was to come, or should we expect someone else?" (Luke 7:19 and 20). This seems strange because John was the one who identified Christ with the words: "…Look, the Lamb of God, who takes away the sin of the world!," and "I have seen and I testify that this is the Son of God" (John 1:29 and 34). Had John developed doubts that Jesus, his "first cousin," was the Messiah? Considering that a number of people close to Jesus misunderstood him, that is possible. Joseph Good suggests another possibility in his book, *Rosh HaShanah and the Messianic Kingdom to Come*:

> As the ancient Jewish scholars and Rabbis began to study the scriptural information about the Messiah, they encountered a serious problem: many of the passages seemed to contradict one another. Often the Messiah is seen as a conquering king…Other passages speak of a

---

3. In Matthew alone, there are at least five occasions when Jesus warned his disciples of his coming trials, his death or his resurrection (implying that he would have to die): in Caesarea Philippi (Matt. 16:13ff); at the Mount of Transfiguration (Matt. 17:9); as he was "going up to Jerusalem from Judea" (Matt. 20:19); in the parable of the tenants (Matt. 21:33–40) and after the Olivet discourse two days before the Passover (Matt. 26:2).

suffering servant. From this paradoxical description of the Messiah came a first-century Common Era (A.D.) rabbinical teaching of two Messiahs.[4]

Good goes on to say that the ancients called the conquering Messiah "Messiah Ben David" and called the suffering Messiah "Messiah Ben Joseph." The Talmud applied Zechariah 12:10 to Messiah Ben Joseph: "...when they look on the one whom they have pierced, they shall mourn for him, as one mourns for an only child..." (NRSV).[5] Good continues:

> This anticipation of two Messiahs by the Jewish people of the first century is the background for the question posed by Yochanan the Immerser (John the Baptist) to *Yeshua* [Jesus] as to whether He was the Messiah (indicating one, singular), or if they were to expect another. His question was specifically whether *Yeshua* would fulfill all of the prophecies concerning Messiah, or whether the Rabbis, who said there would be two Messiahs, were right. *Yeshua's* answer is a paraphrase of various passages that Rabbis identified as referring partially to Messiah Ben Joseph and partially to Messiah Ben David. Therefore, *Yeshua* was expressing, in dramatic language that was clear to His listeners, that He would fulfill all of the Messianic prophecies. Rather than send two Messiahs with two different roles, G-d would send one Messiah in two separate appearances or comings.[6]

Whether or not Joseph Good is correct about the reason for John's question, it is important for us to realize that, at the time of Christ, there were Rabbis teaching that there would be two Messiahs instead of one. It is hard for us to put ourselves in the position of the people of the Old Testament who knew Jesus only from the prophecies, but that is what we must do if we are to understand what they knew about him and what they were expecting. To be sure, there are prophecies in the Hebrew Scriptures that, while not specifically mentioning the Messiah, were nonetheless quite well known as Messianic prophecies. Nevertheless, the fact is that many of the verses the New Testament writers and Christian commentators have understood as Messianic prophecies were not viewed that way by the Jewish commentators. Thus, these did not figure into their understanding of what the Messiah was going to be like and what he would accomplish.[7] For example, we know that Joseph and Mary took Jesus to Egypt to protect him from Herod. In regard to them returning from Egypt, Matthew 2:15 states, "...And so was fulfilled what the Lord had said through the prophet [Hosea]: 'Out of Egypt I called my son.'" To the reader of the New Testament, this seems very clear. However, as the verse reads in Hosea, especially in light of its context, it is difficult indeed to see that it refers to the Messiah.

Hosea 11:1–3 (NRSV)
(1) When Israel was a child, I loved him, and out of Egypt I called my son.
(2) The more I called them, the more they went from me; they kept sacrificing to the Baals, and offering incense to idols.

---

4. Joseph Good, *Rosh HaShanah and the Messianic Kingdom to Come* (P.O. Box 3125, Hatikva Ministries, Port Arthur, TX, 1989), p. 2.

5. Edersheim, *op. cit., The Life and Times,* (Book 2, p. 736). However, even in the Jewish commentaries there is a difference of opinion. Edersheim writes, "[it is unclear] whether the mourning is caused by the death of the Messiah Ben Joseph, or else on account of the evil concupiscence."

6. Good, *op. cit., Rosh HaShanah,* p. 5.

7. Just as Jews today have various interpretations of the Hebrew Scriptures' Messianic prophecies, so ancient Jewish interpreters reached different conclusions about who the Messiah would be and what he would do.

(3) Yet it was I who taught Ephraim to walk, I took them up in my arms; but they did not know that I healed them.

The ancient Jews looked at these verses in Hosea as Jewish history. "When Israel was a child…," barely a few hundred years old, God called the nation out of Egypt. In the Hebrew Scriptures, Israel was called God's "son" (Exod. 4:22, etc.). But when God called them to fellowship with Him, they instead worshipped "the Baals." Scholars know of no Jewish commentator living before Christ who applied Hosea 11:1 to the Messiah. Therefore, no one at the time of Christ was looking for a Messiah who was to spend part of his life in Egypt. How is this "prophecy" explained today? The best explanation seems to be that "Israel" is a type or figure of the "greater Israel," i.e., Jesus Christ, just as David is sometimes a type of the "greater David," Solomon a type of the "greater Solomon," etc. What follows in the next section are some key prophecies about the Messiah that the Jews recognized and upon which they based their expectations of him.

The Messiah the Jews Were Expecting

Genesis 3:15
The Seed of the Woman and His Conflict

Genesis 3:15 says: "And I will put enmity between you and the woman, and between your offspring ["seed"] and hers; he will crush your head, and you will strike his heel." This is a clear prophecy of the coming Messiah. Both ancient Jewish commentators and modern Christian commentators realize that it applies to him. The Lord God is telling the Serpent that there will be a seed of the woman who will eventually come and crush his head. Since the word "seed" is a collective singular (like "deer" or "fish") and can refer to one seed or many, is there any indication that this verse refers to a singular Messiah? Yes. The Hebrew uses the masculine singular in the phrase "his heel," which shows that the understanding of "*he* will crush" is correct.[8] Furthermore, the Septuagint, which was done by Greek-speaking Jews around 250 B.C., uses the masculine singular pronoun *autos* ("he") to refer to the "seed" of the woman. This is highly unusual since Greek grammar requires that the number and gender of the pronoun agree with the noun. The use of the masculine pronoun with the neuter noun indicates that the Jewish translators of the Septuagint knew the verse was referring to their Messiah.[9]

It could well be asked why then the Old Testament Jews did not also recognize the *suffering* Messiah in this verse. The ancient Jews did understand from this verse, from Psalm 2 and from other verses, that the Messiah would be opposed during his life. What they did not understand was the intensity of the opposition that he would face, the personal suffering he would endure, and his death. It could also be asked why the Jews did not see in this verse both the first and second comings of Christ to Israel, as modern Christians do. The simple fact is that the wording of Genesis 3:15 does not demand two comings. The Hebrew is worded in such a way that both parts of the prophecy could be fulfilled

---

8. The ancient Hebrew text was "unpointed," i.e., without many of the vowels the modern text has. Because of this, it is often possible to question the exact translation of the ancient Hebrew. Imagine English written without vowels. What would "ht" mean: "hat," "hit," "hot," "hut" or "hate"? The context would actually be the key to determining the exact meaning. So, in Genesis 3:15 the masculine singular for "his heel" allows us to better see the accuracy of the masculine singular, "he" will crush.

9. For more detail, see Walter Kaiser, Jr., *The Messiah in the Hebrew Scriptures* (Zondervan, Grand Rapids, 1995), pp. 37–42.

in one coming. As worded in the Hebrew and expressed in the KJV, RSV, ASV and other English translations, the seed would "bruise" the head of the Serpent and the Serpent would "bruise" the heel of the seed. This could take place in one coming as the two forces battled each other. We today know it will happen in two, but we know that only by 20/20 hindsight about the first coming of the Messiah, not because of the Hebrew text.

Genesis 22:18
From the Line of Abraham

The Jews understood that the Messiah would be a descendant of Abraham, according to several promises God had made to Abraham. Genesis 12 says that all the "people" (*mishpachah* = clan or family) of the "earth" (*adamah* = land, ground [usually re: Israel]) will be blessed through Abraham. In most English versions of Genesis 18:18, God seems simply to repeat what He had said to Abraham, but the Hebrew text expands the promise of Genesis 12:3 to include all the people of the world. Genesis 18:18 says that all the "nations" (*goyim*) of the "earth" (*erets* = land, earth) will be blessed in Abraham. This wider promise was repeated to Abraham in Genesis 22:18, except this third time it was to be through his "seed" that the nations of the earth will be blessed. By the time of Christ, the Jews had lost sight of the truth that the Messiah was to bless everyone, and therefore held a proprietary view of him that excluded the Gentiles.

Genesis 49:10
Shiloh from the Tribe of Judah

Jacob had twelve sons, and each of them fathered a tribe of Israel. Scripture tells us that the Messiah was to come from a specific tribe:

> **Genesis 49:10 (ASV)**
> The sceptre shall not depart from Judah, Nor the ruler's staff from between his feet,
> Until Shiloh come: And unto him shall the obedience of the peoples be.

The word translated "Shiloh" has been confusing for translators. As the authors of this book, we agree with many commentators who take it as a proper noun, the first proper name of the Messiah given in the Hebrew Scriptures. "Shiloh" is related to the Hebrew root *shala*, which means "to rest" or "to be secure." Thus, Shiloh could be translated as the proper name "Rest-Bringer," or perhaps "Peaceful One." However, there are variant texts, targums and other reputable sources with readings like "until he comes to whom it [the scepter or rule] belongs." The American Standard Version of 1901 and the New International Version represent the two basic ideas of how the verse should be handled:

> ASV: The sceptre shall not depart from Judah, Nor the ruler's staff from between his feet, Until **Shiloh** come: And unto him shall the obedience of the peoples be.

> NIV: The scepter will not depart from Judah, nor the ruler's staff from between his feet, until he comes **to whom it belongs** and the obedience of the nations is his.

The debate about the exact translation of this verse has raged loud and long, and we do not believe it will be settled here. What is settled, however, is that the verse is a prophecy of the coming Messiah, and a clear teaching that he would come through Judah, as both Jewish tradition and modern conservative commentators recognize. Thus, the Messiah would have to come through Abraham, Isaac, Jacob and Judah.

Numbers 24:17
A Star Out of Jacob

Numbers 24 contains a prophecy that was recognized by the ancient Jews to be about the coming Messiah. Interestingly, it was spoken by Balaam, a prophet of dubious character. He was actually hired to curse Israel, but at least was honest enough to speak the words that God gave him rather than invent words just to make money (of course, his encounter with an angel with a drawn sword had vividly reminded him of how short his life could be). He spoke powerful words about the coming Messiah.

> **Numbers 24:16–19 (NRSV)**
> (16) the oracle of one who hears the words of God, and knows the knowledge of the Most High, who sees the vision of the Almighty, who falls down, with his eyes uncovered:
> (17) I see him, but not now; I behold him, but not near—**a star** shall come out of Jacob, and **a scepter** shall rise out of Israel; it shall crush the borderlands of Moab, and the territory of all the Shethites.
> (18) Edom will become a possession, Seir a possession of its enemies, while Israel does valiantly.
> (19) One out of Jacob shall rule, and destroy the survivors of Ir."

Among the Jews, it was known and believed that the "star" and "scepter" referred to the coming Messiah and that he would indeed be a conquering hero. This prophecy foretold that the coming of the Messiah was going to be "not near," i.e., after a long time, and according to our best understanding of biblical chronology, the Messiah's coming was some 1400 years later. Balaam's prophecy is one more example of a prophecy portraying the coming Messiah as one who would fight battles and deliver the people, certainly not one who himself would suffer, particularly an ignoble death such as crucifixion.

2 Samuel 7:12 And 13
The Son of David

God promised David that the Messiah would come through him.

> **2 Samuel 7:12 and 13 (NRSV)**
> (12) When your days are fulfilled and you lie down with your ancestors, I will raise up your offspring ["seed"] after you, who shall come forth from your body, and I will establish his kingdom.
> (13) He shall build a house for my name, and I will establish the throne of his kingdom forever.

This prophecy clearly referred to the ultimate rule of the Messiah, and was taken as such. "Son of David" is a title used many times by the Jews in referring to the Messiah, and it occurs quite a few times in the Gospel records. In Matthew alone, the phrase is so used in 9:27, 12:23, 15:22, 20:30 and 31, 21:9 and 15, 22:42.

Psalm 2
The Messiah Opposed, Fighting and Ruling with a Rod of Iron

Psalm 2 has always been believed to be about God and His Messiah. Verse two says that the rulers of the earth will gather together against Yahweh [God] and His Anointed One [Christ]. Their confederacy will not succeed, however, and the Anointed will end up ruling with an iron scepter and dashing his enemies to pieces like a clay pot. The advice of the Psalm is to "Kiss the Son," (i.e., submit to his rule), because "…Blessed are all who take refuge in him."

Psalm 45
Your Throne Will Last Forever

Jewish and Christian commentators alike agree that Psalm 45 is about the Messiah. It is a very powerful Psalm, and speaks of the authority and power that the Lord God will give His Messiah. The Messiah can be clearly seen in the following verses:

Psalm 45:2–7 and 17 (NRSV)
(2) You are the most handsome of men; grace has been poured upon your lips; therefore God has blessed you forever.
(3) Gird your sword on your thigh, O mighty one, in your glory and majesty.
(4) In your majesty ride on victoriously for the cause of truth and to defend the right; let your right hand teach you dread deeds.
(5) Your arrows are sharp in the heart of the king's enemies; the peoples fall under you.
(6) Your throne, O God, endures forever and ever. Your royal scepter is a scepter of equity;[10]
(7) you love righteousness and hate wickedness. Therefore God, your God, has anointed you with the oil of gladness beyond your companions;
(17) I will cause your name to be celebrated in all generations; therefore the peoples will praise you forever and ever.

It is easy to see from Psalms like this how the people could be very surprised at the comparatively mild-mannered Jesus who told people to bless their persecutors, and who never once talked of getting an army together to conquer the earth. We can also see how the people would be confused when he spoke of his death, even in veiled terms. In John 12:23–36, Jesus was speaking of his death, and the crowd replied, "…We have heard from the Law that the Christ will remain forever…." This verse clearly shows that the people at the time of Christ were not expecting his death, and they were quoting Scripture to substantiate their beliefs. We see the same thing happening today. Many

---

10. The use of "god" in referring to the Messiah does not mean that he is the same as the Father or that there is a Trinity. The Jews used the word "god" to refer to those with God's authority. See Appendix A (Heb. 1:8). That the Messiah was to be subject to the Lord God is clearly set forth in verse 7.

Christians defend their theology by misapplying Scripture verses. The entire Word has to fit together without loose ends.

Psalm 72
The King, the Royal Son

Psalm 72 was considered by the ancient Jews to be about the Messiah. Edersheim writes:

"This Psalm also was viewed throughout by the ancient Synagogue as messianic, as indicated by the fact that the Targum renders the very first verse: 'Give the sentence of the judgment to the King Messiah, and Thy justice to the Son of David the King,' which is re-echoed by the Midrash, on the passage which applies it explicitly to the Messiah…."[11]

This Psalm has some wonderful verses about the Messiah:

Psalm 72:1, 2, 4–15 and 17 (NRSV)
(1) Give the king your justice, O God, and your righteousness to a king's son.
(2) May he judge your people with righteousness, and your poor with justice.
(4) May he defend the cause of the poor of the people, give deliverance to the needy, and crush the oppressor.
(5) May he live while the sun endures, and as long as the moon, throughout all generations.
(6) May he be like rain that falls on the mown grass, like showers that water the earth.
(7) In his days may righteousness flourish and peace abound, until the moon is no more.
(8) May he have dominion from sea to sea, and from the River to the ends of the earth.
(9) May his foes bow down before him, and his enemies lick the dust.
(10) May the kings of Tarshish and of the isles render him tribute, may the kings of Sheba and Seba bring gifts.
(11) May all kings fall down before him, all nations give him service.
(12) For he delivers the needy when they call, the poor and those who have no helper.
(13) He has pity on the weak and the needy, and saves the lives of the needy.
(14) From oppression and violence he redeems their life; and precious is their blood in his sight.
(15) Long may he live! May gold of Sheba be given to him. May prayer be given for him continually, and blessings invoked for him all day long.
(17) May his name endure forever, his fame continue as long as the sun. May all nations be blessed in him; may they pronounce him happy.

This Psalm promises that the Messiah will rescue the afflicted and make them prosper while their oppressors are crushed and made to lick the dust. Thus, it is easy to see why the disciples would want Jesus to become king, or why the crowds would shout "Hosanna" ("Save") when they thought Jesus was the Messiah. They wanted what this Psalm said the Messiah would accomplish. Verse 11 says that the kings of the earth will bow to him. The exaltation of the Messiah is an oft-repeated theme. It shows up again in Psalm 89, which the Jews also correctly applied to the Messiah:

11. Edersheim, *op. cit., The Life and Times*, Part 2, p. 719.

Psalm 89:24, 25 and 27 (NRSV)

(24) My faithfulness and steadfast love shall be with him; and in my name his horn shall be exalted.

(25) I will set his hand on the sea and his right hand on the rivers.

(27) I will make him the firstborn, the highest of the kings of the earth.

Psalm 110
Human Lord, Priest and King

Psalm 110 portrays the Messiah, and is quoted more in the New Testament than any other Psalm. This is especially noteworthy in that the entire Psalm is only seven verses. Verse one depicts the Lord God speaking to His anointed, His Messiah, and picks up the familiar theme of God and His Son conquering the earth: "The LORD says to my Lord: 'Sit at my right hand until I make your enemies a footstool for your feet." This verse gives us very clear evidence that the Jews expected the Messiah of God to be a created human being, not God Himself. "My Lord" is the Hebrew word *adoni*, a word only used of human masters and lords, and *never* God. This makes it very clear that the Jews were not expecting their Messiah to be God Himself, but were expecting a human "Lord."[12] The Jews listening to Peter quote this verse on the Day of Pentecost would have clearly seen the correlation between Peter's phrase "...a man accredited by God..." (Acts 2:22) and "my Lord" of Psalm 110:1, which he quoted shortly thereafter (Acts 2:34), and whom they would have understood to be a created human being.[13]

In this Psalm, a startling truth is revealed: The Messiah will not only be king, but he will be a *priest* also. Not a typical priest, for according to Mosaic Law all priests had to be descendants of Aaron of the tribe of Levi. But *this priest* will be after the order of Melchizedek. "The LORD has sworn and will not change his mind: 'You are a priest forever, in the order of Melchizedek'" (Ps. 110:4). Since Abraham paid tithes to Melchizedek, and Levi was "in the loins" of Abraham at the time, then this priest after the order of Melchizedek will be a greater priest than the Aaronic priests. Zechariah 6:13 also was known by the Jews to refer to the Messiah and showed him as a priest-king.

Although the ancient Jews never saw it as such, Christ understood that this verse referred to the fact that, after his resurrection and ascension, he would sit at God's right hand as "Lord" (Matt. 26:64).

---

12. This verse has been used by some to try to prove the Trinity. See Appendix A for a thorough refutation.

13. This verse has been used by some to try to prove the Trinity. But Anthony Buzzard writes:

Such a theory involves a misuse of the Hebrew language that can easily be cleared up. The two words for "Lord" in the sentence, "the LORD said to my Lord," are significantly different. The first "Lord" is Yahweh. The second word for "Lord" (here, "my Lord") is *adoni*, meaning, according to all standard Hebrew lexicons, "lord," "master," or "owner," and it refers here to the Messiah. If David had expected the Messiah to be God, the word used would not have been *adoni*, but *adonai*, a term used exclusively of the one God. There is an enormous difference between *adoni*, "my master," and *adonai*, the supreme God. The title *adoni* ("my Lord") is, in fact, never applied in the Hebrew Scriptures to the one God. In its 169 occurrences it refers only to superiors (mostly men and occasionally angels) *other than God*. This important fact tells us that the Hebrew Scriptures expected the Messiah to be not God but the human descendant of David, whom David properly recognized would also be his Lord.

Sir Anthony Buzzard, *The Doctrine of the Trinity, Christianity's Self-Inflicted Wound* (Atlanta Bible College, Box 100,000, Morrow, GA, 30260, 1994), p. 24.

Ecclesiastes 1:9
The Miracle Worker

The Jews taught that Ecclesiastes 1:9 ("That which has been is that which will be, And that which has been done is that which will be done. So, there is nothing new under the sun" NASB) showed that the Christ would do the same miracles that had been done in the Hebrew Scriptures, so they were expecting him to be a great miracle worker. This in part explains why Christ spoke so sternly against the cities that did not repent even though many of his miracles had been done there (Matt. 11:20–23), and why he told the Jews that the miracles he did spoke for him (John 10:25).

Isaiah 9:6 and 7
The Messiah's Endless Reign on David's Throne

Jews, both ancient and modern, and Christians alike, realize that Isaiah 9:6 and 7 are referring to the coming Messiah, and these verses, like some others, show the power and authority that God's Messiah will have. In his coming kingdom, which will last forever, there will be peace, justice and righteousness.

> **Isaiah 9:6 and 7 (NRSV)**
> (6) For a child has been born for us, a son given to us; authority rests upon his shoulders; and he is named Wonderful Counselor, Mighty God, Everlasting Father, Prince of Peace.
> (7) His authority shall grow continually, and there shall be endless peace for the throne of David and his kingdom. He will establish and uphold it with justice and with righteousness from this time onward and forevermore. The zeal of the LORD of hosts will do this.

That God's Messiah would rule the earth and bring justice to the nations was something the ancient Jews clearly understood. The fact that they applied verses like this to the Messiah demonstrates that. Because, since the time of Rehoboam, Solomon's son (1 Kings 12), the nation of Israel had been divided into ten northern tribes known as Israel and two southern tribes known as Judah, the promise that the Messiah would reign from David's throne over all Israel was astonishing. It seemed quite impossible to unite them since Israel had been destroyed by the Assyrians and was no longer a nation (2 Kings 17). A particularly eloquent and beautiful prophecy of the two being united is Amos 9:11: "On that day I will raise up the booth of David that is fallen, and repair its breaches, and raise up its ruins, and rebuild it as in the days of old" (NRSV).

By the time of Amos, King David's "tent" had certainly fallen. Israel and Judah were two nations at odds with each other, and Israel in particular had even officially turned away from the worship of Yahweh. Jeremiah 3:18, which spoke of the reuniting, was also correctly applied in the ancient Jewish writings to the time of the Messiah: "In those days the house of Judah will join the house of Israel, and together they will come from a northern land to the land I gave your forefathers as an inheritance." The Jews eagerly anticipated this reuniting. They just did not see that this restoration would occur at his *second* coming to the earth to Israel, an event that, admittedly, was not then clear to them in the Hebrew Scriptures.

A major blessing prophesied in the Hebrew Scriptures was that there would be justice in the Messiah's reign. There has been so little justice executed by the governments of the world that it is very comforting to know that the Messiah's kingdom will be one where justice prevails. There are also many other clear verses stating that the Messiah will rule the earth with justice.

Likewise, there are many verses that speak of peace in the Messiah's kingdom. In that sense, the title "Prince of Peace" fits him well. Zechariah 9:10 is a good example: "…I will cut off the chariot from Ephraim, and the horse from Jerusalem, and the battle bow shall be cut off: and he shall speak peace unto the heathen: and his dominion *shall be* from sea *even* to sea, and from the River *even* to the ends of the earth" (KJV).

Isaiah 11
The Branch of the Lord and His Kingdom

Even a cursory reading of this chapter shows why the Jews applied it to the coming Messiah. Isaiah 11 portrays in very graphic language what the kingdom of the Messiah would be like. It is no wonder that the Jews wanted to be a part of it. That is why, when John, and later Jesus and his Apostles, went about saying, "…Repent, for the kingdom of heaven is near" (Matt. 3:2, 4:17, 10:7, etc.), the people became very excited. That excitement never died in Jesus' followers, so even after his resurrection they asked, "…Lord, are you at this time going to restore the kingdom to Israel?" (Acts 1:6).

Isaiah 11:1–16 (NRSV)
(1) A shoot shall come out from the stump of Jesse, and a branch shall grow out of his roots.[14]
(2) The spirit of the LORD shall rest on him, the spirit of wisdom and understanding, the spirit of counsel and might, the spirit of knowledge and the fear of the LORD.
(3) His delight shall be in the fear of the LORD. He shall not judge by what his eyes see, or decide by what his ears hear;
(4) but with righteousness he shall judge the poor, and decide with equity for the meek of the earth; he shall strike the earth with the rod of his mouth, and with the breath of his lips he shall kill the wicked.
(5) Righteousness shall be the belt around his waist, and faithfulness the belt around his loins.
(6) The wolf shall live with the lamb, the leopard shall lie down with the kid, the calf and the lion and the fatling together, and a little child shall lead them.
(7) The cow and the bear shall graze, their young shall lie down together; and the lion shall eat straw like the ox.
(8) The nursing child shall play over the hole of the asp, and the weaned child shall put its hand on the adder's den.
(9) They will not hurt or destroy on all my holy mountain; for the earth will be full of the knowledge of the LORD as the waters cover the sea.
(10) On that day the Root of Jesse shall stand as a signal to the peoples; the nations shall enquire of him, and his dwelling shall be glorious.

---

14. We will discuss in detail the dramatic Messianic implications of the term "branch" in the next chapter.

(11) On that day the Lord will extend his hand yet a second time to recover the remnant that is left of his people, from Assyria, from Egypt, from Pathros, from Ethiopia, from Elam, from Shinar, from Hamath and from the coastlands of the sea.
(12) He will raise a signal for the nations, and will assemble the outcasts of Israel, and gather the dispersed of Judah from the four corners of the earth.
(13) The jealousy of Ephraim shall depart, the hostility of Judah shall be cut off; Ephraim shall not be jealous of Judah, and Judah shall not be hostile towards Ephraim.
(14) But they shall swoop down on the backs of the Philistines in the west, together they shall plunder the people of the east. They shall put forth their hand against Edom and Moab, and the Ammonites shall obey them.
(15) And the LORD will utterly destroy the tongue of the sea of Egypt; and will wave his hand over the River with his scorching wind; and will split it into seven channels, and make a way to cross on foot;
(16) so there shall be a highway from Assyria for the remnant that is left of his people, as there was for Israel when they came up from the land of Egypt.

This chapter is so beautiful and powerful in its portrayal of the future that it is difficult indeed to adequately summarize it in a few paragraphs. Jesse (v. 1) is King David's father. The everlasting throne had been promised to the seed of David, but other countries, including Syria, Egypt, Ammon and Moab, had attacked Israel and scattered her people. Even during Isaiah's life, the Assyrians attacked Israel and Judah and took many people captive. Isaiah 11 foretold that even if the throne of David looked cut off like a stump, there would come forth from it a "branch," one who would shoot up and bear much fruit as a great ruler of the people.[15]

Verses 2–5 describe his wonderful rule, beginning with the fact that the spirit of the LORD would rest on him. Other verses that the Jews applied to the Messiah foretold that God's spirit would be on him. An example is Isaiah 42:1: "Here is my servant, whom I uphold, my chosen one in whom I delight; I will put my Spirit on him and he will bring justice to the nations."

Verses 4ff portray the Messiah destroying the wicked so that the meek, the poor and the needy will be able to inherit the earth (see also Ps. 37:9–11; Matt. 5:5). During the Messiah's reign wild animals will be friendly toward each other and safe around children, and lions and other carnivores will eat plants again just as they did in the Garden of Eden (Gen. 1:30). This point is made a number of times in Scripture, and Isaiah 65:25 and Hosea 2:18 are good examples. Furthermore, the Lord will gather all the scattered people and bring them back to Israel, and enemy nations will be his subjects. The people of Christ's time knew and believed these prophecies, which explains why they were so anxious for the Messiah to come, and so astounded when he preached a "love your enemies" gospel and then was arrested and finally crucified. No wonder the two disciples on the road to Emmaus were walking away from Jerusalem disheartened, saying, "But we were hoping that it was He who was going to redeem Israel…" (Luke 24:21a - NASB). Nevertheless, let the reader be assured that our God, who "cannot lie," will fulfill all these prophecies. There is a time coming when those of Israel who were meek to believe God and were saved will inherit the land and see these promises fulfilled.

---

15. See Appendix A (Isa. 9:6).

Isaiah 25:8 and 26:19
Death Will Be Swallowed Up

The Bible clearly teaches that the dead will be raised. Some of the Jews at the time of Christ were looking forward to a resurrection and a judgment that would precede the Messiah's kingdom on earth. The following two verses are quoted in the Talmud as referring to the times of the Messiah:

Isaiah 25:8 (NRSV)
he will swallow up death forever. Then the Lord God will wipe away the tears from all faces, and the disgrace of his people he will take away from all the earth, for the LORD has spoken.

Isaiah 26:19 (NRSV)
Your dead shall live their corpses shall rise. O dwellers in the dust, awake and sing for joy! For your dew is a radiant dew, and the earth will give birth to those long dead.

Many of the people who believed in a resurrection looked forward to that day as a time when they would be reunited with their loved ones and get to meet "great" believers like Moses, Job and Daniel. With clear verses like these, how could the Sadducees possibly say that there was not going to be a resurrection (Matt. 22:23; Mark 12:18; Luke 20:27; Acts 23:8)? The answer is that the Sadducees based their beliefs only on the five books of Moses, which they did not believe taught life after death. They had their own philosophy as to why the books of Job, Daniel, Isaiah, Ezekiel, etc., which clearly taught the resurrection, were not actually foretelling a resurrection. Thus, there was genuine confusion at the time of Christ about the resurrection of the dead.

Isaiah 32:15a
The Spirit Is Poured Out from on High

One of the things the Jews were looking forward to when the Messiah came was an outpouring of the spirit of God. Isaiah 32:15a says: "until a spirit from on high is poured out on us…" (NRSV).[16] There are other verses referring to the spirit being poured out that the Jews knew applied to the time of the Messiah. Ezekiel 11:19 and Joel 2:28 also teach this truth. The ancient Jews were expecting that during the time of the Messiah every one of them would become a prophet or prophetess. Joel 2:28 says, "Then afterward I will pour out my spirit on all flesh; your sons and your daughters shall prophesy, your old men shall dream dreams, and your young men shall see visions" (NRSV).

Isaiah 32:15b and 20
The Land Is Healed, the Desert Blooms

Ancient Jews believed that in the days of the Messiah, the curse on the ground would be removed and the land would produce abundantly. Many Scriptures declare this future reality. Isaiah 32:15b says: "…and the wilderness becomes a fruitful field, and the fruitful field is deemed a forest" (NRSV). Also Isaiah 35:6b, "…For waters shall break forth in the wilderness, and streams in the desert" (NRSV).

---

16. See footnote 14 in this chapter.

Although these promises have not come to pass yet, they will happen—the promise of God will not remain unfulfilled.

However, this promise was not to be fulfilled when Christ came as the Lamb of God, but as the Lion of Judah; not as the one whose heel will be bruised, but as the one who will "bruise" the Adversary. Still another verse that was correctly understood as applying to the abundance during the Messianic Age is Joel 3:18: "In that day the mountains shall drip sweet wine, the hills shall flow with milk, and all the streambeds of Judah shall flow with water; a fountain shall come forth from the house of the LORD and water the Wadi Shittim" (NRSV). Ezekiel 47:9 and 12 were two other verses that the ancient Jews knew foretold of abundance in the time of the Messiah.

The Jews who were looking for the Messiah were confused when promises like these were not fulfilled. When Jesus was hanging on the Cross, it certainly looked to them like he did not fulfill the scriptural requirements for the Messiah.

Isaiah 35:5 and 6
The People Healed

Just as there are many verses foretelling that the land will be healed in the kingdom of the Messiah, there are also verses that foretell the healing of the people:

Isaiah 35:5 and 6 (NRSV)
(5) Then the eyes of the blind shall be opened, and the ears of the deaf unstopped;
(6) Then the lame shall leap like a deer, and the tongue of the speechless sing for joy.
For waters shall break forth in the wilderness, and streams in the desert;

Sickness has been a terrible problem since the days of Adam. For most of recorded history, sickness has been chronic and lifespans have been short. The prophecies that healing would be part of the Messianic Kingdom produced great excitement. A verse in Malachi believed by the ancient Jews to apply to the coming of the Messiah said, "…the sun of righteousness [the Messiah] shall rise, with healing in its wings." (Mal. 4:2 - NRSV). This verse seems nonsensical to most Christians because they do not understand "wings." The "wings" referred to are the "corners" of the outer garments worn by the people (see Num. 15:38 and Ruth 3:9 where the same Hebrew word is translated as "corners," not "wings").

The prophecy in Malachi was clearly understood by the Jews. They read and understood the Hebrew text that when the Messiah came, he would have healing in the corners of his garments. And people were indeed healed when, with faith, they touched the "wings" of his garments (Matt. 9:20–22, 14:34–36). The record in Matthew is revealing because it portrays a woman who kept saying to herself, "…If I only touch His garment, I shall get well" (Matt. 9:21 - NASB). This indicated that she believed Jesus was the Messiah, and in fact, because of his healing miracles, many other people believed that also. Jesus certainly healed many people, and because of his healings many believed that he was the Christ. Still, as the record in Acts 3 indicates, not everyone in Israel was healed by Jesus. However, the Bible foretells a time when everyone will be healed.

Isaiah 49:8–10, 22 and 23
Israel Restored, Captives Freed, Favor Bestowed

Isaiah 49 contains some great promises that the Jews recognized as prophecies of the Messianic Kingdom.

Isaiah 49:8–10, 22 and 23 (NRSV)

(8) Thus says the LORD: In a time of favor I have answered you, on a day of salvation I have helped you; I have kept you and given you as a covenant to the people, to establish the land, to apportion the desolate heritages;

(10) they shall not hunger or thirst, neither scorching wind nor sun shall strike them down, for he who has pity on them will lead them, and by springs of water will guide them.

(22) Thus says the Lord GOD: I will soon lift up my hand to the nations, and raise my signal to the peoples; and they shall bring your sons in their bosom, and your daughters shall be carried on their shoulders.

(23) Kings shall be your foster fathers, and their queens your nursing mothers. With their faces to the ground they shall bow down to you, and lick the dust of your feet. Then you will know that I am the LORD; those who wait for me shall not be put to shame.

It does not take too much imagination to see why verses like these would excite the Jews. God promised that Jews would once again rule Israel, and that their covenant blessings would be restored. He further said that all Jewish captives would be freed and get to come back to Israel. And not just freed, but actually escorted home by Gentiles. This is no small feat, because Jews had been taken captive for generations and the "Diaspora" were scattered all over the world. Many Jews were slaves of individuals or of the Roman state or slaves in other countries. Notice how, in contrast to the way Jews were usually the slaves and servants of others, in the Messianic Kingdom they will be favored.

There are many verses that the Jews correctly interpreted about being restored to their land during the time of the Messiah. Ezekiel 48 foretells how the Messiah will divide up the land of Israel among the tribes, and he will get a portion of Israel for himself.[17]

Isaiah 52:13, 53:5 and 10
The Suffering Savior

As we have said, some Jews saw that the Messiah would have to suffer, but they did not see his death and resurrection. Just before what we now clearly see as a classic prophecy about his suffering and death, comes Isaiah 52:13, which speaks of the exaltation of the Messiah: "See, my servant will act wisely; he will be raised and lifted up and highly exalted.[18]

---

17. Edersheim has the following comment on his note on Ezekiel 48:19: "The Talmud (Baba B 122a) has the following curious comment, that the land of Israel would be divided into thirteen tribes, the thirteenth belonging to the Prince (*op. cit., The Life and Times*, Book Two, p. 733).

18. Edersheim comments on what the ancient Jews wrote about the Messiah's suffering and exaltation:

"On the words 'He shall be exalted and extolled,' we read in Yalkut ii. (Para., 338, p. 53c, lines 7 etc. from the bottom): 'He shall be higher than Abraham, to whom applies Gen. 14:22; higher than Moses, of whom Num. 11:12 is predicated; higher than the ministering angels, of whom Ezek. 1:18 is said. But to him there applies this in Zech. 4:7: 'Who art thou, O great mountain?' 'And he was wounded for our transgressions, and bruised for our iniquities, and the chastisement of our peace was upon him, and with his stripes we are healed.' R[abbi] Huna

Isaiah 53:5 and 10

(5) But he was pierced for our transgressions, he was crushed for our iniquities; the punishment that brought us peace was upon him, and by his wounds we are healed.
(10) Yet it was the LORD's will to crush him and cause him to suffer, and though the LORD makes his life a guilt offering, he will see his offspring and prolong his days, and the will of the LORD will prosper in his hand.

Reading Jewish commentaries about these verses gives one a clear picture of the "blindness" (Rom. 11:7 - KJV) that came over Israel regarding their Messiah. This blindness is referred to several times in the Epistles of Paul. Reference is made to the fact that without Christ, the Jews read the Old Testament with a veil over their faces and their minds are "dull" (2 Cor. 3:14). Ancient Jewish commentaries say that Isaiah 52:13 and *some* verses in Chapter 53 refer to the Messiah. But, remarkably, the commentaries do not recognize that *all* of the verses in Chapter 53 refer to the Messiah, nor do they note that there is anything in the context of the chapter that would change the focus of its subject matter. In Chapters 52 and 53, the entire picture of the Messiah is set forth: his sufferings (52:14–53:7), his death (53:8, 9 and 12), his resurrection (53:10 and 11) and his exaltation (52:13, 53:10–12). The natural interpretation of Isaiah 52 and 53 would seem to be that Christ would suffer, die, and then, soon after his resurrection, he would set up his kingdom. Yet the Jews did not understand that. Isaiah 53 does not mention ascension into heaven. There is nothing in this record indicating that Christ would ascend up to heaven instead of conquering the earth and establishing a kingdom. Uncertainty about Christ's ascension is why the disciples asked him after his resurrection if he were going to set up the kingdom "at this time" (Acts 1:6 - KJV).

As we have seen by learning of "Messiah Ben Joseph," some of the ancient Jews did believe there would be a suffering Savior, but their picture of this man was confusing and not based on a clear exegesis of Scripture. Another verse that mentions the suffering of the Messiah is Zechariah 12:10, which says, "…They will look on me, the one they have pierced…." According to the ancient writings, this section of Scripture was applied to Messiah Ben Joseph, and even then disputed as to exactly what it meant. Its genuine interpretation is given in John 19:37—it refers to when Jesus was on the Cross and the soldier came and pierced his side.

Clearly there was confusion about the suffering of the Messiah. Were there really to be two Messiahs, of which only one would suffer? Was the Messiah to suffer for a week, or how long? And for Israel only or for righteous Gentiles as well? And for all Israel, such that both good and evil Israelites would be saved? If you find this confusing, so did the Jews, especially since they read many clear prophecies about a conquering Messiah. There are many Scriptures, and clear ones at that, which speak of the conquests of the Messiah and his wonderful kingdom, so a suffering Savior was not generally expected, as we have seen.

---

says, in the name of R[abbi] Acha: 'All sufferings are divided into three parts; one part goes to David and the Patriarchs, another to the generation of the rebellion (rebellious Israel), and the third to King Messiah…In regard to Isaiah 53, we remember that the messianic name of 'Leprous' (Sanh. 98b) is expressly based upon it. Isaiah 53:10 is applied in the Targum on the passage to the Kingdom of the Messiah"
(*Ibid.*, p. 727).

Isaiah 63
The Conquering Messiah

Isaiah 63 was known by the ancient Jews to apply to the Messiah conquering the Gentile enemies.

Isaiah 63:1–4 (NRSV)
(1) "Who is this that comes from Edom, from Bozrah with garments stained crimson? Who is this so splendidly robed, marching in his great might?" "It is I, announcing vindication, mighty to save."
(2) "Why are your robes red, and your garments like theirs who tread the wine press?"
(3) "I have trodden the wine press alone, and from the peoples no one was with me; I trod them in my anger and trampled them in my wrath; their juice spattered on my garments, and stained all my robes.
(4) For the day of vengeance was in my heart, and the year for my redeeming work had come.

The illustration of the "wine press," found here in Isaiah, is found also in the book of Revelation regarding the Battle of Armageddon (14:19 and 20). Verses like these, which graphically portray the battle that will precede the kingdom, reinforced the people's idea that Christ would be a conqueror. Many verses speak of the destruction of the wicked when the Messiah comes. Isaiah 11:4, already quoted, says: "…with the breath of his lips he shall kill the wicked." Malachi 4:1 says: "'See, the day is coming, burning like an oven, when all the arrogant and all evildoers will be stubble; the day that comes shall burn them up, says the LORD of hosts, so that it will leave them neither root nor branch'" (NRSV). Verses like these also reinforced the idea that only the meek would be left alive to inherit the earth, and that the Messiah's kingdom would be peaceful and prosperous.

The Jews were not expecting the kind and gentle Jesus who died for their sins. They rightly believed that the nations, once conquered, would obey the world-rule of the Messiah. They correctly applied to the Messianic Age verses like Daniel 7:27 ("…His kingdom will be an everlasting kingdom, and all rulers will worship and obey him"). Also, Zephaniah 3:8: "Therefore wait for me,' declares the LORD, 'for the day I will stand up to testify. I have decided to assemble the nations, to gather the kingdoms and to pour out my wrath on them—all my fierce anger. The whole world will be consumed by the fire of my jealous anger."

Isaiah 65:17–25
Blessings in the Messiah's Kingdom

Isaiah 65:17–25 portrays some of what the Jews expected life would be like in the Messiah's kingdom.

Isaiah 65:17–25 (NRSV)
(17) For I am about to create new heavens and a new earth; the former things shall not be remembered or come to mind.
(18) But be glad and rejoice forever in what I am creating; for I am about to create Jerusalem as a joy, and its people as a delight.
(19) I will rejoice in Jerusalem, and delight in my people; no more shall the sound of weeping be heard in it, or the cry of distress.

(20) No more shall there be in it an infant that lives but a few days, or an old person who does not live out a lifetime; for one who dies at a hundred years will be considered a youth, and one who falls short of a hundred will be considered accursed.

(21) They shall build houses and inhabit them; they shall plant vineyards and eat their fruit.

(22) They shall not build and another inhabit; they shall not plant and another eat; for like the days of a tree shall the days of my people be, and my chosen shall long enjoy the work of their hands.

(23) They shall not labor in vain, or bear children for calamity; for they shall be offspring blessed by the LORD—and their descendants as well.

(24) Before they call I will answer, while they are yet speaking I will hear.

(25) The wolf and the lamb shall feed together, the lion shall eat straw like the ox; but the serpent—its food shall be dust! They shall not hurt or destroy on all my holy mountain, says the LORD.

These verses were applied by the ancient Jews to the kingdom of the Messiah, and they portray a time of great prosperity, peace and enjoyment. There will be no more weeping or crying, and the fact that the curse that now plagues the earth will be removed is shown by stating that wild animals will live together in harmony and the carnivores will eat plants. Verses 21–23 portray the blessing of the LORD—that people would live in peace and harmony. Zechariah 3:10 says: "On that day, says the LORD of hosts, you shall invite each other to come under your vine and fig tree" (NRSV).[19]

Jeremiah 3:17
The Nations Honor the Lord

The Scriptures that the ancient Jews applied to the time of the Messiah did not only involve him conquering some of the Gentiles and then enslaving them, but also portrayed the destruction of

---

19. In spite of the obvious blessings portrayed by these verses, they have confused both ancient Jews and modern Christians alike. People become confused because these verses mention death in the Messiah's kingdom, but do not explain it clearly. This problem is magnified because, in the next chapter, Isaiah 66:22 was applied to the Messiah's kingdom. It reads: "As the new heavens and the new earth that I make will endure before me,' declares the LORD, 'so will your name and descendants endure." So it seems that one verse says that there will be death in the Kingdom, while another says there will not be. How can this apparent contradiction be explained?

Many subjects in the Word of God are unclear if only one section of Scripture is read. However, answers to questions can be found by comparing Scripture with Scripture and building a complete understanding as the pieces fit together. First, why does the Word say there will be a new heaven and earth? The answer is that during the Tribulation, and in particular the Battle of Armageddon, the earth as we know it will be greatly devastated. The Messiah will have to make it over, change animal nature, repopulate the seas and the land with fish, animals, plants, etc. And, yes, some people in the Messiah's kingdom will die, but not those who have already died once and been raised from the dead. The people who will die during the Kingdom are those who will be alive during the Tribulation and be among the "fortunate" ones who live through it and then are allowed to enter the Messiah's kingdom as mortals (Matt. 25:31–40). These people will marry, have children and die, just as people do today. In fact, they will have lots of children. The earth's population will explode during the 1000 year reign of the Messiah. The earth will go from having very few people at the end of the Tribulation (Isa. 13:9–12 and 24:1–6) to having people "...like the sand on the seashore" by the end of Christ's Millennial Kingdom (Rev. 20:8). The 1000 year reign of Christ will end with Satan being loosed, the nations being deceived and rebelling against God and Christ, and God raining fire down from heaven and destroying the earth (Rev. 20:7–10). Then there will be another "...new heaven and a new earth..." (Rev. 21:1), complete with a city with streets of gold (Rev. 21:21).

the rebellious Gentiles. Other people, once conquered, choose to participate in the worship of the LORD, many apparently with a more-than-willing heart. There are quite a few verses that foretell this:

Jeremiah 3:17 (NASB)
"At that time they shall call Jerusalem 'The Throne of the LORD,' and all the nations will be gathered to it, to Jerusalem, for the name of the LORD; nor shall they walk anymore after the stubbornness of their evil heart.

Zephaniah 3:9 (NASB)
"For then I will give to the peoples purified lips, That all of them may call on the name of the LORD, To serve Him shoulder to shoulder.

Isaiah 56:7 (NASB)
Even those [foreigners] I will bring to My holy mountain, And make them joyful in My house of prayer. Their burnt offerings and sacrifices will be acceptable on My altar; for My house will be called a house of prayer for all the peoples."

Isaiah 60:3 (NASB)
"And nations will come to your light, And kings to the brightness of your rising.

Zechariah 8:23 (NASB)
"Thus says the LORD of hosts: 'In those days ten men from all the nations will grasp the garment of a Jew saying, "Let us go with you [to Jerusalem], for we have heard that God is with you."'"

Perhaps the earliest reference to the Gentiles worshipping with the Jews is in Genesis 9:27, which says that Japheth will dwell in the tents of Shem. One of the Targums interprets that to mean that the Gentiles will become proselytes.

Jeremiah 30:21
One of Their Own

Jewish theology, both ancient and modern, is aggressively monotheistic. Suggesting to such Jews, who will not even pronounce the name of God, that the Messiah is none other than God Himself come down from heaven (or one of a three-part Godhead) is, to them, absurd and offensive. They were expecting the Messiah to be a "son" of Abraham, Isaac, Jacob, David, etc. He was also expected to have a mother and a family. Other Scriptures affirm this. Jeremiah 30:21 is one of those, and the ancient writings confirm that the Jews applied this verse to their Messiah: "'And their leader shall be one of them, And their ruler shall come forth from their midst; And I will bring him near, and he shall approach Me; For who would dare to risk his life to approach Me?' declares the LORD" [NASB].

Jeremiah 31:31, 33 and 34
The New Covenant

One of the things the Jews realized the Messiah was to do was to establish a new covenant with Israel in place of the one made at the time of Moses.

Jeremiah 31:31, 33 and 34 [NASB]

(31) "Behold, days are coming," declares the LORD, "when I will make a new covenant with the house of Israel and with the house of Judah.

(33) "But this is the covenant which I will make with the house of Israel after those days," declares the LORD, "I will put My law within them, and on their heart I will write it; and I will be their God, and they shall be My people.

(34) "And they shall not teach again, each man his neighbor and each man his brother, saying, 'Know the LORD,' for they shall all know Me, from the least of them to the greatest of them," declares the LORD, "for I will forgive their iniquity, and their sin I will remember no more."

The Jews were looking for a king who would make a new covenant with them.[20] God promised that part of the New Covenant would be that the Law would be written on the hearts of the people. The Jews believed this and saw that this promise was restated in other Scriptures. For example, Ezekiel 11:19 was applied by the ancient Jews to the day of the Messiah: "And I shall give them one heart, and shall put a new spirit within them. And I shall take the heart of stone out of their flesh and give them a heart of flesh" (NASB). So was Ezekiel 36:27: "And I will put my Spirit within you and cause you to walk in my statutes, and you will be careful to observe my ordinances" (NASB). Hosea 3:5 says "…the Israelites will return and seek the LORD their God and David (the Messiah) their king. They will come trembling to the LORD and to his blessings in the last days."

Daniel 2:44
The Kingdom That Will Never End

We have seen that the ancient Jews believed that the Messiah would set up a kingdom. The Jewish writings establish that beyond any doubt, and Zechariah 14:9, applied by the ancient Jews to the kingdom of the Messiah, states: "The LORD will be king over the whole earth…." Daniel 2:44 is one of the clearer verses that speaks of the Messiah's kingdom: "In the time of those kings, the God of heaven will set up a kingdom that will never be destroyed, nor will it be left to another people. It will crush all those kingdoms and bring them to an end, but it will itself endure forever." It is to the Jews' credit that at least they knew what the Messiah's kingdom will be like:

- The Messiah will rule from Jerusalem, from David's throne (Isa. 9:7, etc.).
- Jerusalem will be exalted (Isa. 2:1–4, 62:1–7; Mic. 4:1–8; Zech. 2:12, etc.).
- The land will be restored to both Israel and Judah (Isa. 11:10–16; Jer. 3:18, 23:3–8, 31:8–11, 33:7; Ezek. 11:17, 28:25, 37:15–28; Hosea 1:10 and 11, etc.).
- The wicked will be destroyed but the meek will inherit the earth (Ps. 37:9–11; Ezek. 37:11 and 12; Dan. 12:2 and 3; Zeph. 3:8–12; Mal. 4:1, etc.).
- The house of Israel will know God (Isa. 29:23 and 24; Jer. 31:33 and 34; Ezek. 11:18–20, etc.).
- The nations will be conquered and ruled with a "rod of iron" (Ps. 2:9; Isa. 11:4, 14:2, 49:22 and 23, 60:10–14; Mic. 7:16 and 17; Zech. 14:16–19, etc.).

---

20. Jesus did just that at his last supper. What is not generally understood is that there can be a long time between the making of a covenant and when that covenant is fulfilled. God made a covenant with Abraham for the land of Israel, and today, after almost 4000 years, it has still not been fulfilled. The New Covenant that Christ made at the last supper will not be fulfilled until his kingdom is established on earth.

- The conquered nations will come to Jerusalem to worship (Isa. 2:1–3, 19:18–25, 56:4–8, 66:19–21; Zech. 2:11, 8:20–23, 14:16, etc.).
- There will be justice on earth (Isa. 2:4, 9:6 and 7, 11:1–5, 32:1, 2, 5, 16 and 17; Jer. 23:5 and 6, 33:15, etc.).
- There will be no war (Isa. 2:4, 9:4, 5 and 7; Mic. 4:3 and 4; Zech. 9:9–11; Hosea 2:18, etc.).
- The people of Israel will be healed (Isa. 29:18, 32:3 and 4, 33:24, 35:5 and 6; Jer. 33:6; Mal. 4:2, etc.).
- People will live in safety (Isa. 11:6–9, 32:18, 54:14–17, 60:15–18, 65:17–25; Jer. 23:4–6, 33:6; Ezek. 28:26, 34:25–31; Mic. 5:4 and 5; Zeph. 3:13–17, etc.).
- There will be an abundance of food (Isa. 25:6, 30:23–26, 35:1, 6 and 7, 41:18–20, 51:3; Jer. 31:5, 11–14; Ezek. 47:1, 2, 7–12; Hosea 2:21 and 22; Joel 2:19, 22–26, 3:18; Amos 9:13, etc.)..

What wonderful promises! What a great kingdom to look forward to! It is easy to see that what the Bible foretells about the Messiah's kingdom has not happened yet. The Jews thought Christ would bring it, but we can now see that this kingdom will not be established until his Second Coming to the earth to save Israel. The Jews, however, thinking that the Messiah would come only once and usher in this kingdom at that time, believed Jesus to be a fake, a fraud. He said the kingdom was close, but his actions were not king-like, at least according to them.[21]

Daniel 7:13
Coming in the Clouds of Heaven

Daniel 7:13 and 14 (NASB)
(13) "I kept looking in the night visions, And behold, with the clouds of heaven One like a Son of Man was coming, And He came up to the Ancient of Days And was presented before Him.
(14) "And to Him was given dominion, Glory and a kingdom, That all the peoples, nations, and *men of every* language Might serve Him. His dominion is an everlasting dominion Which will not pass away; And His kingdom is one Which will not be destroyed.

Verse 13 is spoken of in the Talmud where it is said that if Israel is worthy, the Messiah will come in the clouds of heaven, but if Israel is unworthy, then the Messiah will ride in on a donkey. This is an example of how close the Jews could be to the truth and yet miss it. The prophecy was that the Messiah was to be born of a woman; of Abraham, Isaac, Jacob, Judah and David; and that he was to be "from among his brothers." Putting the Scriptures together, Christ would have to be born of a woman and come in a gentle and humble way, and suffer. Yet he would also have to come in the clouds of heaven to conquer and rule. The only way for all these verses to be true is that there would have to be two

---

21. The Jews were not the only ones to misunderstand the prophecies concerning the coming kingdom. Most Christians misunderstand the prophecies of the Messianic Kingdom, but for other reasons. First and foremost, they are taught that "heaven," not the earth, is the future home for all Christians. However, this erroneous idea negates the words of Christ that "…the meek shall inherit the earth…," and makes them into something like "the saved shall inherit the air." See our book: *op. cit., Is There Death After Life?*

separate comings.[22] Of course Jesus understood it that way, and he taught it when he quoted Daniel 7:13 as recorded in Matthew 24:30, 26:64; Mark 13:26 and Luke 21:27.

Amos 5:18
A Time of Trouble

It was not lost on some of the Rabbis that the Hebrew Scriptures foretold a time of trouble when the Messiah came. Edersheim writes: "Amos 5:18 is one of the passages adduced in the Talmud (Sanh. 98b) to explain why certain Rabbis did not wish to see the day of the Messiah."[23] Amos 5:18 says: "Woe to you who long for the day of the LORD! Why do you long for the day of the LORD? That day will be darkness, not light."[24]

Micah 5:2
The Messiah To Come from Bethlehem

The Jews also knew the verse quoted in the New Testament that the Messiah was to be born in Bethlehem. "But you, Bethlehem Ephrathah, though you are small among the clans of Judah, out of you will come for me one who will be ruler over Israel, whose origins are from of old, from ancient times" (Mic. 5:2). Part of this verse has been fulfilled: the Messiah, Jesus, was born in Bethlehem. One day, he will be Israel's king.

Micah 5:3
Israel Conquered by Enemies

Micah 5:3 states: "Therefore Israel will be abandoned until the time when she who is in labor gives birth and the rest of his brothers return to join the Israelites." The Talmud teaches that enemies will occupy Israel for nine months before the Messiah would come.[25] It is true that Israel will be occupied by enemies before the Messiah comes, but the nine month figure is inaccurate (Dan. 7:25; Rev. 11:2, 12:6 and 14, 13:5). Some of the Jews living at the time of Christ saw the Roman occupation as a fulfillment of this, and were expecting the Messiah to come and deliver them. Zechariah 14:2 was another verse that the ancient Jews understood to portray the conquest of Jerusalem before the advent of the Messiah: "I will gather all the nations to Jerusalem to fight against it; the city will be captured, the houses ransacked, and the women raped. Half of the city will go into exile, but the rest of the people will not be taken from the city."

---

22. We believe the same is true regarding his Second Coming. The only way for all the Scriptures to be true regarding his coming again is if his advent is in two parts. First he comes *for* his saints (Christians, who meet him in the air), then he comes *with* his saints (Israel [and Gentile proselytes], who go into the land). Between the two events is the "Great Tribulation," from which Christians will be spared.

23. Edersheim, *op. cit., The Life and Times*, p. 734.

24. Some ancient Jews were not the only ones to wish for the delay of the Messiah. There have also been Christians who have prayed that his Second Coming not be during their lifetime because they, not believing in a pre-Tribulation rapture, thought that they would have to go through the Tribulation just before he comes. See: *The Formation of Christian Dogma* by Martin Werner (Boston, Beacon Press, 1957), p. 43. Knowing the truth of the pre-Tribulation rapture allows us to pray fervently, "Come, O Lord! [Jesus]" (1 Cor. 16:22).

25. Edersheim, *op. cit., The Life and Times*, Book Two, p. 735.

Zechariah 6:12 and 13
The Temple Builder

The ancient Jewish writings universally applied both Zechariah 6:12 and 13 to the Messiah:

Zechariah 6:12 and 13 (NASB)
(12) "Then say to him, 'Thus says the LORD of hosts, "Behold a man whose name is Branch, for He will branch out from where He is; and He will build the temple of the LORD.
(13) "Yes, it is He who will build the temple of the LORD, and He will bear the honor and sit and rule on His throne. Thus, He will be a priest on His throne, and the counsel of peace will be between the two offices." '

One of the ancient names for the Messiah was "the Branch," and one of the things he would do is build a Temple. Obviously, Jesus did not do so during his first coming, but the Scripture will not be broken. When he comes to conquer the world, he will build a Temple. The Temple that he will build, its location and some of the sacrifices and offerings are described in Ezekiel 40–48. Many modern Christians miss this altogether because they interpret the Temple in Ezekiel as an allegory, and say that the Church is the Temple. It is true that the Church is figuratively a Temple, but we are not *the* Temple described in Ezekiel, complete with an altar, sacrifices, priests, storerooms, meathooks, washing basins, etc. The Temple in Ezekiel sits in the center of the land that was promised to Israel and in the Kingdom promised to Christ. When Christ comes back to earth, he will make good the prophecy that he will build the Temple.

Zechariah, like Psalm 110 (which we already covered) shows the Messiah to be a priest-king. Thus, not only will Christ be a King, but as High Priest he will oversee the Temple.

Zechariah 9:9
The King on a Donkey

It was believed by the ancient Jews that the victorious Messiah would ride into Jerusalem on a donkey. Edersheim writes: "We may here add that there are many traditions about this ass on which the Messiah is to ride; and so firm was the belief in it, that, according to the Talmud, 'If anyone saw an ass in his dreams, he will see salvation.'[26] Of course, Jesus did ride into Jerusalem on a donkey, but not after he conquered the Gentile nations. In fact, it was just before he was crucified.

Zechariah 9:9 (NASB)
Rejoice greatly, O Daughter of Zion! Shout *in triumph*, O Daughter of Jerusalem! Behold, your king is coming to you; He is just and endowed with salvation, Humble, and mounted on a donkey, Even on a colt, the foal of a donkey.

The fact that Jesus was riding into Jerusalem on a donkey was not lost on the crowds, who shouted, "…Hosanna to the Son of David!" "Blessed is he who comes in the name of the Lord!" "Hosanna in the highest!" (Matt. 21:9). "Hosanna" means "Save," and "Son of David" was a common Messianic title. The crowds were excited, and expected Jesus to miraculously fulfill the prophecies and "save"

---

26. *Ibid.*, Book Two, p. 736.

them. When he was later arrested, they were disappointed, and shouted "Crucify him" (Matt. 27:22 and 23). Yet the prophecy also contains words that indicate that Christ would not ride into Jerusalem as a conqueror. When he came on the donkey he was to be "humble," and bringing salvation. And he did. He did bring salvation—but not the salvation the Jews were looking for, which was salvation from the Romans. Had he then come in judgment, many of them would not have passed muster. No, he came with salvation by being the humble Lamb of God, who, by paying for the sins of mankind, would offer everlasting life to those deserving of it.

Malachi 4:5
Elijah Will Come First

Malachi 4:5 was quite confusing to the ancient Jews. It says: "Behold, I am going to send you Elijah the prophet before the coming of the great and terrible day of the LORD" (NASB). The Jews did not know what to do with this verse, and so opinions varied. Many believed that Elijah would descend from heaven in the same manner as he was taken up. Others believed that Elijah would be raised from the dead and come back.

The answer to the "riddle" of the coming of Elijah is found in a figure of speech common to both modern language and the Bible. The figure of speech is called *antonomasia*, which Webster defines as "the use of the name of some office, dignity, profession, science, or trade instead of the true name of the person; a grave man is called a *Cato*, an eminent orator, a *Cicero*, a wise man, a *Solomon*." It is common in languages that when you want to show that one person is like another in some way, you often call that person by the other's name. If a child is jumping on a couch, you might say, "Stop it, Tarzan!" Or if someone makes a great shot in basketball, you might say, "Nice shot, Michael Jordan."

In order to transfer the characteristics of one person to another, all that is sometimes needed is to change the name. Thus, the Messiah is called "David" in Ezekiel 37:24 to emphasize that he would sit on David's throne. The kingdom of Judah is called "Sodom" and "Gomorrah" when they were deep in sin (Isa. 1:10). Jezebel called Jehu, the king of Israel, "Zimri" (2 Kings 9:31), to see if she could scare him. Jehu was about to kill her, and Zimri had killed to become king but then reigned for only seven days before he himself was killed. Using a well-known name or title to import meaning is simple and effective. God said "Elijah" would come before the great day of the LORD. Not the Elijah who had lived and died, but someone with his fiery spirit. That person was John the Baptist, as Christ said in Matthew 17:10–13.

Summary of the Evidence of the Hebrew Scriptures

It should be quite clear by now that the Messiah the Jews were expecting and the Messiah who came were very different. The Messiah who came brought no world-wide kingdom, no uniting of Israel and Judah, no destruction of ancient enemies, no ideal world with peace, justice, food and healing. In fairness to them, remember that the fact that Christ would come in two appearings, one as the suffering servant, and another, years later, as the Lion of Judah, is not clearly stated in the Hebrew Scriptures. No single Scripture says something like, "The Messiah will come, suffer, die, be raised and then come again as a conqueror." The virgin birth is not clearly stated, nor is Herod's killing of children around Bethlehem, nor is Christ's trip to Egypt as a child. His death and resurrection are mentioned, but not so clearly that the Jews understood the truth about them, and his ascension into heaven is very unclear. No wonder Jesus said to Peter, who correctly identified him as the Christ, "…this was not revealed to you by man, but by my Father in heaven" (Matt. 16:17).

Do the Jews who rejected Christ have a valid excuse? No, for the Father has always been more than willing to reveal the Messiah to any and all who seek him from the heart. We just saw that many of the Old Testament Scriptures portrayed things about the coming Messiah that should have caused the Jews to see who he was to be and understand his two comings to Israel. For example, he was going to be of the line of David, but also come in the clouds of heaven. He was going to be gentle and have salvation, but also be a fierce warrior, killing his enemies and dashing them with a rod of iron. He was going to be pierced, but also going to conquer his enemies and pierce them with his arrows. Isaiah 52:13–53:12 shows his suffering, death, resurrection and glory. Also, as the Gospels record, some people believed he was the Messiah because of the miracles and healings he performed, and he rebuked the cities that did not accept him, especially those where he did many of his miracles.

A great lesson to learn about the things of God from this study of the Hebrew Scriptures is that, although Scripture may not always be totally obvious, God looks on the heart of each person and promises that those who hunger and thirst after righteousness will be filled. Many in the Old Testament found that out, including the prophets who wrote the Scriptures that reveal the Messiah.

The Messiah Unveiled in the New Testament

The "New Testament" writings, especially the Four Gospels, reveal a perspective of the Hebrew Scriptures that was basically concealed from the Jews living in that time. As 2 Corinthians 3:14 says, and we have noted in this chapter, the Hebrew Scriptures were "veiled," but that veil is taken off in Christ. Therefore, by reading the Gospels, Acts, the Church Epistles and the General Epistles the reader should expect to get a much clearer understanding of the Old Testament prophecies about Jesus Christ. The New Testament writers and Jesus himself explained many verses in the Hebrew Scriptures that were previously unnoticed or unclear. What follows are some important examples of how the Synoptic Gospels clarify both the Old Testament prophecies and how Jesus fulfilled them. These prophecies, and their application in the Gospels, continue the discussion about the Messiah the Jews were expecting. In this portion of the book, we have chosen to discuss the major prophecies concerning Christ that are cited in the Synoptic Gospels, because these prophecies contain some interesting and unique insights into the fulfillment of prophecy in general and how the Gospels view the way Jesus specifically fulfilled them.

Matthew 1:23
The Virgin Birth

The whole context of Matthew 1:23 (KJV), which says, "Behold, a virgin shall be with child…," is Mary giving birth to Jesus while she was still a virgin. To show that the virgin birth had been foretold in Scripture, Matthew quoted Isaiah 7:14. The context of Isaiah 7, however, does not say anything about the Messiah, and seems to talk about a child who would be a "sign" to Ahaz, the king of Judah. Ahaz needed a sign because he was about to be attacked by Israel and Syria, and had not much hope of defeating them. Today, we believe that Isaiah 7:14 is actually a prophecy that had two applications, one immediate as a sign to Ahaz, and the other as a prediction of the virgin birth for the Messiah. The context of the chapter is such that the ancient Jews never understood it to be prophecy, and believed instead that it was just Jewish history. Thus, Matthew 1:23 is an excellent example of how the Hebrew Scriptures are made fully comprehensible by the New Testament writings.

Matthew 2:15
Out of Egypt

This verse is quoted from Hosea 11:1, which we have already mentioned. We will review the main points because this is an important and defining prophecy that argues powerfully for the Messiahship of Jesus, who fulfilled it. Matthew records that Joseph and Mary took Jesus to Egypt to protect him from Herod. In regard to them returning from Egypt, Matthew 2:15 states, "...And so was fulfilled what the Lord had said through the prophet [Hosea]: 'Out of Egypt I called my son.'"

Hosea 11:1–3 (NRSV)
(1) When Israel was a child, I loved him, and out of Egypt I called my son.
(2) The more I called them, the more they went from me; they kept sacrificing to the Baals, and offering incense to idols.
(3) Yet it was I who taught Ephraim to walk, I took them up in my arms; but they did not know that I healed them.

In the Hebrew Scriptures, Israel was called God's "son" (Exod. 4:22, etc.). Scholars know of no Jewish commentator living before Christ who applied Hosea 11:1 to the Messiah. Therefore, no one at the time of Christ was looking for a Messiah who was to spend part of his life in Egypt. How is this prophecy explained today? Israel is a type or figure of the "greater Israel," i.e., Jesus Christ, just as David is sometimes a type of the "greater David," Solomon a type of the "greater Solomon," etc. As we saw in Chapter 4, virtually everything in the Hebrew Scriptures points to Christ, including the nation of Israel itself as the "son" of God. As Israel spent 40 years wandering in the wilderness, so Jesus spent 40 days there. As Israel was called out of Egypt, so was the Christ-child called out of Egypt.

Matthew 2:18
Rachel Weeping for Her Children

This verse quotes Jeremiah 31:15, saying: "...A voice is heard in Ramah, mourning and great weeping, Rachel weeping for her children and refusing to be comforted, because her children are no more." Matthew applies it to the time when Herod killed all the children around Bethlehem. A person reading the New Testament might well think, "Why didn't the Jews realize who Jesus was when Herod killed the children around Bethlehem?" There is a good answer to that question. The context of the verse in Jeremiah is the Babylonian destruction of the towns of Judah. They had put cities to the sword, and carried away captives, so "Rachel," one of the wives of Jacob, was "crying" over her children. But the LORD comforted Rachel by saying that her children will come back from the north country, Babylon.

Jeremiah 31:8, 10, 11, 15 and 16
(8) See, **I will bring them from the land of the north** and gather them from the ends of the earth. Among them will be the blind and the lame, expectant mothers and women in labor; a great throng will return.

(10) "Hear the word of the LORD, O nations; proclaim it in distant coastlands: 'He who scattered Israel will gather them…'

(11) For the LORD will ransom Jacob and redeem them from the hand of those stronger than they.

(15) This is what the LORD says: "A voice is heard in Ramah, mourning and great weeping, Rachel weeping for her children and refusing to be comforted, because her children are no more."

(16) This is what the LORD says: "Restrain your voice from weeping and your eyes from tears, for your work will be rewarded," declares the LORD. "**They will return** from the land of the enemy.

Jeremiah 31:15, like Isaiah 7:14 and Hosea 11:1, seems more like a simple description of Jewish history, so the Jews did not see any Messianic aspect in it. Admittedly, the children murdered by Herod's troops were not going to return to Israel from the North, but this illustrates the principle that a prophecy can be partially fulfilled, or applied in part, to an unrelated situation or event. Matthew "unveils" this Old Testament record and shows that the heart of the prophecy was fulfilled again, as "Rachel" continued to weep for *all* her "children," not just those who had been conquered by the Babylonians. Christ will further fulfill this prophecy as he gathers the children of Israel at his Second Coming and redeems them from their "enemy," death. Truly, the prophetic language of Scripture is marvelously multifaceted and capable of multiple fulfillments.

Matthew 2:23
From Nazareth

The Jews knew that Christ would be born in Bethlehem, but they also thought that he would grow up there. Because the people knew the Messianic prophecies only in part, they were confused when Christ came from Galilee. They asked, "…How can the Christ come from Galilee? Does not the Scripture say that Christ will come from David's family and from Bethlehem, the town where David lived?" (John 7:41 and 42). The Jews would not have been confused by Jesus coming from Galilee if they had known the words "spoken [not written] by the prophets" that, "…He will be called a Nazarene" (Matt. 2:23).

There is no Old Testament reference to the Christ living in Nazareth, a town not mentioned in the Hebrew Scriptures, Talmud or the writings of Josephus. Critics of the Bible often say that Matthew invented the reference to Nazareth in the Hebrew Scriptures, but E. W. Bullinger, in the marginal note in The Companion Bible, properly identified the solution to the apparent problem, as follows: the prophets "spoke," not wrote, about the Messiah coming from Nazareth. "Spoken. It does not say 'written.' It is not 'an unsolved difficulty,' as alleged."[27] So Christ perfectly fulfilled the predictions of the prophets—he was born in Bethlehem and grew up in Nazareth, as recorded in Matthew.

Matthew 13:35
Teaching in Parables

One of the common elements of the Synoptic Gospels is the use of parables (John never records Jesus using them). Even a cursory study of the life of Christ will show that he taught a great many

---

27. Bullinger, *op. cit.,* Companion, p. 1311.

things by way of parables. This was foretold in the Hebrew Scriptures, but not in a way that clearly referred to the Messiah, as a reading of the first four verses of Psalm 78 will show:

Psalm 78:1–4 (NRSV)
(1) Give ear, O my people, to my teaching; incline your ears to the words of my mouth.
(2) I will open my mouth in a parable; I will utter dark sayings from of old,
(3) things that we have heard and known, that our ancestors have told us.
(4) We will not hide them from their children; we will tell to the coming generation the glorious deeds of the LORD, and his might, and the wonders that he has done.

Nevertheless, Matthew again gives us God's understanding of the Old Testament and unveils the deep meaning of the Hebrew Scriptures. Matthew 13:35 is quoting Psalm 78:2 and it says: "This was to fulfill what had been spoken through the prophet: 'I will open my mouth to speak in parables; I will proclaim what has been hidden from the foundation of the world'" (NRSV).

Matthew 21:42
The Cornerstone Rejected by the Builders

Psalm 118:22 and 23 (NASB)
(22) The stone which the builders rejected Has become the chief corner *stone*.
(23) This is the LORD's doing; It is marvelous in our eyes.

With the information provided in the Gospels and Acts, we can look at these verses in Psalms and see that the Messiah was going to be rejected by the Jewish leaders. Yet they were the very ones who should have "built" upon Christ, their Messiah, who came to the lost sheep of the house of Israel. There is no evidence that the Jews understood these verses in any Messianic sense because the context of Psalm 118 does not mention the Messiah. Peter, speaking to the religious leaders in Acts 4:11, also quoted this verse to show that indeed Scripture had foretold that they would reject the Messiah.

Matthew 24:30
Coming in the Clouds of Heaven

In Matthew 24, Jesus Christ taught the chronology of the Tribulation and his return to the earth in judgment. It is apparent that he clearly understood that he would ascend up into heaven to be with his Father, because he told his disciples that he was going to go away and another comforter would come (John 14). Jesus clearly understood that Daniel 7:13, which speaks of the "son of man" coming in the clouds of heaven, applied to his return as conqueror, because he referred to it in that context in Matthew 24:30. The Jews, who did not have the benefit of the New Testament or the life of Christ, were confused as to exactly what Daniel 7:13 meant.

Matthew 26:31
The Smitten Shepherd

Matthew 26:31 quotes Zechariah 13:7: "'Awake, O sword, against my shepherd, against the man who is close to me!' declares the LORD Almighty. 'Strike the shepherd, and the sheep will be scattered, and I will turn my hand against the little ones." Christ referenced this verse when he was about to be arrested, and he used it to show that his disciples would fall away that night. The ancient Jews did not understand that it referred to the sufferings of the Messiah, perhaps because it did not fit their understanding that the "sheep," i.e., *Israel*, would be "scattered." We have no trouble understanding it today with the help of the New Testament. When properly understood, it clearly tells what happened to the Messiah and to his followers.

Matthew 27:35
The Messiah's Garments

Matthew 27:35 quotes Psalm 22:18: "They divide my garments among them, And for my clothing they cast lots" (NASB). This is an excellent example showing that the New Testament writings unveil the Hebrew Scriptures because, even though the parting of Christ's garments could have been a sure sign to the Jews that Jesus was the Messiah, there is no evidence that the Jews understood Psalm 22:18 as applying to the Messiah.

Mark 15:28
Numbered with the Transgressors

Mark 15:28 (KJV) quotes Isaiah 53:12 about the Messiah: "Therefore I will allot him a portion with the great, and he shall divide the spoil with the strong; because he poured out himself to death, and was numbered with the transgressors; yet he bore the sin of many, and made intercession for the transgressors" (NRSV). This verse is in a section of Isaiah that contains some verses that the Jewish writings say point to the suffering of the Messiah, but they do not cite this verse among them. Yet it contains the suffering and death of Christ, as well as another important piece of information. If Christ were numbered with the transgressors, then someone in authority must have done the numbering. Correctly piecing this verse together with others, such as Psalms 118:22 and 23 that say the builders rejected him, shows that the evidence existed to correctly understand that the authorities of his time would reject Christ.

John 3:14
Lifted Up on a Pole

A very interesting record in the Old Testament occurred while Moses was taking the Israelites through the wilderness. Numbers 21:4–9 records that poisonous snakes bit and killed some people, but when Moses put a bronze serpent on a pole and lifted it up, whoever looked at it was healed. The ancient Jews did not see a Messianic type or foreshadowing in this, but Jesus himself said that it foreshadowed his crucifixion. John 3:14 and 12:32 and 33 refer to Christ's being lifted up from the earth. Had the Jews recognized Moses' serpent on a pole foreshadowing Christ, they might have been more inclined to see his sufferings and recognize him at the crucifixion when he was lifted up on a pole.

John 13:18
Betrayed by a Friend

John 13:18 quotes Psalm 41:9: "Even my close friend, in whom I trusted, Who ate my bread, Has lifted up his heel against me" (NASB). The Jews did not apply this verse to the Messiah, but if they had, they would have looked for the Messiah to have a friend who would betray him. We know today from reading the Gospels that the "friend" was Judas Iscariot.

John 15:25
They Hated Me Without a Cause

John 15:25 uses a phrase that occurs in the Old Testament. Psalm 35:19 and 69:4 both use the phrase, but it was not understood to refer to the Messiah. This is another verse that, if properly understood, would have pointed to the Messiah being rejected by his own people. It would not have referred to his natural enemies, the pagan nations, because they had a "cause" for hating anyone who ruled Israel. The ones who would hate the Messiah without a cause would have to come from within Israel.

John 19:36
No Bone Broken

The Passover Lamb was a type of Christ, and in many, many ways foreshadowed the Messiah. One of the specific instructions about the Passover Lamb was that not a bone was to be broken (Exod. 12:46; Num. 9:12; Ps. 34:20). The Jews did not recognize this as typological, but it prophetically pointed to the suffering of the Messiah. Thus, when the Messiah was beaten and finally crucified, it was a miraculous fulfillment of Old Testament prophecy that not even one of his bones was broken.

Acts 2:25–28
Death and Resurrection

Between Christ's resurrection and his ascension, he spent time with the disciples and taught them (Acts 1:1–3). By the Day of Pentecost, Peter had a firm grip on the teachings about Christ in the Old Testament, and demonstrated that by his exposition of Psalm 16:8–11 as recorded in:

Acts 2:25–28 (NASB)
(25) For David says of Him [Christ]: 'I WAS ALWAYS BEHOLDING THE LORD IN MY PRESENCE; FOR HE IS AT MY RIGHT HAND, THAT I MAY NOT BE SHAKEN.
(26) 'THEREFORE MY HEART WAS GLAD AND MY TONGUE EXULTED; MOREOVER MY FLESH ALSO WILL ABIDE IN HOPE;
(27) BECAUSE THOU WILT NOT ABANDON MY SOUL TO HADES [the grave], NOR ALLOW THY HOLY ONE TO UNDERGO DECAY.
(28) 'THOU HAST MADE KNOWN TO ME THE PATHS OF LIFE; THOU WILT MAKE ME FULL OF GLADNESS WITH THY PRESENCE.'

Peter explained what the Jews listening to him did not know, that these verses were about the Messiah, and showed that he would die but not be abandoned to decay in the grave. Thus, he very clearly indicated that Christ would die and then be resurrected. These verses were "veiled" to the Jews who did not apply them to the Messiah.

Acts 2:34 and 35
The Ascension

Peter understood that the Messiah was foretold to ascend into heaven, and he quoted Psalm 110:1 to make his point: "The LORD says to my Lord: 'Sit at My right hand, Until I make Thine enemies a footstool for Thy feet'" (NASB). The Jews knew that this Psalm referred to the Messiah, but they did not understand that sitting "at the right hand" of God referred to the ascension. The ascension can be seen, however, when this verse is pieced together with Daniel 7:13, which tells of the Messiah coming in the clouds of heaven. The ascension is also referred to in Psalm 68:18, a reference that was veiled to the Jews but revealed in Ephesians to be about the ascension: "This is why it [Psalm 68:18] reads: "…When he ascended on high, he led captives in his train and gave gifts to men" (Eph. 4:8).[28]

Acts 3:22
A Prophet Like Moses

Moses foretold that the LORD God would raise up "…a prophet like me from among you, from your countrymen…" (Deut. 18:15 and 18 - NASB), but not many Jews were expecting that prophet to be the Messiah. Peter's sermon in Acts 3 clarified this prophecy. Although the Jews, for the most part, were unaware of it, the Messiah was not only to be a king and priest, but also to be a prophet like Moses.

Acts 13:33
This Day I Have Begotten You

Paul shed light on the chronology of Christ's life when he quoted Psalm 2:7: "I will proclaim the decree of the LORD: He said to me, 'You are my Son; today I have become your Father.'" The ancient Jews applied this to the birth of their Messiah, but the New Testament reveals that its more proper interpretation is his *resurrection*. Once that is understood, the truth that the Messiah would conquer his enemies after his resurrection from the dead becomes plain.

Psalm 2:7–9 (NASB)
(7) "I will surely tell of the decree of the LORD: He said to Me, 'Thou art My Son,
Today [the day of his resurrection] I have begotten Thee.

---

28. Actually, the Lord changes the quotation of Psalm 68:18 in a powerful way when it is brought into Ephesians. Psalm 68:18 reads: "…you led captives in your train: you received gifts from men…." As it is quoted in the Ephesians, the verse says: "…he led captives in his train; and gave gifts to men." Both the original Psalm and the adaptation in Ephesians are very powerful. The emphasis in the Psalms is the conquest of the enemy, and thus the fact that the vanquished foes would bring gifts to appease the conqueror was very important. In the Church Epistles, however, Christ is giving grace in the form of ministries (cp. Eph. 4:7 and 11), and so the Psalm is adapted from receiving to giving, to support Christ's actions. Ephesus was the Roman capital of the province of Asia, so the Roman Triumphal procession would have been in the minds of the readers. In a Triumphal procession, the conquering general "ascended up on high" into a gilded chariot and was known to throw gifts (usually money) to the crowds as he paraded through the streets of Rome.

(8) 'Ask of Me, and I will surely give the nations as Thine inheritance, And the *very* ends of the earth as Thy possession.
(9) 'Thou shalt break them with a rod of iron; Thou shalt shatter them like earthenware.' "

Acts 13:47
A Light to the Gentiles

As the early Church grew and expanded, the traditional separation and hardness toward the Gentiles softened. Formerly Jewish Christians were able to see that there was only one Messiah who had to be the Messiah for all the earth. Paul quotes part of Isaiah 49:6 to show that he must go to Gentiles as well as to Jews. Isaiah 49:6 says: "…It is too light a thing that you should be my servant to raise up the tribes of Jacob and to restore the survivors of Israel; I will give you as a light to the nations, that my salvation may reach to the end of the earth" (NRSV). Thus, God's servant, the Messiah, would be a light for the Gentiles, but it took the Jews some time to soften to the idea. Isaiah 49:6 is not applied to the Messiah in the ancient Hebrew writings.

Acts 15:16 and 17
Repairing David's Fallen Tent

The prophecy in Amos 9:11 and 12 about David's fallen tent being repaired was considered messianic by the Jews, and was eagerly awaited (see Isaiah 9:6 and 7 above). What they did not expect was that the Gentiles coming into the Messianic Kingdom were part of that "repair." However, that was exactly the case, as James made clear to the council gathered in Jerusalem. Romans 10:13 shows that the proper understanding of Joel 2:32 includes the Gentiles when it says, "…everyone who calls on the name of the LORD will be saved…." Thus, the New Testament leaders came to see that God had made the Messiah the Savior for the Gentiles even though the ancient Jews did not interpret the verses that way.

Romans Through Revelation the "Veil" Completely Removed

The remainder of the New Testament finishes removing the veil off the Hebrew Scriptures by explaining certain other verses that were not clear from reading those Scriptures alone. A few of these will be discussed in the remaining chapters of this book when appropriate.

Conclusion

Proverbs 2:1–5 says that to get knowledge and wisdom one must cry out for it and seek it as for hidden treasure. Proverbs 25:2 says, "It is the glory of God to conceal things, but the glory of kings is to search things out" (NRSV). God is true to His Word. There were things about the Messiah that God concealed, but the "kings" among people will search for His hidden riches rather than be distracted by what the world has to offer. It may be difficult to see the Messiah in some of the Hebrew Scriptures, but he is there.

Indeed, this review of the prophecies concerning the coming of the Messiah has shown that behind nearly every character, object and event in the Hebrew Scriptures is the prophetic presence of the coming one, Jesus Christ. Yet the Old Testament is not self-interpreting. It needs the Four Gospels to complete the picture it sketches out, and show us what the real meaning of many of the Scriptures was. It took the personal presence of the One of whom Scripture spoke to bring clarity and focus to this prophetic picture. His two comings, the distinct separation of his sufferings and the glory, his bodily resurrection from the dead—these were all things that were hard to see from the Hebrew Scriptures, but which we can now see clearly. We must now move ahead to the Gospel accounts of the Messiah in person, and see how his life fulfilled many of these prophecies.

PART THREE

The Messiah
in Person

6

The Four Gospels:
The Fourfold Portrait of Christ

In the book of Ephesians, the careful reader will be able to see an important distinction is made:

Ephesians 3:8 (KJV)
Unto me, who am less than the least of all saints, is this grace given, that I should preach among the Gentiles the **unsearchable** riches of Christ;

What we have been exploring in this book so far have been the "searchable" riches of Christ, that is, those things revealed about Christ in the Hebrew Scriptures. In the previous chapter, we learned with 20/20 hindsight about what *could* have been searched out if the Jews had had eyes to see, or had known what we know and believe now. We are continuing to lay the foundation of these "searchable riches" so that when we begin to explore the Church Epistles, we will be able to appreciate the "unsearchable" things that are revealed there, things that not even hindsight into the Hebrew Scriptures could have revealed.

135

One of the most important sections of Scripture are the Four Gospels: Matthew, Mark, Luke and John. These are the only books in the Bible that specifically record the events of the life of Jesus Christ. As such, they set forth the fulfillment of the Old Testament prophecies about Christ's *first* coming. Therefore, the Four Gospels are actually a part of and the conclusion of the "Old Testament."

According to 2 Timothy 3:16, the text of Scripture is "God-**breathed**." This means that it has the very life of God in it, and was originally perfect in every detail. However, it has been "man-handled," that is, man has added things to the Bible that often cause confusion. Perhaps one of the most confusing of these additions has been the page in the Bible between Malachi and Matthew that says "The New Testament." Our experience among Christians is that almost all of them believe that Matthew, Mark, Luke and John are a part of the "New Testament." This error has many significant and harmful ramifications.

The "New Testament" title page was placed there by Church councils and authorities long after the time of Christ and the first-century Church, because of the generally accepted distinction between Scriptures written in the Hebrew language and those written in Greek. This man-made title page actually had nothing to do with the "Testament" or "Covenant" of God. The word *diatheke* is the closest Greek equivalent to the Hebrew word for "covenant," but it means something closer to "will" or "testament." Thus, the New "Testament" would better be translated the New "Covenant," in order to express its continuity with the Old "Covenant." This fact is widely known and believed.[1]

There is much evidence to show that the New Covenant did not start in the Four Gospels, which begin with events before the birth of Christ. Just before his death, Christ said, "…This cup is the new covenant in my blood, which is poured out for you" (Luke 22:20), so the New Covenant could not have started until at least the death of Christ. Actually, the greatest changes in God's dealings with man took place on the Day of Pentecost, as recorded in Acts 2. The following examples make that clear: circumcision became unnecessary, not in the Four Gospels, but on the Day of Pentecost; Temple sacrifice became obsolete, not in the Four Gospels, but at Pentecost; all believers became "priests" and had access to God, not in the Four Gospels, but at Pentecost. The same is true with the

---

1. See Kittel, *op. cit., Theological Dictionary*, Vol. II, pp. 126–134.

The Gospels are part of the Old Covenant even though they were written after it had come to a close. It is important to realize that a portion of Scripture written during one administration or covenant can be about another administration or covenant. Since all Scripture is "God breathed," an accurate account of events can be given either before an administration (prophetically, such as the information about the New Heaven and Earth given in the Old Testament) or after it. The "Old Covenant" (and the Law Administration) was started when God and Israel made a covenant together at Mt. Sinai. This was around 1450 B.C., about 2500 years after Adam. There at Mt. Sinai God gave the Ten Commandments and other laws by which Israel was to govern their lives and society (Exodus chapters 21–23). These were written in a book called, "The Book of the Covenant" (Exod. 24:7). Moses gathered the people, killed sacrifices and sprinkled one-half of the blood on the altar of the Tabernacle, which represented God. Then he read the Book of the Covenant to the people of Israel. They all agreed to obey it, so Moses sprinkled the remaining half of the blood from the sacrifices onto the people and said, "This is the blood of the covenant that the LORD has made with you in accordance with all these words" (Exod. 24:8). Thus what we know as the "Old Covenant" was born. This establishment of the "first covenant" (Heb. 8:7; 9:1, 15 and 18) between Israel and God is noted in Hebrews 9:16–22. Although we commonly speak of Enoch, Noah, Abraham, Joseph, etc., being a part of the Old Covenant, technically they are not, since they predate the making of that covenant. Thus Moses wrote about the Original Paradise, Conscience and Patriarchal administrations after they had come to a close, just as Matthew, Mark, Luke and John wrote the four Gospels after the "Old Covenant" had come to a close. We would not think that Noah was under the Old Covenant and the Law simply because Moses was the one who wrote down the record about Noah. Similarly, we should not be confused into thinking that the Gospels are somehow part of the Grace Administration simply because they were written down during the Grace Administration.

Sabbath laws, keeping the feasts of the LORD and going up to Jerusalem three times a year, etc. Also, the gift of holy spirit was given to *all* believers, not in the Gospels, but on Pentecost.[2]

Exactly when the Four Gospels were written is unknown, and the subject is hotly debated. Most of the estimates range from 50 to 90 A.D. That means the Gospels were written during, or perhaps after, the time when the Apostle Paul was penning the Church Epistles. Nevertheless, the Gospels certainly were not written to take us back under the Old Testament law, but rather to show us the heart of our Savior.

Matthew, Mark and Luke are called the *Synoptic* Gospels because "synoptic" literally means "to view together," and these three books share a similar view of the Lord's life and contain much overlapping information in their narrative accounts of the life of Jesus. John presents a unique and independent view of Christ with less than ten percent of its material paralleled in any of the Synoptics.

The basic synoptic witness of Christ is that Jesus was conceived by divine conception and born of Mary when she was still a virgin. He began his existence as a baby, and grew up in Nazareth of Galilee. At the age of 30, Jesus was baptized by John the Baptist in the river Jordan to inaugurate his earthly ministry. On that occasion, the spirit of God descended on him in the form of a dove, and he went forth in the power of that spirit to the wilderness, to be tempted by the Devil. He successfully resisted those temptations, and went on to Galilee, where he announced his ministry, using the text of Isaiah 61:1 and 2 to describe his mission. He continually validated the Hebrew Scriptures as his standard of faith and practice, and encouraged others to do the same.

There is no mention in the Synoptic Gospels of anything that could be construed as a "pre-existence" or remembrance of a former life in heaven. Jesus is portrayed as a man who walked in the certainty of his unique Sonship and divine calling, displaying a remarkable intimacy with God, whom he referred to as his "Father." No one had ever before presumed to have such an intimate relationship with God. He claimed to act and speak with divine authority and represented God as no one had ever done before. He also manifested the power of God like none before him, healing multitudes, feeding multitudes and casting out demons. He is portrayed as standing in God's stead, doing and saying what God would do and say. He forgave sins and corrected the traditions that had been handed down ("You have heard it said, but I say..."). He asserted authority over the weather, and even the Sabbath. His miracles displayed God's power on a scale that had never been seen before.

Yet he always gave God glory for everything he said and he did. He never claimed to be God, and was even very veiled in his use of Messianic language and claims. The only title he chose to apply to himself was "the Son of Man," which was an ambiguous term that could refer either to the Messianic figure of Daniel 7:13 or it could mean, simply, "a certain one" in Aramaic.

He chose 12 Apostles, and taught them and the people using many stories and parables. He chose the company of common people and sinners rather than the religious leaders and the "righteous" Jews. Because of his many miracles and wonders among the people, he attracted the attention of the authorities, who considered him a false prophet and Messianic pretender. On a number of occasions they plotted to kill him, but because of his popularity with the people they had to await the right

---

2. The Day of Pentecost initiated an administration (often called a "dispensation") of God called "the administration of God's grace" (Eph. 3:2), which was a "Sacred Secret" ("Sacred Secret" is a better translation of the Greek *musterion*, translated "mystery" in Eph. 3:4, 5 and 9; Col. 1:26 and 27) in the past, but revealed by God to the Apostle Paul (Eph. 3:2–13). For more information on this entire subject, we refer you to our website: www.TLTF.org, click Bible teachings/articles/Administrations. Under Bible Teachings you can also click on audio and listen to: "*Administrations in Scripture*" and "*The Purpose Of The Ages.*"

opportunity. Finally, one of his disciples betrayed him to the Temple authorities, who came late at night and arrested him apart from the crowds. His disciples mostly scattered and ran away.

After a mockery of a trial and several episodes of beating and torture, he was taken before the Roman authorities, Herod and Pilate. Though there was no evidence of his having committed a capital crime worthy of death, the Roman procurator Pilate finally gave cowardly consent to his crucifixion, blaming the angry mob. Thus, he died on a tree in the midst of four criminals, on Wednesday, the 14th of Nisan, 28 A.D.[3] One of his disciples, Joseph of Arimathea, received permission from Pilate to take Jesus' body and bury it in a tomb near the place of crucifixion. Three days and three nights passed, and finally, early Sunday morning, Mary Magdalene discovered that the tomb was empty. Shortly thereafter, she spoke with the resurrected Lord. She then told the other disciples, who eventually believed. Jesus made various appearances to his disciples during the next 40 days, made certain promises, gave them some instructions, and then ascended into heaven.

The gospel of John generally agrees with the above account, but it handles so much unique material written in such a different style that it paints a picture of Jesus Christ significantly different from that of the Synoptic Gospels. This is so much the case that we will handle it separately in Chapters 8 and 9, after we focus on the Synoptic perspective of Jesus as a veiled Messiah in Chapter 7.

The Synoptic "Problem"

About ninety percent of Mark is found in Matthew and fifty percent in Luke. Ninety-five percent of Mark is paralleled in either Matthew or Luke or both. Sixty-five percent of Matthew is paralleled in either Mark or Luke or both; and fifty-three percent of Luke is paralleled in either Matthew or Mark or both. What this appears to mean is that each of the three Gospels shares most of its material with one or both of the other two. This is why these three Gospels are called the Synoptic Gospels. This also accounts for what is called "the Synoptic problem." *The Interpreter's Bible* outlines their view of this "problem."

> How did it happen that out of all the remembered deeds and sayings of Jesus these three gospel authors chose much the same material and presented it in much the same order and to a considerable extent in much the same wording—a wording that comes to us, not in the Aramaic in which Jesus regularly spoke, but in Greek? The same problem can be stated from the other side: How did it happen that these authors of the first-century Church, dealing with the Gospel story, with material of the utmost importance to every Christian, continually show striking agreements and tantalizing differences in material selected, order used and wording? This combination of similarities and differences is called the Synoptic problem.[4]

To solve this "problem," New Testament scholars have hypothesized that there was a common source of historical information about Jesus that was drawn upon in the writing of all three Gospels. The theory is that Matthew, Mark and Luke each started with this historical source and added their

---

3. There are many details about the crucifixion that we believe are misunderstood by most Christians. In *op. cit.*, The Companion Bible, Appendix 164, Bullinger does an admirable job of describing why Scripture testifies that there were actually four men, rather than two, crucified with Christ, and other scholars have also attested to this fact. The 28 A.D. date for the death of Jesus Christ has long been a qualified candidate, and we feel it is the proper one. It can also be shown from Scripture that Christ died on a Wednesday, not a Friday, thus giving time for the "three days and three nights" in the grave of Matthew 12:40.

4. *Interpreter's One Volume Commentary on the Bible* (Abingdon Press, Nashville, 1971) pp. 1129 and 1130.

own material to it. This hypothetical source, called "*Q*" after the German word for source (*Quelle*), has never been found, and in our opinion, never will be. Why? Because *there was no such source*. "*Q*" is in reality "*G*," as in "*GOD*," who inspired each of the Four Gospels according to His own purpose and design, and who is the true "source" for each one. This is the simple and elegant solution to the so-called "Synoptic problem." We will now proceed to explore the evidence as to why there are Four Gospels, each written as it is.

Why Four Gospels?

Why are there Four Gospels? The best answer we have is twofold. First, the existence of Jesus Christ required written records attesting to the events of his life, death and resurrection. Had Jesus written an autobiography, his critics would have immediately dismissed it as self-promotion. In accordance with the ancient Jewish method of authentication, wherein "two or three witnesses" were required to establish credibility (Deut. 17:6, 19:15; Matt. 18:16; 1 Tim. 5:19; Heb. 10:28, *et al.*), the record of his life had to come from *others*. Although Mark and Luke may not have been "eyewitnesses," as were the Apostles Matthew and John, their accounts have been recognized by most Christians not only as authentic historical documents, but also as God-inspired records of the life of Christ. For those with eyes to see, faith in the integrity of God's Word and understanding of some of the things we will share in this chapter, these four accounts harmonize perfectly and speak loudly of their divine inspiration. Not only do they fit with each other, they fulfill many aspects of the prophetic portrait of the Messiah that we have been looking at in the previous chapters. As the Christian Apostles and disciples went forth to preach in the book of Acts, they proved from Scripture that Jesus of Nazareth is indeed the Promised Messiah.

But, alas, many serious Bible students and scholars do not believe that the Gospel records are inspired of God. In fact, from our experience we would have to say that the vast majority of Bible scholars have given up the idea of the full inspiration of Scripture, and particularly the Gospels. They believe that the Four Gospels are full of inaccuracies and fictitious sayings that are attributed to Jesus but which are really things made up by later Christians.[5] They have also given up on the idea that the contents of the Gospels can actually be harmonized without contradictions. In our opinion, they have done so in ignorance of the role of faith and trust in the handling of Scripture. They have figuratively analyzed the text to death—not the death of the indestructible text itself, but rather its "death" in their own lives.

Like the secrets of nature, the beauty and order of God's Word is opened up to those who approach it with respect, reverence and humility. As Richard Hays says in *Christianity Today*, a "hermeneutic of trust" must replace the cloud of suspicion that surrounds the New Testament, particularly the Four Gospels.[6] We agree with E. W. Bullinger when he writes: "The Four Gospels are treated in the

---

5. "The Jesus Seminar" is a particularly notorious example of scholarly disbelief. Members of this group believe that more than 60% of the sayings of Jesus in the Four Gospels are inauthentic, and more than that are questionable.

6. "The New Theologians," *Christianity Today*, Feb. 8, 1999, p. 30. Richard Hays (Professor of New Testament at the Divinity School of Duke University) presented a paper at the 1996 conference of the Society of Biblical Literature in which he called for a "hermeneutic of trust" to replace the suspicious view of Scripture that is the cornerstone of much modern scholarship. In his paper, Hays called for, "nothing less than a reverent, humble, Christian reading of the Bible—a stance that is rarely, if ever, articulated in American universities."

"Companion Bible" not as four culprits brought up on a charge of fraud, but as four witnesses whose testimony is to be received."[7]

Luke begins with a personal testimony about how he wrote his Gospel. We think it is important to quote, because it applies not only to the Four Gospel writers, but to all those who were inspired to write Scripture.

Luke 1:1–4 (NRSV)
(1) Since many have undertaken to set down an orderly account of the events that have been fulfilled among us,
(2) just as they were handed on to us by those who from the beginning were eyewitnesses and servants of the word,
(3) I too decided, after **investigating everything carefully from the very first** [*anothen*], to write an orderly account for you, most excellent Theophilus,
(4) so that you may know the truth concerning the things about which you have been instructed.

The above translation of verse 3 ("after investigating everything carefully") places the emphasis entirely on Luke's own personal diligence to ensure that what he is writing is accurate. We have no doubt that God moved Luke, the "holy man of God" that he was, to gather eyewitness accounts of Jesus' life as a part of his being moved by holy spirit to write Scripture (2 Pet. 1:21). But Luke recorded many long discourses, prayers and events that happened 40 years prior, and even "eyewitnesses" begin to forget details in just a few years. We are hardpressed to find real comfort in the accurate recollections of people 40 years after the fact. Obviously, we need to look deeper for the answer to how Luke could be so sure that what he was writing was not only accurate, but that it would minister *certainty* to "Theophilus."

The key is in the Greek word *anothen*, translated in verse three above as "from the very first." Though this is one possible lexical translation, Greek lexicons give the first meaning for *anothen* as "from above," or "from a higher place."[8] It is used of the rending of the veil of the Temple "from the top" to the bottom when Jesus died. This word has a poetic overlay of meaning that is perfectly appropriate to this passage. Luke received his information "from above" at the same time he was investigating the eyewitness accounts of events of "the beginning." He did his best to acquire accurate information, but God gave him the final, inspired account to write, one with the life of God in every word. This is the faith that we must have as we study the text, that the men who penned it were invisibly and powerfully guided to write what God inspired them to write—the truth—for His purposes and from the right perspective. The closer you look, the better it looks.

The second reason there are Four Gospels is that each is written from a different perspective, and together they comprise a very profound, prophetic and precise fourfold pattern for who the Messiah would be that had already been foreshadowed long before by the Old Testament prophets. It is very sad that this truth appears to have been stolen from both the scholar and the average Christian. We

---

7. Bullinger, *op. cit.*, Companion Bible, p. 1381.
8. We checked three: Wm. F. Arndt and F. Wilbur Gingrich, *A Greek-English Lexicon of the New Testament and Other Early Christian Literature* (The University of Chicago Press, Chicago 1979), p. 77; Bullinger, *op. cit.*, Lexicon, p. 21; Joseph Henry Thayer, *The New Thayer's Greek-English Lexicon of the New Testament* (Book Publisher's Press, Lafayette, IN, 1981), p. 52.

hope that this book helps restore confidence in the veracity and integrity of these Gospel records, upon which a large measure of our faith depends.

Indeed, our very salvation depends in large part upon the reliability of these four historical records of the birth, life, death and especially *the resurrection* of Jesus Christ. A deeply held belief in the resurrection as a fact of history is a vital element for our eternal salvation. The closest thing we have to a "formula" for salvation in the New Testament, Romans 10:9, asserts: "That if you confess with your mouth, 'Jesus is Lord,' and **believe in your heart that God raised him from the dead**, you will be saved." Are we not trifling with the bedrock of our salvation when we entertain doubts about the integrity and accuracy of any part of Scripture? But most crucial are those parts that make historical claims upon which our salvation depends!

The Fourfold Paradigm: King, Servant, Man, Son

As mentioned, the second reason there are Four Gospels is that there is a fourfold pattern or paradigm in Scripture regarding the "searchable riches" of Christ, one that has its roots in an important prophetic Hebrew term, the *tsemach*. *Tsemach* means "sprout" or "offspring," and often is translated "Branch." *Tsemach* paints a mental picture of a new sprout or shoot coming up out of a dead-looking stump, and in the Hebrew Scriptures it is used five times in direct prophetic reference to the Messiah and aspects of his life. We saw in the previous chapter that "the branch" was a common term for the Messiah, but five Old Testament verses in particular lay out a fourfold prophetic pattern describing the Messiah's existence to the very end of his redemptive work. The first two verses portray the "Branch" as the King, the third verse as a servant, the fourth as a man, and the fifth as "the Branch of the Lord," i.e., one directly from the LORD.

Jeremiah 23:5
"The days are coming," declares the LORD, "when I will raise up to David **a righteous Branch**, a **King who will reign** wisely and do what is just and right in the land.

Jeremiah 33:15
" 'In those days and at that time I will **make a righteous Branch sprout from David's line**; he will do what is just and right in the land.

Zechariah 3:8
" 'Listen, O high priest Joshua and your associates seated before you, who are men symbolic of things to come: I am going to bring **my servant, the Branch.**

Zechariah 6:12
Tell him this is what the LORD Almighty says: 'Here is **the man whose name is the Branch**, and he will branch out from his place and build the temple of the LORD.

Isaiah 4:2
In that day the **Branch of the LORD** will be beautiful and glorious, and the fruit of the land will be the pride and glory of the survivors in Israel.

Perhaps a visual diagram of these four aspects would be helpful:

	King	
Son	**The Branch** (*tsemach*)	Man
	Servant	

These four terms establish a definitive paradigm or a pattern for the person and work of the coming Redeemer. Of all the terms that we looked at in the last chapter that could have been used to define the life and ministry of the Messiah, it is these four that are singled out and built upon in the Four Gospels. It behooves us as lovers of Christ and students of the Bible to search out the richness of their meaning, both as individual terms and as they relate to one another. They will prove to be a fertile source of insight.

The first thing we see is that they subdivide according to one of the most basic distinctions we can make about any person: who he is and what he *does*. That is, there is an important distinction between a person and his work or function. The same is true of "the offspring," the promised Redeemer. Two of the four terms refer to his **person**—*Son* and *man*, while the other two relate to his **work**—*King* and *servant*. The designation *Son* defines his role in relationship to his Father. *Man* defines him as being a member of the class *homo sapiens*, which says a lot about who he is as a person. *King* describes his function in terms of his position and authority, and *servant* describes his attitude toward the work that he does. Both kings and servants are almost entirely defined by their function or work. Whoever he is as a person, the king derives his authority from his position or function as the sovereign of his realm. The servant's life is entirely defined by his work, which he performs for another person. The purer the servant, the less his personal life is relevant.

Intrinsic to these terms is another important distinction in the life of the Messiah: he is humbled and he is exalted, that is, both "sufferings" and "glory" will characterize his life. Most men drift in the "misty flats" of mediocrity, but this man will be either loved or hated, on top or on the bottom. How accurately the Word of God delineates his experience even before he was born! We will now illustrate the interrelationship of these four roles using a matrix to see the patterns emerge more clearly:

	Person (subjective)	Work (objective)
Exalted	Son of God (John)	King (Matthew)
Humbled	Man (Luke)	Servant (Mark)

Understanding these four aspects of the life and ministry of the Redeemer is absolutely crucial to accurately handling the information contained in the Four Gospel records. Without this insight, cutting the cornerstone squarely would be nearly impossible. In fact, it is significant that there would be *four* sides to his life, considering that he is called *the cornerstone*. A "square" is defined in geometry as a plane figure having four equal straight-line sides, with each adjacent pair forming a right angle. There is a metaphorical richness to this word "square" that is very relevant to this study. When we do not want to do the work required in a particular job, we are tempted to "cut corners." An accountant *squares* accounts to bring them into a state of even balance of debits and credits; a *square* bank statement leaves no remainder unaccounted for, but is in perfect balance with one's checkbook. A carpenter uses a *square* to check for straightness or perpendicularity. In logic or rhetoric, a *square* statement is an unequivocal statement, the words it employs being clearly defined and consistent in their use throughout an argument or speech. In our study of the identity of Christ, we want our conclusions to *square* with all the biblical information and harmonize without any remainder. And because we want to build upon the rock of Christ, we want to make sure we are cutting the cornerstone as accurately as the Bible does.[9]

Each of the Four Gospels—Matthew, Mark, Luke and John—views the person and work of Christ from *one* of these four different perspectives: King, Servant, Man and Son. As we begin to view each of these Gospels, we see that this paradigm is reflected right away in the varied handling of Jesus' genealogy. Each genealogy supports the theme of the Gospel in which it appears in a way that speaks powerfully of God's inspiration to those with eyes to see. We will now present some highlights of this remarkable example of scriptural precision, but we encourage the reader to study this subject in further detail in order to see the pattern for himself.

Matthew, which presents Jesus as a **King** from the line of David, starts out with the "…record of the genealogy of Jesus Christ the son of David…" and then gives the genealogy from Abraham, the one who was promised the land, through King David, who was promised the kingdom in a covenant of salt with God (2 Chron. 13:5). Mark, which portrays Jesus as the **servant** of God, has no genealogy, which makes sense because a servant's genealogy is not relevant. The gospel of Luke, which portrays Christ as a **man**, has a genealogy that traces Jesus back to Adam, the first man. John, which portrays Christ as **the Son** of God, starts out by saying that God, in the beginning, had a plan, purpose or wisdom (the *logos*) that became flesh, that is, the Son "comes from" the Father. The Old Syriac translates John 1:18 this way: "the only begotten Son who is *from* the bosom of the Father." This is a very short genealogy: the Father had a Son, an *only begotten* Son. Thus, we see that the genealogy in each gospel fits the purpose of that gospel.

As we continue to explore each gospel in depth, we find more and more evidence that each gospel represents just one particular aspect of this fourfold paradigm. This goes a long way toward explaining the supposed "discrepancies" and "contradictions" between and among them.[10] **Matthew** has a number of unique characteristics that point to Christ as King. The phrase, "the kingdom of heaven" is associated with the specific reign of the Messiah on earth. It occurs more than 30 times in the gospel of Matthew, but not once in any of the other Gospels, which use the phrase, "kingdom of God." Matthew is the only gospel that records the visit of the Magi, who came to Jerusalem and asked, "…Where is the one who has been born king…?"(Matt. 2:2).

---

9. Because the gospel of John was written late and was a late addition to the New Testament canon, there was some controversy over its acceptance. F. F. Bruce comments on how this Gospel came to be accepted as canonical by the early church "fathers"; To Irenaeus the fourfold character of the gospels is as axiomatic as the four quarters of the world or the four principal winds. (Irenaeus' *Against Heresies*, 3.11.11, cited in F. F. Bruce, *The Gospel of John*, William B. Eerdmans, Grand Rapids, MI, 1983), p. 11.

10. See also Appendix O.

The title, "Son of David," occurs ten times in Matthew and only six times in all the other Gospels combined. There are a number of parables of the Kingdom that are unique to Matthew, and only Matthew records the "sheep and goat judgment," when the king lets the righteous into his kingdom but excludes the unrighteous (Matt. 25). We should note that outside of the Four Gospels there are only a few other places in the New Testament that refer to Christ as a "King."[11] However, the title "King" is amplified to "King of kings" in 1 Timothy 6:15; Revelation 17:14 and 19:16.[12] Yet where he is not specifically called "King," he may still be referred to as being positionally exalted, as in his titles or functions "Lord" or "Head."

The gospel of **Mark** is short, simple and forceful, emphasizing Christ's works more than his words. Commentators have long noticed that Mark focuses more on what Jesus *did* than what he *said*, which makes sense because obedient action is the sign of a good servant. Mark also moves quickly from one event to another. Even the vocabulary reflects this pattern. The Greek word *eutheos* ("immediately") occurs 40 times in Mark but only 27 times in all the other Gospels combined. That statistic is made even more vivid when one realizes that there are only 16 chapters in Mark, but 73 chapters in the other three Gospels combined. A valued servant is humble, and quick to obey. In describing Christ's servanthood, Philippians 2:8 says that he "...humbled himself and became obedient to death—even death on a cross." Appropriately, more than a third of Mark takes place in the last week of Jesus' life placing special emphasis on his obedience and personal sacrifice.

Luke presents the Messiah and his relationships in a way that highlights his humanity as the Last Adam. Luke opens with information on the parents and birth of John the Baptist, giving information we would expect to find in a "human interest" story. It gives details about the birth of Christ and his presentation at the Temple that show that Jesus was subject to the same laws and regulations as every other Jewish child. The gospel of Luke portrays two particularly poignant scenes from his infanthood: the aged believer Simeon living long enough to take the child up in his arms and prophesy over him; and the 84-year-old prophetess Anna who prayed faithfully day and night in the Temple, being blessed by God to see her longed-for Redeemer.

Luke clearly portrays Jesus' great love for all mankind, and describes him as a warm and loving person. Commentators note that the book of Luke portrays Jesus' special concern for the poor, sinners, women and the family more clearly than any other gospel. Uniquely emphasized in Luke is Christ sympathetically acknowledging the Gentiles. It emphasizes forgiveness and also highlights Jesus' prayer life, as well as the value of prayer itself.

The gospel of **John** presents Jesus as the "only begotten" Son of God, and we will be exploring this aspect of his life and ministry in more detail in Chapter 8. Suffice it to say here that Christ's intimacy with his Father is uniquely portrayed in that gospel, as would be predicted of a literary portrait with the theme of Jesus as the *Son* of God. For example, the word "father" occurs as many times in John as in all the other Gospels combined. Theologians have long noticed that John is different from the other Gospels and truly unique. This fits with our expectations, because, as "the only begotten Son of God," Jesus is truly unique.

---

11. Generally, Christ is called "King" only in relationship to *Israel*, to whom God promised to raise up someone to sit on the throne of David. That kingdom is still future. For the Church, Christ is not "King," but "Lord," and "... head over everything for the church" (Eph. 1:22).

12. The fact that both Jesus and God are sometimes referred to as "King," and as "King of kings," has led some to the conclusion that Jesus is God. We find, on the contrary, that this is more evidence for God's exalting Christ to the position of functional equality with Himself, even allowing His Son to share in the titles that describe His own various functions. See Appendix A (1 Tim. 6:14–16).

It should be clear from this brief examination of the evidence that this paradigm is powerfully stamped upon the Four Gospels, and provides powerful evidence of their inspiration. There is absolutely no evidence that these four writers collaborated on their writing to produce this remarkable result. Like all the different writers of the Bible, they each wrote independently of one another, separated by both time and space.

But there is even more evidence of a divine stamp on this fourfold paradigm. It proves to be a consistent pattern throughout the entire Bible. We will point out a few of the most noteworthy examples. In the Hebrew Scriptures, the Tabernacle was a detailed physical representation of the coming Messiah, and had four colors in its scheme: blue, white, crimson and purple (Exod. 25:4). Purple represented royalty, or Kingship. Crimson represented the shedding of his blood as a Servant. Blue represented his humanity, and white reflected the sinless purity and glory of his divine Sonship.[13]

Also related to the Messiah are the four creatures of Revelation 4:6 and 7, which are the same as the four cherubim of Ezekiel 1:10: lion, ox, man and eagle.[14] The lion is "the king of the beasts," and hence represents the Messiah as **King**. Christ is also referred to as the "lion of Judah" in Revelation 5:5. The ox is a beast of burden and is therefore man's **Servant** (see Deut. 5:14). The man is obviously the Messiah as **Man**. The eagle represents Christ as the **Son of God**, because the eagle is the most majestic of all fowl, soaring high in the heavens. It also has the loftiest perspective and the best eyesight of any animal.[15] This truth relates powerfully to the glorious perspective of Jesus Christ adopted by the gospel of John, as will be seen in Chapter 8.

---

13. White is associated with sinlessness. Revelation 7:14 describes the garments of those who endure through the Tribulation, being washed white in the blood of the Lamb. Normal blood will stain fabric permanently, but the Lamb's blood cleanses and turns the fabric white. This is due to the *sinlessness* of his blood (cp. Isa. 1:18). White garments are also associated with glorious angelic visitations (Dan. 7:9; Matt. 28:3; Rev. 15:6 - KJV). In the Transfiguration, Jesus is glorified and is seen in brilliant white garments (Matt. 17:2). White is used also in a pejorative sense associated with religious leaders attempting to cover their own sinfulness (Matt. 23:27; Acts 23:3). Blue is associated with the Law, which was necessary for the proper governance of man's life. Crimson and purple are customarily associated with blood and royalty, respectively, in both the Bible and secular literature.

14. Cherubim are associated with epochal events in the unfolding of redemption history. Lucifer was "anointed as a guardian cherub" (Ezek. 28:14), but fell, making the redemption of creation necessary. Cherubim guarded the east side of Eden, preventing Adam and Eve from eating fruit from the tree of life (Gen. 3:24). Images of cherubim are incorporated into the very design of the mercy seat in the holy of holies in both the Tabernacle and the Temple. In Ezekiel 10 and 41 we see the glory of the LORD leaving and returning to Israel accompanied by the cherubim. Finally, the cherubim are referred to as the "four living creatures" of Revelation 4:6–8, 5:8–14, 6:1–7, 7:11, 14:3, 15:7 and 19:4, and are associated with the intense worship of God and the restoration of Paradise. In some sense, these cherubim point to the Christ and his complete and ultimate destruction of Lucifer, who was once a cherub himself. Biblically, a cherub is a spirit being of great power and majesty, representing the presence and authority of God. It is no accident that the image of a "cherub" in modern times has degenerated into a chubby little Cupid-like creature who is the spiritual equivalent of the Pillsbury® doughboy. The Devil demeans and ridicules what he himself once was.

15. God's creation is replete with examples of minerals, plants and animals that illustrate biblical truths, in this case shedding light on who the Messiah was to be. This phenomenon is not a circumstantial accident, but by deliberate design. For instance, the Devil is called a serpent because he is crafty, stealthy, and highly poisonous. One day, the Messiah will crush his head, the best way to kill a Serpent. Those who embrace an evolutionary model of the origin of life can see "nature" only as an accidental combination and recombination of molecules, and they miss out on the enriched perspective of the natural world as the work of an intelligent Designer, the same one who is the also the Author of the Bible.

The Name of Jesus Christ

Even the elements and combinations of the name of Jesus Christ can be analyzed in terms of this fourfold pattern. There are four permutations of the name "Jesus Christ": "Jesus," "Christ," "Jesus Christ" and "Christ Jesus." The many occurrences of these four terms sort themselves into the same four categories we are studying, with only a few exceptions. "**Jesus**" of Nazareth is **the man** from Galilee. This is the name given him by an angel before he was born, and represents him as a person without supplemental descriptions or titles.[16] In general, the term "Jesus" refers to his earthly life from birth to his being raised from the dead. But we must remember that it is his given name, and therefore it continues to be used throughout the New Testament.

"**Christ**" is equivalent to the term "Messiah," and relates to his work of **service**. In the Greek language, *chrio* means "to anoint," and the English word "Christ" comes from *chrio*. The Hebrew word "to anoint" is *mashach*, and "anointed" is *mashiach*. The word "messiah" is from *mashiach* and means "the anointed one." Thus, the "Messiah" and "Christ" both mean the same thing, "the anointed one," "Messiah" coming from the Hebrew, and "Christ" coming from the Greek.[17]

---

16. The use of the unadorned name of "Jesus" is particularly significant in Philippians 2:10 where we see that every knee must bow at the name *Jesus*—this one who started out as a baby but who is now the highly exalted Lord. Some, like E. W. Bullinger, have correctly noted that nowhere in the New Testament is he ever called only "Jesus" when directly addressed by his followers, and that it is his enemies (John 18:5 and 7, 19:19; Acts 4:18, 5:40, 6:14, 26:9) and demons (Mark 1:24, 5:7) who refer to him as "Jesus" in direct discourse. Some have concluded from this that his followers should never refer to him as "Jesus," either in direct address or otherwise. We regard this teaching as very impractical and legalistic. We have seen firsthand the verbal paranoia that can be generated among those who are exposed to this teaching. One becomes uncomfortable even uttering a verbally naked "Jesus" in any context, and must always quickly clothe it with one of his titles—Christ, Lord, etc.

We cannot imagine that Jesus himself would want his brothers and sisters feeling uncomfortable every time they say his name without any adornment. First of all, there is no biblical injunction against such use of the name "Jesus." It is, after all, his God-given *name*, as distinct from a title or appellation. Second, the resurrected and glorified Lord still identified *himself* as "Jesus" when appearing to Paul in Acts 9:5 (we suppose he did so because it continues to be *his name*). The angel at his ascension referred to him as "Jesus," and Peter uses his simple name three times in his sermon on Pentecost (Acts 2:22, 32 and 36). The disciples refer to "Jesus" when praying to God in Acts 4:27 and 30 (and they weren't struck by lightning). Finally, Paul uses an unadorned "Jesus" throughout his Epistles with a precision and power commensurate with his being a holy man inspired to write Holy Writ (See 2 Cor. 4:11; Eph. 4:21; 1 Thess. 1:10, 2:15, 4:14). Having thus made our point, all we can say is Praise *JESUS!* Thank you, *JESUS!* We love you, *JESUS!*

If he was not called "Jesus" by his followers in direct address, what *was* he called? The most common term was "lord," a title of respect at least equivalent to "Sir," but with a meaning ranging from "Sir" to "master" or "owner" (See Appendix B). Sometimes he was called "Rabbi," mostly in John (8x), a title that was keenly desired by the Pharisees (Matt. 23:7), and equivalent to "Teacher." Against this backdrop of Pharisaical arrogance, Jesus taught his disciples about the use of titles for the purpose of personal elevation. He expressly discouraged them from referring to themselves as "Rabbi," because they were all brothers, and they had only one "Teacher," namely he. In that same context, he also forbade the use of the titles "Father," because there is only one Father (our heavenly Father), and "Master," because he was their only Master. This latter title (Gk. *kathegetes*) was never used of him, and since this is the only use of this word in the New Testament, we cannot be certain of precisely the way Jesus used it since it has a wide range of secular usage. Though he discouraged their use of titles for themselves by identifying himself as their Teacher and Master, he did not seem to expect them to refer to him as such. They continued to refer to him primarily as *Kurios*, and he made no attempt to correct them. The bottom line of this discussion about titles, however, is that they ought not to be used to elevate oneself. Humility must be the mark of Christ's followers (Matt. 23:8–10).

17. The astute reader will have picked up on the fact that since many people in the Bible were anointed, there were many "Messiahs" or many "Christs." When David said that he would not kill King Saul because he would not "...lay a hand on the LORD's anointed..." (1 Sam. 26:9), the Hebrew text reads "the LORD's *mashiach*," or Messiah. Thus, in the

All through the Hebrew Scriptures, "anointing" had great significance. Priests, prophets and kings were all anointed with oil (Exod. 40:13; 1 Sam. 10:1, 16:13; 1 Kings 19:15 and 16), in recognition of the fact that the important work set before them would require divine guidance and help. On occasion, even objects used in the service of God were anointed (Gen. 28:18; Lev. 8:11).

The words "the anointed" thus emphasize the work, function or task for which the person or object was anointed. Acts 10:38 clearly relates his being anointed to the Messianic work for which Jesus of Nazareth was called.

> **Acts 10:38**
> how God anointed Jesus of Nazareth with the Holy Spirit and power, and how he went around **doing good and healing** all who were under the power of the devil, because God was with him.

Another way to understand the distinction between person and function is this: "Christ" relates to the job that needed doing and "Jesus" is the person who did the job.[18] This means that Jesus did not actually become "Christ," i.e., "the anointed one," until he was anointed at his baptism at the age of 30. That is why Peter said that God "made this Jesus…both Lord and Christ" (Acts 2:36). Logically, he would have been *made* "Christ" (i.e., *empowered* to be the Christ) when he was anointed, but was *declared* to be Christ categorically and conclusively at his resurrection when the earthly phase of his Messianic work, and therefore his "sufferings," was finished.

We consider it an inescapable conclusion that "Jesus" would have been unable to do the work of "Christ" had he not been anointed with holy spirit and power, despite being the Son of God by birth. Thus, the term "Christ" rather strictly relates to the *work* that he was called upon to do and highlights the humility with which he would approach it. This is why the Synoptic Gospels portray him as the graciously-enabled adult **servant** rather than the privileged Son (predictably, the baptism of Jesus by John is not included in the gospel of John—See Chapter 8).

"**Jesus Christ**" is the combination of his name that is used most commonly in conjunction with "the Father," and hence it relates to his role as **the Son**. God is "the God and Father of the Lord *Jesus Christ*," never the "Father of the Lord Christ," or "the Father of our Lord Jesus," etc. Generally, "Jesus Christ" is the **person** who is the Son of God seated at the right hand of God with whom we are personally connected. It is "Jesus Christ" with whom we have personal fellowship (1 John 1:3; 1 Cor. 1:9). It is he who gave personal revelation to Paul (Gal. 1:11 and 12). Putting "Jesus" before "Christ" places the emphasis on his person, and therefore his relationships with his Father and his family. Though he is the exalted Lord seated at the right hand of God, he is personally acquainted with every member of his Body, who are his brothers and sisters in the family of God (Heb. 2:11).

"**Christ Jesus**" emphasizes his exalted position at the right hand of God, and is related to the aspect of Messiah as one who **functions** in an exalted position of authority as **King**. The king has authority not from his personal qualities but from his *position*. Anyone can serve as a king and have authority, even if he is a buffoon. "Christ Jesus" also emphasizes the objective aspect of the Messiah's work and accomplishments. The term "Christ" preceding "Jesus" places the emphasis on the legal rights, privileges and responsibilities of believers that have resulted from his finished work. This compound

---

Bible there were many messiahs, but only one true Messiah, just as there are many saviors, but only one true Savior. For more on the use of Savior, see Appendix A (Luke 1:47).

18. Some scholars have noticed this distinction. One says that the word "Christ" appears "when there is reference to the work of redemption." Kittel, *op. cit., Theological Dictionary* Vol. IV, p. 1090.

form of his name is used most often with "in" and "by," again emphasizing not his person but his exalted position. We "rejoice in Christ Jesus" (Phil. 3:3 - KJV), meaning in this case that the source of our joy is his completed *work* on our behalf. This is not to say that having a personal relationship with him is not a source of joy, only that the term "Christ Jesus" does not have that emphasis.

We will conclude this study of the fourfold paradigm by quoting an old, familiar passage in light of what we have just learned. Knowing the extensive biblical depth of this paradigm and what each term means helps us properly interpret a passage such as this:

Philippians 2:6–11

(6) Who, being in very nature [KJV—"in the form of"] God [i.e., as His **Son**, his privileged position], did not consider equality with God something to be grasped [as Lucifer and Adam did],

(7) but made himself nothing, taking the very nature of a **servant** [his daily decision], being made in human likeness [i.e., a **man**, a human being, his "nature"].

(8) And being found in appearance [KJV— "fashion"] as a man, he humbled himself and became obedient to death—even death on a cross!

(9) Therefore God exalted him to the highest place [i.e., as the **King** of kings] and gave him the name that is above every name [i.e, the *Lord Jesus Christ*],

(10) that at the name of Jesus every knee should bow, in heaven and on earth and under the earth,

(11) and every tongue confess that Jesus Christ is Lord, to the glory of God the Father.

The following chart puts all the previous information together in a way that may visually help to establish this scriptural pattern:

	King	Servant	Man	Son
	FOUR GOSPELS			
	Matthew	**Mark**	**Luke**	**John**
Tsemach	Zechariah 9:9; Jeremiah 23:5 A righteous branch, the King	Isaiah 42:1; Zechariah 3:8 My servant, the branch	Zechariah 6:12 The man whose name is Branch	Isaiah 4:2 The branch of the LORD... beautiful and glorious
The cheribum of Ezekiel 1:10 and Revelation 4:6–7	Lion	Ox	Man	Eagle
Tabernacle Colors	Purple	Crimson	Blue	White
Genealogy	From Abraham and David to Christ	None	From Adam, the first man	From the bosom of the Father
Name	Christ Jesus, Lord	Christ, Lord	Jesus, Lord	Jesus Christ, Lord

The Reliability of the Gospels

Through the years, we have heard many people who do not believe in the death and resurrection of Christ call the Bible "a good book" or say that it "contains moral lessons." However, if Christ did not do the miracles the Bible says he did, nor rise from the dead, and if his disciples and the writers of the Bible foisted a huge hoax on mankind by saying he was alive when he wasn't, then the Bible is neither good nor moral. The Four Gospels are the history and account of the life, death and resurrection of Jesus Christ. They testify to what Christ said and did. They also claim to be an authoritative record of his identity: the only-begotten Son of God who died, but was raised from death, and who now sits as Lord of lords at the right hand of God.

Aside from the accuracy of the narrative account of his life, we have many specific prophecies that the Gospels claim are fulfilled in Jesus Christ. The fact that he fulfilled prophecy after prophecy is powerfully persuasive evidence of his Messiahship. As prophesied, he was a descendant of Adam and David. He was born of a virgin in Bethlehem, spent part of his life in Egypt, grew up in Nazareth, etc. In *The Signature of God*, Grant Jeffrey gives the odds of one person being able to fulfill just 17 of all the prophecies that Christ fulfilled. It is: 480,000,000,000,000,000,000,000,000,000,000,000 to 1.

That huge number is really impossible to conceive of, so Jeffrey gives it in the following analogy: imagine that every star and planet in the entire Milky Way galaxy is made of sand, just sand. That would not be as many grains of sand as the above number indicates. So one person trying to fulfill all those prophecies would be like someone having one guess to find one specific grain of sand in an entire galaxy of sand.[19] Good luck!

There is much more reason than just prophecy to consider the Gospel records reliable, however. Scripture records that after his resurrection, Jesus "…gave many convincing proofs that he was alive…" (Acts 1:3). That is the reason why Christianity is around today. Had Jesus not shown himself alive, his disciples would have scattered and there would be no Christianity. This was already starting to happen, as evidenced by the two disappointed disciples who were walking away from Jerusalem when he appeared to them and convinced them he was alive (Luke 24). Mary Magdalene, upon seeing the empty tomb, did not conclude from this fact that there had been a resurrection; instead she thought someone had carried off Jesus' dead body (John 20:10–16). But she, too, was convinced when Jesus personally appeared to her. After Jesus appeared to these disciples, they were convinced of the resurrection but were unable to convince the other disciples. The Apostles were only convinced by Jesus himself, who "appeared to the eleven as they were eating: he rebuked them for their lack of faith and their stubborn refusal to believe those who had seen him after he had risen" (Mark 16:14).

It was Jesus' personal appearance to the Apostles and to the others that convinced them that he was alive and thus was worth living and dying for. Jesus had been unable to convince the Jews to believe in him, and yet Peter, less than two months after the last time Jesus himself had entered the Temple and taught the people, stood up on the Day of Pentecost and addressed many of the same people who had recently shouted, "Crucify him." Peter boldly told the people that they had crucified their Messiah, but that God had raised him from the dead and made him "Lord." The resurrection was not a question in Peter's mind. Standing there with the other Apostles, he told the crowd, "… we are all witnesses of the fact" (Acts 2:32). Of course, the talk of people seeing Jesus alive after his death had gotten around, and on the Day of Pentecost about 3000 people believed. That was a good start, and Christianity spread rapidly after that.

---

19. Grant Jeffery, *The Signature of God*, (Frontier Research Publications, Toronto, 1996), p. 182.

The Bible is a "good book" (actually, it is the *best* book!) and it is a "moral book." It is not built on a hoax or a lie. Jesus is the Promised Messiah, and he died for the sins of all of us just as was foretold in the Hebrew Scriptures, clearly portrayed in the Four Gospels and recounted and expanded upon in Acts and the Epistles. Christianity spread rapidly after the resurrection, and it is still spreading. If Christianity has spread to you, and you are a Christian, we thank God for your salvation and encourage you to continue in the grace of God. Jesus said, "I tell you the truth, anyone who has faith in me will do what I have been doing…" (John 14:12). The Gospels clearly portray what Jesus Christ did. Now we can honor him and his Father by going and doing the same things.

If it has not "spread" to you yet, we urge you to honestly consider the evidence and make the decision to believe it. A person is saved when he personally confesses and believes what Scripture clearly says: "…if you confess with your mouth, 'Jesus is Lord,' and believe in your heart that God raised him from the dead, you will be saved" (Rom. 10:9).

Make Jesus Christ your Lord and Savior, because he is the promised Messiah. His life stands at the very crossroads of eternity. It is he before whom every person who has ever walked the earth must one day stand and acknowledge as Lord. It is he for whom Christians labor, bearing the Good News of his coming to the ends of the earth, that every man would know how to answer the Lord's question: **"…who do you say that I am?"**

7

The Synoptic Gospels:
Open or Veiled Messiah?

In the previous chapter, we presented the "synoptic" witness of the life of Christ, and established the fact that these three Gospels—Matthew, Mark and Luke—basically agree on the identity of Christ as a human being who was empowered at his baptism to be the Savior of the world. These accounts of Jesus' life give no hint of any "pre-existence" or "incarnation," nor that Jesus believed he was "God in human flesh."[1] He even avoided the titles normally associated with the Messiah, and preferred to

---

1. Origen, the early Church "father," recognized that the Synoptic Gospels did not support the idea of Jesus as God. Todt quotes Origen on John 1:6: " 'For none of these [Paul, Matthew, Mark, Luke] plainly declared Jesus' Godhead, as John does when he makes him say, 'I am the light of the world'; 'I am the way, the truth and the life'; 'I am the resurrection.' There is not a single 'Son of Man' saying within the Synoptic tradition which links up with the concept of pre-existence from apocalyptic literature." (H. E. Todt, *The Son of Man in the Synoptic Tradition*, SCM Press, 1965), p. 284.

Dunn affirms the same point: "In not one instance where Jesus is portrayed as the Danielic son of man is there any perceptible implication that Jesus is thereby understood as a pre-existent being hidden in heaven prior to his (initial) manifestation on earth." (Dunn, *op. cit., Christology*), p. 88.

call himself "the son of man," an ambiguous term.[2] It occurs 79 times in the Synoptic Gospels and 12 times in John, and is never used by anyone but Jesus. The ambiguity is found in the fact that in the Aramaic language that Jesus spoke, "son of man" meant simply "a certain one" or "someone."[3] Thus, as with the use of parables, those with ears to hear and true spiritual hunger could discern who he was, while those who looked on the flesh remained in the dark.

Many Christians have traditionally understood the phrase "son of man" to refer to his "human side" as opposed to his "God side." But, in recent years, a variety of scholars have recognized the particular Messianic meaning of the phrase, unknown to the vast majority of Jesus' listeners. It refers not to his humble status as a man, but to one vested with the highest honor and authority who comes to rule the earth in the name of **Yahweh**. Daniel had used this term in his famous Messianic prophecy concerning the end times when the Messiah would rule.

> **Daniel 7:13 and 14 (NASB)**
> (13) "I kept looking in the night visions, And behold, with the clouds of heaven One like a Son of Man was coming, And He came up to the Ancient of Days And was presented before Him.[4]
> (14) "And to Him was given dominion, Glory and a kingdom, That all the peoples, nations, and *men of every* language Might serve Him. His dominion is an everlasting dominion Which will not pass away; And His kingdom is one Which will not be destroyed.

Open or Veiled Messiah?

It is commonly asserted by orthodox Christian teachers and apologists, and believed by most Christians, that Jesus clearly stated during his earthly ministry that he was "God." But many scholars have noted from a careful reading of the Synoptic Gospels that not only did Jesus not assert that he was *God*, he did not openly assert that he was the Messiah, the Son of God![5] If it was not Jesus' practice to assert

---

2. Bruce, *op. cit., Gospel of John*, p. 67, notes 71 and 73:

> The phrase 'son of man' is a Hebrew and Aramaic idiom meaning simply 'a man', 'a human being'. In Aramaic, the language that Jesus appears normally to have spoken, 'the son of man' would have meant 'the Man'. On occasion Jesus may have used this expression as a substitute for the pronoun 'I' or 'me'…In Ps. 8:4 'the son of man' (Heb. ben 'adam) stands in synonymous parallelism with 'man' (Heb. 'enosh), both expressions being used in the generic sense.

3. Trent C. Butler [General Editor], *Holman Bible Dictionary*, "Son of Man,"(Holman Bible Publishers, Nashville, TN, 1991), p. 1291.

4. Note that the "Son of Man" is the Messianic figure who receives all power and authority to rule over the nations. He receives this power from the "Ancient of Days," a clear image of the Almighty God who would delegate it to him. Note the transference of language from the "Ancient of Days" to the "son of man" in Revelation 1:13ff. This is a powerful way to express the exaltation of Jesus to functional equality with God by portraying him in similar language, but certainly not to be taken to supersede the already clearly defined relationship of the Almighty God and His Messiah, the "son of man." See Appendix A (Gen. 18:1 and 2; Rev. 1:13–15).

5. This idea of Jesus veiling his Messianic ministry is not new. In 1901, German theologian W. Wrede wrote *The Messianic Secret*, in which he suggested that Jesus did not make any Messianic claims himself, but that the Church made these claims for him in later years and Mark redacted the idea into his gospel. Scholars since have recognized this "secrecy motif," and have subdivided the secrecy material into at least two categories, his Messiahship and his miracles. Scholars are still debating the issue. Witherington sees "a tension that exists between secrecy and openness" in the gospel of Mark, and attributes this to Mark being a "collector of diverse traditions." Along with virtually every other Christian scholar, he thus fails to understand that the spiritual perspective of Mark, with its emphasis on Christ's *service*, would

that he was Christ or even the "Son of God," then he certainly did not assert his "deity," or that he was "God," as many Trinitarians claim. Many modern scholars agree with this, and have challenged the notion that he understood himself to be and openly declared that he was "God in human flesh."[6] They have even questioned whether he openly declared that he was the promised Messiah. Although Jesus did occasionally declare that he was the Messiah, this was the exception and not the rule, and he did this only when he was with certain select individuals.[7] Scripture reveals that the clear and open presentation of Jesus as the Christ came *after* he was raised from the dead.

> **Acts 2:22, 24, 31–33 and 36 (NASB)**
> (22) "Men of Israel, listen to these words: Jesus the Nazarene, a man attested to you by God with miracles and wonders and signs which God performed through Him in your midst, just as you yourselves know—
> (24) "And **God raised Him up again**, putting an end to the agony of death, since it was impossible for Him to be held in its power.
> (31) he [David] looked ahead and spoke of **the resurrection of the Christ**, that HE WAS NEITHER ABANDONED TO HADES [the grave], NOR DID HIS FLESH SUFFER DECAY.
> (32) "This Jesus God **raised** up again, to which we are all witnesses.
> (33) "Therefore having been exalted to the right hand of God…
> (36) "Therefore let all the house of Israel know for certain that God has made Him both Lord and Christ—this Jesus whom you crucified."

Notice that the signs and wonders associated with his ministry attested to his being "accredited by God" (verse 22), but not necessarily to the fact that he was the Messiah. Prophets like Elijah and Elisha had performed many mighty acts, but were not thought to be the Messiah on that account. Nevertheless, Jesus' signs and wonders were an important part of his ministry. John 20:30 and 31 says that the signs and miracles that he did were written down so that others beside those who

be the very gospel we would expect to emphasize the secrecy motif. The servant labors in obscurity. Ben Witherington, *The Christology of Jesus* (Fortress Press, Minneapolis, 1990), p. 264.

6. Dunn writes: "But if we are to submit our speculations to the text and build our theology only with the bricks provided by careful exegesis, we cannot say with any confidence that Jesus knew himself to be divine, the pre-existent Son of God" (Dunn, *op. cit., Christology*), p. 32.

7. In Matthew 16:15–20, Jesus' identity is the issue. Peter correctly understands Jesus to be the Christ, but Jesus never actually affirms or denies the fact. He says, in effect, "I never told you that, but God apparently did." In John 4:25 and 26 (NRSV), Jesus says, "I am he," meaning the Messiah, but the Samaritan woman would have had different Messianic expectations, and so he would have less concern about revealing his true identity to her. Even during the time of his trial before the High Priest and Pilate, there is doubt among scholars as to whether he was forthcoming about his identity. In Mark 14:61 and 62, Jesus identifies himself to the High Priest. Oscar Cullman argues that when the parallel synoptic passages (Matt. 26:63 and 64; Luke 22:70) are considered and we go back to the Aramaic original, Jesus' answer is not clearly affirmative. This would be consistent with his behavior at other times in his ministry, leaving it to others and God whether or not he was recognized for who he really was. Cullman writes:

> The corresponding Aramaic word by no means indicates a clear affirmation. It is rather a way of avoiding a direct answer and can even mean a veiled denial. In that case, the sense of Jesus' words would be, "You say so, not I." If we may understand his answer to the high priest's trick question in this way, then Jesus neither clearly affirmed nor clearly denied that he was the Messiah.

Oscar Cullman, *The Christology of the New Testament*, (The Westminster Press, Philadelphia, 1963), p. 118.

witnessed them firsthand might have a chance to believe. Jesus upbraided the people of his time for not accepting his miracles.[8] He said that the miracles he did in God's name spoke for him:

> **John 10:24 and 25 (NASB)**
> (24) The Jews therefore gathered around Him, and were saying to Him, "How long will You keep us in suspense? If You are the Christ, tell us plainly."
> (25) Jesus answered them, "I told you, and you do not believe; the works that I do in My Father's name, these bear witness of Me.

He spoke harshly about the cities that witnessed his miracles yet did not repent, even saying that if the people of Sodom had seen the same miracles, they would have repented (Matt. 11:20–24). In this regard, however, Jesus sounded more like a prophet calling the people to repentance than the Messiah, for many of the prophets were miracle workers. However, as Acts 2:31–36 indicates, the decisive and conclusive proof that Jesus of Nazareth was the Messiah ("the Christ") was his *resurrection* and *ascension*. This truth is further established in the following verses:

> **Acts 17:31 (NASB)**
> because He has fixed a day in which He will judge the world in righteousness **through a Man** whom He has appointed, **having furnished proof** to all men by **raising Him from the dead**.

> **Romans 1:4 (NASB)**
> who was declared the Son of God with power by the **resurrection from the dead**, according to the spirit of holiness, Jesus Christ our Lord,

1 Corinthians 1:22 says the "Jews demand miraculous signs" before they will believe that someone is representing God. Accordingly, the Synoptic Gospels all record a time when the Pharisees and the teachers of the Law confronted Jesus and asked for a miraculous sign as the proof that God was with him. In Mark 8:11 and 12, Jesus flatly refuses them and says that no sign will be given to them. In Luke 11:29–32, Jesus says that only one sign would be given to them: the sign of Jonah, but he does not elaborate. Matthew supplies some important information.

> **Matthew 12:40 (NASB)**
> for just as JONAH WAS THREE DAYS AND THREE NIGHTS IN THE BELLY OF THE SEA MONSTER, so shall the Son of Man be three days and three nights in the heart of the earth.

In our experience, most Christians miss the point of this reference to Jonah because they believe that he was *alive* inside the fish. But Jesus was "just as" Jonah, so if Jonah had been alive, then Jesus also would have to have been alive in the grave. The Jews, however, understood that Jonah had been *dead* three days and nights inside the fish, and that God had raised him from the dead. Yet they failed to see the Messianic application of Jonah 1:17, which Jesus quotes here, indicating that he would also be dead for three days and nights, and like Jonah, be raised from the dead.

The "sign" to which Jesus was referring was not actually the fact of him being in the grave for 72 hours ("Look at that! Someone has been dead for 72 straight hours! Amazing!"). What he was

---

8. See Chapter 5 (Eccles. 1:9).

pointing to was the event that would occur at the *end* of that period of time: the Resurrection! What Jesus was saying was that the Resurrection would be the one and only sign that would demonstrate conclusively that he was the promised Messiah. This being the case, we can understand why he would not have made a point to persuade the people of his Messianic identity during his earthly ministry. His primary mission was to be obedient to his Father and keep himself from sin so that he could fulfill his earthly destiny, which was to give his life as a perfect sacrifice for sin.

On the surface, it would appear that the purpose of Christ's ministry was to present himself as the promised Messiah. After all, at his birth the angels had made plain to the shepherds who he was, and they had excitedly passed on this proclamation. This fact had also been clearly announced at the time of his dedication in the Temple shortly after his birth. Simeon (Luke 2:25–35) clearly prophesied of the Messianic ministry that lay ahead for the baby Jesus, including both his sufferings and glory, as prophesied in Genesis 3:15. Anna, too, spoke of him to "…all them that looked for redemption in Jerusalem." In other words, she believed him to be the promised Redeemer (Luke 2:36–38 - KJV). But we must remember that these incidents follow a pattern: these were people who had a heart for God, and so God revealed to them what He was doing and who Jesus was.

With the aforementioned exceptions, it would appear that Jesus' identity as the Son of God was kept a secret from the beginning of his life. His mother and father were obviously discreet about it. Luke 2:19 (KJV) says that "…Mary kept all these things, and pondered *them* in her heart." In other words, she kept her mouth shut about who he was and what he was to do. In the town where Jesus grew up, Nazareth of Galilee, many knew him only as "the carpenter's son," so his true identity had been kept secret while he was growing up. John 8:41 (KJV) indicates that the Pharisees had investigated his background and heard that he was born "of fornication," or out of wedlock. Apparently the rumor was that Mary was already pregnant when she and Joseph were married. Jesus was viewed as a commoner of humble origins, born in a manger, raised in a second-class part of Israel and thought by many to be illegitimate. He would not be able to rely on "the world" to assist him in carrying out his Messianic mission. In fact, the cards were stacked against him.

Mary must have been careful to protect her son's identity. Once, when her 12-year-old son's precocious knowledge of Scripture led him to forget a family caravan appointment, she and Joseph spent three days looking for him throughout Jerusalem (We can hear her now: "Oy vey, I've *lost* the Son of God!"). When she finally caught up with Jesus, she found him in the Temple debating with the rabbis.

Luke 2:46–52 (NASB)
(46) And it came about that after three days they found Him in the temple, sitting in the midst of the teachers, both listening to them, and asking them questions.
(47) And all who heard Him were amazed at His understanding and His answers.
(48) And when they saw Him, they were astonished; and His mother said to Him, "Son, why have you treated us this way? Behold, Your father and I have been anxiously looking for You."
(49) And He said to them, "Why is it that you were looking for Me? Did you not know that I had to be in My Father's *house*?"
(50) And they did not understand the statement which He had made to them.
(51) And He went down with them, and came to Nazareth; and He continued in subjection to them; and His mother treasured all *these* things in her heart.
(52) And Jesus kept increasing in wisdom and stature, and in favor with God and men.

There are several important points to make about this record. It certainly seems to indicate that Jesus knew who his Father was, and therefore knew his own identity as *the Son* of God. It also shows that he felt the urgency of his calling to the point that he was unaware of what his being "lost" in Jerusalem would mean to his mother and adopted father, and even shows some typical pre-adolescent obliviousness to parental stress. The words, "…He continued in subjection to them…" at the end of this record imply that he had somewhat neglected his responsibility to his parents in this instance and that it did not happen again. We are sure there were many such experiences that Jesus had growing up, who "Although He was a Son, He learned obedience from the things which He suffered (Heb. 5:8 - NASB)." Mary, once again, pondered and guarded these things in her heart, knowing that then was not the time for him to be calling a lot of attention to himself. That would come in due time.

Chronologically, there is no further mention made about his identity until the incident recorded in Luke 3:15–22, when some people wondered if John the Baptist might not be the Messiah. John prophesied that one was coming whose sandals he was not worthy to loosen, and this one would be the true Baptizer. As John was baptizing Jesus in the river Jordan, the spirit of God descended upon him and a voice from heaven said, "…You are my beloved Son in whom I am well pleased." Also, John the Baptist gave his testimony about that event:

John 1:30–34 (NRSV)
(30) This is he of whom I said, 'After me comes a man who ranks ahead of me because he was before me.'
(31) I myself did not know him; but I came baptizing with water for this reason, that he might be revealed to Israel."
(32) And John testified: "I saw the Spirit descending from heaven like a dove, and it remained on him.
(33) I myself did not know him, but the one who sent me to baptize with water said to me, 'He on whom you see the Spirit descend and remain is the one who baptizes with the Holy Spirit.'
(34) And I myself have seen and have testified that this is the Son of God."

John's testimony that Jesus is the Son of God came by revelation, not the fact that, as Jesus' first cousin, he had heard it through the family grapevine. Although John said he saw the spirit descend, he made no mention of hearing the voice. There is no absolute biblical evidence that anyone other than Jesus and John saw the holy spirit descend in the form of a dove or that Jesus heard the voice of God, but they might have. *Something* visible and noteworthy occurred there, because one of the qualifications for an Apostle to replace Judas Iscariot was that he be someone who had been a witness at John's baptism of Jesus (Acts 1:22).

As his earthly ministry unfolded, Jesus' behavior was so contrary to the behavior that people were expecting from the Messiah that even his friends and family wanted to "take custody of him," meaning they believed him to be "several sandwiches short of a picnic."

Mark 3:20 and 21 (NASB)
(20) And He came home, and the multitude gathered again, to such an extent that they could not even eat a meal.
(21) And when His own people [NIV—"family"] heard *of this*, they went out to take custody of Him, for they were saying, "He has lost His senses."

We think the most probable explanation for this lack of support from his family is the old adage, "familiarity breeds contempt." It is also likely that they had their own preconceived ideas about the coming Messiah that did not match his behavior. Even later in his ministry, some of his family continued in their unbelief (John 7:5). Jesus realized that he was acting in ways contrary to what was taught about the Messiah, but, in keeping with his knowledge that God would reveal who he was to those whose hearts were pure, he identified those who did God's will as being his true family.

Even the Devils Believed (and Trembled)

The first three chapters of Mark are very revealing about how Jesus was perceived. As we just saw, his family did not believe in him. In Mark 3:22, immediately after his family believed he was insane, the teachers of the law came down from Jerusalem and let it be known that they thought he was a worker of evil—casting out demons by the prince of demons, Beelzebub. In the first three chapters of Mark are three records where evil spirits identify him as the Christ, but he commanded them not to reveal who he was. This is clear evidence that he veiled his Messianic identity.

Mark 1:23–26 (NASB)
(23) And just then there was in their synagogue a man with an unclean spirit; and he cried out,
(24) saying, "What do we have to do with You, Jesus of Nazareth? Have You come to destroy us? **I know who You are—the Holy One of God!**"
(25) And Jesus rebuked him, saying "**Be quiet**, and come out of him!"
(26) And throwing him into convulsions, the unclean spirit cried out with a loud voice, and came out of him.

Mark 1:32–34 (NASB)
(32) And when evening had come, after the sun had set, they *began* bringing to Him all who were ill and those who were demon-possessed.
(33) And the whole city had gathered at the door.
(34) And He healed many who were ill with various diseases, and cast out many demons; and **He was not permitting the demons to speak, because they knew who He was.**

Mark 3:10–12 (NASB)
(10) for He had healed many, with the result that all those who had afflictions pressed about Him in order to touch Him.
(11) And whenever the evil spirits beheld Him, they would fall down before Him and cry out, saying, "You are the Son of God!"
(12) **And He earnestly warned them not to make Him known.**

Thus, as Jesus started his public ministry, the only ones who seemed to know for sure who he was were the Devil and his demons. When Jesus went into the wilderness to be tempted, the Devil certainly knew who he was, but challenged his identity anyway, saying, "…If you are the Son of God…." He said this not because he thought Jesus did not know who he was, but because he hoped to manipulate him to act unwisely in order to *prove* his identity as "the Son of God." Satan attempted to put Jesus on the defensive. However, Jesus made no attempt to assert his identity, but appealed to the same written Word of God that was accessible to all Jews of his day. He claimed no special dispensation, rights or privileges because of his status as the Son of God.

In a transparent attempt to have Jesus skip the suffering part of his godly assignment and cut straight to the glory, the Devil offered Jesus **all the kingdoms of the world** and all the power and glory thereof in exchange for his worship. Incidentally, if Jesus Christ were God, Satan would have obviously known this fact, and this temptation would have been utterly hollow. Satan knew that God "cannot be tempted" (James 1:13). As we saw in Mark, demons also knew who Jesus was and were often quick to try to make trouble for him by prematurely "letting the cat out of the bag" and revealing that he was the Messiah. It was to their advantage to have his secret become public knowledge because then the people would have put tremendous pressure on him to deliver them from the Roman occupation of Palestine. They were looking for a Messiah who was a *political* deliverer. Therefore, Jesus was particularly careful around crowds, as the following record illustrates:

> **Luke 4:40 and 41**
> (40) When the sun was setting, **the people** brought to Jesus all who had various kinds of sickness, and laying his hands on each one, he healed them.
> (41) Moreover, demons came out of **many people**, shouting, "You are the Son of God!" But **he rebuked them and would not allow them to speak, because they knew he was the Christ.**

Note how this record contrasts with the one when he was alone with his Apostles and the demons identified him and he did not shut them up. In fact, he had a brief conversation with the chief demon and permitted them all to go into a herd of nearby swine. It was not as crucial that Jesus silence the demons in this case because he was in a remote place among those who already understood his identity.

> **Luke 8:28 (NASB)**
> And seeing Jesus, he (the demonized man) cried out and fell before Him, and said in a loud voice, "What do I have to do with You, **Jesus, Son of the Most High God?** I beg You, do not torment me!"

Even when they had no opportunity to create trouble for him by announcing his Messianic identity, the demons knew who he was and identified him immediately. The demons spoke the same truth that was later revealed throughout the New Testament: *Jesus is the Christ, the Son of the living God.*

More Reasons for Secrecy

He had other good reasons for keeping it secret beside the problem of people putting pressure on him to be their version of the political Messiah if he revealed his Messianic identity. Perhaps the best reason of all was to fulfill the Scriptures. Isaiah had prophesied of the quiet ministry of the Lord's servant:

Isaiah 42:1–3a (NASB)

(1) "BEHOLD, My Servant, whom I uphold; My chosen one *in whom* My soul delights. I have put My Spirit upon Him; He will bring forth justice to the nations.

(2) "**He will not cry out or raise** *His voice*, **Nor make His voice heard in the street**.

(3a) "A bruised reed He will not break, And a dimly burning wick He will not extinguish…"

Matthew 12 quotes this passage in the very context that we have been studying. Jesus has just healed a crippled man in the Temple on the Sabbath day and the Pharisees do not like it. They begin plotting to kill him, so he warns his followers not to tell anyone who he is:

Matthew 12:15–21 (NASB)

(15) But Jesus, aware of *this* [that the Pharisees were planning to kill him], withdrew from there. And many followed Him, and He healed them all,

(16) and **warned them not to make Him known,**

(17) in order that what was spoken through Isaiah the prophet, might be fulfilled, saying,

(18) "BEHOLD MY SERVANT, WHOM I HAVE CHOSEN; MY BELOVED IN WHOM MY SOUL IS WELL-PLEASED; I WILL PUT MY SPIRIT UPON HIM, AND HE SHALL PROCLAIM JUSTICE TO THE GENTILES.

(19) "HE WILL NOT QUARREL, NOR CRY OUT; NOR WILL ANYONE HEAR HIS VOICE IN THE STREETS.

(20) "A BATTERED REED HE WILL NOT BREAK OFF, AND A SMOLDERING WICK HE WILL NOT PUT OUT, UNTIL HE LEADS JUSTICE TO VICTORY.

(21) "AND IN HIS NAME THE GENTILES WILL HOPE."

As we noted in Chapter 5, the treatment of these verses in the ancient Hebrew writings reveals how selective the Jews were concerning messianic prophecies and this blindness affected the way they experienced Jesus. According to rabbinical literature, the Jews correctly applied Isaiah 42:1 and 4 to the Messiah because they understood the idea that he would proclaim and establish justice on the earth as a function of his Davidic reign as king, but they did not understand how the verses in between (the words in **bold type** in the above passage) were also about the Messiah. They did not understand how he could "lead justice to victory" by being a gentle and quiet servant. This passage from Isaiah is quoted in Matthew in the context of his warning the disciples not to say who he was, and explains why he would urge them to silence.

Jesus perfectly fulfilled this prophecy up until the phrase, "until he leads justice to victory." Though he did *proclaim* justice, he was treated very unjustly and crucified as a common criminal. Not until his resurrection would he be vindicated and begin to "lead justice to victory." Even to this day, this Scripture has not been completely fulfilled, and will not be until Christ puts an end to death after his Millennial reign on the earth (see also 1 Cor. 15:56, which refers to that final victory over death, the ultimate "injustice").

Knowing that his suffering would precede his glory, he was not one to quarrel and shout in the streets. Though he had his confrontations with the scribes and Pharisees, he did not go out of his way to pick a fight. He was very gentle with the people, and he touched, taught, and healed those who were "battered" or "smoldering." Some of the Gentiles did hope in him, and were healed and saved under his ministry. With the aid of the light from Matthew, this prophetic passage from Isaiah 42 is seen to richly portray the Messiah's actual ministry, and helps us understand why it had to be that way to fulfill the Scriptures.

Another reason Jesus veiled his messianic identity was to protect the all-important timing of his death. Luke 4:16–30 records his first public utterance at which he declared the nature of his ministry. He did this by letting Scripture speak for him, quoting Isaiah 61:1 and 2:

Luke 4:18 and 19 (NASB)
(18) "THE SPIRIT OF THE LORD IS UPON ME, BECAUSE HE ANOINTED ME TO PREACH THE GOSPEL TO THE POOR. HE HAS SENT ME TO PROCLAIM RELEASE TO THE CAPTIVES, AND RECOVERY OF SIGHT TO THE BLIND, TO SET FREE THOSE WHO ARE DOWNTRODDEN,
(19) TO PROCLAIM THE FAVORABLE YEAR OF THE LORD."

Having read this, Jesus simply said: "…Today this scripture has been fulfilled in your hearing." He did not say, "I am the Messiah, and these Scriptures are talking about me." He let the people figure out who he was. At first, the crowd's reaction was very favorable, until he suggested that some of them would reject him because "…no prophet is accepted in his home town." On hearing this, the people turned on him and led him to the edge of a cliff, intending to throw him to his death. They did this because they thought he was a false prophet, not because he was claiming to be the Messiah.[9] This experience would have made it clear to Jesus "right out of the gate" that he would have to be very careful about how he identified himself so that he would not be killed before the appointed time.

This spiritual warfare over the timing of his death raged around Jesus, as is abundantly evident in the following record:

John 7:1–9 (NRSV)
(1) After this Jesus went about in Galilee. He did not wish to go about in Judea because the Jews were looking for an opportunity to kill him.
(2) Now the Jewish festival of Booths [Tabernacles] was near.
(3) So his brothers said to him, "Leave here and go to Judea so that your disciples also may see the works you are doing;
(4) for **no one who wants to be widely known acts in secret**. If you do these things, show yourself to the world."
(5) (For not even his brothers believed in him.)
(6) Jesus said to them, "**My time has not yet come**, but your time is always here.
(7) The world cannot hate you, but it hates me because I testify against it that its works are evil.
(8) Go to the festival yourselves. I am not going to this festival, **for my time has not yet fully come**."
(9) After saying this, he remained in Galilee.

This is a remarkable record of familial disloyalty and how the enemy will even attempt to use those closest to us to defeat us. Not only did Jesus' own half-brothers not believe that he was the Messiah, they were unwittingly encouraging him to go to the very place where his life was in serious danger!

---

9. They were angry because he had said to them, "…no prophet is accepted in his home town," thus comparing them unfavorably to non-believing Israelites in the time of Elijah.

They said he should be "going public." His answer to them revealed his commitment to remain in the absolute center of God's will and do everything at the proper time.

As in Luke 4, we again see the fickleness of the crowd, this time at the end of his earthly ministry, as they turned on Jesus after his triumphal entry into Jerusalem. Having their hopes up that he was coming to save them from Roman domination ("Hosanna" means "Save us"), their mood quickly turned ugly when they determined that he was being arrested by the Romans, and concluded that he was impotent against these ungodly civil authorities.

Anticipating the fickleness of the crowd and the spiritual battle waged against him, Jesus walked with great wisdom and self-control. To borrow a phrase from the game of poker, he "played his cards close to the vest." This is no doubt also the reason why he commanded Peter, James and John to keep quiet about what they had seen at the Mount of Transfiguration.

> **Matthew 17:9 (NRSV)**
> As they were coming down the mountain, Jesus ordered them, "**Tell no one about the vision** until after the son of Man has been raised from the dead."

Another reason Jesus concealed his identity was to honor the way the Father has always revealed truth. It is commonly acknowledged that the Bible can be a difficult book to understand. God reveals many truths in a way that requires diligent study and prayer to comprehend them. He does want everyone "…to perceive *and* recognize *and* discern *and* know precisely *and* correctly the [divine] Truth" (1 Tim. 2:4 - AMP). In spite of that, He follows His own advice: He does not cast His pearls before swine (Matt. 7:6) or speak openly to fools so they can despise the wisdom of His Words (Prov. 23:9 - NASB). Rather, He conceals many gems of truth in such a way that only those who "incline their heart to understanding," "cry out for insight" and "…search for it as for hidden treasures" …find the knowledge of God (Prov. 2:1–5 - NRSV).

Proverbs 25:2 states that God conceals truths in His Word: "It is the glory of God to conceal things; but the glory of kings is to search things out" (NRSV). Jesus followed his Father's guidance and revealed truth in the same way his Father did. In Matthew 13, after he taught the crowds in parables, the disciples were perplexed.

> **Matthew 13:10 and 11 (NASB)**
> (10) And the disciples came and said to Him, "Why do you speak to them in parables?"
> (11) And He answered and said to them, "To you it has been granted to know the mysteries of the kingdom of heaven, but to them it has not been granted.

Jesus taught the crowds in parables, but he later expounded to the disciples the truth of what he had said (Mark 4:34). Just as he concealed some truth from the crowds, he veiled his identity so that people who do not incline their hearts "to understanding" would not know. He called himself such things as "the bread of life," "the good shepherd," "the light of the world," "the resurrection and the life," and "the son of man."

This self-assigned title of "son of man" refers to Daniel 7:13–18, which prophesies of the authority and dignity conferred on the Messiah in his glory, two ideas that the resurrection of Jesus confirmed (Acts 7:56). Some of the religious leaders (Matt. 12:39) and some of the crowds (Luke 11:29) asked Jesus for a sign. He told them that the only sign he would give to them was the sign of Jonah. As

Jonah was raised from the dead after three days and three nights in the sea creature's belly, Jesus knew that his Resurrection was the absolute and ultimate proof that he was the Christ of God.

Those whose hearts were hard remained in confusion about his true identity all the way through his life and ministry. In fact, the problem persists unto the present day.[10] Even in the days just prior to his arrest, the crowds understood Jesus to be a prophet (Matt. 21:46) but not necessarily the Messiah.

In spite of the fact that Jesus deliberately concealed his identity as the Messiah from the crowds, Scripture testifies loudly that those with a heart for God found out who he was. The shepherds at his birth, Simeon, Anna, the Magi, the woman at the well, John the Baptist, his disciples, the woman with the issue of blood, Mary and Martha, Joseph of Arimathea and many others came to know that he was the Christ. Readers today do not always recognize those individuals in the Gospels who realized that Jesus was the Messiah. For example, although many of those who called him "Son of David" apparently knew Jesus was Messiah, only those people who know that the "Son of David" is a Messianic title would be aware of that. The woman who touched his garment for healing apparently knew who he was, but a knowledge of the Old Testament is required to understand this.[11]

A further reason that Jesus hid his identity is that he recognized that *God* would have to confirm his Messiahship, and it was not his job to "toot his own horn." Rather than take the Devil's bait and do something that would hasten his being recognized as the true Messiah, he trusted rather in the living God, his Father, to corroborate his calling and the meaning of his life. As a wise man once said, "we boast because we are afraid that no one will notice us unless we do."

Jesus fulfilled prophecy after prophecy, said that he was the Messiah (albeit in mostly veiled terms), and did signs and miracles that should have revealed to the people who he was. Nevertheless, the picture in the minds of most people of what the Messiah would be like was so different from the living Christ that they did not recognize him. Their preconceived ideas came more from "synagogue training" than from the prophecies of Scripture.

There was confusion about the fact that the Messiah would have to die (Matt. 16:21 and 22; John 12:34), about who "Elijah" was (Matt. 17:10) and about Christ's actions on the Sabbath (John 5:18, 9:16).[12] There was false teaching about where Christ would come from (John 7:25–27), and also erroneous ideas about his death (John 12:34). There was little known about his ascension, and when Jesus spoke of it, the people were bewildered (John 7:33–36). There was so much confusion over his crucifixion that most of those who had believed that he was the Messiah (like the two on the road to Emmaus in Luke 24) were not persuaded enough by his signs and wonders to remain convinced of who he was. In fact, the only one who apparently kept his faith in Jesus was Joseph of Arimathea, who was presumably not as much of a witness of his miracles as were his more intimate followers. Nevertheless, Joseph was one who "waited for the kingdom of God," and saw the necessity of Christ's death.[13] His life is a powerful testimony to the importance of having one's faith grounded in the written Word of God, for that is the only thing that will sustain us and keep us within the will of God.

---

10. Cp. Matthew 12:23, 16:13 and 14; John 7:12, 40–43, 9:16, 10:20 and 21.

11. In Malachi 4:2, the Old Testament foretells that the "sun of righteousness," the Messiah, would have healing in his "wings." See Chapter 5 (Isa. 35:5 and 6).

12. Many people teach that Christ actually broke the Sabbath Law, but breaking the Law of God is sin, and Jesus Christ *never* sinned. A careful reading of the Mosaic Law on the subject of the Sabbath will show that what Jesus actually broke was the Sabbath traditions that had been set up by the religious leaders. Since these traditions were so ingrained in the culture, the people thought they were part of the Law and questioned Jesus' Messiahship when he disregarded them. Jesus carefully distinguished between spoken *Torah* and written *Torah*.

13. Joseph of Arimathea is one of the most interesting of all Christ's followers, and is made more compelling by the scant references to him in Scripture. Compiling all the evidence from the Four Gospels, we know he was a good man,

A study of Matthew reveals that Jesus was well into his ministry before he clearly revealed his identity even to his disciples. Note the background of belief in reincarnation among those who struggled to understand who he was.[14]

Matthew 16:13–17 and 20 (NASB)
(13) Now when Jesus came into the district of Caesarea Philippi, He began asking His disciples, saying, "Who do people say that the Son of Man is?"
(14) And they said, "Some *say* John the Baptist; and others, Elijah; but still others, Jeremiah, or one of the prophets."
(15) He said to them, "But who do you say I am?"
(16) And Simon Peter answered and said, "Thou art the Christ, the Son of the living God."
(17) And Jesus answered and said to him, "Blessed are you, Simon Barjona, because **flesh and blood did not reveal *this* to you, but My Father who is in heaven**.
(20) Then **He warned the disciples that they should tell no one that He was the Christ**.

Jesus' statement that God alone had revealed his identity to Peter is further evidence that he was not making a concerted effort to convince even his closest disciples of his Messianic identity, but instead depended upon his Father to defend and support him and reveal who he was. Earlier in the book of Matthew, he had told his disciples that no one could really know who he was, but that only the Father knew him.

Matthew 11:27 (NASB)
"All things have been handed over to Me by my Father; and **no one knows the Son, except the Father**; nor does anyone know the Father, except the Son, and anyone to whom the Son wills to reveal *Him*.

---

wealthy, one of the ruling elders of Israel (serving on the Sanhedrin) and that he had not voted against Jesus in the kangaroo court they held for him. We believe that Joseph knew the prophecy in Isaiah 53:9, that Jesus was to be buried among the rich, and thus had a tomb dug out of the stone somewhere near Golgotha, in a place where rich people were buried. He went to Pilate, a Gentile, to plead for Jesus' body, and in the process made himself ceremonially unclean to keep the Passover that year, a serious sacrifice for a member of the Sanhedrin. By the simple way he buried Jesus, wrapping him only in a linen cloth (Greek *sindon*), we see that he believed that Jesus would not remain in the grave. In contrast, Nicodemus followed after Joseph and buried Jesus properly "according to the Jewish customs," tightly winding his limbs, head and torso with strips of cloth dipped in 75 pounds of spices. All these, plus a neatly folded napkin that had covered his face, were left behind when Jesus was raised from the dead, a monument to Nicodemus' lack of belief in Jesus' resurrection.

The NIV unfortunately misses that Nicodemus came with some people sometime after Joseph had left the scene. It translates John 19:39 as Joseph being "accompanied" by Nicodemus, but the Greek text simply reads that Nicodemus came "also," i.e., as well as Joseph. Matthew, Mark and Luke all agree that the women were watching Joseph bury the body of Jesus, and, noting that he had not done a "proper" job, went off and bought the spices to do the job correctly (Luke 23:55 and 56). Had Joseph and Nicodemus been together, the women would have seen all the spices and never would have gone to buy more.

14. Reincarnation was one of a variety of beliefs about the afterlife prevalent in Jesus' day. The Pharisees were heavily influenced by pagan Greek thinking concerning the immortality of the soul. If a person's soul can exist apart from his body, and represents the "real" part of him, then this soul can take on another body. This is called human "reincarnation." The Pharisees believed that great souls, or spirits, like Elijah, John the Baptist or Jeremiah were not dead but could, in God's purposes, reenter another body. This is the most likely explanation for his disciples thinking that the resurrected Christ was a "spirit." See our book, *op. cit., Is There Death After Life?*

This same truth is recorded in Luke in a parallel passage:

Luke 10:22 (NASB)
"All things have been handed over to Me by my Father, and **no one knows who the Son is except the Father**, and who the Father is except the Son, and anyone to whom the Son wills to reveal *Him*."

John 6:44 adds further proof of the point we are making, that the Father revealed the identity of the Son to those who had ears to hear: "No one can come to me unless the Father who sent me draws him…"

Until this time recorded in Matthew 16, Jesus had not told his disciples outright that he was the Messiah. And after Peter gives the right answer to Jesus' question in Matthew 16:13 (a time Peter got it right), Jesus tells him not to tell anyone!

As we have already noted, the *Resurrection* was in fact the final validation of Jesus' identity as the promised Messiah. Therefore, in the book of Acts, his followers continually preached this truth. Twice in his sermon on the Day of Pentecost, Peter made mention of the following prophecy indicating that God would raise the Messiah from the dead.

Psalm 16:8–10 (NASB)
(8) I have set the LORD continually before me; Because He is at my right hand, I will not be shaken.
(9) Therefore my heart is glad, and my glory rejoices; My flesh also will dwell securely.
(10) For Thou wilt not abandon my soul to Sheol [the grave], **Neither wilt Thou allow Thy Holy One to undergo decay.**[15]

It is commonly believed that the uniqueness of Jesus' ministry was found in his saying and doing new things, but almost all his words were drawn from the Hebrew Scriptures, which all Jews of that time studied and "knew" to some degree. And his works were similar to those done by prophets of old, with the notable exception of the casting out of demons. He was, however, utterly unique in that he was the one and only man born of a virgin and who fulfilled all the prophetic parameters for the Messiah. He also broke almost every stereotype the Jews had for what the Messiah was going to be like. He was also unique in his attitude of authority that came from his intimate relationship with his "Father." And, of course, he was the only human being in all of history ever raised from the dead unto immortality. Now *that's* uniqueness!

Another significant aspect of Christ's ministry was the way in which he called out of Israel those who recognized him for who he was, based on their faith in his words and works and not because of a title he had or because of their social or religious status. In fact, he seemed to make it difficult for the self-righteous religious people even to consider him a holy man, because he often and repeatedly associated with sinners, prostitutes, tax collectors, and other "undesirables." By virtue of their disregarding the Law, these people were apparently outsiders to the blessings of Israel. He

---

15. In this context of his resurrection, we should mention Jesus raising Lazarus from the dead. An often overlooked aspect of this event is its remarkable timing in the unfolding of his ministry. He deliberately waited for four days after Lazarus had died before going to him, when by that time he was already decomposing. Jesus raised him, and then prophetically declared himself to be "the resurrection and the life." This event occurs within two weeks of his own death, serving to build the faith of his disciples in his own resurrection. They missed the point.

discouraged others from following him on any other basis than that they hungered for spiritual truth. He continually directed people's attention to spiritual values. For example, when he blessed the few loaves and fishes so that there became enough to feed a multitude, the people were apparently ready to crown him king. This he tried to discourage, even reproving the crowd for their false motives in following him.

John 6:26 and 27

(26) Jesus answered, "I tell you the truth, you are looking for me, not because you saw miraculous signs but because you ate the loaves and had your fill.
(27) Do not work for food that spoils, but for food that endures to eternal life, which the Son of Man will give you. On him God the Father has placed his seal of approval."

Jesus was a man accredited by God, one in whom He was well pleased. Jesus pleased his Father by always listening to His voice and seeking to honor Him in every possible way. The Gospels paint a portrait of one who did everything he could to direct those who listened to him toward his Father in heaven. He even entrusted the revelation of his identity as the Son of God to Him, never making it an issue, never using it as a shield to defend himself against accusation.

"He made himself of no reputation"

No doubt this commitment to keeping a low profile about his true identity is exactly what Philippians 2:6–8 is referring to, and removes this section of Scripture from the mystical clutches of "kenotic Christology" (from the Greek word *kenosis*=empty).[16] This system of belief, the handmaiden of "the incarnation," teaches that Christ emptied himself of his "pre-incarnate divinity" before he became a human fetus. How much simpler it is to place these verses from Philippians in the specific context of the witness of Christ's life as revealed in the Gospels.

Philippians 2:5–8

(5) Your attitude should be the same as that of Christ Jesus:
(6) Who, being in very nature God, did not consider equality with God something to be grasped,
(7) but made himself nothing [KJV—"of no reputation"], taking the very nature of a servant, being made in human likeness.
(8) And being found in appearance as a man, he humbled himself and became obedient to death, even death on a cross!

The NIV translation of verse 5 is excellent, compared to "Let this mind be in you…" as the KJV is worded.[17] But, almost immediately, we run smack into the blatantly Trinitarian translation, "… being

---

16. Even many Trinitarian scholars have problems with the doctrine of *kenosis*. Although many see it as a "good solution" to the problem of the incarnation and the two natures that would have to exist in Christ, the plain fact is that it never appears in Scripture. Thus, even Trinitarians argue about it amongst themselves. See Appendix A (Phil. 2:6–8).

17. The Greek word "*phroneo*" would be better translated as "inclination of the mind," which is exactly what the English word "attitude" denotes. The "attitude" of an airplane points the plane toward the sky or toward the earth. It is the "inclination" of the plane with relationship to the ground. We believe that instead of "thoughts" or "to think," *phronema / phroneo* is better understood as "the inclinations of the mind" and "to incline the mind." This is easily seen in the use of these words in Romans, Chapter 8.

in very nature God…." The word "nature" is "*morphe*," which refers to his outward form, appearance or circumstances. This word is nearly synonymous with the word *eikon* that we examined in Chapter 2, and we do not think that either one refers to his physical appearance. Remember that verse 5 has already set the context—having his *attitude!* Saying that Christ was in "the form of God" is to assert his identity as the Son of God, the Messiah. Though he had a special relationship with and likeness to his Father, he did not use this fact to elevate himself nor make a point of asserting his true identity in the face of misjudgment. He even had to endure his family thinking that he was insane, and the most influential religious leaders of his day thinking that he was the prince of demons. Even then, he made little effort to set them straight, but began to speak in parables so that those who had ears to hear could draw near if they so willed.

Jesus did not consider "…equality with God something to be grasped." Although Lucifer was the first one to get the bright idea to grasp at equality with God, it is more likely that Adam is primarily in view in this verse because, as we have already seen in Chapters 1 and 2, Adam and Christ are directly paralleled in similar Scriptures. Adam became unthankful for what God had given him (Paradise, an interesting job, a beautiful wife, fruit in abundance, everlasting life, etc.) and believed the lie that God was holding out on him. In fact, if he ate the forbidden fruit, he would be *just like God* (that is, he would gain "equality with God"). Thus, the Serpent defeated him because of his unthankful attitude and his desire to be more like God than he already was. This was very odd considering that he had been made in the *image* of God. In other words, Adam lusted for more than he already had and *grasped at equality with God.*

In contrast to Adam, Jesus began his life as a baby and grew up with the stigma of being thought illegitimate. During his earthly ministry, he suffered many other hardships, yet he chose not to believe that God was holding out on him and making his life miserable. Despite the difficult road he had to travel, he faithfully looked with joy and gratitude to God as his loving Father, refusing to disobey in even the smallest way. He was walking in obedience when he kept his true identity veiled. He was making himself "nothing," or of "no reputation." He was entrusting himself to God, seeking to glorify his Father by everything he did and said.

Jesus did not become bitter because of his lowly birth. He did not complain about being from Nazareth of Galilee, a "second rate" town. He did not allow his being thought illegitimate to define his sense of worth. He did not murmur about working as a carpenter for about 17 years until the time was right to begin his public ministry.[18] He did not become morose when his family doubted who he was. He did not grouse about having to go into the wilderness for 40 days to fast and be tempted by the Devil. He did not become impatient when time after time he was let down by his followers. He did not react angrily when he was accused of being the helper of Beelzebub, the prince of Devils, despite the absurdity of such a devilish misjudgment.

No, Jesus endured it all patiently, trusting his Father who he knew loved him and watched over him. Yes, he was the unique Son of God, but he would have to enjoy the fullness of that status later. For that time, he was called to be a faithful servant, daily and moment-by-moment emptying himself of his own thoughts and desires, keeping his "attitude" fixed upon humbly and lovingly doing the will of his Master, his Father.

---

18. Traditionally, Jewish males began learning a trade at the age of 13, according to the rabbinical saying: "Whoever does not teach his son a trade is as if he brought him up to be a robber" (Kidd. 29). Quoted in Alfred Edersheim's *Sketches of Jewish Social Life in the Days of Christ* (Hodder and Stoughton, NY), p. 190. Therefore, at the age of 30, when he began his public ministry, he would have been working as a carpenter for 17 years.

Throughout the whole course of his life, Jesus never so much as hinted at having any need for independence, nor did he struggle with anything God asked him to do until he came to the Garden of Gethsemane. There, as he contemplated the hideous indignity and humiliation of the next 40 hours, he asked his Father three times if there might not be some other way to accomplish His plan.[19] But when he was assured that the way ahead was the only way, he rose from his knees and walked bravely into the mouth of the waiting dragon.

Those were perhaps the darkest hours any human being has ever had to face, and Jesus knew they would end in his ignominious death by crucifixion. Yet he would do it all without murmuring, without complaining, without asserting his divine authority as the Son of God. "...do you think that I cannot appeal to My Father, and He will at once put at My disposal more than twelve legions of angels?" he asked. "How then shall the Scriptures be fulfilled, that it must happen this way?" (Matt. 26:53 and 54 - NASB).

His commitment was to the written Word of his Father, which only *he* could fulfill. Conversely, it was also within his ability, by disobeying the Word, to make his Father a liar. But Jesus was a righteous Son and obeyed his Father through it all. He renounced the opportunity to accept angelic deliverance and finally embraced his destiny as necessary for the Father's plan to come to pass. The only light at the end of that dark tunnel was shed by the Messianic prophecies that God would not let His holy one see corruption, because He would raise him from the dead like Jonah after three days and three nights.

So by depending on the same Word that got him through the Devil's temptations at the opening of his ministry, he would now be sustained as he trusted in his resurrection to glory. He locked his mind on the joys that lay ahead.

Hebrews 12:2b (NASB)

....Jesus, the author and perfecter of faith, who for the joy set before Him endured the cross, despising the shame, and has sat down at the right hand of the throne of God.

He did not do all that he did by remembering his former glory in heaven. He did not do it by being "God incarnate," or "God Almighty clothed in human flesh." He did it by being the Last Adam, the sacrificial Lamb of God from the human flock, confronting his humanity, facing down his fears, summoning his courage and learning to obey by doing the things he was asked to endure. From this perspective and backdrop, we can now understand the rest of the Philippian passage that describes his high exaltation. The beloved human Son became the ultimate source of pleasure for his Father, who gladly and joyfully lavished upon him everything he so richly deserved.

When in our hearts we let Jesus be humbled and suffer as the true man that he was, to the point that we can grasp that his suffering for us was genuine and unmitigated by "deity," then we can truly rejoice with him as he is honored by his resurrection as he should be honored—as the divine Hero, Agent of everlasting life and the Firstborn of a new and righteous creation. We are then fully able to draw from his example of strength and courage, and walk forth determined to have the same attitude of genuine humility and courage that he epitomized, and go on to do the works that he did.

---

19. It is commonly taught that Jesus was arrested on Thursday night and crucified on Friday morning some 12 hours later. Scripture portrays a much more horrifying picture of a 40-hour period of humiliation, trials, and torture. A thorough study of the subject reveals that he was arrested on our Monday night, crucified on Wednesday afternoon, and raised on Saturday afternoon.

8

The Gospel of John: Great Scott!
He's Back from the Future

We have by now clearly established the significance of the resurrection of Jesus Christ as the great divide between his suffering and his glory. We have also seen that each of the Gospels portrays Christ in a different way for a different purpose, and that the Synoptics agree on their view of Christ as a fully human person prepared and called to be the King of Israel and the Savior of the world.

This Jesus of Nazareth fulfilled many of the Old Testament Messianic prophecies and did the works that were expected of the Messiah. But, after a brief period of popularity, he died a humiliating death on a tree as a common criminal. He was vindicated three days later by his resurrection from the dead, after which he entered into his glory. There is no indication in the Synoptics that Jesus had "pre-incarnate glory" before his birth or that he was "God" or declared himself to be such. How, then, do so many Christians seem to find scriptural support for this belief? Without any doubt, they find it in the gospel of John. Trinitarian scholars are candid in their admission that John is the source of their doctrine:

The Christology of the Church is essentially Johannine. Without the Fourth Gospel, even the Pauline Epistles would not have sufficed as a basis for the Trinitarian doctrine we have today.[1]

In many important ways, John seems to portray Jesus in a much different way than the Synoptics. This is so much the case that some theologians believe that John, who wrote later, must have thought the other Gospels inadequate. Representing this position, Barrett writes:

John alone, however, gives the narrative about Jesus an absolute theological framework, and, though he alludes to the starting-points used by Mark (vv. 1:6–8, 15) and by Matthew and Luke (1:13), he must have regarded them as inadequate, and possibly misleading.[2]

While we obviously do not believe that John thought the other Gospels inadequate (all four are "God-breathed"), it is important to recognize the differences in the Four Gospels and understand why those differences exist. John seems to indicate that the Son of God had some sort of life with God before ever setting foot on the earth, which theologians call a "pre-existence." We understand, however, that John is showing that Jesus Christ is the Plan of God that existed from before his birth. The purpose of John is not historical, but spiritual (or theological). The historical "Jesus" is unified with the exalted "Christ" into a proleptic portrait of "Jesus Christ" that simultaneously brings him down to earth *and* exalts him.

In short, the view of Christ in John is without doubt the "highest" in the New Testament.[3] We must therefore reexamine this unique gospel in light of what we have already established from the Word of God, and see how it fits. Hypothetically speaking, if it cannot be made to fit, then it would have to be considered spurious, that is, "another gospel," and not a part of the canon of Scripture. As a matter of historical fact, this gospel was not met with universal acceptance when it first was introduced.

Though now this gospel has won the favor of all Christians, and is even the first one to be handed out at many 20th Century evangelistic crusades,[4] this was not always the case. In fact, there was so much controversy generated among the Christians of the second and third centuries that this gospel was not immediately accepted into the canon of Scripture. A large part of the cause of this lack of acceptance was the fact that it was quickly adopted by the Gnostics as the springboard for their speculations about Christ. We will have more to say about the influence of the Gnostics in the next chapter and in Chapters 16–18, but suffice it to say now that this enthusiastic Gnostic acceptance made the "Fourth Gospel," as it is often called, suspect. Nevertheless, it was finally acknowledged to be an important document that helps round out the New Testament record and was fully accepted as Scripture when the canon was established by the fourth or fifth century A.D.

---

1. J. Jocz, "*The Invisibility of God and the Incarnation*," Judaica 17, 1961, p. 196.

2. C. K. Barrett, *The Gospel According to St. John* (Westminster Press, Philadephia, PA, 1978), p. 149.

3. Raymond Brown gives a good thumbnail definition of the terms "high and "low" applied to Christology: "In scholarly jargon, 'low' Christology involves the application to Jesus of titles derived from Old Testament or intertestamental expectations (e.g. Messiah, prophet, servant, Lord, Son of God) titles that do not in themselves imply divinity. 'Son of God,' meaning divine representative, was a designation of the king; (See 1 Sam. 16:16; "lord" need mean no more than "master"). 'High Christology' involves an appreciation of Jesus that moves him into the sphere of divinity, as expressed, for instance, in a more exalted use of 'Lord' and 'Son of God,' as well as the designation 'God.'" *The Community of the Beloved Disciple*, (Paulist Press, N.Y., 1979, p. 25).

4. One modern scholar suggests that it should be the last book of the New Testament to be translated and given to new converts in foreign lands: "Perhaps it should be the last of the Gospels to be translated for new churches in non-Christian lands, instead of being the first, as so often happens…The Church today must use and value the Fourth Gospel for what it is and not for what it is not." Anthony T. Hanson, *The Prophetic Gospel: A Study of John and the Old Testament* (T & T Clark, Edinburgh, 1991), p. 371.

Undoubtedly, the difficulties presented by the view of Christ presented in John are real, and may continue to challenge the integrity of the Christian message if the contradictions they appear to present are not resolved. If the traditional view of Christ as "fully God and fully man" is correct, then the obvious question arises: why is this idea not *clearly* and *totally* supported by the Synoptics, the book of Acts and all the other New Testament writings? And if it is the true view of Christ, and necessary for salvation, why was it apparently not a part of the "Apostle's Doctrine" but instead needed several centuries to be formulated?

In the next two chapters, we will explore the ways that the gospel of John rounds out our understanding of the Son of God, Jesus Christ. There is so much unique material in John about the life, words and works of Christ that is not found in the other Gospels that we need to devote two chapters to it. In this chapter, we will examine the gospel itself. In the next, we will focus on the Prologue, particularly the first three verses concerning the *logos*.

Not "Higher" but Harmonious

The gospel of John is often used to try to establish the "deity of Christ" and to assert that Jesus claimed that he was "God." In fact, if the gospel of John were not in the Bible, orthodox Trinitarianism would disintegrate, so dependent is it on what is called the "high Christology" of this gospel. That is, the gospel of John is the basis for almost all Trinitarianism's basic ideas: pre-existence, the incarnation, essential deity, etc. Hanson points out that Johannine Christology has been the mainstay of the orthodox faith of Nicaea.[5] But even a number of modern Trinitarian scholars recognize that John's gospel is in many respects a difficult and problematic part of Scripture, and much care must be exercised in its interpretation.[6]

In certain verses, the gospel of John does seem to indicate that Jesus was in heaven before his birth and "came down" to earth and later "returned to where he was before." This view is unique to John and, if taken literally without understanding the language and customs of the times, can present a host of textual and exegetical problems. J. A. Baker argues that to take literally the idea of pre-existence in John is actually to deny rather than affirm the doctrine of the incarnation:

> It simply is not possible at one and the same time to share the common lot of humanity and to be aware of oneself as one who has existed from everlasting with God…[7]

---

5. *Ibid.*, p. 1, *et al.*

6. Brown, *op. cit., Community*, p. 163: "At various times I have referred to the theology of the Fourth Gospel as challengingly different, volatile, dangerous, and as the most adventuresome in the NT…. Over the centuries John's gospel has provided the seedbed for many exotic forms of individualistic pietism and quietism (as well as the inspiration for some of the most profound mysticism). Brown also writes: "Johannine Christology is very familiar to traditional Christians because it became the dominant Christology of the Church, and so it is startling to realize that such a portrayal of Jesus is quite foreign to the Synoptic Gospels. With justice Johannine Christology can be called the highest in the NT" (*Ibid.*, p. 45).

7. J. A. T. Robinson, 'The Use of the Fourth Gospel for Christology Today'; *Christ and Spirit in the New Testament: Studies in Honor of C.F.D. Moule*, ed. B. Lindars and S. S. Smalley, Cambridge University Press, 1973, pp. 61–78, who quotes (*The Foolishness of God*, Darton, Longman and Todd, 1970, p. 144); Fount 1975, p. 154. Robinson makes the same point even more forcefully in another work: "These ['I am' statements of Jesus] are not assertions about the ego of human Jesus, which is no more pre-existent than that of any other human being. Nor are statements about the glory that he enjoyed with the Father before the world was to be taken at the level of psychological reminiscence. As such, they would clearly be destructive of any genuine humanness…" John A. T. Robinson, *The Priority of John*, (Meyer Stone Pub., Oak Park, IL, 1985), p. 384.

As we pointed out in Chapter 2, if Jesus were aware of being "God" in some way, or could remember his former state of glory in heaven, then his experience of earthly life would be very different from ours. Consequently, our ability to identify with both his overcoming temptation and leaving us a righteous path to follow is seriously compromised. We are then essentially left without a "mediator," but are being asked to be like *God* Himself, instead of developing absolute *trust* in God, our heavenly Father, as Jesus did, and becoming like him as he said we could and should.

Because of its unique and elevated perspective of Christ compared with the rest of the New Testament, some scholars have concluded that the gospel of John has created a mythological view of Christ completely divorced from Jesus as a historical figure.[8] Is it intellectually and theologically honest, then, to erect upon the foundation of a single book of the Bible a theological superstructure that requires a fairly radical reinterpretation of almost the entire New Testament? With the exception of a few "proof texts,"[9] the idea that "Jesus is God" is not consistent with the New Testament when considered as a whole.[10] Not a Christian theologian, but a professor of logic, made the following astute statement regarding what is required for the *logical* interpretation of the Bible:

> Selecting texts to give a one-sided presentation of the truth is a widespread method of propagating erroneous views. Out of the Bible can be drawn phrases or verses that justify everything under the sun, including contradictories. Read in context, the Bible may be a liberal document, but it is not that liberal. What we need to know is if the Bible *as a whole* [emphasis ours] supports a given position.[11]

No part of Scripture demands such a rigorously logical analysis more than the gospel of John, which is acknowledged by many New Testament scholars to be a difficult section to harmonize with the rest of Scripture. Accordingly, it is a well-established hermeneutical principle among biblical interpreters that the difficult verse or passage must be interpreted in light of the clear and simple

---

8. Hanson is one of many scholars who have noted this aspect of John's gospel. Though we do not share his doubts about John's inspiration, we agree with his observation that the focus of John is not history, but theology. He writes:

> The Church has consciously chosen to live with tension…One cannot resist the impression that in his gospel, John was greatly concerned neither with historical accuracy nor with historical verisimilitude and consistency (p. 335). We may be sure that this picture of the God-man is not historically true, but [rather] John's construction. Consequently, our doctrine of the incarnation needs to be modified…the first rule for the Church in its handling of the Fourth Gospel today must be this: do not treat it as a reliable historical record…the Church must admit that the Jesus of the Fourth Gospel is not the Jesus of history. This, it must be confessed, demands something like a revolution in the Church's preaching and in its Christology…Most students of the New Testament acknowledge this, but it is a truth that has still to reach the rank-and-file of clergy and church-goers, as far as these islands [Britain] are concerned, at any rate… (Hanson, *op. cit., Prophetic*, p. 368).

9. Proof texting is isolating verses that appear to support a particular theological or doctrinal position, but by weighting them too heavily, creating contradictions with other verses on the same subject.

10. J. A. T. Robinson underscores this reality with his candid admission in 1961:

> But in practice popular preaching and teaching presents a supranaturalistic [the metaphysical God-man] view of Christ which cannot be substantiated from the New Testament. [Popular preaching] says simply that Jesus was God, in such a way that the terms 'Christ' and 'God' are interchangeable. But nowhere in Biblical usage is this so. **The New Testament says that Jesus was the Word of God, it says that God was in Christ, it says that Jesus is the Son of God; but it does not say that Jesus was God, simply like that (or rather not in any passages that certainly require to be interpreted in this way.** Passages that may be so interpreted are Romans 9:5 and Hebrews 1:8. But see in each case the alternative translations in the Revised Standard Version or the New English Bible).

(John A. T. Robinson, *Honest To God*, (Westminster Press, Philadelphia, 1963) pp. 70 and 71). See also Appendix M.

11. Moulds, A. J., *Thinking Straighter* (University of Michigan Press, Ann Arbor, 1975), p. 46.

parallel verses or passages.[12] The difficult or unusual must not be elevated and established as an altogether higher and better view than the rest of Scripture, as has been done with the gospel of John. Because it apparently presents a Jesus most compatible with Trinitarian orthodoxy, it is not surprising that this is the one gospel that is translated and distributed to potential converts more than any other. We agree with Hanson, however, that it ought to be the *last* one to be fronted,[13] after the basic groundwork of Jesus' identity as a human being has been laid.

John's gospel was not meant to be isolated and elevated above the other Gospels, as if it somehow portrays a truer view of Christ's identity. It was meant to provide a vivid and complete portrait of Christ that would inspire the reader to believe that Jesus Christ is the Son of God (John 20:31). If it is handled as the truest picture of Christ, instead of just one particular aspect of his identity, the other Gospels are demeaned and considered the writings of less enlightened disciples. According to this view, the Synoptic writers had not yet come to a real understanding of the identity of Christ as the pre-existent Son, who was actually an eternal being with a brief earthly mission. Indeed, many Christian teachers and scholars adopt this view of the Synoptic Gospels. But rather than cast off the weight of the biblical evidence in three of the Four Gospels, Paul's and Peter's Epistles, and the remainder of the New Testament, would it not be wiser to patiently and sensitively seek to understand how the gospel of John fits with all the rest?

The radical shift of perspective that we have identified is not unique to the gospel of John, but exemplifies a literary device employed by God elsewhere in Scripture. 1 and 2 Chronicles bears the same relation to Samuel and Kings in the Old Testament as John does to the Synoptic Gospels. Samuel and Kings record the historical narrative from a human, horizontal perspective, while Chronicles is written from God's vertical perspective.[14]

When viewed against the backdrop of the Synoptic Gospels and their contributions to the portrait of Jesus as the promised King, Servant and Man, the real literary beauty and significance of John's gospel becomes marvelously clear. This view of the life and ministry of Christ is written from the standpoint of his *post-resurrection glory*, bridging the chasm between the suffering and the glory of the one person, Jesus of Nazareth, the human Son of God. F. F. Bruce notes that there is no distinction made in John between Christ's suffering and his glory:

---

12. Johannes Munck of Aarhus University, writing in an essay called "The New Testament and Gnosticism," makes a great point about understanding difficult material in light of the clear. His criticism of the methods of those who propose that Gnosticism was antecedent to Christianity can be very appropriately applied to those who elevate John's gospel above the rest of the New Testament:

> They abandon the valuable historical method of beginning with the certain and easily accessible material and then trying to understand the more dubious and difficult material; instead they begin with a construction built of dubious material and proceed to know with staggering certainty what is written in the New Testament and how it is to be understood.

(From *Current Issues in New Testament Interpretation*, a Festschrift in honor of Otto A. Piper, edited by William Klassen and Graydon F. Snyder, Harper and Row, N.Y., 1962, p. 224).

13. Hanson, *op. cit.*, *Prophetic*, p. 368: "The Fourth Gospel may well instead prove to be something like the crown of our doctrine [of incarnation] rather than its basis…How then should this marvelous gospel, a great gift to the Church, but one which, like a delicate piece of machinery, has to be handled with great care. Perhaps it should be the last of the Gospels to be translated for new churches in non-Christian lands, instead of being the first, as so often happens."

14. For example, 1 Samuel 31:4 attributes the death of Saul to his falling on his sword in a battle against the Philistines, while 1 Chronicles 10:4 also mentions the fact of his suicide, but adds the true spiritual cause in verses 13 and 14: "Saul died because he was unfaithful to the LORD; he did not keep the word of the LORD and even consulted a medium for guidance, and did not inquire of the LORD. So the LORD put him to death and turned the kingdom over to David son of Jesse."

Students of the Synoptic Gospels distinguish passages, which speak of the suffering Son of Man from those which speak of his coming in glory. But in this gospel no such distinction is made: the suffering of the Son of Man is caught up into the glory, so that the glory is revealed pre-eminently in the suffering.[15]

By highlighting him as *the Son of God*, the gospel of John completes the cornerstone begun by the Synoptic Gospels in their portrayal of Jesus as a King, Servant, and Man. It also harmonizes perfectly with the view of Christ as the exalted "creator" of the Church that we will see in Chapter 11 when we look at the evidence of Ephesians and Colossians.

Similarities with the Synoptics

Before exploring the differences between the gospel of John and the Synoptics, we should point out the similarities. The fact is, the gospel of John does not present a *totally* different view of Christ. It actually agrees with the Synoptics on many points. For instance, the Synoptics portray the relationship between Jesus and God as so intertwined that to accept the one is to accept the other, and to reject the one is to reject the other. This theme is greatly amplified in John, but is one that is consistent throughout all the Gospels. The Father is known by and through the Son, and the Son is known by and through the Father. To know the one is to know the other, and to know either is to love them both.

> **Luke 10:16 and 22 (NASB)**
> (16) "The one who listens to you [the 70 he sent out] listens to Me, and the one who rejects you rejects Me; and he who rejects Me rejects the One who sent Me [God]."
> (22) "All things have been handed over to Me by My Father, and no one knows who the Son is except the Father, and who the Father is except the Son, and anyone to whom the Son wills to reveal *Him*."

The tenderness and intimacy between the Father and the Son is also pointed out in the Synoptics, but in John this truth takes center stage. We see the idea vividly in the gospel of Mark in Jesus' use of the Aramaic word "*Abba*" when addressing his Father in prayer, for *Abba* communicates intimacy between a father and his children.[16] He also taught his disciples to pray in this fashion, addressing God as *Abba*.

> **Mark 14:36 (NRSV)**
> He said, "Abba, Father, for you all things are possible; remove this cup from me; yet, not what I want, but what you want."

---

15. Bruce, *op. cit., Gospel of John*, p. 63.

16. Holman, *op. cit., Prophetic*, The Aramaic word *abba* is not preserved in the Greek text of John, and is therefore not transliterated into English as it is in Mark 14:36, Romans 8:15 and Galatians 4:6. Nevertheless, in the Aramaic text of John the words *aba* and *abi* occur often, more than in any other Gospel. The Aramaic construction in Mark 14:36, *et al.*, is "*aba, abi*" meaning "Father, my father" or "Father, our father" where the figure *Epizeuxis* (Duplication) is employed, bringing emphasis to the intimacy of the relationship between Father and son (see also Gaebelein's *Expositor's Bible Commentary*, Vol. 8, p. 764). In addition to the intimacy denoted by the word *aba* is the idea of authority inherent in his carrying out of his father's purposes (Gaebelein, Vol. 9, p. 149). Thus, although *Abba* does not come through in the Greek, the entirety of its meaning is exemplified in the gospel of John in the portrayal of Jesus' intimate relationship with his Father and the power and authority that he derived from it.

This verse also shows the willing subordination of the Son to the Father, in the context of his prayerful agonizing in the Garden of Gethsemane about his impending suffering and death. The Synoptics all clearly portray this willing and determined subordination of the Son's will to the Father's (see the parallel passages in Matt. 26:42 and Luke 22:42), but it is developed as a major theme in the gospel of John. Interestingly, the agony of Gethsemane is conspicuously absent from John's account of this time of prayer. In John 17, Jesus prays in the garden not for strength to embrace the will of God, but prays in the light of his glory as if it were already fully realized, and for the empowering of his disciples after his exaltation. As we shall see, Jesus in John is portrayed as completely subservient to his Father, and to portray him in a struggle to do the will of God would be inconsistent with that theme.

The theme of the Son glorifying the Father and vice-versa is also greatly amplified in John, but is clearly seen in the Synoptics as well. They show Jesus giving God all the glory for the things that he did, as in the case of the miraculous deliverance of the Gadarene tormented by the "legion" of demons.

> **Mark 5:18 and 19 (NRSV)**
> (18) As he was getting into the boat, the man who had been possessed by demons begged him that he might be with him.
> (19) But Jesus refused, and said to him, "Go home to your friends, and tell them how much **the Lord** [God, his Father] **has done for you**, and what mercy he has shown you."

In John, just as in the Synoptics, when challenged to produce a miraculous sign as proof of his relationship with God, Jesus gives the people a veiled reference to his future resurrection. The prophecy in John, however, does not refer to Jonah as Matthew and Luke do, but to the temple of Jesus' body.

> **John 2:18, 19, 21 and 22 (NASB)**
> (18) The Jews therefore answered and said to Him, "What sign do You show to us, seeing that You do these things?"
> (19) Jesus answered and said unto them, "[You will] Destroy this temple, and in three days I will raise it up."[17]
> (21) But He was speaking of the temple of His body.
> (22) When therefore He was raised from the dead, His disciples remembered that He said this; and they believed the Scripture, and the word which Jesus had spoken.

In this case, John records Jesus' actual comment about the temple, in which he prophesied that they would destroy the "temple," that is, kill *him*. In contrast, Matthew 26:61 and Mark 14:58 record the false witnesses giving their hearsay testimony at his trial, claiming that he had said that *he* would destroy the actual, physical Temple and rebuild it in three days.

Subordinationism in John

The final similarity we will point out between John and the Synoptics is that they both portray Jesus as a man who is limited in his authority, function and even his intrinsic "goodness." In other words,

---

17. This verse is used to teach that Jesus raised himself from the dead, because he said "I will raise it up," referring to his "body." See Appendix A (John 2:19).

all that he has, God has given him—no more and no less. This theme of the subordination of the Son is greatly amplified in John but apparent in the Synoptic Gospels nonetheless.

> **Matthew 20:23 (NRSV)**
> He said to them, "You will indeed drink my cup, but to sit at my right hand and at my left, **this is not mine to grant**, but it is for those for whom it has been prepared by my Father."

> **Mark 10:18 (NRSV)**
> Jesus said to him, "Why do you call me good? **No one is good but God alone**.

The Synoptics are more apt to simply portray Jesus' words and actions without elaborating on his motivation. However, the gospel of John develops the understanding of Jesus' dependence on his Father, while also making clear Jesus' commitment to glorify Him rather than call attention to himself. In light of the elevated perspective of Christ that John gives, it makes perfect sense to emphasize his subordination, lest his followers get the wrong idea. Ironically, it seems that most Christians *have* gotten the wrong idea—that Christ in John is affirming his identity with God, when he is clearly establishing his dependence upon and trust in one much greater than himself. The idea that Jesus was in some sense God Himself destroys the force of his example of dependence, trust and obedience. If he *were* God, why would he have needed to *depend* on God?

> **John 14:28 (NRSV)**
> You heard me say to you, 'I am going away, and I am coming to you.' If you loved me, you would rejoice that I am going to the Father, **because the Father is greater than I**.

Many scholars recognize that Jesus' subordination to God his Father is a dominant theme within the gospel of John. In fact, there have been many Christians through the centuries who have concluded that Jesus is not actually co-equal but subordinate to the Father. In theological terms, this is called a "subordinationist Christology," and orthodox theologians condemn it as heresy. Nevertheless, they have had a difficult task of explaining how it is that Christ can be "co-equal" with the Father when the Bible never says he is, and instead clearly indicates that the Father is greater than the Son.[18] This is made plain by the following statements made by Jesus and recorded in the gospel of John:

---

18. The *Evangelical Dictionary of Theology* comments that "in the early centuries, the struggle to understand the human and divine natures of Christ often led to placing the Son in a secondary position to the Father" and "this doctrine has continued in one form or another throughout the history of the church." (Walter Elwell, *Evangelical Dictionary of Theology*, Baker Books, Grand Rapids, 1984, p. 1058). We assert that a simple reading of the Bible will clearly show that the Son is inferior to the Father, and that that is not only the "true doctrine," but explains why the concept of subordination keeps coming up in the Church. In his eight volume work on the history of the church, Phillip Schaff remarks about the "heresy" of subordinationism, and the orthodox explanation of it:

> The Nicene fathers still teach, like their predecessors, a certain subordinationism, which seems to conflict with the doctrine of consubstantiality [i.e., that the Father and Son are of one substance]. But we must distinguish between a subordinationism of essence and a subordinationism of hypostasis, of order and dignity.

Scriptural argument for this theory of subordination was found abundant in such passages as these: "As the Father has life in himself, so hath He *given* to the Son to have life in himself; and hath *given* him authority to execute judgment also;" "All things are *delivered* unto me of my Father;" "My Father is greater than I." But these passages refer to the historical relation of the Father to the incarnate *Logos* in his estate of humiliation, or to the elevation of human nature

John 4:34 (NRSV)

"…My food is to do the will of him who sent me and to complete his work.

John 5:19 and 20a (NRSV)

(19) …the son can do nothing on his own, but only what he sees the Father doing; for whatever the Father does, the Son does likewise.

(20a) The Father loves the Son and shows him all that he himself is doing…

John 5:30 (NASB)

"I can do nothing on My own initiative… I do not seek My own will, but the will of Him who sent Me.

John 6:38 (NRSV)

for I have come down from heaven, not to do my own will, but the will of him who sent me.

John 6:57 (NRSV)

Just as the living Father sent me, and I live because of the Father…

John 7:16 (NRSV)

….My teaching is not mine but his who sent me.

John 8:28b and 29 (NRSV)

(28b) "…I do nothing on my own, but I speak these things as the Father instructed me.

(29) And the one who sent me is with me; he has not left me alone, for I always do what is pleasing to him."

John 8:42b (NRSV)

…for I came from God…I did not come on my own, but he sent me.

John 9:4a (NRSV)

We must work the works of him who sent me while it is day…

John 15:15b

…everything that I learned from my Father I have made known to you.

John 16:15a (NRSV)

All that the Father has is mine…

---

to participation in the glory and power of the divine, not to the eternal metaphysical relation of the Father to the Son [Phillip Schaff, *History of the Christian Church* (William B. Eerdmans Pub., Grand Rapids, 1994) pp. 681–683].

Thus, the orthodox church has condemned subordinationism as a heresy and given the explanation that the verses that ascribe inferiority to the Son are only talking about Christ's *function or his earthly relation* to God and not his essence or "metaphysical relation" to the Father. The problem with this explanation is simple and straightforward: no such "explanation" exists in the Bible. We assert that the Bible states a simple truth: that the Father is greater than the Son in every way, and the Son honored the Father and acknowledged that fact. We further assert that the "explanation" the orthodox church offers was made up after the fact to explain otherwise clear verses in light of their unbiblical doctrine. Furthermore, the reason it took centuries to establish orthodox doctrine (often by the point of the sword) was that it was unbiblical. That is also why Church historians have to admit that "subordinationism" has consistently been a problem in the Church. See Appendix C.

We must remember this dominant theme when we come upon some verses in John that appear to be stating that Jesus and God are "equal." These are often seized upon by Trinitarians as proof texts to establish their doctrine, as when Jesus said, "…Whoever has seen me has seen the Father…" (John 14:9 - NRSV), "And whoever sees me sees him who sent me" (John 12:45 - NRSV) or "The Father and I are one" (John 10:30 - NRSV). We must keep in mind that the Bible cannot contradict itself if it is the Word of God. The verses that say Christ is doing God's work and the verses that say the Father and Son are "one" must be teaching a similar truth. Verses that teach the "oneness" of the Father and the Son are not asserting any "sameness of essence" or intrinsic deity for Jesus. Indeed, when viewed in light of the above well-documented subordination, Jesus is seen to be referring to his obedient way of being, and therefore that his words and his works were not his, but came from God, his Father. The two were "one" in purpose because Jesus always lined himself up with his Father. In the case of John 14:9, the very next verse explicitly explains in what sense Jesus meant that if one had seen him, he had seen his Father:

John 14:10 (NRSV)
…the Father who dwells in me does his works.

This is a consistent theme throughout the Four Gospels. Jesus is the Son dependent upon the Father. However, this theme is most markedly observable in the gospel of John. Despite his glorification and divine authority, Jesus in John is portrayed as being utterly dependent upon his Father for everything. In this way, his example is not out of our reach, and in fact he is modeling the proper attitude of any son of God, an identity and privilege he would soon confer on all those who would believe on him. Thus, the example that Jesus Christ set for us as Christians shines bright and clear. If we are going to be like Christ, we must learn the will of God and obey it willingly and promptly. Christ, our example, said, "If you have seen me, you have seen the Father," and that was because he did what God would have done if God had been personally present. The Gospel records give us an example, a target, something to aspire to and to strive for so that we can be like Christ and his Father. Paul wrote to the Corinthian church: "Follow my example, as I follow the example of Christ" (1 Cor. 11:1). Paul had the right idea. Christianity is not a spectator sport where we watch from afar the activities of a few great Christians and comment about how godly they are. Christ prayed about us being "one" as he and the Father were "one." True Christianity strives to make that prayer a reality.

The Fourth Gospel: A Unique Perspective

We will now elaborate on the unique aspects of the gospel of John, which in light of what we have covered so far, will become even more understandable and illuminating. As we have stated, John provides the final aspect of the fourfold cornerstone of the Christian faith: his divine Sonship.[19] There have been *many* men, *many* servants and *many* kings, but there is *only one "begotten Son of God."*[20] Therefore, it makes perfect sense that the gospel of John would be as unique as the one it is portraying. We will now examine many important and unique contributions of this gospel to our understanding of the identity of Jesus Christ. A careful reading of the gospel of John leads us to

---

19. We use the term "divine" in the biblical sense of "authorship" or "origin," and fully recognize the "divinity" of Christ in this sense. But we distinguish "divinity," meaning "of divine origin," from "deity," meaning "identical with God." See Glossary.

20. See the next chapter for more on the term "only-begotten."

the conclusion that its purpose is very different from the purpose traditionally given to explain its writing; that is, to prove that Jesus is a pre-existent divine being, a second person in a triune Godhead incarnated as God in human flesh, etc, etc. The fact is, John clearly states near the end of his gospel that his purpose has been to enable us to believe that Jesus is *the Christ*, the *Son* of God:

John 20:30 and 31 (NRSV)
(30) Now Jesus did many other signs in the presence of his disciples, which are not written in this book.
(31) But these are written so that you may come to believe that **Jesus is the Messiah, the Son of God**, and that through believing you may have life in his name.

This is the same affirmation that Peter gave in Matthew 16:16, which Jesus said *God Himself* had revealed to Peter. John's purpose for writing was also revealed to him by God. This must be kept clearly in view when reading John's gospel, for everything in it will contribute to this goal. When the purpose is so clearly stated, why do so many Christians seem to think that John's purpose is to prove that Jesus is *God Himself*? Hanson's comment below gives us a clear view of how Trinitarians see support for their doctrine in the language of John, language that cannot be found in the Synoptic Gospels. He also acknowledges the importance of viewing the glorious Jesus of John against the historical backdrop of the Synoptic Gospels:

John's Jesus is omniscient, omnipotent, conscious of pre-existence, co-eternity, and consubstantiality with the Father. The human limits of knowledge of a particular culture, or a particular mind-set, of a particular race and geographical environment, which are perceptible in the Synoptic accounts, are ignored in the Fourth Gospel…Jesus appears in [John] as a superman, fully aware of his divine nature, always in control of the situation…Fortunately there are other accounts of Jesus in the New Testament [esp. the Synoptics], and ultimately the pull of the actual Jesus makes itself felt. We are faced with a Jesus who really did not know who touched him (Mark 5:30), a Jesus who discounts any goodness of his own (Mark 10:18), a Jesus who when he comes to Gethsemane is really uncertain about the Father's will for him. Without the Synoptic accounts of Jesus, and above all those of Mark and Luke, the Jesus of the Fourth Gospel rapidly turns into a legendary figure…[21]

This was precisely Augustine's attitude; the incarnation revealed to us a divine being appearing as man who was nevertheless fully equipped with superhuman powers, so that he could manipulate nature and matter exactly as he liked. The Jesus of the first three Gospels has been developed into a figure comparable to the Buddha of the Mahayana Scriptures, in which the original Gautama Sakyamuni has become a divine visitant who can accomplish the most astounding miracles by lifting his finger. We are in the realm of legend and are in full flight towards a positively superstitious attitude towards Jesus.[22]

Hanson is quite correct that the Jesus portrayed in the gospel of John is different from the Jesus of the other three Gospels. But we would expect that. In John, Christ is being set forth as the only begotten Son. The fact that Christ is portrayed differently in John, however, does not mean that he is somehow a different person. Different sections of Scripture focus on different aspects of Christ's

---

21. Hanson, *op. cit., Prophetic*, p. 366.
22. *Ibid.,* p. 365.

life, but he is just one person.[23] In particular, the prologue of John's gospel (1:1–18) is often wrested out of its context and made to mean something never intended by John or God who inspired him. We will be handling the prologue and its concept of the *logos* in the next chapter. But to remain faithful to the text of John, the entire gospel must harmonize with the rest of the New Testament. Accordingly, we must keep clearly in mind that this gospel *makes known the intimate relationship Jesus had and has with his Father, and the glory that results from it.* When we read John's gospel in this light, we see that the way John is inspired to write is perfectly consistent with this theme of Jesus' glorious divine Sonship.

When we refer to his "Sonship," however, we are not just thinking of his first birth in a manger, as is commonly supposed. Indeed, for those who hold to orthodox Christology, his "incarnation" in human flesh represents the defining moment of his "eternal" existence. From this perspective, his resurrection becomes little more than *a return to his former glory*, and is therefore rendered anti-climactic and presupposed. But as we discussed in Chapter 3, the resurrection of Jesus Christ is spoken of in Scripture as his *birth into glory* (see Ps. 2:7; Heb. 1:5; Acts 13:33). This truth is clearly communicated in Romans 1:4, one of the earliest of all New Testament writings, when it refers to Jesus as "…the Son of God **with power**…":[24]

Romans 1:2–4 (NRSV)

(2) [The gospel of God] which he promised beforehand through his prophets in the holy scriptures

(3) the gospel concerning his Son, who was descended from David according to the flesh

---

23. It is important when reading the Bible to pay close attention to what God is focusing on and emphasizing in a particular part of Scripture. For instance, while reading the book of Galatians, one might be tempted to think that Abraham was not like the rest of us. Romans says, "…he did not waver through unbelief regarding the promise of God…" (Rom. 4:20). Yet reading Genesis 16 shows that Abraham did have a weak time in his life and ended up having a child by his wife's slave, Hagar. The proper understanding of the Bible is not to assert that Galatians is wrong and Genesis correct, or vice versa, but to see that the two accounts can be made to harmonize. If God gives you a promise, and you have a weak period but then rise up and claim the promise by faith, God may focus on and emphasize your victory without speaking of the weak time you went through. The example of Manasseh, son of Hezekiah and king of Judah is another good example. Manasseh did a lot of evil as the king, and the book of Kings records the evil that Manasseh did and then records that he died. Chronicles, on the other hand, focuses on a different aspect of Manasseh's life and records that he repented, prayed, tore down the idols he had built and restored the altar of God. The point we are making is that what God reveals in different places of Scripture can be very different, but the diligent workman of the Word will see how they harmonize and use the various records to build a complete picture.

24. Some of the early Christian scribes realized that the Resurrection was the time when Christ was clearly declared to be the Son of God, and that bothered them because it conflicted with their theology. Their easy solution to this problem was to change the texts they were supposed to be faithfully transcribing. Ehrman notes: "Some of the earliest traditions put the Christological moment *par excellence* at his resurrection. For these traditions, God appointed Jesus to be his Son when he vindicated him and exalted him to heaven. A textual corruption of this verse occurs as the addition of the prefix *pro* to *horisisthentos*, implying "that God 'predestined' Jesus to attain his status as Son of God at the Resurrection. This would mean, of course, that Jesus already enjoyed a special status before God prior to the event itself (as the one "predestined") so that the Resurrection was but the realization of a status proleptically [before the fact] conferred upon him. In short, the variation, which cannot be traced beyond the confines of the Latin West, serves to undermine any assumption that Jesus' resurrection effected an entirely new standing before God." Ehrman, *op. cit., Orthodox Corruption*, pp. 71 and 72.

(4) and was **declared** ["appointed," "installed," "constituted"[25]] **to be the Son of God with power according to the spirit of holiness by resurrection from the dead**, Jesus Christ our Lord,

Based upon this reality, the gospel of John is perfectly consistent with the body of the New Testament evidence, and its depiction of Jesus as the "Son" powerfully reflects this post-resurrection emphasis. John's elevated view of Jesus as the glorified Christ magnifies his intimacy with his Father who has so exalted him, and this is one of the most distinctive features of the Fourth Gospel. The glory that he fully realized in his resurrection is projected back throughout his earthly ministry even to the very ground of Creation itself, when God planned his coming "before the foundation of the world." This projecting of his post-resurrection glory back onto the past is accomplished through the figure of speech *prolepsis*, which is "an anticipating; especially the describing of an event as taking place before it could have done so, the treating of a future event as if it had already happened."[26]

It is not surprising that this bold proleptic picture of Christ could be misunderstood and taken literally, thus breaking down the literal, historical and crucial importance of the Resurrection. If he *literally* already enjoyed his resurrection glory before his death, the difficulty of his temptation and suffering would have been radically lessened. But the Fourth Gospel should not be interpreted in a manner that virtually negates the significance of the Resurrection, the watershed event of his life. The Resurrection becomes devalued by the assertion of Jesus' apparently innate glory as a pre-existent divine being. If contradictions with the whole of Scripture arise from literally interpreting a verse, a passage or an entire book, we must start looking for figures of speech. These are legitimate literary devices employed to give vigor and emphasis to verbal communication. In addition to *prolepsis*, John employs a related figure of speech called *heterosis*, which is the exchange of one verb tense for another, in this case, the present for the future.[27]

---

25. Dunn quotes C. E. B. Cranfield's firm conclusion that the Greek word translated "declared," *horisthentos*, means more than "declared" or "shown to be," and actually has the force of "installed." In other words, the Resurrection was in some sense the time in which his Sonship was officially or actually realized. This leads Dunn to conclude:
- that "Jesus' divine Sonship stemmed from his resurrection."
- that "the resurrection of Jesus was regarded [by the earliest Christian communities] as of central significance in determining his divine Sonship, either as his installation to a status and prerogatives not enjoyed before, or as a major enhancement of a Sonship already enjoyed."
- that "there is no thought of a pre-existent Sonship here."
- that "Sonship is seen in eschatological terms: the divine Sonship of which the original formula speaks is a Sonship which begins from the resurrection."
- that "primitive Christian preaching seems to have regarded Jesus' resurrection as the day of his appointment to divine Sonship, as the event by which he became God's Son."

Dunn, *op. cit., Christology*, pp. 34–36.

26. *Websters New Universal Unabridged Dictionary* (Simon and Schuster, NY, 1983, p. 1439). Bullinger further defined *prolepsis* as follows: "An anticipation of some future time which cannot yet be enjoyed; but has to be deferred. From *pro* ("before") and *lepsis* ("a taking,"), i.e., anticipation. The figure is employed when we anticipate what is going to be done, and speak of future things as being already present. Some biblical examples are: Genesis 1:27 speaks of both male and female, though only Adam is in view at the time; Exodus 10:29 describes the final departure of Moses, but Moses spoke to Pharaoh once more. 1 Kings 22:50 speaks of Jehoshaphat's death as if it had already happened; Isaiah 37:22 describes the future rejoicing of Jerusalem; In Isaiah 48:5–7, God spoke of future things from the beginning." E. W. Bullinger, *Figures of Speech Used in the Bible* (Baker Book House, Grand Rapids, MI, 1968 [originally published 1898] pp. 914 and 15).

27. *Heterosis* is also the exchange of one voice, mood, tense, person, number, degree or gender for another. *Ibid.*, pp. 510–534.

The gospel of John, therefore, is a profoundly *literary* portrait of the Messiah that is emphasizing his post-resurrection glorification at the right hand of God. It goes beyond being *prophetic* (i.e., *foretelling* of his future glory) and becomes *proleptic* by portraying him as *already* glorious. The use of these figures of speech *heterosis* and *prolepsis* is not incidental and occasional—it is the very warp and woof of the tapestry of John's gospel. It is important to note that we are not the only ones to notice this literary feature of the Fourth Gospel. A number of scholars have noted this bold and beautiful bent of the gospel of John. We will quote two:

> "…the Jesus of the Fourth Gospel is **the risen Lord retrojected back into the time of the earthly ministry.** We can accept the Jesus of the Fourth Gospel as **a model for the risen Lord**. Almost everything that the Jesus of the Fourth Gospel claims for himself is true as far as the believer is concerned of the Jesus of faith, the risen Lord of the Church apprehensible always by the Church's faith. As such, the language which John uses about him fits him very well. **Interpreted in terms of the risen Lord and not of the historical Jesus, it makes excellent sense.**[28]

> The self-revelation of Jesus in John…stems from a theological interpretation by the evangelist… In the mind of the evangelist **the earthly Jesus speaks as though always fully conscious of his exaltation, which begins with the crucifixion.**"[29]

The reason for these literary devices is to bring emphasis to the reality of Christ's exaltation at the right hand of God since his resurrection. This is consistent with a variety of literary figures and devices employed throughout the Bible that bring an appropriate and vivid emphasis to the subject matter, as well as greatly enhance its value as "the literature of eternity." Misunderstanding figurative language accounts for many errors and misconceptions, because our Western minds assume that we understand what seems to be the plain meaning of language. We do not customarily employ either *prolepsis* or *heterosis* in English, so we would not likely recognize the use of either of these figures unless we were familiar with *biblical* figures of speech.

For instance, one of the only variations of verb tenses we employ figuratively in English is the "historic present," when we use the present tense in relating a story from the past to enliven it. For instance, we might relate an incident from the past in the present tense, by saying "Then he *goes* to the meat market." But to be factual, or literal, we would employ the past tense: "He *went* to the meat market." English speakers and readers have little or no experience with the use of the present or past tenses referring to *the future*, as is done in Hebrew and Aramaic. In essence, this is what is happening in the gospel of John. The perspective from which it is written is actually "Back From The Future." Great Scott!!! There has been a major disturbance of the biblical "time-space continuum," and it is caused by the proleptic nature of the gospel of John. We will come back to this subject after looking at more unique features in John.

John does not use the common Greek word for "pray" (*proseuchomai*), as do the other Gospels, but *erotao*, which implies familiarity with the one being asked.[30] In John, Jesus speaks to or asks of

---

28. Hanson, *op cit., Prophetic*, pp. 367 and 368.

29. R. I. Schnackenburg, *The Gospel According to St. John* (E. T., London and NY, 1968 of German ed. Freiburg 1965, 3 volumes), p. 328.

30. E.g., John 16:26, 17:9, 15 and 20. This point about Jesus having an intimate, conversational relationship with his Father is lost in the NIV. For example, in John 17:1 the NIV reads: "…he looked toward heaven and prayed…." However, the Greek text, and most other versions, have "said" instead of "prayed." The same is true in John 17:9, 15, and 20. The NIV has "pray" or "prayed" while other versions more accurately have "say," "request" or "ask." See Appendix P.

the Father with the simple confidence of a child. The intimacy of their communication is very evident when Jesus prays at Lazarus' tomb (John 11:41 and 42): "…Father, I thank you that you have heard me. I knew that you always hear me, but I said this for the benefit of the people standing here, that they may believe that you sent me." Jesus experienced an invisible intimacy in his relationship with God that explains the works he did. In the case of raising Lazarus, we are given an opportunity to see how close he and his Father are, and that the Father always hears his requests. This was due to the fact that he was accustomed to hearing and obeying God's voice. He "heard" the Father, and the Father, "heard" him.

John's gospel records the *words* of Jesus more than does any other Gospel. The prologue identifies Jesus as the living *Word*, so it makes sense that John would elevate the words of Jesus over his works. This is the opposite of the gospel of Mark, which focuses on his acts. In John 3, Jesus gives a lengthy lecture to Nicodemus late at night. In Chapter 4, he addresses a Samaritan woman on worship and the coming gift of the spirit. Chapter 5 is a discourse about the Sabbath. Chapter 6 is an elaborate discussion of his being the "Bread of Heaven." In Chapters 7 and 8, he addresses the Jews in the Temple, in Chapter 9 the Pharisees. In Chapter 10 he talks about his role as the Good Shepherd of the sheep. In Chapter 11 he raises Lazarus and talks about his being "…the resurrection and the life…." Chapters 13–17 cover his prophetic declarations about the spirit of truth, and include a lengthy high priestly prayer. At various points in the gospel, Jesus calls attention to the importance of his word and God's Word:

- 5:24 - Hears my *word* and believes
- 5:46 and 47 - Believing in him is to believe his *words*
- 8:31 - Continue in my *word* (KJV)
- 12:48 - Receive my *sayings*; the word will judge (NRSV)
- 14:24 - The *word* is not mine but the Father's (NRSV)
- 17:14 - I have given them your *Word*
- 17:17 - Thy *Word* is truth (KJV)
- 17:20 - Those who will believe on Christ through the *word* of his disciples (NKJV)

Because John views Christ from his post-resurrection exaltation, it focuses on Christ in heaven, and speaks of heaven as his place of origin. Accordingly, John uses the language of his "coming from" heaven, and being "sent" from heaven.[31]

John 3:13
No one has ever gone into heaven except the one who came from heaven—the Son of Man.

The Jews would not have taken Christ's words to mean that he "incarnated." It was common for them to say that something "came from heaven" if God were its source. Thus, John the Baptist was a man "sent from God" (John 1:6). When God wanted to tell the people that He would bless them if they gave their tithes, He told them that He would open the windows of heaven and pour out a blessing (Mal. 3:10 - KJV). Of course, everyone understood the idiom being used, and no one believed that God would literally pour things out of heaven. They knew that God was the *origin* of

---
31. See Appendix A (John 3:13).

the blessings they received. Similarly, James 1:17 says, "Every good and perfect gift is from above…," and comes "down from the Father."

Another clear example of this idiom occurs in the context of Christ answering the Pharisees concerning the question of his authority to heal, forgive sins and the like:

Matthew 21:25a
"John's baptism—where did it come from? Was it from heaven or from men?…"

This verse makes the idiom clear: things could be "from heaven," i.e., *from* God, or they could be "from men."[32] The idiom is the same when used of Jesus. Jesus is "from God," "from heaven" or "from above" in the sense that God is literally his heavenly Father and thus his origin.

In the Synoptics, Jesus trusts Judas Iscariot to be one of his Apostles, who proves to be a thief and a betrayer. But in John, Jesus knows the hearts of all men, and who can be trusted and who cannot: "But Jesus would not entrust himself to them, for he knew all men" (John 2:24). This is another example of John's exalted perspective of Christ. He is viewed as having the same knowledge in his earthly ministry as he had after his ascension, when the Apostles invoke the risen Lord in the matter of choosing a replacement for Judas.[33]

Acts 1:24 and 25 (NRSV)
(24) Then they prayed and said, "**Lord, you know everyone's heart.** Show us which one of these two you have chosen
(25) to take the place in this ministry and apostleship from which Judas turned aside to go to his own place."

Another example of proleptic language is in John's recording of Jesus dealing with Judas' betrayal:

John 13:2 and 3 (NASB)
(2) And during supper, the devil having already put into the heart of Judas Iscariot, *the son* of Simon, to betray Him,
(3) *Jesus*, knowing that **the Father had given all things into His hands**, and that He had come forth from God, and was going back to God,

When was "all power" actually put under Jesus? *After his resurrection*, as indicated by his saying in Matthew 28:18: "…All authority in heaven and earth has been given to me."[34] On the subject of the "cross" that Christ bore, John's unique perspective is particularly evident. The Synoptics depict the Cross as "the emblem of suffering and shame" (as the old hymn says), but John compares it to the lifting up of the brasen serpent in the wilderness for the healing of Israel. In fact, Jesus' crucifixion is a kind of lifting up, or exaltation, for the healing and deliverance of believers.

---

32. See also Gamaliel's speech in Acts 5:38 and 39.

33. The word "Lord" in Acts 1:24 refers to the risen Lord Jesus because, in context, it is he who "knows everyone's hearts." We also recognize that the context is continuous from Acts 1:2 and concerns "…the apostles he had chosen." Since Jesus had chosen the original twelve, it seems evident that he would be the one asked about Judas' replacement. See Appendix B (Acts 1:24).

34. Bullinger, a Trinitarian, recognizes that "all authority" was given him only after his resurrection. In his *op. cit.*, Companion Bible in a text note on Matthew 28:18, he writes: "[all authority] is given = has (just, or lately) been given." p. 1380.

John 3:14 and 15 (NRSV)

(14) And just as Moses **lifted up** the serpent in the wilderness, so must the Son of Man be lifted up,

(15) that whoever believes in him may have eternal life.

John 8:28 and 29 (NRSV)

(28) So Jesus said, "When you have **lifted up** the Son of Man, then you will realize that I am he, and that I do nothing on my own, but I speak these things as the Father instructed me.

(29) And the one who sent me is with me; he has not left me alone, for I always do what is pleasing to him."

John 12:32 and 33 (NASB)

(32) "And I, if I am **lifted up** from the earth, will draw all men to Myself."

(33) But He was saying this to indicate the kind of death by which He was to die.

The words "lifted up" are the term for "exalt, elevate or set on high." In John, Jesus' exaltation begins at and centers on the crucifixion, and altogether omits the historical ascension after his resurrection. In a bold, proleptic reinterpretation of the Cross, the gospel of John views it not as a criminal act of sinners against the righteous Son of God, but as a symbol of healing and deliverance for all who believe on him. This is the perspective Peter also communicated:

1 Peter 2:24 (NASB)

and He Himself bore our sins in His body on the cross, that we might die to sin and live to righteousness; for by His wounds **you were healed**.[35]

Another example of John's unique perspective concerns what "cross" Jesus bore. Where the Synoptic Gospels agree that Simon of Cyrene was compelled to take the wooden cross from Jesus as he left the Praetorium, or Pilate's palace, John implies that *Jesus* bore his cross all the way to Calvary.[36] But the "cross" Christ bore in John was the figurative "cross" of our sins and iniquities, as prophesied by Isaiah.[37] Rather than being a blatant contradiction of the other Gospels, which are primarily concerned with recording the historical events of his life, John's is written from a spiritual perspective.

Where the Synoptics contain many examples of Jesus casting out demons, the gospel of John omits this important and unique part of his ministry. Jesus mentions the Devil only in connection with Judas Iscariot or the Pharisees. We can only speculate as to the reason for this omission, but it seems to be related to the perspective of Jesus in his post-resurrection dominion over principalities,

---

35. Note the use of the figure of speech *heterosis*, which attributes our healing to the time in the past when Christ gave his body as a sacrifice on Calvary. In actual fact, we must invoke the power and name of Jesus Christ to heal us *in the present* (see Acts 3:16). However, this figure establishes the fact that the ground on which we stand in faith for healing was established at the Cross, and need not be re-established for each believer every time he has a need.

36. Cp. Matthew 27:32; Mark 15:21 and Luke 23:26 with John 19:17.

37. Isaiah 53:3–6; Colossians 2:14 and 15; Matthew 8:16 and 17.

powers, dominions and authorities. Jesus in John is proleptically positioned *far above* all demonic activity, therefore demonstrating his superiority over demons is rendered quite superfluous.[38]

The "Signs": Springboard to the Spoken Words of *the Living Word*

The core of the gospel of John focuses on eight "signs" that specifically point to Christ as the Son of God. In John, miracles are always called "signs" (Greek *semeion*), emphasizing the spiritual significance of these events more than their being historical events or because of their effects on the people as they are in the Synoptic Gospels. In those records, his miracles attract attention and generate faith in others. In John, however, his miracles provide a springboard for a spiritual discourse—spiritual words spoken by the living Word (the *logos*). This is further evidence that John focuses on the *words* of Jesus.

For instance, in the healing of a royal official's son in Capernaum (4:46–54), Jesus chastises the man for the very fact that he was seeking a miracle, saying, "Unless you people see miraculous signs and wonders…you will never believe." He expected them to understand that his miracles illustrated his intimate relationship with God, his Father. This is also clear from the record of the healing of a crippled man at the pool of Bethesda (5:1–15). Because he healed the man on the Sabbath, the Jews began persecuting him. His answer to them was to relate the miracle to his relationship with God: "…My Father is always at work to this very day, and I, too, am working" (verse 17) and "… the Son can do nothing by himself; he can do only what he sees his Father doing…" (verse 19).

The conclusion of the record involving the healing of the man born blind is the spiritual blindness of the Pharisees (John 9:1–41). The raising of Lazarus after he had been dead four days (11:1–44) is preceded by Jesus declaring himself to be "…the resurrection and the life…." Mary's response to this declaration is to affirm her belief that Jesus was "…the Christ, the Son of God…" (verse 27), echoing the theme of John from 20:30 and 31. In other words, the "sign" is significant because of the words that Jesus and others speak in association with the event itself.

After the feeding of the 5,000 (6:1–15), Jesus again delivered a rebuke to those seeking him with the wrong motive. In this case, it was not only the miraculous sign that was prompting their seeking him, but the "all you can eat" free food he produced (v. 26). After another miraculous event, his walking on the water (6:16–21), a "watershed" discourse follows (6:32–58), separating out those who were willing to view him in more spiritual light. The way Jesus identified the true disciples was through the use of figurative language. He spoke of them "eating his flesh" and "drinking his blood." Those who thought that he was speaking literally were very confused and offended (v. 52, 60 and 61). But obviously he had a figurative, spiritual meaning in mind.[39] We see from these records and others that the gospel

---

38. Yet in John, Jesus is accused on several occasions of *having* a demon. This makes sense because the Devil is insanely jealous of the Lord and tries to degrade and besmirch him in any way possible.

39. Ryken observes: "Assimilating religious knowledge and growing spiritually from it are likewise compared to a process of eating and digestion. Paul fed immature Christians with 'milk' because they were not ready to digest solid food (1 Cor. 3:1 and 2), and Hebrews 5:11–14 repeats the image. Similarly, Peter enjoins his audience to 'long for the pure spiritual milk, that by it you may grow up into salvation' (1 Pet. 2:2 - RSV). God's true shepherds feed the people with knowledge and understanding (Jer. 3:15). Conversely, the absence of hearing the words of the Lord is a famine on the land (Amos 8:11). Assimilating folly or falsehood is likewise pictured as assimilating food into the body (Prov. 15:14). In its ultimate metaphoric reaches, to eat is to participate in God's salvation in Christ." Leland Ryken, *Dictionary of Biblical Imagery* (InterVarsity Press, Downers Grove, IL, 1998), p. 227.

of John contains more of the *words* of Jesus than any other gospel. Indeed, its *focus* is on Jesus' words because they elucidate his glorious relationship with his Father. Many times these words are spoken in figurative language, as in the use of *heterosis* and *prolepsis*.

There are many other unique events, ideas and dialogues in John not mentioned or considered in the Synoptic Gospels. Only in John is it said that Jesus "*lays down* his life," and no one takes it from him. Only John calls Jesus "the *Lamb* of God," because only as the Son of God is he not contaminated by sin nature and thus qualified to be the perfect sacrifice for all mankind. John does not include his genealogy, birth or baptism because none of these events contribute to an understanding of his glorification, which he derives directly from his Father. In John, Jesus' "genealogy," if we want to call it that, is very short: "…the only begotten Son, who is in the bosom of the Father…." (KJV)[40] His ancestry through Mary, his virgin birth and his anointing with holy spirit at his baptism, though historical events, are not relevant to the theme of the gospel, and hence are omitted.

This does not mean that the Jesus portrayed in the gospel of John is not the historical person. It simply means that the purpose of John is not historical, but spiritual (or theological). The historical "Jesus" is unified with the exalted "Christ" into a proleptic portrait of "Jesus Christ" that simultaneously brings him down to earth and exalts him. Thus, we have a clear, "earthly" image of the resurrected and exalted Lord in whom we are to have faith. This is very evident as we look more closely at John's post-resurrection perspective of Christ.

Jesus in John: "Back from the Future"

In previous chapters we have clearly seen the two primary aspects of Christ's life and ministry: suffering and glory. We have concluded from our examination of many Scriptures that these two phases of his coming are quite distinct and separate. His first coming was as the suffering servant, but he was resurrected into his glory. Yet the gospel of John in many respects paints a portrait of Jesus as *already* glorified even *before* his resurrection. He has glory even before he was *born!*

John 17:4 and 5 (NASB)
(4) "I glorified Thee on the earth, having accomplished the work which Thou hast given Me to do.
(5) "And now, glorify Thou Me together with Thyself, Father, with **the glory which I had with Thee before the world was**.

John 12:41 (NRSV)
Isaiah said this because **he saw his glory** and spoke about him.

John 17:24 (NRSV)
Father, I desire that those also, whom you have given me, **may be with me where I am** [he is pictured as already seated in heaven], **to see my glory**, which you have given me because you loved me before the foundation of the world.

---

40. The Old Syriac reading of John 1:18 is "*from* the bosom of his Father." This would harmonize with the emphasis in John upon God being his *origin*, having been "sent" from God. This reading is in the Curetonian manuscript (William Cureton, *Remains of a Very Ancient Recension of the Four Gospels in Syriac* (John Murray, London, 1858), p. 38.

This "prophetic glory" that was his even before his birth was because God's plan was for him to be the *glorious* redeemer of Creation. This plan was so well defined by the body of prophecy spoken and written about the Coming One that it was a virtual certainty. Therefore it could be spoken about as a "reality" long before it was actually fulfilled.[41] In this light, we can properly interpret the following verse, which is often used to "prove" the literal "pre-existence" of Christ.

> **John 8:56–58 (NRSV)**
> (56) Your ancestor Abraham rejoiced that he would see my day; he saw it and was glad.
> (57) Then the Jews said to him, "You are not yet fifty years old, and have you seen Abraham!"
> (58) Jesus said to them, "Very truly, I tell you, **before Abraham was, I am**."

The context of verse 58 is clear from verse 56: it is the "day" that Abraham "saw," which is still in the future. Even in Abraham's time, it was established as a certainty in the mind of God that the Messiah would come and establish "the city with foundations" (Heb. 11:10).[42]

If we accept that John 8:58 is somehow saying that Jesus is an "eternal and divine person" who lived before he was born, then the gospel of John is contradicting the Synoptic consensus (Matt. 1:18; Luke 1:35). But if we accept that the Synoptic view is the literal and historical one, then John's way of portraying the Messiah becomes not only understandable, but profoundly harmonious with the other Gospels. In John, the glory that Jesus has as Messiah is pictured as a present reality, not a future one as it is in the Synoptics (Matt. 16:27, 19:28, 24:30, 25:31; Mark 8:38, 13:26; Luke 21:27). We will cite one verse in particular that clearly shows the perspective of the Synoptics that Jesus entered into his glory *after* the resurrection:

> **Luke 24:26 (NRSV)**
> "Was it not necessary that the Messiah should suffer these things [crucifixion and death] **and then enter into his glory** [via resurrection]?"

The "Mount of Transfiguration" event recorded in the Synoptics foreshadows his resurrected glory (Matt. 17:2ff; Mark 9:2ff; Luke 9:26–36), but, clearly, this glorious experience is related to his imminent suffering and death and subsequent resurrection.[43] Glorification is not the normal state of his existence in the Synoptics, but in John, as Hanson observes, "the Transfiguration is taken as an index of Jesus' real person while on earth…"[44] In the gospel of John, there is no mention at all of the Transfiguration, because it related to his *earthly* sufferings. John's perspective is his heavenly and

---

41. See the discussion of the "prophetic perfect" in Chapter 17.

42. See also Appendix A (John 8:58b).

43. The visionary "presence" of Moses and Elijah is very significant in this record, because each was escorted to his burial by God in a manner that pointed to the special death, burial and resurrection of the Messiah. God Himself buried Moses (Deut. 34:6), and the burial place was kept a secret, presumably to keep the Israelites from idolatrous worship of their dead hero. The burial of Moses' body was apparently the occasion of a major spiritual battle (see Jude 9). Elijah was taken up into the air by a whirlwind and moved by God away from all who knew him, (2 Kings 2:11). The Bible does not mention the place he was set down, but we know he died because only Jesus has been granted immortality (see also Heb. 11:13—"these all died"). If Elijah, a man just like us (James 5:17), went to heaven without dying before Christ came to atone for his sin, then eternal redemption was available without Jesus' sacrifice. See our book, *op. cit., Is There Death After Life?*

44. Hanson, *op. cit., Prophetic*, p. 365.

eternal glory transposed onto his earthly life and ministry.[45] Again, we see John's proleptic perspective of Jesus so anchored in the future that it is spoken of in the present: he is *already* glorious; there is no need to record a Transfiguration. The Ascension is also conspicuously absent from John's gospel for the same reason. Jesus in John is *already* exalted. The Johannine portrait of Jesus is of one who walked the earth with something akin to his future exalted glory even while still carrying out his earthly ministry.

More Proleptic Language

More evidence that John's view is proleptic is the fact that John has no record of Jesus' temptations by the Devil or his agony in the Garden of Gethsemane. The risen Lord is beyond such temptation, and to struggle in the flesh with an assignment from God is unthinkable. The reader may recall from Chapter 6 that we saw a correlation between the eagle and the gospel of John because of the eagle's exalted perspective of the earth. This is in essence what the Jesus of the gospel of John is doing—looking down upon his earthly life and reinterpreting it in light of his exalted position at the right hand of God.

This should not be a complete surprise, though, because we know that Jesus Christ was intimately involved with the inspiration of Scripture after his resurrection (Rom. 1:1; 1 Cor. 1:1; Gal. 1:11 and 12, *et al.*). Thus, in many of the passages in John in which Christ speaks, the words are those of the *risen* Christ, not the earthly Christ of the Synoptics. An example of him speaking in a way that blends an earthly with a heavenly perspective is his prayer, on the eve of his arrest, for those who will believe in him in the future. We will point out the statements in which the risen Christ is speaking, those that point prophetically to his post-resurrection glorification. The other statements are consistent with the Synoptic view and should be considered literal statements that the earthly Jesus actually spoke.

> **John 17:20–24 (NRSV)**
> (20) "I ask not only on behalf of these, but also on behalf of those who will believe in me through their word,
> (21) that they may all be one. As you, Father, are in me and I am in you, may they also be in us, so that the world may believe that you have sent me.
> (22) **The glory that you have given me I have given them** [fulfilled at Pentecost in the gift of holy spirit], so that they may be one, as we are one,
> (23) **I in them** [future, at Pentecost] and you in me, that they may become completely one, so that the world may know that you have sent me and have loved them even as you have loved me.
> (24) Father, I desire that those also, whom you have given me, **may be with me where I am** [he speaks in the present tense as if he is already in his exalted position in heaven], **to see my glory, which you have [HAVE] given me** [past tense; again he is speaking as if he were already raised] because you loved me before the foundation of the world.

This prophetic and proleptic nature of the gospel of John is made even clearer from the many other verses that attribute to Christ during his earthly ministry functions and qualities that properly belong to *God*, and which would actually be delegated to him *after* his resurrection. John, by

---

45. We say "eternal" glory because it began, in the mind of God, at the creation of the present heaven and earth and will continue forever.

revelation, is painting a *prophetic* picture of a post-resurrection Christ that is consistent with that revealed to Paul and written especially in his later epistles—Ephesians, Philippians and Colossians. This Jesus in John is already at the right hand of God, invested with all authority. This is seen in John's occasional use of the present tense in the following Scripture, which reveals that he is writing as if Jesus was already risen:

John 1:18 (KJV)
No man hath seen God at any time; the only begotten Son, **which is** [present tense] **in the bosom of the Father**, he hath declared him.[46]

Another interesting example of John's "Back From the Future" perspective is found in Jesus' discussion with the Samaritan woman concerning the issue of true worship:

John 4:21–24 (NRSV)
(21) Jesus said to her, "Woman, believe me, **the hour is coming** [future] when you will worship the Father neither on this mountain nor in Jerusalem.
(22) You [Samaritans] worship what you do not know; we worship what we know, for salvation is from the Jews.
(23) But the hour is coming [future] **and is now here** [i.e., is so certainly coming that it is spoken of as having already come] when the true worshipers will worship the Father in spirit and truth, for the Father seeks such as these to worship him.
(24) God is spirit, and those who worship him must worship in spirit and truth."

The spiritual worship of which Jesus speaks would actually become available on the Day of Pentecost with the gift of holy spirit. Yet it is spoken of in John as having already arrived. This is typical of the prophetic and proleptic language employed in John's gospel.

At other times, Jesus speaks in the present tense, but he is clearly referring to a future time, sometimes even the end of the age, when the "Day of the Lord" will come:

John 5:22 (NRSV)
The Father judges no one but **has given** all judgment to the Son [When? In the future—Acts 17:31].

John 5:26 (NRSV)
For just as the Father has life in himself, so he **has granted** the Son also to **have life in himself** [this indicates that he already has in the present the resurrection life by which he will one day raise the dead at the end of this age];

---

46. There are many Alexandrian texts that read "God the only Son," or "the only begotten God," and so the NIV and NASB translations are not baseless. However, there is much compelling evidence that this is an example of the orthodox corruption of Scripture, and that the original text reads "only begotten Son." Ehrman points out that the term "only begotten son" occurs elsewhere in John's writings, and always in the form of "only begotten Son." Cp. John 1:14, 3:16 and 18; 1 John 4:9 (KJV) (Ehrman, *op. cit., Orthodox Corruption*, pp. 78–82). Also, Kittel, *op. cit., Theological Dictionary*, Vol. IV, p. 740, footnote 14. See Appendix N.

John 11:25 (NRSV)

Jesus said to her, "**I am** the resurrection and the life [note the present tense]. Those who believe in me, even though they die, will live, [When? In the future— "I will raise him at the last day" (John 6:44)].

Many more examples of prophetic and proleptic language can be found in John, but we do not need to belabor the point here. We assume that the reader will find numerous examples for himself now that it has been pointed out. The words of John's gospel have proven to be words of spirit and life (John 6:63), just as Jesus pronounced them to be in his discourse after the feeding of the five thousand. F. F. Bruce aptly expresses his awe at the literary arrangement of the gospel of John, which has continued to inspire and engender faith in the risen Christ, even though greatly misunderstood:

What Shakespeare does by dramatic insight…all this and much more the Spirit of God accomplished in our Evangelist [John]. It does not take divine inspiration to provide a verbatim transcript; but to reproduce the words which were spirit and life to their first believing hearers in such a way that they continue to communicate their saving message and prove themselves to be spirit and life to men and women today, nineteen centuries after John wrote—that is the work of the Spirit of God. It is through the Spirit's operation that, in William Temple's words, 'the mind of Jesus himself was what the Fourth Gospel disclosed'; and it is through the illumination granted by the same Spirit that one may still recognize in this gospel the authentic voice of Jesus.[47]

The Relationship Between Father and Son in John

There are many sections in the gospel of John that illustrate the intimate relationship between God and Christ, but we have picked two in particular that we feel are especially appropriate in light of what we have been discussing in this chapter and throughout this book. They are John 5:16–32 and John 10:24–36. In the first part of John 5, Jesus healed a crippled man who had been an invalid for 38 years. The man picked up his mat and walked away, but it was the Sabbath, and he ran into some religious leaders who reproved him for carrying his mat on that day. He said to them, "Hey, I just got healed after 38 years (he may also have thought, "something *you* never did for me"), and the man who healed me told me to pick up my mat and go for a walk." The religious leaders asked the man, who told him to pick up his mat and walk, but the man couldn't tell them, not knowing who Jesus was. Later, Jesus found him in the Temple and encouraged him to clean up his life, now that he had been healed. The man then went away and told the religious leaders that it was Jesus who had made him well.

---

47. Bruce, *op. cit., Gospel of John*, pp. 16 and 17). For more on this, see Appendix A (John 3:13).

John 5:16 (NRSV)
Therefore the Jews started persecuting Jesus, because he was doing such things on the sabbath.

One would think that religious leaders, supposedly representing God, would be very blessed that the man had been healed, but these Jews were, to say the least, hard to please. In fact, they decided that because Jesus had done this on the Sabbath day, he was worthy of *death*.[48] Jesus did not hide from the religious leaders even though they were against him, but instead he addressed them directly.

John 5:17 (NRSV)
But Jesus answered them, "My Father is still working, and I also am working."

What was Jesus saying to those religious leaders who should have known the Old Testament backward and forward? In essence, he said to them, "Hey, wake up! Everything my Father, God, has done up until this point, as set forth in the Old Testament, has set the stage for *me*. I am the one of whom the Old Testament is speaking. Now I am here and I am working. The fact that I healed the crippled man should not surprise you, because it was prophesied that I would do such things." As the next verse shows, this great truth did little to change their minds:

John 5:18 (NRSV)
For this reason the Jews were seeking all the more to kill him, because he was not only breaking the sabbath, but was also calling God his own Father, thereby making himself equal to God.

There is no record of *Jesus* saying that he was "equal with God." Notice that this is what the *Jews said that he said*, and that is why they were trying to kill him. We have already seen in Philippians 2:6 that Jesus did *not* think that equality with God was something to be seized. Watch what Jesus says in response to their accusations:

John 5:19 and 20 (NRSV)
(19) Jesus said to them: "Very truly, I tell you, the Son can do nothing on his own, but only what he sees the Father doing; for whatever the Father does, the Son does likewise.
(20) The Father loves the Son and shows him all that he himself is doing; and he will show him greater works than these, so that you will be astonished.

Rather than claiming "equality" [as in *identity*] with God, Jesus spoke of God as his source and of his total *reliance* upon God (see also John 7:16 and 17). If Jesus were trying to convince people he was God, or even if he were openly proclaiming himself to be the Messiah, this would have been a

---

48. It is important to realize that Jesus would never ask a man to break a commandment of God. It was the religious leaders of Christ's day who had actually broken the commandments of God by their traditions (Matt. 15:1–9). Carrying a bedding mat from a place you were lying sick would not have been work, except according to the twisted religious traditions of the time. The man needed to leave the pool of Bethesda, where people went to be healed, and start walking out on the healing he had received. He could not very well have left his mat, or it would have been stolen. Jesus was being loving in telling the man to take his mat, but the religious leaders were so twisted by their dogma that they could not even rejoice with a man who was healed after 38 years of being crippled.

wide open door. Instead, he downplayed his own role and spoke of what the Father was doing and of His love. If Jesus were God, he certainly could do whatever he wanted by himself, but he said he was the *Son of God*, and therefore could only do what the Father showed him. Remember that the context is Jesus having healed the crippled man. In verse 20, Jesus said, in essence, "If you think healing the crippled man was a big deal, just hang around, because I am going to do many greater things than that." What greater things was he talking about? Let's keep reading.

John 5:21
For just as the Father raises the dead and gives them life, even so the Son gives life
to whom he is pleased to give it.

We see here that Jesus anticipated his own resurrection and his future joy of raising others. In verse 21, we must again note the figures of speech *heterosis* and *prolepsis*. Here again is an exchange of the future tense for the present tense, anticipating the day when Jesus would literally have resurrection life to give. Jesus Christ had not yet himself been raised from the dead, and certainly he had not raised anyone else to everlasting life, yet he speaks of giving life in the present tense. He does so to emphasize his faith in the certainty of these things coming to pass, and his references to them in this way are placed in the gospel of John as part of the proleptic portrait of Jesus Christ. He did not doubt his own ability to obey his Father, nor his Father's ability to raise him from the dead and highly exalt him.

John 5:22 and 23 (NRSV)
(22) The Father judges no one but has given all judgment to the Son,
(23) so that all may honor the Son just as they honor the Father. Anyone who does
not honor the Son does not honor the Father who sent him.

In the above verses, we see that it will be Jesus Christ who will judge all men, and that thereby all men will honor the Son even as they honor the Father. That is what we saw in Philippians 2:10 and 11: **every knee will bow, and every tongue will confess that Jesus Christ is Lord, to the glory of God the Father.**

We believe it befits justice that Jesus Christ, the one who was judged, condemned and executed by men, will be the one to finally judge all men. Every unrepentant, evil person who has ever lived, who literally tortured and crucified him or who figuratively did so by persecuting those who have loved him, will one day look in the eyes of the Son of God as their judge, and he will be vindicated.

John 5:24 and 25 (NRSV)
(24) Very truly, I tell you, anyone who hears my word and believes him who sent me
has eternal life, and does not come under judgement, but has passed from death to life.
(25) "Very truly, I tell you, the hour is coming, and is now here, when the dead will
hear the voice of the Son of God, and those who hear will live.

Once again we see here that it is Jesus Christ, as the Promised Seed, who will call people to new and everlasting life.

John 5:26 (NRSV)
For just as the Father has life in himself, so he has granted the Son also to have life
in himself,

Jesus Christ understood that the chief property of a seed is that it has life in itself, and that as the
Promised Seed he would, after his resurrection and exaltation, have life in himself to give to others.
As the next verse says, it is Jesus Christ who will decide who is to live and who is to die. Rest assured
that one day there will be justice for all.

John 5:27–29 (NRSV)
(27) and he has given him authority to execute judgment, because he is the Son of Man.
(28) Do not be astonished at this; for the hour is coming when all who are in their
graves will hear his voice
(29) and will come out—those who have done good, to the resurrection of life, and
those who have done evil, to the resurrection of condemnation.

This is a prophecy of what is commonly known as the resurrections of "the just" and "the unjust."
The Bible clearly says that all people who have ever lived will get up from the dead. Those in the
resurrection of the just will be going to one party, while the majority of those in the resurrection of
the unjust will be going to another party, which is considerably shorter and has no party favors.[49]
Those in the resurrection of the just will be getting up for everlasting life in Paradise. The unrighteous
in the resurrection of the unjust will be getting up for judgment, condemnation and destruction in
the lake of fire.

John 5:30 (NRSV)
"I can do nothing on my own. As I hear, I judge; and my judgment is just, because I
seek to do not my own will but the will of him who sent me.

Because Jesus Christ works in perfect harmony with his heavenly Father, there will be justice for all.

John 5:31 and 32 (NRSV)
(31) "If I testify about myself, my testimony is not true.
(32) There is another who testifies on my behalf, and I know that his testimony to
me is true.

The phrase "another who testifies" about Jesus Christ refers to God, his heavenly Father. The
most important way God testified who Jesus was, was by raising him from the dead (Acts 17:31).
Although the Pharisees to whom Jesus was speaking missed the whole point of the Old Testament
and failed to recognize him as the Messiah, some did cleave unto him as such. How sad that so many
people today have misunderstood the Scriptures and to some degree missed the heart of the Son of
God that is so specifically revealed in the Four Gospels.

---

49. It is known as the "resurrection of the *unjust*" because it is the only resurrection when all the unjust people who
have ever lived will be raised from the dead, judged and condemned. At the same time, people who believed on Jesus
Christ and died during his Millennial Kingdom will be raised from the dead and receive salvation.

There is one other record in the gospel of John that we want to explore, one that graphically illustrates the relationship between God and His Son, Jesus Christ. Almost inconceivably, it is often twisted in an attempt to prove that Jesus is, in fact, God. As we examine it, we will see the great truth contained therein. It was winter, and Jesus was at the Temple in Jerusalem for a Jewish holiday.

John 10:24–30 (NASB)
(24) The Jews therefore gathered around Him, and were saying to Him, "How long will You keep us in suspense? If You are the Christ, tell us plainly."
(25) Jesus answered them, "I told you, and you do not believe; the works that I do in My Father's name, these bear witness of Me,
(26) "But you do not believe, because you are not of My sheep.
(27) "My sheep hear My voice, and I know them, and they follow Me;
(28) and I give eternal life to them, and they shall never perish; and no one shall snatch them out of My hand.
(29) "My Father, who has given *them* to Me, is greater than all; and no one is able to snatch *them* out of the Father's hand.
(30) "I and the Father are one."

Although some people use verse 30 in an attempt to prove that Jesus is God, the context (in particular, verses 28 and 29) clearly shows its meaning. Jesus and his Father are "one" in that no one can pluck any of their sheep out of either of their hands.[50]

John 10:31–33 (NASB)
(31) The Jews took up stones again to stone Him.
(32) Jesus answered them, "I showed you many good works from the Father; for which of them are you stoning Me?"
(33) The Jews answered Him, "For a good work we do not stone You, but for blasphemy; and because You, being a man, make Yourself out *to be* God."

Some quote verse 33 to prove Jesus is God. Note that the verse does not say that Jesus is God, or that he claimed to be God, but rather that *the Jews said* that Jesus was making himself "God." We assert that an accurate translation of John 10:33 would reveal that the Jews said that Jesus was claiming to be "a god," i.e., a representative of God.[51] Because they did not believe he represented God at all, they were actually going to stone him, which indicates that their overall spiritual perception was perhaps somewhat distorted. Let us look at Jesus' reply:

John 10:34–36 (NASB)
(34) Jesus answered them, "Has it not been written in your Law, 'I SAID, YOU ARE GODS'?
(35) "If he called them gods, to whom the word of God came (and the Scripture cannot be broken),

---

50. The Greek word for "one" is *hen*, and means "one single." In Jesus' prayer as recorded in John 17:20–23, he makes it very clear what "one" means. He prayed that all those who believe in him will be "one," even as he and his Father are "one." Obviously, this means one in unity of heart and in purpose. See Appendix A (John 10:30).
51. See Appendix A (John 10:33).

(36) do you say of Him, whom the Father sanctified and sent into the world, 'You are blaspheming,' because I said, 'I am the Son of God'?

In verse 34, Jesus is quoting from Psalm 82, verses 1 and 6. There, as in other Old Testament references, representatives of God were referred to as "gods." This was a common Hebrew usage that all the people understood. Jesus quotes these references, and then says, in essence: "Look, if those Old Testament leaders and judges were referred to as 'gods,' what about me? I am by far the best representative God has ever had. Why do you say I am blaspheming when I say I am the Son of God?"

Psalm 82:1–8 (KJV)
(1) God standeth in the congregation of the mighty; he judgeth among the gods [i.e., those who represent Him].
(2) How long will ye judge unjustly, and accept the persons of the wicked? Selah.
(3) Defend the poor and fatherless: do justice to the afflicted and needy.
(4) Deliver the poor and needy: rid *them* out of the hand of the wicked.
(5) They know not, neither will they understand; they walk on in darkness: all the foundations of the earth are out of course.
(6) I have said, Ye are gods; and all of you *are* children of the most High.
(7) But ye shall die like men, and fall like one of the princes.
(8) Arise, O God [i.e. the Messiah], judge the earth: for thou shalt inherit all nations.

These verses make it very clear that those men whom God had chosen to represent Him to His people in Israel failed miserably to do so, generally speaking. The closing verse is a prophetic plea for the Messiah to come, the perfect representative of God who would vividly mirror His heart to all people. Note how precise Jesus was in choosing just the right verses to make his point. He had rigorously studied the Hebrew Scriptures, which he would hardly have had to do if he were God.

Is not John 10:24–36 a clear record of Jesus himself refuting the idea that he is God? It is also a record of Jesus differentiating between the Son of God and God Himself, something that more Christians today could profit from doing. Had Jesus been God, surely this would have been a wonderful opportunity for him to plainly say so, but he did not. His testimony of himself is perfectly consistent with the stated purpose of the gospel of John: to reveal that Jesus is the *Son* of God. With the understanding of John which we have set forth in this chapter, this gospel now perfectly harmonizes with the rest of the New Testament. The historical "Jesus" is unified with the exalted "Christ" into a proleptic portrait of "Jesus Christ" that simultaneously brings him down to earth and exalts him. How truly awesome is the One who has inspired and revealed in His Word such a breathtaking view of the Lord Jesus, "the Christ, the Son of the living God."

9

"But what about John 1:1?"

John 1:1–3 (KJV)
(1) In the beginning was the Word [*logos*], and the Word was with God, and the Word was God.
(2) The same was in the beginning with God.
(3) All things were made by [*dia*] him, and without him was not anything made that was made.

Without a doubt, misunderstanding these verses at the beginning of the gospel of John has done more to further the cause of Trinitarian orthodoxy than misunderstanding any other section of Scripture. Whenever we challenge the traditional understanding of God and Christ, the first three verses of John's prologue are invariably and almost immediately brought to the forefront of the discussion. Thus, it behooves us as workmen of God's Word to thoroughly consider them. We trust you will see that they harmonize beautifully with the rest of the gospel of John and the whole of Scripture.

The first 18 verses of the gospel of John are commonly called "the prologue," and are a powerful introduction to the rest of the book. Just as the introduction of Matthew starts with a kingly genealogy,

Mark very quickly shows Jesus in the service of the Lord and Luke starts with material about Jesus' human relationships and his genealogy from the first man, Adam, so John introduces us to Jesus as the Plan and Wisdom of God, and His only begotten Son. The prologue introduces and supports the theme of the gospel of John, that Jesus is the Christ, the Son of God. We addressed that in the previous chapter, but now need to look at it again:

John 20:30 and 31
(30) Jesus did many other miraculous signs in the presence of his disciples, which are not recorded in this book.
(31) But these are written that you may believe that Jesus is the Christ, the Son of God, and that by believing you may have life in his name.

The purpose of John's gospel is clearly stated, and therefore the prologue introducing this gospel must also support the theme that Jesus is the Son of God, which it does magnificently. We will see that the prologue establishes right at the beginning of the gospel the proleptic view of Christ that we examined in the last chapter. We will also look at both the Greek and Hebrew concepts of "word," and see that John's use of *logos* is a magnificent blend of Greek and Hebrew thought.

Truly this gospel has universal appeal to humanity because it presents a view of Jesus Christ perfectly consistent with the body of Old Testament prophecies concerning the Messiah. Once understood, the prologue of the gospel of John also harmonizes with the Synoptic Gospels and the testimony of the remainder of the New Testament. Finally, we will address the relationship of the gospel of John to the developing Gnosticism of the late first century. In doing so, we will see that John uses some of the language and concepts of Gnosticism itself for the purpose of opposing it (See the beginning of Chapter 16 for a definition of Gnosticism).

We will now go through the prologue of John, highlighting and commenting on the key phrases. The gospel of John begins with the phrase "In the beginning was the Word (Greek = *logos*)," which powerfully brings the reader's mind back to Genesis 1:1: "In the beginning God…" Before we can examine the idea of the "beginning," however, we must have an understanding of what the *logos* is, which was "in the beginning."

The Meaning of *Logos* in Greek

It is a challenge for the modern translator to even translate the word *logos* into a single Enlish word.[1] *Logos* is derived from *lego*, "to say or speak," and its root, *leg*, means "to gather or arrange." For

---

1. The Bible itself demonstrates the wide range of meaning *logos* has, and some of the ways it is translated in Scripture (NIV) are: account, appearance, book, command, conversation, eloquence, flattery, grievance, heard, instruction, matter, message, ministry, news, proposal, question, reason, reasonable, reply, report, rule, rumor, said, say, saying, sentence, speaker, speaking, speech, stories, story, talk, talking, teaching, testimony, thing, things, this, truths, what, why, word, and words.

Op. cit., A Greek-English Lexicon of the New Testament and Other Early Christian Literature (Arndt and Gingrich's revision of Walter Bauer's work) lists the following as some of the definitions for *logos* (the words in **bold** are translated from *logos*):
- speaking; words you say (Rom. 15:18, "…what I have **said** and done").
- a statement you make (Luke 20:20 – NASB, "…they might catch Him in some **statement**…").
- a question (Matt. 21:24, "…I will also ask you one **question**…").
- preaching (1 Tim. 5:17, "…especially those whose work is **preaching** and teaching").

the Greeks, to speak is to utter the arrangement or gathering of one's thoughts. This is reflected in English, as in "I gather that you are not coming this morning." This meaning then developed into "speak, reckon, think" then into "word" and finally into "reason."

The *logos* is God's expression, His communication of Himself, just as a spoken word is the expression of the inner and unseen thoughts of a person. Thus, *logos* includes the idea of "plan," "purpose," "wisdom" and even "power." *Logos* is the term that God uses to represent His purpose for this new creation, which was eventually realized in the person of Jesus. The translation of *logos* as "word" is a good one-word translation of its meaning, but it falls short of illuminating the richness of "*logos*" in its Greek usage, a richness that sheds light on both the purpose of God and the person of Jesus.

Logos expressed the essential unity of *language* and *thought*, both of which consist, in their most advanced forms, of *words*. When we think, we are talking to ourselves; when we talk, we are thinking out loud. English words such as "dialogue" and "monologue" signify the connection of *logos* with language, while words like "logic" and "logistics" signify its connection with thought. *Logos*, in its earliest usage, did not have to do with words per se, but rather with words that made sense out of and gave meaning to human existence and experience.

In addition to its connection to language and thought, *logos* was also associated with the reality of things. To think and speak, in other words, is to think and speak *about something*. To have and give a *logos* was, in ancient Greece, to have and give a rational account, a reasonable explanation, of something in the world of human experience, whether an object (of nature or human nature) or an event (an act of God or man). The English suffix "-ology" signifies the connection of *logos* with the world of things, things that have become the objects of human interest and study, e.g., biology, physiology, sociology, psychology and theology.

Another defining point of *logos* was its practical connection to human life. Every *logos*, or reasonable explanation of a human experience, was intended to lead to a wise course of action, a rational approach to handling similar experiences in the future. *Logos*, in other words, implied a purposefulness to life based on a reasonable explanation and a rational understanding of human existence.

Logos, then, in its original Greek usage, encompassed human language and thought in its relation to the things of human experience and the purpose of human existence. The biblical usage of *logos* runs parallel to this concept in that "the Word" is God's purpose or plan, His reasonable explanation of, and His rationale for, His creation of all things before they became corrupted in human experience. His rationale constitutes wisdom, that is, a rational understanding of and approach to human life. Sir Anthony Buzzard waxes eloquent:

- command (Gal. 5:14, "The entire law is summed up in a single **command**...").
- proverb; saying, (John 4:37, "Thus the **saying**, 'One sows and another reaps...'").
- message; instruction; proclamation (Luke 4:32, "...his **message** had authority").
- assertion; declaration; teaching (John 6:60, "...This is a hard **teaching**...").
- the subject under discussion; matter, (Acts 8:21, "You have no part or share in this **ministry**..." and Acts 15:6 – NASB, "And the apostles and the elders came together to look into this **matter**").
- revelation from God (Matt. 15:6, "...you nullify the **word of God**...").
- God's revelation spoken by His servants (Heb. 13:7, "...leaders, who spoke the **word of God**...").
- a reckoning, an account (Matt. 12:36, "...men will have to give **account**" at the day of judgment...).
- an account or "matter" in a financial sense (Matt. 18:23, a king settled "**accounts**" with his servants, and Phil. 4:15, "...the **matter** of giving and receiving...").
- a reason; motive (Acts 10:29 – NASB, "...And so I ask **for what reason** you have sent for me").

See Appendix A (John 1:1).

Recent commentaries on John admit that despite the long-standing tradition to the contrary, the term "word" in the famous prologue of John need not refer to the Son of God before he was born. Our translations imply belief in the traditional doctrine of incarnation by capitalizing "Word." But what was it that became flesh in John 1:14? Was it a pre-existing *person*? Or was it the self-expressive activity of God, the Father, His eternal plan? A plan may take flesh, for example, when the design in the architect's mind finally takes shape as a house. What pre-existed the visible bricks and mortar was the intention in the mind of the architect. Thus, it is quite in order to read John 1:1–3a: "In the beginning was the creative purpose of God. It was with God and was fully expressive of God [just as wisdom was with God before creation]. All things came into being through it." This rendering suits the Old Testament use of "word" admirably: "So shall My word be that goes forth out of My mouth; it shall not return to Me empty, without accomplishing what I desire and without succeeding in the matter for which I sent it."[2]

We are now in a better position to see why Jesus is known as "the word (*logos*) in the flesh." Jesus was the ultimate expression of God. God's plan, wisdom and purpose was the *logos*, and when we speak of the Bible, it is called "the Word" because it also is God's expression of Himself. When we speak of a prophecy, we say, it is "the Word of the Lord," both because it is in the form of words and because it is God's expression of Himself. Jesus was the *logos* in the most complete sense. He was the ultimate expression of God and the essence of His plan and purpose. Thus, it is quite correct to say that Jesus was the *logos*, but he was not all of the *logos*. "Jesus" does not equal "the *logos*," he was part of and the ultimate expression of the *logos*. If we see Jesus, we see the Father, but it is also true that if we study the Bible, God's Word, God's expression of Himself in writing, we will see the Father. More dimly, to be sure, because the written Word is not the clear and ultimate expression of God that the Living Word is, but it is the *logos* just the same.

The Hebrew Word for "Word"

As is true with all genuine study of the Bible, the real question is not what *we today* think of these words in John's prologue, but how the *readers in the first century* would have understood them, especially those who had a Semitic understanding.[3] One scholar made the following insightful

---

2. Buzzard and Hunting, *op. cit.*, *The Doctrine of The Trinity.*

3. The gospel of John is now widely viewed as having been originally written in Aramaic, a Semitic language of even greater antiquity than Hebrew, and the language that Jesus himself spoke. It was the language of the Galileans, which included Jesus. One New Testament scholar writes:

> We find then, that, broadly speaking, sayings and discourse material prove to be that which displays the most unambiguous signs of translation out of Aramaic…In the case of John, not all would be willing to find Aramaic sources even behind the discourses: rather the work of a bilingual author has been postulated, in which the more natural Aramaic has left its indelible imprint on the more mannered Greek…John's Greek can be closely paralleled from Epictetus, but in the opinion of most scholars appears to be a *koine* [Greek] written by one whose native thought and speech were Aramaic; there may even be passages translated from that language…this too underlines the description of the gospel as markedly Semitic.

New Bible Dictionary, "Language of the New Testament," by J. N. Birdsall (W. B. Eerdmans, Grand Rapids, MI, 1975), p. 715. The significance of this fact is that if John's gospel is written from a Semitic perspective, then its references to concepts like *logos* should be understood at least in part from a Semitic perspective also. This puts the *logos* concept squarely in what is called "the wisdom literature" of Judaism, wherein *personification* of concepts is a common figure of

comment about the Hebrew view of "word" not emphasizing the rationale or the plan of God, but His power to bring His will to pass upon the earth:

> All over the ancient Orient, in Assyria and Babylon as well as in Egypt, the word, especially the Word of God, was not only nor even primarily an expression of thought; it was a mighty and dynamic force. The Hebrew conception of "the divine word" had an express dynamic character and possessed a tremendous power."[4]

The Hebrew conception of "word" (*dabhar*) was more dynamic than the Greek conception, which is characteristic of the language as a whole. One basic meaning of the root of *dabhar* is "to be behind" and thus be able to drive forward from behind. This is consistent with the Semitic idea expressed by Jesus in Luke 6:45 that "…out of the overflow of his heart his mouth speaks." In other words, what is in the heart drives the mind, then the mouth and finally the actions. Thus, the meaning of *dabhar* developed along a line defined by three points: "speak," "word" and finally "deed."[5] Boman shows that in the Hebrew mind, words were equivalent to deeds, and this fact is integrated into the very construction of the language itself:

> *Dabhar* means not only "word," but also "deed." Abraham's servant recounted to Isaac all the 'words' that he had done (Gen. 24:66) [seen in the literal Hebrew rendering of this verse]. The word is the highest and noblest function of man and is, for that reason, identical with his action. "Word" and "deed" are thus not two different meanings of *dabhar*, but the "deed" is the consequence of the basic meaning inhering in *dabhar*. Our term 'word' is thus a poor translation for the Hebrew *dabhar*, because for us, 'word' never includes the deed within it. The commentators understand as a contrived witticism Goethe's translation of John 1:1… "In the beginning was the deed."[6] Actually, Goethe is on solid linguistic ground because he goes back to the Hebrew (Aramaic) original and translates its deepest meaning; for if *dabhar* forms a unity of word and deed, in our thinking the deed is the higher concept in the unity.[7]

F. F. Bruce is another scholar who recognizes that the key to understanding the significance of the concept of "*logos*" is by tracing its Old Testament roots:

> The true background to John's thought and language is found not in Greek philosophy but in Hebrew revelation. The "Word of God" in the Old Testament denotes God in action, especially in creation, revelation and deliverance.[8]

The Word of God is repeatedly portrayed in the Old Testament as the agent of God's creative power, as the following verses show:

Psalm 33:6a (NASB)
By the word of the LORD the heavens were made….

---

speech. Spirit and Wisdom and *Logos* (Reason or Word) are all figuratively said to have facilitated and participated in the act of creation (cp. Gen. 1:2; Prov. 8:1 and 22ff).

4. Thorlief Boman, *Hebrew Thought Compared With Greek* (Norton, NY, 1960), p. 58.

5. Boman cites a number of other scholars who see the Semitic view of *logos*, specifically Lorenz Durr, W. F. Albright, Herder and Bultmann. *Ibid.*, p. 61.

6. "Im Anfang war die Tat"—"In the beginning was the word, the action." J. W. von Goethe, *Faust*, line 1237. Quoted in Bruce, *op. cit., Gospel of John*, p. 29.

7. Boman, *op. cit., Hebrew Thought Compared*, p. 66.

8. Bruce, *op. cit., Gospel of John*, p. 29.

Psalms 107:20 (KJV)
He sent his word, and healed them, and delivered *them* from their destruction.

In Isaiah, the "word" of God is spoken of as an agent independent of, but fully in the service of, God:

Isaiah 55:11 (NRSV)
so shall my word be that goes out from my mouth; It shall not return to me empty, but it shall accomplish that which I purpose, and succeed in the thing for which I sent it.

This is reminiscent of the personification of wisdom in Proverbs, where "she" is portrayed as God's helper in creation:

Proverbs 8:22, 23, and 30
(22) The LORD brought me [wisdom] forth as the first of his works, before his deeds of old;
(23) I was appointed from eternity, from the beginning, before the world began.
(30) Then I was his craftsman at his side. I was filled with delight day after day, rejoicing always in his presence,

Broughton and Southgate argue that "Word," "Spirit" and "Wisdom" are all personified because they are intimately connected to how God has related to the world as its Creator, and that John's use of *logos* is consistent with this biblical usage.

We can see how John draws on all the Old Testament teaching…Wisdom is personified in Proverbs 8 as saying that she was in the beginning, that she was with God, and that she was His instrument in creation. The Word of God created the heavens (Ps. 33:6), and so did the Spirit as described in Job 26:13 (KJV) [and Gen. 1:2]. The language clearly is of figure and metaphor, of personification, not actual personality. And John is saying exactly the same of the *logos* or Word. No Jewish reader brought up on the writings of the prophets would have deduced from John's introduction that he was alluding to a person who had existed with God from all time. They would see it *instead* as a continuation of the imagery by which the Word or Wisdom or the Spirit—those manifestations of God which are inseparable from Him—are described as putting God's intentions into effect.[9]

Barclay, a respected Greek scholar, also recognizes that the *logos* is intimately connected to both power and wisdom.

First, God's Word is not only speech; it is power. Second, it is impossible to separate the ideas of Word and Wisdom; and it was God's Wisdom, which created and permeated the world, which God made.[10]

---

9. Broughton, James H. and Southgate, Peter J., *The Trinity: True or False?* (The Dawn Book Supply, Nottingham, 1995), p. 247. Broughton and Southgate note that the Spirit of God is also personified. We would add the example of Genesis 1:2, where the spirit is described as a living thing, again in the context of God's creative action: "Now the earth was formless and empty, darkness was over the surface of the deep, and the Spirit of God was hovering [AMP - "brooding"] over the waters."
10. William Barclay, *New Testament Words*, (Westminster Press, Philadelphia, 1974), p. 186.

There is still more evidence for connecting the Semitic understanding of *logos* with "power." The Targums are Aramaic paraphrases of the Hebrew text, and they are well known for describing the wisdom and action of God as His "Word." This is especially important to note because Aramaic was the spoken language of many Jews at the time of Christ, including Christ himself, and thus the people at the time of Christ would have been very familiar with them. Remembering that a Targum is usually a paraphrase of what the Hebrew text says, note how the following examples attribute action to the "word" of the LORD:

Genesis 39:2
And the word of the LORD was Joseph's helper (Hebrew text: "The LORD was with Joseph").

Exodus 19:17
And Moses brought the people "to meet the word of the LORD" (Hebrew text: "And Moses brought the people out of the camp to meet God").

Job 42:9
And the word of the LORD accepted the face of Job (Hebrew text: "And the LORD accepted the face of Job").

Psalm 2:4
And the word of the LORD shall laugh them to scorn (Hebrew text: "The LORD shall laugh at them").[11]

The contrast between the Hebrew text and the Aramaic paraphrases in the verses above show that the Jews had no problem personifying the "Word" of God such that it could act on God's behalf. They also prove that the Jews were familiar with the idea of the "Word" referring to His wisdom and action. This is especially important to note because these Jews were fiercely monotheistic, and did not in any way believe in a "Triune God." They were familiar with the idioms of their own language, and understood that the wisdom and power of God were being *personified* and did not represent actual "persons" in any way.

Thus, "the Word" in John 1:1 represents an intersection of the two differing Hebrew and Greek lines of thought.[12] Although there are similarities, the Hebrew and the Greek languages reflect profound differences in the way the world was perceived. Boman observes:

---

11. These examples are from *A Commentary on the New Testament from the Talmud and Hebraica* by Dr. John Lightfoot (Hendrickson Pub., Peabody MA, 1989) Vol. 3, p. 238.

12. *The* NIV Study Bible note on *logos* (John 1:1) agrees that the "word" represents an intersection of Greek and Hebrew thought, but their Trinitarian bias is revealed in the fact that they say "Word" was a way that the Hebrews referred to *God*, when in fact it consistently refers to the creative activity, purpose and action of God. No Jew would have mistaken "the Word" of God for God Himself: *(continued)*

> Greeks used this term not only of the spoken word but also of the unspoken word, the word still in the mind—the reason. When they applied it to the universe, they meant the rational principle that governs all things. Jews, on the other hand, used it as a way of referring to God. Thus, John used a term that was meaningful to both Jews and Gentiles.

According to the Israelite conception, everything is in eternal movement: God and man, nature and the world. The totality of existence, *olam*, is time, history, life. The history of heaven and earth (Gen. 2:4) is of the same form as the history of Adam (5:1), Noah (6:9), and Shem (11:10); it is referred to in each case by the same word, *toledhoth* [generations]. The fact that God created the world and man once and for all implies that God makes history and brings forth life and that he continues them until they achieve their goal...As *space* was the given thought-form for the Greeks, so for the Hebrews it was *time*...For the Hebrew, the decisive reality of the world of experience was the *word*; for the Greek it was the *thing*. Yet the word had a great significance for the Greek on account of its meaning; on the whole, however, the meaning of the word is independent of the word as spoken or dynamic reality.[13]

As we read the gospel of John with a true understanding of the concept of *logos*, the wonderful love of our heavenly Father is clearly shown. From the very beginning God had a purpose, a plan that He brought to pass in the world in a way that reveals His love and wisdom and clearly expresses Himself. It should be apparent, then, that the use of *logos* in the prologue of John reflects the richness of the biblical usage of the term "Word" when it is used in relation to God and His creative purpose and activity.

While in John 1:1 the *logos* is God's self expression and His wisdom, plan and power, many times in the New Testament the *logos* is *the message* of the coming, the life, the death, the resurrection, the ascension, the exaltation, the lordship and the coming again of Jesus the Messiah. If the *logos* that was "in the beginning" is understood in these terms, then it becomes clear that God had this very series of events in mind when He created the cosmos. "The Word was God" (John 1:1) in that it is God's self-revelation, the account that God chose to give of Himself and His will to all nations.[14]

The *logos* or message of God, as it has been revealed in Jesus, includes the following account of the meaning and purpose of creation: Jesus' coming was prophesied throughout the Hebrew Scriptures; he was finally born a man, and by his free will lived a sinless life; Jesus died on the Cross to mark the beginning of the end of the present age of sin and death, revealing that it is only a matter of time until this age and fallen humanity as it now exists come to an end; Jesus was raised from the dead to reveal that death (the experience that all humans since Adam have held in common) is contrary to God's will and will ultimately be abolished by resurrection; Jesus was exalted as Lord to the right hand of God where he presently exercises this authority; after he comes to gather together the Church, Jesus will come again at the end of this age in judgment, bringing destruction on the unbelieving world and salvation to the community of faith; he will rule for one thousand years on this earth; finally he will destroy Satan and all evil, end the heaven and earth of the present age and begin the new heaven and earth of the age to come, a "new creation."

"In the beginning"

Once we understand that the *logos* is God's self expression, His wisdom, plan and purposes, and that it can include His power and His actions, we are in a position to really understand the full meaning of the phrase, "In the beginning" in John 1:1.

---

13. Boman, *op. cit., Hebrew Thought Compared,* pp. 205 and 206.

14. A better translation of that phrase ("the Word was God") would be "…what God was, the Word was…" (NEB), or "the Logos was divine," (Moffatt). See Appendix A (John 1:1).

It is often simply assumed that "the beginning" referred to here is the origin of creation, identical to the creation described in Genesis 1:1 and 2. However, that assumption is usually made because most Christians believe that in John 1:1, Jesus is the "word" and Jesus was "in the beginning." We trust that by now the reader knows that Jesus did not pre-exist his birth and that he was not with God in Genesis 1:1. We also trust that the reader understands that the *logos* of John 1:1 is not identical to "Jesus." What we will present in this section is that "the beginning" is actually a *double entendre*: it refers to the earliest time when God conceived of the plan of man's salvation, but, like the rest of the gospel of John, it has proleptic overtones, speaking of the future as if it were a reality.[15] Thus, "the beginning" referred to in John 1:1 also refers to the *new* creation of which Jesus Christ is the prototype.

The meaning of "beginning" that immediately comes to mind when John 1:1 is read refers to the time before history when God first conceived of man, and foresaw the possibility that he would fall and need a Savior. This is because of the familiar phrase, "In the beginning God" in Genesis 1:1. John tells us that "in the beginning" God had wisdom and a plan, and was prepared to start acting that plan out so that the people He created and invested His love in could be rescued from death and live with Him eternally. The crowning piece of the plan of God was the creation of Jesus Christ, who was in a very real sense, "the last word."

However, there was much groundwork to be done before he who would perfectly represent God could come. That groundwork was laid in the time period covered by the Old Testament, and so in a very real sense, God's plan was being expressed in wisdom and action all through the Old Testament. The *logos* was being expressed as Abraham set off to sacrifice Isaac, as Moses lifted the serpent up on the pole, as Solomon built the Temple, and as Isaiah penned the verses stating that the Servant of God would be pierced for our transgressions. It was expressed in pieces and parts in history, as people acted, and in prophecy, as people spoke. Then one day, probably in 3 B.C., the types, foreshadowings and prophecies ceased, and the *logos*, the plan, purpose, wisdom and power of God, "became flesh" in the man Jesus Christ. Thus, the word "beginning" in John 1:1 does clearly represent the plan and power of God before our history.

As we have already pointed out, "the beginning" also has overtones of the new creation. We spent a lot of time in the last chapter developing the idea that John was written from the perspective that Jesus was already in glory. This is proleptic language, writing about the future as if it were an accomplished reality. At least two places in the first chapter of John show that it too was written from the perspective that the life of Christ had already been lived and he was now in glory with His father. John 1:14 says, "…We **have seen** his glory…," and John 1:18 says that Jesus "…**is** at the Father's side…." We are not the only ones to consider this possibility that the "beginning" in John 1:1 can refer to the new creation also. Bruce argues for this interpretation:

> It is not by accident that the Gospel begins with the same phrase as the book of Genesis. In Genesis 1:1, 'In the beginning' introduces the story of the old creation; here it introduces the story of the new creation. In both works of creation the agent is the Word of God.[16]

---

15. There are a number of passages in the Bible that have more than one meaning. In his magnificent work titled *op. cit., Figures of Speech Used in the Bible*, Bullinger covers some of these under the figure *amphibologia*, or "Double Meaning." The fact that God so intricately and carefully interweaves two meanings into one word and makes them both correct is more convincing proof that the Bible was not authored by men but by God, and that He has inspired it in such a way that only those who really look into the depth of Scripture will find its great buried treasure.

16. Bruce, *op. cit., Gospel of John,* pp. 28 and 29.

The *Racovian Catechism*, one of the great doctrinal works of the Unitarian movement of the 16th and 17th centuries, states that the word "beginning" in John 1:1 refers to the beginning of the new dispensation and thus is similar to Mark 1:1, which starts, "The beginning of the gospel about Jesus Christ…."

> In the cited passage (John 1:1) wherein the Word is said to have been in the beginning, there is no reference to an antecedent eternity, without commencement; because mention is made here of a *beginning*, which is opposed to that eternity. But the word *beginning*, used absolutely, is to be understood of the subject matter under consideration. Thus, Daniel 8:1 (KJV), "In the third year of the reign of king Belshazzar a vision appeared unto me, *even unto* me Daniel, after that which appeared unto me at the first." John 15:27 (KJV), "And ye also shall bear witness, because ye have been with me **from** *the beginning*." John 16:4b (KJV), "…And these things I said not unto you at **the beginning**, because I was with you. And Acts 11:15 (KJV), "And as I began to speak, the Holy Ghost fell on them, as on us at **the beginning**."

> As then the matter of which John is treating is the Gospel, or the things transacted under the Gospel, nothing else ought to be understood here besides the beginning of the gospel; a matter clearly known to the Christians whom he addressed, namely, the advent and preaching of John the Baptist, according to the testimony of all the evangelists [i.e., Matthew, Mark, Luke and John], each of whom begins his history with the coming and preaching of the Baptist. Mark indeed (1:1) expressly states that this was the beginning of the gospel. In like manner, John himself employs the word beginning, placed thus absolutely, in the introduction to his First Epistle, at which beginning he uses the same term (*logos*) Word, as if he meant to be his own interpreter ["That which is from the beginning…concerning the Word (*logos*) of life." 1 John 1:1].[17]

In this context of the new creation, then, "the Word" is the plan or purpose according to which God is restoring His creation, as we saw in Chapter 3.[18] As such, "the Word" was conceived in the mind of God even before this present creation, and was the center point determining the trajectory of "the diameter of the ages." But "the Word," or this plan, was not fully *revealed* to human understanding until it "became flesh" as the *living* Word, Jesus Christ, God's perfect and ultimate communication to mankind. Thus, the *purpose* of God became the *person* of Jesus, whom the Bible calls "the Christ," the Son of God, the "image" of the invisible God. As E. W. Bullinger notes on John 1:1 in the Companion Bible: "As the spoken word reveals the invisible thought, so the Living Word reveals the invisible God."[19] Paul communicates essentially this same truth, also in connection with the original creation:

17. *The Racovian Catechism* (reprinted by Spirit & Truth Fellowship International®, Martinsville, IN, 46151, 1994). *The Racovian Catechism* was first published in Polish in 1605, translated into Latin in 1609, into English in 1818.

18. Although many theologians and even some translators treat the "word" of John 1:1 as if it were "the pre-incarnate Christ" that is an unwarranted assumption. Note the following from the Ryrie Study Bible:

> Word (Gk., *logos*). *Logos* means "word, thought, concept and the expressions thereof." In the Old Testament, the concept conveyed activity and revelation, and the word or wisdom of God is often personified (Ps. 33:6; Prov. 8). In the Targums (Aramaic paraphrases of the Old Testament), it was a designation of God. To the Greek mind, it expressed the ideas of reason and creative control. Revelation is the keynote idea in the *logos* concept. Here it is applied to Jesus, who is all that God is and the expression of Him (John 1:1 and 14). Note on John 1:1 in *Ryrie Study Bible Expanded Edition* (Moody Press, Chicago, 1995 update).

19. Bullinger, *op. cit.,* Companion Bible, p. 1512.

2 Corinthians 4:6
For God, who said, "Let light shine out of darkness," made his light shine in our hearts to give us the light of the knowledge of the glory of God in the face of Christ.

In the ninth verse of the prologue of John, Jesus Christ is referred to as "The true light that gives light to every man…," reinforcing the idea that Christ is the true light that has shined in the spiritual darkness that has engulfed mankind.

So, the careful reader sees the beauty and depth of the phrase "in the beginning" in John 1:1. We believe the richness of the text is revealed when one sees that it hearkens back to Genesis and reminds us that God has been expressing Himself via His plan, purpose, wisdom and power all through the Old Testament. Yet it also includes the concept of the new creation and the "beginning" of the age when Christ will come and eventually bring everything back into an orderly subjection to God. This proleptic view of the beginning fits with the proleptic view of Christ that occurs throughout the entire gospel of John, which we studied extensively in the last chapter. We believe that it misses the point to say that the word "beginning" refers only to the beginning of time, and not at all to the beginning of the new creation, or vice versa. We think that God worded it the way He did in order to include both perspectives.

"…and the Word was with [*pros*] God"

We will now continue our explanation of the prologue of John, examining the phrase, "…and the Word was with [*pros*] God…." When *pros* occurs in the accusative case, as it does in this phrase, one of its meanings is "with," as most translations have. In order for the Word to be "with" God, each must be a distinct entity. Nothing can be "with" itself. Though there are many ways that the Word could have been "with" God, we feel that, in his Greek-English Lexicon, E. W. Bullinger gives a definition of *pros* that fits very well in the context of John 1:1 and our understanding of the intimate relationship that exists between the logos (Word) and God.

"Implying intimate and closest inter-communion, together with distinct independence."[20]

In John 1:1 we see both the independence of, and intimacy between, the Word and God. Thus, John 1:1 marvelously encapsulates a precise thumbnail description of the essence of the gospel of John, which revolves around the themes of the intimate yet independent and subordinate relationship of the Son to the Father. It is evident that one thing cannot be "with" another thing and be identical to it at the same time. Even Trinitarian scholars recognize this:

John always perceives a distinction between the divinity of the pre-existent Son and that of the Father. If he states "the Word is God," he still speaks of the Word being directed toward God (*pros ton theon*).[21]

---

20. Bullinger, *op. cit., Lexicon*, p. 888.

21. Brown, *op. cit., Community*, p. 53. In another passage, Brown responds to A. C. Sundberg, who wrote two articles for *Biblical Research Journal*, "*Isos To Theo*: Christology in John 5:17–30" (15, 1970, p. 19–31) and "*Christology in the Fourth Gospel*" (21, 1976, pp. 29–37). Brown admits that later theological speculations about the equality of the Son with the Father go far beyond what can be substantiated by the gospel of John:

A classic contrast is between John 10:30 (NRSV), "The Father and I are one," and 14:28 (NRSV), "…the Father is greater than I" [which] shows that the Christ of John still stands at quite a distance from the Christology of Nicaea where the Father is not greater than the Son.

Logically, nothing can be both "identical to" and "with" anything else. Actually, the phrase "… the Word was with God…" is contrary to Trinitarian doctrine. Trinitarians teach that the "Word" in this verse is the pre-existent Christ. Yet they teach that Christ is God. Christ cannot be "with" God and be God at the same time. In order to support Trinitarian doctrine, the verse would have to say, "the Word was with the *Father*." Of course, Trinitarians assert that "God" means "Father" here, but why would God author the very first verse of the gospel in such a way that, when read in a plain and straight forward manner, contradicts the Trinity, if in fact He were trying to present the Trinity as a truth? We are on much more solid ground when we believe that God knew what He was doing and plainly wrote that the Word is different from God so that we would know and understand that truth. Thus, the sense in which "the Word" *was* "God" is limited by this statement that it was also "*with* God," and points to a meaning closer to "represents," "manifests," or "reveals." Hence, the Word was "divine" because it represented and manifested God. In the same way, Jesus, "the Word in the flesh," represented and manifested God, and, in that limited way, was "divine."

Although many use the phrase ("…the Word was with God…") to attempt to establish the doctrine of the pre-existence of Christ, this idea is based upon a supposed identity between "the Word" and Jesus Christ. The argument goes: "The Word was with God in the beginning, and Jesus was the Word, therefore Jesus was there in the beginning." The assumption that "the Word" is the man, Jesus, is reflected in the fact that Bible translators assign the masculine gender to the pronouns referring to Word. The pronouns related to *logos* often get translated "he" when in fact the Greek word *logos*, though masculine in gender, is intrinsically neither male nor female.[22] In 1526, the pronoun associated with *logos* was translated "it" and not "he" by William Tyndale, who provided the translation that formed the basis for the KJV. Although approximately 90 percent of Tyndale's work was preserved in the KJV, his use of the neuter for *logos* was changed to "he." The Wycliffe translation of 1380, the Cranmer Bible of 1539 and the Geneva Bible of 1557 also translated the pronoun associated with *logos* as "it."

But even if the pronoun associated with *logos* could legitimately be translated "he," this could be readily explained by the use of *personification*, and does not necessitate a literal person called "the *logos*." As we have already seen, the use of *personification* of *logos* puts the *logos* concept squarely in what is called the wisdom literature of Judaism, wherein personification of concepts is a common figure. Dunn comments on the use of *personification* in the prologue of John, wherein the usage of *logos* moves from "impersonal personification to actual person," namely Jesus:

> We are dealing with personifications rather than persons, personified actions of God rather than an individual divine being as such. The point is obscured by the fact that we have to

22. The Greek and Hebrew languages assign genders to nouns, just as do Spanish, French, German and many other languages. Thus, every noun in Greek and Hebrew is assigned a gender. In Greek, there are masculine, feminine and neuter nouns, while in Hebrew there are only masculine and feminine. The origin of the gender is ancient, and does not seem to follow a specific pattern. In Hebrew, for example, altar (*mizbeach*) is masculine, while the *menorah* is feminine. An arrow (*chets*) and an ax (*qardom*) are masculine, while a sword (*chereb*) is feminine. A beetle (*chargol*) is masculine, while a bee (*deborah*) is feminine. In Greek, for example, *logos* is masculine, while *rhema* and *euanggelion* (gospel, good news) are neuter and *biblos* (book, scroll; from which we get "Bible") and *didache* (doctrine or teaching) are feminine. "Spirit" (*pneuma*) is neuter, while "comforter" (*parakletos*) is masculine. A chain (*halusis*) is feminine, a rope (*schoinion*) is neuter, while a leather strap (*imas*) and a nail (*helos*) are masculine. When these words are translated into English, we use "it" because they are *things*. If someone asks, "Where is the chain," we say "It is in the garage," not "She is in the garage." Thus, the point should be made that just because *logos* is masculine does not mean that the English pronoun "he" is the proper pronoun to use when associated with it. We assert that "it" is the proper pronoun to use in verses like John 1:2 and 3, etc.

translate the masculine *logos* "he" throughout the poem. But if we translated *logos* as "God's utterance" [or "it"] instead, it would become clearer that the poem did not necessarily intend the *logos* in v. 1–13 to be thought of as a personal divine being."[23]

The "Word" was *with* God in the same sense that "wisdom" was with God. Proverbs 8:29b and 30a says, "…when he [God] marked out the foundations of the earth, Then I [wisdom] was the craftsman at his side…." No one we know of believes that there was a being called "Wisdom" who helped God make the heavens and the earth. Everyone knows that wisdom is personified to make the record interesting and easy to understand. So too, in John 1:1 when Scripture says that the *logos* was "with God," it is a *personification*. God had His plan and power, and "…when the time had fully come…" (Gal. 4:4), Jesus was conceived in the womb of Mary. This means that the person called "Jesus" did not yet exist, as is the case with all human persons, until he was conceived in his mother's womb. Prior to his conception, his existence was not personal, but *prophetic*, as foretold in the Old Testament Scriptures (the "Word"). Before Jesus' conception in the womb of Mary, the *logos* was to Jesus what promise is to fulfillment. When "the *logos* became flesh," the promise was fulfilled in the form of a person. While this understanding will be objectionable, perhaps anathema, to Trinitarian believers, it must be admitted that it is not a denial of Jesus' divine Sonship or Messiahship but, rather, a compelling alternative interpretation of relevant scriptural texts.

All the texts in which Jesus spoke of his heavenly existence with the Father before his coming (which, interestingly, are all found in John's gospel) are best understood in a prophetic light.[24] In other words, Jesus did not speak from *experience* about his "pre-existence" with the Father, but, rather, he spoke out of his faith in the *logos*, which he understood from the testimony of the prophets of Israel. Jesus was so sure of the future fulfillment of God's purpose and promises regarding his resurrection from the dead and his exaltation to God's right hand that he spoke of them as having already taken place. By speaking of God's purpose and promises as if they had already been fulfilled (i.e., proleptically), and then carrying them out by obedience to God's Word, Jesus distinguished himself as "…the author and perfecter of our faith…" (Heb. 12:2), the one whose faith is the model for all believers to follow.

The *logos*, then, as it relates to Jesus Christ, has existed in three stages: first as God's *purpose* "in the beginning," then as God's *promises* to mankind, and finally as God's *person*, Jesus the Messiah, the Son of God.

"…and the Word was God," i.e., "If you've seen me, you've seen the Father"

The words "…and the Word was God…" might seem to supply the premises for a logical syllogism with a necessary conclusion:

- Jesus is the Word [*logos*].
- The Word was God.
- Therefore, Jesus is God.

---

23. Dunn, *op. cit., Christology,* pp. 243, 256 and 259.
24. See Appendix A (John 3:13).

According to standard Christian teaching, this is apparently an open-and-shut case. However, most scholars recognize that the issue is not as cut-and-dried as most Christians think. This is reflected in the various ways the verse is translated. The New English Bible superbly translates the verse as, "…and what God was, the Word was." We also believe that James Moffatt has captured the sense better than most translations when he renders the phrase, "the Logos was divine." The whole of Scripture, the semantic range of the Greek word for "God," *theos*, and the absence of the definite article before *theos* must each be considered. We will quote two scholars who, after analyzing the precision of the Greek words employed in John 1:1, recognize the limitations of concluding from John's prologue that the terms "Jesus" and "God" are in any way identical, equivalent, synonymous or interchangeable:

> Because *logos* has the article [*ho*] preceding it, it is marked out as the subject. The fact that *theos* is the first word after the conjunction *kai* ("and") shows that the main emphasis of the clause lies on it. Had the article preceded *theos* as well as *logos*, the meaning would have been that the Word was completely identical with God, which is impossible if the Word was also "with God." What is meant is that the Word shared the nature and being of God, or, to use a piece of modern jargon, was an extension of the personality of God. The NEB paraphrase, "what God was, the Word was," brings out the meaning of the clause as successfully as a paraphrase can. John intends that the whole of his gospel shall be read in the light of this verse. The deeds and words of Jesus are the deeds and words of God [i.e., "If you have seen me, you have seen the Father"]; if this be not true, the book [i.e., *the* gospel of John] is blasphemous.[25]

> What it does say is defined as succinctly and accurately as it can be in the opening verse of St. John's Gospel. But we have to be equally careful about the translation. The Greek runs: *kai theos en ho logos*. The so-called *Authorized Version* has: "And the Word was God." This would indeed suggest the view that "Jesus" and "God" were identical and interchangeable. But in Greek this would most naturally be represented by "God" with the article, not *theos* but *ho theos*. But, equally, St. John is not saying that Jesus is a "divine" man, in the sense with which the ancient world was familiar [the product of God and man] or in the sense in which the Liberals spoke of him [as a great man, teacher, prophet, etc.]. That would be *theios*. **The Greek expression steers carefully between the two**. It is impossible to represent it in a single English word, but the New English Bible, I believe, gets the sense pretty exactly with its rendering, "**And what God was, the Word was.**"

> In other words, if one looked at Jesus, one saw God—for "…He who has seen Me has seen the Father… (John 14:9 - NASB)." He was the complete expression, the Word, of God. Through him, as through no one else, God spoke and God acted: when one met him, one was met—and saved and judged—by God. And it was to this conviction that the Apostles bore their witness. In this man—in his life, death and resurrection—they had experienced God at work; and in the language of their day they confessed, like the centurion at the Cross, "…Truly this man was the Son of God" (Mark 15:39 - NASB). Here was more than just a man: here was a window into God at work. For "…God was in Christ reconciling the world to Himself…" (2 Cor. 5:19 - NASB).[26]

25. Bruce, *op. cit., Gospel of John,* p. 313. By quoting Bruce, we do not mean to imply that he agrees with our conclusion that Jesus is not God. What he wrote shows that John 1:1 does not have to be understood in a Trinitarian frame of mind.
26. Robinson, *op. cit., Honest to God,* pp. 70 and 71.

Dunn, another modern scholar, also sees the prologue and its use of *logos* as communicating the same truth—that the Word is the image of God or that which can be known of Him. He quotes Philo, a first-century Alexandrian Jew familiar with the sense of *logos* as debated and used in apostolic times:

> To use Philo's favorite sun-and-light symbolism, the *logos* is to God as the corona is to the sun, the sun's halo which man can look upon when he cannot look directly on the sun itself. That is not to say that the *logos* is God as such, any more than the corona is the sun as such, but the *logos* is that alone which may be seen of God.
>
> God is unknowable by man, except in a small degree by the creation, but the *logos* expresses God's ideas to man. There is no idea of personality attached to the *logos*. The *logos* seems to be nothing more for Philo than God himself in his approach to man, God himself insofar as he may be known by man.[27]

Thus, even Trinitarian scholars acknowledge that to say "the Word was God" is not synonymous with saying "Jesus is God." Indeed, the phrase, "…what God was, the Word was" communicates in a nutshell what is about to be developed in the body of the gospel of John—that Jesus perfectly represents and reflects the Father's glory. The phrase, like the gospel itself, portrays him in his post-resurrection glorification in which he shines as the "image of God" (See Chapter 2).

C. H. Dodd is another scholar who sees in the *logos* the meeting of the divine, God's communication of Himself, with the human, the man in whom God most clearly revealed Himself. The *logos* is the "final concentration of the whole creative and revealing thought of God" in "an individual who is what humanity was designed to be in the divine purpose."[28] In other words, Jesus Christ, the living Word of God, is what Man was intended to be, the perfect representative of God.

"through [*dia*] him all things were made"

The pronoun "him" in John 1:3 ("through him all things were made"), can legitimately be translated as "it." It does not have to be translated as "him," and it does not have to refer to a "person" in any way. A primary reason why people get the idea that "the Word" is a person is that the pronoun "he" is used with it. The Greek text does, of course, have the masculine pronoun, because as we have already pointed out, the Greek language assigns a gender to all nouns, and the gender of the pronoun must agree with the gender of the noun. Because the noun controlling the pronouns in verse three is *logos*, the pronouns in Greek are all masculine, but they would only be translated into English as "he" if the noun were speaking of *a person*, not *a thing*. If the *logos* is not a literal person, then the pronoun should be translated as "it."

Once we clearly understand that the gender of a pronoun is determined by the gender of the noun, we can see why one cannot build a doctrine on the gender of a noun and its agreeing pronoun. No student of the Bible should take the position that "the Word" is somehow a masculine person based on its pronoun any more than he would take the position that a *book* was a feminine person or a *desk* was a masculine person because that is the gender assigned to those nouns in the French language. Indeed, if one tried to build a theology based on the gender of the noun in the language, great confusion would result. In Hebrew, "spirit" is feminine and must have feminine pronouns, while in Greek, "spirit" is neuter and takes neuter pronouns. Thus, a person trying to build a theology

---

27. Dunn., *op. cit., Christology*, pp. 226 and 227.
28. C. H. Dodd, *The Interpretation of the Fourth Gospel*, (Cambridge, 1953), p. 282.

on the basis of the gender of the noun and pronoun would find himself in an interesting situation trying to explain how it could be that "the spirit" of God somehow changed genders when the New Testament was written.

Because the translators of the Bible have almost always been Trinitarians, and because "the Word" has almost always been associated with Christ, the pronouns referring to the *logos* in verse three have almost always been translated as "him." However, because the *logos* is the plan, purpose, wisdom and power of God, then the Greek pronoun should be translated into English as "it." To demand that "the Word" is a masculine person and therefore a third part of a three-part Godhead because the pronouns used when referring to it are masculine is poor scholarship.

Viewed in light of the above translation, the opening of the gospel of John reveals wonderful truth, and is also a powerful polemic against the primary heresies of the day. We paraphrase:

> In the beginning there was God, who had a plan, purpose, wisdom and power (i.e., the *logos*) which was, by its very nature and origin, divine. It was through and on account of this reason, plan, purpose and power that everything was made. Nothing was made outside its scope. Later, this plan became flesh in the person of Jesus Christ and tabernacled among us.

Understanding the opening of John this way fits with the whole of Scripture. Just as the word "beginning" in John 1:1 is a *double entendre* referring to both the beginning before history and the beginning of the new creation, John 1:3 continues that mode. John 1:3 also contains overtones of Christ's control over the new creation. God never created anything outside the confines of His wisdom, plan and power, so it surely is true that "…without it (the *logos*) nothing was made that has been made." However, it is also true that John 1:3 points toward the creation of the new order by Jesus Christ. Colossians refers to this when it says, "…all things were created by him and for him" (Col. 1:16).[29] Also, Ephesians 2:15 says that Christ created a "new man" out of Jew and Gentile.

The reader will recall that in Chapter 3 we saw that the Greek preposition *dia* is distinctly associated with Jesus Christ, and particularly his relationship to God's creation—indicating that he is the one *through* whom (better understood as *on whose behalf*) God acted. Thus, he is spoken of as the agent or the means or *the purpose of the ages* and of creation itself. That this word *dia* occurs in the prologue of John used in this sense ties this passage to the other passages in the New Testament that describe *the post-resurrection relationship between Christ and God*, particularly 1 Corinthians 8:6 and Hebrews 1:2 and 3. Jesus Christ is once again being portrayed as "the purpose of the ages," the one *through whom* we have life.

To assume that Christ is the Creator of the Genesis 1 creation is to introduce confusion into what is a clear New Testament theme: God is the Creator of the heavens and the earth (as Scripture states):

Ephesians 3:9
and to make plain to everyone the administration of this mystery, which for ages past was kept hidden in **God, who created all things.**[30]

---

29. See Appendix A (Col. 1:15–20).

30. The NIV correctly omits the words "by Jesus Christ" after the words [God] who created all things. These words were added to the text in an apparent attempt by an orthodox scribe to artificially insert Christ into the actual act of Creation. Christ was not in on the action, but he was the reason for it.

"In him was life, and that life was the light of men"

John 1:4 continues the powerful introduction to the gospel of John, and also continues with phrases that refer to both God and the original creation, and Christ and the new creation. There is no question that in God was life for mankind. The Father is life, and defined life. Christ said, "…the Father has life in himself…" (John 5:26). This is so well known that there is no need to belabor the point. Once Christ was resurrected, however, God gave Christ the job of giving life. Christ even said, "…he has granted the Son to have life in himself" (John 5:26), and because of that, one day the dead will hear Christ's voice and live (John 5:25).

Anyone who has a personal relationship with the Lord Jesus Christ will testify that there is more than just eternal life in the Son, and the same was true for the believers of the Old Testament. In both ancient times and in the new creation since the Age of Grace started, a relationship with God, or with God and Christ meant life and vitality on a day-by-day basis. Psalm 36:9 mentions both life and light, just as John 1:4 does:

Psalm 36:9
For with you [God] is the fountain of life; in your light we see light.

Today, in the Age of Grace, Christ is the one who gives life and is our life, even as Colossians says: "When Christ, who is your life, appears, then you also will appear with him in glory" (Col. 3:4).

"The light shines in the darkness, and the darkness did not overcome it"

John 1:5 (NRSV) can clearly be seen to make a reference to both the original creation and the new creation that is headed up by Jesus Christ. There is no question that when one reads, and the "…light shines in the darkness…," that his mind is drawn back to the primal darkness of Genesis 1 and the time that God spoke the words, "Let there be light!" Furthermore, the light of God shown throughout the Old Testament. It is well known that the word "light" refers not just to physical light, but to knowledge and truth as well. And, all through the Old Testament, try as he might to obscure, blot out or discolor the light, the Serpent did not succeed. The darkness just did not overcome the light.

John 1:5 not only echoes the language of Genesis 1 but can refer to the new creation as well. It is well known that Christ is referred to as the light. For example, when Christ preached in the area of the Galilee, Matthew records:

Matthew 4:16
the people living in darkness have seen a great **light**; on those living in the land of the shadow of death a **light** has dawned.

John records Jesus saying, "…I am the light of the world…" (John 8:12). Thus, anyone who studies the life of Christ and the New Testament can see clearly that John 1:5 can also refer to Jesus Christ and the light that he was, and that shown forth from him. F. F. Bruce comments on John 1:5:

In the first creation, "…darkness *was* upon the face of the deep…" (Gen. 1:2 - KJV) until God called light into being, so the new creation (in which the Word is God's agent as effectively as in the earlier one) involves the banishing of spiritual darkness by the light which shines in the Word. Apart from the light (as is emphasized repeatedly in the body of the Gospel) the world of mankind is shrouded in darkness…Light and darkness are to be understood ethically rather than metaphysically; "light" is a synonym of goodness and truth, while "darkness" is a synonym of evil and falsehood.[31]

This relationship between light and darkness in an ethical context is clearly seen elsewhere in the New Testament, notably in the following passage from Paul's epistle to the Ephesians. The light of Christ shines in the hearts of believers and shows the way to righteous conduct:

Ephesians 5:8–15
(8) For you were once **darkness**, but now you are **light** in the Lord. Live as children of **light**
(9) (for the fruit of the **light** consists in all goodness, righteousness and truth)
(10) and find out what pleases the Lord.
(11) Have nothing to do with the fruitless deeds of **darkness**, but rather expose them.
(12) For it is shameful even to mention what the disobedient do in secret.
(13) But everything exposed by the **light** becomes visible,
(14) for it is **light** that makes everything visible. This is why it is said: "Wake up, O sleeper, rise from the dead, and Christ will **shine** on you."
(15) Be very careful, then, how you live—not as unwise, but as wise,

Christ is the means by which God is making His light shine and establishing a new and righteous creation, because the one spoken of in Genesis 1 has been stained by sin. The process will be completed only when Christ has finished his work of subduing all God's enemies, as described in 1 Corinthians 15:24–28. So again in John 1:5 we see the intricate pattern that God is weaving, using words and phrases that powerfully remind us of His great work at the beginning of time and in the Old Testament, but also pointing at the great work of His Son and the time of the new creation.

"The Word became flesh and dwelt among us, full of grace and truth"

Of all the gospel writers, John is most concerned with emphasizing that Jesus came in the flesh. This is an important theme in the Johannine epistles as well (1 John 4:2; 2 John 7). This will be explained later in this chapter in the discussion of John's relationship to the Gnostics, who took a dim view of "flesh."

It is at this point in the prologue, in John 1:14, that "the Word of God" becomes associated with a particular historical person, Jesus of Nazareth. Up until this verse, the prologue has been dealing with impersonal personification of a concept called the *logos*, but this verse is the transition from personification to actual person.[32] Dunn recognizes that to this point in the prologue there is nothing that would have particularly arrested the attention of a Hellenistic Jew.[33]

---

31. Bruce, *op. cit., Gospel of John*, p. 34.
32. Robinson, *op. cit., Priority*, pp. 379 and 380.
33. Dunn, *op. cit., Christology*, p. 241. Dunn writes (emphasis his): "…we must recognize that *prior to v. 14 nothing has been said which would be strange to a Hellenistic Jew* familiar with the Wisdom tradition or the sort of mystical philosophizing that we find in Philo."

Again we will quote J. A. T. Robinson, who captures our sentiments about this verse:

The Word, which was *theos*, God in His self-revelation and expression, *sarx egeneto* [became flesh], was embodied totally in and as a human being, became a person, was personalized, not just personified. **But that the logos came into existence or expression as a person does not mean that it was a person before.** In terms of the later distinction, it was not that the *logos* was hypostatic [i.e., a person] and then assumed an impersonal human nature, but that the *logos* was anhypostatic until the Word of God finally came to self-expression, not merely in nature and in a people but in an individual historical person, and thus *became* hypostatic… Jesus is genuinely and utterly a man who so competely incarnates [in a figurative sense] God that the one is the human face of the other.[34]

Another scholar weighs in on this point:

For John, Jesus is really man, but in a unique, all surpassing relationship with God. Anyone who knows him knows the Father.[35]

Concerning the personality of the *logos*, another scholar, T. W. Manson, writes:

I very much doubt whether he [John] thought of the *logos* as a personality. The only personality on the scene is "Jesus the son of Joseph from Nazareth." That personality embodies the *logos* so completely that Jesus becomes a complete revelation of God. But in what sense are we using the word "embodies"? I think in the old prophetic sense, but with the limitations that were attached to the prophets removed. The word that Isaiah speaks is the word of the Lord, but it is also Isaiah's—it has become part of him. Not every word of Isaiah is a word of the Lord. For John, every word of Jesus is a word of the Lord.[36]

To us, it makes perfect sense that Jesus so internalized the standard of "It is written" that he was its very embodiment. This speaks highly of his love for the Word of God and his dependence upon it. In everything he said and did, he was looking to obey, properly explain or fulfill the Word of God, his Father. It was in this sense that it could be said of him that he was "the *logos* made flesh," not that he was such *by his mere birth*. He had to *learn* to obey God and His Word (Heb. 5:8), which means that he first had to learn it inside and out.

The *logos* was not "made flesh" through a metaphysical or mystical process by which a pre-existent spirit being transmigrated his eternal consciousness into a temporal human zygote at the moment of conception. The *logos* was "made flesh" through a process that began when God fulfilled His Word to His people by *creating* the long awaited Seed of Promise, the seed of the woman, the one who would be just like his Dad, the "chip off the old Rock." This man, by internalizing the standard of the Word of God that was to guide his life, walked in perfect obedience "in the flesh."

In Chapter 18, we will develop in greater detail the historical development of the doctrine of the incarnation and its mythological overtones.

---

34. Robinson, *op. cit., Priority*, pp. 380 and 381.
35. E. Schillebeeckx, *Christ: the Christian Experience in the Modern World* (E. T., London, 1980), p. 431.
36. T. W. Manson, *On Paul and John*, ed. M. Black (SBT 38, London and Naperville, 1963), p. 156.

"The glory of the only begotten one"

This term "only begotten" in the phrase "only begotten Son" in John 1:18 (KJV) is traditionally understood to refer to his virgin birth, when he was first "begotten."[37] However, it is widely recognized in scholarly circles that "only begotten" is a mistranslation of the Greek word *monogenes*.[38] "Unique" is a profoundly appropriate term to characterize Jesus Christ, the Son of God. His uniqueness begins with the voluminous prophetic utterances about his coming. No other human being has ever been so specifically described and anticipated. Then his virgin birth is indeed another aspect of his uniqueness. Adam was created directly by God, not through the agency of a woman. Others received a child by God's promise, but through the normal process of sexual intercourse. No other human being, even Adam, was ever directly conceived by God Himself, yet carried in a woman's body.

No man ever walked the earth with such commanding presence and authority, nor did as many miracles. No man walked in such moral perfection nor was treated so unjustly. No man showed so much compassion for his fellow man, nor risked his own life and reputation more for the sake of helping those who were downcast and troubled. No man ever represented God so perfectly, and yet died in a manner that seemed to say that he had been cursed of God. Men have been miraculously raised from the dead, but only one has died and been raised with an entirely new and immortal body. And, finally, no man has ever sat where he sits, presiding over the angels at the right hand of God Himself.

Jesus Christ was the only begotten Son of God, and, as we have already seen, that sonship was clearly declared when he was "born" from the dead. That *monogenes* also reflects the post-resurrection glory of Jesus Christ is evident from the qualifying phrase of John 1:18—"…who is at the Father's side…." In other words, Jesus is pictured as being at the Father's side, providing a capstone to the prologue and sealing it with the stamp of his exalted glory. This leads us to the conclusion that from the very first verse the prologue of John has overtones of Christ's present state of being at the right hand of God. Thus, the prologue of John fits with the remainder of the New Testament, including those passages that describe Christ in his post-resurrection glory.

To show the relationship of the language of John, and especially the prologue, to other passages in the New Testament that define the post-resurrection identity of Jesus Christ, we have created a table on the following page. In it we have attempted to correlate the appropriate phrases that address a similar idea. Though it may be incomplete, the general affinity of the themes of these passages can be easily seen, and helps us to harmonize some of the language which, taken by itself, might lead to the erroneous conclusion that Jesus Christ is God, an eternal being, "essential deity," etc., as Trinitarians propose.

---

37. Ehrman argues against the translation of 1:18 as *monogenes theos*, "only begotten God," although it is found in the vast majority of Alexandrian texts:

> Outside of the New Testament, the term simply means "one of a kind" or "unique" and does so with reference to any range of animate or inanimate objects…There seems little reason any longer to dispute the reading found in virtually every witness outside the Alexandrian tradition. The prologue ends with the statement that "the unique Son who is in the bosom of the Father, that one has made him known" (Ehrman, *op. cit., Orthodox Corruption*, p. 81).

38. Robinson explains the origin of the translation:

> Under the influence of the Arian controversy, Jerome [the medieval scholar responsible for the Latin translation of the Bible that became the standard text of Roman Catholicism] translated *monogenes* regarding Jesus as *unigenitus* (John 1:14 and 18, 3:16 and 18; 1 John 4:9; of all others, except Isaac in Heb. 11:17 - all KJV). He preserves the *unicus* of the old Latin [which Luke perpetuated in the AV as "only begotten" yet the word does not derive from *gennao* [birth], but *genos* [genus, kind]; it means "one of a kind." Robinson, *op. cit., Priority*, p. 397, n.156.

John 1:1	Hebrews 1:3	1 Corinthians 8:6	Ephesians 1:17ff	Colosians 1:12ff
From (*para*) the Father, the one true God (17:3)	God	There is one God—out of (*ek*) whom are all things and we unto (*eis*) Him (God)	I keep asking the God of our Lord Jesus Christ (1:17)	Giving thanks unto the Father (v. 12); it pleased the Father (v. 19)
To those who believed in his name he gave the right to become children of God	God appointed him heir of all things, and we are joint heirs with him (Rom. 8:17)		The riches of his glorious inheritance in the saints	Made us adequate to share in the inheritance, brought us into the kingdom of His Son
The Word was God ("...what God was, the Word was" NEB)	The radiance of God's glory; the exact representation of his being	One Lord		The image of the invisible God
The unique Son (*monogenes*)	This day have I begotten (*gennao*) thee (by resurrection, verse 5 - KJV)			The firstborn of the (new) creation; the firstborn from the dead
	God made the ages through (*dia* w/gen) him	We through (*dia* w/gen) him and unto (*eis*) whom are all things		By (*en* w/dative) him all things were created by (*dia*) him and for (*eis*=unto) him
He who comes after me has surpassed me because he was before me	He became so much superior to the angels		Seated him at his own right hand in the heavenly realms far above all	He is before all things; in all things he has preeminence
			Far above all rule (*arches*) authority (*exousia*) power (*dunameos*) dominion (*kurotetos*)	Rulers (*archai*) authority (*exousias*) thrones (*thronoi*) dominions (*kuriotetes*)
	Sustaining all things by his powerful word		He fills everything in every way	In him all things hold together
The Word was with (*pros*) God	Thy throne, O God, is for ever [KJV]			In him all fullness dwells

Prolepsis and *Logos*

If Jesus is not identical to the *logos*, what exactly is the relationship between them? The relationship of Jesus to the *logos* of God can best be described as intimate and prophetic, two important characteristics of the entire gospel of John. Jesus was conceived in the mind of God "in the beginning," and was in view when God created the present heaven and earth.[39] God knew His plan, and throughout the Old Testament communicated it through a body of prophetic language that pointed toward Christ's coming. Jesus refers to this plan in his prayer on the eve of his death:

> **John 17:24**
> "Father, I want those you have given me to be with me where I am, and to see my glory, the glory you have given me because you loved me before [*pro*] the creation of the world.

Peter communicates this same truth in his first epistle:

> **1 Peter 1:20 (NASB)**
> For He was foreknown before [*pro*] the foundation of the world, but has appeared in these last times for the sake of you

John and the Gnostics (Not a First-Century Rock Band)

We will be handling the subject of Gnosticism in greater depth in Chapter 16 on the beginnings of heresy, but the Gnostics deserve some mention with respect to the prologue of the gospel of John. As we have noted, the Gnostics seized upon the gospel of John and borrowed much of its language and many of its themes for their diverse speculations.[40] This fact led many Christians of the time to

---

39. Scripture delineates between the Creation and the foundation of the creation. This is reflected in the usage of two different Greek prepositions used in relationship to the words *katabole*, meaning foundation, and *kosmos*, meaning "world." Some things were prepared in secret from (*apo*) the foundation of the world, and some things before (*pro*) the foundation of the world. This is a matter for further study, but it is interesting that Ephesians 1:4 says that we in the Church were chosen in Christ *before* the foundation of the world. The Church was a part of "...the unsearchable riches of Christ" (Eph. 3:8), which was a part of "the secret" which "for ages past was kept hidden in God..." (v. 9). Arndt and Gingrich, *op. cit., Lexicon*, p. 409.

40. F. F. Bruce comments on the early Gnostic use of the Gospel of John:

In the earlier part of the second century, the Fourth Gospel was recognized and quoted by Gnostic writers at least as much as by those whose teaching came to be acknowledged as more in line with the apostolic tradition. There are affinities to its thought and language in the letters of Ignatius, bishop of Antioch (ca. A.D. 110) and in the collection of hymns called the Odes of Solomon (from about the same period, which have a Gnostic flavor... Hippolytus states that the Gnostic Basilides (ca. A.D. 130) quoted John 1:9 (about the true light coming into the world) as a gloss on the creative word "Let there be light" (Gen. 1:3); if he is right, then that is the earliest known explicit quotation from the Gospel of John.

The Gospel of Truth (ca. A.D. 140), a Gnostic work coming either from Valentinus or from one of his disciples, has several echoes of [John], if not direct quotations...Later, he says, "those who were material were strangers and did not see his form or recognize him. For he came forth in flesh (*sarx*) of such a kind that nothing could block

doubt the credibility of the fourth gospel.[41] By the end of the second century, the gospel of John was accepted as one of the four canonical Gospels. Irenaeus was the first of the "Church fathers" to fully accept it and begin to comment on it.

But we ought to ask why the Gnostics gravitated to this gospel and if the gospel of John addresses Gnostic teaching in any way. John is clearly not a polemical book specifically addressing competing Gnostic teaching, but we believe that part of its inspired genius is the way it subtly corrects the incipient Gnosticism of its day.[42] Though primarily addressed to those who would believe, it was also written to *maintain* belief in the midst of a world full of idolatrous and anti-biblical philosophical systems. One scholar, representing the opinion of many, has noted, upon studying the relationship of John to Gnosticism: "At every crucial point the gospel is in tension with the Gnostic point of view, indeed repudiates it."[43] Thus, the gospel of John is like all Scripture—profitable for doctrine, reproof and correction (2 Tim. 3:16 - KJV). The essence of the teaching of the gospel of John that corrects Gnostic error is contained in the prologue. But before we discuss this, we will first point out earlier scriptural evidence of incipient Gnosticism and why it is very likely that there was a well-established Gnostic version of Christianity that had developed by the time John wrote his gospel.

Because Paul was fighting doctrinal battles with the proto-Gnostics at various points in his epistles, we know that the germs of Gnostic thought had already infected the Christian Church well before John wrote his gospel. In particular, the epistles to the Corinthians, Colossians, Timothy and Titus address teachings of Paul's time that would later develop into full-blown Gnostic religious systems. 2 Peter also addresses some issues. For instance, Paul spoke of the "super-apostles" in Corinth who thought that they had been initiated into a deeper awareness of wisdom and truth than he had, and were therefore more qualified to lead others into a truly spiritual life (2 Cor. 11:5). Paul responded that he was not a trained speaker like those men were, but had the marks of a true Apostle nevertheless (2 Cor. 11:6). Earlier, in 1 Corinthians 2:4, Paul had compared his approach with those who use "wise and persuasive words," as opposed to the demonstration of the spirit.

---

his progress" (31:1-7). Here "flesh" is conceded, but not in the sense of ordinary flesh: this flesh is not material or subject to physical limitations, but is rather as free from them as was Jesus' resurrection body, to which closed doors presented no barrier (John 20:19).

A disciple of Valentinus named Heraclean, who died ca. A.D. 180, is the first known commentator on the fourth Gospel (Bruce, *op. cit., Gospel of John*, pp. 7 and 8).

41. This illustrates the wisdom of avoiding the trap of "guilt by association." Because the Gnostics found John's gospel to their liking, this fact does not bear on the truth or falsehood of the gospel itself. In fact, this reasoning is irrational to the core, and is a variation of the logical fallacy called *Ad Hominem* (to the man). Jesus was accused by the Pharisees of being a fraud because they did not like the people who he associated with. The canonicity of John is determined by careful analysis and comparison with the entire Bible to see if it harmonizes. On this basis, John passes with flying colors. See Appendix K for more about logical fallacies.

42. Robinson observes that John and Paul have distinct approaches to combat Gnostic thinking. This is logical because of the developing Gnostic beliefs of the latter half of the first century. Paul employed many of their own terms and used them against the Gnostic teachers, especially in 1 Corinthians and Colossians. In these epistles, he emphasized that Christianity is the true *gnosis* and Christ is the true wisdom. Throughout his epistles he uses many of the same Greek words the Gnostics used: *pistis* (faith), *sophia* (wisdom), *gnosis* (knowledge), *pneumatikos* (spiritual matters), *musterion* (secret), *apokalupsis* (appearing), *pleroma* (fullness) and *eikon* (image). John's gospel, however is conspicuous in the way it avoids these terms, even *pistis* (faith). It uses *pleroma* only once, and in a different sense than the Gnostics used it. Robinson opines: "[John] seems to wish to give his opponents no handle by using the nouns [he used the verb forms instead]." One scholar suggests that in light of the conspicuous absence of all key Gnostic terms, John must have employed the term *logos* in the belief that it was not tainted by Gnostic overtones. Robinson, *op. cit., Priority*, pp. 105ff.

43. S. C. Neill, *The Interpretation of the New Testament, 1861-1961* (Oxford Press, NY, 1964), p. 210.

What would later become fully developed Gnosticism had its roots in vain speculation that was divorced from both the accuracy of Scripture and the reality of the power of God activated by faith. What would mark the Gnostic system of thought more than anything was their dualistic view of the world: spirit is entirely good and matter is entirely evil. "Spirituality," therefore, involved becoming as far removed from the shackles of matter as possible. Because they held the material world to be sinful and debased, they believed that the true God could have had nothing to do with its creation. Therefore they invented various intermediary deities called "demiurges," who were responsible for the creation of this world, but these were actually evil beings who were responsible for the corruption, degradation and deceit of the material world. Thus, for John to pose the *logos* as intermediary to both God and creation would have corrected this growing Gnostic error. It also provided a way of looking at the relationship between God and creation that appealed to others beside Gnostics who had a problem with too closely associating a transcendent God with an imperfect creation. Unfortunately, some people took that idea too far and tried to show that God did not really wish to come into contact with His creation:

> The *logos* theory was all too warmly welcomed by thinkers strongly imbued with Greek metaphysics, because the *logos* performed the cosmological function of relieving the Father, the supreme God, of the painful necessity of coming in close contact with the world.[44]

For the *logos*, an immaterial reality, to become "flesh," integrates and connects the "spiritual" realm with the "physical" realm in a way that corrects the error of the Gnostic teaching and the tendencies of Greek philosophy. It even explains the quasi-mystical connotation of the phrase "the *logos* became flesh," because John employs a poetic image to show the intimacy of God with His creation, and the extent of His involvement with it. We know from Scripture that He personally conceived Jesus in the womb of Mary. That act of creation marked the beginning of putting His Plan for the Man into action. When modern theologians and Bible teachers make the *logos* refer to a pre-incarnate Jesus, and then take the phrase "the *logos* became flesh" to mean that God became a man, they miss the precise point it is making. John is not propounding a mystical process by which a pre-existent spirit being became clothed in flesh. Rather, it is asserting that the prophetic plan and purpose of God has become a *true* man, "in the flesh," and that as the "purpose of the ages," even creation itself is organized around him.

In John 6:54, Jesus challenges and offends many of his followers by way of figuratively suggesting that they eat his flesh and drink his blood. This apparent exhortation to cannibalism would have horrified the proto-Gnostic readers who did not even want to believe that Jesus had "come in the flesh" at all, much less "eat" his flesh. These proto-Gnostics, the forerunners of the Docetists, were teaching that Jesus was not a true flesh-and-blood human being, because that would necessarily make him evil. They viewed him as essentially a spirit being who took on only the appearance of flesh. This teaching is also known as "Docetism."[45] John addresses the issue in a direct and stern way in his first epistle. Though he obviously spoke in a figurative manner, Jesus' words in John 6:54 are a subtle but devastating jab at Gnostic aversion to the flesh. This is a classic example of the way God employs figurative language to confound those who are taken in idolatry.

---

44. Hanson, *op. cit., Prophetic*, p. 369.

45. The early spread of Docetism among the believers explains the use of the phrase, "Jesus Christ has come in the flesh," in 1 John 4:2 and 3, to combat a false spirit that was introducing error among the believers. Those who were teaching that Jesus Christ was a heavenly messenger and not a true man were in some cases using John's gospel as a springboard for their theological speculations, even as others cloaked in orthodoxy have used it to propound Trinitarian dogma.

"Pre-existence" of human beings was also a feature of Gnostic thought.[46] So it is worth considering the possibility that since this doctrine cannot be supported elsewhere in the New Testament, there is a dual purpose served by employing such language in John. We know from elsewhere in the Gospels that Jesus spoke in *parables*, a particular kind of figure of speech, to reveal those who had a firm desire to understand spiritual things. Such language served to separate out the believers from the unbelievers. The language of the gospel of John has the same deliberate quality as the parables, where the casually interested person or one who has already been deceived by mythology and philosophy could easily become misled by a loose interpretation of the language on a literal level and go off into error.[47] It is highly likely that the language of pre-existence used in John relates to the Gnostic belief in pre-existence and contributed to their early adoption of the gospel.

At this point, it is useful to know some of the details of the Gnostic Redeemer myth, which involved a figure of light. Dart takes excerpts of Bultmann's version of the myth to show its main features:

> The Gnostic myth tells the fate of the soul, humanity's true inner self represented as "a spark of a heavenly figure of light, the original man." In primordial times, demonic powers of darkness conquer this figure of light, tearing it into shreds.
>
> The sparks of light are used by the demons to "create a world out of the chaos of darkness as a counterpart of the world of light, of which they were jealous." The demons closely guarded the elements of light enclosed in humans. "The demons endeavor to stupefy them and make

---

46. Brown, a Trinitarian who himself believes in the pre-existence of Christ, recognizes that "pre-existence" was a favorite subject of the Gnostics: "A common thesis in the Gnostic systems involves the pre-existence of human beings in the divine sphere before their life on earth. In the Fourth Gospel, only the Son of God pre-exists; others become children of God through faith, water, and Spirit during their earthly lives. According to Irenaeus, the Gnostic initiate connected his own status with a theology of pre-existence: 'I derive being from Him who is pre-existent and return to my own place from which I came forth'" (Brown, *op. cit., Community*, p. 151).

Regarding the concept of pre-existence in the Fourth Gospel, Robinson and Dunn have opposing points of view. We side with Robinson, but believe that Dunn's comments are important because they show the common language used by both John and the Gnostic literature. We understand the correspondence between John and the Gnostics because John was inspired to subtly address many of their erroneous beliefs, among which was pre-existence.

Dunn believes that John was "taken for something of a ride" by the "cultural evolution" of the late first century, and was influenced by the Gnostics, accounting for their early and enthusiastic acceptance of his gospel:

> It could be said that the Fourth Evangelist was as much a prisoner of his language as its creator…That is to say, perhaps we see in the Fourth Gospel what started as an elaboration of the *logos*-Son imagery applied to Jesus inevitably in the transition of conceptualizations coming to express a conception of Christ's personal pre-existence, which early Gnosticism found more congenial than early orthodoxy (Dunn, *op. cit., Christology*, p. 264).

Robinson rebuts Dunn, as follows:

> I agree that this happened, but I believe it happened *to* John rather than *in* John, and that he was "taken over" by the gnosticizers. In evidence, I would cite again the Johannine Epistles, which are saying in effect: "If that's what you think I meant, that I was teaching a docetic-type Christology—denying Christ come in the flesh and trying to have the Father without the Son—then this is the very opposite: it is Antichrist."

Robinson, *op. cit., Priority*, pp. 381 and 382.

47. This deliberate usage of opponent's language, mythology and metaphor is evident elsewhere in Scripture. In particular, Jesus employed the image of the afterlife adopted by the Pharisees in contradiction to the Hebrew Scriptures. In Luke 16:19ff (KJV), Jesus spoke a parable to the Pharisees revolving around their conception of "Abraham's bosom," a mythical and unbiblical "place" where the Jewish dead were said to dwell. Since Jesus nowhere else in the Gospels spoke of any other hope for the future except a bodily resurrection and his personal return in glory, it is clear that he did not intend to validate their error. His purpose was to teach that if someone does not believe Moses and the Prophets, even if one returned from the dead, they would still not believe. See the final chapter of our book, *op. cit., Is There Death After Life?*

them drunk, sending them to sleep and making them forget their heavenly home." Some people nevertheless become conscious of their heavenly origin and of the alien nature of the world. They yearn for deliverance.

The supreme deity takes pity on the imprisoned sparks of light, and sends down the heavenly figure of light, His Son, to redeem them. This Son arrays himself in the garment of the earthly body, lest the demons should recognize him. He invites his own to join him, awakens them from their sleep, reminds them of their heavenly home, and teaches them about the way to return.

The redeemer teaches them sacred and secret passwords, for the souls will have to pass the different spheres of the planets, watchposts of the demonic cosmic powers. "After accomplishing his work, he ascends and returns to heaven again to prepare a way for his own to follow him. This they will do when they die." The redeemer's work will be completed when he is able to reassemble all the sparks of light in heaven. That done, the world will come to an end, returning to its original chaos. "The darkness is left to itself, and that is the judgment."[48]

We believe that these Gnostic writings came later and used the prologue as the springboard for their speculations. But if they were contemporaneously written, then it is easy to see how John would be presenting the truth of which the Gnostic writings are the spiritual counterfeit. If somehow the Gnostic writings did come first, John would be addressing their errors in his gospel by employing similar imagery with an entirely different purpose and effect. In any event, we think it is important to recognize that one of the purposes of the gospel of John is to correct Gnostic teaching by setting forth Christian truth that is grounded in the historical reality of the resurrection and exaltation of Jesus, the Christ, the unique Son of God.

The prologue also pierces the elitist program of special enlightenment, subjective experience, spiritual initiation and esoteric knowledge, that was developed by the Gnostics. To *all* who receive him, Jesus Christ gives "...the right to become children of God" (1:12) without any initiation or special knowledge. In John, Jesus is clearly rejected by the Jews, who should have been the "initiated ones," and so God sent him to "the world" instead. He is the Savior for all mankind, not just the elite and enlightened ones.[49] We trust that as more is learned from Gnostic sources, we will gain even more insight into the precise usage of biblical terms and concepts employed by John. We will have more to say about Gnosticism in the historical section of this book, particularly Chapters 16–18.

Conclusion

And so we have seen how marvelously the prologue introduces the content of the gospel of John. It introduces God's plan, power and wisdom in bringing forth His only begotten Son. It introduces the intimate but distinct relationship between the Father and the Son. It introduces the conflict between light and darkness and how darkness is not able to win that conflict. And it introduces

---

48. John Dart, *The Jesus of Heresy and History* (Harper and Row, San Francisco, 1988), p. 40.

49. Phillip Lee wrote an interesting indictment of contemporary Christianity, identifying aspects of Gnostic thought that have re-emerged in the Church today. One is the emphasis on personal religious experiences (at conversion, in worship, etc.) more than doctrine and discipline. Another is subjective knowledge over a knowledge of nature and history. Another is a shift from man's need for deliverance from *sin*, which requires repentance and atonement, to his need for deliverance from *ignorance*, which requires special knowledge and enlightenment. The latter accounts for the name Gnostic, from the Greek word *gnosis*, meaning "knowledge" (*Against the Protestant Gnostics*, Oxford Press, N.Y., 1973), pp. 102–113.

the plan-of-God-become-flesh, whom we know as the Lord Jesus Christ. We have also seen how its language harmonizes with the other passages in the New Testament that describe his post-resurrection identity, as well as subtly introduces its readers to important truths that correct the doctrinal errors of the Gnostics. That it could accomplish all this and more in a few verses is powerful testimony to its divine inspiration. We find it ironic that the Gnostics embraced this gospel despite its repudiation of many of their doctrines, and we find it equally ironic that Trinitarians have embraced John as their favorite section of the New Testament when in fact it not only falls far short of validating "orthodox" Christian teaching, but in fact contradicts it.

Once understood, the gospel of John, including its prologue, presents a clear and compelling portrait of the One who came in fulfillment of the Old Testament prophecies, lived a life of profound submission to his Father (the one true God) and was highly exalted because of his perfect obedience. This post-resurrection glory of the risen Lord is so intimately associated with his earthly ministry that it provides wide literary license for a proleptic portrait of the unique One, the Lord Jesus Christ. Rather than being confused by the language of John, we must work (**as *work*men of the Word** —2 Tim. 2:15) to see its profound harmony with the rest of the New Testament. By so doing, we cannot help but stand in humble awe at the majesty of our God, the glory of our risen Lord and the wondrous perfection of the Word, the *logos*, that so eloquently and profoundly provides the words that give faith, hope, life and light to those who believe them.

PART FOUR

Jesus: Both Lord and Christ

10

The Book of Acts:
"A Man Accredited by God"

The book of Acts forms the biblical link between Jesus Christ coming to fulfill the Old Testament promises to Israel and his beginning the Church (the "Body of Christ") on the Day of Pentecost.[1] It presents a clear and unified witness of the Apostles' view of Jesus Christ, and what they taught as

---

1. Scripturally, the "Body of Christ" is figurative language that refers to the Church, that is, all Christians. Jesus Christ is called the "Head" of his Body, the Church. Thus, in the Church Epistles, Christians are referred to as being "in Christ." Since every human being is born dead in sin, he must be "born again" in order to have life in Christ. That New Birth happens the moment one confesses with his mouth that Jesus is Lord and believes in his heart that God raised him from the dead (Rom. 10:9). It is via the New Birth that one receives spiritual life and a guarantee of living forever in Paradise. At the moment of one's New Birth, he is endowed with holy spirit, "power from on high," "the divine nature," which equips him to be like Jesus Christ and do the works that Jesus did. What did Jesus do in his body during his earthly ministry? He expects those who believe in him to do the same things, and, in fact, he told them that they could (John 14:12). Jesus Christ is called "…the firstborn from among the dead…." As such, he was the Head, but he did not have a body until the Day of Pentecost when the Church, the "one new man" (Eph. 2:15), was born. That spiritual organism has been growing ever since as more and more people are added to it by way of their belief in Christ and resulting New Births. It is the Lord Jesus Christ who pours out the gift of holy spirit into the heart of each new person who believes in him as Lord (Acts 2:33). In that moment it is as if Jesus pulls you from the dead group into which you were born and places you in

"the Apostles' Doctrine." They viewed him as the Son of God, a man sent by God to be the promised Messiah, first to Israel, then to the Gentiles. They were convinced of his Messiahship by his resurrection, which they boldly preached as they fanned out throughout the Mediterranean countries. Nowhere in Acts is there any suggestion that Jesus was "God" in any sense, and this omission is remarkable if this doctrine were in fact a part of apostolic Christianity.

The book of Acts begins with a brief recap of the 40-day period that Christ spent in his resurrected body among the believers. He had ordered them to stay in Jerusalem until they were empowered by the gift of holy spirit. This filling, or "baptism," with the spirit would equip them to be his "witnesses." Having thus given them their marching orders for the next few days, and for their lifetimes, he ascended heavenward in complete defiance of the law of gravity.

One can only try to imagine the shock and wonder that filled the hearts of his disciples when he ascended into heaven before their very eyes. They were transfixed by the sight, pondering its significance. They were still trying to figure out when he would restore the kingdom to Israel, and they were very unclear about what his ascension meant. Almost immediately, an angel disrupted their reverie and reassured them that Christ would be returning to earth in the same way he left them. With this promise ringing in their ears, they headed back to Jerusalem to begin their new job as the Lord's empowered witnesses.

Though the meaning of the ascension understandably befuddled them, as time went on God revealed more and more about what it meant. The pinnacle of this revelation about the ascension is found in Ephesians:

Ephesians 4:7–13 (NASB)
(7) But to each one of us grace was given according to the measure of Christ's gift.
(8) Therefore it says, "WHEN HE ASCENDED ON HIGH, HE LED CAPTIVE A HOST OF CAPTIVES, AND HE GAVE GIFTS TO MEN."
(9) (Now this *expression*, "He ascended," what does it mean except that He also had descended into the lower parts of the earth?
(10) He who descended is Himself also He who ascended far above all the heavens, that He might fill all things.)
(11) And He gave some *as* apostles, and some *as* prophets, and some *as* evangelists, and some *as* pastors and teachers,
(12) for the equipping of the saints for the work of service, to the building up of the body of Christ;
(13) until we all attain to the unity of the faith, and of the knowledge of the Son of God, to a mature man, to the measure of the stature which belongs to the fulness of Christ.

After the ascension, the book of Acts then describes the growth and development of the early Church as Christ gave and guided these ministries to act in his stead, causing spiritual growth in the lives of all those who followed him. But Christ was not just working with these "equipping ministries,"[2]

---

his Body so that you are now part of him. For more detailed teaching on this, listen to our audio teaching: *The Purpose of the Ages* (May/Jun 97) at www.TLTF.org, click Bible Teachings and you will find it under audio.

2. Ephesians 4:11 mentions five specific ministries in the Church that are especially given by the Lord Jesus to prepare and equip Christians for service to God. Scripture does not refer to these ministries collectively by any particular name, so different Christian groups have referred to them in different ways. Some call these five ministries (apostles, prophets, evangelists, pastors, and teachers) "gift ministries," but that is misleading because each Christian has a gift ministry, that

as they are sometimes called. He worked directly with his brethren, like Ananias, "a certain disciple" (Acts 9:10 - KJV), or indirectly with them through those to whom he had specifically entrusted with the ministry of apostle, prophet, etc. What was clear to the first-century believers was that Christ was no longer physically present to do his work, so they were supposed to be doing it. But they were to do it by the power of the holy spirit that he had given them, and in conjunction with his continued leading of them. This they were to continue to do until they saw him reappear through the clouds, which they expected to happen in their lifetime.

Acts 2 records the events on the Jewish feast day of Pentecost that year when the Church began. The initial outpouring of holy spirit upon the disciples of Jesus, and their speaking in tongues in the Temple, caused no small stir.[3] Peter then stood up and addressed the huge crowd assembled there. We will now focus on fifteen verses of his discourse that contain a magnificent exposition of an Old Testament passage that Peter quotes and then explains. It is this teaching that pricked the hearts of about 3,000 people who got born again that day (Acts 2:41). The key points in Peter's speech that led to their New Birth were later capsulized in one classic verse in the Church Epistles. Here it is:

Romans 10:9
That if you confess with your mouth, "Jesus is Lord," and believe in your heart that God raised him from the dead, you will be saved.

We will see that what Peter said in Acts 2 focuses on the two basic components in the above verse: the resurrection of Jesus Christ from the dead and his lordship. It is significant that Peter did not portray Jesus as God nor further state that believing this was a requirement for salvation. In contrast, Peter referred to Jesus as "…a **man** accredited by God…." If Peter held the traditional Trinitarian concept of Christ, his omission is astounding. If Peter believed that those listening to him that day needed to believe that Jesus was God in order to be saved, as is often taught by Trinitarians today, he certainly did not say so. The fact that the Bible states that about 3000 people were saved that day, without hearing anything about the Trinity or Christ being God, is proof that this belief is not a requirement for salvation. Had this been an oral exam to graduate from most seminaries today, Peter would have flunked, yet by God's standards, his sermon is right on:

Acts 2:22
"Men of Israel, listen to this: Jesus of Nazareth was **a man accredited by God** to you by miracles, wonders and signs, which God did among you through him, as you yourselves know.

---

is, a ministry he or she is to carry out in the Body of Christ. "Ministry" simply means "service," and every Christian has been specifically enabled and empowered to serve. These five ministries have also been called "ascension gift ministries," but again, after his ascension Jesus gave each Christian a ministry (Eph. 4:8). The Word of God says that the purpose for these five ministries is "for the equipping" of the believers (Eph. 4:12 - NASB), and many other versions recognize that "equip" or "equipping" is an excellent translation in this verse. Whenever possible, we of The Living Truth Fellowship do our best to use the vocabulary of the Word of God to describe the spiritual realities in the Bible, and so we refer to the five ministries listed in Ephesians 4:11 as "equipping ministries."

3. Traditionally, Christians believe that the original outpouring of the gift of holy spirit occurred in the "upper room." Bible students are beginning to recognize that this is not tenable, because, for one reason, the multitudes involved could not possibly have fit into the upper room. Also, in Scripture, "the house" often refers to the Temple. Consider this note in the NIV Study Bible: "Evidently not the upstairs room where they [the Apostles] were staying, but perhaps someplace in the Temple precincts, for the apostles were 'continually in the Temple' (Luke 24:53 - KJV) when it was open."

We see in this verse that Peter was being very specific to identify the particular Jesus of whom he is speaking—"Jesus of Nazareth." When Peter said Jesus was "…a man accredited by God…," he meant that God supported and energized Jesus. Peter continued:

Acts 2:23
This man was handed over to you by God's set purpose and foreknowledge; and you, with the help of wicked men, put him to death by nailing him to the cross.

Remember that Jesus came specifically to the nation of Israel as their Messiah. And what did they do to him? They killed him, as he prophesied they would. He also prophesied that God would raise him from the dead, and Peter confirmed this in the next verse, when he declared the resurrection of Christ:

Acts 2:24
But God raised him from the dead, freeing him from the agony of death, because it was impossible for death to keep its hold on him.

The first reason it was not possible for death to hold Jesus is because God Almighty, the Creator of the heavens and the earth, who cannot lie, had promised in Old Testament prophecy that He would raise His Son from the dead. That is why "the gates of Hades" (Matt. 6:18) will not be strong enough to retain its captives.[4] It was also not possible because Jesus Christ was a righteous man without sin, who did not deserve the penalty, or "wages," of sin, which is death. Therefore, God could legally and ethically raise him from the dead. Again we see the absolute urgency of his obedience to God, for a single sin would have made it possible for the grave to hold him in its clutches.

Remember that Peter was talking to Jewish people. Who was one of the chief heroes of Judaism? David, and it was David who had prophesied about the future resurrection of the Messiah. By quoting David, Peter really got the attention of those Jews.

---

4. The phrase, "the gates of hell" has been popularized and thrown around in Christianity with little or no understanding of its real meaning. The phrase is usually used in emotional sermons designed to inspire Christians to storm the Devil's stronghold. The Greek word translated "hell" in the KJV is *hades*, and it is transliterated into *"hades"* in the NIV. *Hades* was the Greek word used in the Septuagint to translate the Hebrew word *sheol*. E. W. Bullinger has an extensive study of *sheol* in his lexicon, and concludes: "*Sheol* therefore means the state of death; or the state of the dead, of which the grave is a tangible evidence." Thus *hades* describes a state of being of dead people, equivalent to "gravedom." Biblically, it is not a literal place with literal "gates." Our book *op. cit., Is There Death After Life?* covers the subject of *sheol* in Chapter 4. When Jesus Christ said that "the gates of *hades*" would not be able to prevail against his Church, he was using the phrase in the same way it is used in the Old Testament, where it occurs twice, using the word *sheol*. Job asks, "Where then is my hope? Who can see any hope for me? Will it go down to the gates of death [*sheol*]? Will we descend together into the dust?" (Job 17:15 and 16). In the book of Job, the "gates of *sheol*" are the gates of the grave. When someone dies, it is as if gates were permanently shut behind him. There is no way out, no way back to the land of the living.

King Hezekiah of Judah later used the phrase, "the gates of *sheol*" in exactly the same way Job had many years earlier. Hezekiah almost died from a sickness and was miraculously healed. After the experience, he wrote: "In the prime of my life must I go through the gates of death [*sheol*] and be robbed of the rest of my years?" (Isa. 38:10). A related phrase, "the gates of death," occurs in Job 38:17; Psalm 9:13 and 107:18.

Thus, a study of the way the phrase is used in Scripture reveals its meaning and how Jesus used it. Because Jesus Christ is the resurrection and the life, he could say that he would build his Church and the gates of Hades would not prevail against it. Although the gates of the grave will close over us if we die, we will break through them unto everlasting life when the Lord calls us at his appearing.

Acts 2:25–27

(25) David said about him: 'I saw the Lord always before me. Because he is at my right hand, I will not be shaken.

(26) Therefore my heart is glad and my tongue rejoices; my body also will live in hope,

(27) because you will not abandon me to the grave, nor will you let your Holy One see decay.

How did David know that he would be raised from the dead? Because he believed in the resurrection of the "Holy One" (the Messiah) who would one day raise him to everlasting life.

Acts 2:28

You have made known to me the paths of life; you will fill me with joy in your presence.

Peter made it clear that David knew he would see his Redeemer face to face. Then he launched into an exposition of the verses he had just quoted.

Acts 2:29–31

(29) "Brothers, I can tell you confidently that the patriarch David died and was buried, and his tomb is here to this day.

(30) But he was a prophet and knew that God had promised him on oath that he would place one of his descendants on his throne.

(31) Seeing what was ahead, he spoke of the resurrection of the Christ, that he was not abandoned to the grave, nor did his body see decay.

Peter told the Jews that David had prophesied about the resurrection of the man they had just murdered. Then he boldly stated that the resurrection had been accomplished.

Acts 2:32 and 33

(32) God has raised this Jesus to life, and we are all witnesses of the fact.

(33) Exalted to the right hand of God, he has received from the Father the promised Holy Spirit and has poured out what you now see and hear.

Peter was saying that not only did God raise His Son from the dead, but also that He highly exalted him and gave him holy spirit, which Jesus had in turn given to those who believed in him as Lord. In the next verses, Peter made it plain that David is not in heaven.[5] Then he spoke of Jesus exalted at the right hand of God, another truth prophesied in the Old Testament from which he quoted:

Acts 2:34 and 35

(34) For David did not ascend to heaven, and yet he said, " 'The Lord said to my Lord: "Sit at my right hand

(35) until I make your enemies a footstool for your feet." '

Peter finished this amazing presentation with a resounding crescendo:

---

5. If *David* is not in heaven, great believer that he was, then where is he? He is dead and in "gravedom" awaiting resurrection at the hand of the Messiah. The Bible teaches that all who have died will stay dead until they are resurrected by Christ.

Acts 2:36
"Therefore let all Israel be assured of this: God has made this Jesus, whom you crucified, both Lord and Christ."

The idea that "Jesus is Lord" is clearly explained within Scripture. Acts 2, beginning in verse 22, sets forth the biblical understanding of this concept. On the Day of Pentecost, Peter boldly set forth the truth that Jesus was "…a **man** accredited by **God**…by miracles, wonders and signs which God did among you through him…." He then went on to say that this "man" was handed over to the Jewish leaders, crucified and killed by them. Then God raised him (this man) from the dead and "exalted" him (this man) to His (God's) right hand where he (this man) received from the Father and then poured out to people the promised holy spirit.

What was Peter saying? He was making the claim that Jesus was the Christ prophesied in the Old Testament. After this, Peter concluded by quoting the Messianic prophecy of Psalm 110:

Acts 2:34b–36
(34b) '…The Lord [Septuagint=*kurios*, but Hebrew text=Yahweh] said to my Lord: [Septuagint=*kurios*, Hebrew text=*Adoni*]: "Sit at my right hand
(35) until I make your enemies a footstool for your feet."
(36) Therefore let all Israel be assured of this: **God** has **made** this **Jesus**, whom you crucified, both **Lord** and **Christ**."

Was Peter identifying Jesus as the **Yahweh** of the Old Testament?[6] Hardly. He was instead proving from Scripture that Jesus was the Christ, that is, **Yahweh's** Anointed One. According to Scripture, the Christ (Messiah) had to suffer and rise again. In addition, as the Christ of Old Testament prophecy, Jesus had been exalted to the right hand of God and installed by God as Lord over all. In short, he had entered into his glory (Luke 24:26 and 46).

Psalm 110:1
…The LORD [Yahweh] says to my lord [*adon*]: "Sit at my right hand until I make your enemies a footstool for your feet."

As we saw in Chapter 5, the Jews regarded Psalm 110 as a Messianic prophecy concerning the coming Christ. Psalm 110 also speaks of the coronation of a king, in this case, a king from the line of David. In its original context, it may have been speaking of Solomon, but in its larger context, it was either a foreshadowing or direct foretelling of the future Davidic king, that is, the Messiah or Christ.

Remember that to Peter's audience on the Day of Pentecost, the Hebrew understanding of the text would have been clear. The Messiah (or King) who is being installed in Psalm 110 is referred to as *Adon*, not as Yahweh. Yahweh was the personal (proper) name of God in the Old Testament. On the other hand, *Adon* was a descriptive name meaning "Lord."[7] Unfortunately, both of these terms were translated from Hebrew into the Septuagint (the Greek Old Testament) as *kurios* and then later into English as "Lord."[8] In our English Bibles, they are distinguished only by various means of capitalization within the Old Testament.

---

6. For more information on the name Yahweh, see Appendix L.
7. For specifics on this verse see Appendix A (Ps. 110:1).
8. See Appendix B for a detailed examination of *Kurios*.

No monotheistic Jew living at that time would have taken Peter's statements recorded in Acts 2 to mean that the Messiah (or Christ) was Yahweh, that is, God. This would have been ludicrous to them, and had Peter proclaimed this, no one would have given him the time of day. Instead, Peter clearly set forth that it was, in fact, God Himself, Yahweh of the Old Testament, the God of their fathers, who had raised Jesus from the dead and highly exalted him to the heavenly position of Lord in fulfillment of the Old Testament prophecies concerning the Christ. As Philippians 2 states, God elevated the man He had named "Jesus" (meaning "**Yahweh our Savior**") to the most highly exalted position possible. Thus, his name is above every name.

The Greek term *kurios* (Lord) was used in a variety of ways in New Testament times, as well as in the New Testament itself. Its basic meaning is "Lord," "master" or "owner," always indicating one who has authority. But it does not of itself imply or indicate deity, even though God was called "Lord" and the pagan gods of the East were called "lords." Masters of slaves, property owners, kings, emperors and great teachers could also be called "lords" (*kurios*). In its vocative use (marking the one addressed), the term was often equivalent to "sir" as a respectful way of addressing an honorable person (See Matt. 21:30; John 12:21, 20:15; Acts 16:30). But no matter what language was spoken by the various believers of those times, the understanding of "Jesus is Lord" would have been governed by their understanding of the Messianic fulfillment of Psalm 110. It was only later that this understanding was corrupted.[9]

The point is simply that in Psalm 110, God was not talking to Himself or with the "second person of the Trinity." Instead, Yahweh is pictured as talking with the Messiah, David's "Lord." David foresaw that God would raise the Christ from the dead and install him as Messiah and Lord at His right hand in heaven. David recognized him as his superior, his Lord. As a result, David himself had the hope of a future resurrection.

Since Peter told his audience that Jesus is Lord and that God raised him from the dead, and we know from that and other similar Scriptures in Acts and the Epistles that salvation is dependent upon the confession that "Jesus is Lord," it certainly seems logical that we should desire to know exactly what this statement means. In its note on Romans 10:9, the NIV Study Bible offers a view that is all too often held and promoted in evangelical Christian circles. Under the heading, "Jesus is Lord," we read:

> …the earliest Christian confession of faith (cf. 1 Corinthians 12:3), probably used at baptisms. In view of the fact that "Lord" (Greek *kurios*) is used over 6,000 times in the Septuagint (the Greek translation of the O.T.) to translate the name of Israel's God (Yahweh), it is clear that Paul, when using this word of Jesus, is ascribing **Deity** to him… [emphasis ours].

Can "deity," that is, that Jesus is "God," really be ascribed to him on this basis? No. "Lord" is simply the most appropriate title for Jesus, especially now that he sits at God's right hand.[10] This is one of the many places where the NIV translators have endeavored to imprint their own Trinitarian belief either onto the text itself (via their translation) or onto the understanding of the text (via their study notes). Some examples of other places include: John 1:1 and 18; Romans 9:5; 1 John 5:20.[11] This list could go on and on. In pointing out these examples, we do not mean to denigrate what we consider to be an excellent translation. They are simply indicative of the extent to which the Trinitarian interpretation has colored the understanding of most translators and Bible scholars. So

---

9. See Appendix A (Rom. 10:9).
10. See Appendix B, Uses and Usages of *Kurios*.
11. For our explanation of these verses see Appendix A.

ingrained is it in most Christians' minds that seldom do any of their thoughts about its illogic lead them to seriously seek any alternative.

Another consequence of not seeing the difference between "Lord" and "God" is the fallacious idea that one is not saved unless he believes that Jesus is God. This is in spite of the clarity of Romans 10:9, which says that salvation is dependent upon confessing that Jesus is Lord. There is no verse that says to be saved one must believe that Jesus is "God" or "divine."[12] Furthermore, in all the records in Acts, there is no presentation of the Trinity. For example, as we have seen, about 3,000 Jews were saved on the Day of Pentecost without Peter mentioning the Trinity or that Christ was somehow God. The Roman soldier Cornelius and his household were saved in spite of the fact Peter never mentioned the Trinity. The jailer in Philippi was saved, and Paul's words were short and to the point: "…Believe in the Lord Jesus, and you will be saved…" (Acts 16:31).

Are we to believe that Paul did not really communicate the whole message of salvation to the jailer, and somehow missed saying that this simple jailer really needed to believe that Jesus had two natures incorporated into one body and was a "co-equal and co-eternal being," actually "God in human flesh"? We hardly think so. Surely the fact that Acts portrays thousands of people being saved, yet not once records anyone teaching the doctrine of the Trinity, should be conclusive proof that the Trinity was not a part of early Church doctrine. How many precious Christian saints have been made to doubt their salvation and thus suffer emotional trauma at the hands of those promoting this false doctrine? It is also a lever of intimidation used to tyrannize thinking people by labeling them "cultists" and ostracizing them from fellowship with the Body of Christ.

Acts states clearly that God has exalted Jesus the Christ to His own right hand and installed him as Lord, and the rest of the New Testament agrees. All authority in heaven and on earth has been given to him. Angels, powers and principalities have been made subject to him. He is the Head over all the Church. God has placed all things under his feet, with one exception—Himself. Thus, Jesus is now "Lord," installed and coronated by God in fulfillment of the great biblical prophecy of Psalm 110. To confess "Jesus is Lord" is to bring glory and honor to God (Phil. 2:11). It is to acknowledge the accomplishments of God Himself in bringing about victory over sin, death and Satan. In the life, death and resurrection of Jesus Christ and his exaltation as Lord, God's wisdom and power are revealed.

We also want to point out that in Acts 2:36 Peter says that God "…has made this same Jesus… both Lord and Christ." The context of this statement is his resurrection, therefore the question arises, *when* did God make Jesus the Christ? Had He not made him the Christ before his resurrection? The answer is found later in the book of Acts, when Peter addresses a Gentile audience for the first time:

> **Acts 10:38**
> how God anointed [*chrio*] Jesus of Nazareth with the Holy Spirit and power, and how he went around doing good and healing all who were under the power of the devil, because God was with him.

God anointed Jesus at his baptism, empowering him to be the Messiah, or Christ. But as we recognized in Chapter 7, Jesus was veiled about his Messianic claims, knowing that only resurrection would authenticate his Messiahship. Therefore Peter appropriately speaks of God having "made" (i.e., proven) Jesus the Christ through his resurrection. This further explains why the Gospel (the Good

---

12. See Appendix Q, Do You Have to Believe in the Trinity to be Saved?

News) preached by his disciples in Acts revolves around the truth that Jesus Christ is the Messiah, as verified by his resurrection (see Acts 9:22, 13:34, 17:3 and 31, 18:28).

The Active Christ

When Peter boldly addressed the house of Israel in Acts 2:36, he confronted them with the irony that it was they who had crucified Jesus. In essence, he said to those Jews: "All of your lives you were looking for the Messiah, but when he came face to face with you, you killed him, just like the Old Testament prophecies said you would. God, however, has raised him from the dead and exalted him as Lord and the Anointed One."

Why did the Jews fail to recognize Jesus as the Messiah? Chiefly because they failed to believe in the *sufferings* of the Messiah that had to precede his exaltation and glory. They were looking for a political deliverer, not a man whose blood had to be shed for their redemption. They should have seen in Exodus 12 the suffering of the Redeemer in the types of the Passover Lamb and the other sacrifices. They should have seen his death in Genesis 22, Psalm 22 and Isaiah 53. Graciously, God gave them another chance by way of the message of Peter, and about 3,000 responded affirmatively. Based upon what happened in the days that followed, it appears that most of the religious leaders, however, slunk off in anger and prepared to persecute the disciples just as they had their Master. The believers, however, had been cut to the heart by Peter's words, and prepared to follow in the Apostles' Doctrine.

> **Acts 2:37–41**
> (37) When the people heard this, they were cut to the heart and said to Peter and the other apostles, "Brothers, what shall we do?"
> (38) Peter replied, "Repent and be baptized, every one of you, in the name of Jesus Christ for the forgiveness of your sins. And you will receive the gift of Holy Spirit.
> (39) The promise is for you and your children and for all who are far off—for all whom the Lord our God will call."
> (40) With many other words he warned them; and he pleaded with them, "Save yourselves from this corrupt generation."
> (41) Those who accepted his message were baptized, and about three thousand were added to their number that day.

The book of Acts shows that Jesus had not lied when he told Peter "…I will build my church…." We see Jesus Christ actively and powerfully working to build and support the Church, which is his Body. He pours out the gift of holy spirit to all who believe. He adds to the Church those who call on his name. He heals people. He is supporting the outreach of his Church in many ways: by signs and miracles and by specific guidance and revelation. Records like the vision he gave to Peter on the rooftop show him preparing the hearts of Christians for ever greater works of service. That he personally appeared to Paul on the road to Damascus shows him building his Body and lightening the persecution of Christians at the same time.

He is calling out ministries to provide leadership, sending angels to do his work, defending his causes against the Adversary's forces, and encouraging those who stand for him. On two occasions in Acts, he appeared to the Apostle Paul to encourage him (18:9, 23:11). Thus, the book of Acts is indeed a book of "acts." Jesus is acting powerfully on our behalf, the ascended Christ working hard for his earthbound Church. It is also a book of inspiration and hope for the believer. Although the book of Acts also shows the hard work and suffering involved in the Christian life, it is easy to see how much Christ loves and supports those who give their lives to him.

The book of Acts also records the history of the early Church as believers reached out with the Word, first to the Jews, and then later to the Gentiles. In the early part of the book of Acts, despite Jesus' admonition to his followers to "go unto all nations," the message of salvation by grace through faith in Christ was preached only to Jews. Acts faithfully sets forth the growth of the Church. First the Jews, then the Samaritans (Acts 8), then the Gentiles (Acts 10). It sets forth the actions of the Church as the Lord Jesus began to reveal the truths that set the Church of the Body apart from the "Old Testament." These doctrinal truths are clear in the Church Epistles, which set forth the truth about the "administration of grace," in which all believers, no matter what their nationality or heritage, Jew and Gentile alike, form the One Body of Christ. The truth of the "Sacred Secret" (often mistranslated as the "Mystery") that is set forth in the Church Epistles was unfolded gradually throughout the period covered in the book of Acts.[13] As we shall see, Jesus Christ will one day confirm all of God's promises to Israel (Rom. 15:8). He will also give everlasting life to all Gentiles who call upon his name.

The relationship between God and Jesus Christ is clearly portrayed in Acts. As we have already seen in the record of Peter's sermon in Acts 2, Christ is shown as distinct from God. He is the man approved by God. Nowhere in Acts is there any hint of a "Trinity," and nowhere in Acts is anyone told to believe in the Trinity or that Jesus is God. All through the book of Acts, people get saved when they accept Christ as the Man whom God raised from the dead and made Lord. The disciples call him the servant of God (4:27) and "the man" (17:31). As Stephen was being stoned to death by the Jews, he saw a vision of both God and His Son.

Acts 7:55 and 56
(55) But Stephen, full of the Holy Spirit, looked up to heaven and saw the glory of God, and Jesus standing at the right hand of God.
(56) "Look," he said, "I see heaven open and the Son of Man standing at the right hand of God."

Stephen did not look up into heaven and see a Triune God, he saw God on His throne, just as the elders of Israel and prophets had seen.[14] And at the right hand of God stood the resurrected Christ. Stephen was so blessed and amazed at the vision that he shouted out what he saw, even though no one else could see it.

Conclusion

As the Head of the Church that began on the Day of Pentecost, it was the Lord Jesus Christ who spearheaded the outreach of God's Word as recorded in the book of Acts. He is the Lord who spoke to Ananias about going to see Paul, and the one who spoke to Peter on the rooftop about going to see Cornelius.[15] He is the Lord whose power energized the many signs, miracles and wonders done by those who believed in him and who went forth in the authority of his name.

---

13. For an explanation of why the Greek word "*musterion*" should be translated "Sacred Secret" see our book: *op. cit., Gift of Holy Spirit*, Appendix A, of that book.

14. See Appendix A (Gen. 18:1 and 2).

15. In Acts 10:14, Peter recognizes that the source of the vision was the "Lord" (see Appendix B). But in verse 15, the voice from heaven says, "…Do not call anything impure that God has made clean." When Peter is recounting his vision

The "Apostles' Doctrine" concerning Jesus Christ is as clear. They believed him to be "…a man accredited by God…," the Messiah, the Son of the Living God. Since the early Christians lived in closer proximity to the Lord Jesus and presumably derived their doctrinal understanding "at his feet," why would later Christians want to try to "improve" upon the apostolic witness? Would it not be wiser to attempt to cleave to their same language and understanding? Yet in many, many ways, the Church strayed from its apostolic roots, and this will become more evident in the later chapters of this book when we address the historical development of the Church's doctrine concerning Christ.

Having a biblically accurate view of Christ should help us hold to his "headship" and look to him for the direction of his "Body." Jesus Christ is the same Lord today, and we need to expect and believe that "this same Jesus" is working powerfully in the Church today, just as he did in Acts. As fellow laborers with him, it is incumbent upon us to work with him by acting upon the guidance he gives us, because only with our cooperation can he accomplish his mission of proclaiming the true Gospel to all people. When we obey him and walk with him, we can see the same kind of deliverance in people's lives as there was nearly 2000 years ago.

---

to the circumcision "police" in Acts 11:4-18, he says the same thing. Had God been speaking directly to Peter, He would have said, "Do not call anything impure that I have made clean." The use of the third person here argues for the source of the vision being Jesus Christ and not God Himself.

11

The Church Epistles:
The "Head" of His "Body"

Paul's epistles, called "the Church Epistles," were written to the various churches that he helped to establish. They were intended to be encyclical, meaning that they were passed along from one church to another so that all could learn and be established in the faith. Virtually every Bible commentator recognizes the importance of these documents in the growth of the Christian Church, and Paul is recognized as perhaps the most influential of the Apostles. His view of Christ and the relationship he had with both God and Christ reveal much about "the Apostles' Doctrine."

Paul's epistles confirm what the Gospels and Acts reveal about our risen Lord and Savior, and go on to reveal even more about him. The Gospel records close with Jesus in his resurrected form, and state that he had been given all authority (Matt. 28:18). Jesus clearly demonstrated his loyalty to, and connection with, God by calling God both his "Father" and his "God" (John 20:17). He spoke of things that were still future (John 20:22). Furthermore, he demonstrated his Lordship and authority by changing his form (Mark 16:12), disappearing from one place and appearing in another (Luke 24:31, 36 and 37), and filling the Apostles' nets with fish (John 21:6).

The book of Acts focuses on Jesus in action. He responded to the prayers of the disciples (Acts 1:24–26), poured out the gift of holy spirit (Acts 2:33), added believers to the Church (Acts 2:47), revealed himself in support of his Church (Acts 7:55, 9:3–6), guided and directed his disciples (Acts 9:10–15, 16:7, 22:17–21), provided power for healing (Acts 9:34), and comforted his people in difficult circumstances (Acts 18:9, 23:11). Acts also has teachings by Paul, Peter and others that make known many things about the Lord. He is the Man accredited by God by signs and wonders, who was crucified and then raised from the dead, and the Man whom God has appointed to judge the world.

The Epistles confirm what the Gospels and Acts say about the risen Lord, and add to them. They confirm that Jesus Christ is not dead, but alive, having been raised from the dead by God, something specifically stated more than a dozen times. A clear example is 1 Corinthians 6:14, which reads, "By His power, God raised the Lord from the dead, and he will raise us also." While the book of Acts states that Jesus showed himself alive to his disciples and "…gave many convincing proofs that he was alive…" (Acts 1:3), it is revealed in the Epistles that many more people than that saw him alive.

1 Corinthians 15:3–8 (NRSV)
(3) For I handed on to you as of first importance what I in turn had received: that Christ died for our sins in accordance with the scriptures,
(4) and that he was buried, and that he was raised on the third day in accordance with the scriptures,
(5) and that he appeared to Cephas, then to the twelve.
(6) Then he appeared to more than **five hundred brothers and sisters** at one time, most of whom are still alive, though some have died.
(7) Then he appeared to James, then to all the apostles.
(8) Last of all, as to one untimely born, he appeared also to me.

It was during the latter half of the period covered in the book of Acts that Paul's letters to Christians in Rome, Corinth, Galatia, Ephesus, Philippi, Colosse and Thessalonica were written. These "Church Epistles" are the apex of God's revelation to mankind. Christ had promised his disciples that when the holy spirit came, it would guide them into "all truth" (John 16:13). We believe that the bulk of the "all truth" that Christ was referring to is the information revealed in the Church Epistles.[1] The Church Epistles are specifically addressed to Christians, the Body of Christ, the "called out" (*ekklesia=* people "called out" for some purpose), as the introduction to each of the Epistles shows. Although a particular location is usually mentioned in each introduction, it was well understood in both ancient and modern times that the truths being taught applied to the entire Church worldwide.[2] Note the following examples:

---

1. For more on the "all truth" referring to the Church Epistles, see two books by E. W. Bullinger, *op. cit., The Church Epistles,* pp.10 and 11, and *How to Enjoy the Bible* (Samuel Bagster and Sons, London, 1970) pp.142 and 143. See also Appendix J.

2. In Colossians 4:16, the believers are instructed to have others read the epistle, and they are instructed to read the epistle from Laodicea. Scholars have long believed that the letter to the Laodiceans is actually the Epistle of Ephesians that was being spread from church to church and may have even been sent to Laodicea as well as Ephesus when it was sent out from Paul in Rome.

Romans 1:7 (NRSV)
To all God's beloved in Rome, who are called to be saints: Grace to you and peace from God our Father and the Lord Jesus Christ.[3]

1 Corinthians 1:2 (NRSV)
To the church of God that is in Corinth, to those who are sanctified in Christ Jesus, called to be saints, together with all those who in every place call on the name of our Lord Jesus Christ, both their Lord and ours:

There are great truths in the Church Epistles that were kept "secret" from those who lived before they were written. These truths were "…not made known to men in other generations…," and were "…for ages past kept hidden in God…." They were "unsearchable" in the Old Testament Scriptures.[4] The Church Epistles reveal these "secrets," the basic thrust of which was that instead of there being two groups, Jews and Gentiles, one with special privileges and one without, Christ has now created, and continues to add to, "one new man" (Eph. 2:15) a body of believers called out from among both Jew and Gentile. Other corresponding blessings that were secret include: secure salvation, a position with Christ in the heavenlies, deliverance from the Great Tribulation, being sealed with the gift of holy spirit (a deposit that guarantees life in the age to come), the theretofore unavailable manifestations of speaking in tongues and interpretation of tongues, and a perfectly righteous standing before the Father. The Epistles also show Jesus Christ in his position as Lord and Head of the Church, and define his role as such.

The Church Epistles form the heart of the Christian's curriculum for life today. They are God's revelation to the Church of the Body of Christ that started on the Day of Pentecost, when holy spirit was poured out in New Birth for the first time. The Church will end when the Christians are taken up ("raptured") into the air to be with the Lord.[5] Because the Lord Jesus created a "new man," i.e., the Church that is his Body, it is not surprising that he would have new information concerning this "new man" that he had created, and the Church Epistles contain that vital knowledge.

More Christians today need to recognize the indispensable importance of the Church Epistles, because only by knowing and applying the truth in them can a Christian have the quality of life that God intends him to have. Among many other wonderful things, they contain information about what Jesus Christ is now doing, and particularly what he, as the Head, is doing for us, the Body. It

---

3. The word "saints" means "those set apart by God." It is translated from the Greek word *hagios*, "holy one." It is used of angels and of men. Christians are called "saints" because, having been "born again," they have been made holy by God because of the sanctifying presence of God's gift of holy spirit. It is unfortunate that many Christians think of saints only as especially holy people, and usually those who are already dead. The Epistles do not use the word "saint" that way at all. All Christians are "saints," just as they are "witnesses" and "ambassadors" for the Lord Jesus Christ. The question is, what kind of saints, witnesses and ambassadors are we?

4. It is unfortunate that in most versions of the Bible the Greek word *musterion* is translated "mystery" instead of "Sacred Secret." The important difference is that a "mystery" cannot be known, but a "Sacred Secret" can be. Translating *musterion* as "mystery" has helped promulgate the idea that God and the things of God are essentially beyond human comprehension. For a more detailed explanation of the Greek word *musterion*, see Appendix A (Col. 2:2). Ephesians 3:2–9 says in several different ways that the truths now known were hidden in times past.

5. One of the great scriptural proofs of the uniqueness of the Christian Church is the gathering together of all Christians from the earth, and from their graves, into the *air* to meet the Lord Jesus. In contrast, the believers of the Old Testament will come from their graves and settle on the *land* (Ezek. 37:11–14), fulfilling the prophecy that "…the meek shall inherit the earth…" (Ps. 37:9, 11 and 29; Matt. 5:5).

is interesting that in no ancient biblical manuscript ever found are the Church Epistles in any other order than they are in the Bible today.[6]

Luke 24:51 and Acts 1:9–11 record Jesus leaving the earth and ascending into heaven. The Apostles witnessed his ascension, but only until "…a cloud took him out of their sight" (Acts 1:9 - NRSV). However, even if the sky had been cloudless, Jesus would have disappeared from sight after he had gone up a mile [a little over 1.6 kilometers] or so. Humans simply become too small to see with the naked eye beyond such a distance. There are many clear Scriptures that say that Jesus is now in heaven (Acts 3:21; Eph. 1:20, 6:9; Col. 4:1; Heb. 1:3; etc.) Nevertheless, occasionally people become confused by the wording of Ephesians 4:10, which says that Jesus ascended "…higher than all the heavens…." The noted Bible commentator R. C. H. Lenski writes:

> Christ's ascent "far above" all the heavens must not be interpreted mechanically as implying somewhere beyond all the heavens, beyond the place where God, the angels and the blessed saints dwell; the sense is that the ascension gave Christ his exaltation and supremacy over all the heavens. We have the commentary in Ephesians 1:20 and 21; Philippians 2:9–11. To be far above the heavens is not to be somewhere that is not heaven—where would that be? Christ ascended "into heaven" (Acts 1:11).[7]

Jesus still has a physical body, and so he is located in time and space. Where exactly he is now is not revealed in the Bible, other than to say that he is seated "…at the right hand of God…" (Acts 2:33, Rom. 8:34). Actually, that is figurative language indicating his function as God's "right hand man." This means that he is *busy*, going wherever he needs to go to do whatever he needs to do in carrying out the will of God. Scripture also reveals that he is in us and we are in him, this via the gift of holy spirit that he gave us when we were born again.

Recognizing Our Personal Relationship with Jesus Christ

For those followers of Christ who had the privilege of knowing him "in the flesh," it would have been a difficult, though necessary, transition for them to learn to relate to him as the risen Lord. Though he was now invisible to them (except when making rare personal or visionary appearances), he was intimately involved with them through the gift of holy spirit that he poured out into each of them. Instead of just remembering his words and actions from the time when he was physically among them, they had to learn to think of him as spiritually "with" them, gently but surely guiding each of them as his representatives on the earth.

---

6. To review the importance of the order of the Epistles of Paul, see Appendix J.

7. R. C. H. Lenski, *The Interpretation of St. Paul's Epistles to the Galatians, Ephesians, and Philippians* (Augsburg Pub. House, Minneapolis, MN, 1961), pp. 523 and 524. Another Scripture that confuses people in regard to the whereabouts of Jesus is Hebrews 4:14, which says that Jesus "…has gone through the heavens…." Since the most common use of the words "gone through" (Greek = *dierkomai*) is going all the way through, some teach that Jesus must have gone through heaven and out the other side. However, the Bible never mentions anything "beyond heaven," and since God is in heaven and Christ is with God, Jesus could not have passed all the way through heaven. Acts 13:6 reveals a use of *dierkomai* that is "through part of but still inside." Paul and Barnabas "passed through" the Isle of Cyprus, but were still on it and ministered in the city of Paphos. In the same way, Jesus "passed through" the heavens, i.e., he went through some of heaven, but he is still in heaven, he has not passed out the other side as if there were something beyond.

As more and more people were won to the Lord, the number of those who had actually physically witnessed his earthly ministry became proportionately smaller and smaller. It would have been easy for those who had been with Jesus physically to lord it over the newer believers who had believed without seeing him in the flesh. The gospel of John, written late in the first century when few were left who had actually been with Jesus, addresses this issue. Jesus himself spoke of those who would need to believe in him without seeing him, as they heard the Good News about the Lord.

John 20:29 (NASB)
Jesus said to him [Thomas], "Because you have seen Me, have you believed? Blessed *are* they who did not see, and *yet* believed."

Note that Jesus says that those who have believed without seeing are "blessed," because they are not dependent upon their memories of him nor do they have any status from previous association with him. Paul also forcefully addresses this issue:

2 Corinthians 5:16 (NRSV)
From now on, therefore, we regard no one from a human point of view; even though we once knew Christ from a human point of view, we know him no longer in that way.

This is a powerful point that must be recognized, even though we do not face exactly the same issue that the first-century believers did. We have never had the opportunity to know Christ according to the flesh, except through the Gospel accounts of his earthly life. These accounts are immensely helpful to us to get to know our Savior, but it is not enough to read about his life in the Gospels and try to be like him. We are called to know him personally and intimately via the holy spirit that he has given us.

Many verses in the Church Epistles say that we are "*in* Christ," and therefore it is simply not enough to read *about* him. Having Christ *with* us and *in* us is the perspective of the Church Epistles, not the Gospels, and it is imperative that we become thoroughly acquainted with who we are in Christ and who he is in us. This understanding is available only through a knowledge of the Church Epistles, which call us not to look *back to* Christ in his earthly ministry, but rather to look *up to* him in his heavenly one. Characteristic of this perspective is the following passage from Colossians:

Colossians 3:1–4 (NRSV)
(1) So if you have been raised with Christ, seek the things that are above, where Christ is, seated at the right hand of God.
(2) Set your minds on things that are above, not on things that are on earth,
(3) for you have died, and your life is hidden with Christ in God.
(4) When Christ who is your life is revealed, then you also will be revealed with him in glory.

This is the perspective of the Church Epistles. We are "with Christ," and Christ is even our very life. The following verse in Galatians also shows the "resurrection life" of the believer in Christ:

Galatians 2:19b and 20 (NRSV)
(19b) …I have been crucified with Christ;

(20) and it is no longer I who live, but it is Christ who lives in me. And the life I now live in the flesh I live by faith in the Son of God, who loved me and gave himself for me.

In his resurrection glory, Christ is "re-living" his life in us who believe in him. Rather than living solely under external laws and ordinances, we are given access to a living relationship with him who gave himself for us. Knowing that he is living in us and that we are "in him" makes our obedience that much more available and compelling, because we know that he is at work within us to help us think, speak and live the way he did. What a privilege, and how sad that so few Christians are really taught this "Church Epistle" perspective of the Christian faith.

Jesus Christ, the "Head" of a Spiritual "Body"

One great truth that is clearly revealed in the Church Epistles is that all believers, both Jew and Gentile, have been made into a new man (Eph. 2:15), a "Body" with Christ as the "Head" and all the members of the Church as its parts.[8] Representative of many Scriptures in the Church Epistles teaching this truth are the following:

Romans 12:5 (NASB)
so we, who are many, are one body in Christ, **and individually members one of another.**

1 Corinthians 12:27 (NASB)
Now you are Christ's body, **and individually members of it**.

Ephesians 4:16 (NASB)
from whom [Christ] the whole body, being fitted and held together **by that which every joint supplies, according to the proper working of each individual part**, causes the growth of the body for the building up of itself in love.

Colossians 1:18 (NASB)
He [Christ] is also the head of the body, the church; and He is the beginning, the first-born from the dead; so that He Himself might come to have first place in everything.

Colossians 2:19 (NASB)
and not holding fast to the head [Christ], from whom the entire body, being supplied and held together by the joints and ligaments, grows with a growth which is from God.

---

8. The "new man" from both Jew and Gentile is exactly that: new. Interestingly, there are today many converts to Christianity from Judaism who still hold to the Jewish laws and believe that the law is valid for them because they are Jews. We believe that misses the point of the message in the Church Epistles. What Christ is doing now for Christians is very different than what God did for Jews and Gentiles under the Law. Christians are not to be separated into different congregations, some "Messianic Jews" and some "Gentile congregations." The Epistles contain directives not to be separate from each other or form distinct groups (1 Cor. 1:10–13). They reveal that the Levitical requirements were a shadow of the reality that is Christ (Col. 2:17), and that the Law was done away in Christ. Since the Law was given to Moses, if it was to be done away with, that fact had to be written very clearly, and it was: Christ abolished the Law (Eph. 2:15) and was the end of the Law (Rom. 10:4). Christians are not under the Law (Rom. 6:14 and 15), are dead to the Law (Rom. 7:6), are released from the Law (Rom. 7:6, 8:2) and are not under the supervision of the Law (Gal. 3:25).

Christ is presented as the Head of the Body in which each member has a particular function in harmony with the whole (see Rom. 12:3ff; 1 Cor. 12:12–27). The truth that Christ is Head of his Body, the Church, forms a key doctrinal cornerstone of Ephesians:

> **Ephesians 1:19b–23 (NASB)**
> (19b) …*These are* in accordance with the working of the strength of His might
> (20) which He brought about in Christ, when He raised Him from the dead, and seated Him at His right hand in the heavenly places,
> (21) far above all rule and authority and power and dominion, and every name that is named, not only in this age, but also in the one to come.
> (22) And He put all things in subjection under His feet, and gave Him as **head** over all things to the church,
> (23) which is His **body**, the fullness of Him who fills all in all.

This exaltation as "Head" evokes memories of David's inspired prayer of praise to God at the occasion of the dedication of the Temple.

> **1 Chronicles 29:10b–13 (NRSV)**
> (10b) "…Blessed are you, O Lord, the God of our ancestor Israel, forever and ever.
> (11) Yours, O Lord, are the greatness, the power, the glory, the victory, and the majesty; for all that is in the heavens and on the earth is yours; yours is the kingdom, O Lord, and you are exalted as **head** above all.
> (12) Riches and honor come from you, and you rule over all. In your hand are power and might; and it is in your hand to make great and to give strength to all.
> (13) And now, our God, we give thanks to you and praise your glorious name.

David recognized God as "head" over all things in heaven and earth. In Ephesians, Paul recognizes that God has made Christ to be "Head" over all things *to the Church*, which is his "Body." This presentation of Christ as the Head and the Church as the Body is yet another way to describe that God has delegated authority to the Son, and further delineates Christ's authority and dominion. He has been given authority *in heaven* over the angels ("…all rule and authority and power and dominion…"), and he has been given authority *on earth* over the Church.

Holding the Head

That Jesus is often clearly described as the Head of his Body in the Church Epistles clearly reveals how connected he is to us and we to him. Via holy spirit, each Christian is one with Christ, but it is possible for a Christian to live as if he or she were not connected to the Head. It is a sad fact that many professing Christians do not feel personally supported and guided by the Lord, and worse, some are not aware that they can and should be.

Nonetheless, biblical language is designed to communicate that truth. Surely the fact that Jesus is called the "Head" is to call our attention to the parallel between the workings of the Body of Christ and our physical bodies. Just as one's physical head communicates with and directs his body, so too our spiritual Head, Jesus Christ, directs us in our walk as Christians. Christ gives us guidance and direction, and we communicate back to him our experiences and needs, just as the parts of our physical body communicate back to our head. Nevertheless, as we have just said, some Christians are not connected with the Head, practically speaking, and this is not new. It is noteworthy that some Christians in the first century had also "lost connection with the Head."

> **Colossians 2:18 and 19 (NASB)**
> (18) Let no one keep defrauding you of your prize by delighting in self-abasement and the worship of the angels, taking his stand on *visions* he has seen, inflated without cause by his fleshly mind,
> (19) and not holding fast to the head, from whom the entire body, being supported and held together by the joints and ligaments, grows with a growth which is from God.

Clearly, it is not enough only to be "held fast" to the Head by the gift of holy spirit. The believer must recognize the Headship of Christ in his daily life, and in particular must not be looking to other people for guidance, unless those people are being led by the Lord.[9] As the members of the physical body must be connected to the head to receive nourishment and grow, so the members of Christ's spiritual Body must be practically and personally connected to him in order to grow. This is the view presented by Jesus in John 15:1ff using the figure *prolepsis* that we studied in Chapter 8. Here, instead of the analogy of the body, the Scripture employs a botanical analogy to communicate the same truth—the believer must be connected to the Lord in order to bear fruit:

> **John 15:1, 4, and 5 (NRSV)**
> (1) "I am the true vine, and my Father is the vinegrower.
> (4) Abide in me as I abide in you. Just as the branch cannot bear fruit by itself unless it abides in the vine, neither can you unless you abide in me.
> (5) I am the vine, you are the branches. Those who abide in me and I in them bear much fruit, because apart from me you can do nothing.

The Colossian passage that we quoted above echoes two verses in Ephesians that describe how spiritual growth occurs in the Church Age:

> **Ephesians 4:15 and 16 (NASB)**
> (15) but speaking the truth in love, we are to grow up in all *aspects* into Him, who is **the head**, *even* Christ,
> (16) from whom the whole body, being fitted and held together by that which every joint supplies, according to the proper working of each individual part, causes the growth of the body for the building up of itself in love.

---

9. Christians need to take note of the fact that in Colossians the immediate context of losing connection with the Head is the worship of angels (v. 18). Angel pictures, pins, statues, etc., are very popular in our culture today, but angels work for the Lord and obey him, and they are not to be worshipped. When in Scripture angels were offered worship, they refused it (Rev. 19:10). If an angel pin reminds you that the Lord may send angels to protect you, that is one thing. However, if you think of a "guardian angel" as apart from the Lord, you are not honoring the angel or the Lord. Demons are fallen angels and they do desire your love. The Christian must be careful to give all his heart to the Lord. The book of 1 John closes with the words, "Little children, keep yourselves from idols" (1 John 5:21 - NRSV), which is good advice for any era.

The growth of the Body comes from Christ, who is the Head, working in conjunction with us as we each do our individual part. He is able to do this for us because God has delegated the responsibility and authority to him. He, in turn, has delegated to us the responsibility and authority to serve and represent him.

Colossians 2:9 and 10 (KJV)
(9) For in him [Christ] dwelleth all the fullness of the Godhead bodily,[10]
(10) And ye are complete in him, which is the head of all principality and power:

In the same way Christ has the fullness of God, we have the fullness of Christ.[11] The wording of the King James Version helps to communicate the truth of what has happened to us in Christ: "And ye are complete in him…." The believer is complete in Christ, full in Christ. As the risen Lord, Christ has given us fullness, and we have all spiritual blessings (Eph. 1:3). He is our "all in all," and we need not look to be completed by delving into spiritualism, getting "answers" from psychics or trying to fill a void by exploring any other belief systems outside of Christianity. In the Greek text of Colossians, the phrase "…ye are complete in him…" is a periphrastic perfect, and the essence is, "you have been made full, are so now, and continue so."[12]

Although we have fullness in Christ and all spiritual blessings, we will be able to enjoy this privilege only to the extent that we "hold fast" to him, the Head. If we are men-pleasers or subjugated to denominational politics or serving Christian tradition instead of having a living relationship with the Head, we will have a form of godliness, but deny the power thereof (2 Tim. 3:5 - KJV). If we live in disobedience, either by committing acts contrary to his wishes or by refusing to do what he commands because it makes us uncomfortable, then we will likely not experience the presence of the Lord in our lives. Christ is Head, Lord and Master, but he still allows us to exercise our freedom of will. It is our choice to walk or not walk in the fullness and blessing he has given us. If we do, he promises that he will take an active role in our lives.

Christ the Temple Builder

Another aspect of his present ministry was alluded to in the Old Testament. There was an ancient Jewish prophecy that the Messiah would build a Temple:

Zechariah 6:12 and 13 (NASB)
(12) "Then say to him 'Thus says the LORD of hosts: "Behold, a man whose name is Branch, for He will branch out from where He is, and **He will build the temple of the LORD.**
(13) "Yes, it is He who will **build the temple of the LORD**, and He who will bear the honor and sit and rule on His throne. Thus, He will be a priest on His throne, and the counsel of peace will be between the two offices." '

---

10. For an explanation of this, see Appendix A (Col. 2:9).

11. In a different sense, the Body of Christ is also called the "fullness," as Ephesians 1:22 and 23 shows: "And God placed all things under his feet and appointed him to be the head over everything for the church, which is his body, the fullness of him who fills everything in every way."

12. R. C. H. Lenski, *The Interpretation of St. Paul's Epistles to the Colossians, to the Thessalonians, to Timothy, to Titus, and to Philemon* (Augsburg Pub. House, Minneapolis, MN, 1961), p. 101.

As we elaborated upon in Chapters 5 and 6, one of the ancient names for the Messiah was "the Branch" (*tsemach*), and one of the things that he would do is build a Temple for the LORD. In the future, Jesus will build a physical Temple on the earth, but now he is building a figurative Temple. By analyzing the pattern established by Moses and David for the building of the physical Tabernacle and Temple, respectively, we can glean important insight into the role that Jesus Christ plays as he coordinates the building of a spiritual "temple" in the Church Age. Ephesians makes this very clear:

Ephesians 2:19–22 (NASB)
(19) So then you [the Gentile believers] are no longer strangers and aliens, but you are fellow citizens with the saints, and are of God's household [i.e., the Church],
(20) having been built upon the foundation of the apostles and prophets, Christ Jesus Himself being the corner *stone*.
(21) In whom the whole building, being fitted together is growing into **a holy temple in the Lord**;
(22) In whom you also are being built together into **a dwelling** of God in the Spirit.

The Church is spoken of in this passage as a "holy temple" being built together to become a dwelling place for God. This was precisely the purpose of both the Old Testament Tabernacle and the Temple. Moses received in immense detail the pattern for the building of the Tabernacle. He did not do the actual building, however, but delegated it to others who were equipped with the spirit of God, notably Bezaleel son of Uri (see Exod. 25–31 - KJV). David, too, received in detail the pattern for building the Temple, as described in 1 Chronicles 28 and 29, yet neither was he the one to build it. Solomon, his son and others did the building, in particular Huram-Abi (2 Chron. 2:13), a man of exceptional skill and cunning in craftsmanship. These records concerning Moses and David set a pattern for us to consider in relationship to the present ministry of the Lord Jesus Christ. We can infer that Jesus stands in an analogous position to Moses and David, who are clear types of the Messiah in many ways.

Jesus, then, as the Head of his Body, has received the "blueprint" for the building of a spiritual "Temple" for the Church Age, which is to be the dwelling place of God. As was the case with Moses and David, Jesus is not actually building the Temple by himself, but is directing, overseeing and working in others who are doing much of the actual work. Though we have been showing from Acts and the Church Epistles that Jesus is a "hands-on" Lord, working among his brethren to build the Church, he in fact is delegating most of the work.

For instance, in the case of Paul's conversion on the road to Damascus, Jesus himself confronted him, but sent Ananias to actually do the work of building him up in the faith. Barnabas then took Paul under his wing and introduced him to the believers who had before been afraid of him. Phoebe, Aquila and Priscilla and others are mentioned as being important players in the dramatic conversion of Paul from feared persecutor to beloved Apostle. Jesus was of course intimately involved in Paul's growth process, but delegated most of the work of grafting him into the Church.

God is the Master Architect, who has designed the Church Age with all of its graces, privileges and enablements, and has given the plans to His Son to carry out. The Lord Jesus is like the General Contractor, who has been given the responsibility and authority to see to it that the project gets done. He in turn empowers and employs workers in whom he can work to get the job done. Is not an "irrevocable contract" with his "subcontractors" being clearly communicated in the following verses?

2 Corinthians 5:18–20a (NASB)
(18) Now all *these* things are from God, who reconciled us to Himself through Christ, and gave us the ministry of reconciliation,
(19) namely, that God was in Christ reconciling the world to Himself, not counting their trespasses against them, and He has committed to us the word of reconciliation.
(20a) Therefore, we are ambassadors for Christ, as though God were entreating through us…

What a privilege to be entrusted by God and the Lord Jesus with this ministry of reconciliation and the building up of the Body of Christ. As we stay connected to the Head and heed his instructions for the building of this dwelling place for God, we are a part of "the purpose of the ages." This truth should surely provide ample motivation to continue in faithful service to the one who has entrusted us with so much.

Making Christ Lord

The Church Epistles emphasize the fact that Christ is Lord. The word "Lord" appears more than 200 times in the Church Epistles, and nearly every use refers to Jesus Christ.[13] We have just seen that it is the responsibility of each and every Christian to "hold the Head," which is a way of saying that we are to follow and obey Jesus Christ. "Holding the Head" and "making Christ Lord" are basically synonymous. Just as a person can be a Christian without "holding the Head," so it is possible to be a Christian without really taking the Lordship of Jesus Christ seriously. The word "Lord," as it is used of Jesus Christ, means "ruler, boss, master, owner, one to be obeyed and one to whom allegiance is due." To become saved, a person must confess with his or her mouth that Jesus is Lord (Rom. 10:9), but that is a truth that can be believed in the mind without being lived out in one's life. That is why the Bible calls some Christians "carnal," "worldly" or "unspiritual."

1 Corinthians 3:3 (KJV)
For ye are yet carnal: for whereas *there is* among you envying, and strife, and divisions, are ye not **carnal**, and walk as men? (See also Rom. 8:7; 1 Cor. 3:1 and 4).

When we get born again, we are sealed with holy spirit (Eph. 1:13 and 14), have Christ in us (Col. 1:27), and are each a child of God (1 John 3:1 and 2). However, that does not mean that we have made him our boss and master with all our heart, soul, mind and strength. When we turn away from following him, then Christ is not Lord in an active sense in our lives, and we do not reap the many benefits of fellowship with him.

The Church in Galatia had turned away from the grace of Christ and what he was offering to them, and started to return to the law, led away by false teachers. Paul wrote that they were causing him pain by doing that: "My dear children, for whom I am again in the pains of childbirth until Christ is formed in you" (Gal. 4:19). Paul's reference to Christ being "formed" in the Galatian believers is not a reference to them being saved, but rather to them making Christ "Lord" of their lives by obedience to him in their thoughts, words and deeds. In 1531, Martin Luther lectured on the Epistle to the Galatians at the University of Wittenberg, and his lectures were printed in a commentary in

---
13. See Appendix B on the use and usages of "Lord."

1535. Luther was accurate when he said that Christ being formed in the Galatian believers referred to Christ being formed in their hearts and minds:

> The Apostles are in the stead of parents, as schoolmasters also are in their place and calling. For as the parents beget the bodily form, so they beget the form of the mind. Thus, every godly teacher is a father who engendereth and formeth the shape of a Christian heart, and that by the ministry of the Word. Moreover, by these words, "I travail in birth," he toucheth the false apostles. As though he would say: "I did beget you rightly, through the gospel, but these corrupters have formed a new shape in your heart, not of Christ, but of Moses, so that now your affiance [trust] is not grounded upon Christ, but upon the works of the law. This is not the true form of Christ, but another form altogether devilish. Paul, therefore, goeth about to repair the form of Christ in the Galatians, which is that they should speak, think, and will as God doeth. They who believe this are like unto God, as the affection of their heart is: they have the same form in their mind which is in God, or in Christ. This is to be renewed in the spirit of our mind, and to put on the new man.[14]

Every Christian has an obligation to make Christ his Lord in an active and outward way, not just "in the mind." Christians should look to him for guidance and wholeheartedly obey him. It is because Christ is "Lord" that the Church Epistles introduce us to "the law of Christ" (Gal. 6:2; 1 Cor. 9:21). Before the Day of Pentecost in Acts 2, the only law was from God. However, as Lord, Christ has a law for the Church. Actually, Jesus had already revealed this to his disciples on the night that he was betrayed by Judas. He said, "A new command I give you: Love one another…" (John 13:34). Jesus' "command" before his resurrection and exaltation became his "law" when he sat down at the right hand of God.

Identification with Him

Every Christian is "in Christ," meaning that we are a part of his Body.[15] As our foot is a part of us, every member of Christ's Body is identified with him. The Christian is now, therefore, able to grow up into Christ, and to become like he was in his earthly ministry and do the works that he did. At the end of the Church Age, Christ will exercise his great authority and power and transform each of us into his glorious likeness. We will then be like him, as he is presently in his glorified position at the right hand of God. This tremendous truth is clearly described in Philippians, another one of the Church Epistles:

Philippians 3:20 and 21 (NRSV)
(20)But our citizenship is in heaven, and it is from there that we are expecting a Savior, the Lord Jesus Christ.

---

14. Martin Luther, *Commentary on Galatians* (Kregel Publishing, Grand Rapids, MI, 1979), pp. 276 and 277.

15. The phrase "in Christ" also has the overtones of the covenant culture of Israel. When a covenant was made with someone and his children after him, the children would be beneficiaries of the covenant even though they were not around when it was made. We all benefit from the covenant God made with Noah, for example. Hebrews notes that the covenant Abraham made with Melchizedek was valid concerning the tribe of Levi because Levi was "in" Abraham when it was made. Thus, we get to be included in the experiences and blessings of Christ because we confessed him as Lord and became God's children.

(21) He will transform the body of our humiliation that it may be conformed to the body of his glory, by the power that also enables him to make all things subject to himself.

Only by studying the Church Epistles will we learn that we are identified with Jesus Christ because he first became identified with us. He was made like us in every way (Rom. 8:3; Gal. 4:4; Heb. 2:17) so that we could be made like him in every way. The believer can share with Christ in his suffering (Phil. 3:10), his crucifixion (Gal. 2:20), his death (Rom. 6:3; Col. 3:3), his burial (Rom. 6:4), his resurrection (Eph. 2:6; Col. 3:1), his ascension (Eph. 2:6), his seating at the right hand of God (Eph. 2:6) and his glory (Rom. 8:30). In him we are made righteous (2 Cor. 5:21), sanctified (Acts 26:18; 1 Cor. 6:11; Eph. 5:26 - KJV) and redeemed (1 Cor. 1:30; Col. 1:14). He will give an inheritance to those who deserve it (Col. 3:23–25). We are irrevocably reconciled to God through him (Rom. 5:11) and will have life in the age to come (Rom. 6:23). And on top of all this, upon his return to the earth with us, we will receive rewards and crowns for faithful service to him, sharing in his reign as subjects in his future kingdom (Col. 1:13).

Christ's Active Role in the Church Today

The Church Epistles paint a powerful picture of what Jesus Christ is doing for the Church today. Far from being absent or taking a passive role, the Epistles portray Christ as Head of the Body, feeding, nourishing, directing, defending and blessing his Church. It would be difficult indeed to make a comprehensive list of everything he has done and is doing, but a large number of his current functions are listed below:

- Jesus Christ is Lord (Rom. 14:9; 1 Cor. 1:9, 6:14, 15:57; 2 Cor. 4:5; Gal. 6:14).
- He was declared the "Son of God" by his resurrection from the dead (Rom. 1:4).
- He is the firstborn from among the dead, and therefore our confidence that he can raise us up from the dead (1 Cor. 6:14; 2 Cor. 4:14; Col. 1:18).
- God seated Christ at His right hand, far above all principalities and powers, and made him "Head" of the Church (Eph. 1:20–22; Phil. 2:9–11; Col. 3:1).
- Christ will, in a future administration, be Head of all in heaven and earth (Eph. 1:10) [at this time, all things are not yet subject to him—Heb. 2:8; 1 John 5:19].
- Christ is now functioning as God's co-ruler, and will, at a future time, after the destruction of all evil authority, hand over the kingdom to God (1 Cor. 15:20–28).
- Christ is the image of God (2 Cor. 4:4; Col. 1:15).
- Christ is still Israel's deliverer and servant (Rom. 11:26, 15:8).[16]
- He is our example (Rom. 15:3 and 4; 1 Cor. 11:1; Eph. 5:2, 25–29; Phil. 2:5–8).
- Gives us grace (Rom. 1:5, 16:20; 1 Cor. 16:23; 2 Cor. 8:9, 13:14; Gal. 1:6, 6:18; Eph. 4:7; Phil. 4:23; 1 Thess. 5:28; 2 Thess. 1:12, 3:18).
- Gives us peace (2 Thess. 3:16).
- Gives us access to God (Eph. 2:14 and 18).
- Gives us mercy (1 Cor. 7:25).
- Blesses us (Rom. 10:12, 15:29).

---

16. The way Christ delivers those Israelites who come to him today is by including them in the Church. After the Rapture, he will again work with Israel to rescue and deliver it.

- Loves us (Rom. 8:39; Eph. 5:25–30; Phil. 2:1; 2 Thess. 2:13).
- Accepted us (Rom. 15:7).
- Sanctified us (1 Cor. 6:11; Eph. 5:26 - KJV).
- Has paid for the Church with his life, so we belong to him (Rom. 14:8; 1 Cor. 7:22 and 23; Gal. 3:29, 5:24).
- Is faithful (2 Thess. 3:3).
- We fellowship with him (1 Cor. 1:9).
- Created the things necessary for his Body, the Church, to function, whether in heaven or on the earth (Col. 1:16).[17]
- Created a "new man," the Church, out of Jews and Gentiles (Eph. 2:15).
- As "Head" of his "Body," the Church, he directs the growth of his Body (Eph. 4:16; Col. 1:17 and 18).
- Nurtures and cares for the Church, holds it together and causes it to grow (Eph. 5:29; Phil. 1:19; Col. 1:17, 2:19).
- Directs us (1 Cor. 16:7; 2 Thess. 3:5).
- Has work for us to do (1 Cor. 15:58, 16:10; Col. 4:17).
- Lives his life through us (Gal. 2:20).
- Works with us to be transformed into his image (2 Cor. 3:17 and 18).
- "Writes on our hearts" so that we are literally "letters from Christ" (2 Cor. 3:3).
- Is present with us (2 Cor. 13:5; Col. 1:27; 2 Thess. 3:16).
- Lives in our hearts (Eph. 3:17).
- Listens to and answers our requests (2 Cor. 12:8 and 9).
- Occasionally shows himself to people (1 Cor. 9:1).
- Is present via the power he sends (1 Cor. 5:4; 2 Cor. 12:9).
- Is interceding for us (Rom. 8:34).
- Protects us from the evil one (2 Thess. 3:3).
- Comforts us (2 Cor. 1:5).
- Forgives us (Col. 3:13).
- Redeemed us (Gal. 3:13).
- Set us free from the Levitical Law (Rom. 10:4; Gal. 5:1).
- Increases our love (1 Thess. 3:12).
- Is the "head" of the Christian marriage (1 Cor. 11:3).
- Calls people into their ministries and sends forth his workers (Rom. 1:5; 1 Cor. 1:17; 2 Cor. 1:1, 10:8; Gal. 1:1; Eph. 1:1, 4:8 and 11; Col. 1:1; 1 Thess. 2:6).
- Gives us revelation (2 Cor. 12:1; Gal. 1:12).
- Gives authority to his ministers (2 Cor. 10:8, 13:10; 1 Thess. 4:2).
- Works in and through us (Rom. 15:18; 2 Cor. 13:3; Phil. 1:11, 3:12; Col. 1:29).
- Has made us his ambassadors (2 Cor. 5:20).
- Clears paths for us (1 Thess. 3:11).
- Opens doors for us (2 Cor. 2:12).
- Encourages and strengthens us (1 Thess. 3:13; 2 Thess. 2:17, 3:3).
- Will come again in person (1 Cor. 1:7, 4:5, 15:23, 16:22; Phil. 3:20; Col. 3:4; 1 Thess. 1:10, 2:19; 3:13; 2 Thess. 1:7, 2:1 and 8).

---

17. See Appendix A.

- Will appear and call us up into the air to be with him (1 Thess. 4:15–18).
- Will transform our bodies at his appearing (Phil. 3:21).
- Will rescue us from our dead bodies (Rom. 7:24 and 25).
- Will be glorified and marveled at when he returns to the earth (2 Thess. 1:10).
- Will judge all men on behalf of God (Rom. 2:16; 1 Cor. 4:4; 2 Cor. 5:10).
- Will reward or punish people, according to what they deserve (2 Cor. 5:10; Eph. 6:8; Col. 3:23–25; 1 Thess. 4:6; 2 Thess. 1:8).
- Will commend those who deserve it, now and in the future (2 Cor. 10:18).

The Believer's Role

Just as the Church Epistles reveal many things that Christ is doing, so they also reveal many things that the Christian is supposed to do in order to enter into an intimate relationship with the Lord and serve him. It is imperative that the believer reciprocate by acting in conjunction with the Lord. Christ was very clear in his teaching in John 14 that whoever really loves him will obey him, and that he would then manifest himself to all those who do so. The Church Epistles have many commandments, but the list that follows is specifically related to our responsibilities in relationship with Christ. We are to:

- Confess him as Lord (Rom. 10:9).
- Get to know him (Phil. 3:8).
- Love him (1 Cor. 16:22).
- Understand his will for us (Eph. 5:17).
- "Minister to" (serve) him (Rom. 14:18, 15:16; 1 Cor. 4:1; Gal. 1:10; Col. 1:7, 4:12).
- Please him (2 Cor. 5:9; Eph. 5:10; Col. 1:10).
- Live unto the Lord (Rom. 14:8).
- Be strong in the Lord (Eph. 6:10).
- Clothe ourselves with the Lord (Rom. 13:14).
- Follow the Lord (Rom. 15:5).
- Obey him (1 Cor. 7:22; Eph. 6:5).
- Not sin against him (1 Cor. 8:12).
- Sing and make music in our hearts to him (Eph. 5:19).
- Honor him (2 Cor. 8:19).
- Let the word of Christ dwell in us (Col. 3:16).
- Glory in him (Rom. 15:17; Phil. 3:3).
- Be devoted to him (2 Cor. 11:3).
- Show reverence to him by our godly actions (Eph. 5:21; Col. 3:22).
- Rejoice in the Lord (Phil. 4:4).

It is quite easy to see from the above list that our relationship with our Lord and Head is not to be a one-way relationship. Christ does a lot for us, and we are to give ourselves to him in response.

The Relationship Between God and Christ

Christ has been raised to the right hand of God, been made "Lord," and has been given "all authority." In many ways, he is functionally equal to God, actually carrying out the work of God. The Church Epistles set forth this functional equality. However, they also show that God, the Father, is still the great power behind Christ, and is the only true God. As he did when he was on earth, Christ is still doing the will of his Father, and tapping into His knowledge and power.

It was God who raised Christ from the dead, seated him at His own right hand, exalted him above everything else and appointed him over the Church. The Church Epistles make it clear that there is "one God and Father" (1 Cor. 8:6; Eph. 4:6) and He is carefully held in the highest esteem. It would be a great dishonor to God and to Christ (who in everything he did elevated God) if Christ were to be elevated in such a way that God was set to the side. In fact, God is mentioned more than 400 times in the Church Epistles. [God is clearly declared to be the "Head" of Christ (1 Cor. 11:3), and Jesus gave himself as a sacrifice to God (Eph. 5:2).] As Christians, we were born into a family of which God is the great "patriarch."

Ephesians 3:14 and 15
(14) For this reason I kneel before the Father,
(15) from whom his whole family in heaven and on earth derives its name.

We are called "sons" of God, and we call God, *Abba* (Father) while Jesus Christ is our brother (Rom. 8:29).

Many Scriptures show the relationship between God and Christ today. The two of them are working in tandem, as God is working in and through Christ. Christ never does anything apart from God's will, so he always has God's strength and support. The openings of each of the Church Epistles show the two working together. Consider Romans, for example: "…Grace and peace to you from God our Father and from the Lord Jesus Christ" (Rom. 1:7b). Other verses reveal the same thing: "Peace to the brothers, and love with faith from God the Father and the Lord Jesus Christ" (Eph. 6:23). As well as verses that show God and Christ working together, there are many that show God working through Christ. God reconciled us to Himself through Jesus Christ (2 Cor. 5:18) and adopted us into His family through Christ (Eph. 1:5). God will judge the world through Christ (Rom. 2:16), Paul said his apostolic grace came from God through Jesus Christ (Rom. 1:1 and 5) and glory and thanks go to God through Jesus Christ (Rom. 7:25, 16:27; Col. 3:17).

Once it is understood that God is still working out His will in the world with and through His Christ, then it becomes clear why there are so many things in the Church Epistles (indeed, in the New Testament) that *both* God and Jesus Christ are said to be doing. The following chart highlights some of the things that God and Christ are each doing for us.

Activity	God	Christ
Gives us grace	Romans 5:17, 15:15	Romans 16:20; Galatians 6:18
Gives us mercy	Romans 12:1; 2 Corinthians 4:1	1 Corinthians 7:25
Gives us peace	Romans 15:13 and 33	2 Thessalonians 3:16
Loves us	Romans 5:5	Ephesians 5:25–30; Philippians 2:1
Blesses us	Ephesians 1:3	Romans 10:12, 15:29
Is faithful to us	1 Corinthians 1:9; 2 Corinthians 1:18	2 Thessalonians 3:3
Is our example	Ephesians 5:1	1 Corinthians 11:1
Empowers us	2 Corinthians 13:4; Ephesians 1:19	1 Corinthians 5:4; 2 Corinthians 12:9
Enourages us	Romans 15:5; 2 Thessalonians 2:17	2 Thessalonians 2:17
Strengthens us	Romans 15:5; Ephesians 3:16	2 Thessalonians 2:17
Comforts us	2 Corinthians 1:3 and 4	2 Corinthians 1:15
Forgives us	Ephesians 4:32	Colossians 3:13
Is with us	Romans 15:33	2 Thessalonians 3:16
Places us in the Body	1 Corinthians 12:18, 24 and 28	Ephesians 4:8–12
Calls us to the ministry	1 Corinthians 1:1	Ephesians 4:8–12
Has work for us to do	2 Corinthians 10:13	1 Corinthians 16:10; Colossians 4:17
Gives us revelation	1 Corinthians 2:10	2 Corinthians 12:1; Galatians 1:12
Directs our hearts	2 Corinthians 8:16	2 Thessalonians 3:5
Works in and through us	Galatians 2:8; Philippians 2:13	Romans 15:18; 2 Corinthians 3:18
Will judge us	Romans 2:5 and 14:10	Romans 2:16; 2 Corinthians 5:10
Will reward or chastise us	Romans 2:6	2 Corinthians 5:10; Colossians 3:23–25
Will reign over us	Galatians 5:21; Ephesians 5:5	Colossians 1:13; Ephesians 5:5

Both our Father and our Lord share what we have to give them in response:

We serve	Romans 1:9 , 15:17	Romans 14:18; 1 Corinthians 4:1
We live for	Romans 12:1; Galatians 2:19	Romans 14:8
We are slaves to	Romans 6:22	1 Corinthians 7:22
We give honor to	1 Corinthians 6:20	2 Corinthians 8:19
We rejoice in	Romans 5:11	Philippians 4:4

There is much more that could be said, and further study will reveal more depth in regard to what has been already uncovered, i.e., that Jesus has been given functional equality with God in many things. Nevertheless, Jesus does not have "essential equality" with God, that is, Christ is not "one in essence" with the Father. Jesus Christ is God's Messiah, not God Himself or one part of a "Triune God." God deserves our love, devotion and praise because He is the one true God who planned all things and supplied the power to make them happen. In our hearts, we must keep Him in the highest place and give Him all He deserves. Christ is our risen Lord, who also deserves our praise, love and obedience. In a very real sense, we owe our lives to both of them, and it behooves us, if we are to love them both, that we recognize each of them for their uniqueness and individuality. It does not honor either God or Christ to confuse them or call them something they are not. We give them the highest honor by recognizing them for who they are, the one true God and Father, and His Messiah and Wonderful Son, the one Lord Jesus Christ. The Church Epistles reveal the individuality of each, and their unity of purpose as a "Dynamic Duo" flanking each believer on the path of life.

Jesus Christ, the "Creator" of the Church

In this section, we want to take another look at Colossians 1:15–18, in light of what we have seen in previous chapters about Christ's post-resurrection supremacy over the angels. Understanding the broader context of his post-resurrection glory helps us to interpret these verses accurately, and in accordance with other verses on the same subject, that is, Christ's present supremacy in heaven. These Colossian verses are frequently quoted to support the intrinsic deity of Christ as God and his supposed creation of the heavens and earth in Genesis 1. A closer look at this passage argues powerfully for interpreting them as descriptive of Christ's *post-resurrection* supremacy in heaven. This supremacy was the result of restructured authority between Christ and the angels after his ascension. It also shows that the domain of Christ's reign at present is both in heaven and over the Church, and that with respect to the Christian Church, he is even called its "creator."

Before we consider this very important section of Scripture regarding the relationship between God and Jesus Christ, it is necessary to discuss briefly the relationship among the epistles of Ephesians, Philippians and Colossians, which parallels that of Romans, Corinthians and Galatians. Ephesians sets forth doctrine, Philippians corrects the practical failure of people to adhere to that doctrine and Colossians addresses the doctrinal deviations away from the revelation of Ephesians that led to the practical errors. Just as in Galatians you can read many of the same truths stated in Romans, so in Colossians can you read many of the truths recorded in Ephesians. In fact, many of the Greek constructions are exactly the same. Colossians reiterates the basic truth of Ephesians about the Headship of Jesus Christ in his relation to his Body.[18] If one keeps these truths in mind, especially recalling what he read in Ephesians 2:15, he will be able to "correctly handle" (2 Tim. 2:15) the following section of Scripture, one that has been for many Christians most difficult.

Colossians 1:15–18 (NASB)
(15) And He is the image of the invisible God, the **first-born** of all creation [via his resurrection].
(16) For by [*en*, "in"] Him all things [in context, primarily a new order or hierarchy in heaven] were created, *both* in the heavens and on earth, visible and invisible, whether [angelic] **thrones** or **dominions** or **rulers** or **authorities**—all [these new] things have been created by [*dia*] Him and for Him [he is the ranking functional authority in heaven—God having delegated it to him],
(17) And He is **before all things** [in priority], and in Him all things hold together,
(18) He is also the head of the body, the church; and He is the beginning, the **first-born from the dead**; so that He Himself might come to have **first place in everything**.

The language in this passage of Colossians must be carefully compared to the similar language in Ephesians 1, which sets the doctrinal stage for the Colossian correction of their wrong teaching and thinking regarding Christ. Both passages describe his post-resurrection glorification and empowerment, and contain similar language with respect to his supremacy of his authority over "rulers," "authorities," etc.

Ephesians 1:19b–23 (NASB)
(19) …*These are* in accordance with the working of the strength of His might
(20) which He brought about in Christ **when He raised Him from the dead, and seated Him at His right hand in the heavenly places,**
(21) far above all **rule** and **authority** and **power** and **dominion**, and every name that is named, **not only in this age, but also in the one to come.**
(22) And He put **all things in subjection under His feet,** and **gave Him as head over all things to the church,**
(23) which is His body, the fullness of Him who fills all in all.

By putting side-by-side the corresponding concepts from these two epistles, we can easily see the precise correlation of the subject matter.

---

18. For more information, see Appendix J.

Ephesians 1:17–23, 2:14 (NASB)	Colossians 1:12–19, 2:9 (NASB)
The God of our Lord Jesus Christ, the Father of glory (1:17)	Giving thanks to the Father (1:12); God was pleased (1:19)
When He raised Him from the dead	The first-born of all [the new] creation (1:15); the first-born from the dead
Make [create] the two [Jew and Gentile] into one new man (2:15)	By [*en* w/dative] Him all things were created by [*dia*] Him and for [*eis*=unto] Him (1:16)
Seated Him at His right hand in the heavenly places [*far above all*]	He is before all things [in priority]; in all things He might come to *have first place*
rule [*arches*] authority [*exousias*] dominion [*kuriotetos*] power [*dunameos*]	rulers [*archai*] authority [*exousia*] dominions [*kuriotetes*] thrones [*thronoi*]
He fills all in all	In Him all things hold together
His body, the fulness of Him	all the fulness to dwell in Him (1:19) all the fulness of deity dwells (2:9)

When such a precise doctrinal correlation exists, we do not need to stretch the Colossians passage beyond its intention, particularly in regard to verse 16, which is often cited as proof that Jesus Christ created the heavens and the earth. Clearly the context of these verses is his post-resurrection glorification and not an eternal state as a pre-existent Son, part of a Triune "godhead." Some special note should be given to verse 16, though, because it amplifies the truth of 1 Corinthians 8:6, which we already looked at in depth in Chapter 3. The reader may recall that the Greek preposition *dia* occurs in that verse twice with a similar meaning. Let us look at it again:

1 Corinthians 8:6 (NRSV)
Yet for us there is **one God, the Father**, from whom are all things and for whom we exist, and **one Lord, Jesus Christ**, through [*dia*] whom are all things and through [*dia*] whom we exist.

The Church Epistles show Christ's relation to the Church, his Body, of which he is the Head. As the Church Epistles are the apex of revelation from God to mankind, the book of Ephesians is the apex of the revelation of the Church Epistles. In the last half of Ephesians 2, God sets forth how, through Christ, both Jews and Gentiles have entrée into the Body of Christ, and how, *in Christ*, they have been made "one new man."

Ephesians 2:10–15
(10) For we are God's workmanship **created** in Christ Jesus to do good works, which God prepared in advance for us to do.

(11) Therefore, remember that formerly you who are Gentiles by birth and called "uncircumcised" by those who call themselves "the circumcision" (that done in the body by the hands of men)—

(12) remember that at that time you were separate from Christ, excluded from citizenship in Israel and foreigners to the covenants of the promise, without hope and without God in the world.

(13) But now in Christ Jesus you who once were far away have been brought near through the blood of Christ.

(14) For he himself is our peace, who has made the two one and has destroyed the barrier, the dividing wall of hostility,

(15) by abolishing in his flesh the law with its commandments and regulations. His purpose was to **create** [*ktizo*] in himself one new man out of the two, thus making peace,

The way Christ is "creating" one new man is by filling each member of his Body with all that God has given him. This "creation" is twofold. First, the Lord Jesus "creates" the gift of holy spirit in a person at the moment of his New Birth. Second, as the believer obeys God's Word, he becomes a "new creation," being transformed from the inside out by the inherent power of this divine nature within him. Several passages in the Church Epistles speak of this new creation:

2 Corinthians 5:17 and 18a
(17) Therefore, if anyone is in Christ, he is a **new creation**; the old has gone, the new has come!
(18a) All this is from God…

Ephesians 4:23 and 24 (NRSV)
(23) …to be renewed in the spirit of your minds,
(24) and to clothe yourselves with **the new self, created** according to the likeness of God in true righteousness and holiness.

Colossians 3:10 and 11 (NRSV)
(10) and have clothed yourselves with **the new self**, which is being renewed in knowledge according to the image of its **creator** [Christ]
(11) In that renewal there is no longer Greek and Jew, circumcised and uncircumcised, barbarian, Scythian, slave and free; but **Christ is all and in all!**

At the very least, we can conclude from these verses that Christ is "co-creator" with God of this new creation, which is manifest within each believer and in the collective Body of Christ.

We know that Colossians 1:15 and 16 cannot be saying that Christ is the creator of the original heavens and earth because verse 15 (KJV) says he is "…the firstborn of every creature [or "all creation"]. If he is "…the firstborn of all creation," then he is a created being.[19] The things that are

---

19. The NIV translates this phrase "…firstborn over all creation," because this supports their presupposition that Christ is the creator of the heavens and earth. Were they to admit the standard use of the genitive here, they would be forced to conclude that the verse is saying that Christ is the firstborn of a different creation, and not the Creator himself. They also translate *en* as "by" in verse 16, with the intention of attributing creation to Jesus Christ beyond what is warranted textually. Consider the translation of this verse in the Amplified Version: *(continued)*

spoken of in the above passage as being "created" are not rocks, trees, birds, animals, etc., because those things were created by God. These things—"thrones, powers, rulers and authorities"—are the powers and positions that were needed by Christ to reign over heaven and his Church, and were created by him for that purpose.

In Ephesians 2:15, the NIV uses the word "create," and accurately so, according to the Greek word from which it comes (ktizo). What we see in this verse is that Jesus Christ has created something and, in fact, is still in the process of creating it.[20] What is this "creation" of Jesus Christ? Certainly, in context, it is not the "creation" of Genesis 1:1. The Bible says that what Jesus did was to "…create in himself one new man…." That "new man" is the Church, the Body of Christ (Eph. 1:22 and 23) that was figuratively "born" on Pentecost, the called out of both Jew and Gentile (Eph. 2:15), "God's household" (Eph. 2:19), the "holy temple" (Eph. 2:21), the "dwelling place of God" (Eph. 2:22). This is the "Sacred Secret" upon which Paul elaborates in Ephesians 3.

Colossians 1:13 and 14 (NASB)
(13) For He [God] delivered us from the domain of darkness, and transferred us to the kingdom of His beloved Son,
(14) **in whom** [or "by" or "through" whom] we have redemption, the forgiveness of sins.

In the above verses, we see once again that it is through Christ that God has made redemption available to us.

Colossians 1:15 (NASB)
And He is the image of the invisible God, the first-born of all creation.

If God is invisible, and if Jesus is *the image* of God, then obviously Jesus is *not* God Himself. That Jesus is the "…image of the invisible God…" is the same truth communicated in Philippians 2:6 (NASB), when it says that he was "…in the form of God…." This is not difficult to understand, but many people have been confused by the last half of verse 15: "…the first-born of all creation." Most Christians have been taught that this refers to the "creation" of Genesis 1:1, but verse 16 specifically defines what sphere of creation it is talking about: "…thrones or powers or rulers or authorities…." This fits with the context of Colossians, as it relates to Ephesians.

The "creation" of Colossians 1:15 is the same "creation" of Ephesians 2:15—*the Church!* As we continue reading Colossians 1, we will see more about this creation.

"For it was **in** Him that all things were created, in heaven and on earth, things seen and things unseen, whether thrones, dominions, rulers or authorities; all things were created and exist **through** Him (by His service, intervention) and in and for Him."

20. Whether Christ is creating something in this verse or not depends upon how the Greek word *en* is translated. When it occurs with the dative case, it can carry the meaning of "by," as in active causation (as in the NIV). But otherwise it would be translated "in," which changes the meaning of the verse considerably. In that case, Jesus is not *creating* anything, but is the domain in which the creation occurs. In other words, he is the one through (*dia*) whom and in (*en*) whom God laid out His plans and purposes for the Church Age. In our exegesis of this verse, we are granting the translation of *en* as indicating active agency in light of the parallel Ephesian usage of "create" in the context of the Church (2:14). We disagree, however, that the passage can be handled accurately and honestly by attributing the creation of the heavens and earth to Jesus Christ, in part because to do so completely obliterates the intended parallelism with Ephesians.

Colossians 1: 16 and 17 (NASB)
(16) For by [the text reads "in"] Him **all things** were created, *both* in the heavens and on earth, visible and invisible, whether thrones or dominions or rulers or authorities— **all things** have been created by Him and for Him.
(17) And He is before **all things**, and in Him **all things** hold together.

The figure of speech, *epanadiplosis* ["encircling"] helps us to identify the proper context of "all things," that it refers to the "things" needed to administer in heaven and the Church. Note in the above verse that the phrase "all things" occurs before and after the things that were "created," and thus defines them. The "all things" here are the "things" for the Church, not the "things" of the original creation. The word "all" is used in its limited sense, not in a universal sense.[21] The phrase appears a number of other places in the Church Epistles. Let us consider this phrase as it is used in the following verses:

Ephesians 1:22 and 23 (NASB)
(22) And He put **all things** in subjection under His feet, and gave Him as head over **all things** for the church,
(23) which is His body, the fulness of Him who fills **all** [**things**] in **all** [**things**].

The "all things" of Colossians 1:16 and 17 are the same "all things" of Ephesians 1:22 and 23.[22] As the exalted Lord and Head of the Church, Jesus Christ has now been given all authority over *all* spiritual powers. The "all things" of Colossians 1:16 refers to "thrones, dominions, rulers or authorities" in the spiritual, or angelic, realm as well as in the physical, namely *the Church*. The latter is corroborated in Ephesians 1:22 where it says that Jesus is Head over everything *for the Church*.

In verse 17, we see that Jesus Christ is "before" all things. This word "before" (*pro*), can be used in regard to place, time or superiority.[23] Here in this context, it is clearly referring to his superior rank and position. Jesus Christ is now the pre-eminent one. It is he who is the one in whom God's ultimate purposes for mankind are held together. This leads us to conclude that the whole point of the section is to show that Christ is "before," i.e., "superior to" all things, just as the verse says. If someone were to insist that time is involved, we would point out that in the very next verse Christ is the "firstborn" from the dead, and thus "before" his Church, in time as well as in position.

Colossians 1:18 (NASB)
He is also head of the body, the church; and He is the **beginning** [*arche*], the **first-born** from the dead; so that He Himself might come to have first place in everything.

Here the NASB well translates the Greek word arche as "the beginning." Jesus Christ is the beginning of the Church, over which he has supremacy. He has the prototypical body that all members of his spiritual Body will be given one day, and he was the first "member" of the Church to be established—that is, the *Head!*

---

21. See Appendix A (Col. 1:15 20).

22. "All things" appears also in 1 Corinthians 8:6, another key verse that establishes Christ's identity as God's agent: "yet for us there is but one God, the Father, from whom **all things** came and for whom we live; and there is but one Lord, Jesus Christ, through whom **all things** came and through whom we live."

23. Bullinger, *op. cit., Lexicon*, p. 89.

Let us now consider the word "first-born," which we saw in verse 15 also. So far we have seen that Jesus is the "first-born" of all creation and the "first-born" from among the dead.[24] Let us look at another verse containing this word.

Romans 8:29 (NASB)

For whom He foreknew, He also predestined to *become* conformed to the image of His Son, that He might be the **first-born** among many brethren;

Here we see that Jesus Christ is the "first-born among many brethren." Since the other uses of "first-born" refer to Christ's resurrection, do you think there is any possibility that part of the "all creation" of Colossians 1:15 is those "many brothers" who will be raised "from among the dead"? Bingo! Remember John 5:26, where we read that God gave Jesus life in himself? Jesus Christ is the Promised *Seed*, and as the resurrected Lord at the right hand of God, he gives life to whoever believes in him as Lord. On the Day of Pentecost, he first poured out that life and began the Church of his Body. On that day, he first poured out holy spirit, which is the "deposit guaranteeing" the everlasting life he will one day give to all who believe on him. It was on Pentecost that Jesus Christ began the Church (Acts 2:1ff).

The phrases, "…the first-born of all creation" and "…the first-born from the dead…," encircle the domain of Christ's resurrection authority and dominion. The "creation" being referred to here is the new creation of which Jesus Christ is the prototype. He is the first one to have been born from death into everlasting life with a body perfectly suited to live eternally in heaven or on earth. This places Jesus Christ in a unique and advanced position, supreme above all of God's creations. Indeed, in his resurrected body he has been given the privilege of sharing in all that God is, including His creativity.

Colossians 1:19 and 20 (NASB)

(19) For it was the *Father's* good pleasure for all the fullness [of God] to dwell in Him,
(20) and through Him to reconcile all things to Himself, having made peace through the blood of His cross; through Him, *I say*, whether things on earth or things in heaven.

Praise God for the magnificent gift of His only begotten Son. Praise the Lord Jesus for his faithfulness to be obedient unto death, even the death of the Cross. Praise God for raising him from the dead and exalting him as Lord to His right hand on high. Praise the Lord Jesus for his constant care for us as members of his Body. What a mighty God and what a magnificent Lord we have!

---

24. See Appendix A (Col. 1:15–20).

12

God's Namesake in Action

To truly understand God's Word and put it into practice in our lives, it is imperative that we know all we can of what God reveals in His Word about who Jesus Christ is and what he accomplished for us by his life, death, resurrection, and ascension. It is vital to understand what Jesus Christ will do in the age to come, but it is perhaps even more vital to understand what he is doing *now* in his exalted Lordship. To maximize our limitless spiritual potential, we as Christians must understand Jesus Christ in both his relationship to God and his relationship to us. Because Jesus perfectly represented God by always obeying His Word, he could, and did, say, "...He who has seen Me has seen the Father..."(NASB). If we take Jesus at his word, it seems necessary to know him in order to really know God.

In the previous chapter we discussed the relationship between God and Christ. In this chapter, we will continue this theme by focusing on the truth that God's blood-covenant relationship with man was fulfilled in His Son Jesus, the Christ. "Jesus" (Hebrew *Yeshua*) is his God-given name, and means **"Yahweh our Savior"** or **"Yahweh saves."** Jesus Christ represents a kind of synopsis of all God has done for His people throughout the ages. We will look at how, in both his earthly ministry and in his exalted ministry as Lord, Jesus embodies all the chief attributes of Yahweh given in the Old Testament.

"Idolatry" means man looking to an image, an object of worship, or anything else other than the true God as a source of supernatural wisdom, power, or blessing. It is not "idolatry" to look to Jesus Christ as the exalted Lord, the position to which God has elevated him.[1] It is *God* who chose to exalt Jesus Christ, and when we worship, honor, praise, and glorify "Jesus as Lord" (Rom. 10:9; 1 Pet. 3:15), God gets the ultimate glory (John 5:23; Phil. 2:11).

In regard to the relationship between God and His Son, consider the following verse:

Romans 15:8
For I tell you that Christ has become a servant of the Jews on behalf of God's truth, to confirm the promises made to the patriarchs

Here is one of many verses in Scripture that makes plain the unity of purpose of God and His Son. It was *God* who made the promises to the patriarchs (Abraham, Isaac, Jacob, that is, *Israel*). It is *Jesus Christ* who will make the promises to the patriarchs come true. The reason Jesus is in a position to do so is that God has "…made Him both Lord and Christ…" (Acts 2:36 - NASB) and given him "…All authority in heaven and on earth…" (Matt. 28:18).

When the angel Gabriel spoke to Joseph and Mary, he told them the name that God had picked out for His Son (Matt. 1:21). In the Old Testament, Joshua had the same name and was a clear type of Christ. It was by way of Joshua's leadership that he and the nation of Israel were finally able to claim their inheritance in Canaan, which typified Israel's future Millennial inheritance. However, the "rest" that Joshua gave them was only temporary (Heb. 4:8). Likewise, Jesus is the Agent of salvation for both Jews and Gentiles who believe on him, and for those believers God's rest will be everlasting.

Those who adhere to the doctrine of the Trinity have long recognized that there are verses in the Old Testament that ascribe certain attributes to Yahweh, and corresponding verses in the New Testament that ascribe like attributes to Jesus Christ. This has led them to the erroneous conclusion that Jesus is in fact the Yahweh of Israel. A good example of this is found in the NIV Study Bible concerning Hebrews 1:6, which reads, "And again, when God brings his firstborn into the world, he says, 'Let all God's angels worship him.'" The NIV note on this verse reads as follows: "…This statement, which in the Old Testament refers to the Lord God (Yahweh), is here applied to Christ, giving clear indication of His full deity…."[2]

By "full deity," the NIV translators mean that Jesus is "God the Son." We do not see it that way, and we believe that understanding what we have thus far set forth clears up this error. God exalted His Son as "Lord" and delegated to him the authority and power to function in all the ways that God Himself had been functioning for His people (remember Joseph and the Pharaoh? Gen. 41:44). As he carries out his responsibility as "Lord," Jesus Christ is now functionally equal to his Father. It was Jesus who said that all men should honor the Son even as they honor the Father, and that whoever does not honor the Son does not honor the Father (John 5:23). Is it really honoring Jesus to ascribe to him attributes he never claimed? Is it honoring God the Father to make Jesus "God the Son"? We

---

1. Trinitarians and Unitarians alike will advance this argument. Trinitarians assert that if Jesus is a "creature" (i.e., a created being), then it would be idolatry to worship him. Since he is a legitimate object of worship scripturally, then he must be God (i.e., uncreated). Some Unitarian Christians (especially strong subordinationists) argue that because he is a man, he is obviously a created being and therefore not worthy of worship. The argument presupposes that it is always "idolatry" to worship a created being, and that God will always be "jealous" of any other one being worshiped beside Him. However, when God highly exalts a created being to functional equality with Himself, He is obviously not concerned about the competition, and in fact solicits worship and acclamation for His Son who is worthy of exaltation.

2. NIV Study Bible, note on Hebrews 1:6.

think not. However, in the next section we will see that God Himself highly honored His Son Jesus (*Yeshua*) with **the name above every name**. We will now examine what this means.

God's "Name" and Namesake

The first use of Yahweh is found in Genesis 2:4, and the Ryrie Study Bible (NASB) makes this comment regarding it:

> "…the most significant name for God in the Old Testament. It has a twofold meaning: the active, self-existent One (since the word is connected with the verb "to be," [Exod. 3:14]) and Israel's Redeemer (Exod. 6:6)…[It] is especially associated with God's holiness (Lev. 11:44 and 45), His hatred of sin (Gen. 6:3–7), and His gracious provision of redemption (Isa. 53:1, 5, 6 and 10)." [In short, Yahweh indicates God as Redeemer].[3]

In Exodus 3:14 (NASB), Moses asked God what His name was. His response was "…I AM WHO I AM…" and, "…Thus you shall say to the sons of Israel, 'I AM has sent me to you.'" Actually, "I am" is more properly translated, "I will be." The point God made to Moses was that, in contrast to the many Egyptian gods, He is the only true God, and He is versatile—able to be and do whatever His people needed. Regarding this verse, the Ryrie Study Bible comments on this elaboration of the name of God in the Old Testament: "…The inner meaning of Yahweh,—'I am the One who is'—emphasizes God's dynamic and active self-existence…."

Philippians 2:9 and 10 (NASB) declares that God "…highly exalted Him [Jesus], and bestowed on Him the name which is above every name, that at the name of Jesus EVERY KNEE SHOULD BOW, of those who are in heaven, and on earth, and under the earth." Jesus is Lord over all, even as he said, "…All authority has been given to Me in heaven and on earth" (Matt. 28:18 - NASB). Because of his glorious exaltation to the "right hand of God," his "name" is above every other name. Remember that "Jesus" is *Yeshua* in Hebrew, and means "**Yahweh saves**." Since Jesus was God's appointed agent of salvation who successfully completed the most important job of all time, he now stands in the same relationship to his Body as Yahweh did to the children of Israel. Does this mean that he is the same being? To us, it is obvious that he is not, and to think so misses the point of his exaltation, *which was in response to his carrying out his job so successfully*.

God does not reveal Himself by a sacred or special name in the New Testament. The Greek word translated "God" is *theos*, which is the same word used of pagan deities. In the New Testament, the primary way the one true God is distinguished from false gods is by the addition of the term "Father" in relationship to His "Son." The one true God identifies Himself with His Son, who perfectly revealed Him. Jesus was the *logos*, not as a pre-existent divine being, but by representing God and actually carrying out the will of God all the way to his humiliating death by crucifixion.

In order to identify Himself to the world, God associated Himself with certain Old Testament individuals or groups with whom He had made covenants. In regard to this, the Bible refers to Him as:

"…the LORD the God **of Shem**…" (Gen. 9:26).

"…the God **of Abraham** and the God **of Nahor**" (Gen. 31:53).

"…the God **of the Hebrews**…" (Exod. 3:18).

"…the God **of Abraham, Isaac and Jacob**…" (Exod. 3:6 and 16).

---

3. Ryrie Study Bible (NASB), note on Genesis 2:4.

"…O Lord God **of our fathers**…" (2 Chron. 20:6).

"…the Lord, the God **of your father David**…" (2 Chron. 21:12).

"…the God **of Israel**…" (2 Chron. 29:10, 30:5).

"…the God **of Jacob**…" (Ps. 20:1).

In the New Testament, God has now associated Himself with the one person who perfectly embodies His redemptive character. He is "…the God and Father **of our Lord Jesus Christ**…" (Eph. 1:3). While in the past God has associated Himself with other names, now He identifies Himself with **the name above every name**.

What's in *The* Name?

What we want to consider now is how Jesus' title of "Lord" relates to his current ministry to the Church and to his future ministry in the Millennial Kingdom. To do so, we need to briefly consider the difference between two critical Hebrew words used of God many times throughout the Old Testament. One is *Elohim* and the other is Yahweh. Studying both *Elohim* and Yahweh in the Old Testament will show that God is *Elohim*, the Creator, and that Yahweh is His name *in relationship to* those with whom He has entered into some kind of commitment or covenant. *Elohim* is a more impersonal title, while Yahweh, regarding God's covenant relationship with mankind, is a more personal name.[4]

Genesis 1:1
In the beginning, God [*Elohim*] created the heavens and the earth.

Here in its first use, we see the word *Elohim* inextricably linked with Creation. Throughout the Old Testament, *Elohim* refers to God as "the Creator" relative to man, His creation. In the context of Creation, God is referred to as *Elohim* 32 times in the 33 verses between Genesis 1:1 and Genesis 2:3. If we are to follow the flow of its context, Genesis 2 should actually begin with the following verse:[5]

Genesis 2:4
This is the account of the heavens and the earth when they were created. When the Lord [Yahweh] God [*Elohim*] made the earth and the heavens—

The above verse begins the record of the creation of mankind, and here we find the first use of the word **Yahweh**, which refers to God in His covenant relationship to His creatures. It is significant that God is referred to as Yahweh *Elohim* eighteen times between Genesis 2:4 and Genesis 3:24. The only places in those verses where Scripture does not refer to Him as such are Genesis 3:1, 3, and 5, where Lucifer called Him by the more impersonal name *Elohim*, in line with the thrust of his assault

---

4. See Appendix L for more on the name Yahweh.

5. Genesis 2:4 starts with the words "This is the account of…," marking it as an important break in the flow of the context. The corresponding Hebrew word is *tholedoth*, which often occurs at the beginning of major literary sections. The English reader is not helped to see them because, in most versions, the word *tholedoth* is translated differently. The sections are: (1) 2:4–4:26, (2) 5:1–6:8, (3) 6:9–9:29, (4) 10:1–11:9, (5) 11:10–11:26, (6) 11:27–25:11, (7) 25:12–18, (8) 25:19–35:29, (9) 36:1–8, (10) 36:9–37:1, (11) 37:2–50:26. If the commentators who had first added chapters to the Bible had started Genesis 2 with what is now verse 4, the flow of early Genesis would be easier to see.

on God's personal love for man. The following Old Testament verse refers to God as both *Elohim* and Yahweh, and provides us with a vivid example of the difference between the two:

2 Chronicles 18:31
When the chariot commanders saw Jehoshaphat, they thought, "This is the king of Israel." So they turned to attack him, but Jehoshaphat cried out, and the Lord [Yahweh] helped him. God [*Elohim*] drew them away from him,

What a fabulous truth! Because of His covenant relationship with Jehoshaphat, who had finally realized the folly of his ways and the life-threatening consequences thereof, Yahweh mercifully helped him. But because Yahweh had no relationship with the surrounding Syrian enemy, *Elohim* moved them away.

In the Old Testament, God's name Yahweh is combined with certain other words that are descriptive of His redemptive functions in regard to those with whom He has entered into a committed relationship. Before the birth of Christ, God Himself did everything that needed to be done for His people. When Jesus started his ministry, he clearly demonstrated what God could be to people who trusted and obeyed Him. Now that Jesus has been exalted to the right hand of God and made Lord and Christ, God has delegated to him the tasks that He Himself did in the Old Testament. This is not to say that God has now left the picture, for we have already seen that the relationship between God and His Son is more like a "dynamic duo" working together for the benefit of believers.

What we will see in this chapter is that as the exalted Lord with his delegated authority, Jesus Christ is now performing all these "Yahweh functions" for God's people. After a brief study of the context in which each of these descriptive titles are found, we will expound upon how Jesus Christ as *Lord* is now fulfilling each of these particular functions. Keep in mind as you are reading that you can count on the Lord Jesus Christ, who is invested with all authority as the Head of the Church, to perform these functions for *you* day by day.

Yahweh Who Provides

The first "Yahweh title" is found in Genesis 22:14 (KJV). It is **Yahweh-*Jireh***, which indicates that "Yahweh will see, and therefore provide." This occurs in the context of Abraham attempting to sacrifice Isaac. Yahweh intervened and provided an animal substitute to sacrifice in place of Isaac. It should be noted that Abraham was in the process of obeying Yahweh's direction when additional "orders" came in at the last minute.

We can count on the Lord Jesus to see and provide for us whatever we need to carry out his will for the Church. In his earthly ministry, Jesus Christ believed God to provide actual bread to feed a multitude and changed water into wine to bless a wedding party. We find it very significant that the first miracle recorded in Jesus' ministry was the changing of water into wine at a wedding party. They had run out of wine, and in what appears to be a favor to his mother, he not only produced wine, but a *better* wine than they started with. This incident shows that Jesus is not a Lord who provides only when we are in desperate need or involved in "religious activities." John 10:10 (KJV) says that he came that we might have *life*, and have it more abundantly. That apparently extends even to making sure that, in at least this one occasion, his mother and friends have a good time at a party. If he is willing to provide expensive wine for a poorly catered wedding reception, it is evident that he will provide *the best* for us in other categories as well. As the exalted Lord, he now figuratively is "the bread of life" and provides everything necessary for those who partake of it by believing in him. In his Millennial Kingdom, he will provide abundance beyond our imagination.

Yahweh Who Heals

Another redemptive name is **Yahweh-*Rapha***, which is found in Exodus 15:26. It means "Yahweh who heals." After the miracle of the parting of the Red Sea, the Israelites departed into the desert of Shur, going three days without water. When they finally found water in Marah, they could not drink it because it was bitter. Moses cried out to Yahweh, who showed him a piece of wood. He threw the wood into the water, which then became sweet. Yahweh then promised the Israelites that if they would obey Him, He would not bring on them any of the diseases that He brought on the Egyptians, but would instead heal them.[6] Psalm 105:37 (KJV) says that at this point in their history there was "…not one feeble *person* among their tribes." This healing was an important function in the process of redeeming Israel from bondage, for without it the people would not have survived their ordeal.

When he walked the earth, Jesus healed every person who came to him with faith, and even a few who did not.[7] Since his resurrection and exaltation, the Lord Jesus continues his healing ministry in a greatly expanded scope by empowering his disciples with his spirit, the same spirit that enabled him to heal (Acts 10:38). In Acts 9:34, Peter said to a man named Aeneas, "Jesus Christ heals you," and Aeneas rose up whole. In his Millennial Kingdom, "No one living in Zion will say 'I am ill…'" (Isa. 33:24a).

Yahweh My Banner

Yahweh-*Nissi* means "Yahweh my banner" [protector, avenger]. In this case, a banner is an emblem or insignia representing both God's name and the power behind it to defend His people and avenge His enemies. This term is found in Exodus 17:15 (KJV), where the context powerfully reveals the commitment Yahweh has to protect His people. Amalek had attacked the Israelites in Rephidim, where God had miraculously supplied water from the rock. While Moses held up his staff, Joshua fought against the Amalekites and defeated them. After the Amalekites were defeated, Yahweh declared perpetual war against them and vowed that their memory would be erased from the earth. A related title is **Yahweh** *of Hosts*, referring to the LORD as the leader of the angelic armies that fought for God's people.

This aspect of Yahweh's redemptive character is not apparent in Jesus' earthly ministry, because he came the first time as a sacrificial lamb rather than a warrior. The days of vengeance of our God, Yahweh, and the revelation of the Warrior, Jesus, are reserved for the future. Now is "…the acceptable year of the Lord," and Jesus encouraged his disciples to love their enemies and defer vengeance to God. Nevertheless, even in his earthly ministry we see glimpses of his passion to defend God's honor and protect the believers. On two occasions, consumed by his passion for God's purity and his zeal

---

6. When understood properly, the Bible does not say that God brings sickness upon His people. The true origin of sickness is sin, not God. See our book: *op. cit., Don't Blame God!*

7. The "Gadarene demoniac," for example, was incapable of personal faith because of the way the demons were continually tormenting him, yet Jesus healed him (Luke 8:26–39). In certain circumstances, Jesus accepted the faith of others on behalf of the sick and tormented. Demonized children were healed without personal faith, but the parents were required to have faith in Jesus (Mark 9:14–29; Luke 9:37–43). The centurion's servant did not have faith in Jesus, as far as the Bible records, but Jesus healed him because of the faith of the centurion (Matt. 8:5–13).

to defend God's "house" against those who would make merchandise of it, Jesus cleansed the Temple area of money-changers.

In his love and wisdom, Jesus Christ stood between the evil Pharisees and the woman taken in adultery (John 8:1ff)—his love was the emblem in which she put her trust. When the Apostle Paul sought the Lord's deliverance from his enemies in 2 Corinthians 12:7 and 8, the Lord replied that his "grace is sufficient."[8] In other words, the Lord would not at that time be taking vengeance on Paul's enemies, but would strengthen Paul for the spiritual battle. In the same manner, as the exalted Lord, he stands with and strengthens all the members of his Church, as Paul proclaimed: "…the Lord stood at my side and gave me strength…" (2 Tim. 4:17).

In the future, we will see Jesus arrayed as a mighty warrior commanding an army of angels and redeemed saints when he returns to the earth as described in 2 Thessalonians 1:5–10 and Revelation 19:11–21. In his Millennial Kingdom, "…He will reign on David's throne and over his kingdom, establishing and upholding it with justice and righteousness from that time on and forever…" (Isa. 9:7).

Yahweh Who Sanctifies

In Exodus 31:13 (NASB) (and several other places), we find the redemptive name **Yahweh-*Mekaddishkem***, which means "Yahweh who sanctifies you," that is, sets you apart for His service. The context of this redemptive characteristic was Yahweh's urgent and emphatic command that the Israelites observe the Sabbath and keep it holy in remembrance of the fact that Yahweh is the one who made them holy. In his earthly ministry, Jesus observed the Sabbath, consecrating it with many acts of healing and blessing. In doing so, he opposed those for whom holiness was only an outward act of religious devotion apart from a heart of compassion. Jesus showed the heart of true holiness, as he kept himself from sin both inwardly and outwardly. He kept the Law but did not neglect justice, mercy, and faithfulness (Matt. 23:23).

Jesus chose some of those who believed on him and set them apart, or sanctified them for service to him with its corresponding blessings. Both he and his disciples attracted attention because of their unconventional ways, which were not considered properly "holy." He and his disciples scandalized the religious crowd because they were often found "eating and drinking" with "publicans and sinners" (Matt. 11:19; Luke 5:30–33 - both KJV). Jesus was "set apart" to serve Yahweh, not by avoiding sinners, wearing special clothes, or performing the right rituals. Rather, he was set apart by his burning love for his Father and the awesome mercy he showed toward people. Jesus' walk of holiness was precisely in accordance with what the prophets had revealed about God's heart, in that He desired above all mercy and not sacrifice (Hosea 6:6; Mic. 6:8; Matt. 9:13).

Hebrews 2:11 (NASB) tells us that it is the risen Lord Jesus who now sanctifies all those who believe in him. This sanctification occurs as a result of Jesus baptizing us with holy spirit, thus making us holy within, apart from our outward works. Like Jesus in his earthly ministry, we are *in* the world but not *of* the world, because we have been bought with a price. In his Millennial Kingdom, his purchase of us will be consummated and he will completely set us apart from all our enemies.

---

8. Paul's "thorn in the flesh" has traditionally been understood as some kind of ailment or physical handicap. Such erroneous speculation could be avoided if the biblical usage of "thorn" were consulted first. Numbers 33:55 and Joshua 23:13 reveal a biblical usage of "thorns" figuratively meaning *people* who are actively opposing the will of God. Even a cursory reading of the book of Acts will reveal Paul's continual battles with the Judaizers who opposed his ministry, frequently following him wherever he went and undermining his teaching. See Acts 13:45–50, 14:2, 17:5, 18:12, 20:3, etc. For more information, see F. F. Bosworth, *Christ the Healer,* (Fleming H. Revell Comp. Tarrytown, NY, 1973).

Yahweh Our Peace

In Judges 6:24 (KJV), we find **Yahweh-*Shalom***, which means "Yahweh our peace." The context of this statement is Gideon struggling with his calling to deliver the Israelites from the oppression of the Midianites. Gideon submitted to the LORD an offering of goat's meat and unleavened bread. The angel of the LORD touched the offering and consumed it with fire, indicating that the offering was accepted by the LORD. In response to Gideon's fearful reaction to these events, Yahweh said, "...Peace! Do not be afraid. You are not going to die." In this record, we see that Yahweh brings peace to His people when they are agitated and come to Him with humility.

In his earthly ministry, Jesus often worked with his disciples to assuage their fear. When they were in the middle of a storm, they feared for their lives and woke Jesus, who had apparently failed to see the urgency of the situation and was sleeping in the boat. He calmly rebuked the storm and restored peace to their lives. Near the end of his ministry, Jesus told his disciples, "...my peace I give you..." (John 14:27), and "...in me you may have peace..." (John 16:33). Ephesians 2:14 tells us that as the exalted Lord, "...he himself is our peace...," indicating that we can have peace amidst the strife of this fallen world. In his Millennial Kingdom, our peace will be not only inward, but also outward.[9]

Yahweh Our Righteousness

In Jeremiah 23:6 and 33:16, we find **Yahweh-*Zidkenu***, meaning "Yahweh our righteousness." In that context, Yahweh made a solemn promise that a "righteous branch" from David's line will sit on his throne and do what is just and right for the people. The result of this righteous reign is that people will live in safety.

At his first coming, Jesus declared that "...God did not send His Son into the world to condemn the world, but to save the world through him" (John 3:17). As long as they believed on him, those who did so were assured of their salvation, and thus safe from eternal death. Since the Day of Pentecost, when the Lord Jesus first made available the New Birth, each person who believes in him also receives "the gift of righteousness" (Rom. 5:17). The Lord Jesus Christ has been made righteousness unto each Christian (1 Cor. 1:30), and "...in him we might become the righteousness of God" (2 Cor. 5:21). In his Millennial Kingdom, Jesus will have perfected our righteousness by transforming our "lowly bodies" and giving us a body "like his glorious body" (Phil. 3:21). At that point we will be complete, in that we will be perfected and no longer have a sin nature.

Yahweh Is Present

Another Old Testament redemptive name of God, **Yahweh-*Shammah***, is found in Ezekiel 48:35 and means "Yahweh is present." This title is given as the name of the city of Jerusalem that the Messiah will build after the Battle of Armageddon. This is the city from which Christ will reign in his Millennial Kingdom. Then, it will be absolutely true that the Lord is present. This name foreshadows the "New Jerusalem" of Revelation 21:10–27, where there will be no need for a sun or a moon because God is the light and Jesus Christ is the lamp. Where now we see through a glass darkly, sometimes finding it very difficult to perceive God's presence, there will then be no question.

---

9. As we pointed out in Chapter 5 (re: Gen. 49:10), Shiloh was the first proper name prophetically given to the Messiah, and means "rest-bringer" or "peaceful one."

When he walked the earth, Jesus Christ described himself as the light of the world (John 3:19, 8:12, 9:5, 12:35 and 46). As such, he was always in the right place at the right time with the right people, and for each of them he was everything they needed him to be. Before he ascended, he promised those who would believe on him that he would be with them "…always, even to the end of the age" (Matt. 28:20 - NASB). In the Church Epistles, we often see the phrase "in Christ," which signifies that each Christian is an inextricable part of the Body of Christ. We are "sealed" in Christ (Eph. 1:13), and nothing can separate us from him (Rom. 8:39). In his Millennial Kingdom, he will once again be physically present with us, and we will enjoy sweet fellowship with him.

Yahweh My Shepherd

The last redemptive name we will consider is perhaps the best known. It is **Yahweh-*Roi***, which means "Yahweh my shepherd," and it is found in Psalm 23:1. This most famous of Psalms paints a vivid portrait of Yahweh's redemptive characteristics. In fact, this Psalm incorporates all the above qualities and characteristics:

Psalm 23:1–6
(1) …I shall not be in want [because Yahweh will **provide** for me].
(2) He makes me lie down in green pastures, he leads me beside the still waters [because he is my **peace**],
(3) he restores my soul [because he is the one who **heals** me]. He guides me in paths of righteousness for his name's sake [because he is my **righteousness**].
(4) Even though I walk through the valley of the shadow of death, I will fear no evil, for you are with me [because he is **present**]; your rod and your staff, they comfort me.
(5) You prepare a table before me in the presence of my enemies [because he is my **banner**]. You anoint my head with oil; my cup overflows [because he is my **sanctifier**].
(6) Surely goodness and love will follow me all the days of my life, and I will dwell in the house of the LORD forever [because he is a faithful **Redeemer** and has promised to save me].

In John 10:1ff, Jesus declared that he is the one who feeds and cares for his people—"I am the Good Shepherd"—even to the point of laying down his life for the sheep. In 1 Peter 5:4, referring to his ministry as Lord, Scripture refers to Jesus as "the Chief Shepherd." It is he who cares for his Church today. In his Millennial Kingdom, all those who have ever believed in Christ "…will all have one shepherd…" (Ezek. 37:24).

As we have seen, Jesus Christ's existence began when God fertilized one of Mary's eggs with a perfect sperm He created in her womb. Certainly, therefore, Jesus was not literally alive during the Old Testament. Rather, as God had said to Moses, "…I will be what I will be…" (Exod. 3:14). The one and only true God was everything He needed to be for His people Israel, and in the process established the paradigm for exercising the lordship that He would later give to His Son to fulfill. While He awaited the coming of His Son, God spoke to Israel through the prophets (Heb. 1:1), whose words pointed to the coming one—God's ultimate communication to mankind (Heb. 1:2). The greatest thing God ever did for them was to send the Messiah, Jesus, but Israel rejected and killed him. Then God raised His Son from the dead and highly exalted him as Lord. Now *Jesus Christ* is the "Lord" who provides for you, who heals you, who is your banner, who sanctifies you, who is your peace, who is your righteousness, who is always there with you, and who is your Good Shepherd. In his future Millennial Kingdom, Jesus Christ will be and do all of these things to an even more magnified degree.

The Apostle, Prophet, Evangelist, Pastor, and Teacher

When he ascended to the right hand of God, Jesus gave "equipping ministries" to his church, including apostles, prophets, evangelists, pastors, and teachers.[10] We can see by studying God's Word closely that Jesus Christ exemplified each of these five ministries in his earthly ministry, and continues to energize them in his Body.

In Hebrews 3:1 (NASB), Jesus Christ is called "the Apostle." "Apostle" means "sent one," and Jesus was "sent" by God for the salvation of the world. In John 4:44, Jesus clearly implied that he was "a prophet." Peter confirmed this prophetic ministry when he identified Jesus as the "prophet like" Moses that God would raise up (Acts 3:22). When Jesus preached "the Gospel," he functioned as an evangelist (Matt. 9:35–38), and in Mark 1:38 he clearly made preaching the Gospel his highest priority. He identified himself as the "Teacher" when he said, "…you have one Teacher, the Christ" (Matt. 23:10). The crowds recognized him as such and marveled that he taught with authority, not as the scribes (Matt. 7:29 - KJV). Jesus also said he was the good "shepherd" (John 10:11), which is the same Greek word translated "pastor" in other passages in the New Testament.

Jesus has not changed in his position or way of functioning since he was first seated at the right hand of God. We can be confident that he continues to do all these things and more on our behalf and on behalf of the Church at large. Though it sometimes looks like the Christian Church is in a shambles of division and confusion, the Lord Jesus Christ is ever working to bring his Body into subjection to the will of his Father. Most especially, that means bringing people into an awareness of his lordship of their lives, and a recognition that their lives have been purchased by his sacrifice. The question then naturally arises: are we living for ourselves, or for him who died for us and rose again to empower us to become a son or daughter of God?

---

10. See Chapter Ten, footnote #2, to see why we call them "equipping ministries."

13

Our Fellowship with Jesus Christ

It is clear that the Lord Jesus Christ has both the ability and the willingness to do for each Christian whatever we need to help us function as members in particular in the Body of Christ, the Church. The Lord's goal is to reproduce himself all over the world in the lives of those who call upon his name. Whether or not he is successful is individually proportionate to the degree of intimacy each believer attains with him. One biblical word for such a relationship is contained in the following verse:

> **1 John 1:3**
> We proclaim to you what we have seen and heard, so that you also may have fellowship [*koinonia*] with us. And our fellowship [*koinonia*] is with the Father and with his Son, Jesus Christ.

In the above verse, the Greek word translated "fellowship" is *koinonia*, a word that in its biblical uses clearly refers to sharing, communion and partnership between or among two or more people. Even a brief biblical study of this word shows that the kind of sharing, communion and partnership it involves is impossible without heartfelt verbal communication. Words are the primary means God chose for people to enter into a state of fellowship or a degree of oneness with each other. We see no reason to believe that the same principle would not hold true when it comes to each Christian's relationship with his Lord, Jesus Christ.

1 John 1:3 tells us that Christians have fellowship with both the Father *and* with His Son, Jesus Christ. The question then is, "What degree of fellowship do we have?" Scripture written to the Church clearly encourages us to have intimate fellowship with both God and the Lord Jesus Christ. There is no such exhortation in any Scripture pertaining to the time prior to the Day of Pentecost, as recorded in Acts 2. The reason is that prior to Jesus' life, death and resurrection, he was not yet the exalted "Lord." But now, after Pentecost, of the more than 250 uses of the word "Lord" from Romans through Titus, we submit that nearly all of them refer to Jesus Christ rather than to God.

It is also interesting to note that the phrase "Lord God," so common in the Old Testament, is never found in the Church Epistles. Why not? Because after Christ's resurrection, as 1 Corinthians 8:6 tells us, "…there is but one God, the Father…and…one Lord, Jesus Christ."

Near the conclusion of his earthly ministry, and as recorded primarily in John 14–16, Jesus had much to say to his disciples about his future relationship with them. In the Church Epistles, particularly Ephesians, we see this clarified in detail. Jesus Christ is the *Head* of the Church, which is his *Body*. Ephesians also shows that the relationship between the Head and the Body indicates their oneness. Certainly we would understand vital communication to be a chief element of that oneness. In fact, the "Head" includes the brain, which, as the nerve center of the body, communicates constantly with every cell in the body.

Let us consider some of the things Jesus said to his disciples shortly before his death.

John 14:21
Whoever has my commands and obeys them, he is the one who loves me. He who loves me will be loved by my Father, and I too will love him and show myself to him."

John 15:5 and 7
(5) "I am the vine; you are the branches. If a man remains in me and I in him, he will bear much fruit; apart from me you can do nothing.
(7) If you remain in me and my words remain in you, ask whatever you wish, and it will be given you.

John 16:12
"I have much more to say to you, more than you can now bear.

Certainly the above statements by Jesus Christ to his disciples indicate important future communication between him and them. John 16:12ff makes it clear that Jesus had much more that he intended to say to his disciples after his ascension and his giving them the gift of holy spirit, the connection by means of which he would speak to them. Although we do not see the word "Lord" in the above verses, the relationship therein implies one of a master and an apprentice, or follower. First of all, the disciples knew that Jesus had been their Teacher while they walked with him, and he was simply telling them that even though he had to leave them physically, this teacher-pupil relationship would not end. By way of the gift of holy spirit that he would give them, he would continue to mentor them and train them to walk in his steps. To do this without two-way verbal communication would be difficult.

In Romans 10:9, we learn that to be "saved," that is, born again, one must confess Jesus as "Lord." That is how a person gets started in his relationship with the Master. 1 Peter 3:15 encourages us to "set apart" (look up to him to honor and obey) the Christ as "Lord" so we are prepared to give an answer to every man who asks us the reason for our hope. Not only do we confess Jesus as Lord to get started in our walk with him, but we keep going by setting him apart as Lord on a daily basis. As we choose to be yoked with him and follow his lead, he who walked a walk of perfect faith will give us on-the-job training in the art of trusting God.

The point is that our Lord Jesus Christ wants us, as the members of his Body, to do exactly what he did when he was physically present on the earth. By way of the gift of holy spirit in each believer, he is now able to represent himself around the world, enabling us to do the works that he did. If the Body of Christ is going to be coordinated, it will naturally require that the Head of the Body be in clear communication with each of the parts. This Man, **who was tempted in all ways like we are**, and who is **touched with the feeling of our infirmities**, is a personal Lord and Savior who knows how each part of his Body should function. He has **played every part**, as it were, and thus can help each of us trust God in the drama of life.

Remember that, in John 14:6, Jesus Christ said that he is the only way by which anyone can come to the Father. The basic meaning of his statement was in regard to salvation, that is, that one must recognize that Jesus Christ was the perfect sacrifice for the sins of mankind, and that only by faith in his work can one be saved. We believe, however, that his statement can also be applied to other elements of his relationship with God and with us. In the context of this chapter, what we mean here is that Jesus Christ "crystallizes" God and makes Him more real to us. Jesus is the most vivid, concrete way to know the invisible God, who is spirit.

Can We "Pray" to Jesus Christ?

There is a controversy among some Christians who believe that Jesus is not God about whether or not we can pray to Jesus. The only definitive place to go for an answer to that question is the Word of God. It is important when trying to answer such an important question that we do not base our position upon only one Greek word or one verse. Rather, we must examine the scope of Scripture to see what it says. We believe that the Bible makes it clear that one can certainly pray to Jesus, but does not have to, and we will do our best to show why that is.

There are many points of logic in understanding why we can pray to Jesus. Before we delve into the issue, however, it is important to understand that the basic and fundamental definition of "pray" is "ask." Prayer may also include praise, but prayer is fundamentally asking for something, as is clear from studying the pertinent Hebrew and Greek words, and even looking up "prayer" in an English dictionary. Consider the following eight points:

First: Jesus is Lord of all (Acts 10:36; Rom. 10:12), and has all authority in heaven and earth (Matt. 28:18). How can he be "Lord" in any real sense if we cannot ask him for things? Now that the exalted Lord Jesus has all authority, it makes even more sense that we petition him, even as it made sense that people petitioned him when he was alive in his earthly ministry. Hundreds, even thousands, of people asked Jesus for things when he was on earth. Does it make sense that someone could ask Jesus for something 2000 years ago, but cannot do so now?

Second: We are to have fellowship with the Son (1 John 1:3). How can we have fellowship with Jesus, which clearly indicates being in relationship with him, but not ask him for anything? We have fellowship with God and ask Him for things, and we have fellowship with other Christians and ask them for things, so does it make sense that we are to have fellowship with Jesus but not ask him for anything?

Third: Jesus said that his followers could ask him for things.

John 14:13 and 14

(13) And I will do whatever you ask in my name, so that the Son may bring glory to the Father.

(14) You **may ask me** for anything in my name, and I will do it.

These verses are especially enlightening when we remember that the entire context of John 14 is Jesus telling his disciples that he is going to be with the Father. If we could not pray to Jesus after his ascension to the Father, that would have been the perfect place to say so. He could have said something like: "You have asked me many things while I have been with you, but now I go to my Father, after which you cannot ask me for anything, but must ask Him." Of course that is not at all what he said. On the contrary, he said we could ask him for anything after he was with the Father, and he would do it.

Fourth: The Word of God makes it clear that believers in the early Church thought it normal to talk with the exalted Lord Jesus Christ.

After his ascension, the disciples prayed to Jesus about choosing a replacement for Judas. This was logical because they understood it was Jesus who had originally chosen the Twelve.

Acts 1:24 and 25

(24) Then they prayed [*proseuchomai*], "**Lord**, you know everyone's heart. Show us which of these two **you** have chosen

(25) to take over this apostolic ministry, which Judas left to go where he belongs."

Although some have contended that the Lord in the above verse is God, it is more logical that it refers to Jesus. He was the one who chose Judas, and he was addressed as "Lord" by all the Apostles over and over in the New Testament. Furthermore, as Peter stated in Acts 2:36, the ascended Christ now holds the title of "Lord."

Stephen called upon Jesus, not God, when he was being stoned.

Acts 7:59 and 60a

(59) While they were stoning him, Stephen prayed [*epikaleo* = "calling upon"], "Lord Jesus, receive my spirit."

(60a) Then he fell on his knees and cried out, "Lord, do not hold this sin against them...."

Paul pleaded with the Lord Jesus about his "thorn in the flesh," as is clear from the context of the following verses.

2 Corinthians 12:8 and 9

(8) Three times I pleaded [*parakaleo* = to beseech] with the Lord to take it away from me.

(9) But he said to me, "My grace is sufficient for you, for **my power** is made perfect in weakness." Therefore I will boast all the more gladly about my weaknesses, so that **Christ's power** may rest on me.

Fifth: Verses such as Acts 9:34 and 2 Timothy 4:17 show that as the Head of the Body, the Lord Jesus is actively involved in healing and sustaining its members. It is our contention that any Christian can ask the Lord Jesus to do for him anything that would help him do the works that Jesus did. As Head of the Body, he converses with believers and asks things of them. It is only logical that we would also ask things of him. The New Testament tells us of his personal interaction with Stephen (Acts 7:56); Saul/Paul (Acts 9:1–9, 16:7, 23:11; 2 Cor. 12:9; Gal. 1:12); Ananias (Acts 9:10–16); Peter (Acts 10:9–22;[1] 2 Pet. 1:14); and John (Rev. 1:9–18).

Since Pentecost, many things come to the Body via the Head, Jesus Christ. Below are some of the things Scripture says he now does:

- Pours out the gift of holy spirit (Acts 2:33)
- Gives us grace (Rom. 1:5, 16:20; 1 Cor. 16:23; 2 Cor. 8:9, 13:14; Gal. 1:6, 6:18; Eph. 4:7; Phil 4:23; 1 Thess. 5:28; 2 Thess. 1:12, 3:18)
- Gives us peace (2 Thess. 3:16)
- Gives us mercy (1 Cor. 7:25)
- Blesses us (Rom. 10:12, 15:29)
- Nurtures and cares for the Church, holds it together and causes it to grow (Eph. 5:29; Phil 1:19; Col. 1:17, 2:19)
- Directs us (1 Cor. 16:7; 2 Thess. 3:5)
- Is interceding for us (Rom. 8:34)
- Gives the leadership ministries to the Church (Eph. 1:1, 4:8 and 11)
- Gives revelation (2 Cor. 12:1; Gal 1:12)
- Will transform our bodies at his appearing (Phil 3:21)
- Will judge, reward, and punish people, according to what they deserve (John 5:21 and 22; 2 Cor. 5:10; Eph. 6:8; Col. 3:23–25; 1 Thess. 4:6; 2 Thess. 1:8)

Could it really be that with such an intimate connection to the members of his Body, the Lord Jesus could not be addressed by his Church? Surely we can ask our Lord and Head for whatever we need.

Sixth: One solid piece of evidence that people can pray to Jesus is the phrase, "call upon the name of the Lord." Christians are to call on the name of the Lord Jesus, that is, pray to him for help in life. Through the Old Testament, when people "…called upon the name of the LORD," it was to pray to, appeal to, or ask for help from God.

Abraham was in the habit of praying to God, and though there are many examples in Scripture, one will suffice.

---

1. Some say "the Lord" here was God, but there are good reasons to believe it was Jesus. First, Peter was in the habit of calling Jesus "Lord." Second, he had a history of arguing with Jesus, but never with God. Third, the voice came from "the Spirit" (verse 19) and in direct address after Pentecost, Jesus is "the Spirit" (2 Cor. 3:17; Rev. 2:7; etc.).

Genesis 12:8
From there he went on toward the hills east of Bethel and pitched his tent, with Bethel on the west and Ai on the east. There he built an altar to the LORD and **called on the name of the LORD [Yahweh]**.[2]

Elijah challenged the prophets of Baal as to who was the true God and who was not. He and they each prayed to their god, and the one who answered by fire would be known to be God. They prayed, which in the Hebrew idiom is to "call upon the name."

1 Kings 18:24
Then you **call on the name of your god**, and I will **call on the name of the LORD**. The god who answers by fire—he is God." Then all the people said, "What you say is good."

Naaman, the great Syrian general, who was also a leper, expected Elisha to come out and pray for him. He expresses his thought about prayer as follows:

2 Kings 5:11
But Naaman went away angry and said, "I thought that he would surely come out to me and stand and **call on the name of the LORD his God**, wave his hand over the spot and cure me of my leprosy.

In Psalm 99 we see that when the great men of God prayed to God ("called on the LORD"), He answered them.

Psalm 99:6
Moses and Aaron were among his priests, Samuel was among those who called on his name; they **called on the LORD** and he answered them.

God tells the people that when they pray to Him ("call upon my name"), He will answer.

Zechariah 13:9
This third I will bring into the fire; I will refine them like silver and test them like gold. They will **call on my name** and I will answer them; I will say, 'They are my people,' and they will say, 'The LORD is our God.'"

Just as the Old Testament records people calling upon the name of the LORD God in prayer, so the Church Epistles use the same terminology to record people praying to the Lord Jesus.

1 Corinthians 1:2
To the church of God in Corinth, to those sanctified in Christ Jesus and called to be holy, together with all those everywhere who **call on the name of our Lord Jesus Christ**—their Lord and ours:

---

2. Abraham and others called on the name of their God, Yahweh, (which gets translated as "the LORD" in most English versions). For more on Yahweh, see Appendix L, "The Name Yahweh."

This is clearly the same phrase used in the Old Testament, and is applied to Jesus as well as God. Vincent writes, "It is used of worship, and here implies prayer to Christ."[3] R. C. H. Lenski writes, " 'To call on him' means to praise, bless, thank, worship him, and to ask of him all that we need for body and for soul."[4]

The epistle to the Romans also speaks of calling on the Lord Jesus.[5]

Romans 10:12 and 13

(12) For there is no difference between Jew and Gentile—the same Lord is Lord of all and richly blesses all who **call on him**,

(13) for, "Everyone who **calls on the name of the Lord** will be saved."

There is a lot of important information in these verses. First, we should note that the Lord Jesus "richly blesses" those who call on him, showing that as we ask him, he will answer our prayers. Second, verse 13 is a quotation of Joel 2:32, which is a prophecy of people calling on the name of God for help and deliverance—definitely prayer to God. The fact that the Word of God takes the quote about prayer to God from the Old Testament and applies it to Jesus in the Church Epistles is more very solid evidence that we can pray to Jesus.

The epistle to Timothy also shows believers calling on the Lord.

2 Timothy 2:22

Flee the evil desires of youth, and pursue righteousness, faith, love and peace, along with those who **call on the Lord** out of a pure heart.

Even as Old Testament believers called upon the name of the LORD (Yahweh), we today can "call upon" Jesus, and that means we can pray to him and expect him to answer our requests.

Seventh: It is honoring to God when we honor Jesus.

John 5:22 and 23

(22) Moreover, the Father judges no one, but has entrusted all judgment to the Son,

(23) that all may honor the Son just as they honor the Father. He who does not honor the Son does not honor the Father, who sent him.

The first thing we notice about these verses is that God's intent is that people honor the Son just as they honor Him. More than that, if we do not honor the Son, we do not honor the Father. The pertinent question we must ask ourselves is, "How do we honor the Father?" Surely one way we honor Him is by our praise and thanksgiving to him, and by our prayers to Him. According to Scripture, we are to honor the Son in the same way.

Eighth: There is no verse, and nothing in the scope of Scripture, that forbids us from praying to Jesus. This is important, because God's prohibitions in Scripture are quite plain. Since we can ask both God and other people for things we need, it seems only logical that if we could not ask our

---

3. Marvin R. Vincent, *Vincent's Word Studies in the New Testament*, (Hendrickson Publishers, Peabody, MA, originally printed 1888), Vol. 3, p. 186.

4. R. C. H. Lenski, *The Interpretation of I and II Corinthians* (Augsburg Publishing House, Minneapolis, MN, 1963), p. 26.

5. The context of Romans 10:4–17 shows that the "Lord" in the verse is Jesus, and the same is true of 2 Timothy 2:22.

living Lord Jesus for things, the Bible would say that somewhere. However, no verse prohibits us from asking Jesus for what we need.

Thanking Jesus

Not only can we ask Jesus for things, we can thank him for what he did and is doing for us, and that is only logical. Think about it. Jesus is alive. He is Head of the Body of Christ. He is our Lord. How could we not be able to lift up our voices in praise and thanksgiving for saving our lives? We thank God for all kinds of things, and we thank other people for their acts of kindness to us. We are also able to, and should, thank Jesus Christ for what he did and is doing, even as Paul did.

> **1 Timothy 1:12**
> I thank [*charin*] Christ Jesus our Lord, who has given me strength, that he considered me faithful, appointing me to his service.

Conclusion

There is no question that most of the uses of the different Greek words for "prayer" are in regard to our communication with God, and most of the prayers (upward discourses) in the Church Epistles are directed to God. He is a Father whose love for each of us is boundless, focused, passionate, and relentless. We are to converse with Him regularly and intimately. Nevertheless, it is clear that we can also pray to Jesus for things we need.

We have seen there is clear biblical precedent for calling on the name of the Lord Jesus, i.e., talking with him and praying to him for what we need. But some have taught that for a Christian to talk (or to "pray") to Jesus Christ is a slight to his Father, God. In John 5:23, however, Jesus said that in the future all men will honor the Son just as they honor the Father, and that anyone who does not honor the Son does not honor the Father who sent him. We must remember that it was God who elevated His Son and gave him all authority and the name above every name. Far from being a slight to the Father when we honor the Son, it glorifies the Father and validates the plan He had in sending His Son, and it glorifies Jesus Christ for the magnificent and magnanimous work he did for all mankind. When we honor the Son, the Father ultimately gets the glory.

The Bible does not seem to have any specific commandments as to when or about what a believer should talk to Jesus, as opposed to God. Whether a believer prays to God or Jesus is left up to the individual. However, the vast majority of Scriptures dealing with prayer make it clear that God is the principal source of all things, and therefore should be the chief focus of our worship, praise, and supplication.[6] However, we do see some indication that the Lord Jesus Christ focuses primarily on dealing with the Church, while God not only deals with the Church, but also with bringing to pass His desired ends for the world in general.

The very terminology of Jesus Christ being the "Head" of the "Body" (the Church) indicates that he is inseparably linked to the daily direction of Church affairs. As a human being's head is constantly in touch with each cell of his body, so the Lord Jesus Christ is directly connected to each believer via the gift of holy spirit, and is readily available to direct each individual's function in the Body. Some verses to study in this light are: 1 Corinthians 12:4–6; Ephesians 1:20–23, 4:11, 15 and

---

6. See Appendix P, Greek Words Used for Speech Directed to God and/or the Risen Christ.

16; Colossians 1:16–18. Those verses show the Lord's involvement in setting in place the members of his Body and directing the function of those willing to listen to him.

Those who enthusiastically embrace the idea of praying to the Lord Jesus must recognize that this practice ought not to be carried out to the point of distracting one from the worship of the Father. We are sure that the Lord Jesus would find it ironic indeed if he himself were to become the principal object of Christian worship and adoration, when his entire life and ministry was devoted to the glorification of his Father.

We should also make it clear that we are not saying that a Christian *must* pray to the Lord Jesus as part of his or her Christian walk. Since there is no clear command to pray to Jesus Christ, as there is to God (Eph. 5:19 and 20; Col. 1:3 and 9, 4:3), we are hesitant to transform an inference, no matter how clear, into a doctrine, which would then mandate the practice. On the other hand, we shudder at the idea of any Christian telling another that it is wrong for him to talk/pray to the Lord Jesus. We would particularly hate to see believers judge one another and segregate themselves from other Christians over the issue of whether or not they pray to the Lord Jesus.[7] We think whether or not one prays to Jesus is a matter of individual conscience, and not an issue about which believers ought to tyrannize one another.

Reflecting the Light of the Lord

We have seen that because God, the Creator of all life, is spirit and is invisible, He needed an image that five-senses man could see, hear, and touch. We saw that godless men have throughout history constructed their own images of "God" and worshipped them as such. None of these, however, have come close to communicating God's heart, that is, the reality of who He is, and most have grossly perverted it.

We saw that in God's written Word one can find His true character, because the written Word reveals the living Word, Jesus Christ. Jesus Christ gives definition to God for man. He is the ultimate communication of God's heart. It is Jesus Christ who most vividly "declared" (displayed) God for all to see. But now this wonderful man who, because of his perfect obedience to the will of God, could say to the world, "…He who has seen Me has seen the Father…," is no longer physically living on the earth. How then are those who today hunger and thirst after righteousness to "see" and know God?

God's plan was (and still is) that, through Christ's virgin birth, sinless life, death, resurrection and ascension as Lord over all, he would be able to give everlasting life to all who believe in him. At Christ's appearing, this will be consummated for those believers in the form of new, incorruptible bodies like he now has. Until then, the Lord Jesus has given the gift of holy spirit to each Christian, a deposit guaranteeing our inheritance in the age to come (Eph. 1:14).[8] Not only is this our guarantee of a new, everlasting body, but it also gives us the potential to think, speak and act like Jesus Christ while we are still in this body. As we do, we show the world the image of Jesus Christ, who makes known God, the Father.

---

7. This in fact happened during the Christological controversies surrounding the development of the Socinian movement. The "Adorantists," including the Socinians, were those who believed that true Christians should pray to and worship the Lord Jesus. Others denied this, and said it tended toward idolatry. The two parties had many bitter battles over the issue, but the issue became moot when both parties were persecuted out of existence. See Chapter 19.

8. Refer to our book: *op. cit., The Gift Of Holy Spirit: The Power To Be Like Christ.*

2 Corinthians 3:2–6
(2) You yourselves are our letter, written on our hearts, known and read by everybody.
(3) You show that you are a letter from Christ, the result of our ministry, written not with ink but with the Spirit of the living God, not on tablets of stone but on tablets of human hearts.
(4) Such confidence as this is ours through Christ before God.
(5) Not that we are competent in ourselves to claim anything for ourselves, but our competence comes from God.
(6) He has made us competent as ministers of a new covenant—not of the letter but of the Spirit; for the letter kills, but the Spirit gives life.

2 Corinthians 3:7–16 is a parenthesis, elaborating upon the administration of the Mosaic Law. Watch how verses 17 and 18 relate this current administration of the Church of the Body to its originator, the Lord Jesus Christ. Fellowship with him is the key to transformation, so we can be living epistles and able ministers of the Gospel.

2 Corinthians 3:17 and 18 (NASB)
(17) Now the Lord is the Spirit, and where the Spirit of the Lord is, *there* is liberty.
(18) But we all, with unveiled face beholding as in a mirror the glory of the Lord, are being transformed into the same image from glory to glory, just as from the Lord, the Spirit.

The "mirror" referred to here was in those days a mirror of highly polished metal, usually bronze. As one looked at himself in it, others nearby could see on his countenance the warm, reflective glow of the metal. As we continue to look at *who we are in Christ*, primarily in the Church Epistles, others can see the reflection of his life in our own. In verse 18, the word "transformed" is *metamorphoomai*. As a caterpillar has within itself the potential to change from the inside out and become a butterfly, so each Christian has within himself holy spirit, the potential for his life to grow so that it more clearly manifests the image of the Lord Jesus Christ. As the following verse shows, the Apostle Paul's efforts were directed to helping Christians do this:

Galatians 4:19 (KJV)
My little children, of whom I travail in birth again until Christ be formed [*morphoomai*] in you.

Here Paul is not speaking of the New Birth, when one receives the gift of the spirit of Christ. Rather he is speaking of the Christian's character and lifestyle taking on a form like Christ's. How can this happen? Let us reread these tremendous verses from Colossians.

Colossians 3:1–4
(1) Since, then, you have been raised with Christ, set your hearts on things above, where Christ is seated at the right hand of God.
(2) Set your minds on things above, not on earthly things.
(3) For you died, and your life is now hidden with Christ in God.
(4) When Christ, who is your life, appears, then you also will appear with him in glory.

How do you seek the things that are above? Verse 2 tells you: Set your thoughts and desires on living your real life, which is your spiritual life (v. 3). Why? Because in Christ you are guaranteed everlasting life and its corresponding rewards. You still have an old nature that will be trying to "dance" with you throughout this life, but with holy spirit, your *true* nature, you have the power to tell it to go sit in the corner. You can choose not to live as you used to when you had no choice.

Colossians 3:5–10
(5) Put to death, therefore, whatever belongs to your earthly nature: sexual immorality, impurity, lust, evil desires and greed, which is idolatry.
(6) Because of these, the wrath of God is coming.
(7) You used to walk in these ways, in the life you once lived.
(8) But now you must rid yourselves of all such things as these: anger, rage, malice, slander, and filthy language from your lips.
(9) Do not lie to each other, since you have taken off your old self with its practices
(10) and have put on the new self, which is being renewed in knowledge in the image of its Creator.

The *collective* "new man" that the Lord Jesus is *creating* (Eph. 2:15) from both Jew and Gentile is *individually* a "new man" in each Christian (2 Cor. 5:17). The true nature of this new man is the nature of Christ, which we can and must "put on" in our lives. Whatever we choose to put on, that is, to clothe ourselves with, is what other people see day by day. To put on these qualities is to make a deliberate decision to manifest the character of Christ one thought, one word and one deed at a time. We then walk by faith in Christ who lives in us, trusting that as we walk out upon the water he will make it firm under our feet. Without his continual help and guidance, our attempts to follow him would fall woefully short. But knowing that he has thus empowered us and even commanded us to walk like he walked, we can be assured that we are not alone, and that he is right there to hold us up. Indeed, our fellowship with Jesus Christ is greatly deepened when we are engaged in the struggle to walk like he walked. In the process, we learn to let him be our strength in times of weakness and we see his kindness and brotherly affection manifested in our lives more and more.

Look closely at Colossians 3:10 (above). We are to put on the new man by being renewed in knowledge according to the image of him (Christ Jesus) who created him (the new man). The Lord Jesus poured out into each Christian the gift of holy spirit. As we choose to put new knowledge (the Word) in our minds, that is, put on the mind of Christ, our thoughts will be the seeds of godly words and deeds, energized by the holy spirit in us. Our resulting "good works" will earn for us rewards at the appearing of our Master.

Colossians 3:23 and 24
(23) Whatever you do, work at it with all your heart, as working for the Lord, not for men,
(24) since you know that you will receive an inheritance from the Lord as a reward. It is the Lord Christ you are serving.

Although now we must live bearing the stamp of the First Adam, we have been sealed by the Last Adam, who will one day consummate his work in us, as the following verses illustrate:

1 Corinthians 15:45–49
(45) So it is written: "The first man Adam became a living being, the Last Adam, a life-giving spirit.
(46) The spiritual did not come first, but the natural, and after that the spiritual.
(47) The first man was of the dust of the earth, the second man from heaven.
(48) As was the earthly man, so are those who are of the earth; and as is the man from heaven, so also are those who are of heaven.
(49) And just as we have borne the likeness of the earthly man, so shall we bear the likeness of the man from heaven.

1 John 3:1 and 2
(1) How great is the love the Father has lavished on us, that we should be called children of God! And that is what we are! The reason the world does not know us is that it did not know him.
(2) Dear friends, now we are children of God, and what we will be has not yet been made known. But we know that when he appears, we shall be like him, for we shall see him as he is.

Let us do as Paul stated in Philippians 3, and count all things loss for the excellency of the knowledge of Christ Jesus our Lord. Let us strive with all our might to know him and the power of his resurrection and the fellowship of his sufferings. Moment by moment, let us forget those things that are behind and press toward the mark for the prize of the high calling of God in Christ Jesus, knowing that one day we will be like him.

Philippians 3:20 and 21
(20) But our citizenship is in heaven. And we eagerly await a Savior from there, the Lord Jesus Christ,
(21) who, by the power that enables him to bring everything under his control, will transform our lowly bodies so that they will be like his glorious body.

Colossians 1:15 says that Jesus Christ, the perfect Man, is "…the image of the invisible God, the first-born of all creation" (NASB). As we saw earlier, this "creation" is the previously mentioned creation of Ephesians 2:15, the creation of the Church of the Body of Christ. God raised Jesus from the dead, and now the Lord Jesus is in the process of creating a new race of people who will one day have everlasting life and replace the death-dominated race that the First Adam "created." All those in the Old Testament who ever believed in the coming Christ will one day be joined with the Church to make up this future race of men, the fruit of the Promised Seed (Gen. 3:15).

The one and only Jesus Christ is the Last Adam, the Way, the Truth, the Life—the image of God. Only he showed the world God's heart, while at the same time attaining a perfect redemption for all who believe in him. Only he has blazed a trail for man to get back to God. It is he who has given us the power of holy spirit and the ability to shine as lights in this dark world as he did. As we follow his steps, we bring glory to our heavenly Father, and people may say of us, "Like Father, like son."

14

The Book of Revelation:
"King of Kings and Lord of Lords"

When the Redeemer of mankind began his ministry, he was recognized by John the Baptist, who spoke the now-famous words, "…Behold, the lamb of God who takes away the sin of the world!" Throughout Scripture, it is clear that without the shedding of blood there is no remission of sin. As the Lamb of God, Jesus shed his blood for the sin and sins of all men. The Four Gospels record the first coming of Jesus and chronicles the sufferings of the Messiah as prophesied from Genesis 3:15 onward. Jesus Christ came to the nation of Israel to be their Savior and King, but they killed him.

The book of Revelation shows Jesus' second coming to the earth to save Israel, the very people who, as a nation, once killed him. At his second coming to them, Israel will not miss his true identity, for each person will see him come in glory as the King. The book of Revelation portrays not the *Lamb of God* coming to take away the sin of the world, but the *Lion of Judah* coming to judge the world. Instead of "Behold the lamb," a lamb who came for all but was recognized by few, we read:

Revelation 1:7 (NASB)
BEHOLD, HE IS COMING WITH THE CLOUDS, and every eye will see Him, even those who pierced Him; and all the tribes of the earth will mourn over Him. Even so, Amen.

In Adam and Eve, mankind was given the directive to subdue the earth. "'God blessed them [Adam and Eve] and said to them, 'Be fruitful and increase in number; fill the earth and subdue it. Rule over the fish of the sea and the birds of the air and over every living creature that moves on the ground'" (Gen. 1:28). Implied in that directive, and expanded upon later in Genesis and the Law of Moses, is mankind's responsibility to steward the world in a godly way. That actually started in Eden itself, because God's instructions about the garden were "…to work it and take care of it" (Gen. 2:15).

However, instead of caring for the earth, mankind has, in essence, ruined it. Man's disobedience to God and his abuse of the earth have been continuous (Isa. 24:1–6), and the pleas of God through His prophets for men and women to return to Him and His ways have, for the most part, been ignored. Even God's own Son was horribly abused and eventually tortured and crucified. The book of Revelation portrays God and His Christ taking back the earth for the godly and judging the ungodly for all their ungodly deeds. This event, which is still future, has been foretold many times over the years. The book of Jude refers us to one of the early prophets:

Jude 14 and 15
(14) Enoch, the seventh from Adam, prophesied about these men: "See, the Lord is coming with thousands upon thousands of his holy ones
(15) to judge everyone, and to convict all the ungodly of all the ungodly acts they have done in the ungodly way, and of all the harsh words ungodly sinners have spoken against him."

Enoch, the seventh from Adam, lived many thousands of years ago, but he foretold events that are still future. Many of those events are prophesied in both the Old and New Testaments, and the book of Revelation is the capstone of that prophecy. Before getting into specifics, an overview of the book of Revelation is appropriate. First of all, it needs to be understood that the book of Revelation is not addressed to the Christian Church. Christians can learn many things from the book of Revelation, just as we can learn many things from the Old Testament. However, there is a difference between things that are *for our learning* and things that are written *to us*.[1] The Christian Church, known as the Body of Christ, started on the Day of Pentecost in Acts 2 and will end with the Rapture, which is described in 1 Thessalonians 4. We believe that the book of Revelation is written to those who will be left on earth after the Rapture. E. W. Bullinger concurs:

> Our great fundamental proposition—which we may as well state at once—is that—**The Church is not the subject of the Apocalypse.**…However startling this may sound and may seem to some of our readers, we implore you not to dismiss it, but to test the reasons we shall give by the Word of God itself, and to weigh them in "the balances of the sanctuary." Try to forget all that you have "received by tradition," and ask *from whom* you learned this

---

1. We think most Christians have some understanding of this fact. For example, the Bible says in the Old Testament that to be in the covenant, a male must be circumcised. We today know that that does not apply to Christians. The Bible makes a distinction between that which is addressed **to** us and that which is just **for our learning** (Rom. 15:4—KJV). We today do not have a Temple in Jerusalem or animal sacrifices or require lepers to say "Unclean" when they walk along the street (Lev. 13:45).

or that. Be prepared and ready to unlearn anything that you may have received from men, and learn afresh from the Word of God itself. The first chapter [of Revelation] furnishes us with fifteen proofs of our fundamental proposition.[2]

Whereas the Church Epistles are specifically addressed to the Church of the Body which started on the Day of Pentecost, the book of Revelation speaks of events which will occur on earth after the Church is taken up. Jesus Christ will be dealing with his Church, but his Church will be Jews and Gentiles, not the "one new man" that is the subject of Ephesians 2:15.[3] Revelation shows that Christ is active and still building his Church. In Chapter 1, he is dispensing revelation to angels to take to believers. In Chapters 2 and 3, Christ is authoring letters to assemblies in different towns, strengthening, encouraging, and warning them. Chapter 5 shows Christ taking the scroll from God's hand and preparing to open it and begin the time of "Jacob's trouble" (Jer. 30:7), also called the Tribulation. Starting with Chapter 6, there is a series of judgments. There are seal judgments, trumpet judgments, and bowl judgments. During this time, there is tribulation and then wrath on the earth. Interwoven into the record of this terrible time is information about the believers of the time and those who oppose them, particularly the man known as the Antichrist. Revelation 19 portrays the Battle of Armageddon in which Christ rides down from heaven followed by his armies. After defeating his enemies and reclaiming the earth for God and His people, he raises the righteous dead who come to life and live in his kingdom for a thousand years.

During this thousand years, the Devil is chained and powerless, but at the end of the thousand years he is released and manages to stir up a revolution against Christ's kingdom. This revolt is ended by fire from heaven, which puts a quick end to the enemies of the Lord.[4] At that point God "…will judge the world with justice by the man He has appointed…" (Acts 17:31). All the dead who were not previously raised, either in the Rapture or the first resurrection, are raised and stand before Christ. He had said in John 5:22 that the Father entrusted all judgment to the Son, and this is the Final Judgment. Each and every person will get what he deserves. He had spoken this clearly while he was still with us on earth: "For the Son of Man is going to come in his Father's glory with his angels, and then he will reward each person according to what he has done" (Matt. 16:27). As the Judge, Christ will have the final word on who will live eternally and who will be condemned to die. After destroying all unrighteous people, Christ will reign with God, his Father, even as Revelation 21 describes.

---

2. E. W. Bullinger, *Commentary on Revelation* (Kregel Publications, Grand Rapids, 1984), p. 3. Bullinger's 700 page book is a masterpiece of accurate exposition. He knows the language and the customs involved, and shows clearly that the Church of the Body is not involved in the wrath of God and of the Lamb that is poured out in Revelation.

3. Many people are confused by the word "Church." It is from the Greek word *ekklesia*, which simply means "assembly" or "gathering." It is the context that determines what kind of assembly is being spoken of. When the Church Epistles speak of the "Church," the word refers to saved Christians. In Acts 7:38, Moses was with the "assembly" in the wilderness (the KJV actually has "church") though that assembly was the Jews with Moses. In Acts 19, a mob assembles in Ephesus, and that "assembly" was pagan Gentiles. Most of the time, the reader of the English Bible never sees the flexibility in the word *ekklesia* because the translators translate it according to context. Nevertheless, the point should be clear: when Revelation addresses "the church at Ephesus," or "the church at Sardis," it can be the same as Acts 7:38, where the "church" is a Jewish assembly, and the internal evidence of the letters themselves shows that is the case.

4. Many people are confused about the Battle of Armageddon and this final war. The Battle of Armageddon is the battle *before* the 1000 year reign of Christ (Rev. 19), and the war that ends with fire from heaven occurs *after* the 1000 year reign of Christ (Rev. 20:7–9). Thus, Armageddon is not "the final battle" as so many teach.

The time of the Tribulation and the Judgments, will be a terrible time for God's enemies, but for people who have been waiting for years for justice on the earth, it will be a time to be thankful. Evil people may have gotten away with their wickedness all their lives, but the Day of Reckoning is coming:

Revelation 11:17 and 18
(17) "...We give thanks to you, Lord God Almighty, the One who is and who was, because you have taken your great power and have begun to reign.
(18) The nations were angry; and your wrath has come. The time has come for judging the dead, and for rewarding your servants the prophets and your saints and those who reverence your name, both small and great— and for destroying those who destroy the earth."

The book of Revelation opens in a fashion that shows the distinction between God and His Son, and also points to the exalted position that Christ now holds, having been enthroned in "the highest place" and having been given "...the name that is above every name" (Phil. 2:9). The content of the book of Revelation was passed from "hand to hand." It was held first in the mind of God and then given to Jesus Christ, who in turn made it known to an angel, who then told it to John.

Revelation 1:1
The revelation of Jesus Christ, which God gave him to show his servants what must soon take place. He made it known by sending his angel to his servant John,

This verse establishes the distinction between God and Christ in that, even after Christ's resurrection and glorification, each has a separate mind and separate thoughts. God knew the information contained in the book of Revelation and "gave" it to Jesus. Note that now, as always, Jesus is obedient to God. God gave Jesus the information to share with others, and that is exactly what Jesus did—he "made it known." Often we say that "Christ set a perfect example for us, always obeying the will of God." While that is true, a greater truth is that Jesus is *still* setting a perfect example because he is still perfectly obeying the will of God. This example is in stark contrast to Lucifer's behavior when he once occupied a similar position. Scripture teaches that Christians are to be followers of Christ, and each day every Christian has a decision to make: "Do I follow Christ and do what he wants me to do, or do I do what I want to do?"

The fifth chapter of Revelation shows the Son as the Agent of God. God is portrayed sitting on a throne and holding a scroll with its contents sealed. No one can be found who is worthy to open the scroll until Jesus Christ comes and takes the scroll from God and begins to open it. The song of the 24 elders standing before God points to the great truth of why Jesus Christ is worthy to open the scroll: not because he is God, but rather because with his own blood he purchased men for God (Rev. 5:9). Let us not forget that the reason Jesus shed his blood was that he loved God and His people. What a great example to us as to how we ought to live.

Revelation 6 begins the accounting of the tribulation and wrath that characterizes so much of the book and is a large part of the judgment on the earth. It can be confusing to the uneducated reader as to whether it is God or Christ who is actually doing the judging. As we said, Revelation clearly portrays the distinction between God and Christ. Note how clearly this is set forth in the following verses:

Revelation 5:13b

"...To him who sits on the throne [God] and to the Lamb be praise and honor and glory and power, for ever and ever!"

Revelation 7:10

And they cried out in a loud voice: "Salvation belongs to our God, who sits on the throne, and to the Lamb."

Revelation 11:15

The seventh angel sounded his trumpet, and there were loud voices in heaven, which said: "The kingdom of the world has become the kingdom of our Lord [God] and of his Christ [Jesus], and he will reign for ever and ever."

Revelation 12:10a

Then I heard a loud voice in heaven say: "Now have come the salvation and the power and the kingdom of our God, and the authority of his Christ....

Revelation 20:6b

...they will be priests of God and of Christ and will reign with him for a thousand years.

Revelation 21:22 and 23

(22) I did not see a temple in the city, because the Lord God Almighty and the Lamb are its temple.
(23) The city does not need the sun or the moon to shine on it, for the glory of God gives it light, and the Lamb is its lamp.

Revelation 22:1

Then the angel showed me the river of the water of life, as clear as crystal, flowing from the throne of God and of the Lamb.

These verses speak loudly against any concept of two, and certainly not *three*, "persons" making up "one God." The clear distinction between God and Christ is always maintained, even after the resurrection and glorification of Christ. If Christ is "co-equal and co-eternal" with God as Trinitarians teach, then surely there must be two Gods: the Father and Christ, because the above verses clearly portray two distinct beings. But of course there are not two Gods, there is one God, and these verses make clear that even after the resurrection Jesus is "His [God's] Christ," not another part of God.

Another factor in the above verses that argues against the Trinity's three "co-equal, co-eternal" beings is that there is never any third "person" (the "Holy Spirit"), present with God and His Christ. When all is said and done, only God and Christ sit on the final throne. Surely if the "Holy Spirit" were a "co-equal third person" in "one God," he would be represented in some way as judging or reigning or would at least get some mention by the saints or elders. Please take a minute to re-read the above eight verses and note that if God were actually represented in three persons, then one of them is getting slighted. At these most important times in history, there is never "a third person," the Holy Spirit, portrayed with God and Christ.[5]

As we stated above, the book of Revelation can be confusing as to exactly who is doing the judging of the earth and its people. Some verses seem to say that Christ will judge, while others say that God will be the one to judge. For example, Revelation 6:16 mentions "...the wrath of the Lamb," while 15:7 mentions "the wrath of God." Revelation 14:7 says that the hour of God's judgment has come, while 19:11 says that Jesus Christ judges and makes war. Much of the confusion can be cleared up by understanding the biblical concept of *agency*. Under the heading "Agent," *The Encyclopedia of the Jewish Religion states*:

> The main point of the Jewish law of agency is expressed in the dictum, "A person's agent is regarded as the person himself." Therefore, any act committed by a duly appointed agent is regarded as having been committed by the principal.[6]

The fact is that *both* God and His Christ are involved in the wrath and the judgment, and there are clear verses that indicate this. For example:

Revelation 6:16 and 17
(16) They called to the mountains and the rocks, "Fall on us and hide us from the face of him who sits on the throne [God] **and** from the wrath of the Lamb!
(17) For the great day of **their wrath** has come, and who can stand?"

God is the Author, and Christ is His agent. The example in the Old Testament of Pharaoh and Joseph foreshadowed this tandem sovereignty. In the Joseph record, he acted out Pharaoh's will. So it is here. Jesus is the agent of God's wrath, and is God's appointed judge. Even before his crucifixion, Jesus said, "...the Father judges no one, but has entrusted all judgment to the Son" (John 5:22). Acts 17:31 records that Paul knew and taught the same truth: "For He [God] has set a day when He [God] will judge the world with justice by that man He has appointed...." Of course, "the man" appointed by God as His agent to do the judging is none other than Jesus Christ.

Another interesting example showing Jesus Christ as the agent of God is the Battle of Armageddon, which is called "...the great winepress of God's wrath" (Rev. 14:19). In this battle Jesus is the agent who carries out God's wrath, and "he [Jesus] treads the winepress" (Rev. 19:15). The above examples give us some key information about the relationship between God and Christ. It is easy to see the love and trust that God has for His Son in having given him such great responsibility, making Jesus His agent **to judge and make war** and to administer the ages to come. Surely God has given Jesus the name above every name and has exalted him above all others. At the same time, we clearly see the obedience Jesus demonstrates in that he always did, and still continues to do, the will of God.

The fact that God "...seated him [Jesus Christ] at his right hand in the heavenly realms, far above all rule and authority, power and dominion, and every title that can be given, not only in the present age but also in the one to come" (Eph. 1:20 and 21) is most clearly seen in the book of Revelation. The period of tribulation and wrath that will start in Revelation 6, with Jesus Christ opening the

---

5. For a biblical exposition of "the Holy Spirit," see our book: *op. cit., The Gift of Holy Spirit, The Power To Be Like Christ* and Appendix I.

6. R. J. Z. Werblowski and Geoffrey Wigoder, *The Encyclopedia of the Jewish Religion citing Ned. 72B; Kid 41B* (Adama Books, New York, 1986). See also Appendix D.

seven seals, comes to a close in Revelation 19 as he rides out of heaven on a white horse, with the armies of God following him, and conquers the earth:

Revelation 19:11-15
(11) I saw heaven standing open and there before me was a white horse, whose rider is called Faithful and True. With justice he judges and makes war.
(12) His eyes are like blazing fire, and on his head are many crowns. He has a name written on him that no one knows but he himself.
(13) He is dressed in a robe dipped in blood, and his name is the Word of God.
(14) The armies of heaven were following him, riding on white horses and dressed in fine linen, white and clean.
(15) Out of his mouth comes a sharp sword with which to strike down the nations. "He will rule them with an iron scepter." He treads the winepress of the fury of the wrath of God Almighty.

The Bible is very clear about the authority Jesus will have over the nations: "...He will rule them with an iron scepter..." (Rev. 19:15 is quoting the prophecy of the event in Ps. 2:9). The book of Revelation mentions the thousand year reign of Christ but does not take time to describe what it will be like. It is spoken of extensively in the Old Testament. The picture portrayed throughout the Old Testament of the thousand year reign of Christ is one of peace and security. Although there are many verses that show this, the following is a representative list: justice will prevail on earth (Jer. 23:5 and 6); there will be no war or weapons of war (Mic. 4:1-4); people's homes will be secure (Isa. 32:18); children will be safe from harm (Isa. 11:8 and 9); animals will not kill each other (Isa. 11:6 and 7); there will be no sickness (Isa. 33:24, 35:5-7); there will be plenty of food (Amos 9:13); and even the animals will have more than enough to eat (Isa. 30:23 and 24).[7]

This future time of peace and security is possible, in large part, because the Devil and his demons will be chained and unable to influence mankind. Even this is prophesied in the Old Testament in veiled terms (Isa. 24:21 and 22; Dan. 7:12), but is clearly stated in Revelation:

Revelation 20:1-3
(1) And I saw an angel coming down out of heaven, having the key to the Abyss and holding in his hand a great chain.
(2) He seized the dragon, that ancient serpent, who is the devil, or Satan, and bound him for a thousand years.
(3) He threw him into the Abyss, and locked and sealed it over him, to keep him from deceiving the nations anymore until the thousand years were ended. After that, he must be set free for a short time.

The book of Revelation is the "capstone" of the Bible, clearly showing the fitting conclusion to the odyssey of mankind. It portrays the just reward of the righteous and the punishment of the wicked. It portrays the godly vengeance of Jesus Christ, who, although he "knew no sin," was treated worse than any sinner. It portrays the high position to which God has exalted Christ, even showing him reigning alongside God on the new earth. And, very fittingly, it portrays both God and Christ receiving the worship that they so richly deserve from all the saints, for whom they have each done so much.

---

7. See Chapter 5 (Dan. 2:44).

Changes in the Relationship Between God and Christ

The book of Revelation highlights one of the problems with Trinitarian doctrine—that it leaves one with an essentially "static" (unchanging, invariable) view of Jesus. If Jesus were "God in the flesh," with his dominant nature being deity, he is as changeless as God. Therefore, in essence, Christ never changed, and neither did his relationship with God.

On the other hand, the non-Trinitarian perspective of the Man, Jesus, results in a much more "dynamic" (capable of change and growth) relationship between God and His Son. Jesus grew and developed in "wisdom and stature"—ways in which all of us grow and develop (Luke 2:52). When he received God's gift of holy spirit at his baptism, he was able to relate to his Father on a new and much deeper level. As he walked day by day, his relationship with God deepened, just as ours does as we walk in obedience. Understanding this allows us to relate to the Man, our brother, in an inspiring and refreshing way, for he truly did experience life as we do.

Understanding who both God and Jesus are is critical to understanding their relationship, which has evolved and changed at several key points. We must recognize these changes and the corresponding time factors. The first major change that occurred in their relationship was at the baptism of John, when Jesus was anointed with holy spirit and began his Messianic ministry (Acts 10:38). It was at this point that he literally became "the Christ," or "the Anointed One" and from then on his working relationship with God was catapulted to a new level. Furthermore, because of the work set before him and his willingness to do it, his intimacy with his Father continued to deepen.

The next major change was at his resurrection, when he was given a "glorious body" (Phil. 3:21) and "all authority" in heaven and earth (Matt. 28:18). He ascended to the right hand of God and assumed joint rulership of the creation as "Lord." In this present relationship, he and his Father are in a heavenly partnership, sharing cooperatively such functions as inspiring Scripture (Rom. 1:7; 1 Cor. 1:3; Gal. 1:11 and 12; *et al.*) and directing the leadership of the Church (1 Thess. 3:11). It is important to note that in the Four Gospels, Jesus had not yet been "glorified" (John 7:39). He had to suffer and die before he could be raised and glorified. Jesus' own statements in the Gospels clearly show his total dependence on his heavenly Father.

When the exalted Lord Jesus has fulfilled all the prophecies about his second coming to the earth, including the judgment of all men and the restoration of Paradise, his relationship with God will change one last time. This truth is vividly illustrated in 1 Corinthians 15:24–28. It is a section of Scripture that we believe clearly portrays the changing nature of the relationship between God and His Son, as well as the clear distinction between the two.

> **1 Corinthians 15:24–28 (NASB)**
> (24) then *comes* the end, when He (**Christ**) delivers up the kingdom to the God and Father, when He (**Christ**) has abolished all rule and all authority and power.
> (25) For He (**Christ**) must reign until He (**Christ**) has put all His (**Christ's**) enemies under His (**Christ's**) feet.
> (26) The last enemy that will be abolished is death.
> (27) For HE (**Christ**) HAS PUT ALL THINGS IN SUBJECTION under HIS (**Christ's**) FEET. But when He (**Christ**) says, "All things are put in subjection," it is evident that He (**God**) is excepted who put all things in subjection to Him (**Christ**).

(28) And when all things are subjected to Him (**Christ**), then the Son Himself also will be subjected to the One (**God**) who subjected all things to Him (**Christ**), that God may be all in all.

As we stated, the book of Revelation is the complement to the Old Testament. It is God's account of "…when the times will have reached their fulfillment—to bring all things in heaven and on earth together under one head, even Christ" (Eph. 1:10). Because of the accomplishments of Christ, the "last chapter" of God's Word has been written. We win!!! Amen!! Come quickly, Lord Jesus!

A New Race for a New Age

The book of Revelation does not speak much about the people who will live and reign with Christ forever, it just says that we will. Thus, Revelation is a wonderful conclusion to the odyssey of human history. Remember that the purpose of the Messiah was to redeem mankind from death, and that is exactly what Christ did. We now want to develop the tremendous truth that we introduced in Chapter 1, where we wrote in closing: "God's original plan was to have many sons and daughters living together in Paradise forever. The First Adam was *supposed* to have been the father of that perfect race; the Last Adam *will* be the 'father' of such a race." Because Jesus Christ has blazed for us a trail through the wilderness of sin and death all the way to everlasting life, we who choose to believe in him will be part of this *new race for a new age*. We should acknowledge the world's most famous Bible verse in this connection:

John 3:16
"For God so loved the world that he gave his one and only Son, that whoever believes in him shall not perish but have eternal life.

This hope of everlasting life is to be for each Christian the **anchor of our souls** (Heb. 6:19), that which keeps us from being "…blown about by every wind of doctrine…" (Eph. 4:14 -NRSV) and dashed on the rocks of this tempestuous world with its many unbiblical religious beliefs and ethical systems.[8]

We will now consider a key word in regard to this issue, a word used only four times in the New Testament—Hebrews 2:10, 12:2; Acts 3:15 and 5:31, and we will examine each of these. The word is *archegos*, and it means "the first one in line in a rank or file." We have already looked at the following verse containing one of its four uses:

Hebrews 2:10
In bringing many sons to glory, it was fitting that God, for whom and through whom everything exists, should make **the author** [*archegos*; KJV—"captain"] of their salvation perfect through suffering.

---

8. It is a little known truth that Scripture distinguishes between the concepts "everlasting" and "eternal." God alone has inhabited "eternity" in a state of transcendent, perpetual immortality. Jesus had a beginning at his birth and was given "immortality" in his resurrection (see 1 Tim. 1:17, 6:15). We will be given "everlasting life" when we are either raised from the dead or transformed with new bodies, as clearly described in 1 Thessalonians 4:16 and 17. "Eternal life" is literally "*aionian* life," from the Greek word *aion*, meaning "age." Hence, we are actually given "life in the age to come."

Jesus was the only one who could blaze a trail to salvation, one that all men who chose to do so could follow. Our salvation will not be consummated until he appears again and gives us new, everlasting bodies. In the meantime, we can walk confidently through this minefield of life looking always to him and carefully following his footsteps.

Hebrews 12:1–4
(1) Therefore, since we are surrounded by such a great cloud of witnesses, let us throw off everything that hinders and the sin that so easily entangles, and let us run with perseverance the race marked out for us.
(2) Let us fix our eyes on Jesus, **the author** [*archegos*] and perfecter of our faith, who for the joy set before him endured the cross, scorning its shame, and sat down at the right hand of the throne of God.
(3) Consider him who endured such opposition from sinful men, so that you will not grow weary and lose heart.
(4) In your struggle against sin, you have not yet resisted to the point of shedding your blood.

Jesus is not only the "author" of salvation, but he is also the "author and perfecter" of *faith*, and faith is the key to a person receiving salvation. Jesus is our perfect example of one who always trusted his heavenly Father, no matter what the circumstances were. His faith was in large part based on "…the joy set before him…." As he had the hope of reigning forever with his Father, so we have the hope of reigning forever with both of them. This hope should keep us going in the face of "opposition from sinful men." For Jesus, such opposition included an ignominious death on the Cross. For most of us, the opposition is not as much from sinful men opposing us as it is from internal resistance from our old, sinful nature.

Shortly after the Day of Pentecost and the beginning of the Church of the Body of Christ, Peter and John healed a lame man who had begged daily on the Temple steps. Peter then addressed an astonished group of Israelites, many of whom had been a part of turning Jesus over to the authorities for crucifixion.

Acts 3:15 and 16
(15) You killed **the author** [*archegos*; KJV—"prince"] of life, but God raised him from the dead. We are witnesses of this.
(16) By faith in the name of Jesus, this man whom we see and know was made strong. It is Jesus' name and the faith that comes through him that has given this complete healing to him, as you can all see.

Jesus is the Author of life because he is the first one who overcame death. The fact that he is the "*first* one in line in a rank or file" means that others will follow him on this road to everlasting life. Even in this fallen world, those who have faith in the authority of the name of Jesus can impart to others the kind of life that healed the lame man. Because they healed the lame man, Peter and the other Apostles were arrested and questioned by the Sanhedrin, the ruling body of Judaism, about their angelically-assisted jailbreak. Their reply is both informative and inspirational:

Acts 5:29–31
(29) Peter and the other apostles replied: "We must obey God rather than men!
(30) The God of our fathers raised Jesus from the dead—whom you had killed by hanging him on a tree.
(31) God exalted him to his own right hand as **Prince** [*archegos*] and Savior that he might give repentance and forgiveness of sins to Israel.

Jesus, God's "Prince," will one day in actuality be crowned King and rule his kingdom here on earth. In the meantime, as Lord, he is authorized to give repentance and forgiveness of sin to all who believe in him. When we have *faith* (Heb. 12:2), he gives us *forgiveness of sins* (Acts 5:31). This assures us of *salvation* (Heb. 2:10) and *everlasting life* (Acts 3:15). That is a summary of the four uses of *archegos*, which show Jesus blazing a trail for us to follow into the presence and very life of God. Because of Jesus' faith and obedience, he was the firstborn from among the dead. As the "Promised Seed" of Genesis 3:15, Jesus will produce fruit after his kind, a new race of people who will live forever.

When Will the New Race Begin?

The question we want to look at now is *when* will this new race of people come into existence? Perhaps the fact that, on the Day of Pentecost, quite a number of people were born again at the same time foreshadows what could be called the largest "multiple birth" ever. When Jesus Christ comes again, hundreds of millions (maybe billions) of dead believers will be simultaneously raised to everlasting life, while living believers will also be clothed with immortality. To begin to answer the question of when this will happen, let us consider the following verses:

Galatians 1:3–5
(3) Grace and peace to you from God our Father and the Lord Jesus Christ,
(4) who gave himself for our sins to rescue us from **this present evil age**, according to the will of our God and Father,
(5) to whom be glory forever and ever. Amen.

Let us first note that the Greek word translated "age" is *aion*, from which we get the English word "eon," meaning a period of time. Verse 4, about Jesus rescuing us, sure looks good, but it raises some specific questions. For example: *Why* is this "present age" *evil*? When did "the present evil age" *begin*? When will it *end*, that is, when will Jesus rescue us? To answer the first question, look at the following verse:

2 Corinthians 4:4
The **god of this age** has blinded the minds of unbelievers, so that they cannot see the light of the gospel of the glory of Christ, who is the image of God.

It is not difficult to figure out who the god of this age is. It is Satan, the Devil. But that raises another question: how did *he* get to be the god of this age? Once again God's Word has the answer:

Luke 4:5 and 6
(5) The devil led him [Jesus] up to a high place and showed him in an instant all the kingdoms of the world.
(6) And he said to him, "I will give you all their authority and splendor, **for it has been given to me**, and I can give it to anyone I want to.

No one can give away anything he does not have. Who had the authority over the world? The First Adam had it (Gen. 1:28), and when he disobeyed God's commandment in the Garden of Eden, he relinquished it to Satan. Guess what? That also answers the second question as to *when* this present evil age began. It began when the First Adam lost his original dominion to Satan. This present evil age will end when the Last Adam takes back that dominion by force. In the meantime, each Christian has both the choice and the ability not to conform to this "age," but to be transformed by the renewing of his mind so as to prove the will of God in his life (Rom. 12:2).

When Jesus Christ comes again, he will not only raise to everlasting life all those who have believed in him, he will also provide a place for them to live.

Romans 8:18–21 (NEB)
(18) For I reckon that the sufferings that we now endure bear no comparison with the splendor, as yet unrevealed, which is in store for us.
(19) For the created universe waits with eager expectation for God's sons to be revealed.
(20) It was made the victim of frustration, not by its own choice, but because of him [Satan] who made it so; yet always there was hope,
(21) because **the universe itself is to be freed from the shackles of mortality** and enter upon the liberty and splendor of the children of God.

Jesus Christ, the one born in a manger in Bethlehem and now the exalted Lord, will one day restore the Paradise that the First Adam lost. He will destroy Satan and all evil, and he will create a new heaven, a new earth and a new race for a new and everlasting age. That will complete the mission that was prophesied for him in Genesis 3:15, and which he saw elaborated upon in Isaiah 61:1 and 2. He will then come before his heavenly Father and say, as it were: "Last Adam reporting. Mission accomplished, Paradise regained!" And we can picture God replying, "Thank you, Son. Let's enjoy our family forever."

It is doubtful that you have ever seen a counterfeit thirteen-dollar bill. The reason you have never seen one is that there is no *genuine* thirteen-dollar bill to counterfeit. There is no such thing as a counterfeit without something genuine to copy. The truth of God's Word is that there will be a "new race" for a "new age," and therefore Satan has counterfeited *both* of these ideas. Just as they are inextricably linked together in truth, so are they in the Devil's counterfeits. These counterfeits are encompassed by what is today called "New Age" philosophy. The roots of the "New Age" movement are not new. As a matter of fact, you can find them in Genesis 3. While he was in the Garden tempting Eve to disobey God, the Devil said to her:

Genesis 3:4 and 5
(4) "You will not surely die," the serpent said to the woman.
(5) "For God knows that when you eat of it your eyes will be opened, and you will be like God, knowing good and evil."

Satan lied to mankind then, and he is still promoting the same lie today, a lie that is also at the root of the doctrine of evolution. "You shall be as gods" is the bottom line of New Age philosophy, which propounds that it will be this new race of "god-men" who will usher in a "new age," the "Age of Aquarius"—an age of peace, prosperity, one-world government and everyone living happily ever after. Throughout history, a number of tyrants have attempted to produce this new race according to their own timetable. Perhaps Adolf Hitler is the most well known, but true Communists like Joseph Stalin and Mao Tse Tung also had as their goal a "regenerate" mankind—a new race living in peace on the earth with no "religion" but atheistic, humanistic materialism. Such tyrants were not above genocide and genetic manipulation to help speed up man's "evolutionary destiny" to produce a "master race." As we have seen, there is going to be a master race, but it is only THE MASTER who will ever produce it. There *is* going to be a NEW AGE of true peace and prosperity, and it *will* have a one-world government—headed up by JESUS CHRIST THE KING!

Jesus Christ, the Fulcrum of History

We have now come to the end of our Genesis to Revelation survey of the biblical evidence that there is one God, the Father, and one Lord, the man Jesus Christ, His Son. We have repeatedly made the point that the vivid and compelling view of Jesus thus portrayed greatly facilitates our ability to identify with him and to appreciate the majestic plan of God who sent him. Our minds reel at the immense love of both God and Christ to bring to pass our redemption. Our words fail, but the following passage says it best:

> **Romans 11:33–36**
> (33) Oh, the depth of the riches of the wisdom and knowledge of God! How unsearchable his judgments, and his paths beyond tracing out!
> (34) Who has known the mind of the Lord? Or who has been his counselor?
> (35) Who has ever given to God, that God should repay him?
> (36) For from him and through him and to him are all things. To him be the glory forever! Amen.

In concluding this section of this book, we ask you to consider, from the perspective of Jesus, what his life must have been like, and how that life brought such glory to his Father.

Born in a manger in Bethlehem, he grew up in Nazareth much like thousands of other Jewish boys. In the synagogue, the Temple and at home, Jesus heard the Old Testament Scriptures. What must it have been like for him in the moment that he first understood that *he* was the "promised seed" of Genesis 3:15, the Messiah to Israel and the Redeemer of mankind? Apparently, this realization dawned on him before he was twelve years old, because, in answer to his parents' urgent questioning when they realized they had left him behind at the Temple in Jerusalem, he stated, "…Did you not know that I must be about My Father's business?" Jesus' understanding of his identity led to a corresponding understanding of his purpose in the fulfillment of God's original dream. Jesus came to realize that he, and he alone, could do what was necessary to bring to pass an everlasting family of God in Paradise.

Think of the focus he must have had in his heart through his teenage years when, no doubt, many of his peers were frittering away their time with trivial teenage pursuits. Think of how goal-oriented he must have been throughout his twenties, when many other Jewish young men were consumed in establishing their secular careers. Think of how he steeled his heart throughout his earthly ministry, beginning with the time when he was face to face with the Devil in the wilderness.

Think of his agony in the garden of Gethsemane when he was tempted to the limits of his endurance and asked his heavenly Father if there were any other way than the Cross to redeem mankind. Unlike the first man tempted in a garden (the First Adam), Jesus chose to obey his God. Think of his resolve when, after hearing from his Father that there was no other way than the Cross, he arose and walked forth to meet his executioners.

Think how God must have felt as he watched his only-begotten Son suffer at the hands of evil men. Think about God's fathomless love in sacrificing His Son for you. If you are a parent, you know how you hurt when your child hurts. If it were possible, most parents would gladly take upon themselves the suffering of their children. It took far more love for God, whose love for His Son is beyond our comprehension, to watch Jesus suffer and die than it ever would have taken for God to somehow become a man, if that were even possible, and go through the suffering Himself.

Think of the pressure on Jesus as he was beaten and tortured beyond description and then nailed to the tree, realizing that the destiny of all mankind was riding on his "going the distance" for his Father. Throughout his life, Jesus had built an unwavering trust in the Word of his heavenly Father. In entrusting the mission of the ages to His Son, God had "put all of His eggs in one basket." In essence, all the Old Testament prophecies of Christ's life, death, resurrection and exaltation comprised the "good reputation" God gave His Son to live up to. Because Jesus had *genuine* freedom of will, he could have made one big lie out of all the prophecies about him from Genesis 3:15 through Malachi. In the garden of Gethsemane, Jesus could have turned his back on his Father, just like the First Adam did when he was tempted.

No doubt the angels watched in horror and with bated breath as Jesus hung on the tree. Surely God was doing all He could to help His Son, yet at that point it was up to Jesus alone to be faithful unto death. The entire destiny of mankind was riding on the flesh-and-blood shoulders of the Man from Galilee. At exactly the right moment, when he had fulfilled all of the Word of God that he had hidden in his heart, Jesus breathed his last breath with the words, "It is finished," and gave up his most precious possession—his *life*, entrusting himself to God's promise of resurrection.

What a bittersweet moment that must have been for God and the heavenly host. How horrifying to see the Son of God die, and yet how scintillating to realize that the destiny of mankind was now in the hands of the Creator. There was no question that God Almighty would keep His Word and raise His Son from the dead. There was no question that God would then highly exalt him as Lord, upon whom those who so chose could believe and receive everlasting life. Because, by his free-will obedience, he died and was "planted" in the ground, the Promised Seed would one day bear much fruit after his kind.

The Church Epistles are the apex of God's revelation to mankind, setting forth the "all truth" of God's curriculum for those who believe in the Lord Jesus Christ. Each and every Epistle begins with a greeting from "God the Father and the Lord Jesus Christ," and they illustrate the oneness of God and His Son. As with the gift of holy spirit, which Jesus Christ received from his Father and first poured out to mankind on the Day of Pentecost, so Jesus received the revelation of the Church Epistles and gave it to the Apostle Paul (Gal. 1:11 and 12). The Church Epistles are "the word of Christ" (Rom. 10:17), as he received it from his heavenly Father.

In the Church Epistles, God describes Himself as "the Father of Jesus Christ." What an incredible illustration of God's humility, and also of how highly He reveres His Son and what he accomplished. How God beams with pride as He says, in essence, "I'm *Jesus*' dad." How touched the Lord's heart must have been when he received from his Father this revelation now recorded in the Epistles. This must be the epitome of recognition for the Lord Jesus.

By making Jesus the genetic equal to the First Adam, God equipped His Son to be the Redeemer of mankind. It was Jesus, however, who had to choose to obey the Written Revelation of his Father, and he did. God then kept His Word and raised His Son from the grave. How can we ever adequately thank God our Father and our Lord Jesus Christ for what they have done for us? Certainly, one way we can thank them is to pour out our lives in service to them day by day.

If you are a Christian, God and His Son have equipped you to walk the path of righteousness that Jesus Christ blazed. Via the gift of holy spirit, you have the divine nature of God. You can do the works that Jesus did, and greater works. As you do, know that you will be richly rewarded for these works at his appearing, after which you will live forever with him and all God's people in Paradise. All of this, and its unfathomable yet-to-be-made-known blessings, was made possible by one man, *The Man* who "…became obedient to death—even death on a cross!"

Philippians 2:9–11
(9) Therefore God exalted him to the highest place and gave him the name that is above every name,
(10) that at the name of Jesus every knee should bow, in heaven and on earth and under the earth,
(11) and every tongue confess that Jesus Christ is Lord, to the glory of God the Father.

When the testimony of Scripture is so profoundly clear about the identity of Jesus Christ, we must now examine how it became so radically altered in the historical development of orthodox Christian doctrine. How is it that the vast majority of Christians have believed something fundamentally unbiblical and unintelligible, and which effectively diminishes the accomplishments of the one they sincerely meant to exalt?

PART FIVE

An Historical Perspective

15

The Expansion of Piety

From our perspective today, we stand in awe at the infinite precision, simplicity and beauty of God's Written Revelation, the Bible. It is sad to say that man's respect for and adherence to God's Word has not been commensurate with its inherent perfection. "History" is too often the record of man ignoring or distorting God's Word and repeating his mistakes. However, when man allows God's Word to speak, and then conforms his behavior to it, history becomes "His-Story," that is, the will of God comes to pass in the lives of people.

We have seen that the "Trinity" is not in the Bible. How, then, did this doctrine become the so-called "cornerstone" of the Christian faith for the vast majority of believers during the past sixteen hundred years? This question requires a much more detailed answer than we will attempt to answer in this, the concluding part of this book. For those who would like to explore this subject in greater depth, a bibliography is provided in the back of the book to direct you to more detailed sources of historical documentation. Our focus in this section of the book will be to identify the key factors and historical influences that, in our view, swept away the Christian Church from its biblical and logical moorings. We will begin in this chapter with one of the most fundamental of all human tendencies—to be pious and religious at the expense of truth. We will see how this tendency worked to corrupt the very text of Scripture, compounding errors and progressively establishing them as the "orthodox truth."

The "God-Breathed" Word

The original texts of the books of the Bible were written when men who loved God wrote what God inspired them to write. What we know about the process of inspiration is basically contained in four verses in the New Testament:

2 Peter 1:21
For prophecy never had its origin in the will of man, but **men spoke from God** as they were carried along by the Holy Spirit.

Galatians 1:11 and 12
(11) I want you to know, brothers, that the gospel I preached is not something that man made up.
(12) I did not receive it from any man, nor was I taught it; rather, **I received it by revelation** from Jesus Christ.

2 Timothy 3:16
All Scripture is **God-breathed** and is useful for teaching, rebuking, correcting and training in righteousness,

The precious original documents written by these inspired men have long since disappeared, but the words they contained have been transmitted and translated many thousands of times. "Transmission" is copying the text in the same language. "Translation" is copying the text into a different language. Thank God for all those who have labored throughout the centuries to preserve the text of Scripture. No doubt the vast majority of them sincerely desired to reproduce what they believed God had spoken. However the facts show that whether sincerely or insincerely, many scribes and copyists deliberately changed the biblical text. At this point, let us say that despite these changes, we today have a text of Scripture that is closer to the original than anything since the third century. This is because thousands of textual copies have been made throughout the centuries, and with the advent of computers, these texts have been much more thoroughly compared to produce an accurate representation of the original.

The scribes who changed the text were not the first to do so. In fact, *the first two humans* beat them to it. Please indulge us in a little literary license to colloquially reenact the event (Don't worry, we're using a computer—we won't misrepresent the text).

"Hey, did God[1] really say that you couldn't eat of every tree in the garden," Satan asked, ever so sincerely trying to communicate his concern for the poor creature. After all, Eve wasn't getting to do whatever she liked. The Old Tyrant was being a piker again, holding out on her.

---

1. A close reading of the text in Genesis reveals that it was "the LORD God" (Yahweh *Elohim*) who formed man, planted a garden, made the trees grow, commanded the man not to eat of the one tree, declared that it was not good for a man to be alone and made a woman for him. In fact, from Genesis 2:4 onward, Satan is the first one to refer to God as *Elohim* rather than the more personal and relational Yahweh *Elohim*. This makes sense, because the Adversary is always trying to alienate the LORD God from His people. Sadly, Eve echoed the Serpent and used the more impersonal *Elohim*," revealing either a lack of intimacy in her relationship with her Creator or perhaps a too-willing attitude to be congenial at the expense of truth.

Casting about for the exact words God had told Adam, she finally stated, quite matter-of-factly, without annoyance or discernible excitement: "We may eat the fruit of the trees of the garden," which may not have been *exactly* what God told Adam, but close enough, she thought. Anyway, it was the best she could recall in the pressure of the moment.

Let's talk about this. Actually, she omitted the important figure of speech, *polyptoton*, that God used, which communicated a lot about His heart. God had said, literally, "*Eating*, you may *eat* of every tree in the garden," indicating that He really wanted them to feel free to partake of all the abundance He had provided for them. She omitted that vivid expression of God's excitement and love for them.

"Another thing," Eve added. She seemed to get a little more animated as she thought about the prohibition. She was speaking louder and faster now. "God did say, 'You must not eat fruit from the tree that is in the middle of the garden, and you must not touch it, or you will die.'" She was pretty confident she had that part of it right and even tried to quote God.

But did she quote Him *accurately*? She did all right until she got to "…and you must not touch it…." Where did she get *that*? God had never said anything of the kind. It must have reflected what was in her heart regarding the commandment—that it was too restrictive. The fact is, Eve wasn't very clear at all about what God had said, or about His heart of love for her and Adam. In failing to grasp the details, she failed to grasp the point.

Her husband Adam was no better. In fact, he was really the one to blame, because God had originally spoken the commandment to him, and he then was responsible to tell his wife. Apparently, he did a poor job. But, hey, *only one word* was left out, what could that hurt? Considering the devastation wrought on humanity that was caused by Adam's failure to adhere exactly to God's Word, it is clear that anyone who "modifies" God's Word, even in an attempt to "improve it," does so at his own peril. And beyond that, he endangers those to whom he communicates his spurious representation of God's revelation.

If the first two humans so quickly changed "the text" by adding to it and subtracting from it, it is not surprising that their offspring continue to do the same. Modern research into the history of the transmission of the New Testament text provides clear evidence of human tampering by sincere Christian believers in the centuries after Christ, both intentionally and unintentionally. Although it appears that most of the tampering was done with "good intentions," it nonetheless contributed to the development and establishment of false doctrines.[2]

There are a number of ways errors were introduced into manuscripts. Unintentional changes were caused by copyists making mechanical mistakes in copying words from one text to another. They accidentally skipped words and even whole lines, or omitted words that were repeated in the text but were not copied because the scribe thought he had already written it down. The vast majority of manuscript errors are of this "unintentional" variety.

Most of the "intentional" changes arose out of a copyist's desire to correct or improve the grammar, spelling or logical cohesion of the original. Changes also came from deliberately "adjusting" the text to fit the copyist's theological bias. The difficulty this textual tampering presents is that a translation can only be as accurate as the text from which one is translating. Then these inaccuracies are compounded further as these translations are translated into multitudes of other languages. Bible expositors and teachers then produce endless tracts, tapes and books based on the translations that proliferate these inaccuracies.

---

2. See Appendix N for a list of some intentional changes to the text.

Amazingly, despite the many variant readings and scribal adjustments to the text during the centuries, the majority of textual scholars concur that the original reading of Scripture has not been lost. This is because the greatest tendency in copying the text was to change or *add* material, rather than subtract it. What scholars call "the tenacity of the text" is the fact that the original reading is very likely still preserved in various manuscripts, although they might be a statistical minority. Through the art and science of textual criticism, and much laborious and detailed work comparing possible readings with the whole context of Scripture, the original reading can still be distilled. This requires willingness, however, to let go of favored readings and translations if they are found to contain corruptions.

Some Basic Text Types

To help the reader understand the basics of textual criticism, we will now list some basic text types. Most textual scholars agree that there are at least three basic types of New Testament texts, the Alexandrian, Byzantine, and Western. The text types are named for the geographical location of their discovery or where the greatest number of them ended up.

Most scholars believe that the Alexandrian represents the earliest, most accurate text type. It is the most "concise" text, meaning that it contains the simplest readings. Later texts, like the Byzantine, include "conflations" (where a passage from one text is put together with a passage from another). Later texts also have a tendency to "inflate" the titles and references to Christ. It is for this reason that the King James Version (KJV), translated from a Byzantine text, is considered by some to be more "Christ honoring."[3] Those who object to the 20th century versions of the Bible claim that in a number of instances, these modern versions "deflate" the names and titles of Jesus Christ. Concerning this controversy about the supposed superiority of the KJV, D. A. Carson observes:

> I suppose that no doctrine is more repeatedly thought to be under attack in the non-Byzantine traditions, according to the defenders of the KJV, than the doctrine of the deity of Christ.[4]

But as Victor Perry shows, the Alexandrian Greek text can also be used to support an inflated view of Christ if that is the intention of the translators.[5]

It is true that many modern versions, which are based on the earlier Alexandrian text type, may read "Jesus" instead of "Jesus Christ" or "the Lord Jesus." This is not a matter of "deflating" the

---

3. D. A. Carson, *The King James Version Debate: A Plea for Realism* (Baker Book House, Grand Rapids, MI, 1979). Carson argues against the supposed "heresy" of modern versions:

> None of the text-types distinguished by contemporary textual criticism is theologically heretical in the way that defenders of the KJV sometimes suggest. The second thing to note is the fact that the omission of an individual title or phrase or verse does not constitute evidence for theological heresy. Perhaps the omission was part of the original, and the manuscripts that include the title or phrase or verse are guilty of additions. Beyond that, however, even if the omission were not part of the autograph, the omission *per se* would not prove heterodoxy. One would have to ask why the omission had taken place. The reason might prove to be nothing more than *homoeoteleuton* [e.g., when two sentences have like endings, one may be omitted unintentionally] (p. 63).

4. *Ibid.,* p. 63.

5. Victor Perry, "Problem Passages of the New Testament in Some Modern Translations: Does the New Testament Call Jesus God?" *Expository Times* 87 (1975–76): pp. 214 and 215. This article discusses the places in the New Testament where the Greek can be understood (either by the right choice of witnesses or by the appropriate grammatical interpretation) to call Jesus "God," but this translation is not an open-and-shut case. See Appendix M for a comparison of the various modern versions with respect to the principal "Trinitarian proof texts."

reading of the KJV, but rather a matter of recovering what God originally said when He spoke to the "holy men" who penned the original text, which is called the "autograph." Whether or not it sounds sufficiently pious, it is still God's Word. If we ever feel that the language of Scripture is not elevated enough for us, we might take that as a sign that "the expansion of piety" has expanded its way to our door. Is it not the prerogative of the Author of Holy Writ to assign pronouns, names and titles to His Messiah as it suits *Him*? It is not for us to second-guess Him and try to improve upon His inspiration just because we are driven by sincere religious zeal. History attests to the fact that a large part of the world's cruelty and foolishness can be attributed to misguided religious zealotry. As Romans 10:2 declares so aptly of the Judaizers, "…they are zealous for God, but their zeal is not based on knowledge." This has also been true of many of those responsible for the transmission of the text of Scripture.

This phenomenon of expanding words or phrases referring to Christ is so common that textual scholar James White has dubbed it "the expansion of piety." White also provides a concise explanation of the difference between the Alexandrian and Byzantine text-types:

> Most scholars today (in opposition to KJV-only advocates) would see the Alexandrian text-type as representing an earlier, and hence more accurate, form of text than the Byzantine text-type. Most believe the Byzantine represents a later period in which readings from other text-types were put together ("conflated") into the reading in the Byzantine text. This is not to say the Byzantine does not contain some distinctive readings that are quite ancient, but that the readings that are unique to that text-type are generally secondary or later readings. Since the Byzantine comes from a later period (the earlier texts are almost all Alexandrian in nature, not Byzantine), it is "fuller" in the sense that it not only contains conflations of the other text-types, but it gives evidence of what might be called the "expansion of piety." That is, additions have been made to the text that flow from a desire to protect and reverence divine truths.[6]

The chart on the following page shows the expanded names and titles used of Jesus in the Byzantine texts. The modern English versions like the NASB and the NIV favor the Alexandrian readings as the older and more authoritative.

In his study of the controversy over the supposed superiority of the KJV, Carson also identifies the concept of the expansion of piety without calling it that:

> When an intentional change affects the meaning of the passage, **there is a demonstrable tendency to move the meaning in the direction of the orthodoxy and forms of piety current at the time**, not away from it. By "demonstrable" I mean that even within the Byzantine tradition, the later witnesses are inclined to change things in favor of giving more titles to Christ, not fewer; in favor of using more liturgical phrases and explanatory asides, not fewer.[7]

---

6. James White, *The King James Only Controversy* (Bethany House Publishers, Minneapolis, MN, 1995), p. 43.
7. Carson, *op. cit., King James Debate,* p. 63.

		Alexandrian	**Byzantine**
SCRIPTURE	Matthew 4:18, 12:25 Mark 2:15, 10:52 Luke 24:36	he	Jesus
	Acts 19:10	the Lord	the Lord Jesus
	1 Corinthians 16:22	the Lord	the Lord Jesus Christ
	Acts 19:4	Jesus	Christ Jesus
	Hebrews 3:1	Jesus	Christ Jesus

As James White puts it, these modifications occurred because of a "desire to protect and reverence divine truths…to safeguard the sanctity of the Lord Jesus…leading people to naturally expand the titles used of the Lord, possibly even without their conscious effort to change the text."[8] White goes on to show the same tendency in the present day:

> A number of years ago I was hosting a radio program on which we dealt with various religious groups. An elderly lady called in one week and took us to task for not being "reverent" enough. "Last week you talked about Jesus saying this and Jesus doing that. You need to say, 'the Lord Jesus said this' or 'the Lord Jesus Christ said that.' You need to show more reverence."[9]

Historical evidence concerning the transmission of the New Testament text further proves our assertion that devoted Christians inflated the text because of their sincere desire to elevate Christ, something Trinitarian scholars admit. These "inflations" most likely resulted from sincere and pious scribes thinking they were adding dignity to their beloved Master by inflating his name and titles. We have seen this same tendency at work in artificially elevating Christ in other ways as well, like making him "God the Son" instead of "the Son of God."

While we grant the sincerity, piety and religious zeal of those who took such liberties with the text of Scripture, we think something very valuable was lost. The first thing that was lost was the absolute integrity of the text as it was originally written by "…holy men of God…moved by the Holy Spirit." God's precise purpose in inspiring the text as He did is obscured by these sincere inflations and adjustments. Second, these elevated titles have lead to a proportionate lessening of the Christian's ability to identify with Christ as a true *man*, working against an intimate and personal relationship with Jesus. Furthermore, elevating Jesus beyond the boundaries of God's Word creates a gulf between Jesus and mankind that God never intended (Heb. 2:11). Some attribute "the Virgin Mary's" present status (in the eyes of many Roman Catholics) as co-Redemptrix and Mediatrix between man and the Lord Jesus to the progressive elevation of Christ beyond the reach of the average believer, while Mary at least stayed human. This raises a logical question: why should we need to have a mediator to get to our *mediator*? Even Roman Catholic scholar Oscar Cullman acknowledges the problem:

---

8. White, *op. cit., King James Only,* pp. 43 and 44.
9. *Ibid.,* p. 46.

The question has rightly been raised whether the need for veneration of Mary has not perhaps developed so strongly among the Catholic people just because this confusion has made Jesus Himself remote from the believer."[10]

Scholars are finding more and more evidence for orthodox tampering with the text of Scripture. In 1993, Bart Ehrman, a New Testament textual scholar, published a book titled *The Orthodox Corruption of Scripture*. It is Ehrman's position that the Christological controversies in the centuries before the Council of Nicaea created a climate in which "proto-orthodox" scribes made "corrections" in the text to keep the "heretics" from demeaning, denying or perverting Christ.[11] Their motivation was to make the text say what they already "knew" it meant. Convinced that theirs was the proper interpretation, they were apparently oblivious to the implications of substantially altering the sense of the whole biblical message. Ehrman demonstrates "on a case-by-case basis how proto-orthodox scribes of the second and third centuries modified the texts of Scripture to make them conform more closely with their own Christological beliefs, effecting thereby the 'orthodox corruption of Scripture.'"[12]

Ehrman also writes:

> Naturally the same data relate to the basic doctrinal concerns of early Christianity—theologians and, presumably, lay persons alike: Was Jesus the Messiah predicted in the Old Testament? Was Joseph his Father? Was Jesus born as a human? Was he really tempted? Was he able to sin? Was he adopted to be the Son of God at his baptism? At his resurrection? Or was he himself God? Was Jesus Christ one person or two persons? Did he have a physical body after his resurrection? And many others. The way the scribes answered these questions affected the way they transcribed their texts, and the way they transcribed their texts has affected, to some degree, the way modern exegetes and theologians have answered these questions."[13]

Ehrman identifies three main categories of theological emphasis reflected in these corruptions. The first was the result of the "Adoptionists," who believed that Christ was a man and not God, that he was a full flesh-and-blood human being, neither "pre-existent " nor (for most) born of a virgin. At some point (usually said to be at his baptism), Christ was adopted by God to be His Son and be the Messiah. Proto-orthodox critics argued that this position viewed Christ as a "mere man," and they altered the text in a few places to elevate his "divine" status. In the birth narratives in Luke, verses that refer to Joseph as Jesus' "father" were changed to "relatives," or "his parents" was changed to "Joseph and his [Jesus'] mother."[14]

---

10. Cullman makes this observation in the context of the common practice of improperly distinguishing between the Father and the Son.

Cullman, *op.cit., The Christology of the New Testament*, p. 306, footnote.

11. Ehrman explains that he uses the term "proto-orthodox" in order "to avoid historical anachronism." He writes:

> The doctrine of the Trinity in the finished form that we have it today was not generally agreed upon until the fourth century after Christ. Yet there were controversies about whether Christ was God before that time. To call those involved in the controversies "Trinitarians" in the modern sense of the word is not quite correct, and to call them "orthodox," in the sense that they had arrived at a dominant status, is not correct either. 'Proto-orthodox' conveys the idea that they believed Christ was God before the modern doctrine of the Trinity was completely clarified [the word "proto" means first, original or primitive].

Ehrman, *op. cit., Orthodox Corruption*, pp. 12 and 13.

12. *Ibid.,* p. xiii.

13. *Ibid.,* p. 276, footnote 11 (pp. 281 and 282).

14. *Ibid.,* p. 56.

Acts 10:38 was corrupted in later manuscripts by scribes who did not like the fact that Jesus' anointing was associated with his baptism. In one case, they changed the words in verse 37 from "…after the baptism that John preached…" to read "after the preaching of John." Ehrman explains the reasoning behind this change:

> The change is subtle, but again seems to minimize the connection between the Baptist's activities and Jesus' anointing, making the passage less susceptible to an adoptionistic use. For the orthodox it was less objectionable to concede in a general way that Christ was endowed with God's spirit and power than to associate that endowment with a specific event that transpired at his baptism.[15]

The second group were "Docetic" Christians, or Docetists, who believed that Christ was really God or some sort of spirit-being and not a man. Therefore he only *seemed* to be human or to suffer. In response, proto-orthodox scribes had a tendency to inflate verses of Scripture that emphasized Christ's humanity. One of the interesting apparent corruptions in this category is in Luke:

Luke 22:43 and 44
(43) An angel from heaven appeared to him and strengthened him.
(44) And being in anguish, he prayed more earnestly, and his sweat was like drops of blood falling to the ground.

According to Ehrman, these verses are missing from the earliest and best Greek witnesses.[16] They were added by proto-orthodox scribes to highlight Jesus' humanity.

The last category was the "Separatists," who thought that the "divine Christ" and "Jesus" were two separate beings. They believed that "Christ" was a spirit being that at some point entered into the body of the man "Jesus," remained there throughout his ministry to empower him to do what he did, and departed from him at his crucifixion.

One of the surprising aspects of Ehrman's research is the fact that scribes were just as likely to affirm Christ's humanity as his divinity, and changed the texts inconsistently, evidently in opposition to one or another of these three competing heresies. The effect of these changes was to modify the verses that represented the extremes in the Christological debate in such a way that they were supportive of the proto-orthodox position, or could not be used by "the opposition" against them. Ehrman writes:

> It appears that the scribes were more likely to modify texts that could serve as proof texts for their opposition than those that had, in their original form, little bearing on the debates. That is to say, scribes were more inclined to "correct" or "improve" a passage than to interpolate into it a notion that was previously wanting…"[17]

We must remember that the scribes who made these adjustments to the text were first and foremost human beings, not copy machines. As Ehrman notes:

> It is simply not enough to think in terms of manuscripts as conveyors of data; manuscripts were produced by scribes, and scribes were human beings who had anxieties, fears, concerns,

---

15. *Ibid.*, p. 69.
16. *Ibid.*, pp 187–194. Ehrman's argument concerning this corruption goes into considerable depth along both textual and literary lines. Some modern versions like the NIV acknowledge that these verses are not contained in some early manuscripts.
17. *Ibid.*, p. 277.

desires, hatreds and ideas. In other words, scribes worked in a context, and prior to the invention of movable type, these contexts had a significant effect on how the texts were produced.[18]

There were also political or power issues involved, for whoever controlled the text controlled the direction of the Church. In no small measure, debates over doctrine are debates over power, and deciding what is "correct" to believe means deciding who can wield that power.[19]

Thus, we see how gradually the text was altered to the detriment of truth and biblical accuracy. But understanding this well-established historical tendency in the development of the Christian faith goes a long way toward explaining how doctrinal error could not only arise, but become solidified and "substantiated" by a corrupted text. The "expansion of piety" arises from man's sinful desire to elevate his own ideas above the Word of God. It springs from the same polluted well that Adam and Eve's desire arose for religious works (fig leaf coverings), and all manner of idolatrous practices throughout mankind's history. It also explains how the man Jesus, the Son of God, could have been "inflated" to become God Himself.

The Sacred Name of God

Altering the text to make it more "God-honoring" was not done to the Greek text only. Another example of "the expansion of piety" is the way Jews regarded the sacred name of God in the Old Testament, called the "Tetragrammaton" (literally, "four letters," because it is composed of four letters transliterated Y H W H).[20] This name became so sacred that it was not allowed to be spoken aloud. Because this name appears constantly in the Old Testament, not saying it aloud was very inconvenient. To get around this difficulty, the letters of the sacred name were given vowel markings from a related word considered less sacred. That word was *adonai* (meaning "Lord," as a title, not a proper name). Whenever readers came to the word YWHW, they read *adonai*, lest they should "blaspheme" God by pronouncing His name out loud. Never did God Himself require them to take such measures, but that is how they interpreted Exodus 20:7 (NASB), the third of the Ten Commandments: "You shall not take the name of the LORD your God in vain, for the LORD will not leave him unpunished who takes His name in vain." In order to ensure that they would not take His name in vain, they simply refused to speak His name at all. It is hard to imagine that God intended such an extreme position, considering the fact that His name occurs 6,823 times in the Old Testament. Furthermore, God inspired a Psalmist to say that he would call on "the name of the LORD" in response to His goodness:

Psalm 116:13 and 17
(13) I will lift up the cup of salvation and **call on the name of the LORD**
(17) I will sacrifice a thank offering to you and **call on the name of the LORD.**

We believe that the custom of the Jews is just that, a custom, and that it is not a command of God to not pronounce his name. The prophets of Old spoke openly about their communication with Yahweh. The phrase "Thus, says the LORD [Yahweh]" occurs more than 400 times in the Old Testament. While it is easy to see in the printed text that "LORD" is Yahweh, when the prophets of old spoke, if they did not say Yahweh, there would definitely be a lessening of impact since the word

---
18. *Ibid.,* p. 277.
19. *Ibid.,* p. 274.
20. See Appendix L for a more detailed examination of the sacred name Yahweh.

adonai was used of lesser deities than God. Therefore we believe that the prophets of old did pronounce the name of God, Yahweh, and that the custom to not pronounce it evolved later in Jewish history.

Emendations of the Sopherim

Pious scribes were uncomfortable with readings in the Old Testament that they considered derogatory or blasphemous toward God, so they simply changed the text. E. W. Bullinger lists 134 places where the Sopherim, or scribes, altered Yahweh to *Adonai*, (Lord). Bullinger comments, "Out of extreme (but mistaken) reverence for the Ineffable Name 'Jehovah,' the ancient custodians of the Sacred Text substituted in many places '*Adonai*.'"[21]

The renowned Hebrew scholar, Christian D. Ginsburg, writes: '"In the best MSS [manuscripts] there are remarks in the margin against certain readings calling attention to the fact that they exhibit 'an emendation of the Sopherim.'"[22] He comments that one Midrash, or commentary, "emphatically declares the primitive readings were altered by the Members of the Great Synagogue or the spiritual authorities who fixed the canon of the Hebrew Scriptures."[23] The following examples are some of the emendations, or alterations, cited in Ginsburg's work:

Genesis 18:22 (KJV)
"...but Abraham stood yet before the LORD."

The original reading was "...but the LORD stood yet before Abraham," only that the text was altered. As the phrase to *stand before another* is sometimes used in Scripture to denote a state of inferiority and homage it was deemed derogatory to the Deity to say that the LORD stood before Abraham. Hence in accordance with the above rule to remove all indelicate expressions, the phrase was altered by the Sopherim [pp. 352 and 253].

Numbers 11:15
All the four ancient records and the Massoretic Lists give this passage as exhibiting an alteration of the Sopherim. The three Yemen MSS and the Massorah preserved in the *Maase Ephod* state the text originally was "...kill me I pray thee out of hand if I have found favor in thy sight that I may not see *thy evil*," i.e., the evil or punishment wherewith thou wilt visit Israel. As this might be so construed as to ascribe evil to the LORD, the Sopherim altered it into "...that I may not see *my evil*," which the *Authorized Version* (KJV) and the *Revised Version* render "my wretchedness" [p. 353].

2 Samual 20:1 (KJV) (also; 1 Kings 12:16; 2 Chron. 10:16)
"Every man to his tents, O Israel..."

We are told in the Mechiltha, which contains the earliest record on the subject, that this is not the original reading but that it exhibits an alteration of the Sopherim. Originally the text read, "Every one to his *gods*, O Israel." The rebellion against the

---

21. Bullinger, *op. cit.,* Companion Bible, Appendix 32.
22. Christian D. Ginsburg, *Introduction to the Massoretico-Critical Edition of the Hebrew Bible* (KTAV Publishing House Inc., N.Y., 1966. Originally published in 1898), p. 347.
23. *Ibid.,* p. 350.

house of David was regarded as necessarily involving apostasy from the true God and going over to idolatry. It was looked upon as leaving God and the Sanctuary for the worship of idols in tents. But this impudent challenge of Biehri the man of Belial was regarded as a contemptuous defiance of, and derogatory to, the God of Israel, which apparently escaped with impunity. Hence the Sopherim transposed the two middle letters of the word and *to his gods* became *to his tents*. For this reason, the ancient authorities tell us the expression in question was also altered in the same phrase in 1 Kings 12:16 and 2 Chronicles 10:16, which record a similar event [p. 356].

Job 32:3

"...and yet they had condemned **Job**,"

Exhibits an alteration of the Sopherim. According to the List of these alterations preserved in the *Maase Ephod*, the text originally was "and because they had condemned *God*." The context shows that the original reading is preferable to the emendation. Job's three friends came to prove that God's providential dealing towards the afflicted patriarch were perfectly just, inasmuch as his sufferings were the merited punishment for his sinful life. But instead of vindicating the Divine justice they ceased to answer Job because he was right in their eyes (as the *Septuagint* rightly has it) and they thereby inculpated the conduct of God. The expression, however, "and they condemned God" was considered blasphemous, and hence *Job* was substituted for *God* [p. 361].

Jeremiah 2:11

The ancient records emphatically declare that the original reading here was: "...but my people hath changed *my* glory...," and that the Sopherim altered it into: "...but my people hath changed *his* glory...." The same reverend motive which underlies that alteration with regard to the name of God in the preceding passage determined the change here. The expression *glory* was considered to denote the visible manifestation of the Deity, i.e., the *Shechinah*. To say, therefore, that the Israelites changed this Supreme Glory for an idol was deemed too bold a statement and derogatory to the LORD, hence the alteration [p. 356].

Ezekiel 8:17 (KJV)

"...and lo, they put the branch to **their** nose."

We are told by all the ancient authorities that this is a correction of the Sopherim [scribes] and that it was originally: "...and lo, they put the branch to **my** nose," i.e., face. To understand the alteration here effected it is necessary to examine that context. The LORD here enumerates the great abominations which the house of Judah has committed in His very Sanctuary. He states that they have not only profaned His altar by introducing the idolatrous sun-worship into the Temple of the LORD, "but still further to provoke me to anger they scornfully display the branch which is used as an emblem in this abominable worship into my very nostrils." This bold anthropomorphism was afterwards regarded as derogatory to the supreme Deity and hence in accordance with the prescribed canon was altered by the Sopherim [p. 357].

Malachi 3:9.

The original reading here was: "with a curse you **have cursed**…"—the active participle as is evidence from the parallelism:

Ye have cursed with a curse
And ye have robbed me.

As this cursing was pronounced against God which was blasphemy in the highest degree, the active was changed to the passive [you have been cursed instead of you have cursed me] [p. 363].

The unfortunate thing about these alterations in the text is that, although they were designed to elevate God and protect His holiness, they produce an artificial distance between God and us. God created us to have intimate fellowship with Him, and man's sincere but misguided efforts to elevate God actually remove Him from our presence. He is not "with us" anymore; He is "up there" enjoying His own perfect holiness apart from us. How heartening to know that the LORD God would come down and stand before Abraham. No wonder Abraham is called the "friend" of God, but that close relationship is eroded as words are altered to make God less personal and more an untouchable Monarch.

The same thing happens with the Lord Jesus. We trust that every Christian knows he is the Lord, and God's Christ. He is the one who has been given a name above every name and has sat down at God's right hand. Yet he is also one of us, a man. He was a flesh-and-blood human who was touched with the same infirmities we are, was tempted with the same temptations we are, and suffered just as we suffer. The Bible calls him "Jesus" many, many times in the New Testament. Although he is Lord, we are supposed to relate to him as a "brother" and friend also. Although the famous song says, "I have found a friend in Jesus," for many people Jesus is so elevated and apart from them in their minds that he is not a friend at all. They see him as a master and Lord, a commander and director, a judge and assessor, but not as a "friend."

As we have already seen in this chapter, this artificial elevation of Jesus is evident in the altered Greek manuscripts. The title "Christ" or "Lord" gets added to the name "Jesus" to emphasize his elevated position or give him more reverence. We understand that it is good and proper to give reverence to Christ, but we also realize that it is not proper to change the God-breathed Word to do so. It is our contention that artificial elevation of Jesus is actually detrimental to true fellowship with him.

The Development of Creeds and Baptismal Formulas

A final example of the expansion of piety is clearly seen in the development of what are called "baptismal creeds" in the centuries after Christ. These were spoken by new converts who were being baptized in water and making a public Christian confession. Typically these confessions were simple and to the point in their earliest versions, but then became more involved as time went on, as we would predict in the light of the expansion of piety. Because water baptism came to be practiced as a ritual of initiation into the Christian faith, there also arose correspondingly expanding creedal statements of what constituted true belief. There began to be steadily more all-embracing theological statements associated with it.[24]

The Simple Formula

What is termed the "simple formula" is that which we see mentioned in the book of Acts, which involved only a single element: "to be baptized in the name of Jesus Christ" (or some form thereof). As creed historian F. J. Badcock observes:

> In the earliest days of Christianity it seems clear that the baptismal confession consisted of one clause only: "I believe in Jesus Christ, the Son of God, the Lord," or "Our Lord" or of some formula even briefer than that. Later this was expanded into three clauses: "I believe in God the Father almighty; and in Jesus Christ His (only) Son our Lord; and in the Holy Ghost:"[25] Badcock notes that by the middle of the first century, the form of the creedal statements were at the most no fuller than this, as the Bible clearly shows. This fact is demonstrated in the following verses:

Acts 2:38
Peter replied, "Repent and be baptized, every one of you, **in the name of Jesus Christ** for the forgiveness of your sins. And you will receive the gift of the Holy Spirit.

Acts 8:16
because the Holy Spirit had not yet come upon any of them; they had simply been baptized **into the name of the Lord Jesus**.

Acts 10:48a
So he ordered that they be baptized **in the name of Jesus Christ**....

Acts 19:5
On hearing this, they were baptized **into the name of the Lord Jesus**.

Acts 22:16
And now what are you waiting for? Get up, be baptized and wash your sins away, **calling on his name**.

---

24. Ephesians 4:5 indicates that there is only "one baptism," which is clearly the baptism in holy spirit that John the Baptist prophesied about and that Jesus Christ poured out (Matt. 3:11; John 7:37–39; Acts 1:5, 2:33). Therefore, the continuation of the practice of ritual washing with water for cleanliness from sin and an indication of repentance represents, not the will of the Lord himself, but Christian tradition. Owing to the public nature of these baptism rituals, the recitation of creeds was required as a sensory verification of Christian commitment and salvation. In contrast to this tradition, we see the pattern in the book of Acts clearly marked out: when new believers accepted the Gospel they were filled with holy spirit (the gift) and began to speak in tongues as the Spirit (God, the Giver) gave them utterance, as on Pentecost. Speaking in tongues is God's provision for a sensory validation of the internal reality and presence of His gift of holy spirit, salvation and the evidence of everlasting life or "life in the age to come." See our book: *op. cit., The Gift of Holy Spirit: The Power To Be Like Christ*.

25. F. J. Badcock, *History of the Creeds* (McMillan Co., N.Y., 1938), p. 3.

Romans 6:3

Or don't you know that all of us who were baptized **into Christ Jesus** were baptized into his death?

1 Corinthians 1:13 (by implication)

Is Christ divided? Was Paul crucified for you? Were you baptized **into the name** of Paul?

Galatians 3:27

for all of you who were baptized **into Christ** have clothed yourselves with Christ.

This baptismal formula was consistent with the truth communicated in Acts 4:12 and 16:31–33 and Romans 10:13: that to call on the name of the Lord in faith was to be saved.

The Triple Formula

This simple formula found throughout the New Testament Scriptures gave way to a more developed one that gradually evolved into a Trinitarian formula. Badcock continues:

> How widespread was the use of the simple formula, or how long it persisted, we cannot determine: but by about the middle of the second century a threefold formula appears to have been established both in the East and in the West."[26]

There is record of some objections to its use as late as the third century, and some refused to use it even at the end of the fourth. In its first forms, the triple formula clearly differentiated among "God," "Jesus Christ" and "the Holy Spirit," and was later changed to "Father, Son and Holy Spirit." This is consistent with the places in Scripture where the terms "God," "Jesus Christ" and "holy spirit" are mentioned together in the same verse or immediate context.[27] In fact, the formula cited in Matthew 28:19 ["…baptizing them in the name of the Father, and the Son and the Holy Ghost"] was never carried out in the book of Acts and actually not seen in practice until much later. This fact argues powerfully that this phrase was an inflation to the text from a later time in Christian history when the more Trinitarian "Father, Son and Holy Spirit" formula had been developed.[28]

---

26. *Ibid.*, p. 17.

27. Examples of these abound, e.g., 1 Cor. 2:2–5, 6:11, 12:4–6; 2 Cor. 1:21 and 22, 3:3, 5:5–8, 13:14; Gal. 3:11–14; Eph. 2:20–22, 4:4–6; 1 Pet. 1:2; *et al.* That they occur together or within the same immediate context in no way means that these three are all "one substance," etc. They are one in *purpose*. Jesus Christ always does the Father's will and the spirit, the "spirit of truth," brings us into remembrance of Christ (John 14:26).

28. One scholar summarizes scholarly opinion regarding the triple formula used in Matthew 28:19:

> Critical scholarship, on the whole, rejects the traditional attribution of the tripartite baptismal formula to Jesus and regards it of later origin. But whoever was the author of that tripartite formula, it must have already been in existence before the end of the 1st Century, when the gospel according to Matthew assumed its present form, for it already occurs in the Dialect, which was probably composed in its present form at about the end of the first century. Certainly this tripartite baptismal formula was already in existence during the first part of the second century.

H. A. Wolfson, *The Philosophy of the Church Fathers* (Harvard Univ. Press, Philadelphia, PA, 1976), p. 143.

The Church historian Eusebius quotes Matthew 28:19 as, "Go ye and make disciples of all the nations [and] baptize them in my name."[29] This fact is made much more powerful when one realizes that Eusebius lived from ca. 260–ca. 340, during the heat of the Trinitarian debates. He was a moderate, and had originally sided with Arius who taught that Christ was a created being. However, later Eusebius considered Arius' position heresy. It is quite unthinkable that Eusebius would have missed the opportunity to quote the verse in a way that supported the Trinitarian position if he had had that version of the verse before him. We assert that the fact that Eusebius quoted the verse the way he did is proof that the version he was reading from did not have "in the name of the Father, and of the Son and of the Holy Spirit," which is therefore a later reading. That the reading would have been inflated in this way is perfectly consistent with what we have been identifying as "the expansion of piety."

The oldest known Eastern creed is the Epistola Apostolorum, (Letter of the Apostles). It is the earliest creed known word-for-word that can be dated with some certainty between 150 and 170 A.D. While not a simple formula, it was decidedly non-Trinitarian. It read: "[Faith] in God the Father almighty; in Jesus Christ, our Savior; and in the Spirit, the Holy, the Paraclete; Holy Church; forgiveness of sins.

The Bible mentions the terms "God," "Jesus Christ," and "holy spirit" within three or four verses more than 70 times. But only once do these terms occur even close to the form that Matthew 28:19 puts them: "Father, Son and Holy Spirit." Consider 1 John 4:13 and 14 (NASB): "…He has given us of His Spirit. And we…bear witness that the Father has sent the Son *to be* the Savior of the world." This verse falls far short of providing any kind of Trinitarian "triple formula." All the other occurrences of this supposed "formula" in Scripture use the term "God," not "Father," when it mentions Jesus (Christ) (our Lord) and holy spirit, precluding the possibility that a tri-personal deity is being referred to. The spirit and the Son are apart from "God," and not a part of "God." "God, Jesus Christ and the Holy Spirit" is a transitional baptismal formula, more complex than the simple form of "in the name of Jesus Christ," but not as developed as the fully Trinitarian "Father, Son and Holy Spirit" of the later creeds. This is confirmed by many Patristic sources outside of the New Testament.[30]

Conclusion

More evidence for the phenomenon known as "the expansion of piety" could be marshalled, but we think the point is clear. Sincere devotees of the Christian faith, and the Jewish faith that grounds it, have altered the text of Scripture and added their own requirements and concepts to the original God-breathed Word. This has resulted in a number of important textual corruptions that have served to solidify several prominent doctrines in Christendom, one of which is Trinitarian orthodoxy. Many of these are coming to light now in the scrutiny of modern textual, archaeological and historical research.

Because the text is the tool by which we measure the truth or falsehood of doctrine, the compromising of the text starts a vicious downward spiral. The text is corrupted to support the teaching of error, which is then substantiated by the text. This process will continue until scholars and critics, in light of the whole Scripture, evaluate the particular verses that seem to substantiate particular doctrines. Even if many texts support a given reading, the honest scholar and textual critic must keep looking at all the textual evidence for the reading that best harmonizes with the entire teaching of Scripture.

---

29. Philip Schaff, editor, *Nicene and Post-Nicene Fathers: Vol. 1. "Eusebius: Church History, Life of Constantine the Great, and Orations in Praise of Constantine"* (Hendrickson Publications, Peabody, MA, 1994), p. 138.

30. Badcock, *op. cit., History of the Creeds,* p. 17.

Based on our presupposition that the Bible is the Word of God and therefore cannot contradict itself, it is this reading that is undoubtedly the original, even if it is in a statistical minority.

We have also documented the natural, human tendency over time to inflate and elevate the titles and personhood of the Lord Jesus Christ in response to competing "heresies." We can now see that the line between "orthodoxy" and "heresy" is very thin indeed, and that those considered "orthodox" are those who ultimately prevailed in the political and social struggle within the early Church, rather than necessarily those who were right biblically. It behooves us as we enter a new millennium to look afresh at all the biblical evidence and see which way the preponderance points us.

16

The Beginnings of Heresy:
Gnosticism and Neoplatonism

It is now necessary for us to address Satan's continued assault on the Word of God by way of Gnosticism and its evil stepchild, Neoplatonism. It is our opinion that the influence of these two philosophies greatly altered the course of Christian history and became the sandy foundation of what is now known as Christian "orthodoxy."

Most Bible scholars agree that the Epistles of 1, 2 and 3 John were some of the last parts of Scripture written, late in the first century. A significant amount of the content of these Epistles was directed at combating the progenitors of the Gnostic heresy, which in its embryonic form had by that time infiltrated the Church to quite a degree.[1] When we refer to "Gnosticism" in this discussion, we are referring to the whole range of speculative and syncretistic (derived from many sources)

---

1. Although the true aim of the Epistles of John is to edify believers and deepen their fellowship with the Lord, this can only occur if believers are really standing in the truth and not turned from it by false ideas. A pervasive error entering the Church and turning believers from the faith was Gnosticism. A. E. Brooke, Dean of King's College in Cambridge, writes:

> Nine times at least the writer offers his readers tests by which they may assure themselves about the truth of
> their Christian position. The writer's aim in this ninefold "hereby we know" cannot be only to set forth the true

philosophy that grew up about the same time the Christian Church was developing. There seems to be a growing scholarly consensus that what we call "Gnosticism" is more accurately understood as those systems of religious thought that made a distinction between *a totally transcendent deity* and *the Creator of the world*, the latter identified with the Creator God of the New Testament.[2] In most cases, this "creator" was understood to be a lesser deity, called a "demiurge," who was considered evil. The diversity of these forms of incipient Gnosticism led one scholar to comment: "The plurality of definitions [of 'Gnosticism'] and the inability of any single definition to win a clear consensus has been the problem."[3]

It is noteworthy that the book of Jude was also written to encourage believers to "...contend earnestly for the faith..." (Jude 3 - NASB), which was being opposed by numerous false doctrines, chief among which was Gnosticism. Nowhere was this Gnostic influence more influential than in the area of the identity of Christ. Based upon the truth in 2 Corinthians 4:3 and 4, that the Devil's primary goal is to blind men's minds to the truth about Jesus Christ, it is predictable that this would have been one of the first areas of Satanic attack on the Church.

Gnosticism

The discovery of the Nag Hammadi Coptic Library in Egypt in 1945–46 made possible much greater understanding of Gnostic religious thought, because for the first time scholars could study first-hand sources. Until then, the sum of what was known about Gnostic thought was through the filter of the early Church "Fathers," notably the heresiologist Irenaeus.[4] This discovery complicated the prevailing view, derived from Irenaeus, that a pure and apostolic Christian faith was being attacked by a philosophical system that bore little similarity to orthodox Christianity and threatened to overcome it. For one thing, it was discovered that there were many variations of Gnosticism. This led modern scholars into many schools of thought on how they developed. Another fact revealed by modern research is that Gnostics and "orthodox" believers were more similar in their beliefs and practices than scholars thought. Though Gnostics were given to wild speculation, both they and the developing "orthodox" community shared common concerns. One of these was the elevation of "God" to a status previously unheard of—even beyond "being" itself. From this view, even calling Him the supreme *being* would limit him. Another shared concern was the triadic or Trinitarian nature of the "godhead, as Gnostic scholar Alastair Logan observes:

> ...a concern with **the absolute transcendence of the supreme deity** seems to have been characteristic of second-century philosophy and theology, **pagan and Christian**...The whole problem of how the diversity and plurality of the heavenly world, and hence of our visible world, arose from the perfect unity of the Monad [the Gnostic's "supreme being"] is one which exercised the minds of the Gnostics as it did those of orthodox Christians and pagan

knowledge in opposition to the false *"Gnosis"* of his Gnostic opponents. Clearly his readers had felt the doubts which had grown in force.

The International Critical Commentary, The Johannine Epistles (T&T Clark Ltd., Edinburgh, 1994), pp. xviii–xx.

2. Michael A. Williams, *Rethinking Gnosticism: An Argument for Dismantling a Dubious Category* (Princeton Univ. Press, Princeton, NJ, 1996), p. 26.

3. *Ibid.,* p. 27.

4. "Heresiologist" is the technical term for a Church "father" who directed his energy toward combating "heresy" in the early Church.

philosophers. But over against the tendency of the latter two to develop a single answer, the Gnostics characteristically present a variety of views reflecting various kinds of imagery.[5]

This concept of "absolute transcendence" is very important to note, for it explains later theological developments in the formulation of Christian doctrine. John Dart quotes Kurt Rudolph citing Job 28 and Proverbs 30:1–4:

> In the wisdom genre, **God tended to be more inscrutable for humans**…He is removed into the distance and placed high above earthly concerns so that his acts in history and his acts of creation become veiled.[6]

It is also clear from the Nag Hammadi sources that the Gnostics considered themselves "Christians." They used Christian themes and symbols, but because they were syncretistic (adding unbiblical concepts into their religious "stew"), they were the first to borrow heavily from the Greek philosopher Plato. They apparently provided the philosophical framework for Neoplatonic thought that arose later.[7] Most significantly, the Gnostics were the first to articulate a multi-personal "Godhead," developing a Trinity of Father, Mother and Son. Logan supplies us with critical insight concerning the relationship between second-century "Christian" speculation and Gnostic beliefs, particularly in reference to the origin of the Trinitarian idea:

> One significant task of second-century Christian theology could be said to be to determine the role and identity of Sophia, Wisdom, in relation to the Father, Son and Holy Spirit… Furthermore, **these Gnostics…may with justice be seen as the pioneers in developing an understanding of God as "triadic" or "Trinitarian,"** perhaps even in immanent as well as economic terms. What unites the two [competing] systems of [Gnostic thought], beside the light theme and the Sophia myth, is that **both develop alternative Trinitarian schemes**. Thus, the [one] system, probably mainly under the influence of the female figures of Holy Spirit and Wisdom of Jewish Christianity, but also aware of the speculations of contemporary Middle Platonists and Neopythagoreans on the divine hierarchy, develops a triad of Father, Mother and Son, splitting the Mother into a higher and lower Sophia, the latter of whom it identifies with the Holy Spirit.[8]

The research now shows that the Gnostics derived much of the basis of their philosophy from Jewish and Christian sources, and a variety of respected scholars think that by the time of Irenaeus (180 A.D.) they were as influenced by incipient Trinitarian speculations about the Godhead (Christ

---

5. Alastair H. B. Logan, *Gnostic Truth and Christian Heresy* (Hendrickson Publishers, Peabody, MA, 1996), pp. 75 and 76.

6. John Dart, *The Jesus of Heresy and History: The Discovery and Meaning of the Nag Hammadi Gnostic Library* (Harper and Row, S.F., 1988), p. 57.

7. Logan, *op. cit., Gnostic Truth and Christian Heresy*, p. 22. He writes:

> The world-view of these Gnostics, as with Saturninus, Basilides and Valentinus, is undoubtedly Platonic. It reflects the attempt to derive the Many from the One, and to explain the visible universe as the work of a lower god, the Demiurge, emanated from the transcendent One beyond being, in terms of the inexplicable self-revelation and unfolding of the supreme God as Father, Mother and Son…As the fundamental concept of the self-revelation of the divine triad suggests, it is essentially a Christian scheme.

Because of his theological training, Logan considers the Father, Mother, Son imagery to be a "Christian" scheme. We assert that the evidence is clear that the triadic formula originated with the Gnostics and, through their influence and the later influence of Neoplatonism, profoundly affected the development of "Christian" doctrine.

8. *Ibid.,* p. 32.

being a pre-existent divine being, etc.), as they were a heretical influence.[9] This lends credence to the point that we expanded upon in Chapter 15 when we investigated the expansion of piety—that many errors in both the text and doctrine were the result, not of outside heretical influence, but of sincere theological speculation and religious devotion on the part of the textual custodians of that era who were under the influence of unbiblical philosophical systems. Hawkin cites Bauer, who demonstrated the relativism of the terms "orthodox" and "heretical" in the early Church:

> [Bauer] has given renewed impetus to viewing Christian origins from the standpoint of diversity...Early Christianity [showed] considerable confusion and fluidity...Groups later labeled "heretical" were in fact the earliest representatives of Christianity in many areas (like the Arians, Ebionites, etc.)...The victory of what is now labeled "orthodox" was due almost entirely to the Roman Church.[10]

Although there were many errors taught by later Christians under the direct influence of Gnosticism and Neoplatonism, it is certain from the biblical evidence that there were various forms of incipient Gnosticism thriving in the first century that twisted the Christian message and led believers astray. Alan Richardson calls this phenomenon "the melancholy transformation of the original apostolic *kerygma* [i.e., the Apostles' Doctrine] into the developed Gnostic Catholicism of the second century."[11] A few of the early Church fathers of the 2nd and 3rd centuries, among them Irenaeus, Tertullian, Hippolytus and Epiphanius, were scathing in their remarks about Gnostics, even while they were guilty of many of the same philosophical excesses. As we have discussed, there were many variations of Gnostic thought, some more dangerous than others by virtue of their counterfeit appeal. The attack on Christianity was real, and was addressed by the apostolic Church.

Some common Gnostic beliefs that flew in the face of "the Apostles' Doctrine" were:

- The world was created by lower beings and not by the Supreme Being.
- The physical world and matter were evil, and the "soul" was trapped in a body until death when it could, but not necessarily would, ascend to a higher existence.
- The text of Scripture had a meaning deeper than the actual words, and the Gnostic understanding of the meaning behind the text was the true message that could be learned only by studying the Gnostic secrets.
- Jesus was a spirit being, and although he looked like a flesh-and-blood person, that was not the case; and even when he ate and drank, he did not later excrete any waste.
- God became incarnate and came to earth to call people back to their heavenly home.

These last two points are very significant, in that those errors most profoundly influenced Christian thought. Although most people today do not view Jesus as only a spirit being, many think of him as a God-man, with the "God" part more important, or at least more relevant, than the "man" part. This fact is reflected in the common belief among Christians that Jesus could not have sinned or failed in his mission.

---

9. Dunn, *op. cit., Christology*, p. 99: Regarding the doctrine of the Incarnation being derived from a first-century "Gnostic Redeemer myth": "all the indications are that it was a post-Christian (second century) development using Christian beliefs about Jesus as one of its building blocks."

10. David J. Hawkin, "A Reflective Look at the Recent Debate on Orthodoxy and Heresy in Earliest Christianity," *Eglise et Theologie*, 7 (1976), pp. 367–378. The article centers on the work of Walter Bauer, *Orthodoxy and Heresy in Earliest Christianity* (Fortress Press, Philadelphia, 1971).

11. Alan Richardson, *The Bible in an Age of Science* (Westminster Press, Philadelphia, 1961), pp. 107 and 108.

Another point to note is that Gnostics saw the universe populated by groupings of divine beings that came from the supreme being, or "Monad" (the One). These included dyads, triads, tetrads, ogdoads, etc. The impact of these groupings cannot be overestimated. It was very easy for someone indoctrinated by this belief system to see God as a "Godhead" composed of more than one being. In fact, he who was known as "The Valentinian Gnostic" had been, accordingly, so far as the existing sources permit us to know, the first "Christian" theologian to designate the Father, Son and Spirit specifically as a triad.[12] Logan verifies this point and adds some further insight into the way the Gnostics viewed "the God of the Old Testament" as a lesser God. We can also see their idea of a transcendent God beyond that lesser "God."

> The world-view of these Gnostics, as with Saturninus, Basilides and Valentinus, was undoubtedly Platonic. It reflected the attempt to derive the Many from the One, and to explain the visible universe as the work of a lower god, the Demiurge, who emanated from the transcendent One beyond being, in terms of the **inexplicable** self-revelation and unfolding of the supreme God as Father, Mother and Son....As the fundamental concept of the self-revelation of the divine triad suggests, it is essentially a Christian scheme. It... see[s] the God of the Old Testament as a blind, ignorant and arrogant Demiurge, and thus seek[s] to discover the hitherto **unknown God beyond God**, first revealed by Christ and his proclamation. And it builds its theogony not on the basis of Genesis and the prophets, reflecting the work of and inspired by that Demiurge, but on the basis of [second-century] Christian speculation on Christ and Wisdom such as is found in Hebrews, derived from the Psalms and Wisdom books but interpreted in the light of contemporary Platonic ideas. Above all, it reflects the experience of salvation through a Christian Gnostic initiation ritual based on **baptism in the name of the Gnostic triad**..." [i.e., Father, Mother, Son]."[13]

Another aspect of Gnostic thought was the concept of the "Fullness" (Gr. *Pleroma*), which was speculated to be an intermediate realm populated by various incorporeal spirit entities (i.e., they did not have bodies, which were made of lower stuff—flesh). This provides a strong indication why both John (John 1:16) and Paul (Eph. 1:23 and Col. 2:9) would employ the word "fullness" in connection with Christ. In John, we have received of his fullness; in Ephesians, the Church is his fullness; and in Colossians, **he is all the fullness of God in bodily form**. Perhaps the reason why the only occurrence of the word "Godhead" is in Colossians 2:9 (KJV) is that Colosse was one of the locations in the first century where incipient Gnosticism was particularly influential. What the term "Godhead" meant to the proto-Gnostics is unclear, but biblically it refers to God's power, signifying that Christ sits at His right hand fully endowed with authority and majesty to rule and reign with God.[14] There is no indication that the term implies a substance or state of being in which there can be more than one person. Colossians 2:9 contradicts the Gnostic assertion that there were all manner of beings populating "the Fullness," and asserts that Christ alone is the "fullness" of God in bodily form. The term "bodily

---

12. Martin Werner, *The Formation of Christian Doctrine* (Beacon Press, Boston, MA, 1965), pp. 252 and 253. "*Trias*=Trinitas" was one of a number of numerical concepts employed in Gnostic *pleroma* speculation, where there was, with the trias, also dyads, tetrads, hexads, ogdoads, deltas, and dodekas.

13. Logan, *op. cit., Gnostic Truth and Christian Heresy,* p. 22.

14. Gerhard Kittel, ed., on *theotes,* which occurs only once in the New Testament (Col. 2:9): "The [God] of the Old Testament has attracted to Himself all divine power in the cosmos, and on the early Christian view He has given this fullness of power to Christ as the Bearer of the divine office." Kittel, o*p. cit., Theological Dictionary,* Vol. III, p. 119. See Appendix A (Col. 2:9).

form" is significant because the exalted spirit beings of Gnostic thought had no need for bodies. But Jesus, even now in his exalted state as the Lord, Vice-Regent of the universe, has a body.

Paul's (and John's) writings contain statements that can be best understood in the context of the belief systems influencing the people to whom they wrote. In 1 Timothy 1:4, Paul exhorts his young protégé to command certain men not to devote themselves to myths and endless genealogies. Scholars now recognize the Gnostic influence in these, since the Gnostics had many genealogies in the development of their hierarchy of gods. Later in 1 Timothy, Paul wrote, "For there is one God and one mediator between God and men, the man Christ Jesus" (1 Tim. 2:5). One can hardly imagine Paul needing to write to Timothy about "one God" if Timothy were dialoguing only with monotheistic Jews. The Gnostics, however, had many gods, and to them Jesus was not "the man Christ Jesus," but rather an emanation of the Father—a god, a god-man or a spirit being of some sort. Paul wrote by revelation to support the clear and simple teaching of all Scripture, but it should be obvious that the Gnostic tendencies won out, and the "doctrine of the God-man" Jesus became the standard teaching in Christendom thereafter.

Holding the Truth

Most scholars believe that Paul's Epistles to Timothy were written approximately twenty years before John's Epistles. There are numerous references throughout Paul's Epistles to Timothy that refute Gnostic doctrine, but many of these are not relevant to this book. Suffice it to say that from the beginning of 1 Timothy to the end of 2 Timothy, Paul is almost pleading with his young friend to uphold the standard of the written Word of God in the face of heresy, notably Gnosticism. The following two sections make this plain:

> **1 Timothy 1:3–5**
> (3) As I urged you when I went into Macedonia, stay there in Ephesus so that you may command certain men not to teach **false doctrines** any longer
> (4) nor to devote themselves to **myths and endless genealogies**. These promote controversies rather than God's work—which is by faith.
> (5) The goal of this command is love, which comes from a pure heart and a good conscience and a sincere faith.

> **2 Timothy 4:1–3**
> (1) In the presence of God and of Christ Jesus, who will judge the living and the dead, and in view of his appearing and his kingdom, I give you this charge:
> (2) Preach the Word; be prepared in season and out of season; correct, rebuke and encourage—with great patience and careful instruction.
> (3) For the time will come when men will **not put up with sound doctrine**. Instead, to suit their own desires, they will gather around them a great number of teachers to say what their itching ears want to hear.

It is obvious that Paul was very concerned that Timothy uphold the truth, because as he wrote in 1 Timothy 2:4, God wants "…all men be to saved **and** to come to a knowledge of the truth." The next verse sets forth the focal point of the truth as far as God's Word is concerned:

1 Timothy 2:5
For there is one God and one mediator between God and men, **the man Christ Jesus**,

This succinct statement highlights the primary truth of God's Word from Genesis 3:15 forward. Only a *man* could redeem mankind.[15] Only a man, by living a sinless life and dying on the Cross, could be the bridge between a holy God and sinful mankind. But, as we have seen, this man could not be just *any* man. As a matter of fact, only one man ever born could fit the bill—THE MAN, Jesus Christ. A clear statement like this should go a long way to disprove the Gnostic or Trinitarian belief that Christ is a God-man and not a man.

In the next-to-last chapter of his gospel, John summarizes the reason it was written.

John 20:31
But these are written that you may believe that Jesus is the Christ, the Son of God, and that by believing you may have life in his name.

As we saw in Chapter 6, Matthew's gospel emphasizes Jesus as the King to Israel, Mark's gospel emphasizes Jesus as a servant, Luke's gospel emphasizes him as a man among men, and John's specifically emphasizes Jesus as the Son of God. John's three epistles continue the theme of his gospel, and include a number of truths that specifically combat Gnostic heresy. John's gospel and his three epistles can only be properly understood and appreciated against the backdrop of Gnosticism, which was competing for the minds and hearts of his readers.

1 John 1:1–3
(1) That which was from the beginning, which we have heard, which we have seen with our eyes, which we have looked at and our hands have touched—this we proclaim concerning the Word of life.
(2) The life appeared; we have seen it and testify to it, and we proclaim to you the eternal life, which was with the Father and has appeared to us.
(3) We proclaim to you what we have seen and heard, so that you also may have fellowship with us. And our fellowship is with the Father and with his Son, Jesus Christ.

In verse 1, John writes with the same understanding as he did in the first verse of his gospel. Jesus was the embodiment of the *logos*, the purpose and plan in God's mind, "from the beginning." Verse 3 makes clear that one of John's intentions in writing was that those who read this epistle will "…fellowship with the Father and with his Son, Jesus Christ." Once again we see the "Dynamic Duo," not the "Triune Trio."

In the ensuing verses concluding Chapter 1 and beginning Chapter 2, John goes on to say that through Jesus Christ, Christians can, despite their sin nature, be perfected and walk in the light as he is the light. John then addresses the subject of the spirit of antichrist that was causing some people to lie about Jesus Christ.

1 John 2:18–23
(18) Dear children, this is the last hour; and as you have heard that the antichrist is coming, even now many antichrists have come. This is how we know it is the last hour.

---

15. The Gnostics believed that redemption came from heaven as an event, as we will explore in the next chapter.

(19) They went out from us, but they did not really belong to us. For if they had belonged to us, they would have remained with us; but their going showed that none of them belonged to us.

(20) But you have an anointing from the Holy One, and all of you know the truth.[16]

(21) I do not write to you because you do not know the truth, but because you do know it and because no lie comes from the truth.

(22) Who is the liar? It is the man who denies that Jesus is the Christ. Such a man is the antichrist—he denies the Father and the Son.

(23) No one who denies the Son has the Father; whoever acknowledges the Son has the Father also.

It is interesting that verse 22 says that whoever denies that Jesus is the Christ, the Messiah (that is, the promised seed of Genesis 3:15, the seed of Abraham, the seed of David, a *man anointed with holy spirit*—Acts 10:38) is a liar.[17] The verse goes on to say that the antichrist spirit denies the proper relationship between the Father and the Son. Verse 23 states that whoever denies the Son has not the Father. Nowhere in the above verses is a "third person of the Trinity" mentioned. Trinitarians often quote this section of Scripture to admonish those who deny their doctrine, but it seems to us that Trinitarian doctrine undermines the proper relationship between the Father and the Son and is therefore a prime candidate for the false doctrine that entered the Church under the influence of a "spirit of anti-Christ." In light of all the various aspects of error that this doctrine has introduced, we think it is quite plain that the Church was not under the influence of the true spirit of God when developing its Christological doctrine. John warned the early Church to be alert for the influence of this spirit, but, sadly, it was not alert enough.

The influence of idolatry, deception and temptation is often extremely subtle, and God's people have to some degree succumbed to it in nearly every age and period of their history. It is certainly not a disgrace that, under the difficult times of persecution and deprivation faced by the early Church, they might have embraced some pagan ideas in order to make the Christian message more palatable to a pagan audience. In the light of available historical research, it should be possible for Christian teachers and leaders to recognize the mistake and correct it.

If you are on a long journey and you take a wrong turn, it is wisest and most practical to quickly admit it and get back on the right road. Or, if you realized that your suitcases blew off the roof of your car on the first day of driving, you would stop and go back for them. You wouldn't spend endless amounts of mental energy rationalizing that the loss was a good thing ("We're getting better gas mileage," "The car handles better," etc.). Unfortunately, the longer a situation goes uncorrected and the present condition defended and rationalized, the harder it is to admit that a wrong turn was even made or that something was really lost. Indeed, you may very well become angry at those who suggest that it doesn't make sense to drive around lost or without any luggage. Admittedly this is a metaphor that doesn't exactly fit the situation, but it does invite consideration of some important parallels.

---

16. Logan identifies various Gnostic rituals that involved chrisms (chrismation), or "anointings" for the elect. Interestingly, John identifies this "anointing" as something that the believers have already received. We already have an "anointing", thus interrupting the Gnostic elitism of the *gnostikoi* (the enlightened or anointed ones). Logan, *op. cit., Gnostic Truth and Christian Heresy,* p. 34.

17. "Messiah" comes from the Hebrew word *mashiach,* which means "anointed." "Christ" comes from the Greek word *christos,* which also means "anointed." Thus, linguistically, Messiah = Christ = anointed.

As we continue through 1 John, we notice at the beginning of Chapter 4 that John specifically addresses a primary Gnostic heresy. He does this while at the same time setting forth the criterion to distinguish the spirit of God from the spirit of antichrist.

1 John 4:1–3
(1) Dear friends, do not believe every spirit, but test the spirits to see whether they are from God, because many false prophets have gone out into the world.
(2) This is how you can recognize the Spirit of God: Every spirit that acknowledges that Jesus Christ has come in the flesh is from God,
(3) but every spirit that does not acknowledge Jesus is not from God. This is the spirit of the antichrist, which you have heard is coming and even now is already in the world.

Remember that the Gnostics believed that all matter is evil, and therefore they taught that Jesus Christ was not actually a man of flesh and blood, but rather some kind of phantom or spirit being. In verses 2 and 3, John makes it very plain that anyone who teaches that Jesus Christ was anything other than a 100 percent, red-blooded human being is teaching false doctrine.

The remainder of Chapter 4 contains the same fabulous truth found in the world's most famous verse, John 3:16:

1 John 4:9–15
(9) This is how God showed his love among us: He sent his one and only Son into the world that we might live through him.
(10) This is love: not that we loved God, but that he loved us and sent his Son as an atoning sacrifice for our sins.
(11) Dear friends, since God so loved us, we also ought to love one another.
(12) No one has ever seen God; but if we love one another, God lives in us and his love is made complete in us.
(13) We know that we live in him and he in us, because he has given us of his Spirit.
(14) And we have seen and testify that the Father has sent his Son to be the Savior of the world.
(15) If anyone acknowledges that Jesus is the Son of God, God lives in him and he in God.

God so loved the world that He gave His only begotten Son. Verse 15 agrees with Romans 10:9: Whoever confesses that Jesus is the *Son* of God, God dwells in him. Chapter 5 begins by affirming this same truth:

1 John 5:1
Everyone who believes that Jesus is the Christ is born of God, and everyone who loves the father loves his child as well.

Let us read carefully as we closely examine the following verses:

1 John 5:5–8
(5) Who is it that overcomes the world? Only he who believes that Jesus is the Son of God.

(6) This is the one who came by water and blood [meaning that he was born]—Jesus Christ. He did not come by water only, but by water and blood.
(7) And it is the Spirit who testifies, because the Spirit is the truth.
(8) For there are three that testify: the Spirit, the water and the blood; and the three are in agreement.

Verse 5 says that Jesus is the Son of God. Verse 6 says that he was born of a woman like every other human being since Adam and Eve ("by water and blood"). Then he received the spirit of God upon him. If you are familiar with the KJV, you know that there is a tremendous discrepancy between it and the NIV in verses 7 and 8.

1 John 5:7 and 8 (KJV)
(7) For there are three that bear record **in heaven, the Father, the Word, and the Holy Ghost: and these three are one.**
(8) **And there are three that bear witness in earth:** the spirit, and the water, and the blood: and these three agree in one.

Some time after the fifteenth century, a misguided scribe added to the Greek text of verses 7 and 8 the spurious words (**in bold type**) that you can see are not found in the NIV. These added words are found in no Greek text prior to the sixteenth century. The NIV translators, despite the fact that they were Trinitarians, recognized this and deleted these words. Rather than an "honest mistake," this insertion is very likely a textual forgery, and appears to have stemmed from a Trinitarian's desire to insert in Scripture a doctrine that is simply not there.[18]

The Second Epistle of John is only thirteen verses, but it contains some vital truth regarding the relationship between God and His Son.

2 John 1–4
(1) The elder, To the chosen lady and her children, whom I love in the **truth**—and not I only, but also all who know the **truth**—
(2) because of the **truth**, which lives in us and will be with us forever:
(3) Grace, mercy and peace from God the Father and from Jesus Christ, the Father's Son, will be with us in **truth** and love.
(4) It has given me great joy to find some of your children walking in the **truth**, just as the Father commanded us.

Notice that the word "**truth**" appears five times in those first four verses. What do you think is the primary truth being referred to? The answer is found in verse 3 where the phrase, "the Father's Son" (KJV: "the Son of the Father") appears for the only time in the Bible. John here reiterates the same truth contained in 1 Corinthians 8:6 that there is one God, the *Father* and one Lord Jesus Christ, His *Son*.

2 John 7–11
(7) Many deceivers, who do not acknowledge Jesus Christ as coming in the flesh, have gone out into the world. Any such person is the deceiver and the antichrist.

---

18. See Appendix A.

(8) Watch out that you do not lose what you have worked for, but that you may be rewarded fully.

(9) Anyone who runs ahead and does not continue in the teaching of Christ does not have God; whoever continues in the teaching has both the Father and the Son.

(10) If anyone comes to you and does not bring this teaching, do not take him into your house or welcome him.

(11) Anyone who welcomes him shares in his wicked work.

Here we see that John repeats what he wrote in the first epistle about Jesus Christ being a flesh-and-blood human being. In verse 9, he twice refers to this truth as the doctrine "of [about] Christ." In verse 9, we also once again see *both* the Father and the Son. It is noteworthy that the word "both" precedes the phrase, "the Father and the Son," because "both" indicates *two* separate and individual beings. There is no mention here of any Holy Spirit or a "third" person.

In verse 9, notice the words, "Anyone who runs ahead and does not continue in the teaching of Christ…." Instead of "runs ahead," the NASB reads, "goes too far." We agree with E. W. Bullinger's marginal note that this verse "refers to false teachers who claimed to bring some higher teaching beyond the Apostles' Doctrine." This is in contrast to exhortations like Paul's, for example:

1 Timothy 6:3 and 4a
(3) If any one teaches false doctrines, and does not agree to the sound instruction of our Lord Jesus Christ and to godly teaching.
(4a) he is conceited and understands nothing….

Is it not "conceited" and "running ahead" and "going too far" to assert what Scripture does not—in this case, that Jesus is a "God-man"?

The remains of Gnostic heresy are still found today in the doctrine of the Trinity, which, despite its claims to the contrary, states that Jesus was not really a flesh-and-blood human being like the First Adam was. Rather, he was a "God-man," having both a divine nature and a human nature. He was "100 percent God and 100 percent man."[19] The doctrine also teaches that Jesus had always lived in heaven with God and the Holy Spirit before he was born in the manger. Could such a "pre-existent Jesus" really be the flesh-and-blood Jesus of Scripture? To us, such a Jesus is "another Jesus," according to Scripture:

2 Corinthians 11:4
For if someone comes to you and preaches a Jesus other than the Jesus we preached, or if you receive a different spirit from the one you received, or a different gospel from the one you accepted, you put up with it easily enough.

Keep in mind that one of the great goals of Scripture is to motivate us to make every effort to be like Christ. The more we can identify with him, the easier this will be. It is an unfortunate result of much Christian teaching and worship that Jesus is elevated to such an extent that if someone says, "I am going to think and act like Jesus," he or she is often thought of as being irreverent and ungodly. Although it is true that none of us will attain his state of perfection, it is a goal each of us should have, and a goal toward which we are commanded to strive.

---

19. See the wording of the Chalcedonian definition in Appendix C.

Neoplatonism and the Rise of Trinitarianism

Neoplatonism was an influential philosophical movement that arose from 200 to 500 A.D., and was heavily influenced by Gnosticism. The *Columbia Encyclopedia*, describing "Neoplatonism," says:

> An ancient mystical philosophy based on the later doctrines of Plato, especially those in the *Timaeus*. Considered the last of the great pagan philosophies, it was developed in the third century A.D. by Plotinus. Despite his mysticism, Plotinus' method was thoroughly rational, based on the logical traditions of the Greeks. Later Neoplatonists grafted onto its body such disparate elements as Eastern mysticism, divination, demonology, and astrology. Neoplatonism, widespread until the 7th century, was an influence on early Christian thinkers (e.g., Origen) and medieval Jewish and Arab philosophers. **It was firmly joined with Christianity by St. Augustine, who was a Neoplatonist before his conversion.** Neoplatonism has had a lasting influence on Western metaphysics and mysticism. Philosophers whose works contain elements of Neoplatonism include St. Thomas Aquinas, Boethius and Hegel.[20]

Plotinus and Proclus, who wrote in the third century, were the chief proponents of Neoplatonism. This philosophy was developed from Plato's theories of "Forms," which he believed were the only things that were "real."[21] These "Forms" exist in a divine mind beyond the heavens. Rejecting Gnostic dualism, the metaphysical doctrine that only two substances exist, mind and matter (soul and body, etc.), Plotinus saw reality as one vast hierarchical order containing all the various levels and kinds of existence. In his view, the highest "Form" was "The One," or Monad, beyond being. The lowest level of "Form" was the realm of matter and physical bodies. *The One* emanated its own essence, like light shines through darkness. This emanation created the Divine Mind, or *Logos*. The *Logos*, or divine reason, was the highest form in which forms exist as ideas, and it contains all intelligent forms of all individuals. This in turn generates the World Soul, which links the intellectual and material worlds [don't worry, this makes no sense to us either]. Souls were believed to travel when they leave the body.

As the *Columbia Encyclopedia* pointed out, Neoplatonism profoundly influenced St. Augustine's theology, although he repudiated much of what he had formerly believed and taught when he converted from Neoplatonism. However, his theories about the transcendence of God, the role of faith and the soul's survival after death were particular areas in which he was influenced by his former beliefs. Augustine, in turn, was a major influence in the development of Christian theology in general, and is considered by many to be the greatest theologian of the first millennium of Christian history.

Proclus' views helped shape Christian *negative theology*, which emphasizes the limits of man's ability to comprehend a Supreme Being. He taught that one could not say who or what God was, only what He was *not*. He taught that reality existed in a solitary perfect being, *The One*, who was the source of all truth, goodness and beauty. He contributed to the notion that God was essentially a mathematical abstraction. The triune "God" of traditional Christianity is the result of such reasoning, for "God" is not a unique person but a unique "substance" or "essence," which coexists in the form of three "co-eternal persons." In our view, this reduces the concept of "God" to an incomprehensible and unbiblical abstraction. A good example of such reasoning is the following assertion by two modern Trinitarians:

---

20. *Columbia Encyclopedia* (Columbia Univ. Press, N.Y., 1994).

21. Plato taught that there were invisible and ideal "forms," like truth, beauty, love, etc., that lie behind the visible things of this earthly existence. Thus, we recognize a particular "chair" because there is the ideal form of "Chair," which we know intuitively and can therefore recognize particular chairs.

God is what happens between Jesus and his Father in their spirit…**This makes God an event**, not a being.[22]

To illustrate the reasoning, consider one of the common analogies often proposed to argue for the Trinity: there are three generations of "Smiths"—Tom, George and Bruce. They are three separate persons, but of one "essence," which could be called "Smithness." Thus, Tom, George and Bruce are three persons but one essence. The problem with this "logic" is that "Smithness" does not exist as a person, only as an abstraction. God, however, is clearly represented as a person, a personal being who can be called upon for aid. One cannot call upon "Smithness" to help in a crisis.[23]

The living God is not an abstraction, but is a real being with personality, will and desire. And Jesus Christ is the unique Son of this living God, who is also identified as **the Father of Jesus Christ**. The Trinitarian "God" is not the personal "God" who is one person, but some kind of "Entity" who is manifested as three separate persons. Such a vague and mystical theological construct does not seem possible without the aid of Neoplatonic emphasis on mathematical forms or ideals that have no personal relationships with seekers, nor are they capable of giving revelation or guidance to those who look to them. Thus, the Christian Church by the end of the fourth century had completely redefined who God is.

The principal agents of this transformation were three theologians from Cappadocia. Richard Rubenstein's "*When Jesus Became God*" includes an insightful discussion about the role of the Cappadocians—Basil of Caesarea, Gregory of Nazianzus, and Gregory of Nyssa, Basil's younger brother—on the development of Christian doctrine in the fourth century. These Cappadocians were the main ones to use "creative thinking" (i.e., "Neoplatonically influenced") to arrive at a solution to the problem of the personality of the Holy Spirit, and in the process developed a completely new understanding of the nature of God. Rubenstein explains:

> What was needed to clear up this confusion [about the identity of the Holy Spirit] was something that the Nicene Creed alone could not supply: a doctrine explaining how God could be One and yet consist of two to three separate entities. And the development of this doctrine, Basil recognized, could not take place without new language. It was necessary to create a new theological vocabulary capable of going beyond the bare statement that the Father and Son were of the same essence (*homousios*). That term expressed the Oneness of God, but how to express His multiplicity as well?
>
> The answer was to clarify or redefine key words…The corrective was to distinguish clearly between *ousia* and *hypostasis*, "essence" and "being." The Father, the Son, and the Holy Spirit are three separate beings, each with his own individual characteristics—they are three *hypostases*. But they are one and the same in essence—they are *homoousios*…

---

22. Ted Peters, "God Happens: The Timeliness of the Triune God," *The Christian Century*, April 1, 1998, p. 342. Peters reviewed Robert Jensen's book, *Systematic Theology (Vol. 1): The Triune God* (Oxford University Press, 1998).

23. This thinking of "God" as an "essence" or "substance" has led many Trinitarians to liken the Godhead to H_2O, and the persons of the Godhead as ice, water and steam. But water can be in only one of these forms under the same conditions at the same time (ice below freezing, steam above 212° F [100° C], etc.). Therefore by employing this reasoning they have unwittingly fallen into the historical "heresy" of Sabellianism or Modalism, in which it is asserted that God only manifests Himself as one of the divine persons at a time, and does not coexist as three persons simultaneously.

Gregory of Nyssa summed up the doctrine with characteristic sharpness. God is three individuals sharing one essence. Both the unity and the tripartite division of the Godhead are real. If this seems paradoxical, so be it.[24]

Gregory's enthusiasm for paradoxical doctrinal formulations is evident in the following quote:

The difference of the *hypostases* does not dissolve the continuity of their nature nor does the community of their nature dissipate the particularity of their characteristics. Do not be amazed if we declare that the same thing is united and distinct, and conceive, as in a riddle, of a new and paradoxical unity in distinction and distinction in unity.[25]

Rubenstein recognizes that the Cappadocian solution "altered the Christian understanding of God":

What the Cappaccocian theology did was to make it clear that if Christ was fully divine, God could not be primarily a Father, but must equally be a Son and a Spirit. As Gregory of Nyssa put it, "God is not God because he is Father, nor the Son because he is the Son, but because both possess the *ousia* of Godhead.

Clearly, there was some tension between this idea of a God that is distributed over three equal persons and the notion...that God as the Father is in some sense "greater" than God as the Son and Holy Spirit.[26]

Thus, the most basic New Testament understanding of "...God [as] the Father of our Lord Jesus Christ..." was transformed into an incomprehensible "God" of three equal Persons, none greater or lesser, earlier or later. Trinitarians want to convince us that the Trinity was a doctrine taught by the Apostles, but as we are seeing, history clearly shows that this is not the case. The doctrine of the Trinity as it is now taught by orthodox Christianity was not "the Apostle's Doctrine" but a theological construct. With the advent of this new doctrine, even prayer became challenging to understand. Who was Jesus praying to in the garden of Gethsemane? Why would he need to pray to the Father if as the Son he was a co-equal part of the Godhead? Even the Lord's prayer became problematic, as the following commentator observes:

Was the Lord's prayer addressed only to the *hypostasis* of the Father as "our Father" and the Father of the Son, or to the entire *ousia* of the Godhead? Basil's answer...was to declare that what was common to the Three and what was distinctive among them lay beyond speech and comprehension and therefore beyond either analysis or conceptualization.[27]

Basil's response set the pattern for Cappadocian Trinitarianism, which has now become "orthodoxy." Such rhetoric, typical among those who still echo it, "transports us to realms where words, shorn at last of their semantic burdens, pirouette and regroup into combinations hitherto undreamed of."[28] It

---

24. Richard E. Rubenstein, *When Jesus Became God* (Harcourt, Brace, NY, 1999), pp. 206 and 207.

25. *Ibid.*, p. 207. Rubenstein quotes R. P. C. Hanson, *The Search for the Christian Doctrine of God: The Arian Controversy*, 318–381 A.D. (T. & T. Clark, Edinburgh, 1988), pp. 723 and 724.

26. *Ibid.*, p. 209.

27. *Ibid.*, p. 209. Rubinstein quotes Jaroslav Pelikan, *The Christian Tradition: A History of the Development of Doctrine. Vol, 1, The Emergence of the Catholic Tradition* (100–600) (University of Chicago Press, 1971), p. 223.

28. We first heard this classic phrase in a piece of political polemic by W. F. Buckley addressing the self-contradicting verbiage of an American president, but we think it is most appropriately applied to the Cappadocians and their innovative doctrine.

seems to us that this vague and mystical theological construction was made possible by the influence of Neoplatonic thought, with its emphasis on abstract and mathematical "Forms." The biblical view of a personal relationship with a reasonable God who reveals Himself and His nature to mankind was severely compromised in the process.

The "one God" of the Bible is the "living God," the Father of Jesus Christ. Beginning with Adam, this one true God has always sought a personal relationship with each man and woman. Jesus Christ is the unique Son of this living God, his "Father."

Historians are very aware of the direct link between Neoplatonism and the development of Christian doctrine in the second through fifth centuries, culminating in the Councils of Nicaea and Constantinople in which Trinitarian orthodoxy was formulated.[29] In its article on "Christianity," the *Encyclopaedia Brittannica* considers the following information vital to understanding the history of the Christian faith. Keep in mind that what is important is not that we understand the teachings of Neoplatonism (Thank God!), for they are extremely speculative and virtually incomprehensible. What is important is to recognize that they had a profound influence upon the intellectual and ecclesiastical leaders of their day. We have taken the liberty of emphasizing key portions of the article (and adding a few comments):

Introduction of Neoplatonic Themes in the Johannine Understanding

Christ as the *Logos*, under the influence of Neoplatonic *Logos* philosophy, became the subject of a speculative theology; there thus developed **"a speculative interest in the relationship of the oneness of God to the triplicity of his manifestations."** This question was answered through the Neoplatonic metaphysics of being. The transcendent God, who is **beyond all being**, all rationality and all conceptuality, **divests himself of his divine transcendence**; in a first act of becoming self-conscious he recognizes himself ["Hey! I'm me!"] as the divine *nous* (mind), or divine world reason, which was characterized by the Neoplatonic philosopher Plotinus as the "Son" who goes forth from the Father.

The next step by which the transcendent God becomes self-conscious consists in the appearance in the divine *nous* of the divine world, the idea of the world in its individual forms as the content of the divine consciousness ["Are we having fun yet?"]. In Neoplatonic philosophy both the *nous* and the idea of the world are designated the hypostases [personalities] of the transcendent God. **Christian theology took the Neoplatonic metaphysics of substance as well as its doctrine of *hypostases* as the departure point for interpreting the relationship of the "Father" to the "Son" in terms of the Neoplatonic *hypostases* doctrine.** This process stands in direct relationship with a speculative interpretation of Christology in connection with Neoplatonic *Logos* speculation.

---

29. *The New Catholic Encyclopedia*, in its article on the "Holy Trinity," says the following:

There is the recognition on the part of exegetes and Biblical theologians, including a constantly growing number of Roman Catholics, that one should not speak of Trinitarianism in the New Testament without serious qualification. There is also the closely parallel recognition on the part of historians of dogma and systematic theologians that when one does speak of an unqualified Trinitarianism, one has moved from the period of Christian origins to, say, the last quadrant of the 4th Century. It was only then that what might be called the definitive Trinitarian dogma "one God in three Persons" became thoroughly assimilated into Christian life and thought (McGraw Hill, N.Y., 1967), Vol. 14, p. 295.

The assumption of the Neoplatonic *hypostases* doctrine meant from the beginning a certain evaluation of **the relationships of the three divine figures to one another**, because for Neoplatonism the process of hypostatization is at the same time a process of diminution of being. In flowing forth from his transcendent source, the divine being is weakened with the distance from his transcendent origin. Diminution of being is brought about through approach to matter, which for its part is understood in Neoplatonism as non-being. **In transferring the Neoplatonic *hypostases* doctrine to the Christian interpretation of the Trinity**, there existed the danger that the different manifestations of God—as known by the Christian experience of faith: Father, Son, Holy Spirit—would be transformed into a hierarchy of gods graduated among themselves and thus into a polytheism. Though this danger was consciously avoided, and, proceeding from a *Logos* Christology, the complete sameness of essence of the three manifestations of God was emphasized, there arose the danger of a relapse into a triplicity of equally ranked gods, which would displace the idea of the oneness of God.

Attempts to Define the Trinity

By the third century it was already apparent that all attempts to systematize the mystery of the divine Trinity **with the theories of Neoplatonic *hypostases* metaphysics led to ever new conflicts.** The high point, upon which the basic difficulties underwent their most forceful theological and ecclesiastically political actualization, was the so-called Arian controversy… In his theological interpretation of the idea of God, **Arius was interested in maintaining a formal understanding of the oneness of God.** In defense of the oneness of God, he was obliged to dispute the sameness of essence of the Son and the Holy Spirit with God the Father, **as stressed by the theologians of the Neoplatonically-influenced Alexandrian school.** From the outset, the controversy between both parties took place upon the common basis of the Neoplatonic concept of substance, **which was foreign to the New Testament itself.** It is no wonder that the continuation of the dispute on the basis of the metaphysics of substance likewise **led to concepts that have no foundation in the New Testament**, such as the question of the sameness of essence (*homoousia*) or similarity of essence (*homoiousia*) of the divine persons.[30]

It is interesting to note that the debate over the single "i" difference between these two words (*homoousia* and *homoiousia*) was the origin of the aphorism: "It doesn't make one *iota* of a difference." Logically, however, there is a very great difference between things that are identical and things that are similar. Failing to distinguish the difference has led to a host of other errors in biblical interpretation, most particularly in discerning the difference between literal statements and figures of speech.

From the historical development of the doctrine of the Trinity, we can see that Paul's warning to the church at Colosse to avoid "deceptive philosophy" went unheeded. In fact, after his death, the Church strayed from his teaching and veered toward the deceptive teaching that he warned about His words continue to resonate powerfully through the centuries, still seeking ears that will hear, and still full of latent power to free those who are captivated by unbiblical ideas:

---

30. *Encyclopaedia Britannica* article on "Christianity, Holy Trinity" (1999 edition), pp. 281 and 282.

Colossians 2:8
See to it that no one takes you captive through hollow and **deceptive philosophy**, which depends on human tradition and the basic principles of this world rather than on Christ.

Not only did Paul warn those who came after him to avoid speculative philosophies like Gnosticism, he also warned them that if they did not, the truth would be exchanged for a myth. We must now explore how the deadly combination of piety within and heresy without shook the foundations of the faith and eventually led to the Church's embracing the myth that the transcendent and mysterious God had actually become a human being and lived among us.

17

Jesus Christ: Incarnated or Created?

We now will examine the historical background of the development of what has become the cornerstone of Christian orthodoxy, the doctrine of the "Incarnation." We will see that this doctrine arose neither in a vacuum, nor strictly from the text of Scripture. It was the result of the influence of certain beliefs and attitudes that prevailed in and around the Christian church after the first century. Pagan mythology, Gnostic views of redemption and human pre-existence, and the misunderstanding of Johannine language all contributed to the teaching that God Himself became a man, which is the essence of "Incarnational theology."

Although the "Incarnation" is assumed to be a basic tenet of Christianity, the term is used nowhere in Scripture. This is even admitted by Trinitarian scholars: "Incarnation, in its full and proper sense, is not something directly presented in Scripture."[1] The doctrine of the Incarnation was actually formulated during the next several centuries. *The Oxford Dictionary of the Christian Church* verifies this fact:

> The doctrine, which took classical shape under the influence of the controversies of the 4th–5th centuries, was formally defined at the Council of Chalcedon of 451. It was largely molded

---

1. Dunn, *op. cit., Christology*, p. 4, quoting M. Wiles.

by the diversity of tradition in the schools of Antioch and Alexandria…further refinements were added in the later Patristic and Medieval periods.[2]

The reason the councils and synods took hundreds of years to develop the doctrine of Incarnation is that it is not stated in Scripture, and the verses used to support it can be explained without resorting to a doctrine that bears more similarity to pagan mythology than biblical truth. Teaching the Jews that God came down in the form of a man would have completely offended those living at the time of Christ and the Apostles, and greatly contradicted their understanding of the Messianic Scriptures. As we saw in Chapter 9, this doctrine is derived most prominently from the gospel of John, and in particular from the phrase in John 1:14 (KJV): "And the Word was made flesh…." But was "the Word" synonymous with "the Messiah" in Jewish understanding? Hardly. The Jews would have understood it to mean "plan" or "purpose," that which was clearly and specifically declared in Genesis 3:15—a "seed" of a woman who would destroy the works of the Devil. This plan of God for the salvation of man finally "became flesh" in Jesus Christ. This verse is not establishing a doctrine of Incarnation contrary to all prophetic expectations, nor a teaching of pre-existence. It is a teaching of God's great love in bringing into existence His plan to save mankind from their sin.

Before proceeding, we must define what is traditionally understood by the "incarnation" of Christ. Keep in mind that we strongly affirm the reality and necessity of the virgin birth of Christ as the only way he could have been born without the inherent sin of mankind that would have disqualified him from becoming the Lamb of God. But the traditional "formula which enshrines the Incarnation … is that in some sense God, without ceasing to be God, was made man."[3]

We will quote the *New Bible Dictionary*, a Trinitarian source, for a working definition and explanation of this doctrine:

> It appears to mean that the divine Maker became one of His own creatures, which is a prima facie contradiction in theological terms.[4]

> When the Word "became flesh," His deity was not abandoned or reduced or contracted, nor did He cease to exercise the divine functions which had been His before…The Incarnation of the Son of God, then, was not a diminishing of deity, but an acquiring of manhood.[5]

One wonders how a pre-existent "God the Son" can become a man without any "diminishing of deity," or that he could live a "fully human" life without ceasing to exercise the divine functions he had been exercising since eternity began. Trinitarians say this is part of the "mystery" of the Incarnation. The *New Bible Dictionary* admits that the concept is not developed or discussed in the New Testament:

> The only sense in which the New Testament writers ever attempt to explain the incarnation is by showing how it fits into God's overall plan for redeeming mankind…This evangelical interest throws light on the otherwise puzzling fact that the New Testament nowhere reflects on the virgin birth of Jesus as witnessing to the conjunction of deity and manhood in His person—a line of thought much canvassed by later theology.[6]

---

2. F. L. Cross, ed. *The Oxford Dictionary of the Christian Church* (Oxford University Press, N.Y., 1983), p. 696.
3. *New Bible Dictionary*, (Wm. B. Eerdmans Pub., Grand Rapids, MI, 1975), p. 558.
4. *Ibid.,* p. 558.
5. *Ibid.,* p. 560.
6. *Ibid.,* p. 559.

If the deity of Jesus was not at first clearly stated in words (and Acts gives no hint that it was), it was nevertheless part of the faith by which the first Christians lived and prayed…The theological formulation of belief in the Incarnation came later, but the belief itself, however incoherently expressed, was there in the Church from the beginning.[7]

We disagree with the assertion that the doctrine of the Incarnation was "in the Church from the beginning." Since the doctrine is clearly not in Scripture, how can it possibly be considered a part of "the Apostles' Doctrine"? Because scholars admit that this doctrine is biblically tenuous, we must examine why Christian theologians of the third century and later became so preoccupied with establishing it as the cornerstone of a Trinitarian Christian faith. In doing so, we will see some of the changing assumptions and beliefs that led to the development of this doctrine. We must first establish the fact that the very process of turning from historical truth to mythology was clearly prophesied by the Apostle Paul at the end of his life. This is amazing but not surprising, in light of the many times in Scripture that God has warned His people about being influenced by pagan culture.

Turning from Truth to Fables

"Incarnation," at least in the most common Christian conception, is the belief that Jesus is not a created being, but the invisible God "clothed" in human flesh. To quote a recent book on the identity of Jesus by a popular author, Jesus "thought of Himself as God in human flesh."[8] Thus, in our view, the biblical account of the creation of the Last Adam is exchanged for a myth. The concept of God, or any spirit being, *becoming a baby* is completely inconsistent with biblical truth.[9]

We recognize that the doctrine of the Incarnation is not the *direct* result of the incursion of pagan mythology, as if some Church leaders of the second century made up a story they knew would sound like mythology. We do think, however, that Church leaders of the third and fourth centuries after Christ were not diligent to allow the whole of Scripture to determine Christian doctrine. In the absence of a complete commitment to the whole Bible, they misconstrued the language of the gospel of John and used it to establish a doctrine that does not harmonize with Old Testament prophecy, the Synoptic Gospels and the rest of the New Testament. The result has been to shift the center of the Christian message from the historically documented resurrection to the Incarnation, a very mystical, mythological and mysterious idea.[10] As Maurice Wiles admits, "The Church has always recognized the highly mysterious nature of incarnational belief."[11]—We would argue that this doctrine has done more to weaken the foundation of the rational core of the Christian faith than have all the assaults of so-called "heretics" put together.

The idea that God Himself came and lived among us in the form of a man echoes pagan mythology, and at the very least has left the Christian message open to unnecessary ridicule. A pre-existent divine being taking on human flesh and being raised by regular human parents sounds so mythological that it has often been derided by critics, especially Jews and Muslims. This is even admitted by our Trinitarian source:

---

7. *Ibid.,* p. 558.
8. Tim LaHaye, *Jesus: Who Is He?* (Multnomah Books, Sisters, OR, 1996), p. 80.
9. See Appendix A (Gen. 18:1 and 2).
10. See Appendix G for historical proofs of the Resurrection.
11. Maurice Wiles, *The Remaking of Christian Doctrine* (Westminster Press, Philadelphia, 1978), p. 44.

Such an assertion, considered abstractly against the background of Old Testament monotheism, might seem blasphemous or nonsensical— as indeed, orthodox Judaism has always held it to be.[12]

Robinson discusses the mythological character of the traditional and popular understanding of the Incarnation, or "the Christmas story":

> Traditional Christology has worked with a frankly supranaturalist scheme. Popular religion has expressed this mythologically, professional theology metaphysically. For this way of thinking, the Incarnation means that God the Son came down to earth, and was born, lived and died within this world as a man. From "out there" there graciously entered into the human scene one who was not "of it" and yet who lived genuinely and completely within it. As the God-man, he united in his person the supernatural and the natural: and the problem of Christology is how Jesus can be fully God and fully man, and yet genuinely one person.
>
> The traditional supranaturalistic way of describing the Incarnation almost inevitably suggests that Jesus was really God Almighty walking about on earth, dressed up as a man. Jesus was not a man born and bred—he was God for a limited period taking part in a charade. He looked like a man, he talked like a man, he felt like a man, but underneath he was God dressed up—like Father Christmas...Indeed, the very word "incarnation" (which, of course is not a Biblical term) almost inevitably suggests it. It conjures up the idea of a divine substance being plunged in flesh and coated with it like chocolate or silver plating...The supranaturalist view of the Incarnation can never really rid itself of the idea of the prince who appears in the guise of a beggar. However genuinely destitute the beggar may be, he is a prince; and that in the end is what matters.[13]

Some in the "History of Religions school" have even suggested that the doctrine of the Incarnation was derived from Gnostic redeemer myths.[14] Though the specific Gnostic redeemer myth is now thought to have been developed after the theory of "God became a man" was already established, the mythological character of the doctrine of the Incarnation is evidently derivative and influenced by pagan God-man beliefs of the first few centuries after Christ. The doctrine sounds so similar to many other myths concerning divine beings who came and lived among men that it is hard not to conclude that Christian thinkers employed the language of pagan religions instead of adhering diligently to biblical language (Scripture).

The idea that God or the gods could come down in the form of men was a common view in New Testament times. We see a very clear example of this in the book of Acts, following the healing of a crippled man:

---

12. *Op. cit., New Bible Dictionary*, p. 558.

13. Robinson, *op. cit., Honest to God*, pp. 65 and 66.

14. John Hick stirred a controversy in the 1970's and 80's with the publishing of his book, *The Myth of God Incarnate* (SCM Press, 1977), p. 161. He regarded the doctrine of the Incarnation as something entirely foreign to the whole of New Testament thought, calling it "a dogma that Jesus himself would probably have regarded as blasphemous." Rudolf Bultmann sees so much influence of mythology on the doctrine that he called for a "demythologizing" of Christianity, even including the Resurrection, which he also questioned the historicity of. Modern critic A. N. Wilson is particularly demeaning of what he views as apostolic borrowing from pagan mythology in order to establish the Christian faith as a sufficiently grandiose story that could be competitive with the Greek and Roman fables. See A. N. Wilson, *Paul: The Mind of the Apostle* (W. W. Norton, N.Y., 1997).

Acts 14:11–13

(11) When the crowd saw what Paul had done, they shouted in the Lycaonian language, "The gods have come down to us in human form!"

(12) Barnabas they called Zeus, and Paul they called Hermes because he was the chief speaker.

(13) The priest of Zeus, whose temple was just outside the city, brought bulls and wreaths to the city gates because he and the crowd wanted to offer sacrifices to them.

It is worthy of note that Paul and Barnabas did not take this opportunity to explain that it was not *they* who were gods come in human form, but Jesus (who was supposedly "God made man"). Instead, they argued against the mythological basis of such pagan beliefs and practices:

Acts 14:14 and 15

(14) But when the apostles Barnabas and Paul heard of this, they tore their clothes and rushed out into the crowd, shouting:

(15) "Men, why are you doing this? We too are only men, human like you. We are bringing you good news, telling you to turn from these worthless things to the living God, who made heaven and earth and sea and everything in them.

As this section of Scripture implies, most people influenced by Greek and Roman religion and culture believed in a variety of myths involving the intermingling of gods, men, women, and even animals. For example, the Romans believed that Romulus and Remus were twins born of a mortal mother and Mars, the war god. The story was told that they were set afloat in a basket on the Tiber River. A she-wolf found the babies and raised them. A shepherd found the twins and brought them up to adulthood. The twins decided to build a city at the spot where the wolf found them, but Romulus killed Remus and founded Rome, supposedly in 753 B.C.

The Roman mythological pantheon included a triad, meaning a group of three gods, composed of Jupiter, Mars and Quirinus.[15] Jupiter was the god of the heavens and Mars the god of war, while Quirinus represented the common people (the Greeks had no similar god). By the late 500's B.C., the Romans replaced the archaic triad with another triad of Jupiter, Juno, and Minerva. Juno was associated with Hera [the wife of Zeus], and Minerva with Athena, who sprang fully grown from Zeus' head.

The chief god in the Greek pantheon, Zeus, visited the human woman Danae in the form of golden rain and fathered Perseus, a "god-man." Hercules (Herakles) was the son of Zeus, who fooled Alcmena by impersonating her husband, the general Amphitryon. In his descent into the realms of death, Hercules had become the Saviour of his people.

Another pagan myth particularly closely akin to the idea of the Incarnation is that of Dionysus. A. N. Wilson cites this myth as an example of what he believes is Christian mythologizing by the Apostle Paul:

Dionysus discards his divine nature and walks in the human world disguised…Dionysus, the god disguised in human form, tells him that his efforts to resist the new movement will be

---

15. This triadic motif among pagan mystery religions is well documented, and we will not elaborate upon it here. For example, in Hindu mythology, the chief divinity was Brahman, the supreme World-spirit and the Creator. He was joined by Vishnu, the Preserver, and Shiva, the Destroyer. These three divinities are called the Trimurti, which in Sanskrit means three forms. This entity had three forms, but one essence.

completely worthless; he is not contending against flesh and blood, but against a god. "You are mortal, he is a god. If I were you, I would control my rage and sacrifice to him, rather than kick against the pricks" [From Euripides, *The Bacchae*].[16]

Critics of Christianity like Wilson have a field day with the likeness of the Incarnation to these pagan mythologies, and scoff at the notion that Jesus is "God" made manifest. There are enough things that the critics will find objectionable in the genuine Christian message. Why distort Scripture and thus give them legitimate ammunition?

It seems that believing myths is endemic to the human race. One of the advantages of myths, legends and stories compared to historical truth is that the former can be changed at any time and few will mind as long as it makes a better story. Because myths frequently form the core of a people's identity and their sense of value in the cosmos, they are prone to believe stories that elevate their own status by the intermingling of the divine with their own history.

Mythology was an integral part of the life of the average person in the first century, and many rulers tried to associate their own birth with a god. Because of this mythological backdrop of the pagan religions of his day, the Apostle Paul went to great lengths to communicate the historical and scriptural basis for belief in Christ's suffering, death and resurrection according to prophecies spoken generations before. Instead of myths invented by man and bereft of the possibility of authentication, Paul and the believers of the early Church declared their faith in a Messiah who was a vivid and specifically *prophesied* historical figure. Only the true God could both declare His intentions well in advance and then perform them perfectly in a way that could be verified by eye-witnesses and later students of the Bible.

No one was ever an eye-witness to the fables of mythology, which were kept alive by the naïve credulity of devotees of pagan religions. Nor was the coming of any mythological figure accurately prophesied centuries before in a coherent body of prophetic literature. The Christian faith, therefore, stands alone among all the world's belief systems, which, with the exception of Judaism, are based on unverifiable mythologies. Even the secular "religion" of Evolutionism is based upon a grandiose myth—that the minutely ordered cosmos arose spontaneously by chance from chaos, gradually increased in complexity by a series of small, random mutations, and eventually produced the minds of Charles Darwin and Carl Sagan, who were "smart" enough to conceive of and rationalize such a preposterous fable. In contrast, Christians are expected to ground their faith on a rational, scriptural and historically verifiable foundation, so that their testimony cannot be discredited by later discoveries.

J. A. T. Robinson articulately sums up the sense in which Jesus embodies or "incarnates" God, not as a mythological figure, but as the one whom God sent to perfectly represent Him and do His will:

Jesus is a man who incarnates in everything he is and does the *Logos* who is God. He is the Son, the mirror-image of God, who is God for man and in man. The "I" of Jesus speaks God, acts God. He utters the things of God, he does the works of God. He is his plenipotentiary, totally commissioned to represent him—as a human being. He speaks and acts with the "I" that is one with God, utterly identified and yet not identical, his representative but not his replacement—and certainly not his replica, as if he were God dressed up as a human being. He is not a divine being who came to earth, in the manner of Ovid's metamorphoses,[17] in the

---

16. Wilson, *op. cit., Paul: The Mind of the Apostle*, pp. 75 and 76.

17. Ovid was a great Latin poet who is famous for his narrative poem called *Metamorphoses* (Transformations) that included more than 200 tales taken from the favorite legends and myths of the ancient world. Interestingly, Ovid considered

form of a man, but the uniquely normal human being in whom the *logos* or self-expressive activity of God was totally embodied.[18]

Jesus makes no claims for himself in his own right, and at the same time makes the most tremendous claims about what God is doing through him and uniquely through him. **Jesus never claims to be God personally; yet he always claims to bring God completely.**[19]

A strong argument against the idea that God became man in order to redeem us is that there is not a single prophecy that supports the idea. Nowhere in the body of Prophetic Literature does it say that God ever intended to make Himself into a man in order to redeem mankind. All the prophecies foretold of *a human being* who would be uniquely qualified and empowered to rule and reign and establish righteousness in the earth. For this reason, Satan was continually attempting to destroy the Christ line whenever he was able to determine its course. When Abraham was singled out, Satan escalated the wickedness of Sodom and Gomorrah. When Jacob was identified as the one through whom the Christ would come, he and his children became the object of Satanic attack.

This was the consistent story throughout the Old Testament, and it is clearly seen in the New Testament also. As soon as Herod knew that the baby had been born, Satan inspired him to have the child killed. Would Satan have been so determined to destroy the child if he had known that it was *God Himself* who had made Himself into a baby? Did he think that by killing the baby he could destroy *God*? The fact is, such a notion is completely foreign to the Prophetic Literature, which is radically trivialized by the idea that God meant all along that He would come Himself. Never do we read that a voice thundered down from Mt. Sinai or anywhere else: "Don't make me come down there!"

It is true that the Messianic hope was at its root an anticipation of a human being that could completely represent God on earth. That is why the prophecy so clearly spoke "The Spirit of the LORD will rest on him…." (Isa. 11:2). This human being would certainly have some divine attributes in order to carry out his job, but it is going too far to say, as the *New Bible Dictionary* does, that:

> The ascription by the Old Testament of various titles, functions and relationships to the God head, served to prepare the Jewish mind for the Christian doctrine of a triune Deity, which is necessarily connected with that of the Incarnation.[20]

The fact is, *nothing* prepared the Jewish mind for the idea of a triune godhead, as is evidenced by the millions of monotheistic Jews who still think the idea is nonsensical (See Chapter 5 for a detailed explanation of the Messiah the Jews expected from the prophecies in the Jewish Scriptures).

Can Only God Save?

As the subtle influence of Gnostic doctrine infiltrated the Church, early Church leaders and teachers began to accept the idea that for Christ to have been the Redeemer, it was necessary for him to transcend creation, that is, be an uncreated being, part of an eternal godhead.[21] Their reasoning was that creation could not be redeemed by a creature, but only by God Himself. We will now seek

---

the stories sheer nonsense, and not to be believed. He wrote: "I prate of ancient poets' monstrous lies, Ne'er seen now or then by human eyes." Edith Hamilton, *Mythology: Timeless Tales of Gods and Heroes* (Penguin Books, NY, 1940) p. 21.

18. Robinson, *op. cit., Priority*, pp. 393 and 394.

19. Robinson, *op. cit., Honest to God*, p. 65.

20. *Op. cit., New Bible Dictionary*, p. 558.

21. Dart cites Bultmann's research to support this connection between his idea of "Christianity" [orthodox tradition] and Gnosticism: *(continued)*

to prove that neither of these assumptions is supported by biblical evidence, and that each has led to an unscriptural conclusion that Jesus Christ is God "incarnate." We will further show that this reasoning still prevails in the Christian Church today despite the biblical evidence to the contrary.

We must consider this assumption that Christ had to be "uncreated," "eternal" and "fully God" in light of what will be handled in depth in the next chapter on the rejection of Scripture and logic by the early Church fathers and the Nicene Council. It is our considered opinion that this idea was not derived from the Bible, but was introduced under the influence on the Church of the belief in a transcendent God who was completely detached from the process of creation.[22] Indeed, as we saw in the previous chapter, one of the main earmarks of Gnostic thought was that God was not the Creator of this present creation, which was evil, but that this present cosmos was the work of a lesser, evil deity called a "demiurge." This concept was complete speculation and mythology, but it had an influence on the direction of the Church's teaching. The acceptance of myths into the core of the Christian Gospel sowed the seeds of a disastrous diminishment of the power of the Gospel message. Indeed, the *historical* validity of Jesus of Nazareth being the promised Messiah is the very core of the Gospel and a necessary element for salvation, because we must have faith in our heart that God has *in actual fact* raised him from the dead. That is, we are asked to believe in the validity of an historical event, because that event, like no other, demonstrated and proved that Jesus of Nazareth was who he said he was: the Son of the living God, Christ the Lord.

> **Romans 10:9**
> That if you confess with your mouth, "Jesus is Lord," **and believe in your heart that God raised him from the dead**, you will be saved.

Obviously, we are not expected to just "have faith" in the resurrection without evidence, as if we were children believing in the Easter Bunny or the Tooth Fairy. We see from Acts 1:3 that Christ provided the disciples with many convincing proofs of his resurrection:

> **Acts 1:3**
> After his suffering, he showed himself to these men and gave many convincing proofs that he was alive. He appeared to them over a period of forty days and spoke about the kingdom of God.

This issue of the historical validity of the Christian Gospel, especially the Resurrection, is forcefully advanced in the New Testament as a part of "the Apostles' Doctrine." The Apostle Paul argues in 1 Corinthians 15:12–19 that unless Jesus was *truly* raised from the dead, our faith and preaching are vain (useless and worthless), and we are still in our sins. Any doctrine that compromises this historical

---

Christianity asserts that humanity cannot redeem itself, that is "save" itself from the world and the powers that hold sway in it. In this concept, primitive Christianity was greatly influenced by Gnostic ideas, said Bultmann. "Man's redemption," he wrote, "can only come from the divine world as an event, according to both the Gnostics and the Christians."

Rudolf Bultmann, *Primitive Christianity in its Contemporary Setting* (The World Publishing, Cleveland, 1956), pp. 162–171. Dart, *op. cit., Jesus of Heresy and History*, p. 39.

22. *Ibid.,* p. 57. The following quote from Dart is an example of scholarly belief that the God of the Bible was unknowable: "In the wisdom genre, God tended to be more inscrutable for humans. 'He is removed into the distance and placed high above earthly concerns so that His acts in history and His acts of creation become veiled,'" writes Kurt Rudolph, citing Job 28 and Proverbs 30:1–4.

bedrock of the Christian faith ought to be held in the profoundest suspicion. The resurrection of Christ is the lynchpin of the Gospel, and the affirmation of his Sonship and Messiahship. It is the fact of the Resurrection as the proof of the Messiahship of one Jesus of Nazareth that the early Church propounded. This is the historical truth upon which the Christian Gospel is built.

However, even today it is common to hear respected Bible teachers and commentators say that the essence of the Gospel is that "God became a man and died for our sins." One modern defender of incarnational theology argues that if one does not believe that Jesus is God incarnate, that person will die in his sins. The verse he uses to substantiate this position is found in (surprise!) the gospel of John. We will quote the verse exactly as it appears in his newsletter with his inserted bracket:[23]

John 8:24b (KJV)
…for if ye believe not that **I am** *he* [**God**], ye shall die in your sins.

We strongly disagree with this interpretation, and assert that the real meaning of the verse is clear in light of the stated purpose of the gospel of John: to prove that Jesus is the Christ, the Son of the living God (20:31; cp. Matt. 16:16). In other words, if one chooses to not believe in the atoning sacrifice of Jesus Christ as the Redeemer to mankind, he will die in his sins. To go beyond this simple and easily understandable verse and assert, as orthodox Christianity has, that one must believe that Jesus is God incarnate or he will die in his sins, is, in our view, completely reprehensible. If only one person were discouraged from accepting Christ's sacrifice on his behalf because of this teaching, that would be too many. But, no doubt, some people have thought they were lost in their sins simply because they could not believe in the Trinitarian view that God became a man.

The aforementioned apologist for orthodoxy makes the further comment about the necessity for the Redeemer to be God Himself. His reasoning is essentially the same as the thinking of the Christians under the influence of Gnosticism in the centuries after Christ:

Throughout the Old Testament, God says that He is the only Savior. Obviously this must be true because salvation is an infinite work, including as it must the full payment of the infinite penalty for sin required by God's infinite justice—**something which only God could accomplish.** Consequently, for Jesus to be our Savior, He must be God. Paul called him "God our Savior" (1 Tim. 1:1, 2:3; Titus 1:3 and 4, 2:10 and 13, 3:4) as did Peter (2 Peter 1:1) and Jude (v. 25)…Thus, **God** in His infinite love and grace **became a man** through the virgin birth so that He, as a man, could take the judgment we deserved and make it possible for us to be forgiven.[24]

The logic of this argument begins with the premise that only God can save. Beside the influence of pagan thought, this idea comes from the fact that God is called "Savior" in Scripture. For example:

Isaiah 43:11
I, even I, am the LORD, and apart from me there is no savior.

Because the above verse seems to say that God is the only savior, the argument is that Jesus has to be God in order to save us, and if he is not God, then he did not save us, and we will die in our

---

23. Dave Hunt, *The Berean Call*, April, 1999.

24. Dave Hunt, *In Defense of the Faith* (Harvest House Publishers, Eugene, OR, 1996), p. 50. See Appendix A for our response to some of the verses he cites, many of which involve the Granville-Sharp "Rule."

sins. But this is a fallacious argument because it fails on several counts. First, it fails to recognize the distinction between God as the Author of salvation and Christ as the Agent.[25] God, Christ and others are all referred to as "savior," but that clearly does not make them identical. The term "savior" is used of many people in the Bible. This is hard to see in the English versions because, when it is used of men, the translators almost always translated it as "deliverer." For example:

Nehemiah 9:27
So you handed them over to their enemies, who oppressed them. But when they were oppressed they cried out to you. From heaven you heard them, and in your great compassion **you gave them deliverers** ["saviors"], who rescued them from the hand of their enemies.

This in and of itself shows that modern translators have a Trinitarian bias that was not in the original languages. The only reason to translate the same word as "Savior" when it applies to God or Christ, but as "deliverer" when it applies to men, is to make the term seem unique to God and Jesus when in fact it is not. This is a good example of how the actual meaning of Scripture can be obscured if the translators are not careful or if they are theologically biased.

God's gracious provision of "saviors" is not recognized when the same word is translated "savior" for God and Christ but "deliverer" for others. Also lost is the testimony in Scripture that God works through *people* to bring His power to bear. Of course, the fact that there are other "saviors" does not take away from Jesus Christ, who is the only one who could and did save us from our sins and eternal death.[26]

Second, the term "savior" must be understood in relationship to what people were being "saved" from. The "saving" that God did prior to His Son's coming was rescuing His people from their various bondages and captivities, not the *ultimate* salvation of saving His people from their sins. That job had to wait until the birth of the man who was the Lamb of (from) God, not the God who became a Lamb.

The third problem with this argument is that it fails to take into account a common idiom employed in prophetic utterances, namely that actions are often attributed directly to God when in fact they will be carried out by His agents. Matthew 1:21 (NRSV) says that the name "Jesus" or *Yeshua* means "**Yahweh saves**," and proceeds to give a prophetic utterance based on the name: "…for he will save his people from their sins." His name means "**Yahweh saves**," and yet it says that "he [Jesus] will save." This kind of language has a rich biblical background that must be understood clearly to avoid confusion.

Jesus, *Yeshua*, is the same name as the "Joshua" of Old Testament fame. By studying the relevant biblical records, we learn that Yahweh did not "save" Israel by doing the job Himself, or by becoming Joshua. Joshua "saved" Israel by obeying God and leading the children of Israel out of the wilderness and into the Promised Land. The salvation was wrought by God empowering both Joshua and the people who went forth in faith to claim the victory that God guaranteed for them if they would go get it. Yet leading up to this victorious accomplishment of Joshua's were several prophetic utterances spoken by God Himself, strongly stating that *He* would do the job. For example:

---

25. God is both the *Author* of the plan of salvation and an active player in our salvation. For example, God, the Father, is called "savior" in 1 Tim. 1:1, 2:3, 4:10; Titus 3:4; Jude 25. Jesus Christ is called "savior" because he is the *agent* who carried out God's plan, and without whom it could not have come to pass. See Appendix A (Luke 1:47).
26. See Appendix A (Gen. 16:7–13).

Exodus 23:23, 27, and 28
(23) My angel will go ahead of you and bring you into the land of the Amorites, Hittites, Perizzites, Canaanites, Hivites and Jebusites, and I will wipe them out.
(27) **I will send** my terror ahead of you and throw into confusion every nation you encounter. **I will make** all your enemies turn their backs and run.
(28) **I will** send the hornet ahead of you to **drive** the Hivites, Canaanites and Hittites out of your way.

It seems very clear in verse 23 that God said that He Himself would do the delivering. But, in this same context a few verses later, He says that *the Israelites* will drive His enemies out:

Exodus 23:31
"I will establish your borders from the Red Sea to the Sea of the Philistines, and from the desert to the River. I will hand over to you the people who live in the land and **you will drive them out before you.**

What is going on? Is God the "savior" here or not? The fact is, this is typical of prophetic language.[27] The principle we see over and over in Scripture is this: *God says that "He will do" something that in fact He will empower His servants to do with His help.* More specifically, when God says that He will do something, He means that He will *send* someone with whom He will work to bring His will to pass. In the above case, it was Joshua, but also Moses, Gideon, the other judges, David and many others were the active agents of the salvation that God "wrought."[28] In the case of sending someone to die for our sins, He sent Jesus, the namesake of Joshua. Only rarely in Scripture does God act sovereignly (i.e., without a human agent), and in the case of Jesus, He did not take matters into His own hands, but entrusted His will into the loving and obedient hands of His beloved Son. God, as His manner has always been, sent the perfect person into the battle and worked with him until the job was done. So in a very real sense, both God *and* Jesus "saved" us, as Old Testament heroes saved Israel, and therefore it is appropriate that each should be called "savior."[29]

We agree that Man, in his fallen condition, could never produce a qualified candidate for the job of Messiah, nor initiate anything resulting in the redemption of mankind. Because sin is inherent in mankind, and because the wages of sin is death, the death of a sacrifice was required to atone for it (Heb. 9:22). Animal blood, though provisionally adequate before Christ by the grace of God, failed to satisfactorily meet the requirements of a complete atonement. God, being spirit, has no blood; furthermore, God, who is immortal and eternal, cannot die. Therefore the only solution was that *a man with perfect blood* (that is, a sinless man) *had to die.* But because all men have been tainted by sin, there would be no possibility for a sinless human to exist without some kind of direct, divine

---

27. Perhaps the clearest example of this is in Exodus 17:14b, where God clearly says, "…I will completely blot out the memory of Amalek from under heaven." But He did not mean that He would do so Himself without human agency, as is revealed in Deuteronomy 25:19, when Moses says: "When the LORD your God gives you rest from all the enemies around you in the land he is giving you to possess as an inheritance, you shall blot out the memory of Amalek from under heaven. Do not forget!" 1 Samuel 15 also verifies that the blotting out of the Amalekites was to be accomplished by the Israelites with God's help. They could not sit back and let God do it, even though His utterance in Exodus 17:14 could have been interpreted that way.

28. See Appendix A (Acts 7:45).

29. For a more technical discussion of another fallacy employed in this argument, see Appendix K, "Undistributed Middle."

intervention. However, we must reject the proposition that the *only* way God could satisfy the requirements of redemption was by becoming a man Himself.

Contrary to the assumption that Christ must be God for redemption to be accomplished, we find, upon closer scrutiny, that the *opposite* must be the case—that unless he was a *man*, Jesus could not have redeemed mankind. God's "infinite" (we prefer a less mathematical and more biblical term like "immortal") nature actually precluded Him from being our redeemer, *because God cannot die.* He therefore sent a man equipped for the task, one who could die for our sins and then be raised from the dead to vanquish death forever. This is the clear testimony of Scripture.

> **Romans 5:15**
> But the gift is not like the trespass. For if the many died by the trespass of the one **man** [Adam], how much more did God's grace and the gift that came by the grace of the one **man**, Jesus Christ, overflow to the many!

If it were a major tenet of Christianity that redemption had to be accomplished by God Himself, then this section of Romans would have been the perfect place to say it. But just when Scripture could settle the argument once and for all, it says that redemption had to be accomplished by a *man*. The theological imaginings of "learned men" that only God could redeem mankind are rendered null and void by the clear voice of God Himself speaking through Scripture: a **man** had to do the job. Not just *any* man, but a *sinless* man, a man born of a virgin—THE MAN, Jesus, now The Man exalted to the position of "Lord" at God's right hand.

The crux of the Christian faith is not a mythical and mystical "incarnation" by which God supposedly became a man, but the historical event of a purely righteous man's death on a tree, and then his being raised from the dead by God to everlasting life. It is this simple but powerful truth that began to be exchanged for a "mystery."[30]

Creation, Not Incarnation

Jesus makes clear reference to two distinct categories in John 3:6 when he says that the "Flesh gives birth to flesh, but the Spirit gives birth to spirit." Jesus clearly declared God to be "spirit" (John 4:24). Note that he did not say, "I am spirit," or "God is flesh" or even "The Father is spirit." By thus placing "God" in the category of "spirit," when he himself is clearly a man of flesh and blood, Jesus effectively excluded any possibility that he was God. If God, being spirit, can incarnate Himself as a man, then the clear scriptural distinction between flesh and spirit disintegrates. But God the Creator, who is spirit, can *create* flesh, as He did in Genesis 1. His spirit brooded upon the face of the water, speaking into being things that had not existed before. These things were in "the flesh," but were not He. They were His creation, but He stood apart from them and judged them to be very good.

Creation is the means by which God has brought things to pass outside of that which would occur naturally. He caused a human life to begin in the womb of Mary by an act of supernatural creation, not mystical incarnation (Matt. 1:18; Luke 1:35). He waited for a willing woman to bear this child, a woman whose confession and testimony were befitting the honor bestowed upon her.

---

30. One particularly enthusiastic supporter of incarnational theology strongly affirms that the Incarnation is the foundation of the faith: "He did not become less God because of the incarnation, God manifest in the flesh is the foundation of Christianity. That one should be the God-man is the great mystery of our faith." W. E. Best, *Christ Could Not Be Tempted* (W. E. Best Book Missionary Trust, Houston, TX, 1985), p. 8.

In this way He brought into the world a human being who fulfilled the necessary conditions for becoming the Messiah. That was only the first hurdle. Then He had to work with the growing child to help him maintain his sinless condition until the time he could be anointed with holy spirit and thus be empowered to do the work to which he was called (Acts 10:38). Yes, God had to provide (by creation) the body that could be sacrificed, but Jesus had to obey Him flawlessly for his body to finally be the perfect sacrifice that it needed to be. Thus, God and Jesus each had a responsibility that the other could not perform, and upon which our redemption depended.

Let us reiterate a point we have already made in the first two chapters: the assertion that Jesus was God in human flesh nullifies the absolute necessity of Christ's obedience, because, as God, no temptation he faced would have been genuine. God cannot be tempted, because God cannot sin (James 1:13). It is also axiomatic that God can neither "obey" nor "disobey" Himself. Nor does He need to command Himself to do *anything*, for as God, the perfect moral being, He *always* acts in a timely and perfectly righteous manner.

Another unsolvable problem caused by the "incarnation" is that it destroys the plan that God established of a First Adam and a Last Adam. Romans 5:12–19 clearly defines a critical, logical parallel between Adam and Jesus Christ in the context of the redemption of mankind. A major consequence of the doctrine that God became man is that it destroys this key parallel, for *Adam* is hardly comparable to an eternally pre-existent being. Rather, he was a created being made in the image of the One who created him, God. Adam was not "fully man and fully God," "100 percent man and 100 percent God," "co-equal with God the Father," or "of the same substance as the Father." Adam was a created, empowered being who chose to disobey a direct command of God, with dire consequences to himself and all mankind as a result.

Jesus Christ was also a created being, made a man in the same way that Adam was originally made, that is, a masterpiece of God's creation, given dominion over Paradise and every creature He had made. Jesus could have no intrinsic advantage over Adam, or his qualification as Redeemer would be legally nullified. He was the Last Adam, not the first *God-man*. The differences between Adam and Jesus were circumstantial, not essential: Adam started tall with no navel; Jesus started short with a navel. Adam was created fully formed and fully able to comprehend the voice of God. Jesus had to learn from his parents. Adam did not have to suffer the indignity of a humble birth and be considered illegitimate, the son of common folk. Adam had only to dress and keep the garden and care for his wife. He had to keep from eating the fruit, or die and bring death to all his descendants. Jesus had to drink the cup of suffering and die so he could be raised to conquer death and make it possible for others to eat of the "fruit" of eternal life.

In a head-to-"Head" comparison, Adam had every advantage, yet Jesus overcame where Adam fell. He chose to obey God's will, which was that he present himself as a perfect sacrifice for sin. For the legal requirements of redemption to be satisfied, whatever Adam was, Jesus Christ had to be. Scripture declares very clearly that Jesus was a created human being like Adam was. In fact, they were both the result of God's direct creative activity.

As we have stated, the whole Bible is simply the story of two Adams. Except for the initial genetic perfection that they shared in common, the contrast between them is stark. Here is perhaps another way to summarize Romans 5:12–21:

- Two Adams
- Two created beings
- Two Sons of God

- Two men
- Two gardens
- Two temptations
- Two choices
- Two attitudes
- Two decisions
- Two results
- Two races

Other Problems with the Doctrine of the "Incarnation"

Aside from its mythological character, what are other problems with the idea of God becoming a man? First of all, it is illogical and self-contradictory when we are true to the accurate biblical usages of words. The Bible explicitly states that "God is not a man…," (Num. 23:19), which defines two distinct categories, God and man.[31] In terms of symbolic logic, it could be stated in this way: P is not Q. If Q, then not P. If God is not a man, then if someone is a "man," he cannot be "God."

God's holiness precludes Him from becoming anything other than what He is. Rubenstein points out the illogic of the assertion that "God can do anything."

> Athanasius [a bishop of Alexandria who spearheaded what became the orthodox Trinitarian position] says that God can do anything He chooses to do, and that He chose to turn Himself into a man for the sake of our salvation. Jesus Christ is not one of God's creatures, he insists, but God Himself, incarnated in human form. These sound like clear statements, but, actually, they are hopelessly confused.

> Can God do anything He chooses to do? Of course—*except* those things that are inconsistent with being God. Can He choose to be evil or ignorant? Could He be the Devil—or nothing at all?[32]

Perfection cannot be improved upon or changed. He is not a pantheistic "god" who dwells in everything. He is holy, meaning that He stands apart from and above His creation, yet is intimately involved with it. Therefore, God cannot alter His essential nature, which by definition is perfect, and perfection cannot be improved upon. But even if He could, in doing so He would, by definition, no longer be "God."

If Jesus Christ is "God in human flesh," there are other scriptural casualties. First, it renders the pathos of Gethsemane virtually meaningless, when Jesus prayed three times for **this cup to be removed from me** (Luke 22:42). If he is "of the same substance" as the Father, and an eternally integral part of a "Godhead," then his will is of necessity the same as "God's." If he struggled only in his "human side," as Trinitarians argue, while accepting the assignment in his "divine side," we are certainly left unimpressed by the difficulty he faced, compared to the way we face temptation without the benefit of a "divine" side that is sure to dominate.

---

31. God is also not "a son of man." See appendix H, #7.
32. Rubenstein, *op. cit., When Jesus Became God*, p. 118.

If it were "God's" will that Jesus should die, and Jesus is "God" in human flesh, then it was clearly also his will to die. Why then did Jesus wrestle so intensely with the assignment to sacrifice himself, finally surrendering and saying "...**nevertheless not my will, but thine, be done**"? If this struggle were between his divine and human natures, then why invoke God his Father in prayer in what was really an internal, almost schizophrenic, struggle?[33]

In our considered opinion, attempting to artificially exalt Christ via theological manipulation results in the complete negation of the heroic character of this free act of his will. Unless he was really a man, "...in all points tempted like as *we are...*" (Heb. 4:15 - KJV), with real freedom to turn his back on the assignment, the value of his act as a magnanimous sacrifice (an emptying of his own will and desire) is virtually eliminated. If he were *God*, he could hardly deny himself or disobey his own directive. Seeing Jesus as an empowered human being who had to obey God like we do is the proper context and backdrop for appreciating his heroism. Seeing him as essentially God, endowed with a divine perspective of human events, results in a view that he was only going through the prearranged motions. In that case, his heroic commitment and example collide with his supposed "deity" and sink into a gray and uninspiring sea of inevitability.

Along with the demise of Christ's heroism is the destruction of the logic of Philippians 2:8–11, and a diminishing of his exaltation based upon the merits of his obedience. Scripture here reveals that God highly exalted Jesus Christ *in response to* his humbling himself to be obedient unto death, even a death as humiliating and painful as crucifixion. If Christ were "co-eternal" and "pre-existent" with "God the Father," and if he already occupied the highest position in glory before the "incarnation," then what is the significance of *this* special exaltation relative to his obedience unto death? Was he not simply returning to his former elevated station, one that could hardly be denied him since he willingly gave it up with the understanding that he would be able to return to it? If we are truly concerned about giving Christ his proper due and honoring him appropriately, does it not make more sense to place his accomplishments in a theological framework in which his heroism is *more* apparent rather than *less*?[34] Consider the power of James Moffatt's translation of Isaiah 9:6 in this regard:

Isaiah 9:6
For a child has been born to us, a son has been given to us; the royal dignity he wears, and this the title that he bears—"A wonder of a counselor, **a divine hero**, a father for all time, a peaceful prince!"

Yet another casualty of the "Incarnation" is the significance of his Lordship. Acts 2:36 says that God made Jesus of Nazareth "both Lord and Christ." If Jesus Christ were already "God," then one cannot

---

33. It is interesting that even the devotees of the doctrine of the Incarnation see a problem with the "dual nature" theory of his being. W. E. Best writes: "To say that Christ could have sinned as to his human nature but not as to his divine nature forces me to conclude that there was a conflict between his two natures. This was impossible because his human nature was united to his Divine Person. Thus, there was never any conflict in Christ as there is in the Christian (Rom. 7:15–25)." Best, *op. cit., Christ Could Not Be Tempted*, p. 15.

34. The reader can decide for himself which of the following sounds more logical and scriptural:

a) God Himself became a man, coming down to earth from heaven to do a job. He is treated poorly while trying to do the job, and is killed. He then raises Himself from the dead and goes back to where He came from, declaring Himself victorious.

b) God created a human being, whom God prepared and commissioned to do a job. The man comes from a humble, earthly origin, is treated poorly and killed. Because he did such a good job, however, God raised him from the dead and promoted him to an exalted position in heaven.

comprehend the granting of the title "Lord" to him as anything particularly notable, because he already had every right to the title and had already been exercising it in the Old Testament. Again we find that manmade theological attempts to exalt Christ beyond what is specifically revealed in *Scripture* result in a radical demeaning of the value of his obedience and accomplishments on our behalf. Man, however sincerely, cannot add to Jesus' greatness by making him something that Scripture does not. In fact, any attempt to do so significantly subtracts from the greatness of the biblical message. When we let the Word of God speak for itself and allow every piece of the puzzle to fit together without squeezing it to fit our own traditions or preconceived notions, both God and His Son are glorified, reason is satisfied and the Christian Church is blessed as it builds upon a sound cornerstone.

The "Pre-existence" of Christ

As Paul prophesied, myths began to replace the clear and simple assertions of Scripture. One of the myths that arose was that Jesus Christ existed prior to his birth. This idea led to the necessity of the doctrine of the Incarnation, which attempts to explain how God became a human. In his thorough examination of the doctrine of the Incarnation, James D. G. Dunn recognizes that the concept arose late in the first century through a mistakenly literal interpretation of the gospel of John. Dunn devotes many hundreds of pages to documenting that the doctrine of pre-existence can be substantiated only from John:

> Only in the Fourth Gospel does the understanding of a personal pre-existence fully emerge, of Jesus as the divine Son of God before the world began sent into the world by the Father… at the end of the first century a clear concept of pre-existent divine sonship has emerged, to become the dominant (and often the only) emphasis in subsequent centuries.[35]

Other verses in the New Testament have been used from time to time to attempt to establish the doctrine of pre-existence, but many scholars have concluded that neither Paul nor Peter nor James nor the Synoptics portray Jesus as a pre-existent being.[36]

Without the idea of Christ existing in some form before his birth, there would be no need for the doctrine of an "incarnation." There have been many non-Trinitarians through the ages who have openly stood against the Trinity but who have believed that Jesus was the first of all of God's creation and was the being through whom God created the world. Apparently Arius, the bishop who debated with Athanasius at the Counsel of Nicaea in 325 A.D., held this position.[37] In examining the gospel of John, Chapter 6, we freely admit that there are verses in Scripture that seem to say that Jesus actually existed prior to his birth. However, there is a greater weight of evidence against such an incongruous notion (can one exist before he exists?), and the verses that seem to say he did "pre-exist" can be understood in a way that does not support such a counterintuitive notion. Furthermore, the few

---

35. Dunn, *op. cit., Christology*, p. 61.

36. Raymond Brown is representative as he comments on 1 Corinthians 8:6: "The text is not really clear about his personal pre-existence. It could be a reference to the power of a new creation given to Jesus." And, regarding the phrase in Philippians 2:6 and 7, Brown comments: "Many scholars today doubt that "being in the form of God" and "accepting the form of a servant" refers to incarnation [and therefore pre-existence]." Brown, *op. cit., Community*, p. 46.

37. We say "apparently," because it is hard to know exactly what Arius believed. Since he was declared a "heretic" by the "winners," all his works were burned. Trinitarian theologian McGrath acknowledges this fact: "However, it must be stressed that we know Arius' views mainly in the form in which they have been mediated to us by his opponents, which raises questions about the potential bias of their presentation." Alistair McGrath, *Christian Theology: An Introduction* (Blackwell Publishers, Cambridge, MA, 1997), p. 332.

"pre-existence" verses are outnumbered by many clear verses that teach that Jesus began his life as a seed in the womb of Mary.

The first place the Messiah is mentioned is in the Old Testament, and there is no statement that Jesus was already alive in any form. On the contrary, countless references to the Messiah speak of him in the literal future tense. For example, "I **will** raise up for them a prophet…" (Deut. 18:18), is typical in speaking of the Messiah in a future tense. Another example is in Samuel: "…I **will** raise up your offspring…I **will be** his father, and he **will be** my son…" (2 Sam. 7:12 and 14). Trinitarians say that the Messiah was "God the Son," the second person of the Trinity, who was "co-eternal" (i.e., never created). In that case he would "already" have been the Son, and the use of the future tense is misleading, even inaccurate. Another example is: "…His name **will be** called Wonderful Counselor…" (Isa. 9:6 - NASB). The phrase "**will be called**" shows clearly that the people did not think the Messiah was already around. If the Messiah were already alive, he would have already had a name. There are theologians who believe that Jesus appeared in the Old Testament, but there is no place where the text says that "Jesus" appeared. God and angels came into concretion for people, but never Jesus, for he did not yet exist.[38]

If Jesus did "pre-exist," then the only way that he could become a baby would be to "incarnate." Thus, the fact that the Scripture does not mention any such "incarnation" is a good argument that it never actually occurred. This is made even more apparent when the birth narratives in Matthew and Luke are read, because they clearly indicate that Jesus' life began when God impregnated Mary. For example, the wording of Matthew 1:18 is specific. Most translations read something like: "This is how the birth of Jesus came to be…." The Greek word translated "birth" is *genesis*, which technically means "beginning," and is translated "birth" only when the context demands it. It was apparent that the early copyists were unhappy that the Bible said "the beginning of Jesus Christ," so in many Greek texts they changed "*genesis*," "beginning," to the closely related word, "*gennesis*," which definitely means "birth."[39] Thankfully, there are honest people doing textual work today and it is openly admitted, even by Trinitarians, that the original word used in Matthew was *genesis* ("beginning").

As Peter declared by revelation, "For he was foreknown before the foundation of the world, but has appeared in these last times for the sake of you" (1 Pet. 1:20 - NASB). Christ was in God's *foreknowledge* before the world began, but was not yet a reality. Christians are spoken of in exactly the same way. Romans 8:29 says Christians were foreknown. Ephesians 1:4 (KJV) says Christians were chosen before the foundation of the world. 2 Thessalonians 2:13 says Christians were chosen from the "beginning." 2 Timothy 1:9 (NASB) says the grace of God was granted us from all eternity. Yet no theologians say that Christians "pre-existed," so it is inconsistent of them to take the same wording about both Christ and Christians and arrive at two different conclusions—that Christ "pre-existed," but Christians were only "foreknown."

---

38. Daniel 3:25 is often cited in this connection as evidence that Jesus did make a few cameo appearances in the Old Testament. When Nebuchadnezzar threw Shadrach, Meshach and Abednego into the fiery furnace, they were not only kept alive, they were joined by a fourth man, whom Nebuchnezzar described as "a son of the gods." The *NIV Study Bible*, despite the translators' belief that Jesus was the Lord in the Old Testament, says the following regarding this verse: "Nebuchadnezzar was speaking as a pagan polytheist and was content to conceive of the fourth figure as a lesser heavenly being sent by the all-powerful God of the Israelites." The one that God sent was clearly an angel, as Daniel 3:28 makes plain.

39. For an examination of this and other changes that copyists made to make the text more Trinitarian, see Ehrman, *op. cit., Orthodox Corruption.*

Angel Christology

Many Trinitarian theologians elevate the "high Christology" of the gospel of John and proceed to read into the writings of the Apostle Paul that he understood Christ to be some form of pre-existent, angelic being. But even before Jesus was born, some Jewish rabbis and authors were identifying God's Messiah as an angelic being. For example, the Jewish scholars who translated the *Septuagint*, the Greek translation of the Old Testament, identified Christ as an angelic being in Isaiah 9:6.[40]

The widely held and deeply rooted belief that Christ was a created being was a major obstacle that had to be overcome in order for the Trinity to be accepted by most Christians. In the first place, it is a clear tenet of Scripture that, born as a baby, Jesus *became* the glorified Christ with a new body and *acquired* the position of "Lord" that the Word says he earned by virtue of his obedience to God. It was quite inconceivable to the Jews and early Christians that God Almighty, the Creator of heaven and earth, could undergo growth and change, because the Bible clearly testifies that He is perfect and does not change (Mal. 3:6; James 1:17). Thus, the fact that Christ did grow and change presupposed that he was not God, but a creation of God (Luke 2:52). No wonder centuries of theological debate were required before the Trinity was accepted in the Church! Not only was it non-scriptural, but it flew in the face of another ancient myth that we have been discussing—Jewish Angel-Christology.[41] The doctrine of the Trinity was not accepted immediately, but had to gain ascendancy by replacing the beliefs already in existence.

The battle for the ascendancy of Trinitarian doctrine was fought on many fronts, and the weapons included excommunication and the sword. Doctrinally, the battle raged fiercely. There were many questions that Trinitarians had to either answer or sidestep, and the path was a winding one with many detours. It is not within the scope of this book to cover the whole matter in depth in order to show all that was going on theologically in the early centuries in the Church, but these facts are available to learn from many objective historical sources.

The essence of the Gospel, that God "made" the man Jesus "both Lord and Christ" (Acts 2:36), had to be downplayed, even done away with. If Christ were God in eternity past, and if he were God in the flesh, then it was hardly a "promotion" or "honor" for him to be "made Lord." He was simply returning to the position he occupied previous to his earthly "incarnation" after his guest appearance here on the earth.

To change from the original biblical understanding that Jesus *became* "both Lord and Christ," to the new doctrine of what is actually "God regaining His rightful position as God," yet another new doctrine had to be developed. This was the doctrine of the "two natures in Christ," which is commonly understood as Christ being both "100 percent man and 100 percent God." This new idea of the two natures in Christ also had to overcome obstacles, and it did. Martin Werner writes:

---

40. Werner, *op. cit., Foundation of Christian Doctrine*, pp. 132–139. According to Werner, some of the early references to Christ being an angel are: The *Ascencio Jesaiae*, the Ebionites who recognized Christ as an archangel; Theodotus, who wrote that Christ was "an angel of the [Gnostic] *pleroma*; Apelles the Marcionite, the book of *Jeu* [probably *Jehu*]; the writing *Pistis Sophia*; the writing *Sophia Jesus Christi*, which identifies Jesus as "the angel of Light"; the *Epistula Apostolorum* has Christ as the angel Gabriel appearing to Mary; the widely known *Shepherd Of Hermas* portrays Christ as the angel Michael; *Of Threefold Fruits*; Justin wrote that Christ was the highest angel prince; Clement wrote that Christ appeared as an angel in the Old Testament; Origen wrote that Christ was the angel who guarded Paradise; Methodius of Olympus wrote that Christ was first of the Archangels; the book of Enoch has "the son of man" as an angel; and Novatian and Lactonius referred to Christ as an angel.

41. "Angel-Christology" is a theological term for the belief that Christ is an angel or some created spirit being who existed before he was born on earth.

But the notion of a transformation [that Jesus went from a baby to "Lord"] had been too clearly set forth by Paul and the Synoptics to allow its being completely disregarded. Accordingly, the Church in its theology made a concession to the transformation-scheme when once the Angel-Christology had been definitively repudiated. This took the form of the notion that the "human nature," with which that divine nature had united itself in Jesus, had become deified through the Resurrection and Exaltation.[42]

As we mentioned above, the Church began to accept and teach that only God Himself could redeem mankind. If so, then it follows that an angelic being or a creation of God could not do so. Let us again state emphatically and categorically that the teaching that the redemption of mankind had to be accomplished by God and not by a man is grossly unbiblical. The Bible clearly teaches that the Redeemer had to be a true *man*, and not a hybrid "God-Man."

God Is the Source of the Messiah

There are a number of verses that refer to Jesus coming "from heaven," "from above," "sent from God," etc., and these are all found in the gospel of John. We explored some of the reasons for this language in the Fourth Gospel in Chapter 8, but we will now address the issue further because of the way the gospel of John is used by Trinitarians to establish the doctrines of Pre-existence and Incarnation:

- …no one has ascended into heaven, but He who descended from heaven: *even* the Son of Man" (3:13 - NASB).
- "He who comes from above is above all, he who is of the earth is from the earth and speaks of the earth. He who comes from heaven is above all (3:31 - NASB).
- For He whom God has sent speaks the words of God… (3:34 - NASB).
- "For the bread of God is that which comes down out of heaven, and gives life to the world" (6:33 - NASB).
- "For I have come down from heaven, not to do My own will, but the will of Him who sent Me (6:38 - NASB).
- "*What* then if you should behold the Son of Man ascending where He was before? (6:62 - NASB).
- …I am from above. You are of this world; I am not of this world (8:23).
- …I proceeded forth and have come from God, for I have not even come on My own initiative, but He sent Me (8:42b - NASB).
- "I came forth from the Father, and have come into the world; I am leaving the world again, and going to the Father" (16:28 - NASB).

These verses may seem to be impressive proof that Jesus did "pre-exist" in heaven before his birth, but in Chapter 8 we explained the purpose of such figurative language. Beyond that important truth, however, how would *the people to whom Jesus was talking* understand his words? The Jews were not even expecting God to impregnate a virgin in order to bring forth their Messiah, much less that God Himself would mystically transform Himself into the Messiah. The concept of God having such a direct relationship with a mortal woman was foreign to Jewish thinking. Mary, upon being told she would bear "the Son of the Most High," said to the angel, "How will this be"…"since I am a virgin?" (Luke 1:34).

---

42. Werner, *op. cit., Foundation of Christian Doctrine*, p. 149.

A quick study of Jewish commentaries on the Old Testament verses that Christians use to show the virgin birth in prophecy will demonstrate that the Jews did not then, and do not now, interpret them to mean a virgin birth. That is one reason Christ was accused of being "illegitimate" (John 8:41). James Dunn, himself a believer in the doctrine of pre-existence, wrote in *Christology in the Making: A New Testament Inquiry into the Origins of the Doctrine of the Incarnation*: "We have examples of men who are said to be the offspring of a union between some god and mortal woman (Dionysus, Heracles, Alexander the Great), but this was foreign to Jewish thought, and Jewish writers seem to have avoided the conception completely."[43] Thus, the Jews would not have understood Christ saying that he "came from above" to mean that he was "incarnated." How *would* they have understood him?

If studied in the language and culture in which they were spoken, words or phrases that seem to communicate one truth often communicate something else entirely. This is a common occurrence in verbal intercourse. James Dunn's exhaustive study devoted to the origin of the doctrine of the "Incarnation" was motivated by a desire to understand the words of the New Testament in their original context. He writes: "My concern has been all the time, so far as it is possible, *to let the New Testament writers speak for themselves, to understand their words as they would have intended, to hear them as their first readers would have heard them...*"[44] Unfortunately, Dunn is not sensitive to idiomatic language and falls into the same trap many Trinitarian New Testament scholars do, that of taking figurative language literally, and literal language figuratively. Once again we see that the proper acknowledgement of figures of speech is absolutely crucial for sound biblical exegesis.

There is a common Hebrew and Aramaic idiom that when God is the author of something, the Jews spoke of it as "coming from God," "coming from heaven," "coming down from heaven," etc. For example, the very prologue of John most often used to substantiate the doctrine of Incarnation says in John 1:6 (KJV): "There was a man sent from God, whose name was John." Does this mean that John, too, was a pre-existent divine being who was sent from heaven and became a human by an "incarnation"? Clearly not, but he was "sent from God" in the sense that he was commissioned by God to perform an important function.

There are many other examples of this idiom. God said in Malachi that He would "open the windows of heaven and pour out a blessing," and today we still use the word "Godsend" for a blessing that comes at just the right time. The Bible speaks of the "bread from heaven" referring to manna, but the manna did not float down like snow. Rather, it appeared like frost on the ground. It was said to "come down from heaven" because God was its source. God being the source is the best explanation for Christ's statements that he was sent by God, came from above, etc. The Jews would naturally have understood Christ's statements that way, and there is no evidence at all that they would have expected Christ to be speaking of a literal descent from heaven or an "incarnation."

In regard to the example of John the Baptist as a man "sent from God," consider the following verse:

Matthew 21:25
[Jesus asked the Jews:] John's baptism—where did it come from? Was it from heaven [i.e., was God its source?], or from men?" They discussed it among themselves and said, "If we say, 'From heaven,' he will ask, 'Then why didn't you believe him?'

John's baptism was "from heaven" because God was the source of the inspiration. So too, Jesus "came from heaven" because God was the source of the seed created in Mary. It would be an intrusion

---

43. Dunn, *op. cit., Christology*, p. 20.
44. *Ibid.*, p. 9 (emphasis his).

on the language and the culture of the times to insist that the Bible teaches an incarnation when there is evidence that the words used to "prove" it have an entirely different meaning. We will quote one final example that should suffice to make the point. James 1:17 says that good and perfect gifts are "from above" and "come down" from the Father. Obviously, this verse is saying that God is the source of the wonderful things spoken of. No one believes that unless something literally drops from the sky it is not from God.

The Prophetic Perfect

There is yet another Jewish idiomatic expression that we need to be aware of when studying the verses about Jesus Christ. When something was absolutely going to happen in the future, it is often spoken of as occurring in the past, or as already in existence. This is very well known to Hebrew scholars, and it is called by different names including: "the prophetic perfect," "the historic sense of prophecy," and "the preterite of prophetic vision." The distinguished scholar and author of *Young's Concordance* wrote: "The past is frequently used to express the certainty of a future action."[45] Before Abraham had any descendants, God said to him: "…To your descendants I **have given** this land…" (Gen. 15:18 - NASB). Jude 14 (NASB) speaks of Enoch's prophecy, which literally reads "…the Lord came with many thousands of His holy ones." Of course, the Lord has not yet come, but the event is so certain that it is placed in the past tense. There are many more examples of this in the Bible.

In his magnificent work, *Figures of Speech Used in the Bible*, E. W. Bullinger showed that the Greeks referred to the switch from the literal future tense to the past tense for emphasis of the figure of speech *heterosis*, and we have already introduced the concept of *heterosis* in Chapter 8. As an introduction to the subject of the past being used instead of the future for a future event, Bullinger writes:

> [The past tense is used instead of the future] when the speaker views the action as being as good as done. This is very common in the Divine prophetic utterances where, though the sense is literally future, it is regarded and spoken of as though it were already accomplished in the Divine purpose and determination. The figure is to show the absolute certainly of the things spoken of.[46]

Some of the examples of the Hebrew text speaking of a future event in the past are:

- **Genesis 15:18**. The Hebrew text reads, "…to your descendants I **have given** this land.…" However, this promise was made before Abraham even had any descendants to give the land to. Nevertheless, God states His promise in the past tense to emphasize the certainty of the event. In order to avoid possible confusion, the NIV has, "…To your descendants I **give** this land.…"
- **1 Samuel 2:31**. The Hebrew text is in the past tense and literally reads, about Eli the High Priest, "Lo, the days are coming, and I **have** cut off your arm… [i.e., "your strength"]. Almost all modern versions translate this verse in the future tense so it makes sense to the modern reader. The NIV has, "The time is coming when I **will** cut short your strength.…"
- **1 Samuel 10:2**. The Hebrew text is in the past tense and says, "…you **have found** two men.…" Most modern versions convert the past to the future so the reader is not confused. The NIV

---

45. *Young's Concordance*, Hint #60 in "Hints and Helps" (Wm. B. Eerdmans Pub., Grand Rapids, 1964).

46. E. W. Bullinger, *Figures of Speech Used In The Bible* (Baker Book House, Grand Rapids, MI, 1968. Originally published 1898) pp. 510 and 518.

reads, "When you [Saul] leave me [Samuel] today, you **will meet** two men near Rachel's tomb...."

- **Job 19:27** is one of the great statements of hope in the Bible. Job knew that sometime after he died he would be resurrected to life and be with the Messiah. The Hebrew text makes this future resurrection certain by portraying it as a past event. The Hebrew text literally reads, "...my eyes **have** seen him...[the Redeemer]." The NIV converts the past to the future so the reader will not be confused: "I myself **will** see him with my own eyes...."

- **Proverbs 11:7 and 21** offer an interesting contrast. In verse 7, the past tense of the Hebrew text makes the future destruction of the wicked person a sure thing, reading, "...the hope of the unjust man **has** perished." In contrast, in verse 21 the Hebrew text, speaking of the righteous man, reads, "...the seed of the just **has** escaped." Of course, the actual judgment of the righteous and wicked is still future, and most modern versions say that the hope of the wicked **will** perish while the seed of the just **will** escape. God's justice for both the righteous and the wicked is assured, and the use of the idiom warns of that in a powerful way.

- **Isaiah 11:1** is a great prophecy about the coming Messiah. God foretold the coming of the Messiah from the line of David. He used the prophetic perfect idiom and placed the prophecy of the coming Messiah in the past tense. The Hebrew text reads, "...a shoot **has** come up from the stump of Jesse...." The modern versions use the future tense and read, "A shoot **will** come up from the stump of Jesse...." The coming of the Messiah was absolutely certain, and God represents that certainty in the text.

- **Isaiah 9:6** also speaks of the coming Messiah. To mark the certainty of the future event, the past tense is used in the Hebrew text. The Hebrew text of Isaiah 9:6 reads, "...to us a child **has been** born, to us a son **has been** given, and the government **has been** on his shoulders, and he **has been** called Wonderful, Counselor..." Of course, the birth of the Messiah was future, and the noted commentator Edward J. Young writes:

  We must note again how impressive this fact was to Isaiah. He speaks of the birth as though it had already occurred, even though from his standpoint it was future. We know that Isaiah is not speaking of a past occurrence, for the simple reason that to do so would not yield a good sense. Whose birth, prior to Isaiah's time, ever accomplished what is herein described? To ask that question is to answer it. Furthermore, we must note that the Child whose birth is here mentioned was also the One whose birth had been foretold in chapter 7.[47]

- **Jeremiah 21:9** speaks of the certainty that those people who surrender to the Babylonians will spare their life. The Hebrew text reads, "...whoever goes out and **has** surrendered...will live...." Of course, no one had surrendered yet, and so the modern versions read, "...whoever goes out and surrenders...**will** live...."

The idioms of the Hebrew culture come over into the New Testament text as well. Bullinger explains that the idioms of the Hebrew language and culture are reflected in the Greek text. He writes:

The fact must ever be remembered that, while the language of the New Testament is Greek, the agents and instruments employed by the Holy Spirit were Hebrews. God spake "by the

---

47. Edward J. Young, *The Book of Isaiah* (William B. Eerdmans Pub., Grand Rapids, 1996), Vol. 1, p. 329.

mouth of his holy prophets." Hence, while the "mouth" and the throat and vocal chord and breath were human, the *words* were Divine.

No one is able to understand the phenomenon; or explain how it comes to pass: for Inspiration is a fact to be believed and received, and not a matter to be reasoned about. While therefore, the *words* are Greek, the *thoughts* and *idioms* are Hebrew.

Some, on this account, have condemned the Greek of the New Testament, because it is not classical; while others, in their anxiety to defend it, have endeavored to find parallel usages in classical Greek authors. Both might have spared their pains by recognizing that the New Testament Greek abounds with *Hebraisms*, i.e., expressions conveying Hebrew usages and thoughts in Greek words."[48]

We agree with Bullinger, and would like to add that there is also the possibility that there was an Aramaic original text underlying some of the Greek text and giving it a Semitic flavor. A New Testament example that Bullinger gives is Ephesians 2:6: "And God **raised** us up with Christ and **seated** us with him in the heavenly realms in Christ Jesus." This verse is usually translated in modern versions just as it reads in the Greek—in the past tense. That causes a problem. In the rest of the Bible, the translators have almost always translated the "prophetic perfect" as a future tense so the reader will not be confused, so the average Christian is not used to seeing a future event described in the past tense. Thus when they read that Christians are "seated" in the heavenly realms, they have no training to help them understand that this is a way of stating that in the future we will absolutely be seated with Christ in the kingdom of heaven.[49] Most of them try to "spiritualize" the verse and come up with some way we are seated in heaven now, even though that contradicts what both experience, as well as what the rest of the New Testament says about us being on earth now.

Another clear example of the prophetic perfect in the New Testament occurs in the book of Jude. Jude 14 speaks of Enoch's prophecy, which literally reads, "…the Lord **came** with ten thousands of His holy ones." Of course, the Lord has not come yet, but his coming is so certain that it is placed in the past tense. It can easily be seen how idioms of the language like the "prophetic perfect" put translators in a tough position. If they translate the text literally, many Christians will be very confused. However, if they do not, then the powerful way that God communicates what will absolutely occur in the future is lost.

It is important for us to understand the prophetic perfect. For example, we are studying the Scripture and we come across a reference to the Messiah that is obviously future, (Isaiah 53:5 which speaks of the Messiah already having been pierced more than 700 years before he was born), we are not confused, but understand that God is using the idiom to communicate the certainty of his being pierced.

There are many important examples of the "prophetic perfect" in the Bible, and an exhaustive list would be very difficult to compile. However, the examples listed above should be enough to show that a future event may be spoken of in the past tense to show that it will absolutely come to pass. The fact that the past tense is used for a future event all through Scripture should be evidence that it was commonly understood.

---

48. Bullinger, *op. cit., Figures of Speech*, pp. 819 and 820.

49. This is one of the great differences between Israel and the Christian Church, the Body of Christ. Christians will be raptured up from the earth and meet the Lord in the air. Then, after a time, we will return to earth with Christ to conquer and reign. Israel, on the other hand, will be resurrected and go right to the land of Israel (Ezek. 37:11–14).

Conclusion

It should now be clear that the doctrine of the Incarnation is not biblical and was developed by man, particularly in the third through fifth centuries in conjunction with the doctrines of the Trinity and the dual nature of Christ. Based upon this evidence, we propose that the idea of incarnation give way to a simpler and more biblical explanation of Jesus' origin—that God was his source by the same process of special creation that brought the heavens and the earth into being. We agree that it is important for Christians to believe in the virgin birth of Jesus, because without that teaching, Jesus is merely the offspring of Joseph and Mary, and tainted by the sin of mankind. If so, he would be incapable of being our Redeemer, because he could never present himself as the perfect sacrifice for sins. In that case, Christianity would indeed fall apart. But nothing is lost if a shift is made in Christian thinking from Jesus being the "incarnation" of God to Jesus being the *creation* of God, his Father. How sad that the vast majority of Christians believe the fable that God became a baby. The truth is nearly just the opposite—a *baby* became *the Lord!*

18

The Rejection of Both Scripture and Logic

Let us continue to explore Christological history and examine the roots of Trinitarian orthodoxy. We will see that the Church rejected logic as a tool for investigation of Scripture and the teaching of sound doctrine, and ultimately rejected the Scriptures themselves as the only rule of faith and practice and certainly the only solid ground upon which to build any true theology and Christology.

When God made man "in His own image," He endowed him with the ability to reason—to think, to judge, to analyze and to categorize. It was this ability that enabled man to "name" the animals, which was far more than a mere labeling exercise. It was a task that challenged Adam to invent a complete taxonomy based upon a detailed understanding of the natural order. It was this God-given ability that enabled man to appreciate his surroundings and draw a rational conclusion that the Creator of Paradise was the One to obey. In allowing the Serpent to seduce her by his wily and fallacious logic, Eve was being *irrational* before being *disobedient*.

As Isaac Watts pointed out in his classic textbook on logic, the ability to reason logically is a God-given treasure:

The power of reasoning was given us by our Maker, for this very end, to pursue truth; and we abuse one of His richest gifts if we basely yield up to be led astray by any of the meaner powers of nature or the perishing interests of this life. Reason itself, if honestly obeyed, will lead us to receive the divine revelation of the Gospel, where it is duly proposed, and this will show us the path to life everlasting.[1]

Reason and logic, therefore, ought not to be surrendered to any thief or con artist who tries to swindle us out of it. Unfortunately, the Church was the swindler's handmaiden in the centuries following Christ and the Apostles. Without reason and logic, we are left vulnerable to any appeal that stirs our emotions or tickles our fancy. We need to reason clearly and well to "…correctly handle the word of truth" (2 Tim. 2:15), to defend the Christian faith against competing ideologies and to make wise choices. Would it not be particularly important to reason clearly and well in regard to the cornerstone of our faith? Yet Maurice Wiles hits the nail on the head when he characterizes the historical pursuit of Christology, which has often been approached with more mysticism and speculation than logic:

> Christological doctrine has never in practice been derived simply by way of logical inference from the statements of Scripture.[2]

In other words, too much standard Christian "doctrine" has strayed into some theological domains that could have had placed above their entrances: "Abandon all common sense, ye who enter here" (or, in today's vernacular, "Check your brain at the door"). Somehow the abridgment of logic and reason works in the religious field like no other, because people assume that spiritual matters are already clouded and difficult to understand. For many, reason and logic do not apply to matters of religion and spirituality, and, for them, God is so far superior to logic and reason that we are fools to hold Him to any standards of rationality. Consequently, God can be portrayed as a murderer (He takes people "home"), a child abuser (He inflicts suffering on His children), a propagandist (He encourages blind faith and obedience) or a whimsical tyrant (His "will" is unclear—sometimes He makes you sick and sometimes He heals you). And the response of the vast majority of those who consider themselves "religious" is to just shrug and avoid what they consider "second-guessing God." We have heard many Christians say "God can do anything He wants, He is sovereign."

---

1. Isaac Watts, *Logic*, first published in 1724. Reprinted by Soli Deo Gloria Publications, Morgan, PA, 1996, p. 325. Watts is most well-known for his many Christian hymns marked by unquestionable devotion to Christ ("When I Survey the Wondrous Cross," "Joy to the World," "O God, Our Help in Ages Past," *et al.*) but he was also a logician and a theologian. In fact, his logic text was the preoccupation of his latter life and became the standard textbook for European students of the 18th and 19th centuries. It is evident that there is a close connection between his study of logic and his rejection of the Trinity. Eliot quotes the almost dying words of Watts after having devoted 20 years to intense scriptural study on the nature of God:

> But how can such weak creatures ever take in so strange, so difficult and so abstruse a doctrine as this [the Trinity], in the explication and defence whereof multitudes of men, even men of learning and piety, have lost themselves in infinite subtleties of dispute and endless mazes of darkness? And can this strange and perplexing notion of three real persons going to make up one true God be so necessary and so important a part of that Christian doctrine, which, in the Old Testament and the New, is represented as so plain and so easy, even to the meanest understandings?

William G. Eliot, *Discourses on the Doctrines of Christianity* (American Unitarian Association, Boston, 1877), pp. 97 and 100).

2. Wiles, *op. cit., Remaking of Christian Doctrine*, p. 55.

We see a lot of problems with this perspective, and we don't think it is consistent with what the Bible reveals about God. First of all, He promotes truth and hates lies. He values order, which the physical universe demonstrates in a billion ways. There is a uniformity of all the facts of the universe, so that true knowledge in one field of science is harmonious with that which is known in every other field. The demonstrable facts of chemistry fit with those of physics and biology. Though there are apparent mysteries and paradoxes, there are no contradictions between and among the recognized facts of the cosmos. This indicates that God is rational. As we consider the way God employs the rules of evidence to support belief, we recognize that He appeals to man's mind and does not manipulate his emotions (especially fear) in order to compel belief. Indeed, we find that our experience of the universe is coherent and ordered, and in many, many ways predictable, e.g., we reap what we sow. We find then that there is something fundamentally ordered and logical about the way God has created the heavens and the earth. Interestingly, we are right back to the truth revealed in the prologue of John, that in the beginning was the *logos*, around which God ordered everything that He made.

Logos versus *Muthos* Fact versus Fiction

As we saw in Chapter 9, God inspired the Greek word *logos* as the proper term for communicating His plan, purpose and power for a redeemed creation. There is another important aspect of the *logos* that we thought would be appropriate to present in this chapter on the rejection of reason and logic, since "logic" comes from the word *logos*. In Greek history, the introduction of the *logos* concept represented an entirely new way of perceiving the world when compared to previous, traditional Greek belief. Before the term *logos* first came into prominence in ancient Greece, the Greeks believed that truth was found in *muthos*, a term referring to the stories of the gods and their interactions with humans, as told in the writings of early Greek poets like Homer and Hesiod. *Muthos* was the "revelation" of the gods to men, which is now called "Greek mythology." As evidenced by the content of Greek mythology, *muthos* was the result of the dictates of whimsical yet authoritative gods, who were not under the "bondage" of rational thought. If they wanted a man to be part horse, no problem.

Several centuries before Christ, there arose in Greece a number of thinkers, first the Cosmologists and later the Sophists, who challenged the sacred *muthos* that had ruled Greek culture for centuries. They sought to undermine and overturn the *muthos* with what they called *logos*, by which they meant the reasonable explanation of reality as they perceived it. Their celebration of the power of *logos*, or persuasive discourse, to enlighten minds and elevate lives, facilitated the emergence of democracy in ancient Greece. The *muthos*, which perpetuated the authoritarian rule of kings and wealthy families, who, it was believed, ruled by the will of the gods, was countered by *logos*, which generated the development of discourse and debate as the means of formulating public policy.

The philosopher Plato later attempted to synthesize *muthos* and *logos* in the name of philosophy, and his pupil Aristotle sought to narrow *logos* to what has come to be known in English as formal logic. Despite Plato's and Aristotle's jaded attempts to redefine *logos*, however, its original sense of reasonable explanation and persuasive discourse continued into the first century. So did *muthos*, as revelation that is unaccountable to reason.

When God used the term *logos* to signify the message of Jesus and the kingdom of God, He emphasized the radical difference between the one true God and the gods of ancient Greece. Rather than associating Himself with *muthos*, an association that all Greeks made with their gods, God associated Himself with *logos*, the principle of reason and rationality embodied in persuasive discourse. In other words, the true God was not to be found in mystical experiences that could not be reasonably explained or rationally understood. It is a powerful truth that God wanted people to know that He was not to be found in the mystical practices of paganism. He was, instead, to be found in the spoken message of the Apostles, who testified with reason and rationality to their experience with the crucified and risen Jesus. God is the author of Scripture, and in it He clearly aligns Himself with *logos* and distances Himself from *muthos*.

The term *logos* represented for many Greeks the rejection of *muthos*, which is to say, the rejection of irrationality, superstition and dogma that was accepted merely because it had been handed down by the powers that be. Although idolatry was still firmly entrenched in the Greek culture of the first century, the revelation of a God who addressed humanity's capacity for rational understanding must have had a magnetic appeal for those Greeks who had outgrown the capricious gods of their forefathers.

Tragically, with the passing of the Apostles, Greek Christians with a background in Platonic philosophy rose to power in the Christian community during the second through fifth centuries, and the original import of *logos* was obscured in Christian tradition. Trinitarian theology, which began to develop in the second century A.D. and was formalized into "orthodoxy" in the fifth century, theologically transformed the Jesus of the Apostles into "God the Son, the second Person of the Godhead." Rather than understanding the *logos* as God's rational purpose for His creation, realized in the human person of Jesus, the *logos* ironically became what *muthos* had been, a mystical entity that defied reason.

Trinitarians recognize that their doctrine requires a return to *muthos*, because it asserts a mystical "truth" about a "God-in-three-Persons." Historically, this teaching has been accepted as truth primarily because ecclesiastical authorities have said it is. The Trinity has always rested upon the authority of the Church, and those who promote it today continue to do so primarily by arguing that it is the "historic position of the Church." As Catholic priest James Hughes freely admitted, "My belief in the Trinity is based on the authority of the Church: no other authority is sufficient…I have now proved the Trinity opposed to human reason."[3] It is irrational in that it cannot be reasonably explained or rationally understood, even by the admission of its most ardent proponents:

> One God in three persons, a truth made familiar to us by faith, disconcerts human reason. Divine revelation may guarantee it to us in a certain fashion, which becomes for some of us self-evident, but the intelligence remains disturbed, chained by the will to a truth it cannot see, and its impatience threatens at every moment the sacrifice of one of the two terms, the harmony of which it cannot perceive: either the unity of the divine nature, or the Trinity of the divine persons.[4]

Karl Rahner even aggressively defends the mysteriousness of the concept of the Triune God:

> It is meaningless to deny this mysteriousness, trying to hide it by an accumulation of subtle concepts and distinctions which only seem to shed more light on the mystery, while in fact they feed man with verbalisms which operate as tranquilizers for naively shrewd minds and dull the pain they feel when they have to worship the mystery without understanding it.[5]

According to Rahner, not only are Christians expected to embrace this mystery, they are to stand in the pain of worshiping an incomprehensible deity without any attempt to understand it. Such is

---

3. James Hughes, *Bible Christian for January*, 1839; quoted in John Wilson's *Unitarian Principles Confirmed by Trinitarian Testimonies* (American Unitarian Association, Boston, 1872), pp. 322 and 323.

4. Jules Lebreton, *History of the Dogma of the Trinity* (Benzinger Brothers, NY, 1939), Vol. I, p. xxii.

5. Karl Rahner, *The Trinity* (Herder and Herder, N.Y., 1970), p. 47.

the legacy of the early Church fathers who, when they rejected the authority of reason and Scriptural language, began the long slide down the slippery slope of mysticism.

If "the Father is God," "the Son is God' and the "Holy Spirit is God," and they are all separate "persons," then it seems obvious that there are three Gods, not one. Furthermore, explanations seem inevitably to plunge into theological double-talk about Jesus being "100 percent God and 100 percent man," which, in any comprehensible scenario, amounts to 200 percent, or two 100 percent persons. All of this, of course, results in not only a three-person God, but also a two-person Christ. This departure from reason usually ends with the disclaimer that explanation is futile because God, being infinite, is "beyond" human comprehension.[6]

Things that are beyond human comprehension are necessarily things that cannot be put into words; and for this very reason God has not put them into words. That is, He has not revealed things that cannot be understood. As Moses said, "The secret things belong to the LORD our God, but the things revealed belong to us and to our children forever…" (Deut. 29:29). The "things revealed" about the relationship between God and His Son are intrinsic to His *logos*, that is, "things" that are comprehensible. The Greek word *apokalupsis*, translated "revelation," means the "unveiling" of what was previously hidden from human understanding. Things revealed are things that believers can understand and assimilate into their lives.

In contrast to things God has revealed that can be understood, some of the more ardent proponents of Trinitarianism have said, "If you try to understand the Trinity, you will lose your mind, but if you deny the Trinity, you will lose your soul." In Matthew 22:37, Jesus echoed the *Shema* of Israel (Deut. 6:5), exhorting his followers to love God "with all your mind." The Greek word for "mind," *dianoia*, means "understanding." The Trinitarian definition of God denies people any possibility of the joy of loving God with the simple understanding of Him revealed in His Word. Surely it also at least dilutes their *worship* of Him, the one and only thing we can give to God that He does not have. Since He seeks those who will worship Him "…in spirit and in truth" (John 4:24), it seems logical that He would want to be worshiped for who He is, and not how theology and tradition portray Him.

For all the talk about how we mortals cannot understand God, the fact is that God has plainly revealed Himself in His Word because He wants us to get to know Him and His Son, Jesus Christ. Think about how much God tells us about Himself. His heart's desire is that we know and love Him! In *The Open Church*, James Rutz writes:

> Stained glass windows, steeples and high, vaulted church ceilings got into our lives through Plato, not Christ. Plato wrote again and again about light and space and color as they relate

---

6. Critics of Christianity have a field day with Trinitarian "logic." The following was gleaned from the website of *The Freethinkers of Colorado Springs* and appears in an article called "Trinity" by John P. M. Murphy. He quotes someone by the name of Ingersoll from the 1800's who attempts to "explain the Trinity":

> So it is declared that the Father is God, and the Son God and the Holy Ghost God, and that these three Gods make one God. According to the celestial multiplication table, once one is three, and three times one is one, and according to heavenly subtraction if we take two from three, three are left. The addition is equally peculiar. If we add two to one we have but one. Each one is equal to himself and the other two. Nothing ever was, nothing ever can be more perfectly idiotic and absurd than the dogma of the Trinity. How is it possible to prove the existence of the Trinity? Is it possible for a human being, who has been born but once, to comprehend, or to imagine the existence of three beings, each of whom is equal to the three? Think of one of these beings as the father of one, and think of that one as half human and all God, and think of the third as having proceeded from the other two, and then think of the three as one. Think that after the Father begot the Son, the Father was still alone, and after the Holy Ghost proceeded from the Father and the Son, the father was still alone—because there never was, and never will be but one God. At this point, absurdity having reached its limit, nothing more can be said except: "Let us pray."

to man's upward spiritual striving toward the "unknowable" Divine essence, the "other than," the "touch with the sublime," the "moment of awe."

The early Christians knew that God could be known, that we could meet Him directly, heart to heart, right here and now. In a different sense, we also meet Him in face-to-face, down-to-earth fellowship with other believers. The early Christians saw no need for stained glass and steeples to point us upward to a God just out of reach. "**He is here!**" they said. "**He is among us!**" But walk into any cathedral, and you will immediately be staring upward toward an unreachable apex in the sanctuary. *Permanent awe, permanent frustration.*

Plato insisted that man must go through a number of ascensions and plateaus to meet the divine essence. It takes a lifetime, he warned, and very few will achieve it. Only the gifted will succeed, and that through much suffering. The Catholics adopted the Platonic "Stages of Ascent." They can be found in virtually all their writings on the subject of knowing God.

Plato's brilliant nonsense was enthusiastically picked up, massaged, endorsed and passed on down by generations of heavy-duty Christian thinkers like Origen, Tertullian, and Augustine.[7]

As the idea that God was "unknowable" grew in Christendom, real knowledge of God decreased. He was said to be "triune," which in itself was unknowable. He was said to be in total control of both good and evil.[8] He was said to torture unbelievers in a fictitious place called "hell" for all eternity.[9] The fact is that as a result of these and other false teachings, all kinds of illogical misinformation about God exists in the world today. The greatest way to correct this problem is by reading and understanding the Bible, guided by reason to work through apparent contradictions. As we do so, we will gain increased understanding of who God is and what He does and does not do, and our love for Him and faith in Him will grow.

The Bible says that "…without faith it is impossible to please God…" (Heb. 11:6). "Faith" is the English translation of the Greek word *pistis*, and can almost always be translated "trust" or "confidence."[10] God wants us to have trust and confidence in Him, but we cannot do that if we cannot enter into a relationship with Him. We do not trust those whom we do not know. Trust is a deep feeling or deep assurance that someone will keep his promises and neither fail us nor betray us. It is built by relational experience. This is why people who believe that God is in charge of both good and evil often lose their faith, their trust in God, when some terrible thing happens to them or to someone they love. They feel they cannot trust God anymore, and if what they believed about Him were actually true, they would most certainly be right.

We think it is axiomatic that "faith," or "trust," is tied to "understanding." It is very hard to have confidence in something we do not understand. Too often, this fact gets glossed over in Christendom. We hear ministers and Bible teachers say that we can have faith in God without understanding

---

7. James Rutz, *The Open Church* (The Seed Sowers, Auburn, ME, 1992), pp. 63 and 64.

8. Many books have been written trying to explain how a loving God can do seemingly unloving things like give a baby cancer or "call home" (in plain language, "murder") a mother with small children. The "explanations" these books have offered have never been satisfactory—because *God* does not do those things. The *Devil* is in the business of death and destruction (Heb. 2:14; 1 John 5:19). For a biblical and rational explanation of this issue, read our book: *op. cit., Don't Blame God!*. See Appendix D also.

9. The Bible says the wages of sin is *death*, not eternal "life" in torment. For a complete explanation, read our book: *op. cit., Is There Death After Life?*; or for an exhaustive study, read *The Fire That Consumes*, by Edward Fudge, (Paternoster Press, Carlise, Cumbria UK CA30QS). See Appendix D also.

10. For a more complete study, see "Keep the Faith," Chapter 11 in our book: *op. cit., Don't Blame God!* See Appendix D also.

Him. That type of statement is usually backed up by other statements such as, "I do not understand electricity, but I use it." That misses the point. When we turn on a light, it does not indicate our trust in, or understanding of, electricity, but rather our trust in electricians, as well as in our experience of the results of electricity—that when we flip the switch, the light comes on. The object of our trust is in our *experience* and not "electricity" *per se*, and this is revealed if the light does not come on—we change the bulb or call an electrician. If we truly believed that electricity was a "mystery," we would sit in the dark and philosophize about how sometimes the light works and sometimes it does not. God works to make Himself known and understood by those who seek Him. God has represented His Word as the *logos*, not the *muthos*, because He knows that we can readily enter a trusting relationship with Him only as we understand and obey Him.

Christians are called to present their bodies as living sacrifices (as opposed to the burnt offerings of dead animals under the Old Covenant), which is described as their "reasonable service" (Rom. 12:1 - KJV). The word translated "reasonable" is *logikos*, a form of *logos*. A life of loving servanthood is "reasonable." In other words, in view of the love of God in giving His Son and the love of Christ in giving his life for the salvation of humanity, serving him is a reasonable response to a rational understanding of the Gospel of Christ.

A Mysterious and Unknowable God

As we have seen in the previous chapters, one of the principal ways that Christianity was influenced by Gnostic thought was to consider *God as fundamentally mysterious and outside the realm of reason*.[11] This stream of thought became an unspoken assumption, one not held by the Jews or the early Church of 35–75 A.D.[12] This subtle belief affected the course of Church history and culminated in the formulation of the Nicene Creed at the Council of Nicaea in 325 A.D.

Such an idea flies in the face of Scripture. Jesus Christ came to declare, to make known, his Father (John 1:18). He came to bring knowledge of the true God—His will (John 1:17 and 18), His nature (John 4:24), His desire (John 4:23) and many other things. Jesus said, "...He who has seen Me has seen the Father..." (John 14:9 - NASB), and enabled the people to see what God was like by how he spoke and how he acted. Thus, Jesus perfectly represented the heart of God to mankind. He also revealed secrets (often mistranslated "mysteries") to his disciples (Matt. 13:11; Mark 4:11; Luke 8:10).

We understand that God did not fully reveal His true nature in the Old Testament, but after Christ came, there is no Scripture that says God is withholding from man anything we need to know

---

11. It is very unfortunate that the Greek word *musterion* became transliterated into the Bible and other Christian literature as "mystery" when it actually means "secret." When Christ said in Matthew 13:11 (KJV), "...Because it is given unto you to know the mysteries of the kingdom of heaven, but to them it is not given," the innocent reader believes that the things of God are mysterious, i.e., not really comprehensible except perhaps to a chosen few. If that same verse is read with the words "secrets" in place of the word "mysteries" (like it is in the NIV), it takes on an entirely different meaning. To learn a secret, all one has to do is talk with the one "in the know." Every child has secrets he shares only with others that he really likes. God does the same. The secrets of God are open to those who diligently seek Him and obey Him. The Bible is clear on this point, e.g., Luke 11:9 and 10; Prov. 2:3–5, 25:2; Matt. 13:11–14; John 14:23 and 24.

12. Many orthodox Christians believe and teach that there was a historical continuity between the early Church and subsequent developments in Church History. However, thanks to the work of Harnack, Bauer, Ehrman and others, it is becoming clearer that when we read the Patristic literature (written by the "Church Fathers" of the second through fifth centuries), we see some fundamental differences between their perspective and the "Apostle's Doctrine." We encourage every Christian to read the Patristics for himself and compare them to the Bible to see how little historical continuity exists between the early Christian Church and the later centuries.

about Him. If knowing the nature of the Godhead is important enough to determine whether a person is saved or not, as orthodox doctrine argues, then it is important enough to be clearly defined in Scripture. If God is truly unknowable and inscrutable, as unfortunately many theologians have thought, man would then be consigned to speculation, guesswork and several centuries of "doctrinal development" and "theological reflection" in order to ascertain any real knowledge of God. In His Word, God reveals to us everything we need to know about Him. Thus, He is knowable. God tells us that He is good, holy, just, pure, truthful, faithful, kind, compassionate, merciful, understanding, gracious, able to get angry and much more.

The fact that God is holy, even awesome, does not mean that He is *mysterious*. Scripture contains numerous examples of people wanting to remove themselves from His presence, not because He was mysterious, but because He was *so clearly revealing Himself to them!* From the time Adam hid in Eden, it has been sin in man that has caused him to tremble before a holy God, and invent a variety of forms of religion to cover his spiritual nakedness (Gen. 3:7). This helps to explain why sinful man has invented a theology of mystery, because it keeps God at a more comfortable distance from him. As long as one is unclear about God's nature and will, he is much less accountable to listen and obey. A "mysterious" and abstract God is a distant idea, but a God who has revealed Himself and His will for man is an immediate reality who must be engaged personally.[13]

The fact is, God reveals Himself in both the Old and New Testaments as a God who wants very much for people to know Him and His will for their lives. When God did not reveal things, it was because He wanted to keep His purposes a secret from His enemies (1 Cor. 2:8), because the carnality of His people did not permit Him to reveal much (1 Cor. 2:1, 2 and 6), to protect the immature (John 16:12) or to allow the seeker to prove his sincerity (Prov. 2:1–5).

Not only were the early disciples blessed to have an abundance of revelation given to them, but they were also encouraged, even commanded, by the Lord to "use their heads," or *reason* (logically, if you will) toward the acquisition of spiritual insight. When the two disciples on the road to Emmaus demonstrated their ignorance of the necessity of his suffering, Jesus called them "foolish men" (Luke 24:25 - NASB). "Foolish men" is the Greek word *anoetos*, which is defined as "unreflecting, never applying the *nous* (mind) to moral or religious truth."[14] As a result of failing to think through what Jesus had been teaching all his disciples, they built their expectations on false premises that did not sustain them during the crisis of his crucifixion and death.

Reason divorced from spiritual truth is discouraged by Scripture, as in 2 Timothy 3:7 (KJV), which describes this as "Ever learning, and never able to come to a knowledge of the truth." However, the use of reason to comprehend and expound Scripture is not only encouraged, but the believer is considered a "fool" if he does not do so. "Come now, let us reason together, says the LORD..." (Isa. 1:18). 2 Timothy 2:15 commands us to "correctly handle" the word of truth. Isn't correct *thinking* prerequisite to "correct handling" of Scripture?

---

13. There are many examples of God clearly revealing Himself in the Bible. A good example is Job. Theological speculation seemed to be working pretty well for Job until God showed up. Then Job said, "My ears had heard of you but now my eyes have seen you. Therefore I despise myself and repent in dust and ashes" (Job 42:5 and 6). Too many people have "heard" various ideas about God but have never personally encountered Him in any way. However, because of His loving nature, God will work with people whose theology is in error. Many Christians wrongly assume that because the Lord has given them revelation, or they have done a healing, or they speak in tongues, that what they believe about God must be right. However, both the Word and experience reveal that a person can be wrong in his beliefs and, particularly if he has love and faith, God can still work powerfully with him.

14. Bullinger, *op. cit., Lexicon*, p. 294.

If reason is irrelevant to revelation, then it is curious that Paul's Epistles, which are given by revelation (Gal. 1:11 and 12) are so full of carefully reasoned arguments (Rom. 5–7; 1 Cor. 15, *et al.*).[15] Since orthodox Christians hold these Epistles to be God's revelation, they should acknowledge that reason and revelation are closely related and not mutually exclusive categories. God's very appeal to man to believe in Him and obey His commands is based on His Word's intrinsic reasonableness as well as its consistency with other revealed truth and the physical universe (Rom. 4:1ff; 6:1–7:25, *et al.*).

As we look at the rejection of reason by the Church fathers, the continual influence of *Satan* in Church history should not be underestimated. Genesis 3 makes it clear that the focus of his assault is the Word of God. Along with his frontal assault in the early centuries of the Church, he made an indirect but parallel assault on God's Word by assaulting logic and reason, a powerful tool for understanding Scripture and discerning truth in any category.

Ehrman notes the tendency of proto-orthodox Christians of the second century to dwell on paradox:

> All of the proto-orthodox authors appear to have embraced a paradoxical view of Christ. The paradoxical affirmations were nonetheless strongly characteristic of these forerunners of orthodoxy, and it was precisely such affirmations that later came to be crystallized in the orthodox creeds.[16]

Tertullian

Although a gradual distrust of reason can be found in the writings of other pre-Nicene writers, we will focus on Tertullian, the influential third-century lawyer/theologian. It is widely accepted that Tertullian was the first to use the word "Trinity" (Latin *trinitas*),[17] as well as the idea of "three-in-one" (*tres personae*) and one substance (*una substantia*) in connection with the Trinity.[18] He does so without hesitation or evident humility, nor acknowledging that he is using terms that do not appear in Scripture. His attitude even belies an elitest mentality, since apparently his views were not shared by the majority of the believers of his day:

---

15. Ehrman, *op. cit., Orthodox Corruption,* p. 13. Ehrman shows the value of logic and reason in determining the correct textual reading when the various Greek manuscripts give different readings. Unfortunately, as the Church moved away from reason and logic and accepted a paradoxical view of Christ, readings that violated common sense presented no problem. For example, on page 80 of Ehrman's book, he addresses the difficulties of the textual variant reading of John 1:18 identifying Jesus as the "unique God." He points out the logical difficulty with this reading and why this would not be a problem for second and third-century Christians, who by that time had embraced a fully paradoxical view of Christ:

> By definition there can be only one *monogenes*: the word means "unique," "one of a kind." The problem, of course, is that Jesus can be the *unique* God only if there is no other God; but for the Fourth Gospel, the Father is God as well. Indeed, even in this passage the *monogenes* is said to reside in the bosom of the Father. How can the *monogenes theos*, the unique God, stand in such a relationship to (another) God?…[This] was not a problem for Christians in the second century and beyond, who, with their increasingly paradoxical understandings of Christology, *could* [emphasis his] conceive of ways for Christ to be the unique God himself.

16. *Ibid.,* p. 13.

17. The Latin word for "Trinity" (*trinitas*), occurs for the first time in Tertullian's *Adv. Prax.* 3, quoted in H. A. Wolfson, *The Philosophy of the Church Fathers* (Harvard Univ. Press, Philadelphia, PA, 1976). He quotes Tertullian from *Adv. Prax.* p. 105.

18. Jean Danielou, *The Origin of Latin Christianity* (Westminster Press, Philadelphia, PA, 1977), p. 364.

The simple indeed, I will call them unwise and unlearned—who always constitute the majority of believers, are startled at the dispensation of the three in one.[19]

Tertullian's enthusiastic and arrogant embrace of the three-in-one concept elevated him above the common man. This illustrates the fact that one of the appealing things about teachings that are difficult to grasp is that they elevate the one who can apparently understand and communicate them. When doctrine is agreeable to common sense, common people can understand and apply it. Indeed, one of the greatest accomplishments of the Reformation was that it overturned the scholastic monopoly that kept the Scripture locked away in monasteries obscured by dogma and Latin translations that only the monks could read. Once the common man was allowed to read the Scripture for himself, many unscriptural ideas that had been maintained by Church tradition for hundreds of years fell by the wayside.

Tertullian was a gifted writer and rhetoricist who used reason with devastating effect against his enemies. Yet when expounding upon Scripture, he discarded reason as a tool for truth-finding. His basic view was that because everything one needs to know is found in the Bible, reason is unnecessary. As one historian stated Tertullian's view: "Since God has spoken to us, it is no longer necessary for us to think."[20] Because Tertullian thought that revelation was sufficient, he avoided the rigors of logical thinking, believing that it only tended to heresy. He wrote:

> We want no curious disputation after possessing Christ Jesus, no inquisition after enjoying the Gospel. With our faith, we desire no further belief.[21]

This sounds very humble, but in fact his position was rather arrogant. Remember that he was speaking of "the majority of believers" when he was speaking of those who did not accept his Trinitarian ideas. Tertullian even went so far as to say:

> The Son of God died; it is absolutely to be believed because it is absurd. And he was buried and rose again; the fact is certain because it is impossible.[22]

Tertullian thought this was absurd because of his assumption that the "Son of God" was also "God the Son," and God cannot die. But reason demands that every assumption be rationally evaluated according to Scripture. If it is not, the conclusions that "logically" follow will be grossly illogical.

It is one thing to assert that God, while rational and consistent, can do something that *seems* impossible to men. It is quite another thing to say that God is actually capable of *absurdity*. *The American Heritage Dictionary* says that the word "absurd" implies "obvious departure from truth, reason or common sense."[23] Tertullian's statement is indicative of the theological thinking of his time—that something devoid of truth, reason or common sense should be believed. Worse yet, that it should be believed *because* it makes no sense.

Fideism: The "Pistic Heresy"

Tertullian represented a school of thought called "Fideism" (from the Latin word *fides*, meaning "faith"), which enrolled other influential Christian thinkers like Augustine. This school believed that

19. Wolfson, *op. cit., Philosophy of the Church Fathers*, p. 105.
20. E. G. Bewkes, *The Western Heritage of Faith and Reason*, (Holt, Rinehart, Winston, N.Y., 1971), p. 382.
21. *Ibid.,* p. 448.
22. *Ibid.,* p. 448. See also A. McGiffert, *A History of Christian Thought* (Scribners & Sons, N.Y., 1946), p. 16.
23. *The American Heritage Dictionary,* (Houghton Mifflin Company, Boston, MA, 2000).

it is not necessary for biblical doctrines to conform to logical restraints, teaching that faith is not generated or matured when reason is satisfied. In other words, they believed that if something could be clearly understood, then "faith" could not be involved. Therefore, they rejected logic and reason in order to promote their faith. Doctrine can therefore be illogical and true at the same time, because God is not fundamentally a God of reason, but of mystery. Scripture, however, says no such thing, but rather includes *understanding* as a prerequisite to genuine faith (Rom. 10:17; Matt. 13:19; *et al.*).

In our opinion, this wholesale rejection of reason in favor of faith represents a heretical view of Scripture, one that has had a disastrous effect on the course of Christian history. Indeed, as Gnosticism elevated special mystical "knowledge" (*gnosis*) above Scripture and reason, so the fideists elevated "faith" (*pistis*). For this reason, we have dubbed fideism the "Pistic Heresy." This preoccupation with irrational faith contributed to the widespread acceptance of nonsensical doctrine that greatly undermined the persuasive power and historical validity of the Christian faith.

We must not think that fideism is a phenomenon limited to early Christianity. As this book goes to print, fideism is undergoing a renaissance in the Christian world, marked by widespread distrust of reason in favor of emotion and mysticism in both Christian faith and practice. Theologians of every age seem given to speculative philosophies instead of the clear language of Scripture. British theologian Maurice Wiles' candor is refreshing in regard to the predilections of those in his profession to embrace contradiction and mystery:

> Nonsense is still nonsense, even when people talk it about God. Contradictions remain contradictions and cannot be rescued from their logical impropriety by the magical device of rechristening them paradoxes.[24]

Sometimes it is argued that many of the finest minds in human history employed their reasoning skills in the process of rationalizing the Trinity, but there is a difference between "reasoning," which is often *rationalization* (starting from a conclusion and then finding reasons for it) and *logical* reasoning based on truth. We grant that there is a gigantic volume of inferential reasoning (speculation and reflection) associated with the formulation of Trinitarian orthodoxy. Indeed, this is widely acknowledged by Trinitarian scholars.[25] The question is whether or not this reasoning is scriptural and logical. Too often, the highly educated are the most deceived by their "elevated reasoning," and need more common sense. Some of the most brilliant minds in the world have also been involved in the development of the theory of evolution as well. But, as sociologist Peter Berger observes, "There is some warrant for asserting that the propensity to believe evident nonsense increases rather than decreases with higher education."[26]

We recognize that there are limits to the authority and usefulness of logic. For instance, the Bible is not a logical treatise on the existence of God. It opens with the presupposition that God exists and moves in history. Nevertheless, both the Bible and the Creation described in it provide abundant evidence to support this assumption for those who will to believe. One of the main attributes that the Bible reveals

---

24. Wiles, *op. cit.*, *The Remaking of Christian Doctrine*, p. 31.

25. *Op. cit.*, *The New Catholic Encyclopedia*, in its article on the "Holy Trinity," says the following:

> The controversies that occasioned the early councils stemmed partly from the difficulty of the subject—the Trinity and Christology—and partly from the lack of an accepted terminology [because the Trinitarians did not accept the limitations of biblical language]. Today, the catechism states that in God there are three Persons and one nature, and that in Jesus Christ there is one Person and two natures. **This answer is the fruit of vast theological reflection** (p. 291).

26. Peter Berger, *A Far Glory: The Quest of Faith in an Age of Credulity* (Free Press, Toronto, 1992), p. 163.

about God is that He is love. As such, He cannot compel belief, or faith, although He could certainly do so if He wanted. Rather, He allows for alternative explanations and interpretations of the evidence, as the theory of evolution so clearly demonstrates. Though His hand in Creation is clearly seen, such that man is without excuse to reject it, he is also not compelled to believe it by overwhelming evidence. God, in His wisdom, has required man to take a step in His direction, a step of faith. But this step is supported by a plethora of evidence that God is who He says He is, and that He is there for those who believe. That is different than expecting mankind to take a "leap of faith" into the darkness, without reason to expect God to be there in an understandable and predictable manner.

Dennis McCallum makes a number of insightful comments on fideism in contrast to the role of logical reasoning in the life of a believer:

> Many people believe wishful thinking is exactly what faith is all about. These thinkers, commonly known as fideists, argue that a scientific or rational worldview has to be decisively rejected before a person can properly approach religion.
>
> For the biblical Christian, however, this would be a devastating mistake. The biblical Christian believes that once we abandon reason in matters of faith, we have lost any value that faith may have given us. This is because once reason is abandoned, there is no basis for thinking that anything is actually *true*. Things may be true in a *religious* sense, but this is different from being true in the *real* sense. For example, some people believe that 2 + 2 = 4, no matter where one lives or how one was raised. Yet these same people believe that one God may exist for them, while another may exist for a Hindu. There are two kinds of faith being suggested here. One is reasonable; the other is mystical. One insists on consistency; the other allows contradictions.
>
> Usually, if two lines of evidence lead to conflict, we realize there must be a way to resolve the problem, even if we don't know what it is. But this is totally different from accepting the idea that contradiction is OK, and that both conflicting conclusions are true.
>
> In order to believe that, an altogether different way of thinking would be necessary: a departure from reason into mysticism. Mysticism, in the context of religion, refers to an approach where truth is beyond human comprehension. According to this understanding, we must transcend our normal way of thinking and experience truth rather than try to reason our way to it. The Bible teaches that there is truth that could be called mystical in the sense that it must be experienced in order to be understood (Eph. 3:19). But this truth is compatible with truth as we usually use the word. There is a place for experience in knowing God…but experience is to be added to rational thinking, not replace it.
>
> Unfortunately, when we choose to move entirely out of reason and into mysticism, we also inherit a number of serious problems. First, as already mentioned, we could not be sure that what we "believe" has any connection with reality. Also, if reason indicates that one of our beliefs is not actually true (in the objective sense), we would become uncomfortable. We would have to learn to practice a way of thinking that enables us to put up with contradictions in various areas of mystical faith. For instance, modern science may have some things to say that bother us, and from which we must avert our gaze (such as evolution and the role of cause and effect). There may also be various features of history or modern sociology that cannot be accounted for on the basis of a suprarational faith. We may even have to try to smooth over or look away from certain inconsistencies within our own faith.

Once we permit ourselves to look away from things we suspect are true, we are cultivating the ability to deliberately deceive ourselves. We are conditioning ourselves to feel comfortable with contradictions in our thinking.

This suprarational, mystical thinking controls the religious world today (as it always has). In such thinking, the emphasis is on religious experience and "feeling-states" rather than on objective truth. How else can we explain the fact that many today who would consider themselves Christians are unable to offer a rational defense for their faith or even to explain what their faith is? If there is no reasoned defense, including some objective evidence, it appears that the person has simply chosen to believe something because of personal experience or because it is convenient or traditional. A Muslim, for example, would have to reject a rational worldview when it comes to faith. Muslims believe that Mohammed was the prophet of Allah. But what evidence is there that he was? In the end, there is only the say-so of the prophet himself and the religious experience of the worshiper. While both of these could be considered evidence, neither qualifies as objective evidence.[27]

The renowned fourth century theologian Augustine went even further down the fideistic road, believing that the more unreasonable the object of faith, the more opportunity there was for faith to develop. "We believe in order that we may know, we do not know in order that we may believe." He then goes on to contradict himself: "Who cannot see that thinking is prior to believing? For no one believes until he has first thought that it is to be believed." And again, "We could not believe unless we possessed rational souls."[28]

Following such reasoning to its logical conclusion, a believer would not only accept, but actively seek, mysterious objects of faith, and in the process surrender his sanity and his ability to make rational judgments. This is essentially what happened historically, plunging the Western world into the Dark Ages. Gilson asks:

> Did he [Tertullian] mean that faith is more certain than human reason, and that since only what is incomprehensible to reason can be an object of faith, a crucified God is absolutely certain (by faith) by virtue of its very incomprehensibility?[29]

The answer to Gilson's question is quite obviously "Yes." How else are we to explain Tertullian's acceptance of the following four propositions as simultaneously true?

1. There is only one God.
2. The Father is God.
3. The Son is God.
4. The Father is not the Son.

This is logically equivalent to saying:

1. A man has only one wife.
2. Sue is his wife.
3. Ann is his wife.
4. Sue is not Ann.

---

27. Dennis McCallum, *Christianity: The Faith That Makes Sense* (Tyndale, Wheaton, IL, 1992), pp. 8–11.

28. Wolfson, *op. cit., Philosophy of the Church Fathers*, p. 133. (Quotes from Augustine's *De Praed. est. Sanct. 2.5; Epist. 120.1,3, ad consentium*).

29. Etienne Gilson, *A History of Christian Philosophy in the Middle Ages* (Random House, N.Y., 1955), p. 45.

Thus, by this rejection of logic, or sound reasoning, the Church positioned itself to accept doctrines on the inadequate basis of sincerity, theological and mystical reflection, personal experience, tradition and Church authority rather than what the Word of God actually says.[30] Augustine's statement concerning the authority of the Church is worth mentioning in this connection:

> No Christian ought in any way to dispute the truth of what the catholic [universal] church believes in its heart and confesses with its mouth. But always holding the same faith unquestioningly, loving it and living it, he ought himself as far as he is able to seek the reason for it. If he cannot, let him not raise his head in opposition but bow in reverence.[31]

This certainly sounds to us like a formula for tyranny, manipulation and the subjugation of individual conscience. Such a wholesale submission to authority would perhaps be appropriate in a perfect world, such as during the Millennial reign of Christ on the earth. But in a world corrupted by sin and influenced by Satan, we need both eyes open. One eye is reason. Without it, Christians live in ignorance, superstition and fear. But divorced from faith, *reason* proves insufficient, as history has demonstrated by Aristotle's extremely rational but largely erroneous system of thought.

The other eye is *faith*, based on the written Word of God. Without it, man lives in doubt and despair. Divorced from reason and Scripture, however, faith becomes gullibility, and usually leads to authoritarian intimidation and indoctrination. A classic example of this is the fact that millions of people believe the doctrine called "Transubstantiation," which theorizes that the bread and wine of the Lord's Supper literally become the body and blood of Christ, despite the contradictory testimony of both Scripture and their taste buds. Through the centuries, this doctrine has been challenged by hundreds of theologians, and the primary defense offered is that "you simply have to take it by faith."

First, the Church rejected logic as a necessary and appropriate tool for rightly dividing the Scriptures. Having swallowed this "camel," the Church was hardly able to notice the many "gnats" of subsequent erroneous teaching. With one eye out, it was then vulnerable to a subtle "blind side" attack on the integrity of Scripture as the final rule of faith, which it later also rejected.

In the Nicene debate, Arius, whom Trinitarians still consider to have been a dangerous heretic, is acknowledged by Trinitarian sources as having "consistently rejected nonscriptural words and expressions."[32] Of course they view this as a foolish and unnecessary stand, since the Church, and not Scripture, is the final authority. But in light of the Church's many failures throughout her history, would we not be wise to trust in the language of Scripture and distrust our inferences from it? Should not Arius' reliance on scriptural language be counted to his *credit*?

Rubenstein recognizes that the Arians showed a greater commitment to rational methods, optimism, humility and toleration:

> …There was a rationalist element in Arianism, an insistence on clarity and logic, and on coherent readings of the Gospels, that those schooled in Greek philosophy were particularly

---

30. The Roman Catholic Church, never even partially purged from its Augustinian roots (as the Protestant Church was by Luther, etc. in the Reformation) still plunges ahead today with doctrine completely divorced from Scripture. Two widely known examples are Papal Infallibility and the Assumption of Mary into heaven at her death, wherein Catholic theologians consider Mary to have been born without the sin that the rest of humanity has. All of these ideas blatantly contradict the Bible. Recently, the Pope said that Mary was the first to see Jesus after his resurrection, a clear contradiction of Mark 16:9, which says that Mary Magdalene was the first to see Jesus. Currently, millions of Roman Catholics are petitioning the Pope to invoke Papal infallibility and declare Mary as "Co-Redemptrix, Mediatrix of all Graces and Advocate for the People of God." (*Newsweek Magazine*, August 25, 1997), pp. 48–56.

31. Gilson, *op. cit., History of Christian Philosophy in the Middle Ages*, p. 45.

32. *Op. cit., The New Catholic Encyclopedia*, "Holy Trinity," p. 299.

likely to appreciate.[33] Most of all, Constantius [Constantine's son] would have appreciated the temperament of the moderate Arians: their relatively optimistic view of people's potential to make moral progress and to assist in their own salvation; their capacity (again relative) to tolerate a variety of theological perspectives without declaring their opponents agents of the Devil; and their modest disinclination to claim knowledge of matters beyond human understanding, like the precise relationship between the Father and the Son.

Conversely, the Nicene doctrine, especially as expressed by Latin zealots like Ambrose of Milan and the wild-eyed Sardinian, Lucifer of Caralis, seemed presumptuous in its claim to knowledge of divine relationships. Overly fond of paradoxes, intolerant of other theologies, and inclined to pander to rural prejudices, it did not seem a reasonable faith at all.[34]

Representing this tendency to move away from the language of Scripture, Tertullian had already introduced into the debate extra-biblical terms like "one substance," "person" and "trinity." Contrary to his stated distrust of "philosophy," Tertullian drew from Plato and the Gnostics the terms *homoousia* and *hypostases*, and introduced them as an integral part of Christian doctrine. Thus, what is today called "orthodoxy" became defined and defended by the language of pagan philosophy. Regarding the use of the extra-biblical term *homoousia* ("of the same substance"), the *New Catholic Encyclopedia* admits that it is an unbiblical term:

The *homoousian* formula, in any event, and carrying the intention of at least specific identity (between Father and Son), encountered so much opposition that more than once in the half-century prior to its final reassertion at Constantinople I in 381, it appeared close to being abandoned. To not a few even among the fiercest anti-Arians, introduction into the confession of faith of **a non-biblical device**, albeit to articulate **a biblically inescapable conclusion** was for a long time unacceptable.[35]

The *homoousian* formula is in no way a "biblically inescapable conclusion." It is the refuge of those whose preconceived ideas and theological traditions supersede a genuine commitment to the integrity of Scripture. The fact that those proto-orthodox Christian leaders were finally willing to accept such a non-biblical term is pregnant with significance. First, it was an admission on their part that *they did not believe that the words of the Bible are adequate to clearly reveal its most basic doctrines, especially those upon which salvation depends.*[36] If God is unable or unwilling to clearly communicate something as basic as the nature of His own being, either because of man's inability to comprehend or the intrinsic difficulty of the subject, then man's attempt to help Him by borrowing from a pagan philosopher like Plato looks pathetic indeed.

Because God presumably has a supreme command of language, He must have had the word *homoousian* in His vocabulary and could have inspired its use in Scripture if it had accurately

---

33. The Arians were criticized by their opponents for being influenced by Aristotle, but this criticism "seemed to have consisted more in the rationalistic methods of argument than in the ideas themselves" (*Ibid.,* p. 791). The "rationalistic method" to which reference is made is undoubtedly logic, which was one of Aristotle's chief contributions to philosophical inquiry. Arius, following Aristotle's methods, would have insisted upon consistent definitions of terms, logical necessity between premises and conclusions, etc. Apparently this was not appreciated by Athanasius and others who had piety, not logic, on their side.

34. Rubenstein, *op. cit., When Jesus Became God,* pp. 179 and 180.

35. *Ibid.,* p. 299.

36. The Athanasian Creed so strongly associates belief in the triune nature of God with salvation that for those who reject it salvation is not available. See Appendix C.

communicated the truth about His relationship with His Son. But the fact is that the term is *not* biblical, and furthermore, it confuses the otherwise simple-to-understand relationship between the Father and the Son as two distinct and unique beings. Do we hear echoes of Eve adding to the Word of God?

Are not the proponents of such extra-biblical propositions guilty of just what they decry in "Arians" and other "heretics"—elevating human reason above the revelation of God's Word? Is the Bible the *final authority* or is it not? One ought not to give lip-service to biblical integrity and then proceed to avoid or contradict it when it does not fit his theological presuppositions.

We believe that as a result of the councils of Nicaea, Constantinople and Chalcedon, the Church had finally poked out both its eyes (logic and true faith), and then stumbled blindly into the Dark Ages. The vast majority of Christians view these councils as the Church successfully defending itself from dangerous heresy and establishing correct Christological doctrine. But in light of the way they essentially demeaned the integrity of the Bible as the only rule of faith and practice, might we rather suggest that these councils were instead the unfortunate triumph of essentially pagan philosophy, mystical mumbo-jumbo and authoritarian indoctrination over logical and scriptural methodology? And the legacy of the "orthodoxy" that was established through these councils has been intolerance, arrogance, cruelty and tyranny.

Furthermore, accepting a Trinitarian view of Christ as the very "cornerstone" of the Christian faith, and an unbiblical term (*homoousian*) as a litmus test for both orthodoxy and salvation, and rejecting wholesale the Arian "heresy," ensured that Christology has rarely come up for significant debate.[37] There was a strong challenge to Trinitarian orthodoxy in the early 1600s by the founders of the Unitarian Church (not the same as the present Unitarian Universalist organization), but once again Trinitarians prevailed by the edge of the sword.[38] Considering the persuasive quality of cold steel, dank dungeons and social ostracism, it is certainly understandable how many otherwise courageous Christian leaders did not challenge this illogical and incomprehensible doctrine that had by then been firmly established as the so-called "cornerstone" of Christianity. We think the time has more than come for Christians to reset the cornerstone of the faith upon the bedrock of Scripture and common sense: **there is One God and One Lord**.

---

37. See Chapter 19 for a description of the Socinian movement, as well as a more detailed description of latent anti-Trinitarianism among the reformers and why they retreated into orthodoxy.

38. *Op. cit., The Racovian Catechism*, Introduction, pp. xiv-xviii.

19

Socinianism and the Radical Reformation

Historically, the Christological position that most resembles the one proposed by this book was the Socinian movement in Poland and Transylvania from the late 1550s to the mid-1600s.[1] Socinianism was a fully Christian movement characterized primarily by belief in the unitary being of God and the humanity of Christ. Beyond the doctrinal similarity, the Socinian movement represents the first time since the apostolic age of Christianity that a Christian community arose and developed around the idea of religious freedom. They also had a very developed doctrine of the separation of Church and civil authority, no small task considering how, for more than a thousand years, these had been virtually joined together.

Even in early Reformation Europe, the lines of civil and ecclesiastical authority were blurred as Roman Catholics, Lutherans and Calvinists exerted a profound and often cruel influence in the regions they dominated. As J. P. Moreland observes, when reason and truth are not authoritative,

---

1. In regard to Jesus Christ, one area of disagreement we have with Socinian thought concerns their understanding of the Atonement. They held that it was irrational to believe that one person could die for the sins of mankind. They also taught that there was no such thing as "original sin," which we disagree with. Nevertheless, we find great value in the Socinian writings, as well as those later "Unitarians" who, while dissenting from the Trinity, still affirmed the uniqueness of Jesus Christ as the only Son of God, and were avowedly "Christian."

the only way left to persuade is through political force.[2] The Socinian movement, therefore, with its elevation of reason and Scripture over creeds and traditions, provides us with a rare opportunity to see the value of establishing a Christian community that encourages the free exercise of logic in the pursuit of truth.

Almost miraculously, the Socinian movement arose out of a virtual quagmire of religious tradition and tyranny. Wilbur agrees with our assessment of the state of the Christian Church in the Middle Ages, up to and including the dawning of the Reformation:

> The Church had been for more than a thousand years practically stagnant at the point to which the creeds and councils of the fourth and fifth centuries had brought it. The doctrines of Christianity appealed to the sole authority of tradition. One was not supposed to examine them in the light of reason, or even of Scripture, but humbly to accept them on faith as divine mysteries. Intolerance of divergent opinions in religion was deemed a Christian duty, and persecution of heretics a cardinal civic virtue.[3]

It is very candid of Wilbur to say that "Intolerance of divergent opinions in religion was deemed a Christian duty, and persecution of heretics a cardinal civic virtue." The Romans, of course, persecuted the Christians even as many pagans and unbelievers do today. However, the fact that Christians, both past and present, persecute other Christians, despite Christ saying that we will be known for our love one for another (John 13:35), shows that power and control mean more to many Christians than does obedience.[4] History shows the overt and covert persecution of Unitarian Christians, and our experience is that this persecution continues today, though not as blatantly thanks to the religious freedoms we here in America enjoy.

The use of force by Christians against other Christians started soon after Rome became a Christian empire. Constantine became a follower of Christ in 312 A.D., and it took only a few years for persecution to start—actually it had begun earlier, but now it would not be random violence between disagreeing churches, but organized persecution with the backing of the state. We will quote some excerpts from two other historians familiar with this unfortunate period of Church history:

> An inevitable consequence of the union of the church and state was the restriction of religious freedom in faith and worship, and the civil punishment of departure from the doctrine and discipline of the established church.

> After the Nicene age, all departures from the reigning state-church faith were not only abhorred and excommunicated as religious errors, but were treated also as crimes against the Christian State, and hence were punished with civil penalties; at first with deposition, banishment, confiscation, and, after Theodosius, even with death.[5]

---

2. From a lecture titled, "A Postmodern Proposal," part of a series that J. P. Moreland conducted at the *Xenos Fellowship* in Columbus, Ohio in June, 1998.

3. Earl Morse Wilbur, *The History of Unitarianism: Socinianism and its Antecedents* (Harvard University Press, Boston, 1945), pp. 12 and 13. Dr. Wilbur ably surveys the history of anti-Trinitarian and non-Trinitarian movements, beginning with the second century through the Socinian movement.

4. There are some Christians who justify their intolerance and persecution by stating that non-Trinitarians are not really saved, but a quick review of Romans 10:9 and 13 will show that that is not the case. For the record, despite our many differences with Trinitarian doctrine, we have no interest in persecuting those who hold the belief.

5. Philip Schaff, *History of the Christian Church, Vol. 3, Nicene and Post-Nicene Christianity* (Wm. B. Eerdmans, Grand Rapids, 1994), pp. 138 and 139.

The Christians involved in the great controversy over Christ's divinity would soon find themselves gripped by the urge to persecute their adversaries.

St. Augustine himself advocated violent suppression of the Donatists, justifying the massacres in the name of Christian unity [Donatists were Christians who would not accept the authority of Bishop Caecilian of Carthage, because the one who appointed him had knuckled under to Roman persecution and not stood strong for Christ].

[Athanasius, Bishop of Alexandria and a main opponent to Arius] was equally at home in great houses and poor neighborhoods...and quite prepared to use the violent methods of the streets, when necessary, to accomplish worthwhile goals [ellipsis his].

Constantine had appeared at the council in the role of peacemaker. His decision to enforce what he took to be a theological consensus by exiling Arius, however, meant that the victors in religious disputes might now use the power of the state against their enemies. That was a lesson that all parties to the conflict, including the Arians, were quick to learn.[6]

In the early stages of the Christian empire, there were both pro-Trinitarian and pro-Arian emperors, and so there are records of Arians persecuting the Trinitarians. However, the last pro-Arian emperor was Valens, who died in 378 A.D. For all practical purposes, the widespread practice of any form of Unitarianism in the Eastern Roman Empire died with him and stayed dead for more than 1000 years until the Socinian movement. Theodocius I succeeded Valens. In 380 A.D. he wrote the following edict:

We, the three emperors, will that all our subjects steadfastly adhere to the religion which was taught by St. Peter to the Romans, which has been faithfully preserved by tradition, and which is now professed by the pontiff Damasus, of Rome, and Peter, Bishop of Alexandria, a man of apostolic holiness. According to the institution of the apostles and the doctrine of the gospel, let us believe in the one Godhead of the Father, the Son and the Holy Ghost, of equal majesty in the holy Trinity. We order that the adherents of this faith be called *Catholic Christians*; we brand all the senseless followers of other religions with the infamous name of *heretics*, and forbid their conventicles [assemblies] assuming the name of churches. Besides the condemnation of divine justice, they must expect the heavy penalties which our authority, guided by the heavenly wisdom, shall think proper to inflict."[7]

Theodocius was good for his word: in 381 A.D. he anathematized all Arians and *Pneumatomachoi*.[8] Also in 381 A.D. Theodocius passed laws against the Arians, forbidding them to use churches or assemble in the towns or the countryside. In 383 A.D., that ban was further clarified and the Arians were forbidden to build their own churches or to even meet in private homes. No wonder Maurice Wiles wrote:

---

6. Rubenstein, *op. cit., When Jesus Became God*, pp. 17, 39, 63 and 88.

7. Schaff, *op. cit, History of the Christian Church*, p. 142.

8. The "*Pneumatomachoi*," (a word that loosely translates as "Spirit-haters") was the name given to those Christians who believed that Christ was God, but did not believe that "the Holy Spirit" was God. Remember that the Jews had always taken "spirit" to be either another name for God or a representation of His power, and the late 300s was still early in the formulation of the formal doctrine of the Trinity.

The Arianism which had been so prominent and so powerful a feature of the Eastern empire throughout the fourth century had by the early years of the fifth century virtually disappeared from view.[9]

However, truth never really dies out because there is a God in heaven who continues to support it. Thus, a detailed study of the history of Christianity will show that the doctrine of the Trinity has constantly been questioned, and the true doctrine that **there is one God and one Lord** keeps coming up like weeds through the asphalt—it just cannot seem to be totally suppressed.

One proof that the doctrine of the Trinity keeps giving the Church problems can be seen in the records of the orthodox Church itself. There are seven councils of the Christian Church that are widely held to be "ecumenical," or "world wide." These seven are:

1). **Nicaea I** in 325 A.D., which dealt with the Arian controversy, that is, whether or not Christ was God and therefore unbegotten, or if he was a created being of God.

2). **Constantinople I** in 381 A.D., which dealt with Apollinarianism. The Church, having declared Christ as unbegotten God, now had to deal with theologians who rejected Christ's full manhood. These "new heretics" were reasoning that if Christ were God, then he could not also be a man like us.

3). **Ephesus** in 431 A.D., which dealt with the Nestorian controversy. Having declared Christ as both fully God and fully man and condemning anyone who did not agree, the Church now had to deal with those who could not seem to believe that the God-nature and the man-nature in Christ could together make only one "Person." Nestorius, the Patriarch of Constantinople, began to teach that Christ was composed of two persons, a God-person and a man-person. At the Council of Ephesus, Nestorius and his doctrine were condemned.

4). **Chalcedon** in 451 A.D., which again dealt with the issue of the exact makeup of Christ. Some Christians were again having trouble believing that Jesus Christ could somehow have both a God-nature and a man-nature. They were causing enough division in the Church that the Council of Chalcedon was convened to reassert the "official" doctrine of the Church, i.e., that Jesus was both 100 percent God and 100 percent man and that these two natures come together in Christ in such a way that he was one person.

5). **Constantinople II** in 553 A.D., which had to be convened because once again Christians were having trouble believing that a God-nature and a man-nature could exist in Jesus and yet just be one "person." This is the Nestorian controversy all over again (see Ephesus in 431), and, as before, the "heresy" was condemned and the perpetrators were anathematized.

6). **Constantinople III** in 680–681 A.D., was held because some "Christian heretics" were having trouble believing that there existed in Christ two wills at the same time. Since Christ was said to have both a God-nature and a man-nature, the orthodox teaching of the Church was (and still is) that Jesus Christ actually has two wills, a Divine will and a human will. This view was being challenged, and at Constantinople in 680 and 681, the "official" doctrine of the Church was upheld and the teaching that Christ had only one will was condemned as heresy.

---

9. Maurice Wiles, *Archetypal Heresy: Arianism Through the Centuries* (Clarendon Press, Oxford, 1996), p. 34.

7). **Nicaea II**, in 787 A.D., was over the veneration of icons, or images, in the church.[10]

It is obvious to us from the history of the Church, and the harsh measures that were taken by those in power to suppress "heresy" and oppress the ones who propounded teachings different from what was accepted, that we are not the only ones who have trouble believing the "orthodox" position. We assert that the entire problem is the result of the invention of the doctrine of the Trinity. None of these thorny theological issues even exists if we simply believe the teaching of Scripture, that Jesus was a "man accredited by God." In any case, as we already said, in spite of persecution and pressure, the truth keeps popping out.

The "Unitarian" movement began in opposition to Trinitarian orthodoxy, and Socinianism was a vital part of that movement.[11] Unitarianism is actually considered to have its roots in the 1531 publication of Michael Servetus' book criticizing the doctrine of the Trinity, only fourteen years after Luther posted his 95 theses on the church door at Wittenberg.

A study of the history of the Unitarian movement reveals that the Nicene and Athanasian creeds continued to be the source of much division, confusion and intolerance even throughout the Reformation period of Christianity. At this time, as much as at any other in history, there was a bewildering array of charges and countercharges of "heresy" as the various Christian sects competed for dominance. The Socinians were devout Christians, yet they were persecuted, tortured, exiled and otherwise abused by the proponents of the "orthodox" Christian faith, particularly the dominating Roman Catholics, led by their watchdogs, the Jesuits. And these enforcers were even joined by their

---

10. This record of the seven "ecumenical counsels" can be found in F. L. Cross, *Oxford Dictionary of the Christian Church* (Oxford University Press, Oxford, 1983), p. 993, under the heading "Oecumenical Counsels," and is itself a demonstration of a kind of persecution. A persecution by omission, if you will, that is, not really being honest with history. Notice that the first "Ecumenical Counsel" in the list is the Counsel of Nicaea. The Trinitarians won the day at that counsel. However, any good reference book will confirm that there were only between 220 and 250 bishops present, and only about half a dozen of them represented the Western Church, and the rest represented the Eastern Church. That is not a genuine "ecumenical counsel." However, in 359 A.D., a little more than 30 years after Nicaea, the Emperor Constantius II (337–361 A.D.) called a meeting of the Church in an attempt to settle the Arian dispute, which was still boiling. The joint council of Rimini-Seleucia was a much larger counsel than Nicaea, having about twice as many bishops present, and those bishops represented both the Eastern Church and the Western Church. Rubenstein observes:

> Several later gatherings would be more representative of the entire Church; one of them, the joint council of Rimini-Seleucia (359), was attended by more than five hundred bishops from both the East and West. If any meeting deserves the title "ecumenical," that one seems to qualify, but its result—the adoption of an Arian creed—was later repudiated by the Church. Councils whose products were later deemed unorthodox not only lost the "ecumenical" label but virtually disappeared from official Church history. (Rubenstein, *op. cit., When Jesus Became God*, p. 75).

Rubenstein is not kidding when he says the councils that leaned toward Arianism virtually disappeared from Church History. The council of Rimini gets a small paragraph in *The Oxford Dictionary of the Christian Church*, and was not mentioned in the Church histories we checked, not even in the eight volume *History of the Christian Church* by Philip Schaff. We assert that to exclude Church councils from the history books because what they declared does not line up with the "politically correct" view of doctrine evidences a lack of commitment to the truth. Once again we see the truth of the old saying, "The victors write the history books." It is no wonder most Trinitarian Christians have never heard "the whole story" of the Unitarian challenge to "Trinitarian" orthodoxy.

11. The "Unitarian" movement must be distinguished from what later became the current Unitarian Universalist denomination, which bears little similarity to early Unitarianism and Socinianism. Although these latter movements were solidly based on the integrity of the Scripture, later expressions of the Unitarian faith turned away from the authority of Scripture and the uniqueness of Christ as an object of devotion and worship. He was relegated to the status of a "prophet" or "great moral teacher," but not the unique Son of God. There is a resurgence of interest in "Biblical Unitarianism," through the work of Buzzard and others, that is Christ-honoring and Bible-believing. See Chapter 20, "Modern Trends."

erstwhile Reformation brothers, the Lutherans and the Calvinists, who chose to affirm without much consideration many of the traditional doctrines of the "historic Christian faith." Wilbur's comment on the failure of the Polish Protestants to successfully unite against Rome is sobering:

> The Calvinist wing of the Reformed Church refused to have fellowship with the liberal wing. When the whole Protestant camp needed to stand against the reviving power of Rome, they divided their camp and fell to fighting against each other. By demanding the acceptance of certain speculative dogmas [especially the Trinity] as the thing of first and greatest importance in religion, they sacrificed upon the altar of dogma the chance of success for their whole cause. From this time on, the history of Protestantism in Poland is therefore a record of progressive weakness, gradual decline, slow strangulation and ultimate practical extinction at the hands of Rome."[12]

Freed from the tyranny of the irrational basis of the Trinity as the cornerstone of their faith, the Socinians enthusiastically engaged in dissent and debate about many other doctrinal issues. But when they were not being persecuted and having to defend their teachings, they focused on applying them in the vital, practical issues of conduct and character. As Wilbur put it, they were known for "being at all times far more concerned with the underlying spirit of Christianity in its application to the situations of practical life than with intellectual formulations of Christian thought."[13] In other words, they concentrated on living out their beliefs in the context of Christian community. The "Unipersonality of God" and subordinate rank of Christ may be said to be incidental to the movement rather than essential to it."[14] Of the aspects of the human mind, the will, rather than the emotion or intellect, was the emphasis.[15]

Let us note here that removing the irrational basis of Trinitarian orthodoxy was the key to establishing a faith based on logic and truth, with the result that the Socinians furthered their cause by rational persuasion rather than intimidation and political domination through civil authority, as had so often been the case before. It is our belief that the incomprehensible doctrine of the Trinity has left the Christian Church today tottering on an unstable and irrational foundation. As in the past, this myth still holds sway not by persuasion, but by intimidation or force.[16]

Calvinists, Lutherans and Jesuits united in their persecution of the Socinians because of their refusal to accept the Trinity, and began a deliberate campaign of accusation. They charged that the Socinians were blasphemers, atheists and revolutionary Anabaptists (who were an extreme faction of the "radical reformation" essentially promoting the undermining of the social order and anything approximating loyalty to the King or the State). Wilbur writes:

> There was scarcely any reproach, religious, moral or political, that was not launched against them; and when all had been done to poison the public mind and to arouse popular prejudice, they resorted to means of political persecution.[17]

---

12. *Wilbur, op. cit., History of Unitarianism*, p. 326.

13. *Ibid.*, p. 3.

14. *Ibid.*, p. 4.

15. *Ibid.*, p. 5.

16. Countless numbers of non-Trinitarian Christians of our acquaintance have suffered persecution and ostracism by the orthodox community. Christian seminaries and book publishers are afraid to publish anything that might be considered antagonistic to the "historic faith." Academic publications do continue to publish some controversial materials on this volatile subject, but these rarely filter down to the level of the common churchgoer, who is ignorant of the ongoing scholarly debate on these issues.

17. *Wilbur, op. cit., History of Unitarianism*, p. 339.

Calvinists, Lutherans and Catholics then joined forces to demand of the King that he expel the Socinians from the country (which finally happened in 1660). Providentially, however, Jan Sieninski, a tolerant Calvinist magnate, had a wife who was a zealous "Arian," as the Socinians were sometimes erroneously called.[18] Her heart was heavy due to the persecution of her Unitarian brothers and sisters, and her husband resolved to help. He founded a new town, Rakow, chartered to have wide religious toleration. This city came to be known as an idyllic Christian community, one of the most notable in the history of the Christian Church. The dominant interest of the Racovians was the study of the Scriptures as the guide for life, as well as the discussion of questions of faith and conduct arising out of this. But overshadowing all other elements that helped to shape Socinianism was the tendency to look directly to the Scripture itself as the sole source of religious truth, and to ignore as unimportant whatever could not be traced to this source.[19]

Rakow became a favorite place for European Christian intellectuals to visit and teach. In 1602, a university was founded there, marked by a five year course of academic study, standard cultural training and an early experiment in manual training requiring each student to work at a trade. Special emphasis was placed upon practice in debate on various philosophical or theological subjects in order to prepare students to ably defend their faith. The upper class was required to engage in two such debates each week.

The university attracted some of the best minds in Europe, even drawing faculty away from some of the best Calvinist universities. The Socinians not only valued Scripture, they loved freedom and honored the rights of others to disagree. They held that the Church was not to be an external organization of all who hold accepted doctrine, but a spiritual fellowship of all in whom the spirit of God dwells. Their power was strictly that of influence and persuasion, and even when they had the power of the state on their side, they refused to use it to help establish their movement. This reflected their commitment to reason and Scripture, for they clearly understood that no man should tyrannize another man's conscience, and should allow him the freedom to believe as he might. They emphasized Christian conduct more than belief as that which is ultimately judged by God and Christ.

Rakow also became an important publishing center. In 1605, the *Racovian Catechism* was published in Polish, translated into Latin in 1609, and quickly distributed throughout Europe. It was a notable landmark in the development of Unitarian doctrine, being the earliest attempt of the Socinians to state their position systematically and in detail. It stirred a firestorm of controversy, and was often quoted by opponents of Socinianism.[20] Despite the opposition, the questions it raised stirred interest

---

18. Because it was well known that Church councils had decreed that Arians were heretics, it was a common ploy to label Socinians "Arians" in order to turn popular opinion against them. As will be seen later in this chapter, this epithet was used for the same reason against more orthodox reformers who only minimally challenged orthodox opinion. It was used against them in order to make them stay in line with the orthodox Church.

19. Wilbur, *op. cit., History of Unitarianism*, p. 7.

20. The following is the text of an act of the British Parliament in 1652 banning the *Racovian Catechism* and ordering all copies in England to be burned:

> VOTES of the PARLIAMENT touching the Book commonly called THE RACOVIAN CATECHISM. Mr. Millington reports from the Committee to whom the Book (entitled…*The Racovian Catechism*) was referred, several passages in the said book which were now read. Resolved upon the question by the Parliament, That the book, Entitled *Catechesis Ecclesiarum quo in Regno Polonioe, &c.* commonly called the *Racovian Catechism*, doth contain matters that are blasphemous, erroneous, and scandalous. Resolved upon the question by the Parliament, That all the printed copies of the book…be burnt. Resolved upon the question by the Parliament, That the Sheriffs of London and Middlesex be authorized and required to seize all the printed copies of the book…called the *Racovian Catechism*, wheresoever they shall be found, and cause the same to be burnt at the Old Exchange London, and in the New Palace at Westminster, on Tuesday and Thursday next. Friday, the Second

in the integrity of Scripture and the value of reason in religious thought that eventually affected the Puritan movement, and through it the religious life of the new colonies in America. This Unitarian Christian movement was later dubbed "Socinian" because Faustus Socinus systematized the faith and was the *de facto* leader by virtue of his brilliant command of Scripture. Socinianism, however, was established by and basically arose after the publication of the *Racovian Catechism*.

Latent Non-Trinitarianism Among the Early Reformers

The Protestant Reformation went much farther than was initially intended by the first reformers. It was not intended as a revolution or a revolt from the Church, but was designed to address practical problems and excesses of the Roman Church. Orthodox Christian dogmas were not questioned, nor was there any initial inclination to oppose or revise them. After the reformers had presented their statements for imperial approval at the Diet of Augsburg, Melanchthon, who worked closely with Luther, spoke for the other reformers and made it clear that they did not differ from the Roman Church on any point of doctrine.

In his edition of the Greek New Testament in 1516, the Greek scholar Erasmus laid the foundation for inquiry into the dogma of the Trinity. He had omitted as a textual corruption the strongest proof-text for the doctrine of the Trinity (1 John 5:7); and in his Annotations on the New Testament he also helped to undermine belief in scriptural support for this doctrine.[21] Subsequent versions of the Bible recognize much of Erasmus' work, in particular leaving out part of 1 John 5:7 and 8.

Earl Morse Wilbur, arguably the leading Unitarian historian (now deceased), cites evidence that the early reformers reconsidered the issues of the Trinity and Christ's dual nature in the atmosphere of freedom and religious liberty they at first enjoyed:

> Martin Luther disliked the term *homoousios* as being a human invention, not found in Scripture, and he preferred to say "oneness." "Trinity," he said, has a cold sound, and it would be far better to say "God" than "Trinity." He therefore omitted these terms from his Catechism, and the invocation of the Trinity from his Litany. Hence Catholic writers did not hesitate to call him an Arian.

> In 1521, Melanchthon, in his *Loci Communes* said, "Surely there is no reason why we should spend such pains on these sublime matters: God, unity, trinity, the mystery of creation or the mode of incarnation. Why, what have the scholastic theologians gained in all these centuries by their handling of such themes? How many of them, indeed, seem to tend to heresy rather than to the Catholic doctrine…Paul did not philosophize on the mystery of the Trinity, or the mode of incarnation, or active or passive creation, did he?" He too was accused of being an Arian by Catholic writers.[22]

---

of April, 1652. Resolved by the Parliament, That these Votes be forthwith printed and published. Hen. Scobell, *Cleric. Parliarnenti*. London: Printed by William Field, Printer to the Parliament of England, 1652. Quoted in the frontispiece of: *op. cit., The Racovian Catechism*.

21. Wilbur, *op. cit., History of Unitarianism*, p. 15 note (cp. Henri Tollin, *"Der Verfasser De Trinitatis Erroribus und die seitgenossischen Katholiken,"* Jahrbucher fur protestantische Theologie, xvii (1891), pp. 398–412, *et al.*).

22. Wilbur, *op. cit., History of Unitarianism*, p.15.

Calvin himself, in his *Commentaries on the Gospels*, frankly recognized human limitations in Jesus; and in his earlier career he declared that the Nicene Creed was better fitted to be sung as a song than to be recited as a confession of belief. He disapproved of the Athanasian Creed, disliked the usual prayer to the Holy Trinity, and in his Catechism touched but lightly on the Trinity. He taught that the Holy Spirit is not so much a person in the proper sense of the term as a power of God active in the world and in man. At Lausanne in 1537, therefore, both he and the other Geneva pastors were charged by Pierre Caroli with Arianism and Sabellianism.[23]

In 1525, Farel, Calvin's predecessor at Geneva, wrote in French a list of the chief points of Christian doctrine, and never once mentioned the Trinity or the dual nature of Christ. In Zurich, the renowned Swiss reformer Zwingli declared that Christ was not a proper object of worship, and this view influenced the practice of the Reformed Church.[24]

In the face of such accusations, the leaders of the Reformation chose to pick their battles and concentrate on those particularly odious practices of the Roman Church such as priestly misconduct, indulgences and the like. Regarding this doctrinal "backpedaling," Wilbur writes:

Not only did they [the early reformers] give at least a nominal adherence to the Nicene and Athanasian Creeds, but after a few years, for reasons that will be shown later, when faced by hostile criticism, they took special pains to make their position on this point unmistakably orthodox. But they do show a disposition to question the form in which these doctrines had been stated, and to regard them as not essential to salvation because they are not clearly supported by Scripture authority; and the next step logically would have been to treat them as optional, and let them be ignored or even denied by those that found them superfluous or objectionable.

This next step, however, was not taken, for doctrinal controversy and doctrinal history took such a turn that when the several Protestant confessions within a generation adopted their official standards of faith, they with one consent reaffirmed their acceptance of the traditional views. Freedom of inquiry on these lines was no longer to be possible, the appeal to reason or even to Scripture was to have no standing in opposition to authoritative tradition, and tolerance of dissenting views was to be frowned upon as opening the way to heresy and to the ruin of immortal souls.[25]

The Influence of Socinianism

The persecution of the Socinian movement in Poland accelerated to the point of death by torture and burning at the stake, and their publishing and educational facilities were destroyed, but some of them fled to Holland where there was more toleration of religious diversity. From there, Socinian literature and influence extended to England, especially into the prestigious halls of British academia. McLachan, an historian who has studied the influence of Socinianism in England, notes that there was even competition among the Oxford "divines" to include Socinian literature in their personal libraries despite its being banned.[26] Even when it was illegal to own a copy of this "heretical" work,

---

23. *Ibid.,* pp. 15 and 16.
24. *Ibid.,* p. 16.
25. *Ibid.,* p. 17.
26. H. John McLachan, *Socinianism in 17th Century England* (Oxford University Press, London, 1951). pp. 118–148.

many influential leaders like John Locke and Isaac Newton read and were influenced by Socinian writings.[27] Particularly influential were their ideas on the value of reason to separate truth from error even when analyzing "revelation." That is, the idea that reason and revelation are not separate categories found enthusiastic acceptance among many Christian thinkers.

Both Locke and Newton wrote on theological issues and applied their rational and brilliant minds to discerning Christian truth. Locke even wrote a treatise titled *Rational Christianity*, which many scholars believe to be strongly influenced by Socinian thought. Newton's studies and intellect led him away from orthodoxy and toward a unitary view of God, a fact that has proven an embarrassment to orthodox Christians. Some of his theological works, written in Latin, remain untranslated, buried in British libraries and museums. It seems fairly certain to us that if this intellectual giant who mightily advanced the fields of mathematics and physics had written in support of Christian orthodoxy, his works would be fronted enthusiastically. As it is, he is barely recognized as a theologian, although this was actually his passion, even beyond his more scientific pursuits that brought him fame.

We pray that some Latin scholars whose vision is not obscured by the veil of orthodoxy will take it upon themselves to give to the world the gift of Newton's complete theological works. The mind that discovered calculus and the laws of motion through a careful analysis of the creation of God was undoubtedly divinely guided to see wondrous things from the *Word* of God as well. One can only wonder what order and majesty he found in the countless hours he spent poring over what was recognized by his brilliant mind to be God's communication to mankind.

Socinians were also influential among European and American intellectuals because of their ideas on the separation of church and state, and the value of religious toleration. It could be argued that their ideas helped to break the tyranny of the Church of England over both the religious and the intellectual life of the British Isles. From England, the influence of Socinian thought and its call for radical religious freedom was exported through the Puritans and Pilgrims to the blossoming American Colonies, where the principles of religious toleration were eventually codified in the Bill of Rights. In a very real sense, the American experiment in political and religious freedom owes its very existence to the ideas of the Socinians, who were actually the first to establish in Racow a truly free community. Though their movement was persecuted out of existence, the ideas they represented could not be easily snuffed out, and smoldered beneath the European ground until they burst into flame again in New England.

American Unitarian thought was strongly Socinian at first, respecting the integrity of Scripture and the glorious person of Christ as the unique Son of God. Eventually, however, their enthusiasm for rationalism and toleration clashed with their Christian commitment and they began to adopt a less biblical view of the world. There were also some key Socinian doctrines that bore bad fruit over time. Their rejection of the Atonement and original sin undoubtedly contributed to their diminished appreciation for the spiritual importance of the sacrifice of Christ on the Cross. They also developed an inflated sense of man's value apart from God's grace, and adopted a social gospel more akin to humanitarianism. Eventually, they came to view Christ as a great moral teacher who left a profound and exalted ethical ideal for others to follow, and faithful diligence in this pursuit was the key to one's salvation. This view did not require repentance from sin or conversion (being "born again") through the gift of holy spirit, nor did it recognize the manifestations of the spirit in the Church. Many Socinians viewed miracles as irrational and hence rejected them.

---

27. *Ibid.*, p. 144.

Nevertheless, the legacy of the Socinians continues to be enjoyed wherever there is wholesome and rational Christian dialogue over an open Bible. The Socinian spirit is in evidence where Christians are able to recognize that the marks of their profession are not just adherence to outward traditional creeds, but must also involve the transformation of the inward man such that he authentically loves God and his neighbor, especially his Christian brethren. Finally, the Socinian love of truth and courage in the face of religious tyranny is alive wherever men and women stand on reason and truth against the icons of tradition, where they refuse to be intimidated by the fear of being labeled a "heretic" and where they repay cruelty and prejudice with loving persuasion instead of bloodshed.

20

Modern Trends and Final Thoughts: Ecumenism, Biblical Unitarianism and Trinitarian Renewal

In this chapter, we will be looking at three great trends in the current Christian scene. First, we will consider the "ecumenical movement" that has been steadily gaining ground since its inception in the first part of the 20ᵗʰ Century, and which is reaching a fever pitch among Roman Catholics and Protestants. We will look at a few of the problems we see in this movement, and identify the central place Trinitarian orthodoxy occupies in it. We will then propose a biblical "bottom line" around which Christians can truly unite. We will then discuss a movement away from Trinitarianism among some scholars, as well as what can be called a movement toward "biblical Unitarianism." Finally, we will look at the Trinitarian Renewal movement of the last few years in response to various contemporary challenges to orthodoxy.

Ecumenical "Unity"—Sorry, Trinitarians Only

Since being established as the foundation of orthodoxy in 325 A.D., the Nicene Creed ("one God in three persons") has been the litmus test for what constitutes true Christianity (see Appendix C). In our opinion, those who aggressively promote this creed as the standard of orthodoxy are included in the number of those who "create divisions contrary to the doctrine" we have received from the first-century Apostles (Rom. 16:17). The unbiblical language of this creed has been a divisive stumbling block for many Bible-centered Christians through the centuries, and a *chopping block* for others who died at the hands of those who espoused it. Do we not trivialize their ultimate sacrifice when we say that the Nicene Creed is an acceptable criterion for true Christianity, and that doctrinal precision does not really matter because the important thing is for all Christians to be unified? How can Christians ever expect to be truly unified on concepts that are not clearly and unequivocally biblical?

An important distinction must be made: there are those (the vast majority) who marginally accept the Trinity either because they are not really familiar with the Bible, and trust their teachers and spiritual leaders, or they are intimidated by "the system" and just go along with it. There are others who aggressively uphold the Trinity as the very cornerstone of Christianity, and go out of their way to warn those who even think of straying from historical orthodoxy. In any case, we love our Trinitarian brothers and sisters and welcome opportunities to fellowship with them for our mutual profit. But we are not naïve about what committed Trinitarians are taught to think about those of us who teach an alternate view. Nor are we hopeful that we can develop successful, cooperative, working relationships with them as long as they think us to be heretics.

Many Christians we know are not aware of the fact that admission to the global Ecumenical movement requires adoption of a Trinitarian formula for Christian salvation. We will quote from Robert McAfee Brown, only one of many authors who document this same fact:

> "…all Christian communions throughout the world that confess our Lord Jesus Christ as God and Savior…unite with us…."[1]

> The World Council of Churches is a fellowship of churches which confess the **Lord Jesus Christ as God and Savior** according to the Scripture and therefore seek to fulfill together their common calling to the glory of **one God, Father, Son and Holy Spirit**."[2]

> According to the Vatican Council Decree on Ecumenism, participation in the movement was for "those **who invoke the Triune God and confess Jesus as Lord and Savior…**"[3]

These are just a few representative samples of many declarations of the Trinitarian basis of ecumenical unity. In 1910, an international gathering of missionary societies met in Edinburgh, Scotland to establish a basis of cooperation among themselves in the dissemination of the Gospel around the globe. This came to be known as "the Life and Work movement," whose slogan was *Doctrine divides, service unites.*

However, McAfee notes that the Life and Work movement found its aversion to doctrine to be unworkable in practice:

---

1. Robert McAfee Brown, *The Ecumenical Revolution: An Interpretation of the Catholic-Protestant Dialogue* (Doubleday, Garden City, N.Y., 1967), p. 83.

2. *Ibid.,* p. 37.

3. *Ibid.,* p. 16.

It was not possible to be concerned about service to man without articulating **a doctrine of man**. Nor was it possible to discuss church and state relations without **a doctrine of the church**, let alone **a doctrine of the state**. Consequently, it became apparent that discussion centering exclusively on life and work was a cul-de-sac and must be reconceived to include discussion of the theology [doctrine]…The outcome of the Oxford conference, therefore, was a recommendation that Life and Work be merged with an already existing movement called Faith and Order…and that something like a "world council of Churches" be created out of the two groups.[4]

The Faith and Order movement had an equally difficult time finding any doctrine on which they could universally agree, other than the doctrine of the Trinity. This was in part because the Roman Catholic delegation would not agree to an exclusively biblical standard for doctrine. Their doctrinal positions have admittedly never been derived from the Bible alone, but developed through the authority of the Roman Catholic Church as the "Mother Church." The following statement from a Lutheran/Roman Catholic dialogue held in 1965 on the value of the Nicene Creed shows that the Trinity is fundamental to modern attempts at Christian unity:

The Nicene Faith possesses a unique status in the hierarchy of dogmas by reason of its testimony to and celebration of the Mystery of the Trinity as revealed in Christ our Savior.[5]

Since modern resurgence of interest in "unity" is in line with these earlier attempts at ecumenical unity, we must note that *the least common denominator of the modern unity movement is also a triune conception of God.* Anyone not accepting the Nicene formulation of "one God in three persons" is not welcome at the party.

Social Trinitarianism

The modern Trinitarian renewal movement prominently features the idea that "the being of the… Trinity can provide a model for personal relations in human social order."[6] Supposedly, this is the case because the persons of the triune Godhead are assumed to be in a state of eternal interrelationship:

To speak of God as the communion of the persons of the Father, the Son and the Spirit where each person is constituted in its personal particularity relationally through its relation to the other implies seeing these relations as internal relations, internal to the being of God. To be is for God to be the Father, the Son and the Spirit, to be a communion of persons. Being is therefore always relational. This is indeed a revolution in ontology since it redefines on the basis of earlier Athanasian insights the concept of being as relational being [echoes of Neoplatonic thought?].[7]

This is one reason why modern Trinitarian theologians argue that their view of God as a multi-personal being is a superior conception to the Unitarian view that God is only one person—

4. *Ibid.,* p. 31.
5. "The Status of the Nicene Creed as Dogma of the Church": a theological consultation between representatives of the USA national committee of the Lutheran World Federation and the Bishop's Commission, held July 6 and 7, 1965 in Baltimore, MD. Published jointly, 1965.
6. Colin Gunton, *The Promise of Trinitarian Theology* (T & T Clark, Edinburgh, 1997), p. xix.
7. Christoph Schwobel, Editor, *Trinitarian Theology Today,* "Christology and Trinitarian Thought" (T & T Clark, Edinburgh, 1995), p. 132.

because the "triune" God is never solitary or "alone." This view is represented by the following orthodox apologist in a work defending the Trinity against its detractors:

> That God must have both unity and diversity is clear. The…God of unitarian "Christian" groups would be incomplete in Himself. He would be unable to love, commune or fellowship before creating other beings capable of interacting with Him in these ways. The quality of love and the capacities for fellowship and communion, by their very nature, require another personal being with which to share them. And God could not fully share Himself except with another Being equal to Him. **Yet the Bible says that "God *is* love" in Himself alone.** This could only be true if God Himself consisted of a plurality of Beings who were separate and distinct, yet one.[8]

Clearly, this argument is speculative and makes inferences not supported by Scripture. Further, it asserts that the God of Scripture, "the Father of Jesus Christ," who plainly and specifically reveals Himself as one supreme being and one unique person, not three persons in one being, would be imperfect if His oneness were *true* oneness. We think this kind of "God-is-not-big-enough-as-one" thinking is akin to what the polytheistic nations surrounding Israel thought about Israel's "one God." The notion that "God" is composed of three distinct "selves" loving each other is at best a radical departure from anything suggested by Scripture, and at worst is a completely different idea of God than what the early Jewish Christians, with their monotheistic heritage, would have accepted.

Not all Trinitarians see Social Trinitarianism as such an attractive idea. Trinitarian scholar Morris points out that this view has met with some skepticism:

> The view of Social Trinitarianism (the view that the deity worshiped by Christians is comprised of three ontologically distinct persons, severally exemplifying each of the attributes strictly necessary for being God, or for being literally divine) has had its advocates, and it has had its opponents as well. It has seemed to its critics to involve the simple abandonment of monotheism and the embracing of a world view according to which there are three gods, much as in the pantheons of pagan religion.[9]

Rather than enhancing the idea of the relationality of God, the Social Trinitarianism model diminishes any urgency for God to create beings to love and be loved by. If God is so complete within His triune being, why would he be desirous to have fellowship with created beings who could receive love and respond freely? In the Trinitarian view, God can just "hang out" with "Him-selves." Beside the lack of biblical support, this model fails to recognize the necessity of love requiring an *object*. God creates other beings out of a pure motivation to share with them the life and love that He has within Himself, which is just what His Word says. God, as love, enters the potential pain and rejection that might follow His creating truly free beings with whom He can share His love. He is motivated by a greater possibility: that those He creates might know and love Him for who He is. Thus, God, driven by His desire to love and share His being with creatures equipped to appreciate Him, patterns self-sacrificial love much more powerfully than a self-content, socially fulfilled, tri-personal "Godhead."

Modern attempts to inject life into Trinitarian theology through the social analogy are not compelling and create more problems than they solve, but a growing number of Trinitarian theologians, particularly feminist ones, are attracted to the idea because of its "politically correct" possibilities. They

---

8. Dave Hunt, *In Defense of the Faith* (Harvest House Publishers, Eugene, OR, 1996), pp. 53 and 54.
9. Thomas V. Morris, *The Logic of God Incarnate* (Cornell University Press, Ithaca, NY, 1986), pp. 207 and 208.

believe that because there is community and no hierarchy within the triune Godhead, it is preferable to the monotheistic model. The latter, in their view, exemplifies a hierarchy with an authoritarian domination-submission dialectic, that includes even the seeds of gender domination (the "Father" is "over" the Son). Absent from this discussion among feminist Trinitarians, interestingly, is the problem created by viewing the Holy Spirit as a third male person ("He") instead of an "it," which is strongly indicated by the consistent use of the neuter gender for the Greek word *pneuma*.

Biblical Unitarianism

Bernard Cooke has observed that in recent years some scholars have expressed reservations about Trinitarian doctrine:

> Something is stirring in theological thought, something deep and far-reaching enough to give promise of a basic reconsideration of our Christian theology…Obviously it will not do to repeat unchanged the verbal formulations of the past [re: the Trinity] particularly if, as is just possible, they are less than totally adequate…Contemporary theologians are… questioning the extent to which the idea "trinity" corresponds to the reality of God as revealed in Jesus Christ.[10]

Gunton recognizes that until the recent renewal of interest in the Trinity, it was coming into disrepute:

> The doctrine of the Trinity has in the West come into increasing question…there has long been a tendency to treat the doctrine as a problem rather than as encapsulating the heart of the Christian Gospel.[11]

One of the principal catalysts of the Trinitarian Renewal movement is German theologian Karl Rahner. He summed up the state of Trinitarianism in 1970 by saying:

> Despite their orthodox confession of the Trinity, Christians are, in their practical life, almost mere monotheists. We must be willing to admit that, should the doctrine of the Trinity have to be dropped as false, the major part of religious literature could well remain virtually unchanged.[12]

If most Christians are still "almost monotheists" after many hundreds of years of indoctrination, it is time to consider whether an *actual* "monotheism" is not a more biblical, practical, understandable and easily taught position. In an earlier article, Rahner indicated that he thinks the reason so few people embrace Trinitarianism in their practical life is due to the fact that so little is said about it by theologians and Bible teachers:

> There has been practically no intrinsic development of the classic treatise on the Trinity since the council of Florence.[13]

This same reality is lamented by Christopher Hall in an article called "Adding Up The Trinity." In it, he echoes Torrance's questions and then asks one of his own:

---

10. Bernard J. Cooke, *Beyond Trinity*, The Aquinas Lecture 1969 (Marquette Univ. Press, Milwaukee), pp. 1 and 3.

11. Gunton, *op. cit., Promise of Trinitarian Theology*, p. 31.

12. Rahner, *op. cit., The Trinity*, p. 10.

13. "Some Remarks on the Dogmatic Treatis De Trinitate" in *Theological Investigations*, Vol. 4, Trans. K. Smyth, (Helicomk, Baltimore, 1966), pp. 77–102 (originally published in *Universitas* 1960).

Why have western Christians generally failed to grasp the grammar of the Trinity as the "fundamental grammar of Christian theology"? Why the "strange paucity of Trinitarian hymns in our modern repertoire of praise"? Or for that matter, in evangelical praise songs, hymns and choruses?[14]

What Torrance and Hall think "strange" seems to be a very natural consequence of holding an incomprehensible doctrine of God. Generally speaking, people do not write songs about things they cannot comprehend or articulate. Trinitarian scholars have been forced to face the fact that modern Christian pastors and teachers are not very motivated to teach the Trinity, and when they do, they cannot seem to get it straight and raise more questions than they can answer. How well can such a doctrine serve as the cornerstone of Christian faith if it cannot be adequately articulated by the average parish pastor?

In the April 13, 1998 issue of *Newsweek*, it was reported that Professor Marguerite Shuster of Fuller Theological Seminary in Pasadena, California, analyzed more than 3,000 sermons presented by mainline denominational ministers. Of these, only 20 focused on the Trinity, and in her opinion many of these were only marginally "orthodox." Apparently, very few pastors and Bible teachers even attempt to teach the Trinity, and when they do, they often drift into some "heresy" or another. How can Christians possibly be united around a doctrine that is seldom expounded, much less clarified to the point that leaders can rally their troops to promote and defend it?[15]

Morris candidly provides a reason why so little attention is paid to Trinitarianism despite the modern "renewal":

> Whatever else may be said about the doctrine of the Trinity, it is safe to say that in the history of Christian doctrine there has been no single, universally accepted articulation of the specific way in which it is to be understood. Every attempt to articulate the doctrine in detail has had its detractors and has been viewed as erring in one direction or the other. Articulations stressing the unity of God to the relative de-emphasis of divine threeness have most often been labeled modalist or Sabellian: whereas, those stressing the threefold existence of deity to the relative neglect of divine unity have been castigated as tri-theistic or polytheistic. **It has seemed next to impossible to achieve a balanced presentation of the triune nature of God that is both relatively detailed and also acceptable to most sincere Christians with theological sensitivity.**[16]

Whether due to neglect by its adherents or to its intrinsic weaknesses, the doctrine of the Trinity no longer holds the presupposed and unchallenged position that it did even 30 years ago. As this book has demonstrated, if the reader has paid careful attention to the footnoted sources, there is a growing body of scholarly evidence that supports a non-Trinitarian reading of the Scripture. In the light of textual research, modern English versions of the Bible have overturned some key Trinitarian proof texts. Non-Trinitarian groups like Megiddo Ministries, Hatikfa, The Church of God of the Abrahamic Faith, and the Christadelphians, to name just a few, have persuaded many uncommitted or marginal Christians of their views, and in many cases have won souls for Christ who were unreached by the orthodox Christian community.

---

14. *Christianity Today*, April 28, 1997, p. 28. Hall quotes Thomas Torrance, *The Christian Doctrine of God: One Being, Three Persons* (T & T Clark, 1996).

15. See also Appendix C for a list of historical heresies.

16. Morris, *op. cit., Logic of God Incarnate*, pp. 207 and 208.

At key points in this book, we have highlighted the work of John A. T. Robinson, who candidly expressed dismay at the limitations of orthodox theology. He was often joined in his critique of orthodoxy by his British Anglican colleagues Geoffrey Lampe (*God as Spirit*) and Maurice Wiles (*The Formation of Christian Doctrine*). In his last work, *The Priority of John*, Dr. Robinson reflects on its implications in his notes on the very last page:

> Of course this [the idea that Jesus is not "all there is of God"] has far-reaching implications for a corresponding doctrine of the Trinity. It is clear that patristic and mediaeval theology misused the Fourth Gospel by taking its Christological statements out of context and giving them a meaning that John never intended.[17]

Robinson then quotes Schillebeeckx, who concludes from his own study of the Johannine literature that "there is no basis in Johannine theology for the later scholastic theology of the procession of the Son from the Father within the Trinity per *modum generationis* (birth)."[18] Robinson then comments:

> Such transpositions from the Johannine vocabulary have been the traditional foundation of the doctrine of the Trinity. But if they are removed, it remains to be seen what will be left from the wreckage. In my article "The Fourth Gospel and the Church's Doctrine of the Trinity," I have discussed this problem more fully and attempted to contribute to the reconstruction that lies ahead.[19]

If there is a wreckage, as is certainly very possible, there would be a huge need for sound Christian teaching to shore up the faith of those who have been so indoctrinated into belief in the Trinity that to find out that it was neither biblical nor true would come as a devastating shock. We who by the grace of God know better must prepare our hearts to be servants to the brokenhearted. Those who have loved theology and the tradition of the Church more than the truth of God's Word could be in for a drastic rearrangement of their faith. It has been well said that when a man who is honestly mistaken hears the truth, he either ceases to be mistaken or he ceases to be honest. This may well be the choice for our Trinitarian brethren.

Though truth is more valuable than tradition, the argument to tradition is a strong one. As Gunton observes hypothetically, the Church would have to completely rethink its identity if it found out that its traditional cornerstone is misplaced:

> A church that changes its conception of God as radically as the abandonment of Trinitarianism would entail could scarcely find it possible to claim to be the same church.[20]

Sir Anthony Buzzard, Robinson's cousin, is himself a respected linguist and Bible scholar. He has written an important book called *The Doctrine of the Trinity: Christianity's Self-Inflicted Wound*. Another fine work is Don Snedeker's *Our Heavenly Father Has No Equals: Unitarianism, Trinitarianism and The Necessity of Biblical Proof*. Spirit & Truth Fellowship International has reprinted many of the more important works of biblical Unitarians in New England in the 1800's, before the movement was splintered by the Transcendentalists and turned toward a humanistic perspective. Many of these works are excellent expositions of Bible truth, as well as devastating polemics against Trinitarian

---

17. Robinson, *op. cit., Priority*, p. 397, footnote 156.

18. Schillebeeckx, *op. cit., Christ*, p. 875, n. 57.

19. Robinson, *op. cit., Priority*, p. 397. His article appeared in Twelve More New Testament Studies, Cambridge, pp. 171–180.

20. Gunton, *op. cit., Promise of Trinitarian Theology*, p. 18.

orthodoxy and tyranny. STF also reprinted *The Racovian Catechism*, the most illuminating work of the Socinian movement.

The Messianic Judaism movement, although for the most part ironically Trinitarian, does hold promise for returning to the monotheism of its Jewish roots (Deut. 6:4, *et al.*). Though at this juncture most of the Messianic congregations of our acquaintance have accepted a Trinitarian view, we can imagine that they might be persuaded by the mounting evidence as to the intrusion of Hellenistic thought into the Hebraic understandings that ground Christianity.

If the reader is aware of individual pastors, teachers, televangelists or others who are teaching a non-Trinitarian gospel, please let us know. We would like to serve as a clearinghouse to network together those biblical Unitarians that no doubt dot the landscape but who imagine that they are alone. Perhaps with the aid of the Internet, we can disseminate information and encouragement to those who are standing on the truth of "**one God and one Lord.**" We envision an International Conference of Unitarian Christians that would bring in people from many different non-Trinitarian ministries and denominations to compare notes and share resources. We are confident that God and His Son are moving to restore these important truths to the Christian Church. The time may be short to go into all the nations and make disciples for the Lord, but with a rational Gospel that is simple to communicate and easily accepted, we ought to be able to convert Muslims, Jews and thinking people who have a hard time with Trinitarian orthodoxy and its mystifying terminology. As Christopher Hall admits, "Trinitarian language can be extremely confusing, especially for modern Christians."[21] Now is a good time to preach the simplicity of the Gospel—the Bible is the story of two men: the first man wrecked everything, the second man is fixing it!

Trinitarian Renewal

"Suddenly we are all Trinitarians, or so it would seem," says Gunton, expressing his guarded enthusiasm for the apparent bandwagon that has been gaining momentum.[22] Gunton also identifies a resurgence of interest among orthodox scholars for the Trinity:

> The fact is that the loss of a Trinitarian dimension has gravely impoverished the Christian tradition over recent decades, and one of the hopeful signs has been a renewal of interest.[23]

Robert W. Jenson also belongs to this new Trinitarianism. He shares a conceptual agenda with E. Jungel, J. Mortmann, W. Pannenberg, Duane Larson and the late Catherine M. LaCugna, all of whom have written books about the Trinity in recent years. In the past five years, Thomas F. Torrance, Thomas March, Colin Gunton, Christoph Schwobel, Peter Toon, Millard Erickson, Jung Young Lee, Ted Peters, Alan J. Torrance, Donald Bloesch, Alvin F. Kimel, Charles J. Scalise, Philip Walker Butin, Thomas G. Weinancy and Roderick T. Leupp have authored or edited significant works devoted specifically to the Trinity. Others have explored Trinitarian connections to broader theological, historical, cultural and hermeneutical issues and figures, like Clark Pinnock, *et al.*, *The Openness of God and Flame of Love: A Theology of the Holy Spirit.*

These recent works have attempted to utilize Trinitarian thinking to unite Christian doctrine into a whole system. Therefore, renewed effort has been made among contemporary Trinitarian

---

21. Christopher Hall, *Christianity Today*, "Adding up the Trinity" April 28, 1997, p. 28.
22. Gunton, *op. cit., Promise of Trinitarian Theology*, p. xv.
23. *Ibid.*, pp. xi and xii.

scholars to develop a systematic Trinitarian theology that would demand more than perfunctory and half-hearted allegiance:

> We may say, then, that because the Trinity has been divorced from other doctrines, it has fallen into disrepute, except as the recipient of lip-service.[24]

Schwobel makes the same point in his recent book, which we will quote in several places: Attempts at recovering the doctrinal significance of the doctrine of the Trinity seem fated to founder unless its displacement in the systematic order of the exposition of Christian doctrines is overcome…If the understanding of God as Trinity is constitutive for Christian faith, it cannot be relegated to the place of a mere appendix of the Christian doctrine of God. Rather, it must be conceived as the gateway through which the theological exposition of all that can be said about God in Christian theology must pass. The doctrine of the Trinity is thus elevated from a place of virtual obscurity to a place of central significance in the systematic structure of Christian dogmatics.[25]

Reflection on the Trinity, so it seems, inevitably has repercussions for the whole project of Christian theology and its relation to the cultural situation of the times. Trinitarian theology therefore appears to be a summary label for doing theology that effects all aspects of the enterprise of doing theology in its various disciplines. Because of this, **it is difficult to point to any one area of theological reflection that is not potentially affected by being viewed from a Trinitarian perspective**. This concerns not only major doctrinal topics such as the doctrine of creation, the destiny of humankind, the person and work of Christ, the Church, its ministries and sacraments, and eschatology, but also those areas where doctrinal reflection and non-theological modes of inquiry overlap, such as the conversation with the natural sciences, anthropological inquiries, historical investigation and social theory. In being relevant for the main doctrinal topics, Trinitarian theology also affects the interface these topics have with non-theological forms of inquiry.[26]

Schwobel foresees a time when the Trinity is so anchoring all the major Christian doctrines that "any theological decision taken with regard to the doctrine of the Trinity will have echoes throughout the whole building of Christian doctrinal theology."[27] He goes on to further describe the centrality of the doctrine of the Trinity in nearly all of modern Christendom:

> The resurgence of interest in Trinitarian theology can claim to be taking up some of the seminal insights and proposals of three of the most influential theologians of an earlier generation, Karl Barth, Karl Rahner and Vladimir Lossky…The most significant studies on Trinitarian theology that have shaped the debate in recent years show that **the theological impetus of Trinitarian thinking has spread into all major denominations**. In spite of the diversity of their Trinitarian conceptions, these theologians agree in seeing Trinitarian theology as the primary orientation for their work…There appears in some theological quarters the possibility of a shared appreciation of Trinitarian theology that cannot remain without effect for the way in which the churches learn to conceive the way towards greater communion [i.e., greater unity].[28]

---

24. *Ibid.,* p. 57.
25. Schwobel, *op. cit., Trinitarian Theology Today,* p. 6.
26. *Ibid.,* p. 1 and 2.
27. *Ibid.,* p. 2.
28. *Ibid.,* pp. 2 and 3.

It is certainly clear, then, that there are two large trends in the modern theological scene. One is moving away from Trinitarian thinking and the other is reacting to this retreat with renewed vigor for maintaining the Trinity as not only the "cornerstone" of the faith but also the lynchpin of an entire system of Christian systematic theology. Then, beyond the theological commitment that can be expected to accelerate at seminaries and Bible schools, the ecumenical zeal for uniting Christians around the Trinity will continue to steamroll. Not only that, the Trinity will provide a fruitful opportunity for interfaith dialogue with Eastern Religions like Buddhism and Hinduism that already embrace a belief that is similarly mystical. Where does that leave those of us who are unable to join the party for conscience sake?

We must be prepared to "Bless those who persecute you; bless and do not curse" (Rom. 12:14). As the Trinitarian rhetoric increases, we will have to keep our eyes open for those who are left cold by its unintelligibility and mysticism and be prepared to offer them a rational and biblical alternative. We must also be prepared to endeavor "…to keep the unity of the Spirit through the bond of peace" (Eph. 4:3), and **be especially good to the household of faith** (Gal. 6:10 - KJV). We must now look at the biblical evidence as to who is included in that domain.

Seeking a Biblical "Bottom Line"

Because we too see that there are many reasons to value Christians uniting, we must search for a true standard under which this can legitimately occur. Either God is "triune" or He is not. If He is not, then belief in a triune God is a false standard for unity and will not generate liberty and a healthy diversity. Only *truth* will suffice. Is God a God of truth or of "half-truth?" We agree with half of the Ecumenical formula that we looked at in the beginning of this chapter: *Christians are those who truly invoke Jesus Christ as their personal Savior.* We find this to be a very biblical statement. Peter's sermon on Pentecost contains the first use of a phrase we believe is profoundly important in defining the least common denominator for determining true Christians.

> **Acts 2:20 and 21**
> (20) The sun will be turned to darkness and the moon to blood before the coming of the great and glorious day of the Lord.
> (21) And everyone who **calls on the name of the Lord** [for salvation] will be saved.

This phrase also occurs in Romans in the same context of salvation. Does it not describe those who recognize that Jesus Christ is their *Savior*? In other words, if they were paratroopers jumping out of a plane and their parachutes failed to open, they would cry out to the Lord Jesus for salvation. When Paul went looking for Christians to persecute and imprison, he looked for "…all who call on your [his] name" (Acts 9:14). This is the earliest designation for members of the Body of Christ, and we see no reason to believe that God has changed His mind (see also Rom. 10:11–13). So we see that the biblical phrase for designating members of his Body is *those who call on his name*, or recognize him as Savior. Anything added to this is *creating division and dissension contrary to the* [received] *doctrine* (Rom. 16:17).

This provides us with a practical way of obeying the command of Galatians 6:10: "Therefore, as we have opportunity, let us do good to all people, **especially to those who belong to the family of believers**." We are to *accept* as fellow Christians all those who call on the name of the Lord Jesus. However, the final use of the phrase exhorts us to *fellowship* with those who call on his name *out of a* *pure heart*. Some members of the Body of Christ will be deceived and refuse to be corrected. Biblically speaking, those believers are not "of a pure heart." With these folks there can be no true unity.

2 Timothy 2:22
Flee the evil desires of youth, and pursue righteousness, faith, love and peace, **along with those who call on the Lord out of a pure heart**.

Consider with us the following verses, which clearly express God's heart for all His children—Unitarian Christians, Trinitarians, Arians, Hungarians and Librarians:

Romans 15:5–7 (KJV)
(5) Now the God of patience and consolation grant you to be likeminded one toward another according to Christ Jesus:
(6) That ye may with one mind *and* one mouth [with like passion and speech] glorify God, even the Father of our Lord Jesus Christ.
(7) Wherefore receive ye one another, as Christ also received us to the glory of God.

Once again we see that *Jesus Christ* is the standard for oneness among believers, and that such oneness glorifies both God and Christ. In verse 7, the word "receive" is far from a passive word. The Greek word means to "reach out and take to one's self." It means to overlook differences in background, lifestyle or personality for the sake of the goal of magnifying the one true God.

Each of us must decide for himself whether or not he will respond to God's call to true unity. Spiritually, we are seated together at the right hand of God. With His nature of holy spirit in us, we have limitless potential for practical unity today. Each of us can mine all the treasures of wisdom and knowledge hidden in the depths of the Secret of the One Body. We can be bonded together in the love of God by a common belief of and a passion for the truth. We can see an incredibly diverse group of individuals become one in heart and spread the true Gospel around the world.

A Closing Story

In concluding this historical overview, we would ask the reader to join us in considering that we are now at a point in history when the Church has the opportunity to again have both its eyes open. The Reformation started the process by reasserting the final authority of Scripture. The Enlightenment, the Renaissance and the rise of science revived interest in reason, nature and human freedom. The history of science has demonstrated that when faith in nature's orderliness, integrity and uniformity is combined with rational methodology, the result is the growth of real knowledge and power to shape man's environment. If we can escape the assumption that "religion" must operate by its own set of rules, and can instead come to view God as the Author of both His Word *and* Creation, perhaps we can approach the Word of God as honestly as true science approaches the physical universe. Then we can present, especially to thinking people who have not yet been reached by traditional Christianity, a consistent and rational faith that could cause the Word of God to prevail in our day as it did in the first-century Church.

As long as Christians persist in teaching that God is essentially outside the realm of reason, even to the point that He embraces contradiction and absurdity, many will be limited in their ability to grow in real and practical knowledge of Him. Then various competitive sects and denominations will work only to preserve their own traditions and assumptions instead of discovering truth and building on these discoveries as the scientific community is able to do. A parallel expansion of true spiritual knowledge could happen in the Christian Church if the evidence of Scripture were upheld with the same conviction that scientists have about *their* final authority, the observable facts of nature. In *science*, if a hypothesis is contradicted by the evidence, it is revised. But in theology, even if a hypothesis is not supported by the whole of Scripture, or if it contradicts particular verses, it may well be accepted *anyway*.

"Ockham's Razor" is the philosophical maxim that whenever two or more theories are in competition to explain the same facts, the simpler of them is probably the truth. A good example of this is Copernicus' theory of the sun-centered solar system. One of its most compelling aspects was its elegant simplicity. Traditionally, Christian theologians have favored complexity and mystery over simplicity and clarity. Roman Catholic apologist Cozens even says that what characterizes "heresy" is most often "oversimplification."[29] While we recognize the importance of avoiding *over*simplification, we also think that William of Ockham was onto something. Indeed, we believe that the Christology we are advancing in this book is very simple to understand and communicate, even to a child. This becomes compelling if we think about the fact that God would have us trust Him with child-like simplicity.

In fact, the widespread acceptance among Christians of the doctrine of the Trinity despite the fact that it is admittedly unbiblical and unintelligible, even after more than 1700 years of attempting to rationalize it, reminds us of the children's story titled "The Emperor's New Clothes." The Emperor needed a new wardrobe and summoned tailors to provide it. The "tailors" were actually "con-men" who pretended to labor over an invisible robe that only those who were wise could see. Neither the Emperor nor anyone who came in to "see" this robe would admit that he could not see it, because no one wanted to be called a fool.

Finally the day came for the Emperor to parade his new clothes before all his subjects. As he passed through the crowd, all "oohed" and "aahed," pretending to be impressed with his outfit for fear of being thought a fool. But suddenly, from amidst the din of this massive chorus of adult fools, a small voice of reason pierced the pretentious proceedings. A little boy cried out, "Hey, look, the Emperor is in his underwear!"

At first the crowd reacted with horror, and turned to see who could be so foolish, so insolent and so presumptuous as to challenge what "everybody" believed. When they saw it was a child, one too innocent to be caught up in their pretense, they realized that he had stated what each of them knew in his heart but were silenced by the fear of public scorn. With relief, and then with joy, they laughed and laughed at the absurdity of the whole situation.

So it is in regard to the Church's parade throughout the last 1700 years, clad in its mystical Trinitarian robe, which was fashioned by theologians who told the people that they were fools if they could not "see" that the Trinity was true. Its "emperors" have intimidated Christian people along the way with the threat of social and religious ostracism, and even death. They have then used the resulting acquiescence of the vast majority to reinforce their elitist "wisdom." Among the onlookers, however, there has been a remnant, a steady stream of dissenting voices, men and women not afraid to be thought fools by their fellow men in pursuit of the wisdom of God. Surely God and His Son must weep to think of how many of them through the years have been silenced, not by Scripture or through rational and friendly persuasion, but by intimidation and by the sword.

---

29. M. L Cozens, *Heresies* (Canterbury Books, Shed and Ward, N.Y., 1928), p. 5.

We trust that by way of this book we can add our voices to a growing chorus that cries out for a rational faith in an insane age, a faith that harmonizes reason, Scripture and authentic Christian experience and community. It is our prayer that many Christians will recognize the unbiblical nature of Trinitarian orthodoxy, throw off the shackles of theological tyranny and embrace the simple truth that liberates the mind to worship and serve the one true God, the Father, and the one Lord, Jesus Christ, in spirit and in truth. Amen!

PART SIX

Appendices

An Explanation of Verses Sometimes Used to Support the Trinity

The purpose of this appendix is to present clear explanations of the verses in the Bible that Trinitarians have sometimes used in attempts to "prove" the Trinity and to substantiate that Jesus is God. Since there are an overwhelming number of very clear verses about Jesus Christ's identity and his distinction from God, and since God's Word has no contradictions, these comparatively few verses must fit with the many clear verses, and they do. Serious students of the Bible must acknowledge that every verse that Trinitarians use to try to prove the Trinity can be explained from a non-Trinitarian point of view.

Every lawyer understands "circumstantial evidence," and that is exactly how the case is made for the Trinity. A case is built from circumstantial evidence only when there is not eyewitness testimony or primary evidence. We assert that it is ludicrous to think that God would have Christians build the very foundation of the faith on circumstantial evidence. He would surely state it clearly. Yet there is not a single verse in the Bible that actually states the doctrine of the Trinity, and this fact is openly admitted by Trinitarians. In stark contrast to other doctrines such as salvation, the depravity of man and the need for repentance, which are clearly spelled out, the doctrine of the Trinity is pieced together from different verses and is built from inference.

Can it be that the "foundation" of Christianity is not clearly set forth in Scripture? Would God conceal the truth concerning Himself while providing great detail about less significant issues? And what if every verse used to support the Trinity has another meaning, one that fits more perfectly with the Unitarian view of God found in Scripture? It would mean that there really is no Trinity at all, and that is the conclusion we have come to. The real foundation of Christianity is clearly spelled out in the Bible. God, the Father, is the one God over all, and Christ is God's anointed, the man who was made "Lord and Christ," given a name above every name and who is seated at God's right hand. As you read our explanations of these verses that are sometimes used to prove the Trinity, it will also become apparent that some of them actually show just the opposite.

Because debate has raged about the doctrine of the Trinity since it was first formulated, there is a rich and extensive body of literature expounding our position that Jesus is the Son of God and not "God the Son." Thus, in our own brief explanations, we refer our readers to some of that literature also, with references to books and page numbers where these same verses are explained by other authors who also hold the position that Christ was created by God and is the Son of God. The books we refer to do not always support our position on how a particular verse should be handled, which will become apparent if they are read in full. Sometimes they explain verses differently than we do. However, they all agree that the verses used to support the Trinity do not actually support it at all.

We are certainly thankful for the pioneers who have gone before us and laid a foundation for understanding the Scriptures. They forged ahead with less foundation than we have, with fewer texts and fewer general resources, no computers, phones or other devices that make communication easy, and often in fear of their very lives. When we do disagree with these pioneers, we do so with the utmost respect.

This appendix consists of two parts. The first part contains, in canonical order, the verses sometimes used to prove the Trinity. We begin by quoting the verse, then give our explanation of it. Although we usually quote from the NIV first, that is not always the case. Many times it is more appropriate to quote other versions for reasons that are made obvious in the notes. The second part contains the groupings of some of these difficult verses according to topics. At the end of the appendix is an alphabetical list of the authors and the books to which we refer.

Verses Sometimes Used to Support the Trinity In Canonical Order

Genesis 1:1 (KJV)
In the beginning God created the heaven and the earth.

1. The word "God" is *Elohim*, which is itself a plural form and, like most other words, has more than one definition. It is used in a plural sense of "gods" or "men with authority," and in a singular sense for "God," "god," or "a man with authority, such as a judge." The Hebrew lexicon by Brown, Driver and Briggs, considered to be one of the best available, has as its first usage for *Elohim*: "*rulers, judges,* either as divine representatives at sacred places or as reflecting divine majesty and power, *divine ones,* superhuman beings including God and angels, *gods.*"[1]

1. Francis Brown, S. R. Driver and Charles Briggs, *The Brown-Driver-Briggs Hebrew and English Lexicon* (Hendrickson Publishers, Peabody, MA, reprint 1996), p. 43.

Elohim is translated "gods" in many verses. Genesis 35:2 reads, "…Get rid of the foreign gods you have with you…," and Exodus 18:11 says, "Now I know that the LORD is greater than all other gods…." It is translated "judges" in Exodus 21:6, 22:8 and 9. It is translated "angels" (KJV) or "heavenly beings" (NIV) in Psalm 8:5. That is its plural use, and there is no evidence that anyone thought of these "gods" as having some kind of plurality of persons within themselves.

2. *Elohim* is also translated as the singular "god" or "judge," and there is no hint of any "compound nature" when it is translated that way. An example is Exodus 22:20, which reads, "Whoever sacrifices to any **god** other than the LORD must be destroyed." Another example is Judges 6:31: "…If Baal really is a **god**, he can defend himself when someone breaks down his altar." In Exodus 7:1, God says that He has made Moses a "god" (*Elohim*) to Pharaoh. Again, in Judges 11:24, the pagan god Chemosh is called *Elohim*, and in 1 Samuel 5:7, the pagan god Dagon is called *Elohim*, yet Christians do not conclude that those gods were somehow composite or "uniplural," or that the people who worshipped them thought they were.

Exactly how to translate *Elohim* in 1 Samuel 2:25 has been debated by scholars. The question is whether *Elohim* in the verse refers to a human judge or to God. The KJV says "judge." The versions are divided between them, some translating *Elohim* as a man, others as God Himself. The fact that the scholars and translators debate about whether the word *Elohim* refers to a man or God shows vividly that the word itself does not have any inherent idea of a plurality of persons. If it did, it could not be translated as "god" when referring to a pagan god, or as "judge" when referring to a man. The evidence in Scripture does not warrant the conclusion that the Hebrew word *Elohim* inherently contains the idea of a compound nature.

3. Some teach that the word *Elohim* implies a compound unity when it refers to the true God. That would mean that the word *Elohim* somehow changes meaning when it is applied to the true God so that the true God can be a compound being. There is just no evidence of this. The first place we should go for confirmation of this is to the Jews themselves. When we study the history and the language of the Jews, we discover that they never understood *Elohim* to imply a plurality in God in any way. In fact, the Jews were staunchly opposed to people and nations who tried to introduce any hint of more than one God into their culture. **Jewish rabbis have debated the Law to the point of tedium, and have recorded volume after volume of notes on the Law, yet in all of their debates there is no mention of a plurality in God.** This fact in and of itself ought to close the argument.

No higher authority on the Hebrew language can be found than the great Hebrew scholar, Gesenius. He wrote that the plural nature of *Elohim* was for intensification, and was related to the plural of majesty and used for amplification. Gesenius states, "That the language has entirely rejected the idea of numerical plurality in *Elohim* (whenever it denotes *one* God) is proved especially by its being almost invariably joined with a singular attribute."[2]

The singular pronoun is always used with the word *Elohim*. A study of the word will show what Gesenius stated, that the singular attribute (such as "He," not "They," or "I," not "We") always follows *Elohim*. Furthermore, when the word *Elohim* is used to denote others beside the true God, it is understood as singular or plural, never as "uniplural." To us, the evidence is clear: God is not "compound" in any sense of the word. He is the "one God" of Israel.

4. Scripture contains no reproof for those who do not believe in a "Triune God." Those who do not believe in God are called **fools** (Ps. 14:1). Those who reject Christ are condemned (John 3:18). Scripture testifies that it is for **doctrine, reproof, and correction** (2 Tim. 3:16 - KJV), and there are

---

2. E. Kautzsch, ed., *Gesenius' Hebrew Grammar* (Clarendon Press, Oxford, 1910), p. 399.

many verses that reprove believers for all kinds of erroneous beliefs and practices. Conspicuous in its absence is any kind of reproof for not believing in the Trinity.

> Buzzard, *op. cit., Doctrine of the Trinity*, pp. 13–15, 125 and 126; Charles Morgridge, *True Believer's Defence Against Charges Preferred by Trinitarians*, (Boston: Benjamin Greene, 1837. Reprinted 1994 by Spirit & Truth Fellowship International, 180 Robert Curry Drive, Martinsville, IN 46151), pp. 88–96; Donald R. Snedeker, *Our Heavenly Father Has No Equals*, (International Scholars Publications, Bethesda, MD, 1998), pp. 359–367.

Genesis 1:26 (KJV)
And God said, Let us make man in our image, after our likeness....

---

1. *Elohim* and *Adonim*, Hebrew words for God, occur in the plural. If this literally meant a plurality of persons, it would be translated "Gods." But the Jews, being truly monotheistic and thoroughly familiar with the idioms of their own language, have never understood the use of the plural to indicate a plurality of persons within the one God. This use of the plural is for amplification, and is called a "plural of majesty" or a "plural of emphasis," and is used for intensification (see note on Gen. 1:1). Many Hebrew scholars identify this use of "us" as the use of the plural of majesty or plural of emphasis, and we believe this also.

2. The plural of majesty is clearly attested to in writing from royalty through the ages. Hyndman writes:

> The true explanation of this verse is to be found in the practice which has prevailed in all nations with which we are acquainted, of persons speaking of themselves in the plural number. "Given at our palace," "It is our pleasure," are common expressions of kings in their proclamations (p. 54).

Morgridge adds:

> It is common in all languages with which we are acquainted, and it appears to have always been so, for an individual, especially if he be a person of great dignity and power, in speaking of himself only, to say *we, our, us*, instead of *I, my, me*. Thus, the king of France says, "*We,* Charles the tenth." The king of Spain says, "*We,* Ferdinand the seventh." The Emperor of Russia says "*We,* Alexander," or "*We,* Nicholas" (p. 93).

The plural of majesty can be seen in Ezra 4:18. In Ezra 4:11, the men of the Trans-Euphrates wrote, "...To King Artaxerxes, From your servants...." The book of Ezra continues, "The king sent this reply...Greetings. The letter you sent us has been read and translated...." Thus, although the people wrote to the king himself, the king used the word "us." It is common in such correspondence that the plural is used when someone speaks of his *intentions*, and the use of the more literal singular is used when the person *acts*. Morgridge adds more insight when he says:

> It is well known that Mohammed was a determined opposer of the doctrine of the Trinity: yet he often represents God as saying *we, our, us*, when speaking only of Himself. This shows that, in his opinion, the use of such terms was not indicative of a plurality of persons. If no one infers, from their frequent use in the Koran, that Mohammed was a Trinitarian, surely their occurrence in a few places in the Bible ought not to be made a proof of the doctrine of the Trinity (p. 94).

3. Some scholars believe that the reason for the "us" in Genesis 1:26 is that God could have been speaking with the angels when he created man in the beginning. Although that is possible, because there are many Scriptures that clearly attribute the creation of man to God alone, we believe that the plural of emphasis is the preferred explanation.

4. The name of God is not the only word that is pluralized for emphasis (although when the plural does not seem to be good grammar, the translators usually ignore the Hebrew plural and translate it as a singular, so it can be hard to spot in most English versions). After Cain murdered Abel, God said to Cain, "…the voice of your brother's *bloods* cries to me from the ground" (Gen. 4:10, "bloods" is the way the Hebrew text reads). The plural emphasizes the horror of the act. In Genesis 19:11, the men of Sodom who wanted to hurt Lot were smitten with "blindness." The Hebrew is in the plural, "blindnesses," and indicates that the blindness was total so Lot would be protected. Leviticus tells people not to eat fruit from a tree for three years, and in the fourth year the fruit is "…an offering of praise to the LORD" (Lev. 19:24). The Hebrew word for "praise" is plural, emphasizing that there was to be *great* praise. Psalm 45:15 tells of people who are brought into the presence of the Messiah. It says, "They are led in with joy and gladness…." The Hebrew actually reads "gladnesses," emphasizing the great gladness of the occasion. In Ezekiel 25, God is speaking of what has happened to Israel and what He will do about it. Concerning the Philistines, He said, "… the Philistines acted in vengeance…I will carry out great vengeance on them…" (Ezek. 25:15 and 17). In the Hebrew text, the second vengeance, the vengeance of God, is in the plural, indicating the complete vengeance that the LORD will inflict. Although many more examples exist in the Hebrew text, these demonstrate that it is not uncommon to use a plural to emphasize something in Scripture.

Buzzard, *op. cit., Doctrine of the Trinity*, p. 13; Frederick Farley, *Unitarianism Defined: The Scripture Doctrine of the Father, Son, and Holy Ghost*, (American Unitarian Association, Boston, MA, 1873. Reprinted 1994 by Spirit & Truth Fellowship International, 180 Robert Curry Drive, Martinsville, IN 46151), pp. 25–27; Hyndman, *op. cit., Principles of Unitarianism*, pp. 53 and 54; Morgridge, *op. cit., True Believer's Defence*, pp. 92–96; Snedeker, *op. cit., Father Has No Equals*, pp. 363–366.

Genesis 11:7 (KJV)
…let us go down, and there confound their language, that they may not understand one another's speech.

For an explanation applicable to this verse, see the note on Genesis 1:26.

Genesis 16:7–13 (NRSV)
(7) The angel of the LORD found her by a spring of water in the wilderness, the spring on the way to Shur.
(8) And he said, "Hagar, slave-girl of Sarai, where have you come from and where are you going?" She said, "I am running away from my mistress Sarai."
(9) The angel of the LORD said to her, "Return to your mistress and submit to her."
(10) The angel of the LORD also said to her, "I will so greatly multiply your offspring that they cannot be counted for multitude."
(11) And the angel of the LORD said to her, "Now you have conceived and shall bear a son; you shall call him Ishmael, for the LORD has given heed to your affliction.

(12) He shall be a wild ass of a man, with his hand against everyone, and everyone's hand against him; and he shall live at odds with all his kin."

(13) So she named the LORD who spoke to her, "You are El-roi"; for she said, "Have I really seen God and remained alive after seeing him?"

1. It is believed by some Trinitarians that in the Old Testament "the angel of the LORD" is Jesus Christ before he supposedly "incarnated" as a human. This point is disputed by many, and with good reason. There is not a single verse that actually says that Jesus Christ is the angel of the LORD. The entire doctrine is built from assumption. Why then, if the doctrine is not stated, do so many people believe it? The reason is that it is very awkward for Trinitarians to believe that Jesus is co-equal and co-eternal with God from the beginning of time, and yet he never appears in the Old Testament. Since one cannot miss the active role that Jesus plays today as Head of the Church, is it possible that he could have been around throughout the entire Old Testament and yet never have gotten involved with mankind? A Trinitarian answer to this question is to place Jesus in the Old Testament by assumption: he must be "the angel of the LORD." However, we answer the question by asserting that this is very strong evidence for our position that Jesus Christ did not yet exist during the Old Testament, but was the plan of God for the salvation of man. We believe that physically he *began* when God impregnated Mary (Matt. 1:18). Exactly what are the reasons Trinitarians say that the angel of the LORD is Jesus? Trinitarians differ on the points of evidence (which is to be expected when working from assumptions), but the standard reasons are: he seems superior to other angels; he is separate from the LORD; he is able to forgive sins (Exod. 23:21); he speaks with authority as though he were God; his countenance struck awe in people; he was never seen after Jesus' birth, and, most importantly, he is addressed as God himself. All these points will be considered, and we will start with the last, which is the most essential point of the argument.

2. A study of the appearances of the angel of the LORD reveals that sometimes he is addressed as the angel and sometimes he is addressed as "the LORD" or "God" (see also Judg. 6:12 and 16). The Jewish law of agency explains why this is so. According to the Jewish understanding of agency, the agent was regarded as the person himself. This is well expressed in *The Encyclopedia of the Jewish Religion*:

> **Agent** (Heb. *Shaliah*): The main point of the Jewish law of agency is expressed in the dictum, "a person's agent is regarded as the person himself" (*Ned.* 72b; *Kidd.* 41b). Therefore any act committed by a duly appointed agent is regarded as having been committed by the principal, who therefore bears full responsibility for it with consequent complete absence of liability on the part of the agent.[3]

In the texts in which the angel is called "God" or "the LORD," it is imperative to notice that he is always identified as an angel. This point is important because God is never called an angel. God is God. So if a being is called "God," but is clearly identified as an angel, there must be a reason. In the record in Genesis quoted above, the angel is clearly identified as an angel four separate times. Why then would the text say that "the LORD" spoke to her? It does so because as God's agent or messenger, the angel was speaking for God and the message he brought was God's message. The same basic idea is expressed when "God" is said to "visit" His people, when actually He sends some form of blessing (see the notes on Luke 7:16). God Himself does not show up, but someone unfamiliar with the culture might conclude from the wording that He did. Also, some of the people to whom

3. Werblowsky and Wigoder. *op. cit., Encyclopedia of the Jewish Religion*, p. 15.

the angel appeared, clearly expressed their belief he was an angel of God. Gideon exclaimed, "…I have seen the angel of the LORD face to face!" (Judg. 6:22).

There is conclusive biblical evidence that God's messengers and representatives are called "God" (see the notes on Heb. 1:8). This is important because if representatives of God are called "God," then the way to distinguish God from His representative is by the context. We have already shown that when the angel of the LORD is called "God," the context is careful to let the reader know that the agent is, in fact, an angel.

3. Another piece of evidence that reveals that the angel of the LORD is an angel and not a "co-equal" member of the Trinity is that he is under the command of the LORD. In one record, David disobeyed God and a plague came on the land. "…God sent an angel to destroy Jerusalem…" (1 Chron. 21:15). We learn from the record that it was the angel of the LORD afflicting the people, and eventually "…the LORD was grieved because of the calamity and said to the angel who was afflicting the people, 'Enough! Withdraw your hand.' The angel of the LORD was then at the threshing floor of Araunah the Jebusite" (2 Sam. 24:16). These verses are not written as if this angel was somehow God himself. There is no "co-equality" here. This is simply the LORD giving commands to one of His angels.

4. Another clear example showing that the angel of the LORD cannot be God in any way is in Zechariah. Zechariah was speaking with an angel about a vision he had. The Bible records, "Then the angel of the LORD said, 'LORD Almighty, how long will you withhold mercy from Jerusalem and from the towns of Judah, which you have been angry with these seventy years?' So the LORD spoke kind and comforting words to the angel who talked with me" (Zech. 1:12 and 13). The fact that the angel of the LORD asked the LORD for information and then received comforting words indicates that he is not co-equal with God in power or knowledge. It is unthinkable that God would need information or need comforting words. Thus, any claim that the angel of the LORD is the pre-incarnate Christ who is in every way God just cannot be made to fit what the Bible actually says.

5. It is interesting that two pieces of evidence that Trinitarians use to prove that the angel of the LORD must be the pre-incarnate Jesus are that the Bible clearly states that he is separate from God and that he speaks with God's authority. We would argue that the reason he is separate from God is because he is exactly what the text calls him, i.e., an angel, and that he speaks with authority because he is bringing a message from God. The prophets and others who spoke for God spoke with authority, as many verses affirm. Also, the angel of the LORD speaks about God in the third person. For example, in Genesis 16:11 above, the angel says, "…the LORD has heard of your misery." The angel does not say, "I have heard of your misery," as if he were God. In Genesis 22:12, the angel said, "…Now I know that you fear God…," not "Now I know you fear me." In Judges 13:5, the angel says Samson will be "set apart to God," not "set apart to me." So although the text can call the angel God, which is proper for a representative of God, the angel never said he was God and even referred to God in the third person.

Also, if Jesus were the angel of the LORD who spoke to Moses at the burning bush, then he did not say so in his teaching. Mark 12:26 records Jesus speaking with the Sadducees and saying, "…have you not read in the book of Moses, in the account of the bush, how God said to him, 'I am the God of Abraham, the God of Isaac, and the God of Jacob?'" If Jesus had been the angel in the bush, and was openly proclaiming himself to be "the pre-existent God," he would have used this opportunity to say, "*I* said to Moses." The fact that Jesus said it was *God* who spoke to Moses shows clearly that he was differentiating himself from God.

6. That the angel of the LORD seems superior to other angels is no reason to assume he is somehow part of the Trinity. Many scholars agree that angels differ in power and authority. The Bible mentions archangels in 1 Thessalonians 4:16 and Jude 9, for example. It would not be unusual that this angel would be one with greater authority. Neither is the fact that the angel of the LORD can forgive sins any reason to believe that he is God. God's agents can forgive sins. God gave Jesus the authority to forgive sins, and then he in turn gave the Apostles the authority to forgive sins (see the notes on Mark 2:7).

7. Although it is true that the countenance of the angel of the LORD occasionally struck awe in people, that is no reason to assume he is God. A careful reading of the passages where he appears shows that sometimes the people did not even realize that they were talking to an angel. For example, when the angel of the LORD appeared to Samson's mother, she returned to her husband Manoah with this report: "…A man of God came to me. He looked like an angel of God, very awesome. I didn't ask him where he came from, and he didn't tell me his name" (Judg. 13:6). Note that angels had a reputation for having an awe-inspiring countenance, and the woman thought this "man of God" did too, but she still did not believe he was an angel. When Manoah met the angel of the LORD and the two of them talked about how to raise Samson, Manoah did not discover he was an angel until he ascended to heaven in the smoke of Manoah's sacrifice. Therefore, just because someone's countenance may be awesome, he is not necessarily God.

8. It is also argued that Jesus is probably "the angel of the LORD" because those words never appear after his birth, and it seems reasonable that this angel would appear right on through the Bible. The fact is, however, that the angel of the LORD does appear after Jesus' *conception*, which seems inconsistent with the premise that the angel of the LORD is the "pre-incarnate Christ." The record of Jesus' birth is well known. Mary was discovered to be pregnant with Jesus before she and Joseph were married, and Joseph, who could have had her stoned to death, decided to divorce her. However, "…the angel of the Lord…" appeared to him in a dream and told him the child was God's. Matthew 1:24 states, "When Joseph woke up, he did what the angel of the Lord had commanded him and took Mary home as his wife." Two conclusions can be drawn from this record. First, Jesus was already in Mary's womb when the angel of the Lord appeared to Joseph. From this we conclude that "the angel of the Lord" cannot be Jesus because Jesus was at that time "in the flesh" inside Mary. Second, it should be noted that in the same record this angel is known both as "an" angel of the Lord and as "the" angel of the Lord. This same fact can be seen in the Old Testament records (cp. 1 Kings 19:5 and 7).

There are many appearances of "an" angel of the Lord in the New Testament (cp. Acts 5:19, 8:26, 12:7 and 23). From this we conclude that it is likely that the same angel who is called both "the" angel of the LORD and "an angel" in the Old Testament still appears as "an angel of the Lord" after Christ's birth. When all the evidence is carefully weighed, there is good reason to believe that the words describing the "angel" of the Lord are literal, and that the being referred to is an angel, just as the text says.

Genesis 18:1 and 2

(1) The LORD appeared to Abraham near the great trees of Mamre while he was sitting at the entrance to his tent in the heat of the day.

(2) Abraham looked up and saw three men standing nearby. When he saw them, he hurried from the entrance of his tent to meet them and bowed low to the ground.

---

1. These verses pose a problem for Christians who have been taught that no one has ever seen God. The Hebrew text clearly says that Yahweh appeared to Abraham in the form of a man, and He was with two angels, who also took on human appearance. This is not a problem. God created mankind so He could intimately fellowship with us. It is reasonable that He would occasionally become visible and take on human form to be intimate with His creation. In fact, Scripture records a number of people to whom God appeared: Adam and Eve (they heard His footsteps, Gen. 3:8), Abraham (Gen. 12:7, 15:1, 17:1, 18:1), Jacob (Gen. 28:13), Moses and the elders of Israel (Exod. 24:9–11), Samuel (1 Sam. 3:10), Solomon twice (1 Kings 3:5, 9:2, 11:9), Micaiah (1 Kings 22:19–22), Isaiah (Isa. 6:1–5), Ezekiel (Ezek. 1:26–28), Daniel (Dan. 7:9–14), Amos (Amos 7:7), Stephen (Acts 7:56) and the Apostle John (Rev. 5:1–8).

2. A study of Genesis 18:1 in Christian commentaries reveals that most theologians do not believe that Yahweh can appear in the form of a man. Before we examine why they say that, we must remember that, difficult to believe or not, that is *exactly* what the text says. Many theologians who do not believe that the text can be literal have postulated other explanations. The standard explanations of the verse are: it was actually a dream and not real; it was the pre-incarnate Christ who appeared; it was an angel that appeared carrying the name of Yahweh.

Some theologians teach that the record of Genesis 18:1ff was a dream because of the circumstances, i.e., it was the heat of the day and the time for naps. However, the Bible never says it was a dream, and there certainly was no time when Abraham "woke up." The record of Sodom and Gomorrah is certainly not a dream. The angels left Abraham and went to the city of Sodom where they rescued Lot and his daughters from God's judgment. There is just no solid scriptural evidence that Yahweh's appearance was a dream. Neither would this account for the many other times Yahweh appears.

Many Trinitarian theologians say that Genesis 18:1 is an appearance of the pre-incarnate Christ. The evidence they give for their conclusion is twofold: Yahweh is invisible and no one has or can see Him, so it cannot be He; and the record clearly says it is Yahweh, so it must be the pre-incarnate Christ since "Christ is a member of the Godhead." However, if it could be shown that Yahweh does indeed occasionally appear in the form of a man, then there would be no reason not to take the Bible literally. Furthermore, the fact that Scripture never says that the one appearing is Christ is strong evidence that this is not Christ. And there are at least two occasions where Yahweh and Christ appear together (Dan. 7 and Rev. 5). This seems to us to force the conclusion that Yahweh cannot be Christ.

The major reason to make "Yahweh" of this record into an angel is the same as the reason to make the record a dream or to make Yahweh into the pre-incarnate Christ. It comes from the preconceived idea that Yahweh just cannot appear in human form. Therefore, the temptation here is to make Yahweh of necessity a dream, an angel or Christ. Even though in other records angels are called God, this record is different. We have seen from other verses that angels are occasionally called "God" (see the notes on Gen. 16:7–13). However, a study of the records where the angel of the LORD is called "God" shows that he was always clearly identified as an angel, and it was clear that he was bringing a message from God. This record, and the others mentioned above in which Yahweh appears, are decidedly different. The "man" identified as Yahweh is among other angels, and the entire record identifies Him as Yahweh. And while other records show the angel of the LORD carefully avoiding the use of the first person, "I," "me" and "my," referring to God, "Yahweh" in this record uses the first person over and over.

3. Most Christians have not been taught that God can appear in a form resembling a person. They have always heard, "no one has seen God at any time." In our book *Don't Blame God!*, the language of that phrase is examined and explained. John 1:17 and 18 states: "For the law was given through Moses; grace and truth came through Jesus Christ. No one has ever seen God…" We write:

Please note that **truth**, in its fullness, came not with Moses, but with Jesus Christ. It was he who for the first time in history made God truly understandable. It is not that the Old Testament believers knew nothing of God, but rather that their knowledge and understanding of Him were quite limited ("veiled"). Since **truth** came by Jesus Christ ["For the law was given through Moses; grace and **truth** came through Jesus,"], we believe that the first part of John 1:18—"No man hath seen God at anytime…"—means that no man had "known" God [as He truly is] at any previous time. It is Jesus Christ who reveals, or makes known, God to man.

In many languages, "to see" is a common idiom for "to know." In the Hebrew language, one of the definitions for "see" (Hebrew = *ra' ah*) is "see, so as to learn, to know." Similarly, the Greek word translated "see" in verse 18 (*horao*) can be "to see with the eyes" or "to see with the mind, to perceive, know." Even in English, one of the definitions for "see" is "to know or understand." For example, when two people are discussing something, one might say to the other, "I see what you mean."

The usage of "see" as it pertains to knowing is found in many places in the New Testament. Jesus said to Philip, "Anyone who has seen me has seen the Father" (John 14:9). Here again the word "see" is used to indicate knowing. Anyone who *knew* Christ (not just those who "saw" him) would know the Father. In fact, Christ had made that plain two verses earlier when he said to Philip, "If you really knew me you would know my Father as well" (John 14:7).[4]

Further evidence that "see" means "know" in John 1:18 is that the phrase "No man has seen God…" is contrasted with the phrase "has made him known." The verse is not talking about "seeing" God with one's eyes, it is saying that the truth about God came by Jesus Christ. Before Jesus Christ came, no one really knew God as He truly is, a loving heavenly Father. Jesus Christ made that known in its fullness. Our study has led us to conclude that verses seeming to say that no one has ever "seen" God are either using the word "seen" as meaning "to know," and thus referring to knowing Him fully, or they are referring to seeing Him in all His fullness as God, which would be impossible. We agree with the text note on John 1:18 in the NIV Study Bible, which says, "…since no human being can see God as He really is, those who saw God saw Him in a form He took on Himself temporarily for the occasion."

Another point should be made about the word "seen" in John 1:18. If Trinitarians are correct in that Jesus is "God incarnate," "God the Son" and "fully God," then it seems to us that they would be anxious to realize that "seen" means "known" because it makes no sense to say that no man has seen God with his eyes and then say Jesus is God. Theologians on both sides of the Trinitarian debate should realize the idiom of "seen" meaning "known" in John 1:18.

The Bible also calls God "the invisible God." This is true, and God's natural state is invisible to us. However, that does not prevent Him from occasionally becoming visible. Angels and demons are also naturally invisible, but they can and do become visible at certain times. If angels and demons can sometimes become visible, then God certainly can too. We remind the reader that the Bible plainly says, "Yahweh appeared to Abraham," and to others as well.

It is often stated that the people could not have really seen Yahweh because a person will die if he sees God. This idea comes mainly from the conversation Moses had with God. Moses asked to see the glory of God, and God responded, "…you cannot see my face, for no one may see me and live" (Exod. 33:20). It is clear from the context that the "face" of God was the "glory" of God, because that

---

4. *Op. cit., Don't Blame God!* Chapter Four.

is what Moses asked to see. We would concur that human beings are not equipped to comprehend God in all His fullness, and exposure to all that God is would be lethal. However, we know that God did create mankind so He could fellowship with us, and we assert that the human-like form that He has sometimes assumed in order to be near us is not His fullness in any way.

There are two records very important to this subject because they describe God and also show Jesus Christ with Him. The first is a revelation vision of the future that Daniel the prophet had.

Daniel 7:9, 10, 13 and 14

(9) "As I looked, "thrones were set in place, and the Ancient of Days took his seat. His clothing was as white as snow; the hair of his head was white like wool. His throne was flaming with fire, and its wheels were all ablaze.

(10) A river of fire was flowing, coming out from before him. Thousands upon thousands attended him; ten thousand times ten thousand stood before him. The court was seated, and the books were opened.

(13) "In my vision at night I looked, and there before me was one like a son of man, coming with the clouds of heaven. He approached the Ancient of Days and was led into his presence.

(14) He was given authority, glory and sovereign power; all peoples, nations and men of every language worshiped him. His dominion is an everlasting dominion that will not pass away, and his kingdom is one that will never be destroyed.

The "Ancient of Days" is Yahweh. Note his description as a man. Into his presence comes "a son of man" who is given authority and dominion. It is quite universally agreed among Christians that the "Ancient of Days" is God the Father, and the "son of man" is Jesus Christ, who receives his authority from God. Note that in this passage there is no hint of the Trinity. There is no "Holy Spirit" and no indication that the "son of man" is co-equal or co-eternal with the Father. On the contrary, while God is called the "Ancient of Days," a title befitting His eternal nature, Christ is called "a son of man," meaning one who is born from human parents. This prophecy is one of many that shaped the Jewish belief about their Messiah: he was not foretold as "God in the flesh," but rather a man like themselves who would receive special honor and authority from God. For our purposes in understanding Genesis 18:1, these verses in Daniel demonstrate very clearly that God can and does appear in human form. And because in Daniel's vision He is with the Messiah when He does so, there is no reason to assume that the other times He appears it is actually Jesus Christ.

The other very clear record is Revelation 4 and 5. The length of the record prohibits us from printing it here, but the reader is encouraged to read those two chapters. They portray God sitting on a throne surrounded by elders and creatures who repeat, "…Holy, holy, holy is the Lord God Almighty…." God is holding in His right hand a scroll that is written on both sides but sealed shut with seven seals. An angel calls out to summon those who could open the scroll, but no one was worthy. As John began to weep, an angel comforted him with the words, "…Do not weep! See, the Lion of the tribe of Judah, the Root of David, has triumphed. He is able to open the scroll…." Then "a Lamb" (the context makes it clear it is Jesus Christ) "…came and took the scroll from the right hand of him who sat on the throne." At that point the creatures and the elders fell down before the Lamb and started singing a "new song."

The record is clear. God is described as sitting on a throne and even holding in His hand a scroll that Jesus comes and takes from Him. This record again shows that God can and does occasionally take on human form so that we can better identify with Him.

4. This record and the others like it show a glimpse of what Christians have to look forward to. God loves us and created us to have a deep and abiding relationship with Him. He will not always remain as distant as He now sometimes seems. The Bible tells of a time when "…the dwelling of God is with men, and he will live with them. They will be his people, and God himself will be with them and be their God" (Rev. 21:3).

Deuteronomy 6:4
Hear, O Israel: The LORD our God, the LORD is one.

---

1. It is believed by some that the Hebrew word "one" (*echad*) that is used in Deuteronomy 6:4 and other verses indicates a "compound unity." This is just not true. Anthony Buzzard writes:

> It is untrue to say that the Hebrew word *echad* (one) in Deut. 6:4 points to a compound unity. A recent defense of the Trinity argues that when "one" modifies a collective noun like "cluster" or "herd," a plurality is implied in *echad*. The argument is fallacious. The sense of plurality is derived from the collective noun, not from the word "one." *Echad* in Hebrew is the numeral "one." Isa. 51:2 describes Abraham as "one" (*echad*), where there is no possible misunderstanding about the meaning of this simple word (p. 15).

There is no reference to the word "one" as to a plurality of any kind. It is used of "one" in number, "the first" in a series, "one" in the sense of "the same," and "one" in the sense of "each" or "a certain one." A study of its uses in the Old Testament will reveal its simple meaning and the truth it conveys. It is translated "first" in Genesis 1:5, when God made light on the "first" day. The whole earth spoke "one" language before Babel (Gen. 11:1). Hagar cast her child under "one" of the bushes (Gen. 21:15). In Pharaoh's dream, there were seven ears of grain on "one" stalk (Gen. 41:5). In the plague on Egypt's livestock, not "one" cow died in Israel (Exod. 9:6). Exodus 12:49 (KJV) says that Israel shall have "one" law for the citizen and the foreigner. The examples are far too many to list. *Echad* is used more than 250 times in the Old Testament, and there is no hint in any Jewish commentary or lexicon that it somehow implies a "compound unity."

The history of the Jews is well known. They were infamous in the ancient world for being downright obnoxious when it came to defending their "one God," as civilizations down through the ages found out. Snedeker quotes Eliot:

> One thing, very important, is certain, that if any such hints [that God was a plurality of persons] were conveyed, the Jews never understood them. The presumption is that they knew their own language, and it is certain they understood that the Unity of God was taught by their Scriptures in the most absolute and unqualified manner. Such was their interpretation of Moses and the Prophets at the time when Christ came. In all Palestine there probably could not have been found a single man or woman, who supposed that there was any distinction of persons, such as is now taught, in the Unity of God (p. 293).

2. Deuteronomy 6:4 is one of the strongest texts *against* the Trinity. God is "one," not "three-in-one" or some other plurality. This has been the rallying cry of Jews down through the ages who have stood aggressively against any form of polytheism or pantheism. Jesus quoted this verse as part of the first and great commandment: "…Hear O Israel, the Lord our God, the Lord is one. Love the Lord your God with all your heart and with all your soul and with all your mind and with all your strength" (Mark 12:29 and 30). It is quite inconceivable that Christ would be promoting some form of the doctrine of the Trinity while at the same time quoting Deuteronomy that God is "one" to a Jewish audience who would be sure to misunderstand him. It is much more reasonable to believe that Jesus was simply affirming that if we are to love God with all our heart we must be certain who He is—the one God of Israel.

Buzzard, *op. cit., Doctrine of the Trinity*, pp. 12–15, 126 and 127; Hyndman, *op. cit., Principles of Unitarianism*, pp. 51–53; Snedeker, *op. cit., Our Heavenly Father Has No Equals*, pp. 283–90.

Psalm 45:6
Your throne, O God, will last for ever and ever; a scepter of justice will be the scepter of your kingdom.

This verse is quoted in Hebrews 1:8 and our explanation can be found there.

Psalm 110:1
The LORD says to my Lord: "Sit at my right hand until I make your enemies a footstool for your feet"

Trinitarian commentators frequently argue that "my Lord" in this verse is the Hebrew word *adonai*, another name for God, and is therefore proof of the divinity of the Messiah. But not only is this not a valid argument, this verse is actually one of the great proofs of the complete humanity of the promised Messiah. The Hebrew word translated "my lord" is *adoni* (pronounced "Adon nee"[5]) in the standard Hebrew texts. This word is always used in Scripture to describe human masters and lords, but *never* God. Unfortunately, this has not been clear to most people because they only learn about the Hebrew text from concordances and lexicons. However, Hebrew concordances and lexicons give only root words, not the word that actually occurs in the Hebrew text. Most of the time this will not affect the result of a word study, but occasionally it does, and Psalm 110:1 is one of those times. The root of *adoni* that is found in concordances is *adon* (cp. *Young's Concordance*), and some of the forms of *adon* do refer to God as well as people. Thus, a person using a concordance such as *Young's* or *Strong's* will naturally assert that the second "Lord" in the verse, which refers to the Messiah, can refer to him as God, and be wrong in their assertion. This is one reason why biblical research done by people using only tools such as a *Strong's Concordance* will often be limited.[6] Let us state again that the form of the word "Lord" in Psalm 110:1 is never used of God, so the fact that the Messiah is referred to as *adoni* is very good evidence he is not God. *Focus on the Kingdom* reports:

The Bible in Psalm 110:1 actually gives the Messiah the title that *never describes God*. The word is *adoni* and in all of its 195 occurrences in the Old Testament it means a superior who

---

5. *Adonai* is pronounced "Adon eye," because the "ai" sounds like "eye." *Adoni* is pronounced "Adon nee" because the final "i" is pronounced like a long "e."
6. People wanting to study this for themselves will need to be able to work with the Hebrew text itself and not just the root words. A good source for this is the Bible study computer program, *Bibleworks*.

is human (or occasionally angelic), created and not God. So Psalm 110:1 presents the clearest evidence that the Messiah is not God, but a supremely exalted man.[7]

The difference between *adon* (the root word), adoni ("lord," always used of men or angels) and *adonai* (which is used of God and sometimes written *adonay*) is critical to the understanding of Psalm 110:1. The *Brown, Driver and Briggs Hebrew Lexicon* (BDB), considered by many to be the best available, makes the distinction between these words. Note how in BDB the word *adoni* refers to "lords" that are not God, while another word, *adonai*, refers to God:[8]

(1) Reference to **men**: *my lord, my master*: (*adoni*) [use the KJV].

   (a) *master*: Exodus 21:5; Genesis 24:12 and 44:5; 1 Samuel 30:13 and 15; 2 Kings 5:3, 20 and 22, 6:15.

   (b) *husband*: Genesis 18:12.

   (c) *prophet*: 1 Kings 18:7 and 13; 2 Kings 2:19, 4:16 and 28, 6:5, 8:5.

   (d) *prince*: Genesis 42:10, 23:6, 11 and 15, 43:20, 44:18, 47:18; Judges 4:18.

   (e) *king*: 1 Samuel 22:12.

   (f) *father*: Genesis 31:35.

   (g) *Moses*: Exodus 32:22; Numbers 11:28, 12:11, 32:26 and 27; Numbers 36:2 (2x).

   (h) *priest*: 1 Samuel 1:15 and 26 (2x).

   (i) *theophanic angel* [an angel representing God]: Joshua 5:14; Judges 6:13.

   (j) *captain*: 2 Samuel 11:11.

   (k) general recognition of superiority: Genesis 24:18, 32:5, 33:8, 44:7; Ruth 2:13; 1 Samuel 25:24.

(2) Reference to God: [*adonai*]. Notice that when the word refers to God, it changes from when it refers to men. The vowel under the "n" (the second letter from the left) has changed.[9]

In the above definition, *adoni* and *adonai* have the same root, *adon*, which is the word listed in the concordances and most lexicons. However, the exact words used are different. *Adoni*, the word used in Psalm 110:1, is never used of God. It is always used of a human or angelic superior. The fact that the Hebrew text uses the word *adoni* of the Messiah in Psalm 110 is very strong proof that he is not God. If the Messiah was to be God, then the word *adonai* would have been used. This distinction between *adoni* (a lord) and *adonai* (the Lord, God, LORD [Yahweh]) holds even when God shows up in human form. In Genesis 18:3, Abraham addresses God who was "disguised" as a human, but the text uses *adonai*.

---

7. Anthony Buzzard, ed., *Focus on the Kingdom, "Who is Jesus? God or Unique Man?"* (Atlanta Bible College, Morrow, GA, March 2000), p. 3, Emphasis his. We found 198 uses of *adoni*, but in a personal conversation with Mr. Buzzard he stated that his figure of 195 could understate the situation slightly since it was not the result of an exacting study.

8. Hebrew reads from right to left, so the first letter of the word looks like a glorified "X."

9. Brown, Driver and Briggs, *op. cit., The Brown-Driver-Briggs Hebrew and English Lexicon*, p. 11 (*Adon*, "Lord"). We have changed the punctuation and reference abbreviations to make it consistent with the abbreviations we use for ease of reading. The letters in parenthesis mark their belief as to the exact writer or redactor of that portion of Scripture, something we do not agree with theologically.

Scholars recognize that there is a distinction between the words *adoni* and *adonai*, and that these distinctions are important. The *International Standard Bible Encyclopedia* notes:

The form ADONI ("my lord"), a royal title (1 Sam. 29:8), is to be carefully distinguished from the divine title ADONAI ("my Lord") used of *Yahweh*.[10]

There are several uses of *adonai* that refer to angels or men, giving them an elevated status, but not indicating that the speaker believed they were God. This is in keeping with the language as a whole. Studies of words like *Elohim* show that it is also occasionally used of humans who have elevated status. Examples of *adonai* referring to humans include Genesis 19:18, 24:9 and 39:2. In contrast to *adonai* being used occasionally of men, there is no time when *adoni* is used of God. Men may be elevated, but God is never lowered.

The following 148 verses contain 166 uses of the word (*adoni*)[11] and every one of them either refers to a human lord or an angel. None refers to God: Genesis 23:6, 11, 15, 24:12 (2x), 14, 18, 27 (3x), 35, 36, 37, 39, 42, 44, 48 (2x), 49, 65, 31:35, 33:8, 13,14 (2x), 15, 39:8, 42:10, 43:20, 44:5, 7, 18 (2x), 19, 20, 22, 24, 47:18 (2x), 25; Exodus 21:5, 32:22; Numbers 11:28, 12:11, 32:25, 27, 36:2; Joshua 5:14, 10:1, 3; Judges 1:5, 6, 7, 4:18, 6:13; Ruth 2:13; 1 Samuel 1:15, 26 (2x), 22:12, 24:8, 25:24, 25 (2x), 26 (2x), 27, 28, 29, 31, 41, 26:17, 18, 19, 29:8, 30:13, 15 ; 2 Samuel 1:10, 3:21, 9:11, 11:11, 13:32, 33, 14:9, 12, 15, 17 (2x), 18, 19 (2x), 22, 15:15, 21(2x), 16:4, 9, 18:31, 32, 19:19 (2x), 20, 26, 27, 30, 35, 37, 24:3, 21, 22; 1 Kings 1:13, 17, 18, 20 (2x), 21, 24, 27 (2x), 31, 36, 37 (2x), 2:38, 3:17, 26, 18:7, 10, 20:4; 2 Kings 2:19, 4:16, 28, 5:3, 18, 20, 22, 6:5, 12, 15, 26, 8:5, 12, 10:9, 18:23, 24, 27; 1 Chronicles 21:3 (2x), 23; 2 Chronicles 2:14, 15; Isaiah 36:8, 9, 12; Jeremiah 37:20, 38:9; Daniel 1:10, 10:16, 17 (2x), 19, 12:8; Zechariah 1:9, 4:4, 5, 13, 6:4.

The following 24 uses can be found under (*l'adoni*), "to my Lord." While we in English separate the preposition from the noun or verb following, in Hebrew the preposition is attached directly to the word. Genesis 24:3, 54, 56, 32:5, 6, 19, 44:9, 16, 33; 1 Samuel 24:7, 25:27, 28, 30, 31; 2 Samuel 4:8, 19:29; 1 Kings 1:2, 18:13, 20:9; 1 Chronicles 21:3; Psalms 110:1. All these refer to human lords, not God.

The following 6 references can be found under (*v'adoni*): Genesis 18:12; Numbers 36:2; 2 Samuel 11:11, 14:20, 19:28, 24:3.

The following reference can be found under (*m_adoni*): Genesis 47:18.

Students of Hebrew know that the original text was written in an "unpointed" form, i.e., without the dots, dashes and marks that are now the written vowels. Thus some scholars may point out that since the vowel points of the Hebrew text were added later, the rabbis could have been mistaken. It should be pointed out, however, that the two Hebrew words, *adonai* and *adoni*, even though written the same in unpointed text, sound different when pronounced. This is not unusual in a language. "Read" and "read" are spelled the same, but one can be pronounced "red," as in "I read the book yesterday," while the other is pronounced "reed," as in "Please read the book to me." The correct way to place the vowels in the text would have been preserved in the oral tradition of the Jews. Thus when the text was finally written with the vowels it would have been written as it was always pronounced.

Further evidence that the Jews always thought that the word in Psalm 110:1 referred to a human Messiah and not God come to earth is given in the Greek text, both in the Septuagint and in quotations in the New Testament. It is important to remember that the Septuagint, the Greek translation of the Hebrew Old Testament, was made about 250 B.C., long before the Trinitarian debates started. Yet

---

10. Geoffrey Bromiley, *The International Standard Bible Encyclopedia* (Eerdmans, Grand Rapids, MI, 1979), "Lord."

11. WTT or BHS Hebrew Old Testament, edited by K. Elliger and W. Rudoph of Deutsche Bibelgesellschoft, Stuttgart, fourth corrected edition, copyright © 1966, 1977, 1983, 1990 by the German Bible Society.

the Septuagint translation is clearly supportive of Psalm 110:1 referring to a human lord, not God. It translates *adoni* as *ho kurios mou*.

> The translators of the LXX [the Septuagint] in the 3rd century B.C. attest to a careful distinction between the forms of *adon* used for divine and human reference by translating *adoni* as *ho kurios mou*, "my lord."[12]

When Psalm 110:1 is quoted in the New Testament the same truth about the human lordship of the Messiah is preserved:

> The New Testament, when it quotes Psalm 110:1, renders *l'adoni* as "to my lord" (*to kurio mou*). But it renders *adonai* ([Psalm 110] v. 5 and very often elsewhere) as "the Lord" (*kurios*). This proves that the difference between *adonai* and *adoni* was recognized and reported in Greek long before the Masoretic vowel points fixed the ancient, oral tradition permanently in writing.[13]

It is interesting that scholars have often not paid close attention to the text of Psalm 110 or the places it is quoted in the New Testament, and have stated that it shows that Christ must have been God. The well-known *Smith's Bible Dictionary* contains an article on "Son of God," written by Ezra Abbot. He writes:

> Accordingly we find that, after the Ascension, the Apostles labored to bring the Jews to acknowledge that Jesus was not only the *Christ*, but was *also* a *Divine* Person, even the *Lord* Jehovah. Thus, for example, St. Peter…[Abbot goes on to say how Peter said that God had made Jesus "both Lord and Christ."][14]

We believe Abbot's conclusion is faulty because he did not pay attention to the exact wording of the Hebrew text. Even scholars who contributed to *Smith's Dictionary of the Bible* apparently agree, because there is a footnote after the above quotation that corrects it. The footnote states:

> In ascribing to St. Peter the remarkable proposition that "God hath made Jesus JEHOVAH," the writer of the article appears to have overlooked the fact that *kurion* ("Lord") in Acts 2:36 refers to *to kurio mou* ("my Lord") in verse 34, quoted from Ps. 110:1, where the Hebrew correspondent is not Jehovah but *adon*, the common word for "lord" or "master." St. Peters meaning here may be illustrated by his language elsewhere; see Acts 5:31 [where Peter calls Jesus a "prince," etc.].[15]

The footnote is quite correct, for the word in Psalm 110 is the word for a "lord" or "master" and not God. Thus Psalm 110:1 gives us very clear evidence that the expected Messiah of God was not going to be God himself, but a created being. The Jews listening to Peter on the Day of Pentecost would clearly see the correlation in Peter's teaching that Jesus was a "man approved of God" (v. 22 - KJV), and a created being, the "my lord" of Psalm 110:1 which Peter quoted just shortly thereafter (v. 34). The use of *adoni* in the first verse of Psalm 110:1 makes it very clear that the Jews were not expecting their Messiah to be God, but were expecting a human "lord."

---

12. Buzzard and Hunting, *op. cit.*, *The Trinity, Christianity's Self-inflicted Wound*, p. 28.
13. Buzzard, *op. cit.*, *Focus on the Kingdom*, "*Who is Jesus? God or Unique Man?*," p. 8.
14. H. B. Hackett, *Dr. William Smith's Dictionary of the Bible*, "Son of God" (Baker Book House, Grand Rapids, MI, reprint 1981), Vol. 4, p. 3090.
15. *Ibid.*, Vol. 4, p. 3090.

Proverbs 8:23
I [wisdom] was appointed from eternity, from the beginning, before the world began.

Occasionally, a Trinitarian will use this verse to try to support the Trinity and the pre-existence of Christ by saying that "wisdom" was appointed from eternity, Christ is the "wisdom of God" (1 Cor. 1:24) and, therefore, Christ was from eternity. This position has not found strong support even among Trinitarians, and for good reason. This wisdom in Proverbs was "appointed" (literally, "set up") by God, and is therefore subordinate to God. Carefully reading the verse and its context shows that wisdom was "...brought forth as the first of his works..." (v. 22). If this "wisdom" were Christ, then Christ would be the first creation of God, which is an Arian belief and heretical to orthodox Trinitarians. Therefore many of the Church Fathers rejected this verse as supportive of the Trinity, among them such "heavyweights" as Athanasius, Basil, Gregory, Epiphanius and Cyril. We reject it also, but for different reasons. Taking a concept and speaking of it as if it were a person is the figure of speech *Personification*. *Personification* often makes it easier to relate to a concept or idea because, as humans, we are familiar with relating to other humans. *Personification* was common among the Jews, and the wisdom of God is personified in Proverbs. Christ is considered the wisdom of God in Corinthians because of what God accomplishes through him.

Op. cit., Racovian Catechism, pp. 73–75.

Isaiah 7:14
Therefore the Lord himself will give you a sign: The virgin will be with child and will give birth to a son, and will call him Immanuel.

Some people believe that because Jesus was to be called "Immanuel" ("God with us"), he must be God incarnate. That is not the case, and for a full explanation of this, see the note on Matthew 1:23 below.

Isaiah 9:6b
...And he will be called Wonderful Counselor, Mighty God, Everlasting Father, Prince of Peace."

1. Trinitarians should admit that this verse is translated improperly just from the fact that Jesus is never called the "Everlasting Father" anywhere else in Scripture. Indeed, Trinitarians correctly deny that Jesus is the "Everlasting Father." It is a basic tenet of Trinitarian doctrine that Christians should "neither confound the Persons nor divide the Substance" (Athanasian Creed). Thus, if this verse is translated properly, then Trinitarian Christians have a real problem. However, the phrase is mistranslated. The word translated "everlasting" is actually "age," and the correct translation is that Jesus will be called "father of the [coming] age."

In the culture of the Bible, anyone who began anything or was very important to something was called its "father." For example, because Jabal was the first one to live in a tent and raise livestock, the Bible says, "...he was the father of those who live in tents and raise livestock" (Gen. 4:20). Furthermore, because Jubal was the first inventor of musical instruments, he is called, "...the father of all who play the harp and flute" (Gen. 4:21). Scripture is not using "father" in the sense of literal father or ancestor in these verses, because both these men were descendants of Cain, and all their descendants died in the Flood. "Father" was being used in the cultural understanding of either one who was the first to do something or someone who was important in some way. Because the Messiah will be the one to establish the age to come, raise the dead into it, and rule over it, he is called "the father of the coming age."

2. The phrase "Mighty God" can also be better translated. Although the word "God" in the Hebrew culture had a much wider range of application than it does in ours, the average reader does not know or understand that. Readers familiar with the Semitic languages know that a man who is acting with God's authority can be called "god." Although English makes a clear distinction between "God" and "god," the Hebrew language, which has only capital letters, cannot. A better translation for the English reader would be "mighty hero," or "divine hero." Both Martin Luther and James Moffatt translated the phrase as "divine hero" in their Bibles. (For more on the flexible use of "God," see the notes on Heb. 1:8).

3. A clear example that the word translated "God" in Isaiah 9:6 can be used of powerful earthly rulers is Ezekiel 31:11, referring to the Babylonian king. The Trinitarian bias of most translators can be clearly seen by comparing Isaiah 9:6 (*el* = "God") with Ezekiel 31:11 (*el* = "ruler"). If calling the Messiah *el* made him God, then the Babylonian king would be God also. Isaiah is speaking of God's Messiah and calling him a mighty ruler, which of course he will be.

The phrase translated "Mighty God" in Isaiah 9:6 in the NIV in the Hebrew, *el gibbor*. That very phrase, in the plural form, is used Ezekiel 32:21 where dead "heroes" and mighty men are said, by the figure of speech personification, to speak to others. The phrase in Ezekiel is translated "mighty leaders" in the NIV, and "The strong among the mighty..." in the KJV and NASB. The Hebrew phrase, when used in the singular, can refer to one "mighty leader" just as when used in the plural it can refer to many "mighty leaders."

4. The context illuminates great truth about the verse, and also shows that there is no justification for believing that it refers to the Trinity, but rather to God's appointed ruler. The opening verse of the chapter foretells a time when "...there will be no more gloom for those in distress." All war and death will cease, and "Every warrior's boot...will be destined for burning..." (v. 5). How will this come to pass? The chapter goes on: "For to us a child is born, to us a son is given..." (v. 6). There is no hint that this child will be "God," and reputable Trinitarian scholars will assert that the Jews of the Old Testament knew nothing of an "incarnation." For them, the Messiah was going to be a man anointed by God. He would start as a child, which of course Yahweh, their eternal God, could never be. And what a great ruler this man would grow to be: "...the government will be on his shoulders. And he will be called Wonderful Counselor, Mighty Hero, Father of the Coming Age, Prince of Peace." Furthermore, "...He will reign on David's throne... (v. 7), which could never be said of God. *God* could never sit on *David's* throne. But God's Messiah, "the Son of David," could (Matt. 9:27, *et al.*). Thus, a study of the verse in its context reveals that it does not refer to the Trinity at all, but to the Messiah, the son of David and the Son of God.

Buzzard, *op. cit., Doctrine of the Trinity*, pp. 45 and 51; Farley, *op. cit., Unitarianism Defined: The Scripture Doctrine of the Father, Son, and Holy Ghost*, pp. 47–49; Morgridge, *op. cit., True Believer's Defence Against Charges Preferred by Trinitarians*, pp. 105 and 106; Snedeker, *op. cit., Our Heavenly Father Has No Equals*, pp. 397–403.

Isaiah 11:10

In that day the Root of Jesse will stand as a banner for the peoples; the nations will rally to him, and his place of rest will be glorious.

See the note on Revelation 5:5.

Isaiah 43:11

I, even I, am the LORD, and apart from me there is no savior.

For the usage of Savior in the Bible, see notes on Luke 1:47 and Chapter 17, under the heading "Can Only God Save?"

Isaiah 44:6

"This is what the LORD says— Israel's King and Redeemer, the LORD Almighty: I am the first and I am the last; apart from me there is no God.

See the notes on Revelation 1:17.

Jeremiah 17:5

This is what the LORD says: "Cursed is the one who trusts in man, who depends on flesh for his strength and whose heart turns away from the LORD.

Occasionally, a Trinitarian will argue that Jesus cannot be a man because we are expected to trust Jesus, but not to trust men. We feel that analysis misses the point of this verse, and we remind the reader that the entire verse and its context must be read to get its proper meaning. The immediate context reveals that a person is cursed if he trusts man *and also* turns his heart away from the LORD. But we are not turning our hearts away from God by trusting in His Son Jesus. On the contrary, "… He who does not honor the Son does not honor the Father…" (John 5:23). God is the one who made Jesus our Lord and Head of the Church. Indeed, our hearts would be turning from the LORD if we did *not* trust Jesus. This same logic applies to other servants of God. The people were not cursed when they followed Moses, or Joshua, or David, and trusted in what they said, because these men were acting for God. Exodus 14:31 says the people trusted God and Moses. The husband of the virtuous woman is blessed when he trusts in his wife, as Proverbs 31:11 (KJV) says, "The heart of her husband doth safely trust in her…." Truth is never obtained by taking a piece or a part of a verse and ignoring its context. The entire Bible is God's Word, and it must be handled in a holy and godly way, with diligence and dignity and attention to the entire context. Grabbing a piece of a verse and forcing it to take on a meaning not fitting to the context, just to substantiate a theology, is never appropriate.

Op. cit., Racovian Catechism, pp. 155 and 156.

Jeremiah 23:6b

…This is the name by which he will be called: the LORD our Righteousness.

---

1. When something is "called" a certain name, that does not mean that it is literally what it is called. Jerusalem is also called "the LORD our Righteousness," and Jerusalem is obviously not God (Jer. 33:16). So, calling something "the LORD our Righteousness" does not make it God. Abraham called the mountain on which he was about to sacrifice Isaac "the LORD will provide," and no one would believe that the mountain was Yahweh. Similarly, no one would believe an altar was Yahweh, even if Moses called it that: "Moses built an altar and called it the LORD is my Banner" (Exod. 17:15). Later, Gideon built an altar and called it Yahweh: "So Gideon built an altar to the LORD there and called it The LORD is Peace. To this day it stands in Ophrah of the Abiezrites" (Judg. 6:24). These verses prove conclusively that just because something is called Yahweh, that does not make it Yahweh.

2. The Messiah will be *called* (not will *be*) "the LORD our Righteousness" because God Almighty will work His righteousness through His anointed one, Jesus the Christ. The city of Jerusalem will also be called "the LORD our Righteousness" because God will work His righteousness there, and that righteousness will reach over the entire world (For more on "names" and "called," see the notes on Matt. 1:23).

> Farley, *op. cit., Unitarianism Defined: The Scripture Doctrine of the Father, Son, and Holy Ghost*, pp. 49 and 50; *Op. cit., Racovian Catechism*, pp. 76–78; Snedeker, *op. cit., Our Heavenly Father Has No Equals*, pp. 403–406.

Micah 5:2

"But you, Bethlehem Ephrathah, though you are small among the clans of Judah, out of you will come for me one who will be ruler over Israel, whose origins are from of old, from ancient times."

---

1. "Origins" literally signifies a "going out," hence a beginning or birth, and thus the verse is saying that the birth of the Messiah has been determined, or appointed, from everlasting. In contrast to the Messiah who had an origin, the true God is without origin.

2. The ancient Jews read this verse and realized that it spoke of the birth and birthplace of the Messiah. One of the few things the Jews at the time of Jesus did understand about the Messiah was that he would be born in Bethlehem (Matt. 2:3–6). Yet of the Jews who read, studied, and understood the verse, there is no record that any of them concluded from the wording that Jesus had to be "God incarnate."

3. The context of Micah makes it clear that the "ruler" from Bethlehem will not be God. This ruler will be born, and have "brothers." No Jew ever thought *God* could be born, and the thought of the Creator of the heavens and earth having brothers was absurd to them. These verses are speaking of God's Anointed King, and the Word declares, not that this ruler will be God, but rather that Yahweh will be "his God" (v. 4). Thus, this text of Micah is clear: a child will be born in Bethlehem and the Israelites will be his brothers, but he will grow up to deliver and rule the nation and stand in the strength of Yahweh his God.

Morgridge, *op. cit., True Believer's Defence Against Charges Preferred by Trinitarians*, p. 120; *Op. cit., Racovian Catechism*, pp. 69–71.

Matthew 1:23 (KJV)

Behold, a virgin shall be with child, and shall bring forth a son, and they shall call his name Emmanuel, which being interpreted is, God with us.

---

1. The name can be translated as, "God with us" or "God is with us." We know that God was with the people in Jesus Christ, and Jesus himself said that if one had seen him, he had seen the Father.

2. The significance of the name is symbolic. God was with us, not literally, but in His Son, as 2 Cor. 5:19 (NASB) indicates: "…that God was in Christ, reconciling the world to Himself…." It is important to read exactly what was written: God was *in* Christ, not God *was* Christ. Symbolism in names can be seen throughout the Bible. It is not unique to Jesus Christ. Many people were given names that would cause great problems if believed literally. Are we to believe that Elijah was "God Yahweh," or that Bithiah, a daughter of Pharaoh, was the sister of Jesus because her name is "daughter of Yahweh?" Are we to believe that Dibri, not Jesus, was the "Promise of Yahweh," or that Eliab was the real Messiah since his name means "My God [is my] father?" Of course not. It would be a great mistake to claim that the meaning of a name proves a literal truth. We know that Jesus' name is very significant—it communicates the truth that, as the Son of God and as the image of God, God is with us in Jesus, but the name does not make Jesus God. For more on the fact that calling something does not make it that thing, see the notes on Jeremiah 23:6.

Buzzard, *op. cit., Doctrine of the Trinity*, p. 135; Farley, *op. cit., Unitarianism Defined: The Scripture Doctrine of the Father, Son, and Holy Ghost*, pp. 46 and 47; Morgridge, *op. cit., True Believer's Defence Against Charges Preferred by Trinitarians*, p. 119; Snedeker, *op. cit., Our Heavenly Father Has No Equals*, pp. 355–359.

Matthew 4:10

Jesus said to him, "Away from me, Satan! For it is written: 'Worship the Lord your God, and serve Him only.'"

---

1. It is sometimes stated that since we are to worship only God, and, because we are also supposed to worship Jesus, therefore he must be God. That argument is not valid because, although there is a special worship that is reserved just for God, we can "worship" certain people as well. This is an issue of the heart. There is no special word for "worship" reserved only for God. The special worship due Him comes from the heart. In fact the entire temptation of Christ by the Devil proves that Jesus was not God. God cannot be tempted (James 1:13). Also, if Jesus were God, the Devil would never have asked Jesus to worship him. It was for desiring to be like God (and thus be worshiped like God) that the Devil was thrown out of heaven in the first place (Isa. 14:12–15), and it is unreasonable to think that the Devil would have believed that God could now be persuaded to worship him.

2. In the biblical culture, the act of worship was not directed only to God. It was very common to worship (i.e., pay homage to) men of a higher status. This is hard to see in the English translations of the Bible. The translators usually translate the same Hebrew or Greek word as "worship" when it involves God, but as some other word, such as "bow before," or "pay homage to," when it involves men. Nevertheless, worship is clearly there in the Hebrew and Greek texts. For example:

- Lot "worshipped" the two strangers [they were angels, but Lot did not know it] that came to Sodom (Gen. 19:1).
- Abraham "worshipped" the pagan leaders of the land in which he lived (Gen. 23:7).
- Jacob "worshipped" his older brother when they met after being apart for years (Gen. 33:3).
- Joseph had a dream that his parents and brothers "worshipped" him (Gen. 37:10).
- Joseph's brothers "worshipped" him (Gen. 43:26).
- Joshua fell down and "worshipped" an angel (Josh. 5:14).
- Ruth "worshipped" Boaz (Ruth 2:10).
- David "worshipped" Jonathan (1 Sam. 20:41).
- Abigail "worshipped" David (1 Sam. 25:41).

The above list is just a small sampling of all the examples that could be drawn from Scripture. Checking the references in most Bibles will confirm what has already been pointed out—that the translators avoided the word "worship" when men are worshipping men, but used it in reference to worshipping God. These Scriptures are more than enough proof that "worship" was a part of the culture, and a way of showing respect or reverence. Because of the theological stance that only God should be worshipped, translators have avoided the English word "worship," in spite of the fact that it is clearly in the original text. We assert that not translating what is clearly in the text has created a false impression in the Christian community. It is very clear in the biblical text that men "worshipped" men.

There is a sense, of course, in which there is a very special worship (homage, allegiance, reverent love and devotion) to be given only to God, but there is no unique word that represents that special worship. Rather, it is a posture of the heart. Scripturally, this must be determined from context. Even words like *proskuneo*, which are almost always used of God, are occasionally used for showing respect to other men (Acts 10:25). And the word "serve" in Matthew 4:10 is *latreuo*, which is sometimes translated worship, but used of the worship of other things as well as of the true God (Acts 7:42 - KJV), "…worship the host of heaven…" and Romans 1:25, "served created things"). Thus, when Christ said, "**You shall worship the Lord thy God and Him only shall you worship**," he was speaking of a special worship of God that comes from the heart, not using a special vocabulary word that is reserved for the worship of God only.

Understanding that in the Bible both God and men are worshipped forces us as readers to look, not at the specific word for "worship," but rather at the heart of the one doing the worship. It explains why God rejects the worship of those whose hearts are really not with Him. It also explains why there are occasions in the Bible when men reject the worship of other men. In Acts 10:26, Peter asks Cornelius to stand up. In Revelation 19:10, an angel stops John from worshipping him. In these cases it is not the worship, *per se*, that was wrong, or it would have been wrong in all the other places throughout the Bible. In the aforementioned accounts, the one about to be worshipped saw that it was inappropriate or felt uncomfortable in the situation. Actually, the example of John in Revelation is another strong proof that men did worship others beside God. *If it were forbidden to worship anyone beside God, the great Apostle John would never have even started to worship the angel.* The fact that he did so actually proves the point that others beside God were worshipped in the biblical culture.

It is clear why people fell down and worshipped Jesus while he walked the earth and performed great miracles: people loved him and respected him greatly. It is also clear why we are to worship him now—he has earned our love and our highest reverence. He died to set us free, and God has honored him by seating him at His own right hand above all other powers and authorities.

Broughton, James and Southgate, Peter, *The Trinity, True or False?* (The Dawn Book Supply, 66 Carlton Rd., Nottingham, England, 1995), pp. 194 and 195; Dana, Mary S. B., *Letters Addressed to Relatives and Friends, Chiefly in Reply to Arguments in Support of the Doctrine of the Trinity*, (James Munroe and Co., Boston, 1845. Reprinted 1994 by Spirit & Truth Fellowship International, 180 Robert Curry Drive, Martinsville, IN 46151), p. 21; Morgridge, *op. cit., True Believer's Defence Against Charges Preferred by Trinitarians*, pp. 46–52; Norton, Andrews, *A Statement of Reasons for Not Believing the Doctrines of Trinitarians*, (Boston: American Unitarian Association, 10th edition, 1877), pp. 447 and 448; Snedeker, *op. cit., Our Heavenly Father Has No Equals*, pp. 389 and 390.

Matthew 9:2 and 3
(2) Some men brought to him a paralytic, lying on a mat. When Jesus saw their faith, he said to the paralytic, "Take heart, son; your sins are forgiven."
(3) At this, some of the teachers of the law said to themselves, "This fellow is blaspheming!"

This is a similar record to Mark 2:7 and the explanation can be found there.

Matthew 9:8b
…they praised God, who had given such authority unto men.

Although this verse is sometimes used to "prove" that Christ is God, the verse actually militates against the idea. Scripture states very clearly that Jesus was a *man*. The only "man" with authority in the entire context is Jesus. When the crowd saw Jesus performing miracles, they praised God for giving such power to the man, Jesus. We do the exact same thing today. For example, Christians praise God for giving such a powerful outreach ministry to Billy Graham. We trust that no one would think we Christians are saying that Dr. Graham is God just because we believe God has given him power.

Snedeker, *op. cit., Our Heavenly Father Has No Equals*, p. 306.

Matthew 28:18
Then Jesus came to them and said, "All authority in heaven and on earth has been given to me.

Carefully reading a verse is the only way to begin to properly interpret it. In this case, it is clear that Christ's authority was *given* to him. Many other Scriptures say the same thing: "…God has **made** …Jesus…both Lord and Christ" (Acts 2:36). God "placed" everything under his feet and "appointed" him to be Head of the Church (Eph. 1:22). If Christ were really God, and co-equal and co-eternal with the Father as the Trinitarians teach, then it is illogical to say Christ was *given* authority. God, by definition, *has* authority. The authority Jesus now has is delegated and derived, and is not a function of his "divine nature." The wording of these Scriptures is, in actuality, a refutation of the Trinity. Jesus is that man to whom God gave "all authority."

Dana, *op. cit., Letters Addressed to Relatives and Friends,* p. 215.

Matthew 28:19
Therefore go and make disciples of all nations, baptizing them in the name of the Father and of the Son and of the Holy Spirit,

---

1. Eusebius (ca. 260—ca. 340) was the Bishop of Caesarea and is known as "the Father of Church History." Although he wrote prolifically, his most celebrated work is his *Ecclesiastical History*, a history of the Church from the Apostolic period until his own time. Today it is still the principal work on the history of the Church at that time. Eusebius quotes many verses in his writings, and Matthew 28:19 is one of them. He never quotes it as it appears today in modern Bibles, but always finishes the verse with the words "**in my name**." For example, in Book III of his *History*, Chapter 5, Section 2, which is about the Jewish persecution of early Christians, we read:

> But the rest of the apostles, who had been incessantly plotted against with a view to their destruction, and had been driven out of the land of Judea, went unto all nations to preach the Gospel, relying upon the power of Christ, who had said to them, "Go ye and make disciples of all the nations **in my name**."

Again, in his *Oration in Praise of Emperor Constantine*, Chapter 16, Section 8, we read:

> What king or prince in any age of the world, what philosopher, legislator or prophet, in civilized or barbarous lands, has attained so great a height of excellence, I say not after death, but while living still, and full of mighty power, as to fill the ears and tongues of all mankind with the praises of his name? Surely none save our only Savior has done this, when, after his victory over death, he spoke the word to his followers, and fulfilled it by the event, saying to them, "Go ye and make disciples of all nations **in my name**."

Eusebius was present at the council of Nicaea and was involved in the debates about Arian teaching and whether Christ was God or a creation of God. We feel confident that if the manuscripts he had in front of him read "in the name of the Father, and of the Son and of the Holy Spirit," he would never have quoted it as "in my name." Thus, **we believe that the earliest manuscripts read "in my name,"** and that the phrase was enlarged to reflect the orthodox position as Trinitarian influence spread.

2. If Matthew 28:19 is accurate as it stands in modern versions, then there is no explanation for the apparent disobedience of the Apostles, since there is not a single occurrence of them baptizing anyone according to that formula. All the records in the New Testament show that people were baptized into the name of the Lord Jesus, just as the text Eusebius was quoting said to do. In other words, the "name of Jesus Christ," i.e., all that he represents, is the element, or substance, into which people were figuratively "baptized." "Peter replied, 'Repent and be baptized, every one of you, in the **name** of Jesus Christ for the forgiveness of your sins...'" (Acts 2:38). "...they had simply been baptized into the **name** of the Lord Jesus" (Acts 8:16). "So he ordered that they be baptized in the **name** of Jesus Christ..." (Acts 10:48). "On hearing this, they were baptized into the **name** of the Lord Jesus" (Acts 19:5). We cannot imagine any reason for the Apostles and others in Acts to disobey a command of the risen Christ. To us, it seems clear that Christ said to baptize in his **name**, and that was what the early Church did.

3. Even if the Father, Son and holy spirit are mentioned in the original text of this verse, that does not prove the Trinity. The doctrine of the Trinity states that the Father, Son and "Holy Spirit" together make "one God." This verse refers to three, but never says they are "one." The three things this verse refers to are: God the Father, the Lord Jesus and the power of holy spirit (We say "holy spirit" instead of "Holy Spirit" because we believe that this verse is referring to God's gift of holy spirit that is born inside each believer. It is lower case because it refers to the gift of God and not God. The original Greek texts were all written in what scholars call "uncial script," which uses all capital letters. Thus, although we today make a distinction between "Spirit" and "spirit," in the originals every use was just "SPIRIT." Whether or not it should be capitalized is a translator's decision, based on the context of the verse. For more on the form of the early texts, see the note on Heb. 1:8).

It should be clear that three separate things do not make "one God." Morgridge writes:

> No passage of Scripture asserts that God is three. If it be asked what I intend to qualify by the numeral three, I answer, anything which the reader pleases. There is no Scripture which asserts that God is three persons, three agents, three beings, three Gods, three spirits, three substances, three modes, three offices, three attributes, three divinities, three infinite minds, three somewhats, three opposites, or three in any sense whatever. The truth of this has been admitted by every Trinitarian who ever wrote or preached on the subject."

4. It is sometimes stated that in order to be baptized into something, that something has to be God, but that reasoning is false, because Scripture states that the Israelites were "baptized into Moses" (1 Cor. 10:2).

5. It is sometimes stated that the Father, Son and spirit have one "name," so they must be one. It is a basic tenet of Trinitarian doctrine not to "confound the persons" (Athanasian Creed), and it does indeed confound the persons to call all three of them by one "name," especially since no such "name" is ever given in Scripture ("God" is not a name). If the verse were teaching Trinitarian doctrine and mentioned the three "persons," then it should use the word "names." There is a much better explanation for why "name" is used in the singular.

A study of the culture and language shows that the word "name" stood for "authority." Examples are very numerous, but space allows only a small selection. Deuteronomy 18:5 and 7 speak of serving in the "name" (authority) of the LORD. Deuteronomy 18:22 speaks of prophesying in the "name" (authority) of the LORD. In 1 Samuel 17:45, David attacked Goliath in the "name" (authority) of the LORD, and he blessed the people in the "name" (authority) of the LORD. In 2 Kings 2:24, Elisha cursed troublemakers in the "name" (authority) of the LORD. These Scriptures are only a small sample, but they are very clear. If the modern versions of Matthew 28:19 are correct (which we doubt, see above), then we would still not see this verse as proving the Trinity. Rather, they would be showing the importance of the three: the Father who is God, the Son (who was given authority by God [Matt. 28:18]) and the holy spirit, which is the gift of God.

6. In reading the book of Matthew, we note that there is no presentation of the doctrine of the Trinity. Some prominent Trinitarians doubt that the Apostles were even introduced to the doctrine until after they received holy spirit. It would be strange indeed for Christ to introduce the doctrine of the Trinity here in the next-to-last verse in the book without it being mentioned earlier.

Morgridge, *op. cit., True Believer's Defence Against Charges Preferred by Trinitarians,* pp. 13–15, 28, 98–101; Norton, *op. cit., A Statement of Reasons for Not Believing the Doctrines of Trinitarians*, pp. 215–218; *Op. cit., Racovian Catechism*, pp. 36–39; Snedeker, *op. cit., Our Heavenly Father Has No Equals*, pp. 109–115.

Matthew 28:20b
…And surely I am with you always, to the very end of the age."

Occasionally this verse is used to prove the Trinity because it is said that the only way that Jesus could always be with his Church is if he were God. However, that is an unproven assumption, and is not stated in Scripture. Scripture shows us that there is a use of "with us" that is spiritual in nature, not physical. We must be careful not to underestimate the power and authority God gave Christ when He set him at His own right hand and gave him a name that is above every name. Just two verses before this one, Christ said he had been given "all authority." God gave Christ all authority, and made Christ Head of the Church, so it is only logical to conclude that God also gave Christ the power to stay in communion with his Church.

Snedeker, *op. cit., Our Heavenly Father Has No Equals*, pp. 408 and 409.

Mark 2:7
Why does this fellow talk like that? He's blaspheming! Who can forgive sins but God alone?"

On several occasions the Lord Jesus told the Pharisees that their doctrine was wrong. Mark 2:7 records an instance where this was the case. There is no verse of Scripture that says, "only God can forgive sins." That idea came from their tradition. The truth is that God grants the authority to forgive sins as He pleases. He granted that authority to the Son and, furthermore, to the Apostles. John 20:23 records Jesus saying to them: "If you forgive anyone his sins, they are forgiven…." If the Pharisees were right, and only God can forgive sins, then God, Jesus and the Apostles were all God, because they all had the authority to forgive sins.

Buzzard, *op. cit., Doctrine of the Trinity*, pp. 21 and 22; Morgridge, *op. cit., True Believer's Defence Against Charges Preferred by Trinitarians*, pp. 127 and 128.

Luke 1:35
The angel answered, "The Holy Spirit will come upon you, and the power of the Most High will overshadow you. So the holy one to be born will be called the Son of God.

---

1. There are some Trinitarians who insist that the term "Son of God" implies a pre-existence and that Jesus is God. Once the doctrine of pre-existence was propounded, a vocabulary had to be developed to support it, and thus non-biblical phrases such as "eternally begotten" and "eternal Son" were invented. Not only are these phrases not in the Bible or secular literature, they do not make sense. By definition, a "Son" has a beginning, and by definition, "eternal" means "without beginning." To put the two words together when they never appear together in the Bible or in common usage is doing nothing more than creating a nonsensical term. The meaning of "Son of God" is literal: God the Father impregnated Mary, and nine months later Mary had a son, Jesus. Thus, Jesus is "the Son of

God." "This is how the birth [Greek = "beginning"] of Jesus Christ came about…," says Matthew 1:18, and that occurred about 2000 years ago, not in "eternity past."

2. When the phrase "Son of God" is studied and compared with phrases about the Father, a powerful truth is revealed. The phrase "Son of God" is common in the New Testament, but the phrase "God the Son" never appears. In contrast, phrases like "God the Father," "God our Father," "the God and Father" and "God, even the Father" occur many times. Are we to believe that the Son is actually God just as the Father is, but the Father is plainly called "God, the Father" over and over and yet the Son is not even once called "God the Son"? This is surely strong evidence that Jesus is not actually "God the Son" at all.

3. Anyone insisting that someone is somehow God simply because he is called "Son of God" is going to run into trouble explaining all the verses in the Bible that call other beings "sons of God." The phrase, "son of God" was commonly used of angels in the Old Testament [see Gen. 6:2; Job 1:6, 2:1 (the phrase in these verses is often translated as "angels," but the KJV says "sons"), and used of Israel (Exod. 4:22; etc.)]. In the New Testament, it is used of Christians, those who are born of God (see 1 John 3:1 and 2—occasionally, "sons" gets translated into "children" to be more inclusive, but the original language is clear). A study of Scripture reveals quite clearly that "son of God" does not in any way mean "God."

4. Trying to prove the Trinity from the phrase "Son of God" brings up a point that often gets missed in debates about whether or not the Trinity exists, and that point has to do with words and the way they are defined. The Bible was not written in a vacuum, and its vocabulary was in common use in the culture of the times. Words that are spoken "on the street" every day have a meaning. If someone writes a letter, it is natural for the reader to assume that the definitions of the words in the letter are the definitions common to the contemporary culture. If the person writing uses the words in a new or unusual way, he would need to say that in the letter, or the reader might misunderstand what he was saying.

The word "son" is a good example. We know what the word means, and we know that if there is a father and a son, the son came *after* the father. God is clearly called the Father and Christ is clearly called the Son. Thus, the meaning should be simple and clear. But according to Trinitarian doctrine, the Father and Son are both "eternal." This teaching nullifies the clear definitions of the words and makes the vocabulary "mysterious." There is no place in Scripture where the meanings of the words describing the Son are said to be changed from their ordinary meaning to some "new and special" meaning.

To explain the problem their doctrine has created, Trinitarians say that the Son was "eternally begotten," but that phrase itself creates two problems. First, it is not in Scripture, and leads to the erroneous teaching that the Bible does not contain a vocabulary sufficient to explain its own doctrines. Second, the phrase itself is nonsense, and just lends to the belief that the Bible is basically "mysterious" and cannot be fathomed by the average Christian. After all, "eternal" means "without beginning," and "begotten" means "born," which clearly indicates a beginning. The fact that the two words are inherently contradictory is why we say that combining them makes a nonsense word.

The doctrine of the Trinity has caused a number of problems with the vocabulary of the New Testament. For example, Hebrews 1:2 mentions that Jesus Christ was made "heir" by God. By definition, no one is his own heir. To say that Christ is God and then say that Christ is the *heir* of God is nonsense, and abuses the vocabulary that God used to make His Word accessible to the common Christian and believable to those not yet saved. It changes the simple truth of the Bible into a "mystery" no one can understand.

There are many words that indicate that Jesus was not equal to the Father. Christ was "made Lord"; he was "appointed" by God; he "obeyed" God; he did God's will and not his own; he prayed to God; he called God "my God," etc., etc. Trinitarian teaching contradicts the conclusion that any unindoctrinated reader would arrive at when reading these Scriptures, and insists that the Father and the Son are co-equal. Trinitarians teach that the human nature (but not the God nature) of Christ was subservient to the Father and that is why the Bible is worded the way it is. We believe that teaching twists the clear and simple words of Scripture, and we point out that there is not one verse that says that Christ had two natures. Historians admit that the doctrine of the two natures was "clarified" late in the debates about the nature of Christ (actually six out of the seven Ecumenical Councils dealt in some way with the nature of Christ), and we believe that the only reason the doctrine of the two natures was invented was to support the Trinity.

The Trinitarian concept of the two natures also forces a "mysterious" interpretation of the otherwise clear verses about Jesus' humanity. Interpreting the verses about Jesus is quite simple. He was from the line of David and "…made like his brothers in every way…" (Heb. 2:17). He was "the Last Adam" (1 Cor. 15:45) because, like Adam, he was a direct creation of God. Over and over, the Bible calls him a "man." However, these words are less than genuine if Christ were both 100 percent God and 100 percent man. How can anyone honestly say that Jesus is both *fully* God and *fully* man, and then say that he is like his brothers in every way? The standard "explanation" given is that, "It is a mystery and no one can understand it." We ask the reader to consider carefully the choice before you. We are arguing for reading the words in the Bible and then just believing what they say. We assert that one cannot do that if he believes in the Trinity. Trinitarian doctrine forces the meanings of clear and simple words like "Father," "Son," "heir" and "man" to take on new and "mysterious" meanings.

Buzzard, *op. cit., Doctrine of the Trinity*, pp. 155–157; Morgridge, *op. cit., True Believer's Defence Against Charges Preferred by Trinitarians*, pp. 139–142.

Luke 1:47
…my spirit rejoices in God my Savior.

---

1. Some Trinitarians believe that Christ must be God because they are both called "Savior." There are many references to God the Father being called "Savior." That makes perfect sense because He is the author of the plan of salvation and is also very active in our salvation. For example, God, the Father, is called "Savior" in Isaiah 43:11; 1 Timothy 1:1, 2:3, 4:10; Titus 1:3, 2:10, 3:4; Jude 25. Jesus Christ is called "Savior" because he is the *agent* who carried out God's plan, and without whom it could not have come to pass.

2. The term "savior" is used of many people in the Bible. This is hard to see in the English versions because, when it is used of men, the translators almost always translated it as "deliverer." This in and of itself shows that modern translators have a Trinitarian bias that was not in the original languages. The only reason to translate the same word as "Savior" when it applies to God or Christ, but as "deliverer" when it applies to men, is to make the term seem unique to God and Jesus when in fact it is not. This is a good example of how the actual meaning of Scripture can be obscured if the translators are not careful when they translate the text. God's gracious provision of "saviors" is not recognized when the same word is translated "Savior" for God and Christ but "deliverer" for others. Also lost is the testimony in Scripture that God works through people to bring His power to bear. Of course, the fact that there are other "saviors" does not take away from Jesus Christ, who is the only one who could and did save us from our sins and eternal death.

If all the great men and women who were "saviors" were openly portrayed as such in the English versions, the grace and mercy God demonstrates in saving His people by "saviors" He has raised up would be openly displayed. Furthermore, we believe no reader would confuse the true God with the people He was working through. A good example that shows God raising up "saviors" to rescue Israel through history occurs in Nehemiah in a prayer of confession and thanksgiving to God. The Israelites prayed, "...But when they [Israel] were oppressed they cried out to you. From heaven you heard them, and in your great compassion you gave them deliverers [saviors], who rescued them from the hand of their enemies" (Neh. 9:27). Some other examples of men designated as "savior" are in 2 Kings 13:5; Isaiah 19:20; Obadiah 21. It is incorrect to say that because Christ and God are both called "Savior," they are one and the same, just as it would be incorrect to say that the "saviors" God raised up throughout history were the same individual as Jesus Christ.

Norton, *op. cit.*, *A Statement of Reasons for Not Believing the Doctrines of Trinitarians*, pp. 304 and 305; Snedeker, *op. cit.*, *Our Heavenly Father Has No Equals*, pp. 378–380.

Luke 5:20 and 21
(20) When Jesus saw their faith, he said, "Friend, your sins are forgiven."
(21) The Pharisees and the teachers of the law began thinking to themselves, "Who is this fellow who speaks blasphemy? Who can forgive sins but God alone?"

There are those who believe that only God can forgive sins, but that is not true. For an explanation applicable to this verse, see Mark 2:7.

Luke 7:16 (KJV)
And there came a fear on all: and they glorified God, saying, That a great prophet is risen up among us; and, That God hath visited his people.

---

1. Occasionally, Trinitarians will cite this verse as proof that Jesus is God, because it states that God visited His people. However, that phrase in no way proves the Trinity. Any word or phrase in Scripture must be interpreted in light of both its immediate and remote contexts. In this case, the immediate context alerts us to the truth being presented. The people called Jesus "a great prophet," which tells us right away that they did not think he was God.

2. God "visits" His people by sending them some blessing. This is clear from verses like Ruth 1:6 (KJV), "Then she [Naomi] arose with her daughters in law, that she might return from the country of Moab: for she had heard in the country of Moab how that the LORD had visited his people in giving them bread." In the book of Ruth, Yahweh visited His people by sending them bread, while, in the Gospels, God visited His people by sending them "a great prophet" who raised a widow's son from the dead.

3. A lesson we should learn from this verse and others like it is that God works through His people. When He does, He often gets the credit even when people do the actual work. When God works through people, the Word records things like, "...God has visited His people" (Luke 7:16 - NASB) and "...great things God has done..." (Luke 8:39 - NASB). Americans today use the same language. If an acquaintance gives you some money when you need it and says, "The Lord put it on my heart to give this to you," you might well say to someone else, "The Lord really blessed me today." Neither you nor any other person would believe that you were saying that the person who gave you money was "the Lord." Everyone understands that the Lord works through people, and so our language, like biblical language, reflects that knowledge.

Morgridge, *op. cit., True Believer's Defence Against Charges Preferred by Trinitarians*, p. 118.

Luke 8:39
"Return home and tell how much God has done for you." So the man went away and told all over town how much Jesus had done for him.

---

1. God works His miracles through people. Thus, whenever a miracle is performed, there are thanks for the one who stood in faith and performed the miracle, and also thanks and glory to God who supplied the power and actually did the work. The whole lesson of Hebrews 11, which speaks of the heroes of faith, is that almost always someone has to walk in faith for God's power to work, and the people listed in Hebrews 11 were "commended for their faith" (verse 39). So when Jesus performed miracles, it was not just he, but God acting also, just as it is when we, as Christians, do miracles, healings, etc. In fact, Jesus gave credit to the Father for what he was accomplishing. "The words I say to you are not just my own. Rather, it is the Father, living in me, who is doing his work" (John 14:10b).

2. The note on Matthew 9:8b is applicable to this verse.

Luke 10:18
He replied, "I saw Satan fall like lightning from heaven.

Some people use this verse to try to prove the Trinity or the pre-existence of Christ by saying that Jesus must have existed in the beginning with God because he witnessed the original war between God and Satan, and saw Satan thrown down to earth. However, that is not at all what the verse is saying. First, that interpretation makes no sense in the context. Jesus had sent out the disciples to preach the Good News, and had given them authority over demons. When they returned to report all they had done, they excitedly exclaimed, "...Lord, even the demons submit to us in your name" (Luke 10:17). To fully understand their excitement, we must remember that no one before then had ever exercised authority over demons. Neither Moses, nor David, nor Elijah, nor any Old Testament "heroes" did what these disciples were now doing, and they were excited about it, as well they should have been.

In response to their report, it does not make sense that Jesus would say that he had been around to see Satan cast out of heaven. Such a statement would be totally unrelated to what the disciples said, and also to the following verses, in which Jesus reconfirmed the authority they had and admonished them not to rejoice in their spiritual authority on earth, but that their "...names are written in heaven." Furthermore, there no reason to believe the disciples would have understood any reference to Satan falling from heaven millennia ago. Although it is true that Satan was cast to earth in one sense (Rev. 12:4; Isa. 14:12; Ezek. 28:17), it is also true that he is regularly in heaven. He shows up before God and accuses the believers (Job 1:6, 2:1; Rev. 12:10). The key to understanding Satan's presence in heaven now is to realize that there are two wars between God and the Devil mentioned in Revelation 12.

The first war, long ago, involved the dragon and one-third of the angels (Rev. 12:4). Satan was cast out of heaven, but more in the sense of heavenly authority and position than heavenly location. Scripture testifies that he comes before God regularly. The second war (Rev. 12:7–9), is still future. In this second war, Michael and his angels will fight the Devil and his angels, but the Devil will not be strong enough to retain his place in heaven.[16] He will be cast down to earth and denied any more access to heaven. Not surprisingly, this will cause great rejoicing in heaven among the angels who have had to listen to Satan's accusations.

Revelation 12:10 and 12

(10) Then I heard a loud voice in heaven say: "Now have come the salvation and the power and the kingdom of our God, and the authority of his Christ. For the accuser of our brothers, who accuses them before our God day and night, has been hurled down. (12) Therefore rejoice, you heavens and you who dwell in them! But woe to the earth and the sea, because the devil has gone down to you! He is filled with fury, because he knows that his time is short."

The angels will rejoice when the Devil is forced from heaven, but he will be enraged about being denied access to God, so he will viciously attack the "…woman who had given birth to the male child" (Rev. 12:13; in this verse, the woman is not Mary, but Israel, just as Israel is portrayed as a woman in many Old Testament verses). When the Dragon cannot destroy Israel, he will go after "…those who obey God's commandments… (Rev. 12:17).

God did not destroy the Devil when he rebelled the first time. In fact, because God is just, He has allowed the Devil to stand "before" Him, that is, in His presence, and accuse the believers. That is exactly what is portrayed in the book of Job and Revelation 12:10. However, shortly before the Battle of Armageddon, the Devil will be cast out of God's presence forever.

When Jesus spoke to his disciples about seeing Satan fall like lightning, they rightly believed, as should we, that Satan is regularly in the presence of God in heaven, accusing the believers. Therefore, it would not have occurred to them that Jesus was making a reference to seeing Satan ejected from heaven eons before, because to them (and anyone else reading and believing the book of Job), he had not been.

If Jesus did not mean that he had seen Satan fall from heaven ages ago, what did he mean? The tense of the verb "saw" gives us some help, because it shows us that Jesus was watching for a period of time, but not necessarily long ago. If Jesus had meant to say, "I have seen Satan cast out of heaven long ago," it seems the Greek would be worded quite differently. The NASB gets the tense of the verb correctly when it says, "…I was watching Satan fall from heaven like lightning."

Consider the situation of Jesus and his disciples: Satan was in heaven, standing before God and accusing the believers. Meanwhile, Satan's demons on earth were doing their evil work. Things seemed to be running smoothly enough when suddenly there was a major disruption of a kind that had not happened before. All over Israel demons were being cast out of people and their evil

---

16. A number of authors have written about this future war. A few of the notable ones are: E. W. Bullinger, *op. cit.,* *Commentary on Revelation*, pp. 403–412; Arnold Fruchtenbaum, *The Footsteps of the Messiah* (Ariel Ministry Press, Tustin, CA, 1982), pp. 165 and 166; Henry Morris, *The Revelation Record* (Tyndale House Publishers, Wheaton, IL, 1983), pp. 223–228; John Walvoord, *The Revelation of Jesus Christ* (Moody Press, Chicago, 1966), pp. 191–194.

work was being disrupted—by people! The local demons did not know what to do; they had never encountered people with the authority to cast them out, and they needed guidance. Satan responded by coming quickly from heaven, falling like lightning to try to repair the damage being done to his evil kingdom. God showed this to Jesus to show him the powerful impact that his disciples were having, and no doubt to give him a vision for the kind of things that could happen when thousands upon thousands of people, not just several dozen, would be empowered disciples.

John 1:1
In the beginning was the Word, and the Word was with God, and the Word was God.

---

1. It is imperative that the serious student of the Bible come to a basic understanding of *logos*, which is translated as "Word" in John 1:1. Most Trinitarians believe that the word *logos* refers directly to Jesus Christ, so in most versions of John *logos* is capitalized and translated "Word" (some versions even write "Christ" in John 1:1 - TLB & NLV). However, a study of the Greek word *logos* shows that it occurs more than 300 times in the New Testament, and in both the NIV and the KJV it is capitalized only 7 times (and even those versions disagree on exactly *when* to capitalize it). When a word that occurs more than 300 times is capitalized fewer than 10 times, it is obvious that when to capitalize and when not to capitalize is a translators' decision based on their particular understanding of Scripture.

As it is used throughout Scripture, *logos* has a very wide range of meanings along two basic lines of thought. One is the mind and products of the mind like "reason," (thus "logic" is related to *logos*) and the other is the expression of that reason as a "word," "saying," "command" etc. The Bible itself demonstrates the wide range of meaning *logos* has, and some of the ways it is translated in Scripture are: account, appearance, book, command, conversation, eloquence, flattery, grievance, heard, instruction, matter, message, ministry, news, proposal, question, reason, reasonable, reply, report, rule, rumor, said, say, saying, sentence, speaker, speaking, speech, stories, story, talk, talking, teaching, testimony, thing, things, this, truths, what, why, word and words.

Any good Greek lexicon will also show this wide range of meaning (the words in **bold** are translated from *logos*):

- speaking; words you say (Rom. 15:18, "...what I have **said** and done").
- a statement you make (Luke 20:20 - (NASB), "...they might catch Him in some **statement**...").
- a question (Matt. 21:24, "...I will also ask you one **question**...").
- preaching (1 Tim. 5:17, "...especially those whose work is **preaching** and teaching).
- command (Gal. 5:14, "The entire law is summed up in a single **command**...").
- proverb; saying (John 4:37, "Thus the **saying**, 'One sows, and another reaps...'").
- message; instruction; proclamation (Luke 4:32, "his **message** had authority").
- assertion; declaration; teaching (John 6:60, "...This is a hard **teaching**...").
- the subject under discussion; matter (Acts 8:21, "You have no part or share in this **ministry**...." Acts 15:6 (NASB), "And the apostles...came together to look into this **matter**").
- revelation from God (Matt. 15:6, "...you nullify the **word of God**...").
- God's revelation spoken by His servants (Heb. 13:7, "...leaders, who spoke the **word of God**...").
- a reckoning, an account (Matt. 12:36, "...men will have to give **account**" on the day of judgment...).
- an account or "matter" in a financial sense (Matt. 18:23, ...a king who wanted to settle "**accounts**" with his servants. Phil. 4:15, "...the **matter** of giving and receiving...").

- a reason; motive (Acts 10:29 - NASB), "...I ask **for what reason** you have sent for me").[17]

The above list is not exhaustive, but it does show that *logos* has a very wide range of meaning. With all the definitions and ways *logos* can be translated, how can we decide which meaning of *logos* to choose for any one verse? How can it be determined what the *logos* in John 1:1 is? Any occurrence of *logos* has to be carefully studied in its context in order to get the proper meaning. We assert that the *logos* in John 1:1 cannot be Jesus. Please notice that "Jesus Christ" is not a lexical definition of *logos*. This verse does not say, "In the beginning was Jesus." "The Word" is not synonymous with Jesus, or even "the Messiah." The word *logos* in John 1:1 refers to God's creative self-expression—His reason, purposes and plans, especially as they are brought into action. It refers to God's self-expression, or communication, of Himself. This has come to pass through His creation (Rom. 1:19 and 20), and especially the heavens (Ps. 19). It has come through the spoken word of the prophets and through Scripture, the written Word. Most notably and finally, it has come into being through His Son (Heb. 1:1 and 2).

The renowned Trinitarian scholar, John Lightfoot, writes:

> The word *logos* then, denoting both "reason" and "speech," was a philosophical term adopted by Alexandrian Judaism before St. Paul wrote, to express the *manifestation* of the Unseen God in the creation and government of the World. It included all modes by which God makes Himself known to man. As His *reason*, it denoted His purpose or design; as His *speech*, it implied His revelation. **Christian teachers, when they adopted this term, exalted and fixed its meaning by attaching to it two precise and definite ideas: (1) "The Word is a Divine Person,"** (2) "The Word became incarnate in Jesus Christ." It is obvious that these two propositions must have altered materially the significance of all the subordinate terms connected with the idea of the *logos*.[18]

It is important to note that it was "Christian teachers" who attached the idea of a "divine person" to the word *logos*. It is certainly true that when the word *logos* came to be understood as being Jesus Christ, the understanding of John 1:1 was altered substantially. Lightfoot correctly understands that the early meaning of *logos* concerned reason and speech, not "Jesus Christ." Norton develops the concept of *logos* as "reason" and writes:

> There is no word in English answering to the Greek word *logos*, as used here [in John 1:1]. It was employed to denote a mode of conception concerning the Deity, familiar at the time when St. John wrote and intimately blended with the philosophy of his age, but long since obsolete, and so foreign from our habits of thinking that it is not easy for us to conform our minds to its apprehension. The Greek word *logos*, in one of its primary senses, answered nearly to our word *Reason*. The *logos* of God was regarded, not in its strictest sense, as merely the Reason of God; but, under certain aspects, as the Wisdom, the Mind, the Intellect of God (p. 307).

Norton postulates that perhaps "the power of God" would be a good translation for *logos* (p. 323). Buzzard sets forth "plan," "purpose" or "promise" as three acceptable translations. Broughton and Southgate say "thoughts, plan or purpose of God, particularly in action." Many scholars identify *logos* with God's wisdom and reason.

---

17. Arndt and Gingrich, *op. cit., Greek-English Lexicon of the New Testament*.

18. J. B. Lightfoot, *St. Paul's Epistles to the Colossians and Philemon* (Hendrickson Publishers, Peabody, MA, 1993), pp. 143 and 144. **Bold** emphasis ours, *italics* his.

The *logos* is the expression of God, and is His communication of Himself, just as a "word" is an outward expression of a person's thoughts. This outward expression of God has now occurred through His Son, and thus it is perfectly understandable why Jesus is called the "Word." Jesus is an outward expression of God's reason, wisdom, purpose and plan. For the same reason, we call revelation "a word from God" and the Bible "the Word of God."

If we understand that the *logos* is God's expression—His plan, purposes, reason and wisdom, it is clear that they were indeed with Him "in the beginning." Scripture says that God's wisdom was "from the beginning" (Prov. 8:23). It was very common in Hebrew writing to personify a concept such as wisdom. No ancient Jew reading Proverbs would think that God's wisdom was a separate person, even though it is portrayed as one in verses like Proverbs 8:29 and 30: "…when He marked out the foundations of the earth…I [wisdom] was the craftsman at his side…."

2. Most Jewish readers of the gospel of John would have been familiar with the concept of God's "word" being with God as He worked to bring His creation into existence. There is an obvious working of God's power in Genesis 1 as He brings His plan into concretion by speaking things into being. The Targums are well known for describing the wisdom and action of God as His "word." This is especially important to note because the Targums are the Aramaic translations and paraphrases of the Old Testament, and Aramaic was the spoken language of many Jews at the time of Christ. Remembering that a Targum is usually a paraphrase of what the Hebrew text says, note how the following examples attribute action to the word:

- And the word of the LORD was Joseph's helper (Gen. 39:2).
- And Moses brought the people to meet the word of the LORD (Exod. 19:17).
- And the word of the LORD accepted the face of Job (Job 42:9).
- And the word of the Lord shall laugh them to scorn (Ps. 2:4).
- They believed in the name of His word (Ps. 106:12).[19]

The above examples demonstrate that the Jews were familiar with the idea of God's Word referring to His wisdom and action. This is especially important to note because these Jews were fiercely monotheistic, and did not in any way believe in a "Triune God." They were familiar with the idioms of their own language, and understood that the wisdom and power of God were being personified as "word."

The Greek-speaking Jews were also familiar with God's creative force being called "the word." J. H. Bernard writes, "When we turn from Palestine to Alexandria [Egypt], from Hebrew sapiential [wisdom] literature to that which was written in Greek, we find this creative wisdom identified with the Divine *logos*, Hebraism and Hellenism thus coming into contact."[20] One example of this is in the Apocryphal book known as the Wisdom of Solomon, which says, "O God of my fathers and Lord of mercy who hast made all things by thy word (*logos*), and by thy wisdom hast formed man…" (9:1 and 2). In this verse, the "word" and "wisdom" are seen as the creative force of God, but without being a "person."

3. The *logos*, that is, the plan, purpose and wisdom of God, "became flesh" (came into concretion or physical existence) in Jesus Christ. Jesus is the "…image of the invisible God…" (Col. 1:15) and His chief emissary, representative and agent. Because Jesus perfectly obeyed the Father, he represents everything that God could communicate about Himself in a human person. As such, Jesus could

---

19. Lightfoot, *op. cit.*, *Commentary on the New Testament from the Talmud and Hebraica*, Vol. 3, p. 238.
20. *The International Critical Commentary*: St. John. Vol. 1, p. cxxxix.

say, **If you have seen me, you have seen the Father** (John 14:9). The fact that the *logos* "became" flesh shows that it did not exist that way before. There is no pre-existence for Jesus in this verse other than his figurative "existence" as the plan, purpose or wisdom of God for the salvation of man. The same is true with the "word" in writing. It had no literal pre-existence as a "spirit-book" somewhere in eternity past, but it came into being as God gave the revelation to people and they wrote it down.

4. The last phrase in the verse, which most versions translate as "and the Word was God," should not be translated that way. The Greek language uses the word "God" (Greek = *theos*) to refer to the Father as well as to other authorities. These include the Devil (2 Cor. 4:4), lesser gods (1 Cor. 8:5) and men with great authority (John 10:34 and 35; Acts 12:22). At the time the New Testament was written, Greek manuscripts were written in all capital letters. The upper and lower case letters were not blended as we do today. Thus, the distinction that we today make between "God" and "god" could not be made, and the context became the judge in determining to whom "*THEOS*" referred.

Although context is the final arbiter, it is almost always the case in the New Testament that when "God" refers to the Father, the definite article appears in the Greek text (this article can be seen only in the Greek text, it is never translated into English). Translators are normally very sensitive to this (see John 10:33 below). The difference between *theos* with and without the article occurs in John 1:1: "In the beginning was the Word, and the Word was with "**the** *theos*," and the Word was "*theos*." Since the definite article is missing from the second occurrence of "*theos*" ("God,") the usual meaning would be "god" or "divine." The New English Bible gets the sense of this phrase by translating it, "What God was, the Word was." James Moffatt who was a professor of Greek and New Testament Exegesis at Mansfield College in Oxford, England, and author of the well-known Moffatt Bible, translated the phrase, "the *logos* was divine."

A very clear explanation of how to translate *theos* without the definite article can be found in *Jesus As They Knew Him*, by William Barclay, a professor at Trinity College in Glasgow:

> In a case like this we cannot do other than go to the Greek, which is *theos en ho logos. Ho* is the definite article, *the*, and it can be seen that there is a definite article with *logos*, but not with *theos*. When in Greek two nouns are joined by the verb "to be," and when both have the definite article, then the one is fully intended to be identified with the other; but when one of them is without the article, it becomes more an adjective than a noun, and describes rather the class or sphere to which the other belongs.

> An illustration from English will make this clear. If I say, "The preacher is *the* man," I use the definite article before both preacher and man, and I thereby identify the preacher with some quite definite individual man whom I have in mind. But, if I say, "The preacher is man," I have omitted the definite article before man, and what I mean is that the preacher must be classified as a man, he is in the sphere of manhood, he is a human being.

> [In the last clause of John 1:1] John has no article before *theos*, God. The *logos*, therefore, is not identified as God or with God; the word *theos* has become adjectival and describes the sphere to which the *logos* belongs. We would, therefore, have to say that this means that the *logos* belongs to the same sphere as God; without being identified with God, the *logos* has the same kind of life and being as God. Here the NEB [New English Bible] finds the perfect translation: "What God was, the Word was."[21]

---

21. Barclay, *op. cit., Jesus as They Knew Him*, pp. 21 and 22.

5. It is important to understand that the Bible was not written in a vacuum, but was recorded in the context of a culture and was understood by those who lived in that culture. Sometimes verses that seem superfluous or confusing to us were meaningful to the readers of the time because they were well aware of the culture and beliefs being propounded by those around them. In the first century, there were many competing beliefs in the world (and unfortunately, erroneous beliefs in Christendom) that were confusing believers about the identities of God and Christ. For centuries before Christ, and at the time the New Testament was written, the irrational beliefs about the gods of Greece had been handed down. This body of religious information was known by the word "*muthos*," which we today call "myths" or "mythology." This *muthos*, these myths, were often irrational, mystical and beyond understanding or explanation. The more familiar one is with the Greek myths, the better he will understand our emphasis on their irrationality. If one is unfamiliar with them, it would be valuable to read a little on the subject. Greek mythology is an important part of the cultural background of the New Testament.

The myths were often incomprehensible, but nevertheless, they had been widely accepted as the "revelation of the gods." The pervasiveness of the *muthos* in the Greco-Roman world of the New Testament can be seen sticking up out of the New Testament like the tip of an iceberg above the water. When Paul and Barnabas healed a cripple in Lystra, the people assumed that the gods had come down in human form, and the priest of Zeus came to offer sacrifices to them. While Paul was in Athens, he became disturbed because of the large number of idols there that were statues to the various gods. In Ephesus, Paul's teaching actually started a riot. When some of the locals realized that if his doctrine spread, "…the temple of the great goddess Artemis will be discredited, and the goddess herself, who is worshiped throughout the province of Asia and the world, will be robbed of her divine majesty" (Acts 19:27). There are many other examples that show that there was a *muthos*, i.e., a body of religious knowledge that was in large part incomprehensible to the human mind, firmly established in the minds of some of the common people in New Testament times.

Starting several centuries before Christ, certain Greek philosophers worked to replace the *muthos* with what they called the *logos*, a reasonable and rational explanation of reality. It is appropriate that, in the writing of the New Testament, God used the word *logos*, not *muthos*, to describe His wisdom, reason and plan. God has not come to us in mystical experiences and irrational beliefs that cannot be understood; rather, He reveals Himself in ways that can be rationally understood and persuasively argued.

6. In addition to the cultural context that accepted the myths, at the time John was written, a belief system called Gnosticism was taking root in Christianity. Gnosticism had many ideas and words that are strange and confusing to us today, so, at the risk of oversimplifying, we will describe a few basic tenets of Gnosticism as simply as we can.

Gnosticism took many forms, but generally Gnostics taught that there was a supreme and unknowable Being, which they designated as the "Monad." The Monad produced various gods, who in turn produced other gods (these gods were called by different names, in part because of their power or position). One of these gods, called the "Demiurge," created the earth and then ruled over it as an angry, evil and jealous god. This evil god, Gnostics believed, was the god of the Old Testament, called *Elohim*. The Monad sent another god, "Christ," to bring special *gnosis* (knowledge) to mankind and free them from the influence of the evil *Elohim*. Thus, a Gnostic Christian would agree that *Elohim* created the heavens and earth, but he would not agree that He was the supreme God. Most Gnostics would also state that *Elohim* and Christ were at cross-purposes with each other.

This is why it was so important for John 1:1 to say that the *logos* was *with* God, which at first glance seems to be a totally unnecessary statement.

The opening of the gospel of John is a wonderful expression of God's love. God "…wants all men to be saved and to come to a knowledge of the truth" (1 Tim. 2:4). He authored the opening of John in such a way that it reveals the truth about Him and His plan for all of mankind and, at the same time, refutes Gnostic teaching. It says that from the beginning there was the *logos* (the reason, plan, power), which was with God. There was not another "god" existing with God, especially not a god opposed to God. Furthermore, God's plan was like God; it was divine. God's plan became flesh when God impregnated Mary.

7. There are elements of John 1:1 and other phrases in the introduction of John that not only refer back in time to God's work in the original creation, but also foreshadow the work of Christ in the new administration and the new creation. Noted Bible commentator F. F. Bruce argues for this interpretation:

> It is not by accident that the Gospel begins with the same phrase as the book of Genesis. In Genesis 1:1, 'In the beginning' introduces the story of the old creation; here it introduces the story of the new creation. In both works of creation the agent is the Word of God.[22]

The Racovian Catechism, one of the great doctrinal works of the Unitarian movement of the 14th and 15th centuries, states that the word "beginning" in John 1:1 refers to the beginning of the new dispensation and thus is similar to Mark 1:1, which starts, "The beginning of the gospel about Jesus Christ…."

> In the cited passage (John 1:1) wherein the Word is said to have been in the beginning, there is no reference to an antecedent eternity, without commencement; because mention is made here of a *beginning*, which is opposed to that eternity. But the word *beginning*, used absolutely, is to be understood of the subject matter under consideration. Thus, Daniel 8:1 (ASV), "In the third year of the reign of king Belshazzar a vision appeared to me, even unto me, Daniel, after that which appeared unto me **at the first**." John 15:27 (ASV), "And ye also shall bear witness because ye have been with me **from the beginning**." John 16:4, "…these things I said not unto you **from the beginning** because I was with you. And Acts 11:15 (ASV), "And as I began to speak, the Holy Spirit fell on them, even as on us **at the beginning**." As then the matter of which John is treating is the gospel, or the things transacted under the gospel, nothing else ought to be understood here beside the beginning of the gospel; a matter clearly known to the Christians whom he addressed, namely, the advent and preaching of John the Baptist, according to the testimony of all the evangelists [i.e., Matthew, Mark, Luke and John], each of whom begins his history with the coming and preaching of the Baptist. Mark indeed (Chapter 1:1) expressly states that this was the beginning of the gospel. In like manner, John himself employs the word beginning, placed thus absolutely, in the introduction to his First Epistle, at which beginning he uses the same term (logos) Word, as if he meant to be his own interpreter ["That which is from the beginning…concerning the Word (logos) of life." 1 John 1:1].[23]

While we do not agree with the *Catechism* that the only meaning of beginning in John 1:1 is the beginning of the new creation, we certainly see how the word beginning is a double entendre. In the context of the new creation, then, "the Word" is the plan or purpose according to which God is restoring His creation.

22. Bruce, *op. cit., Gospel of John*, pp. 28 and 29.
23. *Op. cit., The Racovian Catechism*, pp. 63 and 64.

8. To fully understand any passage of Scripture, it is imperative to study the context. To fully understand John 1:1, the rest of the chapter needs to be understood as well, and the rest of the chapter adds more understanding to John 1:1. We believe that these notes on John 1:1, read together with the rest of John 1 and our notes on John 1:3, 10, 14a, 15, and 18 will help make the entire first chapter of John more understandable.

Broughton, and Southgate, *op. cit., The Trinity, True or False?*, pp. 238–248; Buzzard, *op. cit., Doctrine of the Trinity*, pp. 111–119; Morgridge, *op. cit., True Believer's Defence Against Charges Preferred by Trinitarians*, pp. 107–109; Norton, *op. cit., A Statement of Reasons for Not Believing the Doctrines of Trinitarians*, pp. 307–374; Robinson, *op. cit., Honest to God*, p. 71; Snedeker, *op. cit., Our Heavenly Father Has No Equals*, pp. 313–326.

John 1:3 (KJV)
All things were made by him; and without him was not anything made that was made.

---

1. Trinitarians use this verse to show that Christ made the world and its contents. However, that is not the case. What we have learned from the study of John 1:1 above will be helpful in properly interpreting this verse.

John 1:1–3 (Author's Translation)
(1) In the beginning was the Word [the wisdom, plan or purpose of God], and the Word was with God, and the Word was divine.
(2) The same was in the beginning with God.
(3) All things were made by it [the Word]; and without it was not anything made that was made.

2. The pronoun in verse 3 can legitimately be translated as "it." It does not have to be translated as "him," and it does not have to refer to a "person" in any way. A primary reason why people get the idea that "the Word" is a person is that the pronoun "he" is used with it. The Greek text does, of course, have the masculine pronoun, because like many languages, including Spanish, French, German, Latin, Hebrew, etc., the Greek language assigns a gender to all nouns, and the gender of the pronoun must agree with the gender of the noun. In French, for example, a table is feminine, *la table*, while a desk is masculine, *le bureau*, and feminine and masculine pronouns are required to agree with the gender of the noun. In translating from French to English, however, we would *never* translate "the table, she," or "the desk, he." And we would never insist that a table or desk was somehow a person just because it had a masculine or feminine pronoun. We would use the English designation "it" for the table and the desk, in spite of the fact that in the original language the table and desk have a masculine or feminine gender.

This is true in the translation of any language that assigns a gender to nouns. In Spanish, a car is masculine, *el carro*, while a bicycle is feminine, *la bicicleta*. Again, no English translator would translate "the car, he," or "the bicycle, she." People translating Spanish into English use the word "it" when referring to a car or bicycle. For another example, a Greek feminine noun is "anchor" (*agkura*), and literally it would demand a feminine pronoun. Yet no English translator would write "I accidentally dropped the anchor, and *she* fell through the bottom of the boat." We would write, "it" fell through the bottom of the boat. In Greek, "wind" (*anemos*) is masculine, but we would not translate it into English that way. We would say, "The wind was blowing so hard *it* blew the trash cans over," not "the wind, *he* blew the trash cans over." When translating from another language into English, we have to use the English language properly. Students who are studying Greek, Hebrew, Spanish, French, German, etc., quickly discover that one of the difficult things about learning the language is memorizing the gender of each noun—something we do not have in the English language.

Greek is a language that assigns gender to nouns. For example, in Greek, "word" is masculine while "spirit" is neuter. All languages that assign gender to nouns demand that pronouns referring to the noun have the same gender as the noun. Once we clearly understand that the gender of a pronoun is determined by the gender of the noun, we can see why one cannot build a doctrine on the gender of a noun and its agreeing pronoun. No student of the Bible should take the position that "the Word" is somehow a masculine person based on its pronoun any more than he would take the position that a *book* was a feminine person or a *desk* was a masculine person because that is the gender assigned to those nouns in French. Indeed, if one tried to build a theology based on the gender of the noun in the language, great confusion would result.

In doctrinal discussions about the holy spirit some people assert that it is a person because the Bible has "he" and "him" in verses that refer to it. So, for example, John 14:16 and 17 reads:

John 14:16 and 17
(16) And I will ask the Father, and he will give you another Counselor to be with you forever—
(17) the Spirit of truth. The world cannot accept him, because it neither sees him nor knows him. But you know him, for he lives with you and will be in you.

In the Greek language, "spirit" is neuter and thus is associated with the neuter pronoun, "it." So, for example, verse 17 above should be literally translated as: "…The world cannot accept it (the spirit), because it neither sees it nor knows it. But you know it, for it lives with you and will be in you." Any *Analytical Lexicon* will confirm that the pronouns in this verse that refer to spirit are neuter, not masculine.

If the pronouns in the Greek text are neuter, why do the translators translate them as "he" and "him?" The answer to that question is that translators realize that when you are dealing with a language that assigns genders to nouns, it is the context and general understanding of the subject at hand that determines how the pronouns are to be translated into English as we have seen in the above examples (desk, bicycle, car, wind, etc.). It is amazing to us that Trinitarian translators know that the same neuter pronoun can be converted to an English masculine pronoun (e.g., "it" becomes "he") but are evidently not as willing to see that a Greek masculine pronoun could be translated as an English *neuter* pronoun (e.g., "he becomes "it"), if the subject matter and context warrant it. Linguistically, both conversions could be completely legitimate. But any change depends, not on the gender assigned by the Greek language, but rather on the subject matter being discussed. For example, the *logos* is God's plan and should be an it," and "holy spirit," when used as God's gift, should also be translated into English as an "it." To the unindoctrinated mind, plans and gifts are obviously not "persons."

Trinitarian Christians believe "the Holy Spirit" is a masculine being and translate the pronouns that refer to it as "he" in spite of the fact that the noun is neuter and call for an "it," not a "he" in Greek. Similarly, even though the masculine noun calls for the masculine pronoun in the Greek language, it would still not be translated into English as the masculine pronoun, "he," unless it could be shown from the context that the subject was actually a male; i.e., a man, a male animal, or God (who represents Himself as masculine in the Bible). So the question to answer when dealing with "the Word," "the Comforter" and "the holy spirit" is not, "What gender are the noun and associated pronoun in the Greek language?" Rather, we need to ask, "Do those words refer to a masculine *person* that would require a "he" in English, or do they refer to a "thing" that would require the pronoun "it"?" When "holy spirit" is referring to the power of God in action or God's gift, it is properly an "it." The same is true for the "comforter." For a much more exhaustive treatment of the subject of holy spirit see our book: *The Gift of Holy Spirit: The Power To Be Like Christ.*

In Hebrew, "spirit" is feminine and must have feminine pronouns, while in Greek, "spirit" is neuter and takes neuter pronouns. Thus, a person trying to build a theology on the basis of the gender of the noun and pronoun would find himself in an interesting situation trying to explain how it could be that "the spirit" of God somehow changed genders as the New Testament was written.

Because the translators of the Bible have almost always been Trinitarians, and since "the Word" has almost always been erroneously identified with the person of Christ, the pronouns referring to the *logos* in verse 3 have almost always been translated as "him." However, if in fact the *logos* is the plan, purpose, wisdom and reason of God, then the Greek pronoun should be translated into the English as "it." To demand that "the Word" is a masculine person and therefore a third part of a three-part Godhead because the pronouns used when referring to it are masculine, is poor scholarship.

3. Viewed in light of the above translation, the opening of the gospel of John reveals wonderful truth, and is also a powerful polemic against primary heresies of the day. We have already seen (under John 1:1) that Gnostics were teaching that, in the hierarchy of gods, the god *Elohim* and the god Christ were actually opposed to each other. Also active at the time John was written were the Docetists, who were teaching that Christ was a spirit being and only appeared to be flesh. The opening of John's gospel shows that in the beginning there was only one God, not many gods. It also shows that this God had reason, wisdom, a plan or purpose within Himself, which became flesh in Jesus Christ. Thus, God and Christ are not at cross purposes as some were saying, and Christ was not a spirit being as others were saying.

The opening of John reveals this simple truth in a beautiful way: "In the beginning there was one God, who had reason, purpose and a plan, which was, by its very nature and origin, divine. It was through and on account of this reason, plan and purpose that everything was made. Nothing was made outside its scope. Then, this plan became flesh in the person of Jesus Christ and tabernacled among us." Understanding the opening of John this way fits with the whole of Scripture and is entirely acceptable from a translation standpoint.

Op. cit., Racovian Catechism, pp. 86–88; Snedeker, *op. cit., Our Heavenly Father Has No Equals,* pp. 411 and 412.

John 1:10 (KJV)
He was in the world, and the world was made by him, and the world knew him not.

---

1. This verse is a reference to the Father, not to Christ. A study of the context reveals that this section opens in verse 6 by telling us, "There came a man who was sent by God...." We are told, "God is light," and that God's light shown through Jesus Christ and made him **the light of the world**. Though God was in the world in many ways, including through His Son, the world did not recognize Him. He came unto his own by sending His exact image, Jesus Christ, to them, but even then they did not receive God, in that they rejected His emissary. The fact that the world did not receive Him is made more profound in the context as Scripture reveals how earnestly God reached out to them—He made his plan and purpose flesh and shined His light through Christ to reach the world—but they did not receive Him, even though He was offering them the "…right to become children of God" (v. 12).

2. Some scholars make the phrase, "…the world was made by him…," a reference to the new creation only (see Col. 1:15–20 and Heb. 1:2 and 10), but we see it as a double entendre referring to both the original and the new creations (see #7 under John 1:1 above, and Chapter 9).

Op. cit., Racovian Catechism, pp. 89–91.

John 1:14a
The Word became flesh and made his dwelling among us….

---

1. The "Word" is the wisdom, plan or purpose of God (see John 1:1) and the Word "became flesh" as Jesus Christ. Thus, Jesus Christ was "the Word in the flesh," which is shortened to "the Word" for ease of speaking. Scripture is also the Word, but it is the Word in writing. Everyone agrees that the "Word" in writing had a beginning. So did the "Word" in the flesh. In fact, the Greek text of Matthew 1:18 says that very clearly: "Now the beginning of Jesus Christ was in this manner…." Some ancient scribes were so uncomfortable with the idea of Jesus having a "beginning" that they tried to alter the Greek text to read "birth" and not "beginning," but they were unsuccessful. The modern Greek texts all read "beginning" (*genesis*) in Matthew 1:18. "Birth" is considered an acceptable translation of "*genesis*," since the beginning of some things is birth, and so most translations read "birth" in Matthew 1:18. Nevertheless, the proper understanding of Matthew 1:18 is the "beginning" (*genesis*) of Jesus Christ.

In the beginning, God had a plan, a purpose, which "became flesh" when Jesus was conceived. To make John 1:14 support the Trinity, there must first be proof that Jesus existed before he was born and was called "the Word." We do not believe that such proof exists. There is a large body of evidence, however, that Jesus was foreknown by God, and that the "the Word" refers to God's plan or purpose. We contend that the meaning of the verse is straightforward. God had a plan (the Word) and that plan became flesh when Jesus was conceived. Thus, Jesus became "the Word in the flesh."

2. It is quite fair to ask why John would say, "The Word became flesh," a statement that seems so obvious to us. Of course Jesus Christ was flesh. He was born, grew, ate and slept, and Scripture calls him a man. However, what is clear to us now was not at all clear in the early centuries of the Christian era. In our notes on John 1:1, we explain that the Bible must be understood in the context of the culture in which it was written. At the time of John's writing, the "Docetic" movement was gaining disciples inside Christianity ("Docetic" comes from the Greek word for "to seem" or "to appear"). Docetic Christians believed Jesus was actually a spirit being, or god, who only "appeared" to be human. Some Docetists did not believe Jesus even actually ate or drank, but only pretended to do so. Furthermore, some Jews thought that Jesus was an angel. In theological literature, theologians today call this "angel-Christology." John 1:14 was not written to show that Jesus was somehow pre-existent and then became flesh. It was to show that God's plan for salvation "became *flesh*," i.e., Jesus was not a spirit, god or angelic being, but rather a flesh-and-blood man. A very similar thing is said in 1 John 4:2, that if you do not believe Jesus has come *in the flesh*, you are not of God.

Hyndman, *op. cit., Principles of Unitarianism*, p. 113; *Op. cit., Racovian Catechism*, pp. 117–119.

John 1:15
John testifies concerning him. He cries out, saying, "This was he of whom I said, 'He who comes after me has surpassed me because he was before me.'"

This verse is occasionally used to support the Trinity because it is assumed that for Jesus to come "before" John he would have had to exist before John. While it is true that the Greek word "before" (*protos*) can mean "before in time," it can just as easily be "first," "chief," "leader," etc. The "first" and great commandment was not the first given in time, but the first in rank. There are many examples of this in Scripture, including: Matt. 20:27, 22:38; Mark 6:21, 10:44; Luke 11:26. John the Baptist recognized that Jesus was above him in rank, and said so plainly.

Buzzard, *op. cit., Doctrine of the Trinity*, pp. 86 and 87.

John 1:18 (KJV)
No man hath seen God at any time; the only begotten Son, which is in the bosom of the Father, he hath declared *him*.

---

1. As it is written in the KJV, there is no Trinitarian inference in the verse.

2. There are versions such as the NIV and NASB, however, that are translated from a different textual family than the King James Version, and they read "God" instead of "Son."

NIV: "No one has ever seen God, but God the One and Only, who is at the Father's side, has made him known."

NASB: "No man has seen God at any time; the only begotten God, who is in the bosom of the Father, He has explained *Him*."

The NIV and NASB represent theologians who believe that the original text read "*ho monogenes theos*" = "the unique, or only begotten God," while the KJV is representative of theologians who believe that the original text was "*ho monogenes huios*" = "the only begotten Son." The Greek texts vary, but there are good reasons for believing that the original reading is represented in versions such as the KJV. Although it is true that the earliest Greek manuscripts contain the reading "*theos*," every one of those texts is of the Alexandrian text type. Virtually every other reading of the other textual traditions, including the Western, Byzantine, Caesarean and secondary Alexandrian texts, read *huios*, "Son." The two famous textual scholars, Westcott and Hort, known for their defense of the Alexandrian text type, consider John 1:18 to be one of the few places in the New Testament where it is not correct.

A large number of the Church Fathers, such as Irenaeus, Clement and Tertullian, quoted the verse with "Son," and not "God." This is especially weighty when one considers that Tertullian argued aggressively for the incarnation and is credited with being the one who developed the concept of "one God in three persons." If Tertullian had had a text that read "God" in John 1:18, he certainly would have quoted it, but instead he always quoted texts that read "Son."

It is difficult to conceive of what "only begotten God" would have meant in the Jewish culture. There is no use of the phrase anywhere else in the Bible. In contrast, the phrase "only begotten Son" is used three other times by John (3:16 and 18 - KJV; 1 John 4:9 - KJV). To a Jew, any reference to a "unique God" would have usually referred to the Father. Although the Jews of John's day would have had a problem with "only begotten God," Christians of the second century and beyond, with their increasingly paradoxical understanding of Christology and the nature of God, would have been much more easily able to accept such a doctrine.

The reason that the text was changed from "Son" to "God" was to provide "extra evidence" for the existence of the Trinity. By the second century, an intense debate about whether or not Jesus was God raged in Alexandria, Egypt, the place where all the texts that read "God" originated. The stakes were high in these debates, and excommunication, banishment or worse could be the lot of the "loser." Changing a text or two to in order to "help" in a debate was a tactic proven to have occurred. An examination of all the evidence shows that it is probable that "the only begotten son" is the original reading of John 1:18. For a much more detailed accounting of why the word "Son" should be favored over the word "God," see *The Orthodox Corruption of Scripture*, by Bart Ehrman (Oxford University Press, New York, 1993, pp. 78–82).

3. Even if the original text reads "God" and not "Son," that still does not prove the Trinity. The word "God" has a wider application in Hebrew, Aramaic and Greek than it does in English. It can be used of men who have divine authority (See John 10:33 and Heb. 1:8 below). There is no "Trinitarian Formula" in this verse that forces a Trinitarian interpretation.

John 1:30
This is the one I meant when I said, 'A man who comes after me has surpassed me because he was before me.

This verse, spoken by John the Baptist, is actually simple to understand, but has been clouded by Trinitarian theology and often translated with a Trinitarian slant. John the Baptist was speaking to his disciples about Christ, calling him "the Lamb of God" (John 1:29), and speaking to them of the importance of Jesus. John's statement that Jesus was before him, and had surpassed him, was to help his disciples see that Jesus was the Messiah. There is no evidence that John thought Jesus was God, here or anywhere else John testified about Jesus. In fact, in this context, John says, "…I testify that this is the Son of God."

The words "has surpassed me" are well translated. The Greek uses the perfect tense of the verb *ginomai*, "to become," and the word *emprosthen*, which means "to be before, ahead of, or higher in position or rank than someone." "To become" of a higher rank than someone is to surpass him, thus, "has surpassed me" (NIV) is a good translation. No one argues that Jesus had surpassed John the Baptist in every way.

The next phrase of the verse, however, needs to be understood properly. First, when John says, "he was before me," the Greek word "*protos*" can mean first in the sense of time, i.e., earlier, or first in the since of rank, i.e., more important, more prominent. Second, the Greek word translated "was" is the imperfect tense, active voice of *eimi*, the common word for "to be" (which occurs more than 2000 times in the New Testament), so "was" is a good translation. The force of the imperfect is, "he was and continues to be." Jesus was, in the mind of God, and continued to be after his birth, "before" John in rank and importance.

Jesus was before John in both time and rank, but not because he existed in a literal sense before John, but rather because he existed in the foreknowledge of God and in the prophecies, and then, of course, "outranked" John on earth. The existence of Christ in the mind of God is so clear that it need not be disputed. Before the foundation of the world he was foreknown (1 Pet. 1:20); from the foundation of the world he was slain (Rev. 13:8); and before the foundation of the world we, the Church, were chosen in him (Eph. 1:4). The certainty about the Messiah that is expressed in the prophecies about him definitively reveal that all aspects of his life and death were clearly in the mind of God before any of them occurred. That is what John had in mind when he said Jesus "was before" him; Jesus was before John in time and rank in the mind of God, as the prophecies make clear. Thus this verse is similar to other verses that refer to Jesus being before his physical birth, including Jesus himself saying that he was "before" Abraham (John 8:58b; see that verse).

In conclusion, we should note that a number of modern versions translate the last phrase something like, "because he [Jesus] existed before me." That translation would be all right as long as we realize that something can "exist" in the mind of God before it exists in the real world. However, generally, that translation is written due to a Trinitarian slant, and makes the verse more difficult for most Christians to understand than it is if the text reads "was before me."

John 2:19 (NASB)
"...Destroy this temple, and in three days I will raise it up."

---

1. Many verses plainly state that it was *the Father* who raised Jesus, and the Bible cannot contradict itself.

2. Jesus was speaking to the Jews after he had just turned over their tables and driven their animals out of the Temple. This was the first of the two times when he did this, and this occurrence was at the beginning of his ministry. He did it once again at the end of his ministry, and that event is recorded in other Gospels. The Jews were angry and unbelieving, and Jesus was speaking in veiled terms, so much so that the gospel of John has to add, "But He was speaking of the temple of His body," (John 2:21 - NASB) so the reader would not be confused. Since Jesus was standing in the actual Temple when he said, "Destroy this temple," the natural assumption would be the one his audience made, that he was speaking of the Temple where he was standing at the time.

3. The fact that Jesus was speaking in veiled terms to an unbelieving audience should make us hesitant to build a doctrine on this verse, especially when many other clear verses say that *the Father* raised Jesus. For example, 1 Corinthians 6:14 states: "By his power God raised the Lord from the dead...." Jesus was not in a teaching situation when he was speaking. Tempers were flaring and the Jews were against Jesus anyway. It was common for Jesus to speak in ways that unbelievers did not understand. Even a cursory reading of the Gospels will show a number of times when Jesus spoke and the unbelievers who heard him (and sometimes even the disciples) were confused by what he said.

4. We know that Jesus was speaking in veiled terms, but what did he mean? He was almost certainly referring to the fact that he was indeed ultimately responsible for his resurrection. How so? Jesus was responsible to keep himself "without spot or blemish" and to fully obey the will of the Father. In that sense he was like any other sacrifice. A sacrifice that was blemished was unacceptable to the LORD (Lev. 22:17–20; Mal. 1:6–8). Since this event in John was at the start of his ministry, he knew he had a long hard road ahead and that obedience would not be easy. If he turned away from God because he did not like what God said to do, or if he were tempted to the point of sin, his sin would have been a "blemish" that would have disqualified him as the perfect sacrifice. Then he could not have paid for the sins of mankind, and there would have been no resurrection. The reader must remember that Jesus did not go into the Temple and turn over the money tables because he "just felt like it." John 2:17 indicates that he was fulfilling an Old Testament prophecy and the will of God, which he always did. Had he not fulfilled the prophecy spoken in Psalm 69:9, he would not have fulfilled all the law and would have been disqualified from being able to die for the sins of mankind. Thus, his destiny was in his own hands, and he could say, "…I will raise it up."

5. It is common in speech that if a person has a vital part in something, he is spoken of as having done the thing. We know that Roman soldiers crucified Jesus. The Gospels say it, and we know that the Jews would not have done it, because coming in contact with Jesus would have made them unclean. Yet Peter said to the rulers of the Jews, "you" crucified the Lord (Acts 5:30). Everyone understands that the Jews played a vital part in Jesus' crucifixion, so there really is a sense in which they crucified him, even though they themselves did not do the dirty work. A similar example from the Old Testament is in both 2 Samuel 5 and 1 Chronicles 11. David and his men were attacking the Jebusite city, Jerusalem. The record is very clear that David had sent his men ahead into the city to fight, and even offered a general's position to the first one into the city. Yet the record says, "…David captured the stronghold of Zion…." We know why, of course. David played a vital role in the capture of Jerusalem, and so Scripture says he captured it. This same type of wording that is so common in the Bible and indeed, in all languages, is the wording Jesus used. He would raise his body, i.e., he would play a vital part in it being raised.

6. Christ knew that by his thoughts and actions he could guarantee his own resurrection by being sinlessly obedient unto death. That made it legally possible for God to keep His promise of resurrecting Christ, who was without sin and therefore did not deserve death, the "wages of sin."

Op. cit., Racovian Catechism, pp. 362 and 363; Snedeker, *op. cit., Our Heavenly Father Has No Equals*, pp. 413 and 414.

John 2:24
But Jesus would not entrust himself to them, for he knew all men.

---

1. It is obvious from Scripture that Jesus did not know everything, for he grew in wisdom (Luke 2:52), and he did not know certain things (Matt. 24:36). Whenever the word "all" is used, the student of Scripture must be careful to ascertain from the context whether it means "all" in a totally inclusive sense, or whether it means "all" in a more limited sense (see note #5 on Col. 1:15–20). For example, 1 John 2:20 (KJV) says of Christians, "ye know all things." Surely there is no Christian who actually believes that he knows everything. The phrase is taken in a limited sense of "all" according to the context.

2. Trinitarians explain the fact that Jesus did not know certain things by appealing to his "manhood" in contrast to his "Godhood," or "God-nature." However, when there is a verse that can be construed to mean that Jesus knows everything, they abandon that argument and say that his omniscience proves he is God. We think it is reasonable to assert that you cannot have it both ways. Either Christ did not know everything, or he did. There are very clear verses that say he did not, and no verse that actually says that Jesus did know *everything* the same way God does. When a verse seems at first to say Jesus "knew all men," it should be understood in a limited sense according to the context, just as when Scripture says Christians "know all things."

Trinitarians are aware that some verses say that Jesus did not know everything and others say he did. Rather than accept the common use of "all" in a limited sense, they press onward with their doctrine by asserting that Christ had both a God nature and a human nature within himself. They claim that the "God nature" knew everything, but the "human nature" was limited. This argument falls short on many counts. First, Jesus Christ was "…made like his brothers in every way…" (Heb. 2:17, *et al.*), and *we* are not "part God, part human," or "fully God and fully man." In order for the integrity of Scripture to be preserved, Jesus must actually be like we are, i.e., fully human.

Second, there is no place in Scripture where this doctrine of the "dual nature" of Christ is actually stated. Trinitarians are asking us to believe something they cannot prove from the Word of God. We, on the other hand, are asking them to believe something that we can read line by line in the Bible: that Jesus was flesh and bone, not spirit; that he was a man, and that he partook in our humanity. Third, the very concept involves a self-contradiction. God is infinite and man is finite, and so Christ would have to be a finite-infinite being, which we believe is inherently impossible. That is not the Jesus described to us in the Bible. No wonder Tertullian, an early Trinitarian, said, "*Credo quia impossibile est*" (I believe because it is impossible). We realize it is not only "impossible," but also *unscriptural*, so we choose not to believe it.

3. Jesus needed to hear from God to know how to judge (John 5:30), and he knew all men the same way—by hearing from God.

4. In saying that Jesus knew all men, the Bible was confirming that Jesus was in touch with God just as were the prophets of old (but, of course, much more intimately). It was a common belief that prophets knew people's thoughts (Luke 7:39, etc.), and it is substantiated in Scripture that God did show prophets what people were thinking. Nathan knew of David's secret sin (2 Sam. 12:7). Ahijah knew what the wife of Jeroboam wanted, and who she was, even though he was blind and she was wearing a disguise (1 Kings 14:4 and 6). Elijah knew that Ahab had committed murder by framing Naboth (1 Kings 21:17–20), and he knew the information that the king of Israel wanted to know (2 Kings 1:1–4). Elisha knew that Gehazi was lying and knew of the greed in his heart (2 Kings 5:19–27). Daniel knew Nebuchadnezzar's dream, even though Nebuchadnezzar had not revealed it to anyone (Dan. 2:5 and 28ff). By saying that Jesus knew all men, Scripture confirms that he was, like the prophets of old, in communication with God.

Morgridge, *op. cit., True Believer's Defence Against Charges Preferred by Trinitarians*, pp. 124–126.

John 3:13
No one has ever gone into heaven except the one who came from heaven—the Son of Man.

The Jews would not have taken John's words to mean that Christ "incarnated." It was common for them to say that something "came from heaven" if God were its source. For example, James 1:17 says that every good gift is "from above" and "comes down" from God. What James means is clear. God is the Author and source of the good things in our lives. God works behind the scenes to provide what we need. The verse does not mean that the good things in our lives come directly down from heaven. Most Christians experience the Lord blessing them by way of other people or events, but realize that the ultimate source of the blessings was the Lord. We should apply John's words the same way we understand James' words—that God is the source of Jesus Christ, which He was. Christ was God's plan, and then God directly fathered Jesus.

There are also verses that say Jesus was "sent from God," a phrase that shows God as the ultimate source of what is sent. John the Baptist was a man "sent from God" (John 1:6), and it was he who said that Jesus "comes from above" and "comes from heaven" (John 3:31). When God wanted to tell the people that He would bless them if they gave their tithes, He told them that He would open the windows of "heaven" and pour out a blessing (Mal. 3:10 - KJV). Of course, everyone understood the idiom being used, and no one believed that God would literally pour things out of heaven. They knew that the phrase meant that God was the origin of the blessings they received. Still another example is when Christ was speaking and said, "John's baptism—where did it come from? Was it from heaven, or from men?…" (Matt. 21:25). Of course, the way that John's baptism would have been "from heaven" was if God was the source of the revelation. John did not get the idea on his own, it came "from heaven." The verse makes the idiom clear: things could be "from heaven," i.e., from God, or they could be "from men." The idiom is the same when used of Jesus. Jesus is "from God," "from heaven" or "from above" in the sense that God is his Father and thus his origin.

The idea of coming from God or being sent by God is also clarified by Jesus' words in John 17. He said, "As you sent me into the world, I have sent them into the world" (John 17:18). We understand perfectly what Christ meant when he said, "…I have sent them into the world." He meant that he commissioned us, or appointed us. No one thinks that we were in heaven with Christ and incarnated into the flesh. Christ said, "**As** you have sent me…I have sent them…." So, however we take the phrase that Christ *sent* us, that is how we should understand the phrase that God sent Christ.

Buzzard, *op. cit., Doctrine of the Trinity*, pp. 154–157; Norton, *op. cit., A Statement of Reasons for Not Believing the Doctrines of Trinitarians*, pp. 246–248.

John 5:18b
…he was even calling God his own father, making himself equal with God.

---

1. The people in the time and culture of the Bible knew that children often carried the authority of the family. For example, the son of a king had authority. When Christ said that God was his Father, the Pharisees correctly interpreted that to mean that he had God's authority on earth, something that Jesus *was* in fact saying (cp. John 5:17ff).

2. This verse is actually unsupportive of the Trinity. It accurately records that Jesus was saying that God was his father, not that he was himself God, or that he was "God the Son." It is clear that Jesus' authority came from the fact that he was the Son of God, not God Himself.

3. The concept of people being "equal" is found in several places in the Bible. For example, when Joseph was ruling Egypt under Pharaoh, Judah said to him, "…you are equal to Pharaoh himself" (Gen. 44:18). Paul wrote about men who wanted to be considered "equal with us" (2 Cor. 11:12). No Christian we are aware of believes that Joseph and Pharaoh or Paul and his opponents are "of one substance," and make up "one being" simply because they are called "equal." We believe that John 5:18 should be handled like the other verses that mention equality. Jesus was using God's power and authority on earth, and was thus "equal" to God in the same way Joseph, who was using Pharaoh's authority and power, was equal to Pharaoh.

Morgridge, *op. cit., True Believer's Defence Against Charges Preferred by Trinitarians*, p. 43; *Op. cit., Racovian Catechism*, p. 133.

John 6:33
For the bread of God is he who comes down from heaven and gives life to the world."

See notes on John 3:13.

John 6:38

For I have come down from heaven not to do my will but to do the will of him who sent me.

See notes on John 3:13.

John 6:46

No one has seen the Father except the one who is from God; only he has seen the Father.

---

1. For more information on "seeing" God, see our explanation of Genesis 18:1 and 2, which covers God occasionally appearing in human form.

2. Some people infer from John 6:46 that Jesus must be God, or at least that he pre-existed his birth, because he said he had seen the Father. However, this verse has nothing to do with the Trinity or pre-existence. For one thing, his audience would not have understood Jesus' teaching about the Trinity unless it included more information, because they were not expecting a Messiah who was God.

In contrast, it was assumed in the culture that the Messiah would have an intimate relationship with God, so what Jesus was saying to them could, and likely was, properly understood by some of his audience. However, the Biblical record does not focus on the average people in the audience, but upon the religious leaders, which the Bible refers to as "the Jews" (John 6:41 and 52). Since almost all of Jesus' audience would have been Jewish, it is well known to scholars that the phrase, "the Jews" refers to the religious leaders such as top Pharisees and Sadducees in the audience. In this teaching after feeding the 5,000, as in most of his teachings, the religious leaders did not understand Jesus' message.

The key to understanding John 6:46 is knowing that the phrase "seen the Father" does not refer to seeing with the eye, but to "knowing the Father." Jesus knew God, not because he lived with God before his birth, but because God revealed Himself more clearly to Jesus than to anyone else. Jesus made this clear in other teachings, saying, "For the Father loves the Son and shows him all he does…" (John 5:20a).

In both Hebrew and Greek, words translated "see" also mean "to know, to realize." The Hebrew word *ra'ah* is used of both seeing with the eyes and knowing something, or perceiving it (Gen. 16:4; Exod. 32:1; Num. 20:29). Similarly, the Greek word *horao*, translated "see" in John 1:18, 6:46; and 3 John 1:11, can mean "to see with the eyes" or "to see with the mind, to perceive, know." Even in English, one of the definitions for "see" is "to know or understand." For example, when two people are discussing something, one might say to the other, "I see what you mean."

The usage of "see" as it pertains to knowing is found in many places in the New Testament. For example, Jesus said to Philip, "…Anyone who has seen me has seen the Father…" (John 14:9). Here again the word "see" is used to indicate knowing. Anyone who *knew* Christ (not just those who "saw" him) would know the Father. In fact, Christ had made that clear two verses earlier when he said to Philip, "If you really knew me, you would know my Father as well. From now on, you do know him and have seen him" (John 14:7). In this verse Jesus says that those who know him have "seen" the Father.

One of the verses that uses the word "seen" in the sense of "known" is John 1:18.

John 1:18 (RSV)
No one has ever seen God; the only Son, who is in the bosom of the Father, he has made him known.

The phrase "seen God" is parallel to the phrase "has made Him known," and both phrases refer to knowing God. No man fully knew God, but Jesus made Him known. Throughout the Old Testament, what people knew about God was very limited. In fact, 2 Corinthians 3:13–16 refers to the fact that even today, the Jews who reject Christ have a veil over their hearts. The full knowledge, the "truth" about God, came through Jesus Christ (John 1:17). He was the one who "saw" (fully understood) God, and then he taught others—which is what John 1:18 says. Before Jesus Christ came, no one really knew God as He truly is, a loving heavenly Father, but Jesus Christ "saw" (knew) God intimately, because the Father revealed Himself clearly to him.

John 6:62
What if you see the Son of Man ascend to where he was before!

1. This verse is referring to the *resurrection* of Christ. This fact is clear from studying the context. Because the translators have chosen to translate *anabaino* as "ascend," people believe it refers to Christ's ascension from earth as recorded in Acts 1:9, but Acts 1:9 does not use this word. *Anabaino* simply means "to go up." It is used of "going up" to a higher elevation as in climbing a mountain (Matt. 5:1, 14:23, *et al.*), of Jesus "coming up" from under the water at his baptism (Matt. 3:16; Mark 1:10), of plants that "grow up" out of the ground (Matt. 13:7; Mark 4:7, 8 and 32), or of even just "going up," i.e., "climbing," a tree (Luke 19:4). Christ was simply asking if they would be offended if they saw him "come up" out of the ground, i.e., be resurrected, and be where he was before, i.e., alive and on the earth.

2. The context confirms that Jesus was speaking about being the bread from heaven and giving life via his resurrection. Verses such as 39, 40 and 44 confirm this: Jesus repeatedly said, "…I will raise him [each believer] up at the last day." Christ was amazed that even some of his disciples were offended at his teaching. He had been speaking of the resurrection, and they were offended, so he asked them if they would be offended if they saw *him* resurrected, which has been unfortunately translated as "ascend" in verse 62.

Norton, *op. cit., A Statement of Reasons for Not Believing the Doctrines of Trinitarians,* pp. 248–252; Snedeker, *op. cit., Our Heavenly Father Has No Equals*, p. 215.

John 6:64b
…Jesus had known from the beginning which of them did not believe and who would betray him.

1. Some Trinitarians act as if this verse proves that Jesus was God just because the word "beginning" is in the verse. Nothing could be further from the truth. Even a cursory word study will show that the word "beginning" has to be defined by its context. Any good lexicon will show that the word "beginning" is often used to describe times other than the start of Creation. Examples abound: God made them male and female at the "beginning," not of Creation, but of the human race (Matt. 19:4).

There were "eyewitnesses" at the "beginning," not of Creation, but of the life and ministry of Christ (Luke 1:2 and 3). The disciples were with Christ from the "beginning," not of Creation, but of his public ministry (John 15:27). The gift of holy spirit came on Peter and the Apostles "at the beginning," not of Creation, but of the Church Administration that started on the Day of Pentecost in Acts 2 (Acts 11:15). John 6:64 is simply saying that Christ knew from the time he began to choose the Apostles which one would betray him.

2. When this verse is understood in its context, it is a powerful testimony of how closely Jesus walked with his Father. First, there is nothing in the context that would in any way indicate that the word "beginning" refers to the beginning of *time*. Jesus had just fed the five thousand, and they said, "…Surely this is the Prophet who is to come into the world" (6:14). Right away that tells you that the people did not think Jesus was *God*, but a prophet. The people wanted to make Jesus king, but only because he filled their stomachs (6:15 and 26). When he challenged them to believe in him (6:29), they grumbled (6:41). As Jesus continued to teach, the Jews began to argue among themselves (6:52), and even some of Jesus' disciples began to grumble at the commitment Jesus was asking from them (6:60 and 61). Jesus, knowing his disciples were upset with his teaching, did not back off, but rather pressed on, even saying that he knew some would not believe (6:64). The result of this discussion was that some of his disciples left him (6:66). Since some disciples left him after this teaching, it would be easy to say that perhaps Jesus acted unwisely by pressing on with his difficult teaching. Not so. Scripture reminds us that Christ knew from the beginning who would not believe, and even who would betray him. Thus, he also knew that his hard words would not drive any of the true sheep away. The "beginning" being referred to here is the beginning of his ministry. When he started gathering disciples and Apostles and teaching them, God showed him by revelation who would believe and who would betray him.

Snedeker, *op. cit., Our Heavenly Father Has No Equals*, p. 215.

John 8:24b (KJV)
…for if ye believe not that I am *he*, ye shall die in your sins.

Trinitarians occasionally cite this verse to try to show the necessity of believing their doctrine, and unfortunately sometimes even to intimidate those who doubt it. They supply the word "God" after "I am," not from the text, but from the dictates of their doctrine, and make the verse read: "… for if you believe not that I am [God], *ye* shall die in your sins." This is a distortion of the biblical text as a whole, and the gospel of John in particular. The purpose of the gospel is clearly stated in 20:31: "But these are written that you may believe that Jesus is ["God"? No!] the Christ, the Son of God, and that by believing you may have life in his name." In light of the explicitly stated purpose of the gospel of John, teaching that unless one believes in Christ's "deity," he will die in his sins, is particularly unwarranted. The true meaning of the text is that if one does not believe that *Jesus is the Christ*, he will die in his sins, and this teaching can be found in a number of Scriptures in the New Testament. Obviously, if one chooses to not believe in the atoning sacrifice of Jesus Christ, he will die in his sins. We believe the NIV does a good job with this particular text, especially in light of the way Christ was veiling his role as Messiah: "…if you do not believe I am **the one I claim to be**, you will indeed die in your sins." This then fits with other times he said similar things, such as in John 13:19 when he said to disciples at the last supper, "I am telling you this before it [his betrayal] happens, so that when it does happen you will believe that I am He."

John 8:42

Jesus said to them, "If God were your Father, you would love me, for I came from God and now am here. I have not come on my own; but he sent me.

See the explanation for: "I came from God" under John 3:13.

John 8:58b (KJV)

…Before Abraham was, I am.

1. Trinitarians argue that this verse states that Jesus said he was the "I am" (i.e., the Yahweh of the Old Testament), so he must be God. This is just not the case. Saying "I am" does not make a person God. The man born blind that Jesus healed was not claiming to be God, and he said "I am the man," and the Greek reads exactly like Jesus' statement, i.e., "I am." The fact that the exact same phrase is translated two different ways, one as "I am" and the other as "I am the man" (John 9:9), is one reason it is so hard for the average Christian to get the truth from just reading the Bible as it has been translated into English. Most Bible translators are Trinitarian, and their bias appears in various places in their translation, this being a common one. Paul also used the same phrase of himself when he said that he wished all men were as "I am" (Acts 26:29). Thus, we conclude that saying "I am" did not make Paul, the man born blind or Christ into God. C. K. Barrett writes:

> *Ego eimi* ["I am"] does not identify Jesus with God, but it does draw attention to him in the strongest possible terms. "I am the one—the one you must look at, and listen to, if you would know God."[24]

2. The phrase "I am" occurs many other times in the New Testament, and is often translated as "I am he" or some equivalent ("I am he"—Mark 13:6; Luke 21:8; John 13:19, 18:5, 6 and 8. "It is I"—Matt. 14:27; Mark 6:50; John 6:20. "…I am the one I claim to be…"—John 8:24 and 28.). It is obvious that these translations are quite correct, and it is interesting that the phrase is translated as "I am" only in John 8:58. If the phrase in John 8:58 were translated "I am he" or "I am the one," like all the others, it would be easier to see that Christ was speaking of himself as the Messiah of God (as indeed he was), spoken of throughout the Old Testament.

At the Last Supper, the disciples were trying to find out who would deny the Christ. They said, literally, "Not I am, Lord" (Matt. 26:22 and 25). No one would say that the disciples were trying to deny that they were God because they were using the phrase "Not I am." The point is this: "I am" was a common way of designating oneself, and it did not mean you were claiming to be God.

3. The argument is made that because Jesus was "before" Abraham, Jesus must have been God. There is no question that Jesus figuratively "existed" in Abraham's time. However, he did not actually physically exist as a person; rather he "existed" in the mind of God as God's plan for the redemption of man. A careful reading of the context of the verse shows that Jesus was speaking of "existing" in God's foreknowledge. Verse 56 is accurately translated in the King James Version, which says: "Your father Abraham rejoiced to see my day: and he saw *it*, and was glad." This verse says that Abraham "saw" the Day of Christ, which is normally considered by theologians to be the day when Christ conquers the earth and sets up his kingdom. That would fit with what the book of Hebrews says about

---

24. Barrett, *op. cit., Gospel According to St John*, p. 342.

Abraham: "For he was looking forward to the city with foundations, whose architect and builder is God" (Heb. 11:10). Abraham looked for a city that is still future, yet the Bible says Abraham "saw" it. In what sense could Abraham have seen something that was future? Abraham "saw" the Day of Christ because God told him it was coming, and Abraham "saw" it by faith. Although Abraham saw the Day of Christ by faith, that day existed in the mind of God long before Abraham. Thus, in the context of God's plan existing from the beginning, Christ certainly was "before" Abraham. Christ was the plan of God for man's redemption long before Abraham lived. We are not the only ones who believe that Jesus' statement does not make him God:

> To say that Jesus is "before" him is not to lift him out of the ranks of humanity but to assert his unconditional precedence. To take such statements at the level of "flesh" so as to infer, as "the Jews" do that, at less than fifty, Jesus is claiming to have lived on this earth before Abraham (8:52 and 57), is to be as crass as Nicodemus who understands rebirth as an old man entering his mother's womb a second time (3:4).[25]

4. In order for the Trinitarian argument that Jesus' "I am" statement in John 8:58 makes him God, his statement must be equivalent with God's "I am" statement in Exodus 3:14. However, the two statements are very different. While the Greek phrase in John does mean "I am," the Hebrew phrase in Exodus actually means "to be" or "to become." In other words God is saying, "I will be what I will be." Thus the "I am" in Exodus is actually a mistranslation of the Hebrew text, so the fact that Jesus said "I am" did not make him God.

Buzzard, *op. cit., Doctrine of the Trinity*, pp. 93–97; Dana, *op. cit., Letters Addressed to Relatives and Friends*, Letter 21, pp. 169–171; Morgridge, *op. cit., True Believer's Defence Against Charges Preferred by Trinitarians*, pp. 120 and 121; Norton, *op. cit., A Statement of Reasons for Not Believing the Doctrines of Trinitarians*, pp. 242–246; Snedeker, *op. cit., Our Heavenly Father Has No Equals*, pp. 416–418.

John 10:18
No one takes it [my life] from me, but I lay it down of my own accord. I have authority to lay it down and authority to take it up again. This command I received from my Father."

See the notes on John 2:19.

John 10:30 (KJV)
I and *my* father are one.

---

1. There is no reason to take this verse to mean that Christ was saying that he and the Father make up "one God." The phrase was a common one, and even today if someone used it, people would know exactly what he meant—he and his father are very much alike. When Paul wrote to the Corinthians about his ministry there, he said that he had planted the seed and Apollos had watered it. Then he said, "...he who plants and he who waters are one..." (1 Cor. 3:8 - NKJV). In the Greek texts, the wording of Paul is the same as that in John 10:30, yet no one claims that Paul and Apollos

---

25. Robinson, *op. cit., Priority of John*, p. 384.

make up "one being." Furthermore, the NIV translates 1 Corinthians 3:8 as "The man who plants and the man who waters have **one purpose**…." Why translate the phrase as "are one" in one place, but as "have one purpose" in another place? In this case, translating the same phrase in two different ways obscures the clear meaning of Christ's statement in John 10:30: Christ always did the Father's will; he and God have "**one purpose**."

2. Christ uses the concept of "being one" in other places, and from them one can see that "one purpose" is what is meant. John 11:52 says Jesus was to die to make all God's children "one." In John 17:11, 21 and 22, Jesus prayed to God that his followers would be "one" as he and God were "one." We think it is obvious that Jesus was not praying that all his followers would become one being or "substance" just as he and his Father were one being or "substance." We believe the meaning is clear: Jesus was praying that all his followers be one in purpose just as he and God were one in purpose, a prayer that has not yet been answered.

3. The context of John 10:30 shows conclusively that Jesus was referring to the fact that he had the same purpose as God did. Jesus was speaking about his ability to keep the "sheep," the believers, who came to him. He said that no one could take them out of his hand and that no one could take them out of his Father's hand. Then he said that he and the Father were "one," i.e., had one purpose, which was to keep and protect the sheep.

Buzzard, *op. cit.*, *Doctrine of the Trinity*, pp. 135 and 136; Farley, *op. cit.*, *Unitarianism Defined: The Scripture Doctrine of the Father, Son, and Holy Ghost*, pp. 60 and 61; Morgridge, *op. cit.*, *True Believer's Defence Against Charges Preferred by Trinitarians*, pp. 39–42.

John 10:33
"We are not stoning you for any of these," replied the Jews, "but for blasphemy, because you, a mere man, claim to be God."

---

1. Any difficulty in understanding this verse is caused by the translators. Had they faithfully rendered the Greek text in verse 33 as they did in verses 34 and 35, then it would read, "…you, a man, claim to be *a god*." In the next two verses, John 10:34 and 35, the exact same word (*theos*, without the article) is translated as "god," not "God." The point was made under John 1:1 that usually when "God" is meant, the noun *theos* has the definite article. When there is no article, the translators know that "god" is the more likely translation, and they are normally very sensitive to this. For example, in Acts 12:22, Herod is called *theos* without the article, so the translators translated it "god." The same is true in Acts 28:6, when Paul had been bitten by a viper and the people expected him to die. When he did not die, "…they changed their minds and said he was a god." Since *theos* has no article, and since it is clear from the context that the reference is not about the true God, *theos* is translated "a god." It is a general principle that *theos* without the article should be "a god," or "divine." Since there is no evidence that Jesus was teaching that he was God anywhere in the context, and since the Pharisees would have never believed that this *man* was somehow Yahweh, it makes no sense that they would be saying that he said he was "God." On the other hand, Jesus was clearly teaching that he was sent by God and was doing God's work. Thus, it makes perfect sense that the Pharisees would say he was claiming to be "a god" or "divine."

2. We take issue with the NIV translation of "mere man" for the Greek word *anthropos*. The English word "anthropology," meaning "the study of man," is derived from *anthropos*. Spiros Zodhiates writes, "man, a generic name in distinction from gods and the animals."[26] In the vast majority of versions, *anthropos* is translated as "man." The word *anthropos* occurs 550 times in the Greek text from which the NIV was translated, yet the NIV translated it as "mere man" only in this one verse. This variance borders on dishonesty and demonstrates a willingness to bias the text beyond acceptable limits. Unfortunately, the NIV is not the only translation that puts a Trinitarian spin on this verse. The Jews would have never called Jesus a "mere" man. They called him what they believed he was—a "man." They were offended because they believed that he, "being a man, made himself a god (i.e., someone with divine status).

3. For more on *theos* without the article, see the notes on John 1:1 and Hebrews 1:8.

Morgridge, *op. cit., True Believer's Defence Against Charges Preferred by Trinitarians*, pp. 39–42; *Op. cit., Racovian Catechism*, pp. 34–36; Snedeker, *op. cit., Our Heavenly Father Has No Equals*, p. 422.

John 14:11
Believe me when I say that I am in the Father and the Father is in me; or at least believe on the evidence of the miracles themselves.

This verse is sometimes used to prove the Trinity, but it proves nothing of the kind. The exact same language about being "in" is used many times of Christians. We assert that when the same exact language is used both of Christ and of Christians, it needs to be understood the same way. We are "in" Christ, and Christ is "in" us (cp. John 14:4–7, 17:21, 23 and 26). When used in the sense of "in God," or "in Christ," the word "in" refers to a close communion, a tight fellowship. It was part of the covenant language of the day, when people spoke of being either "in" or "cut off from" the covenant.

Morgridge, *op. cit., True Believer's Defence Against Charges Preferred by Trinitarians*, pp. 116 and 117; *Op. cit., Racovian Catechism*, pp. 142 and 143.

John 14:16 and 17
(16) And I will ask the Father, and he will give you another Counselor to be with you forever—
(17) the Spirit of truth. The world cannot accept him, because it neither sees him nor knows him. But you know him, for he lives with you and will be in you.

Some people assert that "the Holy Spirit" is a person because the Bible has "he" and "him" in these verses in John and in some other places. This assertion is invalid because the gender of the noun and pronoun have nothing to do with whether or not a person or thing is actually a person. See notes on John 1:3.

---

26. *Complete Word Study Dictionary*, (AMG Publishers, Chattanooga, TN, 1992), p. 180.

John 16:28–30
(28) I came from the Father and entered the world; now I am leaving the world and going back to the Father."
(29) Then Jesus' disciples said, "Now you are speaking clearly and without figures of speech.
(30) Now we can see that you know all things and that you do not even need to have anyone ask you questions. This makes us believe that you came from God."

These verses are sometimes used to support the Trinity because Jesus said that he came from the Father, and the disciples answered by saying that he was speaking plainly and not using figures of speech. Thus there are two issues to discuss here. First, what did Jesus mean when he said he "came from the Father," and second, why did the disciples say he spoke clearly (using plain language) and not with a figure of speech?

As to the first issue, when Jesus said that he came from God he was using the same kind of language he used in John 3:13 (see the note on this verse in this appendix). The fact that he "came" from God did not mean he was alive with God before he came. We commonly speak of babies "coming" from their parents without meaning that the baby was somehow alive with the parent before it was born. God was Jesus' Father, and He created the perfect sperm that joined with Mary's egg to become Jesus. So it makes perfect sense that Jesus would say he "came from the Father" and mean only what we mean when we say we come from our father.

A child saying he "came from" his parents is very clear language in every culture, so the disciples acknowledged that Jesus was speaking clearly and not using a figure of speech. This is especially true when we consider that Jesus had generally been vague about his being the Son of God, the Messiah. For example, he often referred to himself as "the Son of Man" (Matt. 8:20), which was confusing to the Semitic people he was speaking to because in Hebrew and Aramaic the expression can mean simply, "a human" (Dan. 8:17). When John's disciples came and asked if Jesus were "the one," Jesus did not say "Yes," but only told them that he was healing, preaching, etc. (Matt. 11:2–6). When Peter and the Apostles finally figured out that he was the Christ, he commanded them not to tell anyone (Matt. 16:20). In John 16:28, however, Jesus said he came from the Father, just as anyone would say he came from his parents, so the disciples clearly understood that Jesus was the Christ.

For an explanation of: "…going back to the Father" (v. 28) see note on John 6:62.

John 17:5
And now, Father, glorify me in your presence with the glory I had with you before the world began.

---

1. There is no question that Jesus "existed" before the world began. But did he exist literally as a person or in God's foreknowledge, "in the mind of God?" Both Christ and the corporate Body of Christ, the Church, existed in God's foreknowledge before being alive. Christ was the "*logos,*" the "plan" of God from the beginning, and he became flesh only when he was conceived. It is Trinitarian bias that causes people to read an actual physical existence into this verse rather than a figurative existence in the mind of God. When 2 Timothy 1:9 says that each Christian was given grace "… before the beginning of time," no one tries to prove that we were actually alive with God back then. Everyone acknowledges that we were "in the mind of God," i.e., in God's foreknowledge. The same is true of Jesus Christ. His glory was "with the Father" before the world began, and in John 17:5 he prayed that it would come into manifestation.

2. Jesus was praying that he would have the glory the Old Testament foretold, which had been in the mind of God, the Father, since before the world began, and would come into concretion. Trinitarians, however, teach that Jesus was praying about glory he had with God many years before his birth, and they assert that this proves he had access to the mind and memory of his "God nature." However, if, as a man, Jesus "remembered" being in glory with the Father before the world began, then he would have known he was God in every sense. He would not have thought of himself as a "man" at all. If he knew he was God, he would not and could not have been "…tempted in every way, just as we are…" because nothing he encountered would have been a "real" temptation to him. He would have had no fear and no thought of failure. There is no real sense in which Scripture could actually say he was "…made like his brothers in every way…" (Heb. 2:17) because he would not have been like us at all. Furthermore, Scripture says that Jesus "grew" in knowledge and wisdom. That would not really be true if Christ had access to some type of God-nature with infinite knowledge and wisdom.

We believe that John 17:5 is a great example of a verse that demonstrates the need for clear thinking concerning the doctrine of the Trinity. The verse can clearly be interpreted in a way that is honest and biblically sound, and shows that Christ was a man, but was in the foreknowledge of God as God's plan for the salvation of mankind. It can also be used the way Trinitarians use it: to prove the Trinity. However, when it is used that way it reveals a Christ that we as Christians cannot truly identify with. We do not have a God-nature to help us when we are tempted or are in trouble or lack knowledge or wisdom. The Bible says that Christ can "sympathize with our weakness" because he was "…tempted in every way, **just as we are**…" (Heb. 4:15). The thrust of that verse is very straightforward. *Because* Christ was just like we are, *and* was tempted in every way that we are, he can sympathize with us. However, if he was not "just as we are," then he would not be able to sympathize with us. We assert that making Christ a God-man makes it impossible to really identify with him.

3. Jesus' prayer in John 17 sets a wonderful example for us as Christians. He poured out his heart to his Father, "the only true God" (John 17:3), and prayed that the prophecies of the Old Testament about him would be fulfilled.

4. For Christ's relation to the Plan of God, see notes on John 1:1. For more on Christ in God's foreknowledge, see the note on John 8:58b.

Op. cit., Racovian Catechism, pp. 144–146; Snedeker, *op. cit., Our Heavenly Father Has No Equals,* pp. 424 and 425.

John 20:17 (KJV)
Jesus saith unto her, Touch me not; for I am not yet ascended to my Father: but go to my brethren, and say unto them, I ascend unto my Father, and your Father; and *to* my God, and your God.

---

1. This verse is no problem at all in all the major versions we checked except for the NIV. The translators of the NIV caused a problem by using the word "return" instead of "ascend," and making Christ say, "…I have not yet **returned** to my Father…." The Greek word means, "to go up" and although it occurs 82 times in the Greek New Testament, even the NIV translators have translated it "returning" only in this one place, and as "returned" in the next verse. Christ did not "return" to his Father as if he had been there before, rather he "went up" to his Father. The Trinitarian "problem" in this verse is caused by a mistranslation, but, thankfully, other versions translate the verse more accurately.

2. This verse is one of the strongest proofs in the Bible that there is no Trinity. This event occurred after the resurrection, and Jesus said to Mary that he was ascending to "...my God, and your God." Jesus' statement makes it clear that "God" is both his God and Mary's God. If Jesus *is* God, he cannot *have* a God, for by definition if someone has a "God," he cannot *be* "God." If Jesus had a "God" as he said, then he cannot be part of that God. This is especially clear in this verse, because he and Mary have the same God. If he were God, then he would have been Mary's God, too. He would not have said that he was going up to her God, because "her God," i.e., Jesus himself, was standing right there. One of the most recognized principles of Bible interpretation, and one that is accepted by conservative scholars from all denominations, is that to be properly understood, the Bible must be read in a literal, "normal," or "standard" way, i.e., the words of the Word should be understood the way we understand them in everyday speech, unless figurative language is demanded by the context. Everyone understands the phrase, "my God." Christ used it both before and after his resurrection. He called to "my God" when he was on the Cross. He told Mary he was going to ascend to "my God." He spoke of "my God" to both the churches of Sardis and Philadelphia (Rev. 3:2 and 12). It is hard to see how Jesus can be assumed to be co-equal and co-eternal with God when he calls Him, "my God." The Bible simply means what it says in this verse: God is indeed both our God and Jesus' God.

John 20:28 (KJV)
And Thomas answered and said unto him, My Lord and my God.

---

1. Jesus never referred to himself as "God" in the absolute sense, so what precedent then did Thomas have for calling Jesus "My God?" The Greek language uses the word *theos*, ("God" or "god") with a broader meaning than is customary today. In the Greek language and in the culture of the day, "GOD" (all early manuscripts of the Bible were written in all capital letters) was a descriptive title applied to a range of authorities, including the Roman governor (Acts 12:22), and even the Devil (2 Cor. 4:4). It was used of someone with divine authority. It was not limited to its absolute sense as a personal name for the supreme Deity as we use it today.

2. Given the language of the time, and given that Jesus did represent the Father and have divine authority, the expression used by Thomas is certainly understandable. On the other hand, to make Thomas say that Jesus was "God," and thus 1/3 of a triune God, seems incredible. In *Concessions of Trinitarians*, Michaelis, a Trinitarian, writes:

> I do not affirm that Thomas passed all at once from the extreme of doubt to the highest degree of faith, *and acknowledged Christ to be the true God.* This appears to me too much for the then existing knowledge of the disciples; and we have no intimation that they recognized the divine nature of Christ before the outpouring of the Holy Spirit. I am therefore inclined to understand this expression, which broke out in the height of his astonishment, in a figurative sense, denoting only "whom I shall ever reverence in the highest degree"...Or a person raised from the dead might be regarded as a divinity; for the word *God is* not always used in the strict doctrinal sense" [Michaelis is quoted by Dana, ref. below].

Remember that it was common at that time to call the God's representatives "God," and the Old Testament contains quite a few examples. When Jacob wrestled with "God," it is clear that he was actually wrestling with an angel (Hosea 12:4—For more on that, see the note on Gen. 16:7–13).

3. There are many Trinitarian authorities who admit that there was no knowledge of Trinitarian doctrine at the time Thomas spoke. For example, if the disciples believed that Jesus was "God" in the sense that many Christians do, they would not have "all fled" just a few days before when he was arrested. The confession of the two disciples walking along the road to Emmaus demonstrated the thoughts of Jesus' followers at the time. Speaking to the resurrected Christ, whom they mistook as just a traveler, they talked about Jesus. They said Jesus "…was a prophet, powerful in word and deed before God…and they crucified him; but we had hoped that he was the one who was going to redeem Israel…" (Luke 24:19–21). The Bible is clear that these disciples thought Jesus was a "prophet." Even though some of the Apostles realized that Jesus was the Christ, they knew that according to the Old Testament prophecies, the Christ, the anointed of God, was to be a man. There is no evidence from the Gospel accounts that Jesus' disciples believed him to be God, and Thomas, upon seeing the resurrected Christ, was not birthing a new theology in a moment of surprise.

4. The context of the verse shows that its subject is the fact that Jesus was *alive*. Only three verses earlier, Thomas had ignored the eyewitness testimony of the other Apostles when they told him they had seen the Lord. The resurrection of Christ was such a disputed doctrine that Thomas did not believe it (the other Apostles had not either), and thus Jesus' death would have caused Thomas to doubt that Jesus was who he said he was—the Messiah. Thomas believed Jesus was *dead*. Thus, he was shocked and astonished when he saw—and was confronted by— Jesus Himself. Thomas, upon being confronted by the *living* Christ, instantly believed in the resurrection, i.e., that God had raised the man Jesus from the dead, and, given the standard use of "God" in the culture as one with God's authority, it certainly makes sense that Thomas would proclaim, "…My Lord and my God." There is no mention of the Trinity in the context, and there is no reason to believe that the disciples would have even been aware of such a doctrine. Thomas spoke what he would have known: that the man Jesus who he thought was dead was alive and had divine authority.

5. For other uses of *theos* applicable to this verse, see Hebrews 1:8 below.

Buzzard, *op. cit.*, *Doctrine of the Trinity*, pp. 39–41, 61 and 62, 136 and 137; Dana, *op. cit.*, *Letters Addressed to Relatives and Friends*, pp. 23–25; Farley, *op. cit.*, *Unitarianism Defined: The Scripture Doctrine of the Father, Son, and Holy Ghost*, pp. 62–64; Morgridge, *op. cit.*, *True Believer's Defence Against Charges Preferred by Trinitarians*, pp. 109 and 110; Norton, *op. cit.*, *A Statement of Reasons for Not Believing the Doctrines of Trinitarians*, pp. 299–304; Snedeker, *op. cit.*, *Our Heavenly Father Has No Equals*, pp. 271 and 272, 426–430.

Acts 5:3 and 4

(3) Then Peter said, "Ananias, how is it that Satan has so filled your heart that you have lied to the Holy Spirit and have kept for yourself some of the money you received for the land?

(4) Didn't it belong to you before it was sold? And after it was sold, wasn't the money at your disposal? What made you think of doing such a thing? You have not lied to men, but to God."

---

1. We must understand that both "God" and *pneuma hagion* ("holy spirit") can refer to something other than a separate "person" in the Trinity. Since there is no verse that actually states the doctrine of the Trinity, its existence is built from assumption and by piecing verses together. Verses such as Acts 5:3 and 4 are used as "proof," for the doctrine, but that is actually circular reasoning. The doctrine is assumed, and then, because this verse fits the assumption, it is stated to be proof of the doctrine. However, at best these verses could offer minimal support for the Trinity because there are other completely acceptable ways to handle them, specifically that "the Holy Spirit" is sometimes another designation for God.

2. It is clear in these verses that God and "the Holy Spirit" are equated, and this has caused Trinitarians to claim that this proves their case that God and "the Holy Spirit" are the same. But these verses are clearly an example of Semitic parallelism, which is one of the most commonly employed literary devices in Scripture. "God" is equated with "the Holy Spirit." Obviously, the point is that Ananias did not lie to two different persons, but to one person, God, and the parallelism serves to emphasize that fact.

3. Trinitarians believe that "the Holy Spirit" is the third "person" in the three-person Trinity. Non-Trinitarians say that no "third person" exists. The original texts were all capital letters, so every use was "HOLY SPIRIT." There are times in the English versions when "spirit" is spelled with a capital "S" and times when it has a lower case "s." This is all the work of the translators, because all the early Greek manuscripts were in all capital letters. Thus, whether "HOLY SPIRIT" should be translated as "Holy Spirit" or "holy spirit" must be determined from the context (for more on capitalization and punctuation, see the notes on Heb. 1:8).

To the non-Trinitarian, the holy spirit is either 1) another name for God the Father (in which case it is capitalized), 2) the power of God in operation, or 3) the gift of God's nature (spirit) that is given to each believer. Peter spoke of this gift on the Day of Pentecost when he said, "...ye shall receive the gift of the Holy Ghost" (Acts 2:38 - KJV). Because *pneuma* has several meanings the context of a passage of Scripture must always be studied carefully to determine the correct meaning.

4. God is known by many names and designations in the Bible. *Elohim*, *El Shaddai*, Yahweh, *Adon*, "the Holy One of Israel," "the Most High" and "the Father" are just a few. Since God is "holy" and God is "spirit," it should not surprise us that one of the names of God, the Father, is "the Holy Spirit." The distinguished scholar and author of *Young's Concordance*, Robert Young, wrote: "Spirit—is used of God himself, or the Divine Mind, His energy, influence, gifts."[27] When *pneuma hagion*, "holy spirit," is being used as another name for the Father, it should be capitalized, just as any name is capitalized.

When "holy spirit" refers to the spirit that God gives as a gift, it should not be capitalized. Biblically, "the Holy Spirit" is quite different from "the holy spirit." The record of the birth of Christ in Luke provides a good example of why it is important to recognize whether the "Holy Spirit" refers to the power of God or another name for God. "The angel answered, 'The Holy Spirit will come upon you, and the power of the Most High will overshadow you. So the holy one to be born will be called the Son of God' " (Luke 1:35). This verse and Matthew 1:18–20 make Jesus Christ the Son of the Holy Spirit, yet all the other references to Jesus make him the Son of the Father. Did Jesus have two fathers? Of course not. In the records of Christ's birth, "the Holy Spirit" is another way of referring to God Himself, and not a third person in the Trinity. This eliminates the "problem" of which person in the Trinity actually fathered Jesus. Also in Acts 5:3, "Holy Spirit" is another name for God. For a

---

27. *Op. cit., Young's Concordance*, Hints and Helps # 66.

much more complete explanation of the uses of "holy spirit," see our book: *The Gift of Holy Spirit: The Power To Be Like Christ*. See also Appendix I.

> Buzzard, *op. cit., Doctrine of the Trinity*, pp. 101–107; Farley, *op. cit., Unitarianism Defined: The Scripture Doctrine of the Father, Son, and Holy Ghost*, pp. 96–108; Morgridge, *op. cit., True Believer's Defence Against Charges Preferred by Trinitarians*, pp. 129–138.

Acts 7:45 (KJV)
Which also our fathers that came after brought in with Jesus into the possession of the Gentiles, whom God drave out before the face of our fathers, unto the days of David;

---

1. Although the King James English makes this verse a little hard to understand, it is saying that Jesus was the one who brought the Israelites into the Promised Land. This is a case of mistranslation. The name "Jesus" and the name "Joshua" are the same, and on two occasions the translators of the KJV confused them. This point is well established by William Barclay, a professor and author at Trinity College in Glasgow. He writes:

> The name "Jesus" underlines the real humanity of our Lord. To us the name Jesus is a holy and sacred name, and we would count it almost blasphemy to give it to any child or call any person by it. But in New Testament times it was one of the commonest of names. It is the Greek form by which three Hebrew Old Testament names are regularly represented—Joshua (e.g., Exod. 17:10); Jehoshua (e.g., Zech. 3:1); Jeshua (Neh. 7:7). There are indeed two occasions in the AV [the KJV] in which Joshua is very confusingly called "Jesus." In Acts 7:45, we read that the fathers brought the tabernacle into the land of Palestine with Jesus. In Hebrews 4:8, it is said that if "Jesus" had been able to give the people rest, there would have been no need to speak of still another day. In both cases, "Jesus" is Joshua, a fact which is made clear in all the more modern translations. By the second century, the name "Jesus" was vanishing as an ordinary name. Amongst the Jews it vanished because it had become a hated name by which no Jew would call his son; and amongst the Christians it has vanished because it was too sacred for common use.[28]

2. One of the easiest and most accessible keys to correct biblical interpretation is the context. Examine the context of Acts 7:45, and it becomes exceedingly clear that the verse is not speaking of Jesus.

Acts 7:44-46
(44) "Our forefathers had the tabernacle of the Testimony with them in the desert. It had been made as God directed Moses, according to the pattern he had seen.
(45) Having received the tabernacle, our fathers under **Joshua** brought it with them when they took the land from the nations God drove out before them. It remained in the land until the time of David,
(46) who enjoyed God's favor and asked that he might provide a dwelling place for the God of Jacob.

---

28. Barclay, *op. cit., Jesus As They Saw Him*, pp. 10 and 11.

There is no record anywhere in the Old Testament that shows Jesus with the Tabernacle, and, as Barclay pointed out, all the modern translations read "Joshua."

Acts 7:59
While they were stoning him, Stephen prayed, "Lord Jesus, receive my spirit."

This verse supports the idea of the Trinity only as it appears in some translations. The KJV has the phrase, "calling upon *God*," but puts "God" in *italics* to show that the translators added the word and that it was not in the original text. The truth is that "God" does not appear in *any* Greek text of the verse. Thus, this verse does not support the Trinity.

Acts 20:28b
…Be shepherds of the church of God, which he bought with his own blood.

---

1. There are some Greek manuscripts that read "…the church of the Lord…" instead of "the church of God." Many Trinitarian scholars believe that "Lord" is the original reading, because there is no mention anywhere in the Bible of God having blood. If the Greek manuscripts that read "Lord" are the original ones, then the "problem" is solved. However, it is the belief of the authors that good textual research shows that "the church of God" is the correct reading.

2. Both the American Bible Society and the Institute For New Testament Research in Germany (which produces the Nestle-Aland Greek text) agree that the manuscript evidence supports the reading *tou haimatios tou idiou*, literally, the blood of His own (Son), and not *idiou haimatios*, "his own blood." God paid for our salvation with the blood of His own Son, Jesus Christ.

3. The text note at the bottom of the very Trinitarian NIV Study Bible gets the meaning of the verse correct: "*his own blood*. Lit. 'the blood of his own one,' a term of endearment (such as 'his own dear one') referring to His own Son."

Norton, *op. cit., A Statement of Reasons for Not Believing the Doctrines of Trinitarians*, pp. 184, 199–203; Ehrman, *op. cit., Orthodox Corruption*, pp. 87 and 88; *Op. cit., Racovian Catechism*, pp. 83 and 84; Wilson, *op. cit., Paul: The Mind of the Apostle*, p. 429.

Romans 8:3
For what the law was powerless to do in that it was weakened by the sinful nature,
God did by sending his own Son in the likeness of sinful man to be a sin offering.
And so he condemned sin in sinful man,

This verse has confused some Christians because it refers to Jesus being "…in the likeness of sinful man…" (the Greek is more literally: "…in the likeness of sinful flesh…," as the KJV, NASB, and ESV have). Trinitarians teach that Jesus was not a man like we are because he was both "fully human" and "fully God." But there is another explanation of the verse, one that fits with a non-Trinitarian understanding of Scripture. Carefully reading the verse shows that it does not say Jesus was like "humans," it says that Jesus was like "sinful" humans. He was like we are in that he was a man, but he was different from us "sinful" people because he was sinless. He had no sin nature. Neither did he ever commit sin. The fact that Jesus was not a God-man, but was a human in every sense of the word explains why the verse has to have the adjective "sinful" to describe "man." Jesus was a man, but only "in the likeness" of "sinful" man. If the reason that Jesus was only like man was that he was a God-man, then the presence of the adjective "sinful" is unnecessary.

The word "likeness" is a good translation of the Greek word *homoioma*, which refers to similarity; when things are similar. For example, Romans 1:23 speaks of images (statues, paintings, etc.), that "look like" people, birds, and animals, but of course are not the real thing. Revelation 9:7 refers to locust-creatures that in some ways were "like," or similar in appearance to, horses. Jesus Christ was "in the likeness of" us "sinful" people, but was not himself "sinful."

Romans 9:5b
…Christ, who is God over all, forever praised!…

---

1. The student of the Bible should be aware that the original text had no punctuation, and thus in some instances there is more than one way a verse can be translated without violating the grammar of the text (see the notes on Heb. 1:8). Then how do we arrive at the correct translation and meaning, the one that God, the Author, meant us to believe? In the majority of cases, the context, both immediate and remote, will reveal to us what He is trying to say. The entire Bible fits together in such a way that one part can give us clues to interpret another part. The serious student of the Bible will glean information from the scope of Scripture to assist in the interpretation of any one verse. Romans 9:5 is one of the verses that can be translated different ways, and thus the context and scope of Scripture will help us determine the correct interpretation. Note from the examples below that translators and translating committees vary greatly in their handling of Romans 9:5:

- RSV: to them belong the patriarchs, and of their race, according to the flesh, is the Christ. God who is over all be blessed forever. Amen.
- Moffatt: the patriarchs are theirs, and theirs too (so far as natural descent goes) is the Christ. (Blessed for evermore be the God who is over all! Amen.)
- KJV: Whose *are* the fathers, and of whom as concerning the flesh Christ *came*, who is over all, God blessed for ever. Amen.
- NASB: whose are the fathers, and from whom is the Christ according to the flesh, who is over all, God blessed forever. Amen.
- NIV: Theirs are the patriarchs, and from them is traced the human ancestry of Christ, who is God over all, forever praised! Amen.

Although the exact wording of the above translations differs, they fall into two basic categories: those that are worded to make Christ into God, and those that make the final phrase into a type of eulogy or doxology referring to God the Father. The RSV and Moffatt are outstanding examples of the latter.

2. In *The Doctrine of the Trinity*, R. S. Franks, a Trinitarian and the Principal *Emeritus* of Western College in Bristol, writes:

It should be added that Rom. 9:5 cannot be adduced to prove that Paul ever thought of Christ as God. The state of the case is found in the R.V. margin…He [Paul] never leaves the ground of Jewish monotheism. It has been pointed out that Rom. 9:5 cannot be brought in to question this statement. On the contrary, God is spoken of by the Apostle as not only the Father, but also the God of our Lord Jesus Christ"[29]

3. There is good evidence from both the immediate remote contexts that the last phrase of this verse is a eulogy or doxology to God the Father. "God over all" and "God blessed forever" are both used of God the Father elsewhere in the New Testament (Rom. 1:25; 2 Cor. 11:31; Eph. 1:3, 4:6; 1 Tim. 6:15). In contrast, neither phrase is ever used of Christ. It would be highly unusual to take eulogies that were commonly used of God and, abruptly and without comment or explanation, apply them to Christ.

4. Asking why the words are even in the text gives us a key to understanding them. Paul is writing about the way that God has especially blessed the Jews. The verses immediately before Romans 9:5 point out that God has given them the adoption, the glory, the covenants, the law, the worship, the promises, the patriarchs and even the human ancestry of Jesus Christ. How blessed they are! No wonder a eulogy to God is inserted: "…God, who is over all, be blessed forever! Amen."

5. The entire context of Romans 9:5 is describing God's blessings to the Jews, who have a heritage of being aggressively monotheistic. An insert about Christ being God seems most inappropriate. This is especially true when we understand that Paul is writing in a way designed to win the Jews. For example, he calls them "…my kindred according to the flesh" (v. 3 - NRSV), and says he has sorrow and anguish in his heart for them (v. 2 - NRSV). Would he then put into this section a phrase that he knew would be offensive to the very Jews for whom he is sorrowing and who he is trying to win? Certainly not. On the contrary, after just saying that Christ came from the line of the Patriarchs, something about which the Jews were suspicious, a eulogy to the Father would assure the Jews that there was no idolatry or false elevation of Christ intended, but that he was part of the great blessing of God.

Buzzard, *op. cit., Doctrine of the Trinity*, pp. 131 and 132; Farley, *op. cit., Unitarianism Defined: The Scripture Doctrine of the Father, Son, and Holy Ghost*, pp. 67–69; Morgridge, *op. cit., True Believer's Defence Against Charges Preferred by Trinitarians*, pp. 111–114; Norton, *op. cit., A Statement of Reasons for Not Believing the Doctrines of Trinitarians*, pp. 203–214; Snedeker, *op. cit., Our Heavenly Father Has No Equals*, pp. 434–440.

Romans 10:9
That if you confess with your mouth, "Jesus is Lord," and believe in your heart that God raised him from the dead, you will be saved.

---

1. Christ is Lord, but "Lord" is not "God." "Lord" (the Greek word is *kurios*) is a masculine title of respect and nobility, and it is used many times in the New Testament. To say that Jesus is God because the Bible calls him "Lord" is very poor scholarship. "Lord" is used in many ways in the Bible, and others beside God and Jesus are called "Lord."

- Property owners are called "Lord" (Matt. 20:8, "owner" = *kurios*).
- Heads of households are called "Lord" (Mark 13:35, "owner" = *kurios*).
- Slave owners are called "Lord" (Matt. 10:24, "master" = *kurios*).
- Husbands are called "Lord" (1 Pet. 3:6, "master" = *kurios*).

---

29. R. S. Franks, *The Doctrine of the Trinity*, (Gerald Duckworth and Co., London, 1953), pp. 34–36.

- A son calls his father "Lord" (Matt. 21:30, "sir" = *kurios*).
- The Roman Emperor is called "Lord" (Acts 25:26, "His Majesty" = *kurios*).
- Roman authorities are called "Lord" (Matt. 27:63, "sir" = *kurios*).

The problem these verses cause to anyone who says Christ is God because he is called "Lord" is immediately apparent—many others beside Christ would also be God (for a concise study of the uses of "lord" in the New Testament, see Appendix B).

2. We must recognize that it was God who made Jesus "Lord." Acts 2:36 says: "…God has **made** this Jesus…both Lord and Christ." If "Lord" equals "God," then somehow God *made* Jesus "God," which is something that even Trinitarians do not teach, because it is vital to Trinitarian doctrine that Jesus be co-equal and co-eternal with the Father. The fact that the Bible says God *made* Jesus "Lord" is an argument *against* the Trinity.

Romans 10:13
"…Everyone who calls on the name of the Lord will be saved."

The context of this verse in Romans makes it clear that the "Lord" referred to in this verse is the Lord Jesus Christ. However, this verse is a quotation from Joel 2:32 in the Old Testament, and in Joel the "LORD" is Yahweh. That has caused some Trinitarians to say that Jesus is God. The argument is not valid, however. There is nothing in the context or scope of Scripture that shows that Yahweh and Jesus Christ are the same being. What it shows is simple and straightforward: In the Old Testament, one called upon Yahweh for salvation, and now we call upon Jesus Christ for salvation. This does not show an identity of persons, rather it demonstrates a shift of responsibility. This responsibility that Jesus now has was foreshadowed in the Old Testament record of Joseph: the people would go to Pharaoh for their needs to be met, but after Pharaoh elevated Joseph to second-in-command, he told them, "Go to Joseph" (Gen. 41:55). No one would conclude that Pharaoh and Joseph were the same being, and there is no reason to conclude that Jesus and God are both "God" just because Jesus now has some of the responsibilities that God had until He exalted Jesus.

Part of the confusion surrounding this issue is that in the Old Testament, many versions do not print the name Yahweh, but instead say "LORD." Although God never commanded it, it was the custom of the Jews, out of reverence for God, not to pronounce the name of God, so they wrote "LORD" when the Hebrew text said Yahweh. Many Christian Bibles do not have God's name clearly translated, but have "LORD" where the Hebrew has Yahweh. This confuses many Christians who see "LORD" in both the Old and New Testaments, and assume it is the same person. Also, many Christians who have some training in the Scriptures have been taught that Yahweh in the Old Testament was Jesus Christ. So, instead of seeing Yahweh in Joel and "Lord" in Romans, and then realizing that the Lord Jesus is now doing what Yahweh did, they erroneously believe the same person is acting in both places.

God made Jesus Lord and gave him all authority. This verse and others show that Jesus has taken on many of the jobs God used to do. We understand that perfectly in our culture, because we know what it means to get a promotion and take over a job someone else used to do. With the promotion and new job often comes a new title. Thus, "this same Jesus" was made "Lord" and "Christ" and was given all authority, including raising the dead and judging the people (John 5:21–27). The verses in the Old Testament that speak of God's authority are often quoted in the New Testament and applied to Christ because God gave the authority to Christ.

Snedeker, *op. cit., Our Heavenly Father Has No Equals*, pp. 403–406.

Romans 15:12
And again, Isaiah says, "The Root of Jesse will spring up, one who will arise to rule over the nations; the Gentiles will hope in him."

See the note on Revelation 5:5.

---

1 Corinthians 8:6
yet for us there is but one God, the Father, from whom all things came and for whom we live; and there is but one Lord, Jesus Christ, through whom all things came and through whom we live.

---

1. Trinitarians say that this verse supports their position because of the final phrase in the verse, i.e., that all things came through Jesus Christ. But what the verse actually says is that all things came "from" God, "through" Jesus. This testimony stands in contradiction to Trinitarian doctrine because it places Jesus in a subordinate role to God. According to this verse, he is not "co-equal" with the Father.

2. The context is the key to understanding what the phrase "…through whom all things came…" means. There is no mention in either the immediate or the remote context about the Creation of all things in the beginning. Therefore it would be unusual for this verse to mention God's original Creation of Genesis 1:1, which it is not. Rather, it is speaking of the Church. God provided all things for the Church via Jesus Christ. The whole of 1 Corinthians is taken up with Church issues, and Paul starts 8:6 with "for us," i.e., *for* Christians. The very next two verses speak about the fact that, for the Church, there are no laws against eating food sacrificed to idols. Verse 8 says, "But food does not bring us near to God; we are no worse if we do not eat, and no better if we do." This revelation was new for the Church. The Old Testament believers did not have this freedom. They had dozens of food laws. The verse is powerful indeed, and states clearly that Christians have one God who is the ultimate source of all things, and one Lord, Jesus Christ, who is the way by which God provided all things to the Church.

3. This verse, when properly understood, is actually strong evidence that Jesus Christ is not God. Polytheism was rampant in Corinth, and Scripture is clear that "…there is no God but one" (1 Cor. 8:4). Then the text continues with the statements that although there may be many gods and lords, for Christians there is but one God, the Father, and one Lord, Jesus Christ. If the doctrine of the Trinity is correct, then this text can only be construed as confusing. Here was the perfect opportunity to say, "for us there is only one God made up of the Father, Son and Holy Ghost," or something similar, but, instead, Scripture tells us that only the Father is God. That should stand as conclusive evidence that Jesus is not God.

Hyndman, *op. cit., Principles of Unitarianism*, pp. 58–63; Morgridge, *op. cit., True Believer's Defence Against Charges Preferred by Trinitarians*, pp. 35–36.

---

1 Corinthians 10:4b (KJV)
…they drank of that spiritual Rock that followed them: and that Rock was Christ.

---

1. This verse is only a problem if it is misunderstood or mistranslated. Some Trinitarians use it to teach that Christ was actually *with* the Israelites, following them around. However, the Old Testament makes no mention of Christ being with the Israelites in the wilderness. And if he had been, he certainly would not have been "following" them.

2. The word "follow" means "to go after," and that can mean either in time or space. The Israelites did "drink," i.e., *get* nourishment, from knowing about the Christ who was to come after them. The very Trinitarian NIV translates the word "follow" as "accompanied," as if Jesus were accompanying the Israelites on their journey. The Greek word usually translated "follow" is *akoloutheo*. It appears in the Nestle-Aland Greek New Testament 90 times. Even in the NIV it is translated as some form of "follow" (like "follows," "following," etc.) 83 times. The NIV translates *akoloutheo* as "accompanied" only twice, here and in Mark 6:1, and we submit that the NIV does so here because of the translators' Trinitarian bias and not because the context calls for it. Although it is true that *akolutheo* can be translated as "accompany," it should not be translated that way here, but would be better translated as "followed." The vast majority of translations agree. As we have said, there is no verse in the Old Testament that records Jesus Christ traveling with the Israelites, so the translation "accompanied" does not fit with the rest of Scripture. Christ was the hope of Israel, and people who looked forward to him were strengthened by their anticipation of their coming Messiah.

3. Since this verse mentions the Israelites in the desert, the desert wanderings become the "remoter context" against which one must check any interpretation. As we have already noted, there is no reference that can be brought forward to show that Christ was either with the Israelites or was somehow following them around. Are there verses that show that the Israelites were looking forward to the Messiah? Yes, many. The Passover Lamb foreshadowed the Messiah. The manna anticipated Christ being "...the true bread from heaven." The Tabernacle, with all its offerings, foreshadowed Christ in many ways, including being the place where people would meet God. The High Priest was a type of the Great High Priest, Jesus Christ. It was in the wilderness where that great prophecy of the coming Messiah was given: "...A star will come out of Jacob; a scepter will rise out of Israel...," and "...their kingdom will be exalted" (Num. 24:17 and 24:7). There is no question that the lesson from these verses is that the people looked forward to the coming of the Messiah and "drank," i.e., got strength and nourishment, from knowing that he was coming.

Buzzard, *op. cit.*, *Doctrine of the Trinity*, pp. 52 and 53; Snedeker, *op. cit.*, *Our Heavenly Father Has No Equals*, pp. 440 and 441.

---

1 Corinthians 10:9
We should not test the Lord, as some of them did—and were killed by snakes.

---

1. The reason this verse is a problem verse is that the Greek manuscripts differ. Some texts read "Christ," while others read "the Lord." As it is translated in versions like the NIV, AMP, NASB and others that take the word "Lord" as original, there is no problem at all. This verse is only a problem in some versions that have "Christ" instead of "the Lord."

2. The subject of textual criticism is very involved, and it is common that scholars differ in their opinions as to which texts are more original and which texts have been altered. In this case, there are early texts that read "Lord," and some that read "Christ," so the job of determining the original reading from textual evidence becomes more difficult. We agree with the conclusion of Bart Ehrman

(*The Orthodox Corruption of Scripture*) that "Lord" is the original meaning, and refer anyone who wants to examine the textual argument to his work.

3. Every translator will testify to the importance of *context* in determining the correct translation of Scripture. We feel the context makes it clear that "Lord" is the correct reading. Although there are dozens of times that the Israelites were said to tempt "God" or "the LORD" in the Old Testament, there is not even a single reference to tempting Christ. By reading the verse carefully, we obtain a vital clue to its meaning and the proper translation. The verse says that when the Israelites tempted the LORD, they were "destroyed by serpents." This phrase allows us to find the exact record in the Old Testament that is being referred to. In Numbers 21:5 and 6, the Israelites "spoke against God" and then "…the LORD sent venomous snakes among them…." In the record of this event in the Old Testament, the words "God" and Yahweh are used, but "Christ" is never mentioned. Furthermore, there is no Scripture anywhere in the Old Testament that says "Christ" poured out his "wrath," and certainly not by sending serpents. Thus, if some Greek texts read "the Lord" and others read "Christ," the context points to "Lord" as the correct interpretation.

> Ehrman, *op. cit., Orthodox Corruption*, pp. 89 and 90; Norton, *op. cit., A Statement of Reasons for Not Believing the Doctrines of Trinitarians*, pp. 473 and 474; Snedeker, *op. cit., Our Heavenly Father Has No Equals*, pp. 441 and 442.

---

1 Corinthians 12:4–6

(4) There are different kinds of gifts, but the same Spirit.
(5) There are different kinds of service, but the same Lord.
(6) There are different kinds of working, but the same God works all of them in all men.

---

1. There is no mention here of the "Trinity." The verses speak of three: God, Christ and the spirit, but do not speak of a Trinitarian formula. We put "spirit" with a lower case "s" because it refers to God's gift of holy spirit that is born in each believer. For more on this use of "spirit," see the notes on Acts 5:3 and 4, Appendix I and our book: *The Gift of Holy Spirit: The Power To Be Like Christ*.

2. We find it significant, especially in light of Trinitarian doctrine, that the three mentioned in this verse are "spirit," "Lord" and "God" instead of "spirit," "Lord" and "*Father.*" Morgridge writes:

> Three objects are distinctly mentioned—God, Christ and the Spirit. If Christ and the Spirit were persons in the Trinity, the distinct mention of them would be superfluous, they being included in "God." But as one of the objects mentioned is called "God," it follows that neither of the other two can be God; for we know that "there is none other God but one." If the three objects were the three persons in the Trinity, why is the name "God" given to one of them only?

We agree with Morgridge that the mention of "God" as one of the three, precludes the other two from being "God." The language of the text is plain and simple. There are three distinct things being mentioned, and any attempt to force them together into "one" distorts the simple truth being communicated by the Word of God.

> Morgridge, *op. cit., True Believer's Defence Against Charges Preferred by Trinitarians*, pp. 101 and 102.

> **2 Corinthians 5:19**
> that God was reconciling the world to himself in Christ, not counting men's sins against them. And he has committed to us the message of reconciliation.

1. As this verse is translated in the NIV, it does not have a Trinitarian meaning. Some Trinitarians use the concept from some other translations that "God was in Christ" to prove the Trinity. If the Trinity were true, then God could not be "in" Christ as if Christ were a container. If the Trinity were in fact a true doctrine, then this would be a wonderful place to express it and say, "God was Christ."

2. The fact that in some versions the verse reads that "God was in Christ" is evidence against the Trinity. If the phrase "God was in Christ" means that Christ is God, then when the Bible says that Christ is "in" Christians (Col. 1:27), it would mean that Christians are Christ. Since we know that Christ being "in" Christians does not make us Christ, then we also know that God being "in" Christ does not make Christ God. The correct understanding of the verse is that God was in Christ in the sense that God placed His spirit in Christ, and Christ is in us in the same way—via the gift of holy spirit.

Snedeker, *op. cit., Our Heavenly Father Has No Equals*, pp. 442 and 443.

> **2 Corinthians 12:19b**
> …We have been speaking in the sight of God as those in Christ; and everything we do, dear friends, is for your strengthening.

1. The Greek text contains a difficult construction, and reads, "God in Christ," which has caused some to believe it is a reference to the Trinity. Not at all. If anything, it tends to refute the Trinity (see the notes on 2 Cor. 5:19).

2. This verse is translated in several different ways by Trinitarian translators. It is noteworthy that some Trinitarians do not believe this verse is referring to the Trinity, and how they translate it. A good example is the NIV, quoted above, which is especially meaningful because the NIV translation favors the Trinitarian position in most instances.

> **2 Corinthians 13:14**
> May the grace of the Lord Jesus Christ, and the love of God, and the fellowship of the Holy Spirit be with you all.

1. This closing verse of the epistle of 2 Corinthians is a doxology, and is typical of how Paul closes his Epistles. Galatians, Philippians and both Thessalonian epistles close with "The grace of our Lord Jesus Christ…." The close of Ephesians includes "…love with faith from God…." There is no reason to conclude that a closing doxology would not incorporate three wonderful attributes: the love of God, the grace of Christ and the fellowship of the spirit.

2. There is no presentation of the Trinity in this verse. Three different things are mentioned, but they are never said to be "one," or "of one substance," or "making up one God," or anything like what would be needed for a Trinitarian formula. There are many times that three things are mentioned together in the Bible, yet Trinitarians do not make them "one" just because they are mentioned together. For example, "Peter, James and John" are often mentioned together, but that fact does not make them "one." Abraham, Isaac and Jacob are also often mentioned together, and that fact does not make them "one." If three things are actually "one," there must be a clear verse that says so, and as even Trinitarians will admit, there is no such verse that articulates that God, Jesus and the spirit equal "one God."

3. Although this verse is used by some to support the Trinity, a careful reading shows that it actually contradicts it. The three mentioned in the verse are "God," "Jesus Christ" and the "Holy Spirit" (which we believe should be accurately translated as "holy spirit"). Yet the Trinitarian position is that "God" is composed of the Father, Christ and the Spirit. So the fact that the verse mentions "God" separate from Christ and the holy spirit is strong evidence that they are indeed *separate from* "God" and that there is no Trinity (see also the note on 1 Cor. 12:4–6).

4. This verse does not mean that we have fellowship with the "person," the Holy Spirit, who is part of the Trinity. It refers to the fellowship that Christians have with each other because of the presence of God's gift, holy spirit, in each of us. The "fellowship of the spirit" is a phrase that is also used in Philippians 2:1, and the text note on this verse in the NIV Study Bible is fairly accurate. It says: "…The fellowship among believers produced by the Spirit, who indwells each of them…." We would replace "Spirit" with "spirit," (because we believe it refers to God's gift) and translate "who" as "which" ("spirit" is neuter in the Greek text), but the point is made beautifully. The fellowship of the spirit is the fellowship Christians enjoy with other believers because of the presence of the spirit in each of us (For more on God's gift of holy spirit, see the notes on Acts 5:3 and 4).

Dana, *op. cit., Letters Addressed to Relatives and Friends*, pp. 213 and 214; Morgridge, *op. cit., True Believer's Defence Against Charges Preferred by Trinitarians*, pp. 101 and 102; Snedeker, *op. cit., Our Heavenly Father Has No Equals*, pp. 115–118.

Ephesians 1:22 and 23
(22) And God placed all things under his feet and appointed him to be head over everything for the church,
(23) which is his body, the fullness of him who fills everything in every way.

There are some Trinitarians who assert that the last phrase of verse 23 proves the Trinity. Not so, for there is no mention of any Trinitarian concept such as "three-in-one." This verse clearly teaches that God was the one who "appointed" Christ to be over the Church. Surely if Christ were a co-equal part of God, he needed no such appointment, because by nature he would already have been over the Church. The way to properly understand this verse is to read it with a standard sense of the word "appointment." If Christ were "appointed" to the position of "Head" over the Church, then it is obvious that he would not have been "Head" without the appointment, which could not be true if Christ were God.

Again the *context* is the great key in discovering what a verse is saying. The context of the last phrase is plainly given in the words immediately before it: "…the church, which is his body…." Christ does indeed fill everything in every way for his Church, as other verses in the New Testament verify. We know, however, that Christ's authority stretches even beyond his Church, for God gave "all authority" to him (Matt. 28:18). Thus, it is possible, although the context of this verse would not demand it, that it refers to the wide-ranging authority that God gave to Christ. This verse does not prove the Trinity, it simply confirms what other Scriptures teach, i.e., that Christ is the Head of his

Body, the Church, that God has set everything under his feet, that he is Lord and that he has been given all authority.

Ephesians 3:9
and to make plain to everyone the administration of this mystery, which for ages past was kept hidden in God, who created all things.

This verse is not a problem in most translations, because most do not have the phrase, "by Jesus Christ," at the end of the verse. Apparently this phrase was added to some Greek manuscripts as debates about the Trinity caused some scribes to "augment" their position by adding to the Word of God, or it could have been a marginal note that was accidentally copied into some manuscripts. It is not well supported in the textual tradition. *A Textual Commentary on the Greek New Testament* notes that the omission of the phrase is "decisively supported" by the texts, as well as by the "early patristic quotations" (i.e., the places where the Church Fathers quoted the verse). For more information about how Trinitarian information was added, see the notes on 1 John 5:7 and 8.

Ephesians 4:7 and 8
(7) But to each one of us grace has been given as Christ apportioned it.
(8) This is why it says: "When he ascended on high, he led captives in his train and gave gifts to men."

---

1. Verse 8 is a quotation from the Old Testament, where the context is referring to what God did, so there are some who say that if the verse is applied to Christ, then Christ must be God. However, it is common for a verse to be interpreted one way in the Old Testament and then applied or interpreted differently in the New Testament. Examples of this are quite abundant, and this is not disputed by theologians. Thus, it is not unusual that an Old Testament quotation would be accommodated to Christ.

A lot has been written on the subject of accommodating Old Testament verses to New Testament circumstances, and we refer interested readers to any good theological library. One illustration of this is the title, "the First and the Last," (see the notes on Rev. 1:17). Another is the prophecy in Hosea 11:1. Hosea is speaking of Israel coming up out of Egypt, but in Matthew 2:15 God accommodates the meaning to Christ coming out of Egypt as a child. Another good example is Jeremiah 31:15. In that prophecy, "Rachel," the mother of Benjamin, was weeping because her children, the Israelites, were taken captive to Babylon. She was told not to weep because "…They will return from the land of the enemy" (31:16). However, the verse about Rachel weeping was lifted from its Old Testament context and accommodated to the killing of the children in Bethlehem around the birth of Christ (Matt. 2:18).

Another example occurs in the accommodating of Psalm 69:25 to Judas. In Psalm 69, David is appealing to God to deliver him from his enemies. He cried to God, "Those who hate me without reason outnumber the hairs of my head…" (v.4). He prayed, "Come near and rescue me; redeem me because of my foes" (v.18), and he continued, "May their place be deserted; let there be no one to dwell in their tents" (v.25). Peter saw by revelation that Psalm 69:25 could be accommodated to Judas, and spoke to the disciples around him: "…it is written in the book of Psalms, 'May his place be deserted; let there be no one to dwell in it…'" (Acts 1:20).

Since it is clear that prophecies in the Old Testament are brought into the New Testament and accommodated to the New Testament circumstances, it is easy to understand that some prophecies of God working in the Old Testament are pulled into the New Testament and applied to Christ. That is completely understandable because now Christ has "all authority" and has been made Head over the Church. He has been set above all principalities and powers, and given a name above every name. So, when God accommodates a prophecy or a Scripture about Himself to Christ, it does not mean that Christ is God any more than Hosea 11:1 being accommodated to Christ means that Christ is actually the nation of Israel.

2. For more information that pertains to God working through Christ and Christ taking on the responsibilities that were God's, see Luke 7:16 (God "visited" His people through Jesus), Luke 8:39 (God works through people) and Romans 10:13 (Jesus is given responsibilities that God had in the Old Testament).

Op. cit., Racovian Catechism, pp. 158–160.

Ephesians 5:5
For of this you can be sure: No immoral, impure or greedy person—such a man is an idolater—has any inheritance in the kingdom of Christ and of God.

---

1. Using this verse, some Trinitarians try to make Christ into God by what is known as the "Granville Sharp Rule." The following explanation is lengthy, but it is necessary to show that this "rule" has been properly analyzed and shown to be invalid for proving the Trinity. Granville Sharp was an English philanthropist, who began to study the grammar of the New Testament in order to demonstrate that his Trinitarian beliefs were correct and that Christ was God. From his study of the New Testament, he declared that when the Greek word *kai* (usually translated "and") joins two nouns of the same case, and the first noun has the definite article and the second does not, the two nouns refer to the same subject. This is the principle behind the "rule," but there are a large number of exceptions to it that must be noted.

There are problems with the Granville Sharp "Rule." First, it is impossible to prove that it was a rule of grammar at the time of the Apostle Paul. Nigel Turner, a Trinitarian, writes:

> Unfortunately, at this period of Greek we cannot be sure that such a rule is really decisive. **Sometimes the definite article is not repeated even when there is a clear separation in idea.**[30]

Buzzard writes about Titus 2:13, also supposedly an example of the Granville Sharp rule:

> A wide range of grammarians and Biblical scholars have recognized that the absence of the definite article before "our Savior Jesus Christ" is quite inadequate to establish the Trinitarian claim that Jesus is here called 'the great God' " (p. 130).

The point is, that when Scripture refers to "…our great God and Savior, Jesus Christ," it can refer to two separate beings—1) the Great God and 2) the Savior, Jesus Christ. Andrews Norton wrote a clear evaluation of the Granville Sharp Rule as it applies to the Trinity in *A Statement of Reasons for Not Believing the Doctrines of Trinitarians*. [For the ease of the reader, we have taken the liberty to translate into English some of the Greek words he uses.] Norton writes:

> The argument for the deity of Christ founded upon the omission of the Greek article was received and brought into notice in the last century by Granville Sharp, Esq. He applied it to

---
30. Moulton-Howard-Turner, *Grammar, Vol. 3*, p. 181. Emphasis ours.

eight texts, which will be hereafter mentioned. The last words of Ephesians 5:5 may afford an example of the construction on which the argument is founded: "in the kingdom of Christ and God." From the article being inserted before "Christ" and omitted before "God," Mr. Sharp infers that both names relate to the same person, and renders, "in the kingdom of Christ our God." The proper translation I suppose to be that of the Common Version [the King James], "in the kingdom of Christ and of God," or, "in the kingdom of the Messiah and of God."

The argument of Sharp is defended by Bishop Middleton in his *Doctrine of the Greek Article*. By attending to the rule laid down by him, with its limitations and exceptions, we shall be able to judge of its applicability to the passages in question. His rule is this:

> When two or more attributives, joined by a copulative or copulatives, are assumed of [relate to] the same person or thing, before the first attributive the article is inserted, before the remaining ones it is omitted" (pp. 79 and 80).

By attributives, he understands adjectives, participles and nouns, which are significant of character, relation, and dignity.

The limitations and exceptions to the rule stated by him are as follows:

> I. There is no similar rule respecting "names of substances *considered as substances*." Thus, we may say "the stone and gold," without repeating the article before "gold," though we speak of two different substances. The reason of this limitation of the rule is stated to be that "distinct real essences cannot be conceived to belong to the same thing;" or, in other words, that the same thing cannot be supposed to be two different substances.

In this case, then, it appears that the article is not repeated, *because its repetition is not necessary to prevent ambiguity*. This is the true principle which accounts for all the limitations and exceptions to the rule that are stated by Bishop Middleton and others. It is mentioned thus early, that the principle may be kept in mind; and its truth may be remarked in the other cases of limitation or of exception to be quoted.

> II. No similar rule applies to proper names. "The reason," says Middleton, "is evident at once; for it is impossible that *John* and *Thomas*, the names of two distinct persons, should be predicated of an individual" (p. 68).

This remark is not to the purpose [i.e., "is not correct"], for the same individual may have two names. The true reason for this limitation is, that proper names, when those of the same individual, are not connected by a copulative or copulatives, and therefore that, when they are thus connected, no ambiguity arises from the omission of the article.

> III. "Nouns," says Middleton, "which are the names of abstract ideas, are also excluded; for, as Locke has well observed, 'Every distinct abstract idea is a distinct essence, and the names which stand for such distinct ideas are the names of things essentially different'" (*Ibid.*).

It would therefore, he reasons, be contradictory to suppose that any quality were at once apeira [without experience] and *apaideusia* [without instruction, stupid, rude]. But the names of abstract ideas are used to denote personal qualities, and the same personal qualities, as they are viewed under different aspects, may be denoted by different names. The reason assigned by Middleton is therefore without force. The true reason for the limitation is that *usually* no ambiguity arises from the omission of the article before words of the class mentioned.

> IV. The rule, it is further conceded, is not of universal application as it respects *plurals*; for, says Middleton, "Though *one* individual may act, and frequently does act, in several capacities, it is not likely that a *multitude* of individuals should all of them act in the *same* several capacities: and, by the *extreme improbability* that they should be represented as so acting, we may be forbidden to understand that second plural attributive of the persons designed in the article prefixed to the first, however the usage in the singular might seem to countenance the construction" (p. 90).

> V. Lastly, "we find," he says, "in very many instances, not only in the plural, but even in the singular number, that where attributives are in their nature *absolutely incompatible*, i.e., where the application of the rule would involve a contradiction in terms, there the first attributive only has the article, *the perspicuity of the passage not requiring the rule to be accurately observed*" (p. 92).

It appears by comparing the rule with its exceptions and limitations that it in fact amounts to nothing more than this: that when substantives, adjectives, or particles are connected together by a copulative or copulative, if the first have the article, it is to be *omitted* before those which follow, when they relate to the same person or thing; and it is to be *inserted*, when they relate to different persons or things, EXCEPT when this fact is sufficiently determined by some other circumstance. The same rule exists respecting the use of the definite article in English.

The principle of exception just stated is evidently that which runs through all the limitations and exceptions that Middleton has laid down and exemplified, and is in itself perfectly reasonable. When, from any other circumstance, it may be clearly understood that different persons or things are spoken of, then the insertion of omissions of the article is a matter of indifference.

But if this be true, no argument for the deity of Christ can be drawn from the texts adduced. With regard to this doctrine, the main question is whether it were taught by Christ and his Apostles, and received by their immediate disciples. Antitrinitarians maintain that it was not; and consequently maintain that no thought of it was ever entertained by the Apostles and first believers. But if this supposition be correct, the insertion of the article in these texts was wholly unnecessary. No ambiguity could result from its omission. The imagination had not entered the minds of men that God and Christ were the same person. The Apostles in writing, and their converts in reading, the passages in question could have no more conception of one person only being understood, in consequence of the omission of the article, than of supposing but one substance to be meant by the terms "the stone and gold," on account of the omission of the article before "gold." These texts, therefore, cannot be brought to disprove the Antitrinitarian supposition, because this supposition must be proved false before these texts can be taken from the exception and brought under the operation of the rule. The truth of the supposition accounts for the omission of the article.[31]

---

31. Andrews Norton, *A Statement of Reasons for Not Believing the Doctrines of Trinitarians* (American Unitarian Association, Boston, 10th ed., 1877), pp. 199–202.

Norton makes some great points and shows the irrelevance of the Granville Sharp Rule in "proving" the Trinity. Because no ambiguity between Christ and God would arise in the minds of the readers due to the omission of the article, it can be omitted without a problem. Likewise, there was no need for a second article in Matthew 21:12 in the phrase, "all the [ones] selling and buying," or in Ephesians 2:20 in the phrase, "the apostles and prophets," because no one would ever think that "sold" and "bought" meant the same thing, or that "apostles" and "prophets" were somehow the same office. The same is true all over the Bible. There is no need for a second article if no confusion would arise without it. The "rule" therefore begs the question. It can be made to apply only if it can be shown that an ambiguity would have arisen in the minds of the first century readers between Christ and God. Because the whole of Scripture clearly shows the difference between Christ and God, and that difference would have been in the minds of the believers, the Granville Sharp "Rule" is not a valid reason to make Christ God.

2. Ephesians 5:5 mentions the kingdom of Christ and of God. There is a time coming in the future when the earth as we know it now, with all its wickedness, disease and death, will be destroyed and it will be made into a place of justice, peace and happiness. Christ taught about this future earth when he said, **The meek will inherit the earth** (Matt. 5:5). The future Kingdom that will be set up on earth has many names in Scripture. It is called the "kingdom of heaven" (Matt. 4:17, etc.) and the "kingdom of God" (Mark. 1:15, etc.). In what is known as "the Lord's Prayer," Jesus called it "your [i.e., the Father's] kingdom" (Matt. 6:10). Jesus again called it the Father's kingdom in Matthew 13:43. As well as calling it his Father's kingdom, Jesus called it his own kingdom in Luke 22:30, and it is called "…the kingdom of his dear Son" in Colossians 1:13 (KJV). The reason both God and Christ are named as having the kingdom is apparent. In the Millennial Kingdom, Christ will rule with God's authority, and in the Final Kingdom there will be two rulers (Rev. 21:22–22:1). From the above evidence, it is quite fitting and proper to call the future kingdom "the kingdom of Christ and of God." Since it is so well attested that the kingdom will be the kingdom of God, a phrase well known in Scripture, there is no reason to remove "God" from Eph. 5:5 by grammatical juggling (the Granville Sharp Rule would make the word "God" a double reference to Christ and remove the Father from the verse), and every reason to see that He should be in the verse along with Jesus Christ.

Buzzard, *op. cit., Doctrine of the Trinity*, pp. 130 and 131; Norton, *op. cit., A Statement of Reasons for Not Believing the Doctrines of Trinitarians*, pp. 199–203.

Philippians 2:6–8 (NASB)
(6) who, although He existed in the form of God, did not regard equality with God a thing to be grasped,
(7) but emptied Himself, taking the form of a bond-servant, *and* being made in the likeness of men.
(8) And being found in appearance as a man, He humbled Himself by becoming obedient to the point of death, even death on a cross.

---

1. These verses in Philippians are very important to Trinitarian doctrine (although they have also caused division among Trinitarians) and they must be dealt with thoroughly. There are several arguments wrapped into these three verses, and we will deal with them point by point. First, many Trinitarians assert that the word "form," which is the Greek word *morphe*, refers to Christ's inner nature as God. This is so strongly asserted that in verse 6 the NIV has, "…being in very nature God…." We do not believe that *morphe* refers to an "inner essential nature," and we will give evidence that it refers to an outer form. Different lexicons have opposing viewpoints about the definition of *morphe*, to such a degree that we can think of no other word defined by the lexicons in such contradictory ways. We will give definitions from lexicons that take both positions, to show the differences between them.

Vine's Lexicon has under "form": "properly the nature or essence, not in the abstract, but as actually subsisting in the individual…it does not include in itself anything 'accidental' or separable, such as particular modes of manifestation." Using lexicons like *Vine's*, Trinitarians boldly make the case that the "nature" underlying Jesus' human body was God. Trinitarian scholars like Vine contrast *morphe*, which they assert refers to an "inner, essential nature," with *schema*, (in verse 8, and translated "appearance" above) which they assert refers to the outward appearance. We admit that there are many Trinitarian scholars who have written lexical entries or articles on the Greek word *morphe* and concluded that Christ must be God. A Trinitarian wanting to prove his point can quote from a number of them. However, we assert that these definitions are biased and erroneous. In addition, we could not find any non-Trinitarian scholars who agreed with the conclusion of the Trinitarian scholars, while *many* Trinitarian sources agree that *morphe* refers to the outward appearance and not an inner nature.

A study of other lexicons (many of them Trinitarian) gives a totally different picture than does *Vine's Lexicon*. In Bullinger's *Critical Lexicon*, *morphe* is given a one-word definition, "form." The scholarly lexicon by Walter Bauer, translated and revised by Arndt and Gingrich, has under *morphe*, "form, outward appearance, shape." *The Theological Dictionary of the New Testament*, edited by Gerhard Kittel, has "form, external appearance." Kittel also notes that *morphe* and *schema* are often interchangeable. Robert Thayer, in his well-respected lexicon, has under *morphe*, "the form by which a person or thing strikes the vision; the external appearance." Thayer says that the Greeks said that children reflect the appearance (*morphe*) of their parents, something easily noticed in every culture. Thayer also notes that some scholars try to make *morphe* refer to that which is intrinsic and essential, in contrast to that which is outward and accidental, but says, "the distinction is rejected by many."

The above evidence shows that scholars disagree about the use of the word *morphe* in Philippians. When scholars disagree, and especially when it is believed that the reason for the disagreement is due to bias over a doctrinal issue, it is absolutely essential to do as much original research as possible. The real definition of *morphe* should become apparent as we check the sources available at the time of the New Testament. After all, the word was a common one in the Greek world. We assert that a study of the actual evidence clearly reveals that *morphe* does not refer to Christ's inner essential being, but rather to an outward appearance.

From secular writings we learn that the Greeks used *morphe* to describe when the gods changed their appearance. Kittel points out that in pagan mythology, the gods change their forms (*morphe*), and especially notes Aphrodite, Demeter and Dionysus as three who did. This is clearly a change of appearance, not nature. Josephus, a contemporary of the Apostles, used *morphe* to describe the shape of statues (*Bauer's Lexicon*).

Other uses of *morphe* in the Bible support the position that *morphe* refers to outward appearance. The gospel of Mark has a short reference to the well-known story in Luke 24:13–33 about Jesus appearing to the two men on the road to Emmaus. Mark tells us that Jesus appeared "in a different form (*morphe*)" to these two men so that they did not recognize him (16:12). This is very clear. Jesus did not have a different "essential nature" when he appeared to the two disciples. He simply had a different outward appearance.

More evidence for the word *morphe* referring to the outward appearance can be gleaned from the Septuagint, a Greek translation of the Old Testament from about 250 B.C. It was written because of the large number of Greek-speaking Jews in Israel and the surrounding countries (a result of Alexander the Great's conquest of Egypt in 332 B.C. and his gaining control over the territory of Israel). By around 250 B.C., so many Jews spoke Greek that a Greek translation of the Old Testament was made, which today is called the Septuagint. The Septuagint greatly influenced the Jews during the New Testament times. Some of the quotations from the Old Testament that appear in the New Testament are actually from the Septuagint, not the Hebrew text. Furthermore, there were many Greek-speaking Jews in the first-century Church. In fact, the first recorded congregational conflict occurred when Hebrew-speaking Jews showed prejudice against the Greek-speaking Jews (Acts 6:1).

The Jews translating the Septuagint used *morphe* several times, and it always referred to the outward appearance. Job says, "A spirit glided past my face, and the hair on my body stood on end. It stopped, but I could not tell what it was. A form (*morphe*) stood before my eyes, and I heard a hushed voice (Job 4:15 and 16). There is no question here that *morphe* refers to the outward appearance. Isaiah has the word *morphe* in reference to man-made idols: "The carpenter measures with a line and makes an outline with a marker; he roughs it out with chisels and marks it with compasses. He shapes it in the form (*morphe*) of man, of man in all his glory, that it may dwell in a shrine" (Isa. 44:13). It would be absurd to assert that *morphe* referred to "the essential nature" in this verse, as if a wooden carving could have the "essential nature" of man. The verse is clear: the idol has the "outward appearance" of a man. According to Daniel 3:19, after Shadrach, Meshach and Abednego refused to bow down to Nebuchadnezzar's image, he became enraged and "the form (*morphe*) of his countenance" changed. The NASB says, "his facial expression" changed. Nothing in his nature changed, but the people watching could see that his outward appearance changed.

For still more documentation that the Jews used *morphe* to refer to the outward appearance, we turn to what is known as the "Apocrypha," books written between the time of Malachi and Matthew. "Apocrypha" literally means "obscure" or "hidden away," and these books are rightly not accepted by most Protestants as being part of the true canon, but are accepted by Roman Catholics and printed in Catholic Bibles. Our interest in them is due to the fact that they were written near the time of the writing of the New Testament, were known to the Jews at that time and contain the word *morphe*. In the Apocrypha, *morphe* is used in the same way that the Septuagint translators use it, i.e., as outward appearance. For example, in "The Wisdom of Solomon" is the following: "...Their enemies heard their voices, but did not see their forms..." (18:1). A study of *morphe* in the Apocrypha will show that it always referred to the outer form.

There is still more evidence. *Morphe* is the root word of some other New Testament words and is also used in compound words. These add further support to the idea that *morphe* refers to an appearance or outward manifestation. The Bible speaks of evil men who have a "form" (*morphosis*) of godliness (2 Tim. 3:5). Their inner nature was evil, but they had an outward appearance of being godly. On the Mount of Transfiguration, Christ was "transformed" (*metamorphoomai*) before the Apostles (Matt. 17:2; Mark 9:2). They did not see Christ get a new nature, rather they saw his outward form profoundly change. Similarly, we Christians are to be "transformed" (*metamorphoomai*) by renewing our minds to Scripture. We do not get a new nature as we renew our minds, because we are already "partakers of the divine nature (2 Pet. 1:4), but there will be a change in us that we, and others, can tangibly experience. Christians who transform from carnal Christians, with all the visible activities of the flesh that lifestyle entails, to being Christ-like Christians, change in such a way that other people can "see" the difference. 2 Corinthians 3:18 (KJV) says the same thing when it says that

Christians will be "changed" (*metamorphoomai*) into the image of Christ. That we will be changed into an "image" shows us that the change is something visible on the outside.

We would like to make one more point before we draw a conclusion about "*morphe.*" If the point of the verse is to say that Jesus is God, then why not just say it? Of course *God* has the "essential nature" of God, so why would anyone make *that* point? This verse does not say, "Jesus, being God," but rather, "being in the form of God." Paul is reminding the Philippians that Jesus represented the Father in every possible way.

So what can we conclude about *morphe*? The Philippian church consisted of Jews and converted Greeks. From the Septuagint and their other writings, the Jews were familiar with *morphe* referring to the outward appearance, including the form of men and idols. To the Greeks, it also referred to the outward appearance, including the changing outward appearance of their gods and the form of statues. The only other New Testament use of *morphe* outside Philippians is in Mark, and there it refers to the outward appearance. Also, the words related to *morphe* clearly refer to an outward manifestation or appearance. We assert the actual evidence is clear: the word *morphe* refers to an outward appearance or manifestation. Jesus Christ was in the outward appearance of God, so much so that he said, "…He who has seen Me has seen the Father…." Christ always did the Father's will, and perfectly represented his Father in every way.

Schema, as Kittel points out, can be synonymous with *morphe*, but it has more of an emphasis on outward trappings rather than outward appearance, and often points to that which is more transitory in nature, like the clothing we wear or an appearance we have for just a short time. As human beings, we always have the outward form (*morphe*) of human beings. Yet there is a sense in which our *schema*, our appearance, is always changing. We start as babies, and grow and develop, then we mature and age. This is so much the case that a person's outward appearance is one of the most common topics of conversation between people when they meet.

Like the rest of us, Christ was fully human and had the outward form (*morphe*), of a human. However, because he always did the Father's will and demonstrated godly behavior and obedience, he therefore had the outward "appearance" (*morphe*) of God. Also, like the rest of us, his appearance (*schema*) regularly changed. Thus, in Philippians 2:8, *schema* can be synonymous with *morphe*, or it can place an emphasis on the fact that the appearance Christ had as a human being was transitory in nature. The wording of Philippians 2:6–8 does not present us with a God-man, with whom none of us can identify. Rather, it presents us with a man just like we are, who grew and aged, yet who was so focused on God in every thought and deed that he perfectly represented the Father.

2. After saying that Christ was in the form of God, Philippians 2:6 goes on to say that Christ "…did not consider equality with God something to be grasped" (NIV). This phrase is a powerful argument *against* the Trinity. If Jesus were God, then it would make no sense at all to say that he did not "grasp" at equality with God because no one grasps at equality with himself. It only makes sense to compliment someone for not seeking equality when he is not equal. Some Trinitarians say, "Well, he was not grasping for equality with the Father." That is not what the verse says. It says Christ did not grasp at equality with *God*, which makes the verse nonsense if he were God.

3. The opening of verse 7 contains a phrase that has caused serious division among Trinitarians. It says, "But made himself of no reputation…" (KJV), "but made himself nothing" (NIV), "but emptied himself" (NASB, RSV, NRSV). The Greek word that is in question is *kenos*, which literally means, "to empty." For more than a thousand years, from the church councils in the fourth century until the nineteenth century, the orthodox position of the Church was that Christ was fully God and fully man at the same time in one body. This doctrine is known as the "dual nature of Christ," and has to be supported with non-biblical words like *communicatio idiomatum*, literally, "the communication of the idiom." This refers to the way that the "God" nature of Christ is united to the "man" nature of Christ in such a way that the actions and conditions of the man can be God and the actions and conditions of God can be man. Dr. Justo Gonzalez, an authority on the history of the Christian Church, notes, "The divine and human natures exist in a single being, although how that can be is the greatest mystery of the faith."[32] Biblical truth is not an "incomprehensible mystery." In fact, God longs for us to know Him and His truth (see the notes on Luke 1:35).

The doctrine of the dual nature of Christ has been the standard explanation for the miracles of Christ, such as multiplying food, knowing the thoughts of others, raising the dead, etc. This explanation is maintained in spite of the fact that the prophets in the Old Testament were also able to do these things. The doctrine of Christ's dual nature has caused a serious problem that is stated well by John Wren-Lewis:

> Certainly up to the Second World War, the commonest vision of Jesus was not as a man *at all*. He was a God in human form, full of supernatural knowledge and miraculous power, very much like the Olympian gods were supposed to be when they visited the earth in disguise."[33]

Our experience in speaking to Christians all over the world confirms what Wren-Lewis stated: the average Christian does not feel that Christ "...had to be made like his brothers in every way..." (Heb. 2:17), but instead feels that Christ was able to do what he did because he was fundamentally different. We believe that the teaching of the dual nature is non-biblical and robs power from people who might otherwise seek to *think* and *act* like Christ. This artificially separates people from the Lord Jesus.

In Germany in the mid-1800's, a Lutheran theologian named Gottfried Thomasius began what has now developed into "Kenotic Theology." This thinking arose out of some very real concerns that some Trinitarians had about dual nature theology. First, dual nature theology did not allow Christ's full humanity to be expressed. Second, it seemed to turn Christ into an aberration: very God and very man at the same time. Third, "if Jesus were both omniscient God and limited man, then he had two centers, and thus was fundamentally not one of us". Kenotic Theology (which has since splintered into a number of variants) provided a "solution" to these problems. Since Philippians 2:7 (NASB) says Christ "emptied Himself," what he must have "emptied" was his God-nature, i.e., sometime before his incarnation, Christ agreed to "self-limitation" and came down to earth as a man only.

Trinitarian theologians have vehemently disagreed among themselves about Kenotic Theology, and some orthodox theologians have even called its adherents "heretics." The central criticisms of Kenotic Theology are: First, being only a little more than a hundred years old, it is simply not the historic position of the Church. Second, orthodox theologians say that it is not biblical, and that Philippians 2:7 does not mean what kenotic theologians say it means. And third, Kenotic Theology forces God to change—God becomes a man—which causes two problems for orthodox Trinitarians: God cannot change, and God is not a man.

We agree with the Kenotic theologians who say that dual nature theology does not allow Christ's humanity to be expressed, and that it creates a "being" who is really an aberration and "fundamentally not one of us."[34] However, we also agree with the orthodox Trinitarians who take the biblical stance that God is not a man, and that God cannot change. We assert that it is Trinitarian doctrine that

---

32. Justo Gonzalez, *A History of Christian Thought* (Abingdon Press, Nashville, 1992), pp. 222 and 223.
33. Robinson, *op. cit., Honest to God*, p. 66.
34. Elwell, *op. cit., Evangelical Dictionary of Theology*, pp. 600 and 601.

has caused these problems, and that there simply is *no solution* to them as long as one holds a Trinitarian position. We assert that the real solution is to realize that there is only one True God, the Father, and that Jesus Christ is the "man accredited by God" who has now been made "both Lord and Christ" (Acts 2:22 and 36). Then Christ is fully man and is "one of us," and God is God and has never changed or been a man.

4. While Trinitarians have argued among themselves about the meaning of Philippians 2:6–8, an unfortunate thing has occurred—the loss of the actual meaning of the verse. The verse is not speaking either of Christ's giving up his "Godhood" at his incarnation or of his God-nature being willing to "hide" so that his man-nature can show itself clearly. Rather, it is saying something else. Scripture says Christ was the "image of God" (2 Cor. 4:4), and Jesus himself testified that if one had seen him, he had seen the Father. Saying that Christ was in the "form" (outward appearance) of God is simply stating that truth in another way. Unlike Adam, who grasped at being like God (Gen. 3:5), Christ, the Last Adam, "emptied himself" of all his reputation and the things due him as the true child of the King. He lived in the same fashion as other men. He humbled himself to the Word and will of God. He lived by "It is written" and the commands of his Father. He did not "toot his own horn," but instead called himself "the son of man," which, in the Aramaic language he spoke, meant "a man." He trusted God and became obedient, even to a horrible and shameful death on a cross.

The Philippian Church was doing well and was supportive of Paul, but they had problems as well. There was "selfish ambition" (1:15, 2:3) and "vain conceit" (2:3), arguing and lack of consideration for others (2:4 and 14) and a need for humility, purity and blamelessness (2:3 and 15). So, Paul wrote an exhortation to the believers that, "Your attitude should be the same as that of Christ Jesus" (2:5). He then went on to show how Christ did not grasp at equality with God, but was completely humble, and as a result God "highly exalted him." The example of Jesus Christ is a powerful one. We do not need to make sure people notice us or know who we are. We should simply serve in obedience and humility, assured that God will one day reward us for our deeds.

Buzzard, *op. cit., Doctrine of the Trinity*, pp. 48–50; Dana, *op. cit., Letters Addressed to Relatives and Friends*, Letter #2, pp. 16 and 17; Farley, *op. cit., Unitarianism Defined: The Scripture Doctrine of the Father, Son, and Holy Ghost*, pp. 76–78; Norton, *op. cit., A Statement of Reasons for Not Believing the Doctrines of Trinitarians*, pp. 191–193; *Op. cit., Racovian Catechism*, pp. 119–121; Snedeker, *op. cit., Our Heavenly Father Has No Equals*, pp. 443–446.

Colossians 1:15–20

(15) He is the image of the invisible God, the firstborn over all creation.

(16) For by him all things were created: things in heaven and on earth, visible and invisible, whether thrones or powers or rulers or authorities; all things were created by him and for him.

(17) He is before all things, and in him all things hold together.

(18) And he is the head of the body, the church; he is the beginning and the firstborn from among the dead, so that in everything he might have the supremacy.

(19) For God was pleased to have all his fullness dwell in him,

(20) and through him to reconcile to himself all things, whether things on earth or things in heaven, by making peace through his blood, shed on the cross.

---

1. As with all good biblical exegesis, it is important to note the context of the verses and why they would be written and placed where they are. Reading the book of Colossians reveals that the Colossian Church had lost its focus on Christ. Some of the believers at Colosse had, in practice, forsaken their connection with the Head, Jesus Christ, and some were even being led to worship angels (2:18 and 19). The situation in Colosse called for a strong reminder of Christ's headship over his Church, and the epistle to the Colossians provided just that.

There is no definitive reason to believe that the believers in Colosse were Trinitarian. A thorough reading of Acts shows that no Apostle or teacher in Acts ever presented the Trinity on their witnessing itineraries. Instead, they presented that Jesus was "…a man approved of God…" (Acts 2:22 - KJV), God's "servant Jesus" (Acts 3:13), God's "Prince" (Acts 5:31), the one God anointed (Acts 10:38), the Son of God (Acts 9:20), etc. Acts has no presentation to new Christians that Jesus was God, nor was there any formal presentation of the Trinity, and Colosse was reached with the Word during the Acts period. This is important background, because Trinitarians read Colossians about Christ creating, and think it refers to Jesus creating the earth in the beginning. But if a person who is not a Trinitarian reads the same passage of Scripture, he will come away with a completely different understanding it.

2. These verses in Colossians clearly teach that Jesus is not God. We know that because they open with Christ being "…the image [*eikon*] of the invisible God…." If one thing is the "image" of another thing, it is, by definition, not the thing itself. Christ is the "image" of God, and therefore not God. If he were "God," the verse would simply say so. The Father is plainly called "God" many times in the Bible (John 6:27; Rom. 1:7; 1 Cor. 15:24), and never called the "image" of God. In contrast, Jesus is called the "image" of God precisely because he is not God. Jesus was the image of God in many ways, and lived and acted like God Himself would have if He had been on earth, which is why he could say, "…Anyone who has seen me has seen the Father…" (John 14:9 and 10).

There are Trinitarian theologians who assert that the word *eikon* (from which we get the English word "icon," meaning "image," or "representation") means "manifestation" here in Colossians, and that Christ is the manifestation of God. The evidence of Scripture makes it clear that they choose to define *eikon* as "manifestation" in this one verse to support their belief in the Trinity. The word *eikon* occurs 23 times in the New Testament, and it is clearly used as "image" in the common sense of the word. It is used of the image of Caesar on a coin, of idols that are manmade images of gods, of Old Testament things that were only an image of the reality we have today, and of the "image" of the beast that occurs in Revelation. 2 Corinthians 3:18 says that Christians are changed into the "image" of the Lord as we reflect his glory. All these verses use "image" in the common sense of the word, i.e., a representation separate from the original. 1 Corinthians 11:7 says, "A man ought not to cover his head, since he is the **image** and glory of God…." Thus, just as Jesus Christ is called the image of God, so men are called the image of God. We are not as exact an image as Christ is because we are marred by sin, but nevertheless the Bible does call us the "image" of God. Thus, the wording about being the image of God is the same for us as it is for Christ.

We maintain that the words in the Word must be read and understood in their common or ordinary meaning unless good reason can be given to alter that meaning. In this case, the common meaning of "image" is "likeness" or "resemblance," and it is used that way every time in the New Testament. If the word "image" took on a new meaning those few times it referred to Christ, the Bible would have to let us know that. It does not, so we assert that the use of "image" is the same whether it refers to an image on a coin, an image of a god, or for both Christ and Christians as the image of God. In closing this point, we want to reiterate that calling Jesus the "image" of God is very strong evidence that he is *not God*.

3. People are often confused by Colossians 1:16 because it says "For by him [Jesus] all things were created…." When we read the word "create," we usually think about the original Creation in Genesis 1:1, but there are other ways the word is used in Scripture. For example, Christians are "new creations" (2 Cor. 5:17). After the resurrection, God delegated to Christ the authority to create, and when we read the Epistles we see evidence of Jesus creating things for his Church. For example, Ephesians 2:15 refers to Christ creating "one new man" (his Body, the Church) out of Jew and Gentile. In pouring out the gift of holy spirit to each believer (Acts 2:33 and 38), the Lord Jesus has created something new in each of them, that is, the "new man," their new nature (2 Cor. 5:17; Gal. 6:15; Eph. 4:24).

Not only did Jesus create his Church out of Jew and Gentile, he had to create the structure and positions that would allow it to function, both in the spiritual world (positions for the angels that would minister to the Church—see Rev. 1:1, "his angel") and in the physical world (positions and ministries here on earth—see Rom. 12:4–8; Eph. 4:7–11). The Bible describes these physical and spiritual realities by the phrase, "…things in heaven and on earth, visible and invisible…" (1:16). Jesus was not around in the beginning to create the heavens and the earth, but he did create the "all things" that pertain to his Body, the Church. Colossians 1:16 must be read carefully with a knowledge of both vocabulary and figures of speech if we are going to understand it properly. The study of legitimate figures of speech is an involved one, and the best work we know of was done in 1898 by E. W. Bullinger, titled *Figures of Speech Used in the Bible*.[35]

Once we understand that Jesus created things for the church, we are in a position to more fully understand verse 16, both how the word "all" is used in the verse, and how the figure of speech *epanadiplosis* is used. First, the student of the Bible must be aware that when the word "all" (or "every" or "everything") is used, it is often used in a limited sense. People use it this way in normal speech all over the world. I had an experience of this just the other day. It was late at night and I wanted a cookie before bed. When I told my wife that I wanted a cookie, she said, "The kids ate all the cookies." Now of course our kids did not eat all the cookies in the world. The implied context was the cookies *in the house*. This is a good example of "all" being used in a limited sense, and the Bible uses it that way too. For example, when Absalom held a council against his father, David, 2 Samuel 17:14 says that "…all the men of Israel…" agreed on advice. "All" the men of Israel did not agree with Absalom, but all the men who were there with him did. Another example is Jeremiah 26:8, which says that "all the people" seized Jeremiah to put him to death, but the context makes it clear that "all the people" only meant the people who were present at that time. The last example we will give is 1 John 2:20 (NJKV), which says of Christians, "you know all things." Surely there is no Christian who actually believes that he knows everything. The phrase is using a limited sense of "all," which is determined by the context.

The point we are trying to make is that whenever the word "all" occurs, the reader must determine from the context whether it is being used in the wide sense of "all in the universe," or in the narrow sense of "all in a specific context." We believe the narrow sense is called for in Colossians 1:16, that Jesus created "all" things for his Church, not "all" things in the universe (For more on the limited sense of "all," see the note on John 2:24).

Verse 16 also contains the figure of speech, *epanadiplosis*, which we refer to as "encircling" in English. E. W. Bullinger notes that the Romans called it *inclusio* (p. 245), and he gives several pages of examples from the Bible documenting the use of the figure. He writes: "When this figure is used,

---

35. Bullinger, *op. cit., Figures of Speech Used in the Bible*.

it marks what is said as being completed in one complete circle…" With that in mind, note that the phrase "all things were created" is repeated twice in the verse, once close to the beginning and once close to the end, thus encircling the list of created things: "For by him **all things were created**: things in heaven and on earth, visible and invisible, whether thrones or powers or rulers or authorities; **all things were created** by him and for him." The things that are "created" in this list are not the earth and trees and sky that God created in the beginning, but rather the "thrones, powers, rulers and authorities," which are the positions that Christ needed to run his Church, which he created for that purpose. The figure of speech "encircling" identifies the "all things" that Christ created and show us that "all" has a narrow sense, and refers to the things Jesus needed to administer the Church. The Colossian believers had lost their focus on Christ as the Head of the Church, and Colossians 1:16 elevates Christ to his rightful position as Lord by noting that he was the one who created the powers and authorities in the Church.

4. The phrase in verse 17 that "He is before all things…" was to show the Colossians that Jesus has been elevated by God above everything else, certainly far above the "angels" that some people were worshipping (Col. 2:18), and the rules of the world (Col. 2:20). Some people have used the phrase to try to prove that Jesus existed before everything else. However, the word "before" (here *pro*) can refer to time, place, or position (i.e., superiority). This leads us to conclude that the whole point of the section is to show that Christ is "before," i.e., "superior to" all things, just as the verse says. If someone were to insist that time is involved, we would point out that in the very next verse Christ is the "firstborn" from the dead, and thus in his new body and in the presence of God "before" his Church in time as well as in position.

5. Colossians 1:19 contains the phrase, "For God was pleased to have all his fullness [Greek is *pleroma*] dwell in him," which has confused some people because they wrongly think that if Jesus had God's fullness, he must be God. It is important that we keep in mind that the problem in Colosse was that people had "…lost connection with the Head…," (Col. 2:19), and people needed to be reminded about how important and exalted Jesus really was. One way to elevate Christ was to point out that the fullness of God resided in him. We should immediately notice that this phrase tells us that Jesus is not God, because if he was, the fullness of God would not "reside" in him (the Greek "dwell," or "reside," is *katoikeo*; "reside, live, dwell, inhabit"). The fullness of God does not "reside" in God, any more than the fullness of who we are "resides" in us. Our identity and fullness does not just "live" in us, it is us. That the fullness of "God" is said to "reside" or "live" in Christ is proof that Jesus is not God. We see this elsewhere in the New Testament. For example, Ephesians 3:19 (KJV) says, "And to know the love of Christ, which passeth knowledge, that ye might be filled with all the fulness of God." Here is Paul's prayer that each Christian be filled with all the fullness [*pleroma*] of God, so it is quite clear that a person can be filled with the fullness of God and not be God.

The verse clearly shows that "God" and Jesus are separate, and that Jesus is not God. If the Trinity were true and Jesus were God, this verse would make no sense, and would even confuse people. We can see this because "God" "was pleased" to have "his" fullness dwell in Christ. If Christ were God, then the verse would be saying that it pleased God to have his fullness dwell in himself, which makes no sense. Furthermore, there would be no need for God to "have" his fullness dwell in Christ, because if Christ were God, the "fullness" would already be inseparable from him.

Buzzard, *op. cit., Doctrine of the Trinity*, pp. 51 and 52; Dana, *op. cit., Letters Addressed to Relatives and Friends,* Letter #25, pp. 221–227; *Op. cit., Racovian Catechism*, pp. 91–94; Snedeker, *op. cit., Our Heavenly Father Has No Equals*, pp. 446–450.

Colossians 2:2
My purpose is that they may be encouraged in heart and united in love, so that they may have the full riches of complete understanding, in order that they may know the mystery of God, namely, Christ,

1. This verse, although not usually considered a Trinitarian verse, is occasionally used to show that the mystery of God is Christ (i.e., that Christ is both God and Man, and thus a "mystery"). The verse was a subject of hot debate early in the Christian era, and there is ample evidence from the Greek manuscripts that scribes changed the text to fit their theology. Bruce Metzger writes, "The close of Colossians 2:2 presents what is, at first, a bewildering variety of readings; the manuscripts present fifteen different conclusions of the phrase."[36] In almost all 15 of them, the possibility that Christ could be God is eliminated. The KJV represents a good example: "That their hearts might be comforted, being knit together in love, and unto all riches of the full assurance of understanding, to the acknowledgement of the mystery of God, and of the Father, and of Christ."

2. There is now a wide concurrence of belief among scholars that the original Greek text read "*tou musteriou tou theou Christou*," but the exact translation of that phrase is debated. It can be translated the way the NIV is: "...the mystery of God, namely, Christ." However, it can just as easily be translated "the mystery of the Christ of God." We believe the latter is the most probable translation for reasons that will be given in points 3 and 4 below.

3. It is difficult to make "Christ" into a "mystery" in the biblical sense of the word. In Greek, the word "*musterion*" does not mean "mystery" in the sense of something that cannot be understood or comprehended by the mind of man. It means a "sacred secret," something that was hidden but is then made known. This point cannot be overemphasized for the correct interpretation of the verse. *Vine's Expository Dictionary of New Testament Words* under "mystery," has this to say about *musterion*: "...not the mysterious, but that which...is made known in a manner and at a time appointed by God." This is actually very clear in Colossians 1:26 and 27, which speak of the "mystery" that has now been "made known" to the believers.

Thus, a biblical "mystery" can be understood, in contrast to the Trinitarian "mystery," which is beyond comprehension. A quick study of the other uses of "*musterion*" in the Bible will show that once a "sacred secret" is revealed, it can be understood. But the "Trinity" and the "two natures" cannot be understood at all. Trinitarian theology speaks of the "mystery" of Christ in the sense that his incarnation and dual nature are impossible for us to understand. The Greek text, however, is implying no such thing. 1 Timothy 3:16 does refer to the "secret of godliness," and this text is plainly discernible. Even today, although the Word openly proclaims personal godliness through the Savior, Jesus Christ, this fact remains a secret to the world and, unfortunately, even to some Churchgoers.

4. The difficulty in translating the verse, "the secret of God, namely Christ," can be plainly seen. Although some of what Christ accomplished for us can be called a secret, and some of the things he went through were certainly hidden from the Jews, the Man Jesus Christ is the great subject of the Bible from Genesis to Revelation. We believe that it is much more accurate to translate Colossians 2:2 as, "the secret of the Christ of God." We believe this because there is a "sacred secret" in the New Testament that is clearly set forth in the Church Epistles. The word "*musterion*," i.e., "sacred secret," is

---

36. Bruce Metzger, *The Text of the New Testament, Its Transmission, Corruption and Restoration* (Oxford University Press, N.Y., 1992), p. 236.

used to refer to the "administration of God's grace" in which we are living now. Ephesians 3:2 and 3 should read, "Surely you have heard about the administration of God's grace that was given to me for you, that is, the sacred secret [*musterion*] made known to me by revelation, as I have already written briefly." Thus, when Colossians refers to "the [sacred] secret of the Christ of God," it is referring to the Grace Administration, which was a sacred secret hidden before the foundation of the world, but revealed to Christians today (see Eph. 3:2–9; Col. 1:27 and Gal. 1:11 and 12, and keep in mind that the word translated in many versions as "mystery" should be "sacred secret").

5. Trinitarians are very open about the fact that the doctrine of the Trinity is a "mystery" that is beyond human comprehension. But with the correct biblical definition of "mystery" as "sacred secret," i.e., "something that anyone can understand once it has been revealed or unveiled," one can ask, "Where does the idea that the Trinity is mysterious and beyond comprehension come from?" That concept is found nowhere in Scripture. There is not a single verse from Genesis to Revelation that a Trinitarian can produce to show that one God exists in three persons and that this is a mystery beyond human comprehension. Yet they continue to say things like, "You can't understand it because it is a mystery." We maintain that the reason the Trinity is a "mystery beyond comprehension" is that it is an invention of man and not actually in the Bible at all.

Dana, *op. cit., Letters Addressed to Relatives and Friends*, pp. 167 and 168; Farley, *op. cit., Unitarianism Defined: The Scripture Doctrine of the Father, Son, and Holy Ghost*, pp. 12–18; Norton, *op. cit., A Statement of Reasons for Not Believing the Doctrines of Trinitarians*, p. 476.

Colossians 2:9
For in Christ all the fullness of the Deity lives in bodily form,

---

1. The word "Deity" or "Godhead" is a translation of the Greek word *theotes*. In *A Greek English Lexicon*, by Liddell and Scott, the classic lexicon of the ancient Greek language, it is translated as "divinity, divine nature." In making their case, Liddell and Scott cite Greek authors Plutarch and Lucian, and also reference Heliodorus and Oribasius using the phrase *dia theoteta* = "for religious reasons." The Greek word occurs only once in the Bible, so to try to build a case for it meaning "God" or "Godhead" (which is an unclear term in itself) is very suspect indeed. Standard rules for interpreting Scripture would dictate that the way Paul used *theotes* in Colossians would be the same way the Colossians were used to hearing it in their culture. There is no reason to believe that Paul wrote to the Colossians expecting them to "redefine" the vocabulary they were using. Christ was filled with holy spirit "without measure," and God gave him authority on earth to heal, cast out demons, forgive sins, etc. Thus, it makes perfect sense that Scripture would say that Christ had the fullness of the "divine nature" dwelling in him. In fact, the same thing is said about every Christian (2 Pet. 1:4).

2. The word "fullness" demonstrates that the verse is speaking of something that one could also have just a *part* of. It makes no sense to talk about the "fullness" of something that is indivisible. God is indivisible. We never read about "the fullness of God the Father" because, by definition, God is always full of His own nature. Therefore, the verse is not talking about Christ being God, but about God in some way providing Christ with "fullness." What this verse is saying is made clear earlier in Colossians: "…God was pleased to have all his fullness dwell in him" (Col. 1:19). That is true. John 3:34 adds clarification: "For the one whom God has sent speaks the words of God, for God gives the Spirit without limit."

3. The fact that Christ has "all the fullness" of God does not make him God. Ephesians 3:19 says that Christians should be filled with "…all the fullness of God," and no one believes that would make each Christian God.

4. If Christ were God, it would make no sense to say that the fullness of God dwelt in him, because, being God, he would always have the fullness of God. The fact that Christ could have the fullness of God dwell in him actually shows that he was *not* God. 2 Peter 1:4 says that by way of God's great and precious promises we "…may participate in the divine nature…." Having a "divine nature" does not make us God, and it did not make Christ God. The note on 2 Peter 1:4 in the NIV Study Bible is almost correct when, referring to the divine nature, it states: "…we are indwelt by God through His Holy Spirit…" (we would say "holy spirit", referring to God's gift). Likewise Christ, who was filled with holy spirit without limits, had the fullness of "Deity" dwelling in him.

5. The context is a key to the proper interpretation of the verse. The Colossians had lost their focus on Christ (see Col. 1:15–20 above). Colossians 2:8 shows that the people were in danger of turning to "hollow and deceptive philosophy" rather than being focused on Christ. What could philosophy and traditions offer that Christ could not? The next verse is a reminder that there is no better place to turn for answers and for truth than to Christ, in whom all the fullness of God dwells. There is nothing in the context here that would warrant believing that Paul is writing about the Trinity. He is simply saying that if you want to find God, look to Christ. Christ himself had said he was "the Way" and "the Truth," and that "no man comes to the Father except through me."

Dana, *op. cit., Letters Addressed to Relatives and Friends,* Letter #23, pp. 137 and 138; *Op. cit., Racovian Catechism,* pp. 142–144; Snedeker, *op. cit., Our Heavenly Father Has No Equals,* p. 450.

---

2 Thessalonians 1:12

We pray this so that the name of our Lord Jesus may be glorified in you, and you in him, according to the grace of our God and the Lord Jesus Christ.

---

1. Some Trinitarians try to force this verse to "prove" the Trinity by what is known as the Granville Sharp Rule of Greek grammar. We have shown that this is not a valid proof of the Trinity (see Eph. 5:5, "The Granville Sharp Rule").

2. It is easily established in Scripture that both God and Jesus Christ give grace. The phrase "the grace of God" is well attested to, and there are plenty of verses in the Old and New Testament that reveal the grace of God. That Jesus Christ also gives grace is obvious in Scriptures such as 2 Corinthians 8:9; Galatians 1:6, 6:18; Ephesians 4:7; Philippians 4:23, etc. Also, it is well known from the salutations at the beginning of the Epistles that both God and Jesus Christ send their grace and peace to Christians. One example will do, although many could be given: "To all in Rome who are loved by God and called to be saints: Grace and peace to you from God our Father and from the Lord Jesus Christ" (Rom. 1:7). Since it is so plain in the Bible that both God and Christ give us grace, there is no reason to try to make the two of them into one, and thus remove the Father from the verse.

---

1 Timothy 3:16

Beyond all question, the mystery of godliness is great: He appeared in a body, was vindicated by the Spirit, was seen by angels, was preached among the nations, was believed on in the world, was taken up in glory.

---

1. Although the above verse in the NIV does not support the Trinity, there are some Greek manuscripts that read, "God appeared in the flesh." This reading of some Greek manuscripts has passed into some English versions, and the King James Version is one of them. Trinitarian scholars admit, however, that these Greek texts were altered by scribes in favor of the Trinitarian position. The reading of the earliest and best manuscripts is not "God" but rather "he who." Almost all the modern versions have the verse as "the mystery of godliness is great, **which** was manifest in the flesh," or some close equivalent.

2. In regard to the above verse, Bruce Metzger writes:

["He who"] is supported by the earliest and best uncials…no uncial (in the first hand) earlier than the eighth or ninth century supports *theos*; all ancient versions presuppose *hos* or *ho* ["he who" or "he"]; and no patristic writer prior to the last third of the fourth century testifies to the reading *theos*. The reading *theos* arose either (*a*) accidentally, or (*b*) deliberately, either to supply a substantive for the following six verbs [the six verbs that follow in the verse], or, with less probability, to provide greater dogmatic precision [i.e., to produce a verse that more clearly supports the Trinitarian position]."[37]

3. When properly translated, 1 Timothy 3:16 actually argues against the Trinity. "…by common confession great is the mystery of godliness: He who was revealed in the flesh, Was vindicated in the Spirit, Beheld by angels, Proclaimed among the nations, Believed on in the world, Taken up in glory" (NASB). This section of Scripture beautifully portrays an overview of Christ's life and accomplishments. It all fits with what we know of *the man*, Jesus Christ. If Jesus were God, this section of Scripture would have been the perfect place to say so. We should expect to see some phrases like, "God incarnate," "God and Man united," "very God and very man," etc. But nothing like that occurs. Instead, the section testifies to what non-Trinitarians believe—that Christ was a man, begotten by the Father, and that he was taken up into glory.

Buzzard, *op. cit., Doctrine of the Trinity*, pp. 144 and 152; Dana, *op. cit., Letters Addressed to Relatives and Friends*, p. 137; Farley, *op. cit., Unitarianism Defined: The Scripture Doctrine of the Father, Son, and Holy Ghost*, pp. 69 and 70; Morgridge, *op. cit., True Believer's Defence Against Charges Preferred by Trinitarians*, pp. 82 and 115; Snedeker, *op. cit., Our Heavenly Father Has No Equals*, p. 451.

---

1 Timothy 5:21
I charge you, in the sight of God and Christ Jesus and the elect angels, to keep these instructions without partiality, and to do nothing out of favoritism.

---

1. Some Trinitarians try to force this verse to "prove" the Trinity by what is known as the Granville Sharp Rule of Greek grammar. We have shown that this is not a valid proof of the Trinity (see Eph. 5:5, "The Granville Sharp Rule").

2. It is important to read the Bible thoroughly to find keys that help with the interpretation of a verse in question. In this case, we find that it was common in the biblical culture to charge someone "in the sight of God" (see note #2 on 2 Tim. 4:1). Given that fact, and given that Paul definitely

---

37. Bruce Metzger, *A Textual Commentary on the Greek New Testament* (United Bible Society, New York, 1975), p. 641.

charges Timothy by both God and Jesus Christ in 1 Timothy 6:13, there is no reason to remove God from this verse by making the word "God" a second reference to Jesus Christ.

3. This verse has an element that is very hard to explain if the Trinity is true, and makes perfect sense if it is not. Paul charges Timothy by God, by Christ and by "the elect angels." This fits beautifully with what we teach; i.e., that there is the one God, and there is the man Jesus who has been made "Lord and Christ," but there is no "person" called "the Holy Spirit." If there were a Trinity composed of three co-equal, co-eternal "persons," why would Paul charge Timothy by the "elect angels" and leave the "Holy Spirit" out of the picture?

---

1 Timothy 6:14–16
(14) to keep this command without spot or blame until the appearing of our Lord Jesus Christ,
(15) which God will bring about in his own time—God, the blessed and only Ruler, the King of kings and Lord of lords,
(16) who alone is immortal and who lives in unapproachable light, whom no one has seen or can see. To him be honor and might forever. Amen.

---

1. It is stated by Trinitarians that since God is called "King of kings and Lord of lords," as is Christ, that Christ must be God. However, simply because the same title is used for two individuals does not mean that they are actually somehow one being. Before any conclusion is drawn about the title, we should search all of Scripture to see if we can determine how the title is used. A thorough search reveals that the phrase "king of kings" simply means "the best king." In Ezra 7:12, Artaxerxes is called "the king of kings" because he was the most powerful king at the time. Consider also Ezekiel 26:7: "For this is what the Sovereign LORD says: 'From the north I am going to bring against Tyre Nebuchadnezzar king of Babylon, king of kings, with horses and chariots, with horsemen and a great army." God again calls Nebuchadnezzar "king of kings" in Daniel 2:37. Nebuchadnezzar was the most powerful king of his day, and the Bible calls him "king of kings." Thus, Scripture shows us that having the title "king of kings" does not make a person God. In the Bible, other powerful kings had that title, and no one denies that Jesus Christ is a powerful king and thus is also worthy of it.

2. In the Semitic languages, the genitive case was often used to express the fact that something was the "best." Thus, "the best king" was designated as "the king of kings," etc. When Daniel revealed King Nebuchadnezzar's dream, Nebuchadnezzar called Daniel's God a "God of gods," and that was long before Nebuchadnezzar realized much about the true God. He was simply stating that since Daniel's God could interpret dreams so well, he was "the best god." When Noah spoke of the future of Canaan, he foretold that Canaan would be "a servant of servants" (Gen. 9:25 - KJV). We use the same terminology in our English vernacular to express the greatness of something: "The sale of sales" is the biggest sale, and "the deal of deals" is the best deal.

3. When properly interpreted, 1 Timothy 6:14–16 is a strong refutation of the Trinity. Unfortunately, the Greek text has been translated with two different slants. A few versions, including the KJV, make the verse read such that Christ shows the Father to the world: "...he [Jesus Christ] shall shew *who is* the blessed and only Potentate... [i.e., God]." The vast majority of the versions and most of the commentators, however, state that the verse reads differently. They testify that the verse can be very naturally translated to read that God will bring about the appearing of our Lord Jesus Christ. And this is exactly the testimony of the rest of Scripture—there will come a day when God will send Jesus back to earth (Acts 3:20). The NASB does a good job of translating the Greek text and staying faithful to the meaning: "...until the appearing of our Lord Jesus Christ, which He will bring about at the proper time—He who is the blessed and only Sovereign, the King of kings and Lord of lords; who alone possesses immortality and dwells in unapproachable light; whom no man has seen or can see. To Him *be* honor and eternal dominion! Amen."

The NIV carries the same meaning but, by substituting "God" for "He," makes the verse a little easier for the reader: "...until the appearing of our Lord Jesus Christ, which God will bring about in his own time—God, the blessed and only Ruler, the King of kings and Lord of lords, who alone is immortal and who lives in unapproachable light, whom no one has seen or can see. To him be honor and might forever. Amen."

In both these versions, the ending eulogy refers to God. God alone is the one who is immortal and dwells in unapproachable light, whom no man has seen or can see. Those words cannot be made to refer to Christ, who, although he occasionally takes on some of the titles or attributes of God, cannot accurately be referred to as ever dwelling in unapproachable light or as one whom no man can see.

The reason these verses so strongly testify against the Trinity is now clear. There are clearly *two beings* involved—"God" and Christ. And of the two, "God" is the "blessed and only ruler," and He will bring about Christ's return. If Christ were God, or an equal part of a "Triune" God, these verses would not differentiate between "God" and Christ by calling "God" the "only ruler."

4. Jesus Christ has been given "all authority" by God. Jesus Christ is the Head of the Body of Christ, the one who will raise and judge the dead, and be the ruler of the next ages. He is called "King of kings and Lord of lords," and as God's vice-regent he is indeed that, but notice should be taken of the fact that Christ is never given the title, "God of gods." That title is reserved for God alone, especially since Christ is not above God. Even after his resurrection and in his glorified body, he still called God, "my God" (John 20:17).

Buzzard, *op. cit., Doctrine of the Trinity*, p. 48; Dana, *op. cit., Letters Addressed to Relatives and Friends,* pp. 15 and 212; Snedeker, *op. cit., Our Heavenly Father Has No Equals,* pp. 383 and 452.

---

2 Timothy 4:1
In the presence of God and of Christ Jesus, who will judge the living and the dead, and in view of his appearing and his kingdom, I give you this charge:

---

1. Some Trinitarians try to force this verse to "prove" the Trinity by what is known as the Granville Sharp Rule of Greek grammar. We have shown that this is not a valid proof of the Trinity (see Eph. 5:5, "The Granville Sharp Rule").

2. There is no logical reason for this verse to have a double reference to Christ by making the word "God" refer to Jesus Christ, thus removing "God" (normally understood to be the Father) from the verse entirely. A study of Scripture reveals that charging someone by God was common in biblical times. For example, the High Priest charged Jesus "before God" to say whether or not he was the Christ (Matt. 26:63), and other examples could be cited. In another place, Paul charged Timothy by both God and Christ: "In the sight of God, who gives life to everything, and of Christ Jesus, who while testifying before Pontius Pilate made the good confession, I charge you to keep this command without spot or blame..." (1 Tim. 6:13 and 14).

A study of the books of Timothy will show that Paul charges Timothy three times. The other two times he mentions both Christ and God in his charge (1Tim. 5:21, 6:13). Because it was a custom to charge people before God, and because Paul charges Timothy by both God and Christ in the other places, it is unreasonable for Trinitarians to assert that the word "God" is referring to Christ, and therefore leave God out of the verse altogether. It is much more reasonable to believe that Paul is consistent throughout Timothy and that he does indeed charge Timothy by both God and Jesus Christ, the "Dynamic Duo."

Titus 2:13
while we wait for the blessed hope—the glorious appearing of our great God and Savior, Jesus Christ,

---

1. Scholars debate the exact translation of this verse, and the two sides of that debate are seen in the various translations. Some scholars believe that "glory" is used in an adjectival sense, and that the verse should be translated as above in the NIV. Versions that follow suit are the KJV and the AMP. Many other versions, such as the Revised Version, ASV, NASB, Moffatt, RSV, NRSV, DRB, NEB, etc., translate the verse very differently. The NASB is a typical example. It reads, "looking for the blessed hope and the appearing of the glory of our great God and Savior, Christ Jesus." The difference between the translations is immediately apparent. In the NIV, etc., we await the "glorious appearing" of God, while in the NASB and other versions we await the "appearing of the glory" of God our Savior (this is a use of "Savior" where the word is applied in the context to God, not Christ. See the note on Luke 1:47), i.e., we are looking for the "glory" of God, which is stated clearly as being "Jesus Christ." Of course, the glory will come at the appearing, but Scripture says clearly that both the glory of the Son and the glory of the Father will appear (Luke 9:26). God's Word also teaches that when Christ comes, he will come with his Father's glory: "For the Son of Man is going to come in his Father's glory..." (Matt. 16:27). Keeping in mind that what is revealed in other places in the Bible about a certain event often clarifies what is being portrayed in any given verse, it becomes apparent from other Scriptures referring to Christ's coming that the Bible is not trying to portray God and Christ as one God. In this case, the glory of God that we are waiting for is Jesus Christ.

2. It has been stated that the grammar of Titus 2:13 forces the interpretation that Jesus is God because of the Granville Sharp Rule of grammar. That is not the case, however. The Granville Sharp rule has been successfully challenged, and an extensive critique of it occurs in this appendix in the notes on Ephesians 5:5. The point is that when Scripture refers to "our Great God and Savior, Jesus Christ," it can mean two beings—both the "Great God," and the "Savior," Jesus Christ. The highly regarded Trinitarian Henry Alford gives a number of reasons as to why the grammar of the Greek does not force the interpretation of the passage to make Christ God.[38]

3. The context of the verse helps us to understand its meaning. The verse is talking about saying "no" to ungodliness while we wait for the appearing of Jesus Christ, who is the glory of God. Its purpose is not to expound the doctrine of the Trinity in any way, nor is there any reason to assume that Paul would be making a Trinitarian reference here. It makes perfect sense for Scripture to call Christ "the glory of God" and for the Bible to exhort us to say "no" to ungodliness in light of the coming of the Lord, which will be quickly followed by the Judgment (Matt. 25:31–33; Luke 21:36).

Buzzard, *op. cit.*, *Doctrine of the Trinity*, p. 129; Norton, *op. cit.*, *A Statement of Reasons for Not Believing the Doctrines of Trinitarians*, pp. 199–203, 305 and 306; Snedeker, *op. cit.*, *Our Heavenly Father Has No Equals*, pp. 452–457.

---

38. *The Greek New Testament* (Chicago, Moody Press, 1968 edition, Vol. 3), pp. 419–421.

Hebrews 1:2
but in these last days he has spoken to us by his Son, whom he appointed heir of all things, and through whom he made the universe.

1. The Greek word translated "universe" (or "world" in many translations) is the plural of the Greek word *aion*, and actually means "ages." There are other Greek words that mean "world," such as *kosmos* and *oikoumene*, and when the Devil tempted Jesus by showing him all the kingdoms of the "world," these words are used. This verse is referring to the "ages," not the "world." *Vine's Lexicon* has, "an age, a period of time, marked in the N.T. usage by spiritual or moral characteristics, is sometimes translated 'world;' the R.V. margin always has 'age.'" *Bullinger's Critical Lexicon* has:

> "*Aion* [age], from *ao, aemi*, to blow, to breathe. *Aion* denoted originally the life which hastes away in the breathing of our breath, life *as transitory*; *then* the course of life, time of life, life in its temporal form. *Then*, the space of a human life, an age, or generation *in respect of duration*. The time lived or to be lived by men, time as moving, historical time as well as eternity. *Aion* always includes a reference to the filling of time"[39]

Since most translators are Trinitarian and think that Jesus was the one who made the original heavens and earth, they translate "ages" as "world" in this verse. But the actual word in the Greek text means "ages," and it should be translated that way.

2. Trinitarians use the verse to try to prove that Jesus Christ created the world as we know it, but the context of the verse shows that this cannot be the correct interpretation. Verses 1 and 2 show that God spoke through Jesus "in these last days," whereas He had spoken "in the past" in various ways. If indeed it were through Jesus that the physical world was created, then one of the ways that God spoke in the past was through Jesus. But that would contradict the whole point of the verse, which is saying that God spoke in other ways in the past, but "in these last days" is speaking through the Son.

3. Since verses 1 and 2 say that it was "God" who spoke through prophets and through His Son, it is clear that God is the prime mover and thus different from the Son. These verses show that the Son is subordinate to God and, as a "mouthpiece" for God, is compared to the prophets.

4. The fact that God appointed the Son to be "heir" shows that God and the Son are not equal. For the Son to be the "heir" means that there was a time when he was not the owner. The Bible was written using common words that had common and accepted meanings in the language of the time. The doctrine of the Trinity forces these words to take on "mystical" meanings. Yet there is no evidence in Scripture that the writer changed the meaning of these common words. We assert that if the Bible is read using the common meanings of the words in the text, there is simply no way to arrive at the doctrine of the Trinity. The word "heir" is a common one and, because death and inheritance are a part of every culture, it occurs in every language. Any dictionary will show that an heir is one who inherits, succeeds or receives an estate, rank, title or office of another. By definition, you cannot be an heir if you are already the owner. No one in history ever wrote a will that said, "My heir and the inheritor of my estate is…ME!" If Christ is God, then he cannot be "heir." The only way he can be an heir is by not being the owner.

That Christ is an "heir" is inconsistent with Trinitarian doctrine, which states that Christ is co-equal and co-eternal with the Father. If Christ were God, then he was part owner all along, and

---

39. Bullinger, *op. cit., Lexicon*, under "world."

thus is not the "heir" at all. These verses teach that God is the original owner, and will give all things to His heir, Jesus Christ. It is obvious from the wording of these first two verses that the author of Hebrews does not consider Christ to be God.

5. The entire opening section of Hebrews, usually used to show that Christ is God, actually shows just the opposite. More proof of this is in verses 3 and 4. After Christ sat down at the right hand of God, "...he became as much superior to the angels..." as his name is superior to theirs. "God" has always been superior to the angels. If Christ only *became* superior after his resurrection, then he cannot be the eternal God. It is obvious from this section of Scripture that "the Man" Christ Jesus was given all authority and made Lord and Christ.

6. Since *aionas* means "ages" and not "world," it is fair to ask in what sense God has made the ages through Jesus. First, it must be understood that the word "made" is extremely flexible. It is the Greek word *poieo*, which, both alone and in combination with other words, is translated more than 100 different ways in the NIV, and thus has a wide range of meaning. Some of the ways *poieo* is translated are: accomplish, acted, appointed, are, be, bear, began, been, bring, carry out, cause, committed, consider, do, earned, exercise, formed, gain, give, judge, kept, made, obey, performed, preparing, produce, provide, put into practice, reached, spend, stayed, treated, was, win, work, wrote, and yielded. Although most people read *poieo* in Hebrews 1:2 as referring to the original Creation, it does not have to mean that at all. The context dictates that the "ages" being referred to are the ages after Christ's resurrection. In verse 2, Christ became heir after his resurrection. In verse 3, he then sat at God's right hand after his resurrection. Verses 5 and 6 also refer to the Resurrection. The context makes it clear that God was not speaking through His Son in the past, but that He has spoken "in these last days" through His Son, and "given form to" the ages through him (note #1 on Heb. 1:10 below provides more evidence for this).

Broughton, and Southgate, *op. cit., The Trinity, True or False?*, pp. 286–298; Hyndman, *op. cit., Principles of Unitarianism*, pp. 123–127; Norton, *op. cit., A Statement of Reasons for Not Believing the Doctrines of Trinitarians*, pp. 194–196; *Op. cit., Racovian Catechism*, pp. 93 and 94; Snedeker, *op. cit., Our Heavenly Father Has No Equals*, pp. 457–459.

Hebrews 1:8
But about the Son he says, "Your throne, O God, will last for ever and ever, and righteousness will be the scepter of your kingdom.

---

1. The English language makes a clear distinction between "God" and "god." Thus, in English Bibles, the heavenly Father is called "God," while lesser divinities, people with God's authority on earth and important people such as kings, are also called "god" (2 Cor. 4:4; John 10:34 and 35; Acts 12:22). The Hebrew and Aramaic languages cannot make the distinction between "God" and "god." Since Hebrew and Aramaic have only capital letters, every use is "GOD." Furthermore, although the Greek language has both upper case and lower case letters as English does, the early Greek manuscripts did not blend them. It was the style of writing at the time of the New Testament to make manuscripts in all capital letters, so the Greek manuscripts were, like the Hebrew text, all upper case script. Scholars call these manuscripts "uncials," and that style was popular until the early ninth century or so when a smaller script was developed for books.[40]

---

40. Metzger, *op. cit., Text of the New Testament,* pp. 8–10.

Since all texts were in upper case script, if we translated Genesis 1:1 and 2 as it appeared in the Hebrew manuscripts, it would read:

IN THE BEGINNING GOD CREATED THE HEAVENS AND THE EARTH NOW THE EARTH WAS FORMLESS AND EMPTY DARKNESS WAS OVER THE SURFACE OF THE DEEP AND THE SPIRIT OF GOD WAS HOVERING OVER THE WATERS.

Actually, Bible students should be aware that in both the early Hebrew and Greek manuscripts there were no spaces between the words, no punctuation marks, no chapters and no verses. The original texts of both the Old and New Testament were capital letters all run together, and it looked like this:

INTHEBEGINNINGGODCREATEDTHEHEAVENSANDTHEEARTHNOWTHE EARTHWASFORMLESSANDEMPTYDARKNESSWASOVERTHESURFACEOFTHE DEEP AND THE SPIRIT OF GOD WAS HOVERING OVER THE WATERS

Of course, the entire Bible was hand-printed exactly the same way, with every letter in upper case and no spaces between any words. As you can imagine, that made reading very difficult, and so it was common to read aloud, even when reading to yourself, to make it easier. That is why Philip the Evangelist could hear the Ethiopian eunuch reading the scroll of Isaiah (Acts 8:30). Such a text was hard to read and practically impossible to teach from. Imagine not being able to say, "Turn to Chapter 5, verse 15." Therefore, divisions in the text began to appear quite early. However, because scribes lived far apart and hand-copied manuscripts, the divisions in the various manuscripts were not uniform. The first standardized divisions between verses came into being around 900 A.D., and the modern chapter divisions were made in the 1200s.

It should now be very clear that there was just no way to distinguish between "God" and "god" in the early texts, and so it must always be determined from the context whether or not the word "GOD" is referring to the Father or to some lesser being. Although it was usual that the presence of the definite article in the Greek text alerted the reader that the "GOD" being referred to was the Father, this was not always the case (see the note on John 10:33). For example, in 2 Corinthians 4:4, the word "*theos*" has the definite article, but the verse is referring to the Devil. Context is always the final judge of whether *theos* should be translated "God" or "god."

2. The Semitic languages, and both the Latin and Greek spoken by the early Christians, used the word "God" with a broader meaning than we do today. "God" was a descriptive title applied to a range of authorities, including great people, rulers and people acting with God's authority. In John 10:33, when the Jews challenged Jesus and said he was claiming to be "a god" (mistranslated in most versions as "God"; see our note on that verse), he answered them by asking them if they had read in the Old Testament that people to whom the Word of God came were called "GODS" (and we use all caps here because the earliest texts did. It is hard to escape the modern notion that "God" refers to the True God and "gods" referred to lesser deities).

Any study of the words for "God" in both Hebrew and Greek will show that they were applied to *people* as well as to God. This is strange to English-speaking people because we use "God" in reference only to the true God, but both Hebrew and Greek used "God" of God, great men, other gods, angels and divine beings. It is the context that determines whether "God" or a great person is being referred to. This is actually a cause of occasional disagreement between translators, and they sometimes argue about whether "GOD" refers to God, the Father, or to a powerful person or representative of God. One example of this occurs in Exodus 21:6, which instructs a master whose servant wishes to serve him for life to bring the servant "to *Elohim*." The KJV, the NIV and many others believe that the owner of the servant is supposed to bring the servant before the local authorities, and so they translate *Elohim* as "judges" (see also Exod. 22:8 and 9 for more examples). Other translators felt that the master was required to bring the servant to God, so they translated *Elohim* as "God."(e.g., NRSV) Thus, the verse will read, "God" or "judges," depending on the translation.

Hebrews 1:8 is like other verses in that just because the word "*theos*" ("GOD") is used does not mean that it refers to the Father. It could easily be referring to "god" in the biblical sense that great men are called "god." The Septuagint uses the word *theos* for God, but also for men in places like Psalm 82 where men represent God. The context must be the determining factor in deciding what "GOD" refers to. In this case, in Hebrews which we are studying, the context is clear. Throughout the entire context from Hebrews 1:1, Christ is seen to be lesser than God the Father. Therefore, the use of "*theos*" here should be translated "god."

3. The context must determine whether Christ is being referred to as the Supreme Being or just a man with great authority, so it must be read carefully. In this case, however, one need not read far to find that Christ, called "God," himself has a "God." The very next verse, Hebrews 1:9, says, "…therefore God, your God, has set you above your companions…." Thus, Christ cannot be the supreme God, because the supreme God does not have a God. Furthermore, Christ's God "set" him above others and "anointed" him. This makes it abundantly clear that the use of *theos* here in Hebrews is not referring to Christ being the supreme God, but rather a man with great authority under another God. Andrews Norton writes:

> Here the context proves that the word "God" does not denote the Supreme Being, but is used in an inferior sense. This is admitted by some of the most respectable Trinitarian critics. Thus, the Rev. Dr. Mayer remarks: "Here the Son is addressed by the title *God*: but the context shows that it is an official title which designates him as a king: he has a kingdom, a throne and a scepter; and in verse 9 he is compared with other kings, who are called his fellows; but God can have no fellows. As the Son, therefore, he is classed with the kings of the earth, and his superiority over them consists in this, that he is anointed with the oil of gladness above them; inasmuch as their thrones are temporary, but his shall be everlasting."[41]

4. The verse is a quotation from Psalm 45:6 and 7. The Jews read this verse for centuries and, knowing the flexibility of the word "God," never concluded that the Messiah would somehow be part of a Triune God.

5. We must note that the verse in the Greek text can also be translated as, "Your throne, O God." However, because the verse is a reference from the Old Testament, and because we believe that God, the Father, is calling His Christ a "god" (i.e., one with divine authority), there is no need to translate the verse other than, "…Your throne, O god, will last for ever and ever…."

> Broughton, and Southgate, *op. cit., The Trinity, True or False?*, pp. 196 and 197; Buzzard, *op. cit., Doctrine of the Trinity*, pp. 35; Dana, *op. cit., Letters Addressed to Relatives and Friends*, pp. 205 and 206; Farley, *op. cit., Unitarianism Defined: The Scripture Doctrine of the Father, Son, and Holy Ghost*, pp. 71 and 72; Morgridge, *op. cit., True Believer's Defence Against Charges Preferred by Trinitarians*, pp. 110 and 111; Norton, *op. cit., A Statement of Reasons for Not Believing the Doctrines of Trinitarians*, pp. 301 and 302; Snedeker, *op. cit., Our Heavenly Father Has No Equals*, pp. 459–463.

---

41. Andrews Norton, *Statement of Reasons*, p. 301.

Hebrews 1:10
"...In the beginning, O Lord, you laid the foundations of the earth, and the heavens are the work of your hands.

---

1. This verse is quoted from the Old Testament (Ps.102:25), where it applied to Yahweh, and the author of Hebrews is lifting it from the Psalms and applying it to Jesus Christ. The subject of the verse changes from Yahweh (Old Testament) to Jesus Christ (New Testament). It makes sense, therefore, that the action being attributed changes also. Many Old Testament verses testify that God created the original heavens and the earth (Gen. 1:1, etc.) However, both the Old Testament and New Testament tell us that there will be a new heaven and earth after this one we are currently inhabiting. In fact, there will be two more. First, the heaven and earth of the Millennium, the 1000 years Christ rules the earth, which will perish (Isa. 65:17; Rev. 20:1–10), and then the heaven and earth of Revelation 21:1ff, which will exist forever. The context reveals clearly that Hebrews 1:10 is speaking of these *future* heaven and earth. If we simply continue to read in Hebrews, remembering that the original texts had no chapter breaks, Scripture tells us, "It is not to angels that He has subjected **the world to come, about which we are speaking**" (Heb. 2:5). This verse is very clear. The subject of this section of Scripture is not the current heaven and earth, but the future heaven and earth. The reader must remember that the word "beginning" does not have to apply to the absolute beginning of time, but rather the beginning of something the author is referring to (see the note on this on John 6:64). When this verse is referring to the work of the Father, as it is in the Old Testament, it refers to the beginning of the entire heavens and earth. When it is applied to the Son, it refers to the beginning of his work, not the beginning of all Creation, as Hebrews 2:5 makes clear.

2. Although we ascribe to the explanation above, a number of theologians read this verse and see it as a reference to the Father, which is a distinct possibility. Verse 10 starts with the word "and" in the Greek text, so verse 9 and 10 are conjoined. Since verse 9 ends with, "...your God, has set you [the Christ] above your companions by anointing you with the oil of joy," these theologians see the reference to "the Lord" in the beginning of verse 10 as a reference back to the God last mentioned, i.e., the Father. Norton explains this point of view:

> Now the God last mentioned was Christ's God, who had anointed him; and the author [of the book of Hebrews], addressing himself to this God, breaks out into the celebration of his power, and especially his unchangeable duration; which he dwells upon in order to prove the stability of the Son's kingdom...i.e., thou [God] who hast promised him such a throne, *art he who laid the foundation of the earth*. So it seems to be a declaration of God's immutability made here, to ascertain the durableness of Christ's kingdom, before mentioned; and the rather so, because this passage had been used originally for the same purpose in the 102nd Psalm, *viz.* [Author uses KJV] To infer thence this conclusion, "*The children of thy servants shall continue, and their seed be established before Thee*. In like manner, it here proves the Son's throne should be established *forever and ever*, by the same argument, *viz.*, by God's immutability."[42]

Theologians such as Norton say that as it is used in the Old Testament, the verse shows that the unchanging God can indeed fulfill His promises, and they see it used in exactly the same way in

---

42. *Ibid.,* pp. 214 and 215.

Hebrews: since God created the heavens and the earth, and since He will not pass away, He is fit to promise an everlasting kingdom to His Son.

Authors who believe that the verse refers to the Son:

Broughton, and Southgate, *op. cit., The Trinity, True or False?*, pp. 289–295; Buzzard, *op. cit., Doctrine of the Trinity*, pp. 161 and 162; *Op. cit., Racovian Catechism*, pp. 95–105.

Authors who believe that the verse applies to the Father:

Hyndman, *op. cit., Principles of Unitarianism*, p. 137; Morgridge, *op. cit., True Believer's Defence Against Charges Preferred by Trinitarians*, p. 122; Norton, *op. cit., A Statement of Reasons for Not Believing the Doctrines of Trinitarians*, p. 214.

Hebrews 2:16 (KJV)
For verily he took not on *him the nature of* angels; but he took on *him* the seed of Abraham.

---

1. This verse is occasionally used to prove the Trinity, but if so, it is only because a mistranslation is not recognized. Any student of the Bible should know that the words in the KJV that are in *italics* were added by the translators. The translators wanted readers to know what was in the Greek text and what was not, so they kindly placed the words they added in *italic* script. This is much more honest than some versions that add all kinds of things without giving the reader a hint of it. Without the *italics*, the verse in English becomes somewhat of an enigma, because it is not clear how Christ did not "take on" angels, but did "take on" Abraham's seed. The solution is in the translation of the Greek text, and the modern versions (including the NKJV) get the sense very nicely: "For surely it is not angels he helps, but Abraham's descendants" (NIV). "For surely it is not with angels that he is concerned but with the descendants of Abraham" (RSV).

2. Correctly translated and read in its context, this verse beautifully portrays how the man, Jesus Christ, "helps" us. He was human like we are, a lamb from the flock, and without spot or blemish so he could accomplish God's purpose by being the perfect sacrifice and thus atone for our sins. This allows us to be totally free from fear of death because Christ showed us that death is not permanent for those who believe in him. God can and will raise us from the dead. And, because he was like us in every way, "he is able to help those who are tempted." Because in the context, it so clearly states that Jesus was "...like his brothers in every way..." (v. 17), there can be no reference to the Trinity in this verse. If the Trinity is correct and Jesus had both an eternal nature and human nature, he is hardly like us "in every way."

Hebrews 4:8
For if Joshua had given them rest, God would not have spoken later about another day.

As it is translated above, this verse does not support the Trinitarian position at all. In some versions, the name "Joshua" was mistranslated as "Jesus," which makes it sound as if Jesus were in the Old Testament. The names "Jesus" and "Joshua" are the same in Hebrew and Greek, and the translators of the KJV, for example, confused the names. This is easily discernible by reading the context, and every modern version we are aware of, including the New King James Version (NKJV), has the name "Joshua" in the verse, clearing up the misconception that somehow "Jesus" led the Israelites across the Jordan into Canaan (see the notes on Acts 7:45).

Hebrews 7:3
Without father or mother, without genealogy, without beginning of days or end of life, like the Son of God he [Melchizedek] remains a priest forever.

---

1. There are some Trinitarians who teach that Melchizedek was actually Jesus Christ because this verse says he was without Father or mother, beginning or end of life, etc. This cannot be the case, and misses the point of this entire section of Scripture. Knowing the Old Testament, specifically the Law of Moses, and then knowing about the genealogy of Jesus, the Jews did not believe that Jesus could be a high priest. The Law of Moses demanded that priests be descendants of Aaron and of the tribe of Levi. Of course, Jesus Christ came from the tribe of *Judah*. This "problem" is actually clearly set forth in the book of Hebrews itself: "For it is clear that our Lord descended from Judah, and in regard to that tribe Moses said nothing about priests" (v. 14).

What is the solution to this problem? This section of Hebrews shows that if Melchizedek can be a priest recognized by the great patriarch Abraham, and he had no priestly genealogy, then Christ can be a priest when he has no priestly genealogy. The Jews were very aware of the "qualifications" for the priesthood, and if someone claimed to be a priest but could not produce the required genealogy, he was disqualified (see Ezra 2:62). Thus, when this verse says Melchizedek had no genealogy or beginning or end, the Jews understood perfectly that it meant he did not come from a line of priests. They never thought, nor would they believe, that he had no father or mother or birth or death. They understood that if Melchizedek could be a priest to Abraham without being a descendant of Aaron, the first priest, then so could Jesus Christ.

2. Jesus Christ cannot be Melchizedek. Hebrews 7:3 says that Melchizedek was without Father or mother and without genealogy (i.e., without one given in Scripture). However, Jesus did have a father, God, and a mother, Mary. He also had a genealogy, in fact, two—one in Matthew and one in Luke. Furthermore, this verse says that Melchizedek was "like the Son of God." If he was "like" the Son, then he could not "be" the Son of God.

Buzzard, *op. cit.*, *Doctrine of the Trinity*, p. 35; Snedeker, *op. cit.*, *Our Heavenly Father Has No Equals*, p. 464.

Hebrews 13:8
Jesus Christ is the same yesterday, today and forever.

---

1. There is nothing in the context to warrant believing that this verse has anything to do with a "plurality of persons," "one substance in the Godhead" or any other Trinitarian concept. The verses around verse 8 tell believers not to be fooled by strange new doctrines. The verse preceding it says to "remember" the leaders and "imitate" them. The verse just after it says, "Do not be carried away by all kinds of strange teachings...." The context makes the intent of the verse obvious. Believers were being led astray by new teachings, and the author of Hebrews was reminding them that Jesus Christ does not change. The truth about him yesterday is the same now and will be the same in the future.

2. Although some people try to use this verse as if it said that Jesus Christ has existed from eternity past, the very wording shows that is not the case. A study of the word "yesterday" in Scripture shows that it refers to something that happened only a short time before. It stretches the grammar beyond acceptable limits to try to make this verse say that Christ has always existed.

3. It has been widely recognized by theologians of many backgrounds that this verse is referring to the fact that Christian truth does not change. Morgridge writes: "This passage refers not to the nature, but to the doctrine of Christ. With this exposition agree Adam and Samuel Clark, Calvin, Newcome, Whitby, Le Clerk, and the majority of expositors."

Morgridge, *op. cit., True Believer's Defence Against Charges Preferred by Trinitarians*, p. 123; Norton, *op. cit., A Statement of Reasons for Not Believing the Doctrines of Trinitarians*, p. 269.

---

1 Peter 1:11 (KJV)
Searching what, or what manner of time the Spirit of Christ which was in them did signify, when it testified beforehand the sufferings of Christ, and the glory that should follow.

The fact that this verse says the "Spirit of Christ" was upon people in the Old Testament has caused people to believe that Christ himself was present in the Old Testament. But, as we will see, such is not the case. In the first place, the phrase "Spirit of Christ" never appears in the Old Testament. The "spirit of the LORD" or "the spirit of God" appears over and over, but never the "Spirit of Christ."

The spirit that people receive from God takes on different names as it refers to different functions. This can be abundantly proven. God always gives His spirit, and then it is named as it functions. When it is associated with wisdom, it is called the "spirit of wisdom" (Exod. 28:3 (KJV); Deut. 34:9; Eph. 1:17). When it is associated with grace, it is called the "spirit of grace" (Zech.12:10; Heb. 10:29). When it is related to glory, it is called the "spirit of glory" (1 Pet. 4:14). It is called the "spirit of adoption" when it is associated with our everlasting life (Rom. 8:15, which is translated as "spirit of sonship" in some versions). It is called "the spirit of truth" when it is associated with the truth we learn by revelation (John 14:17, 16:13). When it came with the same power as it was brought to Elijah, it was called "the spirit of Elijah" (2 Kings 2:15). These are not different spirits. All the names refer to the one gift of holy spirit that God gives. Ephesians 4:4 states clearly that there is "one spirit," and that spirit is God's gift of holy spirit given to some people in the Old Testament and to all believers today.

When Peter mentions that "the spirit of Christ" was upon prophets as they "predicted the sufferings of Christ and the glory that would follow," it is easy to see that the spirit is called the "spirit of Christ" because it is associated with Christ and foretold of Christ, not because Christ was actually alive during the Old Testament.

Op. cit., Racovian Catechism, pp. 146–148.

---

2 Peter 1:1b
…To those who through the righteousness of our God and Savior Jesus Christ have received a faith as precious as ours:

---

1. Some Trinitarians try to force this verse to "prove" the Trinity by what is known as the Granville Sharp Rule of Greek grammar. We have shown that this is not a valid proof of the Trinity (see Eph. 5:5, "The Granville Sharp Rule").

2. This verse is generally translated one of two ways: "...Our God and Savior, Jesus Christ..." (Revised Version, RSV, NIV, etc.) and "...God and our Savior Jesus Christ... (KJV). Although it is possible that the word "God" (Greek = *theos*) is here being used in its lesser sense, i.e., of a man with divine authority (see Heb. 1:8 above), it is more likely that it is referring to the true God as distinct from Jesus Christ. This is certainly the way the context is leading, because the very next verse speaks of them separately.

Alford recognizes that two beings are referred to in the verse and writes, "Undoubtedly, as in Titus 2:13, in strict grammatical propriety, both "God" and "Savior" would be predicates of Jesus Christ. But here as there, considerations interpose, which seem to remove the strict grammatical rendering out of the range of probable meaning."[43]

3. There is absolutely no reason to force this verse to make Jesus Christ into God. It is the opening verse of the epistle, and reading all of the Epistles will show that it is customary in the New Testament to introduce both God and Christ at the opening of each one. Furthermore, it is through the righteousness of both God and Christ that we have received our precious faith. It was through God in that it was He who devised the plan of salvation and was righteous in His ways of making it available to us. It was through Christ in that by his righteous life he carried out the plan so that we can have what we now have. Both God and Christ had to be righteous in order for us to enjoy our current status in the faith, and we think the evidence is conclusive that they are both present in the verse.

Broughton, and Southgate, *op. cit.*, *The Trinity, True or False?* p. 202; Buzzard, *op. cit.*, *Doctrine of the Trinity*, p. 129.

---

1 John 3:16
This is how we know what love is: Jesus Christ laid down his life for us. And we ought to lay down our lives for our brothers.

There is no Trinitarian inference in the above verse or in 1 John 3:16 as it is translated in most versions. However, the King James Version reads as if "God" laid His life down for us. It reads: "Hereby perceive we the love *of God*, because he laid down his life for us: and we ought to lay down *our* lives for the brethren." The problem is caused by mistranslation. However, the informed reader will see the solution, even in the KJV text itself. In the KJV, words in *italics* were added by the translators. In this case, the translators added "*of God*," and thus caused the difficulty.

---

1 John 5:7 and 8 (KJV)
(7) For there are three that bear record <u>in heaven, the Father, the Word, and the Holy Ghost: and these three are one.</u>
<u>(8) And there are three that bear witness in earth,</u> the spirit, and the water, and the blood: and these three agree in one

---

43. Henry Alford, *The Greek Testament* (Moody Press, Chicago, Vol. 4), p. 390.

1. Some English versions have a shorter rendition of 1 John 5:7 and 8 than the KJV quoted above. The King James Version has words that support the Trinity that most modern versions do not have. How can this be? The reason that there are different translations of this verse is that some Greek texts contain an addition that was not original, and that addition was placed into some English versions, such as the KJV (the words added to some Greek texts are underlined in the quotation above). The note in the NIV Study Bible, which is well known for its ardent belief in the Trinity, says, "…the addition is not found in any Greek manuscript or NT translation prior to the 14ᵗʰ century."

Most modern versions are translated from Greek texts without the addition. We will quote the NIV: "For there are three that testify: the Spirit, the water and the blood; and the three are in agreement." We agree with the textual scholars and conclude from the evidence of the Greek texts that the statement that the Father, the Word and the Holy Spirit are "one" was added to the Word of God by men, and thus has no weight of truth.

There are many Trinitarian scholars who freely admit that the Greek text from which the KJV is translated was adjusted in this verse to support the Trinity. The Greek scholar A. T. Robertson, author of the unparalleled work, *A Grammar of the Greek New Testament in Light of Historical Research*, and the multi-volumed *Word Pictures in the New Testament*, writes:

> At this point [1 John 5:7] the Latin Vulgate gives the words in the Textus Receptus, found in no Greek MS. save two late cursives (162 in the Vatican Library of the fifteenth century, [No.] 34 of the sixteenth century in Trinity College, Dublin). Jerome did not have it. Erasmus did not have it in his first edition, but rashly offered to insert it if a single Greek MS. had it, and 34 was produced with the insertion, as if made to order. Some Latin scribe caught up Cyprian's exegesis and wrote it on the margin of his text, and so it got into the Vulgate and finally into the Textus Receptus by the stupidity of Erasmus."[44]

Robertson shows how this addition entered the text. It was a marginal note. Since all texts were hand-copied, when a scribe, copying a text, accidentally left a word or sentence out of his copy, he would place it in the margin in hopes that the next scribe would copy it back into the text. Unfortunately, scribes occasionally did not make the distinction between what a previous scribe had left out of the last copy and wrote in the margin, and marginal notes that another scribe had written in the margin to help him understand the text. Therefore, some marginal notes got copied into the text as Scripture. Usually these additions are easy to spot because the "new" text will differ from all the other texts. However, there are times when people adore their theology more than the God-breathed original, and they fight for the man-made addition as if it were the original words of God. This has been the case with 1 John 5:7 and 8, and we applaud the honesty of the translators of modern versions who have left it out of their translations.

The famous textual scholar, F. F. Bruce, does not even mention the addition in his commentary on 1 John (*The Epistles of John*). *The International Critical Commentary* does not mention it either. The conservative commentator R. C. H. Lenski, in his 12 volume commentary on the New Testament, only mentions that it is proper to leave the addition out. He writes: "The R. V. [Revised Version] is right in not even noting in the margin the interpolation found in the A.V. [KJV]." Henry Alford, author of the *The Greek Testament*, a Greek New Testament with extensive critical notes and commentary, writes:

…OMITTED BY ALL GREEK MANUSCRIPTS previous to the beginning of the 16ᵗʰ century;

---

44. A. T. Robertson, *Word Pictures in the New Testament* (Baker Books, Grand Rapids, 1933, reprinted 1960, Vol. 6), pp. 240 and 241).

ALL the GREEK FATHERS (even when producing texts in support of the doctrine of the Holy Trinity: as e.g., by [abbreviated names of Church "fathers"] Clem Iren Hipp Dion Ath Did Bas Naz Nys Ephih Caes Chr Procl Andr Damasc (EC Thl Euthym);

ALL THE ANCIENT VERSIONS (including the Vulgate (as it came from Jerome, see below) and (though interpolated in the modern editions, the Syriac;

AND MANY LATIN FATHERS (*viz.* Novat Hil Lucif Ambr Faustin Leo Jer Aug Hesych Bede) [Emphasis his].[45]

2. With the spurious addition gone, it is clear that there is no reference to the Trinity in 1 John 5:7 and 8. The context is speaking of believing that Jesus is the Son of God (v. 5 and 10). There are three that testify that Jesus is the Son of God: the spirit that Jesus received at his baptism, the water of his baptism and the blood that he shed.

Scripture says, "We accept man's testimony, but God's testimony is greater because it is the testimony of God, which he has given about his Son" (1 John 5:9). This verse is so true! How often people accept man's testimony and believe what men say, but do not believe what God says. We need to accept the testimony of God that He has given about His Son, and agree with the testimony of the spirit, the water and the blood, that Jesus Christ is the Son of God.

> Farley, *op. cit., Unitarianism Defined: The Scripture Doctrine of the Father, Son, and Holy Ghost*, pp. 28–33; Morgridge, *op. cit., True Believer's Defence Against Charges Preferred by Trinitarians*, pp. 70–87; Sir Isaac Newton, "*An Historical Account of Two Notable Corruptions of Scripture*," reprinted in 1841 (John Green, 121 Newgate Street, London), pp. 1–58; Norton, *op. cit., A Statement of Reasons for Not Believing the Doctrines of Trinitarians*, pp. 185 and 186; *Op. cit., Racovian Catechism*, pp. 39–42; Snedeker, *op. cit., Our Heavenly Father Has No Equals*, pp. 118–120.

---

1 John 5:20 (KJV)
And we know that the Son of God is come, and hath given us an understanding, that we may know him that is true, and we are in him that is true, *even* in his Son Jesus Christ. This is the true God, and eternal life.

---

1. Many Trinitarians claim that the final sentence in the verse, "This is the true God," refers to Jesus Christ, since the closest noun to "This" is "Jesus Christ." However, since God and Jesus are both referred to in the first sentence of the verse, the final sentence can refer to either one of them. The word "this," which begins the last sentence, is *houtos*, and a study of it will show that the context, not the closest noun or pronoun, must determine to whom "this" is referring. The Bible provides examples of this, and a good one is in Acts 7:18 and 19 (KJV): "Till another king arose, which knew not Joseph. The same (*houtos*) dealt subtilly with our kindred, and evil entreated our fathers, so that they cast out their young children, to the end they might not live." It is clear from this example that "the same" (*houtos*) cannot refer to Joseph, even though Joseph is the closest noun. It refers to the other king earlier in the verse, even though that evil king is not the closest noun.

If it were true that pronouns always referred to the closest noun, serious theological problems would result. An example is Acts 4:10 and 11(KJV): "Be it known unto you all, and to all the people

---

45. Alford, *Greek Testament*, p. 503.

of Israel, that by the name of Jesus Christ of Nazareth, whom ye crucified, whom God raised from the dead, *even* by him doth this man stand here before you whole. This [*houtos*] is the stone which was set at nought of you builders, which is become the head of the corner." If "This" in the last sentence refers to the closest noun or pronoun, then the man who was healed is actually the stone rejected by the builders that has become the head of the corner, i.e., the Christ. Of course, that is not true.

An even more troublesome example for those not recognizing that the context, not noun and pronoun placement, is the most vital key in determining proper meaning, is 2 John 1:7 (KJV): "For many deceivers are entered into the world, who confess not that Jesus Christ is come in the flesh. This is a deceiver and an antichrist." The structure of this verse closely parallels the structure of the verse we are studying. If one insists that the final phrase of 1 John 5:20 refers to Jesus because he is the closest associated noun, then that same person is going to be forced by his own logic to insist that Jesus Christ is a deceiver and an antichrist, which of course is absurd. Thus we conclude that, although the last phrase of 1 John 5:20 may refer to Jesus Christ, it can just as easily refer to God, who appears in the phrase "Son of *God*" and, via the possessive pronoun "his," in the phrase "*his* Son Jesus." To which of the two it refers must be determined from studying the words in the verse and the remoter context.

2. Once it is clear that the last sentence in the verse can refer to *either* Jesus or God, it must be determined which of the two it is describing. The context and remoter context will determine to whom the phrase "true God" applies. The result of that examination is that the phrase "true God" is used four times in the Bible beside here: 2 Chronicles 15:3; Jeremiah 10:10; John 17:3 and 1 Thessalonians 1:9. In all four of these places, the "true God" refers to the Father and not the Son. Especially relevant is John 17:3, which is Jesus' prayer to God. In that prayer, Jesus calls God "the only true God." These examples are made more powerful by the consideration that 1 John is a late epistle, and thus the readers of the Bible were already used to God being called the "true God." Add to that the fact that John is the writer of both the gospel of John and the epistles of John, and he would be likely to use the phrase the same way. Thus, there is every reason to believe that the "true God" of 1 John 5:20 is the heavenly Father, and there is no precedent for believing that it refers to the Son.

3. From studying the immediate context, we learn that this very verse mentions "him that is true" two times, and both times it refers to the Father. Since the verse twice refers to the Father as "the one who is true," that is a strong argument that "the true God" in the last part of the verse is the same being.

4. Not all Trinitarians believe that the last sentence in the verse refers to the Son. A study of commentators on the verse will show that a considerable number of Trinitarian scholars say that this phrase refers to the Father. Norton and Farley each give a list of such scholars. In his commentary on 1 John, Lenski writes that although the official explanation of the Church is to make the sentence refer to the Son:

> This exegesis of the church is now called a mistake by a number of commentators who believe in the full deity of Jesus as it is revealed in Scripture but feel convinced that this *houtos* clause speaks of the Father and not of His Son."[46]

> Buzzard, *op. cit., Doctrine of the Trinity*, pp. 137 and 138; Farley, *op. cit., Unitarianism Defined: The Scripture Doctrine of the Father, Son, and Holy Ghost*, pp. 72–75; Norton, *op. cit., A Statement of Reasons for Not Believing the Doctrines of Trinitarians*, pp. 196–199; *Op.*

---

46. R. C. H. Lenski, *The Interpretation of I and II Epistles of Peter, the Three Epistles of John, and the Epistle of Jude* (Augsburg Pub. House, Minneapolis, MN, 1966), p. 543.

cit., Racovian Catechism, pp. 78–89; Snedeker, *op. cit., Our Heavenly Father Has No Equals*, pp. 466–468.

Jude 4
For certain men whose condemnation was written about long ago have secretly slipped in among you. They are godless men, who change the grace of our God into a license for immorality and deny Jesus Christ our only Sovereign and Lord.

---

1. As it is written above and in most other versions, the doctrine of the Trinity is not stated or implied in this verse in any way.

2. However, there are a few texts that add the phrase "the only Lord God" in close proximity to "Jesus Christ," and this has caused some Trinitarians to force this verse into a proof of the Trinity by using the grammar and the Granville Sharp Rule. This falls short on two counts. First, the Granville Sharp Rule cannot be shown to "prove" the Trinity (see the extensive note on Eph. 5:5). Second, modern textual research has shown that the word "God" in the phrase "the only Lord God" was not in the original text, but was added as the centuries progressed. Textual critics and translators recognize that fact and thus modern translations read in ways similar to the NASB ("…our only Master and Lord, Jesus Christ").

Revelation 1:8
"I am the Alpha and the Omega," says the Lord God, "who is, and who was, and who is to come, the Almighty."

---

1. These words apply to God, not to Christ. The one, "…who is, and who was, and who is to come…" is clearly identified from the context. Revelation 1:4 and 5 reads: "…Grace and peace to you from him who is, and who was, and who is to come, and from the seven spirits before his throne, **and** from Jesus Christ, who is the faithful witness, the firstborn from the dead, and the ruler of the kings of the earth…." The separation between "…him who is, and who was, and who is to come…" **and** Christ can be clearly seen. The one "…who is, and who was, and who is to come…" is God.

2. This verse is made slightly more ambiguous in the KJV because the word "God" is left out of the Greek text from which the KJV was translated. Nevertheless, modern textual research shows conclusively that it should be included, and modern versions do include the word "God."

3. Because of the phrase, "…the Alpha and the Omega…," many feel this verse refers to Christ. However, a study of the occurrences of the phrase indicates that the title "Alpha and Omega" applies to both God and Christ. Scholars are not completely sure what the phrase "the Alpha and the Omega" means. It cannot be strictly literal, because neither God nor Christ is a Greek letter. Lenski concludes, "It is fruitless to search Jewish and pagan literature for the source of something that resembles this name Alpha and Omega. Nowhere is a person, to say nothing of a divine Person, called 'Alpha and Omega,' or in Hebrew, 'Aleph and Tau.'"[47]

Although there is no evidence from the historical sources that anyone is named "the Alpha and Omega," Bullinger says that the phrase "is a Hebraism, in common use among the ancient Jewish Commentators to designate the whole of anything from the beginning to the end; e.g., 'Adam

---

47. R. C. H. Lenski, *The Interpretation of St. John's Revelation* (Augsburg Pub. House, Minneapolis, MN 1963), p. 51.

transgressed the whole law from Aleph to Tau' (Jalk. Reub., fol. 17.4)"[48] The best scholarly minds have concluded that the phrase has something to do with starting and finishing something, or the entirety of something. Norton writes that these words, "denote the certain accomplishment of his purposes; that what he has begun he will carry on to its consummation" (pp. 479 and 480).

Since both God and Jesus Christ are "the Alpha and the Omega" in their own respective ways, there is good reason to believe that the title can apply to both of them, and no good reason why that makes the two into "one God." The titles "Lord" (see Rom. 10:9 above), "Savior" (see Luke 1:47 above) and "king of kings (see 1 Tim. 6:14–16 above) apply to both God and Christ, as well as to other men. As with "Lord," "Savior" and "King of kings," this title fits them both. God is truly the beginning and the end of all things, while Christ is the beginning and the end because he is the firstborn from the dead, the Author and Finisher of faith, the Man by whom God will judge the world, and the creator of the new ages to come (see Heb. 1:10 above).

> Hyndman, *op. cit., Principles of Unitarianism*, pp. 93–95; Norton, *op. cit., A Statement of Reasons for Not Believing the Doctrines of Trinitarians*, pp. 479 and 480; Snedeker, *op. cit., Our Heavenly Father Has No Equals*, pp. 385–389.

Revelation 1:11
"…Write on a scroll what you see and send it to the seven churches: to Ephesus, Smyrna, Pergamum, Thyatira, Sardis, Philadelphia and Laodicea."

Some texts in the Western tradition add the words, "I am the Alpha and Omega" to this verse, but textual scholars agree that the phrase is an addition to the text, and thus versions like the NIV, NASB, etc., do not have the addition (see the notes on Rev. 1:8).

Revelation 1:13–15 (NASB)
(13) and in the middle of the lampstands one like a son of man, clothed in a robe reaching to the feet, and girded across His breast with a golden girdle.
(14) And His head and His hair were white like white wool, like snow; and His eyes were like a flame of fire;
(15) and His feet *were* like burnished bronze, when it has been caused to glow in a furnace, and His voice *was* like the sound of many waters.

---

1. Many theologians have noticed the similarities between this description of Christ in Revelation, and the description of the "Ancient of Days" (i.e., God) in Daniel 7:9 and Ezekiel 43:2. Thus, based on the similarities between the two descriptions, these verses are used to support the Trinity. One of the reasons that more Trinitarians do not advance these verses in Revelation as a "proof" of the Trinity is that most Christians are unprepared to really understand the argument. That God appeared in the form of a human being is very new information for most people, and quite a few are unwilling to accept it. Nevertheless, the Trinitarian argument goes like this: God appeared in the Old Testament with a certain physical description. Christ has much the same description; therefore Christ must be God.

---

48. Bullinger, *op cit., Commentary on Revelation*, pp. 147 and 148.

Most Christians have not been shown from Scripture that God appeared in a form resembling a person. They have always heard that "no one has seen God at any time" and that God is invisible. A thorough explanation of God's appearing in the form of a man is given in the notes on Genesis 18:1 and 2 above.

2. When God became visible to Daniel (7:9), He had hair "white like wool," and from Ezekiel (43:2 - NASB) we learn that His voice "…was like the sound of many waters.…" This description is the same for Jesus Christ in Revelation 1:13–15, and thus the two are compared. Although we realize that these descriptions are similar, we would note that many things that are similar are not identical. Police are very aware of this. If you went to the police with the description of a man and said, "He has white hair and a deep voice," that would be helpful, but more would be needed to establish identity, since that description can fit more than one person.

To see if Christ is the same as, or identical with, God, we must study the records, and indeed, the entire scope of Scripture. Daniel, Chapter 7 is about the succession of empires through time. By the time we get to verse 9, Daniel described a vision he had of something that is still future to us. He described God preparing for the Judgment. Daniel also foresaw Jesus Christ taking the kingdom from his God, the Ancient of Days.

> **Daniel 7:13 and 14 (NASB)**
> (13) "I kept looking in the night visions, And behold, with the clouds of heaven One like a **Son of Man** was coming, And He came up to the **Ancient of Days** And was presented before Him.
> (14) "And to Him was given dominion, Glory and a kingdom, That all the peoples, nations, and *men of every* language Might serve Him. His dominion is an everlasting dominion Which will not pass away; And His kingdom is one Which will not be destroyed.

In the book of Revelation, God and Christ are both present. Chapter 4 and the opening of Chapter 5 describe God on a throne with a scroll in His right hand. Then Jesus Christ, the Lamb of God, "… came, and He took *it* out of the right hand of Him who sat on the throne" [i.e., God] (5:7 - NASB). Again, there are clearly two present: God and Christ. Nothing in the context indicates in any way that these two are somehow "one." There is no reason to assume that. Two is two. Furthermore, why is it so amazing that the risen Christ has an appearance similar to the one that God chooses to take on when He appears to us? Since God can take on any form He wants, why would He not take on a form that he knew would be similar to His Son? This similarity does not prove identity in any way, but it does show the functional equality of Jesus Christ and God.

> **Revelation 1:17**
> When I saw him, I fell at his feet as though dead. Then he placed his right hand on me and said: "Do not be afraid. I am the First and the Last.

1. The phrase, "…the First and the Last," is a title that is used five times in the Bible, twice in Isaiah of God (44:6, 48:12) and three times in Revelation of the Son (1:17, 2:8, 22:13). Trinitarians sometimes make the assumption that since the same title applies to both the Father and the Son, they must both be God. However, there is no biblical justification on which to base that assumption. When the whole of Scripture is studied, one sees that the same titles are used for God, Christ and men. Examples include "Lord" (see Rom. 10:9 above) and "Savior" (see Luke 1:47 above) and "King of kings" (see 1 Tim. 6:14–16 above). If other titles apply to God, Christ and men without making all of them into "one God," then there is no reason to assume that this particular title would mean they were one God unless Scripture specifically told us so, which it does not.

2. In the Old Testament, God truly was "the First and the Last." The meaning of the title is not specifically given, but the key to its meaning is given in Isaiah 41:4, in which God says He has called forth the generations of men, and was with the first of them and is with the last of them.

Isaiah 41:4
Who has done this and carried it through, **calling forth the generations** from the beginning? I, the LORD—with the first of them and with the last—I am he.

Thus, the Bible connects the phrase "…the First and the Last" with calling forth the generations. While God was the one who called forth the generations in the Old Testament, He has now conferred that authority on His Son. Thus, it is easy to see why the Lord Jesus is called "…the First and the Last…" in the book of Revelation. It will be Jesus Christ who will call forth the generations of people from the grave to enter in to everlasting life. God gave Jesus authority to raise the dead (John 5:25–27). His voice will raise all dead Christians (1 Thess. 4:16 and 17), and he will change our bodies into new glorious bodies (Phil. 3:20 and 21). However, even when Jesus said he had the authority to raise the dead, he never claimed he had that authority inherently because he was God. He always said that his Father had *given* authority to him. While teaching about his authority, Jesus Christ was very clear about who was the ultimate authority: "…the Son can do nothing by himself…the Father judges no one, but has entrusted all judgment to the Son…For as the Father has life in himself, so he has granted the Son to have life in himself. And he has given him authority to judge…" (John 5:19, 22, 26 and 27). If Jesus had the authority to raise the dead because he was in some way God, he never said so. He said he had his authority because his Father gave it to him. With the authority to raise the generations came the title associated with the existence of the generations, and thus after his resurrection Jesus Christ is called "…the First and the Last."

Morgridge, *op. cit., True Believer's Defence Against Charges Preferred by Trinitarians*, p. 122; *Op. cit., Racovian Catechism*, pp. 157–163; Snedeker, *op. cit., Our Heavenly Father Has No Equals*, p. 469.

Revelation 3:14
"To the angel of the church in Laodicea write: These are the words of the Amen, the faithful and true witness, the ruler of God's creation.

1. As it is translated above, there is no Trinitarian inference in the verse. It agrees perfectly with what we know from the whole of Scripture: that God has made Jesus both Lord and Christ.

2. In the KJV, the word "ruler" (Greek = *arche*) is translated "beginning." The word *arche* can mean "beginning," "first" or "ruler." When most people read the KJV, they say that Jesus Christ is the "beginning" of God's original creation, and this has caused some people to say that the verse is Trinitarian, because Jesus would thus have been before everything else. If that interpretation is correct, then this verse would be a strong argument against the Trinity because then Christ would be a created being. "Arianism" is the doctrine that Christ was the first of all of God's created things and that God then created everything else through Christ, and the way the KJV translates the verse can be understood as Arian.

3. It is possible (and some scholars do handle the verse this way) to understand the word "beginning" as applying to the beginning of the new ages that Christ will establish. If that were so, the verse would be similar to Hebrews 1:10 (see above). Christ, being the "firstborn from the dead," would be the beginning of God's new creation. Although it is certainly possible from a textual standpoint to handle the verse that way, the context of the verse is Christ ruling over his people. He is reproving and disciplining them (v. 19) and granting places beside him with the Father (v. 21). Thus, the translation of *arche* as "ruler" is a good translation and best fits the context. No one can argue with the fact that Christ is the ruler over all of God's creation.

Broughton, and Southgate, *op. cit., The Trinity, True or False?*, pp. 286–293; Snedeker, *op. cit., Our Heavenly Father Has No Equals*, p. 470.

Revelation 5:5
Then one of the elders said to me, "Do not weep! See, the Lion of the tribe of Judah, the Root of David, has triumphed. He is able to open the scroll and its seven seals."

Jesus Christ is called the "Root of David" two times in the book of Revelation (here and 22:16), while in two other places he is called the "Root of Jesse" (Isa. 11:10; Rom. 15:12). Jesse was the father of David (Ruth 4:22; 1 Chron. 2:12–15), so the phrases are basically equivalent, however, the name "Jesse" is more closely associated with the whole royal lineage and the people of God, while "David" is more directly associated with the kingdom.

In order for us to understand the phrases: "Root of Jesse" and "Root of David," we must understand how the word "root" was used in the Bible and in the biblical culture. It is used literally of the root of a plant or tree, as many verses show (Matt. 3:10; Luke 17:6). In both Hebrew and Greek, the word "root" is also used to portray strength, stability, the foundation of something, and the source of nourishment (Isa. 27:6; Ezek. 31:7; Hosea 9:16; Matt. 13:21; Mark 4:17). Furthermore, in both Hebrew and Greek it is used to portray the source of something (1 Tim. 6:10; Heb. 12:15).

When the Bible calls Jesus Christ the "Root of Jessie" or "the Root of David," it is saying that Jesus Christ is the strength and stability, as well as the source of nourishment, for the kingdom of God and the people of God. Trinitarians assert that as "God," Jesus is the creator of the people of God and is therefore their root, or source. Jesus, however, never even hinted that he was the creator of people. He himself is often referred to as the "son" of David. In John 15, Jesus refers to himself as the vine (not "root"), and the people as the branches. He made it clear that unless one remained in the vine, he would bear no fruit. Similarly, a plant that is cut off from its root, its source of strength and nourishment, dies. In that sense, Jesus saying he is the vine and we are the branches, or Jesus being our "root," are very similar. From the context and scope of Scripture we can conclude that when Scripture says that Jesus is the "Root of David" it is saying that Jesus is the foundation of stability, strength, and nourishment for the Kingdom of God and the people of God.

There is another possibility that we must consider when studying these verses. The Greek word *rhiza*, usually translated "root," can also mean "shoot" or "sprout." Furthermore, the Hebrew word *sheresh*, normally translated "root," can also refer to a sucker on a stump or the growth of new plant out of the ground (cp. Isa. 53:2). Scholars such as R. C. H. Lenski assert that "shoot" is proper translation of *rhiza* and *sheresh* in the verses referring to the Messiah being from Jesse or David. In that case, the Messiah is the shoot that comes up from the stump of Jesse and David, which is certainly true.

The kingdom of Israel, represented by Jessie or David, was cut off so completely by its captors, the Assyrians, Babylonians, Persians, Greeks, and Romans, that it did not look as if there would ever be a kingdom of Israel again. Only a "stump" remained of the once powerful kingdom. Nevertheless, a "shoot" came up from that stump of Jessie and David to reestablish the kingdom of Israel.

There is still another possibility. Since both "root," and "shoot" can be the meaning of the original text, and since both meanings are true of Jesus Christ and important for understanding who he is and what he does, it is possible that God is employing the figure of speech *Amphibologia*. We sometimes refer to this figure as "double entendre" and it occurs when one thing is said, but it can be taken two ways, both of which are true. Jesus is both a shoot from Jessie and David, and also the "root" of the people of Israel, their source of strength and stability.

Revelation 21:6
"...It is done. I am the Alpha and the Omega, the Beginning and the End. To him who is thirsty I will give to drink without cost from the spring of the water of life.

---

1. For commentary on the phrase "Alpha and Omega," see Revelation 1:8 above.

2. The exact meaning of the phrase "...the Beginning and the End..." is not given. Scholars give differing explanations of the phrase, but the meaning must be closely associated with the concepts of "Alpha and Omega" and "First and Last" because these titles are associated together (see Rev. 22:13 below). We have seen from the study of the title "Alpha and Omega" that it refers to the start and finish of something, and we have seen from the title "First and Last" (Rev. 1:17) that Christ will raise up the generations of people unto everlasting life. It is clear why Christ would be called the "Beginning and the End" in association with these concepts. He is the firstborn from the dead, and he will be the one to call the last people out of their graves, he is both the Author and Finisher of faith, he is the Man by whom God will judge the world and he is the one who will then create and bring to completion the next ages (see the notes on Heb. 1:10). There is no compelling reason to assume Jesus is God simply because of the title, "the Beginning and the End."

Op. cit., Rachovian Catechism, pp. 161–163.

Revelation 22:13
I am the Alpha and the Omega, the First and the Last, the Beginning and the End.

This verse refers to Jesus Christ for commentary on the phrase "Alpha and Omega," see the notes on Revelation 1:8; on "the First and Last," see the notes on Revelation 1:17; on "the Beginning and the End," see the notes on Revelation 21:6.

Revelation 22:16
"I, Jesus, have sent my angel to give you this testimony for the churches. I am the Root and the Offspring of David, and the bright Morning Star."

See the note on Revelation 5:5.

Topical Guide to the Verses Sometimes Used to Support the Trinity

This guide takes the verses listed above and outlines them by categories. Individual explanations for these verses are in the Canonical Index above. The reason for a topical Guide is to allow students to better study the verses that fall under specific categories. A second reason is to allow people to find answers to verses that may not be listed above, but fall under a general heading. For example, some Trinitarians insist that because Jesus is called "Lord," he is God. We explain why that thinking is not valid in our explanation of Romans 10:9 above, however, we do not feel it is necessary to list every place in the New Testament where Jesus is called "Lord." An interested person can find "Lord" below in the topical index and know where to look for our explanation.

I. Verses that are used to support the idea of multiple personalities in God

A. The Plural of Majesty

Genesis 1:26, 11:7.

B. "Uniplural" nouns and pronouns

1. *Elohim* (God). See notes on Genesis 1:1.
2. *Echad* ("one"). See notes on Deuteronomy 6:4.

C. Oneness of being

John 10:30, 14:11.
2 Corinthians 5:19, 12:19b.
Colossians 2:9.
1 John 5:7 and 8.
Revelation 1:13–15.

D. Holy spirit is called "he," and thus thought to be a "person"

John 14:16 and 17.

II. Verses in which Christ is thought to be called "God"

Isaiah 9:6b.
Luke 7:16, 8:39.
John 1:18, 10:33, 20:28.
Acts 7:59, 20:28b.
Romans 9:5b.
1 Timothy 3:16.
Hebrews 1:8.
1 John 3:16.
1 John 5:20.

III. The Granville Sharp Rule

Ephesians 5:5 (see complete notes).
2 Thessalonians 1:12.
1 Timothy 5:21.
2 Timothy 4:1.
Titus 2:13.
2 Peter 1:1b.
Jude 4.

IV. Falsely equating "Lord" and "God"

Romans 10:9.

V. Verses that are sometimes used to ascribe eternality or pre-existence to the Messiah

Proverbs 8:23.
Isaiah 11:10.
Micah 5:2.
Luke 10:18.
John 1:1, 14a, 15, 30, 3:13, 6:33, 38, 62 and 64b, 8:42 and 58b, 16:28–30, 17:5, 20:17.
Acts 7:45.
Romans 15:12.
1 Corinthians 10:4b and 9.
Hebrews 1:2 and 10, 2:16, 4:8, 7:3, 13:8.
1 Peter 1:11.
Revelation 3:14, 5:5, 22:16.

VI. Verses that are used to equate God and Christ because of worship due them

Matthew 4:10.

VII. Father, Son and Holy Spirit are mentioned together

Matthew 28:19.
1 Corinthians 12:4–6.
2 Corinthians 13:14.

VIII. Verses that show God and Christ sharing the same names, titles, descriptions and functions, thus supposedly making Christ identical with God

A. Jesus is called names that lead people to believe he is God

"Immanuel" Isaiah 7:14; Matthew 1:23.
"Mighty God" Isaiah 9:6b.
"The Lord our Righteousness" Jeremiah 23:6b.

B. Functions and Authority

Forgiving sins. Matthew 9:2 and 3; Mark 2:7; Luke 5:20 and 21.
Power to heal. Matthew 9:8b.

Being present with the people. Matthew 28:20b.
Having "all" authority. Matthew 28:18.
Raising himself from the dead. John 2:19, 10:18.
Having all knowledge. John 2:24.
Having equality with God. John 5:18b.
Creating the world. John 1:3 and 10; 1 Corinthians 8:6; Ephesians 3:9;
Colossians 1:15–20; Hebrews 1:2 and 10.
Being trusted by men. Jeremiah 17:5.
Filling everything. Ephesians 1:22 and 23.

C. Verses that show that Jesus and God have the same titles

Lord: Romans 10:9.
Savior: Isaiah 43:11; Luke 1:47.
King of kings: 1 Timothy 6:14–16.
Lord of lords: 1 Timothy 6:14–16.
The Alpha and the Omega: Revelation 1:8 and 11, 21:6, 22:13.
The First and the Last: Revelation 1:17, 22:13.
The Beginning and the End: Revelation 21:6, 22:13.
Son of God: Luke 1:35.

IX. Verses that supposedly support the idea of an incarnation

John 1:14a, 3:13, 6:33, 6:38.

X. Verses that supposedly ascribe God's nature to Christ

Philippians 2:6–8.
Colossians 2:9.

XI. Verses that show that Jesus has taken on some of the responsibilities the Old Testament assigned to God

Romans 10:13.
Ephesians 4:7 and 8.

XII. Verses that equate holy spirit with God

Acts 5:3 and 4.

XIII. Verses supposedly teaching that Christ is a "mystery"

Colossians 2:2.

XIV. Verses that supposedly teach Christ is "the angel of the Lord"

Genesis 16:7–13.

XV. Verses that supposedly show Christ appearing in the Old Testament

Genesis 18:1 and 2.

Selected Bibliography

Although there is a much larger body of literature from which to draw information, the following is large enough to provide substantial confirmation of the information in this appendix and add occasional insight as well.

Broughton, James and Southgate, Peter. *The Trinity, True or False?* The Dawn Book Supply, 66 Carlton Rd., Nottingham, England, 1995.

Buzzard, Anthony, editor. *Focus on the Kingdom, "Who is Jesus? God or Unique Man?,"* Atlanta Bible College, Morrow, GA, March 2000.

Buzzard, Sir Anthony and Hunting, Charles. *The Doctrine of the Trinity: Christianity's Self-inflicted Wound.* Atlanta Bible College and Restoration Fellowship, Morrow, GA, 1994 [In working with Buzzard's book, we have found that occasionally the pagination differs slightly].

Dana, Mary S. B. *Letters Addressed to Relatives and Friends, Chiefly in Reply to Arguments in Support of the Doctrine of the Trinity.* James Munroe and Co., Boston, 1845. Reprinted 1994 Spirit & Truth Fellowship International, 180 Robert Curry Drive, Martinsville, IN 46151.

Ehrman, Bart. *The Orthodox Corruption of Scripture.* Oxford University Press, NY, 1993.

Farley, Frederick. *Unitarianism Defined: The Scripture Doctrine of the Father, Son, and Holy Ghost.* American Unitarian Association, Boston, MA, 1873. Reprinted 1994 by Spirit & Truth Fellowship International, 180 Robert Curry Drive, Martinsville, IN 46151.

Hyndman, J. S. *Lectures on the Principles of Unitarianism.* Alnwick: 1824. Reprinted 1994 by Spirit & Truth Fellowship International, 180 Robert Curry Drive, Martinsville, IN 46151.

Morgridge, Charles. *True Believer's Defence Against Charges Preferred by Trinitarians.* Boston: Benjamin Greene, 1837. Reprinted 1994 by Spirit & Truth Fellowship International, 180 Robert Curry Drive, Martinsville, IN 46151.

Newton, Sir Isaac. *An Historical Account of Two Notable Corruptions of Scripture.* London: John Green, 1841.

Norton, Andrews. *A Statement of Reasons for Not Believing the Doctrines of Trinitarians.* Boston: American Unitarian Association, 10th edition, 1877.

Rees, Thomas. *The Racovian Catechism.* English translation, London; 1818. Latin translation, 1609. Polish, 1605. Reprinted 1994 by Spirit & Truth Fellowship International, 180 Robert Curry Drive, Martinsville, IN 46151.

Snedeker, Donald R. *Our Heavenly Father Has No Equals.* International Scholars Publications, Bethesda, MD, 1998.

B

Use and Usages of *Kurios* ("Lord")

The Greek word *kurios* is a key word in any study of the identity of Christ. Therefore, we have analyzed its many New Testament uses in their contexts and identified four principal usages, which we have indicated by number in the table below.

1. This usage denotes God, the Father of our Lord Jesus Christ and the Creator of the heavens and earth. In each case where *kurios* refers to God, there are indications in the context that it is specifically referring to Him.

2. This usage refers to the Lord Jesus Christ. A "2" indicates the totality of his life and ministry, without respect to before or after his resurrection, or any other subdivision.

2a. This usage refers specifically to his pre-resurrection ministry, for when he was referred to as "lord," the meaning fell considerably short of its meaning *after* his resurrection and ascension. As Matthew 28:18 and Acts 2:36 indicate, God made Christ "Lord" after his resurrection. Philippians 2:6–11 indicates that God honored Jesus with the title of "Lord" as His response to Jesus' obedient suffering. And Romans 14:9 says that because "Christ died and lived again," that he is "…Lord of both the dead and of the living." The lordship he exercised prior to this was analogous to the authority he had as their Teacher, Master, and Rabbi (see Mark 9:5, 11:21; John 13:13).

2b. This usage refers specifically to his post-resurrection, fully-realized Lordship (with a capital L). The Resurrection changed the respectful student/teacher relationship of the disciples with Jesus into the believers' servant/Lord relationship.

In some cases, we have found that both God and Jesus Christ are included in the meaning of *kurios*, and, instead of forcing a definition toward one or the other, we simply include them both. This is consistent with the biblical figure of speech *amphibologia*, which is the layering of one or more truths upon another wherein the same word or words can have more than one meaning. In English, we call this a "double entendre." When we assign both 1 & 2, we see this as a foreshadowing of the concept of "the Dynamic Duo," or God and His Christ functioning together.

3. This usage refers to the owner or master of something or someone. This usage has overtones that apply to the Lordship of Jesus Christ over the believers, because we are not our own, but we belong to him, who purchased us with his own blood (1 Cor. 7:22 and 23, *et al.*). Yet, in this usage, no specific reference is made to Jesus.

4. This usage is when *kurios* is used as a title of respect, equivalent to the English word "sir." Before Mary recognized Jesus at the garden tomb, she called him "*kurios*," thinking he was the gardener (John 20:15). The KJV and the NIV both appropriately translate it as "sir." In some cases, as in John 4, it is hard to say whether the person calling Jesus *kurios* is doing so out of general respect or from specific knowledge of who he was. In those cases, we have assigned both a "4" and another usage.

The Aramaic equivalents to the Greek word *kurios* are *mara* or *marya*. *Mara* with a possessive pronoun like "our" or "my" refers to Jesus, except in a few cases that refer to God (Luke 1:28, 2:29; John 12:38; Rom. 10:16, 11:3; Rev. 4:11). When *mara* is used with a genitive phrase (like Lord of the harvest—Luke 10:2), it also refers to God. *Marya*, the Old Testament word used in the Peshitta for Yahweh, can be used of either God or Jesus Christ in the New Testament, and therefore must be determined by the context of each occurrence. When *marya* refers to Jesus Christ, it generally refers to his post-resurrection Lordship, following the pattern of *kurios*. Where neither *mara* nor *marya* occur in the Aramaic Peshitta text in verses that contain *kurios*, we have indicated the translation of the Aramaic word inside quotes ("Jesus," "God," etc.).

When we are in doubt as to which usage is correct, we indicate such by the word "or" inside the parenthesis. If there are two uses of *kurios* in the same verse with different usages, we note that by separate sets of parentheses, e.g., (1) (2a).

In some cases the word "Lord" occurs in the KJV but not in more modern versions based on better manuscript evidence showing that *kurios* is not in the text (e.g., Acts 9:29; Rom. 1:3).

Matthew

1:20	(1)
1:22	(1)
1:24	(1)
2:13	(1)
2:15	(1)
2:19	(1)
3:3	(1 & 2)
4:7	(1)
4:10	(1)
5:33	(1)
6:24	(4)
7:21	(2)
7:22	(2)
8:2	(2)
8:6	(2a)
8:8	(2a)
8:21	(2a)
8:25	(2a)
9:28	(2a)
9:38	(1)
10:24	(3)
10:25	(3)
11:25	(1)
12:8	(2a)
13:27	(4)
13:51	(2a) Not in NIV
14:28	(2a)
14:30	(2a)
15:22	(2a)
15:25	(2a)
15:27	(2a)
15:27	(3)
16:22	(2a)
17:4	(2a)
17:15	(2a)
18:21	(2a)
18:25	(3)
18:26	(4) Greek texts omit
18:31	(3)
18:32	(3)
18:34	(3)
20:8	(3)
20:30	(2a)
20:31	(2a)

20:33	(2a)
21:3	(2a)
21:9	(1)
21:30	(4)
21:40	(3)
21:42	(1)
22:37	(1)
22:43	(2b)
22:44	(1)
22:44	(2)
22:45	(2b)
23:39	(1)
24:42, 43	(2a)
24:45	(2b)
24:46	(3)
24:48	(3)
24:50	(3)
25:11	(3)
25:18-24, 26	(3)
25:37	(2b)
25:44	(2b)
26:22	(2b)
27:10	(1)
27:63	(4)
28:2	(1)
28:6	(2a) Some texts omit

Mark

1:3	(1 & 2)
2:28	(2a)
5:19	(1)
7:28	(2a & 4)
9:24	(2a) Some texts omit
11:3	(2a)
11:9	(1)
11:10	(1) Not in NIV
12:9	(3)
12:11	(1)
12:29	(1)
12:30	(1)
12:36	(1)
12:36	(2b)
12:37	(2b)
13:20	(1)
13:35	(3)

16:19	(2b)
16:20	(2b)

Luke

1:6	(1)
1:9	(1)
1:11	(1)
1:15	(1)
1:16	(1)
1:17	(1)
1:25	(1)
1:28	(1)
1:32	(1)
1:38	(1)
1:43	(2)
1:45	(1)
1:46	(1)
1:58	(1) Ar: "God"
1:66	(1)
1:68	(1)
1:76	(1)
2:9	(1)
2:9	(1)
2:11	(2a)
2:15	(1)
2:22	(1)
2:23	(1)
2:24	(1)
2:29	(1)
2:39	(1)
3:4	(1 & 2)
4:8	(1)
4:12	(1)
4:18	(1)
4:19	(1)
5:8	(2a)
5:12	(2a)
5:17	(1)
6:5	(2a)
6:46	(2a)
7:6	(2a)
7:13	(2a) Ar: "Jesus"
7:31	(2a) Not in NIV
9:54	(2a)
9:57	(2a) Not in NIV

Luke, *continued*

9:59	(2a)
9:61	(2a)
10:1	(2a) Ar: "Jesus"
10:2	(1)
10:17	(2a)
10:21	(1)
10:27	(1)
10:40	(2a)
11:1	(2a)
11:39	(2a)
12:36	(3)
12:37	(3)
12:41	(2a)
12:42	(2a & 3) Ar: "Jesus"
12:43	(3)
12:45	(3)
12:46	(3)
12:47	(3)
13:8	(4)
13:15	(2a) Ar: "Jesus"
13:23	(2a) Not in Ar.
13:25	(4)
13:35	(1)
14:21	(3)
14:22	(3)
14:23	(3)
16:3	(3)
16:5	(3)
16:8	(3)
16:13	(3)
17:5	(2a)
17:6	(2a) Not in NIV
17:37	(2a)
18:6	(2a)
18:41	(2a)
19:8	(2a)
19:16	(3)
19:18	(3)
19:20	(3)
19:25	(4)
19:31	(2a)
19:34	(2a)
19:38	(1)
20:13	(3)

20:15	(3)
20:37	(1)
20:42	(1 & 2b)
20:44	(2b)
22:33	(2a)
22:38	(2a)
22:49	(2a)
22:61	(2a)
24:3	(2b)
24:34	(2b)

John

1:23	(1 & 2)
4:1	(2a) Some texts omit
4:11	(2a or 4)
4:15	(2a or 4)
4:19	(2a or 4)
4:49	(2a or 4)
5:7	(2a or 4)
6:23	(2a)
6:34	(2a)
6:68	(2a)
8:11	(2a)
9:36	(2a or 4)
9:38	(2a)
11:2	(2a) Ar: "him"
11:3	(2a)
11:12	(2a)
11:21	(2a)
11:27	(2a)
11:32	(2a)
11:34	(2a)
11:39	(2a)
12:13	(1)
12:21	(4)
12:38	(1)
13:6	(2a)
13:9	(2a)
13:13	(2a)
13:14	(2a)
13:16	(3)
13:25	(2a)
13:36	(2a)
13:37	(2a)
14:5	(2a)

14:8	(2a)
14:22	(2a)
15:15	(3)
15:20	(3)
20:2	(2a)
20:13	(2a)
20:15	(4)
20:18	(2b)
20:20	(2b)
20:25	(2b)
20:28	(2b)
21:7	(2b)
21:12	(2b)
21:15	(2b)
21:16	(2b)
21:17	(2b)
21:20	(2b)
21:21	(2b)

Acts

1:6	(2b)
1:21	(2a)
1:24	(2b)
2:20	(1 & 2b)
2:21	(1 & 2b)
2:25	(2b)
2:34	(1 & 2b)
2:36	(2b)
2:39	(1)
2:47	(2b)
3:19	(1)
3:22	(1) Ar: "God"
4:26	(1)
4:29	(1)
4:33	(2b) Ar: "Jesus Christ"
5:9	(1)
5:14	(2b)
5:19	(1 & 2b)
7:31	(1)
7:33	(1)
7:49	(1)
7:59	(2b) Ar: "while he was praying"
7:60	(2b)
8:16	(2b)

Acts, *continued*

8:22	(2b) Ar. "God"
8:24	(2b) Ar: "pray to God"
8:25	(2b) Ar: "word of God"
8:26	(2b)
8:39	(2b)
9:1	(2b)
9:5	(4)
9:10	(2b)
9:11	(2b)
9:13	(2b)
9:15	(2b)
9:17	(2b)
9:27	(2b)
9:28	(2b) Ar: "Jesus"
9:31	(2b)
9:35	(2b) Ar: "God"
9:42	(2b)
10:4	(4)
10:14	(2b)
10:33	(1) Ar: "God"
10:36	(2b)
11:8	(2b)
11:16	(2b)
11:17	(2b)
11:20	(2b)
11:21	(2b)
11:23	(2b)
11:24	(2b)
12:7	(2b)
12:11	(2b)
12:17	(2b)
12:23	(2b)
12:24	(2b) Ar: "God"
13:2	(2b) Ar: "God"
13:10	(2)
13:11	(2b)
13:12	(2)
13:47	(1 & 2b)
13:48	(2b)
13:49	(2b)
14:3	(2b)
14:23	(2b)
15:11	(2b)
15:17	(1) (2x)

15:26	(2b)
15:35	(2b) Ar: "God"
15:36	(2b) Ar: "the word of God"
15:40	(2b) Ar: "the word of God"
16:14	(2b)
16:15	(2b)
16:31	(2b)
16:32	(2b)
17:24	(1)
18:8	(2b)
18:9	(2b)
18:25	(2b)
19:5	(2b)
19:10	(2b)
19:13	(2b)
19:17	(2b)
19:20	(2b) "the faith of God"
20:19	(2b) "serving God"
20:21	(2b)
20:24	(2b)
20:35	(2b)
21:13	(2b)
21:14	(2b)
22:8	(4)
22:10	(2b)
22:19	(2b)
23:11	(2b)
25:26	(4) Ar: "concerning him to Caesar"
26:15	(4)
26:15	(2b)
28:31	(2b)

Romans

1:4	(2b)
1:7	(2b)
4:8	(2b) Ar: "God"
4:24	(2b)
5:1	(2b)
5:11	(2b)
5:21	(2b)
6:11	(2b) [KJV]
6:23	(2b)

7:25	(2b)
8:39	(2b)
9:28	(1 & 2b)
9:29	(1)
10:9	(2b)
10:12	(2b)
10:13	(2b)
10:16	(1)
11:3	(1)
11:34	(1)
12:11	(2b)
12:19	(1 & 2b) Ar: "God"
13:14	(2b)
14:4	(2b)
14:6	(2b)
14:8	(2b)
14:9	(2b)
14:11	(1 & 2b)
14:14	(2b)
15:6	(2b)
15:11	(1)
15:30	(2b)
16:2	(2b)
16:8	(2b)
16:11	(2b)
16:12	(2b)
16:13	(2b)
16:18	(2b)
16:20	(2b)
16:22	(2b)
16:24	(2b) [KJV]

1 Corinthians

1:2	(2b)
1:3	(2b)
1:7	(2b)
1:8	(2b)
1:9	(2b)
1:10	(2b)
1:31	(1 & 2b)
2:8	(2b)
2:16	(1)
3:5	(2b)
3:20	(1)
4:4	(2b)

1 Corinthians, *continued*

4:5	(2b)
4:17	(2b)
4:19	(2b)
5:4	(2b)
5:5	(2b)
6:11	(2b)
6:13	(2b)
6:14	(2b)
6:17	(2b)
7:10	(2b)
7:12	(2b)
7:17	(2b)
7:22	(2b) (2x) Ar: "God"
7:25	(2b) Ar: "God"
7:32	(2b)
7:34	(2b)
7:35	(2b)
7:39	(2b)
8:6	(2b)
9:1	(2b)
9:2	(2b)
9:5	(2)
9:14	(2b)
10:9	(1) Ar: "Christ"
10:21	(2b)
10:22	(2b)
11:11	(2b)
11:23	(2b)
11:27	(2a)
11:29	(2b)
11:32	(2b)
12:3	(2b)
12:5	(2b)
14:21	(1)
15:31	(2b)
15:57	(2b)
15:58	(2b)
16:7	(2b)
16:10	(2b)
16:19	(2b)
16:22	(2b)
16:23	(2b)

2 Corinthians

1:2	(2b)
1:3	(2b)
1:14	(2b)
2:12	(2b)
3:16	(2b)
3:17	(2b)
3:18	(2b)
4:5	(2b)
4:14	(2b)
5:6	(2b)
5:8	(2b)
5:11	(2b)
6:17	(1)
6:18	(1)
8:5	(2b)
8:9	(2b)
8:19	(2b) Ar: "God"
8:21	(2b) Ar: "God"
10:8	(2b)
10:17	(1 & 2b)
10:18	(2b)
11:17	(2b)
11:31	(2b)
12:1	(2b)
12:8	(2b)
13:10	(2b)
13:14	(2b)

Galatians

1:3	(2b)
4:1	(3)
5:10	(2b)
6:14	(2b)
6:18	(2b)

Ephesians

1:2	(2b)
1:3	(2b)
1:15	(2b)
1:17	(2b)
2:21	(2b)
3:11	(2b)
4:1	(2b)
4:5	(2b)

4:17	(2b)
5:8	(2b)
5:10	(2b)
5:17	(2b) Ar: "God"
5:19	(2b)
5:20	(2b)
5:22	(2b)
6:1	(2b)
6:4	(2b)
6:7	(2b)
6:8	(2b)
6:9	(3 & 2b)
6:10	(2b)
6:21	(2b)
6:23	(2b)
6:24	(2b)

Philippians

1:2	(2b)
1:14	(2b)
2:11	(2b)
2:19	(2b)
2:24	(2b)
2:29	(2b)
3:1	(2b)
3:8	(2b)
3:20	(2b)
4:1	(2b)
4:2	(2b)
4:4	(2b)
4:5	(2b)
4:10	(2b)
4:23	(2b)

Colossians

1:3	(2b)
1:10	(2b) Ar: "God"
2:6	(2b)
3:13	(2b) Ar: "Christ"
3:16	(1 & 2b) Most Greek texts: "God"; Ar. "God"
3:17	(2b)
3:18	(2b) Ar: "Christ"
3:20	(2b)
3:22	(3 & 2b)

Colossians, *continued*

3:23	(2b)
3:24	(2b)
4:1	(3 & 2b)
4:7	(2b)
4:17	(2b)

1 Thessalonians

1:1	(2b)
1:3	(2b)
1:6	(2b)
1:8	(2b)
2:15	(2b)
2:19	(2b)
3:8	(2b)
3:11	(2b)
3:12	(2b) Ar: "he"
3:13	(2b)
4:1	(2b)
4:2	(2b)
4:6	(2b)
4:15	(2b)
4:16	(2b)
4:17	(2b)
5:2	(1 & 2b)
5:9	(2b)
5:12	(2b)
5:23	(2b)
5:27	(2b)
5:28	(2b)

2 Thessalonians

1:1	(2b)
1:2	(2b)
1:7	(2b)
1:8	(2b)
1:9	(2b)
1:12	(2b)
2:1	(2b)
2:2	(1 & 2b)
2:8	(2b)
2:13	(2b)
2:14	(2b)
2:16	(2b)
3:1	(2b)

3:3	(2b)
3:4	(2b)
3:5	(2b)
3:6	(2b)
3:12	(2b)
3:16	(2b)
3:18	(2b)

1 Timothy

1:2	(2b)
1:12	(2b)
1:14	(2b)
6:3	(2b)
6:14	(2b)
6:15	(1)

2 Timothy

1:2	(2b)
1:8	(2b)
1:16	(2b)
1:18	(2b)
2:7	(2b)
2:19	(1 & 2b)
2:22	(2b)
3:11	(2b)
4:8	(2b)
4:14	(2b)
4:17	(2b)
4:18	(2b)
4:22	(2b)

Philemon

1:3	(2b)
1:5	(2b)
1:16	(2b)
1:20	(2b)
1:25	(2b)

Hebrews

1:10	(2b) Not in Ar
2:3	(2b)
7:14	(2b)
7:21	(1)
8:2	(1) Ar: "God"

8:8	(1)
8:9	(1)
8:10	(1)
8:11	(1)
10:16	(1)
10:30	(1 & 2b)
12:5	(1 & 2b)
12:6	(1 & 2b)
12:14	(2b)
13:6	(1 & 2b)
13:20	(2b)

James

1:1	(2b)
1:7	(1)
1:12	(2b) Some texts omit; Ar: "God"
2:1	(2b)
3:9	(1)
4:10	(1)
4:15	(1)
5:4	(1)
5:7	(2b)
5:8	(2b)
5:10	(1)
5:11	(1)
5:14	(2b)
5:15	(2b)

1 Peter

1:3	(2b)
1:25	(1 & 2a) Ar: "God"
2:3	(2b)
3:6	(3)
3:12	(2b)
3:15	(2b)

2 Peter

1:2	(2b)
1:8	(2b)
1:11	(2b)
1:14	(2b)
1:16	(2b)
2:1	(2b)
2:9	(2b)

2 Peter, *continued*

2:11	(1 & 2b)
2:20	(2b)
3:2	(2)
3:8	(2b)
3:9	(2b)
3:10	(1 & 2b)
3:15	(2b)
3:18	(2b)

Jude

4	(2b)
5	(1) Ar: "God"
9	(1)
14	(2b)
17	(2b)
21	(2b)
25	(2b)

Revelation

1:8	(1)
4:8	(1)
4:11	(1)
6:10	(1)
7:14	(4)
11:4	(1 & 2b)
11:8	(2b)
11:15	(1) Ar. "God"
11:17	(1)
14:13	(2b)
15:3	(1) 15:4 (1)
16:7	(1)
17:14	(2b)
18:8	(1) 19:6 (1)
19:16	(2b)
21:22	(1)
22:5	(1)

22:6	(1)
22:20	(2b)
22:21	(2b)

Orthodoxy, Heresy, Heterodoxy

Creeds Used to Establish "Orthodoxy"

Before we can really discuss the concepts of "orthodoxy, heresy and heterodoxy," we must be clear on what these terms mean, beginning with "orthodoxy." "Orthodoxy" comes from the Greek words *ortho* (right) and *doxa* (opinion), and therefore means "right opinion or belief." A dictionary definition of "orthodox" is "conforming to an established doctrine." We believe that the Bible is God's "Established Doctrine." If we use the Word of God as the only standard for truth, all doctrines established by men that disagree with it must be discarded as not truly "orthodox." It is obvious that today there are many beliefs and opinions considered to be "Established Doctrine," but which are totally unbiblical. When "orthodoxy" is not real orthodoxy, then "heresy" is not real heresy.

History shows us that many times the "orthodox doctrine" of the Christian Church has been wrong. For instance, for centuries the Church taught that the earth was the center of the solar system, but that was proven wrong by Copernicus. Even modern Roman Catholic doctrine states that Mary was born without original sin, lived sinlessly and was "assumed" into heaven (now that *is* an assumption). Protestants reject this, and are therefore considered "unorthodox" by the Roman Catholic Church, even though the idea is without biblical substantiation. Our point is this, that heresy and orthodoxy are today determined more by "tradition" and "majority rule" than by the standard that should determine it, "the Apostles' Doctrine."

In order to avoid attacking a straw man, we are reproducing in full the text of the Apostles' Creed, the Nicene Creed, the Athanasian Creed and the definition of Chalcedon, the sum of which have been traditionally used to establish Christian belief about the being of God and Christ. This way, the reader can see for himself whether or not these creeds communicate the truth of God's Word that we have endeavored to bring to light in this book. In a few places, we have taken the liberty of **highlighting in bold** those phrases that anathematize those who cannot accept the language of the creed.

The Nicene Creed

This is a statement of faith that is the only ecumenical creed accepted as authoritative by the Roman Catholic, Eastern Orthodox, Anglican and almost all mainline Protestant churches. The creed was most likely issued by the Council of Constantinople in 381 A.D., hence the more accurate term for it is the "Niceno-Constantinopolitan Creed." What is called the "Filioque clause" in the section on the Holy Spirit was added later (about the sixth century) as a part of the creed of the Western Church (i.e., Roman Catholic). This phrase attributes the origin of the Holy Spirit to the Son as much as to the Father. To this day, Eastern Orthodox churches reject the clause because they consider it erroneous, and an unauthorized addition to a previously agreed upon document.

> We believe in one God, the Father, the Almighty, maker of heaven and earth, of all that is seen and unseen.

> We believe in one Lord, Jesus Christ, the only Son of God, eternally begotten of the Father, God from God, Light from Light, true God from true God, begotten, not made, one in Being [*homoousian*] with the Father.

> Through him all things were made.

> For us men and for our salvation he came down from heaven by the power of the Holy Spirit.

> He was born of the Virgin Mary, and became man.

> For our sake he was crucified under Pontius Pilate; he suffered, died, and was buried.

> On the third day he rose again in fulfillment of the Scriptures; he ascended into heaven and is seated on the right hand of the Father.

> He will come again in glory to judge the living and the dead, and his kingdom will have no end.

> We believe in the Holy Spirit, the Lord, the giver of life, who proceeds from the Father and the Son.

> With the Father and the Son he is worshipped and glorified.

> He has spoken through the Prophets.

> We believe in one holy catholic and apostolic Church.

> We acknowledge one baptism for the forgiveness of sins.

> We look for the resurrection of the dead, and the life of the world to come.

> Amen.

The Apostles' Creed

This creed is still used in baptismal ceremonies and public worship by most Protestants and Roman Catholics. It can be dated definitively to the eighth century, but it probably originated from earlier baptismal creeds.

> We believe in God, the Father almighty, creator of heaven and earth.
>
> We believe in Jesus Christ, his only Son, our Lord.
>
> He was conceived by the power of the Holy Spirit and born of the Virgin Mary.
>
> He suffered under Pontius Pilate, was crucified, died, and was buried.
>
> He descended to the dead.
>
> On the third day he rose again.
>
> He ascended into heaven, and is seated at the right hand of the Father.
>
> He will come again to judge the living and the dead.
>
> We believe in the Holy Spirit,
>
> the holy Catholic Church,
>
> the communion of saints,
>
> the forgiveness of sins,
>
> the resurrection of the body,
>
> and the life everlasting. Amen.

The Athanasian Creed

This is a Latin creed used by the Western Church, unknown to the Eastern Church until the 12th century. It is generally accepted that the Athanasian Creed was not written by Athanasius (who died in 373), but was probably composed in southern France during the fifth century. It is worthy of note that this creed not only helped establish the Trinity as "orthodox doctrine," but it made belief in it a requirement for salvation and anathematized those who reject it, as will be evident in the **bold** portions of the text that follows:

> Whosoever will be saved, before all things it is necessary that he hold the Catholic Faith. Which Faith except everyone do keep whole and undefiled, **without doubt he will perish everlastingly**. And the Catholic faith is this: That we worship One God in Trinity and Trinity in Unity, neither confounding the Persons, nor dividing the Substance.
>
> For there is one Person of the Father, another of the Son, another of the Holy Ghost. But the Godhead of the Father, of the Son, and of the Holy Ghost, is all one, the Glory equal, the Majesty co-eternal. Such as the Father is, such is the Son, and such is the Holy Ghost. The Father uncreate, the Son uncreate, and the Holy Spirit uncreate.

The Father incomprehensible, the Son incomprehensible, the Holy Ghost incomprehensible. The Father eternal, the Son eternal, and the Holy Ghost eternal. And yet they are not three eternals but one eternal. As also there are not three incomprehensibles, nor three uncreated, but one uncreated, and one incomprehensible. So likewise the Father is Almighty, the Son Almighty, and the Holy Ghost Almighty. And yet they are not three Almighties but one Almighty.

So the Father is God, the Son is God, and the Holy Ghost is God. And yet they are not three Gods, but one God. So likewise the Father is Lord, the Son Lord, and the Holy Ghost Lord. And yet not three Lords, but one Lord. For like as we are compelled by the Christian verity to acknowledge every Person by himself to be both God and Lord, so are we forbidden by the Catholic Religion, to say, there be three Gods, or three Lords.

The Father is made of none, neither created nor begotten. The Son is of the Father alone, not made, nor created, but begotten. The Holy Ghost is of the Father and of the Son, neither made, nor created, nor begotten, but proceeding. So there is one Father, not three Fathers; one Son, not three Sons; one Holy Ghost, not three Holy Ghosts. And in this Trinity none is afore, or after other; none is greater, or less than another; But the whole three Persons are co-eternal together and co-equal. So that in all things, as is aforesaid, the Unity in Trinity and the Trinity in Unity is to be worshiped. **He therefore that will be saved must thus think of the Trinity**.

Furthermore, **it is necessary to everlasting salvation** that he also believe rightly the Incarnation of our Lord Jesus Christ. For the right Faith is, that we believe and confess, that our Lord Jesus Christ, the Son of God, is God and Man; God, of the Substance of the Father, begotten before the worlds; and Man, of the Substance of his Mother, born in the world; Perfect God and perfect Man, of a reasonable soul and human flesh subsisting; Equal to the Father, as touching His Godhead; and inferior to the Father, as touching his Manhood. Who although he be God and Man, yet he is not two, but one Christ; One, not by conversion of the Godhead into flesh, but by taking of the Manhood into God; One altogether; not by confusion of Substance, but by unity of Person.

For as the reasonable soul and flesh is one man, so God and Man is one Christ; who suffered for our salvation, descended into hell, rose again the third day from the dead. He ascended into heaven, he sitteth on the right hand of the Father, God Almighty, from whence he shall come to judge the quick and the dead. At whose coming all men shall rise again with their bodies and shall give account for their own works. And they that have done good shall go into life everlasting; and they that have done evil into everlasting fire. This is the Catholic Faith, which **except a man believe faithfully, he cannot be saved**.

Definition of Chalcedon

Therefore, following the holy fathers, we all with one accord teach men to acknowledge one and the same Son, our Lord Jesus Christ, at once complete in Godhead and complete in manhood, truly God and truly man, consisting also of a reasonable soul and body; of one substance (*homoousios*) with the Father as regards his Godhead, and at the same time of one substance with us as regards his manhood; like us in all respects, apart from sin; as regards his Godhead, begotten of the Father before the ages, but yet as regards his manhood begotten, for us men and for our salvation, of Mary the Virgin, the God-bearer (*Theotokos*); one and the same Christ, Son, Lord, Only-begotten, recognized in two natures, without confusion, without change, without division, without separation; the distinction of natures being in no way annulled by the union, but rather the characteristics of each nature being preserved and coming together to form one person and subsistence, not as parted or separated into two persons, but one and the same Son and Only-begotten God the Word, Lord Jesus Christ; even as the prophets from earliest times spoke of him, and our Lord Jesus Christ himself taught us, and the creed of the Fathers has handed down to us.

Heresy

Because of our Unitarian beliefs, we (the authors) have for many years been considered "heretics" by the "orthodox" Christian community. Although we have tried very hard to get along with and to work within traditional ministries and churches, we have often been excluded from Christian groups and even been considered unsaved. Having thus endured the pain of rejection by other Christians, one would think that we would be quick to get rid of the idea of "heresy" altogether. But we cannot do away with an idea that is intrinsically biblical, even if it would take the pressure off us. The godly thing to do is to be clear on what truly constitutes "orthodoxy" (*right* belief), so that "heresy" (*wrong* belief) can be meaningfully defined. As we have seen in the historical section of this book, when "orthodoxy" is not real orthodoxy, then "heresy" is not real heresy.

What is a true "heretic?" According to God's Word, it is one who teaches and/or practices error and thereby introduces division into the Body of Christ.

> **Titus 3:10**
> Warn a divisive person once, and then warn him a second time. After that, have nothing to do with him.

The words "a divisive person," come from the Greek word *hairesis*, which is transliterated into English as the word "heresy." It literally means "one who chooses," but the implication is *one who asserts his own choice above God's Word and draws disciples after him* (cp. Acts 20:30). In other words, it refers to those who choose to be factious and to elevate their teaching above that which can be established biblically, and who promote this teaching to the point of making disciples. We think that many people who accept the doctrine of the Trinity do so because they have been taught that if they are true Christians they must believe it, and yet they do not aggressively teach it to others because they cannot even understand it themselves. They are not "heretics" just because they accept it. However, those who aggressively *teach* Trinitarian orthodoxy cause divisions in the Body of Christ by their insistence that a person cannot be a *true* Christian without believing it. Such people are within the purview of the following key verses on this subject:

> **Romans 16:17 and 18**
> (17) I urge you, brothers, to watch out for those who cause divisions and put obstacles in your way that are **contrary to the teaching you have learned**. Keep away from them.
> (18) For such people are not serving our Lord Christ, but their own appetites. By smooth talk and flattery they deceive the minds of naive people.

Clearly, the standard for determining a heretic is *one who causes divisions* by teaching things that are contrary to the "Apostles' Teaching" (see Acts 2:42). Therefore, the crucial issue is *what constitutes Apostolic Teaching*. We think it is obvious that the Apostles never believed or taught the Trinity.

It is an ironic general fact of Christian history that when Trinitarians have been the ruling party in countries without separation between church and state, they have held their position by intimidation, violence and force. When Unitarian Christians have had the upper hand, they have used force less and shown themselves to be more tolerant of other beliefs (a fact that worked toward the demise of the Unitarian movement in America during the 1800's). Rubenstein notes that the Arians (the "heretics") were better able to "tolerate a variety of theological perspectives without declaring their opponents agents of the Devil."[1]

Romans 16:17 addresses the issue of the proper Christian treatment of heretics. Because people who teach wrongly are still, biblically, our "neighbors," we are commanded to love them regardless of the fact that they are teaching error. Simply because a person goes to Church or acts in a pious manner does not necessarily mean that he is a Christian or a Christ-like person. The Pharisees may have seemed religious to many, but when the light of Jesus Christ was shined into the secret places of their hearts, the evil inside them was clearly revealed. We assert that when Christians persecute, torture and execute those whose only "crime" is having a different belief about the Lord Jesus Christ, their acts reveal the evil and hate inside them beneath their false piety.

We do not have to fellowship with those we believe are teaching error or who persecute us, but we are commanded to love them, which would certainly forbid us persecuting them in response. But *how* we are to love them is different from how we would if they were teaching and practicing the truth. God's Word has clearly spoken: we are to avoid having fellowship (full sharing) with them until they change. We are not to "unify" with them just because they are professing Christians.

What it means to "avoid" a fellow Christian is not entirely clear, and must be determined according to the dictates of one's own conscience in accordance with his sometimes complex and obligatory social relationships. We can have many kinds of relationships, even relatively close friendships, with others of even non-Christian faiths, yet we are exhorted in Galatians 6:10 (KJV) to be especially good to the household of faith (i.e., fellow Christians). To be obedient to God's Word, then, there must be *some* sense in which we reserve our most intimate relationships for those whom we can trust to give us sound biblical counsel and manifest the genuine love of God and Christ toward us.

The testimony of both Scripture and history is that "...Evil companionships (communion, associations) corrupt *and* deprave good manners *and* morals *and* character" (1 Cor. 15:33 - AMP). This means that when people who hold the truth come into an intimate relationship with those who do not, the convictions of those who hold the truth are more likely to be diminished than the deceived ones are to be converted. We are fundamentally responsible for the choices we make concerning those we allow to influence us. Therefore, we ought not to be influenced by those whose "opinions" and "judgments" are going to lead us in the wrong direction, even if standing for what we believe means we are criticized for being "narrow-minded," "judgmental" or "arrogant." To be obedient, we must wait until God reveals to us, or we are convinced by our own experience, that we can safely commit ourselves in an intimate relationship to another person whose faith and Christian commitment are known. Such a person is then in a position to deeply influence our beliefs, our attitudes and our behaviors in a godly direction.

---

1. Rubenstein, *op. cit., When Jesus Became God*, p. 179.

The Bible contains a *variety* of verses that recommend avoiding intimate fellowship with those who habitually teach and/or practice error. There is *no* verse that tells believers to unify in spite of false doctrine, nor to just "agree to disagree," which is a modern way of saying "quit trying to persuade someone as if there were such a thing as truth." In fact, Scripture says just the opposite:

1 Corinthians 1:10
I appeal to you, brothers, in the name of our Lord Jesus Christ, that all of you agree with one another so that there may be no divisions among you and that you may be perfectly united in mind and thought.

In a clear example of Jesus rejecting the idea of universal acceptance, he tells his disciples to "leave" the Pharisees, who were "blind guides." Note these other clear verses on the subject.

Matthew 15:14
Leave them; they are blind guides. If a blind man leads a blind man, both will fall into a pit."

2 Thessalonians 3:14 and 15
(14) If anyone does not obey our instruction in this letter, **take special note** of him. **Do not associate** with him, in order that he may feel ashamed.
(15) Yet do not regard him as an enemy, but **warn him** as a brother.

(See also Matt. 16:6, 11 and 12; 1 Cor. 5:9–11; 2 Cor. 6:11–18; 1 Tim. 1:3 and 4; 2 Tim. 4:14 and 15; Titus 1:9; 2 John 7–11).

Notice that the commandment in 2 Thessalonians 3:14 is for the sake of helping the other more than just keeping ourselves pure. The goal of not associating with someone is to exert godly "peer pressure" on him so that he would realize the seriousness of his choice to the point of being "ashamed" and repentant. Today, the prevailing attitude of unlimited toleration runs counter to this biblical directive. There is little or no social pressure applied in a godly direction. In fact, it seems like the only ones who are "avoided" these days are those who are unenlightened enough to insist that there is a standard of belief and practice necessary for an intimate relationship with another Christian.

Although it seems easier to get along with everyone and pretend that doctrine does not matter, fidelity to the text of Scripture demands that we do our best to uphold the truth. The fact that God gives people the freedom to have their own opinions does not mean that we ought not to try to influence them in the direction of God's Word. In fact, God says that is exactly what we *should* do. Clearly, men like Jesus, Paul, *et al.*, were committed to "persuading" everyone they could to embrace the truth. The biblical model for Christian unity is given in Ephesians 4:4–6, which clearly links doctrine and unity. True Christian unity is not achieved by surrendering all of one's convictions, but by engaging in loving and rational dialogue in the hope of arriving at likemindedness on God's Word.

Heterodoxy

We acknowledge the fact that not all teachings are crucial for the fruitful practice and communication of the Christian Gospel. On some topics, the biblical evidence is not conclusive, or the practical consequences are not especially harmful, and reasonable believers can come to different conclusions without compromising the integrity of the Gospel. In these areas, there is room for "heterodoxy," that is, a variety of competing interpretations, none of which must be established as "right" for Christianity to be the liberating and powerful experience that it ought to be. One example of heterodoxy could be the day of Christ's birth. Some denominations believe that Christ was born on December 25 and some do not. Salvation and the fruitful practice of Christianity do not hinge on our Lord's birthdate.

Historical Heresies

In this section, we will provide the reader with an overview of some of the teachings that have been considered heretical by the historic Christian church. There have been many "heretical" positions because the doctrine of the Trinity is so difficult to explain or articulate in a way that will preclude such "misunderstandings." This is admitted by Trinitarian scholars, such as Thomas Morris[2] and Adolph Harnack, who writes:

> Unfortunately, this Trinitarian theology that is so vital to Christianity is very hard to formulate in any detail without falling into one pitfall or another, as readers of Augustine's *de Trinitate* will discover.[3]

One Unitarian scholar observes that Trinitarians promote their doctrine most successfully when they just state it plainly with no attempt to explain its paradoxes:

> One or other among them [Trinitarians] rejects the Trinitarian meaning from each single passage brought in support of it. But this diversity, while it weakens the force of that particular argument, is itself even more fatal to the doctrine. **It cannot be so stated that the mass of its supporters will accept the statement.** Some dangerous heresy has always been detected, lurking under the disguise of every possible interpretation; and those have uniformly succeeded best who have simply **stated the bald dogma, in the most paradoxical form possible, and have left the explanation as a "mystery," to shift for itself.**[4]

The following are some of the main beliefs that have been condemned as heretical by "orthodoxy" since it was first established. In some cases, we note whether these views are still represented by contemporary groups, or whether scholars mention them as still being a contemporary issue.

Adoptionism

Christ was a fully flesh-and-blood human being, not pre-existent or, for most adoptionists, born of a virgin. They teach that Christ was not born the Son of God, but was adopted as such at some point later in his life (his baptism, his resurrection, etc.).

Appollinarianism

This is the heresy debated at the Council of Constantinople I (381 A.D.) which asserts that Jesus was not fully human. He was believed to be fully divine and therefore could not at the same time be fully human.

---

2. See the quote in Chapter 20 by Morris, *op. cit.*, *The Logic of God Incarnate*, pp. 207 and 208.
3. Adolf Harnack, *Lehrbuch der Dogmengeschichte* [The History of Dogma], (Mohr, Tubingen, 1909), II, p. 295.
4. Joseph H. Allen, *Ten Discourses on Orthodoxy* (Wm. Crosby and H.P Nichols, Boston, 1849), pp. 58 and 59.

Arianism

The belief that Jesus was the first of all created beings, pre-existent but eternally subordinate to God, being of different substance from the Father (*heterousios*). Jehovah's Witnesses are generally in this category.

Semi-Arianism

The belief that the Son was "like" (*homoiousios*) the Father but not of one substance (*homoousios*) with him. The two words being distinguished by a single "i" led to the popular expression, "It makes not an *iota* of a difference."

Docetism

This was the teaching that Jesus only *appeared to* be a man, but was really some kind of angel or spirit being. The doctrine of the two natures established at the Council of Chalcedon supposedly corrected this error by asserting that Christ was 100 percent man. But as a result of their understanding of the orthodox position that Jesus the man is somehow also "God," most Christians persist in what J. A. T. Robinson calls a "supranaturalistic" view of Christ that is, in essence, "docetic":

> In fact, popular supranaturalistic Christology has always been dominantly docetic. That is to say, Christ only appeared to be a man or looked like a man: 'underneath' he was God.[5]

Monophysitism

This is the view held by the Eastern Orthodox churches, that Jesus was only one person with one nature, a blend of humanity and deity. Hanson suggests that the Jesus portrayed in the gospel of John "is moving towards Monophysitism. His Jesus is a monophysite figure in the sense that he seems to be a blend of divine and human…where the Transfiguration is taken as an index of Jesus' real person while on earth."[6] Cullman sees this same thinking in the average Roman Catholic, even though the Church has condemned it as heresy:

> Despite its official condemnation, Monophysitism still dominates the religious thinking of the average [Roman] Catholic. Jesus and God are often no longer distinguished even by terminology. The question has rightly been raised whether the need for veneration of Mary has not perhaps developed so strongly among the Catholic people just because this confusion has made Jesus himself remote from the believer.[7]

Cullman's observation that Jesus and God are not distinguished even in terminology seems to be an accusation that would apply to Trinitarianism in general. The customary distinction is between the "Father" and the "Son," not between "God" and "Jesus." The position of the Orthodox Church is that Christ has two different natures, with two wills, one human and one "God," that coexist in

---

5. Robinson, *op. cit., Honest to God*, p. 66.
6. Hanson, *op. cit., The Prophetic Gospel*, p. 366.
7. Cullman, *op. cit., Christology of the New Testament*, p. 306.

him. We believe that Scripture testifies to Christ as the Last Adam, a man like us, having one nature and therefore one will.

Monotheism (Formal)

This concept is held by those like Jews, Muslims and Unitarians, who believe that God is only one person. Rahner accuses virtually all Christians of this heresy: "…despite their orthodox confessions of the Trinity, Christians are, in their practical lives, almost mere 'monotheists.'"[8]

Monotheism (Serial)

In American Church history, the Protestant majority has remained Trinitarian chiefly by practicing serial monotheism—focusing now on one/now on another member of the Holy Trinity. Apparently this is a practical accommodation to confusing Trinitarian terminology that can be avoided if one does not try to talk about all three persons in one breath.

Nestorianism

This is the view held by Nestorius and debated at the Council of Ephesus in 431 A.D. This view held that Christ is composed of two separate "persons," one a "God person," and the other a "human person." Nestorianism was condemned and the "orthodox" belief that Christ was one person, both 100 percent God and 100 percent man, was upheld.

Patripassianism

Also called "Sabellianism" and "Modalistic Monarchianism"; the view that Christ was actually God the Father in the flesh.

Sabellianism or Modalism

So called because God is thought to have three modes of being rather than existing simultaneously and eternally as three distinct persons. Sabellius taught that the Godhead was a monad, expressing itself in three operations: as Father, in creation; as Son in redemption; as Holy Spirit, in sanctification. The Oneness Pentecostals are criticized for taking this position, because for them Jesus is the Father, the Son and the Holy Spirit. Michael Servetus, in his critique of the Trinity, proposed a semi-Sabellian idea that Christ and the Holy Spirit are merely representative forms of the one Godhead, the Father. Swedish mystic Emanuel Swedenborg also taught a form of this doctrine.

This heresy is committed still by many Trinitarian apologists, when they use the famous analogy of ice, water and steam being "three in one." But because the same H_2O molecules can only be in one form (ice, water or steam) at one time and under the same conditions, the argument is actually Sabellian. Many Christians who advance this analogy to propound the Trinity would be shocked to find that they were falling into a heresy that was long ago condemned.

---

8. Rahner, *op. cit., The Trinity*, p.10.

Separationism

The view that a spirit being called "Christ" came into the man Jesus at his baptism, and left him again before his crucifixion. Thus, "Jesus" and "Christ" were separate individuals.

Subordinationism

This is the view that Jesus is subordinate to God and therefore not eternally co-equal. Eastern Orthodox Churches teach that Christ has a subordinate rank to the Father while still maintaining his deity. More extreme forms forbid "prayer" to Jesus Christ as inappropriate and even devilish.

Tri-theism or Polytheism

The three persons of the Godhead are considered as three separate "Gods," or are spoken of as "three" more than they are spoken of as "one." They are said to be united in one substance, so they are technically "one God." "Social Trinitarianism," especially popular today, emphasizes the fellowship and interaction of each of the three divine persons to the point that critics say monotheism is compromised. Says Gunton:

> One danger of the concept of communion—and especially of a "social" analogy of the trinity—is of a form of tri-theism which appears to relate the three persons in such a way as to suggest that they have distinct wills...we may accept the principle, so influential in the West in particular, that the acts of the triune God in the world are undivided. But this principle, like so many others—including the *homoousion*—can be the source of confusion unless it is carefully qualified...The concepts of *homousios* and *perichoresis* [that each of the persons "envelops the other"], are vital devices **to ensure that trinitarian language does not lapse into tritheism**.[9]

Most Trinitarian Christians are actually practicing "Tri-theists." They think of God, Christ and "the Holy Spirit" as separate beings, not as "one God." This is undoubtedly due to the impossibility of holding both ideas in the mind simultaneously. Either God is "one" or He is "three." To say He is truly both defies logic and common sense and cannot be practically grasped or applied.

---

9. Gunton, *op. cit., Promise of Trinitarian Theology*, p. 198.

D

Divine Agents: Speaking and Acting in God's Stead

The Bible records a number of instances where an *agent* of God is referred to as "God" or "the LORD" Himself, and in many of these cases the agent (usually an angel) actually speaks and acts in God's stead. This is an important biblical phenomenon that foreshadows the coming of Christ. Jesus Christ represented God in a manner that went beyond the way the prophets represented Him. Christ claimed to act in God's stead in a way that the prophets never said that they did: "…I **always** do what pleases him" (John 8:29), "…I do exactly what my Father has commanded me…" (John 14:31). Christ spoke as one who knew God and His will intimately through personal acquaintance.

He also claimed to speak and act with authority he had directly received from God Himself, whom he identified as his "Father." His miracles, his command of the elements and demons, and his assertion that how people related to him determined their final destiny all speak of his unique and complete manifestation of God in the human sphere. As we have explored in Chapter 2 and throughout this book, Jesus Christ is the very image of God and therefore God's ultimate communication of Himself. Yet it is clear that he is not God Himself, if only because he is God's ultimate *agent*.

Many orthodox Bible commentators view some Old Testament accounts of angelic manifestations as appearances of Jesus in his "pre-incarnate" state, but in the following list we will cite evidence that even Trinitarian commentators recognize that this is an inference and not by any means conclusive. These examples of "God-manifestation" are qualitatively different from the speaking for God that prophets have always done.[1] The prophets have spoken for God, but not manifested His presence or been identified with God so powerfully and intimately that to see them was to "see" God. Isaiah, Jeremiah and others were recognized as God's spokesmen, but were never identified with God Himself. The following are examples of angels actually standing in the place of God such that afterward the human beings involved said they had encountered God Himself. Their identity as angels is unmistakably preserved in Scripture despite the fact that they were making God's very presence and power manifest.

The concept of agency is simply that an agent or representative speaks and acts on full behalf of the one who sent him. This is commonly practiced in modern times in what is known as power of attorney. In the Roman world an agent of the Emperor was called the Imperial legate, although the standard usage of the word "legate" today refers to a representative of the Pope. According to the Jewish understanding of agency, the agent was regarded as the person himself. This is well expressed in *The Encyclopedia of the Jewish Religion*:

> Agent (Heb. *Shaliah*): The main point of the Jewish law of agency is expressed in the dictum, "a person's agent is regarded as the person himself" (*Ned.* 72b; *Kidd.* 41b). Therefore any act committed by a duly appointed agent is regarded as having been committed by the principal, who therefore bears full responsibility for it with consequent complete absence of liability on the part of the agent.[2]

Modern agency usually means that an agent, not the principal, is present. In the Bible, it is occasionally less clear that an agent is speaking and not the principal, and most of us are not used to seeing an agent speak without identifying himself as an agent. Therefore, we thought it a significant enough aspect of this study on *One God & One Lord* that we should provide examples such that the reader could become familiar with it.

Hagar and the Angel
(Gen. 16:7–14)

The beginning point for this idea of angels manifesting God's presence is found in Genesis 16:7–10, 13 and 14. Charles Ryrie calls this use of "The angel of the LORD…" a "theophany, a self-manifestation of God." The angel speaks as God, identifies himself with God, and claims to exercise the prerogatives of God. Ryrie also recognizes that the idea that this "angel" is the preincarnate Son of God is an "inference," i.e., that it is not directly stated:

> Since the angel of the LORD ceases to appear after the incarnation, it is often *inferred* that the angel in the O.T. [Old Testament] is a preincarnate appearance of the Second Person of the Trinity [emphasis ours].[3]

---

1. Broughton and Southgate, *op. cit., The Trinity, True or False?*, p. 64ff. Broughton and Southgate coined the term "God-manifestation" to represent these occasions when angels stood in for God.

2. *Op. cit., The Encyclopedia of the Jewish Religion*, Werblowsky and Wigoder, p. 15.

3. *Op. cit.,* The Ryrie Study Bible, in the notes on these verses. Ryrie argues that in each of these "theophanies," God Himself is present and acting, missing the point of the angelic agency. It is often argued that Jesus is probably "… the angel

The NIV Study Bible acknowledges the principle of divine agents being identified with God Himself. Recognizing this principle also leads the editors to back away from the traditional interpretation—that the angel was really Jesus in his "pre-incarnate" divine state:

> …Since the angel of the Lord speaks for God in the first person (v. 10) and Hagar is said to name "the LORD who spoke to her: 'You are the God who sees me,'"(v. 13) the angel appears to be both distinguished from the Lord (in that he is called "messenger"—the Hebrew for "angel" means "messenger") and identified with him. Similar distinction and identification can be found in 19:1, 21, 31:11 and 13; Exodus 3:2 and 4; Judges 2:1–5, 6:11, 12, and 14, 13:3, 6, 8–11, 13, 15–17 and 20–23; Zechariah 3:1–6, 12:8. Traditional Christian interpretation has held that this "angel" was a pre-incarnate manifestation of Christ as God's messenger-Servant. It may be, however, that, as the Lord's personal messenger who represented him and bore his credentials, the angel could speak on behalf of (and so be identified with) the One who sent him…Whether this "angel" was the second person of the Trinity remains therefore uncertain….[4]

We are glad that the authors of the NIV Study Bible allow for the possibility that the one talking to Hagar *could be* an angel, but we believe that is not stating the case strongly enough. The Bible says, "**The angel** of the LORD said to her…." Angels are quite common in the Old Testament, and are messengers of God, certainly not God themselves (and being "the second person of the Trinity" is being "God"). In order to make the jump from "a messenger *for* God" to being "God—the pre-incarnate Jesus Christ," there would have to be some clear scriptural evidence that showed that was the case, but that evidence does not exist. The concept of agency, that the agent speaks on full behalf of the "sender," explains the records more than adequately.

In Genesis 16, the angel of the LORD addressed Hagar—"…I will so increase your descendants that they will be too numerous to count." She replied, "…I have now seen the One who sees me," as though she were talking to God, but the record makes it clear she was speaking to an *angel* of God acting as God's agent, not to God Himself.

Sodom and Gomorrah
(Gen. 19:1–24)

God is said to have destroyed Sodom and Gomorrah, but actually sent two angels to do the job. The two angels arrived at Sodom in the evening (v. 1). They informed Lot that "**we** are going to destroy this place. The outcry to the LORD against its people is so great that he has sent us to destroy it" (v. 13). The angels grasped Lot's hand and the hands of his wife and of his two daughters and led them safely out of the city for Yahweh was merciful to them (v. 16). Lot called the angels "my lords" (v. 18), asking

---

of the LORD…" because those words never appear after his birth, and it seems "reasonable" to Trinitarians that this angel would appear right on through the Bible. The fact is, however, that the angel of the Lord does appear after Jesus' *conception*, which seems inconsistent with the premise that the angel of the Lord is the "pre-incarnate Christ." The record of Jesus' birth is well known. Mary was discovered to be pregnant with Jesus before she and Joseph were married, and Joseph, who could have had her stoned to death, decided to divorce her. However, "an angel of the Lord" appeared to him in a dream and told him the child was God's. Matthew 1:24 states, "When Joseph woke up, he did what the angel of the Lord had commanded him and took Mary home as his wife." Thus, Jesus was already in Mary's womb when the angel of the Lord appeared to Joseph. From this we conclude that "the angel of the Lord" cannot be Jesus because Jesus was at that time "in the flesh" inside Mary.

4. *Op. cit, The* NIV Study Bible, Note on Genesis 16:7.

them if he could retreat to Zoar instead of to the mountains. God spoke via the angels: "He [God, singular, not "they," the angels] said to him [Lot]" that his request was granted (v. 21). Then **Yahweh** rained on Sodom and Gomorrah brimstone and fire, and **He** overthrew those cities, etc. (v. 24). These Scriptures combine to portray a beautiful picture of agency. Of course God is the one who supplied the power and authority, but the angels actually did the work. We use the same kind of language today. The owner of a construction company might be showing off some of the buildings his company had built. He might well say, "I built that building," and everyone would understand that he did not actually do the physical work, but was the planner and the authority behind the job.

Jacob's Dream
(Gen. 31:11–13)

This is another record that clearly identifies the speaker as an angel. Jacob said to his wives, "The angel of God said to me in a dream…I am the God of Bethel…" This is powerful proof that the concept of agency was not confusing to the people who knew the customs and the culture. Jacob was comfortable saying that an angel said, "I am the God of Bethel." Jacob knew nothing of a Trinity, and there is certainly no evidence that Jacob would have recognized that he was talking to the Messiah. Jacob understood the idea of agency and was comfortable with it.

Jacob Wrestles With "God"
(Gen. 32:24–30)

In Genesis 32, Jacob wrestled with "**a man**" until daybreak (v. 24), but verse 28 says he had "…struggled with God and with men…." In verse 30, Jacob said he "…saw God face to face…." From Genesis alone we would have to assume that this was one of the times in which God Himself took on the form of a man in order to better relate to mankind.[5] However, the book of Hosea speaks of the same record and lets us know that the one who wrestled with Jacob was an angel. Hosea 12:3 and 4 states: "…as a man he [Jacob] struggled with **God**, He struggled with **the angel** and overcame him…." Thus, the one who is called "God" in Genesis is identified as an angel in Hosea, a clear example of agency.

Moses and the Burning Bush
(Exod. 3:2, 4, 6 and 16)

Exodus 3:2 says, "…the **angel** of Yahweh appeared to him [Moses] in flames of fire from within a bush…." Yet the record then goes on to say that "God" and "Yahweh" spoke to Moses. The reader has to pay attention in this record because, although the angel is said to be in the fire, the record never actually says the angel speaks. It is possible that this is an example of agency where the angel spoke for God, or it could be that the angel was involved with the fire and when Moses drew near the bush, then Yahweh Himself spoke.

---

5. For times that God Himself comes in the form of a man see Appendix A (Gen. 18:1 and 2).

Angelic Accompaniment in the Wilderness and into the Promised Land

Understanding the concept of agency allows us to better understand the records of the Lᴏʀᴅ accompanying the Israelites in the wilderness. Some records indicate an angel was in the pillar of fire, while others indicate that it was God in the pillar of fire.

Exodus 13:21a (NASB)
And **the Lᴏʀᴅ** was going before them in a pillar of cloud by day to lead them on the way, and in a pillar of fire by night to give them light….

Exodus 14:19 (NASB)
And **the angel** of God, who had been going before the camp of Israel, moved and went behind them; and the pillar of cloud moved from before them and stood behind them.

Exodus 23: 20–23
(20) "See, I [God] am sending **an angel** ahead of you to guard you along the way and to bring you to the place I have prepared.
(21) Pay attention to him and listen to what he says. Do not rebel against him; he will not forgive your rebellion, since my Name is in him.
(22) If you listen carefully to what he says and do all that I say, I will be an enemy to your enemies and will oppose those who oppose you.
(23) **My angel** will go ahead of you and bring you into the land of the Amorites, Hittites, Perizzites, Canaanites, Hivites and Jebusites, and I will wipe them out.

Exodus 23:21 gives us more evidence of the custom of agency. God said that His "Name" was "in" the angel. A study of the culture and language shows that the word "Name" stood for "authority." Examples are very numerous, but space allows only a small selection.Deuteronomy 18:5 and 7 speak of serving in the "name" (authority) of the Lᴏʀᴅ. Deuteronomy 18:22 speaks of prophesying in the "name" (authority) of the Lᴏʀᴅ. In 1 Samuel 17:45, David attacked Goliath in the "name" (authority) of the Lᴏʀᴅ, and he blessed the people in the "name" (authority) of the Lᴏʀᴅ (2 Sam. 6:18). In 2 Kings 2:24, Elisha cursed troublemakers in the "name" (authority) of the Lᴏʀᴅ. These Scriptures are only a small sample, but they are very clear. God told the Israelites to obey the angel because God's name, i.e., His authority, was in him, and thus the angel represented God.

The Israelites and the Angel
(Judg. 2:1–4)

In reading Judges 2, one might think that it was God Himself speaking.

Judges 2:1–3
(1) "…I brought you up out of Egypt and led you into the land that I swore to give to your forefathers. I said, 'I will never break my covenant with you,

(2) and you shall not make a covenant with the people of this land, but you shall break down their altars.' Yet you have disobeyed me. Why have you done this?
(3) Now therefore I tell you that I will not drive them out before you; they will be **thorns** in your sides and their gods will be a snare to you."

This is a clear example of an angel standing in for God Himself. Verse 1 opens with, "**The angel** of the LORD went up from Gilgal to Bokim and said…." And verse 4 says, "When the angel of the LORD had spoken these things…." So the record clearly identifies that it was an angel who was actually speaking. He was speaking for God.

Gideon and the Angel
(Judg. 6:11, 12, 14, 16 and 22)

The record of Gideon is another clear example of an angel acting as an agent of God. The one talking with Gideon is clearly identified as an angel in the record:

Judges 6:11 and 12
(11) **The angel** of the LORD came and sat down under the oak in Ophrah that belonged to Joash the Abiezrite, where his son Gideon was threshing wheat in a winepress to keep it from the Midianites.
(12) When **the angel** of the LORD appeared to Gideon, he said, "The LORD is with you, mighty warrior."

These verses are very clear, but in verse 14 "the LORD" turned to him and spoke to him, and in verse 16 "the LORD" talked to him. To English readers this can be confusing, but it did not confuse Gideon. He recognized that it was an angel who was speaking to him, and in verse 22 he said, "…Ah, Sovereign LORD! I have seen the angel of the LORD face to face!" Gideon had no trouble understanding that the angel could represent God.

Manoah and the Angel
(Judg. 13)

The record in Judges 13 is very interesting because when the angel first showed up, he was not recognized as an angel at all. Both Manoah and his wife thought he was a man of God (Judg. 13:3, 6 and 21). Finally, they realized it was an angel: "…Manoah realized that it was the angel of the LORD." However, no sooner had he recognized that he had been speaking to an angel, not a man, that he exclaimed, "We are doomed to die…We have seen God!" (v. 22). The fact that the record makes it clear that he knew what he saw was an angel shows us that he understood that he did not see God, but God's representative. An intriguing fact about this record is that as long as Manoah thought he was with a man of God who was representing and speaking for God, he was comfortable, but when he realized he was talking to an angel, he became afraid. This is a good example of people being uncomfortable in the presence of *God*. God often wants to get closer to us than we, as humans and sinners, want Him to get.

The Angel and Joshua the High Priest
(Zech. 3:1–7)

Zechariah 3:6 and 7

(6) The **angel** of the LORD gave this charge to Joshua:

(7) "This is what the LORD Almighty says: 'If you will walk in my ways and keep my requirements, then you will govern my house and have charge of my courts, and I will give you a place among these standing here.

This record in Zechariah is similar to dozens of others in Scripture where men or angels speak in the name of the LORD.

Before the Lord or Before the Judge?

The concept of agency can cause translators some real difficulties. The Hebrew word *Elohim* is flexible and can refer to "the Supreme God" (which is how it is used most often), "a god," "gods" (because *Elohim* is plural), "angels" or "heavenly beings" or "judges." This has caused the translators some problems in verses such as Exodus 21:6, as the following translations show:

- KJV: Then his master shall bring him unto the judges…
- NIV: then his master must take him before the judges…
- NASB: then his master shall bring him to God…
- RSV: then his master shall bring him to God…

The situation in Exodus was that a slave was to be released after seven years of service, but in some cases the slave did not want to be released. In those cases the master was to bring him "to the *Elohim*" to become a slave forever. Because the judges represented God as his agents on earth, they are called by His name, "*Elohim*." There is a sense in which all four of the above translations are correct. The judges did in fact represent God, *Elohim*, and if they did not, there was no reason to bring the slave to them in the first place, because the vow was to be binding before the LORD. So there is reason to translate *Elohim* as "God" here. On the other hand, the actual representatives of God were the judges, and they were the ones who actually witnessed the slave's commitment. They were the tangible, flesh and blood representatives of God on the earth. For that reason, "judges" is the better contextual translation of *Elohim* in Exodus 21:6, 22:8 and 9.

Conclusion

We have shown that there are times when someone acting as God's agent is called "God" or is said to speak as "God." The above verses demonstrate that both angels and men represent God on earth. Instead of squeezing these verses to prove the doctrine of the Trinity, which is clearly not taught in the Old Testament, we should instead understand them according to the culture of the times. The concept of agency was even more common then than it is now, because our swift means of direct communication, such as telephone and travel by car and airplane, have made the actual practice of agency less necessary. Instead of veiled references to the Trinity, what these verses clearly show that we have a loving, trusting God who allows angels and people to represent Him.

E

Names and Titles of Jesus Christ

"Jesus" is not a Hebrew name, but an English development from the original Hebrew. The oldest name of the man who appears in English Bibles as "Joshua" was *Yehoshua* (Cp. the Hebrew of Exod. 17:9), which means "Yahweh saves." Around the time of Judah's exile to Babylon (ca. 586 B.C.), *Yehoshua* was often shortened to the term we now see more generally, *Yeshua*. Because Joshua was a well-known hero, *Yehoshua* or *Yeshua* was a common name in Jewish culture. In fact, there are four people named Joshua mentioned in the Old Testament (Josh. 1:1; 1 Sam. 6:14; 2 Kings 23:8; Hag. 1:1).

The Greek-speaking Jews translated *Yeshua* into *Iesous* [pronounced: Ē-ā-soos], which became a common name among them. Then, when the Hebrew Old Testament was translated into Greek about 250 B.C., producing what we now call the *Septuagint*, the Old Testament occurrences of *Yehoshua* were translated into *Iesous*, which only contributed to the popularity of *Iesous* among the Greek-speaking Jews. Thus, it is no surprise that there is another "Jesus" in the New Testament (Col. 4:11), and tradition says that the name of the criminal released by Pontus Pilate instead of Jesus Christ was "Jesus Barabbas."

Before the birth of Jesus, an angel told Mary (Luke 1:31) and Joseph (Matt. 1:21) to call the baby "Jesus." The original "Joshua" (Yahweh Saves) brought some "salvation," deliverance, to Israel in the flesh. Now Jesus (Yahweh Saves) would bring the fullness of deliverance to God's people: physical, mental, emotional, and spiritual deliverance that would last forever.[1] Unfortunately, we do not know exactly what name the angel told Joseph and Mary to call the child, because we do not know whether the angel spoke Hebrew or Aramaic to them. If he spoke Hebrew, we do not know whether he used the longer and more original "*Yehoshua*," or the shorter "*Yeshua*." Furthermore, the earliest manuscripts of both Matthew and Luke are in Greek and read "*Iesous*," which must have been acceptable to the early Christians because there was no attempt to alter the early manuscripts to try to "recapture" the Hebrew name.

As Christianity spread after the death and resurrection of Jesus Christ, "Jesus" became a rare name. The Christians [in English speaking countries] would not use it because it seemed like sacrilege, and the Jews would not use it because of its association with the one the Christians called Messiah. Thus, it is no surprise that by the time Colossians was written (ca. 64 A.D.), the "Jesus" in Colossians 4:11 was being called "Justus."

The Greeks chose *Iesous* as the translation of *Yeshua* for a number of phonetic reasons that are too lengthy to discuss in this small article. However, we should note that there was no "Y" sound in the Greek language, and the *iota* (i) was as close as they could get to the Hebrew sound produced by the Hebrew *yod* (ʾ), the first letter of "Joshua." As the English language developed, an initial "i" eventually often developed into what we today have as a "J." That is why the English versions have "Joshua," "Jerusalem," "Judah," and many other "J" words in the Old Testament despite the fact that Hebrew does not have a "J" or a "J" sound.

There is a movement in Christianity today to return to the more Hebrew pronunciation of "*Yeshua*" instead of "Jesus." We do not feel that is necessary. First, as we pointed out, we really do not know the exact name the angel said to call the Christ. Also, if the first century Jewish and Gentile Christians found *Iesous* acceptable, we see no reason to take offence at it, or a transliteration of it, twenty centuries later.

Jesus Christ is the subject of the Word of God from Genesis 3:15 to Revelation 22:21. As such, he is known by many descriptions, names and titles. All of these together paint a rich and vivid portrait of Jesus Christ, the Son of the living God. This is not intended to be an exhaustive list, but these are given for the purpose of providing the reader with the most notable scriptural names or titles of Christ.

---

1. In both Hebrew and Greek, the word we often translate as "salvation" also means "deliverance." Some Trinitarians assert that naming Jesus, "Yahweh Saves," means that Jesus was God, but that is not so. It simply means that Jesus would be the agent of God's salvation, even as Joshua had been the *agent* of God's salvation many years before.

Advocate (1 John 2:1 - NASB)

Alpha and Omega (Rev. 22:13)

Author and finisher of faith (Heb. 12:2 - KJV)

Battle Bow (Zech. 9:10)

Bread (of heaven, of life) (John 6:35)

Bright Morning Star (Rev. 22:16)

Chosen One (Luke 23:35)

Christ/ Messiah/Anointed One (KJV)
    (Matt. 1:16; Acts 4:26)

Coming One (Rom. 5:14)

Counselor (Isa. 9:6)

David's Lord (Acts 2:34)

Door (John 10:7)

Faithful and True (Rev. 3:14)

First and Last (Rev. 22:13)

First fruits (1 Cor. 15:23)

Firstborn of all creation (Col. 1:15)

Firstborn from the dead (Rev. 1:5)

Head (Eph. 4:15)

High Priest (Heb. 3:1)

Holy One (Ps. 16:10)

Image of God (Col. 1:15)

Immanuel (Isa. 7:14)

Jesus of Nazareth (Acts 3:6)

Judge (Acts 10:42)

King (Matt. 21:5)

King of kings (Rev. 19:16)

Lamb (Rev. 17:14)

Lamb of God (John 1:29)

Last Adam (1 Cor. 15:45)

Lion of Judah (Rev. 5:5)

Light (John 1:7, 8:12)

Living One (Rev. 1:18)

Lord (John 13:13; Rom. 10:9)

Lord of lords (Rev. 17:14)

Master (Matt. 23:8)

Mediator (1 Tim. 2:5; Heb. 12:24)

Mighty Hero (Isa. 9:6)

Nazarene (Matt. 2:23)

Our Passover (1 Cor. 5:7)

Prince of Peace (Isa. 9:6)

Prophet (John 7:40)

Rabbi (John 3:2)

Redeemer (Job 19:25)

Righteous One (1 John 2:1)

Rising Sun (Luke 1:78)

Root of David (Rev. 5:5)

Ruler of God's Creation (Rev. 3:14)

Savior (Titus 2:13)

Scepter (Num. 24:17)

Seed (Gen. 3:15)

Servant (Matt. 12:18)

Shepherd (John 10:11)

Shiloh (Gen. 49:10 - KJV)

Son of Abraham (Matt. 1:1)

Son of David (offspring of David) (Matt. 1:1)

Son of God (John 1:49)

Son of Man (John 1:51)

Son of Mary (Mark 6:3 - KJV)

Star (Num. 24:17; Rev. 22:16)

Teacher (John 3:2)

Tent Peg (Zech. 10:4)

Stone/Rock (Rom. 9:32)

Cornerstone/Capstone/Foundation Stone
    (Acts 4:11)

Sun of Righteousness (Mal. 4:2)

The Amen (Rev. 3:14)

The Apostle (Heb. 3:1)

The Beginning and the End (Rev. 1:8)

The life (John 14:6)

The Light of the World (John 8:12)

The rock (1 Cor. 10:4)

The Spirit (2 Cor. 3:17 and 18)

The true vine (John 15:1)

The truth (John 14:6)

The way (John 14:6)

The Word of God (Rev. 19:13)

Unique one (John 3:16) (mis-translated as
    "only begotten" - KJV)

Wonderful (Isa. 9:6)

F

Satan vs. Christ: Head to Head

In the Word of God, there are similarities and distinctions between Satan and Christ that are not immediately apparent. In many ways, Satan is now a counterfeit Christ, attempting to present himself as the true light and thereby lure people away from God. Placing the attributes of Satan and Christ in a side by side comparison, helps us to understand their "Head-to-head" conflict (see Gen. 3:15 and 16; 2 Cor. 4:4, 11:13-15; Eph. 6:10ff).

		Satan	Christ
Similarities	**Light**	Masquerades as an angel of light (2 Cor. 11:14)	"...I am the light of the world" (John 8:12, 9:5)
	Star	The morning star (son of the morning—Isa. 14:12)	The bright morning star (Rev. 22:16)
	Derived authority (*exousia*)	All the kingdoms of the world (Luke 4:5 and 6)	All authority...has been given to me (Matt. 28:18)
	Prince	Prince of this world, prince of darkness (John 12:31 - KJV)	Prince of peace; prince of life (Isa. 9:6b; Acts 3:15 - KJV)
	Angelic helpers	Took 1/3 of angels (Rev. 12:4, 7-9) called demons	He is the Lord of angels (Heb. 1:6; Rev. 1:1)
	Committed human servants	You belong to your father, the Devil, and you want to carry out your father's desire. (John 8:44)	The servants of Christ; "Follow my example as I follow the example of Christ." (1 Cor. 11:1)
	A "god"	"god" of this age (2 Cor 4:4)	Your throne, O god... (Heb. 1:8)
	Wounded in battle	Crushed head (Gen. 3:15)	Bruised heel (Gen. 3:15)
	Administrator/orchestrator	Systematic purveyor of deception (John 8:44; 2 Cor. 11:3)	Orchestrates the activities of the Body; fills each believer with holy spirit (Eph. 1:22 and 23, 4:16).
	Kingdoms	Kingdoms of the world (or demons) (Isa. 23:17; Luke 4:5, 11:18)	Kingdom of His dear Son (Col. 1:13)

Differences between Satan and Christ

Satan	Christ
"Born" (via creation) as a perfect spirit being (Ezek. 28:13-15 - KJV)	Born a human being; not "a spirit"; "born" from the dead with a new body (Luke 2:7, 24:39; Rom. 9:5; Acts 13:32-35; Phil. 3:21)
Given a "body" designed to help rule Creation (Ezek. 28:12 - 17)	Given a body fit to serve by living and dying for others; then at the Resurrection given a body fit to rule and reign forever. (Phil. 2:6-11)
Ungodly character: vain, prideful, unthankful (Isa. 14:13 and 14; Ezek. 28:15; John 8:44)	Godly character: meek, lowly in heart (Phil. 2:6-8; Matt. 11:29)
Started high and brought low (Isa. 14:12-15; Ezek. 28:12-17)	Started low and brought high (Phil. 2:6-11)
Subject to superior authority of Christ (Rev. 20:2 and 10)	Head of all principalities, powers, rulers (Phil. 2:9-11; Col. 1:15-19; Eph. 1:20-23)
Brings all identified with him to ashes (Ezek. 28:18; Rev. 20:10; Matt. 25:41-46)	Brings all those identified with him to glory (Heb. 2:10; Phil. 3:21; Matt. 25:31-38)

Beyond a Reasonable Doubt:
23 Arguments for the Historical Validity of the Resurrection of Jesus Christ

If true, the Resurrection of Jesus Christ from the dead is the single most important event in the history of mankind, and therefore the one most crucial to establish as an authentic historical event. In fact, the Resurrection is the very linchpin of the Christian faith, holding together every claim and every blessing. If the Resurrection could be proven a fraud, Christianity would disintegrate as a total fabrication with little redeeming merit. Jesus would not even be an example of a "good moral teacher," as some maintain, for his most important prediction-that he would be raised from the dead-would be found a lie.

As Christians, our very salvation depends in large part upon the reliability of the four historical records of the birth, life, death, and especially *the Resurrection* of Jesus Christ. A deeply held belief in the Resurrection as a fact of history is a vital element for our eternal salvation. Romans 10:9 asserts: "That if you confess with your mouth, 'Jesus is Lord,' and **believe in your heart that God raised him from the dead**, you will be saved." We are trifling with the bedrock of our salvation when we entertain doubts about the historical accuracy of any part of Scripture. But most crucial are those parts that make historical claims upon which our salvation depends.

Therefore, those who argue that the historicity of the Resurrection is not provable and even unnecessary are contradicting the testimony of the Apostolic witnesses. Indeed, the Apostle Paul's entire ministry was built upon the foundation of the Resurrection, and it was his personal encounter with the risen Christ that caused him to develop an unassailable conviction in the reality of this event. In the following verses, we have **highlighted in bold type** Paul's statements of the consequences to the Christian faith if the Resurrection of Christ did not, in fact, happen.

> **1 Corinthians 15:14–20**
> (14) And if Christ has not been raised, **our preaching is useless and so is your faith**.
> (15) More than that, **we are then found to be false witnesses about God**, for we have testified about God that he raised Christ from the dead. But he did not raise him if in fact the dead are not raised.
> (16) For if the dead are not raised, then Christ has not been raised either.
> (17) And if Christ has not been raised, **your faith is futile; you are still in your sins**.
> (18) Then those also who have fallen asleep in Christ **are lost**.
> (19) If only for this life we have hope in Christ, **we are to be pitied more than all men**.
> (20) But Christ has indeed been raised from the dead, the firstfruits of those who have fallen asleep.

Later in his life, Paul's public testimony to the Resurrection of Jesus Christ and his proclamation of the Gospel in Ephesus caused such an uproar that the Roman authorities took him into protective custody lest he be killed by the Jews. After several appeals according to Roman Law, Paul found himself standing before King Agrippa, his last level of appeal before the Emperor himself.

Given permission to speak freely, Paul launched into a passionate account of his life, culminating with his encounter with the risen Christ on the road to Damascus. When Paul then verified the Resurrection from Old Testament prophecy, the governor, Festus, interrupted him and told him he was crazy. The truth of Paul's brilliant reply remains emblazoned across the pages of human history.

> **Acts 26:25 and 26**
> (25) "I am not insane, most excellent Festus," Paul replied. "What I am saying is true and reasonable.
> (26) The king is familiar with these things, and I can speak freely to him. I am convinced that none of this has escaped his notice, because **it was not done in a corner**."

Amen! And that is why, taken together, the following historical proofs of the Resurrection of Jesus Christ present evidence that is *beyond a reasonable doubt*.

1. The Resurrection narratives have the ring of historical truth

The Resurrection narratives bear unmistakable signs of being historically accurate. The earliness of these accounts, at a time when hostile witnesses were present, would have made a fabrication unlikely and dangerous. There is agreement on the main facts and great variety in the witnesses given, yet they are not a mere repetition of some standardized story with all the discrepancies worked out. Indeed, the accounts of Christ's resurrection appearances are clearly independent of one another, as their surface dissimilarities suggest. Deeper scrutiny, however, reveals that these appearances are non-contradictory. Henry Morris writes:

> It is a well-known rule of evidence that the testimonies of several different witnesses, each reporting from his own particular vantage point, provide the strongest possible evidence when the testimonies contain superficial contradictions that resolve themselves upon close and careful examination. This is exactly the situation with the various witnesses to the resurrection.[1]

2. The Apostle Paul's life and ministry is a strong witness of the Resurrection

At the time Paul met the resurrected Christ, he was an ardent antagonist to the Christian faith. A highly educated man, he was not easily persuaded of anything that appeared contrary to or inconsistent with the Mosaic traditions. It could be said that he would have been the *last* person on earth to accept the idea of a crucified and resurrected Messiah based on the Jewish expectations of the time. The fact that he became so fully persuaded of the Resurrection of Christ that he completely dedicated his life to his risen Lord is powerful evidence of the reality of the Resurrection. Canon Kennett writes:

> Within a very few years of the time of the crucifixion of Jesus, the evidence for the resurrection of Jesus was, in the mind of at least one man of education [the Apostle Paul], absolutely irrefutable.[2]

3. The empty tomb is a historical given

No reputable New Testament historian doubts the historical fact that the tomb in which Christ was placed after his crucifixion was empty. Therefore, there are only three explanations for it. Either his enemies took the body, his friends took the body, or Jesus was raised from the dead. The first possibility is extremely unlikely, because his enemies would have certainly displayed his body if they could have, in order to humiliate his disciples, quell the rumors of his resurrection, as well as to cut short any new religious movement that threatened their Mosaic traditions.

It is equally unlikely that his friends would have taken his body, because after his crucifixion they were profoundly disappointed and discouraged men who did not believe that he would be resurrected. It is absurd to think that under these conditions they would invent a scheme in which they would steal away the body to fabricate a story they obviously did not believe.

4. The disciples were devout Jews

The disciples were Jews who took seriously their Jewish privileges and obligations. Therefore, it is unthinkable that they would have been party to making up a new religion for personal gain. To a first-century Jew, such an act was equivalent to lying against the God of Israel, as Paul argues in 1 Corinthians 15:12–19 (where he called it "bearing *false witness*," contrary to one of the Ten Commandments). For a first-century Jew, lying against God and perverting His revelation would mean risking one's salvation and future participation in the Messianic Kingdom. Would such a person risk divine retribution for a few years of prestige as a leader of a new religion? The answer can only be an emphatic "*No*."

---

1. Henry Morris, *The Defender's Bible* (World Publishing, Grand Rapids, 1995), p. 1576.
2. *Op. cit., New Bible Dictionary*, p. 1087.

5. The testimony of women

The presence of women at the tomb is strong evidence that the biblical record is true. Women had virtually no credibility in the first-century Jewish culture, and their testimony in a court of law was considered worthless. For example, if a man was accused of a crime that only women witnessed, he could not be convicted on that basis. If the account of Jesus' resurrection were a fable added later in an attempt to authenticate Christianity, why would the record have *women* be the first to see him and testify to the empty tomb, unless it had really happened that way? Women bringing testimony of his resurrection that is then denied by the male disciples makes the latter look bad, and these men were the first leaders of the Christian Church. A fabricated story added later by the Church would certainly have painted their first leaders in a more favorable light.

6. Jewish propaganda presupposes the empty tomb and the missing body

The Jewish Temple authorities paid those who had seen the tomb empty to lie and say that the disciples had stolen the body, and they even murdered many of those who preached about his resurrection. With such a powerful incentive to squash the new movement, they would have stopped at nothing to produce Jesus' dead body if they could have. The fact that they did not means they could not because he was risen.

7. His enemies would have produced his dead body to silence the believers

If he did not rise from the dead, what became of his body? If his enemies stole it and never showed it openly, that would have encouraged the very rumors of a resurrection that they were very anxious to prevent. But the decisive proof that his enemies did not take the body is that they surely would have quickly produced it with great fanfare, for they stopped short of nothing to discredit the story. As William Lane Craig argues, "This is historical evidence of the highest quality, since it comes not from the Christians but from the very enemies of the early Christian faith."[3]

8. There was no veneration of the tomb

If Jesus was not resurrected, why is there no record of his disciples venerating his tomb as so often happens to religious leaders? Though God forbade it, the practice continued among the Israelites to the point that God Himself disposed of the bodies of Elijah and Moses lest their followers venerate their gravesites.

9. A non-Christian historian testifies in support of the Resurrection

Josephus, the first-century Jewish historian, wrote about Jesus Christ and the growth of Christianity as follows:

> And when Pilate, at the suggestion of the principal men amongst us, had condemned him to the cross, those that loved him at the first did not forsake him; for he appeared to them alive again the third day; as the divine prophets had foretold these and ten thousand other wonderful things concerning him. And the tribe of Christians, so named from him, are not extinct at this day.[4]

---

3. William Lane Craig, *Reasonable Faith: Christian Truth and Apologetics* (Crossway Books, Wheaton IL, 1994), p. 277.

4. Translated by William Whiston (originally published in 1737), *The Life and Works of Flavius Josephus* (The John C. Winston Co., Philadelphia, 1957), p. 535.

Though some have tried to dismiss this corroborating secular testimony as fraudulent, this is unlikely because Josephus' writings were well received at the time of their writing by both Jews and Romans. He was even made an honorary Roman citizen.

There is no record of any objection being raised to this passage by early detractors of Christianity, and had this been a fraudulent and late insertion into the writings of Josephus, this fact would have been openly debated in the literature of the day. Because this did not happen, the silence of the critics is damning to their cause.[5]

10. No alternative explanations in the early non-scriptural sources

There is no alternative explanation for the rise of the Christian Church given in early historical sources that would even attempt to give the "real" story. In the event that the story was fabricated, surely some critic or disgruntled "ex-christian" would have attempted such an alternative explanation. But the only adequate explanation for the rise of the Church that has ever been given is that the early Christians believed Jesus had been raised from the dead.

11. The biblical records of the Resurrection appearances give a unified witness

The Four Gospels and the Apostle Paul give a unified witness of eleven resurrection appearances. Because these records are harmonious and non-contradictory, the burden of proof is upon those who would say that they do not tell the truth.

The eleven resurrection appearances, in their likely order, are as follows:

1. To Mary Magdalene (Mark 16:9; John 20:11–18)
2. To the other women (Matt. 28:8–10)
3. To Peter (Luke 24:34; 1 Cor. 15:5)
4. To the two men on the road to Emmaus (Mark 16:12; Luke 24:13–35)
5. To eleven of the disciples (except Thomas-Luke 24:33–49; John 20:19–24)
6. To the twelve a week later (John 20:24–29; 1 Cor. 15:5)
7. To seven disciples by the Sea of Tiberias (John 21:1–23)
8. To five hundred followers (1 Cor. 15:6)
9. To James (1 Cor. 15:7)
10. To all the Apostles [this could be speaking of the Ascension # (11)] (1 Cor. 15:7)
11. To the twelve at the ascension (Acts 1:3–12)[6]

---

5. For more on the authenticity of Josephus' reference to Jesus, see Josh McDowell, *The New Evidence That Demands A Verdict* (Thomas Nelson Publishers, Nashville, 1999), pp. 55–57.

6. Traditionally, Judas Iscariot is excluded from the number witnessing his ascension because of the record in Matthew 27:5 that seems to indicate that Judas went and "hanged himself" shortly after the crucifixion. It seems more likely, however, that Judas was received back into the company of the disciples in the period between his repentance and the Ascension, which he witnessed. After he saw Jesus ascend, Judas, with all hope of the restoration of a Davidic kingdom lost, went and killed himself. His absence then precipitated the need to replace him, which became the first order of business after the Resurrection (see Acts 1: 16–26). If Judas had killed himself before the Resurrection, it is logical to assume that Jesus himself would have been involved in choosing his replacement, since he chose the original Twelve. The fact that Judas was received back into the company of the disciples after his betrayal of Jesus speaks volumes about the forgiveness of the Lord Jesus, as well as the unity and brotherhood that must have marked the fellowship of the disciples.

12. The idea of Christ's new body was a totally foreign concept

The disciples had enough trouble believing that Christ would die and then be raised, and would never have even conceived of the idea of the Messiah having a different body. It is virtually inconceivable that early Christians fabricated such a story, which even today sounds like science fiction to many doubters.

13. Modern scholars and historians admit that there is strong evidence of his bodily resurrection

J. P. Moreland confirms this and quotes other scholars:

> Almost no New Testament scholar today denies that Jesus appeared to a number of his followers after his death. Some scholars interpret these as subjective hallucinations or objective visions granted by God which were not visions of a physical being. **But no one denies that the believers had some sort of experience.** The skeptical New Testament scholar Norman Perrin admitted: "The more we study the tradition with regard to the appearances, the firmer the rock begins to appear upon which they are based." Dunn, professor of divinity at the University of Durham, England, agrees: "It is almost impossible to dispute that at the historical roots of Christianity lie some visionary experiences of the first Christians, who understood them as appearances of Jesus, raised by God from the dead."[7]

Thomas Arnold, former Professor of History at Rugby and Oxford, and one of the world's greatest historians, made the following statement about the historical evidence for the Resurrection of Jesus Christ:

> I know of no one fact in the history of mankind which is proved by better, fuller evidence of every sort, to the understanding of a fair enquirer, than the great sign which God hath given us that Christ died, and rose again from the dead.[8]

Simon Greenleaf is one of the most highly regarded legal minds ever seen in America. He was an expert on the laws of evidence, and the founder of the Harvard Law School. He analyzed the accounts in the Four Gospels of the Resurrection of Christ in terms of their validity as objective testimonial evidence, and concluded:

> It was therefore impossible that they could have persisted in affirming the truths they had narrated, had not Jesus actually risen from the dead, and had they not known this fact as certainly as they knew any other fact.[9]

14. The conviction of his followers in the Resurrection

Those who first published the story that Jesus had risen from the dead believed it to be a fact. They rested their faith not only on the fact of the empty tomb, but on the fact that they themselves had seen Jesus alive after his burial. He was seen not once or twice, but at least ten recorded times; and not just one at a time, but in groups of two, seven, ten, eleven, and five hundred.

---

7. J .P. Moreland, *Scaling the Secular City* (Baker Book House, Grand Rapids MI, 1987), pp. 171 and 172.
8. Thomas Arnold, *Sermons on Christian Life, Its Fears and Its Close* (London, 1854), p. 324.
9. Simon Greenleaf, *The Testimony of the Evangelists* (New York: 1874), p. 28.

15. The martyrdom of his followers for their belief in the Resurrection

The first-century believers preached and acted with conviction about the truth of his resurrection, many of them even dying because of their belief. If his friends had stolen the body to make it look like he had been resurrected, they would have known that they were believing a lie, and men do not become martyrs for what they know to be false.

16. The unanimous testimony of eye-witnesses, who could not all have been deceived or deluded

Some critics say that the early Christians had a vision or an hallucination of Christ after his death, in the same way people today claim to have "seen" the pop icon Elvis Presley. Could it not have been an ecstatic vision? A dream? A fantasy of an excited imagination? Perhaps an apparition? None of these is at all probable, for different groups of people do not keep on seeing the same hallucination. 500 people in a crowd would not all dream the same dream at the same time.

Some modern Christian apologists have argued that it is irrelevant whether or not Christ actually was *physically* raised, because his "spirit" went to be with God. God then supposedly gave Christ's followers a "vision" of Christ continuing to live "spiritually" at God's side. Such a mystical and spiritualistic concept would not have satisfied the Hebraic mind of the disciples, however, who believed the dead to be dead until raised in a bodily, physical resurrection.[10] It would also have placed the Christian faith on a subjective, mystical basis without historical claims and would not account for the early disciples' energetic witness of the bodily resurrection of Christ.

17. The unb elief of the disciples concerning his resurrection

With the exception of Joseph of Arimathea, the followers of Jesus did not believe that he would die and then be resurrected. They were not expecting the event, and when it happened they did not believe it at first. They considered it an "idle tale" (Luke 24:11- KJV). They did not believe it until they had to, when they were directly confronted by the risen Lord. Henry Morris writes:

> One thing is certain: the disciples could not have fabricated the story of the resurrection from their own imaginations. On the contrary, they somehow failed to anticipate it even after such an abundance of prophetic preparation for it, both from the Scriptures and from Christ. It took the strongest of evidences to convince them it had actually taken place.[11]

18. The idea of a resurrected Messiah was a hard sell to the Jews and absurd to the Greeks

The picture of Jesus was not in keeping with current conceptions of what the Messiah would be like (a theocratic ruler who would deliver Israel from Gentile oppression) and it would have been hard to convince others of its truth. The Greeks, with their doctrine of the immortality of the soul, thought the idea of a bodily resurrection absurd and unnecessary (cp. Acts 17:32). If the disciples had invented an event or a doctrine around which to build a new religion, it would have been more in line with the standard expectations of the day.

19. He could have gotten out of the tomb only by resurrection

The "swoon" theory has proposed that Jesus was not really dead when they buried him, and that he "came to" again. But in that case, weak and exhausted, encased in heavy grave wrappings, he could scarcely have moved, much less removed the heavy stone door and gotten out of the tomb.

---

10. See our book: *Op. cit., Is There Death After Life?*
11. Morris, *op. cit., Defender's Bible*, p. 1574.

Furthermore, the Roman authorities had sealed the door, and even if he had been successful in moving the stone, the guards would have rearrested him and further humiliated him. Since there is no record of such an event, it must not have happened, because his enemies would have made much of such a bizarre happening.

20. The very existence and growth of the Christian Church makes no sense if he was not raised

Some critics say that the Resurrection was a later addition to the story of Christ, invented years later by the Church to glorify a dead hero. But it is known, from historical records outside Scripture, that the sect known as Christians came into existence in the reign of Tiberius, and that the thing that brought them into existence was their belief that Jesus had risen from the dead.

The Resurrection was not a later addition to the Christian faith, but the very cause and incentive for it. They rested their faith, not on historical records, but on what they had seen with their own eyes. The records were the *result* of their faith, not the cause of it. Christianity hinges on the historical fact of Christ's resurrection, for without it the entire faith is found fraudulent. Had there been no resurrection, there would have been no New Testament, and no Christian Church.

21. The disciples had nothing to gain by fabricating a story and starting a new religion

His followers faced hardship, ridicule, hostility, and martyrs' deaths. In light of this, they could never have sustained such unwavering motivation if they knew what they were preaching was a lie. Religion had its rewards for them, but those rewards came from a sincere belief that what they were living for was true.

22. The unanimous testimony of the early Christian leaders

If the empty tomb and resurrection was a fabrication, why did not at least one of the disciples break away from the rest and start his own version of Christianity? Or why did not at least one of them reveal the claim as a lie? The Temple authorities were willing to pay good money to anyone who would provide such information. Or if money was not alluring enough, what about the possibility of proving the Resurrection a lie in order to draw disciples away to follow some enterprising would-be cult leader? History has shown that this role is a popular one, and this would have been a golden opportunity.

Without the strong and persuasive evidence of the Resurrection, the continued unity of the early Christian leaders is inexplicable in light of the human tendency to want to promote oneself. The assumption that they were all committed to the truth of their message is the only adequate explanation of their continued unity and the lack of any revelation of fraud. Those who lie for personal gain do not stick together very long, especially when hardship decreases the benefits.

23. All of the alternate explanations proposed for the Resurrection lack credibility

In light of the evidence of the empty tomb, the Resurrection appearances and the rise of the Christian Church, a reasonable person should conclude that the Resurrection of Jesus Christ is a well-established historical fact. In a court of law, such evidence would compel conviction unless contradictory evidence could be brought forward to introduce "**a reasonable doubt**." But all alternate explanations and theories are extremely doubtful and counter-intuitive.

Therefore, Christians are being rational, sensible, and fully consistent with common sense when they rest their faith on this well-established historical event. Not only is there compelling historical evidence to back the belief, but extravagant benefits in the future are promised to those who believe it. According to the Bible, the only sure promise of everlasting life for mankind, both individually and collectively, depends upon belief in the Resurrection of Jesus Christ. As Halley writes: "What a Halo of Glory this simple belief sheds on human life. Our hope of resurrection and life everlasting is based, not on a philosophic guess about immortality, but an historic fact."[12]

---

12. Henry H. Halley, *Halley's Bible Handbook*, Twenty-Fourth Edition (Zondervan Publishing House, Grand Rapids, MI, 1965), p. 557.

47 Reasons Why Our Heavenly Father Has No Equals or "Co-Equals"

There are many verses that, if read and believed in a simple, straightforward manner, should clearly convince any unbiased person that God and Jesus are two completely different and distinct beings. There are also many logical reasons that should cause us to doubt the doctrine of the Trinity. What follows is a list of some reasons to believe that the Father is the only true God of Scripture and has no equal.

Reasons to Doubt that the Trinity Exists

(**1**) The word "Trinity" is not in the Bible.

(**2**) There is no clear Trinitarian formula in the Bible.

(**3**) Trinitarians differ greatly in their definitions of the Trinity. The Eastern Orthodox Church differs from the Western traditions regarding the relation of the Holy Spirit to the Father and the Son. Some television evangelists differ greatly from the Reformed Churches in their concept of Christ's divinity while he was on earth. Oneness Pentecostals say the classic formula of the Trinity is completely wrong. Yet all these claim that Christ is God and that the Bible supports *their* position. Surely if the Trinity were a part of Bible doctrine, and especially if one had to believe it to be saved,[1] it would be clearly defined in Scripture. Yet there is no Trinitarian formula in the Bible and Trinitarians themselves cannot agree on a definition. If one is to believe in the Trinity, how is he to know which definition is correct, since none appears in the Bible?

(4) The Trinitarian contention that "the Father is God, the Son is God, the Holy Spirit is God, and together they make one God" is not in Scripture and is illogical. Trinitarians teach that Jesus is both 100 percent man and 100 percent God. We say that God can do the impossible, but He cannot perform that which is inherently contradictory. God is the inventor of logic and mathematics, disciplines He created to allow us to get to know Him and His world. It is the very reason why He said that He is "One God," and why Jesus said that the witness of two was true and then said that he and His Father both were witnesses. God cannot make a round square, and He cannot make 100 percent + 100 percent = 100 percent, without contradicting the laws of mathematics He designed.

Verses that Show a Difference Between the Nature of God and the Nature of Christ

(5) God is spirit (John 4:24), yet even after his resurrection Jesus said of himself that he was not a spirit, but flesh and bone (Luke 24:39).

(6) Jesus is very plainly called a man many times in Scripture: John 8:40; Acts 2:22, 17:31; 1 Tim. 2:5, etc. In contrast to this, the Bible says, "God is not a man..." (Num. 23:19), and "...For I am God, and not man..." (Hosea 11:9).

(7) Numbers 23:19 also specifically says that God is not "a son of man." In the Gospels, Jesus is often called "a son of man" or "the son of man." If God became a human being who was called "the son of man" this creates a contradiction. Some occurances of the phrase "son of man" in the Gospels are Matthew 12:40, 16:27 and 28; Mark 2:10, 8:31; John 5:27. In the Hebrew Scriptures, the "son of man" is also used many times speaking of people (Job 25:6; Psalm 80:17, 144:3; Ezek. 2:1, 3, 6 and 8, 3:1, 3, 4, 10, 17 and 25). Human beings, including Jesus Christ, are called "son of man," and are thus carefully distinguished from God, who is not a "son of man."

(8) God was not born, but is eternal. In contrast to the eternal God, Christ was "begotten," that is, he had a beginning. Matthew 1:18 (KJV) reads 'Now the birth of Jesus Christ...." The word translated "birth" in the original text was *genesis*, or "beginning." Some scribes changed this to *gennesis* [with a double "n" and the second "e" long] because they were uncomfortable saying Jesus had a "beginning." Although it is true that a legitimate meaning of *genesis* is "birth," that is because the birth of something is understood as its beginning. If Jesus pre-existed his birth, as Trinitarians teach, the use of "beginning" in Matthew is misleading. Scripture teaches that the beginning of Jesus was his conception and birth. Thankfully, even modern Trinitarian scholars recognize that the original reading was *genesis*, although it is translated as "birth" in almost all translations.

(9) Jesus is called the "Son of God" more than 50 times in the Bible. Not once is he called "God the Son."

(10) Man (Adam) caused mankind's problems, and Romans 5:19 says that a man will have to undo those problems: "For just as through the disobedience of the one **man** the many were made sinners, so also through the obedience of the one **man** the many will be made righteous." Some

---

1. To understand this subject see Appendix Q "Do You Have to Believe in the Trinity to be Saved?"

theologians teach that only God could pay for the sins of mankind, but the Bible clearly teaches that only a man could do it.

(11) Jesus, the man, is the mediator between God and men. 1 Timothy 2:5 says: "For there is one God and one mediator between God and men, the man Christ Jesus." Christ is clearly called a "man," even after his resurrection. Also, if Christ were himself God, he could not be the mediator "between God and man."

Verses that Show that God Is Greater than Christ

(12) Jesus called the Father "my God" both before and after his resurrection (Matt. 27:46; John 20:17; Rev. 3:12). Jesus did not think of himself as God, but instead had a God just as we do. For example, he told Mary Magdalene to go to the brothers and tell them, "…I ascend to My Father and your Father, and My God and your God" (John 20:17 - NASB). Thus Jesus' God is the same God as our God, the Father.

(13) Jesus said, "…my Father is greater than I" (John 14:28 - KJV). In direct contrast to these clear words from Jesus, the orthodox formula of the Trinity says that the Father and the Son are "co-equal."

(14) It was God who **made** Jesus "Lord." Acts 2:36 says: "…God has made this Jesus…both Lord and Christ." "Lord" is not the same as "God." "Lord" (the Greek word is *kurios*) is a masculine title of respect and nobility, and it is used many times in the Bible. If Christ were God, then by definition he was already "Lord," so for the Bible to say he was "made" Lord could not be true. To say that Jesus is God because the Bible calls him "Lord" is very poor scholarship. "Lord" is used in many ways in the Bible, and others beside God and Jesus are called "Lord."

1. property owners are called Lord (Matt. 20:8, *kurios* is "owner")
2. heads of households were called Lord (Mark 13:35, owner = *kurios*).
3. slave owners were called Lord (Matt. 10:24, master = *kurios*).
4. husbands were called Lord (1 Pet. 3:6, master = *kurios*).
5. a son called his father Lord (Matt. 21:30, sir = *kurios*).
6. the Roman Emperor was called Lord (Acts 25:26, His Majesty = *kurios*).
7. Roman authorities were called Lord (Matt. 27:63, sir = *kurios*).

(15) In the future, the Son will be subject to the Father. 1 Corinthians 15:28 says: "When he has done this, then the Son himself will be made subject to him [God] who put everything under him, so that God may be all in all." Trinitarian dogma contradicts this by making Jesus eternally equal to the Father.

(16) Jesus recognized that the Father was the only true God. In prayer, he said to God "…that they might know you, the only true God, and Jesus Christ whom you have sent" (John 17:3). For Jesus to have prayed this way surely meant that he did not consider himself to be "the only true God."

(17) Jesus was "sanctified" by God. John 10:36 (NASB) says: "do you say of Him, whom the Father sanctified and sent into the world, 'You are blaspheming,' because I said, 'I am the Son of God'?" Jesus was sanctified by God, but God does not need to be sanctified.

(18) Philippians 2:6–8 has been mistranslated in many versions, but properly rendered, verse 6 says that Christ "…did not consider equality with God something to be grasped." Jesus Christ was highly exalted by God because he did not seek equality with God like Lucifer had many years earlier. The statement makes no sense at all if Christ were God, because then Christ would have been praised for not seeking equality with himself.

(19) It was clear that Jesus did not consider himself equal with the Father. In John 5:19, he said, "…the Son can do nothing by himself; he can only do what he sees his Father doing…" (cp. v. 30 and 8:28 and 12:49).

(20) There is only one who is "good," and that is God. In Luke 18:19, Jesus spoke to a man who had called Him "good," asking him, "Why do you call me good?…No one is good—except God alone." If Jesus had been telling people that he was God, he would have complimented the man on his perception, just as he complimented Peter when Peter said he was "…the Christ, the Son of the living God." Instead, Christ gave him a mild rebuke. Christ was not teaching the people that he was God.

(21) 1 Corinthians 3:23 (NASB) makes it clear that God is greater than Christ, just as Christ is greater than we are: "and you belong to Christ; and Christ belongs to God."

(22) If God is greater than Christ, then God is his leader just as Christ is our leader. This is exactly what the Bible teaches: "Now I want you to realize that the head of every man is Christ, and the head of the woman is man, and the head of Christ is God" (1 Cor. 11:3). It is obvious from this verse and 1 Corinthians 3:23 (above) that the Trinitarian formula that Christ and God are "co- equal" is not biblical.

(23) When the disciples prayed to God in Acts, they called King David God's "servant" (4:25). Later in that same prayer they called Jesus "your holy servant" (4:30). It is very obvious that the first century disciples did not believe Christ was God, but thought of him, like David, as a servant of God. (cp. Matt. 12:18 and Acts 3:26, which also refer to Jesus as God's "servant").

(24) It was God who did miracles and wonders *through* Christ. (Matt. 9:8; Acts 2:22, 10:38). If Christ were God, the Bible would simply say that Christ did the miracles himself without making reference to God. The fact that it was God supplying the power for the miracles shows that God is greater than Christ.

(25) There are many verses indicating that Jesus' power and authority was given to him by the Father. If he were the eternal God, then he would have always had those things that the Scripture says he was "given." Christ was given "all authority" (Matt. 28:18). He was given "a name above every name" (Phil. 2:9). He was given work to finish by the Father (John 5:36). He was given those who believed in him by the Father (John 6:39, 10:29). He was given glory (John 17:22 and 24). He was given his "cup" [his torture and death] by the Father (John 18:11). God "seated" Christ at His own right hand (Eph. 1:20). Christ was "appointed" over the Church (Eph. 1:22). These verses and others like them make no sense if Christ is "co-equal" with the Father, but make perfect sense if Christ was the Messiah, "a man accredited by God."

(26) Despite all the people who speak of the "Deity of Christ," the phrase never appears in the Bible, nor is Christ ever called "Deity." "Deity" is from the Latin "*Deus*," which means "God," and the phrase, "the Deity of Christ," as it is popularly (but not biblically) used, means "the 'Godness' of Christ." However, Christ is not God, he is Lord, as many clear verses show. Colossians 2:9 says that in Christ the "…fullness of deity dwells bodily." (NRSV) This verse is stating that God (the Deity) placed all His fullness in Christ, which is quite different from saying that Christ is Deity. Earlier in Colossians, the concept is made clear: "…God was pleased to have all his fullness dwell in him" (Col. 1:19). That is true. John 3:34 says: "For the one whom God has sent speaks the words of God, for God gives the Spirit without limit." The fact that Christ has "all the fullness" of God does not make him God. In Ephesians 3:19, the Bible says that Christians should be filled with "…all the fullness of God," and no one believes that this makes Christians God. Furthermore, if Christ were God, it would make no sense to say that the fullness of God dwelt in him, because, being God, he would always have the fullness of God. The fact that Christ could have the fullness of God dwell in him shows that he was not God.

2 Peter 1:4 says that through the great and precious promises "…you may participate in the divine nature…." Having a "divine nature" does not make us God, and it did not make Christ God. The New International Version Study Bible note on 2 Peter 1:4 says that it means only that "we are indwelt by God through His Holy Spirit." Likewise Christ, who was filled with holy spirit without limits, had the fullness of Deity dwelling in Him.

(27) Ephesians 4:5 and 6 says there is "**one Lord**, one faith, one baptism; **one God** and Father of all…." The "one Lord" is Jesus. The "one God" is the Father. There are clearly two separate beings represented here, not "one God" composed of Jesus and his Father. Furthermore, there is no verse that says that Jesus and the Father are "one God."

(28) 1 Corinthians 8:6 says, "yet for us there is but one God, the Father…and there is but one Lord, Jesus Christ…." If there is one God and one Lord, then there are two, and they are not the same.

(29) Jesus called the Father, "the only God" (John 5:44). The New American Standard Version goes so far as to translate it as "…the *one and* only God." Jesus would not have said this had he believed he himself were God also.

(30) Christ made a distinction between speaking against him and speaking against the Holy Spirit. Luke 12:10: "And everyone who speaks a word against the Son of Man will be forgiven, but anyone who blasphemes against the Holy Spirit will not be forgiven." If both the Holy Spirit and Christ were co-equal persons in one God, then there would be no difference between speaking against Christ and speaking against the Holy Spirit.

(31) Christ said his doctrine was not his own. John 7:16: "…My teaching is not my own. It comes from him who sent me." Christ could not have said this if he were God because the doctrine would have been his.

(32) Jesus and God have separate wills. Luke 22:42: "…not my will, but yours be done" (cp. John 5:30).

(33) Jesus counted himself and his Father as two, not "one." John 8:17 and 18: "In your own Law it is written that the testimony of two men is valid. I am one who testifies for myself; my other witness is the Father…." Jesus confirmed this truth in John 14:1 when he said: "Do not let your hearts be troubled. Trust in God; trust **also** in me." There are literally hundreds of Scriptures like these that set forth Jesus and God as separate and distinct beings. "…Whoever continues in the teaching has **both** the Father and the Son" (2 John 9). The Scripture clearly recognizes the Father and the Son, but not "**both**" of them as "one God."

(34) The Bible always portrays God and Christ as two separate beings. Examples are far too many to list, but a few are: When Stephen saw them just before his death, he saw "…the Son of Man standing at the right hand of God" (Acts 7:56); the Church Epistles are authored by both God and Christ; both God and Christ rule in the eternal city of Revelation (Chapter 21).

(35) The Bible makes it clear that Jesus is an "heir" of God, and a joint-heir with us (Rom. 8:17 - KJV). If Christ is a "person" in the "Godhead" and co-eternal with the Father, then he cannot be an heir, because, as God, he is full owner of all and there is nothing he could "inherit." He simply would share eternal glory. By making Christ a co-heir with believers and an heir of God, the Bible makes it clear how much Christ is like us. We inherit from the Father, and Christ does too.

(36) The Bible is clear that Jesus is the "image of God" (Col. 1:15; 2 Cor. 4:4). If Christ is the image of God, then he cannot be God, because you cannot be an image of someone and the real person at the same time. If you see a photograph of us, you see our image and you can learn a lot about us from it, but the image is not the real us. Christ is the image of God. We learn a lot about God from seeing Christ, but the simple fact that he is God's *image* proves he is not God.

(37) "The **only** wise God" receives His glory *through* Jesus Christ (Rom. 16:27: "to the only wise God be glory forever through Jesus Christ"). To reference "God" apart from Christ and say at the same time that God was the "only" God is very clear. Jesus is not, and is not part of, the "only" God.

Trinitarian Doctrine Teaches that God and Christ (and the Holy Spirit) Make Up "One God," but the Bible Teaches They Are Two Distinct Beings

Verses that Highlight Jesus' Humanity and Thus His Difference from God

(38) Jesus grew in wisdom, but God is all wise (Luke 2:52 - KJV: "And Jesus increased in wisdom…"). Also, Jesus "learned obedience" (Heb. 5:8). God does not need to learn.

(39) Jesus had limited knowledge. For example, Mark 13:32 says: "No one knows about that day or hour, not even the angels in heaven, nor the Son, but only the Father." [Although some Greek texts omit "nor the Son," Trinitarian textual scholars now admit the phrase was in the original text of Mark. It was Trinitarian scribes who tried to have this phrase taken from the Bible because it disagreed with their theology and they could not explain it.] Even after his resurrection, Jesus still receives knowledge from God as Revelation 1:1 indicates: "The revelation of Jesus Christ, which God gave him…."

(40) Scripture teaches that it was fitting that God should "make" Jesus "perfect through suffering" (Heb. 2:10). God is, and has always been, perfect, but Jesus needed to attain perfection through his suffering.

(41) Jesus received the holy spirit at his baptism. If Jesus were God and the holy spirit were God, then God would have been anointed by God. What purpose would this have served? We know why people are anointed, but what power could God give to Himself? Jesus was given holy spirit just as believers are today.

(42) Jesus was "…tempted in every way, just as we are…" (Heb. 4:15), yet the Bible is clear that God cannot be tempted: "…for God cannot be tempted by evil…" (James 1:13).

(43) At times of weakness or difficulty, angels ministered to and strengthened Jesus. Luke 22:43 says: "An angel from heaven appeared to him and strengthened him [in the garden of Gethsemane]." Men need to be strengthened; God does not (cp. Matt. 4:11; Mark 1:13).

(44) Scripture teaches that Jesus died. God cannot die. Romans 1:23 and other verses say that God is immortal. Immortal means "not subject to death." This term applies only to God.

(45) Hebrews 4:15 says that when Jesus was on earth, he was "just as we are." None of us would have the feelings, the doubts, the fears, etc., that we do if we were God. To say that God feels like I do is to make a mockery of God. Jesus was the expected Messiah of God, the Last Adam, a "man accredited by God," as Acts 2:22 says.

(46) Hebrews 2:10 and 11 say that Jesus is not ashamed to call us his "brothers," because we have the same Father he does. The Bible teaches that we are "brothers" of Jesus and "sons of God." The Bible never says or even infers that we are "brothers of God."

(47) We are commissioned to do "greater works" than Jesus. This would be absurd if Christ were God, because then we disciples would be commissioned to do greater works than God does. John 14:12 (NASB) says: "...he who believes in Me [Jesus], the works that I do shall he do also; and greater *works* than these shall he do...."

God is God because of certain attributes that He has. If Jesus Christ were God, he would have to have the attributes of God. Most theologians agree that these attributes are: unoriginated, self-existent, immortal, unchanging, omniscient, all wise, all good, all-powerful and omnipresent. But Jesus denied every one of these.

He was not unoriginated: Christ was begotten of God. "...the Father has life in himself, so he has **granted** the Son to have life in himself" (John 5:26).

He was not self-existent: "...I live because of the Father..." (John 6:57).

He was not immortal. Jesus died and God resurrected him (See #44 above).

He was not unchanging. He grew and learned, and he died and rose in a new and different body.

He was not omniscient. There were things he did not know (See #39 above).

He was not all wise. Jesus "grew in wisdom" (See #38 above).

He was not all good. He said the only one good was God (See #20 above).

He was not all-powerful. Whereas "...nothing is impossible with God" (Luke 1:37), Christ said "...the Son can do nothing by himself..." (John 5:19).

He was not omnipresent. After Lazarus died, Jesus told his disciples, "...I am glad I was not there..." (John 11:15).

The attributes of God are what make Him God, just as there are certain attributes that make a man what he is. There is a common saying that "if it walks like a duck and quacks like a duck, then it's a duck." This could easily be applied here. God "walks and quacks" like God. Jesus "walks and quacks" like a man, and Scripture says very **clearly that he is a man**. We assert that the Bible is clear in its teaching about who God is and who Christ is, and we ask Christians to carefully consider what they believe and why.

We also think that believing that Jesus is God, "the Holy Spirit" is God, and the Father is God actually demeans the **only true God**. Making God one of three co-equal "persons" takes from Him His exalted position as the only true God, the Creator of the universe, the Author of the plan of Salvation, the Father of Jesus Christ, and *our* one God.

Besides robbing God of His exalted position as God supreme, believing that Jesus is God also demeans him. One cannot appreciate how great Jesus really was until you make an effort to live like he did for even one day. His courage, mental tenacity, love and great faith are unparalleled in human history. His true greatness is lost if you believe he is God, for "...with God all things are possible." Believing Jesus is God also demeans God because Jesus himself said, "...my Father is greater than I."

Believing that Christ is God also means that he could not have sinned [which makes sense given that "God" cannot sin]. Christ must have been able to sin, for Scripture says he was "...tempted in every way, **just as we are**...." Christ went through life like each human does, with doubts, fears and concerns, and with the possibility of sin. To believe that Jesus could not have sinned makes it impossible for us to identify with him.

By restoring the Father to His unique and singular position as God, we give Him all the worship, credit, respect and awe He deserves as **the one true God**. By restoring Christ to his position as the man accredited by God, the only-begotten Son of the Father, the Last Adam, the one who could have sinned but voluntarily stayed obedient, the one who could have given up but loved us so much that he never quit, the one whom God highly exalted to be our Lord, we give Jesus Christ all the worship, credit, respect and awe that he deserves, and we can draw great strength and determination from his example.

I

34 Reasons Why the "Holy Spirit" Is Not a "Person" Separate From the Only True God, the Father

Unless otherwise noted, Scripture in this appendix is taken from the King James Version.

The doctrine of the Trinity depends upon the reality of a "third person" called "the Holy Spirit" to complete a supposed multi-personal Godhead. Without such a separate person who is "co-eternal" and "co-equal" with the Father and the Son, the "Triune" God disintegrates. It is therefore wise to consider the reasons why this idea is not supported by logical scrutiny nor the weight of scriptural evidence.

Before exploring the reasons why this teaching is not biblically sound, we should first consider its practical consequences. We must obviate the common objections that we are merely splitting hairs over unprovable doctrines, that truth is not at stake and that one teaching is equivalent to another as long as each is sincerely believed and God is approached with humility and love. It is our assertion that the teaching that "the Holy Spirit" is a separate "person" from God, the Father, is not true and results in some serious practical disadvantages to living the Christian life, namely:

- Confusion about the distinction between "the Giver" and "the gift" results in misunderstanding of many verses of Scripture that become unintelligible, and the truth is exchanged for a man-made myth.
- A lack of recognition of the permanence of the gift of holy spirit in the life of a believer results from the confusion about the coming and going of a "person."[1]
- Worship, praise, prayer, song and liturgy are directed toward an imaginary "third person" in the traditional Christian "Godhead," but it ought to be directed primarily to God, the Father and secondarily to the Lord Jesus Christ. The **only true God, the Father,** seeks those who will worship Him "…in spirit and in truth [reality]…" (John 4:23), in other words, worship Him for who He really is.
- Improperly discerning and understanding what the gift of holy spirit is, many Christians naively assume that virtually all spiritual manifestations are from the true God, and too often fail to discern the genuine from the counterfeit, and are therefore led into error.[2]
- Failing to understand that "…the spirits of the prophets are subject to the prophets," and instead being taught to be "controlled" by the Holy Spirit, many become influenced by demons, even while thinking that they are being "led by the spirit" of God.
- Many are not walking in the power of the spirit because they are waiting for a "person" to move them, while God is waiting for them to utilize by faith that which they have already been given.

We are now ready to examine the principal reasons for denying the Trinitarian assertion that "the Holy Spirit" is a separate person from the Father, the one God of Scripture. These are drawn from our own ruminations and from the work of James H. Broughton and Peter J. Southgate, *op. cit., The Trinity: True or False?* 1995, Anthony Buzzard, *op. cit., The Doctrine of the Trinity; Christianity's Self-Inflicted Wound,* 1994, Charles Morgridge, *op. cit., The True Believer's Defence,* 1837, Fredric A. Farley, *op. cit., The Scripture Doctrine of the Father, Son and Holy Ghost,* 1873 and *Op. cit., The Racovian Catechism,* 1609.

(1) God is said to have a throne (1 Kings 22:19; Dan. 7:9), inhabit heaven as His dwelling place (1 Kings 8:30, 39, 43 and 49), and yet "…heaven and heaven of heavens cannot contain…" Him (1 Kings 8:27). So how can He be said to have a throne and a dwelling place and yet be uncontainable? Psalms 139:7 indicates that God's *spirit* and His *presence* can be equivalent terms. God is therefore omnipresent by His "spirit," which is not a separate "person." This presence can also be extended by His personal ministers and agents, whether Christ, angels, or believers. None of these is a separate person who is also "God" in some multi-personal Godhead, but rather empowered agents who are equipped to do the will of God.

(2) Exodus 23:20–22 mentions the angel of God's presence that would go before Israel in the wilderness. God has permitted angels to speak as if they were God Himself, and even to use His personal name, YAHWEH. A few examples of this principle are Manoah and his wife (Judg.13:21 and 22), Jacob wrestling (Gen. 32:24–30; Hosea 12:3–5), Moses (Exod. 3:2–4, 6 and 16) and Gideon (Judg. 6:12, 13, 16 and 22). What is sometimes attributed to Jesus or to "the Holy Spirit" in the Old Testament is better explained by this principle of God manifesting Himself by means of an angelic messenger who speaks for Him in the first person ("I the LORD," etc.) and manifests His glory.

---

1. See our booklet: *25 Reasons Why Salvation is Permanent for Christians.*
2. See our book: *Op. cit., The Gift of Holy Spirit—The Power to be like Christ.*

(3) Although the Hebrew word for "spirit" (*ruach*), can refer to angels or evil spirits, which are persons or entities with a personality, the Hebrew usage of "the spirit of God" never refers to a person separate from, but a part of, God Almighty. Neither does the phrase, "the spirits of God" occur, which would refer to separate spiritual entities within a multipersonal God.

- Zechariah 6:5 refers to the "…four spirits of the heavens…" riding in chariots, but the NIV text note supplies an alternate reading of "winds," which makes more sense in the context—the four winds of heaven going North, East, etc.).
- Revelation 1:4 refers to the "seven Spirits" before the throne of God. Are these seven "Holy Spirits," or sentient entities, within the "Godhead?" The context provides the answer: they are the seven flaming torches before the throne (4:5 - NRSV) and the seven horns and seven eyes of the slain Lamb (5:6). These are likely the same "spirits" mentioned in Isaiah 11:2 in connection with the Messiah: the spirit of the LORD, the Spirit of wisdom, the spirit of understanding, the spirit of counsel, the spirit of might, the spirit of knowledge and the spirit of the fear of the LORD. These "spirits" are undoubtedly symbols of the intense power of insight and judgment with which the Lamb will judge and reign over the earth during the Millennium.

(4) As with the Hebrew word, *ruach*, the Greek word for spirit (*pneuma*) also has many different meanings, the correct one also being determinable only from the context of each occurrence. Although Greek has both upper and lower case letters, the early manuscripts employed either one or the other. Therefore, no accurate distinction can be made in the original manuscripts of the Bible between upper case "Holy Spirit," a proper noun referring to God, and lower case "holy spirit," referring to an impersonal force. Compounding the problem is the fact that the article "the" was often added by translators, leading the reader to think that "*the* Holy Spirit" is referring to a separate person, a third person of "the Holy Trinity" as taught by traditional Christian orthodoxy.

(5) Scholars admit that the concept of the Trinity cannot be substantiated in the Old Testament. In particular, "the Holy Spirit" as any kind of independent or distinct entity has no place in Old Testament revelation. Therefore, they say, the concept must be derived from the New Testament. With the exception of a few comparatively difficult verses in the gospel of John that are often misunderstood, the New Testament also gives no certain and incontrovertible indication of a "Holy Spirit" as a personal being co-equal with the Father and the Son. This is a rather glaring omission if the Triune God is supposed to provide the foundation of Christian orthodoxy, yet the "tri-unity" of God cannot be clearly established even with New Testament revelation. Thus it makes sense to understand "holy spirit" in the New Testament just as it was understood in the Old Testament, either God Himself or His presence and power.

(6) The Greek word for "spirit," *pneuma*, is neuter, as are all pronouns referring to the spirit, making them necessarily impersonal. New Testament translators knew this grammatically, but groundlessly translated references to the coming "spirit of truth" as "he," instead of "it" because of their Trinitarian prejudice (e.g., John 14:17). If they had consistently translated the neuter pronouns of John 14 through 16 as "it," "its," "itself" and "which" instead of "he," "his," "him," "who," or "whom," the case for the "personality of the Holy Spirit" would largely disappear from Christian belief. Such a major theological doctrine with such important implications for foundational Christian theology cannot depend on a few pronouns, but rather should be founded upon the weight of the biblical evidence considered as a whole, apart from tradition and prejudice.

(7) Any translation from one language to another must recognize the relative unimportance of gender. For the most part, languages that assign a gender to nouns do so in a rather arbitrary manner. For instance, the Spanish word for car is masculine, *el carro*, while a bicycle is feminine, *la bicicleta*. Yet no one would translate into English "the car, he…" or "the bicycle, she…" Either word would require the neuter "it" to reflect the impersonal nature of the object. A writer or a poet might employ such a figurative expression in the use of pronouns, but any reader acquainted with the objects referred to would recognize the figure of speech employed. Such poetic *personification* is employed in reference to "the Comforter."

(8) The figure of speech *Personification* is common in Scripture, and is defined as attributing *personal* qualities, feelings, actions, etc., to things that have no real personality or personal consciousness. Wisdom is personified as such in Proverbs 8 and 9, yet no sensible person would seriously consider that a literal person named "Wisdom" helped God create the world, as Proverbs 8:29 and 30 says. The spirit of God is personified as "the Comforter" in John 14:16 and 26, 15:26, 16:7. Therefore, personal pronouns are appropriate to agree with the personal nature of the figurative title. It is clear from John 16:13 that this Comforter is *sent*, does "not speak of himself" and is instructed ("…whatsoever he shall hear, *that* shall he speak…").

(9) The "Comforter," more properly translated as "Counselor," is said by Jesus to fill the void created by his going to the Father (John 14:12). By this spirit he would still be present: "…I will come to you" (14:18); "I am in you" (14:20 - NIV); and I will "show myself" (14:21 - NIV). By this spirit his work with them would continue: It "will teach you"(14:26 - NIV); It "…will remind you of everything I have said…" (14:26 - NIV); It "will testify about me" (15:26 - NIV); It "…will convict the world of guilt…" (in preparation for his judgment—16:8 - NIV); It "…will guide you into all truth…" (16:13 - NIV); It "…will bring glory to me by taking what is mine and making it known to you" (16:14 - NIV).

All of these statements point to the role of the gift of holy spirit in continuing the work that Jesus started, and even empowering his followers for greater works. This spirit is not independent and self-existent, but is "the mind of Christ" within the believer, influencing, guiding, teaching, reminding and pointing the believer to follow his Lord and Savior. This spirit is certainly not "co-equal" when by its very design it serves the risen Lord and Christ. Yet because it carries the *personal* presence of Christ into the life of every believer, the use of *Personification* is highly appropriate. As a practical matter, holy spirit in us will not lead us anywhere that the Lord himself would not lead us if he were personally present. We can study Christ's life and his priorities in the written Word to verify whether the "spirit" leading us in is fact the spirit of the Lord Jesus Christ or whether it is "another spirit." For instance, he whose basic commitment was "it is written" will not be leading his followers away from relying on Scripture as the only rule of faith and practice.

(10) The "soul" or the "spirit" of *man* is often personified like the spirit of *God is*. "Why art thou cast down, O my soul?…" (Ps. 42:5). "…I will say to my soul, Soul, thou hast much goods laid up…" (Luke 12:19). "…the spirit indeed *is* willing…" (Matt. 26:41). The spirit of Titus "was refreshed" (2 Cor. 7:13). Yet no one would argue that the "spirit of man" is a separate person from the man himself. The figure of speech *Personification* is universally and readily recognized, and in the case of "the Comforter" ought to be recognized as well.

(11) The spirit of man bears the same relation to man as the spirit of God bears to God (1 Cor. 2:11). As the spirit of man is not another person distinct from himself, but his human consciousness or mind by which he is able to be self-aware and contemplate things peculiar to himself, so the spirit of God is not another person distinct from God. It is that consciousness and intelligence that is essential and peculiar to Him whereby He manifests and reveals Himself to man. As the spirit of man means the man himself (the essence of a man is his *mind*), so the spirit of God means God Himself. The parallel usage of mind and spirit is seen in the Apostle Paul's citation of Isaiah 40:13 (NRSV) ("Who has directed the Spirit of the LORD, or as his counselor has instructed him?") and in Romans 11:34 and 1 Corinthians 2:16 where "spirit" is rendered "mind."

(12) If the "Spirit of truth" in John 14:17 is a person, then "the spirit of error" in 1 John 4:6 must also be a person, since the two are directly contrasted. The fact is that each "spirit" represents an influence or a power under which a person acts, but neither is a person in itself.

(13) 1 Corinthians 2:12 directly opposes the "spirit of the world" with "…the spirit which is of God…." As the "spirit of the world" is not a person separate from "the world," neither is the "spirit of God" a person separate from God. Each is an influence emanating from a source that produces certain attitudes, behaviors or "fruit."

(14) The "breath" of God and the "spirit" of God are synonymous terms (Job 4:9 - NIV; Ps. 33:6, 104:29 and 30; John 3:8; Job 27:3). It is as inconceivable that the breath of God could be a person distinct from God as that the breath of a human could be a person distinct from a human. It is especially absurd to speak of one self-existent and eternal person as "the breath" of another such person.

(15) The "spirit of God" is synonymous with the "hand" and "the finger" of God (Ezek. 3:14; Job 26:13; Ps. 8:3; Luke 11:20). It is nonsense to call a "co-equal and co-eternal person" the "hand" and finger" of another such person. In fact, as a man's hand and finger are subordinate and submissive to the will of a man, so the spirit of God is subordinate to the will of God. As what is done by the hand of a man is done by the man himself, so what is done by the spirit of God is done by God Himself. His spirit is his will in action, performing that which He "sends" it to perform.

(16) The "spirit of your Father," is synonymous with "the holy spirit," and is said to speak in our stead on certain occasions when we might be brought before men for possible persecution or trial (Matt.10:19 and 20; Mark 13:11; Luke 12:11 and 12). On the same topic, Luke 21:15 says that Christ will give us "…a mouth and wisdom, which all your adversaries shall not be able to gainsay nor resist." Rather than saying that a person called "the Holy Ghost" will speak through us, these verses teach that we will be inspired by the supernatural power of God and Christ to speak as they give us guidance.

(17) If the spirit is a sentient (able to sense, be self-aware), separate and distinct being with personality, then Jesus either did not know this or was very inconsistent in giving "Him" proper due. In Matthew 11:27, Jesus asserts that "…no man knoweth the Son, but the Father; neither knoweth any man the Father, save the Son…" If "the Holy Spirit" is a person distinct from the Father, and is also omniscient and almighty "God," then would He not also have to know the Father and the Son? Jesus' statement, then, would not have been true, and in fact would be a lie.

The same is true for Jesus' assertion in Matthew 24:36 that *no one* knew the hour of his Second Coming except the Father. How could "the Holy Spirit" be kept in the dark about this very important prophetic event? Are we to believe that it is possible for one member of the Godhead to keep a secret from another member while sharing the same eternal and divine "essence" of "Godself?"

(18) If the spirit of God is a unique and separate person, and having "spirit" is prerequisite to having a unique and separate personality, then the person called "the Spirit of God" must have his own "spirit" peculiar to himself and distinct from the Father and Son. We would then be forced to the absurd belief in "the spirit of the Spirit." If "the Holy Spirit" has no spirit of His own, then He could not be said to have a separate "personality."

If "God" is three co-equal persons, the third person can no more be "the spirit" of the first person, than the first person can be "the spirit" of the third person. To avoid this absurdity, "the spirit of God" cannot have a separate personality, but must be the power, influence, sufficiency, fullness or some extension of the Father, the real and unitary person called *the one true God*.

(19) The spirit of God is said to be divisible and able to be distributed. God took of the spirit that was upon Moses and put it upon the 70 elders of Israel (Num. 11:17–25). Joel 2:28, quoted by Peter on the day of Pentecost, says that God "…will pour out of my Spirit…" (Acts 2:17). Understood literally, the Greek says "some of," or "'part of' my spirit." The footnote in Weymouth's Translation reads "literally 'of' or 'from' my spirit—a share or portion." Though we cannot conceive of how a *person* might be so divided, we can understand that the spirit of God, as the *power* of God, might be distributed among many. 1 John 4:13 echoes this truth in saying, "We know that we live in him and he in us, because he has given us **of** his Spirit" (NIV).

(20) Many words associated with God's spirit give it the attributes of a liquid, which by definition cannot refer to a person. This liquid language is consistent with the spirit being His presence and power. We are baptized (literally "dipped") with and in it like water (Matt. 3:11; Acts 1:5). We are all made to "drink" from the same spirit, as from a well or fountain (1 Cor. 12:13). It is written on our hearts like ink (2 Cor. 3:3). We are "anointed" with it, like oil (Acts 10:38; 2 Cor. 1:21 and 22; 1 John 2:27). We are "sealed" with it as with melted wax (Eph. 1:13). It is "poured out" on us (Acts 10:45; Rom. 5:5 - NIV). It is "measured" as if it had volume (2 Kings 2:9; John 3:34). We are to be "filled" with it (Acts 2:4; Eph. 5:18). This "filling" is to capacity at the New Birth and to overflowing as we act according to its influence.

Even the use of spirit as "wind" implies a liquidity, for air masses behave as a fluid, flowing from areas of higher to lower pressure. All this figurative language must be designed to point us to the truth that the spirit of God is the invisible power and influence of God. It comes into our lives to buoy us up, to help us, to comfort us, to unite us and anoint us for the work to which He has called us. As liquid seeks the lowest level, so the spirit of God comes to us in our lowly and needy state, beneath our sins and iniquities, our faults and our failures to lift us up to stand in all the grace and truth that Christ brought.

(21) The "holy spirit" is clearly said to be given by God to men. A divine "person" cannot be given or bestowed by another divine person, because to be given is to be under the authority of another. If "the Holy Spirit" is co-equal with the Father, He cannot be under His authority.

(22) By definition, the spirit *of* God is derived *from* God. What comes *from* God as its source cannot also *be* "God," without the term "God" being reduced to a formless and incomprehensible abstraction. Nothing and no one can be both a source of a thing and the thing itself.

(23) In biblical usage, "the Holy Spirit" is a synonymous term for "God." In Acts 5:3 (NIV), Peter says Ananias lied to "the Holy Spirit." In verse 4 Peter says he lied to "God." This is an example of the common Semitic parallelism of equivalent terms, and is not evidence that Ananias lied to two separate persons. If that were the case, why would verse 4 not say that Ananias lied to "the Father" instead of to "God." Neither is this parallelism evidence that another divine person called "the Holy Spirit" is also "God" and therefore part of a triune "Godhead."

(24) "The holy spirit" is equivalent to "the power of the Most High," as Luke 1:35 (NIV) clearly indicates by another use of parallelism (cp. Luke 24:49; Acts 1:8, 10:38; Rom. 15:13, 18 and 19; 1 Cor. 2:4 and 5). The context is the conception of Jesus Christ. Matthew 1:18 (NIV) also records that Mary "…was found to be with child through 'the Holy Spirit.'" Yet all through the New Testament are references to the fact that *God* is the Father of our Lord Jesus Christ. If "God" is "the Father," and "the

Holy Spirit" is also "the father" of the baby Jesus, there is a potential paternity suit. Trinitarianism leads to much unnecessary confusion by asserting a separate personality of "the Holy Ghost," and cannot explain away the logical conclusion that according to that view the Son has *two* "Fathers," or two separate persons fathering Jesus.

(25) The "Holy Spirit" (properly "the gift of holy spirit") is used synonymously and interchangeably with "The Spirit of the Lord…" (Luke 4:18, etc.); "…the Spirit of his Son…" (Gal. 4:6); "… the Spirit of Jesus Christ" (Phil. 1:19). We have access to the Father by the spirit (Eph. 2:18); in Christ and through faith in him we have access with confidence to God (Eph. 3:12).

(26) Many Trinitarians assert that "the Holy Spirit" comes and permanently dwells within a believer when he accepts Jesus Christ as his Savior. But many also teach that the Holy Spirit comes upon a believer *after* he is born again. They also pray for "the Holy Spirit" to attend their meetings, and welcome "Him" to come as He desires. This puts them in the difficult position of having to explain how a Christian can have the person of "the Holy Spirit" simultaneously dwelling in him and coming and going from Christian meetings.

The simple answer to this dilemma is that there are two usages of "the spirit" that must be distinguished. One is "the gift of God's nature that is permanently received when a person is born again." The other is "the power and influence of God" as He manifests His presence in His Creation (Gen. 1:1) and among His people (2 Chron. 5:14). In contrast to the permanent gift, this can wax and wane according to the faith of those present and the will of God in the situation. The gift of God's nature, holy spirit, is not always being energized into manifestation. God, "the Holy Spirit," (the Giver) energizes the spirit within believers as they act in faith (Acts 2:4).

(27) John 7:39 says that the Holy Spirit was not yet given, and in Acts 1:4 and 5 (NIV) Jesus tells his disciples to wait for "…the gift my Father promised…" that would come "in a few days." If the Holy Spirit is a person, and He was present in the Old Testament, then how is it possible for Him to be spoken of as "not yet given." It is also confusing to contemplate how the gift of a "person" is even possible, and the only answer Trinitarians can provide is that this is part of the "mystery" of the Trinity.

This "mystery" is solved when we understand that the spirit of God we receive is not a separate person, but rather the gift of God to empower His people. In the Old Testament, this empowering was temporal, hence David could pray that it not be removed from him (Ps. 51:11). It was also measured out differently to different people, hence Elisha could pray to receive a "double portion" (2 Kings 2:9). It was not given to all, and therefore its presence was noteworthy (Gen. 41:38). Since Pentecost, when the spirit was said to have "come," it is now in all believers permanently and without measure, as it had been given to Jesus Christ. He who had the spirit "without measure" (John 3:34), enabling him to do his Messianic work, poured out this same spirit on Pentecost (Acts 2:33 - NIV). And it is he, the true Baptizer, who fills each believer who comes to him for salvation (Matt. 3:11; Eph. 1:23).

(28) The only verse that would indicate that there might be three persons sharing one name is Matthew 28:19: "…baptizing them in the name of the Father, and of the Son and of the Holy Ghost." This verse is quoted in a different form by the early Church Fathers, notably Eusebius (340 A.D.), who quotes the verse at least 18 times as follows: "baptizing them in my name." This agrees with the testimony of the book of Acts and Paul's Epistles, which associate only the name of Jesus Christ with baptism. Even if the verse reads as found in modern versions today, it does not validate the "Holy Spirit" being a separate person from God.

Arguments from Omission

(29) The Holy Spirit is never worshiped as are the Father and the Son, neither does any verse of Scripture command such worship. This is surprising if the Holy Spirit is truly a co-equal and co-eternal member of a triune "God" worthy of worship. If "God" is worthy of worship, and "God" exists in three persons, then shouldn't each "God" person be worthy of worship? Then why is this idea not found in the Scripture?

(30) In the opening of their New Testament Epistles, every one of the writers identifies himself with God the Father and the Lord Jesus Christ, but not one does so with "the Holy Spirit." If they were ignorant of the truth of a "tri-personal" God, and this truth constitutes the foundation of the Christian faith, then their Apostleship was incomplete at best, and at worst they were teaching error. Their failure to clearly teach a three person Godhead proves the assertion that the doctrine of the tri-personal God and a third person in an eternal Godhead was not believed or practiced by the Apostles. In fact, the doctrine was not codified until the fourth century in the Athanasian creed.[3] Since it was not believed nor practiced by the Apostles, and the Apostles were commissioned by the Lord Jesus himself, then it is logical to assert that the doctrine was not believed nor practiced by the Lord Jesus either.

(31) Lacking sufficient Scriptural justification, the orthodox view of "the Holy Spirit" was fully developed in the fourth century after Christ and the Apostles, contemporaneously with the rise of Neoplatonic philosophy,[4] which posited an abstract God "beyond being," in which a variety of divine persons could be "one" in "essence." This was basically a regurgitation of Gnostic philosophy,[5] which had been vigorously opposed by the first century Apostles but later embraced by many of the "Church Fathers" who helped to establish "orthodoxy."

(32) In the Church Epistles, (Romans through Thessalonians), the Apostle Paul sends personal greetings from "God the Father and the Lord Jesus Christ." If "the Holy Spirit" were an integral and personal part of a triune Godhead, then why does "He" not send "His" personal greetings as well? The only good answer is that there is no such person, for as an inspired writer of Scripture, Paul was on intimate talking terms with God and the Lord Jesus. If there were a third person involved, wouldn't Paul have surely known about it and included "Him" in his greetings to the churches? When Paul does include additional persons in his greetings, salutations and adjurations, he names "the elect angels," not "the Holy Spirit" (1 Tim. 5:21; cp. Luke 9:26 and Rev. 3:5).

(33) In the NIV translation, Philippians 2:1 and 2 refers to "fellowship **with** the Spirit," yet 1 John 1:3 says that "…our fellowship *is* with the Father, and with his Son, Jesus Christ." Why is the Holy Spirit left out? A better translation of Philipians 2:1 is the Young's Literal Translation (YLT), which renders the phrase "fellowship of spirit," pointing to the fellowship among believers who share a common spirit and who therefore ought to be able to get along with each other.

(34) In the eternal city of Revelation 21 and 22, both God and Jesus Christ are prominently featured. Each is pictured as sitting on his throne (Rev. 22:1). If "the Holy Spirit" is a "co-eternal" member of a triune Godhead, it is strange indeed that He seems to have no seat of authority on the final throne. This is consistent with the biblical truth that **there is one God, the Father, and one Lord, Jesus Christ,** and no such separate person known as "the Holy Spirit.

---

3. See Appendix C for the entire text of the Athanasian creed.
4. See Chapter 16 for more on Neoplatonism.
5. See Chapter 16 for more on Gnosticism.

By restoring the Father to His unique and singular position as God, we give Him all the worship, credit, respect, and awe He deserves as the **one true God**. By restoring Christ to his position as The Man accredited by God, the only-begotten Son of the Father, the Last Adam, the one who could have sinned but voluntarily stayed obedient, the one who could have given up but loved us so much that he never quit, the one whom God highly exalted to be our Lord, we give Jesus Christ all the worship, credit, respect, and awe that he deserves, and we can draw great strength and determination from his example.

The Order and Structure
of the Church Epistles

The Epistles of Paul are not haphazardly thrown into the Bible, rather they are the very Words of the Lord. In 1905, E. W. Bullinger (1837–1913), a scholar of the first rank and a descendant of the great Swiss reformer Heinrich Bullinger (1504–1575), penned a book on the Church Epistles that is still one of the greatest books ever written about them. We quote freely from his book: (*The Church Epistles*, E. W. Bullinger, Eyre & Spottiswoode, London, 1905)[he uses the King James Version].

It is a serious blow to Inspiration when the importance of one part of Scripture is exalted above another. To do this is to reduce the Bible to the position of any other book, and practically to deny that the whole is made up of "the words which the Holy Ghost teacheth." This is done in the present day when… *The Teaching of Jesus* is exalted above the Teachings of the Holy Spirit by Paul, as though there were a rivalry between the two. The words of Christ and the words of Paul are equal in weight and importance, inasmuch as both are recorded and given to us by the same Holy Spirit; and are therefore equal in authority. That authority is Divine: and no difference can be made between them without jeopardizing the very essence of Inspiration. That there is a difference is clear. But this difference arises from failing to rightly divide the word of Truth as to the various Dispensations of which it treats (page 9).

The seven churches to which the Holy Spirit addressed His epistles by Paul are Romans, Corinthians, Galatians, Ephesians, Philippians, Colossians and Thessalonians. In these epistles we have the perfect embodiment of the Spirit's teaching for the churches. These contain the "all truth," into which the Spirit of Truth was to "guide" us…These contain the "things of Christ" which the Spirit was to receive and show unto us (page 12).

In all the hundreds of Greek manuscripts of the New Testament, the order of these seven epistles addressed to churches is exactly the same (page 13).

That order therefore must present to us the line of study marked out for the churches by the Holy Spirit: a complete course which shall begin and finish the education of the Christian: a curriculum which contains everything necessary for the Christian's standing and his walk: the "all truth" into which the Spirit guides him (page 14).

The Seven Epistles to the Churches

A) **ROMANS.** "Doctrine and Instruction." The Gospel of God: never hidden, but "promised afore." God's justification of Jew and Gentile individually—dead and risen with Christ (i.–viii. [1–8]). Their relation dispensationally (ix.–xi. [9–11]). The subjective foundation of the mystery [Sacred Secret].[1]

    B) **CORINTHIANS.** "Reproof." *Practical* failure to exhibit the teaching of Romans through not seeing their standing as having died and risen with Christ. "Leaven" in practice (1 Cor. 5:6).

        C) **GALATIANS.** "Correction." *Doctrinal* failure as to the teaching of Romans Beginning with the truth of the new nature ("spirit"), they were "soon removed" (i. 6 [1:6]), and sought to be made perfect in the old nature ("flesh") (iii. 3 [3:3]). "Leaven" in doctrine (v. 9 [5:9]).

A) **EPHESIANS.** "Doctrine and Instruction." The Mystery [Sacred Secret][2] of God, always hidden, never before revealed. Jews and Gentiles collectively made "one new man" in Christ. Seated in the heavenlies with Christ.

    B) **PHILIPPIANS.** "Reproof." *Practical* failure to exhibit the teaching of Ephesians in manifesting "the mind of Christ" as members of one Body.

        C) **COLOSSIANS.** "Correction." *Doctrinal* failure as to the teaching of Ephesians. Wrong doctrines which come from "not holding the Head" (ii. 19 [2:19]), and not seeing their completeness and perfection in Christ (ii. 8–10 [2:8–10]).

A) **THESSALONIANS.** "Doctrine and Instruction." Not only "dead and risen with Christ" (as in Romans), not only seated in the heavenlies with Christ (as in Ephesians); but "caught up to meet

---

1. For an explanation of why the Greek word "musterion" should be translated "Sacred Secret" see our book: *op. cit.*, *Gift of Holy Spirit*, read the first half of Appendix A.
    2. See footnote #1.

the Lord in the air, so to be for ever with the Lord." In Romans, justified in Christ; in Ephesians., sanctified in Christ; in Thessalonians., glorified with Christ. No "reproof." No "correction." All praise and thanksgiving (page 21).

K

Logical Fallacies Employed in Trinitarian Theology

"Logic," from the Greek word *logos*, is the science of correct reasoning, and provides tools for analyzing the form and content of arguments. Logic addresses the relationship of premises (or evidence) to conclusions, and helps us determine whether our reasoning is straight or crooked. That is, does our conclusion necessarily follow from the premises, or have we "jumped" to conclusions. The disciplines of logical reasoning are fast becoming a thing of the past, an artifact of a classical education. Feelings, emotions and rhetoric (persuasive speech) are most often the basis of what passes for "reasoning" today. But, if we are ever to "…**correctly** handle the word of truth" (2 Tim. 2:15), we are going to have to learn to *think* correctly.

One of the best ways to understand and apply the basics of logic is by becoming familiar with logical fallacies, that is, examples of faulty reasoning. What follows are the main types of fallacious reasoning that we have encountered in the course of researching this book. Though the systems of classifying fallacies vary from author to author, we find that there is general agreement among teachers of logic that fallacies come in two general forms: formal and informal. The "formal" fallacies revolve around the syllogism form, which involves a major premise, a minor premise and a conclusion.

"Formally" fallacious logic involves some transgression of the proper form of syllogistic reasoning. "Informal" fallacies are those employed in everyday speech, and for the most part involve different ways of slanting or avoiding evidence en route to a conclusion.

Accent

The fallacy of accent is employed whenever an emphasis is placed on a written or spoken communication in a way that materially alters its original or intended meaning. To interpret any piece of literature logically, one must be sensitive to the context and original meaning intended by the author and not alter that meaning by misplaced emphasis. This misplaced emphasis can occur quite subtly. Without changing a word, a piece of written material can be made to say something entirely different from what was intended by the author. A common form of this fallacy is the altering of punctuation, which is particularly significant for biblical research because the original text of Scripture contained no punctuation marks. For instance, the addition of a comma can dramatically alter the simple sentence, "God made man," (as in God *created* man) to "God, made man" (as in God *became* man). What a big difference!

Likewise, "Woman without her man would be lost" is a seemingly straightforward sentence, but watch how the meaning can be dramatically changed by the addition of a period and a comma: "Woman. Without her, man would be lost."

Luke 23:43 (NASB) says, "And He said to him, 'Truly I say to you, today you shall be with Me in Paradise,'" indicating that Jesus will be with the malefactor in Paradise later that same day. But if the comma is moved to the other side of "today," an entirely different emphasis results: "…Truly I say to you today, you shall (in the future) be with me in Paradise." This is, in fact the correct rendering (see our book: *Is There Death After Life?*).

"Proof texting" is a common way that the fallacy of accent is employed. By isolating verses that appear to support a particular theological or doctrinal position, and by weighting them too heavily, contradictions are created with other verses on the same subject. For instance, with the exception of a few "proof texts," the idea that "Jesus is God" is not consistent with the New Testament when considered as a whole. Not a Christian theologian, but a professor of logic, made the following astute statement regarding what is required for the *logical* interpretation of the Bible:

> Selecting texts to give a one-sided presentation of the truth is a widespread method of propagating erroneous views. Out of the Bible can be drawn phrases or verses that justify everything under the sun, including contradictories. Read in context, the Bible may be a liberal document, but it is not that liberal. What we need to know is if the Bible **as a whole** [emphasis ours] supports a given position.[1]

It is a well-established hermeneutical principle among biblical interpreters that the difficult verse or passage must be interpreted in light of the clear and simple parallel verses or passages. The difficult or unusual must not be elevated and established as an altogether higher and better view than the rest of Scripture, as has been done with the gospel of John, for example. Because it apparently presents a Jesus most compatible with Trinitarian orthodoxy, the gospel of John is the one that is translated and distributed to potential converts more than any other. But has this been done honestly and logically, or by employing the *fallacy of accent?*

---

1. A. J. Moulds, *Thinking Straighter* (University of Michigan Press, Ann Arbor, 1975), p. 46.

Equivocation

This fallacy is employed when terms crucial to an argument are not used in the same sense throughout the argument. It could also be called "changing the rules in the middle of the game."

Equivocation can be clearly seen in the following argument:

Major premise: Every square is four-sided.
Minor premise: Your jaw is square.
Conclusion: Your jaw is four-sided.[2]

The reason the conclusion is invalid is that in the argument, the word "square" is used in two different ways. In geometry, a square is a four-sided polygon with equal sides and four 90° angles. In popular usage, a "square" jaw means something closer to "angular." In the reasoning process, it is crucial that words be used precisely in the same sense when reasoning from one premise to another to a conclusion.

One person cannot be "God" and "the *Son* of God" without equivocating the term "God." Trinitarians use the term "God" in the sense of "the Father" as distinct from "the Son" and "the Holy Spirit." But, in calling Christ "God," they use the term "God" in the sense of "the second person of the Trinity." Thus, although the word "God" is the same, it is given two different meanings.

Often, Trinitarians equivocate the term "God" to mean a "triune God" composed of three persons. The editors of the NIV Study Bible equivocate the term "God" in this fashion when they handle 1 Corinthians 15:24–28. The passage clearly separates "God" from "Christ," and asserts that Christ will *submit* to God for eternity "…so that **God** may be all in all." But, because of their doctrinal position that the Father and the Son are equal, neither can be "over" the other. Therefore, they minimize the Son's submission to a matter of "administrative function," and say that "*The triune God will be shown to be supreme and sovereign in all things.*"

To see the equivocation in the Chalcedonian formula of one person and two natures, look at the following argument:

Major premise: Jesus Christ is God (divine, deity, etc.).
Minor premise: God cannot be tempted (James 1:13).
Conclusion: Jesus Christ was tempted in all points (Heb. 4:15).

It should be clear that there is something wrong with the argument, because the conclusion does not follow from the premises. The logical conclusion that should be drawn from the premises is that Jesus Christ cannot be tempted. Let us restate the argument in proper syllogistic form.

Major premise: Jesus Christ is God.
Minor premise: God cannot be tempted (James 1:13).
Conclusion: Jesus Christ cannot be tempted.

But now the logical conclusion of these premises creates a dilemma, because it contradicts Hebrews 4:15, which says that Jesus Christ was tempted in all points. One possible solution is that the term "tempted" is being used in an equivocal sense. We must therefore look at the definition of the word "tempted" and see if it is being distributed throughout the argument in the same sense. We find that the word "tempt" in the minor premise and the conclusion is the same concept, based

---

2. Robert J. Kreyche, *Logic for Undergraduates* (Holt, Rinehart, Winston, N.Y., 1961), p. 192.

on the Greek word, *peirazo* (to pierce or cut). The only other possibility is that the term "God" is being equivocated, as follows:

Major premise: Jesus Christ is God [the Son who became a human being while retaining his divine nature].

Minor premise: God (the Father) cannot be tempted (James 1:13).

Conclusion: Jesus Christ was not tempted in his divine nature, but he was tempted in his human nature because he became a man.

In the major premise, "God" is used in the sense of divine, deity, sharing the attributes of God, etc. In the minor premise, "God" refers to the Creator and the Father of Jesus Christ. This is a clear example of equivocating the term "God." This standard orthodox argument also equivocates the term "man." Jesus Christ is not an *authentic* man in this argument, because a "man" by definition does not have a "divine" nature.

To clarify orthodoxy's equivocation of "man," consider the following argument:

Major premise: Jesus Christ is a man (1 Tim. 2:5; Acts 2:22).

Minor premise: God is not a man (Num. 23:19).

Conclusion: Jesus Christ is God.

The word "man" does not have the same meaning in the above premises. In the first case, "man" is descriptive only of the part of his being that was human, because Trinitarians argue that Jesus was both a man and God at the same time: a God-man. So, anything that is asserted about him being a "man" is qualified by saying that he was also God. In equivocating the terms "man" and "God," Trinitarians create a separate category of being for Jesus Christ and remove him from the normal and customary meaning of both terms as understood biblically and experientially. What is asserted about Jesus Christ could not be asserted about Adam, who was truly the archetypal "man." Unless Jesus' nature is completely comparable to Adam's, he cannot properly and without equivocation be categorized as "man." "100 percent God and 100 percent man" is 200 percent logical equivocation.

Law of Non-Contradiction

This law is completely fundamental to logical and rational thinking, as every student of philosophy knows. It states that "A" and "not A" cannot both be true at the same time and in the same relation. For instance, biologically speaking, Mark can be a father to his son and a son to his father, but he cannot be both a son and a father to the same person at the same time. So, regarding his relationship to his son, he cannot be both his son's (biological) father and *not* his son's father at the same time. He must be one or the other.

This law of non-contradiction is often jettisoned in theological discussions involving the Trinity or the natures of God and Christ. For instance, Jesus cannot be both a man and not-man at the same time and in the same relationship to what defines a man. If we define "man" in a way that makes "man" distinguishable from "God," as a member of the species *homo-sapiens* with various physical and mental limitations, Jesus Christ cannot be a man and not-man at the same time. If he is "man" and "God" at the same time, and if we preserve the integrity of the definitions of these terms, Jesus is a logical contradiction. The only way out of this dilemma is to propose a third category of being called "God-man," which of necessity renders him incapable of being included in either the category of "man" or "God." Though some may find this theologically and mystically compelling, it is logically contradictory if the integrity of biblical language is upheld (as in, "God is not a man"—Num. 23:19).

Logical Identity

Logical "identity" is established by the following principle: whatever is true of A must also be true of B, and whatever is true of B must also be true of A. One point of dissimilarity disproves identity. The stakes get higher when this principle is violated in connection with the identity of God. Scripture identifies the term "God" with the term "Father." *God* is the *Father* of our Lord Jesus Christ. That means that whatever is true of God must also be true of the Father of our Lord Jesus Christ. And whatever is true of the Father of Jesus Christ must be true of God also. Logically speaking, "God" cannot be both the Father of Jesus and Jesus himself, if language is to retain any meaning.

Straw Man

Attacking a straw man occurs when an opponent's position is misrepresented in order to make it more easily refuted. This is very hard to avoid, and points up the need for dialogue with those with whom we disagree. Even if we cannot agree, we can at least represent each other's position fairly and rebut it honestly. We have endeavored to do this throughout this book, and we invite those who disagree with us to let us know if we have misrepresented "orthodox" teaching.

Often, when Trinitarians hear our argument that Jesus is not God, they immediately respond by assuming that we are saying that Jesus is a "mere man." This is a straw man argument because it is easy to refute the claim that Jesus was merely a man like the rest of us. On the contrary, the Gospels are full of evidence of his uniqueness as the *monogenes* ("one of a kind," traditionally translated "only-begotten"). It is not demeaning to be made a man in the same way that Adam was made a man in the original creation. He was the crowning achievement of that Creation. The issue is whether Jesus is to be compared to a fallen man, with the implication that he is then a partaker of man's sinful nature. He had a fully human nature because God originally made man in His image. Man was made to reflect God's life and goodness, and share in His attributes. So for Jesus to be "the image of God" is to say that he is completing the destiny originally designed for Adam in the original creation, which Adam forfeited. There is nothing "mere" about that!

Undistributed Middle

This is a "formal" fallacy that relates to the proper form of syllogistic reasoning, which we must examine before discussing the undistributed middle. An argument can be logical in its form and yet lead to a false conclusion if one or both of the premises are false. The classic Roman Catholic argument for their veneration of the Virgin Mary is a good example:

> **Major premise:** Mary is the mother of Jesus.
> **Minor premise:** Jesus is God.
> *Conclusion:*   Therefore, Mary is the mother of God.

Protestants accept the premises but deny the conclusion. Such reasoning is illogical. We also deny the conclusion, but we do so because the argument is based on a false premise, not because the argument itself is invalid. At least Roman Catholics are consistent and logical in asserting their conclusion.

Seeing the proper form of syllogistic logic in symbols will help us understand the fallacy of the undistributed middle.

Correct form	Undistributed Middle
Major premise: A is B	**Major premise:** A is B
Minor premise: B is C	**Minor premise:** C is B
Conclusion: A is C	*Conclusion:* A is C

The undistributed middle is an illogical argument because the conclusion does not necessarily follow from the premises. It is like arguing: everything worthwhile is difficult to achieve; digging a giant hole from Maine to China is difficult to achieve; therefore digging such a hole is worthwhile. This is essentially the same reasoning as is sometimes employed by Trinitarians who argue in this fashion:

Major premise:	God is the Savior.
Minor premise:	Jesus is the Savior.
Conclusion:	Jesus Christ is God.

The reason this argument is fallacious is that just because Jesus and God share a common title, name or attribute (Savior, Lord, etc.) does not make them *identical*. For example, consider this argument based upon the same major premise:

Major premise:	God was the Savior of Israel.
Minor premise:	Men who delivered Israel from enemies were saviors.
Conclusion:	Men who delivered Israel from enemies were God.

Conclusion

Jesus Christ said that the Word of God is truth. God specifically says in Scripture that He wants men to come to a knowledge of this truth. If Christians are going to do so, then there must be an appreciation of what is logical and what is not. Otherwise, nonsense masquerading as spiritual truth will go undetected and the quality of people's lives will suffer as a result of believing it.

L

The Name Yahweh

Throughout the last century, there has been much debate about the "real" name of God. Some people insist that the real name of God is *Jehovah* and that we should use only that name when speaking of Him. Others insist that "Yahweh" best represents the name of God. The linguistic evidence is clear that "Yahweh" is to be preferred over Jehovah, and either one is to be preferred over the word, LORD, which is simply a generic title. God has a name, and He has not only let us know what it is, He Himself has used it more than 6,000 times in the Bible. It is important to know that the ancient Hebrew language was written without vowels (with the exception of two letters, *aleph* and *ayin*, which are often called consonantal vowels). For that reason, the exact pronunciation of many Hebrew words has been hotly debated by scholars down through the centuries, but none more so than the name of God.

The name of God is made up of four Hebrew consonants, and for that reason it is often referred to as the "Tetragrammaton" (literally, "four letters"). The four consonants are *yod*, *heh* (pronounced "hay"), *waw*, *heh*, or *YHWH*. The first letter of God's name, the *yod*, is the smallest letter in the Hebrew alphabet and was made famous when Christ said that not a "jot" or "tittle" would disappear from the Law until all was fulfilled (Matt. 5:18 - KJV). The "jot" of Christ's statement (according to the Greek text) was the *yod* of the Hebrew alphabet and looks something like an apostrophe, and Christ was saying that not the smallest letter in any word in the Law will disappear until it was fulfilled.

It became a custom in Judaism not to pronounce the name of God because it was considered too holy. When a reader of the Hebrew text came to the name of God, he **saw** *YHWH* but **said** *Adonay* ("Lord"). Obviously, with no vowels in the word and no recorded history of pronunciation, the actual pronunciation was lost in antiquity. The best we can do now is try to reconstruct the way it would have been pronounced. The question about the sacred name thus becomes twofold: how to transliterate it into English (and other languages), and how to pronounce it?

There is no letter "J" in Hebrew, nor does Hebrew have any letter that makes the sound made by the English "J." There is a "J" in Latin, but it was pronounced as a "Y." Because the Latin "J" sounds like the Hebrew "Y" (*yod*), the Hebrew words that started with the "Y" sound were all transliterated into Latin with a "J" to keep the pronunciation the same. Thus, when one reads in his Bible words with a "J," that is not the way the Hebrew text reads. "Jerusalem" in both Hebrew and Latin is pronounced with a "Y" sound as "Ye-rus-a-la-yim." "Jacob" is pronounced as "Ya-a-qob," "Jonah" as "Yo-nah" and Joshua (which is the name translated as both "Joshua" and "Jesus" in the New Testament) as "Ye-ho-shu-a," which becomes shortened to "Ye-shu-a."

Like the Hebrew and Latin, the Greek has no "J" or "J sound." But unlike Hebrew and Latin, the Greek does not have a "Y" either. So, when the Hebrew was translated into Greek, the letter "I" was chosen to represent the *yod* of the Hebrew. Thus, in Greek, Jerusalem is "Ie-ro-so-lu-ma," and "Jesus" is "I-e-sous" (pronounced "E-A-Soos." The Greek "I" is usually pronounced like a long "e").

Because Jews would never pronounce the name of God, the Hebrew scribes of the Middle Ages took the vowels from *Adonay* ("Lord") and put them with the Hebrew letters *YHWH* to remind them to say *Adonay* when they saw the sacred name. When this hybrid Hebrew word was transliterated into Latin, using the Latin "J" for the *yod* and the vowels from the Hebrew *Adonay* (which do not translate exactly into Latin), Latin scribes arrived at *Jehovah* as the name of God. Of course, it would be pronounced the way any Latin "J" would be pronounced, as "Yehovah."

However, **Jehovah** would not be the correct way to bring the name of God over into English. First, there simply was no "J" and no "J" sound in Hebrew or Greek. Even if we were going to bring the Latin *Jehovah* over into English, we should still preserve the pronunciation and say "*Yehovah*." Second, the vowels that were brought into the Latin *Jehovah* were from the Hebrew word *Adonay* and were not related to *YHWH* at all. Third, in the English language, the letter "J" (and the "J sound") was the last letter added to the alphabet. In the late Middle Ages when two "I's" appeared together, scribes often added a "tail" to the last one. During the 1600's, it became customary that when an "I" appeared at the beginning of a word, it was given a tail. Thus, the letter we now know as "J" developed, and the modern sound we now associate with the "J," which was to some degree used earlier, became associated with it.

Using the Septuagint, other ancient sources, and the best understanding of scholars as to how the vowels and consonants of ancient Hebrew were put together, modern scholars say that the name of God was probably pronounced **Yahweh**. Scholars have long noticed the connection between Exodus 3:14 (KJV), "...I AM THAT I AM...," (better translated, "...I will be what I will be...") and Yahweh. The main thrust of "...I will be what I will be..." was that God was a covenant God to the Hebrews and, unlike the nations that had a god for every possible need, God would be for His people whatever they needed. They needed no God but one.

Although the Jews do not pronounce the name of God, we believe they misapply the Scriptures they use as evidence for not doing so. For example, Exodus 20:7 is the third of the Ten Commandments, and it says, "You shall not misuse the name of the LORD [**Yahweh**] your God [*Elohim*]…," but we hardly see how *saying* God's name is misusing it. Similarly, Leviticus 24:16 is used to show that God's name must not be spoken. That verse says, "anyone who blasphemes the name of the LORD [**Yahweh**] must be put to death.…" Again, we see no reason to interpret that verse as a command not to say the name of God. Anyone reading the Hebrew Text, without the custom of saying "LORD" while actually reading **Yahweh**, would say the name of God more than 6000 times! Surely, if God did not want his name to be spoken, He would not have had it written so often. He could have just as easily written, "the LORD," if that is what He wanted people to say. Furthermore, He told Moses, "…This is my name forever, the name by which I am to be remembered from generation to generation." (Exod. 3:15). If we do not pronounce His name, how can it be the name by which He is to be remembered?

Christians should make an effort not to offend people, but there are times when people are offended by things that are godly. When someone's offense is rooted in ungodliness or harmful tradition, Christians must feel free to move ahead in their Christian activities without being curtailed by the offense the other person is feeling. Such is the case with the name Yahweh. We are aware that some people are offended by the use of the name, "Yahweh." However, as we have said, we believe that not saying God's name is a traditional practice with no basis in Scripture, and that it has harmful consequences. It hinders us from knowing God as a personal God by replacing His name with a title. It causes confusion for Bible readers, especially those who are never taught that "LORD" is different from "Lord" in the Hebrew text, and it certainly hinders the understanding of the Bible among anyone who is listening to it being read, such as children, or people listening to a recorded reading. It even causes translators to have to place the word "the" in the Bible when there is none in the Hebrew text, in order to make "Yahweh" into "*the* LORD."

Another problem caused by calling Yahweh "LORD" is that there are other individuals in the Bible called "lord." Furthermore, there are times when God calls Himself "Lord," using other Hebrew words for Lord. Calling Yahweh "LORD" does not properly set apart His personal name as the text clearly does. We believe that God had His name Yahweh written in the text so people would see it and say it, and we believe that it makes it easier to recognize the true God for who He is and what He does when we read the Hebrew Scriptures and say "Yahweh." Throughout this book we have noted the occurrences of the Tetragrammaton by the use of small capital letters (LORD), and there are occasions where we have actually used the transliteration **Yahweh**.

Modern Versions and Trinity "Proof Texts"

The following table appeared in an article by Victor Perry, titled "Problem Passages of the New Testament in Some Modern Translations: Does the New Testament Call Jesus God?"[1] This article discusses the places in the New Testament where the Greek *can* be understood (either by the right choice of witnesses or by the appropriate grammatical interpretation) to call Jesus "God," but this translation is not an open-and-shut case. We reproduce here the table Perry created to show which versions support the translation of Jesus as "God" in these "Trinitarian proof texts."

Please note that no verse is rendered in a Trinitarian way in every version. This is more evidence that the Bible does not support the Trinity, especially when we compare the above verses with all the verses that clearly separate Christ and God. It can also be seen from this table that James Moffatt, a Trinitarian (considered a "liberal" by his Trinitarian colleagues), has translated all but one of these verses in a way that supports a non-Trinitarian view. He did so because he was diligently handling each verse in its context, both immediate and remote, without a theological axe to grind. He is still widely respected among scholars and considered to be one of the finest Bible scholars and exegetes of the 20th Century, and the grandfather of the modern English versions. The reader is encouraged to read Moffatt's translation of the Bible (Kregel Pub., Grand Rapids, MI, 1994). For proof of Moffatt's

---

1. Expository Times 87, (1975–76), pp. 214 and 215.

Trinitarianism, tempered by a commitment to honestly portray Jesus' humanity, we offer the following excerpt from a lecture he gave at Yale in 1940:

> Dogmatic definitions of the Trinity have their place and value, but the right focus for seeing the divine humanity of the Lord is missed when insufficient regard is paid to the moral ideal revealed in his person and teaching on earth.

From "*Jesus Christ the Same,*" from the Shaffer Lectures for 1940 at Yale University, (Abingdon Cokesbury Press, N.Y., 1940), p. 90.

In the chart below a "†" indicates that the version adopts a translation that calls Jesus God, and "x" denotes that the version adopts the opposite view.

	John 1:1	John 1:8	Acts 20:28	Romans 9:5	2 Thessalonians 1:12	Titus 2:13	Hebrews 1:8	2 Peter 1:1
KJV	†	x	†	†	x	x	†	x
RV	†	x	x	x	x	†	†	†
RV mg		†	x	x		x		x
RSV	†	x	x	x	x	†	†	†
RSV mg		†	x	†		x	x	†
NEB	†	x	x	x	x	†	†	†
NEB mg		†	x	†		x	x	
Moffatt	†	x	x	x	x	x	x	†
Goodspeed	x	x	†	x	x	†	x	†
TEV	†	†	x	x	x	†	†	†
TEV mg		x	x	†				
NIV	†	†	†	†	x	†	†	†
NIV mg		x	x	x	†			
MLB	†	x	†	†	x	†	†	†
NWT	x	x	x	x	x	x	x	x
NASB	†	†	†	x	x	†	†	†

Abbreviations:

mg	margin
RV	Revised Version of 1881
RSV	Revised Standard Version
NEB	New English Bible
TEV	Good News for Modern Man: Today's English Version
MLB	Modern Language Bible
NWT	New World Translation
NASB	New American Standard Bible

Textual Corruptions Favoring the
Trinitarian Position

Through the centuries, changes were made to the Greek text that skewed it in favor of the Trinitarian position. Today, Trinitarian scholars recognize these changes, and therefore they are not included in the modern Greek texts produced by the United Bible Society and the Institute for New Testament Research in Germany, which produces the Nestle-Aland text.

It is important for Christians to know something about the history of the modern New Testament. None of the original documents written by the Apostles exist, and scholars do not believe that any first copies of the originals exist. What do exist are more than 5000 handwritten manuscripts of the Greek New Testament from the 2nd century onward. Some of these are as small as a piece of a verse, while others are almost the complete New Testament. The modern New Testament is translated from a text that was pieced together from more than 5000 Greek manuscripts that have come down to us, as well as manuscripts in other languages such as Latin.

When the Lord gave the revelation of the New Testament to the various writers—Paul, Peter, Matthew, etc., they either wrote, or dictated to a scribe who wrote, what we would consider "the original text." This original was copied and sent to churches around the world. It was also translated into the various languages spoken by Christians, primarily Latin, Greek and Aramaic.

Until the invention of movable type and the printing press (around 1450 A.D.), all copies of the Bible were made by hand. A copy of the entire Bible could take a year to write, paper was expensive, and many people could not read or write, so most copies were made by professional scribes. They usually wrote as someone else dictated, and often to a group of scribes. It is easy to see how errors could arise. The speaker could misread a sentence or the scribe could hear incorrectly. Sometimes the scribes did not take their work seriously enough, and that caused many errors in copying. One of the most notable examples of this was in Miniscule Codex 109. The scribe was copying the genealogy in Luke, and instead of copying the columns of names from top to bottom, he copied them across. Thus, in his copy of the Bible, almost everyone has the wrong father, the start of the human race is not God but Phares, and God ends up as the son of Aram!

Honest mistakes can almost always be easily detected. They are usually in the category of spelling or grammatical errors, or they fit some kind of standard mistake pattern such as skipping a line or copying a line twice, or they are obvious in other ways such as in the above example about the genealogy in Luke. A much more serious problem occurred when scribes *deliberately changed* the text to make it agree with their theology. Although this is very serious, most Christians are unaware that these changes were made. Most ministers do not mention the subject. They have trouble getting people to believe the Bible at all, and usually do not want to introduce any idea that might cause people to doubt the Scriptures. Another reason for their silence is that few ministers, and even fewer churchgoers, are prepared to do textual research, which requires sifting through the manuscripts and arguments to be able to discern genuine Scripture from errors and forgeries.

Christians need to be aware that of the more than 5000 handwritten Greek manuscripts, no two of them are exactly the same. However, most of the differences are *very* minor, like spelling and/or punctuation. Other differences, however, are not minor, cannot be easily resolved, and have caused arguments among Christians as to that which is actually Scripture. This is one of the major reasons there are differences between versions such as the New International Version and King James Version.

Scholars today have computers that they use to compare the various texts. Compared to even a hundred years ago, it is now much easier to sort the manuscripts, determine the dates they were produced, and discover where, when and how changes and errors were introduced. As scholars have compared the texts in their efforts to reconstruct the original, a startling pattern has emerged. It is apparent that Trinitarian scribes consistently changed the text to make it more Trinitarian.[1] The evidence shows that these changes were not accidental, but made purposely. This appendix is a sampling of some of the clearer changes that have been made to Greek manuscripts to support the Trinitarian position. Most Trinitarian scholars today have recognized all of the examples given below as errors produced by prejudiced scribes. For that reason, they do not appear in either the Greek text produced by the United Bible Society or the one produced by the Institute for New Testament Research in Germany. Nevertheless, the extent of this list shows very clearly that as the New Testament was transmitted, scribes would change the text to support their theological position.

The impact of these changes cannot be overestimated. Scholars today, doing computer analysis of the more than 5000 Greek texts available to them, recognize these changes to the text. In the earlier centuries of Christianity, however, a variant manuscript could have "won the day" in a debate and

---

1. We recognize that in the early centuries there were many competing belief systems, and scribes from most of them seem to have altered texts in favor of their own beliefs. However, this appendix is focusing on Trinitarian issues, so that is what is emphasized.

further established Trinitarian doctrine, resulting in excommunication, banishment or death for the "heretic" who lost the debate. The changes also illustrate an attitude toward the text that would astound most Christians today. The idea of changing the Word of God to make it say what one wants it to say is appalling to most Christians. Misreading it or misunderstanding it is one thing, but few Christians would actually take a pen and change the text so that it agreed with their teaching. Yet that is what history shows us Trinitarian scribes did.

The best way to use this appendix is in conjunction with different Bible versions. For even further study, most of the examples below can be found in *The Orthodox Corruption of Scripture*, by Bart Ehrman (New York, Oxford University Press, 1993). Also, they can in large part be verified in the critical apparatus of the United Bible Societies Greek Text UBS 4, or the Nestle-Aland Greek New Testament.

Matthew 1:18
Matthew records the "beginning" of Jesus Christ. Trinitarians who were uncomfortable with "*genesis*" (beginning, origin, birth) changed it to "*gennesis*" ("birth").

Matthew 24:36
Scribes were uncomfortable with the fact that the text said that Jesus did not know the future, so the phrase "nor the Son" was omitted from "No one knows about that day or hour, not even the angels in heaven, nor the Son, but only the Father." That omission is reflected in the KJV, but scholars now recognize it belongs in the text, and the modern Greek text includes it, as do most modern versions.

Mark 1:10
That the spirit came "*eis*" ("fully to" or "into") was changed to "*epi*" (upon). The difference between "into" and "upon" was clear to some early Christians. The spirit coming "into" Christ made it more likely that Christ was "adopted" as God's Son than if the spirit simply came "upon" him. So the "*eis*" was changed to "*epi*." The Trinity is so firmly established today that even though the Greek texts read "into," the NIV reads "on." The Amplified Bible does read "into," and has a note saying that the Greek text reads that way.

Mark 3:11
"…You are the Son of God" was altered by scribes to read "You are God, the Son of God" to help support the Trinitarian position.

Luke 2:26
That Simeon would see "the Lord's Christ" was changed to read "Christ, namely God."

Luke 2:33
Copyists changed "Father" to "Joseph" in many manuscripts. They thought this would "clear up" any possible confusion about the father of Jesus.

Luke 2:41
"Parents" was changed by scribes to read "Joseph and Mary," lest someone become confused about Jesus' "real" parents.

Luke 2:43

"Parents" was changed to "Joseph and his mother," or other similar readings. Also, "the boy Jesus" was changed to "the boy, the Lord Jesus," because if Jesus were God, then he had to be Lord from his birth.

Luke 2:48

"Father and I" was altered to either "we," or "Joseph and I," or "your relatives," etc., lest anyone be confused about the real father of Jesus.

Luke 3:21

Scribes changed "Jesus," who came to be baptized, to "the Lord," because of the emphasis that the word "Jesus" placed on his humanity.

Luke 4:22

"Isn't this Joseph's son?" was omitted entirely, or was changed to "Isn't this a son of Israel."

Luke 7:9

Scribes changed "When Jesus heard this" to "When God heard this," to make Jesus into God.

Luke 8:28

"…Jesus, Son of the Most High God…" was changed to "Jesus, the Most High God" so that there would be clear "proof" that Christ was God.

Luke 8:40

"Now when Jesus returned" was changed to "when God returned."

Luke 9:20

You are "the Christ of God" was changed to you are "Christ, God."

Luke 9:35

Scribes altered the phrase "the one who has been chosen" to "in whom I am well pleased." This is a subtle change, but it takes the emphasis off the fact that Jesus was *chosen* by God, which some people recognized does not make sense if Jesus is God.

John 10:33

Scribes added the definite article to the word *theos*, "god," in manuscript "p66." *Theos* without the article means "god" and is translated as such in verses like John 10:34 and 35; Acts 12:22, 28:6. Adding the definite article changes "god" to "God." Most modern translators ignore the fact that the Greek text reads "god" and not "God," and thus "God" is what appears in almost every modern version.

John 14:9

"…Anyone who has seen me has seen the Father…" was modified by scribes to avoid the modalist interpretation that Christ was a form of God and not a member of the "Godhead." They modified the text by adding the word "also" after the word "Father." This is a change that supports what has become the modern Trinitarian position against the position now held by Oneness Pentecostals, but the change in the text is recognized by modern scholars and thus was not included in the modern Greek text.

John 19:5 (KJV)

"Behold the man" was either omitted entirely or changed to "Behold a man" to avoid the fact that Jesus was known as a man.

John 19:40

Scribes changed "Jesus' body" to "God's body."

Acts 2:30

"One of his [David's] descendants" was changed to "of the fruit of his heart," i.e., *like* David, to avoid the idea that Jesus had a human descent.

Acts 10:37

"…the baptism that John preached" was changed to "after the preaching of John" to disassociate the anointing of Jesus (v. 38) with his baptism. It was at his baptism that the spirit came on Jesus and he was "anointed" (and thus became "Messiah" or "Christ"). Most Trinitarians are uncomfortable with Jesus not becoming the Christ until his baptism, so some scribes simply disassociated the two events by removing the baptism from the verse.

Acts 13:33

"By raising up Jesus" was changed to "by raising up Jesus Christ." This change to the text avoided the "problem" that Jesus was not thought by some to be the Christ until his resurrection.

Acts 20:28

"Keep watch over yourselves and all the flock of which the Holy Spirit has made you overseers. Be shepherds of the church of God, which he bought with his own blood." This verse has been represented in many ways in different Greek texts, making it obvious that scribes were changing the text. The challenge to modern scholars is to try to discover the original reading among all the variant readings. The major variant readings are:

1. "…the church of God which He purchased with the blood of His own (Son)."

2. "…the church of God which He purchased with His own blood."

3. "…the church of the Lord which He purchased with His own blood."

4. "…the church of the Lord and God which He purchased with His own blood."

There is no reference anywhere in the Bible to "the blood of God." This reading, already suspect on textual grounds, thus becomes suspect on logical grounds also. The scholars who author the United Bible Society Greek Text, as well as those who author the Nestle-Aland Greek New Testament, all agree that "*tou haimatos tou idiou*" (reading #1 above) is original. As the Trinitarian debate raged, it would have been quite easy for a scribe to change "*tou haimatos tou idiou*" (the blood of his own) to "*tou idiou haimatos*" (his own blood, #2 above) by moving a word and omitting the article "*tou*." However, the textual evidence indicates that once the reading, "His own blood" was created, other scribes were uncomfortable with the idea of God having blood, and thus "God" was changed to "Lord" (#3 above). This reading makes sense, but the textual evidence is clear that this was a later change and not original. Then, scribes copying the verse had another problem: some of the texts they were to copy from read "God" and some of them read "Lord," so rather than choosing one or the other, "the Lord and God" was created (reading #4) as a conflation of #2 and #3.

It is interesting that although the Greek text from which the NIV was translated read as #1 above, the translators nevertheless translated it as if the Greek read as #2, strongly supporting their Trinitarian position. Nevertheless, in the notes at the bottom of the NIV Study Bible, the commentators admit that the phrase refers to the blood of God's Son, and not God Himself. They write, "*his own blood.* Lit. 'the blood of His own [one],' a term of endearment (such as 'his own dear one,' referring to His own Son)."

1 Corinthians 5:7
The original text read "...Christ, our Passover Lamb, has been sacrificed." In some texts, scribes added the words "for us" at the end of the phrase to avoid the implication that Jesus' own sins might be included.

1 Corinthians 15:45
"The first man Adam" was changed by scribes to read, "the first, Adam" to get rid of the word "man," since by grammatical implication Christ would then have to be a man also.

1 Corinthians 15:47
"...the second man from heaven" was changed in various ways: "the second man, the Lord from heaven" or "the second, the Lord from heaven" or "the second man is spiritual," etc. The variety of ways this verse has come down to us today shows that it was not just one or two scribes changing the text but rather a number of unscrupulous scribes who thought their theological position was more important than the authority of the Word of God. Any verse stating that Jesus was a man was "a thorn in the side" of the developing Trinitarian position, and attempts were made to expunge these from the text. Thankfully, through modern scholarship, the original reading is agreed upon by scholars.

Galatians 2:20
"...by faith in the Son of God..." was changed in several ways, such as: "in God, Christ," or "in God, the Son."

Ephesians 3:9
"...God, who created all things" was changed to "God who created all things through Jesus Christ."

Colossians 2:2
This verse, although not usually considered a Trinitarian verse, is occasionally used to show that the mystery of God is Christ (i.e., that Christ is God and Man, thus a mystery).

> **(KJV)** reads:
> That their hearts might be comforted, being knit together in love, and unto all riches of the full assurance of understanding, to the acknowledgment of the mystery of God, and of the Father, and of Christ.

> **(NIV)** reads:
> My purpose is that they may be encouraged in heart and united in love, so that they may have the full riches of complete understanding, in order that they may know the mystery of God, namely, Christ.

This verse was a subject of hot debate, and there is ample evidence that scribes changed the text to fit their theology. The Greek texts reflect some fifteen variations, which are listed in

The Text of the New Testament, by Metzger and Ehrman.[2] It is interesting, however, that in almost all of them the possibility that Christ could be God is eliminated. The KJV represents a good example of that.

It is now widely conceded that the original was probably *"tou musteriou tou theou Christou,"* but how to translate that phrase is debated. It can be translated the way the NIV is. It can also be translated "the mystery [Sacred Secret][3] of the Christ of God," and this is the most probable translation. It is difficult to make "Christ" into the mystery [Sacred Secret] of God. Remember that, in Greek, the word *"musterion"* does not mean "mystery" in the sense of something that cannot be fully understood. The meaning of *"musterion"* is actually "Sacred Secret." Thus, although Trinitarian theology speaks of the "mystery" of Christ in the sense that how the Godhead exists or how the two natures co-exist in Christ is a mystery, that is not at all what this verse is saying. Furthermore, "Christ" cannot be considered a "Sacred Secret," because he is the great subject of the Word of God from Genesis to Revelation. A quick study of the other uses of *"musterion"* in the Bible will show that once a "Sacred Secret" is revealed, it can be understood. But the "Trinity" and the "two natures" cannot be understood.

The question that will help solve the translation problem is: "Is there a 'secret' in the New Testament that could be considered the 'secret of the Christ of God?'" The answer to that question is a definite "Yes." The word *"musterion"* is used to refer to the Age of Grace in which we live. Ephesians 3:2 and 3 reads, "Surely you have heard about the administration of God's grace that was given to me for you, that is, the mystery [*musterion*, "Sacred Secret"] made known to me by revelation, as I have already written briefly."

Thus when Colossians mentions *the Sacred Secret of the Christ of God*, it makes perfect sense to see this as a reference to the Grace Administration, which was a Sacred Secret hidden before the foundation of the world but revealed to Paul by Christ. For scriptural documentation on this point, see Ephesians 3:2–9; Colossians 1:27; Galatians 1:11 and 12.

1 Timothy 3:16 (NASB)
"Who" was changed to "God." This change was very obvious in the texts and is openly admitted by Trinitarian scholars. The change produced a very powerful Trinitarian argument, because the altered text reads, "God was manifested in the flesh," instead of "[Jesus] who was manifested in the flesh," which is the correct and recognized reading.

Titus 3:6
"Jesus Christ our Savior" was changed to "Jesus Christ our God."

Hebrews 1:3
Scribes altered the phrase "purification for sins" to "purification for our sins" to avoid the parallel between Christ and the Levitical priests who provided purification for their own sins as well as those of the people.

---

2. Bruce Metzger and Bart D. Ehrman, *The Text of the New Testament: It's Transmission, Corruption and Restoration, Forth Edition* (Oxford University Press, NY, 2005), p. 334.

3. For an explanation of the word "mystery", which comes from the Greek word *"musterion"*, and why the Greek word *"musterion"* should be translated "Sacred Secret", see our book: *op. cit., Gift of Holy Spirit*, Appendix A, the first half of the appendix explains it.

Hebrews 2:18
Although the verse reads, "Because he himself suffered when he was tempted…," the words "when he was tempted" were omitted by some scribes. As the theology that Jesus was God developed, so did the doctrine that Jesus was not able to sin. Thus a reference to him being tempted became a problem, and omitting the phrase in the text was a simple solution.

Hebrews 13:20
"Our Lord Jesus" was changed to "Our God Jesus."

1 Peter 4:1
"Christ suffered" was changed to "Christ suffered for us." As the doctrine of the Trinity developed, it became more and more important for Trinitarians to show his perfection and godhood in life. Thus the words "for us" were added by scribes, lest someone think that somehow his suffering might have benefited him in some way.

1 John 3:23
The text reads "…that we should believe in the name of His Son Jesus Christ and love one another.…" In some texts, the scribes omitted "Son" so that the text would read "believe in his [i.e., God's] name, Jesus Christ," thus equating Jesus with God.

1 John 5:7 and 8
This text was markedly changed to reflect the Trinitarian position. Reading the KJV and the NIV shows the differences:

1 John 5:7 and 8 (KJV)
(7) For there are three that bear record in heaven, the Father, the Word, and the Holy Ghost: and these three are one.
(8) And there are three that bear witness in earth, the Spirit, and the water, and the blood: and these three agree in one.

1 John 5:7 and 8 (NIV)
(7) For there are three that testify:
(8) the Spirit, the water and the blood; and the three are in agreement.

The phrase, "the Father, the Word, and the Holy Ghost: and these three are one," was added by Trinitarians. The NIV, a very Trinitarian Bible, omits the phrase, and the NIV Study Bible has this note about the verse: "The addition is not found in any Greek manuscript or New Testament translation prior to the 14th century."

Anyone who studies the Reformation carefully knows that in the 1500's there was a tremendous Unitarian revival, and the Trinitarian position was being challenged. A response to that challenge was to add a Trinitarian phrase in 1 John. Thankfully, modern Trinitarian scholars recognize that addition, and newer versions omit the phrase. Nevertheless, the fact that Trinitarian scholars were so willing to add to the Word of God to win their debate should cause us to examine other "clearly" Trinitarian verses very carefully.

Jude 5
"…the Lord delivered his people out of Egypt…" was changed to "Jesus delivered" in a few manuscripts to make Jesus exist in the Old Testament

Conclusion

It is important to repeat again that all the above changes have been discovered and excluded from the newest versions of the Greek New Testament and from almost all modern versions. Christians owe a debt of gratitude to the men and women who work to computerize the texts to make them easy to work with and compare. Gratitude is also owed to the honest scholars who work the texts and draw their conclusions from the textual evidence rather than from tradition. These men and women could "fudge" their data to cloak the Trinitarian changes to the text and thus, in some cases, further their own theology. But the modern versions of the Greek New Testament attest to their honesty in trying to restore the original text. We have cited them throughout this book (NIV, NASB, NRSV, etc.).

How To Eliminate Apparent Bible Contradictions

Many Christians agree that the Word of God is "the Truth." Yet from one Bible come thousands of differing interpretations about exactly what "the Truth" is. It was never God's intention that people read the same document and come away with different ideas about what it is saying. God wants us all to be likeminded about His Word:

> **1 Corinthians 1:10**
> I appeal to you, brothers, in the name of our Lord Jesus Christ, that all of you agree with one another so that there may be no divisions among you and that you may be perfectly united in mind and thought.

One of the major reasons why people have different ideas concerning what the Bible says is that they use different rules or standards for interpreting it. We believe that the following principles, called "canons of interpretation" are essential to understand and apply if there is to be any hope of Christians getting to the truth when they read the Bible.

1. The Bible was written for believers, not for skeptics.

The Bible was not written for unbelievers, but for those willing to search diligently for the truth. Some of the language of Scripture is written with the specific intent of confounding those who either do not have ears willing to hear or for those unwilling to be diligent in their study (Prov. 2:1–5, 25:2; Matt. 13:10–13). To arrive at the truth, one must have faith in God and trust in the integrity of His Word. It is important to be diligent in study and realize that God does not honor study for study's sake. God will not open the understanding of those who are merely curious. The Christian must have a heart both to know and act on the knowledge he finds in Scripture. Prayer and faith that God will work in us are necessary for properly understanding the Bible and seeing its awesome precision and harmony.

2. The original text was perfect, and the Bible we have today is complete.

The Bible is the revealed Word of God, perfect in its original writing, including all books of the Old and New Testament, commonly recognized as the true canon of Scripture. Though there were more than 40 "writers," there is but one "Author," God. Since the canon of Scripture (the books that are recognized as authentic and authoritative) has been established by men, the possibility remains open that some text or book might have been added or removed from what God originally "breathed." From our study, we are satisfied that this is not the case. The burden of proof, therefore, is upon those who doubt that the accepted canon of Scripture is indeed authoritative. They would have to show irreconcilable contradictions with the whole of Scripture. As far as we know, no one has ever done so, and all extra-biblical documents brought forth by critics of the canon as "left out of the original" have within them clear contradictions of the God-breathed text.

3. Principles of interpretation vary according to the literary form of the text involved.

The Bible contains language used for every purpose for which language is designed. There is narration, lists, salutations, conversation, poetry, song, fiction, parable, allegory, history, prayer, etc. Principles of interpretation vary according to which of these literary forms a passage is written in. For example, we would not employ the same rules of interpretation to the content of a parable as we would a section of narrative.

The Bible is an accurate and inspired record of many events that were not inspired by God, and thus Scripture quotes the words of many men and women who were not speaking for God. The reader must carefully note *who* is speaking and/or acting. Unless God or Jesus Christ is speaking, or a passage is in narrative form, what is said or done by others may not be directly inspired by God. For example, the Pharisees said Jesus was Beelzebub, but of course that is not true. *What they said* was not true, but *that they said it* is true. What is inspired is the biblical witness itself, not necessarily every word and event that it bears witness of.

4. The original text was God-breathed and without error or contradiction.

The Bible, as the Word of God, cannot contradict itself. No teaching can be right if it creates contradictions with the clear teaching of other Scriptures. The student must never take the position that there are contradictions or errors in the Word, but if faced with an apparent contradiction or error must continue to work until the pieces of the Word of God fit together perfectly like a well-cut jigsaw puzzle. Patience, prayer and continued study may be necessary, and the pieces should never be "squeezed into place." Time is not important, but handling the Word honestly is.

5. Apparent contradictions or errors are due to transmission errors, mistranslation or misunderstanding.

Since the original text was perfect, apparent contradictions must be properly noted and attributed to one of the following three causes, and then they can be explained.

    a. Our failure to understand the original meaning of what is written (remedied by #6 below).

    b. An error in translation as translators attempted to reproduce the meanings from one language into another (remedied by #7 below).

    c. An error resulting from the transmission of the text, as scribes who copied each manuscript made various mechanical mistakes or theological alterations to the text (remedied by #8 below).

6. Properly understanding the context is essential for proper interpretation.

The Bible must be read carefully, with appropriate attention paid to each detail of the context, because God has a purpose for what is said, who says it, where it is said, when it is said, how it is said, to whom it is said and why it is said. Logic demands that words and verses must not be wrested out of context and made to mean something foreign to the original meaning of the text.

7. There is no "perfect version."

No version or translation can properly be called "the Word of God" as it was originally given by holy men of God (2 Pet. 1:21). Every translation is inherently limited. It is impossible to translate from one language to another and get the sense of the original exactly correct, as any translator of any language will attest. Words in the original can contain figurative or cultural meanings that simply cannot be brought into English, or cannot be brought into English without a lengthy explanation (which is the purpose of a Bible Commentary). Furthermore, the exact understanding of English words may vary from person to person and region to region (which is why different English dictionaries have varying meanings for the same word). If possible, therefore, a wide variety of translations must be consulted, and it is most helpful to develop a familiarity with the original languages.

8. No Hebrew, Greek or Aramaic manuscript is "God-breathed."

Scholars do not believe that any of the "original autographs," the texts actually written by Moses, David, John, Paul and others, exist today. Therefore, no one manuscript or Greek, Aramaic or Hebrew text is "God breathed," as the original was. Furthermore, no text assembled by a textual committee or text editor is "the Word of God." However, we believe that the information exists to assemble a text that is extremely close to the original. Modern research, especially now that it is being aided by computers, is ongoing to construct a text that is as close to the original as possible. At this time, to build a text resembling the original, alternative readings from a variety of text families must be consulted in search of the reading that is most likely to be the original, integrating that reading with both the context and the whole scope of Scripture.

9. It must be recognized that the great subject of the "Old Testament" is Jesus Christ.

The subject of the Bible from Genesis 3:15 to Revelation 22:21 is Jesus Christ, the Messiah. The "Old Testament [Covenant]" points to his coming and provides many symbols, types and foreshadowings of his life and ministry.

    a. "The Old Testament" is a misnomer. The word "Testament" is in itself misleading. We get "testament" from the Latin word *testamentum*, which was the Latin translation of the Greek word *diatheke*. A "testament" is a statement or declaration (often given shortly before death).

A covenant, on the other hand, is an agreement between two parties. The Greeks had no covenants and thus had no word for covenant. Any Hebrew reading "the Old Covenant" would immediately think, "Since this is a 'covenant,' if I accept it, what am I agreeing to do?" There are many covenants established by God in the course of redemption history. Each must be carefully noted as to whether it was conditional or unconditional, and whether it has been fulfilled in part or in whole. Because "the Old Covenant" actually refers to the Mosaic covenant that was fulfilled when Christ instituted a new covenant at his death, the Four Gospels are actually part of "the Old Covenant." Thus, when referring to the books from Genesis to Malachi, "The Hebrew Scriptures" (or Tanakh) is the technically correct term.

b. The Four Gospels actually complete "The Old Testament" and record the inauguration of "The New Testament [Covenant]." Of course, there are a few verses in the Gospels that record events after the death and resurrection of Christ. The New Covenant had been technically instituted, but because the covenant promises had not been fulfilled, the people lived as if they were under the Old Covenant. It is often the case with covenants that there is a period of time between when they are actually instituted and when the promises made come to pass. God made a covenant with Abraham for the land, and it still has not been fully realized. Jonathan made a covenant with David, but died before any of the covenant promises came to pass. Just because the New Covenant was ratified "in Christ's blood" does not mean that immediate changes went into effect.

c. The "New Testament [Covenant]" is initiated by the shedding of Christ's blood, is partially enjoyed by the Church, and is fulfilled in the Millennial Kingdom when God's promises to Israel that are now held in abeyance are fulfilled.

10. The words in the Word must be carefully studied to determine if they have a unique *biblical* meaning.

As the Author of Holy Scripture, God can use words in a unique manner. Therefore, the words of God's Word may need to be understood according to a unique *biblical* usage. One must first assume that God uses the words in the Word in their standard usage of the day, but after thorough study, we may find that God has assigned a special meaning to a word.

a. Almost every word has a semantic range of usage that must be considered in order to determine what meaning (or meanings) is appropriate. When there are several possible meanings of a word, the context must determine the appropriate one.

b. Some words or phrases have more than one meaning that fits in the context, bringing a poetic richness to biblical language. These meanings do not contradict, but layer one truth upon another. This is apparent in modern language in the commonly employed figure of speech called *double entendre*.

c. A word may occasionally be used in two different ways in the same verse. Diligent attention must be paid to the nuance of meaning demanded by the context.

d. Where the Bible has already defined a term, it need not define it again, and its meaning should be kept consistent in the interpretation of various passages in which it occurs, unless the context will not permit it.

11. The Bible should be understood literally whenever possible.

The Bible should be understood to communicate literal and historical fact whenever and wherever possible. However, if understanding something literally creates a contradiction with a known fact or another Scripture, a figure of speech is likely being employed.

   a.   As used by God in the Bible, figures of speech are usages of words or sentences that emphasize a particular truth. They are used for the purpose of giving additional force to the truth conveyed, emphasis to the statement of it, or depth to its meaning. If a word or words are used in a figure of speech, then that figure can be named and described, and the purpose of its use determined. As workmen of the Word, we are bound to diligently examine the figure of speech for the purpose of discovering and learning the truth that is thus emphasized. The study of figures of speech in the Bible is highly technical and quite exact. Calling something "a figure of speech" is never to be the refuge of those who simply do not want to believe the literal truth of a passage of Scripture. Some theological systems employ an allegorical interpretation of the Bible. This is not the proper way to handle God's Word, and leads to false interpretations.

   b.   Figures of speech are identified in three categories: 1) idioms, 2) grammar and 3) syntax. Idioms are words or phrases peculiar to a particular language, often closely related to customs and history of a people. Figures of syntax include illustrative figures, types of rhetoric and changes in meaning. The names are derived from the Greek and Latin systems.

   c.   Identification of the figures of speech used in a particular verse can be crucial to its correct interpretation, and the presence and force of figures ought always to be considered by the Bible student.

12. The customs and culture of the biblical world must be understood.

The Bible is written within the culture and thought forms of the Middle East. Its language sparkles with references to the everyday life and customs of the times in which it was written. While these references were well known to those who lived in Bible times, we must become familiar with their manner of life, idioms, customs and culture in order to arrive at the proper understanding of Scripture as it would have been understood in Bible times.

13. A knowledge of the structure of a passage can be valuable for interpretation.

God's Word is the most intricate piece of literature that has ever been written, and scholars have long noticed that much of it has an easily discernible structure that adds beauty, helps with interpretation and testifies to the greatness of the Author, God. The structure of a passage of Scripture can clarify the main ideas, correspondence, parallelisms and contrasting ideas. Structure occurs in two basic forms:

   a. Alternation: b. Introversion:

   A   A

       B   B

   A   B

       B   A

   E. W. Bullinger's Companion Bible and his book: *How To Enjoy The Bible* are good sources for more structure in Scripture.

14. *Identical* things must be distinguished from *similar* things.

The Bible often repeats the information contained within it. For example, the Four Gospels record many of the same events. Chronicles and Kings often repeat the same records. The Prophets often speak of things also recorded in other places in the Old Testament. Thus, there are many times when the same event is recorded with slightly differing details, or two different events are recorded that may, at first reading, appear to be the same event. The Bible must be carefully analyzed to determine that which is *similar*, but not *identical*, and that which may at first seem only *similar*, but which is in fact *identical*.

    a.   Things equal to the same thing are equal to (or *identical* with) each other.
    b.   The same individual, place or reality (like the New Birth) may be called by different names.
    c.   Sharing *similar* attributes does not create identity, only *similarity*.
    d.   Sharing the same name does not create identity (e.g., both "Joshua" and "Jesus" = *Yeshua*).

15. God, like any other author, can use "literary license."

God is the Author of the Bible, and therefore may employ literary license, changing the chronological order of a narrative or breaking up a narrative into a thematic presentation of events or concepts. "Scripture build-up" or "narrative development" describes the process of putting all the pieces together from various narratives into a complete picture.

    a.   1 & 2 Samuel and 1 & 2 Kings are written from one perspective. 1 & 2 Chronicles covers the same basic events, but is written from another point of view and emphasizes different details.
    b.   The Four Gospels break up the entire literary portrait of the Savior into four prophesied perspectives: King, Servant, Man, Son. Matthew, Mark, Luke and John are written from each of these perspectives, respectively.
    c.   The Church Epistles are written from the perspective of doctrine (right belief and practice), reproof (where not believing or practicing rightly) and correction (where teaching error). Romans (faith), Ephesians (love) and Thessalonians (hope) are doctrinal epistles. 1 & 2 Corinthians and Philippians are reproof epistles. Galatians and Colossians are correction epistles.

16. The word "all" can be used in a universal or limited sense.

The word "all" or "every" is used in the Bible just as it is used in everyday speech and writing, either to mean "all without exception" or "all within a particular category." The context will determine the meaning.

    a.   Sometimes general statements are contradicted by particular experiences or other Scriptures. There are many proverbs that indicate that the righteous will prosper, but other verses say that sometimes the righteous suffer and the wicked prosper. The *general* statement is a "truism," though not necessarily true in every case.
    b.   For example, the statement that "all men are liars" should not be taken to mean that Jesus, as a man, was a liar, or that women are therefore not liars.

17. The Bible is full of small words with big meanings.

    a.   Prepositions and conjunctions are especially important for directing the flow of thought in a context, and failure to notice their effect sometimes leads to serious misinterpretation.
    b.   The biblical usage of the noun cases, especially the genitive ("of"), is important to discern properly.

c. The use of the article "the" must be carefully noted, especially when used with the words "holy spirit."

d. The emphasis of the word "also" must be properly placed.

e. The use of "but" and "not" must be recognized for the degree of contrast or negation they signify in a passage.

18. Time, and time words, are essential to proper interpretation.

Time words must be carefully noted in regard to whether an event occurs in the past, the present or the future. Similarly, the use of abstract biblical terms like "sanctification" or "justification" should be identified as to whether they are in the beginning, the middle or the end of a process (or perhaps some combination of the three), and whether the process is ongoing or has been completed in the past.

a. Sometimes two or more events happen simultaneously even if they are recorded at different times or in different books.

b. Sometimes a record is out of chronological order in a particular book, because chronology is of secondary importance in the relating of the narrative. The material may be organized thematically rather than chronologically.

19. It is important to understand biblical prophecy.

Prophecy as foretelling of the future must be distinguished by two criteria: prophecy that is conditional and prophecy that is unconditional. Prophecy must also be examined in light of whether it has been partially or completely fulfilled in the past, partially or completely fulfilled in the present or is totally reserved for the future. Sometimes prophecy can be fulfilled in more than one way at more than one time.

20. It is necessary to distinguish between a believer's permanent spiritual standing before God and his "walk," his state of relationship with God.

The believer's spiritual standing before God and his experiential "walk" must be distinguished. His standing is the position he has as a son of God that he has obtained by grace because of his faith in Christ's accomplishments on his behalf. His "walk" is his actual behavior and experience, including his attitudes, words and actions (Rom. 12:1; Eph. 4:1). For example, a Christian is righteous in the sight of God because of the saving work of Christ (which is why believers are called "saints" (literally "holy ones"), while at the same time he may be lacking righteousness in his walk because his actions do not line up with the Word and will of God.

21. It is essential that the reader determine "to whom" a particular Scripture is addressed.

Not every verse in the Bible is to be applied to every person in every age. For example, we do not sacrifice animals today because the verses commanding that are not addressed to us. As Christians, we must be careful to note those Scriptures that are addressed to us and distinguish them from those not addressed to us. Even though we can learn from the entire Bible, we are not necessarily to obey every command in it.

a. Administrations (sometimes called "Dispensations") must be divided accurately, and basic changes in God's dealings with man discerned. These changes affect God's commandments and what is and is not sin, dietary restrictions, the regulations of civil government, the mode of worship, financial giving, Church leadership, etc.

    b.   Because of differing expectations, commandments, etc., interpretation and application of Scripture must be determined in light of to whom each section of Scripture is addressed, whether it be Jews, Gentiles or the Church of God (1 Cor. 10:32).

    c.   To whom a particular book is addressed must be noted; sometimes this can change even in the middle of a particular passage (e.g., Rom. 11:13).

22. Difficult verses must be interpreted in light of clear verses.

The Bible contains many verses on many subjects, and some of them are easy to understand, while others are more difficult. Usually, it is the case that there are many more clear verses on a subject than difficult verses. Proper exegesis requires that difficult verses must be interpreted in the light of the many clear verses on the same subject. The scope of the entire Bible must be the final judge of what constitutes truth and error.

P

Greek Words Used for Speech Directed to God and/or the Risen Christ

The following words occur in the general category of "prayer," and encompass the entire range of verbal interaction between man and God and/or Jesus Christ. They reveal what we discussed in Chapter 13, that God, the Father of Jesus Christ is practically the sole object of "prayer" in the pure sense. This striking biblical pattern clearly refutes any "co-equality" of Christ with God as an equivalent Source or Provider to whom "prayer," "worship" and "praise" is commanded in Scripture. However, the New Testament reveals some important exceptions to this clear general pattern, which are noted in the columns labeled "Lord" and "Jesus." These show that because of the exalted "Lordship" of Jesus Christ, his first-century followers considered him also to be a legitimate object for all sorts of verbal communication, from conversation to invocation in a crisis. This information ought not to be considered contradictory to the general theme of Scripture, but further evidence that God and the Risen Christ are presently functioning as a "Dynamic Duo."

The following chart shows the various Greek words used and the object of the words spoken.1 In some cases, each word comprises a wide semantic range, so the numbers of occurrences will relate only to that aspect of the meaning of the word that pertains to speech or prayer directed to God or Jesus. Some of the words occur so frequently that precise numbering proved impractical. In those cases, we simply say "many." Some words occur in the Four Gospels, and while not referring to the Risen Christ *per se*, they paint a verbal picture of the relationship that the believers had with Jesus, a relationship that continued after his Ascension. Though invisible, he continued to be considered a palpable presence in their lives. Some of the words are also used in connection with Jesus praying and speaking to God, revealing much about the intimacy of his relationship with his Father. His prayer life was marked by the use of conversational terms more than formal terms for "prayer" in the stricter sense of the term. We indicate when we are including uses of each word in the Four Gospels with the abbreviation (+FG).

---

1. We are indebted to James Vehonsky for contributing the idea and format for the following chart, which first appeared in an unpublished manuscript titled "Should We Pray to Jesus Christ?" Vehonsky reaches a different conclusion than we do, that "prayer" to Jesus is inappropriate and unsupported scripturally. The complete manuscript can be obtained by writing him at 8827 South Park, Tacoma, WA 98444.

To some extent, our difference of opinion with Vehonsky revolves around the terms "can" and "should." He has titled his work "*Should...?*" and we have titled ours "*Can...?*" We would agree with him that Scripture does not specifically *encourage* prayer to Jesus Christ enough to say that we *should* do so. However, the practice was normative among the earliest Christians and ought not to be *forbidden* or *discouraged* either. We find that biblically sensitive believers can come to different conclusions in this area and ought to respect one another's conscience as Romans 14 teaches.

	God	Unspecified	Others	Lord	Jesus
eucharisteo (verb); thanks	20	7	1	0	0
eucharistia (noun); thanks	5	10	0	0	0
charis (noun) grace, favor, thanks (translated "thanks" 11x in the NIV) (+FG)	7	2	1 (Luke 17:9)	0	1 (1 Tim. 1:12) Paul *thanks* Christ for giving him a ministry
lego (verb) to say, to speak, to talk to, to answer (includes *eipon*, the aorist form of *lego*)	Matthew 27:46; Acts 4:24; Many	Many	Many	Acts 22:19 Paul *speaking* to Jesus who appears during prayer	Acts 7:59 Stephen *saying* to Jesus; Revelation 5:9
proseuchomai (verb) pray	3	Many	0	Acts 1:24 The Apostles pray to the Lord Jesus regarding Judas' successor	0
proseuche (noun); prayer	5	Many	0	0	0
deomai (verb) pray, request, (+FG)	2	4	8	4	4
deesis (noun) prayer (+FG)	4	14	0	1 (1 Pet. 3:12) referring to God	0
euche (noun) vow, prayer	0	3	0	0	0
euchomai (verb) ask (+FG)	2	5	0	0	0
aiteo (verb) ask (+FG)	22	9	30	0	6 (Including the FG)
aiteema (noun) request, the thing asked for (+FG)	1	1	1	0	0
erotao (verb) to inquire, ask (+FG)	6 (Christ to God)	1	32		24
parakaleo (verb) beseech, appeal to, plead with (+FG)	1 (Matt. 26:53)	0	90	(2 Cor. 12:8) Paul *pleaded* the Lord (Jesus)	17
epikaleo (verb) to call upon (+FG)	3	1	15	8	3 (Acts 7:59 - NASB) Stephen *called upon* the "Lord Jesus"
krazo (verb) to cry in supplication (+FG)	2	10	26	6 (Acts 7:60 - NASB) Stephen *cried out* to Jesus	11
anthomologeomai (verb) to thank, to praise	1 (Luke 2:38 - NASB)	0	0	0	0
enteuxis (noun) petition, pray	2 (1 Tim. 2:1 - NASB, and 4:5)	0	0	0	0

Do you have to believe in the Trinity to be saved?

According to orthodox Trinitarian doctrine, if a person claims to be a Christian but does not believe in the Trinity, he is not saved.[1] Is that the truth? Not from the evidence in the Bible. In fact, the evidence in Scripture is that a person can be saved without even knowing about the Trinity. Before we discuss the issue further, however, we need to know the definition of the Trinity according to orthodox theologians. This is important because some Christians think they are Trinitarians simply because they believe in the Father, the Son, and a being called "the Holy Spirit." But that is not the Trinity. The doctrine of the Trinity is that the Father is God, the Son is God, the Holy Spirit is God, and together these "three Persons" make one God; and these three are co-equal and co-eternal, the Son having been "eternally begotten" of the Father, and Jesus being simultaneously 100% God and 100% man.

We of The Living Truth Fellowship have encountered Trinitarians who say that a person will be saved if he believes that Jesus is both 100% God and 100% man, even if he does not believe the

---

1. Let us say at the outset, which we will restate later in this appendix, that some Trinitarians do not believe the official position of orthodox Christianity, which is that a person must believe in the Trinity to be saved.

full doctrine of the Trinity. First, that is not the doctrinal position of the orthodox church, and second, the Bible never says that believing Jesus is both 100% God and 100% man is necessary for salvation. Non-Trinitarians assert that a person can be saved without believing in the Trinity, and demand, as did Martin Luther during the Reformation, that we be convinced from Scripture that what the Trinitarians teach is true. Perhaps a good question to begin this study is, "When did God start requiring that a person believe in the Trinity to be saved?"

The Old Testament

The Old Testament does not teach the Trinity, or even set forth that the Messiah would be God. Therefore it is unreasonable to think that someone back then had to believe it to be saved.[2] There is no evidence of anyone knowing about, or believing in, the Trinity in all the Jewish literature before Christ, including the Old Testament, the Jewish targums and commentaries, the Apocrypha or other apocryphal literature, or the Dead Sea Scrolls.

It is well known that the foundational tenet of the Old Testament faith was, "Hear, O Israel: The LORD our God is one LORD" (Deut. 6:4 - KJV), and the Jews fiercely defended that faith against polytheism of all kinds. There are some singular verses that Trinitarians today say point to the doctrine of the Trinity underlying the revelation of the Old Testament, but none expound it clearly enough that anyone would have formulated the doctrine of a Triune God from them, and there is no historical record that anyone did (which is good evidence for the validity of our point that all those verses have a non-Trinitarian explanation).

Trinitarian scholars are aware of the fact that the Old Testament does not teach the Trinity. The distinguished Trinitarian scholar Bertrand de Margerie writes:

> "…contemporary exegetes [Bible teachers] affirm unanimously that the Old Testament did not bring to the Jewish people a clear and distinct Revelation of the existence of a plurality of persons in God. In this they agree with the clear and frequent affirmation of Fathers such as Irenaeus, Hilary, and Gregory of Nazianzus: that the doctrine of the Trinity is revealed only in the New Testament."[3]

So Trinitarians admit that the Trinity is not revealed in the Old Testament, and thus both Trinitarians and non-Trinitarians agree that before Jesus' ministry a person did not have to believe in the Trinity to be saved.

The Four Gospels

We have seen that both Trinitarians and non-Trinitarians agree that a person living during the Old Testament did not have to believe in the Trinity to be saved because there was no presentation of the Trinity in the Old Testament for them to believe. However, Trinitarians hold that during the ministry of Jesus, and afterward, a person had to believe in the Trinity to be saved. This means that

---

2. Some people would assert that Isaiah 9:6 sets forth that the Messiah would be God, but there are other ways that verse can and should be understood, and there is no record of any Jew expecting the Messiah to be God. Besides, Isaiah was written almost 750 years before Christ, and the vast majority of the Old Testament believers lived and died before that time. See Appendix A for an explanation of Isaiah 9:6 that fits within the monotheistic framework of the Old Testament.

3. Bertrand de Margerie, *The Christian Trinity in History*, Translated by Edmund J. Fortman. (St. Bede's Publications, Petersham, Mass. Originally published in French in 1975, copyrighted 1982), p. 3.

if Jesus or the Apostles wanted anyone to be saved, they had to teach the person more than was in the Old Testament. If the Trinitarians are correct, we should see a clear presentation of the Trinity in Scripture, but we do not, nor is there any record that Jesus, or anyone else, ever taught the doctrine of the Trinity to anyone in order to get him saved.

To know what people during the time of Jesus had to do to be saved, all we have to do is read the Gospels. Before we go any further, however, we should understand what the Jews at the time of Jesus were expecting in a Messiah. The Messiah the Old Testament portrayed was a human empowered by God. He would be from the line of Abraham (Gen. 22:18), from the tribe of Judah (Gen. 49:10), a descendant of David (2 Sam. 7:12 and 13), a Lord under Yahweh, the God of Israel (Ps. 110:1),[4] and he was to be one of their own people: "Their leader will be one of their own; their ruler will arise from among them…" (Jer. 30:21). Although they did understand these things about their Messiah, the first-century Jews were not expecting their Messiah to be born of a virgin, which is why the angel had to instruct Mary about it (Luke 1:34 and 35). Nor did they expect him to die (Matt. 16:21 and 22; John 12:32–34). They were correct, however, in that they were not expecting a God-man, a "Person" of the Godhead, a part of a Triune God.

When it came to the first century Jews not expecting the Messiah to die, Jesus worked very hard to correct that misunderstanding, teaching over and over that he must die (Matt. 16:21, 17:9, 20:19 and 28, 26:2, 12 and 27–32). But there is not one single account of Jesus correcting anyone's belief that he was a fully human Messiah. Never did he say he was part of the Trinity, or that a person had to believe in the Trinity to be saved. Furthermore, the first century Jews believed that "the Spirit of God" or "the Holy Spirit" was not a separate Person in the Trinity, but was another name for God, just as Yahweh, *Elohim*, or *El Shaddai*, were other names for the one true God. When Genesis 1:2 mentions "the Spirit of God," Jews correctly believed it was another name for God or a reference to His invisible power at work. Yet there is no record of Jesus ever trying to "correct" them and show that the Holy Spirit was a third Person in the Trinity. That is very solid evidence that they did not have to believe in the Trinity to be saved.

If Jesus had taught that a person had to believe in the Trinity to be saved, the perfect time for him to have done so would have been when a young man came to him and asked, "…Teacher, what good thing must I do to get eternal life?" (Matt. 19:16). If this young man had to believe in the Trinity to be saved, this was the time to say so. Instead, Jesus said, "…If you want to enter life, obey the commandments" (Matt. 19:17). Jesus further instructed the man that if he wanted to be "perfect" (which Mark 10:21 equates as having treasure in heaven) he should sell his worldly possessions and follow him (Matt. 19:21). Jesus never said to the man that belief in any aspect of the Trinity was necessary for salvation.

Another time Jesus could have easily taught the Trinity, or even that he was God, was when he traveled through Samaria, the district north of Jerusalem and south of Galilee. The Samaritans were not Jews, but foreigners who had been brought into the area and had adopted some parts of the Jewish religion. The Jews regarded them as horrible pagans and pretenders, and had nothing to do with them. When Jesus met the woman at the well in Samaria, she said she knew the Messiah was coming (John 4:25). However, her understanding of the Messiah would have come from the Old Testament and what her tradition taught, so when Jesus said, "…I who speak to you am he" (John 4:26), she never would have concluded that he was somehow God, or part of a Triune God. If she needed to

---

4. Psalm 110:1, when properly understood, is one of the great pieces of evidence in Scripture that Jesus was human and not "God." See Appendix A, Psalm 110:1.

believe that to be saved, Jesus would have taught it to her, as well as to the people from Samaria who came to meet him after the woman told them about him (John 4:41). However, there is no hint in Scripture he ever mentioned the Trinity. Did he ignore their need for salvation? Of course not. What is evident from this record is that a person did not have to believe in the Trinity to be saved.

Another example of a person being saved without believing in the Trinity is the immoral woman who anointed Jesus' feet with her tears while he was eating. All Jesus said to her was, "…Your sins are forgiven" and "…Your faith has saved you; go in peace" (Luke 7:48 and 50). Are we to believe that somehow this Galilean Jewess knew that Jesus was part of a Triune God, and by knowing that she gained salvation? Such an assumption would be to stretch the record beyond credible limits. The woman was a sinner, not a theologian, and if she went to synagogue at all, which is questionable, she would have known about the Messiah only from what the Old Testament taught. There is no reason to believe that she somehow pasted together statements Jesus had made to build a case for the Trinity, and then believed it. She, like millions of Old Testament believers before her, was saved without believing in the Trinity.

Theologians build the doctrine of the Trinity with verses pulled from all over the Bible, but only a few actually spoken by Jesus can even be used to support it, and none of those mention "the Holy Spirit" in any decisive sense as being a distinct "Person."[5] Furthermore, each statement Jesus made that modern Trinitarians use to paste together their case for a Trinity has an alternative, non-Trinitarian explanation. This is important, because although a person who already believes in the Trinity might think that what Jesus said supported the doctrine of the Trinity, someone who never heard of the Trinity would understand what Jesus said in a totally different way.

A good example of this was when Jesus said, "…if you do not believe that **I am the one I claim to be**, you will indeed die in your sins" (John 8:24). Some Trinitarians see this statement as supporting the Trinity, but someone who did not know that doctrine would understand the statement in light of what he knew and believed, especially if what Jesus said made sense in terms of the beliefs he already held. In the case of John 8:24, the Jews he was speaking to were expecting a human Messiah and that people who rejected him would die in their sins. What Jesus said fit their understanding perfectly. Jesus had to have known that, so if he was trying to say that anyone who did not believe in the Trinity was unsaved, he did a poor job of making his point. He certainly never stated that if someone does not believe in the Trinity, he would die in his sins.

If a person did need to believe in the Trinity to be saved, we would expect that Jesus would have been at least as aggressive in teaching that as he was about correcting other erroneous beliefs of his day. For example, we mentioned earlier that Jesus plainly taught his disciples that he had to die, even though they were not expecting it. He also corrected the Sadducees concerning the Resurrection very plainly, telling them, "You are in error" (Matt. 22:29). Time after time he openly corrected the errors believed by the people around him. In the Sermon on the Mount he corrected many erroneous teachings, including the people's misunderstanding about love, revenge, adultery, divorce, and anger, often saying, "You have heard that it was said…But I tell you…" (Matt. 5:21–44). But never in that important teaching that spans three entire chapters in Matthew does he correct their ideas about him being a real human being, or teach them about the Trinity, which he would have were it necessary

---

5. Some people might claim that Matthew 28:19, about baptizing in the name of the Father, Son, and "Holy Spirit" is proof of the Trinity, but it clearly is not a teaching of the co-equality and co-eternality of the three. A first century person knew of the "holy spirit" as the spirit that God gave, which was spirit life and power (Num. 11:17), not a "Third Person" of a Trinity. See our book: *Op. cit., The Gift of Holy Spirit: The Power to be Like Christ.*

to believe that to be saved. After all, which is the more important theological mistake, being wrong about anger, or taking an oath, or praying in public, or being wrong about the true nature of God?

If the Trinity were a true doctrine, and especially if a person has to believe it to be saved, we would have expected Jesus to say something in the Sermon on the Mount such as this:

"You have heard that it was said" that God is One, "but I tell you" that God is a Trinity, one God made of three distinct Persons.[6] "You have heard that it was said" that the Messiah will be one from among you, "but I tell you" he will be more than that, he will be God incarnated in human flesh. "You have heard that it was said" that the holy spirit is the invisible spirit power of God, "but I tell you" that Holy Spirit is much more than that, he is the third Person in a Triune Godhead."

Are we to believe that Jesus openly and plainly corrected errors in people's understanding about many different issues while never correcting people's erroneous thinking that he was the human Messiah they expected, and not a "Person" in a Triune God, especially if their error meant they were not saved? That makes no sense. He did not even correct his closest disciples about the Trinity. When Jesus asked Peter, "…Who do you say I am?" (Matt. 16:15) …Peter answered, "You are the Christ, the Son of the Living God" (Matt. 16:16). Peter believed Jesus was the Christ he had been taught about in synagogue and was expecting, not God in the flesh who was part of the Trinity. Yet Jesus did not correct Peter, but instead complimented him on his insight, saying he was "Blessed" (Matt. 16:17).

Jesus never taught the doctrine of the Trinity or told anyone he had to believe it to be saved. Furthermore, he never corrected anyone's belief that he was the human Messiah they expected and not part of a Triune God. When he taught about himself from the Old Testament, as he did in Nazareth when he quoted from Isaiah (Luke 4:18 and 19), he never even hinted that there was more to believe about him than the Old Testament Scriptures taught. Nor did he ever correct anyone's understanding about the Holy Spirit. All this is conclusive evidence that Jesus did not teach that a person had to believe in the Trinity to be saved.

The Book of Acts

The book of Acts records the teachings of the Apostles and disciples as they spread the good news of Jesus. It is reasonable that if the doctrine of the Trinity were a truth not revealed in the Old Testament but necessary for Christian salvation, it should be clearly taught in Acts. After all, many Trinitarians believe that for an unbelieving Jew or pagan Gentile to be saved, he must believe in the Trinity. The book of Acts, then, is a proving ground for what unbelievers need to know in order to be saved. So what do we see in Acts? In all the sermons in the book of Acts there is not one presentation of the Trinity.

What Acts does record very clearly is that Jesus was a man, the servant of God, who was God's anointed ("Messiah" in Hebrew, "Christ" in Greek), who died, whom God raised from the dead and exalted, and who will be the future King and Judge of all mankind. Furthermore, those who hear and believe that message get saved without hearing anything about the Trinity. Time after time Paul and others went into Jewish Synagogues and taught from the Old Testament about the Messiah, explaining that Jesus was the Messiah the Old Testament spoke of, and that teaching was enough

---

6. The "You have heard that it was said" and "but I tell you" are in quotes because that is the exact format Jesus used in the Sermon on the Mount (cp. Matt. 5:21, 22, 27, 28, 31 and 32, etc.).

to get people saved. There is not one record of Paul or others saying that what the Old Testament taught about the Messiah was not enough for salvation.

What follows are summations of teachings in the book of Acts when believers preached the Word of God in order to get people saved. Almost every record listed below includes something that a speaker actually said to convince the audience about Jesus. If a record in Acts simply notes that someone such as Paul taught, but it does not record what he said, or if the purpose of the conversation was not about getting someone saved, the record is not included in the list below. Each will show that there was no presentation of the Trinity, or that believing it was necessary for salvation.

Acts 2:14–36. Peter spoke to the crowd of unsaved Jews in the Temple on the Day of Pentecost, just 50 days after Jesus was crucified. These Jews did not live in Israel, but had come to Jerusalem from the far reaches of the Roman Empire, including Parthia, Mesopotamia, Egypt, Libya, Rome, Crete, Arabia, and from parts of what today is the nation of Turkey (Acts 2:9–11). They had not heard Jesus or the Apostles teach. All they knew about the Messiah was from the Old Testament and traditions about him, none of which included the doctrine of the Trinity or Jesus being God. Thus it is fair to conclude that if they needed to believe in the Trinity to be saved, someone would have to teach them about it. On Pentecost, however, Peter presented Jesus as a "man approved of God" who was crucified and whom God raised from the dead, much of which he backed up by quoting the Old Testament. Peter never mentioned the Trinity or Jesus being God, **yet about three thousand people got saved that day.** This is conclusive evidence that on the Day of Pentecost, the start of the Christian Church, a person did not have to believe in the Trinity to be saved.

Acts 3:12–26. Peter spoke to a crowd that had gathered in the Temple because a lame man had been miraculously healed. This crowd gathered inside the Temple, so they would have been Jews or interested Gentiles who were not saved. That means that they had either not heard, or had rejected, earlier presentations about Jesus being the Messiah, including the one taught close to the very spot where they were standing on the Day of Pentecost.[7] Peter taught these unsaved men and women that the God of Abraham, Isaac, and Jacob glorified "His servant Jesus." He further taught that Jesus had died and God had raised him from the dead. He also quoted Deuteronomy 18:15, that Christ was to be "a prophet like me [Moses]." There was nothing in Peter's teaching about the Trinity or Jesus being God, and yet so many people were saved that the number of **Christians in Jerusalem grew to 5,000 men**, not counting the women and children (Acts 4:4).

Acts 4:8–12. Peter spoke to the Jewish rulers and elders, and taught that although they had crucified Jesus of Nazareth, God raised him from the dead. He did not make any presentation of the Trinity or Jesus being God. These were mostly the same men who were at Jesus' trials, and there is no record in Scripture that any of them believed what Peter said and got saved.

Acts 5:29–32. Peter and the Apostles were again brought before the Jewish rulers, and Peter again presented to them that although the Jews had killed Jesus, God had raised him from the dead and set him at his right hand as "Prince and Savior" (Acts 5:31). Nothing Peter said referred to a Trinity of co-equal, co-eternal beings in a Godhead. The vocabulary of "God" raising up Jesus and setting him at His right hand fit exactly with what these leaders already believed about the Messiah from the Old Testament, because Peter spoke of two separate beings, a ruler (God) and His "right hand man" (Jesus), not one Being in three persons. This is confirmed by the fact that Jesus is then referred to as the "Prince," not "God." As when Peter was before the rulers earlier, there is no record that

---

7. Tradition teaches that the Pentecost experience happened in the Upper Room, but it happened in the Temple, as a close study of Acts will show, and as more and more scholars are attesting in their writings.

any of them got saved, but if they had believed Peter, they would have been saved without knowing anything of the doctrine of the Trinity.

Acts 7:2–53. Stephen made a presentation to the Jewish rulers, and gave a history of Israel. Like Peter had done (Acts 3:22), he quoted Deuteronomy 18:15 that the Messiah would be a prophet from among the people. He asserted that they had killed the "Righteous One," and then spoke about the vision he had that Jesus was at the right hand of God, something the Jews would have clearly understood to mean that Jesus was now God's second in command. Stephen was trying to win the Jews to the Christian faith, and he did so without mentioning the Trinity or that Jesus was God. Furthermore, no one in his audience would have ever thought that Jesus was "co-equal" to the Father when Stephen spoke of him being raised by God and now at God's right hand.

Acts 8:30–39. Philip the Evangelist was told by an angel to meet, and speak with, a eunuch from Ethiopia, which he did. The Ethiopian was reading from the book of Isaiah, and Philip began there and told him the good news about Jesus. The eunuch believed and was baptized with no hint that Philip tried to teach him about the Trinity or that Jesus was God. Actually, if you think about it, how could Philip have presented the Trinity? All the Ethiopian had were Scriptures from the Old Testament. How would he have reacted if Philip had said, "Well, we know the Hebrew Scriptures present Jesus as a Messiah from the line of David, but actually he was God incarnate, 100% man and 100% God, and you have to believe that to be saved"? Because the Old Testament never said the Messiah would be a God-man, the eunuch would have dismissed Philip as being very misguided in contradicting the Scriptures. What we learn from the record of Philip and the eunuch is that the eunuch got saved without ever knowing about the Trinity.

Acts 9:3–6, 17 and 20. The Apostle Paul became a Christian when the Lord Jesus himself appeared to him on the road to Damascus. Paul was a trained Rabbi and was expecting the Messiah, but he had resisted the Christian teaching that Jesus was that Messiah. Meeting Jesus proved that Jesus was the Messiah he had been expecting, but there is nothing Jesus, or Ananias who prayed for Saul, said about the Trinity or Jesus being God, so there is no reason to believe Saul had to believe it to be saved. Furthermore, immediately after being saved, Paul went into the Synagogue and taught. Like all new converts, Saul would have been very enthusiastic about his new beliefs, but there is no mention that he mentioned the Trinity. Instead, he taught what he himself had just come to know, that Jesus was "the Son of God."

Acts 10:34–43. At the house of Cornelius in Caesarea, Peter taught the Gentiles gathered there that Jesus died, but God raised him from the dead. He taught how God had anointed Jesus with holy spirit (there is no article "the" in the Greek text), made him Lord, and appointed him as Judge. He did not mention the Trinity or say that Jesus was God, but the Gentiles who listened to Peter were saved and filled with the power of holy spirit right in the middle of his teaching.

Acts 13:16–41. Paul spoke in a synagogue in Antioch of Pisidia, a Roman province in what today is the country of Turkey. He addressed the Jews and God-fearing Gentiles who were gathered there, and taught a very effective salvation message. He gave a short history of the Jews, showing that Jesus, a descendant of David, was the Savior, crucified by the Jews, raised from the dead by God, and that he showed himself alive to many of his disciples who testify about him. He further taught that God now offers forgiveness of sins through him. Many people were saved. There is no mention that Paul taught any of the concepts of the modern Trinity, such as that Jesus was God, or incarnated, or co-equal with the Father.

Acts 15:1–29. In this record, a dispute arose between Paul and members of the Pharisees who claimed circumcision and observance of the Law was necessary for salvation. A council at Jerusalem was convened specifically for the purpose of discussing what was necessary for the Gentiles to be saved—Gentiles whose belief system had no conception of a Trinity. The decision of the council was to "…not make it difficult for the Gentiles who are turning to God" (15:19) and "…not to burden you with anything beyond the following requirements" (15:28), which were to abstain from food offered to idols, blood, strangled animals, and sexual immorality. Neither the doctrine of the Trinity nor the divinity of Christ was mentioned as necessary for salvation.

Acts 16:30 and 31. Paul and Silas were put in jail in Philippi and were miraculously released when an earthquake hit the area. The jailor asked, "…Sirs, what must I do to be saved?" This is a very important question for this study, because if someone must believe in the Trinity to be saved, Paul should have said something about it. Instead, Paul responded, "…Believe in the Lord Jesus, and you will be saved—you and your household."

Acts 17:1–4. In this record, Paul arrived in Thessalonica, went into the synagogue, and "… reasoned with them from the Scriptures, explaining and proving that the Christ had to suffer and rise from the dead. 'This Jesus I am proclaiming to you is the Christ…'" (Acts 17:2–4). Paul taught from the Scriptures, which in a synagogue at that time were only the Old Testament. Thus, Paul could not have mentioned anything about the Trinity, which, as we have seen, was not in the Old Testament. Instead, Paul showed that the Messiah had to suffer, die, and rise from the dead, all easily shown from the Old Testament, and then he made the case that Jesus was the Messiah. The result was that some of the Jews were won to the faith, along with a "large number" of Gentiles, including a number of the prominent women of the city. There was no mention of the Trinity, yet many were saved.

Acts 17:10–13. Paul and Silas traveled from Thessalonica to Berea, went into the Synagogue, and spoke to the Jews. This is a very important record for our study because it specifically states that the Jews of Berea were more noble than the Jews of Thessalonica because they searched their Scriptures, the Old Testament, to see if what Paul and Silas were saying was true. However, we have already seen that the Trinity is not in the Old Testament, so the what people of Berea would have seen was that Jesus fulfilled the Messianic prophecies, believed he was the Messiah, and gotten saved. They would not have seen that Jesus was one Person in a Triune God.

Acts 17:22–31. Paul went to Athens and spoke to the Greeks. He taught the Resurrection and lordship of Christ and said: "For he [God] has set a day when he will judge the world with justice by the man he has appointed…." Paul said God proved His point by raising Christ from the dead. Paul's short message was effective, because there were a few men who believed. They got saved without ever hearing anything about the Trinity.

Acts 18:1–5. Paul went to Corinth, and as in many other cities, went into the synagogue to speak about the Lord Jesus. Scripture is clear that Paul was "…testifying to the Jews that Jesus was the Christ" (Acts 18:5), and there is no mention that he taught the Trinity.

Acts 18:24–28. Apollos was an eloquent man who knew the Scriptures. He also had been given instruction by Aquila and Priscilla, who themselves had been personally taught by Paul. He helped the believers by publicly showing from the Scriptures that Jesus was the Christ, something he would have shown from the Old Testament. There is no mention of any aspect of the Trinity.

Acts 22:3–21. Paul spoke to a crowd at the Temple in Jerusalem. His testimony was cut short, but nothing he said even hinted at the doctrine of the Trinity. He spoke of "God" (not "the Father") and the Righteous One (the Messiah), which would have agreed with what the Jews believed from the Old Testament, that there was one God, and His Messiah, not that the Messiah was somehow also God.

Acts 25:13–21. Governor Festus was speaking with King Agrippa. This is a very important record for our study, because neither of the two men was saved. Festus was relating to Agrippa what Paul had said to him, and why the Jews were angry at Paul. Festus says that Paul is disputing with the Jews about "…a dead man named Jesus who Paul claimed was alive." Festus did not believe what Paul said, but he understood that Paul was saying Jesus had been raised from the dead. This record conforms completely to the other places in Acts that record what Paul taught about Jesus, which was that he died on the Cross, but God raised him from the dead. The evidence from this record is clearly that Paul was not teaching the Trinity, which would have been so different from what Festus had ever heard that he surely would have mentioned it to King Agrippa.

Acts 26:2–23. Paul told King Agrippa that Jesus of Nazareth was raised from the dead and proclaimed as a light to "…his own people and to the Gentiles." Paul was trying to get King Agrippa saved, and pressed him to believe, saying, "King Agrippa, do you believe the prophets? I know you do" (Acts 26:27). Agrippa realized Paul was trying to get him to be a Christian, and responded, "…Do you think that in such a short time you can persuade me to be a Christian?" (Acts 26:28). Agrippa could have become a Christian that very day had he believed Paul's message, yet Paul never mentioned the Trinity, a pre-existent Christ, or that Jesus was God. Anything foreign to the Old Testament such as that would only have confused King Agrippa. Paul's message of salvation came from "the prophets," who did not mention the Trinity.

Acts 28:23. In this short but powerful record that closes the book of Acts, Paul is trying to convince the Jews of Rome "about Jesus" from the Law and the Prophets, which we know do not present the Trinity. Had Paul tried to convince those Jews that Jesus was both man and God using the Old Testament, they would have considered him out of his mind. What we need to pay close attention to is that a person could be saved by believing only that Jesus of Nazareth was the one who fulfilled those things that the Old Testament clearly taught about the Messiah: that he would suffer and die, be raised from the dead and be exalted to second in command under God Himself.

Paul and the Jews in Acts

There is another way that Acts reveals Paul was not teaching the Trinity: The Jews and even some Jewish Christians who still followed the Mosaic Law constantly harassed the Apostle Paul. In some cases they even followed him from city to city and stirred up the people against him (Acts 17:13). When Paul was in Jerusalem, James told him about all the Jewish Christians who were still zealous for the Law (Acts 21:20), and when Paul was in the Temple, Jews who knew him shouted, "…Men of Israel, help us! This is the man who teaches all men everywhere against our people and our law and this place…" (Acts 21:28). The Jews accosted Paul about all kinds of issues, including differences about the Law, circumcision, and Jesus being the Messiah, but they never once accused him of going against their monotheistic teaching and speaking about a Triune God.

Anyone who has studied the history of the Jewish nation under Greek and Roman domination knows that the Jews were so fiercely monotheistic that there had been riots and rebellions over the issue of idols, and even the Roman eagle, in Israel. Had Paul been teaching that their God was not One God, but a part of a Trinity, that surely would have aroused their anger and come up as an issue in the book of Acts. After all, it would have been at least as important as circumcision, which comes up in both Acts and the Epistles. The fact that at no time in Acts or the Epistles is there any Jewish opposition to the Trinity is very good evidence that it was not being taught by early Christians and was not essential to salvation.

Conclusion from Acts

After reading and studying the entire book of Acts and looking for evidence about how a person gets saved, we must conclude that no one had to believe in the Trinity. Furthermore, Acts is the record of the rise and expansion of the Christian Church, so what holds true in Acts should be true for the entire Church Age.

Romans through Revelation: The Rest of the New Testament

We have now seen that a person did not have to believe in the Trinity to be saved during Old Testament times, and we have also seen from the Four Gospels and Acts that people got saved without believing in the Trinity or even that Jesus was both God and man. In studying the Epistles we see more of the same; that there is no clear expression of the doctrine of the Trinity from Romans through Revelation, and no evidence anyone had to believe it to be saved. God's plan of salvation through faith in Christ is presented many times without a single verse saying a person has to believe in the Trinity to be saved.

Scholars freely admit that the Trinity is never presented as a complete doctrine in the New Testament, but rather is built from scattered verses. The *Evangelical Dictionary of Theology* states, "In the NT there is no explicit statement of the doctrine…."[8] The *New Bible Dictionary* says: "…it is not a Biblical doctrine in the sense that any formulation of it can be found in the Bible…."[9] The *Holman Bible Dictionary* is very clear: "The New Testament does not present a systematic presentation of the Trinity. The scattered segments from various writers that appear throughout the New Testament reflect a seemingly accepted understanding that exists without a full-length discussion."[10] Theologians admit that the New Testament does not state what the Trinity is, i.e., that the Father, Son, and Holy Spirit are three co-equal, co-eternal "Persons," together making one God, and that Jesus is both 100% God and 100% man. Furthermore, there is no clear teaching that a person must believe in the Trinity to be saved.

If a person had to believe in the Trinity to be saved, we would expect to find that clearly stated in the book of Romans. Theologians commonly teach that the theme of Romans is God's plan of salvation. Some assert that the theme is justification by faith, and that certainly is a major aspect of the epistle, but the NIV Study Bible well states what is generally thought of as the major theme of Romans: "…Paul's primary theme in Romans is the basic gospel, God's plan of salvation, and righteousness for all mankind, Jew and Gentile alike (1:16 and 17)."[11]

We agree with orthodox theologians that the plan of salvation and righteousness for all mankind is the theme of Romans, but it never presents the doctrine of the Trinity or states that a person has to believe Jesus is God to be saved. Could it be that the one book in the New Testament whose theme is salvation never clearly teaches how to get saved? The answer to that question is an obvious "No."

---

8. Walter Elwell, ed. *Evangelical Dictionary of Theology* (Baker Books, Grand Rapids. 1984), p. 1112.
9. J. D. Douglas, ed. *New Bible Dictionary*, 2nd Ed. (Tyndale House, Wheaton, IL. 1982), p. 1221.
10. Trent Butler, ed. *Holman Bible Dictionary* (Holman Bible Pub., Nashville, TN. 1991), p.1372.
11. NIV Study Bible (Zondervan Bible Publishers, Grand Rapids, MI, 1985), p. 2161.

Romans 10:9 is perhaps the clearest presentation of how to get saved in the Epistles:

Romans 10:9
That if you confess with your mouth, "Jesus is Lord," and believe in your heart that God raised him from the dead, you will be saved.

This instruction does not require one to even know about, much less believe, the Trinity in order to get saved. However, according to orthodox Trinitarian doctrine, simply obeying the above verse will not get a person saved, because to be saved he must believe that Jesus is not just "Lord," but "God," 100% man and 100% God, and co-equal and co-eternal with the Father.

It is safe to say that Paul penned the book of Romans to the people in Rome in the confidence that if they believed and acted on what they read, especially Romans 10:9, they would be saved. It is also safe to say that Paul knew that Rome was filled with Jews who had only the Old Testament and traditions about the Messiah to rely on, and Gentiles who knew nothing about the Jewish Messiah at all. It is also important for us to remember that the first century Jews and Gentiles would have thought about Jesus being "Lord" in terms of their culture. Although modern Trinitarians assert that in the context of Romans, "Lord," means "God," no Roman Jew or Gentile in the first century would have believed that. "Lord" was a term for boss, owner, husband, or ruler. The Romans had many "lords," and they were not "God." Without clearer instruction on the matter, no Roman would have read "Lord" and thought it meant "God, the creator," especially since Romans 10:9 also says "God" raised this "Lord" from the dead. A simple and straightforward reading of the verse presents two beings: God and the Lord Jesus, whom God raised from the dead. There is no Trinity, and no mention that the God and the Lord in the verse are both parts of the same Triune God, and that a third "Person" in the Trinity is missing from the verse.

Could it truly be that a non-Christian could read the book of Romans, believe its message, and not be saved? We say, "No." The book of Romans clearly shows that Jesus was the Messiah, that he died for the sins of mankind, and that God raised him from the dead, and anyone who believes it is saved. There is just no logical way to read Romans, knowing that it was addressed to the first century people in Rome to get them saved, and say that they would have to believe in the Trinity to be saved.

Perhaps the next best book after Romans to study to see if a person must believe in the Trinity to be saved is Hebrews. The content of Hebrews tells us that it was addressed to Jews (or Jewish Christians) who were intimately familiar with the Old Testament. Every chapter is packed with Old Testament references, and there is much discussion about the Law. Hebrews teaches that obeying the Law will not get people saved, but what will is faith in Jesus, the one who died for our sins and is now our living High Priest, elevated even higher than angels.

The Jews fiercely held to the Law, which was given by Moses. To persuade them to let it go and move on to something else, God would have to offer something "better," and that is a major theme in Hebrews.[12] Hebrews teaches that God has done something in Jesus that is "better" than what He had done in the Law.[13] Jesus is specifically said to be better than angels (1:4); he brings a better hope (7:19); guarantees and mediates a better covenant that is founded on better promises (7:22, 8:6); is a better sacrifice than those offered under the Law (9:23); reminds people of better possessions

---

12. The NIV text note on Hebrews says, "Hebrews could be called 'the book of better things....'" NIV Study Bible (Zondervan Bible Publishers, Grand Rapids, MI, 1985).

13. The verses referred to as "better" use the word "better" in the KJV. Other versions may use "better," or another word such as "superior."

in the future, including a better future country (10:34, 11:16); offers a better resurrection (11:35), brings something better for us than the Old Testament believers had (11:40); and his blood speaks better than the blood of Abel's sacrifice (12:24). Hebrews also shows (without specifically using the word "better") that Jesus was a greater High Priest than Aaron (4:14–5:10) and ministers in a better sanctuary (9:11–14).

Clearly, the book of Hebrews is trying to get people saved or to understand their salvation, and change their attitude toward the Law. It follows the pattern for salvation that we see in Acts and Romans in that it shows that Jesus died for the sins of the people, was raised by God, and is Lord. It never says that believing the Old Testament prophecies about the Messiah is not enough to get someone saved, never says the prophecies about the Messiah were telling only a part-truth about God and the Messiah, never presents the doctrine of the Trinity, and certainly never states that a person has to believe in the Trinity to be saved.[14]

In conclusion, without addressing each epistle in the New Testament, it is enough to say that they set forth the same plan of salvation as Acts, and never teach that a person must believe in the Trinity to be saved. If the book of Acts and the New Testament Epistles, the very foundation of the Christian Church, do not say that a person must believe in the Trinity to be saved, then Christians should take that as the true doctrine of the Church and not insist that a person has to believe in the Trinity to be saved.

The Creeds of Christendom: The Doctrine Develops

We can see the developing and increasing influence of the doctrine of the Trinity in the increasing complexity of the creeds of Christendom, and the clarity with which they promote the Trinity.[15] A creed is a formal and fundamental statement that clarifies a position, and determines who is "in" and who is "out" of the community defined by the creed. It is a type of statement of beliefs. The creeds are important because their content reveals what issues were being debated at the time the creed was written. For example, if a creed mentions baptism, that was important to the group. If it does not, then likely baptism was a non-issue, either because everyone agreed about it without debate, or because it was not important to the group.

One of the earliest creeds in Christendom is the well-known Apostles' Creed. Its date is not known, but we assume from its simple structure and content that it pre-dated the theological debates that raged in the fourth century. The later creeds are much more complex and specifically address the issues of their time. The Apostles' Creed does not mention the Trinity or any fundamental part of the doctrine of the Trinity, such as Jesus or the Holy Spirit being God. Christians who confess the Apostles' Creed believe that Jesus is the Son of God and the Lord, who died and whom God raised from the dead, much like the teachings we find in the book of Acts. It seems conclusive that the authors of the Apostles' Creed did not consider belief in the Trinity necessary for salvation.

The Nicene Creed was developed in the fourth century, likely in 381 by the Council of Constantinople, and by that time much of the Trinitarian doctrine was more clearly developed. It

---

14. Some theologians argue that Hebrews 1:8 says Jesus is God, but that would not be the natural way a Hebrew would read the verse. The word "God" in Hebrew, Aramaic, and most other Semitic languages, was not used exclusively of the Father God, but was also used of angels, judges, or people representing God, and that is the clear context here, because 1:9 says that the "God" in verse 8 has his own "God," which is certainly true of the Lord Jesus, who, as a man with God's authority, would be called "god" but still have a God over him. For more on Hebrews 1:8, see Appendix A, Hebrews 1:8.

15. To see these creeds go to Appendix C where each is listed in full.

states that the Son was "eternally begotten" and one Being with the Father. It also mentions that the Father, Son, and Holy Spirit are to be worshipped and glorified. Despite the clear Trinitarian doctrine of the Nicene Creed, it does not state that a person must believe in the Trinity to be saved. This makes sense in light of the time period in which it was written. At that time many people in the church believed in the Trinity, but many did not. Although many Christians have heard of Emperor Constantine, who presided over the Council of Nicaea in 325 A.D. and was a Trinitarian, most people are not aware that his son Constantius, who was the Roman emperor after him (337 to 361), was not a Trinitarian, and actually was known to persecute Trinitarian bishops. The point is that the doctrine of the Trinity was not settled in the Church yet, so it makes sense that a creed published in the late 300s would include the doctrine of the Trinity but not demand that one had to believe it to be saved.

By the time the Athanasian Creed was written, likely in the late fifth or early sixth century, more than a hundred years after the Nicene Creed, the situation in Christendom had changed. Trinitarians had become firmly in control of the Church, and non-Trinitarians were routinely persecuted, which is why, looking backward through history, there seemed to be so few of them during the Middle Ages. In contrast to the earlier creeds, the Athanasian Creed plainly states that a person had to be a Trinitarian to be saved. It was written in Latin, so English translations of it differ slightly, but it clearly reflects the conflict going on in the Church during the fourth and fifth centuries about the formulation of, and belief in, the Trinity. We know that because the one subject it covers in great detail is the Trinity, and how its members relate to each other. The Athanasian Creed clearly states that a person who does not believe in the Trinity, or the incarnation of Jesus, or that Jesus is both God and man, is not saved, and this man-made document expressed what became the uncompromising teaching of the Orthodox Church.

The Athanasian Creed, and pronouncements similar to it, proliferated through the Middle Ages and were maintained by the Roman Catholic Church, and then by the Protestant Church. Although there was a great resurgence of non-Trinitarian believers at the time of the Reformation, they were persecuted and even put to death by both Roman Catholics and Protestants. Many of their writings were burned, but thankfully a few survived and are available today, giving us a window into non-Trinitarian thought during the Reformation.

The constant persecution of non-Trinitarians resulted in their becoming a miniscule minority through the Middle Ages and Reformation, and in the modern church, something that most churchgoers greatly misinterpret. Most people believe there are so few non-Trinitarian believers because their doctrinal position is weak, but that is drawing the wrong conclusion. The truth is that most who openly shared their faith were killed or persecuted, or were told the Trinity was a mystery they could not understand, and so the vast majority of them learned to be quiet about what they believed. The persecution of non-Trinitarians continues today, and the vast majority of them keep their beliefs to themselves so they will not be ejected from Christian meetings, called "unsaved" (or worse), and rejected by other Christians they have befriended.

The Modern Church
The Sinner's Prayer

Like the Medieval Church doctrine, the modern Orthodox Church doctrine is that a person must believe in the Trinity to be saved, but on a practical level there is some serious double-mindedness going on in the Church. This is true, first when it comes to evangelism and winning new converts, and second, in assuring that long-time Christians believe in the Trinity and are actually saved.

When it comes to evangelism, Trinitarian evangelists and pastors teach the salvation message in a simple way, just as was done in Acts, and believe their teaching saves people. For example, Trinitarians all over the world say they get people saved by having them pray what is referred to as "the sinner's prayer." Although it varies somewhat from church to church, it goes something like this:

> "Heavenly Father: I come to you in prayer asking for the forgiveness of my sins. I confess with my mouth and believe with my heart that Jesus is your Son, and that he died on the Cross at Calvary that I might be forgiven and have Eternal Life in the Kingdom of Heaven. Father, I believe that Jesus rose from the dead and I ask you right now to come in to my life and be my personal Lord and Savior. I repent of my sins and will Worship you all the day's of my Life. Because your word is truth, I confess with my mouth that I am Born Again and Cleansed by the Blood of Jesus! In Jesus' Name, Amen."[16]

This prayer clearly shows the double-mindedness of Trinitarians because thousands of them use it to get people saved in their churches, while at the same time their doctrine says it will not get someone saved because it does not teach the Trinity. We non-Trinitarians say that based on the teaching of the New Testament, anyone who prayed and believed the above prayer is saved. We say that this practice of the Trinitarians is correct, and it is their doctrine that is in error.

The second evidence for double-mindedness among Trinitarians concerns long-time members of the Church who do not believe the Trinity because they either do not know what it is, or they do not understand it and thus do not really "believe it," they just more or less ignore the whole doctrinal position. The Living Truth Fellowship is openly non-Trinitarian, and we have been in many discussions and debates with Trinitarians since our inception. Our experience is that a significant percentage of those who attend Trinitarian churches openly confess that they do not know what the Trinity is, or when questioned, cannot define it accurately. In our experience, many churchgoers think the Trinity is simply that there are three beings, the Father God, the Son, and a being called "the Holy Spirit."

Many of the supposed Trinitarians we have encountered do not even believe that Jesus is God, much less that he is one of three Persons in the Trinity, all of whom are co-equal and co-eternal and who together make up the One God of Christian orthodoxy. If orthodox Trinitarian doctrine is correct, imagine the sad plight of these churchgoers on the Day of Judgment. They would stand before the Judgment Seat, expecting to live forever with Jesus because they believe God raised him from the dead and have confessed him as Lord. But instead of being granted everlasting life, the Righteous Judge condemns them to everlasting death, saying they were not really saved because they did not believe in the Trinity.

We assert that if the pastors of local churches really believed that a person had to believe in the Trinity to have everlasting life, they would teach it in great detail; regularly have sermons, classes and seminars on it; make sure that all the elders and deacons were well versed about it; and sit with new converts and any new members of their church to confirm that the person was actually saved. The actions of Trinitarian churches around the globe are speaking louder than their manual of doctrine. It seems clear that, in reality, leaders in the modern church do not really think a person has to believe in the Trinity to be saved.

---

16. This particular prayer was taken from a website near the top of the list of search results when Google was searched for "the sinners prayer," a search that returned more than 500,000 results, which is indicative of how many churches use the sinner's prayer to bring people to salvation.

We of The Living Truth Fellowship have encountered a number of people in the Church today, including pastors, who believe that the Trinity is true but admit that it is not clearly presented in the Bible, and thus say that one need not believe it to be saved. These Trinitarian Christians have seen that there is no command to believe in the Trinity, and admit non-Trinitarian believers into their churches and fellowships as brothers and sisters in Christ.

The Manifestations (or "Gifts") of the Spirit and Salvation

The modern Church is waking up to the spiritual power Christians have, and many in different denominations are manifesting the power of God by speaking in tongues, prophecy, words [messages] of knowledge and wisdom, and healing. More and more Christians are seeing that the verse, "I would like every one of you to speak in tongues…" (1 Cor. 14:5), is for all Christians. Although speaking in tongues used to be considered something done only by Pentecostals and Charismatics, now people from very diverse denominations and groups are speaking in tongues, even in the Roman Catholic Church (these are referred to as "Charismatic Catholics").

It is widely admitted that the power to speak in tongues comes from God to those who are saved. Speaking in tongues, then, should be one of the great proofs of who is, and who is not saved, and if non-Trinitarians are not saved, they should not be able to speak in tongues. But many non-Trinitarian groups have members who do speak in tongues. In fact, Trinitarian and non-Trinitarian groups are similar when it comes to speaking in tongues, because some do and some do not. However, if speaking in tongues is an evidence of the presence of the spirit, and thus salvation, which we assert that it is, the fact that people who have accepted Jesus as their Lord, but who are non-Trinitarians speak in tongues is very solid evidence they are saved.

Conclusion

Most Christians assert that the Bible teaches the way of salvation. However, if orthodox Trinitarian doctrine is correct, the Bible does not clearly teach how to be saved because it never clearly teaches the Trinity. Could it be that we have to teach a "more complete" message to get people saved than did Jesus, Peter, or Paul? Could it really be the case that a person must believe in the Trinity to be saved, even though there is not one clear presentation of it in the entire New Testament? Certainly not. We assert that the message of Peter, Paul, and others was enough to get their audiences saved and there is no evidence that God, after the book of Acts, somehow changed the rules so that now a person must believe in the Trinity to be saved.

The book of Acts makes it clear that when the early Christians presented Jesus Christ to the unsaved, they taught that he was a "man approved of God" who was crucified but whom God raised from the dead and who now is our Lord. This simple message has been getting people saved for some 2000 years now, and there is no evidence in Scripture or in the practices of churches around the world that one has to believe in the Trinity to be saved. We reject the decision made by men in the Church, somewhere around 500 A.D., that a person must believe in the Trinity to be saved, even though that decision and belief has been supported by Church tradition for centuries now. It is the Word of God, not tradition, that lives and abides forever.

Like the great reformers of the Protestant Reformation, who demanded to be convinced from Scripture that a doctrine is true, we demand that Trinitarians show us from Scripture that a person needs to believe in the Trinity to be saved. If they cannot do so, we respectfully submit that they retract this doctrine. Christians will never be able to achieve what our God wishes, that "…we all reach unity in the faith…" (Eph. 4:13), until Trinitarians stop demanding that to be considered Christian a person must believe something that cannot be proven from the Bible. It would be a wonderful thing if Trinitarians would draw their doctrine as well as their practice from the Word of God and welcome non-Trinitarian Christians as part of the family of God.

Epilogue

In the above study we have shown from Scripture that a person does not have to believe in the Trinity to be saved. However, there is another point we feel compelled to make. If the Old Testament does not teach the Trinity, if Jesus never taught it, if no one in the book of Acts ever taught it, and if the Epistles do not clearly set it forth, can it really be that the Trinity is right doctrine? Can it be that the very foundation of the Christian faith is a doctrine that is never once set forth clearly in Scripture, but is gathered from isolated texts? God very clearly sets forth the foundational tenets of the Christian faith, including salvation, redemption, righteousness, the character of God (that He is love, light, merciful, etc.), the fallen nature of man and the need for a Savior, and the work of the Messiah. Which makes more sense, that God is clear about the foundational tenets of the Christian faith except the most important one, the Trinity, which must be gathered from isolated texts, or that the Trinity is actually a man-made doctrine, built from verses that can each be explained in a non-Trinitarian way? To us, the answer to that question is clear.

Going strictly by the evidence in Scripture, the correct biblical doctrine is the one that can be clearly seen in the Old Testament and was confirmed again and again in the New Testament. There is one God. He is spirit, so His invisible power and nature are known as the holy spirit (or the Holy Spirit). God had a Son, the Messiah, who we know as the Lord Jesus Christ, who was of the lineage of Abraham and David, born of a virgin, lived a sinless life, died for our sins, was raised from the dead, and ascended to the right hand of God. All of this was taught in the Old Testament and confirmed many times in the New Testament without once being corrected to include the idea of a Triune God. There is no reason not to believe that simple message is the correct biblical doctrine.

Glossary

Arianism The doctrine of Arius, a Greek-speaking priest and theologian from Alexandria condemned as a heretic (ca. 336 A.D.). He believed that Jesus was not of the same substance as God and held instead that he was only the highest of created beings.

Arian Of or pertaining to the doctrine of Arius, but also used as a pejorative against anyone who seemed unsupportive of Trinitarian orthodoxy.

Body The entire structure and substance of an organism; the necessary medium for the possession and manifestation of life, whether organic or spiritual. The "Body" of Christ refers to the spiritual "organism" comprised of all Christians with Christ the Head.

Christ The Messiah, the promised one, who was anointed with holy spirit and power. Jesus of Nazareth literally became the Messiah when he was anointed at the baptism of John, as Acts 10:38 corroborates. The ultimate proof that he was the Christ was that he was raised from the dead and ascended to the right hand of God. Orthodoxy teaches that Christ was the eternal being who became a God-man with two natures and two wills; he died for the sin of mankind and then returned to his former state in glory.

Corporeal Of or pertaining to the physical body; of a material nature; tangible.

Deity A god or goddess; the essential nature of a Supreme Being. Jesus Christ is *functionally* equal to God, but does not share the same "essence," because he, in essence, is a "human being," not a "spirit being" like God.

Divinity (a) Being or having the nature or essence of God; (b) Of, relating to, or emanating from, or being the experience of a deity [i.e., God was *the origin of* Jesus, and we *experience* God through him]; (c) In service or worship of a deity; sacred, holy.

2. Super human; god-like [in his exalted position as Lord, Jesus Christ is truly "god-like"].

Essence That in which the real character of a thing consists; the attribute or attributes that make a thing to be what it actually is. [Jesus Christ is not *actually* "God," but the Son of God, a human being].

Flesh The soft tissue of the body of a vertebrate, covering the bones and consisting mainly of skeletal muscle and fat; the body as distinguished from the mind or soul; sinful nature of man; the physical realm as opposed to spirit.

God The sovereign, eternal and Supreme Being; the Creator of the heavens and the earth; the covenant God of the Old Testament (Yahweh) and the Father of Jesus Christ.

Holy Spirit, the The gift of God's nature especially as first poured out in the New Birth on the Day of Pentecost; God's power in action; another name for God; misunderstood to be a mysterious third person in a triune godhead.

Homoousia Originally used in Greek of the same substance (e.g., two ice cubes made of water); was modified for Christian use becoming "identity of being or essence; consubstantiality; identity in nature."

Homoiousian Similarity of being or essence

Heteroousian Difference of being or essence

Hypostasis The mode of being by which any substantial existence is given an independent and distinct individuality; that in which the self-subsistent reality of a thing consists, as distinguished from the substance or being in which the mode inheres (Well, now, *that* certainly clears things up!). A non-biblical word borrowed from Plato to explain the supposed differentiation of the godhead into separate "persons." Hence, the three persons of the Trinity are called "three hypostases or subsistences."

Identical, identity Sameness of essential or generic character in different examples or instances; sameness in all that constitutes the objective reality of a thing. A and B are identical if all that is true of A is true of B, and vice versa.

Incarnate Invested with flesh or bodily nature and form, especially with human nature and form.

Incarnation Literally, a "clothing" or state of being "clothed" with flesh; a taking on of, or being manifested in, a fleshly body; traditionally, the union of both divinity and humanity in Jesus Christ.

Jesus The human being conceived by the creative activity of God and born of the Virgin Mary. Uniquely designed by God to be the Christ, the Savior of the world, he by the freedom of his will maintained his Messianic qualifications by his perfect obedience. In trinitarian orthodoxy, the God-man who was unable to sin who died for the sins of mankind.

Judgment The faculty of labeling, making distinctions or placing in categories.

Logic The science of correct reasoning; the study of the principles of reasoning; the form or structure of propositions as distinguished from their content. Also related to the ideas of method and validity in deductive reasoning.

Matter That which occupies space, can be perceived by one or more senses, and constitutes any physical body or the universe as a whole. In physics, any entity displaying gravitation and inertia when at rest as well as when in motion.

Mode In philosophy, the particular form or manner in which an underlying substance or some permanent aspect or attribute of it, is manifested.

Modal In philosophy, of or pertaining to mode or form as opposed to substance. Modalism is the Christology that sees one God manifest in three forms, rather than three distinct persons.

Mystery Anything that defies comprehension or arouses curiosity because it is unexplained and inexplicable. The theological refuge of those who attempt to justify contradictories. Unfortunately the word used to translate the Greek word *musterion* [which we translate Sacred Secret and to understand why see Appendix A in our book: *The Gift of Holy Spirit: The Power To Be Like Christ*].

Mysticism The process or method of ascertaining understanding of ultimate realities by non-rational means, notably by experience, intuition or meditation; opposed to the use of logic and reason in spiritual matters; confused and groundless speculation; superstitious self-delusion.

Nature The set of essential characteristics (qualities) or attributes of any given individual or class of individuals, that is, the set of characteristics which that individual must have in order to be included in its class.

Person A self-conscious, self aware, individual being; a separate and unique personality capable of independent action; used in a creative sense as one of the three modes of being in the trinitarian godhead.

Prolepsis A figure of speech that anticipates a future event and treats it as if it had already happened. From *pro* "before" and *lepsis* "a taking," i.e., "anticipation." E. W. Bullinger: "An anticipation of some future time which cannot yet be enjoyed; but has to be deferred." *Proleptic*: of or pertaining to *prolepsis*.

Reason, reasoning The faculty or capacity for rational thought, inference or discrimination. The intellectual process of seeking truth or knowledge from either fact or logic.

Redemption Salvation from sin and its consequences through Christ's substitutionary sacrifice; the recovering of mankind from all the consequences of the Fall; the payment in full as ransom for sin.

Similar, similarity Having characteristics in common; very much alike; comparable. If A and B are similar, many qualities of A must be shared by B. In other ways, A and B may be very dissimilar.

Sound argument An argument in which the premises are true and the conclusion necessarily derives from them. Also called a valid argument.

Spirit A "substance" intangible and immaterial, as opposed to "flesh," which nevertheless allows for personality, attributes, individuation and free will. There are many different biblical usages of "spirit," which must be determined by the context of each occurrence. These include angels, demons, the gift at Pentecost, man's "soul," attitudes, and emotions, etc. (See our book: *The Gift of Holy Spirit: The Power To Be Like Christ*).

Spiritual Of, relating to, consisting of or having the nature of spirit; not tangible or material.

Substance In theology, the divine essence or personality as considered common to each member of the Trinity.

Tangible Capable of being touched; discernible by touch.

Theology Man's study of God based on his own ideas, reason, reflection, observations, logic, etc.

Trinity A three-fold personality existing in one divine being or substance; the union in one God of Father, Son and Holy Spirit as three infinite, co-equal and co-eternal persons; one God in three persons.

Bibliography

Alford, Henry. *The Greek Testsment*. Moody Press, Chicago, 1968.

Allen, Joseph H. *Ten Discourses on Orthodoxy*. Wm. Crosby and H.P. Nichols, Boston, 1849.

Arndt, Wm. F. and Gingrich, F. Wilbur. *A Greek-English Lexicon of the New Testament and Other Early Christian Literature*. The University of Chicago Press, Chicago, 1979.

Badcock, F. J. *The History of the Creeds*. McMillan Co, NY., 1938.

Barclay, William. *Jesus As They Saw Him*. Harper and Row, NY., 1962.

Barclay, William. *New Testament Words*. Westminster Press, Philadelphia, PA, 1974.

Barrett, C. K. *Essays on John*. London and Philadelphia, 1982.

Barrett, C. K. *The Gospel According to St. John*. Westminster Press, Philadephia, PA, 1978.

Bauer, Walter. *Orthodoxy and Heresy in Earliest Christianity*. (orig. pub. 1907), translated by a team from the Philadelphia Seminar on Christian Origins and edited by Robert A. Kraft and Gerhard Krodel. Sigler Press, Mifflintown, PA, 1996.

Berger, Peter. *A Far Glory: The Quest of Faith in an Age of Credulity*. Free Press, Toronto, 1992.

Best, W. E. *Christ Could Not Be Tempted*. W. E. Best Book Missionary Trust, Houston, TX, 1985.

Bewkes, E. G. *The Western Heritage of Faith and Reason*. Holt, Rinehart, Winston, NY, 1971.

Bishop, Wm. S. *The Development of Trinitarian Doctrine in the Nicene and Athanasian Creeds*. Longman, Green & Co., NY, 1910.

Boman, Thorlief. *Hebrew Thought Compared With Greek*. Norton, NY, 1960.

Bosworth, F. F. *Christ the Healer*. Fleming H. Revell Comp. Tarrytown, NY, 1973.

Broughton, James and Southgate, Peter. *The Trinity, True or False?* The Dawn Book Supply, 66 Carlton Rd., Nottingham, England, 1995.

Brown, Raymond E. *The Gospel and Epistles of John: A Concise Commentary*. The Liturgical Press, Collegeville, MN, 1988.

Brown, Raymond E. *The Community of the Beloved Disciple*. Paulist Press, NY, 1979.

Brown, Robert McAfee. *The Ecumenical Revolution: An Interpretation of the Catholic-Protestant Dialogue*. Doubleday, Garden City, NY, 1967.

Bruce, F. F. *The Gospel of John*. Wm. B. Eerdmans, Grand Rapids, MI, 1983.

Bullinger, E. W. *The Church Epistles*. 1991 reprint Johnson Graphics, Decatur, MI, 1905.

Bullinger, E. W. *A Critical Lexicon and Concordance to the English and Greek New Testament*. Zondervan Grand Rapids, MI, 1976.

Bullinger, E. W. *Commentary on Revelation*. Kregel Pub., Grand Rapids, MI, 1948.

Bullinger, E. W. *Figures of Speech Used In The Bible*. Baker Book House, Grand Rapids, MI, 1968— originally published 1898.

Bullinger, E. W. *How to Enjoy the Bible*. Samuel Bagster and Sons, London, 1970.

Bullinger, E. W. *Number In Scripture, Its Supernatural Design And Spiritual Significance*. Kregel Publications, Grand Rapids, MI, 1971.

Bullinger, E. W. *The Witness of the Stars*. Kregel Pub., Grand Rapids, MI, 1972.

Bultmann, Rudolf. *The Gospel of John*, translated by G. R. Beasley-Murray. Westminster Press, Philadelphia, 1971.

Bultmann, Rudolf. *Primitive Christianity in its Contemporary Setting*. The World Publishing, Cleveland, 1956.

Butler, Trent C., general editor. *Holman Bible Dictionary*. Holman Bible Publishers, Nashville, TN, 1991.

Buzzard, Anthony, editor. *Focus on the Kingdom*. Atlanta Bible College, GA, 2000.

Buzzard, Anthony F. and Hunting, Charles F. *The Doctrine of The Trinity: Christianity's Self-Inflicted Wound*. International Scholars Press: An imprint of University Press of America, Lanham, MD, 1998.

Carson, D. A. *The King James Only Debate: A Plea for Realism*. Baker Book House, Grand Rapids, MI, 1979.

Columbia Encyclopedia. Columbia University Press, NY, 1994.

Cooke, Bernard J. *Beyond Trinity*, The Aquinas Lecture 1969. Marquette University Press, Milwaukee.

Cozens, M. L. *Heresies*. Canterbury Books, Shed and Ward, NY, 1928.

Craig, William Lane. *Reasonable Faith: Christian Truth and Apologetics*. Crossway Books, Wheaton IL, 1994.

Cross, F. L., editor. *The Oxford Dictionary of the Christian Church*. Oxford University, Press NY, 1983.

Cullman, Oscar. *The Christology of the New Testament*. Westminster Press, Philadelphia, 1963.

Custance, Arthur. *The Seed of the Woman*. Brockville, Ontario, Doorway Publications, 1980.

Danielou, Jean. *The Origin of Latin Christianity*. Westminster Press, Philadelphia,1977.

Dana, Mary. *Letters Addressed to Relatives and Friends*. James Munroe and Co., Boston, 1845, reprinted 1994 by Spirit & Truth Fellowship International, 180 Robert Curry Drive, Martinsville, IN, 46151.

Dart, John. *The Jesus of Heresy and History*. Harper and Row, San Francisco, 1988.

de Margerie, Bertrand. *The Christian Trinity in History*, Translated by Edmund J. Fortman. St. Bede's Publications, Petersham, MA. Originally published in French in 1975, copyrighted 1982.

Dunn, James D. G. *Christology in the Making*. Wm. B. Eerdmans, Grand Rapids, MI, 1989.

Edersheim, Alfred. *Sketches of Jewish Social Life in the Days of Christ*. Hodder and Stoughton, NY.

Ehrman, Bart D. *The Orthodox Corruption of Scripture*. Oxford University Press, NY, 1993.

Eliot, William G. *Discourses on the Doctrines of Christianity*. American Unitarian Association, Boston, 1877.

Elwell, Walter. *Evangelical Dictionary of Theology*. Baker Books, Grand Rapids, 1984.

Encyclopaedia Brittannica. 1999 edition.

Farley, Frederick. *Unitarianism Defined: The Scripture Doctrine of the Father, Son, and Holy Ghost*. American Unitarian Association, Boston, MA, 1873. Reprinted 1994 by Spirit & Truth Fellowship International, 180 Robert Curry Drive, Martinsville, IN, 46151.

Franks, R. S. *The Doctrine of the Trinity*. Gerald Duckworth and Co., London, 1953.

Fudge, Edward. *The Fire That Consumes*. Providential Press, Houston, TX, 1982.

Gilson, Etienne. *A History of Christian Philosophy In The Middle Ages*. Random House, NY, 1955.

Ginsburg, Christian D. *Introduction to the Massoretico-Critical Edition of the Hebrew Bible*. KATV Publishing House Inc., NY.

Gonzalez, Justo. *A History of Christian Thought*. Nashville, Abingdon Press, 1992.

Good, Joseph. *Rosh Hashanah and the Messianic Kingdom to Come*. Port Arthur, TX, Hatikva Ministries, 1989.

Gunton, Colin. *The Promise of Trinitarian Theology*. T & T Clark, Edinburgh, 1997.

Hackett, H. B. *Dr. Williams Smith's Dictionary of the Bible*. Baker Book House, Grand Rapids, MI, reprint 1981.

Halley, Henry H. *Halley's Bible Handbook*, Twenty-Fourth Edition. Zondervan Publishing House, Grand Rapids, MI, 1965.

Hamilton, Edith. *Mythology: Timeless Tales of Gods and Heroes*. Penguin Books NY, 1940.

Hanson, Anthony T. *The Prophetic Gospel: A Study of John and the Old Testament*. T. & T. Clark, Edinburgh, 1991.

Harnack, Adolf. *History of Dogma*, by E. B. Speirs and James Millar. Williams and Norgate, London, 1898.

Hawkin, David J. *A Reflective Look at the Recent Debate on Orthodoxy and Heresy in Earliest Christianity*. Eglise et Theologie, 7 ,1976.

Hick, John. *The Myth of God Incarnate*. 1st Edition, Westminster Press, Philadelphia, 1977.

Hunt, Dave. *In Defense of the Faith*. Harvest House Publishers, Eugene, OR, 1996.

Hyndman, J. S. *Lectures on the Principles of Unitarianism*. Alnwick, 1824. Reprinted 1994 by Spirit & Truth Fellowship International, 180 Robert Curry Drive, Martinsville, IN, 46151.

The International Critical Commentary. "The Johannine Epistles." Edinburgh, T&T Clark Ltd., 1994.

Interpreter's One Volume Commentary on the Bible. Abingdon Press, Nashville, 1971.

Jay, E. G. McGill. *Son of Man; Son of God*. University Press, Montreal, 1965.

Jeffery, Grant. *The Signature of God*. Frontier Research Publications, Toronto, 1996.

Kaiser, Walter Jr. *The Messiah in the Hebrew Scriptures*. Zondervan, Grand Rapids, 1995.

Kautzsch, E., editor. *Gesenius' Hebrew Grammar*. Clarendon Press, Oxford, 1910.

Kittel, Gerhard. *Theological Dictionary of the New Testament*. Wm. B. Eerdmans, Grand Rapids, MI, 1964.

Klassen, William and Snyder, Graydon F. eds. *Current Issues in New Testament Interpretation*: A Festschrift in Honor of Otto A. Piper. Harper and Row, NY, 1962.

Kot, Stanislaus, translated by Earl Morse Wilbur. *Socinianism in Poland*. Star King Press, Beacon Hill, Boston, 1957.

Kreyche, Robert J. *Logic for Undergraduates*. Holt, Rinehart, Winston, NY, 1961.

LaHaye, Tim. *Jesus: Who Is He?*. Multnomah Books, Sisters, OR, 1996.

Lebreton, Jules. *History of the Dogma of the Trinity*. Benzinger Brothers NY, 1939.

Lee, Phillip. *Against the Protestant Gnostics*. Oxford University Press, NY, 1987.

Lenski, R. C. H. *The Interpretation of St. John's Revelation*. Augsburg Pub. House, Minneapolis, MN, 1963.

Lenski, R. C. H. *The Interpretation of St. Paul's Epistles to the Colossians, to the Thessalonians, to Timothy, to Titus, and to Philemon*. Augsburg Pub. House, Minneapolis, MN, 1961.

Logan, Alastair H. B. *Gnostic Truth and Christian Heresy*. Hendrickson Publishers, Peabody, MA, 1996.

Luther, Martin. *Commentary on Galatians*. Kregel Publishing, Grand Rapids, MI, 1979.

Manson, T. W. *On Paul and John*, editor, M. Black. Studies in Biblical Theology 38, London and Naperville, 1963.

McCallum, Dennis. *Christianity: The Faith That Makes Sense.* Tyndale House, Wheaton, IL, 1992.

McGiffert, Authur C. *A History of Christian Thought.* Scribners & Sons, NY, 1946.

McGrath, Alistair. *Christian Theology: An Introduction.* Blackwell Publishers, Cambridge, MA, 1997.

McLachan, H. John. *Socinianism in Seventeenth Century England.* Oxford University Press, London, 1951.

Metzger, Bruce and Ehrman, Bart D. *The Text of the New Testament: It's Transmission, Corruption and Restoration*, Forth Edition. Oxford University Press, NY, 2005.

Moffatt, James. The Bible. Kregel Pub., Grand Rapids, MI, 1994.

Moffatt, James. *Jesus Christ the Same*: from the Shaffer Lectures for 1940 at Yale University. Abingdon Cokesbury Press, NY, 1940.

Moreland, J. P. *Scaling the Secular City.* Baker Book House, Grand Rapids MI, 1987.

Morgridge, Charles. *True Believer's Defence Against Charges Preferred by Trinitarians.* Boston: Benjamin Greene, 1837. Reprinted 1994 by Spirit & Truth Fellowship International, 180 Robert Curry Drive, Martinsville, IN, 46151.

Morris, Henry. *The Defender's Bible.* World Publishing, Grand Rapids, 1995.

Morris, Thomas V. *The Logic of God Incarnate.* Cornell University Press, Ithaca, NY, 1986.

Moulds, A. J. *Thinking Straighter.* University of Michigan Press, Ann Arbor, 1975.

Navas, Patrick. *Divine Truth or Human Tradition.* AuthorHouse, Bloomington, IN 2007.

Neill, S. C. *The Interpretation of the New Testament, 1861-1961.* Oxford Press, London, 1964.

New Bible Dictionary. Wm. B. Eerdmans, Grand Rapids, MI, 1975.

Newton, Sir Isaac. *An Historical Account of Two Notable Corruptions of Scripture.* London: John Green, 1841.

Norton, Andrews. *A Statement of Reasons for Not Believing the Doctrines of Trinitarians.* American Unitarian Association, Boston, 10th Edition, 1877.

Rahner, Karl. *The Trinity.* Herder and Herder, NY, 1970.

Rees, Thomas. *The Racovian Catechism.* English translation, London: 1818. Latin translation, 1609. Polish translation, 1605. Reprinted 1994 by Spirit & Truth Fellowship International, 180 Robert Curry Drive, Martinsville, IN, 46151.

Richardson, Alan. *The Bible in an Age of Science.* Westminster Press, Philadelphia, 1961.

Robertson, A. T. *Word Pictures in the New Testament.* Baker Books, Grand Rapids, MI, 1933, reprinted 1960.

Robinson, John A. T. *Honest to God.* Westminster Press, Philadelphia,1963.

Robinson, John A. T. *The Priority of John.* Meyer Stone Pub., Oak Park, IL, 1985.

Rubenstein, Richard. *When Jesus Became God.* Harcourt, Brace and Company, NY, 1999.

Rutz, James. *The Open Church.* The Seed Sowers, Auburn, ME, 1992.

Ryken, Leland. *Dictionary of Biblical Imagery.* InterVarsity Press, Downers Grove, IL, 1998.

Schaff, Phillip. *History of the Christian Church, Vol. 3, Nicene and Post-Nicene Christianity.* Wm. B. Eerdmans, Grand Rapids, 1994.

Schnackenburg, R. I. *The Gospel According to St. John*. E. T. London and NY, 1968 of German edition Freiburg, 1965, 3 volumes.

Schillebeeckx, E. *Christ: the Christian Experience in the Modern World*. E. T., London, 1980.

Schwobel, Christoph. *Trinitarian Theology Today*, "Christology and Trinitarian Thought." T & T Clark, Edinburgh, 1995.

Schwobel, Christoph. *Trinitarian Theology Today: Essays on Divine Being and Act*. T & T Clark, Edinburgh, 1995.

Snedeker, Donald R. *Our Heavenly Father Has No Equals*. International Scholars Publications, Bethesda, MD, 1998.

Thayer, Joseph. *The New Thayer's Greek-English Lexicon of the New Testament*. Book Publisher's Press, Lafayette, IN, 1979.

The New Catholic Encyclopedia. McGraw Hill, NY, 1967.

Watts, Isaac. *Logic*. first published in 1724. Reprinted by Soli Deo Gloria Publications, Morgan, PA, 1996.

Werblowski, R. J. Z. and Wigoder, Geoffrey. *The Encyclopedia of the Jewish Religion*. Adama Books, NY, 1986.

Werner, Martin. *The Formation of Christian Doctrine*. Beacon Press, Boston, MA, 1965.

Whiston, William. translator. *The Life and Works of Flavius Josephus*. The John C. Winston Co., Philadelphia, 1957, originally published in 1737.

White, James. *The King James Only Controversy*. Bethany House Publishers, Minneapolis, MN, 1995.

Wilbur, Earl Morse. *The History of Unitarianism: Socinianism and its Antecedents*. Harvard University Press, Boston, 1945.

Wiles, Maurice. *The Remaking of Christian Doctrine*. Westminster Press, Philadelphia, 1978.

Wiles, Maurice. *Archetypal Heresy: Arianism Through the Centuries*. Clarendon Press, Oxford, 1996.

Williams, Michael A. *Rethinking Gnosticism: An Argument for Dismantling a Dubious Category*. Princeton University Press, Princeton, NJ, 1996.

Wilson, A. N. *Paul: The Mind of the Apostle*. W. W. Norton, NY, 1997.

Witherington, Ben. *The Christology of Jesus*. Augsberg Fortress Press, Minneapolis, 1990.

Wolfson, H. A. *The Philosophy of the Church Fathers*. Harvard University Press, Philadelphia, PA, 1976.

Young's Analytical Concordance to the Bible. Wm. B. Eerdmans, Grand Rapids, 1964.

Zodhiates, Spiros. *Complete Word Study Dictionary*. AMG Publishers, Chattanooga, TN, 1992.

What is The Living Truth Fellowship?

The Living Truth Fellowship is an international community of Christian believers connected by the love of God, the spirit of God, and a common belief of the truth as it is revealed in the written Word of God. We desire to make known that truth to as many people as possible. As a legal entity, we are a non-profit, tax-exempt United States (Indiana) corporation: The Living Truth Fellowship, Ltd. The name of our ministry contains an intentional double entendre. The Word of God is the truth (John 17:17), and because it contains the very life of God (Eph. 4:18), it is the living truth (John 6:63; Heb. 4:12). As such, the word "living" is an adjective. But God intends that His truth be practiced, that is, He wants us to make "living" a verb by being living epistles of His truth. In that sense, being "verbal" means more than just speaking the Word; it also means doing it.

Our Father desires that we put His truth in our "inner parts" (Ps. 51:6) so that we might not sin against Him (Ps. 119:11). God looks on the heart of each person, and He does not measure the quality of one's life by how much Bible he knows, but by how much knowledge of the truth he practices in his relationships, that is, how much of the heart of God does he manifest. We can objectively measure the quality of our lives by the quality of our relationships with people (Mark 12:28–31; 1 John 4:20 and 21).

Jesus Christ is our supreme example. In John 17:17, he said: "your word is truth," and he exerted a lifelong effort to learn it precisely. But Jesus also LIVED the truth so flawlessly that he could say, I AM the truth (John 14:6). In other words, he BE true. And those are the two sides of the coin of truth, if you will: doctrinal and practical, propositional and relational. Without both sides, that coin won't spend, that is, people won't "buy" what we have to offer.

Our mission is to provide accurate biblical teaching so as to make known the Lord Jesus Christ, The Living Truth, and thus facilitate a worldwide community of mature Christians committed to following him by living the truth of God's Word and sharing it with others.

We accomplish that mission by way of live teachers, camps and conferences for all ages and categories of people, books, newsletters, audio and video teachings, and internet outreach via our website. Those who choose to partake of and participate in these aspects of our ministry are free to utilize our resources as they see fit, whether by starting their own local fellowship or using our work in an already established group of Christians. Our goal is to provide avenues for individual Christians to exercise their unique callings in the Body of Christ.

The basis of all our belief and practice is the Bible, which is the revealed Word of God, flawless in its original writing by those 40 or so believers who wrote during a period of about 1500 years "…*as they were* moved by the Holy Spirit" (2 Pet. 1:21 - NKJV). An honest look at the Bible reveals a coherence that is impossible for those writers to have achieved by collaboration. So-called "errors" or "contradictions" are due to man's subsequent interference in the transmission of the text, or to mistranslations, or to misunderstandings of what is written. We seek truth rather than the religious traditions of men.

Our goal in setting forth the Scriptures is to enable each believer to understand them for himself so he can develop his own convictions, become an effective communicator of God's Word, and fulfill his individual ministry in the Body of Christ. Jesus said that knowing the truth would set one free (John 8:32), and our teachings have practical benefit in terms of one's quality of life—spiritually, mentally, emotionally, and physically.

One of our goals is to teach the Word to "…faithful men who are able to teach others also" (2 Tim. 2:2 - NKJV). We plan to produce seminars and courses of study whereby those who so choose can become able ministers of the Gospel of Jesus Christ. We will ordain to Christian ministry those whom our faith community recognizes as meeting this criterion, whether by training in our ministry or via an ordination they received elsewhere that we recognize.

Further Study Material

Other Books, Booklets, and Audio Teaching Seminars available from:

The Living Truth Fellowship
7399 N. Shadeland Ave., Suite 252
Indianapolis IN 46250
Phone # (317) 721-4046
Email: admin@tltf.org
Website: www.tltf.org
YouTube Channel: www.youtube.com/justtruthit
Vimeo Channel: http://www.vimeo.com/JustTruthIt

Books

The Gift of Holy Spirit: The Power To Be Like Christ

Is There Death After Life?

Don't Blame God! A Biblical Answer to the Problem of Evil, Sin, and Suffering

Booklets

Beyond a Reasonable Doubt—23 Arguments for the Historical Validity of the Resurrection of Jesus Christ

How To Eliminate Apparent Bible Contradictions

23 Reasons to Believe in a Rapture before the Great Tribulation

25 Reasons Why Salvation is Permanent for Christians

34 Reasons Why the Holy Spirit is Not a Separate "Person" From the Only True God, The Father

47 Reasons Why our Heavenly Father has no Equals or "Co-Equals"

What Is True Baptism?

Audio Teaching Seminars available on our web site:

Romans (18 hrs)

Jesus Christ, the Diameter of the Ages (6 hrs)

CPSIA information can be obtained
at www.ICGtesting.com
Printed in the USA
BVHW010831170619
550808BV00018B/585/P